ON THE OI

Max Hastings was born in 1945 a
in libraries and on the battlefield since he left school. A scholar at Charterhouse and University College, Oxford, he has reported from more than fifty countries for the London *Evening Standard* and BBC TV's *24 Hours* and *Panorama*. He has seen action in the Middle East, India, southern Africa, Vietnam, where he flew on several air force ground attack sorties, and the Falklands. In 1982 he was named Journalist of the Year for his dispatches from the South Atlantic. His book *The Battle for the Falklands* became a bestseller and won the *Yorkshire Post* Book of the Year award, as did *Overlord*. *Bomber Command* was awarded the Somerset Maugham Award in 1979. Max Hastings is editor of the *Daily Telegraph*.

Also by Max Hastings (available in Papermac)

THE KOREAN WAR

MAX HASTINGS

ON THE OFFENSIVE

BOMBER COMMAND

OVERLORD

D-Day and the Battle for Normandy 1944

DAS REICH

The march of the 2nd SS Panzer Division
through France, June 1944

PAN BOOKS

Bomber Command first published 1979 by Michael Joseph Limited,
a division of the Penguin Group
First published by Pan Books in this edition

Overlord first published 1984 by Michael Joseph Limited,
a division of the Penguin Group
First published by Pan Books in this edition

Das Reich first published 1981 by Michael Joseph Limited,
a division of the Penguin Group
First published by Pan Books in this edition

This omnibus edition published 1995 by Pan Books
an imprint of Macmillan General Books
Cavaye Place London SW10 9PG
and Basingstoke

Associated companies throughout the world

ISBN 0 330 34607 5

The publishers wish to thank the following for permission to
reproduce in *Overlord* substantial extracts from material to which
they hold the copyright:

Eyre & Spottiswoode, London Henry Holt & Co., New York	*A Soldier's Story* Omar Bradley
Sidgwick & Jackson, London	*A General's Life* Omar Bradley
Oxford University Press	*The Complete Poems of Keith Douglas*
Hamish Hamilton London McGraw Hill, New York	*Montgomery: Master of the Battlefield* Nigel Hamilton
Chatto & Windus, London Universe Books, New York	*A Nurse's War* Brenda McBryde
Secker & Warburg, London	*The 8.15 to War* Peter Roach *Typhoon Pilot* Desmond Scott
William Kimber, London	*Flamethrower* Andrew Wilson

The Trustees of the Liddell Hart Centre for Military Archives

Every effort has been made to contact the copyright owners of quoted material, and the publishers wish to apologize for any omissions to the above list.

1 3 5 7 9 8 6 4 2

A CIP catalogue record for this book is available from the British Library

Printed and bound in Great Britain by
Cox & Wyman Ltd, Reading, Berkshire

BOMBER COMMAND

For Charles,
who will one day be as moved as I am

How can I live among this gentle
Obsolescent breed of heroes, and not weep?
Unicorns, almost,
For they are falling into two legends
In which their stupidity and chivalry
Are celebrated. Each, fool and hero, will be an immortal

– Keith Douglas, 1942

Contents

List of Illustrations

*Imperial War Museum
†Speer Archives

Foreword

Bomber Command's offensive against Germany in the Second World War was one of the most remarkable passages of arms in history. It began when Winston Churchill could see no other road to victory, as England stood alone in 1940. It was undertaken with almost messianic fervour by a generation of senior airmen determined to prove that strategic air power could make a unique and decisive contribution to war. It ended in a controversy, moral and strategic, which has been raging ever since.

The cost was very high. 55,573 aircrew*, almost all officers and NCOs, among the finest and most highly trained material in the British Empire, were killed. A further 9,784 were shot down and taken prisoner. The sacrifice was greater than the British Army's total loss of officers in the First World War. Bomber Command's casualties amounted to almost one-seventh of all British deaths in action by land, sea and air from 1939 to 1945. The pitiful prospects of surviving a tour of bomber operations were only matched in hazard on either side by the German U-boat crews. Germany's losses in the bomber offensive were also awe-inspiring. All statistical estimates are unreliable, but somewhere between 300,000 and 600,000 people, most of them civilians, were killed by the bombs of the RAF and the USAAF. A further five million were 'de-housed'. By 1945 the major city centres of the Third Reich had been razed to rubble.

But was this *decisive* in making possible Allied victory, as leading airmen have claimed ever since, or merely *catastrophic*, as that very perceptive scientific civil servant Sir Henry Tizard feared would prove to be the case, as far back as 1942?

In his post-war memoirs, Bomber Command's C-in-C Sir Arthur Harris argued that 'in spite of all that happened at Hamburg, bombing proved a comparatively humane method. For one thing, it saved the flower of the youth of this country and of our Allies from being mown down by the military in the field, as it was in Flanders in the war of 1914–18.'[1]

Harris's claim deserves the most careful consideration from a Western Allied point of view, if not for the reasons that he himself would advance. The Second World War cost Britain 400,000 dead, America 300,000. It cost Germany at least 5,000,000, Russia at least 20,000,000. If there had been no bomber offensive from 1941 to 1944, while Ger-

* Royal Air Force: 38,462, (69.2 per cent); Royal Canadian Air Force: 9,919 (17.8 per cent); Royal Australian Air Force: 4,050 (7.3 per cent); Royal New Zealand Air Force: 1,679 (3.0 per cent); other Allied air forces: 1,463 (2.7 per cent).

many was being reduced in the terrible war of attrition in the east, would it have been possible for the Allies to justify the interminable delay before opening the Second Front in Europe? Would it also have been possible to avoid the enormous casualties that would have followed a D-Day in 1943?

It is unlikely that important new evidence will be found about the nature of what was done to Germany by the bomber offensive. Each generation of historians can only seek to reinterpret the post-war reports of the American and British bombing survey units, and the testimony of vital witnesses such as Albert Speer. But there are a succession of fascinating, interwoven questions that still surround Bomber Command: beyond what was done, why was it done? How was it done? What was it like to do it? What was it like to be a victim of it? I have tried to examine all these aspects, chiefly with the help of first-hand accounts from those who took part. It is a decade since the last significant book on the bomber offensive appeared, and in the interval all the relevant official files have at last been released for public scrutiny; and the Speer memoirs and other important studies have been published.

This is not the comprehensive story of the offensive, for it deals only incidentally with the American contribution. Nor is it an exhaustive account of everything that was done by Bomber Command, for which it is necessary to turn to the four volumes of the Official History, published almost twenty years ago. I have omitted or dealt very briefly with legendary episodes, such as the Dambusters' Raid, which have been fully described in the past. Instead, I have pieced together some less widely known epics of courage and endurance. I have tried to look at the key issues of the offensive as they appeared at the time, with generous use of contemporary material, much of it hitherto unpublished. Thirty-five years after the event, I think that most men's memories have gained in frankness what they have lost in precision. The mood of almost childlike bravado in some of the war stories published in the 1950s has faded.

Because Bomber Command's losses were so terrible, those who survived have always been specially sensitive to criticism of the campaign. Yet only a charlatan would seek to entangle the men who flew the aircraft in the strategic controversy. Even one of the most cynical critics of the air force, Professor D. C. Watt, has written in his essay *The R.A.F. View of History*[2]: 'We do not think less of Leonidas's three hundred Spartans at Thermopylae because, reviewed objectively, their deaths had little effect one way or another on the Persian invasion of Greece.'

As far as possible in this book, I have separated the story of the aircrew from that of the struggle in Whitehall, Washington and High Wycombe. It is impossible to describe everything that every unit did, because Bomber Command was an enormous organization, so I have chosen six more or less typical line squadrons, whose experience illustrates the nature of the bomber offensive at various stages, and examined their men and their operations in some detail. Through their stories, it may become possible to understand something of what it was like to fly in the darkness over Germany.

I have quoted extensively from unpublished letters, diaries and manuscripts, and interviewed almost a hundred former aircrew, together with many former senior officers and civil servants. Each section of my draft manuscript was read by a former officer who took part in the events described. This is no protection against error, and indeed some senior officers concerned took the strongest exception to my judgements and comments. But it was intended at least to ensure that I clearly understood the Service view of what took place.

At the strategic level, I must express my deep gratitude to the former Commander-in-Chief of Bomber Command, Sir Arthur Harris; to his former Group commanders, Air Vice-Marshal Donald Bennett, the late Air Chief Marshal Sir Ralph Cochrane, and Air Vice-Marshal E. B. Addison; and to the former Director of Bomber Operations at the Air Ministry, Air Vice-Marshal S. O. Bufton. These are only the most prominent of the distinguished airmen who have given me time and help. They will find much to disagree with in what I have written, but I hope that they will accept that I have tried honestly to review their achievements, recognizing the extraordinary conditions and difficulties amidst which they fought.

As for those who flew, it was deeply moving to sit through long evenings in suburban bungalows, listening to very ordinary middle-aged men describing the quite extraordinary things that they did as young aircrew over Germany. I am grateful that my generation has been spared the need to discover whether we could match the impossible sacrifices that they made.

MAX HASTINGS
Jerpoint House
Co. Kilkenny
January 1979

[illegible]

Prologue

Norfolk and Heligoland Bight, 18 December 1939

On Monday, 18 December 1939, Leading Aircraftsman Harry Jones of 37 Squadron, Bomber Command, ate his last breakfast in England for five and a half years at home in Feltwell with his wife Mary. The war was already more than three months old, yet the Joneses' lives still possessed the tidy discipline of suburban commuters. Feltwell was a tiny Norfolk village on the edge of the empty horizons of the Fens, where they rented a small flat. Every morning, LAC Jones kissed Mary, boarded his squadron bicycle, and pedalled for ten minutes down the road to the airfield where 37 Squadron was based. A rigger by trade, he spent his working days tending the airframes of the twin-engined Vickers Wellington I bombers with which Feltwell was equipped. The previous day, Sunday, he was in the hangars carrying out a routine sixty-hour check on his aircraft, and sorting out some trouble with an oleo leg. Today he would be home again at lunchtime for steak and chips with a poached egg on top. Mary, a pretty, jolly, bespectacled farmer's daughter who defied her family's direst warnings about servicemen by marrying Harry fourteen months before, was spending the morning putting the finishing touches to her Christmas pudding.

Harry Jones loved the Royal Air Force. The son of a Birmingham brewery worker, like so many other boys of his generation he had yearned to be a pilot. The day in 1935 that he reported to the recruiting office just short of eighteen years old, this first ambition was brought back to earth with a bump: 'You've got to be a gentleman to fly, my lad!' So Harry Jones did the next best thing and became a rigger. In 1938 he was posted to Feltwell.

For sixpence a day extra pay, however, ground crew could volunteer for occasional flying duties. After five weeks training on drum-fed Lewis guns at North Coates, LAC Jones qualified to wear the brass winged bullet of an air gunner on his arm and to fly when required in the rear turret of one of the squadron's Wellingtons. The privilege of flying had to be fitted in with routine ground duties, of course. Non-commissioned aircrew volunteers were invariable targets for persecution by a station's senior NCOs, who regarded them as 'spoilt brats' trying to escape fire drill, guard details and other real airman's business. It was not unusual for Harry Jones and his kind to return from a six-hour exercise and find themselves rostered for a 24-hour guard duty while their pilots adjourned to bed or the mess. The Other Ranks' cookhouse closed according to ground duties schedules, and remained impervious to special pleading from aircrew late for breakfast after a night flight. The Royal Air Force was a young service, demanding technical flair, imagination, initiative. Yet its hierarchy and routines were still those devised for the armies, and the baser human material, of an earlier age. It was a frustrating paradox, but one which didn't trouble Harry Jones. He loved to fly, he loved 37 Squadron and the Wellingtons and the smell of high-octane fuel and, yes, perhaps even the bull and brass-polishing and cracking discipline of a pre-war RAF station.

37 was one of 3 Group's six operational squadrons at the outbreak of war. Like the rest of Bomber Command, none of them had so far been permitted to attack any land target on enemy territory, while the British Government cautiously debated the future of aerial bombardment. When it was suggested that the RAF might bomb the Ruhr, Whitehall declared with affronted decency that factories were private property. Even after the German *blitzkrieg* on Warsaw, Allied politicians still fervently hoped to avoid provoking such an assault on their own civilians. Since 3 September, 3 Group had flown, and bled, in three ineffectual attacks on naval targets off the German coast and a number of other minor sorties. But 37 Squadron itself had yet to engage the enemy for the first time. The squadron's only casualties since the outbreak of war had been the crew of an old Harrow, which crashed while lost on an exercise. After the first fortnight, when the squadron was shuttled round England in a fever of panicky diversions to avoid an expected German attack, they came home to Feltwell and stayed there. The war, and even the training for it, returned to its usual gentlemanly pace. Once or twice the squadron took part in desultory affiliation exercises with Fighter Command's Spitfires. After the most recent, in November with a flight from Tangmere, the fighter pilots reported that they could have wiped out 37 Squadron in ten minutes. Nobody believed them. Rivalry with Fighter Command and ill-concealed disdain for its flamboyant habits precluded close co-operation in training. Bomber Command was full of pride in itself, one mess of the most delightful flying club in the world. Tangmere could save their line-shoots for the Luftwaffe. A Wellington could take care of itself. 37 Squadron settled back into Norfolk village life, marching on Sundays to church for the sermons of the local vicar, 'Jubilate Joe'. An official request was sent to the station to make less noise on take-off, because an aged local resident was dying in a cottage close to the flight path.

But at 8.15 am on that 18 December, as Harry Jones cycled up to 'A' Flight hangar, Feltwell's usual disciplined Monday morning calm was already shattered. Six aircraft had been taxied in from their dispersals and were being warmed up on the stands by the ground crews. Armourers were traversing turrets and checking bomb loads. 'Come on, Jonah, you're flying!', somebody shouted. Jones hurried into the hangar and checked the roster in the Flight Book on the table. He was down for duty as rear gunner with Sergeant Ruse.

Amidst the hustle of aircrew pulling on flying clothes and seizing maps and equipment, they drew flying rations of sandwiches and chocolate, to be returned intact if the exercise was for any reason uncompleted. Jones had no time to talk to the other four members of the crew before he swung himself into the turret of Ruse's aircraft behind his twin Browning .303s. The Wellington began to move forward across the grass, past the squadron commander Joe Fogarty, standing as always beside the runway, saluting as 'A' Flight rolled past one by one. They bumped towards take-off. At last Jones called to Ruse on the intercom: 'What's going on, skipper?'

'They've found the German navy, and we're going to Wilhelmshaven to attack them. . . .'

The operation of which 37 Squadron was about to become a part had been conceived months before the war, by the Air Ministry's Directorate of Plans. Among the thick file of alternative attacks to be carried out by Bomber Command, Western Air Plan 7B called for the bombing of the German fleet in or around its base at Wilhelmshaven. In the immediate aftermath of the outbreak of war, while the Government shrank from authorizing an assault on German industry, it seized enthusiastically upon WAP 7B. The German navy was obviously a legitimate target, surrounded by water and therefore safe from the risk that ill-aimed bombs might fall on civilians. Bomber Command was impatient to flex its muscles. On 4 September, fourteen Wellingtons of 3 Group and fifteen Blenheims of 2 Group carried out the first of a series of attacks on the German navy in its bases. The Blenheims attacked the pocket-battleship *Admiral Scheer* in the Schillig Roads with great gallantry at low level, hitting the ship four times. None of the bombs exploded. Five Blenheims were lost. The Wellingtons, bombing the *Scharnhorst* and the *Gneisenau* in the Elbe at higher level, scored no hits on their targets, but lost only two of their own number.

The concept of the self-defending bomber formation, fighting its way over enemy lines to attack vital targets miles behind any battlefield, lay at the core of the theory of strategic air power. The power-operated gun turrets now fitted to the Wellingtons and Whitleys of Bomber Command represented a major British breakthrough in armament technology, and it was believed that they gave the RAF's bombers a decisive margin of protection against an attacking fighter. Group and Bomber Command headquarters studied closely the reports on the events of 4 September, and professed themselves very encouraged by the failure of German Me109 fighters to close with the Wellingtons. Although in reality one Wellington and one Blenheim were destroyed by fighters, it was believed at Bomber Command that enemy anti-aircraft fire – 'flak' – had accounted for all the RAF losses. Tactics were adjusted accordingly. Henceforth attacks would be carried out at higher levels.

On 3 December, after a prolonged lull provoked by digestion of the lessons of September, by lack of suitable targets and weather, and by the general lack of urgency about prosecuting the war that characterized all British activities at this period, a formation of twenty-four Wellingtons from 3 Group carried out a second abortive operation against German cruisers off Heligoland and returned without loss, despite a series of German fighter attacks. These relatively large British forces had failed to damage the enemy, but Bomber Command was encouraged by their very survival. Even when a third 'armed patrol of the Schillig Roads' by twelve Wellingtons on 12 December ended in tragedy, with the loss of half the force, there was no weakening of confidence at the top. It was believed that most if not all the losses had been inflicted by flak and not fighters, despite repeated attacks by Me109s.

'The failure of the enemy', noted Air Commodore Norman Bottomley, Bomber Command's Senior Air Staff Officer and the future Deputy Chief of Air Staff in 1944, 'must be ascribed to good formation flying. The maintenance of tight, unshaken formations in the face of the most powerful enemy action is the test of bomber force fighting efficiency and morale. In our service, it is the equivalent of the old "Thin Red Line", or the "Shoulder to Shoulder" of Cromwell's Ironsides. . . .'

There can be no doubt that these raids were deliberately conceived as a means of testing Germany's defences and Bomber Command's tactics, rather than as a serious assault on German sea power. There is no other way to explain the Command's lack of concern about the failure of its aircraft to sink or damage a single enemy ship. Even after the experience of 12 December – which he himself compared to the Charge of the Light Brigade – 3 Group's AOC, the cheerfully energetic and popular Air Vice-Marshal, John 'Jackie' Baldwin, was impatient to get his squadrons once again to grips with the enemy.

At 3 pm on the afternoon of 17 December, Baldwin telephoned on the scrambler to Air Commodore Bottomley at Bomber Command HQ at High Wycombe, to urge a further operation against the German fleet:

> The Group Commander pointed out the importance of seizing the very first suitable day in view of the few such occasions which were likely to present themselves under winter conditions. He stated that from the point of view of preparation, the details of the plan had been thoroughly considered by all concerned, and he was satisfied that if Monday the 18th of December were given as zero day, there would be no undue haste in planning and preparation right down to the crews engaged.[1]

Air Chief Marshal Sir Edgar Ludlow-Hewitt, C-in-C Bomber Command, concurred. He approved Baldwin's proposal to mount a new attack on the German fleet at Wilhelmshaven on the 18th, subject only to a proviso that the Wellingtons bomb from at least 10,000 feet, which should take them above effective flak. Group-Captain Goodwin, SASO at 3 Group HQ, drafted orders for the operation to be carried out by twenty-four Wellingtons. Nine aircraft would come from 149 Squadron at Mildenhall, including that of the formation leader, Wing-Commander Richard Kellett, who had also led the 3 December sweep; nine would come from 9 Squadron at Honington; the remaining six from 37 Squadron at Feltwell. 'Task: to attack enemy warships in the Schillig Roads or Wilhelmshaven', began the Operation Order. 'Great care is to be taken that no bombs fall on shore, and no merchant ships are to be attacked. Formations shall not loiter in the target area, and all aircraft are to complete bombing as soon as possible after the sighting signal has been made.'

'Not only did I have all the leaders into the Operations Room the night before the mission went out,' wrote Baldwin to Ludlow-Hewitt a few days later, 'but I personally explained to each of them my ideas on formation flying and what I meant by mutual assistance, and they all professed that they agreed and understood.'

Late in the afternoon of Sunday the 17th, the order went out to the squadrons taking part in the operation to stand-by at two hours' notice for take-off from 0730 hrs on the morning of the 18th. Pilots and observers were briefed by squadron and station commanders. Part-time crew members such as Harry Jones were thought to need no enlightenment beyond their time of take-off, and many of them learnt this only the next morning.

Before dawn on the 18th, a Whitley of 4 Group, from 78 Squadron at Dishforth in Yorkshire, flew out across the North Sea, approaching the island of Heligoland at 0800 in patchy cloud, ideal cover for a daylight bomber operation. The crew signalled their weather report, and turned homewards towards England. 3 Group HQ passed the final readiness order to the Wellington squadrons: take-off would be at 0930; squadrons would take up formation over King's Lynn before crossing the North Sea. The attack against Wilhelmshaven was on.

Most of 9 Squadron's officers were out playing rugger on their home pitch at Honington the previous afternoon, when word reached 'Donkeydrop' Horsefall, the adjutant, that nine crews would be required for operations the next day. 3 Group's young pilots probably had fewer illusions about the likelihood of their own survival than their senior officers. It was an affectionate cliché of Bomber Command since long before the war that it was a club of which a member landing at any airfield in England would meet someone he knew. 9 Squadron had heard all about the losses of 12 December. They perceived that this would be a hard war, in which it was unlikely that those who were in at the beginning would remain to see the end, and of course they were perfectly correct. Perhaps the very uncertainty about the nature of the battle that they would be called upon to fight made duty harder for these young men of December 1939 than for those who came after them, to whom at least the reality was brutally apparent.

Within the year, attrition would destroy the continuity and character of 9 Squadron's officers' mess as inexorably as it attacked that of every other unit in the RAF. But in these days before the slaughter began in earnest, Honington's welcoming leather armchairs and white-jacketed mess servants knew their thirty-odd brash young men as intimately as any public school prefects' club or university junior common room: James Smalley, big and untidy, bringing showgirls down from London to their parties and bewildering colleagues on idle evenings by sitting quietly knitting on a sofa: Parrot, who had been a ladies' hairdresser; Bill Macrae, a wild, brave, passionately alcoholic Canadian short-service officer who delighted in stunting his lumbering Wellington over the churches of Norfolk, lifting his wingtip at the last second before crashing into the spires; Peter Grant, fair-haired and elegant, almost a Hollywood caricature of the sporting young English public school boy, a general's son who joined the RAF after failing to get into Cambridge. Half the mess secretly envied his stylish approach to life on the ground and in the air. The previous winter he drove in the Monte Carlo Rally in his own Talbot 10 with Appleby, a fellow-pilot chum from 37 Squadron. Everybody remembered the squadron CO standing roaring with laughter outside the mess as Peter's Wellington came in at nought feet over the rugger pitch, scattering players to all points of the compass. Spirited flying, the CO believed, bred spirited fighters. There was less interest in education for war. Charlie Vann, another squadron pilot, took his leave in Spain in the midst of her civil war, to see what real fighting looked like. He ended up in front of the Group AOC for going abroad without permission. Vann was an exception. Most officers were happy to let Command dictate the leisurely pace and nature of their training and showed little professional curiosity.

They were, on average, three or four years older than the twenty and twenty-one year olds who would be the mainstay of Bomber Command at the height of its offensive five years later, but then that later generation was older by so many seasons' experience of war. These young men of 9 Squadron and their kin were the innocents. Even their faces in the inevitable squadron photographs look somehow different from those who followed in 1943, 1944 and 1945: Challes, Fordham, Lines, Allison, Bailey – these were young men who cut their hair short and cultivated rakish little moustaches, precursors of the later handlebars. They drank at The Angel in Bury St Edmunds and The Bell at

Thetford – always beer. Once a month they climbed into formal messkit for Dining-In nights, and when they were paid they cashed a cheque for five pounds and sped off to London crammed into somebody's car for a night of noisy, gauche wickedness that usually ended unconscious on a bed at the Regent Palace Hotel. In the early summer of 1939, 9 Squadron represented the RAF at the Brussels International Air Exhibiton, where they exchanged warily chivalrous compliments with their Luftwaffe counterparts, and were then sent to stage a 'Show The Flag' flight the length of France and back. Even since the outbreak of war, there had been plenty of social diversions. That autumn the Duke of Grafton did his bit for the war effort by inviting the whole of Honington officers' mess to Euston, his stately home near Thetford. Then, one winter morning, the first contingent of Women's Auxiliary Air Force girls, the WAAFs, arrived at the airfield, creating unprecedented excitement and causing the Station Commander to make one of his rare public appearances to supervise the rigging of barbed-wire entanglements round their quarters. The only discordant note, forerunner of many more social upheavals to come, was struck when the most glamorous and sought-after of the girls ended up, of all places, in the arms of a non-commissioned sergeant pilot.

Even by the standards of the other two services, the young pre-war RAF pilot was the least long-sighted of warriors. At least a few of the young men who joined the British army and the Royal Navy did so because they aspired to end up as generals or admirals. Those who came to the RAF did so because they passionately, single-mindedly, unashamedly wanted to fly. The Hendon Air Displays, the barnstormers of the 1920s and 1930s, the hugely publicized exploits of Lindberg, Hinckler, Amy Johnson, all these had seized the imagination of their generation. Above all, perhaps, they captured that of young grammar-school boys, of modest, conventional lower-middle-class backgrounds from which they yearned to escape. Some day there is an intriguing essay to be written on the social origins of senior British airmen of this period, and the effects of these on their attitudes to the other two services. It is enough here to say that pre-war RAF officers' messes offered young men a unique opportunity to be paid for living the life of gentlemen fliers, and yet public school boys seemed slower to take it up than Lord Trenchard and his colleagues had hoped. There was a rueful pre-war air force chestnut about the young man who told his mother he had become a pianist in a brothel rather than reveal that he had joined the RAF.

But they behaved as English public school boys of the period were expected to behave. One messnight, they locked a racehorse in James Smalley's bedroom, and bravely faced the difficulties the next morning when it was found impossible to get it out again. They were woken in the morning by civilian batmen who had already run their baths, and who uncomplainingly collected the debris of the previous night's revels, ironed the clothes while their owners soaked, then made the beds while the pilots strolled to the mess for ham and eggs. There was usually some flying in the morning, then after lunch squash and tennis and time to clean up before tea. They spurned the vulgarity of a bar – drinks were brought to the ante-room by a waiter summoned by the bell, and signed for by chit (only in the sergeants' mess was it necessary to pay cash). The pre-war stations had been built to standards of spacious solid comfort that ate deep into the RAF estimates even when aircraft design and production were being cut to the bone.

That December of 1939 the war had still made very little impact on Honington. Three armoured cars arrived to take over the station's defence against invasion, and slit trenches had been dug everywhere. The hangars were draped in huge camouflage nets. Dining-In nights in full messkit had been abandoned. Blue bulbs were substituted for the white ones in every socket, a lurid contribution to the blackout. Every morning aircrew spent an inordinate amount of time hanging around the hangars waiting for orders that never came. Peter Grant and a handful of others had been sent on one abortive operation against the Kiel Canal at the very outbreak of war, from which they had returned almost drained of petrol and utterly exhausted, with a bleak inkling that operational flying would be at best very dreary and at worst terrifyingly dangerous. They had been ordered to bomb at extreme low level to avoid risking hitting the neighbouring land, and had lost two aircraft. Since September, however, operations had been ordered again and again, only to be cancelled before take-off. These were the months of the 'Bore War'.

At the evening briefing of 17 December nine captains were detailed. Guthrie, Pett and Macrae, and Allison, Challes and Lines, would fly in two vics – V formations – of three, on the left of the big diamond formation led by six aircraft of 149 Squadron. Peter Grant, with sergeants Ramshaw and Purdy, would fly on the right of the diamond with three aircraft from 149. 37 Squadron would bring up the rear. Wireless silence was to be observed, although leaders would maintain a listening watch on 3190 Kilocycles. The only communication within the formation was to be by Aldis signal lamp. Each aircraft would carry three 500-pound Semi Armour-Piercing bombs.

At 0930 on the morning of 18 December they took off on schedule from Honington at two-minute intervals. They rendezvoused according to plan with 149's aircraft led by Kellett, and took up formation over the coastal town of King's Lynn. Then, mostly in silent apprehension, they settled to keep station on the long-haul across the North Sea.

Feltwell's six aircraft were late taking off, and caught up the formation over the sea. Some of 37 Squadron were lucky. An observer, Sergeant

Butcher, had been found the previous day to be suffering from mumps. His crew was withdrawn from the operation. Others were less fortunate. LAC Jack Graves was in bed in his barrack room when an NCO put his head in to call: 'Come on, you lucky lads, you're "On" this morning!' As the sleepy gunners roused themselves and dressed, Greaves, a wireless operator/gunner who had been posted to Feltwell only a few days before and was not yet attached to a crew, made himself busy in the accumulator charging room. He had heard enough about daylight sweeps to know that this was not a good morning on which to make his operational debut. Then he heard the Tannoy calling 'LAC Greaves to "A" Flight Office'. A stocky, sharp little flight-lieutenant, 'Cheese' Lemon, had a sick wireless-operator. Greaves was to replace him.

Sergeant Herbert Ruse, the pilot of Harry Jones's aircraft, joined the RAF as a technical apprentice at Trenchard's famous Halton school at the age of sixteen, in 1930. A Suffolk butcher's son, he decided that the air force could not be worse than sweating for school certificate at Sudbury grammar school, and discovered too late that the discipline at Halton exceeded that of the most remorseless civilian establishment. In 1936 he was a metal rigger when he was offered the chance to train as an NCO pilot under the ungenerous scheme of the period which allowed selected ground crew to fly for five years before returning to ground duties in their original ranks. But Herbie Ruse thought that if he became an experienced bomber pilot, there might be a career for him in civil aviation. He qualified and was posted to Feltwell in September 1937. That December Sunday of 1939 he was at home in Long Melford when he was telephoned to return to the station: 'Some practice do,' they said. At briefing he was surprised to learn that they were to bomb above ten thousand feet, for he could never remember any crew scoring hits in bombing practice on a target as small as a ship from that height. Enemy fighters were an unknown quantity. In fighter affiliation exercises, the gunners would call exultantly: 'Got him, skip!' But neither he nor they had any scientific means of judging whether they were right. They had seldom fired live ammunition in the air, and on exercises they trained to attack in succession in pairs, making a series of runs over the target to judge their own errors. On this occasion, plainly there would be no opportunity for these refinements.

As Ruse's Wellington climbed slowly over Norfolk, Harry Jones in the rear turret tested his twin guns, while Corporal Fred Taylor the wireless operator/gunner fired a few rounds from the front turret. 37 Squadron had been practising a new formation, flying 'stepped-down' in pairs above each other, rather than in the vics customary in other squadrons. Herbie Ruse's only concern was to keep station with Flying Officer Thompson in the Wellington beside him, to bomb when he did, to change course as he did. Sergeant Tom May, in the second-pilot's seat beside Ruse, had no need to trouble himself with dead-reckoning navigation on this trip. It was simply a case of follow-my-leader. 37's aircraft were over the North Sea before they took up station at the rear of Kellett's formation, and throughout the flight they lagged some way behind. As the day grew around them, they noted with concern that the broken cloud over England had cleared completely. It was now a bright, crystal-clear morning with visibility approaching fifty miles, ideal conditions for an enemy interception.

They had climbed to 15,000 feet, and were becoming acutely conscious of the numbing December cold that was spilling through the draughty turrets, blowing relentlessly down the unheated fuselage, seeping into their hands and feet, closing its grip on their tautening limbs as the hours went on. They could now see the island of Heligoland before them. They were approaching German waters, the familiar naval battle grounds of the First World War, where Beatty's battle-cruisers and the Royal Navy's dashing submarine captains had played tip-and-run with the German High Seas Fleet for so long. They would be making a landfall close to the Danish–German frontier, then turning on a long leg southwards, down the German coast, searching for enemy naval units. In the leading aircraft some miles in front of them, Wing-Commander Kellett, who had made his name before the war chasing long-distance flying records, was for the first time carrying as a member of his crew a naval officer, Lieutenant-Commander Rotherham, to identify suitable targets.

In his lonely turret in the tail of Ruse's Wellington, Harry Jones tightened the twenty-foot scarf Mary had knitted for him as close as he could around his throat, to fight the dreadful cold. The turret was even more cramped than was usual in Wellingtons, for after acute difficulty with the ammunition feeds, 37 Squadron had improvised a system of canvas trays to hold the folded belts beneath the guns, and in consequence the gunners were hemmed in by .303 rounds up to their knees. Herbie Ruse was not one of those captains who tried to enforce silence on the intercom on long flights. Jones chatted for a few minutes to Fred Taylor, at the front gun, gazing down at the dirty grey sea below them, occasionally traversing his turret. It was moving sluggishly, the hydraulic oil already thickening at the unaccustomed height and temperature. Jones stamped his feet on the ammunition below him as he struggled to keep circulation moving.

Two hours out from Mildenhall, in the midst of the North Sea, Flight-Lieutenant Duguid of 149 Squadron, leading the second vic of the forward section, began to have trouble maintaining the revolutions on his starboard engine. Accurate formation flying was no longer possible as his speed dropped. His observer signalled his two wingmen by Aldis lamp to close up on Kellett's vic just ahead, when he himself dropped back. His no. 2, Riddlesworth, obediently closed up on Kellett. His no. 3 apparently failed to see Duguid's signal, and with what can only be described as remarkable lack of imagination, followed the ailing Wellington down and on to the homeward track. The two aircraft landed at Mildenhall at 1.25 pm that afternoon. There were now twenty-two aircraft remaining in the formation.

At 12.30 pm, three hours out from Norfolk, Kellett sighted the north German coast, a smudge fifty miles ahead across the gin-clear sky. For the next one-and-a-half hours, his force would be within range of German fighter aircraft. The long run southwards brought them over Wilhelmshaven as far as possible from the concentration of flak ships among the Friesian Islands. But the price of the dog's leg was that the German defences had maximum warning of their coming.

Yet, in the event, it was German flak which saved the formation from the first fighters into the air. Six Messerschmitt Me109 single-engined night-fighters scrambled to approach the Wellingtons as they closed the Jade Roads. But as the fighters made their first attack, the anti-aircraft batteries on shore opened a furious bombardment on the Wellingtons. The Me109s* broke away, and hung off the flanks of the formation, expecting the barrage to stop. In fact, however, as the Wellingtons approached Wilhelmshaven, the ground fire intensified. The fighters waited for their turn.

To Harry Jones in his turret, the black puffs hanging in the air around them looked like buckets of coal that some madman was hurling into the sky. Ruse's aircraft bucked in the concussions, but the formation was too high for effective flak, just as Ludlow-Hewitt had hoped. Jack Greaves, in the front turret of 'Cheese' Lemon's aircraft, thought that if this was German flak, there was nothing to it. He was relieved, for there was no room in the turret for his parachute, and he felt acutely vulnerable to any sudden disaster to the aircraft.

The most serious consequence of the flak was that it caused the formation, and especially 9 Squadron, its port section, and 37 in the rear, to open ranks and lose their delicate cohesion. Both Squadron-Leader Guthrie of 9 and Squadron-Leader Hue-Williams of 37 were some distance ahead of their sections, and those at the rear were straggling. As Kellett in the leading aircraft opened his bomb doors on the approach to Wilhelmshaven, many of his crews were already dangerously scattered across the sky.

The fact that the Wellingtons had now survived an hour inside German fighter range without loss was the result of an extraordinary series of lapses by the Luftwaffe. The British pilots were only sketchily aware

* As an abbreviation readily understood by a lay audience, henceforth I shall refer to Messerschmitt fighters as Me109s and 110s, although their correct designation was Bf109 and Bf110.

that their own country possessed the capability to detect the approach of enemy aircraft by radar, and certainly had no notion that the Germans did also. In the upper reaches of Bomber Command, it was known that the Germans had been carrying out radar experiments parallel with those of the RAF, but there was a widespread tacit reluctance to believe that Hun technology could already have matched the British achievement. In reality, on this 18 December, at about the same time that Kellett sighted the north German coast fifty miles ahead, the Wellingtons were picked up by the Luftwaffe's *Freya* radar station among the sand dunes of the offshore island of Wangerooge, and by the naval radar station on Heligoland. Yet it was an hour before the fighters made their first effective attack. 53 doomed men among the 114 in the British formation were granted that much extra life because of simple disbelief on the part of the Germans that the Royal Air Force could flaunt itself in the face of the Luftwaffe on a brilliant winter's day that promised only a massacre.

Despite the adequacy of their technology, the Germans had failed to match the British in marrying radar to an effective fighter direction system. The naval radar report was only hesitantly passed through their own HQ exchange to the Luftwaffe at Jever. When the young lieutenant commanding the air-force's own radar station telephoned Jever direct, he was caustically dismissed: 'Tommies approaching in weather like this? You're plotting seagulls or there's interference on your set!'[2] The Luftwaffe officer then tried to telephone the CO of the neighbouring Me110 squadron direct, only to learn that he was absent at headquarters. Kellett's men, now cruising majestically down the coast of Schleswig–Holstein, had gained a few more minutes. Only after a visual sighting report by German naval observers, whose message was duplicated in transmission and reached HQ as a warning of forty-four approaching enemy aircraft, did the Luftwaffe at last grasp the reality of attack. Belatedly the fighters began to scramble.

Even as the Messerschmitts were climbing to engage the Wellingtons, the Germans suffered another moment of bewildered astonishment. The bombers came high over Wilhelmshaven, over a battleship and cruiser lying in Bau Haven, with bomb doors open. Yet not a bomb fell. As the flak still splashed and blackened the sky around them, the British aircraft turned slowly westwards towards the North Sea and home. The formation's orders not to bomb if there was any danger of hitting the shore gave Kellett no discretion. He concluded that the warships were too close to land to risk attack. As an operation of war against the German navy, the Wellingtons' mission was thus a total, indeed a grotesque failure. Yet as the bombers cruised away from Wilhelmshaven and emerged from the flak barrage, a few minutes before 1.30 pm, the destruction began.

In the Luftwaffe's previous encounters with Wellington formations, they had probed the bombers' strengths and weaknesses with some circumspection. Two important conclusions emerged from the fighter pilots' reports. First, although the Wellington's rear turret could be very effective against attacks from astern, the guns were incapable of traversing to a full right-angle with the aircraft, and Wellingtons were thus unable to make any reply to an attack from the beam. Second, through a criminal omission on the part of the Air Ministry, the aircraft lacked self-sealing tanks. If hit in a fuel tank, especially that in the port wing, a Wellington could be transformed within seconds into a flying bonfire. Even if the tanks did not ignite, rapid loss of fuel would almost certainly bring down a crippled aircraft on a long run home. The Luftwaffe fighter squadron commanders urged their pilots to knock out the Tommies' rear turret at long range, where the Wellington's .303s were useless, then close in for the kill.

Many of the men flying the bombers had joined the RAF in the early and mid-1930s, before the era of the 350-mph cannon fighter. As they lumbered westwards at less than 200 mph over the north German island towards the open sea, a succession of stabbing, slashing assaults by the Me109s and 110s began. P/O Speirs of 149 Squadron was flying no. 3 in the leading section behind Kellett, when a twin-engined Me110 dived across the formation hosing fire that suddenly lanced into the fuselage of Speirs's aircraft. There was an explosion to the rear of the cockpit close to the wing root, almost certainly in a fuel tank. The Wellington fell away from the formation, flames pouring from the fuselage, to plunge headlong into the sea 10,000 feet below. There were no parachutes. Riddlesworth, the only survivor of Duguid's vic after the other two aircraft turned back, now closed up to take Speirs's place behind Kellett. The three Wellingtons began twenty minutes of desperate fighting against a procession of Messerschmitts. The 109s seemed to follow the 110s into attack. As they flew over Schillig Point, to their dismay the British could see a further squadron of fighters taking off to join the battle.

'The enemy pressed home their attacks in a splendid manner,' wrote Kellett in his report, striking a curiously gallant note in describing an ill-matched slaughter. But at last an Me109 gave the British their chance. Tiring of beam attacks and difficult deflection shots, the German swung in to attack Riddlesworth from dead astern. This was the situation for which the RAF had developed 'mutual supporting fire'. All three Wellington rear gunners in the lead vic ripped into him. Spuming smoke, the fighter curled away to the sea. The pilot escaped from his sinking cockpit only to drown under the weight of his flying gear. Kellett's three aircraft, with the advantage of being in the van of the formation and aided by some disciplined and determined flying, pressed on towards England.

But behind them, the bomber force was crumbling. In 9 Squadron's section on the port side of the formation, the fierce little Canadian Bill Macrae cursed his gunner as he twisted and banked the Wellington under attack and heard no sound of answering fire from his own rear turret: 'I'm trying, skip, but my fingers are too stiff to get the guns to bear!' shouted the frozen, desperate gunner, who was wounded moments later. Fabric was flapping from great gashes torn in the wings and fuselage, and fuel leaking from the tanks. In Pett's aircraft nearby, the first burst from a Me109 wounded the rear gunner. Heathcote, the second pilot, scrambled down the fuselage and dragged the gunner out. He emptied burst after burst into the attacking fighters until at last the guns clicked dead. The ammunition trays were empty. Heathcote crawled forward to the front gunner, wounded in the thigh, and took over his turret instead. Sergeant Pett threw the aircraft into a tortured dive to sea level to shake off the Messerschmitts. Miraculously he succeeded. With his bleeding gunners and his rudder controls partly jammed, he nursed the Wellington home to a forced landing at Sutton Bridge in Lincolnshire. Macrae made an emergency landing at the coastal airfield of North Coates.

These were the only two aircraft from the port section to reach home. S/Ldr Guthrie, whom Baldwin was to charge with 'lack of interest' in his report, flew his blazing aircraft headlong into the North Sea. Douglas Allison, a quiet, serious Londoner, dropped away with his port engine on fire, and no trace of himself or his crew was ever found. The Wellington of Challes, beside him, broke up in mid-air after being hit amidships by fire from an Me110. Lines, the last of the section, vanished shortly afterwards, probably at the hands of an Me110 of the Luftwaffe's 2 Squadron ZG 76.

The starboard section of the big diamond – two vics of three, led respectively by S/Ldr Harris of 149 and F/Lt Peter Grant of 9 Squadron – held formation under attack better than their counterparts on the port side. Grant had just given the order to close bomb doors after leaving Wilhelmshaven when the first wave of fighters fell on them. It was the first time that they had seen an Me110, and as they droned steadily west they were shocked by the ruthless ease with which the Germans took station abreast of them, and hammered fire into the bombers with impunity, the Wellingtons' turrets traversed to their impotent maximum of 80 degrees. Glancing out of the cockpit, Grant was dismayed to see fuel spuming out of his holed tanks. He began urgently pumping what remained into those that seemed unhit: 'There was absolutely nothing that we could do except sit there being picked off one by one . . .'[3] On Grant's port side Sergeant Ramshaw, his aircraft hit repeatedly by attacks which came almost certainly from the Messerschmitt of Gordon Gollob – later to become a famous ace with 150 alleged victories – was appalled to find all his turrets jammed and his rear gunner mortally wounded. Defenceless, he dropped his

Wellington under the rest of the section and flew on homewards, clinging beneath the shelter of their guns, fuel pouring from his tanks. In Harris's aircraft in front of them, fire cut into the front turret, one round smashing through the sole of the gunner's boot, another burst damaging sections of the geodetic frame and an elevator. Behind Harris, Briden was staggering onwards in an aircraft heavily damaged and losing fuel fast.

It was the performance of this starboard section and that of Kellett in the lead which later caused one of the German fighter squadron commanders to note in his report the 'tight formation and excellent rear gunners of the Wellington bombers'. One Me110 had already been compelled to pull out of action and make an emergency landing with its crew wounded by turret fire from a Wellington. The German squadron CO himself forced-landed with a badly damaged aircraft, and most of his fighters had been hit by the British guns. But the fact remained that none of the 110s was totally destroyed, and as the German also stated in his report: 'The Wellingtons' maintenance of formation and rigid adherence to course made them easy targets to find.'

While the leading sections of the British force fought a savage battle for survival, it was at the rear, among the aircraft of 37 Squadron, that disaster became almost absolute. Even before Kellett's formation closed Wilhelmshaven, the second pilot of 'Cheese' Lemon's aircraft reached down to open the bomb doors. On a Wellington, the appropriate control was set beside the flap lever. He accidentally put on full flap. The results were dramatic. The Wellington soared abruptly upwards, causing chaos among the crew and uproar on the intercom. The aircraft then stalled and began to dive steeply towards the earth, as Lemon and his second pilot struggled to regain control.

By the time they had done so, they were alone, very low, over the sea. 'Christ, we've lost everything now. We're on our own,' thought Greaves. It was at this moment that the rear gunner, Kidd, shouted: '109s!' Lemon clung desperately to the waves as the gunner called out the attacks: 'They're coming in . . . now . . . left! Now, right, right! He's overshooting!' They were hit repeatedly in the fuselage, the aircraft still streaking along with spray breaking on the perspex of the front turret, where Greaves tried in vain to bring his gun to bear. 'If we go down now, we've had it,' he thought, struck by the ghastly vision of the aircraft plunging unhesitating to the sea bottom if Lemon lost control for a moment. The observer in the astrodome was commentating on the German attacks. Suddenly, as one of the fighters closed again, there was a cry of choked astonishment from the rear turret: 'Christ! He's gone straight in!' The German's wingtip seemed to have touched the water, and in an instant vanished. The other fighter broke away. They were alone. There was an outburst of nervous hilarity on the intercom about the German's sudden collision with the North Sea.

Then Lemon cut in: 'Come on, cut the chatter, we've got to get home.' Silent, exhausted by fear, they settled for the long run back to Feltwell, flying all the way almost at sea level. Greaves swore that he could taste the salt. After their half-hearted debriefing on landing at 3.30 pm, they waited for the next Feltwell aircraft to return. Yet by evening, none had come.

As the rear section of the Wellington force, 37 Squadron were the first and easiest targets for the German fighters. The experiment with the 'stepped down' formation in pairs must be considered a failure, by results. Lemon had been flying as wingman to S/Ldr Hue-Williams. In the chaotic nightmare of the battle, as each bomber struggled for its own survival, men could spare only momentary glances for the plight of others. Peter Grant glimpsed Hue-Williams's aircraft diving for the sea, starboard wing on fire. Hue-Williams's second pilot was the same Appleby who drove so gaily to Monte Carlo with Grant that spring. There were no survivors.

Just north of Wangerooge a second pair – Wimberley and Lewis – broke away westwards in an attempt to make a low level escape for home over the sandbanks. They were at once spotted by Lieutenant Helmut Lent in his Me110. Lent had scrambled from Jever with his armourer still lying on the wing loading cannon shells into the magazines – the man was scarcely able to roll to the ground before Lent accelerated to take off. After one abortive beam attack on the blindspot of Wimberley's Wellington, the impatient Lent closed astern and abruptly silenced the rear gunner. His second burst set fire to the aircraft, which dived and crashed in the sea close to Borkum Island. 'Pete' Wimberley was picked up by a German patrol boat, the only survivor. Lent turned in pursuit of Lewis, now struggling ten feet above the sea to escape in the same style as Lemon. The fighter pilot, unlike his colleague in the Me109 which attacked Lemon, made no mistake. After a single burst, the Wellington caught fire and broke up as it hit the water. There were no survivors. Lent later became one of the most celebrated German aces of the war.

Herbie Ruse, concentrating on keeping formation with F/O Thompson as the middle pair of the 37 Squadron section, was one of the few British pilots to drop bombs that day. Thompson opened his bomb doors, apparently on his own initiative, as they approached a German vessel a few miles west of Schillig Point. Ruse followed suit, and Tom May, himself a former seaman who had joined up during the Slump, took position forward by the bomb release. 'He's going for that ship!' called May. 'He's going to overshoot!' 'Are you sure it's naval?' asked Ruse, as he struggled to hold the aircraft steady amidst a new surge of flak. Then as Thompson's bombs fell away, May released their own. The aircraft rose as the weight vanished. They saw the sticks splash harmlessly into the sea at the same moment that Herbie Ruse spotted a German fighter underneath them 'climbing like a lift'. Thompson put his nose down and dived steeply northwestwards, Ruse close behind him. The pilot of the leading Wellington had obviously decided that they must make a run for it on their own. Although Ruse instinctively regretted breaking away from the formation, 37 Squadron's section was a straggling litter of aircraft. This might be their only hope.

The Wellington was racing downwards at an incredible 300 mph, shaking in every rivet. Harry Jones was irrelevantly startled to see red roofs on the coast to port of them: 'The roofs can't be red!' he muttered. 'Those are German houses. We have red roofs in England.' Then he saw a German fighter streaking towards them at a closing speed of more than 100 mph. 'My God, isn't it small!' he thought, as so many thousands of air gunners would think in their turn in the next five years as the slim silhouette of the fighter swung in, guns winking, to attack. At 600 yards Jones touched his triggers. The Brownings fired single rounds and stopped. They were frozen. He tried to traverse the turret. It was jammed by the cold. Fighting with the cocking handles, he glimpsed Thompson's Wellington sliding by beneath them, its tail shot to pieces. Its rear turret had simply disappeared, and with it Jones's friend Len Stock, a little instrument-repairer from North London. There were no survivors from Thompson's aircraft.

Jones was still wrestling with his guns when the fighter came in again. There was a violent explosion in the turret and a savage pain in his ankle and back. 'Skip, I've been hit!' he called down the intercom. 'Can you do anything back there? No? Then for God's sake get out of the turret,' answered Ruse. Jones dragged himself up the fuselage towards the rest bed, half-conscious, with his back scored by one bullet, his ankle shattered by a second. The Wellington I was equipped with a bizarre mid-under turret known to the crews as 'the dustbin'. Because of its fierce drag on the aircraft's speed in the firing position, it was lowered only in action. Now Tom Holly, the wireless operator, was struggling to bring it to bear as the Messerschmitts raked the Wellington yet again. Fred Taylor bent over Harry Jones, morphia in hand, trying to lift his leg on to the rest bed. A burst smashed through the port side of the fuselage, shattering Taylor's head and back. Jones had persuaded the quiet northern boy to put aside his wartime scruples and get married only a few weeks before. Now Taylor collapsed on him, dying. The next burst caught Tom Holly as he struggled to pull himself out of the dustbin turret, jammed and useless. Hit in the face and side, Holly fell dead, draped half in, half out of the gun position.

Herbie Ruse could smell the cordite from the explosions in the fuselage, and feel the Wellington being cut to pieces as he laboured to keep it in the air, still diving towards the sea with the revolutions counter gone mad and the engines in coarse pitch. Calmly, he wound back the actuating wheel controlling the aircraft's trim, so that if he himself was hit and fell from the controls, the Wellington should automatically seek to recover from the dive. Then the elevator controls collapsed, and he knew that the aircraft was doomed. Beside him Tom May fought to help pull back the control column. Jones, lying behind them, was astounded to see a burst of fire tear up the floor between May's legs as he stood straddled in the cockpit. May was hit only once, slightly wounded in the buttock. They saw the sand dunes of an island rushing up to meet them. It was Borkum, just a few miles east of neutral Dutch waters. With a grinding, wrenching, protracted shriek of metal and whirlwind of sparks from the frozen ground beneath, Ruse brought the Wellington to rest. There were a few seconds of merciful silence. May jettisoned the canopy and jumped down. Ruse was about to follow when he heard Jones's painful cry: 'I'm trapped!' As flames began to seep up the fuselage, Ruse hoisted Jones off the floor. 'My God, you're heavy, Jonah,' he complained. Then he half-dragged, half-carried the gunner out of the wrecked aircraft. The three men lay silent, in pain and exhaustion behind a dune in the sandy, frozen waste as their aircraft burned. At last a German patrol arrived to greet them with the time-honoured cliché: 'For you the war is over!' The rear section of the Wellington formation had ceased to exist.

It is a measure of the fierceness of the struggle that continued for almost thirty minutes around Kellett's Wellingtons that of those aircraft which survived, 9 Squadron claimed six certain 'kills' and six 'probables' among the German fighters, 149 Squadron the same, and Lemon of 37 Squadron a single. Their turrets were strewn with cartridge cases, their wings, tanks and fuselages holed repeatedly. Almost all had jettisoned their bombs in the sea. Three aircraft remained of the leading section under Kellett. The port and rear sections had vanished entirely. On the starboard side, Sergeant Ramshaw was still tucked in underneath, streaming fuel, while immediately ahead of Peter Grant, Briden of 149 Squadron was also heavily damaged and losing fuel fast.

Then, perhaps ninety miles west of Wilhelmshaven, Grant glanced up for a moment to find that 'quite suddenly, there were just a few Wellingtons flying alone in the clear sky'.[4] The German fighters had reached the limit of their endurance. They retired, to claim thirty-four victories, twenty-six of which were confirmed by the Reich Air Ministry. They had lost two Me109s, a further one which was written off after crashlanding, and almost all the Me110s which took part in the action were more or less damaged. In reality, ten British aircraft had already been totally destroyed out of the original twenty-four. It was not an impressive performance by the Germans. Even after their belated interception, they made repeated ineffectual long-range attacks. If their tactics had been better, it would have been remarkable if any

British aircraft survived at all. But for the British, by any objective assessment, it had been a disastrous day.

As the remnants of the formation lumbered home, the Wellingtons of Briden and Ramshaw were steadily dropping back. There was no longer any merit in radio silence. Briden called Harris, his section leader: could they take the shortest possible route home, because he was losing petrol very fast? Forty miles out from the English coast, a few minutes after 3 pm, Briden's engines spluttered and died. The Wellington glided smoothly down towards the icy sea below, cartwheeled to starboard as it touched, then settled. Harris circled above it, watching the crew struggling around their dinghy. He ordered his own crew to throw out their dinghy to assist. After a struggle, they set it free. But it inflated as it fell away from the aircraft, struck the tail and jammed there. With his rudder controls crippled, Harris with difficulty flew on to make a forced landing at Coltishall. Lifeboats put out from Cromer and Sheringham to Briden's last reported position, but the North Sea in December is not a welcoming refuge. Like so many men who ditched in her waters in the next five years, neither Briden nor his crew were ever seen again. They had been warned in training that they might expect to survive for fifteen minutes under such conditions.

Sergeant Ramshaw of 9 Squadron was more fortunate. His engines died at last just short of Grimsby. Lilley, his rear gunner was already critically wounded when they ditched and was lost with the aircraft. Ramshaw and the remainder of his crew were picked up by a trawler and by nightfall lay in Grimsby hospital.

Thus the twelve surviving aircraft – ten, discounting the two which had not attacked – came home. Soon after 4 pm, after almost seven hours in the air, the eight remaining in the formation touched down. At Honington, only Peter Grant and Sergeant Purdy landed. Grant told his tale to the CO and the Adjutant in the officers' mess, then went exhausted to bed. An officer who put his head into the mess a little later found it deserted but for the CO, who sat bowed and old, alone by the fireplace.

Slaughter of these proportions at this, still squeamish, moment of the war provoked an unprecedented upheaval and post-mortem both at 3 Group and at Bomber Command. Ludlow-Hewitt, a C-in-C already well known for his sensitivity to casualties, flew in person to Norfolk to hear first-hand accounts of the operation. Group-Captain Hugh Pughe-Lloyd, a 3 Group staff officer who had commanded 9 Squadron until a few weeks before, said in one of a mass of reports inspired by the disaster: 'I dislike the course taken to the target. On this occasion we make a landfall near the German-Danish frontier and run the whole way down it, giving the enemy all the warning he can get.' This was almost the only instance of open criticism of the planning of the operation.

Most senior officers studied the events of 18 December and drew much more hopeful and face-saving conclusions. They readily accepted that Wellingtons must be provided with beam guns and self-sealing tanks. But granted these measures, it seemed to them that the elements of Kellett's formation which stuck rigidly together as ordered had fared astonishingly well. Only one of Kellett's own section of four aircraft had been lost, and an impressive list of enemy fighters destroyed was accepted. Of the six aircraft on the starboard side, it seemed reasonable to assume that all would have survived the battle had they been fitted with self-sealing tanks.

Why therefore had the port and rear sections of the formation fared so badly? Air Vice-Marshal Baldwin's report to Ludlow-Hewitt contained no breath of criticism of the strategic and tactical concepts underlying the operation:

> I am afraid [he wrote firmly on 23 December] there is no doubt that the heavy casualties experienced by 9 and 37 Squadrons were due to poor leadership and consequent poor formation flying. Squadron-Leader Guthrie is reported as being almost a mile ahead of his formation. For some unknown reason Hue-Williams, who, I thought, was a very sound leader, appears to have done the same thing . . .
>
> I have not by any means given up hope of being able to drive home the lessons learnt. . . . I have already taken steps to prevent a repetition, but I was allowing a certain period to elapse before pinning results on to individual actions, although instances of bad leadership have already been pointed out to all units.

3 Group's summary of the lessons to be derived from the events of 18 December concluded: 'There is every reason to believe that a very close formation of six Wellington aircraft will emerge from a long and heavy attack by enemy fighters with very few, if any, casualties to its own aircraft.'

3 Group's Operational Instruction No. 21 of 23 December 1939 stated: 'With the intention of combining useful training and operations, sweeps will continue to be carried out. . . . If enemy aircraft are encountered, gunners will be able to practise shooting at real targets instead of drogues . . .'

On 2 January 1940, Air Vice-Marshal A. T. Harris, the future C-in-C of Bomber Command, then serving as AOC of 5 Group, told HQ at High Wycombe that so long as three bombers were in company in daylight, the pilots 'considered themselves capable of taking on anything'.

Peter Grant was sent to lecture to a Bomber Command gunnery school on the realities of facing fighter attack in daylight. On his return, he was reprimanded for having given 'an unpatriotic talk likely to cause dismay and demoralization'.

The Germans at Wilhelmshaven were unaware that Ruse had dropped his bombs in the sea before crashing, and were therefore bewildered to find that his Wellington had apparently flown the operation unloaded. The only logical conclusion that they could reach about the behaviour of Kellett's formation was that the British had been carrying out some suicidal form of exercise, which was indeed not far from the truth.

On the night of 18 December, there was a knock on the door of Mary Jones's little flat in Feltwell. It was 37 Squadron's adjutant, struggling to mask his embarrassment in harshness: 'You know your husband's not coming back, don't you?' That night Mary dreamt of Harry's golden hair floating on the sea. She was quickly gone from Feltwell. The station made it apparent that it was anxious to rid itself of its dreadful crop of widows as hastily as possible. It was weeks before she heard confirmation of German radio claims that Harry, with May and Ruse, was a prisoner. It was Christmas 1945 before the Joneses sat down together to eat the pudding that she had made that winter of 1939, and which she stored so hopefully through the six Christmases of war that followed.

Most of the other men who survived 18 December were killed on operations in the years that followed. Bill Macrae, 9 Squadron's tough little Canadian, died perhaps most pathetically of all, on collecting a Distinguished Flying Cross from Buckingham Palace a few weeks after the Wilhelmshaven raid. After a celebration with his crew, he took off from Weybridge to fly home to Norfolk, and almost immediately crashed into the ground.

But if it had not been Weybridge, the odds were overwhelming that it would have been Cologne, Hanover, Berlin, or Frankfurt, some night in the five years that were to come. The Wilhelmshaven raid was merely a blooding, a minor incident in the first weeks of a long war. Its importance was that it struck a major blow at the strategic and tactical concepts on which the Royal Air Force had based itself for twenty years – although its leaders declined to see the battle in these terms. The Wilhelmshaven raid was the beginning of the confrontation between the theory and practice of warfare that would dominate the long campaign of Bomber Command.

I

In the Beginning, Trenchard

British Bomber Policy, 1917–40

'From the time when the first experiments were made in air power during the First World War until the great Bomber Command attack on Dresden and the discharge of the first atomic bombs by the USAAF thirty years later, the whole development and direction of strategic bombing was a highly and continuously controversial matter. . . . The controversy raged over the whole field of the offensive which embraced questions of strategic desirability, operational possibility, economic, industrial and moral vulnerability, and legal and moral responsibility. . . .'

– *Official History of the Strategic Air Offensive against Germany 1939–45*[1]

One clear May morning in 1917, a formation of German Gotha bombers droned high over the Kent coastal town of Folkestone and the neighbouring army camp of Shornecliffe. In the few minutes that followed, their bombs killed 95 people and injured 175. The seventy-four British aircraft which took off to intercept them were able to shoot down only one Gotha. Three weeks later, on 17 June, twenty-one Gothas mounted a second daylight attack. Seven bombers attacked small towns in Kent and Essex, while the remaining fourteen flew on in diamond formation to attack London itself. 162 people were killed and 432 injured. A third attack on 7 July killed 65 people and injured 245. It was the inauguration of strategic air bombardment, the first significant attempt by an air force to take advantage of this third dimension of warfare to pass above protecting armies and navies and strike direct at the nation of the enemy.

The consternation, indeed panic, provoked by the German attack was considerably greater among British politicians and in the press than among Britons at large. All governments in wartime are nervous about the effects of unexpected shocks on national morale, and the Gothas came at a moment when mounting war-weariness was apparent in Britain. The bombings seemed to signal the inception of a new, ghastly age, vividly foretold as far back as 1908 by England's most celebrated contemporary prophet, H. G. Wells, in his book *The War in the Air*. Extraordinary efforts were made to strengthen the air defences, especially around London. Fighters were recalled from France. Guns and searchlights were deployed for the first time in depth. Lloyd George, the Prime Minister, appointed himself and one of the Empire's foremost heroes, the rehabilitated Boer General Smuts, as a committee of two, to study how best Britain's air forces could be reorganized to meet the German threat; above all, to consider whether the national interest was best served by maintaining the air forces as subordinate corps within the British Army and Royal Navy. In the event, Smuts conducted the inquiry single-handed, with the assistance of army and Royal Flying Corps officers. The Smuts Report, as it became known, inspired the creation of the Royal Air Force as an independent service alongside the army and navy. More than this, Smuts sowed the germ of the seed of the vast British strategic air offensive in the Second World War.

Somewhere in the midst of his rather cursory investigation, Smuts became captivated by the vision of air power. He was fascinated by the concept of a New Force in warfare – this, at a moment when in France the Old Forces were achieving the most spectacular and ghastly débâcle in their history. His report, completed on 17 August 1917, formed the foundation on which British airmen would build a complete theory of warfare in the next twenty years:

> An air service [Smuts wrote to the War Cabinet] can be used as an independent means of war operations. Nobody that witnessed the attack on London on 11 July could have any doubt on that point. . . . As far as can at present be foreseen there is absolutely no limit to the scale of its future independent war use. And the day may not be far off when aerial operations with their devastation of enemy lands and destruction of industrial and populous centres on a vast scale may become the principal operations of war, to which the older forms of military and naval operations may become secondary and subordinate.
>
> The magnitude and significance of the transformation now in progress are not easily recognized. It requires some imagination to realize that next summer, while our Western Front may still be moving forward at a snail's pace in Belgium and France, the air battle front will be far behind on the Rhine, and that its continuous and intense pressure against the chief industrial centres of the enemy as well as on his lines of communication may form an important factor in bringing about peace.

Here indeed was a vision, and one which sent as great a shock of anger and scorn through the ranks of the generals and admirals as of excitement and enthusiasm through those of the airmen. At another time, the combined hostility of the War Office and the Admiralty would have been enough to kill the Smuts Report without notice. But in the autumn of 1917 the political stock of the leaders of the two established services had sunk to a very low ebb indeed in the eyes of the British Government. Service objections to Smuts's recommendations were interpreted as rearguard actions to prevent any transfer of forces from their own commands. Lloyd George overruled them. He approved the creation of an 'Independent Air Force' to begin bombing operations against Germany at the earliest possible moment. He authorized the build-up of a powerful fighter force in England to meet the German bomber threat. He decreed the union of the Royal Flying Corps and the Royal Naval Air Service to form the new Royal Air Force from 1 April 1918. The RFC's commander, Sir Hugh Trenchard, was brought back from France to become the first Chief of Air Staff.

To the Government's satisfaction, this extraordinary wave of activity produced results. The Germans abandoned daylight bombing in the face of stiffening opposition, and for the rest of the war troubled England with only desultory night attacks by Gothas and Zeppelins. Although the merger of the RFC and the RNAS provoked such heat at high level, on the squadrons themselves it was accomplished without excessive ill will. Trenchard, who had earlier opposed the creation of a Royal Air Force as an independent service, now surprised and confused everybody by the fierce single-mindedness with which he nurtured the fledgling against the army and navy's rapacious designs. His initial tenure as Chief of Air Staff was short-lived, for he quarrelled with the Air Minister and returned to France to command the Independent Air Force – the Allies' embryo strategic bombing force – for the remaining months of the war. The 543 tons of explosives his aircraft dropped on Germany before the armistice made only a pinprick impact on the enemy, but enormously enlarged Trenchard's vision of air power. At the end of the war, after a change of Air Minister, Trenchard returned to England not only as Chief of Air Staff, but as the messiah of the new form of warfare. His passionate belief in the potential of a bomber offensive against an enemy nation was to dominate the Royal Air Force for more than twenty years.

At the armistice, the RAF was larger than the British Army had been in 1914. But in the first months of peace, this vast organization was almost totally dismantled. Like the other two services, the air force found its annual financial estimates cut to the bone. Indeed, throughout the 1920s it would have been difficult for the RAF to resist total dismemberment but for Trenchard's invention of the new scheme of 'Air Control' for some of the wilder frontiers of the Empire, notably Iraq. Trenchard persuaded the Government that rather than maintain expensive standing garrisons of troops and dispatch punitive expeditions against recalcitrant tribesmen, the RAF could keep them at bay with occasional prescriptions of air attack. In the next twenty years, the RAF's only operational experience was gained dropping bombs, usually without opposition, on the hillside villages of rebellious peasants. Local Political Officers remained sceptical of Air Control and its achievements, but Trenchard and his followers were convinced that, in the years between the two world wars, it was only their well-publicized activities abroad which sufficed to save the RAF from extinction at home.

Between 1920 and 1938 the air force commanded only an average 17 per cent of Britain's paltry defence budget. The RAF share fell to a low of less than £11 million in 1922, and never passed £20 million a year until the great drive for rearmament began, in 1935. There was no question in Trenchard's mind of trying to do everything, of seeking a balanced force. With such tiny resources, he concentrated them where he believed that they mattered – on his bomber squadrons. He was convinced that fighters had no chance of effectively countering a bomber attack, and he grudged every fighter unit that he was compelled to keep in being as a sop to public and political opinion. Trenchard's air force was to be devoted decisively to strategic rather than tactical ends.

> In my view [he wrote, in an important and controversial memorandum to his fellow Chiefs of Staff in May 1928] the object of all three services is the same, to defeat the enemy nation, not merely its army, navy or air force.
>
> For any army to do this, it is almost always necessary as a preliminary step to defeat the enemy's army, which imposes itself as a barrier that must first be broken down.
>
> It is not, however, necessary for an air force, in order to defeat the enemy nation, to defeat its armed forces first. Air power can dispense with that intermediate step, can pass over the enemy navies and armies, and penetrate the air defences and attack direct the centres of production, transportation and communication from which the enemy war effort is maintained. . . . The stronger side, by developing the more powerful offensive, will provoke in his weaker enemy increasingly insistent calls for the protective employment of aircraft. In this way he will throw the enemy on to the defensive and it will be in this manner that air superiority will be obtained, and not by direct destruction of air forces.

In the bitter struggle to retain a *raison d'être* for the RAF as an independent service, Trenchard argued that aircraft provided an opportunity to wage an entirely new kind of war. The army and the Royal Navy greeted his prophecies with memoranda in which conventional courtesies did little to mask withering scorn. But Trenchard was uncrushable. Although often completely inarticulate at a conference table, 'Boom' (a nickname his remarkable voice had earned for him) possessed much personal presence and the power of inspiring great affection. Through the 1920s he gathered around himself in the middle ranks of the air force a body of passionate young disciples, not only captured by his vision of air power, but devoted to the old man himself. Portal, Harris, Cochrane and Slessor were among the most prominent. The Hon. Ralph Cochrane, for example, who would be Harris's outstanding wartime Group commander, met Trenchard in Egypt one day in 1921. Cochrane had joined the Royal Navy in 1908 and flew airships on convoy escort during the First World War. He once tried to hit a German submarine with four 8-lb bombs without successfully convincing either himself or the enemy of the efficacy of air power. He was still an airship man when 'Boom' entered his life. 'Young man,' said the fatherly Trenchard, 'you're wasting your time. Go and learn to fly an aeroplane.' Within a few years of this Damascene conversion Cochrane was a flight commander in Iraq, where Harris was converting Vernon troop carriers into bombers on his own initiative, and experimenting with the prone position for bomb-aiming.

In the years between the wars, air power and the threat of bombing offensives against great cities became matters of growing public debate and concern. They provoked an enormous literature, much of it fanciful, on bombers and air defence, on air-raid precautions and the morality of bombing. It is generally accepted that the godfather of air power was the Italian General Guilo Douhet, whose book *The Command of the Air* was published in 1921. Douhet ranks alongside Trenchard and Billy Mitchell in America, the most important advocates of assault on the heart of a nation by self-contained, self-defending bomber formations. Captain Basil Liddell Hart and Colonel J. F. C. Fuller would come to be regarded as the foremost British military thinkers of the twentieth century, and in later life became formidable opponents of Bomber Command's strategic air offensive. But in 1920 Fuller foresaw that in the next war 'Fleets of aeroplanes will attack the enemy's great industrial and governing centres. All these attacks will be made against the civil population in order to compel it to accept the will of the attacker. . . .'[2] Liddell Hart wrote in 1925, in his book *Paris, or the Future of War*:

> A modern state is such a complex and interdependent fabric that it offers a target highly sensitive to a sudden and overwhelming blow from the air. . . . Imagine for a moment London, Manchester, Birmingham and half a dozen other great centres simultaneously attacked, the business localities and Fleet Street wrecked, Whitehall a heap of ruins, the slum districts maddened into the impulse to break loose and maraud, the railways cut, factories destroyed. Would not the general will to resist vanish, and what use would be the still determined fractions of the nation, without organization and central direction?[3]

Here, from a soldier, was a prophecy that Trenchard himself might have hesitated to match. The concept of limitless terror from the air grew throughout the 1920s. In 1925 the Air Staff were asked by the Government to project the casualties in the event of an attack on Britain by the air force of France, with whom British relations were then strained almost to breaking point. They answered: 1,700 killed and 3,300 wounded in the first twenty-four hours; 1,275 killed and 2,475 wounded in the second twenty-four hours; 850 killed and 1,650 wounded in every twenty-four hours thereafter. This was merely a crude projection of casualties suffered during the German surprise attack of 1917. The War Office was highly critical of the Air Staff's figures, but the public – to whom such forecasts eventually filtered through – was appalled. There were further anxious questions from politicians. Trenchard and his colleagues declared insistently that the only effective precaution against bomber attack was the possession of a British bomber force capable of inflicting comparable damage on an enemy. Fighter defence was useless. As late as 1934 the RAF's fighter squadrons were still outnumbered two to one by bomber units, and depended heavily on reservists and auxiliaries to provide aircrew on mobilization. The Battle of Britain would make the fighter pilot the most glamorous figure in the RAF, but in the years between the wars the bomber crews considered themselves the elite of the service.

The most celebrated writers of the day launched forth upon the horrors of air attack with the passion a later generation would bring to those of the atomic bomb. Beverley Nichols and A. A. Milne denounced its barbarity. *The Times* declared in 1933 that 'it would be the bankruptcy of statesmanship to admit that it is a legitimate form of warfare for a nation to destroy its rival capital from the air'. Bernard Shaw reflected gloomily on 'cities where millions of inhabitants are dependent for light and heat, water and food, on centralized mechanical organs like great steel hearts and arteries that can be smashed in half an hour by a boy in a bomber'.[4] The Royal Navy, which still clung to the conviction that war could be waged with chivalry, was foremost in the assault on the RAF and its weapons. Admiral of the Fleet Lord Beatty wrote a letter to *The Times*. Admiral Sir Herbert Richmond delivered a lecture to the Royal United Services Institution in which he declared disdainfully that 'frightfulness, expressly repudiated in the case of sea warfare, appears to be a fundamental principle in the air'.

There was also, however, a highly articulate air lobby, championing the cause of the new force. The airmen themselves argued – as they would reiterate repeatedly for the next half century – that in the age of industrialized mass slaughter it was ridiculous to draw an artificial line at some point between a tank factory and the front line, where the tank and those responsible for it became morally acceptable targets. A body called 'The Hands Off Britain Air Defence League' was distributing pamphlets in 1933: 'Why wait for a bomber to leave Berlin at four o'clock and wipe out London at eight? Create a new winged army of long range British bombers to smash the foreign hornets in their nests!'

> Air Power has its dreams [wrote one of the RAF's foremost public advocates, a civil servant at the Air Ministry, Mr J. M. Spaight]. It knows that its qualities are unique. The armoury of the invincible knight of old held no such weapon as that which it wields. It dreams of using its powers to the full. It dreams of victory achieved perhaps by a swift, sudden, overwhelming stroke at the heart and nerve centre of a foe, perhaps by a gathering wave of assaults that will submerge the morale and the will to war of the enemy people, perhaps by ventures as yet but dimly apprehended. Its mystery is half its power. . . .[5]

In one passage of his book *Air Power and Cities*, the lyrical Mr Spaight recommended an interesting moral compromise to validate air bombardment of cities: 'The destruction of property not strictly classifiable as military should be legitimized under strict conditions designed to prevent loss of life, eg by confining bombardments of establishments tenanted only by day (as many large factories are) to the hours of darkness. . . .'

In the last decade before the Second World War, it is no exaggeration to say that the threat of aerial bombardment and the difficulties of defence against it became a public obsession in Britain and France – in Germany propaganda was already too dominant for any similar neurosis to develop. Americans could view the development of air power with detachment, conscious that no likely enemy bomber force possessed the range to reach their shores. For the rest of the civilized world, a horrifying vision was conjured up by the apostles of air power. Baldwin, Britain's former Prime Minister and a prominent member of the Coalition Cabinet, confirmed the worst fears of many people when he addressed the House of Commons on 10 November 1932, winding up a debate on international affairs:

> I think it is well for the man in the street to realize that there is no power on earth that can protect him from being bombed. Whatever people may tell him, the bomber will always get through. The only defence is in offence, which means that you have to kill more women and children more quickly than the enemy if you want to save yourselves. I just mention that . . . so that people may realize what is waiting for them when the next war comes.
>
> One cannot help reflecting that, after the hundreds of millions of years during which the human race has been on this earth, it is only within our generation that we have secured the mastery of the air. I

certainly do not know how the youth of the world may feel, but it is not a cheerful thought to the older men that, having got that mastery of the air, we are going to defile the earth from the air as we have defiled the soil during all the years that mankind has been on it. This is a question for the younger men far more than for us. They are the men who fly in the air.

'By 1933, and even more by 1934, Baldwin had developed what can best be described as the "Armada Complex" ' in the words of a political historian of these years.[6] 'The Defence of the Realm – particularly from the air – was his personal and almost total obsession.'

Thus the Royal Air Force and its bombers stood at the very heart of the political and public debate between the wars. Yet in 1941, after two years in action, it was to come as a paralysing shock to Britain's leaders to discover that Bomber Command was not only incapable of bombing a precise objective, but even of locating a given enemy city by night. The theory of the self-defending daylight bomber formation had been tested and found wanting over the Heligoland Bight and would finally be proved untenable by the American 8th Air Force. Seldom in the history of warfare has a force been so sure of the end it sought – fulfilment of the Trenchard doctrine – and yet so ignorant of how this might be achieved, as the RAF between the wars.

As a bomber squadron commander, Wing-Commander Arthur Harris explored such techniques as marking a target at night with flares, but was compelled to abandon the experiment because the flares then available were quite inadequate for the task. Harris and his contemporary Charles Portal, who would be Chief of Air Staff for much of the war, competed fiercely year after year for squadron bombing trophies, but the exercises for which these were awarded bore as much relation to the reality of wartime bomber operations as a funfair rifle-range to the front line at Stalingrad. Although efforts were made to improve the quality of weather forecasting, there was no attempt to face the fact that wartime operations would inevitably take place in differing conditions for much of the year, that indeed the weather would dominate the conduct of the entire bomber offensive. Before 1939 crews simply did not fly in bad weather. Cross-country flying exercises over England taught them nothing about the difficulties of navigating at night for long distances over blacked-out countries, for they grew accustomed to following railway lines and city lights. In the last two years before the war, 478 Bomber Command crews force-landed on exercises in England, having lost their way. Realistic training might have been carried out over the Atlantic or the North Sea, but the loss of aircraft and crews that would undoubtedly have ensued was quite unacceptable in the climate of peace.

These were the years when if there was to be any hope of striking effectively against Germany when war came, it was vital to build a comprehensive intelligence picture of the German economy. But as late as 1938, the British Secret Service budget was only equal to the annual cost of running one destroyer. Economics were scarcely comprehended outside the ranks of a few specialists. A very small branch of Air Intelligence was created to study targeting under a retired squadron leader. The Secret Service officer Major Desmond Morton controlled the Industrial Intelligence Centre, but devoted the weight of his limited resources to the study of arms-related industries rather than to assessing the broad industrial potential of the German economy.

Until the mid-1930s at least, the Air Staff showed no awareness of the speed with which aircraft technology was changing. Specifications were issued for biplanes a few miles an hour faster than those already in service, when designers were already feeling their way towards the 400 mph, retractable-undercarriage, monoplanes that would dominate the war. Because there had been no scientific analysis of the problems of destroying a modern aircraft, there was no understanding of the need for heavy calibre automatic weapons on both fighters and bombers – the inadequate .303 machine-gun was the basis of all RAF armament at the outbreak of war, and until the end of the war in Bomber Command. Barnes Wallis, the Vickers designer who later became famous as the creator of the dambusting bomb and other remarkable weapons, notes that it was not until after the outbreak of war that there was any understanding in the RAF of the need for big bombs because there had been no analysis of the problems of destroying large structures.[7] Most senior officers preferred to see a load of ten 200-lb bombs on an aircraft rather than one 2,000-lb bomb, according to Wallis, because they thus increased the chance of hitting a target at least with something. For the first three years of the war, the RAF used an explosive markedly inferior to that of the Luftwaffe, having failed to develop anything comparable for itself in twenty years of peace. When Wallis first proposed the creation of really big bombs in the 1930s, Air Ministry 'experts' replied that they doubted whether it was possible properly to detonate large quantities of explosive in a bomb, and argued that it would probably fizzle out with a mere damp-squib effect. Likewise, the development of bombsights was lamentably sluggish. The early Mark 7 automatic bombsight, with which the RAF went to war, lacked any facility for taking account of an aircraft's gyrations on its bombing run, and required a pilot to make an absolutely steady approach to the target – a suicidal concept under operational conditions.

The RAF trained for more than two decades guided only by a Trenchardian faith that it would somehow be 'all right on the night'. The Air Staff stand condemned for failure to inspire advanced aircraft design – the Spitfire, the Hurricane and the Mosquito are the most famous examples of aircraft that reached production only thanks to independent initiatives by British manufacturers. In his anxiety to create a strong organizational base for the new RAF, Trenchard devoted a surprisingly generous proportion of his budget to the building of solid, elegant stations and the staffing of an overweight Air Ministry, while almost totally neglecting research and development. There were three Air Ministry officials for every aircraft in squadron service, and in the 1920s one-fifth of the RAF's budget was spent on buildings. It is possible to blame the politicians for all the quantitative shortcomings of the RAF at the outbreak of war, but the airmen themselves must accept overwhelming responsibility for the qualitative failures.

Much of the above has been often remarked. Yet there has never been a satisfactory explanation of *why* these huge omissions were made by men who, contrary to later allegations, were neither knaves nor fools. Many of them stemmed directly or indirectly from a reluctance openly to discuss the real nature of a strategic bomber offensive. Both in those years and up to the present day, RAF officers have asserted that they were planning for an attack on the industrial infrastructure of the enemy, by destroying his factories and vital installations. Air Vice-Marshal Sir John Steel, later Bomber Command's first C-in-C, declared in 1928 that 'there has been a lot of nonsense talked about killing women and children. Every objective I have given my bombers is a point of military importance which the guns would shell if they could reach it. Otherwise the pilots, if captured, would be liable to be treated as war criminals.' Both the pre-war plans of Bomber Command and the early operations of war undertaken by its crews invariably specified strategic targets: factories, rail yards, power stations.

Yet it is impossible to accept the airmens' declarations at face value. Trenchard said in 1919 that 'at present, the moral effect of bombing stands undoubtedly to the material effect in a proportion of twenty to one', and ever since it had been the prospect of destroying the enemy's morale, bringing about the collapse of his will to resist by bombing, that lay at the heart of the airmen's vision of a bomber offensive. Most of them understood perfectly well that attack upon an enemy nation and its morale meant the killing of civilians, but they were reluctant to say so, and even at the height of their offensive in the Second World War, their political masters remained persistently deceitful about revealing the nature of what was being done to Germany. In 1927 and even 1937, it seemed unthinkable to make the kind of mathematical projection carried out as a routine daily exercise at Bomber Command headquarters in 1943, in which 'Effort' measured 'tons of bombs claimed dropped per built-up acre attacked', 'Efficiency' measured 'acres of devastation per ton of bombs claimed dropped', and 'Success' was calculated by 'acres of devastation per acre of built-up area attacked'.

No scientific study had been conducted in 1917 (of the sort that would be made so thoroughly and with such startling conclusions in the Second World War) of the effects on British morale and productivity of the German air attacks. Airmen merely remembered the shock and outcry among the civilian population, and the political panic which had ensued. The notion had bitten deep of a 'soft centre' at the heart of a nation behind its shield of armies and navies, that air forces might and must attack.

> In air operations against production [wrote the future Chief of Air Staff, Group-Captain John Slessor, in 1936] the weight of attack will inevitably fall upon a vitally important, and not by nature very amenable, section of the community – the industrial workers, whose morale and sticking power cannot be expected to equal that of the disciplined soldier. And we should remember that if the moral effect of air bombardment was serious seventeen years ago, it will be immensely more so under modern conditions.[8]

Perhaps the central conscious or subconscious reason that the RAF devoted so little thought to the successful execution of a precision air attack between the wars was that, on the evidence of the 1917 experience, no very accurate aim seemed necessary to provoke the desired moral collapse. In a memorandum of 1938 the Air Staff distinguished two forms of bombing against: '(1) the "precise target", eg a power station . . . (2) the "target group", of considerable area in which are concentrated many targets of equal or nearly equal importance on which accurate bombing is not necessary to achieve valuable hits, eg parts of cities, industrial towns, distribution centres or storage areas'. If a few tons of German bombs had caused a major political crisis in London in 1917, it seemed reasonable to assume that many times more bombs on such a 'target group' as Berlin would provoke a veritable cataclysm. It is also worth remembering that when airmen conceived a future enemy moral collapse in which a crazed and deprived civilian population roamed the streets shooting and looting and demanding peace behind the back of their own armies, they were not weaving a fantasy but remembering the reality of Germany in 1918, albeit forgetting the military collapse that simultaneously took place.

Yet at a time when fierce public controversy raged around the legitimacy of air bombardment, when they were attempts to outlaw the very existence of the bomber at the international conference table, it would have been unthinkable publicly to debate a strategic air offensive in terms of terrorizing a nation into suing for peace. And this, for all the talk of 'centres of production and communication', was really the point at issue. The RAF's belief in attacking industrial areas stemmed not from realistic analysis of the prospects of smashing enough industrial plant to break the German economy (although much lip-service was paid to that end), but from belief that the will of industrial workers would collapse when bombs rained around their factories and homes. The pre-war RAF was geared to the execution of a strategic terror bombing campaign and this was at the core of the Trenchard doctrine.

Perhaps the central flaw of this concept was that it was already obsolete. It rested upon the old assumption of armies as professional bodies, behind which lay the unprotected and undisciplined civilian heart of the nation, divorced from the battle and thus totally unconditioned to take part in it. Yet the essence of warfare since the mid-nineteenth century was that the world had left behind the era of the *condottieri* and entered upon the new age of the nation in arms. The historic gulf between fighting man and civilian had ceased to exist. The age when Jane Austen's characters could act out their private dramas with scarcely a glancing reference to the great European wars taking place beyond the park gates had vanished. Among the great western powers, it had become impossible to conduct a major war without the support and participation of an overwhelming consensus within the nation. In a fascinating paper which he wrote as Minister of Munitions as far back as 1917, Winston Churchill dismissed the arguments for morale bombing before Trenchard and the airmen had even developed them:

> It is improbable that any terrorization of the civil population which could be achieved by air attack would compel the Government of a great nation to surrender. Familiarity with bombardment, a good system of dug-outs or shelters, a strong control by police and military authorities, should be sufficient to preserve the national fighting spirit unimpaired. In our own case, we have seen the combative spirit of the people roused, and not quelled, by the German air raids. Nothing that we have learned of the capacity of the German population to endure suffering justifies us in assuming that they could be cowed into submission by such methods, or indeed, that they would not be rendered more desperately resolved by them. Therefore our air offensive should consistently be directed at striking at the bases and communications upon whose structure the fighting power of his armies and his fleets of the sea and of the air depends. Any injury which comes to the civil population from this process of attack must be regarded as incidental and inevitable.
>
> . . . But the indispensable preliminary to all results in the air, as in every other sphere of war, is to defeat the armed forces of the enemy.[9]

If Churchill's paper had been made a basic text at the RAF Staff College between the wars, much heartbreak and failure in the first four years of the bomber offensive might have been avoided. The airmen might have addressed themselves intensively to the problems of ground and naval air support, instead of allowing their obsession with an independent role for the RAF to distort the thinking of a generation. They might have focused on the decisive problem of air warfare, the defeat of the enemy's air force, and thus conceived the need for a long-range fighter in 1933 rather than 1943. Instead, their thinking was directed towards means of by-passing the enemy's defences, either by the power of the bomber's guns in daylight, or by using the cover of darkness, in order to attack his allegedly vulnerable heart. The RAF might also have avoided the fatal disparity between their public commitment to precision bombing – which their line aircrew would offer so much devotion and sacrifice to fulfilling when war came – and the half-articulated faith in terror bombing in the higher ranks of the service. The decisive gulf between the alleged function of Bomber Command as a precision-bombing force, and its real nature as an area-bombing one, would be revealed at the end of 1941. Harris, who then became C-in-C with a mandate to conduct a full-blooded area campaign, was far more truly Trenchard's disciple than those diligent staff officers at the Air Ministry who continued throughout the war to try to direct Bomber Command's efforts to the destruction of selected key industrial targets.

In the last five years, and most dramatically in the last two years before the outbreak of war, the face of the British and German air forces changed beyond recognition. As the political sky darkened, the Cabinet approved a succession of Royal Air Force rearmament programmes that tripped upon each other in the haste with which one was overtaken by the next. Air defence loomed larger and larger in Government priorities until by 1938 the RAF share of the combined services budget had risen to 40 per cent from its inter-war average of 17 per cent. Yet the bomber still seized the lion's share of the available cash: under Scheme A, approved in July 1934, RAF strength in Britain would expand by April 1939 from 316 to 476 bombers, from 156 to 336 fighters. Schemes C, F, H succeeded each other in May 1935, February 1936 and February 1937 respectively. Then in December 1937 there was a sudden check: Sir Thomas Inskip, Minister for the Co-Ordination of Defence, declined to accept Scheme J, by which the Air Staff proposed an increased strength of 1,442 bombers and 532 fighters by April 1941. Inskip argued that the total cost would be too great, and that the proportion of fighters was too low. After prolonged debate, in April 1938 the Cabinet finally accepted Scheme L, by which the RAF would reach a strength of 1,352 bombers and 608 first-line fighters by April 1940. Airmen argue that Inskip was an indifferent minister who forced these measures through – at the cost of severe delays in creating a four-engined bomber force – merely for financial and political reasons, because fighters are cheaper than bombers. But modern historians of the Battle of Britain are disposed to believe that it was Inskip's insistence on higher priority for fighter production that gave Fighter Command the tiny margin of strength by which it achieved victory against the Luftwaffe in 1940. In September 1939, Britain entered the war with 608 first-line fighters against the 1,215 of the Luftwaffe, and with 536 bombers against 2,130.

But more important than mere numbers were the aircraft types in production and coming off the drawing board. It is impossible to overstate the significance of production policy decisions taken before the outbreak of war in both Britain and Germany, decisions that would have a decisive effect on the struggle in the air right through to 1945. Although the Luftwaffe achieved overwhelming superiority over the RAF in both quantity and quality in the mid-1930s, in the last two years before war, British designers were creating aircraft that Germany proved disastrously unable to match in 1942, 1943, even 1944. In 1936 the Air Staff issued specifications P13/36 and B/12/36 for four-engined heavy bombers and twin-engined 'heavy-medium' bombers that brought into being, in 1941, the Stirling, the Halifax, the Manchester and its ultimate modification, the Lancaster. Whatever debate is possible about the proportion of national resources ultimately devoted to heavy-bomber production, and about the manner in which the bomber force was employed, it is difficult to dispute the value to the British war effort of possessing heavy aircraft with capabilities no other nation in the world could match, although the best brains in German industry struggled to do so.

The heavy bomber was the visible expression of the RAF's determination to make a contribution to the war independent of the other two services, as was the weakness of its air-ground and air-sea coordination techniques. Germany and France, on the other hand, had throughout the 1930s devoted their resources to producing light and medium bombers primarily for army support, and both the German Army and the Luftwaffe were deeply imbued with the doctrines of mobile warfare preached by De Gaulle, Guderian and Liddell Hart. From the Stuka in 1939 to Hitler's obsession with the jet Me262 as a fighter-bomber in 1944, German planes were preoccupied with tactical air power. Yet they would pay the price in due time for their lack of an adequate four-engined long-range bomber.

The American Flying Fortress, designed as a strategic bomber, achieved remarkable performance and carried enormous defensive armament only at the cost of carrying a severely limited bombload. The early Flying Fortress also lacked the power-operated turrets which proved a vital advance in aircraft defence – albeit still insufficient to make the day bomber self-defending.

But in Britain, until the new generation of 'heavies' began to come off the production line – and with aircraft of such radical design there were inevitable serious teething troubles – the RAF was obliged to go to war with stop-gap bombers of much less satisfactory pedigree – the twin-engined Hampden, Blenheim, Whitley and Wellington, and worst of all the single-engined Battle. The Battle was an unwanted aircraft in 1933, yet such was the pressure to increase the RAF's numbers in the last days of peace that its production was even accelerated: 3,100 Battles were produced before the end of 1940. As the pre-war expansion schemes reached their climax with Scheme M, approved in November 1938, there was no possibility of meeting the requirements with new designs. Instead, bombers such as the Battle and the Blenheim, already known to be quite outclassed for modern warfare, continued to pour off the production lines. It seemed better to have something than to have nothing, at least in Whitehall. Those who would be flying the Battles and Blenheims in action were not consulted.

In 1936 the old area organization of the Air Defence Of Great Britain was abolished and replaced by functional commands: Bomber, Fighter, Training and Coastal. Bomber Command's squadrons were redeployed, moving from the stations in southern England that they had occupied throughout the 1920s when the Government was looking with such alarm towards France, taking up the eastern airfields closest to Germany, from which they would fight the Second World War, and ranging southwards from 4 Group in Yorkshire to 2 and 3 Groups* in Norfolk.

It is extraordinary how rapidly the nature of air war changed in the last years of peace, so much so that few airmen themselves understood what had happened. In March 1939, chafing noisily from his retirement, Trenchard deplored 'the continuous clamouring for defence measures' from an ignorant and optimistic public. Yet the German Me109 and the British Spitfire could now overtake bombers at interception speeds of better than 150 mph. Most important of all, the birth of radar had overnight transformed the power of the defence to plot an attacking bomber and direct fighters to intercept it. The dominance that radar was to achieve over aerial warfare between 1939 and 1945 cannot be overemphasized, nor can the contribution of Watson-Watt, its inventor, and Sir Henry Tizard, the brilliant scientific civil servant whose Committee for the Scientific Survey of Air Defence was largely responsible for bringing Britain's radar network into being. It was Tizard who personally presided over the critical 'Biggin Hill Experiment' in 1938, when the fighter station was used as a laboratory for creating the Fighter Direction organization, linking radar to the defending aircraft, which made victory possible in the Battle of Britain.

*A Bomber Command Group comprised anything between six squadrons of sixteen aircraft in 1939 and eighteen squadrons of twenty aircraft in 1945.

Yet it is important to notice that Fighter Command's brilliant achievement in 1940 only became possible in a situation in which disaster had befallen British strategy. While the Luftwaffe was trained and equipped for mobile operations from improvised airstrips, the RAF had become deeply wedded to the concept of controlled operations from secure bases. The performance of the 261 Hurricane fighters supporting the 160 Battles of the Advanced Air Striking Force in the Battle of France in 1940 was not impressive. Divorced from Fighter Command's sophisticated warning and direction system, which could only operate in defence of Britain itself, the British fighter squadrons were at a loss. Had the Battle of France continued for even a few more weeks instead of ending so abruptly in disaster, the RAF's inability to support the British Army effectively might have been even more embarrassingly exposed.

The composition of the Royal Air Force in 1939 reflected the twenty-year struggle about its purpose: there was a substantial bomber force designed to pursue the airmen's strategic offensive theories, and a fighter arm equipped with short-range, slightly-built and lightly-armed aircraft called into being almost entirely by public and political pressure, organized solely for the defence of Britain. And whereas politicians, scientists and civil servants had taken the keenest interest in the development of Fighter Command, Bomber Command was the subject of much less public concern, and the airmen were left to develop it largely as they saw fit. Professor R. V. Jones, the scientist who would play so prominent a part in the key radar intelligence discoveries of the war, was one of those who noted Bomber Command's shortcomings in the last days of peace:

> I was . . . astonished by the complacency that existed regarding our ability to navigate at long range at night. The whole of our bombing policy depended on this assumption, but I was assured that by general instrument flying, coupled with navigation by the stars, Bomber Command was confident that it could pinpoint targets in Germany at night, and that there was therefore no need for any such radio aids as I had proposed. . . .[10]

Yet the prospect of war concentrates minds wonderfully. In the last months of peace, as urgent inquiries began to flow to the airmen from Whitehall about their state of readiness, about tactical and strategic plans on the outbreak of war, the first tremors of awareness of its desperate plight became apparent within Bomber Command. In the wake of Munich, the C-in-C and the Air Ministry advised the Government that it would be in Britain's interests to accept any restrictions on bombing that could be internationally agreed. The Joint Planners confirmed this advice on 24 October 1938. A scheme was devised for a raid on Munich by two stand-by squadrons of bombers if the crisis exploded without warning: the Staff predicted 100 per cent losses. In May 1939 the AOC of 3 Group reported to Bomber Command HQ that 'Dead Reckoning navigation by day above cloud can only be expected to get aircraft within fifty miles of the target.' In July, Bomber Command's C-in-C Sir Edgar Ludlow-Hewitt was writing: 'As things are at present, the gunners have no real confidence in their ability to use this equipment efficiently in war, and captains and crews have, I fear, little confidence in the ability of the gunners to defend them against destruction by enemy aircraft.' After a generation in which, at Trenchard's insistence, the RAF had dismissed the need to make provision for fighter escorts for bomber formations, only months before the outbreak of war Ludlow-Hewitt sprang a thunderbolt:

> 'Experience in China and in Spain seems clearly to indicate that with the aircraft in use in these two theatres of war at present, Fighter Escorts are considered absolutely essential for the protection of Bomber aircraft. So far as I am aware this policy runs counter to the view long held by the Air Staff.'

It did indeed. There had never been any Bomber Command counterpart of Fighter Command's Biggin Hill experiment, designed to test equipment under operational conditions. Ludlow-Hewitt pressed in vain for the creation of a Bombing Development Unit. He met Sir Henry Tizard for the first time only on 4 July 1939. More and more airmen were becoming convinced that most, if not all, Bomber Command's operations would have to be carried out at night, yet the art of night bombing in the RAF was scarcely more technically advanced than blindfold practice at a coconut shy.

As his *coup de théâtre*, final judgement on the RAF's twenty-year commitment to a strategic bomber offensive, Ludlow-Hewitt informed the Air Ministry before the outbreak of war that if his Command was ordered to undertake an all-out offensive against Germany, he anticipated that his medium bombers – the Blenheims – would be destroyed in three and a half weeks. The heavy bombers – Hampdens, Whitleys and Wellingtons – would be totally destroyed in seven and a half weeks. The Chief of Air Staff, Sir Cyril Newall, reluctantly bowed to the inevitable. On 23 August 1939 he wrote to Ludlow-Hewitt that since it had already been agreed that the odium of inaugurating the air war should be left to the Germans.

> Our plans must to some extent be dependent on the initial reaction of the enemy . . . it would be manifestly unwise to expend a high proportion of our best aircraft and crews at the beginning, when there are so many unknown factors in air warfare of which we have to

gain experience. This would be all the more undesirable during a phase when for political reasons we are confined to a course of action which is neither economical nor fully effective. . . .

This 'course of action' committed Bomber Command to attack only definable military targets where there was no reasonable risk of bombs falling on civilians. The British Government hoped fervently to avoid provoking a mass air assault upon their own people. Instead of seeking to convince the politicians that their scruples were misguided, the airmen themselves gratefully assented to a policy that would avoid instantly exposing the inadequacy of Bomber Command at the outbreak of war. The chief tasks of the bomber force, it now appeared, would be precisely those for which no effective preparation had been made at all: attack on the German navy at sea and close support of the British Army in France under Western Air Plan 4b.

Both among his contemporaries and among historians, Sir Edgar Ludlow-Hewitt has incurred hostility and even scorn for his outbreak of realism at one of the most critical, if inglorious, moments of his service's history. A teetotal Christian Scientist of acute humanitarian sensitivities, he insisted upon being informed personally whenever an aircraft under his command was lost, and invariably spoke personally to the responsible Station Commander. As the RAF prepared to plunge into war, many of his young staff officers were convinced that the austere Ludlow lacked the steel in his soul to lead Bomber Command in battle. And indeed he was replaced on 4 April 1940, before the war began in earnest. But Ludlow-Hewitt was a highly intelligent man, who made a great contribution by speaking so frankly about the shortcomings of his command. In all forces at war, there is a fear that voicing unpleasant truths may be construed as defeatism. In Bomber Command in the next six years, there would be long periods when men shrank from discussing the emperor's absence of clothes, of which many of them were silently aware. Most fighting men believe that it is preferable to do something, however undesirable, rather than merely to stand passive. Ludlow's reluctance to lead Bomber Command on the course which had been set since its birth seemed unmilitary, even old-womanish. His departure from Bomber Command in 1940 was greeted with relief, a sense that at last the real business of conducting the war in the air could begin.

Yet whose judgement was justified by events? It is worth comparing Ludlow-Hewitt's relentlessly pessimistic minutes with a memorandum written four days after the outbreak of war by one of the young turks, John Slessor, Director of Plans. Slessor said:

Although our numerical inferiority in the air is a most important factor it should not be allowed to obscure other potent considera-

> tions. We are now at war with a nation which possesses an imposing façade of armed might, but which, behind that façade, is politically rotten, weak in financial and economic resources, and already heavily engaged on another front [Poland]. The lessons of history prove that victory does not always go to the big battalions. At present we have the initiative. If we seize it now we may gain important results; if we lose it by waiting we shall probably lose more than we gain. . . .

It was fortunate for the crews of the first generation of Bomber Command that Ludlow-Hewitt had his way and Slessor did not get his.*

It is one of the small ironies of history that the British, who had forged a strategic bomber force with the specific intention of striking at the urban centres of the enemy, left to the Germans, who had prepared their air force for an army support role, the dubious honour of laying waste the first city blocks. 'Some amazing stories of the opportunities forgone by Great Britain in observance of the law will be told some day,' declared an editorial in *The Aeroplane* of 29 March 1940. 'Pilots, confronted with perfect targets, have had to keep the law, grind their teeth in chagrin, and hope for a change in the temper of the war.' The writer may have been thinking of Wing-Commander Kellett and his Wellingtons cruising over the German warships in Bau Haven. But in this matter moral restraint and operational expediency marched together. It was to be May 1940 before Bomber Command began to discover in earnest that even when 'confronted with perfect targets', it was entirely another matter to hit them.

At the outbreak of war, Britain hastened to accept President Roosevelt's appeal to the belligerents to renounce the bombing of civilian targets. Bomber Command launched the spasmodic series of attacks on the German fleet; flew scores of monotonous weather, maritime reconnaissance and mining sorties; and sent the Whitleys and Hampdens forth over Germany night after night, inundating the enemy with propaganda leaflets. The CO of 51 Squadron in desperation entered some of his crews for navigation courses at Southampton University. Slessor, the Director of Plans, pressed for more aggressive policies. Although he noted carefully in his memorandum to the Chief of Air Staff on 7 September 1939 that 'indiscriminate attacks on civilian populations as such will never form part of our policy', he urged that Bomber Command commence bombing oil plants and power stations in the Ruhr. In the spring of 1940 he put forward a proposal for adapting the RAF's old Iraqi Air Control techniques by 'proscribing' listed German industrial cities, leafleting the population in warning, and then commencing air bombardment.

*As Slessor himself conceded with disarming grace in his memoirs thirty years later.

But throughout the long months of the Phoney War that ended in May 1940, Government, public and senior airmen alike were very content to stand passive. 'We are fighting for a moral issue,' declared a *Daily Mail* editorial in January 1940, denouncing proposals for bombing Germany. 'We should do nothing unworthy of our cause.' At an Air Ministry conference as late as 28 April 1940, when the battle of Norway was already all but lost, the Vice-Chief of Air Staff, Air Marshal Peirse, said that since a German bomber effort against Britain would be four times as heavy as anything Bomber Command could mount, 'it would therefore be foolish to provoke such an attack needlessly unless Bomber Command could promise decisive results'.

In the first months of war the nature of the air force that Trenchard had created was clearly revealed by its deployments. The bulk of the British Army was in France, where it was expected that sooner or later, the great German blow would fall. But whatever their differences on other issues, the airmen were united in their determination that they would not spend the war acting as long-range artillery for the British Army, or for that matter for the Royal Navy. The 'Advanced Air Striking Force' that went to France under the command of Air Marshal Sir Arthur 'Ugly' Barrett comprised ten squadrons of Battles – 160 aircraft, well known to be the 'expendables' of Bomber Command. The overwhelming weight of the Command's striking power remained at its stations in England, poised for a strategic offensive against Germany. In September 1939 the average daily availability of aircraft stood at 280 out of a total strength of 349 – 77 Wellingtons, 61 Whitleys, 71 Hampdens, 140 Blenheims. The Blenheim 'medium' bombers were notionally available for operations as part of the Advanced Air Striking Force, and indeed during the spring of 1940 a number were moved to France. But when the German onslaught descended with the full weight of the Luftwaffe behind it, it was on the Battle and Hurricane squadrons of Barrett's force that responsibility fell for the direct support of the British army, and tragically inadequate they proved to be. Bomber Command, like Fighter Command, was indeed 'conserved' for the future rather than destroyed in the Battle of France, but as the British army waded into the Channel from the beaches of Dunkirk, the broken battalions which cursed the RAF for its absence could not be expected to understand the airmen's excellent and historically inevitable reasons why.

The RAF's misfortune was that it had believed its own publicity. For twenty years it luxuriated in the conviction 'We are, *ergo* we are capable of a strategic bombing offensive.' It failed to recognise the principle that any theory or weapon of war is effective only if the means are available to exploit it appropriately. Now, in the first years of war, the RAF became the victim of its own pre-war propaganda. The British army and the Royal Navy vented their spleen upon the air marshals for their inability to fulfil the promises of peace. In reality, the RAF's strengths were considerable and its qualitative shortcomings were little worse than those of its enemies. In September 1939 the Luftwaffe possessed no bomb larger than 1,100 lb, and was chronically short of hardware because Hitler had halted bomb production in expectation of a short war. Luftwaffe aircraft were experiencing acute technical problems with oxygen equipment and guns freezing at high altitude. The Germans possessed no power-operated turrets for their bombers, their fighter cannon were quite inadequate, and they lacked sufficient reserves of aircraft to back up the imposing strength of their first-line. Above all, the Luftwaffe's He111, Do17 and even Ju88 bombers were no more capable than Bomber Command's Hampdens, Whitleys and Wellingtons of operating successfully in daylight at acceptable cost *unless local air superiority had first been obtained* by the defeat of the defending fighter force. At night the Luftwaffe possessed the capability to 'bomb on the beam' by radio navigation aids of the kind that Bomber Command so signally lacked. But while Germany won the first air battles of the war, she would lose the Battle of Britain even when operating bombers under massive fighter escort at short range from their bases.

Bomber Command and its leading airmen, however, would be judged not by comparison with the Luftwaffe but by the standard of their own pre-war promises. The core of Trenchard's thesis was that it was unnecessary first to defeat the enemy's air force in order to wage an effective bomber offensive, and – by implication revealed in the RAF's conduct of its own affairs between the wars – that it was not necessary to concentrate much attention where the bombs fell on enemy territory in order to achieve the desired results. Now, the airmen perceived with bleak clarity that they had made no attempt to reconcile their ends with the means available to achieve these. Nothing would persuade them to renounce their purpose before the Government or the other two services. But by the spring of 1940, the Air Staff's confident strategy of twenty years' standing had been replaced by a courageous yet empty determination to make the best of a bad job, and pray for the time to build the means to pursue their great strategic ambitions.

Only Trenchard's sublime faith flew on unshakeable. In 4 April 1940 one of his protégés, Sir Charles Portal, succeeded Ludlow-Hewitt as Commander-in-Chief of Bomber Command. Trenchard wrote to congratulate Portal on his first month in his post, and on the achievements of British air power '. . . though I am sorry that you could not use it where I and others think it probably would have ended the war by now.' Britain, Trenchard still believed, had missed a unique opportunity to achieve immediate victory with a single devastating blow from the air at the heart of Germany. Even after eight months of war, the powers and limitations of bomber forces remained an enigma to the 'father of the RAF', to most of the British public and to their politicians.

On 10 May 1940 the German invasion of France and the Low Countries swept away the Phoney War. The overture was ended. The realities of air power were about to reveal themselves.

II

82 Squadron, Norfolk, 1940–41

With broken wing they limped across the sky,
Caught in late sunlight with their gunner dead,
One engine gone – the type was out of date –
Blood on the fuselage turning brown from red. . . .

So two men waited, saw the third dead face,
And wondered when the wind would let them die.

– John Bayliss, 'Reported Missing'

Strolling out on to the tarmac at Watton and scanning the sky early on the morning of 17 May 1940, Wing-Commander the Earl of Bandon was beginning to wonder where his squadron had got to. At 4.50 am, twelve Blenheims of 82 Squadron had taken off for Gembloux in central Belgium to attack a German armoured column. On this clear, beautiful summer's day, they should have been home for breakfast.

The Battle of France was already a week old, but so far 82 Squadron had escaped astonishingly lightly. In the desperate flurry of anti-shipping strikes that were ordered throughout April to impede the German invasion of Norway, they had sunk nothing but lost only one aircraft. The Blenheims were not called upon to take part in the airfield attacks by 3 and 5 Groups which cost Bomber Command most of the thirty-one aircraft lost over Scandinavia, and which achieved so little even after the Air Ministry withdrew its initial decree ordering RAF aircraft to attack only with machine-guns rather than bombs, to protect innocent bystanders. Since the German onslaught in the west began on 10 May, 82 Squadron had operated only once, against the Maastricht bridges on 12 May, where they saw for the first time the incredible power of German light flak, but somehow came home to tell the tale. They missed the terrible battle of 14 May, when Barratt's Advanced Air Striking Force lost forty out of seventy-one Battles, attempting to break the German bridgehead at Sedan. The same evening, Wing-Commander Basil Embry lost seven of the twenty-eight 2 Group Blenheims he led in the desperate effort to stem the tide with support from England.

On 17 May, Paddy Bandon was not himself leading 82 Squadron because his navigator was away in London being interviewed for a commission. In any event, although Bandon often flew, he was modest enough usually to let one of his experienced flight commanders lead the formation, for he was conscious of his own imperfections as a Blenheim pilot. He had spent the year before the war at the Air Staff College, hearing 'Ugly' Barratt lecture on the 'great fist' of air power, Ludlow-Hewitt argue the superiority of the offensive over the defensive, Group-Captain Robert Saundby declaring the importance of economy of force, of not 'wasting' fighters as bomber escorts. Even in 1938 the students learnt nothing of radar, although there was much discussion of such theories as the invincibility of the Lysander Army Co-Operation aircraft, which was thought to be too slow for modern fighters to engage – a year later the surviving Lysander pilots would cast convincing doubts on the validity of this concept. After Staff College, Bandon was posted to the Air Ministry, and at the outbreak of war hoped for command of a fighter squadron. But at thirty-six he was too old. Instead, although he had never dropped a bomb or flown a Blenheim in his life, in the predictable manner of service bureaucracies Bandon was sent to take over 82 Squadron, one of 2 Group's seven Blenheim units, stationed at Watton in Norfolk, only a few miles from 37 Squadron's Wellingtons at Feltwell.

Like most other pre-war squadrons, 82 was a family in arms, a group of men scarcely changed since 1937. Like most of his service colleagues, they fell in love with Paddy at first sight. There was something rather stylish about having an earl, even an Irish one, as Squadron CO. When he had the charm of Paddy Bandon, the effect was irresistible. He was a mischievous extrovert with a boundless talent for enjoying life, in the front line of every party, finest shot at the squadron partridge shoots with which they passed the winter of 1939–40, chain-smoking compulsively, racing round the airfield in a little black Morgan two-seater with his uncontrollable spaniel Fluff and his flamboyant black moustache, to the impotent fury of Vincent, the station commander, who had already reprimanded Bandon for scruffiness. The week before Gembloux, an 82 Squadron pilot named Charlie Breese forgot to put down the wheels of his Blenheim before landing, and was at once put under open arrest by the enraged station commander for needlessly wrecking an aircraft. He was confined to his quarters with another disgraced pilot, 'Atty' Atkinson, and allowed out only to fly operations. At last the two were summoned to appear before the group commander. Paddy Bandon drove them to headquarters in Huntingdon himself, and stood behind the AOC while that dignitary delivered a fierce reprimand, making faces at the hapless Atkinson and Breese in the hope of reducing them to hysterics. Paddy Bandon's popularity was instantly understandable – but it was a matter for general astonishment that he eventually retired from the RAF as an air chief marshal.

At 8.20 am that 17 May, the handful of aircrew who were not flying and the ground crews waiting for the return of their charges wandered out into the sunlight when they heard a distant aircraft on the circuit. As the Blenheim approached, they could detect the erratic beat of its single remaining engine. A red Very light lanced into the sky from the cockpit. The ambulance and fire tenders bumped hastily across the grass towards the runway. The aircraft wobbled down, bounced, then coasted along the ground until the propeller abruptly stopped. The pilot, Sergeant Morrison, climbed stiffly down from the hatch with his observer and gunner. They sank down on the grass.

'Where's everybody else, Morrison?' asked Paddy Bandon.

Shortly before lunch, three crews who had been on another mission that morning arrived over Watton, puzzled by the curious emptiness of the field beneath them. The pilots – Atkinson, Breese and Hunt – had been guiding three fighter squadrons to France (with written orders that 'There is to be no fighting on the way', but no proposals about what to do if the Luftwaffe thought otherwise). Now, returning from Lille with their Blenheims loaded with looted champagne, they landed to be ordered to report at once to the CO's office. There was a groan at the prospect of trouble from Shoreham Customs about their cargo. They walked into Paddy Bandon's office to find him sitting at his desk, the sparkle of his eyes for once quite dead. 'Well, chaps,' he said. 'We're now 82 Squadron. Yes, just us.' The formation of Blenheims had missed their rendezvous with a hastily organized fighter escort, and pressed on alone. They were opened up to face the flak approaching Gembloux when they were attacked by fifteen Me109s from the vast air umbrella covering the German advance. Sergeant Morrison was the only pilot to bring his aircraft home. Before lunch that day orders came from Group to disband the squadron. It was only after a fierce struggle by Paddy Bandon that the order was rescinded, and they began to rebuild the wreckage of 82.

In the days that followed, as the German armies swept across France, and Britain entered her season of unbroken disaster, half-trained crews were sent to them from the Operational Training Units with 200 or 300 hours' flying experience against the 600 that would become a minimum later in the war. Atkinson began to teach them the rudiments of formation flying. A few survivors of Gembloux trickled back from France, among them Miles Delap who had distinguished himself in March by sinking Bomber Command's first U-boat. Paddy Bandon was touched when his own navigator and two others returned from London with the promise of their commissions, but at once offered to forgo officer training to stay at Watton and keep 82 Squadron alive. An Irish gunner who had gone to the glasshouse for desertion was released at the end of his sentence and asked to be allowed to return to flying duties. He too came back, to be killed like so many others in the weeks that followed.

The so-called heavy aircraft with which the RAF entered the war – the Hampden, Whitley and Wellington – were adequate night-bombers of their generation, chiefly deficient in navigation equipment and crew comfort. But the 'mediums' – the Battle and the Blenheim – were suicidally ill-fitted for their role as daylight tactical bombers. Cruising at 180 mph, the Blenheim was almost 200 mph slower than the fighters which it must inevitably encounter. Armed with a single .303 in its rear turret, a fixed rearward-firing gun in the port engine nacelle designed solely as a 'frightener' and a clumsy rear-firing gun under the cockpit, it was quite incapable of surviving an efficient fighter attack. Lightly built, it could stand little punishment. It packed a negligible 1,000-lb punch in its bomb bay, and could achieve less than half the rate of climb of a German fighter. Under attack, a Blenheim's only chance of survival was to find cloud or to attempt a hedge-level escape. Quite unknown to the survivors of 82 Squadron and the bewildered young trainees who arrived at Watton to fill the vacuum after Gembloux, Portal as C-in-C of Bomber Command had been fighting a losing battle with the Air Ministry, since the day before the German invasion of the west began, about the employment of the Blenheims.

> I am convinced [he wrote on 8 May] that the proposed use of these units is fundamentally unsound, and that if it is persisted in, it is likely to have disastrous consequences on the future of the war in the air. . . . It can scarcely be disputed that at the enemy's chosen moment for advance the area concerned will be literally swarming with enemy fighters, and we shall be lucky if we see again as many as half the aircraft we send out each time. Really accurate bombing under the conditions I visualize is not to be expected, and I feel justified in expressing serious doubts whether the attacks of 50 Blenheims based on information necessarily some hours out of date are likely to make as much difference to the ultimate course of the war as to justify the losses I expect.

The Air Staff could not rationally dispute Portal's judgement. But even after the Wilhelmshaven raids, it was unthinkable to admit that the RAF possessed no bomber capable of operating in daylight with acceptable losses. For the remainder of the Battle of France, Portal ceased to have any effective voice as C-in-C of Bomber Command. He became merely a fireman, struggling to meet the minute-by-minute demands of the British Government and the Air Ministry. It had long ago been decided that the RAF should seek to support the army by attacking German communications rather than forward positions. Whether or not this policy made any sense from the outset, within days of 9 May most of Barratt's Battles, which were intended to execute it, had been wiped out by the brilliantly deployed Luftwaffe screen of flak and fighters covering every potential target. The Air Ministry sought as far as possible to reserve the night bombers for operations against

German installations and communications far behind the lines. In reality, it was unimportant what targets were chosen, since it rapidly became clear that Bomber Command was incapable of hitting any pinpoint accurately in the hours of darkness, and was unable to break through the defences in daylight.

Only 2 Group's Blenheims, however tragically inadequate, could be risked on daylight ground-support operations in the face of the Luftwaffe. No ground-to-air communications existed to make their strikes effective. Efforts to provide them with fighter support were only spasmodically successful. But they were all that the RAF had. 82 Squadron were much bewildered at morning parade on 21 May. Beside their ordered ranks, a handful of scarecrows fell in, dressed in fragments of uniforms, bandages, tin helmets. These were the survivors of 18 Squadron, newly evacuated from France. Their commanding officer requested that his three remaining aircraft should be attached to 82 for operations that day. They flew with fighter escort to attack a reported Panzer division laagered in a French wood. Instead they found a British Red Cross column. Somehow they came home intact, but for one 18 Squadron Blenheim, whose unusual camouflage markings were mistaken by a nervous Hurricane pilot for those of a Ju88. It was shot down without survivors. On the 22nd, Atkinson led them against German armour at Samar near Boulogne, losing one aircraft. There was then another momentary lull after a determined intervention by Portal, who pointed out that operations in France were 'draining away the Blenheim crews at the rate of between one and two squadrons per week . . . It is the height of unwisdom to throw the Blenheims away in an attempt to do the work of artillery . . .'

But the supreme crisis of Dunkirk swept away all reservations. 2 Group were once again flung into the battle. The great pall of black smoke hanging a thousand feet high over the beaches made it almost impossible to pinpoint German batteries accurately before attack, but gave the Blenheims vital cover when they dived away from the pursuing Messerschmitts. Again and again, they flew home clinging to the waves, holed from nose to tail, desperately seeking to sidestep the German fighters. Basil Embry, who would escape to become a legendary 2 Group commander later in the war, was among scores of Blenheim pilots shot down at this period. 6 June was a bleak day for 82 Squadron, when they came home with an aircraft missing and most of the others holed, a gunner draped dead in his turret. The crane that drew up alongside the wreck at Watton to winch the corpse out of his position was one of their grimmest memories of that summer. Honry and Mackenzie were killed on 8 June. On 13 June they went to strafe a tank laager at Le Gault. They had just opened bomb doors when the Me109s fell on them. Within minutes they lost Breese, Williams and Merritt. They were all carrying the standard bombload of two 250-lb, nine 40-lb and a can of incendiaries. One of Breese's 40-lb bombs was still hung up when his aircraft crashed, and exploded on impact.

A few days later a new crew crashed on take-off, and an Me109 poured fire into Atkinson's Blenheim as he bombed. His observer threw himself to the floor to bring the ventral gun to bear, meeting a burst that ripped through the aircraft and himself, lifting the man bodily into the air. French flak hit them in the bomb bay as they hedgehopped home, flying low so that the great columns of refugees could see the RAF roundels and escape being obliged to dive into the ditches. Somehow they got home to Watton.

There were days when they flew in formations drawn from the whole of 2 Group. 'Mac' McFarlane joined the RAF as a Direct Entry Observer in 1938, and now at twenty was the most experienced on 82 Squadron. Three of his pre-war training course survived the war. One morning his Blenheim was in the midst of a long train of thirty-six aircraft, in vics at 8,000 feet, attacking an airfield near Bethune. To his astonishment and dismay, the formation leader took them over the airfield once without bombing, and began a long, slow turn for a second run over the target. The Me109s and 110s were already scrambling. Wellings, McFarlane's pilot, went into a vertical dive as an Me110 flashed by so close that they saw the crews' white faces staring up at them. McFarlane was struck by the fire axe at the stern of the aircraft breaking loose and falling upon him. The compass dial cracked and the air speed indicator reached a mad, screaming 350 mph. A line of holes stitched across the port wing, and there was a sudden explosion as black smoke poured from the engine. The pilot struggled to force back the yoke with McFarlane's assistance. They pulled out of the dive over a wood. In a series of jolting concussions, they lost the ventral gun nacelle, the bomb doors, the trailing aerial and the tailwheel in the tree tops. But the fire was out and the Messerschmitt had vanished. They went home across the fields, sending an old Frenchman diving from his tractor into the corn as they roared over him, then over the coast and skimming the waves of the Channel. Their hydraulics were gone, and over Watton they fired a red Very light. On their second attempt, they made a successful belly landing and walked away from the wreckage.

The German bombing of Rotterdam, although it killed a thousand Dutch civilians rather than the 30,000 reported across the world at the time, seemed a convincing justification for the Royal Air Force to lift some of its restrictions on bombing military targets inside Germany. On 15 May Portal was authorized to attack rail and oil installations east of the Rhine. As the summer of 1940 melted into autumn, Bomber Command's attentions were divided between German airfields in France and the Low Countries, the gathering concentration of invasion barges in the coastal ports, and the oil installations which Portal had become convinced were the key to striking at the German war machine. While 3, 4 and 5 Groups flew night after night over Germany accomplishing little but also losing very few aircraft, 82 Squadron, like the rest of 2 Group, was now called upon to fight by day and by night.

The results of their efforts were predictably indecisive. 'Object of strike: Attack 1(a) (ii) 28a Mannheim Rhenonia Oil Works', reads a characteristic photographic intelligence report of the period, for an attack on 25 June 1940. 'Photograph does not appear to show all the target, but no evidence of damage is visible.' Their losses were also predictably crushing. Under the terms of their new orders, they were not required to press on with a daylight attack unless there was adequate cloud cover en route, but it was left to each pilot to make his own decision, and more and more often they flew on missions independently rather than in formation. On 2 July twelve 82 Squadron aircraft took off. Ten turned back for lack of cloud cover, but of the two which went on, one was lost. The figures were the same for 7 July and 11 July. Three aircraft had thus been lost for six sorties completed. On the 13th, nine Blenheims took off and two more were lost. On the 18th, only two aircraft attacked of the twelve which took off.

On 29 July, Bill Keighley was the pilot of one of four aircraft which were sent in daylight to attack oil refineries at Hamburg. A psychologist had just come down to study 82 Squadron's morale, and reported that he was astonished to find it so buoyant. If he had talked to Flight-Lieutenant Keighley, the young officer would have told him that he did not expect to last the course. At that time, indeed, nobody on 82 seemed to know when a tour of operations was supposed to finish, because no one had ever completed one. Keighley had arrived at the squadron on 20 June and had since noticed that the crews who fared best were those who allowed themselves to think least. On this, his ninth and last operation with Bomber Command, he set course conscious of all sorts of ill omens, because he had taken off through a covey of Norfolk's ubiquitous partridges, downing them all. A man who disliked killing things, he felt that they were in for a bad day.

He had been an engineer in his father's business in Darlington until 1936, when on his third application he was accepted for a short-service commission. He operated the RAF's full range of obsolete medium bombers before the war, the Fairey Gordon, the Wellesley, the Battle and finally the Blenheim, but he reached 82 with very little experience of flying with a full bombload. Like other pilots, he had developed a healthy respect for the Blenheim's alarming accident rate. Banking before adequate airspeed had been obtained on take-off killed scores of novices. There had always been a deep-seated RAF belief that an uncomfortable pilot – indeed preferably a pilot in an open cockpit – remained a wide-awake pilot. There was no danger of falling asleep in a Blenheim, with a generator too weak to support a proper heating system, and crews in winter reduced to flying encased in water-filled 'Ever-Hot' bags to escape freezing. The Blenheim's windscreen was of unstressed glass that could and did shatter under the impact of a passing pigeon. It was not an aircraft to give confidence to the inexperienced.

After flying eastwards across the North Sea, Keighley turned south on the dogleg approach to Hamburg. The clouds had evaporated and the sky ahead was completely clear. Only one of his colleagues risked an attack on 29 July, closing in to bomb, missing the target, then narrowly escaping the pursuing gaggle of Messerschmitts. Keighley decided instead to divert to their secondary target, Leuwarden airfield in northern Holland. They attacked from 2,000 feet and had turned across the coast for home when the gunner reported two Me110s closing fast. Pulling the 9-lb boost lever that gave the engines a burst of extra power at the cost of very rapid fuel consumption, Keighley drove the Blenheim at its 265 mph maximum speed towards a friendly island of cloud. It was quickly clear that he would lose the race. Still minutes short of safety, the first bursts of fire began to clatter through the fuselage, and as Keighley pushed the aircraft into a steep dive for the sea, he heard the gunner's agonized cry: 'I'm hit! I can't see!' The turret never fired and there was sudden silence on the intercom. The German fighters swung in again. Keighley felt as if he was in a corrugated iron shed with someone bouncing dried peas on the roof. Cannon fire rippled into the fuselage. The windscreen shattered, the engine nacelles were riddled.

Then suddenly they were in cloud, and oblivious of the splinters in his leg and back Keighley muttered exultantly: 'We've made it!' In the crowded five minutes of the action, the observer, apparently paralysed, hung over the ventral gun without firing a shot. The aircraft broke from the cloud bank to find itself alone in the peaceful sky, and for a moment Keighley sank back, exhausted with relief. Then the propeller sheared from the port engine and spun glittering away towards the sea. The oil pressure on the starboard engine began to drop rapidly as oil poured from a fractured line. 'There's no future in this,' thought Keighley, and swung resignedly back towards the German coast. He saw the Texel ahead, and threw out his maps and the radio frequency list while they were still losing height over the sea. They crashlanded in a cornfield, where they found the gunner dead. Keighley and his observer were taken away in a German ambulance, having been inspected by the very cocky young Luftwaffe Me110 pilot who had brought them down. Keighley spent six weeks in hospital before being transferred to wait out the next five years in a prison camp.

In the autumn of 1940, as the threat of invasion hung over England, 82 Squadron's aircrew were pushed through a punishing, unyielding cycle of operations against barges and oil installations interspersed with long, dreary Invasion Stand-By duties. The Blenheims were moved to the satellite airfield of Bodney, leaving 21 Squadron in sole possession of Watton, and the crews now lived in a nearby mansion requisitioned by the RAF, Claremont Hall. The house had been taken over complete with furniture and fittings, and the young men revelled in the unaccustomed elegance, whenever they were allowed to enjoy it. Every night the stand-by crews had to sleep in their aircraft, with one officer dossing down alone in the woodman's cottage by the flarepath that served as a Flight Office. They carried revolvers on the ground and in the air.

When they were stood down for a few hours, they hired a coach to go to a dance hall, or made for The George in Fakenham or the Samson and Hercules in Norwich, 2 Group's unofficial headquarters. Meeting crews from other squadrons was a grim business: 'How's old so-and-so?' 'Oh, didn't you know? He bought it on Thursday. . . .' Girls were passed from dead pilots to their successors with the fatalism that became part of the harsh legend of Bomber Command. They always seemed to know the targets, and at this time when Fifth Column mania was rife, more than one pilot began to study the blonde beside him at the bar with the most extravagant suspicions.

Bodney itself was alive with game, and the autumn days were soon peppered with reckless gunfire as pilots and ground crews emptied pistols and rifles at hares, rabbits, partridges and pheasants, frequently narrowly missing the Church Army canteen van parked beside the trees that lined the field. The airmen commuted to and fro between Watton and Claremont Hall on trucks that often went home with the spoils of sport hung ready skinned or plucked over the tailgate. Even after Gembloux, even after the deadly stream of losses throughout the summer, 'Mac' McFarlane was surprised how he and many of the others could still treat everything that happened to them as a great lark, glorified 'cops and robbers': 'To us kids, it was all a marvellous game at first.'

But the squadron's spirits slipped when Paddy Bandon vanished to 2 Group headquarters staff, and in his place came a chilly, ruthless officer who feared nothing himself and had no sympathy for others who obviously did. The new CO was given to cutting remarks about his pilots in the mess, muttering as he watched through the window a Blenheim taking off for an operation: 'Well, I suppose *he'll* find some excuse to creep back before he's half way across the Channel.' One day the CO returned from a strike with the underside of his Blenheim scarred with shrapnel from the explosion of his own bombs beneath him. He called out all the crews to gaze at it: '*That* is the way I expect crews to bomb, and *that* is the height at which I expect them to attack!' he announced furiously. The squadron shrugged its shoulders. Even when crews were being lost faster then they could unpack, they did not shrink from doing the job. But they shared no enthusiasm for a man who was obviously indifferent to his own survival. When he went missing soon afterwards, he was unregretted.

In his place came 'Black Mac' – Wing Commander John Macdonald – sent down from 4 Group to pull the squadron together, no mean task when it was being decimated weekly, when some crews went so rapidly that the Squadron Office did not bother to enter their names in the operational record book. They were not so much demoralized as brutally fatalistic. 'Where are my quarters, please?' asked a big, red-headed former Church of England parson who arrived in the sergeants' mess one afternoon having put aside his dog collar to become an air gunner. 'I wouldn't worry if I was you,' said Bill Magrath blithely, a hardened young veteran of twenty. 'You won't be here a week.'

The planning of operations was a cottage industry. McFarlane, first into the Briefing Room one evening, was summoned to the big map by Vincent, the station commander. He pointed to the flags stuck at intervals across northern Europe: 'Well, you're first. Take your pick.' McFarlane settled for a German aerodrome. In the event, they found it empty, and on their own initiative searched for something better. They unloaded their bombs on a steelworks close to the Dutch border, took a photograph, and came home to show it to the Intelligence Officer. He was horrified: 'Good God, you might have killed women and children.' With the perverse irony of the times, they were taken off operations for three days in punishment.

The short, savage encounters with the enemy, lasting perhaps two or three hours, seemed to create a quite different atmosphere from that of the night bomber stations later in the war, when crews were flying over Germany for eight, nine, ten hours or longer. Bodney in 1940 was more akin to a Royal Flying Corps field in France in the First World War, with its frightful losses and carefully contrived callousness. All these men were still pre-war regulars or reservists or auxiliaries, not yet the wartime volunteers from every corner of civilian life. Afterwards, it was the very squandering of relatively experienced crews in the first year of war that left some men with bitter memories. But at the time they gave themselves willingly enough. There was still a dogged amateurishness about their approach to war that would not survive many more months. It was 'not done' to think too much about personal safety, and dinghy drill always developed into a party. For a long time parachutes were seldom worn because they were uncomfortable, and the use of oxygen was thought rather 'sissy' until a crew passed out at 20,000 feet. There was only one neurosis common to aircrew throughout the war. Rather sheepishly, some met it by installing a piece of armour plate under their seat; others by putting a steel helmet beneath themselves as they approached the target. There is no evidence that this ever saved life or even manhood, but it made them feel better.

On the ground, 'Uncle Duggie' – Flight Lieutenant Douglas, the intelligence officer – was their confidant. A greying veteran of the Royal Flying Corps twenty-five years before, he worried about their fortunes far more than they did themselves, and felt the pain more deeply when losses mounted. The adjutant of a neighbouring squadron had already cracked under the strain, and spent his time writing poetry and drinking a bottle of whisky a day. At Bodney, the villagers counted the aircraft taking off and coming home each day, and profoundly pitied the aircrew. The landlord of The Flying Fish at Watton gave a party one night for the NCOs (who still lived rigidly segregated from their officers). He played his favourite Caruso records for them, and was a little disappointed by their indifference. They preferred to sing their own songs: 'Craven A', 'Moriarty', 'Eskimo Nell', or the simple ditties they made up for themselves round the mess piano:

Keep the home fires burning,
While the props are turning,
Keep the beacon flashing bright
Till the boys come home.
Then when ops are over,
We shall be in clover,
Keep old Duggie up all night,
Till the boys come home. . . .

One night they would glimpse a new face, and the next day it would be gone. Somebody would ask: 'Who on earth was that?' There was Gadsby, who arrived and was shot down within twenty-four hours. Spencer came with his crew, saw his observer volunteer to fill in for a sick man that afternoon, and vanish for ever before unpacking. One officer terrified his crew by flying with a Bible open in his lap, and on the ground sought to convert his colleagues before it was too late. The pilot's father wrote to the CO and said that he was beginning to think that his son was unsuited to operational flying. The CO agreed. The boy disappeared. 'Mac' McFarlane, who had been with the Squadron since October 1939, at twenty developed a chronic tic on the side of his face. The squadron landed after an operation and walked to the 'Green Goddess' aircrew bus past a Blenheim whose gunner stood slumped against the fuselage, sobbing helplessly. One pilot was remembered as 'Ten Minute' Jenkins, because he came to the squadron, took off on his first operation, and was dead within ten minutes of crossing the Belgian coast. A few pilots went on month after month, untouched and apparently invulnerable like the gentle, red-haired Rusty Wardell, who was studying medicine in his spare time. But Wardell would not see August out.

The transition from the prejudices of peace to the harshness, the intrinsic vulgarity of war was taking a long time. When the first WAAF was posted to the Operations Room at Watton, the station commander felt compelled to make a blushing apology for the language of his staff. 'Oh, that's nothing,' she replied indifferently. 'Before I was here I worked in a racing stable.' 'Atty' Atkinson was sent to instruct at the Blenheim Operational Training Unit at Upwood. He devoted himself to trying to winkle out some instructors with immense flying experience, who made it clear that they had no intention of venturing anywhere near an operational squadron if they could avoid it. Word had already gone round that a posting to 2 Group was close to a sentence of death. At the OTUs, the routines of peace seemed uncharged. The day came when senior staff were asked for recommendations for decorations. Atkinson put in a name. Station headquarters threw up their hands in dismay: 'Oh, you can't possibly ask for a gong for him! He's got one already!' The list was rewritten on the time-honoured principle of Buggins's Turn.

August 1940 at Bodney started badly, with a succession of aborted operations in the face of cloudless skies, while over southern England Fighter Command fought for its life against the massed assaults of the Luftwaffe. On the 8th, three crews were detailed 'to make a photographic reconnaissance of the Dutch and Belgian and French coasts with or without the assistance of cloud cover'. Two of them were lost. Another aircraft was shot down on the 10th. On the morning of the 13th, the squadron was ordered to mount a 'maximum effort' formation attack on the German airfield at Aalborg in northern Denmark.

It remains a mystery why the Blenheims were this day ordered to carry out an operation known to be suicidal, with negligible prospects of inflicting significant damage. As far back as 24 April, Portal had minuted the Air Ministry in the most forceful terms about the hazards of attacking the Scandinavian airfields: 'It seems to me the height of folly to throw away the experienced . . . crews on the bombing of aerodromes which, I think you will agree, shows the least result for loss of equipment expended on it.' 82 Squadron would be operating at the very limit of their endurance. They were warned not to try to get back to Bodney, and to put down wherever they could in northern England. But they knew that if they used 9-lb boost for even a few minutes under battle conditions, they would be quite unable to reach the English coast. More seriously, the navigator of the leading aircraft was an inexperienced newcomer.

'Mac' McFarlane and his crew were deeply disgusted that after so many months of operations they were ordered to fly again on an outing such as this. But by one of those freaks of remission sometimes granted by the gods, as they were in the very act of running up their engines for take-off a mechanic ran out waving his arms in the 'Wash Out' signal. They had been stood down from operations and transferred to instructing duties. Another crew took their aircraft. In the radio hut beside one of the hangars, the wireless operators invariably tuned to Lord Haw-Haw's German news broadcasts in English. Later that morning, McFarlane was in the hut when the bulletin came through: 'This morning eleven aircraft of the Blenheim type approached Aalborg in Denmark. Six were shot down by anti-aircraft fire and five by fighters.' The airmen burst into noisy laughter. It was only towards tea, when the empty airfield still lay in silence, that the terrible reality sank home to them.

Bill Magrath, the young cynic who had warned a new arrival not to bother about his quarters, was navigating for Sergeant Donald Blair that morning. Magrath was a country solicitor's son from Northern Ireland who joined the RAF in August 1939. Like all the other young men given immediate NCO rank in the air force at this time, he had to suffer the fierce hostility of the old sweats in the sergeants' mess, whose attitude was ultimately responsible for the creation of separate Aircrew NCOs' messes on so many stations. When Magrath first walked in and ordered whisky, there was a dead silence. Then a senior warrant officer announced witheringly: 'We don't serve whisky to boys.' New NCOs who were foolish enough to take off their jackets to play table tennis were ruthlessly crushed for their impropriety. For some months, NCO aircrew were still obliged to ask to be excused ground duties by the senior warrant officer before taking off on operations. One station CO in 2 Group was so enraged when an NCO pilot arrived late for briefing that he sent him out of the room and refused to let him fly that day.

By 13 August, Magrath had completed six sorties – three against invasion barges, the usual targets for 'freshmen', and three against oil installations. On one of the latter night trips, over Amsterdam, anti-aircraft fire turned the Blenheim on its back and blew a hole in the perspex through which all their navigation equipment was sucked out. Somehow they regained control and found their way home through the balloon barrage up the Thames estuary. On the morning of the 13th, Magrath was called for operations in the spacious former married quarters at Watton where he had been living alone since his room-mate was killed the previous week. In the operations room each of them was handed the usual buff envelope containing details of their target and the relevant maps. They took off into a cloudless sky, although at briefing it had been stressed that if there was less than five-tenths cloud the operations would be aborted. They took up station in the midst of the formation of four stacked vics of three aircraft, and set out across the North Sea, towards that very killing ground which had proved so fatal to 3 Group eight months before.

They were approaching the Danish coast when Greenwood, in the rear turret, said: 'Hello, he's off again.' A sergeant pilot had suddenly dropped his aircraft out of the formation and was turning for home. It had been noticed on previous operations that this man's aircraft was jinxed by repeated problems requiring his return to base. On this occasion, he would claim at his subsequent court-martial that he discovered he had insufficient fuel to complete the operation and get home, and he would be acquitted. The remaining eleven aircraft cruised on. Magrath perceived to his consternation that his fears about the observer of the leading aircraft were justified – he had brought them across the North Sea on a course that crossed the southern rather than the northern coast of Denmark. They were now faced with a run up the entire length of the country to attack.

They crossed the shoreline at 8,000 feet in clear sunshine, and flew steadily northwards. They were still twenty miles short of Aalborg when the first Me109s attacked. The fighters raked the formation continuously until they broke away to allow the flak to open fire as they neared the airfield. Half the Blenheims jettisoned their bombs as soon as the fighters engaged. Don Blair dived for the ground with an Me109 on his tail, and levelled out over the sea with one engine on fire. Bill Magrath was knocked unconscious by the shock of their ditching, and woke to find himself floating in the North Sea in his Mae West. Greenwood, their gunner, had three bullet wounds in his legs. Blair had vanished. They were picked up by a Danish fishing boat. Every single aircraft in the formation was shot down. For once Lord Haw-Haw reported the literal truth. Nine aircrew out of thirty-three survived as prisoners, one of whom, Sergeant Johnnie Oates almost died of his wounds. Oates was hedgehopping to escape the German fighters after bombing when his port wingtip touched a fence post and the Blenheim cartwheeled into the ground. His navigator was thrown clear with shock and a broken wrist. When the ambulance came, Oates insisted that the navigator be put on a stretcher. He himself sat on the floor. Only when they reached the hospital did he learn that his own back was broken.

Bill Magrath had a smashed hip, a broken shoulder, a broken leg and was blind in one eye. Yet on 20 November 1941 he escaped from a transit camp in Rouen where he had just learned that plans for his medical repatriation had been cancelled, and began an extraordinary journey across France via Paris and Marseilles, to the Pyrenees. Still as lame as he would remain for the rest of his life, he walked across the freezing January cold of the mountains into Spain and thus home to England. He was awarded the Military Medal for his escape, but he also discovered that having been passed 'unfit for further aircrew duties', he was automatically reduced to sergeant's rank, and lost the warrant officer's pay he would have retained for the rest of the war had he remained in a POW camp. He remained a sergeant until he was later commissioned as an Air Traffic Control Officer.

The Aalborg operation was a disaster reflecting almost Crimean stupidity on the part of those at Bomber Command and Group who ordered it. At last, however, the staff were being compelled to accept the futility of daylight deep penetrations beyond the range of fighter cover. For 82 Squadron, the Aalborg raid did not signal the end of daylight operations, but a change in the pace of their war that lasted most of that winter. The losses had been too savage for any force to continue on its course unchecked. Night after night, aircraft flew against the barge concentrations along 'Blackpool front', the invasion coast west of Dunkirk. Even after the Germans began to disperse their fleet on 20 September, following the indefinite postponement of *Sealion*, the attacks went on. Bomber Command flew southwards across the Channel while their counterparts of the Luftwaffe droned north towards London. Some nights, 82 Squadron had to provide crews for the oddly-named 'Cheadles', nuisance raids on a triangular course against selected Luftwaffe airfields in France. They dropped empty beerbottles, for like most of the RAF for the rest of the war, they thought these made a noise that upset bystanders beneath. They shot up any targets they could see, and frequently came home more shaken than the Junkers and Dornier crews in their billets below.

New faces came to replace the ghosts of Aalborg: Sam Elworthy, a polished, brilliant New Zealand-born barrister and graduate of Trinity, Cambridge, to command 'A' Flight with instant distinction; 'Messy' Messervy, an Australian who took over 'B' and enlivened mess parties by setting fire to his long fair hair and then pouring beer over it. Messervy would later be transferred abruptly to Photographic Reconnaissance – where he would die – when it was discovered that he had no night vision. John McMichael, a coal merchant's son from Bedford who had joined the RAF during the Slump, was not amused to notice, as more and more crews ditched in the sea, that it was still left to personal initiative to supply dinghy rations. After an 82 Squadron crew came down beside a convoy off Yarmouth and floated impotent in a dinghy while their gunner, with a broken arm, drifted away to drown, McMichael wrote to the Air Ministry suggesting that every dinghy should be equipped with a quoit on a rope that could be tossed to a drifting man. A civil servant wrote back to say that this was impossible, since it would cost the service 12s 6d for every aircraft.

The even tenor and less dangerous atmosphere of the squadron's winter operations were shattered abruptly on the night of 4 December, when they were sent in appalling weather to attack Essen steelworks. At briefing it was suggested jovially that if the fog continued to close in, on their return crews could bale out as a last resort. In the event,

Messervy force-landed at Mildenhall, grazing the mess chimney. Two crews crashed in the fog, killing everybody aboard. One crew was lost without trace in the North Sea. McMichael baled out over King's Lynn, suffering the disconcerting experience of descending with his own abandoned aircraft circling round him. His gunner came down on Marham cookhouse, where for some minutes the occupants mistook him for a mine. One sergeant pilot retained sufficient fuel to circle until dawn, when he landed safely at Bodney.

It is difficult to exaggerate the dedication with which most crews strove to complete these ill-conceived operations. Sergeant Ted Inman and his observer, Ken Collins, spent New Year's Day 1941 circling Ostend for an hour in a snowstorm in a vain effort to locate their target. Peter Tallis in a few weeks on 82 Squadron developed an extraordinary reputation for completing attacks when everybody else had abandoned them, pressing on to the Dutch coast in broad daylight when others had returned for lack of cloud cover. One day early in January Tallis was halfway across the Channel when his aircraft suffered an electrical failure. He simply went home and immediately set off again in a spare one. A few men, not surprisingly, cracked. On one trip a cannon shell took off the head of an observer. The gunner crawled forward to drag the body down the fuselage so that the pilot would not be compelled to sit behind a headless corpse all the way home, but it was to no purpose. The pilot never flew an operation again. The steady drain of losses continued. Moller crashed on take-off, one of several pilots who suffered the fatal consequences of oiling-up their idling engines during the interminable wait on the flarepath for the signal to go. One night Ju88s followed 21 Squadron home to Watton next door, and shot up a succession of Blenheims as they landed. Those of 82's aircrew who survived a few weeks became accustomed to duty with burial parties: 'You soon got the knack.'

The spring of 1941 brought the onset of one of the most horrific phases of 2 Group's operations, the anti-shipping strikes in the North Sea and the Channel. At a moment when Britain stood passive on almost every front, the Prime Minister was determined that she should assert herself at the very gates of the 'island fortress'. The Royal Navy sent out its torpedo boats night after night, and fought convoys through the eastern Channel Narrows at terrible cost not because this was the only possible route for British shipping, but because it had become a matter of national prestige to keep the way open. Bomber Command's Hampdens took off every night to mine the approaches to Germany's harbours – 'gardening', as it was called, would become one of the undisputed successes of the RAF's war. Finally, it fell to 2 Group's Blenheims to attack enemy shipping in daylight wherever and whenever targets could be found. In the spring and summer of 1941, at terrible cost, the pilots did so.

Day after day, sometimes in formation and sometimes in pairs, 82 Squadron took off in search of German convoys, invariably bristling with light flak and guarded by a screen of flakships. The Blenheims came down in a slow dive from 5,000 feet, through the flickering hail of fire to the very tips of the waves. As the ship raced up before them, the pilot called: 'Now!' to his observer in the nose. Away went the aircraft's 250-lb bombs with five-second delay fuses. The Blenheim lunged upwards to avoid the ship's masts and climbed away for home. This at least was the theory. In reality, again and again the attacking aircraft never recovered from its dive, but plunged into the sea streaming smoke from a score of cannon hits. Sea-level attack was not a figure of speech. Blenheims were known to come home with propeller tips and even the entire airframe bent by contact with the water. One 82 Squadron pilot misjudged his run and smashed into the mast of a German ship, ripping open the perspex nose of his aircraft and the body of his observer who had been staring through it. Another was so appalled by the spectacle of his wingman diving through the barrage to bomb that when the time came for him to follow, he froze at the controls and circled, paralysed. Eventually he came home, never to fly an operation again.

2 Group's squadrons were detailed in rotation for the notorious 'Channel Stop' duties, attacking German coastal convoys. On average, a unit lasted a fortnight before being withdrawn, decimated. As the shipping strikes intensified, the usual crop of passengers from Bodney who flew on occasional operations died away abruptly. The orderly room clerk was joyriding in one aircraft that vanished into the sea. When Ken Collins asked Caesar, the engineering officer, if he would like to come on a trip one day, Caesar shook his head decisively: 'All my previous chauffeurs have gone for a burton. . . .'

One day in April the squadron was attacking a convoy off the German coast in formation, led by Sam Elworthy, who had now become CO. He and a sergeant pilot hit two 3,000-ton tankers before the Me109s swept in, slashing at the Blenheim of a new pilot on his first operation. Somehow they escaped, but the novice was nursed home by Elworthy with his gunner dead, having had the unnerving experience of watching one of his propellers fall off. In the middle of April, the squadron was suddenly transferred to the RAF station at Lossiemouth on the north-east coast of Scotland, to attack shipping off Norway. They took off in formation and then as they approached the enemy coast broke off in pairs, each sweeping a sector of sea for a few dangerous minutes before turning hastily for home whether they had bombed or not, in the hope of anticipating the scrambling Messerschmitts. A crew which ditched on these operations knew that their slender hope of survival in the Channel was extinguished altogether in the North Sea. It was on one of these sorties that the dedicated Tallis, on his last operation with the squadron, vanished without trace and defied all efforts to find him. Elworthy was especially depressed by his loss. A few days later Ian Spencer, on his first trip with the squadron, came home hours late with his aircraft shot to pieces and somehow dragged it into a belly-landing at Lossiemouth. At he sat exhausted in his cockpit in the midst of the runway, the station commander's staff car raced up. The furious group-captain jumped out and began berating Spencer for making a mess of his airfield. Sam Elworthy arrived at this moment, and did not mince words about the station commander's sense of priorities. Only when Spencer checked the wreck later did he find that one 250-lb bomb was still hung up in its bay, and the aileron was held on only by the Bristol Aircraft Company's name tag.

One day, under the leadership of a somewhat reckless flight commander, the squadron strayed hopelessly off course on a daylight operation and missed Norway altogether. Fumbling their way home, they broke cloud a few feet above the Firth of Forth, rapidly approaching the Forth Bridge. As they blundered into the balloon barrage around Edinburgh the formation broke up, every man for himself. They landed all over eastern Scotland, on airfields or farms according to where their fuel ran out. Around Lossiemouth snowstorms were common, and more than one crew became detached from formation, and was obliged to feel its way home, sheepish and lonely.

In May they returned to Bodney. Elworthy was promoted to a staff appointment at Group headquarters, where he continued his efforts to persuade Air Vice-Marshal Donald Stevenson, AOC of 2 Group, that his command was being slaughtered to no purpose on the anti-shipping operations. Many wartime Bomber Command officers attracted controversy, but few such universal dislike as Stevenson. He was christened 'Butcher', not with the rueful affection with which the name was later attached to Harris, but with bitter resentment. An arrogant, ruthless man with no apparent interest in the practical problems facing his crews, Stevenson seemed to regard 2 Group's operations solely in the light of their value to his own advancement. 'A ship hit is a ship sunk!' he declared emphatically, as he compiled wilfully and grossly exaggerated statistics of his Group's achievements. Losses did not disconcert him at all. When Paddy Bandon tried to convince him that morale was suffering severely from the futile attrition over the Channel, Stevenson seized an inkwell and hurled it at the wall, 'Churchill wants it!' he declared incontrovertibly.

Yet for all his commitment to the struggle, the Prime Minister was greatly disturbed by 2 Group's losses. In August 1941, for example, of 77 Blenheims that attacked shipping, 23 were lost. In a total of 480 sorties, 36 aircraft were gone in a month. In one of a series of 'Action This Day' minutes to the Chief of Air Staff about Bomber Command casualties, Churchill wrote on 29 August:

The loss of seven Blenheims out of seventeen in the daylight attack on merchant shipping and docks at Rotterdam is most severe. Such losses might be accepted in attacking *Scharnhorst*, *Gneisenau* or *Tirpitz*, or a southbound Tripoli convoy, because, apart from the damage done, a first-class strategic object is served. But they seem disproportionate to an attack on merchant shipping not engaged in vital supply work. . . . While I greatly admire the bravery of the pilots, I do not want them pressed too hard.

The next day Churchill drafted a message to the crews: 'The devotion of the attacks on Rotterdam and other objectives are beyond all praise. The Charge of the Light Brigade at Balaclava is eclipsed in brightness by these almost daily deeds of fame.' From the pen of a man with the Prime Minister's profound sense of history, it could have been no accident that he compared 2 Group's achievements with another futile British sacrifice. Yet Stevenson was unshakeable. One day while Elworthy was still commanding 82 Squadron, he was appalled to be ordered by the AOC to prepare his crew for a daylight attack on Krupps of Essen. It was the only occasion of the war on which Elworthy wrote a 'Last Letter' to his wife. He felt compelled to make one further effort to remonstrate with Stevenson. 'Oh well, if you feel that strongly about it, you needn't feel you have to fly yourself,' replied the group commander blithely. To Elworthy's overwhelming relief, the operation was later cancelled on higher authority. To Bomber Command's overwhelming relief, in December 1941 Stevenson was at last removed as AOC of 2 Group.

On 9 May, 82 Squadron flew down to St Eval in Cornwall. They were briefed that evening for a dawn attack on La Rochelle. As darkness fell, the crews were dismayed to see all the ground crews quit the airfield. 'Where are we going? God, you wouldn't catch us here at night if you paid us. Didn't you know? The Stukas never miss this place.' The Blenheim crew wrote it all off as a 'lineshoot' and were sleeping soundly when the pandemonium of an air raid alarm descended. They were in the shelter when a voice called down: 'Any 82 pilots here? You're wanted to disperse the aircraft.' Amidst the hail of falling bombs, nobody moved. The Blenheims were neatly lined up beside the hangars for the German bomb-aimers. At dawn there were four serviceable aircraft to go to La Rochelle. The rest of the crews went home by train.

They were back in the West Country only two days later, at Portreath this time, for a low-level daylight attack on U-boats alleged to be tied up alongside the quays at St Nazaire. That morning of 13 May they passed over a German convoy minutes before they reached the French coast. Their spirits sank, for they knew that now they would be expected. They were not mistaken. King, their new CO, flew into the curtain of flak and dived straight into the sea before they reached the docks. He was not leading the formation because he was still gaining Blenheim experience. He had been with them barely a week. From all over the harbour light flak hosed up. Sergeant Dusty Miller suddenly found holes appearing all over his Blenheim. He pulled away over the cranes with his port engine on fire, released his bombs above the ships tied up alongside the quays, then bellylanded in a field just outside St Nazaire. He and his crew set fire to the remains of the Blenheim, and started walking. They were on the road for three weeks, until they reached unoccupied Vichy France. There they were rash enough to assume that they would be given help, and gave themselves up. They were imprisoned in St Hippolyte fort near Nîmes for their pains, and it was from here that Miller and his gunner made successful escapes and walked across the Pyrenees into Spain. They were back in England within two months of being shot down.

On 29 May, 82 Squadron's new CO, Wing-Commander Lascelles, led three crews on an operation over the Heligoland Bight. None returned. He was the squadron's seventh commanding officer in eleven months, and the third to be killed. 'Atty' Atkinson, back on operations, took over 82 with orders for Malta. Ken Collins, the observer who had been with 82 since Christmas Eve 1940, looked around at the ghosts of all those who had gone in those five months and said in astonishment to Ted Inman, his pilot: 'We're invincible!' But Inman shook his head: 'I'm surprised we've lasted as long as we have. We've got to go some time.' Less than a week after arriving in Malta, Collins said 'Bombs gone!' over an Italian convoy, and the next thing that he remembered was awakening on the deck of an enemy destroyer. His aircraft and crew had exploded in mid-air. It was his thirty-ninth operation. He had always said that he did not mind being killed, but dreaded capture or the loss of a limb. Now, he had a leg amputated in Tripoli Hospital. He was just twenty.

'Atty' Atkinson went on to become a legend in 2 Group, the only man to survive two anti-shipping tours from Malta. When he finally came home at the end of the year, the seventeen survivors of his command fitted comfortably into a single Catalina. Dusty Miller, after his escape from Spain, boarded a merchant ship at Gibraltar to find that it was carrying 82 Squadron ground crews on their way home from the Mediterranean.

'How's the old squadron, then?' he asked eagerly.

'The old squadron? There's only one left, and he's been sent home "Lacking moral fibre". . . .'

It had been a futile, ghastly year for 2 Group, unredeemed by any sense of technical advance or strategic success. The Blenheims were thrown into the battle because they were there. Little tangible achievement was expected. It merely seemed vital that Britain be seen to be continuing the fight with every instrument at her command, however feeble. For the most part, the crews went extraordinarily uncomplainingly. One of Atkinson's pilots wrote to him from a German prison camp:

> Dear Atty,
> I'm sorry I failed to return on the 26th, but a destroyer picked me off going in to attack, and the merchantman got my second engine, which complicated matters a little. This left me no choice but to fall in the drink about three miles from the convoy. . . .

Much has been said and written about Fighter Command in 1940. Yet the sacrifice of 2 Group of Bomber Command was also the stuff of which legends are made and the scale of their losses far exceeded those of the Spitfire and Hurricane pilots. It was their tragedy that few of them were left to tell of it.

III

10 Squadron, Yorkshire, 1940–41

'I wish Jim had joined the RAF,' said Mrs Leonard. 'I'm sure it could have been managed. You know where you are with them. You just settle down at an RAF station as though it was business with regular hours and a nice crowd.'

Evelyn Waugh, *Men at Arms*

Bomber Command launched its first attack of the war against a land target on the night of 19 March 1940, when twenty Hampdens from 5 Group and thirty Whitleys of 4 Group attacked the German seaplane base of Hornum, on the island of Sylt, a few miles west of the German–Danish coast.

Seven of the Whitleys came from 10 Squadron at Dishforth in Yorkshire, led by their flamboyant squadron commander, Bill Staton. The crews were full of excitement and apprehension to be carrying a live bombload at last. There had been so many months of dreary 'nickelling' – dropping propaganda leaflets over Germany, an exercise which they heartily agreed with Arthur Harris had done no more than 'provide the enemy with five years free supply of lavatory paper'. They might grudgingly have admitted that it also provided Bomber Command with an insight into the difficulties of navigating at night over blacked-out Europe, without great hazard to themselves. They lost one crew. In the mood of the day, these men were commemorated by the unveiling of an oak plaque in the station church at Dishforth. Henceforward, they would be expected to do their dying with rather less ceremony. But in those first months 10 Squadron were allowed to adjust themselves very gently to war.

'Bombs my foot!' said Good King Wence, 'them to be leaflets, Stephen!'

as *Punch* put it that Christmas of 1939. For the night bombers, there were no Gembloux or Aalborg operations, no sudden slaughters or sunlit dramas. Instead, there was only the beginning of the long, slow escalation of the bombing war to its terrible crescendo in 1943 and 1944. The Whitleys, the Wellingtons and the Hampdens, blundering blindly through the night skies over Germany in 1940 and 1941, were the pathfinders for all that followed, for good or ill.

The only pilot in 10 Squadron with any notion of the reality of war was their CO, Bill Staton. A huge, burly rhino of a man, still indecently fit at forty-two, he had flown Bristol Fighters with the Royal Flying Corps in the First World War, become an ace and won the Military Cross, and still bore the great scar across his head where a chair was broken over it at a mess party in 1917. Everything about Staton was larger than life. The squadron called him 'King Kong' because of his size. He was destined for a brewer's engineer if the First War had not intervened, but for more than twenty years now the RAF had been his life, and he threw himself into it heart and soul. A former captain of the air force shooting team, he spent his off-duty hours combing the hills for pheasants and grouse for the mess. He scoured the country houses of the area borrowing portraits and furniture to make the officers' quarters the best appointed in 4 Group. Muscular Christianity personified, he presided every morning at a ten-minute voluntary service outside the hangars. Pipe between his teeth and black labrador Sam at his heels, he loped inexhaustibly from squadron offices to dispersals, mess binges to aircrew funerals.

Above all, this enormous, bombastic figure seemed to his crews to regard the war as a marvellous entertainment laid on for his benefit. He flew at every possible opportunity. He seemed to have no understanding of the meaning of fear. After so many months of 'nickelling', he was first into the air on take-off for Sylt at 7.30 that evening of 19 March 1940, equipped as usual for every possible contingency, a canvas bucket beside his seat filled with shaving tackle and his private escape kit.

As his Whitley approached the target, the German flak began to hose into the sky, red, yellow and white – even the 'Flaming Onions' Staton remembered so well from the First War, wads of wire-linked phosphorus. His novice crew hung tense in their seats as Staton cruised blithely into the barrage. There was a rumour that the Germans possessed a beam capable of cutting the magnetoes of British aircraft, and Staton had made up his mind to test this theory by circling for fifteen minutes to see what happened. Scorning evasive action, he drove the Whitley bucketing through the gunfire over Sylt with its terrified crew. Donaldson, the navigator, shouted to his CO after one burst: 'Can't get the rear gunner to answer, sir!'

'He's probably dead!' said Staton cheerfully. At last, to the other men's great relief, they dropped their bombs and turned for home. On the ground they found that 10 Squadron and its commander were heroes. The press had been summoned to Dishforth and the next day's *Daily Mirror* told the story of 'Crack 'Em' Staton and his leadership of the raid on Sylt. In the squadron record book it was recorded confidently that 'From Captains' reports it is very evident that considerable damage has been done to Hornum.' A day later a Whitley from 77 Squadron at Driffield flew over Dishforth and inundated the station with leaflets: 'Congratulations to CRACK'EM AND CO (the heroes, and leaders, of Sylt) – from an admiring Driffield.' The four other squadrons which had sent aircraft to Hornum were somewhat put out by the epidemic of publicity that had descended on Dishforth.

Yet in the days that followed, Bomber Command was compelled to assess the reality of the raid on Sylt. Of the fifty aircraft which took part forty-one, including all those from 10 Squadron, claimed to have bombed the target, and only one had been lost. Many pilots at debriefing had given circumstantial details of hits on slipways, hangars and workshops. Yet the two photographic reconnaissance Blenheims from 82 Squadron that examined Hornum with the utmost thoroughness after the raid were unable to find evidence of any damage whatever to the base installations. The staff at Bomber Command considered every possibility, including that of the Germans having done an astonishing overnight repair job. But on 10 April the Command report on the Sylt raid concluded with stilted but inescapable dismay: 'The operation does not confirm that as a general rule, the average crews of our heavy bombers can identify targets at night, even under the best conditions, nor does it prove that the average crew can bomb industrial or other enemy targets at night. . . .' An entirely untruthful communiqué was issued to the press, announcing that the reconnaissance photographs of Sylt were of too poor quality for proper damage assessment.

Neither the Air Staff nor Bomber Command had any ready answers to the very serious problems revealed by the Sylt raid. Instead as the tide of war rushed over them in the weeks that followed, they were compelled to launch their forces where they could, as best they could. In April 10 Squadron was sent to attack the Norwegian airfields, which few of its pilots proved able to find, and fewer still to bomb effectively. In May they were thrust into the Battle of France, seeking railway junctions and bridges behind the lines with negligible success. Then the order came to commence bombing Germany itself – the oil installations and marshalling yards whose names like Gelsenkirchen and Hamm became bywords and eventually wry jokes in that first year of the bomber offensive. In the morning the crews who had felt their way through the German sky in the darkness awoke and turned on the radio in their huts to listen to the urbane voice of the BBC reporting that 'Last night, aircraft of Bomber Command . . .', and they were touchingly delighted to hear themselves spoken of. If the BBC said that they had attacked the marshalling yards at Hamm, well, they couldn't be making quite such a mess of it as they sometimes thought.

Bomber Command possessed seventeen squadrons of aircraft suitable for use as night bombers in September 1939: this slowly expanding force of Wellingtons, Whitleys and Hampdens would constitute the backbone of the bomber offensive until well into 1942. The Hampden was the most urgent candidate for replacement: cruising at only 155 mph, 10 mph slower than the other two, this grotesque-looking flying glasshouse could stand little punishment, lacked power-operated turrets, and could carry only a 4,000-lb maximum bombload. The Wellington, with a 4,500-lb bombload, would never carry the weight to compare with the later heavy bombers, but after modifications to improve its speed and ceiling, it continued as a sturdy makeweight with Bomber Command until 1943. Both the Wellington and the Whitley were exceptionally strong aircraft – later wartime design sacrificed structural strength to load and performance. Early in May 1940, 10 Squadron thankfully exchanged their Whitley IVs – equipped with the grossly inadequate Tiger radial engine – for the Whitley V, powered by the excellent Rolls Royce Merlin. The new model cruised to Germany at 165 mph and could carry 8,000-lb over short distances, but coming home against the prevailing westerly wind often took longer than the loaded outward trip. The Whitley looked for all the world like a rather pedantic middle-aged pipe-smoker, with its jutting chin mounting a single Vickers K gun, and its extraordinary tail-high attitude in flight. On its debut in 1937, *Flight* magazine wrote: 'The Whitley is as kind to its crew as it is likely to be unkind to any enemy down below.' Yet in reality the essential weakness of all Bomber Command's early wartime aircraft was their mass of inadequate ancillary equipment prone to technical failure and their utter lack of basic comfort for crews compelled to live in them for ten hours at a stretch. Each aircraft carried a crew of five:* two pilots; a navigator (the old classification of observer was abolished and by the end of 1940 a bomber navigator was recognized as one of the most important members of every crew); a wireless operator, who usually spent much of the trip with his 1155 set in pieces in front of him, or struggling to coax more power out of the Whitley's inadequate generators; and a rear gunner, who nursed his four Brownings in a power-operated turret mounted between the twin booms of the tail.

The cold was appalling. They flew layered in silk, wool and leather, yet still their sandwiches and coffee froze as they ate and drank, vital systems jammed, limbs seized, wings iced-up for lack of de-icing gear. The navigator gave the pilot a course on take-off, and then relied absolutely on being able to establish pinpoints from the ground below at intervals in the six- or seven-hour flight – 'groping', Staton called it. On a clear night it was possible to shoot the stars with a sextant if the pilot was willing or able to fly straight and level for long enough. It was sometimes possible for a skilled wireless operator to pick up a loop bearing from England, but a novice could put an aircraft on a 180-degree reciprocal course if he misjudged the signal, and the Germans

*In British bombers throughout the war the senior pilot was captain of the aircraft whatever his rank, unlike the Luftwaffe, where the navigator, who was also a qualified pilot, was captain. British squadrons were invariably commanded by pilots except in 4 Group later in the war, where a number of navigators and even gunners became squadron COs.

frequently jammed the wavelengths. On rare occasions the weather report before take-off was accurate, and it was possible to allow for the wind strength when navigating in the air. More often, the predictions were quite wrong, and the winds were blowing the aircraft off course and speed. Checking drift by dropping a flare or incendiary was a chancy business, and impossible in cloud. In these nursery days of the offensive, efforts were made to send out the bombers in moonlight, to assist navigation and bombing. In the event, cloud often blanketed the ground for part or all of the operation. Approaching a target wreathed in cloud, there were only two possibilities: to descend to recklessly low level to seek visual identification – which cost many crews their lives – or to bomb on ETA – Estimated Time of Arrival over the target, judged from the last pinpoint, perhaps hundreds of miles back. This was the commonest course among mediocre crews, who had their own saying: 'He who bombs on ETA lives to fly another day.' It was a practice that created errors not of yards, or even miles, but of scores and hundreds of miles. ETA attack was the subject of a savage Bomber Command memorandum to all Groups on 14 June 1940, reiterating that 'bombs are not to be dropped indiscriminately'. But again and again at this period, Germany was genuinely unaware that Bomber Command had been attempting to attack a specific target or even a specific region. There was merely a litter of explosives on farms, homes, lakes, forests and – occasionally – on factories and installations from end to end of the Third Reich.

Peter Donaldson, the navigator who had flown with Bill Staton on the night of the Sylt raid, took off at 8.30 pm on the evening of 27 May to attack a German aerodrome in Holland. His pilot was a 10 Squadron officer named Warren. They were on course, flying steadily across the North Sea, when they encountered a sudden magnetic storm. Flashes of lightning danced on the wings. The aircraft rocked and bucketed as the pilots struggled to maintain control. After a few minutes Warren asked Donaldson for a new course to escape the weather. The last light had gone now, and as their ETA at the Dutch coast came and went, they began to search the sea below for a pinpoint. At last, they saw the Rhine estuary below. Flak curled up towards them. They tracked steadily up the thread of the river, then turned to starboard and began to search for the German airfield that was their target. Suddenly Rattigan, the second pilot, called from the nose: 'This is it! I've got it!' The Whitley lifted as the bombs fell away. 'Give me a course for base,' said Warren.

At first light as their ETA Dishforth approached, they dropped through the cloud. They saw below them a city, and the sea beyond. They were obviously on the west coast of England. Two Spitfires suddenly wheeled curiously across them. They identified the port of Liverpool below. Warren turned to the crew and said flatly: 'According to my calculations, we can only have bombed something inside England. Christ, what are we going to do?' They flew miserably home to Yorkshire. Their magnetic compass had been thrown hopelessly out of true by the storm. They had picked up the Thames estuary in place of the Rhine, and dropped a stick of bombs with unusual precision across the runway of Fighter Command's station at Bassingbourn in Cambridgeshire. Their captain was demoted to second pilot, and known to the mess for ever after as Baron Von Warren. The ordnance experts were dismayed to discover that a stick of Bomber Command bombs had done scarcely any damage at all to Bassingbourn, and thus presumably would have done little more to Germany. Two Spitfires flew over Dishforth and dropped Iron Crosses. It had been a comic episode that might easily have been a tragedy, yet in the context of those days and the equipment with which they were operating, it was astonishing that it did not happen more often.

And beyond navigation problems, they were increasingly aware of the imperfections of their bomb-aiming. During an attack on oil installations at Bremen, Bill Staton organized one of the first attempts to mark a target with flares and Very lights in the hands of his best crews. He himself made six runs over the city at less than a thousand feet, while one of his sergeant pilots tried to decoy the searchlights. Staton's aircraft was riddled. As the battered Whitley crossed the North Sea, he offered his crew the option of ditching rather than attempting a forced landing. When they somehow reached the end of the runway at Dishforth, they counted 700 holes in the aircraft.

They were still deeply concerned about the risk of hitting civilians. The Government's 'Revised Instruction' to the Air Ministry in June 1940 insisted that 'the attack must be made with reasonable care to avoid undue loss of civil life in the vicinity of the target'. Their orders emphatically stated that if they could not identify their target they were to come home with their bombs. Crew after crew crashed attempting the difficult landing with an explosive load aboard, and it was months before they introduced the concept of 'last resort' targets – those bizarre creatures SEMO and MOPA, 'Self-evident Military Objective' and 'Military Objective Previously Attacked', to be bombed if the primary and secondary targets could not be located. One of 10's pilots, Pete Whitby, found a bomb hung up over an oil plant they were attacking one autumn night. It freed itself a few moments later to fall in the midst of Hanover. He and his crew flew home deeply worried by the thought that it might have landed on women and children. One night over Coblenz, a flight commander named Pat Hanafin made four runs and then called to his second pilot to drop the bombs. 'No, no, we're too near the hospital,' the man shouted from the nose. In these days when only a fraction of crews could find a given city, hospitals were still individually marked on every navigator's maps.

That idyllic summer of 1940 they were driven out relentlessly night after night, orders and bombloads being changed at a moment's notice, briefings and cancellations falling over each other as crisis followed crisis. In the wake of Dunkirk, relations between the British army and the RAF plumbed bitter depths. Two of Pat Hanafin's crew rash enough to walk into a Harrogate pub full of soldiers fell out again shortly afterwards, badly beaten up. The incident was repeated everywhere that soldiers and airmen met. The weather mocked their confusion. 'Temperature 85 degrees. Another glorious summer's day,' recorded the squadron operations book on 9 June. The next day Italy declared war, and Bomber Command was ordered forth in the hope of making Mussolini regret his decision. 3 Group's Wellingtons, taking off from staging points in France, were eliminated from the operation when the French drove lorries across the runway to prevent them from taking off – they feared Italian reprisals. 10 Squadron flew from Guernsey in the Channel Islands, to bring Turin just within range.

Pat Hanafin was a Cranwell-trained regular RAF officer who had asked to be posted from his staff job to operations when the invasion of Norway began. He requested Group to send him anywhere but to 10 Squadron, because his bull terrier had once savaged Staton's labrador Sam, and he did not think Staton was the sort of man to forget it. But to his surprise, Staton requested him as a flight commander. The trip to Turin was his seventeenth in less than two months. The cold was murderous. They were fired on by French flak. A few miles short of the Alps, they flew headlong into black cumulus clouds. The lightning eddied around them until suddenly there was a great flash which ripped through the Whitley. It blew the rear gunner backwards out of his turret into the fuselage with the left side of his body paralysed. It burned the wireless operator's hands, cut both engines, and put the aircraft into a vertical dive, laden with ice. Somehow Hanafin regained control before they reached the ground, but they lacked the fuel to climb the Alps once more, even if they still possessed the will. They turned back for Guernsey.

Those of 10 Squadron who reached Italy that night looked down at the great pale ghosts of the Alps in the moonlight with wonderment that would strike so many Bomber Command crews following their course in the next four years. Most were numbed by the relentless cold, for they had little experience of the hazards above 10,000 feet. The Whitley's oxygen supply was inadequate for long flights at high altitude. The exactor controls, which enabled the pilot to vary the engine pitch, were chronically prone to freezing, leaving the engines trapped in fine pitch and the aircraft unable to climb. When the lines froze, the fluid inside them began to leak through pinpoint holes until pressure was gone. Crews learned to unscrew the exactor system and refill it with coffee, urine – anything to restore pressure. Only a handful of pilots claimed to have found Turin that night, despite the indifferent Italian blackout. One aircraft failed to return. The others had strawberries and cream for breakfast in the summer sunshine of Guernsey, then flew home, a little thawed, to Yorkshire.

They were now operating from the new station of Leeming, although until its buildings and tarmac runways were completed they were obliged to fly before each operation to nearby Topcliffe or Linton for briefing and bombing-up. Shortly after the fall of France, Sid Bufton arrived to become their commanding officer. Bufton had been transferred from a staff job at the Air Ministry to the Advanced Air Striking Component a few weeks after the outbreak of war. One May morning he was having a haircut in a French barber's shop when the Luftwaffe appeared overhead and began to rain bombs upon them. He escaped from France on 17 June at the final French collapse, and came home looking for command of a fighter squadron. Instead he was sent to Leeming, where he astonished the adjutant by making his first appearance crawling through the hangar window, having been unable to find the door. He was a former Vickers engineering pupil who had learnt to fly with the RAF in Egypt in 1927. A quiet, earnest, thoughtful man, in sharp contrast to Bill Staton, he inherited Staton's preoccupation with the problem of marking targets at night, which would become the major concern of his war.

The strain of constant operations was telling on them all. Night after night they forged out into the blackness, over the flakships off the Dutch coast where they knew that the German night fighters had begun to fly standing patrols, on towards the empty darkness of Germany. Each captain chose his own route. In the moonlight they could sometimes see the silver thread of a river, and on clear nights the finest ground detail. Once Peter Donaldson picked out a German riding a bicycle. His new pilot, Ffrench-Mullen, was one of those who often flew the outward leg at a thousand feet or less, in his determination to find the target. The searchlights would flick on suddenly: first one, two, three then perhaps a dozen until the night sky was cut open by a great tent of light visible for miles. These were mere gestures compared with the great cones of seventy or eighty lights defending the cities of Germany two years later, but they were quite frightening enough. The flak would start to come up, in all the colours of the rainbow. Cold-blooded captains stooged around the target area until they saw another aircraft pinned by the lights and gunfire, then made their run, but this was too callous for most. Some pilots like Pat Hanafin fired recognition cartridges in the hope of bluffing the defences into silence. Peter Donaldson would man the forward Vickers K gun and lie behind the perspex screen in the nose, blasting off pan after pan of ammunition at the lights or simply at the German countryside to relieve the tension. The smell of cordite filling the cockpit made the crew feel that at least they were hitting back. Some pilots made run after run over the target before bombing, or like Sid Bufton dropped only part of their load on each attack. There was a vogue for making a silent approach, gliding in with the engines cut from 10,000 to 5,000 feet, but most crews were too nervous about being unable to start up again to risk this. Some, hazy about their position, bombed the blazes below in the hope that their predecessors had been on target. In reality, these were usually the decoy fires that the Germans were already setting nightly.

10 Squadron's operations that autumn took on outlandish overtones at the behest of Bomber Command. In August, for the first time, the Whitleys carried in addition to their bombload a clutch of 'Razzles', phosphorus-coated strips that they dropped on the fields of Germany, allegedly to set fire to the ripening crops and summer-dry woods under the terms of Western Air Plan 11. 'Razzles' had to be transported in milk churns of water in the fuselage to avoid spontaneous combustion in the aircraft, then released down the flare chute at suitable moments. 'Razzling' ended abruptly after a few weeks when there proved to be no great blazes in the fields of Germany, but Whitleys had repeatedly come home damaged by 'Razzles' which lodged in their tails and caught fire. The next extravagance was the 'W' mine, a small explosive device which was also carried in a milk churn, this time to be dropped in Germany's rivers, to drift down and explode against locks and small craft. 'W' mines were also short-lived. Instead, for some months aircraft carried quantities of tea bags, to be thrown out over Holland as a propaganda exercise to demonstrate that beleaguered Britain still possessed sufficient comforts to be generous with them.

Bomber Command's losses were still less than 2 per cent of sorties dispatched, perhaps one aircraft every two or three nights of operations from 10 Squadron, a fraction of the casualties that would become commonplace in 1942 and 1943. But as the old sense of a familiar and well-loved flying club faded, as each squadron saw its pre-war personality vanish and die, the pain was acute. A pilot from 10's sister unit at Dishforth, 51 Squadron, wrote to a former colleague in July:

> I'm afraid you wouldn't know 51 if you went back now. Of the pilots at the beginning of the war, only Gillchrist, Otterley and Murray are left in A Flight and Bill Emery in B. Baskerville, Fennell, Gould, Birch and Johnny Crampton are missing – have been for months. Turner, Peach, Milne, Hayward and Johnny Bowles are prisoners. Teddy Cotton is in dock with a compound fracture of the thigh, having run out of petrol and hit the Pennines coming back from Oslo in dirty weather. Marvin is at Torquay recovering from a broken leg acquired by baling out two nights later, also out of petrol coming back from Oslo. But I expect you have been watching the casualty lists. . . .

It was the same at 10 Squadron. The excitement of flying over Germany in the innocent days of 'nickelling' had been overtaken by new sensations: fatalism, callousness, reluctant intimacy with the mingled smell of burning paint, fabric, rubber, petrol and human flesh from a crashed aircraft. Above all they had learnt the reality of fear.

> In a matter of seconds we were in a box barrage, the first warning of which was a heavy thump underneath our tail. [Wrote a Whitley pilot after a winter night of 1940 over Kiel[1]] Almost instantaneously black puffs of smoke materialized around us. Plainly visible, like clenched fists against the faint light of the night sky, they crowded in upon the aeroplane from all the sides. I had just time to think that this was how the hero comes in to bomb on the films, before fear broke its dams and swept over me in an almost irresistible flood. Concentrating all my energies, I forced myself to sit motionless in my seat next to the pilot, fighting back an insane impulse to run, despite the fact that in an aircraft you cannot run because there is nowhere you can run to, unless you can take it with you. As the gunfire got heavier, light flak joined in and I gazed fascinated, as if at a deadly snake, when a stream of incendiary shells came up in a lazy red arc which rapidly increased speed as it got nearer and at last flashed past a few inches above the wing on my side, two feet from the window. As the shells went by, they seemed to be deflected by the air flow over the wing and to curve round it, describing a fiery red line round its upper contour. By now the aircraft was becoming filled with the fumes of cordite from the bursting flak shells. It seemed each second must be our last, and that we must surely disintegrate in a blinding flash at any moment, or come tumbling down flaming from a direct hit. We sat the aircraft in that box barrage for ten minutes, and did not get out of it until we had flown out of range. . . .

Some men cracked, and were treated much more generously than their successors a year or two later. Three able and experienced pilots who had been with the squadron since before the war proved thoroughly unhappy on operations and were quietly transferred to instructing duties elsewhere. One or two members of ground crew, who had volunteered for aircrew duties before the war, applied to remuster in their original earthbound trades. Tom Sawyer, one of the flight commanders, found his navigator literally frozen with fear one night over the target, unable to move a muscle or speak a word for more than an hour.

Every trip was fraught with some kind of incident. Pat Hanafin's Whitley was peppered with holes from the rifles of nervous Home Guards as he crossed the English coast on the way home from Turin early one morning. He was then beaten up by Hurricanes, to whom he could not identify himself because 4 Group had run out of two-star recognition cartridges that were the colours of the day. Hanafin decided to forced-land at White Waltham, a little Berkshire airstrip that he knew well. But as he made his approach, he found the runaway blocked with derelict cars to forestall a German landing. He eventually got down with his fuel tanks all but dry. Others were less lucky. Smith crashed in Norfolk on his way back from Amsterdam. Parsons ditched in the sea off Lympne, and only three of his crew were picked up. Cairns overshot the runway at Leeming on the way back from Ostend and crashed in the middle of the Great North Road. He was pulled from the burning wreck by his wireless operator. A few nights later he climbed out of his aircraft after a trip to Hamburg and turned cheerfully to Sid Bufton: 'Well, sir, that was my thirtieth "op" and I'm nineteen tomorrow!'

They were very young and they took their fortunes very lightly. Few were drunken neurotics, most were rather conscientious boys striving to fulfil that eternal maxim of the English public school: achievement must be apparently effortless. It is a crime to be *seen* to *try*. That autumn, Sid Bufton's 23-year-old brother wrote a letter to his girlfriend from Scampton, where he was flying Hampdens with 83 Squadron. It is worth quoting at length, because it reflects so perfectly the mood of so many young men of Bomber Command, that first year of the strategic offensive. 'Jenny darling,' wrote John Bufton,

> At last, a spot of time to sit back and answer your last two letters! I can hardly read one of them 'cos I was reading it in the bath after a hard day's work on Friday and I was so tired that it fell in the water and got badly smudged!
>
> I wonder if you were very disappointed at getting my telegram and letter about the weekend? I was mad at having to send them, but there was no way out. Maybe we'll have better luck next weekend. Trouble with us here is that weekends are precisely the same as any other time now.
>
> Poor Jenny, I'm so sorry you were so upset by my last letter. Perhaps I shouldn't have been so blunt in what I wrote, but I only wanted to put things to you as fairly as I could. You've got such wonderful faith, dear, in my chances and I mustn't upset you by being pessimistic. Anyway, I'm not pessimistic – I've rarely felt happier and more set on a job in my life, and my chances are as good as anyone else's. But I'm not ass enough to assume *I'm* going to be okay and everyone else will be unlucky, as it's a sheer gamble in the game, but damn good fun while it lasts.
>
> Way back, Jen, my idea of the future was pretty idealistic. We've talked about it so often in peace time, and were agreed on what we wanted out of life, and it was a grand outlook. But now it seems such

a myth! Like one of those dreams that can't possibly come true. We'll get married and be awfully happy – I know you'll do everything to make it seem what we both want – there'll be a cloud over it all for both of us, dear, a cloud that we can't hope to brush aside. For you, it will be the realization that you've given everything in your life to give me a fleeting happiness, and that in accepting it I'm condemning you to great unhappiness ahead, when you could have been *almost* as happy elsewhere, otherwise, with a future both safe and bright.

If the chances were very good, I wouldn't dream of writing like this, but I'm no dreamer, Jen, and the facts are that immediately ahead is the winter, with all the danger that filthy weather invariably brings to flying (your pullover will help immensely there!). Despite this, our bombers are bound to become even more active than they have been in the summer months, and we'll hit harder and wider and more often than ever before. We're the only active force operating against Germany, and as it's the only way of striking directly we'll be exploited more and more, especially as the force grows. The RAF, fighters and bombers combined, will undoubtedly win this war in time, but the end isn't nearly in sight yet, and before it's all over the losses will be enormous. I wonder how many people ever wonder what the average flier's outlook on life is in these times? In most cases it's vastly different from what it was a few months ago. It's almost entirely fatalistic. There seems no point in making any plans about the future. The present is all that matters, and in this day-to-day existence there are three things that occupy one's energies most of all:

(1) Intensive attention to one's machine and equipment, ready for the next trip, so that nothing is left to chance.

(2) Getting enough sleep and exercise.

(3) Getting 'social glow' in the Saracen's Head and keeping mentally fresh!

Doesn't sound very ambitious, but I'll bet anything that 95 per cent of the RAF take these as their guiding principles, because only by doing so can they have the most chance of hitting the target and getting back OK. . . .

Why am I writing all this, Jen? Well, it's the answer to what you asked in your letter: you say 'Do I really want to marry you?' Yes darling, 'course I do, and we'll go through with it in that spell of leave that may come through when I've done enough trips to qualify. But I don't feel much of a man taking you up on such a bad bargain, lovely tho' it'll be for me. In the meanwhile, darling, you'll make me easier in mind if you'll promise this – until we're married, if I should be unlucky enough to go up as 'missing', don't wait too long. . . . If I could only be sure, Jen, that your future was assured I'd be content, whatever happens.

> *If* anything happens to me, I'll want you to go and have a perm, do up the face, put the hat on and carry on – it'll take a lot of guts but I know you'll tackle it in the right way. And remember that I'd be wanting you to get happily married as soon as you could. And don't worry for me these nights more than you can help. It may buck you up to know that I'm feeling bung full of confidence in my own ability, but if I'm to be unlucky, well, I'm prepared for anything. Over the last three months I've got used to the idea of sudden accidents – they've happened so often to friends and acquaintances that the idea doesn't startle one much now. Realizing fully what one is up against helps one along a lot. I'm not really windy about anything now. Anyway, there's too much to do to get windy. I'm longing to see you again, Jenny, and we must make it soon! Keep writing, and when you come up, wear your hat, please, and the smile that cheers me up!

John Bufton never married, for he was killed a month later.

At 10 Squadron, Peter Donaldson, the navigator who had survived Sylt and the bombing of Bassingbourn, was shot down in the sea and taken prisoner with the rest of Ffrench-Mullen's crew on 9 July. The steady drain of casualties continued. On 16 August they were sent to the Zeiss works at Jena. 'This place has never heard the sound of gunfire since the Napoleonic War,' declared Staton in his usual ringing tones at briefing – he was now station commander at Leeming. 'Make sure it hears it tonight. I don't want to see anybody back who bombs above 4,000 feet!' Pete Whitby was flying as a second pilot. His Whitley was approaching Jena at 6,000 feet when the searchlights seized it. They broke away amidst intensive flak, and turned to try again. On their second run at 10,000 feet, shortly after midnight, they had just bombed when their port engine was hit and burst into flames. The fire died, but so did the engine. They settled down to a long struggle home against the headwind, throwing out everything ditchable down to the guns and ammunition.

Tall, fair, lazily good-looking, Whitby had worked in the wool trade in Europe until at the age of twenty he decided to go into the RAF. He was over-age for a short-service commission, but his father wrote to their local MP, Winston Churchill. Whitby got his commission. Since he joined Bomber Command, he had divided his energies between flying and horses, which he loved. He kept an old steeplechaser at Thirsk to ride in off-duty moments in the occasional point-to-point race, and a mare named Myrtle Green at Catterick.

Their ailing Whitley was hit again by flak as they staggered towards the Dutch coast. The wing caught fire and they jettisoned the hatches and leaned out into the slipstream, struggling to suppress the flames. At 3 am they crashlanded in a field just west of Breda. After walking and hiding from German patrols for twenty-four hours, they were taken prisoner. Pete Whitby's father received a telegram, then a note from 10 Squadron:

> Ref 105/6/41/Air
>
> Dear Mr Whitby,
> It is my unhappy duty to inform you that your son, F/O Whitby, is missing. The aircraft of which he was Second Pilot failed to return from operations over enemy territory on the night of 16th/17th August.
>
> S.O. Bufton

Pete Whitby remained a prisoner for the duration, and came home in 1945 to find that his mare Myrtle Green had bred him four foals and run up a bill for £600 for fodder while he was the guest of the Third Reich.

> One was attuned to getting the chop [said Bufton[2]]. You were resigned to dying every night. You looked round your room before you went out, at the golf clubs in the corner, the books on the shelves, the nice little radio set, the letter to one's parents propped on the table. . . .
>
> One night I saw a Whitley coned by dozens of searchlights on the way back from Cologne, and then shot down in flames. I came back and found that Sergeant Hoare was missing. He was the only 4 Group casualty that night, so I knew that it must have been him that I had seen go. But all that night I kept thinking that I heard the beat of his engines approaching the airfield.
>
> Then I realized that it was only the hot-water pipes in the hut. . . .

On 12 December 1940, 10 Squadron sent ten aircraft among 134 from Bomber Command to attack Mannheim. It was a clear night, and most of them came home to report that they had found the target without difficulty. Yet the significance of 'Operation Rachel', as the raid was codenamed, lay in the fact that this was the first occasion on which an entire city was the deliberate target of an attack. It was planned on the direct orders of the Prime Minister as a reprisal for the formidable German raid on Coventry a month earlier that had laid waste the centre of the city. The Mannheim operation was an isolated episode that winter, but it was a foretaste of much that was to come.

The Battle of Britain and the German blitz on British cities had changed the mood of the war in the air. To the fighter pilots on both sides, it might sometimes have seemed a chivalrous 'duel of eagles'. To those below on the ground it was the very rain of sudden death and terror that they had awaited and feared for so long. Both sides had accidentally bombed each other's city centres on several occasions since September 1939, and sought to make maximum propoganda capital out of their sufferings, but now it was no longer a matter of accidents. After the first bombs fell on central London on 24 August, the Prime Minister ordered Bomber Command to Berlin on the night of the 25th. In November the Luftwaffe's Kampfgruppe 100 marked Coventry for devastation using the *X-Gerat* beam system more than two years in advance of any comparable British technique. 400 German aircraft followed in the main wave. Their attack totally destroyed 20,000 houses, killed almost 600 people and injured a thousand more.

At Leeming, Staton pinned photographs of blitzed London, Coventry, Southampton on the wall of the operations room and stabbed a finger at them as he briefed the crews: 'Go now and do likewise to the Hun!' The night after the 14 November attack he turned to the crews and asked who lived in Coventry. Bob Dodd put up a hand. He was invited to choose his own target from the four the squadron were detailed to attack that night. Instead of Hamburg or Cologne, however, young Dodd chose Eindhoven aerodrome in Holland, simply because he thought it would be the cushiest. For the most part, these were boys who flew out over Europe, pressing the bomb release as they were ordered without anger, and with little thought for what lay far beneath in the darkness. But as the rage of the Press mounted, and with it the conviction of the Government that the British public demanded vengeance, so Bomber Command's anxiety about the avoidance of civilian targets in Germany diminished.

Sir Charles Portal, the C-in-C, was one of the earliest and most important advocates of Bomber Command's offensive against the synthetic oil plants on which Germany was overwhelmingly dependent. In twentieth-century war, cutting off a nation from its fuel supplies would clearly be a decisive blow, and this had long been recognized in Western Air Plan 5(c). But as the nights of 1940 went by and the results of Bomber Command's sorties were examined, Portal's doubts about the feasibility of 'precision' bombing mounted.

All through the summer of 1940 there was a surge of directives from the Air Ministry, each overtaking the last with bewildering speed as the Government and the Chiefs of Staff sought to hold back the floodgates of strategic disaster. The first reports from Germany on the effects of British bombing were absurdly optimistic, but warmly welcomed in Whitehall. The Air Ministry directive of 4 June 1940 ordered Portal to press on with the oil attacks. On dark nights when this was impracticable he was instructed to hit targets which would contribute to the 'continuous interruption and dislocation of German war industry', particularly in areas where the German aircraft industry was concentrated, notably Hamburg, Bremen, Frankfurt and the Ruhr. In the next paragraph, however, the directive stated emphatically: 'In no circumstances should night bombing be allowed to degenerate into mere indiscriminate action, which is contrary to the policy of His Majesty's Government.'

The next directive, on 20 June, relegated oil targets to third priority, below attacks on the German aircraft industry aimed at 'reducing the scale of air attack on this country', and below attacks on communications between Germany and her army's forward areas. On 4 July, these in turn were displaced by a new priority: attack on German shipping in port and at sea. Then on 13 July the aircraft industry was reinstated as the primary target, with oil as the secondary. Portal was told to concentrate the attacks of his force on fewer targets 'with a view to complete destruction rather than harassing effect'. To this end, fifteen key installations were listed for priority attention: five aircraft assembly plants, five depots and five oil refineries.

Portal replied to the 13 July directive with a sharp note commenting that of the ten aircraft industry targets, 'only three can be found with any certainty in moonlight by average crews'. He added, in a most significant subordinate clause, that 'since almost all the primary first priority targets are isolated and in sparsely inhabited districts, the very high percentage of bombers which inevitably miss the actual target will hit nothing else important and do no damage'. Portal said that he believed in dispersing attacks over the widest possible area of Germany: 'It largely increases the moral effect of our operations by the alarm and disturbance created over the wider area.'

Here was the seed of the attack on the morale of the German people, of area bombing: a district was to be chosen for bombardment in which was concentrated the highest possible proportion of vital industrial installations. Every hit would be of value, to be sure, but the attack could be launched with the prospect that many bombs which missed industrial targets – the overwhelming majority of those dropped – would hit the homes and shops and cinemas and cafés of the industrial workers and their families upon whom the German war effort must depend. In the eighteen months that followed – and for that matter throughout the next five years – there would be hesitation and much fierce debate about the policy of launching great forces of bombers wholesale against the cities of Germany. But already, in July 1940, the idea had taken root. As will become apparent, it had the wholehearted support of the Prime Minister, whose natural combativeness craved revenge for the laying waste of Coventry and Southampton, and indeed for the rape of Western Europe. But there is a certain irony that it should have been Portal, the cool, calmly reasoning committee chairman whom some considered to lack the iron resolution that marks great captains, who proved to be Trenchard's first true disciple in the Second World War. It was Portal who suggested, on 1 September 1940, that twenty German towns might be 'proscribed', just as Slessor had proposed earlier – warned by radio that they would be attacked indiscriminately one by one, following each occasion on which a British town was devastated by the Luftwaffe. It was under Portal that a note was circulated to all Bomber Command aircraft captains, reminding them that '. . . in industrial areas there are invariably a very large number of targets. In view of the indiscriminate nature of the German attacks, and in order to reduce the number of bombs brought back . . . every effort should be made to bomb these.' It was an instruction carrying the obvious inference that it was now preferable to attack anything in Germany than to attack nothing.

The Air Staff were not only surprised and dismayed by Portal's attitude, but determined to resist his proposals. On 5 September the VCAS, Sir Richard Peirse, wrote to Churchill that he thought there was 'little doubt that the reason for the effectiveness of our night bombing is that it is planned; and relentless until the particular target is knocked out or dislocated, whereas German night bombing is sporadic and mainly harassing'. In the Air Ministry's latest directive to Portal on 21 September the priorities for Bomber Command were restated: 'precision' attacks on invasion barges, the German aircraft industry and submarine works, German communications and oil resources would continue. The only comfort for Portal's convictions was a final paragraph authorizing occasional morale attacks on the German capital ' . . . although there are no objectives in the Berlin area of importance to our major plans . . .'

In the words of Frankland and Webster, the official historians of the British strategic air offensive, there was now general agreement that

> . . . if there was to be any strategic bombing at all, civilians would be killed; hospitals, churches and cultural monuments would be hit. The Air Staff, as represented by its Vice Chief, Sir Richard Peirse, believed that what was inevitable was also desirable only in so far as it remained a by-product of the primary intention to hit a military target in the sense of a power station, a marshalling yard or an oil plant. Bomber Command, as represented by its Commander-in-Chief, Sir Charles Portal, now believed that this by-product should become an end-product. He believed that the time had come to launch a direct attack on the German people themselves. He believed that this course had been justified by previous German actions, and that it would be justified as a strategy in the outcome.[3]

Portal's biographer is unable to accept the official historians' interpretation of the C-in-C's attitude:

> It seems to carry the suggestion that Portal favoured the deliberate killing and maiming of civilians as a major strategy . . . Portal was

not at this time, however, nor did he ever become an advocate of killing civilians. He became, while it was the most practicable policy, an advocate of destroying industrial towns.[4]

Some of the moral issues that are forever entangled in the story of Bomber Command will be discussed in more detail later. Here it is sufficient to say that to his colleagues and contemporaries it seemed that Portal's recommendations amounted to commencing indiscriminate air warfare, and a significant minority opposed them for this very reason. Yet to most of those around him in the RAF Portal seemed absolutely right and the Air Ministry absolutely wrong. Every morning at High Wycombe they studied the results of the previous night's operations, in which a hundred or more crews had stumbled through the night sky over Germany, searching for an oil plant or a factory which Portal suspected that they seldom reached. After months of this the power of the Third Reich was visibly undiminished. Yet in England the Luftwaffe had bombed recklessly from Birmingham and Coventry to Plymouth and London, and all around lay the ruins and the corpses. No one in England that winter of 1940 cared to suggest aloud that morale was cracking under the Blitz, and indeed it never did. But deep in his heart, each man knew the terror of hearing the bombs whistling down, the shuddering crump and the roar of falling masonry, the agony of expectation before the explosion. If Englishmen were thus moved by air bombardment, it seemed reasonable to expect that Germans would be still more so. Much of the reasoning that led to the mass morale bombing of Germany took place in the silence of men's minds, and was never articulated in minutes or memoranda.

On 4 October 1940, Sir Cyril Newall was retired as Chief of Air Staff and replaced by Sir Charles Portal. Sir Richard Peirse, one of the foremost advocates of 'precision' bombing, became C-in-C of Bomber Command. Portal could now unquestionably have secured the launching of an area bombing campaign. Churchill would not only have endorsed such a proposal, but was urging it himself throughout the winter of 1940 and spring of 1941: 'We have seen what inconvenience the attack on the British civilian population has caused us,' he wrote to the Air Ministry on 2 November 1940, 'and there is no reason why the enemy should be freed from all such embarrassments.'

But Portal made no effort immediately to test his faith in area bombing. For the next year he allowed Bomber Command to continue on the course which had been set in May 1940, attempting precision attacks on chosen industrial objectives. Only when this policy was universally agreed to have failed would it finally be abandoned.

From October 1940 until early March 1941 oil remained the first priority of Bomber Command whenever the weather allowed. The attacks on invasion barges continued into the winter. It is unlikely that the loss of an estimated 12 per cent of their fleet played a decisive part in the German cancellation of the invasion of England. But it is important not to underestimate Bomber Command's contribution, compelling Hitler to acknowledge that the RAF still possessed striking power to match the defensive strength of its fighters. There is little doubt that in 1939 the Nazi leaders believed that Goering's Luftwaffe could prevent any enemy aircraft from attacking the Reich. Bomber Command's incursions into Germany in 1940 and 1941 may have been erratic and materially ineffectual. But they played a part in asserting the reality of Britain's survival in the minds of the German people and their rulers.

Portal's concern with attacking German morale was embodied only as a secondary priority in the Air Ministry directive to Peirse of 30 October 1940, ordering him to attack Berlin and other German towns.

> . . . with such regularity as you may find practicable. . . . As many heavy bombers as possible should be detailed for the attack, carrying high-explosive, incendiary and delay-action bombs with perhaps an occasional mine. The aim of the first sorties should be to cause fires, either on or in the vicinity of the targets so that they should carry a high proportion of incendiary bombs. . . . The objectives considered most suitable for these concentrated attacks are the sources of power, such as electricity generating stations and gas plants, and centres of communication; but where primary targets such as the oil and aircraft industry objectives are suitably placed in the centres of the towns or populated districts, they also might be selected.

Portal always suffered from a measure of intelligent indecision and now he was divided between his hopes that the attack on German oil would provide a 'quick death clinch' with Germany, as he put it, and his doubts about Bomber Command's ability to bring this about. He was still undecided in December 1940 when the Lloyd Committee on German oil resources made its remarkable report, asserting that Bomber Command had already achieved a 15 per cent cut in enemy fuel availability. This had allegedly been achieved by the dropping of only 539 tons of bombs, 6.7 per cent of Bomber Command's effort since the summer.

Since in reality the Germans were scarcely aware that their oil resources were supposed to have been the object of a systematic bomber assault, it is a measure of the inadequacy of British economic Intelligence that the Lloyd Committee could reach these conclusions. It is even more remarkable that Portal and the airmen allowed themselves to accept them. Yet not only did they do so, but they allowed the report to become the basis for Bomber Command's continued attack on oil throughout the spring of 1941, despite the Prime Minister's scepticism. They were simply desperate for good news of bombing, and when it came they received it uncritically. To allow themselves to believe the truth seemed a betrayal of scores of careers dedicated to the fulfilment of the Trenchard doctrine.

It is often suggested that in August 1941 Bomber Command received a quite unexpected thunderbolt when it was learnt that only a tiny proportion of crews were bombing within miles of their targets. Yet throughout the winter of 1940 there were few grounds for illusions at High Wycombe about what was taking place over Germany. As early as October Peirse, the urbane advocate of British 'planned' bombing, reckoned that somewhere around one in five of his crews found their primary target on a given night. Projections for the success of the oil offensive required at least 50 per cent of sorties to be successful. Arthur Harris at 5 Group, perpetually sanguine, continued to assert his faith in his crews' navigation. But Coningham at 4 Group, who only a few months earlier said that he expected the same precision from night bombing as from day, now admitted that 'for my part, I have little idea of what the Whitleys do, and it causes me considerable anxiety'. Most significant, however, were the results of the first careful analysis of target photographs. Gelsenkirchen oil refineries, the objects of repeated attacks, appeared virtually undamaged. Mannheim, to which 10 Squadron and so many others had been dispatched for the Coventry retaliation attack of 16 December, was scarcely scarred. It was concluded that it had become a matter of urgency to equip every possible aircraft with night cameras, in order to determine decisively who did and did not reach his target. Yet in the face of the overwhelming evidence of its crews' inability to achieve success, Bomber Command was launched once more upon the oil offensive. Peirse's squadrons continued to struggle in futility over Germany – now receiving much increased oil imports from Rumania – all that winter and through the spring of 1941.

It was the rapid escalation of the Battle of the Atlantic which at last diverted Bomber Command from the oil offensive. In the face of mounting U-boat successes and the strategic threat posed by German capital ships, on 9 March 1941 Peirse received a new directive from the Air Ministry, ordering him to concentrate all his resources on the task of supporting the Royal Navy in the war at sea, by attacking the U-boat bases at St Nazaire, Bordeaux and Lorient in France, by mining the German approaches, and by bombing the ports and construction yards. Portal's letter to Peirse on the new policy, dated 1 March 1941, was a sad throwback to the worst traditions of the RAF. Its temper may have been influenced by his own disappointment at the failure of Bomber Command: 'A very high proportion of bomber effort will inevitably be required to pull the Admiralty out of the mess they have got into. . . .' That summer, it would have been more credible to inquire whether Bomber Command, at this sorry point of its fortunes, was capable of affording the Admiralty any useful support at all in the vital struggle to save Britain from starvation.

We attacked Lorient from the north [wrote a novice Whitley pilot, Denis Hornsey[5]]. Having taken over the controls just beforehand I throttled back the engines and began a glide towards the target at 12,000 feet. My intention was to drop the bombs at 8,000 feet. Richards, who had gone forward to map read, guided me in to the target, the rough position of which I could detect myself from a cone of searchlights and a smattering of light flak immediately ahead. Nearby the Germans were shooting at some parachute flares dropped by previous visitors, and somewhere underneath lay our objective, four submarines reputedly lying close together in the dry docks.

'Steady, steady,' came Richards's voice. 'Keep as you are going, Skipper,' he added, dropping the official bombing patter in his excitement. 'The docks are right ahead.'

'OK,' I said. Then remembering my duty, I called up the rear gunner. 'Skipper calling rear gunner. Skipper calling rear gunner. Keep your eye open for fighters.'

'OK, Skipper,' the rear gunner replied. 'There's some searchlights after us,' he went on laconically. 'Bang on our tail.'

He had no sooner said this than the searchlights were upon us and the inside of the cabin was suddenly illuminated as by an arc lamp. I sat motionless at the controls for a moment, wondering whether they would flick over us or not, and while I did so Richards's voice came through again.

'Running up! Running up!' he was saying imperturbably. 'Bomb doors open! Bomb doors open!'

I repeated the patter and concentrated on the bombing approach. I had opened the bomb doors as directed and was now gliding the aircraft at a steady speed down to our bombing height of 8,000 feet. The searchlights were still on us, and it could not be long before we received attention from fighters or anti-aircraft guns if we remained in them.

'Drop the bombs in one stick,' I ordered Richards. 'We're still in the searchlights.'

The last statement was redundant, for Richards could scarcely be unaware that we were now coned by about twenty beams with others swinging across the sky to join in. It was high time we took evasive action.

'Skipper calling bomb-aimer. We'll have to let the bombs go. Can't hold out much longer,' I said breathlessly, feeling more and more apprehensive as the seconds ticked by.

'OK, skip, we're coming on the target now.'

'Let the bloody things go then,' I said.

'OK. Bombs gone,' Richards replied.

I thankfully closed the bomb doors and opening up the engines, pulled hard back on the stick to go into a steep climb. Climbing steadily for a few minutes, minutes which seemed like an age, I felt as naked in that bright light as if I was standing unclothed in the middle of Piccadilly. Then I tried some diving and climbing turns to left and right, but we were still held relentlessly in the beams as if impaled by twenty or thirty silver lances. All this having availed nothing, it was essential to get out of the searchlights with no more delay, for every second increased the risk of being shot down. Certain that our course and height must have now been accurately plotted by the enemy, I put the aircraft into a dive. I did this automatically and instinctively, without conscious thought, but as the needle of the air speed indicator crept round its dial I watched it without comprehension. I was in a mock sweat and almost exhausted by my efforts.

'Shall I fire at the searchlights, skipper?' came Richards's voice.

'Yes, have a go. You too, rear gunner.'

'No, no,' cried Barney, 'you'll give away our position.'

The noise of the guns came over the intercom.

'Got one,' said Richards triumphantly, ignoring the wireless operator's protest.

My intense concentration during these manoeuvres was interrupted by Franklin tapping my shoulder. He leaned over me from behind and pointed to the altimeter, which was showing only, 3,000 feet. We were still going down fast in a steep dive at 260 mph, very fast indeed for a Whitley. I had become so engrossed in trying to get out of the searchlights that I had forgotten how near we must be getting to the ground. Nodding as if to indicate that I was fully aware of our position and that everything was going to plan – I was enough of a Captain to remember such necessities – I pulled hard back on the stick to flatten out of the dive. We shot out of the beams like an orange pip squeezed from one's fingers, into blessed darkness and relative safety. My unintentional dive had taken us across the headland north of L'Orient and out over the sea.

'Hurrah!' said Richards. 'We're out!'

Night after night that spring and summer of 1941, 10 Squadron and the rest of Bomber Command poured their bombloads into the smokescreens shielding 'Salmon' and 'Gluck' – the *Scharnhorst* and the *Gneisenau* at Brest – and the U-boats at L'Orient and Bordeaux from the eyes of the bomb-aimers. Peirse protested to Portal that his pilots were wasting hundred of tons of explosives on a task for which they had never been intended and were not trained or equipped. Yet air attack on enemy warships had always been an obvious, vital strategic role for

Bomber Command. If this, too, was beyond its capabilities, to what was it suited? For what was it equipped and prepared?

10 Squadron spent the early spring bombing Germany during occasional breaks in the weather and standing-by for hours, acutely bored. By the end of February there had been only two nights on which the sky was clear enough to attack oil targets – just 221 sorties had taken place of the 3,400 estimated to be necessary to have decisive effect on German oil supplies. Often aircraft taxiing out from the dispersals had to weave a path through a sea of mud, becoming bogged down and having to be towed out at predictable cost in temper and tiredness. One day in March an 'oil expert' came down from Group to lecture at Leeming on the importance of what they were doing. His talk merged into the haze of information and misinformation that was crowded into their idle hours: lectures on escaping, on evasive action in the air, on searchlights and the growing defensive belt reaching down across northern Germany into Holland, on the significance of the appearance of the first radar-equipped night-fighters over Holland. One day Trenchard came, a charming, paternal old gentleman, who endeared himself at once. Listening to him lecturing them all in a great semi-circle outside a hangar was like hearing Moses himself, after so many years in which they had learned to think of him as the exalted prophet of bombing.*

Most of their operations were simply very monotonous. But difficult though it may be to grasp today, many aircrew still enjoyed the business of flying an aircraft, and managed to gain great pleasure from what they were doing operation after operation in these days before the odds against their own survival became overwhelming. Pilots revelled in the occasional clear, bright night when they sat in their cockpits watching the shooting stars, with an overwhelming sense of the vastness of the universe. They knew nothing of the intense debates about their own doings that were taking place at Group and at High Wycombe. They would have been dismayed if they did, for they believed that they were doing a good job. It had taken eighteen months of war for High Wycombe to grasp a simple but remarkable truth about night bomber operations, that the airmen themselves were the last people to know what they had or had not achieved. They were not wantonly dishonest – perhaps sometimes a little optimistic, but generally gauchely frank about their own efforts. In a memorandum to the Air Ministry at about this time, Trenchard made the point that the level of debriefing was still abysmal, usually left in the hands of staff

*Even among conscript aircrew later in the war, the old man cast a powerful spell. Visiting 76 Squadron in 1942, he walked into the mess tent set for lunch in his honour, sidestepped his intended place among the 'Brass', and sat down instead with the young pilots below the salt. He noticed one man wearing the single ribbon of the DFC, and glanced down at his own vastly decorated chest: 'Don't worry, my boy,' he boomed. 'Once you've got one, they grow on you like measles.' They loved him.

officers who had no idea how to ask crews the right questions, and who invariably overstated their claims. In the years to come, skilled interpretation of night photos and improved debriefing enabled the Command to form a somewhat more accurate image of what had taken place on operations. But throughout the war, part of the unique character of the bomber offensive was that the men who carried it out were totally dependent on their commanders for information about the success or failure of what they were doing. An infantry platoon commander, over a period of weeks or months, could achieve some notion of his army's gains or losses by noticing whether he himself was moving forwards or backwards. A convoy escort officer could judge a great deal from the rate of sinkings around him. But a bomber pilot, with rare exceptions such as the great firestorms of Hamburg and Dresden, had to wait for the next bulletin from High Wycombe to learn whether his comrades were dying to good purpose or in vain. It was absolutely necessary for him to believe that his commanders' view of the bomber offensive was accurate. For if it was not, then he was flying out each night to risk his life and the lives of his crew for nothing.

The men who survived those primitive operations of 1940 and 1941 would look back on them afterwards as almost lunatic in their crudeness compared with what came later. The little clusters of boys around the Whitleys and Hampdens in the photographs still look like young 'Clubland Heroes': hair plastered down, breathing health and willingness and energy from every pore. The superb propaganda films made about Bomber Command at this time had perhaps captured their imagination as well as that of Britain. They themselves were secretly rather impressed by *F for Freddie* and *Target for Tonight*. At briefing, they were given their target, perhaps a post office or power station, and solemnly handed street maps of the relevant city to guide their way. They drew their flying rations and parachutes and boarded the truck for the dispersals. Two airmen waited with the battery cart. For fifteen minutes they ran up the Merlins, then began the long bumpy journey to the taxi lamp at the end of the runway, among the seagulls in the dusk. They waited for the green flash from the control caravan then rumbled away down the runway. The undercarriage came up and the wireless operator signalled briefly: 'G-George on course,' then lapsed into silence. They picked up Flamborough Head below them, and settled back for the long haul across the North Sea to the Zuider Zee. Bob Dodd of 10 Squadron described a typical night[6]:

> The weather was ten-tenths cloud and we had navigated on Dead Reckoning to ETA target. We broke cloud (*hoping* there was no high ground) so as not to waste the trip, and found a river. After following it for a while we decided we had found our position on the southern border of Germany. We bombed a small town and our incendiaries

set fire to the church, which appeared to have a wooden spire and burned fiercely. Houses were also burning. Since we had come down to about 1,000 feet, we had a clear view. When we returned to base and were able to evaluate the wind direction and speed, we calculated that we had attacked Epinalle in Vichy France. This was later confirmed by our Intelligence Officer. Our Dead Reckoning position with no wireless fix was so far out that we were attacked by flak over Birmingham. Our Dead Reckoning position was over the North Sea. I entered in the log: 'Base-Mannheim-Base. Village bombed ten miles south of Epinalle'.

One night in March 1941, in his Whitley high over the North Sea on the way to Germany, a navigator named George Carter settled down to pass the trip writing a letter to his girlfriend on sheets torn from the log. 'Dear Nicole', he wrote, putting '2020 hours' in brackets after her name, then 'Bound for Berlin':

As you can see from the address, I am on the job. It is the first time I have been to the 'Big City' and as I have nobody else to tell the great news, I tell you. We are at present sixty-four miles off the English coast, a lovely night, moon as near as dammit full. We are punching the old kite along at about 8,000 feet to get full benefit of a favourable wind over this long sea crossing (three hours) and I have not a lot to do. I started to write this note in ink but the reduced pressure up here has forced it all out and the pen won't work, so I'm reduced to pencil now.

I shall have to break off for a while now as I have to work out some wireless bearings and switch on one of the auxiliary tanks, and check our drift by flame float. It's getting cold – 0° on the clock now, and a cold white moon lighting up the plane. . . .

2137. Here I am again after getting drift, about two dozen loop bearings and three sights on astro (I think my sight must be wrong, it gave our position about 180 miles south of where we ought to be, maybe dropping it last night had something to do with it).

I hope we knock the blazes out of the target (which incidentally is the post office in the centre of the city). Before, I have always felt sorry for the people down below, but the other night I came over Portsmouth on the way home and saw it afire. I saw an explosion about 2,000 feet high. So now I feel different about it, and I shall not be too careful to hit the post office. I have got one bottle, one brick and one piece of concrete to throw out with some personal messages to the Hun.

0120. Well, that was Berlin that was. Their AA was mustard – shook me rigid. We appear to be doubtful about our position so some work must be done. . . .

0330. I managed to get back on track and now we're in the middle of the North Sea going home. The wind changed from the met forecast and I found myself well to the south of my track, and with a bit of wangling we are OK, touch wood! You see, we have only just enough juice to get us to Berlin and back. . . .

The flak over Berlin was very accurate and the searchlights held us at 18,000, AA going off all around us – I bet we're full of holes. The shells keep bursting in front of us, and me being in front with the bomb sight, kept getting the smoke in my eyes. Was I scared? I'll say I was scared! I let our bombs go in the middle of the city. I hope they helped our war effort. I could not see where they landed. . . .

It was still the Stone Age of bombing, but this would now be elevated to Britain's principal weapon of war.

IV

Crisis of Confidence, 1941–42

'Then shall the right aiming thunderbolts go abroad; and from the clouds, as from a well-drawn bow, shall they fly to the mark' Wisdom v:21

–from the Air Ministry handbook *Bomber Command*, 1941

What took place in the mind of Winston Churchill to cause the man who wrote in 1917 'it is improbable that any terrorization of the civil population which could be achieved by air attack would compel the Government of a great nation to surrender', to become, by the end of 1941, the foremost political advocate of bombing cities? 'The bombers alone provide the means of victory,' he wrote on 3 September 1940. From the outset Churchill was doubtful of the efficacy of the Air Staff's 'precision' attacks on oil and communications. He demanded retaliation for the blitz on Britain, an attack on German morale that was no more than a euphemism for bombing the cities of Germany. On 20 October 1940, in the midst of the Luftwaffe's night attacks on Britain, he minuted the Air Minister Sir Archibald Sinclair:

> I am deeply concerned with the non-expansion, and indeed contraction of our bomber force which must be expected between now and April or May next, according to present policy. Surely an effort should be made to increase our bomb-dropping capacity during this period. . . . Is it not possible to organize a second-line bomber force which, especially in the dark of the moon, would discharge bombs from a considerable and safe height upon the nearest large built-up area of Germany, which contains military targets in abundance? The Ruhr, of course, is obviously indicated. . . . I ask that a whole-hearted effort shall be made to cart a large number of bombs into Germany by a second-line organization such as I have suggested, and under conditions in which admittedly no special accuracy could be obtained.

Most men found during the course of the war that whatever moments of rage and passion they might suffer at the sight of a blitzed building or in the heat of battle, as the months and years went by it was impossible to sustain a white-hot hatred for the enemy. War became a job, a routine of its own, as much as peace. But Winston Churchill never for a moment lost his passion, his detestation of all things that belonged to the enemy. The force of his hatred for the German people and their leaders contributed immensely to his triumph as a war leader. His determination that Britain should survive and finally destroy the nation that had brought such misery upon the world never faltered. It would not have occurred to him to permit the maltreatment of a prisoner, or to tolerate excess in the government of captured German territory. Once Germans ceased to be enemies in arms, he had no further interest in them. But as he gazed out across the map of Europe at the Third Reich during the six years of war, he sought to bring fire and slaughter without scruple upon the German people. It is doubtful whether at any time after the fall of France he debated whether killing German civilians was a moral exercise. He was concerned only with what was strategically desirable and tactically possible. After the war, in a note to a former staff officer of Bomber Command, Churchill scribbled: 'We should never allow ourselves to apologize for what we did to Germany.'[1] Whatever he may have written elsewhere for public consumption, there is no reason to suppose that Churchill ever suffered a moment's private misgiving about the course and consequences of the strategic air offensive.

It is important to dwell on Churchill's personal attitude to the bombing of Germany, because it will be necessary to emphasize the extent to which the elevation of Bomber Command to its prime place in the British war effort was his personal decision, in the face of intense and important opposition. The bomber offensive would consume a lion's share of Britain's industrial resources – the exact proportion will never be known, but Mr. A. J. P. Taylor suggests more than one-third.[2] Alternative claims on production were pressed with fierce determination. To give some impression of the debate that took place, it is helpful to take certain events out of order, and to consider as an entity discussions that took place between August 1941 and the spring of 1942. In these months the future of the strategic bomber offensive was decided. Once the great Allied commitment had been made, it has been insufficiently recognized to what extent the Chiefs of Staff in 1944 and 1945, in greatly changed circumstances, were the prisoners of the vast investment in industrial effort and national prestige which had already been made in the strategic bomber forces. In early 1942 the destruction of Germany's cities was still many months away. But their ultimate fate had already been decided.

Throughout the winter of 1940–41 and into the spring, the Prime Minister followed closely the progress of the bomber offensive – the raid on Mannheim, the attacks on the *Scharnhorst* and the *Gneisenau*, the debate between Portal and the Air Ministry and subsequently between Peirse and Portal about bombing policy. He was aware of the shortcomings in the results that had been achieved. He was disturbed by 2 Group's losses in the RAF's continuing effort to maintain some sort of daylight bomber effort, and by the inability of Bomber Command to do decisive damage even against the coastal invasion barge concentrations, whose photographs he studied personally. But it is doubtful whether he understood the full extent of the failure: the near-farce of many sorties; the overwhelming majority of crews who never came within miles of the target; the repeated attempts to bomb on ETA; the paltry fruits of the immense effort against the oil plants. Then one morning in August 1941 he was presented with a report by Mr D. M. Butt of the Cabinet Secretariat on the current performance of Bomber Command against targets in France and Germany. Its conclusions seem to have been a great shock to him, and would have decisive repercussions for the future of the bomber offensive.

Mr Butt was directed to carry out his independent investigation by Lord Cherwell, the Prime Minister's personal scientific adviser and the most powerful *eminence grise* in Downing Street. Cherwell had been doubtful for some time about the results being achieved by British bombing, and Mr Butt's conclusions exceeded his worst fears. On any given night of operations, it was already understood that around a third of all aircraft returned without claiming to have attacked their primary target. So Mr Butt analysed only the target photographs and reports relating to the remaining two-thirds of crews who had allegedly bombed their targets, during the preceding two months of June and July 1941. He reported that of these, only one-third came within five miles of the aiming point. Against the Ruhr this proportion fell to one-tenth. At a moment when perceptive airmen already foresaw the end of moonlit bombing operations as German night-fighter activity intensified, Mr Butt found that moonlight was indispensable to the pilots of Bomber Command: two crews in five came within five miles of their targets on full-moon nights; this ratio fell to one in fifteen on moonless ones.

The Royal Air Force was not disposed to make much of the Butt Report. Sir Richard Peirse, who had already achieved a reputation for assertive overconfidence about the work of his Command, found its conclusions incompatible with the degree of damage he believed had been done to Germany, and thus simply unacceptable. Air Vice-Marshal Carr, now AOC of 4 Group, argued that 'lack of a photograph of the precise target should not be regarded as conclusive proof that the aircraft failed to attack its proper objective.' Air Vice-Marshal Saundby, SASO at High Wycombe, noted that the weather had been especially bad in the months studied by Butt, and also suggested rather improbably that squadron commanders tended to give cameras to those crews in whom they had least confidence. All this reflected a natural exasperation on the part of the airmen, who found themselves being reminded by a Whitehall civil servant of a situation of which they had been broadly aware for many months.

But however thoroughly Bomber Command's doings were understood within the ranks of the Royal Air Force, Butt came as a major revelation to one man: the Prime Minister. On 3 September 1942 he dispatched a personal note to the Chief of Air Staff with a copy of the report: 'This is a very serious paper, and seems to require your most urgent attention. I await your proposals for action.'

The submission of the Butt Report marked the low-water mark in the wartime fortunes of Bomber Command. Since September 1939 its crews had sought to attack warships in harbour and at sea, oil installations and factories, power stations and airfields, by day and by night. In almost all these things, they were now being asked to accept, they had failed. The *Scharnhorst* and the *Gneisenau* had been slightly damaged. One brave pilot's efforts won him the Victoria Cross and closed the Dortmund–Ems Canal for ten days in 1940. 100,000 tons of coastal shipping were sunk by air-dropped mines. A wide variety of industrial plants bore superficial scars. The Focke–Wulf aircraft factory in Bremen and a number of other important factories had begun to disperse their operations, more in anticipation of the future than because of the damage of the past. A few thousand German civilians had been killed, and immense labour was being diverted to the construction of air raid shelters. Flak and searchlight defences were being greatly strengthened. Some oil plants had been temporarily shut down by bomb damage, but at no cost to the German war economy. It was fortunate for the airmen that they did not know more than this; of the huge slack capacity in the German economy, the single-shift working that still prevailed in most major factories. Far fewer women were employed than in England. Germans had more to eat (and would continue to do so almost until the end of the war), could buy a far wider range of consumer goods and possessed vastly more machine tools than the British. What the German armed forces lacked in equipment was the result of maladministration and not of any shortage of manufacturing capacity or raw materials. The German economy had been geared for a short war, and had scarcely even begun to exert itself. It has been said that if Britain had understood in 1941 how powerful and how effortless was the German industrial machine, what enormous untapped potential it possessed, how widely its resources were dispersed, no one could have contemplated the overwhelming task of attempting to crush it by bombing. But the Air Ministry and the Ministry of Economic Warfare did not know this. They believed that Germany was under immense strain. Perhaps most important of all, the airmen were still imbued with the mystic faith which sustained them through the interwar years, that the mere act of bombing was having effects upon the enemy out of all proportion to any hits achieved on economic objectives. The chronic lack of clear thinking that had dogged bombing policy since the end of the First World War persisted even in the face of the most convincing evidence. When the airmen pressed their case for the bomber assault upon the German nation, they believed that they were battering a door already loose upon its hinges.

But even if the exact realities of the situation in Germany and the failure of initial bomber offensive were not known, before the Butt Report reached Whitehall, Bomber Command and the massive industrial commitment to heavy bombers were already being assailed in powerful quarters. The Americans in particular, with their own observers in Germany, were deeply sceptical. Their military attaché in London, General Raymond Lee, recorded in his diary a meeting that August of 1941:

> I lunched at the Dorchester as the guest of Colonel Larner, who had Moore-Brabazon, the [junior] Air Minister, and four Air Marshals, together with Royce and myself. . . . As soon as the coffee was served, Moore-Brabazon began to talk about how essential it was that the British should have hundreds and hundreds, if not thousands, more long-range bombers with which to bring Germany down. Finally, he turned to me and asked me what my opinion was. I told him that I was no expert, but so far as my observation went, the British had no proof yet that their bombing had been any more effective than the German bombing of England, and that I thought they were asking the United States for a good deal when they wanted it to divest itself of all its bombers, and devote a lot of production capacity to the construction of more bombers, thereby committing the United States to the policy of reducing Germany by bombing, without affording sufficient proof that this was possible. I pointed out that the Luftwaffe under the most favourable conditions had failed to paralyse the British or reduce this country to impotence in over a year of attack, at very short range, and when its energies were not engaged elsewhere. So why, I asked, should the RAF believe they could bring down Germany at a greater range and with its targets very much more dispersed than those in England and protected by very much better anti-aircraft defences now than the British had here last year. I built on absolutely sure ground here because I have had a little time to study the statistics on the damage done to Britain in the seven months between 1 June and 31 December 1940, and it is really surprisingly small. . . .[3]

It was the American air attaché in London who reported to Washington as late as April 1942: 'The British public have an erroneous belief, which has been fostered by effective RAF publicity, that the German war machine can be destroyed and the nation defeated by intensive bombing.

Throughout the war the Royal Navy waged an unceasing battle against the Air Ministry not only for a larger share of industrial resources, but also for the services of the greatest possible numbers of the long-range aircraft being built, for anti-submarine operations and reconnaissance. Both parties to the dispute stooped to unseemly depths in the pursuit of their cases, and the Royal Navy diminished its own credibility as a judge of the effective use of air forces by insisting that Bomber Command should waste effort first on the abortive bombing of the *Scharnhorst* and the *Gneisenau*, and subsequently on the impenetrable concrete-encased U-boat pens of the French ports. 'Our fight with the Air Ministry becomes more and more fierce as the war proceeds,' wrote Admiral Whitworth at the height of the controversy. 'It is a much more savage one than our war with the Huns, which is very unsatisfactory and such a waste of effort.'[4] However, some shrewd and able naval officers, fighting impossible odds in the far corners of the world, understandably deplored the immense concentration of resources upon Bomber Command.

'It certainly gives us furiously to think when we see that over 200 heavy bombers attacked one town in Germany,' wrote Admiral Willis, second-in-command of the Eastern Fleet, to Admiral Cunningham in the Mediterranean, a few months after the Japanese entered the war. 'If only some of the hundreds of bombers who fly over Germany (and often fail to do anything because of the weather) had been torpedo aircraft and dive-bombers the old Empire would be in better condition than it is now. . . . .'[5]

Professor Pat Blackett did not impress airmen, because he was an adviser to the Admiralty. But he was also one of the most distinguished defence scientists of his generation. Blackett pointed out that in 1941 British bombers killed German civilians no faster than the German defences had been killing highly-trained British aircrew. Computing brutal realities, he concluded that the future British bomber offensive could not expect to kill more than one German for every five tons of bombs dropped.

> I say emphatically [he wrote in 18 February 1942] that a calm dispassionate review of the facts will reveal that the present policy of bombing Germany is wrong; that we must put our maximum effort first into destroying the enemy's sea communications and preserving our own; that we can only do so by operating aircraft over the sea on a very much larger scale than we have done hitherto, and that we shall be forced to use much longer range aircraft. The only advantage that I see in bombing Germany is that it does force the enemy to lock up a good deal of his effort on home defence. . . . The heavy scale of bombing will only be justified in the concluding stages of the war when (or if) we are fortunate enough to have defeated the enemy at sea and to have command of it.

But it was not only the Admiralty and its advisers who questioned the bomber offensive. Few men could claim a more intimate knowledge of air technology than A. V. Hill, one of the founding fathers of British radar, and also Independent Conservative Member of Parliament for Cambridge University. Hill felt sufficiently strongly about the error that he believed was being made in concentrating such great resources upon Bomber Command that on 22 February 1942 he took the unpopular course of denouncing in the House of Commons 'the brave adjectives about big and beautiful bombs, and the fate which will await Berlin next year – it is always next year – from them'. He went on:

> Such adjectives do not impress the enemy at all. He quietly does some simple arithmetic and smiles. . . . Past controversies about the independence of the Royal Air Force have had one most unfortunate result, the exaggeration of the importance of bombing an enemy country. Against an ill-defended enemy bombing, no doubt, can quickly produce disastrous results, but so can other forms of offensive action – against an ill-defended enemy. In the present struggle none of the protagonists is ill-defended now against attack from the air. . . . The idea of bombing a well-defended enemy into submission or seriously affecting his morale – of even doing substantial damage to him – is an illusion. We know that most of the bombs we drop hit nothing of importance. The disaster of this policy is not only that it is futile, but that it is extremely wasteful, and will become increasingly wasteful as time goes on.

A few months earlier the House of Commons aired an agony of protests about the discovery that Professor Solly Zuckerman and a team of biologists had been carrying out experiments about the effects of explosives on live animals. The House was somewhat less moved by Hill's speech. Flight-Lieutenant Boothby MP rose to say that 'in Bomber Command we have fashioned a most formidable weapon of offence'. He deplored statements that might erode confidence in bombing: 'It is tough to ask these chaps to undergo great dangers and perils, which they do cheerfully and bravely, unless they are convinced, as they are at present, that it is worth doing . . .'

In the War Cabinet criticism of the bomber offensive was muted by a mixture of deference on a matter so close to the Prime Minister's heart, and inability to suggest any alternative strategy. The Air Minister, Sir Archibald Sinclair, argued in October 1940 that

> . . . our small bomber force could, by accurate bombing, do very great damage to the enemy's war effort, but could not gain a decision against Germany by bombing the civil population. . . . Unless we get a decision we achieve nothing by promiscuous bombing. Except

> when he uses mines, it is uncertain to what extent the enemy is deliberately choosing to bomb the civil population when he might hit military targets. When he cannot see to hit the latter he bombs centres of population, and we are now doing the same. . . . In so far as the Germans may have been led away by their theories of total war into attacking our civilian population instead of concentrating upon our aircraft and air engineering factories, it is very lucky for us.

But when bombing policy changed, Sinclair changed with it. He was a man in deep personal thrall to the Prime Minister – 'Head of school's fag', as he was sometimes unkindly described in political circles – and as Air Minister he was always the RAF's political representative rather than its master. He became an assiduous public apologist for area bombing, whatever his earlier private misgivings.

Yet as this low point of the bomber offensive in the winter of 1941–42 there would have been the deepest concern at the Air Ministry if it had been known that Captain Harold Balfour, Sinclair's Parliamentary Under-Secretary and a man of wide personal experience of air matters, had also become sceptical about Bomber Command. On 24 January 1942, in a confidential memorandum to Sinclair that is unmentioned in any of the official histories, Balfour reviewed past hopes for British bombing:

> The fact is that this plan has not been fulfilled. . . . Night defences have on both sides increased in quantity and efficiency. As regards accuracy, I believe we calculate that only some 10 per cent of bombs fall in the target area.
>
> The public are more and more questioning the effectiveness of bombing policy and beginning to wonder whether bombs can bring Germany's effort to a standstill and thus be a deciding factor in winning the war.

Balfour was convinced that as Britain faced crisis in the Middle and Far East, bombers must be diverted from the assault on Germany: 'It may be that the believers in bombing Germany to destruction, though right if war were confined to the Western battlefield only – are wrong having regard to the war in the East which has to be won and may continue long after victory in the West if the deteriorating position cannot be checked before then.'

Balfour kept his misgivings to himself. But Sir Stafford Cripps, Lord Privy Seal and Leader of the House of Commons, made a speech in the House of Commons at the beginning of 1942 which caused widespread astonishment, interpreted as a vote of no confidence in the strategic air offensive:

> Another question which has been raised by a great number of members is the question of policy as to the continued use of heavy bombers and the bombing of Germany. A number of hon. members have questioned whether, in the existing circumstances, the continued devotion of a considerable part of our effort to the building up of this bombing force is the best use that we can make of our resources. It is obviously a matter which it is almost impossible to debate in public, but if I may, I would remind the House that this policy was initiated at a time when we were fighting alone against the combined forces of Germany and Italy and it then seemed that this was the most effective way in which we, acting alone, could take the initiative against the enemy. Since that time we have had an enormous access of support from the Russian armies . . . and also from the great potential strength of the United States. Naturally, in such circumstances, the original policy has come under review. I can assure the House that the Government are fully aware of the other uses to which our resources can be put, and the moment they arrive at a decision that the circumstances warrant a change, a change in policy will be made.

Cripps's statement caused momentary alarm at the Air Ministry and in America, where at that very moment the British delegation were devoting their utmost effort to ensuring that the American air forces joined Bomber Command in mounting an even more ambitious combined offensive against Germany. But in reality, while Cripps had made his own scepticism clear, for all his grandiose titles he had no influence on the vital decisions, and no information from the Prime Minister that could possibly have justified his hopes.

Another impotent critic was Lord Beaverbrook. Not in the least afraid of speaking his mind to Churchill, after a relatively brief period of real power as Minister of Aircraft Production, by the end of 1941 his influence had waned greatly. His fierce comments on the bomber offensive, like the speech of Cripps, are important because they were made, not because they influenced policy.

> The events of the past eight months [wrote Beaverbrook on 7 February 1942] have shown that the achievements of our powerful and growing bomber force have been in no way commensurate with its potentialities, with the man hours and materials expended on its expansion, nor with the losses it has sustained. . . . The aircraft in these operations could have been performing vital services in other theatres of war. . . . The policy of bombing Germany, which in any event can yield no decisive results within any measurable period of time, should no longer be regarded as of primary importance. Bomber squadrons should be flown forthwith to the Middle and Far East.[6]

Beaverbrook, who had been at the heart of air warfare policy-making (and at loggerheads with the Air Ministry) since 1940, was better informed than most of his Cabinet colleagues about the reality of the bomber offensive. Many ministers knew little or nothing about the struggle taking place over Germany beyond what they read in the newspapers. Ordinary members of the House of Commons and of the British public knew scarcely anything. It will become apparent later that real debate about the strategic air offensive did not develop even in well-informed circles until long after area bombing began, because so few people had any knowledge of it. Very early on, it had been agreed by the War Cabinet that there should be no public admission of changes in bombing policy. At a meeting on 24 March 1941,

> Several ministers reported that many people in the country believed that, although the enemy was attacking the civil population . . . we were still deliberately refraining from attacks on the German civilian population. No minister suggested that we should alter our policy to the extent of ceasing to attack military objectives. But it might be wise to take steps to bring home to our people that attacks such as those which we had carried out on Mannheim and Hanover had already resulted in inflicting grave injury on the civilian population of those towns: and that as the strength of our bomber force increased, the civilian population of Germany would increasingly feel the weight of our air attack.
>
> The general view of the War Cabinet was that it was better that acts should speak louder than words in this matter. . . .

Therefore although the making of war policy remained in Britain a much more open business than in any Axis state, the debate about the future of the bomber offensive was conducted almost entirely within a very small circle headed by the Prime Minister. Politicians such as Captain Balfour, even those with Cabinet rank such as Cripps and Beaverbrook, were entirely eclipsed by the power of the service chiefs in deciding the course of the war. Even the Chiefs of Staff became frequently no more than a rubber stamp for decisions already taken in Downing Street, in consultation with the Air Ministry. Major-General Sir John Kennedy, the Director of Military Operations, noted without pleasure that 'the bombing policy of the Air Staff was settled almost entirely by the Prime Minister himself in consultation with Portal, and was not controlled by the Chiefs of Staff'.[7]

The purpose of all the foregoing has been to show that in the critical months of decision for the future of the bomber offensive there was a formidable body of dissent in the service departments and in Whitehall which held that strategic bombing had proved a failure, and that, as the war widened and Britain's resources were stretched more tightly around the world, it was a grave error to reinforce the huge commitment to Bomber Command. Yet none of this made any impact on the decisive debate of this period: between the Chief of the Air Staff and the Prime Minister himself.

In the months that followed the fall of France in 1940, there is no dispute about the reasons for the emphasis thrust upon Bomber Command. Britain possessed no other means of taking the war to Germany. The campaign in North Africa would remain at best a sideshow and at worst a strategic irrelevance. The Royal Navy had embarked upon the long struggle to keep the Atlantic sea lanes open, but although this was to be one of the decisive battles of the Second World War, it was also a defensive one. The war could not be won without victory in the Atlantic, but victory in the Atlantic could not win the war. Churchill, with his boundless belligerence, perceived this clearly. He sought to attack Germany with whatever means were at Britain's command. 'In the fierce light of the present emergency,' he wrote to Beaverbrook at the Ministry of Aircraft Production on 8 July 1940:

> . . . the fighter is the need, and the output of fighters must be the prime consideration till we have broken the enemy's attack. But when I look around to see how we can win the war I see that there is only one sure path. We have no Continental Army which can defeat the German military power. The blockade is broken and Hitler has Asia and probably Africa to draw from. Should he be repulsed here or not try invasion, he will recoil eastward, and we have nothing to stop him. But there is one thing that will bring him back and bring him down, and that is an absolutely devastating, exterminating attack by very heavy bombers from this country upon the Nazi homeland. We must be able to overwhelm him by this means, *without which I do not see a way through.**

This is one of Churchill's most moving papers, because it reveals so clearly his knowledge of his own unreason. Reason dictated that Germany must triumph, that there was no means by which the enemy could possibly be defeated. Britain stood alone and impotent. Bomber Command was the sole remaining tool for offensive action. All Churchill's earlier and later writings suggest that he never rationally believed that the bomber alone could win the war. Yet in July 1940, if he did not make himself believe this, he could advocate nothing but surrender. He chose to commit himself totally to galvanizing ministers and mobilizing industry, goading air marshals and sweeping aside army and naval protest, to create the most powerful possible bomber

*Author's italics.

offensive with the utmost expedition. The moment that the first, vital fighter priorities had been met, the best brains and the greatest factories in Britain were directed towards the bomber campaign. He chafed constantly at the delay between decision and production:

> Prime Minister to the Air Minister, Minister of Aircraft Production and Chief of Air Staff:
>
> 30 December 1940
>
> I am deeply concerned at the stagnant condition of our bomber force. . . . I consider the rapid expansion of the bomber force one of the greatest military objectives now before us. . . .

While the Prime Minister pressed the claims of the bomber offensive with all his remorseless energy, a euphoria gripped the Royal Air Force, which never entirely died for the rest of the war. In the wake of the Battle of Britain, with the nightly operations of Bomber Command in the papers and on every newsreel, with the guidance of the Air Ministry's large and energetic public relations department, the airmen achieved a public and political recognition beyond the wildest dreams of the pre-war years. They gained a priority in production capacity and a primacy in strategic debate little short of intoxicating to senior RAF officers who had grown up amidst the constant real and imagined snubs of the army and the Royal Navy. By mid-1941 the first of the new heavy bombers, the Stirlings and Halifaxes with their five-ton bombloads to the Ruhr and 200-mph cruising speed, were coming into squadron service. The Air Staff now advanced the plan that was to remain a touchstone among the bomber enthusiasts for the remainder of the war. They proposed the creation of a force of 4,000 first-line heavy aircraft to bomb Germany, against the existing daily availability of something less than 500 of all types.

It was, in effect, a demand that the RAF should be permitted to take over the British war economy, of which it was already appropriating such an enormous share. Each Halifax required 76,000 man-hours to build, compared with 52,000 for a Whitley and 15,200 for a Spitfire, and even this figure took no account of the mass of sophisticated radar technology that would soon be in service. There was no possibility of creating a force of 4,000 heavy bombers from Britain's industrial resources alone – it was doubtful whether it could be done even with large-scale support from American factories. But the Air Ministry now embarked on a series of increasingly fantastic statistical calculations about the weight of explosives that it was necessary to drop upon the Third Reich in order to bring it to its knees, and the 4,000-bomber plan was the basis for the first of these. To the airmen its lure was irresistible, a scheme on a scale of which they never lost sight even when all hope of Britain fulfilling it had gone.

From the beginning, the 4,000-bomber plan was greeted with a kind of fascinated awe in Whitehall. Sinclair minuted Portal on 16 June 1941, explaining something of the consternation it had caused among those who might be called upon to find the resources to transform it into reality. Ministers were 'reluctant to commit themselves to so big a concentration of effort upon one means of winning the war'. But it is an indication of the Prime Minister's unshakeable determination to persevere with the bomber offensive that on 7 September, only days after the Butt Report reached his desk, he wrote:

> In order to achieve a first-line strength of 4,000 heavy and medium bombers, the RAF require 22,000 to be made between July 1941 and July 1943, of which 5,500 may be expected to reach us from American production. The latest forecasts show that of the remaining 16,500, only 11,000 will be got from our own factories. If we are going to win the war, we cannot accept this position. . . .

Since no man knew better than the Prime Minister that bomber production forecasts invariably failed to be met,* it is unnecessary to take this note too literally, or to regard it as evidence of Churchill's commitment to the 4,000-bomber plan. It was one of the innumerable galvanizing memoranda that he wrote to drive the production departments to greater efforts. There is much to suggest that by September 1941 he had already set aside the concept of winning the war by bombing alone. The desperate circumstances of 1940 forced him to grasp at desperate expedients. But now the whole pattern of the war was changing out of recognition. England was safe from invasion for the foreseeable future, left to stagnate in her backwater by the conquerors of Europe. The Wehrmacht had 'recoiled eastward' as Churchill had anticipated, and was now deep in Russia. It was too early to anticipate the scale of Germany's Napoleonic disaster in the east, but any man with Churchill's sense of history must have cherished hopes that mounted with every day of winter. The Prime Minister feared as deeply as any of his generation the prospect of sending a new British army to the Continent to engage in a prolonged struggle to the death with Germany, which could inflict casualties on both sides to make the Somme a pleasant memory. Historically, England had always striven to avoid committing major land armies to the Continent, had sought instead to win her wars by blockade, naval action, and moral and

*Heavy-bomber production was delayed at several critical periods by industrial action. For those who believe that the war was a halcyon era of British unity, it is worth recalling that wartime production lost by strikes in the metal, engineering and shipbuilding industries alone rose from a low of 163,000 days in 1940 to a high of 1,048,000 days in 1944. See the *Manpower* volume of the official history of wartime production for details.

financial support to her allies. In the winter of 1941, it became increasingly apparent that even if the Russians could not defeat the German army, the titanic struggles in the east must seriously weaken it. The likelihood of America entering the war was growing rapidly.

Yet even if she did so, the Allies would be compelled to adopt an indirect strategy for many months to come. Churchill wrote towards the end of 1942:

> In the days when we were fighting alone we answered the question 'How are you going to win the war?' by saying, 'We will shatter Germany by bombing.' Since then the enormous injuries inflicted on the German army and manpower by the Russians, and the accession of the manpower and munitions of the United States, have rendered other possibilities open. . . . We look forward to mass invasion of the Continent by liberating armies, and general revolt of the populations against the Hitler tyranny. All the same, it would be a mistake to cast aside our original thought – which, it may be mentioned, is also strong in American minds, namely, that the severe, ruthless bombing of Germany on an ever-increasing scale will not only cripple her war effort, including U-boat and aircraft production, but will also create conditions intolerable to the mass of German population. . . . We must regard the bomber offensive against Germany at least as a feature in breaking her war-will second only to the largest military operations which can be conducted on the Continent until that war-will is broken. . . .[8]

Churchill conceived the bomber offensive battering Germany like the siege artillery of old, until the crumbling walls and the starvation, squalor and weariness within made it much easier for the assaulting armies to try the breach. It was precisely because some of the RAF's foremost bomber enthusiasts understood this intention – that they should be the long-range guns of the army until the invasion of Europe could begin – that they fought so fiercely to elevate their campaign into something more, indeed into a battle to destroy Germany by bombing alone, to reduce the invasion to the mere disembarkation of the Allied armies of occupation. The American official historians wrote of the USAAF in the war that it was

> . . . young, aggressive, and conscious of its growing power. It was guided by the sense of a special mission to perform. It had to justify the expenditure of billions of dollars and the use of almost a third of the army's manpower. It sought for itself, therefore, both as free a hand as possible to prosecute the air war in accordance with its own ideas, and the maximum credit for its performance.[9]

These words apply with equal force to the RAF and to Bomber

Command. Seldom in history have men been so devoted to justification of a strategic theory in the midst of war. Only in the unique circumstances of the Grand Alliance from 1941 to 1944, when the bulk of its armies were idle or preparing themselves for the future, when such Allied land operations as took place were the merest sideshows to the great struggle taking place in Russia, could the airmen have achieved and maintained such independence of action in the face of the hostility and disbelief of the generals and admirals.

At the end of September 1941, Portal sent Churchill a paper which 'seeks to show that judging from our own experience of German attacks, the strength required to obtain decisive results against German morale may be estimated at 4,000 heavy bombers and that the time taken would be about six months'. Churchill dealt brusquely with this formidable assertion:

> It is very disputable whether bombing by itself will be a decisive factor in the present war. On the contrary, all that we learnt since the war began shows that its effects, both physical and moral, are greatly exaggerated. . . . The most that we can say is that it will be a heavy and I trust a seriously increasing annoyance.

Churchill's attitude – his apparent ambivalence to the bombing – was to confuse and irk the airmen until the end of the war. At one moment he seemed to be offering them his utmost support, at the next to be damning their pretensions, Yet, in his turn, the Prime Minister was exasperated by the airmen's attempts to transform a pragmatic decision to throw the largest possible weight of explosives at the German people into a scientific theory of war. He was always mistrustful of statistics and mathematical forecasts, from whatever source. In reading his flood of minutes and letters, it is essential to bear in mind the context in which they were written. Each day, he dictated an enormous correspondence. Much of it was unreasoned and unreasonable – barbed questions and comments to service departments on a huge range of strategic, tactical and technical issues. Churchill sought to urge, to provoke, to test argument. His immense energy in searching out the darkest corners of bureaucracy was part of his genius as a war leader. It is most significant that unlike Hitler, who shared his interest in *minutiae*, Churchill rarely allowed his own moments of crankiness to divert the war effort. A core of common sense sustained him even at the height of his own extravagances, and it was this which was constantly offended by the special pleading of the service departments. The following year, when Admiral Tovey dispatched a paper to the Admiralty condemning the bombing of Germany as 'a luxury not a necessity', Churchill dismissed him as curtly as ever he handled the airmen, remarking shortly that the paper 'damns itself'.[10]

But Portal was nettled by Churchill's sharp rebuff in September 1941, and by its apparent inconsistency. He reminded the Prime Minister that only weeks before he had approved a review of strategy by the Chiefs of Staff which stated that 'it is in bombing on a scale undreamt of in the last war that we find the new weapon on which we must principally depend for the destruction of economic life and morale'. On 7 October 1941 the Prime Minister answered Portal at length:

> We all hope that the air offensive against Germany will realize the expectations of the Air Staff. Everything is being done to create the bombing force on the largest possible scale, and there is no intention of changing this policy. I deprecate, however, placing unbounded confidence in one means of attack, and still more expressing that confidence in terms of arithmetic. It is the most potent method of impairing the enemy's morale we can use at the present time. If the United States enters the war it would have to be supplemented in 1943 by simultaneous attacks by armoured forces in many of the conquered countries which were ripe for revolt. Only in this way could a decision certainly be achieved. Even if all the towns of Germany were rendered largely uninhabitable, it does not follow that the military control would be weakened or even that war industry could not be carried on. . . . The Air Staff would make a mistake to put their claim too high. . . . It may well be that German morale will crack, and that our bombing will play a very important part in bringing the result about. But all things are always on the move simultaneously, and it is quite possible that the Nazi war-making power in 1943 will be so widely spread throughout Europe as to be to a large extent independent of the actual buildings in the homeland. . . . One has to do the best one can, but he is an unwise man who thinks there is any *certain* method of winning this war, or indeed any other war between equals in strength. The only plan is to persevere. . . .

This was a brilliant commentary on the reality of war, expounding principles of universal application to its conduct. Churchill was not withdrawing his support from the bomber offensive, indeed he would confirm the commitment of great resources to it in the months that followed. He was serving notice of the moderation of his own expectations.

But what now was Bomber Command to seek to achieve? Since the autumn of 1940, the Air Staff had tacitly conceded that daylight operations against Germany were not a feasible proposition, although many airmen nourished long-term hopes of their resumption. There might be occasional precision attacks by day or by night when opportunity arose and when certain targets demanded urgent attention, but the Butt Report had conclusively demonstrated that the majority of Bomber Command's crews could not find and hit a precise target at night.

> For the first time in air force history [wrote the official historians] the first and paramount problem of night operations was seen at the highest level to be not merely a question of bomb aiming, though that difficulty remained, but of navigation. While the bombers were still not within five miles of the aiming-point, it was a matter of academic interest as to whether a bomb could be aimed with an error of 300, 600, or 1,000 yards.

Left to themselves, it is reasonable to suppose that the airmen would have continued to dispatch bombers to attack precise targets in Germany, maintaining their private conviction that even if these missed their targets by miles, the trauma of air bombardment would somehow cause Germany to crumble. But now they were compelled to face the reality of the Butt Report and the illogic of bombing strategy. A new policy had become inevitable.

V

The Coming of Area Bombing, 1942

'Moderation in war is imbecility'
Admiral of the Fleet Lord Fisher

The decision was taken at the end of 1941 that, since a city was the highest common factor which most crews could identify on a given night under average conditions, Bomber Command would abandon its efforts to hit precision industrial targets and address itself simply to attacking the urban areas of Germany. Although spasmodic precision attacks would take place for the rest of the war, of the total tonnage of bombs dropped by Bomber Command throughout its campaign, three-quarters were directed against urban targets. The area attack was thus by far the most significant of Bomber Command's war.

The Prime Minister had always been doubtful about the RAF's alleged 'precision' offensive, the search for vital economic arteries, what Harris would later scornfully call 'panacea' targets. The concept of attacking whole cities rather than individual installations held no moral terrors for Churchill, although, as the War Cabinet had agreed in March 1941, there was no need to announce publicly any change in policy. Portal had been one of the earliest advocates of attacking German morale, and in the wake of the Butt Report he required no convincing that the way to do this was to launch the heaviest possible attack on urban areas.

Throughout 1941 this process had been getting under way. Although specific aiming-points were given to every crew, it was thoroughly if tacitly understood that most were merely carting explosives to the surrounding city areas. Now this reality would be recognized and the campaign greatly intensified. The only lingering division of opinion within the Royal Air Force lay between those who accepted the need to embark on area bombing merely as a necessary tactical expedient until the means to undertake a new precision attack became available, and those who regarded the policy as an end in itself. Much more will be heard from both these factions.

As far as it is possible to discover, there was no moral debate in Downing Street or the Air Ministry about the launching of the offensive on the cities. No one acquainted with the reality of war had ever supposed that it was possible to conduct any sort of bombing campaign without incidental civilian casualties. Whether it was morally any different to kill civilians incidentally, as Bomber Command had done hitherto, or deliberately as they would now begin to do, was a very nice question indeed. Churchill himself in his 1917 memorandum argued that the killing of civilians should remain an unavoidable side-effect rather a deliberate policy. The Americans were to justify their bombing operations in these terms throughout the war, even when the civilian death toll from their attacks reached extravagant heights. The British official historians have little patience with moral hair-splitting on this issue:

> There was, for example, a school of thought which maintained that, although it was morally permissible to attack specific targets such as factories, oil plants and railway centres even at an incidental risk to life and property, it was immoral to attack that life and property. In other words, the implication was that targets in or near towns could be attacked but that towns themselves could not. . . . It was, indeed, an argument which was generally put forward without operational factors in mind or even in sight. . . .[1]

This seems facile, for it is simply to assert that in warfare moral debate is irrelevant when operational requirements are at stake. Civilized nations, including the western Allies in the Second World War, have customarily waged war by a code which assumes that while all war corrupts, total war corrupts totally. They have sought thus to modify the worst excesses of the slaughter, most especially by avoiding the deliberate killing of non-combatants. The airmen of the Second World War argued that the Royal Navy's blockade in the First World War had killed civilians by starvation as surely as did their own bombs a generation later. Likewise, coastal bombardment by naval squadrons inflicted severe civilian casualties, but had always been an accepted feature of warfare. Extreme apostles of air warfare such as Mr J. M. Spaight in his book *Bombing Vindicated*, published in 1944, argued that 'The justification of air bombardment is that it is essentially *defensive* in purpose. You kill and destroy to save yourself from being killed or destroyed. . . . It would be suicide, normally, for a bomber formation to approach its target at a height at which precision of aim would be certain.' Yet a significant number of people felt that by embarking on a systematic attack against cities occupied largely by non-combatants in the traditional sense, the Allies sacrificed something of their own moral case and that they contributed substantially to the widespread moral collapse that took place in the Second World War, most especially in the treatment of prisoners and civilians. More of this will be heard later, in 1942 and 1943, as the nature of the Allied air offensive slowly became clear to the public in Britain and America.

The official historians dismiss the moral question overhanging area bombing with the simple assertion that by the winter of 1941 the only choice offered to the Royal Air Force was between area bombing and no bombing at all. Yet there was a third choice – to persist, in the face of whatever difficulties, in attempting to hit precision targets, supported by the growing range of radio and radar navigational and bomb-aiming targets that were already in the pipeline. There was also a fourth, and more realistic alternative: faced by the fact that Britain's bombers were incapable of a precision campaign, there was no compulsion upon the Government to authorize the huge bomber programme that was now to be undertaken. Aircraft could have been transferred to the Battle of the Atlantic and the Middle and Far East where they were so urgently needed, and many British strategists would have wholeheartedly defended the decision to move them. There was a genuine moral and strategic dilemma facing the Government in the winter of 1941 about future bombing policy. Thus there were alternatives to the area campaign, albeit at great cost to the *amour propre* of the RAF.

But in those icy months of debate, when Britain lay scarred by the Luftwaffe's blitz, labouring amidst the trauma of almost total catastrophe on every front, conscious of the appalling suffering that Nazi Germany was inflicting upon the world, the directors of the Allied war effort could scarcely be expected to perceive all these issues quite as clearly as they appeared to a generation of liberals thirty years later. The moral opposition to area bombing came from a small, if articulate, minority. The people of Britain might not be crying aloud for vengeance upon the women and children of Germany with quite the fervour that some British politicians supposed, but it is most unlikely that they would have opposed area bombing if they had been allowed to vote on it. Mr Geoffrey Shakespeare, Liberal MP for Norwich, wrote to Sir Archibald Sinclair in May 1942: 'Incidentally I am all for the bombing of working class areas of German cities. I am Cromwellian – I believe in "slaying in the name of the Lord", because I do not believe you will ever bring home to the civil population of Germany the horrors of war until they have been tested in this way.'

Whatever reaction Shakespeare's remarks may inspire today, they were perfectly acceptable among any but the most radical company in 1941 and 1942. The enthusiastic publicity accorded to the bomber offensive played an important role in keeping hope alive among the British people until at least June 1944.

Between the delivery of the Butt Report and the beginning of the concentrated attack on Germany's cities in the early spring of 1942, there was a pause. At the very moment when the Air Staff were brought face to face with the failure of their efforts, Bomber Command's casualties began to rise alarmingly. In the first eighteen nights of August 1941, 107 aircraft were lost. In September, 76 aircraft were missing and another 62 crashed inside England, out of 2,621 dispatched. In

October, 68 were missing and 40 crashed out of 2,501 dispatched. On the night of 7 November, 37 aircraft were lost out of 400 dispatched. 12.5 per cent of those sent to Berlin, 13 per cent of those sent to Mannheim and 21 per cent of those sent to the Ruhr failed to return. Only those sent to targets in France came home relatively unscathed.

Including those aircraft which crashed inside England, the entire front line of Bomber Command had been statistically wiped out in less than four months. Throughout 1941, an aircraft was lost for every ten tons of bombs dropped. Bomber Command would suffer far more severely in 1943, but by then the scale of the war had expanded enormously. In 1941 it was unthinkable to continue operations at this rate of attrition when the Butt Report made it clear that no significant results were being achieved. There was also a serious loss of confidence in Sir Richard Peirse's direction of Bomber Command. He seemed to have little grasp of operational realities, and he was a convenient scapegoat. On 13 November 1941 the Air Ministry instructed him to curtail drastically the scale of sorties against Germany, especially in bad weather. The War Cabinet, stated the directive, 'have stressed the necessity for conserving our resources in order to build a strong force to be available by the spring of next year'. That winter, the most significant of Bomber Command's operations were again launched against the *Scharnhorst* and the *Gneisenau*, to little effect, but with a dramatic fall in loss rates. The bomb figures fell from 4,242 tons dropped by Bomber Command in August 1941 to 1,011 tons in February 1942.

It is true that the strength of Bomber Command gained little on paper from this respite, because it suffered a constant drain of squadrons transferred to Coastal Command to support the Battle of the Atlantic, and to prop up Britain's ailing fortunes in the Middle and Far East. There was also the abrupt loss of the expected American contribution to British bomber strength, when the United States entered the war and at once appropriated almost all domestic aircraft production for her own needs. But in these months the Whitleys and Blenheims were being rapidly phased out, and the new generation of 'heavies' was beginning to arrive. American Venturas and Bostons were replacing the unlamented Blenheims. Later there would be the Mosquito, Geoffrey De Haviland's superb all-plywood light bomber and night fighter which the Air Minsitry had spurned in their enthusiasm for all-metal airframes, but which De Havilands developed on their own initiative into the two-seat aircraft capable of carrying a 4,000-lb bomb to Berlin at 265 mph. It was already apparent that the twin-engined Avro Manchester was a disappointment, but Acro's designer Roy Chadwick conceived the notion of solving its lack of power problems by stretching the wings and adding two more engines to the same fuselage. The result was the Avro

Lancaster, which promised to be one of the outstanding successes of wartime aircraft design when it entered service. The new four-engined Short Stirlings and Handley-Page Halifaxes would look inadequate in 1943 and 1944 – Stirling's pitiful 16,500-foot ceiling was quite inadequate for operations over Germany – but in 1941 and 1942 they were a vast improvement on what had gone before.

The spring of 1942, for which the air marshals were delaying, promised not only better weather and the first substantial deliveries of four-engined bombers from the factories, but above all the means to navigate with improved accuracy over Germany. The scientists had devised a radio-pulse system, codenamed *Gee*, by which the navigator of an aircraft could fix his position by reference to three transmitting stations in England. *Gee* had been tested over Germany in 1941, effectively if dangerously, since one set had already been lost with an aircraft, compromising its security. The scientists believed that when *Gee* was issued in quantity to Bomber Command early in 1942 it would take the Germans six months to devise effective jamming methods, and by the autumn they hoped to introduce still more advanced British devices. At this early stage, some of the scientists and airmen had hopes that *Gee* would prove accurate enough to become a blind-bombing device. Even if it did not, for the first time the bomber crews would have the means to find their way to Germany however severe the cloud masking pinpoint landmarks. Now that the immense technological needs of the air war had been identified, the scientists of the Telecommunications Research Establishment were giving birth to the range of equipment that by the end of the war would make Bomber Command overwhelmingly the most technically complex weapon in the hands of the Allies. Even now, at the end of 1941, with *Gee* in prospect the airmen could wait for the spring without impatience.

They possessed a new policy – the destruction of Germany's industrial cities by fire. They had been promised the means to undertake this. They lacked only a basis by which they might measure their achievements. In March 1942 the Prime Minister's Scientific Adviser, Lord Cherwell, provided this. His paper was not the basis for the bomber offensive – the critical decisions that were to influence British strategy so profoundly for the remainder of the war had already been taken and most of the immense industrial resources required had been committed. But Cherwell's report provided the final rationalization for the programme Bomber Command was undertaking. It became a significant landmark in the history of the bomber offensive.

> The following [Cherwell wrote to the Prime Minister on 30 March 1942] seems a simple method of estimating what we could do by bombing Germany.
>
> Careful analysis of the effects of raids on Birmingham, Hull and

elsewhere have shown that, on the average, one ton of bombs dropped on a built-up area demolishes 20–40 dwellings and turns 100–200 people out of house and home.

We know from our experience that we can count on nearly 14 operational sorties per bomber produced. The average lift of the bombers we are going to produce over the next fifteen months will be above three tons. It follows that each of these bombers will in its lifetime drop about forty tons of bombs. If these are dropped on built-up areas they will make 4,000–8,000 people homeless.

In 1938 over 22 million Germans lived in fifty-eight towns of over 100,000 inhabitants, which, with modern equipment, should be easy to find and hit. Our forecast output of heavy bombers (including Wellingtons) between now and the middle of 1943 is about 10,000. If even half the total load of 10,000 bombers were dropped on the built-up areas of these fifty-eight German towns the great majority of their inhabitants (about one-third of the German population) would be turned out of house and home.

Investigation seems to show that having one's house demolished is most damaging to morale. People seem to mind it more than having their friends or even relatives killed. At Hull signs of strain were evident, though only one-tenth of the houses were demolished. On the above figures we should be able to do ten times as much harm to each of the fifty-eight principal German towns. There seems little doubt that this would break the spirit of the people.

Our calculation assumes, of course, that we really get one-half of our bombs into built-up areas. On the other hand, no account is taken of the large promised American production (6,000 heavy bombers in the period in question). Nor has regard been paid to the inevitable damage to factories, communications, etc., in these towns and the damage by fire, probably accentuated by breakdown of public services.

Sir Charles Portal and Sir Archibald Sinclair reported that they found Lord Cherwell's paper 'simple, clear and convincing', although they noted that for his projections to be fulfilled, bomber production forecasts would have to be met, 50 per cent of sorties would have to be effective, the loss-rate would have to remain within reasonable proportions, and strategic diversions would have to be avoided. These were large reservations. But the airmen were not about to quarrel with the Prime Minister's scientific adviser when he offered his energetic support to the bomber offensive, whatever their private uncertainties about some of his reasoning. 'Lord Cherwell's minute', in the words of the official historians, 'had done no more and no less than to acknowledge a "design and theme" for the air offensive.'[2]

Cherwell, the erstwhile Professor Lindemann, had been close to the

Prime Minister throughout his years in the wilderness in the 1930s, and his fertile mind provided Churchill with many scientific defence ideas with which to belabour supine pre-war governments. Unfortunately, however, Lindemann concentrated his attention on air defence, almost the only area of military preparation in which, under the guidance of Sir Henry Tizard, great strides were being made. Churchill induced the Government to give Lindemann a seat on the Committee for the Study of Aerial Defence, where he at once made himself insufferable. Tizard and his colleagues concluded after much heart-searching that they must risk pouring all the resources at their command into the development of radar. Lindemann's fatal weakness was that he rarely found it possible to believe in an idea unless he was at least a midwife at its delivery. 'He suffered from the didactic approach that he himself knew everything worth knowing, and that anything outside his field of knowledge must be wrong,' said Barnes Wallis.[3] Within weeks of his appointment to the Committee, he caused chaos and dismay by insisting that the priority given to radar should be set aside, and that the Government instead concentrate on two brain-children of his own, aerial mines to be cast in the path of oncoming bombers and infra-red beams. His interference was intolerable. Tizard and others resolved the situation in the classic civil service manner, by dissolving the Committee for Aerial Defence and forming a new body, without Lindemann on it. Momentarily, 'The Prof' was eclipsed. But at the outbreak of war he was foremost among those who shared the rewards of personal loyalty to Churchill. He followed his master first into an office at the Admiralty, then into Downing Street with a peerage and in 1942 a seat in the Cabinet as Paymaster-General. He never lost Churchill's confidence, and wielded immense power for the remainder of the war.

Cherwell was a man of much arrogance, great personal wealth, at ease in the company of the mighty all his life, full of charm when he chose to exercise it. He possessed personal courage, demonstrated by his experiments with spinning aircraft in the First World War. He was a clever man, but had never been quite in the top flight of scientists, and certainly lacked that superlative brilliance which alone can justify sublime conceit in pursuit of one's own prejudices. Above all, Cherwell was personally vengeful. He never forgot a defeat. Sir Henry Tizard was a doomed man from the day that Cherwell achieved power. The outstanding scientific civil servant of his generation had inflicted on Cherwell the most humiliating reverse of his career, and he would never be forgiven for this.

In the winter of 1940 Tizard delivered himself into Cherwell's hand. He made a serious error of judgement in declining to acknowledge the existence of the navigational beams by which the Luftwaffe was bombing Britain with alarming accuracy. He was never allowed to forget this, and by the spring of 1942 his influence was waning fast. But in one of his last important interventions in the direction of the war,* he expressed his deep misgivings about Cherwell's 'de-housing' paper.

Tizard had already shown his scepticism about the weight of resources being devoted to bombing in a memorandum to the Ministry of Aircraft Production dated 12 December 1941, commenting on heavy aircraft plans: 'The war is not going to be won by night bombing,' he said. 'This programme assumes that it is.' Now, on 15 April 1942, he wrote to Lindemann: 'I am afraid that I think that the way you put the facts as they appear to you is extremely misleading and may lead to entirely wrong decisions being reached, with a consequent disastrous effect on the war. I think, too, that you have got your facts wrong. . . .'

Tizard went on to say that he feared that while the RAF's proposed massive bomber force was being assembled the war might be lost elsewhere for lack of sufficient defensive weapons. He was thinking especially of the Battle of the Atlantic. He also mistrusted Cherwell's sums. He reckoned that Bomber Command could only hope for 7,000 bombers by mid-1943, not Cherwell's 10,000. He questioned the crews' ability to find and hit Cherwell's fifty-eight towns. He doubted that the next generation of radar navigation and bombing aids would be available much before the spring of 1943. He thought that it was unreasonable to expect more than 25 per cent of bombs lifted to reach their target. All this, he recognized, 'would certainly be most damaging, but would not be decisive unless in the intervening period Germany was either defeated in the field by Russia, or at least prevented from any substantial further advance'.

> I conclude therefore
>
> (a) that a policy of bombing German towns wholesale in order to destroy dwellings cannot have a decisive effect by the middle of 1943, even if all heavy bombers and the great majority of Wellingtons produced are used primarily for this purpose.
>
> (b) That such a policy can only have a decisive effect if carried out on a much bigger scale than is envisaged in [Cherwell's paper].

Cherwell crushed his critic with considerable scorn. 'My dear Tizzard,' he wrote, 'many thanks for your note. I would be interested to hear what you think wrong with my simple calculation, which seemed to me fairly self-evident. . . . My paper was intended to show that we really can do a lot of damage by bombing built-up areas with the sort of air force which should be available.'

His own calculations had not been made for statistical analysis, but 'partly to save the Prime Minister the trouble of making arithmetical calculations'. Whatever disparities there might be between his figures

*Tizard left Whitehall to become President of Magdalen College, Oxford.

and reality, if Bomber Command concentrated its utmost efforts on Germany's cities, the effects would be 'catastrophic'.

Here was the very heart of the debate about area bombing. No one could reasonably argue that Bomber Command could pour explosives on to Germany over a period of years without doing terrible damage. No one with the slightest experience of bombing could dispute that it is a terrifying business to endure it. The reasoned critics of the bomber offensive did not deny that Bomber Command could raze to the ground areas of Germany – they questioned what contribution this would make to final victory, as against applying similiar resources to other sectors of the war effort. Every pound of explosives carried to Germany by Bomber Command cost at least a pound sterling to deliver. No one by this stage of the war disputed that tactical air superiority and tactical bombing were critical in the execution of any naval or military operation, and every aircraft that could be produced was vitally needed on the battlefield.

Tizard was a man who hated headlong confrontation, which ran against a lifetime's habit of academic circumspection. 'I should like to make it clear', he wrote mildly and probably insincerely[4] to Cherwell, 'that I don't disagree fundamentally with the bombing policy.' He merely doubted whether it could be effective unless carried out on a scale beyond Britain's means. He might have expressed himself more forcefully had he known the full extent of the misinformation on which Cherwell founded his original paper. The basis for Cherwell's projection of the effects of the bombing of England on to Germany's cities was a report, to be known as 'The Hull and Birmingham Survey', then being compiled by two scientists, Professor Bernal and Professor Zuckerman. Throughout their investigations, Bernal and Zuckerman had been answering a stream of questions from Cherwell's office, and feeding him on request with fragments of data. But the impression which Cherwell gave in his paper, that he founded his conclusions on a study of Bernal and Zuckerman's completed investigations, was false. Their report did not appear until 8 April 1942, ten days after Cherwell submitted his paper. Professor (now Lord) Zuckerman has described[5] his astonishment when he first saw Cherwell's minute, years after the war, and found that it drew on 'Hull and Birmingham' to argue directly opposed conclusions to those which the survivors had reached. Zuckerman and Bernal wrote: 'In neither town was there any evidence of panic resulting either from a series of raids or from a single raid . . . In both towns actual raids were, of course, associated with a degree of alarm and anxiety, which cannot in the circumstances be regarded as abnormal, and which in no instance was sufficient to provoke mass anti-social behaviour. There was no measurable effect on the health of either town.'

But Zuckerman and Bernal did not have the ear of the Prime

Minister, and nor did Tizard, Blackett or the distinguished scientists who opposed the bomber offensive. Most of Tizard's apprehensions and predictions proved entirely well-founded. Yet Lord Cherwell, always a devoted advocate of levelling Germany, retained his influence until the end of the war. At Bomber Command headquarters, measurement of acres of built-up area demolished became the standard method of computing the progress of the strategic offensive.

It is important to emphasize, however, that although all the principals were now in agreement about launching a major air attack on Germany's cities, there was still great unspoken confusion about the results to be sought from doing so. Lord Cherwell hoped to create a nation of refugees, and no doubt also a good many corpses under the rubble, although he was too genteel to say so. The airmen's aims were more complex and divided. In a paper of 19 September 1941 justifying the 4,000-bomber plan, the Air Ministry's Directorate of Bomber Operations said that 'It must be realized that attack on morale is not a matter of pure killing . . . It is an adaptation, though on a greatly magnified scale, of Air Control.' Presumably, therefore, DB Ops hoped that after a dose of mass destruction there would be moral collapse in Germany in fear of worse to come, perhaps on the lines suggested by Liddell Hart a generation earlier, with mobs of starved and crazed civilians roaming the streets demanding peace. Sir Charles Portal probably shared this long-term aspiration, but hoped in the short term for drastic reductions in German war production caused by absenteeism and flight from the cities, compounded by direct destruction of industrial plant. Sir Norman Bottomley, Deputy Chief of Air Staff, had composed a long memorandum in his days as SASO at High Wycombe in September 1940, in which he urged that Bomber Command's aim be 'primarily to destroy the enemy's will to win the war, leaving the destruction of his means to win the war as an incidental or indirect task'.

Sir Arthur Harris, who would shortly become the man charged with executing the area bombing policy, claimed in his post-war memoirs that he always regarded morale as a subordinate target. He says that he chiefly sought the direct destruction of German ability to produce. He was convinced by evidence suggesting a direct correlation between acres of concentrated urban devastation and lost industrial man-hours: 'The destruction of factories, which was nevertheless on an enormous scale, could be regarded as a bonus. The aiming-points were usually right in the centre of the town.'[6]

If all this leaves some confusion in the mind of the reader, it also suggests an extraordinary vagueness of thought on the part of the airmen. The concept of a Trenchardian thunderbolt fascinated them. But as far as it is possible to discover, they never recorded a common assent about the exact nature of what they hoped to achieve by area bombing, beyond the destruction of punitively large areas of German real estate. The importance of this lack of rigorous thinking, the absence of a definable and measurable goal for the bomber offensive, cannot be overstated. If a precise definition of success was not arrived at, nor was a yardstick of failure. Admirals could be sacked for failing to sink or save ships, generals for failing to win or hold ground. But nowhere was it suggested in the winter of 1941–42 that if Germany failed to collapse by a given date in the face of air attack, then the bomber offensive would have to be judged a failure. Even in Cherwell's 'de-housing' paper, there was no definition of a precise number of refugees that it was necessary to create to achieve decisive results. For all the talk about morale, no one tried to sketch a realistic political scenario for the overthrow of the Nazi leadership and crumbling of the German armies in the field.

After the war some airmen argued that they failed to achieve decisive success because they were denied the 4,000 bombers they had demanded to defeat Germany. Yet in 1942 they never made the undertaking of the area offensive conditional on being given such forces, and indeed no general or admiral in history has been granted all the forces he deemed desirable to achieve victory.

At the end of the day, Britain's huge area-bombing offensive was launched on the basis of no more concrete expectation – on the part of the air marshals, at any rate: the Prime Minister's view will be considered below – than that if a large enough weight of bombs was poured on to Germany, something vital must give somewhere.

The Air Ministry directive issued to Bomber Command on 14 February, St Valentine's Day 1942, was the blueprint for the attack on Germany's cities, and removed the constraints on bombing policy. The winter injunction to conserve forces was withdrawn. 'You are accordingly authorized to employ your forces without restriction,' wrote Bottomley, Deputy Chief of Air Staff. Annex A, appended to the directive, listed Bomber Command's new targets. Under the heading 'Primary Industrial Areas' came Essen, Duisburg, Düsseldorf and Cologne. 'Alternative Industrial Areas' included Lübeck and Rostock, Bremen and Kiel, Hanover, Frankfurt, Mannheim, Stuttgart and Schweinfurt. The directive ordered continuing harassing attacks on Berlin 'to maintain the fear of attack over the city and to impose ARP measures'. Above all, the directive stressed that during the six months' effective life of *Gee* – TR 1335, as it was referred to – Bomber Command must seek to concentrate the weight and density of its attack as never before. Operations 'should now be focused on the morale of the enemy civil population and in particular, of industrial workers'. It had been recognized for some months that incendiary bombs – 4-lb thermite sticks – had a special part to play as fire-raising weapons. Essen was suggested for the earliest bombardment. The remainder of the cities on the list would follow. Lest there be any confusion about objectives,

Portal wrote to Bottomley on 15 February: 'Ref the new bombing directive: I suppose it is clear that the aiming-points are to be the built-up areas, not, for instance, the dockyards or aircraft factories. . . . This must be made quite clear if it is not already understood.'

The Air Ministry directive was addressed to Air Vice-Marshal Baldwin, acting C-in-C at High Wycombe. Peirse was gone. He had inspired little sympathy or affection among his subordinates at Bomber Command, and little faith in his judgement in high places. He also paid the price for having been the man in command at the lowest ebb of Bomber Command's fortunes. There was now a new policy, new equipment. It was concluded that it would be best to find a new C-in-C, untarnished by the failures of the past.

One evening in December 1941, during the first great conference between the leaders of the British and American war efforts, Sir Charles Portal sought out Air Marshal Arthur Harris, head of the permanent RAF delegation in the United States and asked him to take over Bomber Command. Harris accepted. Portal said: 'Splendid! I'll go and tell Winston at once.'[7] On 22 February 1942, a week after the issue of the Air Ministry directive unveiling area bombing, Harris became Air Officer Commanding-in-Chief at Bomber Command headquarters, High Wycombe. He was just short of fifty and he remained in the post until the end of the campaign. In the thirty months of war that were already passed, Bomber Command had lost 7,448 aircrew killed in action and accidents or taken prisoner. By May 1945 this figure would have reached 72,350. The bomber war had scarcely begun when Harris became C-in-C. Henceforth, his name would be indelibly associated with its fortunes.

Arthur Travers Harris was the son of a member of the Indian civil service, conventionally privately-educated in England until he fell out with his parents over their wish that he should enter the army. He then took the usual path of disgruntled young Edwardian Englishmen, and departed for the Colonies. At the age of sixteen he arrived in Rhodesia with five pounds in his pocket. In the six years that followed, he tried his hand at farming, gold mining and driving horse teams. Rhodesia was kind to him, and he returned her welcome with lifelong affection. At the outbreak of war in 1914, he joined the Rhodesia Regiment as a boy bugler and fought through the fierce hardships of the German South-West African campaign. When this ended in 1915, he found his way back to England, determined that he had had enough of footslogging. He joined the Royal Flying Corps and was shortly afterwards posted to France. He finished the war as a major with the Air Force Cross. In the next twenty years he commanded bomber squadrons exercising Trenchard's Air Control scheme in the further outposts of the Empire, and served from 1933 to 1937 in staff posts at the Air Ministry. Unlike Portal or Ludlow-Hewitt, he was not regarded as an obvious high-flier, destined for the highest ranks. But he advanced steadily to command of 4 Group in 1937, to head the RAF Purchasing Mission in America in 1938, then to command the crack 5 Group in the early days of the war. It was there that he made a reputation as a forceful director of bomber operations.

Sir Arthur Harris, as he now became, possessed something of the earthy, swaggering ruthlessness of an Elizabethan buccaneer. A broad man of medium height, his piercing eye gave him immediate presence in any company. 'There are a lot of people who say that bombing cannot win the war,' he declared to a newsreel interviewer a few weeks after taking over at High Wycombe, in the crisp, clipped tones that cowed so many wavering staff officers. 'My reply to that is that it has never been tried yet. We shall see.' He gave no sign of fearing God or man, and in Washington his outbursts of frankness left behind a trail of savaged American military sensitivities. He was an early convert to the concept of strategic bombing, and ranked among Trenchard's most dedicated disciples. He had devoted much energy between the wars to means of improving bomb-aiming and target-marking.

His dry, cutting, often vulgar wit was legendary throughout the RAF, as was his hatred of the British Army and the Royal Navy. He was fond of saying that the army would never understand the value of tanks until they could be modified to 'eat hay and shit'. A man of boundless energy, he spent much of the war racing his Bentley at breakneck speed between High Wycombe and the Air Ministry, and was the bane of motor-cycle policemen on the London road. 'You might have killed somebody, sir,' said a reproachful constable who stopped him late one night.

'Young man, I kill thousands of people every night!' snapped Harris. He seemed to like the ogre-ish role that fortune had cast for him. His contemporaries called him 'Bert', but his crews called him 'Butcher', 'Butch' for short. His subordinates at High Wycombe were deeply in awe of him, and there was little scope for dissent at his councils. He was a man of startling directness, and his temper cannot have been improved by the ulcers from which he suffered throughout the war. Saundby, his SASO, once sent him a memorandum, painstakingly describing ten alternative methods of attacking a target. Harris returned it with a scrawled endorsement: 'TRY FERRETS'.

From the beginning of the war, he was convinced that given the vast shortcomings of Britain's armed forces compared with those of Germany, a bomber offensive was inevitable:

> I could . . . see only one possible way of bringing pressure to bear on the Boche, and certainly only one way of defeating him; that was by

> air bombardment. It consequently looked as if it was going to be a straight fight between our own and the enemy's production of heavy bombers. . . .
>
> If we could keep ahead of the Germans, I was convinced, having watched the bombing of London, that a bomber offensive of adequate weight and the right kind of bombs would, if continued for long enough, be something that no country in the world could endure.
>
> It was, of course, anybody's guess what effort would be required and over what period the offensive would have to be continued.[8]

Harris was naturally an ardent advocate of the 4,000-bomber plan, which it was apparent would never be fulfilled. Some compromise with the Royal Navy's demands for heavy aircraft and the insistent needs of other theatres had to be made, and Harris would have nothing like the resources he hoped for until at least 1943. But he would fight until the last day of the war to ensure that Bomber Command achieved the utmost possible strength, and the attainment of an order of battle of 1,600 heavy bombers in his operational squadrons by April 1945 was a tribute to his determination and force of personality. Area bombing was not his creation, but he applied himself to executing the policy with an energy and single-mindedness that prevailed long after less committed airmen turned their minds to other strategies.

At the time that he became C-in-C, Harris knew Churchill scarcely at all. In 1940, when he was commanding 5 Group, he had once been summoned to the Prime Minister's occasional retreat at Ditchley, but he had been granted only a few words. Now, however, the apparent intimacy between Harris and Churchill began to attract widespread attention and intense jealousy, not least among the admirals, who were enraged to hear of the airman being invited to drive the few miles from High Wycombe to Chequers for dinner and presumably a great deal of special pleading for his Command. The precise relationship between the C-in-C and the Prime Minister remained a matter of curiosity and controversy throughout the war and afterwards. General Sir Bernard Paget thought that 'Bert Harris was the sort of buccaneer whom Churchill particularly liked. . . .[9] But Major Desmond Morton, the secret service officer who had been one of Churchill's intimate circle since before the war, believed quite otherwise:

> Curiously enough, I think he *never* cared for Harris as a person. I do not know why not, though I know why *I* did not. . . . My own distaste . . . was based on what I thought, rightly or wrongly, of his personality. He seemed to me to be a bit of a boor (not bore) with little or any sort of fine thoughts or sign of anything distinguished in his mind or person. I am always attracted by anyone who seems to be

trying to be, and behave like a gentleman in any way, I found nothing of this sort in Harris. I do not condemn Harris absolutely. He did many great things doubtless. It is not easy (if possible) to become a Marshal of the Royal Air Force without doing many notable things well. But in my opinion many of the things he did and said and did well, were done and said in a manner lacking refinement'.[10]

Morton's shrewd assessment received endorsement many years later, with the publication of *The Long Sunset*, memoirs of Churchill's last Private Secretary, Anthony Montague Brown. In his old age, Churchill said privately of Harris: 'I admired his determination and his technical ability. He was very determined and very persuasive on his own theme. And the Prof. backed him up . . . [He was] a very considerable commander. I said so many times. But there was a certain coarseness about him.'

Whatever the admirals' fears about Churchill's relations with Harris, the airman never gained the Prime Minister's confidence for his grand vision of victory by air bombardment alone. And whatever the truth of Morton's suspicions about the Prime Minister's personal attitude, there is no doubt that many of those in high places reacted to Bomber Command's C-in-C like the fastidious major.

But Harris's style, the stories about his rudeness and extravagance, contributed immensely to his popularity with his overwhelmingly lower-middle-class bomber crews. They endeared him to them, though they never saw him, with a warmth that a more distant, discreet, patrician figure such as Portal never inspired. Harris was a real leader. From beginning to end, he succeeded in seeming to identify himself totally with the interests of his men.

Yet for all his bluntness and supposed pragmatism, it is impossible to accept that Harris was a realist about operational difficulties. From the beginning of the war, he had refused to accept the inadequacy of Bomber Command's navigation, even when most of his colleagues did so. He was foremost among the self-deluded about the early achievements of bombing. In October 1940 one of the most fanciful Intelligence reports quoted 'well-informed industrialists' assessments that 25 per cent of Germany's productive capacity had been affected by bombing'. Harris wrote to Peirse expressing his delight about 'the accuracy with which our aircraft hit military objectives as opposed to merely browning towns . . . These summaries serve to impress upon one . . . the by now patent fact that the Air Ministry Publicity department is half-witted.'

Harris complained, as he was to do repeatedly when he became C-in-C, that the Press gave inadequate recognition to Bomber Command's achievements:

> What a riot of publicity would attend such results had they been secured by the Army, and what a catastrophic spate of words if the Navy had succeeded in doing a thousandth as much! Yet when the bombers begin to win the war – and we are the only people that can win it, and we are winning it – what happens? Nix!

Harris suggested that the only possible explanation for the Publicity Department's passivity was that its staff 'are all long since dead, and nobody's noticed it! Naturally enough, nobody would!'

On 1 February 1941, when the Air Ministry was deeply concerned about Scientific Intelligence's discovery that the Germans were bomb-aiming by radio beam, Harris as Deputy Chief of the Air Staff wrote crossly:

> Are we not tending to lose our sense of proportion over these German beams? . . . We use no beams ourselves but we bomb just as successfully as the Germans bomb, deep into Germany. . . . I do not agree that the beams are in fact a serious menace to this country, or that they have proved to be in the past. They are simply aids to navigation, and it is within our experience that such aids are not indispensable to the successful prosecution of bombing expeditions. I could go further and say that they are not even really useful. . . . Long may the Bosche beam upon us!

This was the man who was now called upon to lead Bomber Command's first major operations under the influence of *Gee*, who would resist to the utmost the creation of the Pathfinder Force, who would fight every attempt to transfer the attentions of Bomber Command from area to precision bombing, and who in 1944 professed his astonishment, when he was overruled and compelled to dispatch his aircraft on precision operations, to find that they were perfectly capable of carrying them out.

Harris was an inflexible man, chronically resistant to negotiation and compromise, who treated those who disagreed with him as mortal enemies. He seemed driven, in the words of one historian,[11] by an 'elemental tenacity of purpose'. This was a quality that would earn him many enemies and abrupt dismissal at the end of the war. But it is a most useful characteristic on the battlefield. Harris was a nerveless commander of great forces, and the history of warfare shows that such men are rare. His very insensitivity rendered him proof against shocks and disappointments. He possessed the considerable gifts of clarity of speech and purpose, and from the moment that he became C-in-C at High Wycombe, he infused these into his entire Command. He was never afraid of taking decisions. He made his officers at every level feel that they were now part of a great design instead of merely running a ramshackle air freight service exporting bombs to Germany. If his superiors ever lost confidence in him, or considered that he was failing to meet their hopes and wishes, it was their business to replace him, as so many wartime C-in-Cs were replaced.

When Harris took command, there had been twenty-two directives from the Air Ministry to Bomber Command since the outbreak of war, repeated changes of policy as the planners groped in the darkness for Germany's economic jugular. Harris was determined that there should be no more of this, no more 'panacea targets' such as oil plants or aircraft factories. He believed that there were no short cuts to defeating Germany from the air. It was necessary to concentrate all available forces for the progressive, systematic destruction of the urban areas of the Reich, city block by city block, factory by factory, until the enemy became a nation of troglodytes, scratching in the ruins. This conviction would become his obsession. Given time and technique – and at the beginning of 1942 it was plain that he could expect years – he would demonstrate to the world the force of properly handled strategic air power, and the unique place of the Royal Air Force in the Allied war effort.

Thus Bomber Command became committed to area bombing, and the Government committed to Bomber Command an industrial capacity eventually equal to that devoted to the entire British army, along with the cream of Britain's wartime high technology.

It remains only to emphasize that the Prime Minister, while he supported the strategic air offensive, shared few of the airmen's extravagant expectations for it. In 1940 he had supported Bomber Command from necessity. Yet now, with the German army mired in Russia and with America not only an ally but committed to a strategy of 'Germany first', why did he persist with a bomber attack in which he had limited strategic faith? The need to sustain the morale of the British people by visible action is a partial answer. But by far the most convincing reason is that the Prime Minister had already become determined to postpone the opening of a Second Front in Europe until the last possible hour. There was no longer any doubt that the Allies would ultimately win the war. The questions were how soon, and at what cost? Already the Americans with their military innocence and huge resources were pressing for an early invasion of northern Europe to get to grips with the enemy. The Prime Minister was resisting this proposal with all the force at his command. He thwarted first proposals for an invasion in 1942, then others for 1943. He was determined that when the Allies landed in France, it should be under conditions of overwhelming advantage. There must be no great campaign of attrition, such as would be inevitable against an unbroken German army.

Churchill never shared the airmen's faith that the bomber offensive could eliminate the need for a land campaign to defeat the enemy. But the bombers could enable the western Allies to delay aggressively, while Russia fought out the huge battles that broke the Wehrmacht, that caused the Axis by early 1944 to deploy 240 divisions in the East against 50 in France and the Low Countries. Neither the Russians nor the Americans could flatly be told that the British proposed to fight no campaign in Europe for years to come. If the bomber offensive, fuelled by publicity and boosted with American support, and given formidable but not extravagant supplies of aircraft, met with even moderate destructive success, this would provide convincing evidence of Britain's commitment to the struggle at a very tolerable cost in British lives. Bomber Command's 56,000 dead represented, at the end, the lowest possible stake that Britain could be seen to throw on the tables of Europe, when the Russians were counting their dead in millions. The strategic air offensive might thus be interpreted as the greatest panacea of all. Yet if this was indeed in Churchill's mind when he authorized the area campaign at the beginning of 1942, then Bomber Command fulfilled his hopes in the next two years far more satisfactorily than those of the Royal Air Force.

VI

50 Squadron, Lincolnshire, 1942

Across the road the homesick Romans made,
The ground-mist thickens to a milky shroud;
Through flat, damp fields call sheep, mourning their dead
In cracked and timeless voices, unutterably sad,
Suffering for all the world, in Lincolnshire.

And I wonder how the Romans liked it here;
Flat fields, no sun, the muddy misty dawn,
And always, above all, the mad rain dripping down,
Rusting sword and helmet, wetting the feet
And soaking to the bone, down to the very heart . . .

Henry Treece, 'Lincolnshire Bomber Station'

1. Harris Conducts an Overture

1942 was the pivotal year for the Allies in almost every theatre of war. The tide turned at Stalingrad; the Japanese were defeated at Midway; the North African diversion was at last brought within sight of conclusion by the defeat of the Afrika Korps; the Atlantic lifelines were held open in the face of horrifying losses. At this critical time, when the Allies were not yet prepared to confront the Germans in Western Europe, the bomber offensive might have made a central contribution had it been ready to do so. But Bomber Command was still hesitantly gathering its strength. In June, its most effective month, only 6,485 tons of bombs were dropped against the 15,271 that would fall in the same month of 1943 and the 57,267 tons of June 1944. Thirteen of the squadrons mustered and equipped with such exertions were detached to Coastal Command and the Middle East, leaving just thirty (with an establishment of sixteen aircraft each) in Harris's front line. He strained credibility when he claimed to the War Cabinet that he controlled only 11 per cent of the RAF and Fleet Air Arm's front line, for this ignored the vast resources needed to produce, support and operate heavy aircraft compared with fighters. But bomber production was lagging, Stirling and Halifax output had been delayed by repeated teething troubles, and the twin-engined Manchester was proving grossly underpowered. Only the Lancaster showed signs of fulfilling the hopes of the pre-war visionaries of heavy bombers.

Yet in 1942 the mould of the offensive was formed, the image in which Bomber Command would fight and send so many men to die and in which it would be etched into history. With hindsight, it is possible to see that there were two wars between 1939 and 1945. The first was the last war of a past generation. The second was emphatically the first of the new era. Technology was coming of age: radar and the atomic bomb, the jeep and the high-performance aircraft. Somehow even the faces in the photographs look different. A Bomber Command group from, say, Honington in 1939 merges imperceptibly into the sepia shades of Camels and 'Archie' and the old Royal Flying Corps. But then study the faces of the Lancaster crews of Harris's Bomber Command (ironically, for he himself was anything but a modern man): so many of the young faces are already those of the knowing, professional young technocrats of the post-war era, children who have lost their innocence thirty times over Germany, who will vote for the Welfare State in 1945, who are the most highly trained front-line fighters in the history of warfare.

By 1942 most of the pre-war generation of regular aircrew had been killed off, promoted to non-operational posts, or left languishing behind German barbed wire. Now, in the spirit of Kitchener's New Armies of 1915, the first flower of the volunteers of 1939 were reaching the squadrons. These were the romantic young idealists, almost to a man aspiring fighter pilots, many of them the colonials who would make such an enormous contribution to Bomber Command – New Zealanders, Australians, Canadians. They had trained all over the world for two years or more – some in America, others in Canada, Rhodesia, South Africa.[1] The pilots and navigators represented the highest skills – most of the latter had been eliminated from pilot training courses. Bomb-aiming had at last been recognized as a specialist trade for which men were specifically trained. Gunners, wireless operators and flight engineers were taught what they needed to know to use their equipment, and little more.

At the Operational Training Units they were brought together. There was no more arbitrary assembling of men for odd operations: it was clearly understood that the fate of Bomber Command hung on the integrity and mutual confidence of the operational crews, and every possible step was taken to allow like-minded souls to fit together. In the first few days at OTU, a milling herd of assorted aircrew was left to crew up by natural selection:

'I hear you want a gunner? Can you fly a Wimpey without making me throw up?'

'We're looking for a wireless operator and you're the only bloke here who doesn't look as if he's got DTs. . . .'

'Our driver flew into a hill this morning so we wondered if you might do us for a new one. . . .'

The accident rate at OTUs was appalling.* Some courses lost as

*5,327 officers and men were killed and a further 3,113 injured in RAF training accidents 1939–45.

many as 25 per cent of their trainees before graduation four or five months after arrival. Tour-expired aircrew posted to instruct rapidly learned that flying pupils in tired and often under-maintained bombers was anything but a rest-cure. But at least men were learning new tactical and technical skills at OTU that a year before they were compelled to teach themselves over Germany.

At the end of their training, these rather bewildered but intensely willing young men went to their stations. Little huddles of blue-clad humanity clutching their gas-masks and kitbags stood on some East Anglian railway platform to be collected by a nonchalant MT driver in a three-quarter-ton truck. If they were destined for 5 Group, they fetched up at Newark or the old garrison town of Lincoln. If they were going to 50 Squadron early in 1942, they found themselves driving down the Fosseway, the old Roman road south-west from Lincoln to Swinderby, the big pre-war station for which 50's ageing Hampdens took off for Germany. Here, amidst the flat, rich fields of East Anglia, something more than half of them would be making their final homes.

5 Group had always been considered – not least by 5 Group – Bomber Command's crack division. 50 was one of its outstanding squadrons. In 1941 its commanding officer was one of the legendary leaders of Bomber Command, Gus Walker. By early 1942 Walker had been succeeded by Wing-Commander 'Beetle' Oxley, a rather more pedestrian figure. The corpulent Oxley was an excellent and forceful administrator, but flew only a minimum of operations himself. At his briefings, crews would sometimes shout that half-serious, half-mocking taunt at groundlings: 'Get some in!' Oxley would say, 'Piece of cake tonight, chaps. Last time I was over Mannheim it was only defended by two men and a dog', which caused a good deal of derisive laughter, since everybody knew that he was harking back to some primeval date in 1940. But Oxley knew how to drive men, and he detested the enemy. Every new crew at 50 Squadron was given a CO's pep-talk on 'the need to work up Hun-hate'. Oxley's passionate dedication to the business of killing Germans had become a sort of legend in 5 Group, and not only there. A 50 Squadron gunner shot down early in 1942 was astonished by one of the first questions put to him by a fascinated German interrogator at Dulag Luft: 'Who is this man Oxley?'

50 Squadron in 1942 bred and trained a long succession of outstanding pilots and crews, including many who went to form the Dambusters a year later. Henry Maudslay, the quiet, gentle Old Etonian son of a rich West Country family, was a former Coastal Command 'Kipper Fleet' pilot. Like his 50 Squadron colleague 'Hoppy' Hopgood, he would die over the Mohne Dam. Les Knight, a little Australian, completed his tour with 50 and burst the Eder dam before his luck ran out over the Dortmund–Ems canal one night in 1943. The rumbustious 'Trev' Trevor-Roper, with his Oxford accent and Billingsgate vocabul-

ary, was a sergeant gunner at Swinderby before he was commissioned and became Guy Gibson's rear gunner.

Micky Martin, who with Gibson, Willie Tait and Leonard Cheshire would be regarded as the four great RAF bomber pilots of the war, transferred to 50 from the Australian 455 Squadron when 455 were posted to Coastal Command. The son of a well-established Australian medical family, Martin was sent to England early in 1939 to sow his wild oats before settling down to train as a doctor. Single-minded in anything he attempted, he managed to get through a thousand pre-war pounds in eight weeks, much of it on horses – he rode in amateur races himself. He then applied to join the RAF as a fighter pilot, and after some bureaucratic problems he was accepted and abandoned his flat in Mayfair for initial flying training. By early 1942 he had completed part of a tour of operations in 455 with his all-Australian crew. Foxlee and Simpson, his gunners, Bob Hay, his bomb-aimer, and Jack Leggo, his navigator, eventually became almost as famous as Martin himself. Aweing English colleagues with their reckless life-style on the ground, they made a reputation for brilliance and utter determination in the air. In 1942 Martin was one of a select band of like-minded spirits. By 1945 this wild man was a rare phenomenon. He lived.

Like every squadron in the RAF, 50 also had its private celebrities, known to every man on the station but few outside it, and mostly destined for unmarked graves in Germany. There was Charlie Stone, the tough, flippant former architectural student who was their tame cartoonist; Drew Wyness, cheerful and handsome, married to an enviably beautiful model; Jock Abercrombie, who once flew Ed Murrow to Berlin and brought him home a shaken reporter; Paul Crampton, who suffered every possible mishap and near-disaster as he lurched through his tour; Flash Southgate; Micky Moores; Hughie Everitt, with his unnaturally flawless uniform and crisp salute; the three American gunners in Canadian uniforms who each earned more in a week than 'Beetle' Oxley – Swinderby knew them all intimately.

It is important to stress the extraordinarily high calibre of the human material that came to Bomber Command. The majority had matriculated and would have been at university or working in one of the professions, if they were not in the RAF. Their imaginations had recoiled from the prospect of trudging through the war in the infantry, and they had been captured by the vision of flying, the glamour that only faded from the blue uniform as they climbed into their lonely cockpits at dusk.

Ken Owen was a 50 Squadron navigator, one of almost half his sixth form at Pontypridd Grammar school who volunteered for the RAF at the outbreak of war: 'We tended to be the gilded youth of our generation: we belonged to the local tennis and cricket clubs, and our fathers knew the local bank manager. . . .'[2] Owen had reached Swinderby after the usual tortuous paperchase through service bureaucracy. He left university at the end of his first year when he was summoned to attend an aircrew selection board at Penarth, outside Cardiff. There was a prolonged, searching medical examination which eliminated many of the queue on the first day as colour-blind, slightly deaf or slow-reflexed. The next day they sat an intelligence test which emphasized spatial judgement. In the afternoon they went before an interview board. A few days later, Owen was among the successful candidates who found themselves summoned by letter to St John's Wood reception centre in north London. Here, like so many RAF volunteers through the war, he spent a dreary fortnight among men falling asleep in rows at lectures on cricket and similar time-fillers until they were packed off to Elementary Flying Training school near Carlisle. Owen was washed out of pilot training within a fortnight, and posted to learn to be a navigator. At an OTU in Shropshire, he joined a crew and graduated on the old Blenheim. They reached Swinderby bursting with enthusiasm to get into the air, and were deeply crestfallen when the flight commander said off-handedly: 'Oh, nobody's going to let you near an operational aircraft yet', and made them fly day and night training exercises for a fortnight before they took off on a trip to Germany.

They flew their first operation to Kassel in a curious daze, almost euphoric in the sense of unreality. It was bright moonlight and the flak was intense, but excitement somehow numbed apprehension. It was only afterwards, remembering, looking ahead to the next time and knowing what was to come, that fear began to seep in. Over the North Sea their feet froze while they sweated profusely under their arms. A few trips later, over the Dortmund–Ems canal, their rear gunner Jackie Smith suddenly shouted: 'Corkscrew port!' and the aircraft shook as the cannon shells hammered home from the German fighter. When they pulled out of the dive and found themselves alone, there was still silence from the rear gunner. Owen felt his way aft. Jackie Smith with his curly hair and big black eyes lay hunched over his guns, dead.

For the rest of the crew, there was no more excitement in flying operations, only the grim sense of a job to be done from which there was no honourable escape. The early weeks of 1942 passed in a round of mining sorties, blind groping over Germany in impossible weather, and the abortive efforts to find and sink the *Scharnhorst* and *Gneisenau* in the Channel on their break-out from Brest on 12 February. It was a routine of its own with no sense of the days of the week or any punctuation beyond the next leave or the end of the tour. To a post-war generation, the bomber offensive may conjure up images of terrified German women and children huddled in their shelters as distant British aircraft rained down death from above. To the crews of Bomber Command, Germany was not a place of innocent *gasthausen* and beer cellars where buxom girls smiled and drinkers stamped their feet to the accordion music, but a terrifyingly hostile environment where British airmen died in their hundreds every night. If they thought at all about what lay far beneath them, they imagined the flak gunners and searchlight crews in their coalscuttle helmets pumping up 88 mm shells and those deadly beams of light that made a man feel 'as if reproving fingers were pointing at him, as if he himself were a naughty boy suddenly discovered in the dark of a larder'. Even the most sensitive young Englishman found that 'he felt no guilt or dismay at dropping bombs, simply because his fear entirely submerged any more noble or humane emotion'.[3] A fascinating anonymous report in the Air Ministry files dated 21 June 1942 analysed aircrews' letters opened by the censors: 'They illustrate the effect of airmen's remoteness from their attacks on human beings. Expressions of satisfaction that the Germans are having to undergo the punishment they have hitherto meted out to others are found in almost all letters, but there is an absence of vindictiveness or fanaticism in the phrases used. . . .'

Their own nation's propaganda had been perfectly effective in making them visualize the Germany below them as the arsenal of Nazi Europe, the cradle of the Gestapo and the Luftwaffe's pioneer *blitzkriegs*, of Hitler himself and his thousands of hysterical arm-raising followers. The opening of Bomber Command's area offensive came at a moment when 30,000 people in Britain had already been killed by German bombing, when vast areas of the City of London, of Coventry and Southampton and a score of other towns lay in ruins. The crews of Bomber Command were very young, and sprung from a generation accustomed to defer to authority. They had been trained and ordered to fly to Germany and release their bombload at a given point. They were told that by doing so they were making a vital contribution to the war effort. With great fear in most of their hearts, they went out each night to do no more and no less than they were ordered. The notion of killing German civilians individually or in bulk troubled only a tiny handful.

One of the first proposals to reach Sir Arthur Harris in the days after he took up his post at High Wycombe in February 1942 came from the Foreign Office. It wished to revive the old idea of proscription: to name publicly, on the radio, twenty German towns that would be subjected to saturation attack by Bomber Command, and hope for panic among the population, a mass exodus of refugees, and a rising tide of terror across the Third Reich. But whatever Harris's long-term plans for Germany's cities, he understood that Bomber Command as yet possessed quite inadequate resources for the sort of wholesale destruction that the Foreign Office wanted. He needed time, and he had no intention of encouraging the Germans to concentrate their defences around a limited number of preordained targets. In the months to come, Bomber

Command's most useful purpose would be to divert resources from Germany's offensive war effort to the defence of her own cities. To bring this about, Harris proposed to skirmish across the widest possible front.

But as Bomber Command fought off its critics, and most especially the demands of the Royal Navy for transfer of aircraft that would have caused its virtual dissolution, Harris also understood that his forces needed some spectacular successes. In his early months at High Wycombe, he stage-managed a succession of operations which, whatever their strategic shortcomings, were brilliantly successful public-relations efforts for the bomber offensive. On 9 March he sent 235 aircraft to hit the Renault works at Billancourt, which produced 14,000 trucks a year for the *Wehrmacht*. They attacked in a new pattern, led by a wave of flare-droppers, followed by a wave of bombers carrying maximum incendiary loads to fire the centre of the target, followed in turn by the main force with high-explosives. It was another step towards evolving a target-marking routine, shortly to be followed by a development codenamed *Shaker*, which exploited *Gee* as a blind-marking aid in the leading aircraft. 470 tons of bombs were dropped on Billancourt. When the photographs of the Renault works came in the next morning, they were hailed as a triumph. 'All aircraft bombed the primary,' exulted 50 Squadron record book. The concentration of bombs around the aiming-point was judged exceptional. Immediate post-raid euphoria was dampened somewhat when the final damage assessments were in a few weeks later, suggesting that the plant had lost less than two months' production and that French civilian casualties had been high. But by then Harris's forces had moved on to greater things.

On 28 March, 234 aircraft attacked the old north German Hanse town of Lübeck. In the weeks following his arrival at High Wycombe, while Harris sent his aircraft to grope through the haze over Essen and other cities of the Ruhr in obedience to the February Air Ministry directive, he had been searching for an area target that they could find, strike and utterly destroy. 'I wanted my crews to be well "blooded", as they say in foxhunting, to have a taste of success for a change,'[4] he said. Lübeck was on the coast and thus a relatively simple navigation problem. It was lightly defended and had not even been incorporated in the major German civil defence schemes because it seemed an unimportant target. But it was on the Air Ministry's February list. Above all, as had been pointed out by Bomber Command's town-planning advisers, it was an old, closely-packed medieval town that would burn far better than the spacious avenues of any modern metropolis. Lübeck was built 'more like a fire-lighter than a human habitation', to quote Harris. 'The inclusion of such a relatively unimportant place as Lübeck, which happened to be especially inflammable, in the target lists', remark the official historians, 'showed the extent . . . to which a town might become a target mainly because it was operationally vulnerable.'[5] Lübeck, then, did not attract the attention of the bombers because it was important, but became important because it could be bombed.

The attack was led by ten Wellingtons equipped with *Gee*, who laid flares over the city. They were succeeded by a wave of forty fire-raising aircraft loaded with incendiaries. Then came the main force, armed with incendiaries and the huge 4,000-lb high-explosive 'cookies' that were to become the heavy weapons of the new generation of heavy bombers. They struck at very low level, in clear skies. The raid was an overwhelming success. The *Gee* aircraft found the target, the incendiaries created huge fires, and the old town of Lübeck was no more. 1,425 houses were totally destroyed and 1,976 badly damaged. 312 people were killed. 12 aircraft were lost of 191 that claimed to have attacked. Of the six aircraft that took part from 50 Squadron, apart from one which returned early with technical trouble, the squadron record book noted almost unprecedentedly that 'all aircraft were successful in the task'. The Ministry of Economic Warfare in London estimated that Lübeck would take six or seven weeks to resume full industrial production. The bombers' achievement was hailed as a personal victory for the leadership of Sir Arthur Harris.

Bomber Command had begun to establish the emphasis on concentration that was to dominate the offensive – aircraft seeking to bomb within the shortest possible space of each other, saturating the German defences and fire-fighting system. Timing over the target had become vital. Routeing across the North Sea to surprise the night-fighters was developing into an art. The days of individual attack 'by guess and by God' were ending. But it was still difficult to assess the full potential of *Gee*, because the hundred or so crews who were now equipped with the device were taking time to learn to use it effectively. The navigator operated the set from a receiver mounted to the right of his table behind the pilot. By timing the radio pulses received from three English ground stations whose signals appeared as lines on a cathode ray tube, he could determine the aircraft's position on charts marked with special *Gee* grids. Accuracy depended heavily on individual proficiency and it was clear from the continuing attacks on the Ruhr that the device was not proving sufficiently precise to become a blind-bombing system. But *Gee* was a vast improvement on Dead Reckoning, and added greatly to the confidence of the crews.

At Swinderby that spring, however, enthusiasm for the delights of new navigational aid was qualified by dismay about exchanging their Hampdens for Manchesters. Initially, everybody was excited by the prospect of the new aircraft with its much more sophisticated equipment and seven-man crew – two pilots, navigator, bomb-aimer, wireless-operator, mid-upper and rear gunners. Then the first reports seeped in of the unreliability and lack of power in the Vulture engines, the poor rate of climb and lack of ceiling. The Manchester could not, in fact, reach the Hampden's fully-loaded maximum height of 20,000 feet. Tolley Taylor, one of 50's sergeant pilots, took his new aircraft for a spin and came back to report that it was 'ideal for going out to lunch': very comfortable, properly heated at last after the icy Hampden, pleasant to fly. But apart from lack of performance, its weak undercarriage punished heavy landings by instant collapse. Under each engine nacelle ran a Y-shaped coolant pipe that proved lethally vulnerable to local shrapnel bursts. The squadron's aircraft serviceability rate fell dramatically. But until the new Lancaster reached them later in the year, the Manchester was all that there was. They set themselves to learn how to get the best out of it.

After the usual assortment of 'Gardening' operations and desultory raids on the Ruhr and some of the less dangerously defended German cities, towards the end of April they were committed to the second of Harris's devastating eradication attacks, on the north German coastal town of Rostock. The ingredients were the same as for Lübeck: a lightly defended tinderbox old city. It was a seven-hour round trip, well beyond *Gee* range. The force was divided, part being directed to attack the city itself, others the Heinkel aircraft factory beyond the southern suburbs.

This time the attack was continued over four nights. On the first two, 23 and 24 April, results were disappointing. But the third and fourth raids, by 128 and 107 aircraft respectively, were greeted at High Wycombe as triumphs to match the destruction of Lübeck. The centre of Rostock was left ablaze. 50 Squadron were among the contingent from 3 and 5 Groups briefed to attack the Heinkel works at low level. Oxley assured them at briefing that they were due for another walk-over against negligible defences. In reality, the Germans had brought up every flak gun they could muster from the length of north Germany by the third night. The defences were fierce. But when the photographs were analysed the next day, the crews were informed that they had staged one of the most accurate precision attacks of the war. Goebbels declared almost hysterically: 'Community life in Rostock is almost at an end.' The Ministry of Economic Warfare reported: 'It seems little exaggeration to say that Rostock has for the time being ceased to exist as a going concern.' Thousands of people had fled in panic from the blazing ruins, public buildings were levelled and the surrounding towns and villages became vast temporary refugee camps.

At 50 Squadron, there was another verse for the intelligence officer's long epic verse, set to the tune of Noel Coward's 'Mad Dogs and Englishmen':

When the sirens moan to awake Cologne
They shiver in their shoes;

In the Berlin street they're white as sheets
With a tinge of Prussian blues;
In Rostock the Wardens knock and yell 'Put Out That Light'
When Hampdens from Swinderby go out in the moonlight, out in the moonlight, out on a moonlight night.[6]

'Thus, by the end of April 1942,' wrote the official historian, 'Bomber Command, under the vigorous leadership of Air Marshal Harris, had shown, not only to Britain's Allies, but also to her enemies the tremendous potential power of the long-range heavy bomber force.'[7]

But they add immediately, almost in contradiction, that Bomber Command 'had yet to win a major victory against a major target'. German production in both Lübeck and Rostock returned to normal with astonishing speed. Far from losing the six to seven weeks' output estimated by the Ministry of Economic Warfare, Lübeck was operating at between 80 and 90 per cent of normal within days, and even the severely damaged Heinkel factory made a miraculous recovery within weeks. If the destruction of the two Hanse towns had been a test of Bomber Command's technique for firing cities, it had also been a forewarning – albeit unknown in London or High Wycombe – of the extraordinary resistance of industrial plant to bombardment. Only the medieval hearts of Lübeck and Rostock lay irrevocably dead and still, rotting in their own remains.

But Sir Arthur Harris exploited publicity brilliantly to further his policies. The attacks on Lübeck and Rostock had been blazoned across Britain. Now, in May 1942, Harris conceived a further, extraordinarily imaginative stroke: a force of one thousand British bombers, the greatest concentration of air power in the history of the world, would attack a single German city in a single night.

There was, of course, no military magic about the figure of a thousand aircraft. It was the potential effect on popular imagination, on the politicians and on the Americans and the Russians that fascinated Whitehall. Portal grasped the beauty of 'The 1,000 Plan' at once, and gave Harris his full support to muster this enormous force, double the strength of Bomber Command's front-line squadrons. The Prime Minister, with his great sense of theatre, was won over immediately. Only the Admiralty, in the midst of the Battle of the Atlantic, was exasperated by such gimmicky enterprises as it struggled to fight its convoys through. The First Sea Lord absolutely refused to allow Coastal Command aircraft to be diverted to the operation. Harris was compelled to raise his force almost entirely from his own squadrons at maximum effort, and from his Operational Training Units. It was a remarkable logistical achievement that, on the night of 30 May 1942, 1,046 Bomber Command aircraft took off for Cologne. They had been crowded on to the stations of eastern England, where ground crews worked to bring the OTU aircraft to operational standard and staff brief OTU pupils and instructors. Only at the last moment did the weather determine that Cologne rather than Hamburg was the target. At his headquarters at High Wycombe, Harris had listened to the forecast in silence. Then, with his unerring eye for drama, he gave his orders:

> The C-in-C moved at last. Slowly he pulled an American cigarette carton from his pocket, and, flicking the bottom with his thumb, selected the protruding Lucky Strike. . . . He continued to stare at the charts and then slowly his forefinger moved across the continent of Europe and came to rest on a town in Germany. . . . He turned to the SASO, his face still expressionless:
> 'The 1,000 Plan tonight.'
> His finger was pressing on Cologne.[8]

50 Squadron put up seventeen aircraft that night. At briefing, when the CO announced that there would be more than a thousand aircraft over the target, there was a moment of awed silence. They were alarmed by the prospect of collision, but they were told that Bomber Command's operational research scientists had computed that statistically there should be no more than two aircraft colliding in the target area. Somebody piped up: 'That's fine – but do they know which two?', and the gale of tense laughter passed into the legend of the bomber offensive. Then they walked out into the dusk of a beautiful summer evening, and took off through clear skies for Cologne.

They attacked in three waves, led by the Wellingtons of 3 Group. Almost uniquely, 3 Group's AOC, Air Vice-Marshal 'Jackie' Baldwin, whom we last saw writing the post-mortem report on the Wilhelmshaven raid two and a half years earlier, flew in person as a passenger in one of his own aircraft. Senior officers were generally forbidden to fly on 'ops' for common-sense security reasons, although this dangerously increased their isolation from the realities of war over Germany. Behind 3 Group came the Stirlings, and last of all the Manchesters and Lancasters of 5 Group, for in these days the 'heavies' were usually left to bring up the rear on the theory that they were best able to withstand punishment over the thoroughly awakened defences. But on the night of 30 May, crews in the later waves crossed northern Germany, skirting the heavy flak around München-Gladbach, unable to accept the reality of the vast red glow in the sky ahead of them. Some crews thought that a great forest or heath must have caught fire, others that the Germans had created an enormous dummy fire to draw the bombers. Only as they drew near did they perceive the incredible truth, that this was the city of Cologne, ablaze from end to end.

Micky Martin was due over target forty-five minutes after H-Hour.

From miles away, he could see the huge fires lighting the sky ahead, dwarfing the pathetic flickers of flak and searchlights. Martin came in low at 4,000 feet, his crew gazing on the glowing red core of the city, broken by the silver thread of the Rhine, the shimmering white spangles of blazing incendiaries, the great silhouette of the cathedral, its twin towers still lingering amidst the miles of rubble around the Rhine bridge. Many of the flak batteries had run out of ammunition, for transport could no longer cross the city from the dumps to the guns. Searchlights were meandering wildly like drunken men. Some pilots felt as if their own aircraft were on fire with the city, as the red glow danced up and down on their wings. Three times Martin swung over Cologne awed, like so many airmen that night, by the devastation below. They had never seen anything remotely like it. Between 0047 and 0225 that morning, 3,330 houses were utterly destroyed, more than 2,000 badly damaged, more than 7,000 partly damaged. 12,000 fires raged among the breached water mains, severed power cables, exploded gas mains and wrecked telephone system. 36 factories were totally destroyed, 70 more badly damaged, more than 200 partially damaged. The docks and railway system had been savaged. The tram system remained totally out of action for a week and dislocated for months to come. 85 soldiers and members of civil-defence teams had been killed along with 384 civilians. Almost 5,000 people required first aid. 45,000 people had lost their homes.

This was a mere token of the destruction Bomber Command would achieve in 1943 and 1944, and indeed the lasting damage to Cologne proved astonishly slight in relation to the forces employed. But in 1942 it seemed to the airmen that Britain had achieved the power to unleash Armageddon. Micky Martin hesitated before deciding where it was still worth dropping bombs, and finally let them fall across the battered railway station. The crew chattered excitedly on the intercom. They would see many such urban funeral pyres in the next three years, but no man who was there ever forgot this baptism at Cologne.

Tolley Taylor's was one of the few aircraft which had the ill luck to be hit that night. Running in to bomb at 12,000 feet, shrapnel struck the starboard engine, setting it on fire. He pressed the feathering button to shut off power, and after a frightening half-minute falling steeply through the sky, the fire went out and he regained control at around 9,000 feet. 'Stand by to bale out,' he ordered. The gunners slipped out of their turrets, the hatches plummeted away from the aircraft and a rush of air swept through the fuselage. As they turned out of the target, Taylor peered at his gauges. They were losing height and could cruise at barely 110 mph. But they were still flying. They might make it. He ordered the crew to free every ounce of spare weight. They began to hurl out guns, ammunition, armour plate, the Elsan portable toilet – anything movable whirled away into the slipstream as they staggered painfully across the Channel. After more than six hours in the air they force-landed at Tempsford, the base of the Special Duties squadrons which operated the cloak-and-dagger flights to occupied Europe. Taylor pushed his way into the debriefing room, full of unaccustomed cubicles and unfamiliar blackened faces. 'Terrific prang! Weren't the fires great?' he said eagerly to the pilot beside him. 'There weren't any fires where I've been,' said the other young man bleakly. Taylor and his crew flew home to Swinderby the next day in a Whitley, in time for the general celebrations.

'OVER 1,000 BOMBERS RAID COLOGNE,' proclaimed *The Times*. 'Biggest Air Attack Of the War. 2,000 Tons of Bombs in 40 Minutes.'

Bomber Command lost forty aircraft on the Cologne operation, an acceptable 3.8 per cent of those dispatched, all the more astonishing in view of the number of OTU crews involved. Two of 50 Squadron's Manchesters failed to return, one of them piloted by a quiet, diffident young man named Leslie Manser. His aircraft was badly damaged over the target, and he faced a long, difficult struggle to bring it home. At last it became clear that he could no longer keep it in the air, and he ordered the crew to bale out, waving away the parachute his flight engineer offered him as he fought to hold the Manchester steady while they jumped. He was killed with the aircraft, but was awarded the Victoria Cross for his sacrifice, which was in no way diminished by the fact that it was so frequently required from the pilots of Bomber Command aircraft.

Harris staged two further massive raids, on Essen and Bremen, before it became necessary to dismantle his '1,000' force to avoid serious damage to the training and logistics of the Command. Neither was a significant success. The weather frustrated the Essen raid by 956 aircraft on 1 June – an experiment with the *Shaker* marking technique, German radio did not even recognize Essen as the target, and reported 'widespread raids over western Germany'. 31 aircraft, or 3.2 per cent, were lost. On 25 June 904 aircraft attacked Bremen, doing some damage to the Focke–Wulf plant at the cost of 44 aircraft, or 4.9 per cent, missing, and a further 65 more or less seriously damaged.

Bomber Command settled to spend the remainder of the summer pounding Germany on a wide front, at less spectacular intensity and with results that could not compare with the dramatic devastation of Cologne. But Harris could bide his time now. In four months as Commander-in-Chief, he had established his own reputation; delighted the Prime Minister whose sense of drama matched his own; and made an immense contribution to British propaganda at a time when the nation's fortunes in the Middle and Far East were at their lowest ebb. The British public and their politicians had been almost universally awed by the scale and vision of power presented by the

'1,000' raids. The Prime Minister proclaimed after the bombing of Cologne: 'Proof of the growing power of the British bomber force is also the herald of what Germany will receive city by city from now on.' Harris said: 'We are going to scourge the Third Reich from end to end. We are bombing Germany city by city and ever more terribly in order to make it impossible for her to go on with the war. That is our object; we shall pursue it relentlessly.'

Amidst the terrible scars of the Luftwaffe's blitz on Britain, there is no doubt that the nation derived deep satisfaction from Harris's words and deeds. Unlike some of his service and political masters, he was never a dissembler or a hypocrite. He gave unequivocal notice of his intentions. Whatever criticism may be made of the strategic substance of Harris's campaign, it is essential not to underestimate the power and value to England of his remarkable military showmanship at this, one of the grimmest phases of the war for the Grand Alliance.

2. *Operations*

In July 1942, to the relief of 50 Squadron the Manchesters were retired after their brief and alarming months in service. In their place came the four-engined Avro Lancaster, indisputably the great heavy night-bomber of the Second World War. Pilots have a saying about an aircraft: 'If it looks right, it is right.' The Lancaster looked superb, its cockpit towering more than nineteen feet above the tarmac, the sweep of its wings broken by the four Rolls-Royce Merlin engines with their throaty roar like a battery of gigantic lawnmowers. The green and brown earth shadings of the upper surfaces gave way to matt black flanks and undersides, the perspex blisters glittering from the ceaseless polishing of the ground crews. The pilot sat high in his great greenhouse of a cockpit, the flight engineer beside him – second pilots had been scrapped in the spring of 1942 to economize on aircrew. Beyond sat the navigator, bent over a curtained-off table in almost permanent purdah in flight, his work lit by a pinpoint anglepoise lamp. Behind him was the wireless operator, his back to the bulk of the main spar between the wings, a waist-high barrier in the midst of the fuelage. The space beyond, in the rear of the aircraft, was clear and roomy when the aircraft left the production line, but as the electronic war intensified, the interior became more and more crowded with equipment: the big, squat case of the *Gee* equipment, linked to the receiver beside the navigator; the Distant Reading Compass, wired to a repeater on the pilot's windscreen; the Air Position Indicator gear; the flare chute; the rest bed for a wounded man; the 'tramlines' carrying the long linked belts of machine-gun ammunition to the rear gunner's four Brownings and the two in the mid-upper turret; the Elsan toilet which most crews used with much caution after a 50 Squadron gunner left most of the skin of his backside attached to the frozen seat one icy night over Germany. Beneath the fuselage, the bomb bay lay long and narrow. In the nose, the bomb-aimer stretched behind the forward blister searching for pinpoints to assist the navigator until they approached the target, or occasionally manned the twin front guns to frighten the light flak gunners on low-level operations. Gunners trained the power-operated Brownings to the right and left with a twist of the grips to which their triggers were fitted. The British hydraulic turret was one of the outstanding design successes of the bomber war; although unfortunately it was fitted with the inadequate .303 machine-gun. The last hopes of equipping Bomber Command with .5s, as Harris had demanded for so long, vanished when America entered the war and her own needs eclipsed British hopes of .5 imports from American factories.

The Lancaster inspired affection unmatched by any other British heavy bomber. The Stirling was easier to fly, a gentleman's aircraft, according to Stirling pilots. But its lamentable ceiling made it the first target of every German gunner and night-fighter pilot, provoking the callous cheers of the more fortunate Lancaster crews when they heard at briefings that the clumsy, angular Stirlings would be beneath them. The Halifax was a workhorse of no breeding and alarming vices in the air. The British never took to the American Flying Fortress, although Bomber Command experimented with a handful in 1941 and 1942; its virtues only became apparent in the hands of the Americans with their lavish supplies of aircraft and men, when the day-bombing offensive came into its own at the beginning of 1944.

But the Lancaster, cruising at 216 mph, intensely durable and resistant to punishment by the standards of the lightly armoured night-bombers, beautiful to the eye and carrying the bombload of two Flying Fortresses at a ceiling of 22,000 feet, ranks with the Mosquito and the Mustang among the great design successes of the war. 50 Squadron, like the rest of Bomber Command, took to it at once. Throughout 1942, while the numerical strength of Harris's forces expanded scarcely at all, the effectiveness of his aircraft and equipment was being steadily transformed. In May 1942 there were 214 Wellingtons, 62 Halifaxes and 29 Lancasters among the front line of 417 aircraft. By January 1943 there were only 128 Wellingtons left, and 104 Halifaxes and 178 Lancasters among the total of 515 first-line aircraft. In the interval the bomb-carrying capacity of the Command increased by more than a third.

The mood of this new Bomber Command was utterly different from that of 1939. Most squadrons were no longer billeted amidst the solid brick comforts of the pre-war airfields, but were learning to live with Nissen huts and chronic mud, to fly from hastily concreted strips now carpeting eastern England, as the island was transformed into a gigantic aircraft-carrier. The old spirit of the officers' mess as home, the idea of the squadron as a family, had been replaced by that of a human conveyor belt, a magic lantern show of changing faces. Bomber Command dickered briefly with committing crews to tours of 200 operational hours, but this stopped abruptly when it was found that some men flew home with their wheels down in order to prolong 'ops' to their limit. Now there was a thirty-trip standard before men were posted to notionally less dangerous instructing jobs. Operational aircrew might fly six or seven times a month, unless the weather was very bad. A first-class CO could create a squadron spirit, but the aircrew had become passing three- or four-month guests on their own stations, leading a parallel yet utterly different life from that of the huge permanent ground-support staff, who remained at one base year after year, drinking in the same pubs and servicing aircraft in the same hangars.

The aircrew, as befitted men who were statistically not long for this world, spent their last months fattened with whatever comfort wartime England could provide for them, unheard-of luxuries such as extra milk, fruit juice, sugar and real eggs. They were warmed by sun-ray lamps in the medical quarters, dosed with halibut-oil capsules and protected from all but the most essential duties when not flying. The former pressure on non-commissioned aircrew had been lifted. Now they usually occupied their own mess separate from that of non-flying NCOs, and enjoyed much the same comforts and privileges as their commissioned counterparts. A crew drank, womanized, often even went on leave together as a close-knit entity, regardless of individual rank. A commissioned navigator called his sergeant-pilot 'Skipper' in the air without a hint of resentment. They were all too close to death to trouble about formalities over Germany now. Throughout 1942, the loss-rate, including fatal crashes in England, seldom fell much below 5 per cent, one aircraft in twenty on every operation. A crew faced thirty trips. It needed no wizard of odds to read the chances of their mortality, even if each man deep in his heart believed that it would be another's turn until the instant that he plunged headlong out of the night sky, the flames billowing from his aircraft.

But unlike the days in France a generation earlier, when these men's fathers queued below the red lamps before they went over the top, brothels seldom flourished around the bomber stations. Many aircrew preferred to relax with drink and each other rather than with women. For those who craved female company, local girls, lonely soldiers' wives and station WAAFs found it difficult to refuse boys who were likely to be dead within a month. It was chiefly remarkable, in the almost frenzied celebrations that accompanied a 'stand-down' or a 'good prang' or the end of a crew's tour or somebody getting a 'gong', that so many aircrew went to their fate as innocent as they had emerged from the cradle. A nineteen-year-old who was given his opportunity by a sentimental WAAF still blushes to recall that he turned her down because he had been warned by the medical officer to keep his strength up for operations. A survivor from the crew of a pilot who was awarded a posthumous Victoria Cross for his efforts to save his aircraft over France never forgot that on their last night together, the boy admitted sheepishly that he had never kissed a girl in his life.

By that summer of 1942 the strange inverted timetable of night-bomber operations had become a routine. The crews awoke in their huts as the Lincolnshire ground mists slowly cleared from the runways, and wandered across to the mess for a late breakfast in the patchy sunshine. By 11 am, they were playing cricket or lounging on the grass around the flight offices, waiting to hear if operations were 'On' for that night. Some days – the good days – they were at once 'stood down'. They dashed for a bus to Nottingham or piled into their cars, illicitly fuelled with 100-octane aviation spirit. Often – very often – they were ordered to prepare for an 'op' that was cancelled at five, six, seven o'clock after they had dressed and been briefed and their aircraft bombed-up. This they hated most of all, because by evening they had already been fighting the battle against fear and anticipation all day, and they had overcome the worst. 'Ops scrubbed' was only an illusory reprieve, because if they did not fly their first or fifth or twentieth trip that night, it would only be waiting for them tomorrow. More often than not, it was the prospect of bad weather over England in the early hours that caused cancellations, rather than cloud over Germany. There had already been some appalling nights when bombers crashed all over East Anglia in impossible visibility, and exhausted crews were compelled to abandon their aircraft and bale out over their own bases rather than risk descending to ground level.

If 'ops' were 'on', the armourers began the long, painstaking routine of bombing-up the aircraft. Knowing their fuel and bombload in the morning, crews could quickly assess the rough distance and perhaps the nature of their target. That summer, Harris was still unwilling to commit his force headlong against Berlin or the Ruhr amidst the stiffening German defences. As he waited for more aircraft and the new generation of navigation and bomb-aiming devices, he advanced with caution. 50 Squadron and the rest of Bomber Command made spasmodic trips to Duisburg, Düsseldorf and other Ruhr targets, but generally bombed less perilous and more easily located ones: Bremen, Osnabrück, Kassel, Nuremberg. They were burning thousands of houses and not a few factories, but Harris was biding his time for the punishing attacks on the industrial heart of Germany.

After taking their aircraft for a brief air test before lunch, gazing down at the chequer board of airfields visible in every direction around them in the naked light of day, some crews tried to sleep on the

THE AVRO LANCASTER I (Four 1,280 h.p. Rolls-Royce Merlin XX Motors)

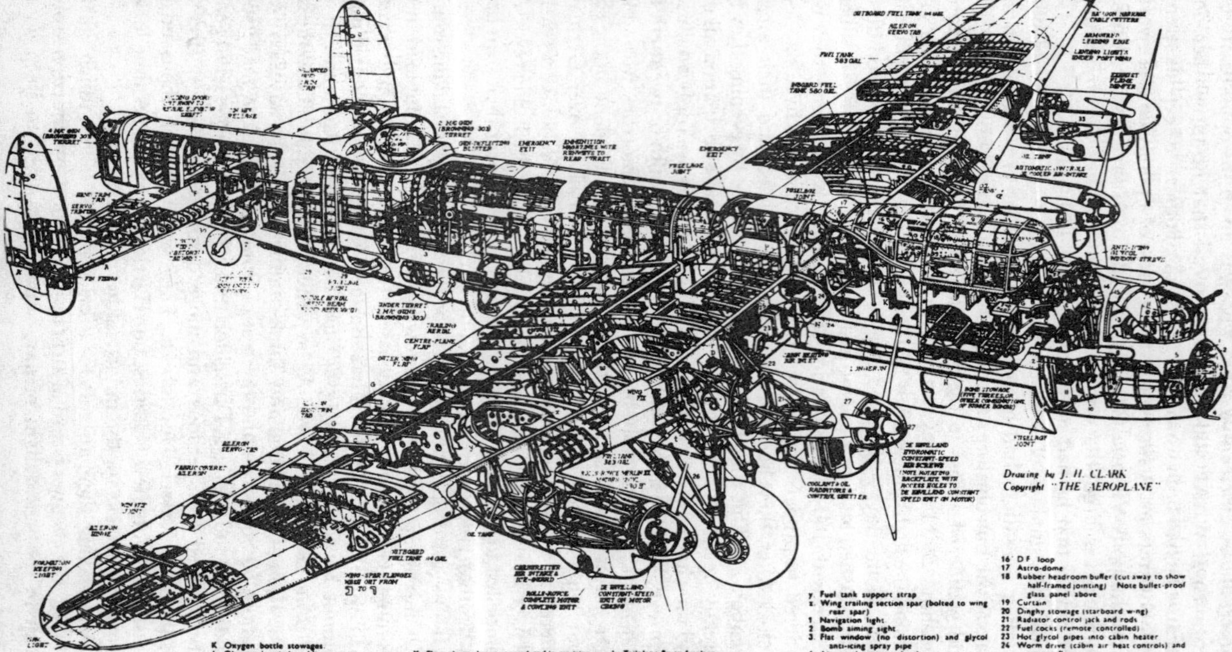

Drawing by J. H. CLARK
Copyright "THE AEROPLANE"

A Rudder and elevator trim
B Control column stops and seat raising cam.
C Aileron control
D Throttle controls
E Rudder bars
F Rudder and elevator control rods
G Aileron trim cables to screw rod
H Service piping along bomb bay
K Oxygen bottle stowages.
L Observer's window blister.
M Bomb lock units in floor.
N Longeron joint flanges and holes.
P Spar flange reinforcement.
Q Hydraulic reservoir.
R Signal pistol.
S Armoured doors.
T Rest bunk and 1½ oxygen bottles underneath.
U Spar webs extended into former frames
V Spar flanges
Y. Flare chute shown stowed and in position.
Z. Tail gun ammunition magazine and runways.
a Under-turret magazines.
b Top turret magazines.
d. Vacuum flasks stowages.
e Dead-man's handle (puts rear turret fore and aft to extricate gunner through sliding door).
f. Elsan lavatory
g. Tailwheel leg spigoted into tailplane.
k Tailplane fix to fuselage.
m. Elevator hinge bracket
n. Bomb door op., jack and mud brushes (and at front end)
p. Hinged leading edge.
q. Starboard fuel tank (580 gal.) space
r. Glycol tank
t. Undercarriage and motor bracket.
w U c radius rod and jack anchorages
x Fuel tank structure (swash-plate former
y. Fuel tank support strap
z. Wing trailing section spar (bolted to wing rear spar)
1 Navigation light
2 Bomb aiming sight
3. Flat window (no distortion) and glycol anti-icing spray pipe
4 Air-speed pressure head
5 Glycol pump for "3"
6 Bomb aimer's body rest.
7 Emergency exit
8 Ventilator
9 Camera (through floor).
10 Pump
11. Glycol tank (window spray) and step
12 Bomb aimer's squint into bomb bay
13. Detail of front turret mounting ring
16 D F loop
17 Astro-dome
18 Rubber headroom buffer (cut away to show half-framed jointing) Note bullet-proof glass panel above
19 Curtain
20 Dinghy stowage (starboard wing)
21 Radiator control jack and rods
22 Fuel cocks (remote controlled)
23 Hot glycol pipes into cabin heater
24 Worm drive (cabin air heat controls) and air overflow
25 Service pipes along leading edge
26 U c door op link rod
27 Spinner and back plate fixing to airscrew hub
28 Wing-tip joint
29 Downwards identification lamps
30 Tailwheel leg hinge
31 Taboo track and rollers
32 Aerial spring suspension

afternoon of an 'op'. Many never succeeded. It was these long hours of preparation and expectation that ate into men's courage and nerves as much as anything that was done to them in the air. Many felt that it was the contrast between the rural peace of afternoon England and the fiery horror of early morning Germany that imposed much greater strain on bomber crews than the even tenor of discomfort and fear on a warship or in a tank. They had time to remember vividly each earlier trip. They gazed around them at the familiar hangars; the 'erks' – the ground crews – pedalling their bicycles round the perimeter track to the dispersals; the fuel bowsers beside the distant aircraft, silhouetted against the flat horizon. The panorama took on a strange unreality. They were called upon to fly over Germany in the midnight hours when human enterprise and resistance is naturally at its lowest ebb. The very young, under twenty, and the older men over thirty, seemed to suffer most, although the latter were often invaluable ballast in a crew. Those in their early twenties proved able to summon up remarkable reserves of resilience.

After the traditional bacon and eggs in the mess, they went to briefing. The old informality of Hampden days, when a cluster of pilots and navigators assembled around the central table in the Ops Room, had vanished with the coming of the 'heavies'. Now each specialist was independently briefed by his respective squadron chief: signals leader, navigation leader and so on. Then they gathered together, more than a hundred young men, arrayed crew by crew on the bench seats of the Briefing Room facing the central stage, the map still hidden by a curtain until the heart-stopping moment when the CO walked forward and pulled it away to reveal the target. 'Funf', the Swinderby 'Met' man, talked to them about the weather. The Intelligence Officer briefed them about the importance of the target from notes sent down to him by High Wycombe. He gave them the latest information on the German defences. The 'Kammhuber line', named by the British after the German general who had created it, now the coastal breadth of Germany, Holland and Belgium. It was almost impossible for a British bomber to avoid. But within its network of interlocking radar-controlled night-fighter and searchlight zones, each 'box' could control only one fighter to one interception at a time. Bomber Command's constantly intensifying 'streaming' technique, pushing the British aircraft along a single course through the defences in the shortest possible time, sought to defeat this outer line of German defences by saturating them. Little was as yet known about the new *Lichtenstein* radar mounted in the fighters themselves, although Scientific Intelligence at the Air Ministry was working towards an astonishingly comprehensive picture.

The station commander stood up to wish them luck, and strode out trailing his attendant staff officers. The crews shuffled to their feet, chattering and gathering up maps and notes.

> They were a queer conglomeration, these men – some educated and sensitive, some rough-haired and burly, and drawn from all parts of the Empire, Great Britain, Canada, New Zealand and Australia. . . . Some of them were humming, some were singing, some were laughing, and others were standing serious and thoughtful. It looked like the dressing room where the jockeys sit waiting before a great steeplechase. . . .[9]

They stripped themselves of personal possessions and gathered up parachutes, escape kits, mascots. Swinderby's station commander chatted easily to them as they prepared. Sam Patch was a popular 'station master', at his relaxed best talking to crews, never above stopping his car to offer a crowd of NCOs a lift as they walked back from the local pub on a stand-down night. Waiting for transport to the dispersals was one of the worst moments. Stan Gawler, one of the rear gunners, was always loaded down with dolls and charms with which he decorated his turret. One night he forgot them, and his crew endured a nightmare hour over Hamburg. Peggy Grizel, a young WAAF Intelligence Officer, never failed to be moved by the ways in which each man fought down his fear. Henry Mossop, a Lincolnshire farm boy, lay calmly on the grass looking out into the dusk, smoking his pipe. A young New Zealander sat down with anybody who would listen and talked about his home. Macfarlane, one of 'Beetle' Oxley's successors as CO insisted on having 'The Shrine of St Cecilia' played on the mess gramophone, and after the record was broken one afternoon, dashed into Lincoln to buy another copy before operating that night.

At the dispersals, they lay smoking on the grass until the time came to swing themselves up into the fuselage. There was a familiar stink of kerosene, with which the erks washed out the dirt of every trip. As the sky darkened around them, the pilot and flight engineer ran up the great Merlins one by one. The pilot slid back his window and gave 'thumbs up' to the ground crew by the battery cart. Port-outer: Contact. He lifted the cover from the starter button and pressed it down, waiting for the puff of grey smoke shot with flame, the cough and roar as it fired. At last, with all four engines running, he checked the oil pressure and tested the throttles, checked revolutions and magneto drop. The navigator spread his maps. The gunners crammed themselves into the turrets they could not leave for the next six or seven hours.

The rear gunner faced the loneliest and coldest night of all. Gazing back all night into the darkness behind the aircraft, he often felt that he inhabited another planet from the tight little cluster of aircrew so far forward in the cockpit. Even after electrically heated suits were introduced, they often broke down. Many gunners cut away their turret doors to dispel the nightmare of being trapped inside when the aircraft was hit – they were wedged impossibly tightly in their flying gear. It was difficult even to move freely enough to clear jammed guns with their rubber hammers. There was no chance of wearing a parachute – it was stowed beside them. Some carried a hatchet to give themselves a forlorn chance of hacking their way out of a wreck. The cold was intensified by the removal of a square of perspex to provide a central 'clear view panel' to the night sky, a refinement pioneered by Micky Martin's gunner, Tammy Simpson, among others. Behind the cockpit a powerful heater system had been installed, but there was a perpetual war in most crews about the temperature at which this was maintained, the wireless operator by the hot-air outlet being permanently roasted, the bomb-aimer shivering amidst the draughts through the front gun vents.

At the dispersals, the flight-sergeant fitter handed his pilot Form 700 on his clipboard, to sign for the aircraft, then slipped away to the ground. The flight engineer reported: 'Engineer to pilot. Rear hatch closed and secure. OK to taxi.' The pilot signalled to the ground crew to slip the chocks, and closed his window. The wireless operator made a test signal to the airfield Watch Office. 'Receiving you loud and clear. Strength Niner.' All over the airfield in the dusk, the Lancasters broke into movement. Twenty tons of aircraft, perhaps five tons of fuel and five more of bombs, bumped slowly round the perimeter to the end of the runway for take-off.

> The control officer flashed a green ray for a split second, which was the signal that this plane was designated for take-off [wrote an American spectator as he watched for the first time a Bomber Command take-off for Germany]. Its roaring grew louder and louder as it dragged its heavy tail towards the starting point like a slow, nearly helpless monster. About twenty yards away we could just discern a vast dinosaurish shape; after a moment, as if stopping to make up its mind . . . it lumbered forward, raising its tail just as it passed us, and turning from something very heavy and clumsy into a lightly poised shape, rushing through the night like a pterodactyl. At this instant, a white light was flashed upon it and a Canadian boy from Vancouver who was standing beside me, put down its number and the moment of departure. It vanished from sight at once and we stood staring down the field, where in a few seconds a flashing green light announced that it had left the ground. . . .
>
> A great calm settled over the place as the last droning motors faded out in the distance and we all drove back to the control room where a staff hang onto the instruments on a long night vigil. . . . I went to sleep thinking of the . . . youngsters I had seen, all now one hundred and fifty miles away, straining their eyes through a blackness relieved only by the star-spangled vault above them.[10]

A critical measure of a squadron's efficiency was its rate of 'Early Returns', aircraft which turned back over the North Sea with technical trouble. It was always a matter of nice judgement whether pressing on with a jammed turret or malfunctioning oxygen equipment represented courage or foolhardiness. Every crew could expect an Early Return once in a tour. To come home more often suggested accident-proneness or something worse. 50 Squadron had a tradition of pressing on: one night, for instance, an aircraft hit a servicing gantry on take-off. At Swinderby control, they waited for the pilot to request permission to land. Instead there was silence. He simply flew on to complete the trip. Some captains took a vote among the crew whether to turn back. Bill Russell, Oxley's successor as CO, had no patience with the hesitant. One night a sergeant pilot reported from dispersal that he was suffering magneto drop on one engine and could not take off. It was the man's third attack of 'mag drop' in a month. Russell ran down the control tower steps, drove furiously to the Lancaster, and ordered the pilot out. He flew the aircraft to Cologne himself, in his shirtsleeves. The pilot was court-martialled and dismissed from the service.

Every night over the North Sea, after the gunners fired their test bursts and they had climbed slowly to cruising height and synchronized their engines, the crew would hear the immortal cliché of Bomber Command down the intercom: 'Enemy Coast Ahead.' The flight engineer checked the aircraft black-out. Henceforth, each man became only a shape in the darkness, each part of the aircraft only recognizable by feel or momentary flash of a penlight torch. The instruments glowed softly. The engines roared distantly through the helmet earpieces. Stale air pumped through the constricting oxygen masks. They watched the gunfire lacing the sky from the flakships off the Dutch coast, the brief flicker of explosions and the pencil cones of searchlights sweeping the darkness. From here to Germany, each pilot had his own conviction how best to survive. Some captains on 50, like Jock Abercrombie, flew straight and level all the way to the target. Some changed their throttle settings constantly or desynchronized their engines. Others, like Micky Martin, weaved or changed course repeatedly every moment that they were within range of the defences.

To fly a heavy bomber called for quite different skills from those of a fighter pilot. Airmen say that contrary to popular mystique, there was no special temperament that equipped one man to fly a Spitfire and another a Lancaster: the job made the man. Pilot trainees who showed outstanding virtuosity in handling an aircraft were generally sent to Fighter Command. Only a handful of men in Bomber Command could throw a four-engined bomber through the sky with absolute assurance, or indeed wished to. Most wartime pilots, even after two years' training found it a strain coping with the technical problems of taking off, flying and landing a heavy aircraft in one piece, before they began to come to terms with the enemy. Handling a machine as big as a Lancaster required a good measure of brute physical strength. Hundreds of crews were lost in mishaps in which the enemy played no part: freak weather, collision, bombs falling on friendly aircraft below, botched landings by tired young men. The first six trips accounted for a disproportionate share of casualties. Those who survived that long became statistically slightly more at risk again in mid-tour, when they began to think that they knew it all, and on their last trips when they had grown tired and stale.

To survive, brilliant flying was less important than an immense capacity for taking pains, avoiding unnecessary risks, and maintaining rigid discipline in the air. Canadians were highly regarded as individual fliers, but incurred intense criticism as complete crews, as squadrons, as (eventually) their own No. 6 Group, because they were thought to lack the vital sense of discipline. A 50 Squadron gunner who was sent one night as a replacement with an all-Canadian crew came home terrified after circling the target while they sang 'Happy Birthday To You' down the intercom to their 21-year-old pilot. Later in the war, 6 Group became notorious for indifference to radio-telephone instructions from the Master Bomber over the target.

A pilot such as Micky Martin was daring in the air, but also very careful. He and his crew checked every detail of their own aircraft before take-off, far more meticulously than routine demanded. Martin personally polished every inch of perspex on his cockpit canopy. At 20,000 feet over Germany at night, a fighter was no more than a smear at the corner of a man's eye until it fired. Martin studied the techniques for improving his own vision, moving his head backwards and forwards constantly, to distinguish between the reality and the optical illusion beyond the windscreen. He taxied the aircraft to the butts before each trip so that his gunners could realign their Brownings. Every man who survived Bomber Command agrees that luck was critical: however brilliant a flier, he was vulnerable to the Russian roulette of a predicted flak barrage. But a careful crew could increase their chance of survival a hundred per cent.

It was difficult for so many young men who flew perhaps a dozen trips without a glimpse of a fighter, without being struck by flak, without becoming lost: operations began to take on the tedium of an eternal drive on a darkened motorway. Reflexes numbed, vigilance flagged, because this was human nature. Careful pilots banked gently every few moments to enable their gunners to search the sky beneath the aircraft. No good captain tolerated chatter on the intercom: it was sacred, reserved for the paralysing second when the rear gunner shouted: 'Fighter port! Corkscrew port – now!' Then they would heel into the mad, stomach-churning routine of fighter evasion, the gunner who could see the enemy directing the pilot who could not, the aircraft screaming in torment, the smell of vomit so often wafting up from a navigator or bomb-aimer overcome by fear and the violence of their movement, the fuselage shuddering as the gunners fired. The first seconds were vital: so often, if the fighter was observed he would break away to seek easier meat. A pilot's confidence in throwing his aircraft through the sky was critical. Some, in their fear of causing the bomber to break up, banked cautiously and died. Others – the ones who lived – recognized that the danger of a wing collapsing was nothing to that of a fighter's cannon. Steep bank to port, full left rudder, fall sideways for a thousand feet, wrench the aileron controls to starboard, soar into climbing turn to the right, then opposite aileron and dive again. . . .

> Anyone who had not done plenty of practice flying by instruments might well have been terrified by the result of all this. The speed varied between 200 and 90 mph, the altimeter lost and regained 1,000 feet, the rate of descent and ascent varied between 1,000 and 2,000 feet a minute, the horizon level just went mad and the rate of turn and skid needles varied from a maximum to port to a maximum to starboard every half minute. The physical exertion for each pull at the bottom of each dive was about equal to pulling on a pair of oars in a boat race.[11]

Micky Martin and other highly skilled pilots almost cartwheeled their Lancasters, banking savagely on to one wingtip as they raced the upper engines and cut the lower. They knew that the bomber's gunners had precious little chance of shooting down a well-armoured German fighter, that almost their only hope of survival lay in escape. Some crews believed that it was best not to fire their own guns until they were certain the fighter had seen them, lest they betray their position. The true value of the gunners was as look-outs. If they saw the German first, they could survive. If they did not, they were probably dead men. Gunners smeared lanolin on their necks to fight the aches and soreness of constantly scanning the sky. They were taught never to gaze into the flames of a target, which damaged their night vision. They took caffeine tablets to stay awake and faced instant dismissal from most crews if they were caught dozing. Yet boredom, monotony, the corrosion of cold and fatigue were deadly enemies. Again and again, a bomber was surprised.

One night in December 1942, 50 Squadron were out on a harassing raid over north Germany, part of a drive to force the Germans to spread their defences more thinly by launching pinprick attacks on scores of small towns, an assignment which uncharacteristically troubled some crews. Norman Goldsmith's crew were armed to the teeth – the flight engineer was carrying a Thompson gun – because they had been ordered to go in low and beat up anything in sight. 'Mitch' Mitchell, the wireless operator, was enjoying himself playing the new game of '*Tinsel*' tuning to German night-fighter frequencies and then blasting the ether with engine noise from a microphone specially fitted in one of the Lancaster's nacelles. He was bent over his headphones listening to the rage of the German controller when he was hammered on the shoulder by the mid-upper gunner. He looked out of the astrodome to see the starboard wing on fire. A German fighter had slid up beneath the fuselage and fired one deadly burst, badly wounding the rear gunner and injuring the mid, mortally damaging the aircraft, 'Bale out,' ordered Goldsmith. Mitchell and Jim Farrell, the Australian navigator, were the only survivors who reached the sodden fields of north Holland alive.

As they cruised across Europe, most pilots worked to gain height, bouncing the aircraft upwards in precious thermals, winning every foot of sky they could put between themselves and the enemy, so often invisible far below the cloud layers. Martin was exceptional in that he preferred to go in low, skimming the waves so that his Lancaster came home coated in salt spray and dirt, running along roads and railway lines to dodge the enemy balloon barrage, although on one notable night on the way home from Kassell, he flew with a balloon cable streaming from his wing. Little Toby Foxlee blazed the front guns at German flak the moment the enemy opened fire; his belts were loaded with continuous tracer instead of the usual one in five, as a simple 'frightener' to throw the gunners' nerve. Martin liked to operate at around 4,000 feet, because this was just beyond the maximum height at which German light flak could be effective, and yet was low for the heavier 88 mm flak. He would climb to bomb, then slip back to deck level for the long run home. For most crews, however, height represented safety, and they valued every foot of it. They had learned that it was vital to stay in the stream. If they were a minute or two early approaching the target, they flew a dogleg to lose time. If they were late, they pushed up their revs as much as they dared. A lone aircraft was instantly vulnerable.

Every pilot responded differently to sudden crisis. Martin found that he became ice-cold. He and his crew had achieved an almost telepathic mutual understanding and instinct for danger. Others were less fortunate. Tolley Taylor had a flight engineer who became literally paralysed with fear on his first trip to Essen, and clung motionless to the window-catch from the enemy coast to touch-down, compelling Taylor to cope with the fuel system as well as flying the aircraft. Stewart Harris, a navigator, fought down his terror during a bad flak barrage over Wilhelmshaven by gobbling his flying rations; the following night he collapsed, in delayed reaction, at a pub in Lincoln, although he operated again the night after. 'Are you hurt, Phillips?' 'King' Cole asked his flight engineer, as the man sat pale beside him after a near-miss. 'No, sir, but I'm very frightened. . . .' Even some pilots were known to become numbed into momentary paralysis by a sudden night-fighter attack, unable to move the controls. Every good captain checked his crew every few minutes of every trip: 'Rear gunner OK?' 'Yes, skip.' 'Mid-upper OK? 'OK, skipper', and so on. But there were many bad captains and bad crews, and they died still ignorant of the folly of omission that had killed them.

At the climax of every trip came the long run-up to bomb, through the dazzling web of lights, the flicker of flak, the curling, twisting pattern of tracer, the glow of fires and incendiaries in all the colours of the rainbow. The bomb-aimer lay in the nose over his Mark XIV bombsight, wired to the primitive grey computer box beside him. The navigator and wireless operator frequently abandoned their cubby-holes to join the gunners searching the sky for fighters at this most vulnerable moment of all. The whole crew held their breath as the bomb-aimer called off 'Left . . . left . . . right a bit . . . steady.' Then there was the sudden 'twang' from beneath them, and 'Bombs gone' from the nose. 'Was this fighting?' V. M. Yeates asked himself as he released his bombs over the German lines in France a quarter of a century before. 'There was no anger, no red lust, no struggle, no straining muscles and sobbing breath; only the slight movement of levers and the rattle of machine-guns. . . .'[12] For a few seconds they held course until the photo-flash fell from the aircraft and exploded to light the sky for their aiming-point picture, without which the trip could not count towards their tour. Then they swung away from the glowing, splitting shambles below and thanked God once more, unless there had been some heart-stopping hang-up, the bomb-aimer had been dazzled at a critical moment, or they were compelled to bank sharply to avoid a converging aircraft. Then they would hear an unhappy voice announce: 'We're going round again.' With the exception of a few phenomena like Martin, no man circled a target more than once in 1942 unless from dire necessity. By that summer, one crew in three was bombing within three miles of the aiming-point. It was not enough, yet it was a considerable improvement on 1941.

1942 was the year in which the dominant threat to a bomber over Germany became the night-fighter rather than the flak gun. The British computed that there were now 12,000 heavy anti-aircraft guns and 3,276 searchlights defending Germany. The Luftwaffe's flak units had almost doubled their strength from 255,000 men in 1940 to 439,000 in 1942. Flak damaged many aircraft and drove the bombers to fly high, but it destroyed few. Fighters, on the other hand, seldom sent a damaged victim home. The overwhelming majority of British bombers attacked were shot down. In 1942, German night-fighter strength rose from 162 to 349 aircraft, almost all Ju88s and Me110s. Over the target the bomber crews had learned to welcome heavy flak, for it indicated that the fighters were elsewhere. Creeping fear grew on the nights when the target was lit by scores of searchlights, yet the guns were silent. On these nights, the British knew that somewhere in the darkness fighters were searching the sky for a hapless Lancaster, or tuning their *Lichtenstein* radar sets to catch one in their electronic grasp.

Crews cherished some strange illusions about protecting themselves. One was that switching on their IFF – Identification Friend or Foe transmitter, controlled by a six-position dial above the wireless operator's head and designed to provide a recognition blip for British radar on the way home – somehow jammed the German searchlight control system if an aircraft was coned. Since late 1941, Dr R. V. Jones and his colleagues of Scientific Intelligence had been urging Bomber Command that not only was IFF profitless over Germany, but like all transmissions which could be monitored by the enemy, its use represented a positive threat to bombers' safety. Yet High Wycombe remained unconvinced for years to come, arguing that if pilots believed IFF benefited them, their illusions should be cherished for the sake of morale. 50 Squadron's signals leader was still teaching the technique in 1942, and most aircrew accepted it implicitly. It was the same with 'Scarecrows', the shells the crews believed that the Germans fired to frighten them, resembling exploding bombers. There were no such projectiles as 'Scarecrows'. What the men saw were indeed exploding British aircraft. But to this day many aircrew will not accept this. The truth was sometimes too frightening.

The occupants of a stricken aircraft had a one-in-five chance of escaping alive. Fighting the G-forces of a diving or spiralling, uncontrollable descent, they had to ditch the hatches, reach their parachutes and somehow struggle clear before the bomber struck the ground. They tried desperately to avoid baling out in the immediate target area, for they had heard too many stories of bomber crews killed by enraged civilians or soldiers, a fate not unknown to Luftwaffe airmen in the London blitz. Luftwaffe men on the ground in Germany often showed astonishing fellow-feeling for baled-out RAF crews, saving them from mobs, treating them with real kindness. When Stewart Harris of 50 Squadron became a prisoner, he was forced to travel through Düsseldorf with the three men of his Luftwaffe escort. The city had suffered appallingly at the hands of Bomber Command. The mother of one of the escort came to meet them at the station. Her own home and the factory in which she worked had already been destroyed. Yet she brought four packed lunches.

It was not unknown for Bomber Command crews to take occasional passengers on operations. Some were authorized – station commanders or reporters. Others were quite illicit – members of ground crew and in extremely isolated cases, WAAFs. The Germans sought to make propaganda capital out of an episode early in 1942 when they claimed to have found a dead WAAF in a shot-down Stirling.[13] It was often far more frightening to be a passenger, without the pressure of duty to suppress fear, than to be a crew member. One night Micky Martin took Group-Captain Sam Patch, Swinderby's station commander, on a trip to the Ruhr. Patch stood behind Martin's seat. Crossing the Belgian coast, Martin scented night-fighters – the searchlights were wavering uncertainly, a sure sign that they were seeking to avoid their own aircraft. He saw a line of tracer curving across the sky to port. 'If you turn round and look now, you'll probably see an aircraft blow up,' he said to Patch. Sure enough, on the German's third burst a few seconds later, a Wellington exploded. Every crew became hardened to seeing others go down, and felt that guilty surge of gratitude that it was another man's turn to die. Martin changed course to fly south of Liege and avoid the night-fighters. The diversion brought them late over the target, which was already burning fiercely. Martin circled three times at his customary 4,000 feet, terrifying yet fascinating Patch. When they came home, he said that he had never before understood how a crew could be frivolous, drunken, apparently irresponsible on the ground, yet utterly close-knit and professional in the air.

In those days, they still came home in their own way, by their own routes, instead of being locked into the stream all the way out and back, as they were a year later. Crews were tired now, aching and stiff and stale. They drank their coffee and ate their flying rations, but those who wished to remain alive did not relax in their cockpit or turrets. If the pilot could not resist the urge to urinate, he did so into the tin below his seat – he could never leave the controls. The wireless operator, in his shirtsleeves by the heater, might read a book or filter music from his radio down the intercom if the captain allowed, but the navigator was still checking fixes and peering into his *Gee* scope, which from August 1942 began to flicker with the green 'grass' of German jamming as soon as the aircraft crossed the enemy coast. The flight engineer juggled the fuel tanks, computing consumption constantly to check the notoriously inaccurate petrol gauges. Some captains allowed crews to smoke, puffing out of the edge of their oxygen masks: Tolley Taylor got through a steady forty cigarettes on every outward trip, twenty more coming home. Most pilots rigidly discouraged the practice, and rear gunners who dragged surreptitously to ease their lonely vigil came home with their boots stuffed with fag-ends to conceal the evidence.

By now, approaching the Channel homewards, some pilots were nursing damaged engines or flak-torn controls, losing height over France and struggling to get across the sea before forced landing at Manston or Woodbridge, the bombers' emergency landing strips. In some aircraft, in the darkness of the fuselage a bomb-aimer or wireless operator struggled over the body of a wounded gunner on the rest-bed, doing his pathetic best to repair terrible wounds made by shrapnel or cannon fire with morphia and sulphanilamide, in the feeble light of a torch. Others had thrown out everything movable, yet were still drifting helplessly downwards towards the North Sea or the Channel. They had a good chance of surviving ditching, a fair chance of being spotted if their navigator could still take a fix and their wireless operator still tap out a Ditching signal. But often a crew could not give their position, and lingered for hours or days in their dinghy before rescue or death overtook them.

The lucky crews, those whose aircraft were still unwounded, glimpsed other bombers going home, and thought about the girls or the wives with whom they might be drinking that night, at the Black Bull or the Baron of Beef. They droned on towards Lincolnshire, hoping that for once they would not be stacked waiting to land for half an hour or more, or diverted because a damaged aircraft had crashed on the runway. An aircraft that crashed in England was never included in Bomber Command's official casualty figures, however many of its crew were killed or wounded, and these added at least 15 per cent to the published loss figures for most of the war.

Their hearts rose at the red wink of the distant beacon. They heard the comforting thump as the undercarriage locked home, and prayed that no unseen joint in the aircraft's structure had been fatally damaged, to crumple as they landed. Then they were in the circuit, losing height and power as they slipped on to the runway, bumping heavily as their tired pilot let them down with a moment's imprecision, then idling along the black rubber-streaked concrete, switching open the bomb doors and gathering up their equipment. After an interminable night's flying to La Spezia and back, Stewart Harris clambered out of the fuselage and opened his flybuttons with boundless gratitude above the tailwheel. 'God, this is good!' he exclaimed deeply to the shadowy figures beside him in the darkness.

'Nice to see you back, too, Harris,' chuckled Sam Patch, stepping aside to reveal the Group commander behind him. The trucks bore them to the headquarters building for debriefing. They climbed wearily out, inhaling the blessed fresh air, then walked into the brightly-lit room with the blinking, dazed look of men woken at the wrong moment of the morning. A young WAAF scribbled her industrious notes about the trip as they lit their cigarettes and drank their tea. A cluster of brass – the station commander, a handful of staff officers, the padre and the doctor – hovered in the background. A WAAF chalked their landing time on the long, wide crew blackboard on the wall of the Ops Room. They had survived. Tomorrow night, or perhaps the one after, they would do it all again.

VII

Protest and Policy, 1942–43

1. Dissent

On 12 October 1942, a memorandum from the Assistant Chief of Air Staff (Policy) was circulated to Command and Group AOCs throughout the RAF. It was a commonplace document in the paperchase of wartime instructions, but it sought to clarify and codify the reality of what had already been taking place over Europe for many months:

> 1. The following rules govern our bombardment policy in British, Allied or Neutral territory occupied by the enemy:
>
> Bombardment is to be confined to military objectives, and must be subject to the following general priciples:
>
> (1) the intentional bombardment of civilian populations, as such, is forbidden.
>
> (2) It must be possible to identify the objective.
>
> (3) The attack must be made with reasonable care to avoid undue loss of civilian life in the vicinity of the target.
>
> 2. German, Italian and Japanese territory:
>
> Consequent upon the enemy's adoption of a campaign of unrestricted air warfare, the Cabinet have authorized a bombing policy which includes the attack of enemy morale. The foregoing rules do not, therefore, apply to our conduct of air warfare against German, Italian and Japanese territory.

Behind the circumlocutions, therefore, Britain was also pursuing a policy of unrestricted air warfare. On operational grounds alone, the Prime Minister and the senior officers of the RAF felt no doubt about its advisability, and to the vast majority of the British people the crimes of the Nazi regime across Europe justified the most terrible counter-offensive. Harris, to his credit, was always in favour of telling the British public exactly what he was seeking to do to the Germans, and indeed no one who read his statements in the course of the campaign had much cause to plead ignorance about area bombing. But the Government was more squeamish. From beginning to end of the war, ministers prevaricated – indeed, lied flatly again and again – about the nature of the bomber offensive.

'Have instructions been given on any occasion to British airmen to engage in area bombing rather than limit their attentions to purely military targets?' Richard Stokes MP asked the Air Minister in the House of Commons on 31 March 1943.

'The targets of Bomber Command are always military, but night-bombing of military objectives necessarily involves bombing the area in which they are situated,' replied Sir Archibald Sinclair.

'Is the Right Hon. Member aware that a growing volume of opinion in this country considers indiscriminate bombing of civilian centres both morally wrong and strategic lunacy?' Stokes asked the Deputy Prime Minister on 27 May 1943.

'No, there is no indiscriminate bombing,' replied Mr Clement Attlee, amidst rousing cheers. 'As has been repeatedly stated in the House, the bombing is of those targets which are most effective from the military point of view.'

In the wake of the blitz on Britain, the Government could have made a powerful and popular case for the area bombing of Germany had they chosen to do so, but by taking refuge in deceit they were contributing mightily to the post-war controversy about the bomber offensive. If ministers in 1942 were ashamed of what they were doing, so the argument would go, they must indeed have had something to be ashamed of. But during the war itself, while service departments and scientists mounted a fierce campaign against Bomber Command on strategic and practical grounds, the civilian opponents of bombing represented only a tiny, articulate minority.

In the House of Commons, Richard Stoke, the Labour MP for Ipswich, was the most determined. His own background was anything but that of an armchair pacifist. A barrister's son, he was educated at Downside and Trinity College, Cambridge, and had won the Military Cross and Croix de Guerre as a Gunner major in the First War. Stokes never questioned the necessity for tactical bombing in support of military operations, but from 1942 to 1945 he was a constant thorn in the Government's flesh on the matter of the area bombing of cities and other contentious strategic issues:

'Will the Secretary of State say whether the policy of limiting the objectives of Bomber Command to targets of military importance has, or has not, been changed to the bombing of towns and wide areas in which military targets are situated? he demanded of the Air Minister in the House of Commons on 1 December 1943.

Sir Archibald Sinclair: 'I would refer the Hon. Member to the answer which I gave him to a similar question on 31 March. There has been no change of policy.'

Stokes: 'Within what area in square miles was it estimated that the 350 blockbusters recently dropped on Berlin fell?'

Sinclair: 'The answer to that question would be of value to the enemy.'

Stokes: 'Would not the proper answer be that the Government does not dare give it? Does not my Right Hon. Friend admit by his answer that the Government are now resorting to indiscriminate bombing including residential areas?'

Sinclair: 'The Hon. Gentleman is incorrigible. I have indicated a series of vitally important military objectives.'

Sinclair was rescued from further bombardment on this occasion by a succession of loyal members who asked when there could be more bombing raids on Germany. The House passed on to a question about why airmen were forbidden to send pyjamas to service laundries. The Commons was overwhelmingly hostile to the handful of critics who returned again and again to sniping attacks on the deeds of the Royal Air Force. When Mr McGovern asked the Air Minister on 6 May 1942 'whether instructions to the RAF who raided Lübeck and Rostock included instructions to impede and disorganize the German effort by the destruction of workmen's dwellings?' Sinclair set his mind at rest:

> The objectives of our bomber offensive in Germany are to destroy the capacity of Germany to make war and to relieve the pressure of the German air force and armies on our Russian allies. No instruction has been given to destroy dwelling houses rather than armament factories, but it is impossible to distinguish in night-bombing between the factories and the dwellings which surround them.

Even among diehard Tories, there was some feeling of repugnance about the destruction of so much beauty and culture in Germany in the course of the bomber offensive. One of the most interesting letters in Sir Archibald Sinclair's personal correspondence files came on 26 November 1943 from the Marquess of Salisbury, head of the great Cecil family which had played so large a part in English public life for four centuries. It was handwritten, and marked 'Confidential':

> My dear Sinclair,
> Forgive a somewhat critical note. Your praise of the valour and skill of the air force in their attack on Berlin is abundantly deserved. They are splendid. But Sir Arthur Harris's reply gives one a shake. These attacks are to go on 'until the heart of Nazi Germany ceases to beat'. This would seem to bring us up short against the repeated Government declarations that we are bombing only military and industrial targets. Perhaps that is all that Harris contemplates, and I shall be delighted if you tell me so. But there is a great deal of evidence that makes some of us afraid that we are losing moral superiority to the Germans, and if Harris means not merely that incidental casualties to women and children cannot be avoided, but also that the residential heart of Berlin is to cease to beat, then a good many people will feel that they have been let down – though in writing this I speak in

> the name of no committee. Of course the Germans began it, but we do not take the devil as our example. Of course all these criticisms may be groundless, but if not, issue fresh confidential orders, I *hope*.
>
> Yours Very Sincerely
> SALISBURY
>
> Please remember that we can say nothing in public for obvious reasons.

This was a difficult letter for Sinclair. Salisbury could scarcely be fobbed off with the usual platitudes about 'hoping for an early end to the war to end this regrettable destruction'. His eldest son Lord Cranborne was Lord Privy Seal in the Government. Sinclair passed the letter to Sir Norman Bottomley, the Deputy Chief of Air Staff, for comment.

> To be strictly accurate [suggested Bottomley], our primary object is the progressive destruction and dislocation of the German military, industrial and economic system and *the undermining of the morale of the German people*.* There is no need to inform Lord Salisbury of the underlined phrase, since it will follow on success of the first part of the stated aim.

Thus Sinclair replied to Lord Salisbury on 29 November 1943:

> Our aim is the progressive dislocation of the German military, industrial and economic system. I have never pretended that it is possible to pursue this aim without inflicting terrible casualties on the civilian population of Germany. But neither I, nor any responsible spokesman on behalf of the Government, has ever gloated over the destruction of German homes.
>
> We have resisted a policy of reprisals . . . although there were those who wanted us to select certain small German towns and villages for deliberate destruction . . . we refused, and adhered fully to the principle that we would attack none but military targets.

Most of the British Press supported the bomber offensive with gusto. 'These first blasts of the whirlwind that Hitler, who sowed the wind at Warsaw and Rotterdam, has now to reap have raised the spirits of the fighters for freedom everywhere,' proclaimed a *Times* leader after the 1,000 Raid on Cologne. On 11 March 1943 Harold Balfour declared emphatically that Britain was bombing only military targets: 'I can give the assurance that we are not bombing the women and children of Germany wantonly.' The *Sunday Dispatch* attacked this statement as

*Bottomley's emphasis

weak-kneed: 'It is right that the German population should "smell death at close quarters". Now they are getting the stench of it.' To the intense satisfaction of the Air Ministry, the influential American *Time* magazine was calling for a growing air attack on Germany. Some commentators exceeded even the apostolic enthusiasm of the airmen for bombing Germany. The *Sunday Express* criticized the Air Staff when the weight of bombing seemed to be flagging. Peter Masefield, air correspondent of *The Sunday Times*, argued on 6 June 1943 that 'If the present bomber offensive could be multiplied by four, her war production would be completely halted. That conclusion emerges from a deliberately conservative examination of the damage done by the big bombers.' The Director of Bomber Operations noted drily on his copy of the cutting: 'I consider rather a rosy picture is painted, as it assumes that every load falls on the target and does fresh damage.'

Propaganda and public relations had begun to loom large in the minds of the directors of the war. The airmen, even more than the other two services, monitored public opinion intently. A report was sent to the Air Ministry analysing a sample of civilian letters opened by the censor in the wake of the 1,000 Raid on Cologne: 'There are those who are pleased, and those who regret that so much suffering should have to be inflicted. There are those who fear reprisals. Many of the letters contain two or more of these elements. Predominant is satisfaction, but many women express regret. . . .' A tiny lobby group calling themselves The Bombing Restriction Committee distributed leaflets on the streets headed 'STOP BOMBING CIVILIANS!' Their purpose, they declared, was 'to urge the Government to stop violating their declared policy of bombing only military objectives and particularly to cease causing the deaths of many thousands of civilians in their homes'. Much more typical of popular opinion was Brigadier Cecil Aspinall-Oglander's distaste for the media's raucous delight in the achievements of the bomber offensive.

> Britain and her Allies and well-wishers must all be devoutly thankful that the RAF is at last able to repay Germany in her own coin [the Brigadier wrote to *The Times* on 1 May 1942] and to inflict upon her cities the same devastation that she has inflicted on ours. But it must offend the sensibilities of a large mass of the British population that our official broadcasts, when reporting these acts of just retribution, should exult at and gloat over the suffering which our raids necessitate . . . Let us at least preserve the decencies of English taste. An Englishman does not exult when a criminal is condemned to the scaffold, nor gloat over his sufferings at the time of his execution.

At the end of 1943, Portal produced a subtle proposal: rather than proscribe German cities for destruction, Britain might now declare certain cities immune from attack, in the hope of provoking a panic-stricken flight of refugees towards them. Sinclair was enthusiastic, for his own reasons:

> There might . . . be cities which would remain on the list because they contain no industries of war importance, but possess buildings or works of art of exceptional historic or aesthetic value. This would appeal to an important section of public opinion which is concerned about the destruction of such monuments in the bomber offensive.

The Air Staff eventually rejected this idea, chiefly on the grounds that it was impossible to ensure that the listed cities would not be bombed by mistake. It is significant that Sinclair was so eager to appease the cultural critics. The airmen were far more concerned about attacks on their strategy.

> What are we doing to try to educate *The Times*? [Slessor, as an Assistant Chief of Air Staff, minuted Bottomley on 9 September 1942] The policy of the paper seems to be, while giving the inevitable lip-service to the exploits of the Air Force, to carefully cut them down as being of no value apart from their contribution to land and sea operations. Fortunately the *Daily Telegraph* continues to champion the cause of Air Power. . . .

It was not only the effect of newspaper criticism on politicians and the public that the airmen feared, but a faltering of morale on the bomber stations if crews began to believe that they were being sent to their deaths to no purpose. A 1942 issue of the Russian propaganda paper *Soviet War News*, normally distributed free to service establishments, was banned from all RAF stations when it was found to contain an article entitled 'Air bombing cannot decide the war'.

Britain's most distinguished military thinkers of the pre-war era, Major-General J. F. C. Fuller and Captain Basil Liddell Hart, mounted one of the most significant offensives against Bomber Command. Both men had long since turned away from their uncriticial worship of air power in the 1920s. They had been the outstanding theoreticians of the art of *blitzkrieg*, mobile warfare spearheaded by tanks and tactical aircraft, and Germany's Panzer leaders unashamedly adopted their gospel. Yet now both these men perceived an overwhelming flaw in the concept of a strategic bomber offensive intended to break the enemy's will to fight, when viewed against the background of the Allied doctrine of Unconditional Surrender, promulgated in January 1943. To what purpose could one terrorize the enemy's population into demanding peace from its leaders, if there were no terms to be made? Fuller was appalled by the rising tide of systematic destruction. In August 1943, for example, he drafted an article for the London *Evening Standard*, edited by the radical socialist Michael Foot, in which he heaped insult upon insult against the instigators of the bomber offensive: '. . . the worst devastations of the Goths, Vandals, Huns, Seljuks and Mongols pale into insignificance when compared to the material and moral damage now wrought. . . .'

Foot wrote to Fuller to say that he lacked the nerve to publish the article.[1]

Basil Liddell Hart drafted a private 'Reflection' in the summer of 1942, in the wake of the 1,000 Raid on Cologne:

> It will be ironical if the defenders of civilization depend for victory upon the most barbaric, and unskilled, way of winning a war that the modern world has seen. . . . We are now counting for victory on success in the way of degrading it to a new low level – as represented by indiscriminate (night) bombing and indiscriminate starvation. . . . If our pounding of German cities, by massed night-bombing, proves the decisive factor, it should be a sobering thought that but for Hitler's folly in attacking Russia (and consequently using up his bomber force there, as well as diverting his resources mainly into other weapons) we *and* the Germans would now be 'Cologning' each other's cities with the advantage on Germany's side, in this mad competition in mutual devastation. . . .

Liddell Hart attacked the bomber offensive in newspaper articles and in his books of the period, but like Fuller he was quite without political influence. Fuller had been discredited in English public life by an eccentric flirtation with the Italian Fascists in the 1930s. Liddell Hart was almost obsessively personally hostile to Churchill. In his papers he noted a conversation with General Sir Frederick Pile, Britain's flak defence chief, in which Pile allegedly told him that 'Winston is pinning all his faith to the bombing offensive now. The devastation it causes suits his temperament, and he would be disappointed at a less destructive ending to the war. . . .' Liddell Hart's own brother-in-law Barry Sullivan was serving with the RAF in Malta, and wrote from the island expressing the fear that the Government 'has become Frankenstein, dominated by its own creation – the monster of Bomber Command'.[2]

Liddell Hart's opponents would have argued that he was living in a fantasy world in which warfare could still be conducted as an academic chess-game, rather than the reality, in which the Allies and the Axis were fighting to the death for the survival of freedom against the imminent threat of tyranny. No member of Churchill's government would accord Liddell Hart or Fuller any more respect than was due to private pundits without posts or power. Until the end of the war, they cried in the wilderness.

Most of Britain's churchmen supported the bomber offensive throughout the war, for much the same reasons that Dr Garbett, the Archbishop of York, advanced for refusing to join protests against area bombing in 1943: 'Often in life', he said, 'there is no clear choice between absolute right and wrong; frequently the choice has to be made of the lesser of two evils, and it is a lesser evil to bomb a war-loving Germany than to sacrifice the lives of our fellow-countrymen who long for peace, and to delay delivering millions now held in slavery. . . .'

George Bell, Bishop of Chichester, was unable to accept this compromise. Throughout the war, he was the most persistent and the most celebrated critic of the bomber offensive, to the impotent fury of the British Government. He supported the struggle against Nazi Germany and tactical bombing operations, but he was unrelentingly hostile to area bombing:

> I desire to challenge the Government [he told the House of Lords on 9 February 1944 in a characteristic speech] on the policy which directs the bombing of enemy towns on the present scale, especially with reference to civilians who are non-combatants, and non-military and non-industrial objectives. . . .
>
> I fully realize that in attacks on centres of war industry and transport the killing of civilians when it is the result of bona fide military activity is inevitable. But there must be a fair balance between the means employed and the purpose achieved. To obliterate a whole town because certain portions contain military and industrial establishments is to reject the balance. . . .
>
> The Allies stand for something greater than power. The chief name inscribed on our banner is 'Law'. It is of supreme importance that we, who, with our Allies, are the Liberators of Europe should so use power that it is always under the control of law. It is because the bombing of enemy towns – this area bombing – raises this issue of bombing unlimited and exclusive that such immense importance is bound to attach to the policy and action of His Majesty's Government. . . .

Bell was the most brilliant and the most articulate of the moral critics of the bomber offensive. It is widely held that his campaign later cost him the archbishopric of Canterbury. But in the midst of war, as Britain's leaders struggled with their enemies and their allies, their own exhaustion and dwindling resources, it seemed to them intolerable to be assailed from the flanks by the darts and pinpricks of men who shared no part of their enormous responsibilities. At no time after the fall of France did the Allied warlords consider restricting the bomber offensive for moral reasons. At no period did the offensive's moral critics extend beyond a tiny minority of English men and women. It may be argued that it is a tribute to the survival of the spirit of democracy in wartime that they were able to speak as freely as they did in attacking Bomber Command. Harris believed that the Government made a major error in failing to answer them more frankly: 'In the House of Commons he [Sinclair] should have been far more forthright than he was. . . . There was nothing to be ashamed of, except in the sense that everybody might be ashamed of the sort of thing that has to be done in every war. . . .'[3]

Sinclair himself told the House of Commons on 4 March 1942: 'The talk about the futility of bombing is dangerous . . . Well armed, highly-trained and inflexibly determined, they are the only force upon which we can call on this year, 1942, to strike deadly blows at the heart of Germany.'

2. *Casablanca: The Airmen Victorious*

It was ironic that just as Harris's '1,000 Raids' were thrilling and aweing the British public, a worm of doubt about area bombing was beginning to gnaw the minds of some powerful members of the Air Staff. Sir Wilfred Freeman, the Vice-Chief of Air Staff, was especially irked by the gulf between Bomber Command's real achievements and the public claims made for them. He submitted a memorandum to Portal on the subject on 16 September 1942.

> There is an increasing tendency among Commanders-in-Chief to compete for publicity [wrote Freeman]. This is in itself contrary to the best traditions of the service. More serious, however, is the fact that in their efforts to attract the limelight they sometimes exaggerate and even falsify facts. The worst offender is C-in-C Bomber Command. . . . This is not the first occasion on which there have been complaints of the way in which Bomber Command exaggerates its achievements.

Harris would have claimed that the fastidious Freeman entirely missed the point about the value of the bomber offensive in 1942. Bomber Command's principal task and principal achievement had been to impress the British people and their Allies, rather than to damage the enemy. But as U-boat sinkings rose in the Battle of the Atlantic, as calls for heavy aircraft intensified from every theatre of war, was this still enough to justify Bomber Command's huge claim upon the war effort?

The airmen resisted the navy's demands for more heavy aircraft, partly on the spurious grounds that it would take months to convert bombers to an anti-submarine role, and fit them with ASV radar.

Likewise, when H2S centimetric radar was introduced – one of the decisive technological breakthroughs of the war – the Admiralty lost its fight for first priority to Bomber Command, and Scientific Intelligence were overruled when they suggested that Coastal Command should be equipped first, because H2S sets lost at sea would be in no danger of capture. Thus, one of the first H2S sets fitted to a bomber was indeed captured by the Germans, and the secrets of its cavity magnetron revealed.

Harris's argument against the diversion of heavy aircraft to the Atlantic battle was put forward in his long paper to the War Cabinet of 28 June 1942, reviewing the work of Bomber Command:

> While it takes approximately some 7,000 hours of flying to destroy one submarine at sea, that was approximately the amount of flying necessary to destroy one third of Cologne. . . . The purely defensive use of air power is grossly wasteful. The naval employment of aircraft consists of picking at the fringes of enemy power, of waiting for opportunities that may never occur, and indeed probably never will occur, of looking for needles in a haystack. . . .

He was a master of rhetoric. Why search for submarines over hundreds of thousands of square miles of ocean, he urged, when Bomber Command could destroy the very factories in which they were built? The admirals could never match his force in debate. Yet it is only necessary to study the course of a single convoy battle in 1942 or 1943 to perceive the extraordinary influence that a heavy aircraft could exert. It was not the submarines that were sunk, but the mere appearance of an aircraft that forced U-boats to dive and frequently thwarted major wolfpack attacks. Adequate numbers of long-range aircraft in 1942 could have turned the tide in the Battle of the Atlantic months earlier. But to spirits such as Lord Cherwell, who supported Harris vigorously, the distant splash of plummeting depth-charges held none of the magic of firing the heart of Germany:

> It is difficult to compare quantitatively the damage done to any of the forty-odd big German cities in a 1,000-ton raid with the advantages of sinking one U-boat out of 400 and saving three or four ships out of 5,500 [Cherwell wrote to Churchill on 28 March 1943]. But it will surely be held in Russia as well as here that the bomber offensive must have more immediate effect on the course of the war in 1943. . . .

The importance of keeping Russia in the war now dominated Allied thinking. No one had forgotten the near-catastrophe that followed the Bolsheviks' negotiated peace with Germany in 1917. In 1942 the War Cabinet cherished the conviction that Moscow needed to be persuaded of British sincerity and support for the Russian struggle. The Russians were understandably contemptuous of the fuss the British made about their Arctic Convoy losses when the Soviet armies were losing hundreds of thousands of men in a single battle. From 1942 onwards, Stalin made his view apparent that only by opening a Second Front in north-west Europe could the Allies make a significant impact on the war in the east. Instead, Churchill offered him the bomber offensive. 'I am deeply conscious of the giant burden borne by the Russian armies and their unequalled contribution to the common cause,' the Prime Minister wrote to Stalin on 6 April 1943. 'I must emphasize that our bombing of Germany will increase in scale month by month. . . . Throughout the war, Stalin was sent updated copies of Harris's celebrated 'Blue Books', the C-in-C's personal photograph albums of the wrecked cities of Germany. Beyond a few platitudes congratulating Churchill on the bombing of Berlin, the Russian never seemed much impressed. But the need to support Russia remained a constant chord in the theme of those in Britain and America arguing the case for intensifying the bombing of Germany.

On 3 November 1942, Sir Charles Portal submitted a paper to the Chiefs of Staff on the prospects for the bomber offensive.

> I am convinced [he wrote] that an Anglo-American bomber force based in the United Kingdom and building up to a peak of 4,000 to 6,000 heavy bombers by 1944 would be capable of reducing the German war potential well below the level at which an Anglo-American invasion of the continent would become practicable.

With such a force at their command, Portal promised, six million German homes could be destroyed, 'with a proportionate destruction of industrial buildings, sources of power, means of transportation and public utilities'. 25 million Germans would be made homeless. There would be 'civilian casualties estimated at about 900,000 killed and 1,000,000 seriously injured'. If, as Portal's biographer argues, his purpose in mounting the bomber offensive was never to kill German civilians as such, then he was now hoping to achieve the most dramatic by-product in the history of strategy.

Sir Alan Brooke, the Chief of the Imperial General Staff, was openly sceptical about Bomber Command's ability to fulfil these promises: 'Experience had shown that built-up areas could stand much more knocking about than had been anticipated,' he said. And the First Sea Lord was never less than scathing about the bomber offensive. Yet on 31 December 1942 the British Chiefs of Staff jointly endorsed Portal's proposals, and recommended that 'we should aim at a force of 3,000 British and American heavy and medium bombers operating from the United Kingdom by the end of 1943'.

Portal unveiled his plan weeks before the great Allied conference at Casablanca. Whatever strategic proposals the service chiefs were considering at this time, Winston Churchill approached Casablanca with one overriding priority: to dissuade the Americans from launching a second front in northern Europe in 1943. The British could scarcely suggest to their allies, still in the first flush of impatience to confront the Nazi war machine, that more delay provided time for the Russian army and the Wehrmacht to destroy each other. But the concept of using 1943 to wage a great bomber offensive specifically to pave the way for the second front gave purpose to prevarication. It was for this reason that the British Chiefs of Staff supported Portal's paper, and for this reason that the bomber offensive remained at the forefront of the British war effort in 1943.

The British went to Casablanca with the knowledge that they would have powerful support for their indirect strategy: from the American airmen. Since 1939 the Americans had been studying British bombing with intense interest. The United States Army Air Force envied the RAF's independent status, and cherished hopes of establishing its own place as a third force, separate but equal, alongside the army and navy. The American airmen's commitment to air power – and specifically to strategic bombing – matched that of the British.

But they favoured entirely different methods for doing so. Unmoved by Bomber Command's failures in 1939 and 1940, they believed that the B-17 Flying Fortress was uniquely capable of carrying out an unescorted daylight offensive against Germany: cruising at 260 mph, heavily armed, heavy armoured, and capable of reaching a 33,000-foot ceiling. More important still, they considered that the Norden bombsight gave them the tool to carry out a precision campaign against the key elements of the German economy. The Americans rejected the concept of area bombing, of attacking enemy morale, not least because they believed that it had proved ineffective. In 1942, Major Alexander Seversky, one of the foremost American proponents of air power, was already writing:

> Another vital lesson – one that has taken even air specialists by surprise – relates to the behaviour of civilian populations under air punishment. It had been generally assumed that aerial bombardment would quickly shatter popular morale, causing deep civilian reactions. . . . The progress of this war has tended to indicate that this expectation was unfounded. . . .
>
> These facts are significant beyond their psychological interest. They mean that haphazard destruction of cities – sheer blows at morale – are costly and wasteful in relation to the tactical results achieved. Attacks will increasingly be concentrated on military rather than on random human targets. Unplanned vandalism from

> the air must give way, more and more, to planned, predetermined destruction. More than ever the principal objectives will be the critical aggregates of electric power, aviation industries, dock facilities, essential public utilities and the like.[4]

Americans believed that the German blitz on Britain might have succeeded had it been properly planned. They argued throughout the war, and indeed through Vietnam a generation later, that incidental civilian casualties in the course of precision bombing were acceptable in a way that deliberate slaughter was not. The 8th Air Force flew its first mission to Rouen marshalling yards on 17 August 1942. From then until the end of the year, the Fortresses flew a further twenty-six operations over Europe, losing only thirty-two aircraft in 1,547 sorties, a missing rate of under 2 per cent. American gunners submitted a flood of claims for enemy fighters destroyed, surpassing even the wild estimates of the RAF early in the war. On 27 August 1942, Ira Eaker, commanding the 8th Air Force, was already predicting that 40 per cent of his Fortresses' bombs could be dropped within five hundred yards of the aiming-point. He believed that ten bomber groups in 1942 reinforced by a further ten by June 1943 would be adequate 'coupled with the British night-bombing effort, completely to dislocate German industry and commerce and to remove from the enemy the means for waging successful warfare'. General Carl 'Tooey' Spaatz endorsed Eaker's enthusiasm. The USAAF's great bubble of optimism, matching that of the RAF two years earlier, was airborne. It would be a year before it was brutally exploded.

An uncommitted observer would quickly have perceived that no radical conclusions could be drawn from the early American bomber operations in the autumn of 1942. The formation attacks did some damage to their targets, but they also scattered bombs among the French civilian population in an alarming manner. The Norden sight, so impressive in clear American summer skies, became entirely useless in overcast European ones. From October 1942 to January 1943 almost half of all American bomber sorties were uncompleted. Above all, not a single 8th Air Force aircraft crossed the border of Germany. The Americans operated during this working-up period entirely against short-range targets under Spitfire escort, which the British advised the Americans was essential. The build-up of the 8th Air Force was also persistently delayed. Throughout the autumn and winter of 1942, as fast as bomber groups could be equipped and assembled in England, they were transferred to support Allied operations in North Africa. By January 1943, Eaker could muster scarcely eighty bombers at his British bases.

Yet by the coming of the Casablanca Conference, the British airmen were as eager as the Americans to make common cause of their enthusiasm for the 8th Air Force's slender achievements. A number of British airmen, including even Sir Arthur Harris himself, were so impressed by the American experience that they began a renewed flirtation with the concept of daylight bombing. On 11 December 1942 Harris wrote to the AOC of 4 Group:

> I think everybody is much too apprehensive about daylight operations. . . . I have never been apprehensive about the ability of the heavy bomber to look after itself in daylight vis a vis the fighter. . . . I want daylight operations started as soon as you are ready against lightly-defended targets. . . . There is not the least doubt in my mind that if we and all the available Americans started daylight attacks against the less heavily defended targets in Germany by big formations of heavy bombers now, we should knock the German fighter force out of the sky in two or three months, by the simple process of shooting them down. . . . It has all along been our experience that whenever the rear gunner, even at night, sees the enemy fighter first, he either destroys it or the fighter refuses to come in and attack.[5]

While this note severely damages Harris's claims to be a realistic judge of the operational facts of life over Germany, it also indicates the mood that prevailed among some British airmen after the early American sorties. The British fell over themselves to be complimentary. The notes survive for a public speech of Sir Archibald Sinclair, delivered on 12 October 1942. He eulogized 'the prodigies of' – the word 'accurate' is here crossed out, and 'daylight' substituted – 'daylight bombing which the US Bomber Air Force have already begun to achieve'. On 17 October, eight squadrons of Lancasters staged a daring daylight attack on the Schneider Armament Works at Le Creusot, and returned with the loss of only one aircraft. Bomber Command was now equipped and trained for night operations, and no abrupt change of policy was possible. But some British airmen were thinking furiously.

The Americans, for their part, were largely indifferent to what Bomber Command did or did not do over Germany, provided that the USAAF had its chance to win the war by a precision-bombing offensive before Allied armies landed in France. Spaatz and Eaker might have no faith in area bombing, but they had no intention of saying anything publicly that might endanger the solid front presented by Allied airmen to their naval and military counterparts. General 'Hap' Arnold, Commanding General of the USAAF, was to display growing concern and indeed anger about the lack of co-ordination between Bomber Command and the 8th Air Force, but Spaatz and Eaker were at pains to take no controversial part in a debate on issues so close to the hearts of British airmen. Throughout the war, the two generals enjoyed almost continuously harmonious relations with the British. They understood each other's difficulties perfectly. Harris's struggle with the Royal Navy was mirrored by the USAAF's difficulties with Admiral King, the Chief of Naval Operations, who was fighting for priority for the Pacific. As early as July 1942, Eisenhower was indicating that he hoped to use the 8th Air Force to support ground operations, a prospect totally at odds with the ambitions of the American airmen.

Harris sought to support the American airmen in their inter-service struggles with as much loyalty as they offered him in his difficulties with British colleagues and with Arnold in Washington. In the file of Harris's correspondence with the Prime Minister there is an undated memorandum from the winter of 1942–43 headed 'Most Secret and Strictly Personal', in which Harris urges Churchill to support Eaker and Spaatz in their difficulties with the US Navy and Army. 'My American air friends are despondent,' he wrote. Among his fellow airmen, Harris laboured constantly for a united front: 'We can defeat the enemy if we are not defeated by our friends,' he wrote to Arnold in August 1942.

Thus the Allied airmen came to Casablanca in January 1943 united in their determination to fight for a mandate for the growth of the bomber offensive. In the event it did not prove necessary to do so. Once the British had got their way about the major strategic decision taken at the conference, the postponement until 1944 of Operation *Overlord* – the invasion of northern Europe – in favour of Operation *Husky* – a step-by-step advance through Sicily and Italy – it was apparent that the Allies must continue the bombing campaign as the only major offensive against Germany. Churchill withdrew his objections to the American daylight attack, which he personally believed was doomed, after an appeal by Ira Eaker. It was agreed that the goal of the Combined Bomber Offensive, as it would henceforth be known, should be 'to weaken Germany's war-making capacity to the point to which invasion would become possible'.

In reality, of course, this was the airmen's phrase: the soldiers would never have acknowledged the implication that invasion could not take place until strategic bombing had achieved some definable and decisive effect on Germany; the armies would be launched upon the invasion when the generals and statesmen saw fit, and their only major concern was that tactical air supremacy should be maintained around the battlefield. If Sir Charles Portal had ever believed that the war could be won by bombing alone, he no longer did so. At Casablanca he said emphatically that it was necessary 'to exert the maximum pressure on Germany by land operations; air bombardment alone was not sufficient'.

The Casablanca Directive – CCS 166/I/D from the Combined Chiefs of Staff to Air Marshal Harris and General Eaker – ordered them to embark on the demolition of a range of German target systems as essential preliminaries to D-Day. First on the list, with the Battle of the Atlantic still foremost in the Allies' concerns, came submarine yards and bases. Then followed the German air force, its factories and depots. After these, ball-bearings, of which it was thought that Germany could be deprived with limited bomber effort against a handful of vital targets; oil; synthetic rubber and tyres; and military transport. The opening phrase of the directive reflected the intended marriage of British and American bombing policies:

> Your primary aim will be the progressive destruction and dislocation of the German military, industrial and economic system, and the undermining of the morale of the German people to a point where their capacity for armed resistance is fatally weakened. . . .

After the preamble, most of the detailed thinking in the directive about the German economy was American. It had been essential for the British to defer to the Americans' precision-bombing ambitions in order to gain their own objectives at Casablanca. In the months following the conference, an Operational Committee produced what became known as the Eaker Plan, intended to transform the Casablanca Directive into realistic orders for Bomber Command and the 8th Air Force. The Eaker Plan reflected some of that general's astonishingly vivid projections. If the 8th Air Force could be built up to a strength of 1,746 aircraft by 1 January 1944, and 2,702 aircraft by 1 April 1944, Eaker promised that German submarine construction could be reduced by 89 per cent; fighter construction by 43 per cent; bomber construction by 65 per cent; ball-bearings by 76 per cent; synthetic rubber production by 50 per cent. 'These figures', he added, 'are conservative and can be absolutely relied upon.'

The plan drawn up by the Operational Committee was endorsed by Portal and Harris in April 1943, with only minor reservations about the prominence given to the submarine bases on the French coast, which had already proved virtually invulnerable to bombing.

> This plan [said its authors] does not attempt to prescribe the major effort of the RAF Bomber Command. It simply recognizes the fact that when precision targets are bombed by the Eighth Air Force in daylight, the effort should be completed and complemented by RAF bombing attacks against the surrounding industrial area at night. Fortunately the industrial areas to be attacked are in most cases identical with the industrial areas which the British Bomber Command has selected for mass destruction anyway. . . .

Harris wrote to Eaker on 15 April 1943:

I am in complete agreement with the policy recommended. The effect of linking up precision bombing of selected targets in daylight by an adequate force of the VIII Bomber Command with intensified night-bombing by the RAF will unquestionably cause damage to *matériel* and morale on a scale which the enemy will be unable to sustain.

As regards the detailed presentation, there are naturally some points on which I would lay slightly varied emphasis if I were presenting the case to my own Chief of Staff, but these are of no consequence compared with the major aim, which is to build up the bomber forces in Britain at the maximum pace, and to the size necessary to achieve our common purpose.

At Casablanca it was decided that the Chiefs of Staffs' authority for the conduct of the Combined Bomber Offensive should be nominally vested in Sir Charles Portal. The allocation of targets and 'the effective co-ordination of the forces involved' was to be ensured 'by frequent consultation between the Commanders in Chief'. General Arnold in Washington was thoroughly uneasy about this cosy arrangement. On 22 April 1943 he wrote to Portal:

It occurs to me that the time has arrived for the establishment of somewhat more formalized machinery for the closest possible co-ordination, or rather integration of the two bomber efforts. The increasing complexity of their operations would appear to me as soon to be beyond the capabilities of the commanders, in person, to co-ordinate.

To the British, Arnold's note and many others that would follow it represents the very Trojan horse that they were determined to keep from their gates. Harris, with his experience of America as head of the RAF delegation in Washington, was one of the first to foresee and prepare to repel American attempts to incorporate Bomber Command in some joint Allied command structure. On land it was inevitable that the Americans would overwhelmingly dominate the war effort. At sea the British still played the principal part in the Mediterranean and were equal co-partners in the Atlantic only because the US navy was so heavily committed in the Pacific. In the air, in 1943 America would build 9,615 heavy bombers against Britain's 3,657; 9,450 twin-engined aircraft against Britain's 5,565; 10,392 single-engined fighters against Britain's 8,151. Even to achieve their own existing levels of aircraft production, the British were now compelled to rely entirely on America for transport aircraft, and very heavily for tanks, ammunition and landing-craft. In 1944, American dominance in the air would be even more dramatic.

Bomber Command represented Britain's last entirely independent contribution to the Allied war effort, gripping the imagination of the British people and much of Occupied Europe. As the enormous build-up of American air power developed in 1943 and 1944, the British were determined to ensure that Harris's forces were not submerged. High Wycombe always regarded the Casablanca Directive as a general mandate for the future of the bomber offensive, rather than as a specific instruction to be strictly obeyed. A number of staff officers at the Air Ministry were already impressed by the American concept of precision bombing, and sought to press their views upon Portal and Harris. But Bomber Command's C-in-C considered Casablanca merely an authorization to continue what he was doing already, and Sir Charles Portal made no attempt to make him think otherwise.

Arnold's proposals for integrating the British and American bomber offensives were rejected. Probably at Harris's instigation,[6] certain phrases in the draft directive for the Combined Bomber Offensive which was now being refined from the Casablanca Directive were altered, to make an already vaguely worded document woollier still. It was a measure of Churchill's waning emphasis on the bomber offensive that when the final proposals based on Casablanca and the Eaker Plan, and now christened *Pointblank*, came before the Washington summit of May 1943 for approval, the Prime Minister nodded them through with the brief assertion that it was unnecessary further to discuss bombing policy, since there was virtual British and American agreement. On 10 June 1943 the *Pointblank* Directive was formally issued to Bomber Command and the 8th Air Force. It was to be the basis of the strategic bomber offensive – at least in the minds of the Chiefs of Staff – until the invasion.

The American airmen had got what they wanted: their orders to embark upon a precision-bombing offensive. From the beginning of 1943, 8th Air Force strength grew steadily from a daily average of 73 heavy bombers available in February to the 279 dispatched on a single operation in May. The Americans' hopes and ambitions for the destruction of German industry were based on the same blend of ignorance, optimism and astonishing statistical projections as those of the British, unrelieved by the RAF's additional hopes for damaging enemy morale. The first priority of the 8th Air Force was to destroy the German air force in production. With unbounded courage and hope its leaders addressed themselves to their task.

But just as the Americans would ignore the phrases about attacking German morale embodied in *Pointblank*, so Sir Arthur Harris proposed to disregard the implication which the directive's creators certainly intended, that Bomber Command should address itself specifically to areas in which the key German target systems were found. Long before Casablanca or even before Cologne, Harris conceived his campaign for the systematic laying-waste of Germany's cities, and he never had the slightest intention of being deflected from it. In *Pointblank* 'he was able to discover a mandate for pursuing the policy upon which he was in any case resolved . . . For most of 1943 there was no combined offensive, but, on the contrary, a bombing competition.'[7] Harris was in many ways a much more shrewd political animal than has generally been recognized. Although he sometimes damaged his own cause by his appalling exaggerations, he understood one prime principle of bureaucratic manoeuvre: that by agreeing to a course of action loudly and often enough in public, it is possible in reality to do something entirely different. Harris's letters to Eaker were effusive in their expressions of common purpose. Harris was certainly sincere in wanting to see a large American strategic bomber force irrevocably committed to the assault on Germany. But beyond this, he treated the *Pointblank* Directive as a harmless plaything for the Ministry of Economic Warfare and the Air Staff.

In 1943 he would have a devastating strike force under his command. He would use it to hit the cities of Germany. His only concession to *Pointblank* was that when his aircraft attacked an urban centre, he was at pains to catalogue for the Air Ministry and for the Americans the aircraft factories or aero-engine plants or oil refineries which it contained, and which were scheduled for destruction in *Pointblank*.

There is one more essential dimension of the Combined Bomber Offensive in 1943: while the soldiers regarded the strategic air offensive at best as subordinate, at worst as irrelevant to grand strategy, both Harris and Spaatz still believed that in the year left to them before D-Day, their forces could defeat Germany without a land campaign. To both men and to many of their subordinates, the role allotted to them in *Pointblank* as mere harbingers of the invasion forces fell far short of their hopes. The lasting significance of Casablanca and of *Pointblank* was that it confirmed the air forces' claims upon a huge share of their nations' resources for the bomber offensive. Now Harris and Spaatz, each in his own way, set out to prove that by air power alone they could bring Germany to its knees.

3. The Tools of Darkness

In Winston Churchill's *History of the Second World War*; it is remarkable that even long after the event, he retained his contempt for the techniques of the Luftwaffe in 1940, and especially for the German *Knickebein* navigational beams:

> With their logical minds and deliberate large-scale planning [he wrote] the German Air Command staked their fortunes in this

> sphere on a device which . . . they thought would do us in. Therefore they did not trouble to train the ordinary bomber pilots, as ours had been trained, in the difficult art of navigation. A far simpler and surer method, lending itself to drill and large numbers producing results wholesale by irresistible science, attracted alike their minds and their nature. The German pilots followed the beam as the German people followed the Führer. They had nothing else to follow.[8]

Yet the techniques of which Churchill wrote with such scorn, *Knickebein* and *X-Gerat* and the 'pathfinder' concept of Kampfgruppe 100 of the Luftwaffe, were precisely those which Bomber Command sought in vain to match throughout 1940 and 1941. Only in 1942 did *Gee* come into service, and by August it was being jammed by the Germans everywhere beyond the coastline of Occupied Europe. Only at the beginning of 1943 was Bomber Command at last equipped with the new generation of radio and radar aids that made it possible to strike with real force at Germany, to bring the bomber offensive out of its cottage-industry phase into the age of automated mass destruction.

It might be thought that once area bombing was introduced, 'browning' a city became a relatively simple exercise. But until the very end of the war it remained a very difficult test of navigating and bomb-aiming skill. A modern British historian argues that 'the one gleaming lesson of twentieth-century warfare is that strategy follows, and does not precede, the scientist and the technician'.[9] It is patently true that the bomber proved unable to play a decisive part in war until armed with devastating scientific weapons, yet one may also claim that the strategic air offensive proves the reverse of the argument. Many of the new tools that became available in 1943 only did so because Bomber Command's needs were belatedly identified, just as were those of Fighter Command in 1936. The scientists at the Telecommunications Research Establishment at Malvern applied themselves to solve the proven operational problems of 1940 and 1941. The fruit of their labour was a remarkable triumph for British technology – until the end of the war the Americans were almost totally dependent on British electronic devices to wage their own air offensive.

It was Harris's good luck that at the beginning of 1943 he could take advantage of the new generation of equipment just as his force of heavy bombers began its major expansion. In the words of the official historians: 'The air attack on Germany in 1943 increased so much in weight and efficiency that it became something quite different from anything that had preceded it.'[10] Harris himself acknowledged that in 1942 he had merely scratched at the roof of Germany: 'So ended a year of preparation', he wrote in his memoirs, 'in which very little material damage had been done to the enemy which he could not repair from his own resources, but in which we had obtained or had in near prospect what was required to strike him to the ground, and learned how to use it.'[11]

The first vital innovation to match the techniques of the Luftwaffe had been introduced in August 1942: the Pathfinder Force was born. Henceforth, on almost every operation of the offensive, the 'Main Force' squadrons of Bomber Command were preceded to their target by the PFF, dropping aerial route markers to guide the stream across Germany, then marking the target by a range of increasingly sophisticated techniques, some visual, some 'blind' by radar.

The creation of the Pathfinders was preceded by one of the most bad-tempered debates of the war between the Air Ministry and Harris. He had nursed a contempt for staff officers since his days as Deputy Chief of Air Staff early in the war. He believed emphatically that subordinates should know their place, which was executing the orders of their superiors:

> My first impression on arriving at the Air Ministry was that the staff of every department was fantastically bloated. Junior officers were to my mind quite needlessly named directors of this and that, and they all imagined themselves as commanders in the field of the commands they were supposed to direct – a very nice job, too, because they thought – mistakenly – that they were running the show without having to take the responsibility for the results.
>
> I looked upon C-in-Cs in the field as responsible people who were not to be bothered by the trumpery opinions of young Jacks-in-office. . . .[12]

Harris reserved his most virulent disdain for the Air Ministry's Directorate of Bomber Operations, whose staff acted as the Chief of Air Staff's personal advisers and agents in all matters relating to bombing policy. The Director in 1942 was Air Commodore J. W. Baker, shortly to be succeeded by his then Deputy, Group-Captain S. O. Bufton, whom we last met commanding 10 Squadron at Leeming in 1940. Ever since his nights over Germany in a Whitley, and subsequently commanding 76 Halifax Squadron, Bufton had been preoccupied by the problems of target location and marking. Back in 1941 he asked for barometrically-fused flares to ignite above the target. He and his crews experimented with such desperate gambits as firing coded Very cartridges when an aircraft positively identified the target. Now, at the Air Ministry, Bufton became convinced that Bomber Command's squadrons must have a specially trained 'Target-Finding Force' to lead them across Germany. It is significant that Bufton was dedicated to the concept of precision bombing, and had the gravest doubts about the value of area attack. He enjoyed close relations with the American 8th

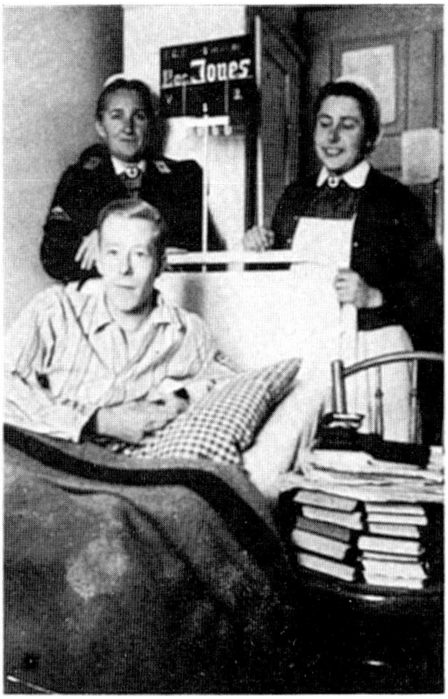

Harry Jones of 37 Squadron in a German hospital after being shot down on 18 December 1939

F/Sgt Herbert Ruse *(on the left)* of 37 Squadron being briefed for an operation. On the right is the squadron CO, W/Cdr Joe Fogarty

(above) Marshal of the RAF Lord Trenchard

(above right) Sir Edgar Ludlow-Hewitt, C-in-C of Bomber Command 1937–40

(below left) Sir Richard Peirse, C-in-C of Bomber Command 1940–42

(below right) Sir Archibald Sinclair, Secretary of State for Air 1940–45. He was leader of the Liberal Party until he went to the House of Lords as Viscount Thurso

A Halifax of Bomber Command sets out for Germany

The face of the enemy: Germany's armament workers continued to produce the tools for the survival of the Third Reich almost until the end, their will unbroken by bombing. Here a factory group is addressed by Albert Speer

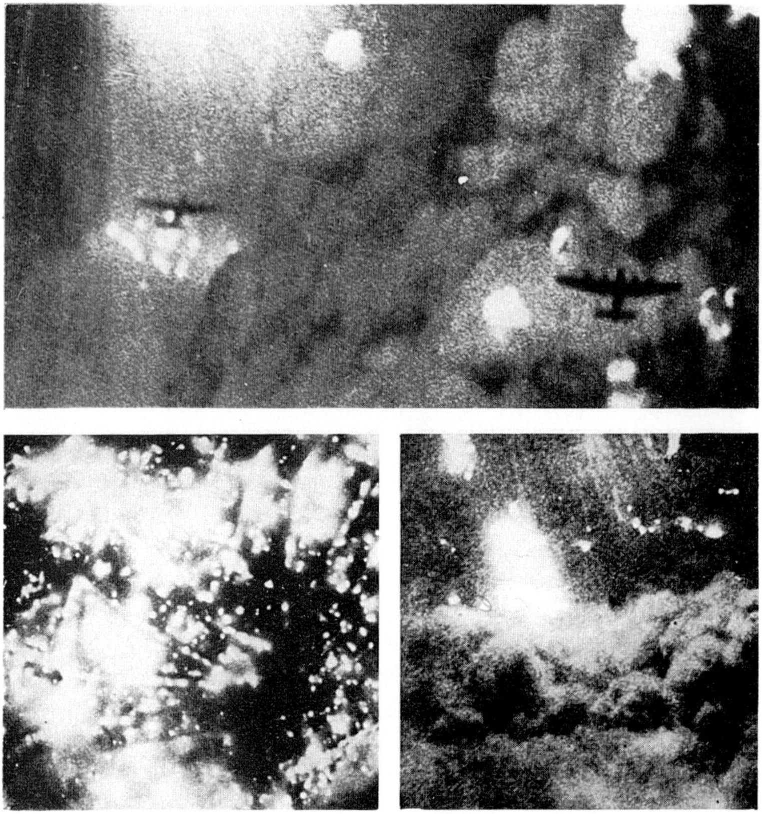

Night images of Germany: the sort of views the crews of Bomber Command saw beneath them over their targets; flak trails, the pinpoints of burning incendiaries on the ground and, in one photo, aircraft below are clearly visible

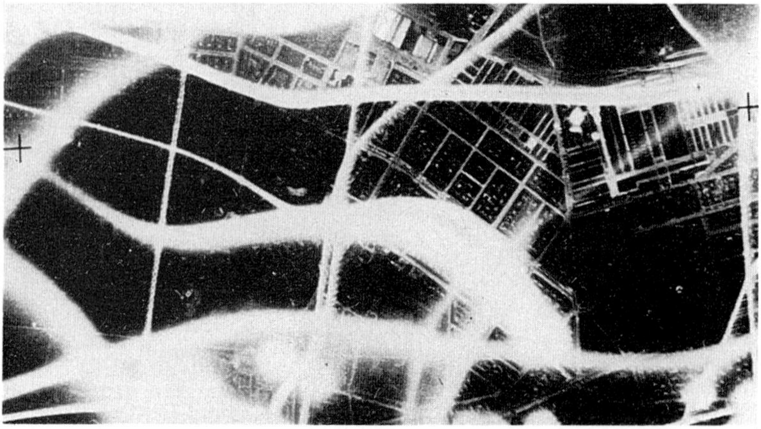

Albert Speer *(on the right)* with Field-Marshal Erhard Milch, the man responsile for aircraft production until his fall from grace in 1944

The Prime Minister with Lord Cherwell *(on the left)*, Sir Charles Portal and the First Sea Lord, Sir Dudley Pound

Magrath (82 Squadron)

Staton (10)

Donaldson (10)

Lindaas (76)

Maze (76)

Hornsey (76)

Newton (76)

Cheshire (76)

Eclipse: the C-in-C of Bomber Command with his wife and daughter on their way to South Africa soon after the end of the war. Harris did not share the honours that fell to other service leaders in the wake of victory, and never concealed his bitterness that his men were denied their own Campaign Medal

Air Force, perhaps not least because of his faith in its objectives, if not its tactics. He was prominent among those at the Air Ministry who regarded area attack as a necessary last resort only until the techniques became available to make Bomber Command a precision-bombing force. It was partly because the creation of a 'Target-Finding Force' might bring this day closer that Bufton advocated it so passionately. It was perhaps for the same reason that Harris fought the proposal tooth and nail. He had no intention of opening the door an inch to the 'panacea merchants'.

Harris's stated reason for opposing Bufton was that morale would suffer throughout Bomber Command if an elite force was created within it:

> I wanted six Pathfinder forces – one in every group. Having only one, we were told to send all the best crews to it. Imagine the feelings of squadron commanders on being told to hand them over! Portal had no right to overrule me on the advice of a junior staff officer whose only qualification was that he had dropped a few leaflets on Europe at the beginning of the war.[13]

'I don't think that the formation of a First XV at a school makes the small boys play rugger any less enthusiastically,' remarked Sir Henry Tizard, in answer to Harris's objections. Throughout the early summer of 1942 there was a series of acrimonious meetings at High Wycombe. Harris and his group commanders were hostile, but, as Bufton pointed out, not one of them had operational experience over Germany. It was a new and entirely unwelcome experience for the C-in-C, who kept dissent at High Wycombe to a minimum, to be thus harried by a junior officer. The morning after one fierce conference, as Bufton walked up the steps of the Air Ministry in King Charles Street, Harris's Bentley drew up at its usual relentless rush, and the C-in-C sprang out, noticing the staff officer without enthusiasm as he passed: 'Morning, Bufton. And what are you going to do to me today?'

Harris began to lose the battle when the file was passed to Freeman, the Vice-Chief of Air Staff. A consensus clearly emerged at the Air Ministry that whatever the problems of a 'Target-Finding Force', it offered better prospects than the existing system of 'Raid Leaders' evolved in the spring, using arbitrarily-selected line squadrons to mark for the Main Force with incendiaries. In July 1942 Harris learnt that he had lost his case.

But there were still some rearguard actions that the C-in-C could win. First, he would not have the new Group called a 'Target- Finding Force'. They would be considered primarily as route guides, 'Pathfinders'. When a proposal was put forward that they should be commanded by the dashing spirit of 2 Group, Basil Embry, Harris would have none of it. His critics said that it was because he feared that Embry would prove as self-willed as himself. In any event, Harris's choice for the command of PFF – No. 8 Group, as it became – was a young Australian group captain named Donald Bennett. Bennett served under Harris in flying-boats before the war, left the RAF to fly for Imperial Airways, and created a reputation as one of the most brilliant technical airmen of his generation: an outstanding pilot, a superb navigator who was also capable of stripping a wireless set or overhauling an engine. Bennett spent the early months of the war as one of the directors of the trans-Atlantic ferry, flying aircraft from America to Britain. After his return to the RAF he commanded a Halifax squadron until he was shot down attacking the *Tirpitz* in a Norwegian fjord, and made a successful escape through Sweden. He was still only thirty-two, twenty years younger than his fellow group commanders. The important reservations about Bennett were that he had no large-scale administrative experience, yet he would be immediately responsible for a hundred aircraft and their huge supporting organization, ultimately for nineteen squadrons. He was a difficult and arrogant 'loner' who gained much respect but very little personal affection everywhere that he went. He made no secret of his satisfaction and conviction that his appointment represented the eclipse of the 'gentlemen' and the arrival of the 'players'. Yet Harris overcame widespread service objections to get Bennett his job, and kept him in it until the end of the war. In a letter to the Prime Minister soon after 8 Group was formed, Harris described its new commander as 'one of the most efficient and finest youngsters I have ever come across in the Service'.

PFF would never get all the resources that it believed it needed. According to Bennett himself,[14] 4 and 6 Groups loyally sent him the best crews they could muster, but the other Group AOCs were half hearted, to say the least, in providing their share of men for secondment to PFF. Bennett and Harris fought a tough battle with the Treasury and the Air Ministry to gain some special recognition for PFF crews, who it was decided should do forty-five trips instead of the usual thirty in their tour, to make the most of their experience. In the end, in addition to the Pathfinder badge which was always genuinely coveted by the aircrew, Pathfinders were granted a step-up in rank and pay for as long as they were on 'ops', to be dropped when they finished their tours. They did not, however, get the pick of the aircraft. The five squadrons of Pathfinders that were operational by the beginning of 1943 flew the general Bomber Command mixture of Stirlings, Halifaxes, Lancasters and the new Mosquitoes.

In the last months of 1942 the concentration of bombs dropped by Harris's forces improved marginally with the introduction of the Pathfinders, despite appalling operating weather. A few Main Force crews still ignored the PFF markers and sought their own identification of the target as a matter of pride and genuine conviction that their own judgement was better; but the vast majority were immensely relieved to see the Target Indicators glowing at the heart of a city, marking the aiming-point. Inevitably now, when PFF marked the wrong place, the whole of Bomber Command likewise went awry. There was an embarrassing night when they were sent to Saarbrücken, but the Pathfinders marked nearby Saarlouis in error, and the unfortunate town was duly devastated, while Saarbrücken scarcely received a bomb. The Pathfinder Force developed and was trained to mark for the area offensive and not – as Bufton and others had hoped – to pave the way towards precision bombing. There would be many nights of scattered marking and thus scattered bombing; blind-marking techniques through cloud never reached a satisfactory degree of effectiveness, even with the new generation of radar aids. But the Pathfinders contributed immensely to the enhanced capability of Bomber Command in 1943.

By far the most important rivals at the turn of 1942–43 were two new radar aids, H2S and *Oboe*. H2S was the first airborne radar set that could paint a shadowy image of the ground below on a cathode ray tube for its operator in an aircraft above. It held out the prospect of identifying targets through cloud, although like *Gee* – and as Tizard emphatically warned – it would never prove the talisman, the precious blind-bombing tool which the airmen always sought. H2S sets came into use gradually through 1943, and were issued initially to Pathfinder units. They suffered considerable teething trouble, and always performed best in the vicinity of bodies of water which showed up clearly on their screens. But, unlike *Gee*, they operated on a 10-cm waveband that could not be jammed by the German defences.

The second device was indeed a vital blind-bombing aid. *Oboe* was a brilliantly sophisticated variation of the system by which the Germans had bombed England in 1940. An aircraft flew at the end of a beam laid by a ground station, like a conker on a string whirled around a child's head. Its bombs or markers were released at the exact point of intersection with another beam from a second ground station. There was no scope for visual error. The device proved accurate to a remarkable 600 yards on tests over Lorient and St Nazaire in December 1942. *Oboe* suffered only two limitations: Bomber Command possessed only two sets of ground stations, and could thus control only twelve *Oboe* aircraft an hour over the target. It was necessary to have Pathfinder heavy bombers constantly available to 'back up' the *Oboe* markers if there was any lapse in the visibility of these during the Main Force attack. The second difficulty was more serious: owing to the curvature of the earth, *Oboe* beams could only reach aircraft at limited range from their English ground stations. They could get to the Ruhr, but not much further. Until the Allied advance into Europe in 1944, British attacks on more distant targets had to rely on *Gee*, H2S and pilot judgement for their success. As will become apparent, these were not enough.

But beyond *Oboe*, Harris was now being equipped with the perfect aircraft to carry it, the twin-engined De Havilland Mosquito, which could mark from 28,000 feet to get the utmost range from the device. Since the prototype Mosquito showed its 350 mph promise, rival Commands of the RAF had been struggling fiercely for priority on supplies. It became the best night-fighter of the war, and it could also take a 4,000-lb bomb to Berlin while giving ordinary German fighters only the flimsiest chance of catching it. Mosquito casualties over Germany were negligible, a fraction of those suffered by the 'heavies'. The aircraft was a delight to fly. In its bomber role it carried no armament, relying solely on speed for survival. From 1943, it became a vital element in Bomber Command operations, first spearheading the Pathfinder force, later carrying out diversionary raids and Intruder operations against German fighter airfields.

There is a school of thought which argues that if Bomber Command had been equipped with an enormous force of Mosquitoes, these could have struck Germany for a fraction of the cost of the heavy-bomber offensive. But apart from the difficulties of reversing the heavy-aircraft programme at this stage, it is doubtful if there were enough carpenters in England physically to build an all-Mosquito force. The requirement for pilots and navigators would have been enormous. To suggest that the Mosquito could single-handed have solved the problems of Bomber Command is an improper use of hindsight. But the RAF made maximum use of all the 'Mossies' that it could get.

The winter of 1942–43 saw other, less dramatic innovations in tactics and equipment. It had at last been recognized that bright moonlight made bombers too vulnerable to fighters, and now the 'Met' men sought broken cloud and dark nights for operations. For the first time, the Pathfinders were given specially-designed Target Indicators, vari-coloured projectiles that were big enough and bright enough to be seen from great height amidst the smoke and haze of a burning city. The 'plate rack' principle of sending aircraft in to attack at varying heights came into general use. The 'streaming' policy for concentrating aircraft over the target was intensified. Bombers were being fitted with *Boozer* to give early warning of gun and searchlight radar, and with *Monica*, which detected other aircraft closing in. The first of the immense range of radio counter-measures against the German defences was being employed by Group-Captain Addison's 80 Wing, which would ultimately flower into a fully-fledged Group – No. 100.

Now, at the beginning of 1943, Harris wrote: 'At long last we were ready and equipped.'[15] He identified the start of his real strategic offensive as the night of 5 March 1943, when 442 aircraft of Bomber Command attacked Essen under *Oboe* marking laid by the Pathfinder

Force. The winter months of sporadic skirmishing against Berlin, and the impenetrable U-boat pens at Lorient and St Nazaire were over. He was free to launch the first of the three great 'battles' which made 1943 the most famous and the bloodiest year of the British air offensive: the Ruhr, Hamburg and Berlin. These represented the central thrusts of the campaign, Bomber Command's attempt to bring a devastating concentration of force to bear on selected regions of Germany. March 1943 to March 1944 would be Harris's year of astonishing independence and personal power.

VIII

76 Squadron, Yorkshire, 1943

'If you live on the brink of death yourself, it is as if those who have gone have merely caught an earlier train to the same destination, and whatever that destination is, you will be sharing it soon, since you will almost certainly be catching the next one'.

F/Lt Denis Hornsey, 76 Squadron, 1943

1. The Ruhr

Although history now remembers the Ruhr as one of Harris's three great 'battles' of 1943, the crews of Bomber Command who carried out its forty-three major attacks between 5 March and 12 July had no such privilege of hindsight. They only knew that they flew night after night to some of the most heavily defended targets in Germany. Some of these – Stettin, Berlin, Munich, Stuttgart – were not even in the Ruhr. The campaign was by its nature incapable of yielding any visible proof of victory. The American official historians have written:

> The heavy bomber offensive was an impersonal sort of war, and monotonous in its own peculiar way. . . . Rarely was a single mission or series of missions decisive; whatever earlier they had taught of sudden paralysis of a nation by strategic bombardment, in actual practice the forces available in 1942–43 were quite inadequate for such Douhet-like tactics.[1]

To the bomber crews, the only reality was the intensity of the struggle. In the four and a half months of the Battle of the Ruhr, Harris lost almost a thousand aircraft missing over Germany and crashed in England. His men learnt to hate and fear the ferocity of the defences of 'Happy Valley', most especially the wall of flak and light surrounding Essen and the great Krupp works. They were riddled by gunfire and mauled by the German night-fighter force, now approaching its zenith. They made bomb run after bomb run struggling to avoid the urge to flinch and turn aside before reaching their aiming-point, the instinct which created a chronic 'creep-back' of bombs falling short or wide on every raid. In the dense mass of heavy aircraft closing on the target, they learned to fear collision, sometimes even to know the terror of seeing another aircraft directly above them with its bomb doors open. They came to take for granted the vast conflagrations reaching across the cities of Germany which seemed the wonder of the age at Cologne a year before.

Yet it was characteristic of the bomber offensive that each squadron, cut off on its lonely airfield somewhere down the length of eastern England, lived in its own private world and knew little of what went on outside except from the bulletins of Group and High Wycombe. Bomber Command could sometimes have a disastrous night, losing scores of aircraft, yet a squadron came home unaware of anything amiss, having attacked in a wave that missed the night-fighters. Conversely, on one trip a squadron for no definable reason could lose four, five, six aircraft – far above Bomber Command's average.

76 Squadron, one of 4 Group's Halifax units stationed at Linton-on-Ouse in Yorkshire, lost a steady one and occasionally two aircraft a night throughout the Battle of the Ruhr. In 1943 as a whole, its crews operated on 104 nights and lost 59 aircraft missing, three times their average operating strength. Sometimes weeks went by without a crew successfully completing a tour.

Harris's assault on the Ruhr began where he had skirmished just a year before, when he took command at High Wycombe: Essen. Led by eight Pathfinder *Oboe* Mosquitoes, 443 aircraft began their attack at 9 pm on the moonless night of 5 March 1943. 76 Squadron's aircraft were among the first wave, attacking from Zero plus two minutes to Zero plus twenty. The Wellingtons and Stirlings followed from Z+15 to Z+25, and last came the Lancasters, from Z+20 to Z+40. They carried a bombload of one-third high explosive to two-thirds incendiaries, for by now it was conclusively established that fire was an infinitely more effective destroyer of towns than blast. The HE was intended only to open up the city, literally to blow apart its windows and walls and doors to make way for the fires. At Bomber Command, the attack was considered an extraordinary success. 153 aircraft bombed within three miles of the aiming-point. 160 acres of Essen had been laid waste for the loss of only fourteen aircraft. But one of the fourteen came from 76 Squadron, and after debriefing a young WAAF Intelligence officer, Pam Finch, noted in her diary: 'They all seem rather badly shaken up.'

Three nights later, they were over Nuremberg, where the markers went down two minutes late, and as they exploded a great mass of bombs deluged them, as aircraft that had been lingering nervously overhead thankfully unburdened themselves. The night after, they were at Munich. The squadron operational record book noted coolly: 'Opposition not up to usual standard.' Then the losses began to creep up. Flight-Sergeant Gallantry baled out over the English coast on the way home from Stuttgart. An aircraft was lost over Essen and another crashed on landing. Two crews were missing after the raid on Berlin on 29 March, one of them that of Sergeant Cursley, who had been a pre-war 'erk' in Singapore, and was on his twenty-ninth trip. It was a night of heavy rain, icing and low cloud, and only three of eleven crews claimed to have attacked. Just three of Bomber Command's 481 aircraft dispatched bombed within three miles of their aiming-point.

On 7 April, Pam Finch, the WAAF Intelligence girl, went to a cocktail party at the house of Linton's station commander with a Canadian pilot named 'Morty' Mortensen. He claimed to be awed by the honour of 'Groupie's' hospitality: 'Now I'm sure to get the chop!' A week later, the squadron went to Pilsen. Pam Finch looked out at the moon and made a wish for 'Morty' to come back. The raid was a failure. The Pathfinders mistook a lunatic asylum for the Skoda works, and a rain of bombs descended on the empty countryside around it. The 'missing' rate was 11 per cent, the highest of the Battle of the Ruhr. 'Being that the raid was carried out in perfect moonlight, heavy losses were to be expected,' noted the Squadron Record Book. Three new crews failed to return from 76 Squadron. One of them was Mortensen's.

On 10 April, Group-Captain John Whitley, Linton's popular station commander, was himself shot down on a trip to Frankfurt. It was uncanny how often senior officers were lost when they made their rare sorties as passengers in bombers. Whitley's successor was lost over Mülheim only two months later. But Whitley himself astonished and delighted everybody by reappearing at Linton large as life only weeks after he was 'Posted Missing to No.1 Depot Uxbridge', as records put it. A prudent man, he always carried a set of civilian clothes with him on operations, and when his aircraft was shot down by a night-fighter over France, he was well-prepared both mentally and physically for the epic adventure that followed. Many aircrew were understandably dazed and disorientated in the first, vital hours after being blown from the sky. But if they were fortunate enough to land in Occupied Europe rather than in Germany itself, those with the will and the luck to survive the first hours on the ground uncaptured often made it to England. With the help of the Resistance, Whitley walked and bicycled across France to the Pyrenees, and came home to receive a well-earned DSO.

On 20 April they went to Stettin. It was a test of new tactics. They flew at sea level across the North Sea in the moonlight, then swept across Denmark low enough to see the windows opening as astonished Danes craned to watch the great stream of bombers roar overhead. One aircraft crashed into a windmill on almost the only hill on the route. All 76's Halifaxes came home. But the next trip they lost a crew over Duisburg, and another over Essen on 30 April. This was a chaotic night, demonstrating the havoc that weather and ill-luck could wreak upon schedules. A Halifax became bogged on the runway, and the three aircraft behind were unable to take off in time to reach the target on schedule. Two of those who got airborne returned early, and only six of those dispatched from 76 Squadron claimed to have attacked.

May began with an attack on Dortmund, one of the most severely punished targets of the battle. On the 11th they went to Duisburg again, another highly successful operation. 572 aircraft were dispatched, and 410 bombed within three miles of the aiming-point. All that early summer, Harris's squadrons seldom bombed less than 300 aircraft strong, often 600 or more. By a characteristic twist of fate, all 76's twelve aircraft came home safe from Duisburg that night, yet 78 Squadron with whom they shared Linton lost three Halifaxes. The mid-upper gunner of one aircraft suddenly parachuted over the target for no evident reason. Pam Finch noted in her diary: 'The Group Captain thinks the man was temporarily insane.'

On 27 May they were bombing on ETA through ten-tenths cloud over Essen. Two nights later, they went among 719 aircraft to Wuppertal. It was a most effective attack, marked by *Oboe*. Intelligence estimated that 118,000 people had been made homeless. Yet some of 76's crews were unhappy about the trip, because they were told by their own Intelligence Officer, 'The Colonel', at briefing that part of their purpose was to catch thousands of refugees who were believed to have poured into Wuppertal after the Dambusting operation a fortnight earlier temporarily flooded areas of the Ruhr. Somehow, bombing refugees didn't seem quite what they thought they were there for. But they all went and came home safely except one aircraft which crashed on force-landing at Watton.

There was a brief respite in June, when they moved from the pre-war comforts of Linton to the wartime austerity and Nissen-hutted mud lakes of Holme-on-Spalding Moor. Their bitterness about the transfer was heightened by the knowledge that it was caused by a political decision to give the most comfortable pre-war North Yorkshire bases to the newly formed Canadian 6 Group. At Holme, the winter cold sometimes induced NCOs to sleep on sofas in the mess rather than in their quarters, and men hoarded coal under their beds in the fierce contest for warmth. It was from Holme that they fought the last action of the Ruhr battle, flying to Krefeld and Gelsenkirchen, Cologne and Aachen, although this last operation became another fiasco for 76 when a pilot crashed on take-off, his Halifax blocking the runway and compelling the eleven aircraft behind him to return wearily to their dispersals.

76 was an exceptionally international squadron even by the standards of Bomber Command. Its little group of Norwegian aircrew added a distinctive character and an underpinning of fierce determination. They were drawn from the steady trickle of escapees from occupied Norway. They had come to England to fight, and unlike, for instance, some of the Free French, they were single mindedly dedicated to doing so. 'The Norwegians never cared about the economic importance of a target,' said one of 76's COs in 1943,[2] 'they just wanted to know how many Germans per acre . . .' They lived in their own private

world not because they were unfriendly, but because their experience set them a dimension apart from their young English colleagues. The Norwegians were more serious, less playful in the mess. On evasion exercises on the moors, they were always back first, while the others idly allowed themselves to be captured. They flew with Norwegian flags pinned in the cockpits. They clustered together in their strange forage caps, sharing avidly the occasional letter from home. They seldom turned back early from an operation, whatever technical trouble their aircraft developed. Hulthin, one of the Norwegians who was later killed when his aircraft collided with a night-fighter en route to Kassel on his twenty-sixth trip, was notorious for his calm readiness to circle a target until he was certain of his aiming-point.

'Target ahead, skipper,' said his navigator, as they approached Hamburg one night.

'I see it, navigator.'

'Rear gunner here, skip. What's it look like?'

'Remember the last time?'

'Yes, skip.'

'Well, it's ten times worse.'

Hulthin and two other Norwegians, Lindaas and Goertz, were known to the squadron as 'Pip', 'Squeak' and 'Wilfred' after the cartoon characters. 'Squeak' – Lindaas – was a charming, fair-haired, blue-eyed 21-year-old. All the Norwegians were well-off by RAF standards because they received flying pay of eight shillings per hour operational in addition to their £28 a month salary. Lindaas told his crew when they joined him that since they were all in it together, he would divide his flying pay between them. They became the richest crew on the squadron.

At twenty-four, Fred Beadle the rear gunner was the oldest man in Lindaas's aircraft. One night they were on their way home from Frankfurt when the cloud thickened dramatically. The aircraft suddenly started to ice up, and within minutes the pilot lost control. Weighed down by their great frozen burden, they fell through the sky. The intercom had iced up, and Beadle knew nothing until he realized that they were plunging steeply for the ground. He pulled himself out of his turret and slid forward to the cockpit. Only Lindaas and the flight engineer were left – the rest of the crew had already baled out. The flight engineer tried to buckle a parachute on Lindaas. The Norwegian pushed it away. Beadle and the other man jumped. Only when they came home after two years in a prison camp did Beadle learn that Lindaas's brother had already been shot by the Gestapo. Lindaas considered that he himself was a dead man if he landed alive in Germany. He preferred to crash with the aircraft.

As the intensity of Bomber Command's raids on the cities of Germany grew, so did the hazards of parachuting over enemy territory.

Many men reached prison camp with terrible stories to tell. A gunner who landed near Kassel was held for five days in a pigsty without food or water by a civilian policeman. Another was attacked by a mob in the streets of Frankfurt, and only saved by a Luftwaffe patrol who pulled him into a basement and later smuggled him out in one of their tunics. Fred Beadle was lucky. He landed near Frankfurt in a snowstorm. Knowing that he had no hope of escape, he hid his parachute, walked into a nearby village, and sat on a doorstep in the early morning darkness, watching the flames of his wrecked aircraft in the distance, until a woman emerged from a door opposite. 'Morgen,' he said, straining his knowledge of German. 'Englander!' she shouted in horror, and ran inside, slamming the door. Eventually soldiers appeared and took him to the local civic office. Children had found his parachute. Villagers fingered his fleece-lined flying clothes and the cigarettes and chocolate emptied from his pocket. 'Churchill propaganda!' said a girl scornfully. Late in the afternoon a truck came to take him, none the worse for wear, to Dulag Luft for interrogation and on to prison camp.

In the opinion of much of 76 Squadron, John Maze should have been an early candidate for 'the chop'. Immensely tall, easy and languid, he proved a remarkable survivor. Night after night, he lifted his Halifax, the long-suffering T-Tommy, off the runway with a sudden wrench as if it was a fighter. Then he set his auto-pilot for the long haul across the North Sea, chatting on the intercom, singing 'I like coffee, I like tea' or some such little ditty, until they approached the German flak belt. Maze's greatest problem on operations was his height, crammed into the Halifax cockpit, until he managed to get hold of a high Lancaster seat and had it fitted in his aircraft. Then Hulthin borrowed T-Tommy while Maze was on leave, and wrecked it on take-off for Aachen. Maze flew the rest of his tour in acute discomfort, and his chief memory of bomber operations was constant exhaustion. But blessed with that gift of luck which was a pilot's most priceless possession, he lived.

He was the son of the distinguished French-born painter Paul Maze, and indeed his real name was Etienne – he only called himself John in the RAF. He had been educated at Stowe and Oxford, where he joined the Air Squadron. In November 1941 he was sent to America for flying training. Like so many pilots of the period, he found when he came home that nothing he had been taught prepared him for the reality of operations. In Georgia they were drilled like Marine Corps recruits, and three of every five trainees were rejected. But they flew only in clear skies, and night-flying practice consisted of cruising between beacons. Maze reached Linton and began operations in April 1943.

Rather than weaving constantly on the way to the target, he used his auto-pilot, because he concentrated on flying accurately in the midst of the stream, hoping thus to avoid exposing his aircraft. He was always experimenting in the air: opening and closing the radiator flaps, increasing speed and losing height coming home. Despite the discomfort, he valued his six feet six inches flying the Halifax, notoriously the most heavy-handed of all the wartime heavy bombers. In an emergency, he had the reach to throw the aircraft fiercely across the sky. The only crisis that Maze encountered in his first twenty trips came when they were coned on the way home from Wuppertal, and his drastic evasive action tore them free.

On their twenty-first trip, a normally cushy run to Milan for which the 'erks' threatened to paint an ice-cream cone on the nose of T-Tommy instead of the usual bomb in the morning, they were crossing the French coast at 20,000 feet when they saw a sudden streak of tracer, and an aircraft fell in flames in front of them.

'Good God! That was a fighter in front,' shouted the astonished Maze. 'Keep a sharp look-out, chaps. Somebody's bought it just ahead. Keep looking down, Rammy' – this to the rear gunner. 'They can see us perfectly in this light.'

Maze was acutely sensitive to the difficulty of seeing another aircraft in darkness. One night when the entire crew were keeping a sharp look-out, he was horrified to glance up and see another bomber glide across them only feet above the cockpit. The two Halifaxes had been quite oblivious of each other. But on this night he still declined to unlock T-Tommy's auto-pilot. The first that the crew knew of the fighter attack was a cannon shell bursting in the rear turret, putting the guns out of action. A second smashed into the controls in the tail, a third into the bomb bay. Maze snatched the controls and flung the Halifax into a dive amidst the appalling din in the fuselage. The tracer fell away to starboard, then they were corkscrewing.

'Can you see him, Rammy?' asked Maze urgently.

'Get-weaving, skipper, he's coming in from the port,' shouted the rear gunner.

They straightened out at last and Maze ordered the bomb-aimer to jettison their load. 'Give me a course for home, Dave,' he said to the navigator. 'Have a look aft, will you, Willie. The elevator is almost impossible to control.' They had lost the trimming tab control, and the rear gunner was lying slightly wounded on the rest bed in the darkness of the fuselage. They were back over the sea now, heading towards England. The flight engineer knotted the dinghy rope round the control column, then he and the bomb-aimer joined Maze's straining efforts to force back the stick and maintain height. The Halifax lurched and bucked across the sky, losing height with every lunge. The rear gunner, slightly cut in the leg, began to apologize down the intercom for failing to spot the fighter more quickly.

'Shut up, Rammy!' snapped the preoccupied Maze. 'I've no time to listen to you now.'

'Is that an aerodrome coming up, Dave?' he asked the navigator, as he hung with fierce concentration to the yoke.

'It could be Ford, skipper.'

Maze began to talk urgently into the R/T: 'Hallo, Ford, hallo, Ford, I am in difficulty, may I have permission to land?'

There was an eternity of silence, then: 'Hallo, hallo. You may land.'

There was no chance of circling to make an approach. Maze merely plunged for the runway. After a final heave on the stick with half the crew straining at the dinghy rope, they lurched on to the tarmac, bounced and steadied. The Halifax's cargo of frightened, exhausted young men stumbled out on to the tarmac in the darkness to face an angry Control Officer who berated them for landing without permission. They had touched down not at Ford, but at nearby Thorney Island, miraculously avoiding three training aircraft which were simultaneously practising circuits and bumps.

Maze's crew had one more bad night. They lost an engine over Munich, and for several minutes feared vividly that they could not remain airborne, while Maze put them into a steep dive to extinguish the flames. Sometimes this tactic succeeded, sometimes it bellowed the flames into melting off the wing. Somebody muttered urgently over the intercom: 'Let's bale out and walk home over the Alps.' But Maze said: 'For goodness sake – it's a hell of a lot worse down there than it is up here!' No one baled out. After eleven hours in the air, they came home. John Maze, just 21, became one of the few 76 Squadron pilots to complete a tour in 1943. He was posted to become ADC to Sir Arthur Harris.

At the end of the Battle of the Ruhr, Bomber Command had flown 18,506 sorties, and lost 872 aircraft missing over Germany – 4.7 per cent – plus a further 16 per cent damaged. On some nights, 30 per cent of all aircraft dispatched came back damaged or failed to return at all. They had poured 58,000 tons of bombs on to Germany, more than the Luftwaffe dropped on Britain throughout 1940 and 1941, more than Bomber Command dropped on Germany in the whole of 1942. The photographs of cities that they had attacked revealed thousands of acres of industrial and residential devastation. High Wycombe computed that up to the end of 1942, 400 acres of urban Germany had been razed by bombing. In 1943, this figure would rise to 26,000 acres. Crews were coming faster and faster from the training machine, as were aircraft from the production line. Harris's daily availability of bombers rose from 593 in February to 787 in August 1943. Yet which was being punished more severely, Germany or Bomber Command? Who was winning the extraordinary contest between bombs and concrete? The rate of attrition on both sides was becoming awesome, yet the struggle seemed as far as ever from any decisive conclusion.

2. *Hamburg*

Holme-on-Spalding Moor was a bleak, unfriendly sort of place, where it was widely felt by the aircrew that the village had turned its back on the war. The locals resented the RAF's domination of their bowling alley. Wives and girlfriends who lodged nearby were treated with ill-concealed disdain, scarlet women from the cities. Every six weeks or so, for those aircrew who survived there were seven days' leave. Some men went home, others hastened with their crews to the blacked-out joys of London. They were crestfallen to discover how little they knew about how to be sinful. Most ended their evenings at the RAF Club or the YMCA. On evenings off from Holme, there were cheap taxis to York and the pleasures of Betty's Bar and The Half Moon. In the officers' mess, more often than not they would merely drink a few pints and go quietly to bed after a game of darts. Only a few relentless spirits went to the village every night and drank themselves to oblivion like a gunner, 'The Pommified Aussie', who had to be retrieved with monotonous regularity from the police station. Most men waited until there was some excuse for a binge, and then threw themselves into the traditional excitements of wartime bomber stations: great choruses of 'Do You Know the Muffin Man?', as one by one they tiptoed across the mess floor with a pint of beer on their heads; frenzied games of 'Flarepath', diving across the floor between two lines of human beacons clutching flaming newspapers. But, often in 1943, they were too tired for games.

In the morning they hung about the Flight Office playing with the station's stray mongrel, 'Flak', or perhaps teasing somebody about 'Calamity Kate', the decorative WAAF clerk who was widely believed to be a passport to 'the chop' for any man who took her out.

> Then despite a very gloomy picture painted by the Met Office, we learned that the raid was 'on'. Our system for finding this news in advance was for all the pilots to put a penny in a box, the contents of which were given to the Wing Co's confidential clerk. In return for this small consideration, we were given 'the gen' and could make our plans accordingly.
>
> The atmosphere in the Flight Office would be very tense until the news came through. Completely contrary to the popular impression given in books and films, there would be a relieved cheer, loud laughter and a babble of excited talk if we were not to operate that day. If we were to do so, the pilots would merely make some casual remark and quickly slip away to get themselves, their aircraft and crews ready. Later we would return to learn what the target would be – not without some secret dread in our hearts that it might again be Berlin or the Ruhr.[3]

On the evening of 24 July 1943, they were briefed to take part in the most effective attack of the war by Bomber Command, on Hamburg. They had been to the great north German port before. But this time, they were told, it would be different. First, 791 aircraft would be taking part in 'Operation Gomorrah'. Second, and much more important, this time it would be easy. They were to be equipped with a brilliant scientific device that would fog the radar screens of Germany – guns, night-fighters and all. It was codenamed *Window*, and consisted simply of bundles of narrow metal foil strips, to be pushed down a special chute by the wireless operator and flight engineer at intervals during the run over Germany. It is a measure of the crews' faith in the scientists that they were at once excited and delighted by the vision of chaos among the defences, convinced that they were being given a weapon that would turn the odds dramatically. 'Why haven't we had it before?' asked Bamber, one of the flight commanders. 'Er . . . good question,' said the man from 4 Group Operational Research.

Window had been devised and reported effective by the spring of 1942, but at a meeting to discuss its future, Lord Cherwell made one of his periodic baleful interventions. If it would work against German radar, he pointed out, obviously it would work against our own. What happened if the Germans launched a new blitz against Britain? Cherwell's remarks threw Fighter and Anti-Aircraft Commands and Herbert Morrison's Ministry of Home Security into confusion. They successfully opposed the introduction of *Window* by Bomber Command, despite a belated effort by Tizard, from the wilderness, to have them overruled. But by the autumn of 1942, the Luftwaffe had become a negligible threat to Britain. The official historians remark tartly on the curious failure of Sir Arthur Harris to 'exert himself to secure the introduction of a measure which was expected so greatly to favour the offence at the expense of the defence'.[4] Once again, Harris had been slow to respond to technological possibilities. Only in the summer of 1943, when the losses of his force to radar-directed night-fighters had become intolerable, did he move at last with real urgency to press for the introduction of *Window*.[5] The Prime Minister personally overruled Morrison and Fighter Command's objections. 'Let us open the window!' he declared majestically. On the night of 24 July, Bomber Command did so with remarkable results.

76 Squadron was now a three-flight unit with an establishment of thirty aircraft. On the night of the 24th, twenty-four crews were briefed for Hamburg. Despite the clear night, three returned early. The remaining twenty-one approached the target dazzled by the vision before them. Searchlights wandered lost across the sky like drunken men. The city's fifty-six heavy and thirty-six light flak batteries were firing desperate blind box barrages, helpless in their inability to take

radar predictions on the aircraft above. The night-fighters had failed utterly to locate the bomber stream.

It was a brief moment of triumph for the bomber in its ceaseless duel against the fighter, and the crews savoured it, as they had the great thrust against Cologne more than a year before. The attack on Hamburg was the most perfectly orchestrated since the war began. Two minutes before zero hour at 1 am, twenty Pathfinder aircraft dropped yellow Target Indicators blind on H2S, under ideal conditions since Hamburg's coastline gave the city an exceptionally sharp radar image. They were followed by eight Pathfinders carrying red TIs, which were aimed visually. A further fifty-three Pathfinders backed up visually with green TIs. The Main Force, bombing from Zero + 2 minutes to Zero + 48, were ordered to overshoot the markers by two seconds, in an effort to reduce the 'creepback', a pronounced feature of recent attacks.

The raid was an overwhelming success. 306 of the 728 aircraft which claimed to have attacked dropped their bombs within three miles of the aiming-point. Vast areas of Hamburg were devastated for the loss of only twelve bombers. The next day, north Germany awoke to find a bewildering array of metal-foil strips littered like errant Christmas decorations over hedges and houses and farmland, being chewed by cows and draped whimsically over telegraph wires. But the Luftwaffe scientists were not puzzled. They had understood the principles of *Duppel*, or *Window*, for as long as Bomber Command, but had flinched from employing it for the same reasons. They knew no antidote.

One of the twelve aircraft lost on the night of the 24th came from 76 Squadron, and another, piloted by a rather wild young man named Mick Shannon, crashed on landing back at Holme. Shannon was having a terrifying tour. The next night, when they went to Essen, his aircraft was hit by flak, shearing off a propeller which spun smashing into the fuselage. In the mid-upper turret was Waterman, a professional poacher in civilian life, and one of the finest shots on the squadron. He normally flew with 'A' flight commander, Bamber, but was filling in for a sick man. Now, Waterman baled out over Germany before Shannon decided that he could save the aircraft, and staggered home to bellyland at Holme. Such incidents, in which part of a crew baled out in the immediate crisis following an aircraft being hit, were not uncommon. If a man did not jump within seconds, he knew that he might never have the chance to jump at all. Ten days later, Shannon was hit yet again over Mannheim. But this time no one jumped. Neither he nor his crew ever came home.

In daylight on 25 and 26 July, Ira Eaker's 8th Air Force flew 235 sorties to Hamburg to stoke the fires lit by Harris. On the night of the 25th, Mosquitoes staged a nuisance raid on the city, further to exhaust the defenders and the air-raid services. Then, on the 27th, Bomber Command went back. This was an entirely new technique: absolute devastation by repeated attack, saturating the fire services. 787 aircraft were dispatched, by a different route from that taken on the 24th. 722 bombed Hamburg, and of these 325 were within three miles. Fires were still blazing from the earlier attacks. Now these were redoubled by the new wave of flame and smoke, crashing masonry, roaring conflagration.

But the Luftwaffe responded to *Window* with remarkable speed and flexibility, assisted by their scientists' instant understanding of the crisis. They knew that, overnight, the ground-controlled interception of individual bombers had been eclipsed. Only weeks before, they had created the first 'Wild Boar' squadrons, of single-engined fighters which were vectored into the bomber stream over the target by radio running-commentary, as infornmation seeped in from observer posts all over Germany about the bombers' direction and changes of course. Now, these 'freelances' were rapidly reinforced. The 'Wild Boars' became the basis of the Luftwaffe's immediate counter-attack, and formidably effective they proved, although costly in fighter accident losses. British 'spoof' raids by small forces of aircraft 'windowing' in a manner that suggested the Main Force, together with deceptive routing to the target, often held off the fighters until the bombers had attacked. But then, even amidst their own flak and searchlights, the fighters came in. A handful of Me109s piloted by experts proved capable of shooting down a succession of bombers each in a single night once they had locked into the stream. Until the very end of the war, the Luftwaffe maintained their counter-offensive with all the energy and brilliance that their supplies of fuel and trained pilots allowed. Some airmen argue that in defeating the German radar network with *Window*, Bombar Command showed the Germans the way to a much simpler and deadlier means of controlling fighter defence.

On the night of 29 July, 777 aircraft went to Hamburg again. Thirty of them were lost, including one from 76 Squadron. The casualties were creeping up as the Luftwaffe recovered from *Window*. On the night of 2 August, the fourth and last of Bomber Command's great attacks of the battle, 740 aircraft were dispatched in appalling weather to Hamburg. A further thirty were lost.

Yet Harris had already gained his triumph in the Battle of Hamburg and this last operation was all but redundant. Twenty-two square kilometres of the dcity had been engulfed in the fantastic firestorm that began on the night of the 27th, the second raid. This was the harbinger of Dresden, Darmstadt and other, lesser infernoes of 1944 and 1945. As the fires reached incredible temperatures – 1,000 degrees centigrade and more – they sucked in air and bellowed themselves into hurricanes of flame and smoke that tore through the heart of Hamburg amidst winds of 150 mph. Private hoards of coal and coke in the cellars fuelled the fires from every house. Thousands suffocated, then their bodies were incinerated in the cellars in which they had perished. Air-raid shelters became vast crematoria. 42,000 Germans were estimated to have died. A million refugees fled the city. In one week, Bomber Command had killed more people than the Luftwaffe had achieved in the eight months of the blitz in England in 1940–41. In Hamburg, 40,385 houses, 275,000 flats, 580 factories, 2,632 shops, 277 schools, 24 hospitals, 58 churches, 83 banks, 12 bridges, 76 public buildings and a zoo had been obliterated. Goebbels said that it was 'a catastrophe, the extent of which simply staggers the imagination'. For the first time in the war, Bomber Command had profoundly shaken the Nazi leadership. Since 24 July, Harris's aircraft had flown 3,095 sorties, and poured 9,000 tons of explosives and incendiaries on to Hamburg for the loss of 86 aircraft.

If other cities were to be pounded as relentlessly as this, the consequences for Germany must have been appalling. No industry, no urban area could stand repeated punishment on this scale. By dawn on 3 August 1943, Hamburg seemed an empty city, 'sunk in a great silence of death'. But Bomber Command was not to repeat the severity of its attack on Hamburg against the other major cities of Germany until 1945. Harris's staff never appeared to grasp the full significance of their success in July 1943, that it was repetition which made possible the climactic destruction. High Wycombe was always nervous about sending aircraft again and again to a target in a manner which allowed the Luftwaffe to anticipate them. Hamburg was in north Germany, and thus required a relatively short penetration inside night-fighter range. But those cities which lay deep in enemy territory – most notably Berlin – could always put up formidable resistance if the Germans correctly predicted the target or were aided by clear skies. To Harris's staff, it seemed more profitable to strike a target at intervals of some weeks rather than to return immediately. Barnes Wallis was deeply frustrated that Bomber Command never sent a high-level bombing force to hit the Mohne dam while repairs were being carried out in the weeks after the attack of May 1943. He argued that extreme precision would have been unnecessary – even a few hits by conventional HE bombs would have prevented the Germans from making the rapid repairs which they in fact completed, and thus would have helped to justify the great sacrifice by 617 Squadron.[6] Whether or not this is true, High Wycombe never gave enough attention to the importance of reinforcing the successes of Bomber Command.

From August until the Battle of Berlin in late November, Harris's aircraft embarked upon the series of deepening penetrations that came to be known as 'The Road to Berlin', although many of the targets – Mannheim, Nuremberg, Munich – lay far from the German capital. At the end of August, they went to Berlin itself: from the first day of the bomber offensive to the last, the most terrifying target of all to the crews.

This was our first raid on Berlin [a 76 Squadron flight engineer named Ferris Newton wrote in his diary]. As we had all heard such stories about the place, we were not at all happy about going. Everyone sat around the kite waiting for start-up time, and nobody hardly spoke a word.

We were first wave in. Berlin's 35-mile area was dotted with light, so that it was hard to distinguish the burst of anti-aircraft shells below from the coloured markers dropped by the Pathfinders. First thing we have to do is fly through a wall of searchlights – hundreds of them in cones and clusters. Behind that all is an even fiercer light. It's glowing red and green and blue, and over that there are myriads of flares hanging in the sky. There is flak coming up at us now. All we see is a quick red glow from the ground – then up it comes on a level – a blinding flash.

There is one comfort, and it's been a comfort to me all the time we have been going over, and that is that it is quite soundless. The roar of your engines drowns everything else. It's like running straight into the most gigantic display of soundless fireworks in the world. The searchlights are coming nearer now all the time. There's one cone split and then it comes together again. They seem to splay out, then stop, then come together again, and as they do there's a Lancaster right in the centre. We start weaving. George puts the nose down and we are pelting away at a furious rate. As we are coming out of the searchlight belt, more flak is coming up from the inner defences.

'Hello, skipper.'

'Hello, navigator.'

'Half a minute to go.'

'OK. Thanks for reminding me.'

'Keep weaving, George, there's quite a lot of light stuff coming up as well – falling off a bit low.'

'Hello, engineer, will you put the revs up?'

'Engineer to pilot. Revs up, skipper.'

'OK. Keep weaving, George. A lot of searchlights and fighter flares left.'

'Hello, bomb-aimer. OK when you are. Bomb doors open.'

'OK, George – right – steady – a little bit longer yet . . . – right a little bit – right – steady – bombs still going . . . OK, bombs gone.'

'Keep weaving, there's some flak coming up. I can actually see ground detail, skipper . . . Oh, it's a wizard sight!'

'OK, Andy, don't get excited – keep your eyes open.'

'Engineer to pilot. Jerry fighter just passed over the top of us port to starboard.'

'OK, engineer, keep your eyes open, gunners.'

'Hello, skipper, will you turn on to Zero 81.'

'Zero 81, right navigator.'

We are out of it and now we are through. I turn and get a glimpse of that furious glowing carpet of light and explosions, that's all I can see of Berlin.

As we approached England we got a diversion message to Catfoss, of all places. Flying time for the trip, 8 hours 50 minutes. This raid had been the heaviest on Berlin up to date, at a cost of 58 aircraft out of 700 (this does not include two aircraft which collided on the circuit at Catfoss: damn hard luck, that, all the way to Berlin and back, then get it on your own circuit . . .

On the night of 18 August, 597 aircraft were sent to Peenemunde on the Baltic, the German V-weapon research establishment. The crews were sobered to be told at briefing that this was a visual 'Radio-location laboratory and aircraft testing site', and that if they failed to destroy it, they would be sent back again and again until they did so. They bombed after a timed run from an offshore island to the target, and the concentration was exceptional. Widespread damage was done to the workshops and scientists' living quarters. The night-fighters, diverted by a Mosquito 'spoof' raid on Berlin, were slow to grasp the British intentions, but caught up with the last stages of the attack on Peenemunde. Forty aircraft failed to return. For once, however, 76 Squadron was lucky. Its twenty Halifaxes went in with an early wave, and all returned unscathed except a navigator wounded by a shrapnel fragment. Afterwards, there was some doubt how seriously the raid had delayed the V-weapon programme, but fortunately for the crews, High Wycombe was satisfied. It was decreed there need be no return visit.

Some nights they were fortunate, and were sent to Italy, which was reckoned to be a pushover unless one had a technical failure or very bad luck, and the crews had their awe-struck view of the Alps in darkness. One night over Turin, Group-Captain John Searby presided for the first time as 'Master Bomber', a technique first employed by Guy Gibson on the Dams raid, guiding the crews by radio-telephone as they approached the target, pointing out the best markers and attempting to concentrate the attack. The Master Bomber never commanded a raid in the fullest sense of being in charge of the huge force of aircraft – Leonard Cheshire was among those who believed that there should have been an airborne commander of every operation, empowered for instance to send everybody home if the weather was hopeless. But the Master Bomber's calm voice across the ether, directing aircraft as he circled above them, could be enormously helpful in keeping an attack on course or preventing a fiasco when markers fell in the wrong place.

76 Squadron was still losing a steady one or two aircraft a night against the German targets, and Hanover now inspired almost as deep a fear as Berlin. The behaviour of bereaved families often seemed

strange to the men on the stations. Relatives would conduct a long and savage correspondence with a squadron CO about the absence of, say, a fountain-pen from their son's personal effects, returned to them by the RAF Central Depository at Colnebrook. Sometimes a family became deeply embittered by their son's loss, and sought to attribute blame.

Death drifted through the huts and hangars in the most erratic fashion. An aircraft code letter, P-Peter or R-Robert, would suddenly become deadly for a succession of crews who owned it. A certain bunk would take on the deadly properties of the Black Spot. Alf Kirkham and his crew found that throughout their tour at Holme, the next-door hut was doomed. Every week, new faces arrived to occupy it, and at once vanished.

Kirkham was one of 76 Squadron's stars, a sergeant pilot who completed a distinguished tour on Halifaxes, was commissioned and twice decorated before doing a further tour on Mosquitoes. He was unhappy about 76's enthusiasm for flying operations with the auto-pilot locked in, which he believed was a formula for disaster. Always a 'press-on type', he had gone round three times at Peenemunde as converging aircraft forced him to bank at the critical moment of each bomb-run. On the ground, he cut a swathe through WAAFs, the girls of York and occasional senior officers' daughters. His crew was one of the few to shoot down a night-fighter, apparently a Luftwaffe novice who was so intent on stalking another aircraft that he did not notice Kirkham's Halifax beside him until the gunners blew him apart, a sitting duck. But at the end of August, over München-Gladbach, as they turned out of the target a fighter fell on them. It was Kirkham's turn to struggle for his life.

> We were hit by cannon shells and tracer immediately. The navigator was badly wounded, a bullet hit me in the right leg, the starboard inner engine was knocked out, the RT packed up completely and we caught fire. I feathered the damaged engine, but another attack knocked out a lot of my instruments and also my call lights so that I had no communication with the gunners. I took violent evasive action, so much so that if anyone had baled out I wouldn't have blamed them, as they could have thought that we were out of control. The control column worked well but I had little rudder control, and my right leg did not seem to be much help. By juggling the throttles and using a lot of bank I was able to corkscrew, but maintaining height was out of the question. I remember seeing the engineer being violently sick and using the fire-extinguisher at the same time . . .
>
> The steep dive blew out the flames, but I was getting pretty desperate. Eventually we did a stall turn with a very nearly 90-degree bank, and fell out of the sky. We lost the fighter. We set a rough course for home and checked our damage. I could hold height, but

the aircraft was very difficult to fly. The navigator could not possibly bale out, so I decided to crash-land and offer the crew the chance to bale out over England. We encountered flak and searchlights a lot of the time, and at 8,000 feet they were quite accurate.

We eventually hit the coast at Bradwell Bay in Essex, and I saw two searchlights indicating an aerodrome. I found I had fair control at 105 mph, but I couldn't hold the aircraft at speeds below this. There were no flaps available, and the undercarriage didn't work, and it appeared that I would have to fly the plane onto the ground at a very high speed . . . By this time all the crew had vanished to their crash-landing positions behind the main spar, and it seemed very lonely.

As we hit the deck, I throttled back and switched off. We ran along for a long time on our belly, but I was pleasantly surprised to see that there was no sign of fire . . .[7]

Yet although many crews suffered nights as terrifying as that of Alf Kirkham, there were also a surprising number who went through a tour without any incidents at all. Ferris Newton, the flight engineer who described his first trip to Berlin, was in a crew captained by twenty-year-old Sergeant George Dunn. They endured a series of frightening experiences at OTU, where they were forced to bale out of a doomed Wellington over Scotland, and four crews out of sixteen in their course were killed. But on 76 Squadron their gunners never fired a shot in anger; they were only once hit by a small piece of shrapnel; and only once suffered a mechanical defect, a hydraulic leak on the way home from Peenemunde. This in no way made flying operations less frightening or less difficult, but is an odd aside on the flukes of war.

They were an exceptionally close-knit crew both in the air and on the ground. Ferris Newton himself owned a little pub near Leeds named The Old Ball, run by his wife Catherine, and at every spare moment they piled into his battered Morris 8, with bodies protruding from its sunshine roof, and dashed away to 'The Ancient Knacker' on petrol bought with stockpiled cigarettes. Reg McCadden, the commissioned navigator, was a Northern Irishman who had been dive-bombed on an auxiliary cruiser in August 1940, and decided that henceforth if there was going to be any bombing done around him, he would be doing it. Andy Maitland, their young bomb-aimer, was passionately enthusiastic about bomber operations. He became a compulsive 'hours chaser', one of the few who survived, completing more than ninety trips and ending the war with a permanent commission in Pathfinders.

'I can see the streets! I can see the streets!' he shouted in excitement as he lay over his bombsight on their first trip over Germany.

'F--k the streets, just bomb and let's get out of here,' said a furious and much more typical voice down the intercom.

In October 1943, just before the Halifaxes entered a period of even more appalling losses in the Battle of Berlin, reaching a climax in January and February 1944 when they were losing 11 per cent of aircraft dispatched to Germany, Ferris Newton wrote in his diary:

> The target was Kassel with a spoof attack on Hanover . . . This being our last trip, we got a really marvellous send-off by everyone. A whole crowd of people on the officers' mess site waving like mad . . . At the ACP caravan at the end of the runway, S/Ldr Bennett and others all giving us the thumbs-up sign . . .
>
> Needless to say we were first back, for the only time. As we touched down we all gave a loud shout through the intercom, and as George had it on 'Transmit', all and sundry heard what we said, not that anybody cared.
>
> After debriefing I gave Catherine a ring, just to tell her I was back and finished. That was about three o'clock in the morning . . . Back at Holme we were having our second breakfast in the officers' mess kitchen, so we could be with the rest of the crew. There were only three of us who were not commissioned by this time . . .

Completing a tour on Halifaxes in 1943 was a matter for unusual celebration. That early morning of 4 October, as Ferris Newton and his crew rejoiced in their personal victory over the percentages, a WAAF in the operations room at Holme was deleting four missing 76 Squadron aircraft from the list of nineteen crews who had taken off a few hours before – twenty-eight more of Harris's men gone. In Kassel, they were counting the bodies of 5,200 people.

3. Courage

Throughout the war, morale on British bomber stations held up astonishingly well, although there were isolated collapses on certain squadrons at certain periods – for example, during the heavy losses of the Battle of Berlin. Morale never became a major problem, as it did on some 8th Air Force stations in the face of the terrible losses of 1943 and early 1944. An RAF doctor seconded to study fliers' spirit at one American station reported in dismay: 'Aircrew are heard openly saying that they don't intend to fly to Berlin again or do any more difficult sorties. This is not considered a disgrace or dishonourable.' Partly the Americans found the appalling business of watching each other die on daylight sorties more harrowing than the anonymity of night operations. Partly also, they were far from their homes, and many did not feel the personal commitment to the war shared by many Englishmen.

But most of the crews of Bomber Command fought an unending battle with fear for most of their tours, and some of them lost it. Even today, the Judge-Advocate General of the Forces is implacably unhelpful on inquiries relating to the problems of disciplinary courts-martial and 'LMF' – 'Lacking Moral Fibre' – cases among wartime aircrew. I believe that around one man in ten was lost to operational aircrew at some point between OTU and completing his tour for morale or medical causes, merely because among a hundred aircrew whom I have interviewed myself, almost all lost one member of the crew with which they served at some time, for some reason. Few of these cases would be classified by any but the most bigoted as simple 'cowardice', for by now the Moran principle that courage is not an absolute human characteristic, but expendable capital every man possesses in varying quantity, has been widely recognized. But in 1943 most cases of men relieved of operational duty for medical or moral reasons were treated by the RAF with considerable harshness. There was great fear at the top of the service that if an honourable path existed to escape operations, many men would take it. 'LMF could go through a squadron like wildfire if it was unchecked,' says one of the most distinguished post-war leaders of the RAF, who in 1943 was commanding a bomber station. 'I made certain that every case before me was punished by court-martial, and where applicable by an exemplary prison sentence, whatever the psychiatrists were saying.'[18]

Command was enraged when stories emerged at courts-martial of doctors in Glasgow or Manchester who for five pounds would brief a man on the symptoms necessary to get him taken off operations: insomnia, waking screaming in his quarters, bed-wetting, headaches, nightmares. Station medical officers became notoriously unsympathetic to aircrew with any but the most obvious symptoms of illness. The Air Staff faced a constant dilemma about the management and treatment of aircrew, who were intensively trained to fly, yet for little else. Regular officers were exasperated by the appearance and off-duty behaviour of many temporary officers and NCOs. In their turn, the relentless pursuit of ambition by some career airmen even in the midst of war did not escape the scornful notice of aircrew, especially when they observed some regulars carefully tucked into Flying Training Command or staff jobs rather than flying with operational squadrons.

The Air Ministry considered that morale and disciplinary problems were closely linked. In a 1943 report which attacked the practice of holding All Ranks dances at bomber stations, which noted that Harris's men had the highest rate of venereal disease in the RAF and No. 6 Group's Canadians a rate five times higher than anyone else's, the Inspector-General of the RAF noted with displeasure:

Aircrew were becoming more and more divorced from their legitimate leaders, and their officers are forgetting, if they ever learnt them, their responsibilities to their men. Aircrew personnel must be disabused of the idea that their sole responsibility is to fly . . . their leisure hours must be more freely devoted to training and hard work . . .

The Air Ministry never lost its conviction that gentlemen made the best aircrew, and a remarkable staff memorandum of late 1942 expressed concern about the growing proportion of Colonials in Bomber Command and suggested: 'There are indications in a number of directions that we are not getting a reasonable percentage of the young men of the middle and upper classes, who are the backbone of this country, when they leave the public schools.'

When Ferris Newton was interviewed for a commission, the group captain had already noted without enthusiasm that he owned a pub, and inquired whether this catered to the coach trade. Yet the Commonwealth fliers, especially, believed that it was their very intimacy with their crews, their indifference to rank, that often made them such strong teams in the air. An Australian from 50 Squadron cited the example of a distinguished young English ex-public school pilot who was killed in 1943. This boy, he said, was a classic example of an officer who never achieved complete cohesion with his crew, who won obedience only by the rings on his sleeves and not by force of personality: 'He simply wouldn't have known how to go out screwing with his gunners in Lincoln on a Saturday night.' In his memoirs Harris argues that the English made the best aircrew, because they had the strongest sense of discipline. This was a matter of opinion.

To the men on the stations, the RAF's attitude to their problems often seemed savagely unsympathetic. One day on a cross-country exercise before they began operations, the bomb-aimer of Lindaas's crew at 76 Squadron fell through the forward hatch of the aircraft, which had somehow come loose. The rest of the crew thought at first that he had fallen out completely. Only after several moments did they realize that he was clinging desperately beneath the aircraft. Only after several more moments of struggle did they get the dinghy rope around him, and haul him back into the aircraft. When he returned to the ground, he said flatly that he would never fly again. He was pronounced LMF, and vanished from the station. Normally in such cases, an NCO was stripped of his stripes, which had been awarded in recognition of his aircrew status, and posted to ground duties. Only in incontrovertible cases of 'cowardice in the face of the enemy', as at one 5 Group station where one night three members of a crew left their aircraft as it taxied to take-off, was the matter referred to court-martial. A further cause of resentment against Permanent Commissioned Officers was that if they wished to escape operations, they could almost invariably arrange a quiet transfer to non-operational duties, because the service was reluctant to instigate the court-martial that was necessary to strip them of rank.

It was very rare for a case to be open and shut. The navigator of a Whitley in 1941 ran amok and had to be laid out with the pilot's torch over Germany. The man disappeared overnight from the squadron – normal procedure throughout the war, to avoid the risk that he might contaminate others. But the pilot recounting this experience[9] added: 'Don't draw the obvious conclusion. The next time I saw the man's name, he was navigating for one of the Dambusting crews.' Many men had temporary moral collapses in the midst of operational tours. The most fortunate, who were sensitively treated, were sent for a spell at the RAF convalescent home at Matlock in Derbyshire. A post-war medical report argues that many such men sincerely wanted to be rehabilitated and return to operations to save their own self-respect, while genuine LMF cases proved on close study to be those who should never have survived the aircrew selection process.

But the decisive factor in the morale of bomber aircrew, like that of all fighting men, was leadership. At first, it is difficult to understand what impact a leader can have, when in battle his men are flying with only their own crews over Germany, far out of sight and command. Yet a post-war 8 Group medical report stated emphatically: 'The morale of a squadron was almost always a direct proportion to the quality of leadership shown by the squadron commanders, and the fluctuations in this respect were most remarkable.' A good CO's crews pressed home attacks with more determination; suffered lower losses; perhaps above all, had a negligible 'Early Return' rate. Guy Gibson, the leader of the Dambusters, was one kind of legendary Bomber Command CO. Not a cerebral man, he represented the apogee of the pre-war English public schoolboy, the perpetual team captain, of unshakeable courage and dedication to duty, impatient of those who could not meet his standards. 'He was the kind of boy who would have been head prefect in any school,' said Sir Ralph Cochrane, his commander in 5 Group.[10]

For the first four months of 1943, 76 Squadron was commanded by Leonard Cheshire, another of the great British bomber pilots of the war, one of a quite different mould from Gibson, but even more remarkable. Cheshire, the son of a distinguished lawyer, also read law at Oxford, then joined the RAF shortly before the outbreak of war. In 1940 he began flying Whitleys over Germany. By 1943, with two brilliant tours already behind him, he was a 26-year-old wing-commander. There was a mystical air about him, as if he somehow inhabited another planet from those around him, yet without affectation or pretension. 'Chesh is crackers,' some people on the squadrons said freely in the days before this deceptively gentle, mild man became famous. They were all the more bewildered when he married and brought back from America in 1942 an actress fifteen years older than himself.

Yet Leonard Cheshire contributed perhaps more than any other single pilot to the legend of Bomber Command. He performed extraordinary feats of courage apparently on impulse, yet studied the techniques of bombing with intense perception and intelligence, later pioneering the first precision marking of the war as leader of 617 Squadron. At 76 Squadron there was a joke about Cheshire, that 'the moment he walks into the bar, you can see him starting to work out how much explosive it would need to knock it down'. He was possibly not a natural flying genius in an aircraft like Micky Martin, but, by absolute dedication to his craft, he made himself a master. He flew almost every day. If he had been on leave and was due to operate that night, he would go up for two hours in the morning to restore his sense of absolute intimacy with his aircraft. He believed that to survive over Germany it was necessary to develop an auto-pilot within himself, which could fly the aircraft quite instinctively, leaving all his concentration free for the target and the enemy. As far back as 1941 he had written a paper on marking techniques. He was always an advocate of low-level bombing.

Cheshire himself wrote, 'I loved flying and was a good pilot, because I threw myself heart and soul into the job. I found the dangers of battle exciting and exhilarating, so that war came easily to me.'[11] Most of those he commanded knew themselves to be frailer flesh, and he dedicated himself to teaching them everything that he knew. He had never forgotten that Lofty, his own first pilot on Whitleys, taught him to know every detail of his aircraft, and he was determined to show others likewise. He lectured 76's crews on Economical Cruising Heights, Escape and Evasion techniques, and methods of improving night vision. They knew that he was devoted to their interests. On a trip to Nuremberg they were detailed to cross the French coast at 2,000 feet. He simply told Group that he would not send them at that height. It would be 200 feet or 20,000. He made his point.

A CO who flew the most dangerous trips himself contributed immensely to morale – some officers were derisively christened 'François' for their habit of picking the easy French targets when they flew. Cheshire did not have his own crew – only Jock Hill, his wireless operator. Instead, he flew as 'Second Dickey' with the new and nervous. Perhaps the chief reason that 'Chesh' inspired such loyalty and respect was that he took the trouble to know and recognize every single man at Linton. It was no mean feat, learning five hundred or more faces which changed every week. Yet the ground crews chorused: 'We are Cheshire cats!' because the CO spent so much of his day driving round the hangars and dispersals chatting to them and remembering exactly who had sciatica. It was the same with the aircrew. A young wireless operator, who had arrived at Linton the previous day, was climbing into the truck for the dispersals when he felt Cheshire's arm round his shoulder. 'Good luck, Wilson.' All the way to the aircraft, the W/Op pondered in bewildered delight: 'How the hell did the CO know my name?' They knew that when Cheshire flew, it was always the most difficult and dangerous operations. He would ask them to do nothing that he had not done himself. It was Cheshire who noticed that very few Halifax pilots were coming home on three engines. He took up an aircraft to discover why. He found that if a Halifax stalled after losing an engine it went into an uncontrollable spin. After a terrifying minute falling out of the sky, Cheshire was skilful and lucky enough to be able to recover the aircraft and land and report on the problem, which he was convinced was caused by a fault in the rudder design.

Handley Page, the manufacturers, then enraged him by refusing to interrupt production to make a modification. Only when a Polish test-pilot had been killed making further investigations into the problem which Cheshire had exposed was the change at last made. His imagination and courage became part of the folklore of Bomber Command. He left 76 Squadron in April 1943 and later took command of 617, the Dambusters squadron. By the end of the war, with his Victoria Cross, three Distinguished Service Orders, Distinguished Flying Cross and fantastic total of completed operations, he had become a legend.

Yet at 76 Squadron, from the spring of 1943 onwards, there were a substantial number of LMF cases, matched by an 'Early Return' rate from operations which by autumn sometimes exceeded 25 per cent of aircraft dispatched, and which caused Sir Arthur Harris to make an almost unprecedented personal visit to Holme in October to remind aircrew in the most forceful terms of their duty. 76 Squadron's morale had slumped. They felt neglected by the promotion and commissioning authorities, bruised by the transfer from the comforts of Linton to the gloominess of Holme, generally disgruntled with the Royal Air Force. It had been an impossible task to find a successor as CO to match Cheshire when he left in April, but it was unfortunate that he was followed by an officer who had difficulty making himself liked or respected. On his occasional operational sorties, the new CO's aircraft was jinxed by repeated bad luck. When he went to Stuttgart, he was obliged to return early with a glycol leak, having lost an engine. Three nights later he had to come home with an engine failure, and crashed at Linton. On a subsequent occasion, the CO committed the oldest crime in the pilot's book by flying a 'red on blue' – a 180 degree Reciprocal Course which took him northwards towards the Atlantic for thirty-two minutes before he realized his error and was obliged to return to Linton and abort the operation. A month later he ran out of petrol on the way home from Mont Beliard, and crashed in a potato field near Scunthorpe. Although the CO completed a number of operations without incident, two of them to Berlin, his troubles were a matter of some mirth to most of the squadron. He was a regular officer who had flown fifty-eight Blenheim operations out of Aden but had no previous European experience. But by 1943 no one was disposed to make any allowances. The crews were not sufficiently afraid of his anger or sufficiently interested in his good opinion to complete an operation if they felt disinclined to do so. His appeals to their courage and determination were treated as cant.

Yet whatever the quality of leadership and morale on a squadron, there was seldom any Hollywood-type enthusiasm for take-off on a bomber operation. One summer evening at Holme, 76 Squadron's crews were scattered at the dispersals, waiting miserably for start-up time before going to Berlin, the most hated target in Germany. The weather forecast was terrible, and the CO had been driving round the pans chatting to crews in an effort to raise spirits. Then, suddenly, a red Very light arched into the sky, signalling a 'wash out'. All over the airfield a great surge of cheering and whistle-blowing erupted.

A 76 Squadron pilot who later completed a second tour on Mosquitoes said that his colleagues on the light bombers 'simply could never understand how awful being on heavies was'. Some men found the strain intolerable. There were pilots who discovered that they were persistently suffering from 'mag drop', so easily achieved by running up an engine with the magnetoes switched off, oiling up the plugs. After two or three such incidents preventing take-off, the squadron CO usually intervened. One of the aircrew at 76 Squadron returned from every operation to face persecution from his wife and his mother, both of whom lived locally. 'Haven't you done enough?' the wife asked insistently often in the hearing of other aircrew. 'Can't you ever think of me?' In the end the man asked to be taken off operations, and was pronounced LMF.

A 76 Squadron wireless operator completed six operations with one of the Norwegian crews before reporting sick with ear trouble. He came up before the CO for a lecture on the need for highly-trained and experienced aircrew to continue flying, and was given a few days to consider his position. At a second interview, he told the CO he had thought over what had been said, but he wanted a rest. He felt that having volunteered 'in' for aircrew duties, he could also volunteer 'out'. He was reduced to the ranks, stripped of his flying brevet, posted to the depot at Chessington which dealt with such cases, and spent the rest of the war on menial ground duties. So did Alf Kirkham's rear gunner:

> After our first few trips together, which were very rough indeed [wrote Kirkham[12]], he simply did not like the odds. He decided that he wanted to live, and told me that nothing anyone could do to him would be worse than carrying on with operations. He was determined to see the war out, and as far as I know he was successful.

Marginal LMF suspects, along with disciplinary cases who had broken up the sergeants' mess, been discovered using high-octane fuel in their cars, or been involved in 'avoidable flying accidents', were sent to the 'Aircrew Refresher Centres' at Sheffield, Brighton or Bournemouth – in reality open-arrest detention barracks – where they spent a few weeks doing PT and attending lectures before being sent back to their stations, or in extreme cases posted to the depot, having been found 'unfit for further aircrew duties'. They were then offered a choice of transferring to the British army, or going to the coal mines. By 1943 the 'Refresher Centres' were handling thousands of aircrew. One 76 Squadron rear gunner went from Sheffield to the Parachute Regiment, and survived the war. His crew was killed over Kassel in October.

A pilot who joined 76 Squadron in the autumn of 1943 wrote:

> There was something lacking in the atmosphere . . . The camaraderie between the aircrew was there just the same, and between aircrew and groundcrew too. But the atmosphere of a squadron, like that of a ship, is hard to define. There are happy ships and happy squadrons. Our squadron was not happy, I thought . . .

This officer, F/Lt Denis Hornsey, was among very many men who spent their war in Bomber Command fighting fear and dread of inadequacy, without ever finally succumbing. At the end of the war Hornsey wrote an almost masochistically honest and hitherto unpublished account of his experiences and feelings.[13] At thirty-three, he was rather older than most aircrew and suffered from poor eyesight – he wore corrected goggles on operations – and almost chronic minor ailments throughout the war. He hated the bureaucracy and lack of privacy in service life, and was completely without confidence in his own ability as a pilot. After flying some Whitley operations in 1941, he was returned to OTU for further training, and his crew were split up. He then spent a relatively happy year as a staff pilot at a navigation school. He felt that he was an adequate flier of single or twin-engined aicraft and repeatedly requested a transfer to an operational station where he could fly one or the other. But by 1943 it was heavy-aircraft pilots who were needed. Everybody wanted to fly Mosquitoes. Hornsey was posted to Halifaxes. He knew that he was by now being accompanied from station to station by a file of unsatisfactory reports. He began his tour at 76 Squadron with two 'Early Returns', which made him more miserable than ever. Fear of being considered LMF haunted him almost as much as the fear of operations.

> Each operation, in my experience, was a worse strain than the last, and I felt sure that I was not far wrong in supposing that every pilot found it the same. It was true that it was possible to get used to the strain, but this did not alter the fact that the tension of each trip was

'banked' and carried forward in part to increase the tension of the next. If this were not so, the authorities would not have thought it necessary to restrict a tour to thirty trips.

There were men who were stronger than Hornsey, even men who enjoyed operational flying, but his conscious frailty was far closer to that of the average pilot than the nerveless brilliance of a Martin or Cheshire. The day after 76 Squadron lost four aircraft over Kassel and George Dunn's crew completed their tour, Hornsey recorded a conversation in the mess:

> 'What chance has a man got at this rate?' one pilot asked plaintively. 'Damn it all, I don't care how brave a chap is, he likes to think he has a *chance*. This is plain murder.'
>
> 'Better tell that to Harris,' someone else suggested.
>
> 'You needn't worry,' I said, 'you represent just fourteen bombloads to him. That's economics, you know.'
>
> As it transpired, operations were cancelled at the eleventh hour, when we were all dressed up in our kit ready to fly. It was too late then to go out, so I went to the camp cinema and saw 'Gun for Hire', a mediocre film portraying what I would have once thought was the dangerous life of a gangster. Now, by contrast, it seemed tame.
>
> That night, I found it difficult to settle down. There was much going on inside my mind that I wanted to express. I felt lonely and miserable, apprehensive and resigned, yet rebellious at the thought of being just a mere cog in a machine with no say in how that machine was used.
>
> But I was getting used to such attacks, which I had learned to expect at least once in the course of a day, as soon as I found myself at a loose end. As I could now recognize, without fear of it adding to my mental discomfort, they merely signified an onset of operational jitters. So composing myself as best I could, I went to sleep as quickly as I could.

Hornsey's tragedy was that he was acutely imaginative. He pressed the Air Ministry for the introduction of parachutes that could be worn at all times by bomber aircrew, so many of whom never had the chance to put them on after their aircraft was hit. He made his crew practise 'Abandon aircraft' and 'Ditching' drill intensively, and protested violently when he found the remaining armour plate being stripped from his Halifax on Group orders, to increase bombload.

The men who fared best were those who did not allow themselves to think at all. Many crews argued that emotional entanglements were madness, whether inside or outside marriage. They diverted a man from the absolute single-mindedness he needed to survive over Germany. When a pilot was seen brooding over a girl in the mess, he was widely regarded as a candidate for 'the chop list'. Hornsey, with a wife and baby daughter, was giving only part of his attention and very little of his heart to 76 Squadron.

Cheshire argued emphatically that what most men considered a premonition of their own death – of which there were innumerable instances in Bomber Command – was in reality defeatism. A man who believed that he was doomed would collapse or bale out when his aircraft was hit, whereas in Cheshire's view if you could survive the initial fearsome shock of finding your aircraft damaged, you had a chance. Yet by the autumn of 1943, many men on 76 Squadron were talking freely of their own fate. One much-liked officer came fresh from a long stint as an instructor to be a flight commander. 'You'd better tell me about this business, chaps,' he said modestly in the mess. 'I've been away on the prairies too long.' After a few operations, he concluded readily that he had no chance of survival. 'What are you doing for Christmas, Stuart?' somebody asked him in the mess one day. 'Oh, I shan't be alive for Christmas,' he said wistfully, and was gone within a week, leaving a wife and three children.

'The line between the living and the dead was very thin,' wrote Hornsey. 'If you live on the brink of death yourself, it is as if those who have gone have merely caught an earlier train to the same destination. And whatever that destination is, you will be sharing it soon, since you will almost certainly be catching the next one.'

On the night of 3 November 1943, Hornsey's was one of two 76 Squadron aircraft shot down on the way to Düsseldorf. He was on his eighteenth trip with Bomber Command. It is pleasant to record that he survived and made a successful escape across France to England, for which he was awarded a DFC perhaps better deserved and more hardly earned than the Air Ministry ever knew.

At the end of 1943, 76 Squadron's CO was 'screened' and awarded the usual DSO handed out to squadron commanders at the end of their stint, regardless of operations flown. In his place came Wing-Commander 'Hank' Iveson, a pilot of much experience who had flown Whitleys and Halifaxes in 1941. Iveson began by sacking the most persistent 'Early Runners', whose crews were broken up and returned to OTU for reassignment. When the new Mark III Halifax arrived at Holme with a fearsome reputation for accidents, Iveson and his three flight commanders flew its first operation themselves. Despite the restriction on squadron COs flying too many trips, Iveson did fifteen in the next six months. He lectured the crews intensively on every aspect of operations, emphasizing three-engine flying, which had caused so many accidents. Within a month this big, bluff, jovial man who confessed that he found bomber operations 'fascinating', had drastically reduced the Early Return rate, and done much to rebuild morale. But even Iveson could do nothing about the losses.

IX

The Other Side of the Hill

Germany 1940–44

'Reports . . . from towns recently attacked make one's hair grow grey.'

Josef Goebbels, March 1945[1]

1. The Destruction

Albert Speer became Minister of Armaments in Hitler's government just two weeks before Sir Arthur Harris took command at High Wycombe, in February 1942. Only thirty-six, he proved the outstanding excutive appointment of the Nazi regime. It was Harris's misfortune that throughout his campaign, he was confronted by an adversary who had a superb grasp of the German economy and a brilliant talent for improvising. Harris began his offensive just as German industry was awakening from the comfortable routines that had continued into the third year of the war. Thenceforth, the rising tenor of bombing was matched step for step by Speer's mobilization of Germany's resources. Only in the last six months of the war did precision attacks on the synthetic oil plants achieve the Allies' aim of severing the jugular vein of the Reich. By then, the victim was already moribund from injuries inflicted on the battlefield.

The Allies' major misunderstanding from start to finish was they saw Hitler's Germany as an armed camp, solely dedicated since at least 1939 to the business of making war. They thus assumed that any damage done by bombing represented a net loss to the German war effort. In reality, Hitler in the 1930s created a formidable military machine, but he had never rearmed in depth. Because he regarded war as an instrument of policy to be used and discarded as a matter of short-term expediency, he sought to employ the *minimum* possible economic resources to enable the Wehrmacht and the Luftwaffe to achieve a given objective, whether this was the destruction of Poland or the invasion of Russia. Unlike the British, Hitler in 1940 and 1941 did not see the war as a life-or-death struggle, because the possibility of Germany's utter defeat did not enter his mind. The worst that he then envisaged was the frustration of his immediate goals.

While the Allies saw Germany as a military monolith, Hitler was always intensely nervous about maintaining his domestic political support, much more so than proved necessary. He was determined to preserve standards of living. Until the end of 1941, he tried to provide both guns and butter for the German people, and to a remarkable extent he succeeded. Short-term munitions contracts were placed with German industry in preparation for his great strategic thrusts, then cancelled the moment victory appeared to be in sight. Faced with the Luftwaffe's shortage of bombs in Poland in September 1939, Hitler only reluctantly authorized further bomb production on 12 October.[2] In the late summer of 1941, while Bomber Command was struggling to reduce German munitions production, Hitler was pursuing the same end: he ordered substantial reductions in the scale of arms output, because he believed that victory in Russia was already within sight. The consequences for the Germany army that winter were privations to match the tragedy of the British army in the Crimea.

Yet at the beginning of 1942, the year of the Thousand Bomber raid on Cologne, when Britain had been geared to total war and the most stringent rationing for more than two years, German consumer spending was at much the same level as in 1937. Britain had recognized from the beginning that she was fighting for survival, and strained every sinew to tool and arm accordingly. Already by September 1939 she was producing more tanks than Germany. In 1940, the year when the overwhelming strength of the Luftwaffe was pitted against Fighter Command, Britain was building aircraft faster than the Reich. In 1941, German aircraft production was a pitiful 10 per cent higher than in 1940.[3] Vast numbers of British women had been brought into industry, but Hitler resisted pressure to follow suit, because he feared the effects upon the German way of life. Goering's 'Four Year Plan', begun in 1936 allegedly to put the German economy on a war footing, was in reality only a limited programme to reduce the nation's dependence on imported raw materials.

Far-sighted men in the government understood that Hitler's economic policy was fraught with danger. General Georg Thomas, head of the *WiRuAmt*, the 'War Economy and Armaments Branch' of OKW, pleaded in vain for rearmament in depth. When the huge drain of casualties on the eastern front began, the Luftwaffe above all suffered acute shortages of aircraft and spares. Goering's squadrons lost 3,000 aircraft missing and a further 2,000 damaged in the first ten months of the Russian campaign, together with thousands of the most experienced aircrew. The ceaseless struggle for personal power among the Nazi leaders precluded the much more co-ordinated economic controls and policies adopted as a matter of course in Britain and America. 'The whole structure of the German administrative body was one of competing individuals and competing machines,' writes the economic historian Professor Milward,[4] 'which by 1942 represented a powerful collection of vested interests, each unwilling to relinquish its control of its own small part of the war economy.'

The prospect of imminent defeat concentrated British minds wonderfully in 1940. There was no parallel confrontation with reality in Germany until at least 1943, but the Russian counter-offensive of November 1941 caused Hitler to concede that the days of the 'blitzkrieg economy' were ended. Fritz Todt's appointment as Minister of Munitions signalled the beginning of the reorganization and mobilization of German industry that was continued by Speer on Todt's death in an air crash in February 1942.

As Hitler's architect and a member of the inner circle of his intimates, for the next two years Speer worked with the overwhelming advantage of Hitler's personal support. He acted on the authority of the Führer Command directive 'Armament 1942', issued to Todt on 10 January 1942. To achieve the massive increase in production that he sought, Speer expanded Todt's system of industry-wide committees of businessmen, who were made responsible for meeting output targets by settling priorities, enforcing co-operation between companies, assigning raw materials. 'Directive Committees' were created to take responsibility for specific weapons, and 'Directive Pools', for the allocation of supplies.

Yet while Hitler had in principle accepted that arms production was now the overwhelming economic priority, it was another matter for Speer to make him accept the consequences of this decision. The new Minister fought an uphill struggle to induce the Führer to cut back on domestic consumer production, and to import Germany's consumer needs from the Occupied Territories. Although in April 1942 90 per cent of German industry was still working only a single shift, Speer was immediately concerned by the shortage of labour which remained his overwhelming problem throughout the war. Conscript workers from the Occupied Territories were inadequate substitutes for native skilled workers drafted into the Wehrmacht. Speer and General Erhard Milch, State Secretary of the Air Ministry and the man responsible for aircraft production, were continuously at loggerheads with Sauckel, the Plenipotentiary for Labour, about manpower. In the first half of 1942 the aircraft industry was allocated 403,000 additional workers, but only 60,000 ever reached the assembly lines. Shortage of men – for the army, the factories, construction and reconstruction work – was the nightmare of the directors of the German war effort until the end.

The British official historians of the strategic air offensive suggest that part of the German achievement must be attributed to 'the strong controls which could be employed in a totalitarian state'. Yet Speer himself and a succession of economic historians have marvelled at the inefficiency and lack of central control in the German war economy compared with that of Britain. In a speech to manufacturers on 6 October 1943, Speer commented acidly on the difficulties of preventing German industry from dissipating its energies on irrelevant production. He noted that in the preceding year, the Reich had produced

120,000 typewriters, 200,000 domestic radios, 150,000 electric blankets, 3,600 refrigerators, 300,000 electricity meters, 512,000 pairs of riding boots and 360,000 spur straps. 'It remains one of the oddities of this war that Hitler demanded far less from his people than Churchill and Roosevelt did from their respective nations,' Speer was later to write.[5] By the end of 1943, Britain had reduced her pre-war army of domestic servants by two-thirds, yet in Germany 1.4 million workers were still employed in household service, and Hitler was so anxious to maintain living standards that he decreed the import of a further half-million Ukrainian girls to reinforce this total. At the end of 1943 there were still six million Germans employed in consumer industries. Speer's efforts to cut back consumer output were repeatedly frustrated by Hitler's personal veto. Eva Braun intervened to block an order banning permanent waves and the manufacture of cosmetics.

Germany was inevitably doomed to lose a battle of production against the western Allies – they ultimately achieved a superiority of 9 to 2 in *matériel*. But almost until the end of the war, Speer's factories were producing more tanks and arms than there were men left in the Wehrmacht's combat divisions to use them. In the two and a half years following Speer's appointment, Germany increased her production of tanks sixfold; of ammunition, weapons and aircraft threefold. It is highly doubtful whether further increases of arms production would significantly have improved her strategic position. Manpower, always manpower, was Germany's central problem. 'Until the last six months of the war,' reported the United States Strategic Bombing Survey, 'the army was never critically short of weapons and shells.'

But where in all this was the Allied bombing of Germany? In 1943, Harris's great year of area attack, 200,000 tons of bombs fell on the Third Reich, five times the weight which had been dropped in 1942. In a minute to the Prime Minister dated 3 November 1943, Harris listed nineteen German cities which he claimed were 'virtually destroyed', meaning that they had become 'a liability to the total German war effort vastly in excess of any assets remaining.' These were: Hamburg, Cologne, Essen, Dortmund, Düsseldorf, Hanover, Mannheim, Bochum, Mülheim, Koln Deutz, Barmen, Elberfeld, München Gladbach/Rheydt, Krefeld, Aachen, Rostock, Remscheid, Kassel and Emden. He also listed a further nineteen which were 'seriously damaged': Frankfurt, Stuttgart, Duisburg, Bremen, Hagen, Munich, Nuremberg, Stettin, Kiel, Karlsruhe, Mainz, Wilhelmshaven, Lübeck, Saarbrücken, Osnabrück, Münster, Rüsselsheim, Berlin and Oberhausen. In 1943, Bomber Command stated that 36 per cent of production had been lost in twenty-nine towns attacked.

In reality, the German armaments production index rose from 100 in January 1942 to 153 in July, 229 in July 1943, 332 in July 1944. The USSBS estimated after the war that in 1943 9 per cent of German production had been lost as a result of bombing, and a further 17 per cent in 1944, mostly in the latter part of the year. Speer said: 'The total damage suffered by the armament programme as a result of air attack during the year 1943 was not considerable.' There was such enormous slack capacity in the economy to be diverted from consumer production that damage on this scale could readily be absorbed by the German war machine.

In 1942 it would have seemed incredible to most people in Britain had they known the relative comfort and normality of life in Germany. In 1943 the bombing of German cities swept away that illusory tranquillity for ever, and brought the German people face to face with the manner of suffering they had inflicted upon so many others. Hitler's Reich suffered a catastrophe:

> Hamburg had put the fear of God into me [said Speer]. At the meeting of Central Planning on 29 July, I pointed out: 'If the air raids continue on the present scale, within three months we shall be relieved of a number of questions we are at present discussing. We shall simply be coasting downhill, smoothly and relatively swiftly. . . .' Three days later I informed Hitler that armaments production was collapsing and threw in the final warning that a series of attacks of this sort, extended to six more major cities, would bring Germany's armaments production to a total halt.
>
> 'You'll straighten all that out again,' he merely said. In fact Hitler was right.[6]

Speer himself was astonished by the speed of Hamburg's recovery. The British official historians, weighing the various estimates made at the end of the war, suggest that 1.8 months' production was lost. Textile and food output suffered more than armaments. In 1943 thirty U-boats under construction were destroyed by bombing in all parts of Germany; the majority of these were lost in the damage of shipyards in the Battle of Hamburg. The Battle of the Ruhr, according to Webster and Frankland, the official historians, cost the region between one and one-and-a-half months' loss of output. Recalling the huge attacks on Essen, Krupps lost a total of three months' production from all air attacks up to and including the spring of 1944. The firm began to believe that it was intended to serve as a decoy for the bombers, since although its production of locomotives, tank bodies and artillery was important, it was nothing like as pivotal to the German war economy as the Allies obviously believed.

The Americans, meanwhile, fared no better. The detailed story of the 8th Air Force's attempts to 'sever Germany's jugular' by destroying the ball-bearing factories at Schweinfurt does not belong here. It is enough to say that their first attack on 17 August 1943 cost them a paralysing loss of 60 of the 376 aircraft dispatched. Production fell by a disturbing, yet not fatal 38 per cent. But the attack also awakened the Germans to the extreme vulnerability of their ball-bearing supplies, and by the time of 'Second Schweinfurt' on 14 October 1943, much had been done towards marshalling reserve stocks from all over Germany, and preparing to disperse production. Schweinfurt's output fell by 67 per cent after the 8th Air Force's extraordinarily gallant second attempt, but the Americans lost another 60 Flying Fortresses out of 291 dispatched. They now suffered a major trauma about the future of their daylight operations, and, to Speer's overwhelming relief, Schweinfurt was not attacked again until 1944, by which stage its relative importance to German industry had been reduced. Harris refused to allow his bombers to have anything to do with the Schweinfurt operations in 1943, which he dismissed as a further example of 'panacea-mongering'. The American failure greatly strengthened his hand in resisting further demands from the Ministry of Economic Warfare for precision attacks on allegedly exposed sectors of the German economy. Bomber Command only went to Schweinfurt in February 1944, when the pressure on Harris had become irresistible. By then it was too late.

The Americans also spearheaded the assault on German aircraft production, notably by their attacks on airframe plants. Here, too, in the autumn of 1943, they suffered overwhelming defeat. German aircraft production advanced by huge strides until the first serious check imposed by the 8th Air Force's 'Big Week' in February 1944. Even after this it reached new peaks. As Dr Frankland has said of the American assault on German aircraft production in 1943: 'The bombers were committed to a race between the destruction of the German air force in production by the bombers, and the destruction of the bombers by the German fighters in being. The result was a decisive victory for the German fighters in being.'[7]

After the war, Speer professed himself astonished by the inconsistency of the Allied air attack. 'The vast but pointless area bombing,' he said,[8] had achieved no important effect on the German war effort by early 1944. But at intervals the bombers stumbled on a blind spot, a genuine Achilles' heel, only to turn aside and divert their attack elsewhere when they had done so. He marvelled at the American failure to repeat the two Schweinfurt attacks, at whatever cost. He was amazed that the British, having achieved remarkable success at Hamburg, neither returned to that city in sufficient force to prevent its recovery nor attempted to inflict the same treatment on any other city save Berlin, where the odds were impossible. He cited the example of the Dams Raid in May 1943. The Ministry of Economic Warfare in London correctly judged that the Mohne and the Sorpe dams were the key to the Ruhr water supplies. But after destroying the Mohne, 617 Squadron used its remaining mines to wreck the Eder dam, which was quite irrelevant. Bomber Command merely judged it more easily breachable with Barnes Wallis's special mines than the Sorpe. It was the same profoundly flawed reasoning process which sent the bombers to Lübeck: a target was attacked because it was destructible, not because it was vital.

Throughout the war Speer's efforts were crippled by the lack of coherent economic thinking by the Nazi leadership. But he recognized that the Allies were as incapable as Hitler of assessing the fatal weakness of the German war machine. The RAF had discussed bombing electricity generating plants in the 1930s, yet no serious attempt was made against Germany's power supplies by Bomber Command. The British assumed that they were too sophisticated and too widely dispersed to succumb. Speer was astonished that the Allies only began their major attack on the synthetic oil plants in the spring of 1944, and even then Harris took no part. For a few weeks, it seemed that the German economy faced imminent collapse. But Speer exhorted his managers. On past experience, the Americans would persist for a few weeks and then change policy: 'We have a powerful ally in this matter,' he said. 'That is to say, the enemy has an air force general staff as well.' His optimism was justified. It was another six months before the air attack on oil was pressed home.

Two further aspects of the British bomber offensive must be considered here. The first is the significant myth, fostered by the British official historians, that it contributed to the Luftwaffe's lack of bomber aircraft in 1944, and thus to its inability to intervene against the Allied armies on and after D-Day. It is perfectly true that Milch and Speer made great efforts to stop bomber production and concentrate exclusively on fighters from the summer of 1943. 'Gentlemen,' Milch told his staff after Hamburg, 'we are no longer on the offensive. For the last one and a half or two year we have been on the defensive. This fact is now recognized even at the highest levels of the Luftwaffe command.'[9] Galland, General of Fighters, fought determinedly for increases in the defences of Germany. Speer was in despair about the effort he considered wasted on bombers, each of which cost nine times the labour and resources of a fighter to build.

But they were all defeated by Hitler's overriding obstinacy. Until June 1944 he absolutely refused all proposals for the halting of bomber production, and by insisting that the jet Me262 meet the requirements of a bomber, delayed its appearance as a revolutionary fighter until too late. Hitler complained insistently about the Luftwaffe's inability to produce an adequate heavy bomber to carry out retaliatory raids upon England. All that Speer could do in the face of Hitler's obsession was to increase fighter production enormously, while maintaining that of bombers at a more or less static level. 'Milch's and my proposals that the manufacture of bombers be radically reduced in favour of increased fighter plane production was rejected until it was too late,' says Speer.[10]

Why was it, therefore, that whereas in September 1940 the Luftwaffe front line included 1,871 bombers and 1,162 fighters, by September 1944 the squadrons in Western Europe were reduced to 209 bombers against 2,473 fighters? The answer is that there was a long and disastrous series of design and development failures, beginning in the 1930s, when Goering, in his determination to create a tactical air force, ordered the destruction of the prototypes of the Do19 and Ju89 bombers. Germany entered the war with some superb aircraft. But after 1939 only the FW190 fighter appeared, to take the Luftwaffe into the next generation. Early in the war, immense development work was wasted on the Ju288 and the FW191, which was intended to carry five tons of bombs and to replace the Ju88. Most futile of all was the Heinkel He177, an extraordinary aircraft with four engines geared to two propellers which Milch christened 'the dead racehorse' in bitter judgement on the millions of hours wasted on flogging it. Several hundred were produced at enormous cost, but proved a total operational failure.

The German aircraft industry was burdened with an impossible number of unproven and competing development projects – at the end of 1941 there were forty different types under active development or in production. The advanced version of the Ju88, the best Luftwaffe light bomber and night-fighter, required 50,000 design changes on the production line, and its problems were resolved only in 1943. Early in the war, in anticipation of the new generation of bombers, the production lines of the old He111 and Do17 had been running down. Yet, in the event, even in 1944 the Heinkel and the Ju88 were the only bombers that the Luftwaffe could get. They were still being produced in quantity, and destroyed in large numbers on the Russian front. There were still more than 1,400 serviceable bombers and dive-bombers on the Luftwaffe strength in June 1944, but few of these were adequate for their task. Speer was always a production rather than a development expert, and he sought to expand the output of what was available rather than risk slowing production to introduce new models. Germany's best scientists and engineers were working on an impossibly extensive range of advanced weapons: the V-1 and V-2, the acoustic torpedo and half a dozen alternative jet aircraft. But if Germany had been able to build a satisfactory new bomber, Hitler would have insisted that the Luftwaffe should be given it, whether his airmen wanted it or not.

It is important to make one further point in this context: the overwhelming tactical lesson of the war was that no bomber could operate effectively unless air superiority had been gained. By early 1944 the Allies possessed the capability for creating such an overwhelming air umbrella over the invasion that there was never the remotest possibility that the Luftwaffe could have intervened effectively against the Allied armies. German airmen like to point out that while they put up nineteen aircraft in support of every German division attacking France in 1940 and twenty-six aircraft for every division invading Russia a year later, on D-Day the Allies launched 260 aircraft for every division landing.[11] Such was the pathetic plight of the Luftwaffe that its pilots flew only 319 sorties in northern France that day, and lost a thousand aircraft in Normandy alone in the month that followed. But the German air force had been brought to this pass by strategic and technical failures at home, followed by defeat in the air by the Allied air forces, not destruction in the factories. The fact that the Allies attained such absolute dominance of the skies, and yet faced a further eleven months of bitter fighting before final victory, raises other questions about the limitations of air power which fall beyond the scope of this book.

The final issue about the effectiveness of the 1943–44 area-bombing campaign is that of its effect on the morale of the German people. When Bomber Command's great attacks on the cities began, the German leadership was deeply alarmed. 'Hitler had repeatedly exclaimed that if the bombings went on, not only would the cities be destroyed, but the morale of the people would crack irreparably,' wrote Speer.[12] 'Hitler was succumbing to the same error as the British strategists on the other side who were ordering mass bombings.'

After Hamburg, Milch said:

> It's much blacker than Speer paints it. If we get just five or six more attacks like these on Hamburg, the German people will just lay down their tools, however great their willpower. I keep saying, the steps that are being taken now are being taken too late. There can be no more talk of night fighters in the East, or of putting an umbrella over our troops in Sicily or anything like that. The soldier on the battlefield will just have to dig a hole, crawl into it and wait until the attack is over. What the home front is suffering now cannot be suffered much longer.[13]

Since April 1942, Goebbels had been advocating reprisals, which the Luftwaffe was entirely incapable of carrying out:

> I now consider it absolutely essential that we continue with our rigorous reprisal raids. I also agree that not much is to be accomplished with raids on munitions centres. Like the English, we must attack centres of culture, especially those which have only little anti-aircraft. Such centres should be attacked two or three times in succession and levelled to the ground; then the English probably will

no longer find pleasure in trying to frighten us by their terror attacks.[14]

By March 1943, Goebbels was recording in his diary:

> Reporting from the Rhineland indicate that in some cities people are gradually getting rather weak in the knees. That is understandable. For months the working population has had to go into air raid shelters night after night, and when they come out again they see part of their city going up in flame and smoke. The enervating thing about it is that we are not in a position to reply in kind. . . . Our war in the east has lost us air supremacy in essential sections of Europe, and we are completely at the mercy of the English.[15]

Goebbels and his colleagues were intensely concerned to convey to the German people the notion that the British had unilaterally instituted terror bombing. British monitoring services noted that in one week of June 1943, 15 per cent of all German radio news output was given up to denunciations of the Allied air attack on German culture. In July a book was published under the auspices of the Propaganda Ministry, discussing the origins of strategic bombing, and entitled *England's Sole Guilt*. A plan was put forward for leafleting England with photographs of the grotesquely broken bodies of shot-down Bomber Command aircrew. A Party Chancellery directive[16] reminded newspaper editors that 'the concept of "terror raid" is intended to reflect the criminal behaviour of the enemy. . . . Therefore a German attack must never be called a "terror raid". Counter-measures of the German Air Force are to be designated as "retaliation measures".'

Yet, astonishingly, the Nazi leadership's fears and caution proved entirely unnecessary. The morale of the German people remained unbroken to the end, despite growing awareness that the war must be lost, and despite the increasing indifference of their Führer to their fate. Hitler refused to visit bombed cities, for all the imprecations of Goebbels and Speer. The Propaganda Ministry reacted nervously to every symptom that might suggest an impending moral collapse: reports from the Schweinfurt area of a decline in the general exchanging of the 'Heil Hitler!' salute; a growing resignation to subterranean life – 'Bunker fever' – as raids intensified; dismay about the news from the Russian front. But even in the ruined cities people queued to pay their taxes at temporary offices. After 'Big Week' in February 1944, Speer and Milch marvelled at the manner in which the aircraft workers laboured on temporary assembly-lines created in the open air in freezing winter weather, the heated factories having been reduced to rubble. Workers everywhere went back to their plants even after the firestorms. They repaired damage, restored production – even made their own shattered homes somehow habitable – with less assistance than the British authorities provided for their own people during the Blitz. The 1940 German attack on Coventry destroyed 100 out of the city's 1,922 acres. In 1943, Krefeld lost 40 per cent of its housing in one night, yet continued to man its factories. Somewhere in the ruins of Hamburg, the vast majority of the million refugees who fled in the immediate wake of the firestorm returned and took up residence to live again within weeks, even with 6,200 of the city's 8,382 acres apparently totally destroyed, according to the reconnaissance photographs that were studied with such fascination at High Wycombe. What was done in Germany in the face of the bombing between 1942 and 1944 was not an economic miracle – Speer was extremely able, but he was not a genius. It was a triumph for the courage and determination of the German people in the face of the utmost suffering, paralleling that of the British in 1940. The chauvinistic assumption upon which the RAF founded its area-bombing campaign, that Germans were liable to moral collapse in a way that the British proved in 1940 they were not, was shown to be totally unfounded. In 1943, Dr Goebbels' department noted a marked stiffening of national morale in the face of raids, matched by the growth of an unprecedented popular hatred for the enemy.

> In the burning and devastated cities we daily experienced the direct impact of war [wrote Speer]. It spurred us to do our utmost. Neither did the bombings and the hardships that resulted from them weaken the morale of the populace. On the contrary, from my visits to armament plants and my contacts with the man in the street, I carried away the impression of growing toughness. It may well be that the estimated loss of 9 per cent of our production capacity was amply balanced out by increased effort.[17]

The British official historians looked back at 1943 and declared: 'For the first time in the war, Germany herself . . . began to pay the price of the fearful deeds which she had perpetrated and was yet to perpetrate, against others.[18]

Beyond dispute, the area offensive punished Germany terribly. It destroyed centuries of construction and of culture, the homes and property of Germans who for the first time glimpsed the cost of Nazism. At the end of 1942 Goering had said: 'We will have reason to be glad if Germany can keep the boundaries of 1933 after the war.' By the end of 1943 production in every critical area of war industry – tanks, U-boats, guns, aircraft – was still expanding at a gigantic rate. But it had become apparent to the German people that they were beyond the hope of mercy. After three years of terrible sacrifice, this was the principal achievement of Bomber Command.

2. The Defences

For the first year of the British bomber offensive that began in May 1940, the Luftwaffe which was responsible for every aspect of the air defence of the Reich relied principally upon flak and searchlights. In 1939 the German air force possessed only one experimental night-fighter squadron equipped with Me109s – this was the first unit to engage 3 Group's Wellingtons on 18 December 1939. In June 1940, Goering himself admitted that the lack of night-fighters was 'the Luftwaffe's Achilles' heel'. That summer, the unsuitable 109s were withdrawn from night operations and progressively replaced by twin-engined Me110s. But their crews roamed the moonlit skies of Europe conducting visual searches for British bombers with almost the same sense of helplessness as afflicted many of the men in the Hampdens and Whitleys', of which they destroyed a bare handful.

But with the appointment of General Josef Kammhuber as General of Night Fighters in October 1940, Germany began to create the great defensive system against the bomber which came within an ace of victory in 1944. Through the winter of 1940–41, as his resources allowed, Kammhuber progressively extended a belt of searchlights and sound-locators across northern Germany and the Low Countries, between fifty and a hundred miles inland from the coast. Fighters patrolled sectors of this line, seeking to attack bombers which been detected and illuminated. Kammhuber himself recognized that these were inadequate stop-gap measures until more sophisticated equipment came into service. By the time Hitler ordered the transfer of all searchlights from Kammhuber's belt to the direct defence of Germany in the spring of 1942, the new and much more deadly *Himmelbett* system, based on a chain of radar-guided fighter 'boxes', had been established the length of the European coast from north Germany to Belgium, and around the most important cities of Germany.

Dr R. V. Jones has described[19] how British Scientific Intelligence, through 1941 and 1942, progressively unravelled the mysteries of what they came to call 'The Kammhuber Line'. Each overlapping night-fighter 'box' was equipped with a *Freya* radar set, which provided early warning of Allied bombers and their course, although not of their height. But as the fighters scrambled and gained altitude to meet them, a bomber was picked up by a short-range *Würzburg* radar – the early model was effective up to something over twenty miles, which determined the radius of each 'box'. A second *Würzburg* meanwhile tracked the German fighter. On the ground, in the T-shaped control huts that now stood at intervals from Ostend to Denmark, the ground controllers plotted the position of fighter and bomber by green and red dots projected on to the *Seeburg* evaluation screen. At first, they sought to trap the bomber in the cone created by their supporting searchlight battery, for the fighter to attack. Later, in 1942, when *Lichtenstein* airborne radar had been fitted to the night-fighters, they sought to guide the fighter to the point within the two miles of the bomber at which the *Lichtenstein* could take over for the final approach.

The brilliant British commando raid on Bruneval in March 1942 enabled the British to seize a *Würzburg* for examination, and the scientists were impressed by its quality and precision. German standards of manufacture in electronics remained higher than those of the Allies throughout the war. But they lagged in design and application. British scientists and airmen preferred their own simpler techniques of tracking both fighter and bomber on the same radar screen. The German system also suffered the overwhelming limitation that each 'box' could direct only one interception at a time. It was in this knowledge that the British evolved their 'streaming' techniques, pushing the bomber force through a single 'box' at the utmost speed and density, to saturate the defences. The German control stations *Jaguar*, *Delphin*, *Lowe*, *Eisbar*, *Seidler* and the rest achieved a formidable total of successes, especially after the introduction in 1942 of the improved 'Giant *Würzburg*', with its range approaching fifty miles. But with the coming of the massive British attacks of 1942 and 1943, although the night-fighters were inflicting terrible losses on Bomber Command, it was evident that the Kammhuber Line was being hopelessly swamped by the scale of the offensive.

Kammhuber's greatest misfortune was that, on Hitler's orders, in October 1941 he was ordered to abandon his experimental 'intruder' operations against British bomber airfields. Hitler considered that only aircraft shot down over Germany were of value in convincing the German people that they were being defended. From late 1940 onwards, the general had been dispatching his largest force he could spare – never more than twenty Ju88 fighters, equipped with cannon and small bombs – to attack British bombers at their most vulnerable moments, as they took off and landed at their airfields. In 1940–41 they had been responsible for two-thirds of the Luftwaffe's night-fighter victories. Kammhuber was convinced that this promised to be the most effective means of causing casualties and chaos to the British bomber offensive. Bomber Command shared his opinion. By 1943 the marshalling and dispatch of Harris's huge force had become an exercise of the utmost complexity, calling for precision timing at every airfield in eastern England. If Kammhuber's 'intruders' had been allowed to continue their operations, the consequences could have been overwhelming. But High Wycombe's nightmares went unfulfilled. With the exception of a single isolated incursion in October 1943, the Luftwaffe left British airfields in peace. It was the greatest missed opportunity of the bomber war, and like so many other major tactical errors, this was a personal decision of the Führer.

It was only in the wake of the Battle of Hamburg that Germany's leaders began to perceive the scale of the threat to the Reich, and for that matter the enormous requirement for aircraft in total war. Ernst Udet, the former First World War flying ace who controlled aircraft production in the first years of the war, made a series of disastrous errors and omissions before his suicide in November 1941. Milch, who took over his responsibilities, struggled to make good shortages and to gear the aircraft industry for all-out effort. He insisted that work should be delayed on the Me262 jet in order to get the Me109F into urgent production. Yet in 1942 when he told Goering that he proposed to build a thousand fighters a month, the Reichsmarshal laughed heartily: 'Where would we use them all?'

But by late 1943 the Luftwaffe was losing more than a thousand aircraft a month, most of them on the Russian front. In June that year, the Luftwaffe's front-line strength on all fronts stood at some 7,000 aircraft. Until late 1944, when fuel shortages made the figures irrelevant, it hovered between 6,000 and 7,000. Yet for the night defence of Germany there were rarely more than 350 fighters, in six *Geschwaders* of four or five squadrons each. On a good night in 1943 or early 1944, the Luftwaffe could hope to mount between 200 and 250 sorties against a bomber attack. When the American Flying Fortresses began their massive daylight operations, the 8th Air Force from England and the 15th Air Force from Italy, the pressure on the Luftwaffe's home defence units became intolerable. Instead of the 400 or 500 day-fighters that were vital to meet the huge American formations on acceptable terms, there were never more than 300. To reinforce them, night-fighters and their highly trained crews were flung into the struggle, intensifying the pressure on aircraft serviceability, and losing a steady stream of experienced aircrew and their precious *Lichtenstein* sets. Again and again Milch, Speer, Kammhuber and Galland pleaded for increased resources for night defence, but until the summer of 1944 they were resolutely denied.

It was the Luftwaffe's misfortune to be under the command of Hermann Goering. For all his pleasure in the trappings of power, deep within himself this indolent sybarite regarded the war as a terrible error which had sown the seeds for Germany's destruction. Even as his own air fleets were launching their great attack on England in 1940, he crushed the bounding optimism of Jeschonnek, his Chief of Staff, about the prospects for an early British surrender:

'Do you think that Germany would give in if Berlin was in ruins?'

'Of course not,' said Jeschonnek.

'Then you think the British are different? That is where you are wrong. . . .'

Goering's sense of doom became overwhelming when Hitler launched the invasion of Russia. For the remainder of the war he took refuge in drugs and delusions, exhibiting spasms of energy only when he felt his empire threatened by the expanding operations of Speer or Milch. The Luftwaffe was left without a dominant voice in the struggle around Hitler's throne. Goering was discredited and despised among his senior colleagues, but Hitler would not dismiss him because of 'The Fat Man's' wide public popularity, and Goering would not voluntarily abandon power. The Reichsmarshal quarantined himself from all unacceptable realities. When the news of the first '1,000 Raid' was brought to him, he declined to believe it. He rejected reports of the American Mustang long-range fighter engaging the Luftwaffe over Germany, because he would not acknowledge that such an aircraft could be built. At a meeting at his Castle Veldenstein in the autumn of 1941, Goering brushed aside the proposals of Kammhuber, Molders and Galland for the defence of Germany: 'This whole phoney business won't be necessary any more once I get my squadrons back to the west.'[20] He continued to delude himself that the return of the vast Luftwaffe forces from the eastern front was imminent, just as he promised Hitler in 1942 that he could supply the beleaguered Sixth Army at Stalingrad from the air. The night-fighters, meanwhile, were starved of numbers and aircrew, fuel and equipment.

'The defence of the Reich follows the latest bomb crater,' the pilots muttered cynically.[21] By 1943, pupils under training were finding themselves scrambled with their instructors to meet bomber attacks. When the former bomber pilot Major Hajo Hermann formed his first 'Wild Boar' squadrons in July that year, he found himself obliged to recruit among failed bomber pilots and disgraced aircrew rejected by other line units. When the *Lichtenstein* AI radar began to be fitted to night-fighters, the scientists had to overcome resistance from senior Luftwaffe officers who believed that its protruding aerials would have an unacceptable effect on speed and performance. From 1941 onwards the fuel allocation for aircrew training was quite inadequate, and the quality – though not the courage – of the Luftwaffe's pilots began the steady decline that continued until late 1944, when they were reaching line squadrons with only 150 hours' flying experience. It is generally accepted by former bomber pilots as well as by the Luftwaffe that the enormous scores claimed by a handful of pilots such as Lt.-Col. Helmut Lent – the veteran of Wilhelmshaven who was credited with 102 victories before he was killed in 1944 – were not far from the reality. A small minority of superb airmen such as himself, Major Heinz-Wolfgang Schnaufer (121 victories), Prince Lippe-Weissenfeld (51 victories) and Prince Sayn-Wittgenstein (83 victories) accounted for the overwhelming majority of bombers shot down by night-fighters, while hundreds of 'green' pilots landed night after night without a kill, even at the height of the 'Battles' in 1943–44.

After Goering, General Hans Jeschonnek, the Luftwaffe's Chief of

Staff, bore much responsibility for the shortcomings of the defence of Germany, which he seemed to recognize by his suicide on hearing the news of the British raid on Peenemunde in August 1943. Jeschonnek was entirely in thrall to Hitler. He directed the Luftwaffe as he believed that the Führer wished, without thought for strategic or tactical reality. In the spring of 1942, in the face of fierce warnings about the long-term consequences for the Luftwaffe, Jeschonnek stripped training units and reserves of every man and aircraft to support the new offensive in Russia. 'The Luftwaffe must attack and not defend,' said Goering at the end of 1941, and Jeschonnek supported the fantasies of the Reichsmarshal and his Führer to the end of his life. Since the beginning of the war, the Luftwaffe had regarded flak and searchlights as the principal defence against strategic air attack, with fighters in a subsidiary role. Now, despite overwhelming evidence that the night-fighter was the decisive weapon in meeting the bomber offensive, there was still no major shift of priorities.

In July 1943, Kammhuber was replaced as GOC XII Air Corps after Hitler rejected his proposals for a massive new radar programme to meet the American air armadas which the general anticipated. Hitler dismissed his forecasts as fantasy, and in November Kammhuber was also removed from his post as General of Night Fighters and sent to Norway. Hajo Hermann, creator of the 'Wild Boars', replaced him.

But in the face of an ever less favourable balance of forces, in late 1943 and early 1944 the German night-fighter force came close to the decisive defeat of Bomber Command, just as the Luftwaffe's day-fighters almost achieved the defeat of the 8th Air Force. It is almost impossible to overvalue the ingenuity and determination with which the German defenders responded to the bomber offensive. Their knowledge of Bomber Command, chiefly derived from prisoner interrogation, was so comprehensive that they proposed to make a film depicting the planning and launching of a British attack, using actors to play the principals, for the training of Luftwaffe units. The script was written and fell into the hands of the Allies in May 1945.

The 'Wild Boar' concept created by Hermann was short-lived, for the difficulties of operating single-engined fighters without blind-flying equipment at night proved overwhelming, and losses in landings and accidents became prohibitive. But the 'Wild Boars' had shown the way to the new approach of fighting the bombers, and the courage of the pilots who dived into their own searchlights and flak – which often ignored orders not to fire above a given height – to engage the bombers excited the respect of the British. The 'Wild Boars' were rapidly eclipsed by the 'Tame Boars', twin-engined fighters which were scrambled to orbit a visual beacon as soon as the approximate course of the bomber force was known. The British discovered that the Germans could often predict a raid by monitoring wireless operators' signals from all over eastern England during their morning air test, and 100 Group began to broadcast fake test signals on days when Bomber Command was not operating, to confuse the issue. But careful study of the weather predictions usually enabled the Germans to judge whether conditions were right for Harris to attack.

As the British approach Germany, the ground controllers directed the 'Tame Boars' into the stream by radio running-commentary. In the final stages of interception, the air turbulence created by hundreds of aircraft warned the fighters that they were close to the British. On a clear night, they then searched visually for the bombers. In moonless conditions they relied upon AI radar – by early 1944 they were being equipped with the *Lichtenstein* SN2, which was impervious to *Window* jamming. The blind spot of the British bombers below the fuselage had always been known to fighter pilots, but they had often been unable to exploit it – until the Autumn of 1943 an ingenious fitter at a Luftwaffe airfield devised the prototype of the deadly *schrage musik* – 'jazz music' – a pair of fixed upward-firing cannon mounted behind the fighter's cockpit. The pilot had only to slide beneath the bomber and fire a short burst which was almost invariably lethal. A few lucky British survivors who came home to report that they had been flying peacefully over Germany until the world collapsed and they found themselves upside down in a wingless fuselage were treated as 'line-shooters'. It was not until the end of the war that British aircrew learned of the existence of *schrage musik*. It has been a matter of debate ever since whether the Canadian 6 Group, which alone fitted ventral turrets to many of its Lancasters to cover the blind spot, were justified in sacrificing speed and adding weight to do so.

But the most dramatic transformation of the bomber war in 1943 and 1944 was brought about by the decision of both sides to turn night into day. After years of rigorously blacked-out cities and oceans of darkness across Europe broken only by islands of light around a target, the most dazzling firework display in history now exploded every night over Germany. British Pathfinders dropped flares to light the target for their markers, while high above them Luftwaffe aircraft were laying their own lines of parachute flares to illuminate the bombers for fighter attack. On cloudy nights when the British were bombing blind, the searchlights arched upwards, seeking to turn the clouds into a layer of light against which the attackers were silhouetted for the fighters: 'The enemy bombers crawl across them like flies on a table cloth,' Milch told Speer with satisfaction.[22] From five Divisional 'Battle Opera Houses', the Luftwaffe controllers maintained their running commentary to the fighters, based on information from ground observer stations that was processed and retransmitted inside one minute. The British adopted the most elaborate methods to halt their voices, by jammers mounted in the 'ABC' aircraft of Addison's newly-formed electronic counter-measures force, 100 Group, or by interference from the huge British monitoring station at Kingsdown in Kent, where German-speaking men and women attempted to deceive the fighters into breaking off or landing. When the Germans began to play selected music to direct the fighter pilots instead of voice transmissions, the British sought to match it. As the Germans strengthened their transmissions and altered their frequencies, the British followed them.

But for all the enormous effort that was mounted, Bomber Command never succeeded in totally breaking the controllers' communications with the fighters. When the Luftwaffe failed to intercept, it was almost invariably because the ground controllers had been deceived by the bombers' course changes, or by the 'spoof' force of Mosquitoes *Windowing* to resemble a Main Force attack. The Germans never got the measure of the Mosquitoes, even with the introduction in 1943 of a limited number of Ju88s boosted with nitrous oxide that were specifically intended for Mosquito interception. In the night-fighter squadrons, a pilot who shot down a Mosquito was allowed to count it as two 'victories'.

By the end of 1943 the radar war was also reaching a new pitch of intensity. The Germans were impressed, almost awed, by their examination of captured British H2S sets and of the cavity magnetrons that they contained. But having grasped the principle upon which the H2S aircraft dropped their blind markers, they embarked upon the herculean task of altering the H2S silhouette of the countryside around some key targets, for example by laying great strips of metal on rafts on the lakes around Berlin. They also devised *Naxos*, a night-fighter radar which from early 1944 could home on H2S transmissions from British aircraft, and which at last caused Bomber Command to order that sets should only be switched on at short intervals over enemy territory. Just as British bombers were fitted with *Monica*, which gave radar warning of aircraft approaching from the rear, so the Luftwaffe in turn fitted its fighters with *Flensburg*, which homed on *Monica*, and eventually led to its withdrawal. The Germans also began plotting the radar 'flames' from Allied IFF transmissions, about which Dr Jones and British Scientific Intelligence had been warning Bomber Command in vain for more than two years. Many crews were still convinced that IFF was capable of interfering with German radar, and kept their sets switched on from take-off to landing. Yet only in the spring of 1944 did the irrefutable evidence of Scientific Intelligence – supported by 'Ultra' intercepted German signals, of which the Luftwaffe's were throughout the war the most readily decipherable – compel Bomber Command to accept the reality of the threat and order crews to discontinue IFF emissions over enemy territory.

Yet whatever tactical antidotes Bomber Command could devise, by the winter of 1943 darkness no longer offered effective protection for the bomber, just as a few months earlier it had ceased to provide any safety for the cities of Germany. The night-fighter had achieved an alarming tactical dominance. It was the good fortune of the British that the leaders of Germany still had no grasp of the significance of the Luftwaffe's achievement. The bulk of the Reich's resources for the war against the bomber continued to be devoted to flak, searchlights and smoke generators. Something like a million people, albeit many of them women and schoolboys, were manning the defences each night. 10,000 of Germany's excellent 88-mm guns which, as Sir Arthur Harris has often remarked, would otherwise have been deployed against the advancing Russian tanks, were placed around the cities, supported by thousands more light flak guns. Their chief value was that they were alleged to boost the morale of the civilian population, and they encouraged the bombers to fly high and bomb wide. In 1940 the Luftwaffe computed that it expended 2,313 heavy and 2,458 light flak shells for every bomber destroyed, a ratio which increased later in the war.[23] One-third of the entire German optical industry was working to produce anti-aircraft defence equipment, half the electronics industry was building radar sets, most of them for the flak and the 7,000 searchlights supporting the guns. All this was a formidable drain on German industry, and its value to the Allies must not be underestimated. Fifteen years after the war, Speer read the American official history of the USAAF's strategic bomber offensive, which expresses doubts about its achievement. He wrote in his secret diary in Spandau prison:

> It seems to me that the book misses the decisive point. Like all other accounts of the bombing that I have so far seen, it places its emphasis on the destruction that air raids inflicted on German industrial potential and thus upon armaments. In reality the losses were not quite so serious. . . . The real importance of the air war consisted in the fact that it opened a second front long before the invasion of Europe. That front was the skies over Germany. . . . The unpredictability of the attacks made the front gigantic. . . . Defence against air attacks required the production of thousands of anti-aircraft guns, the stockpiling of tremendous quantities of ammunition all over the country, and holding in readiness hundreds of thousands of soldiers. . . . As far as I can judge from the accounts I have read, no one has yet seen that this was the greatest lost battle on the German side. . . .[24]

It is essential to quote this passage in any account of the bomber offensive, because the most enthusiastic defenders of the achievements of bombing, including Sir Arthur Harris himself, cite it among the principal testimony supporting their case. But in his memoirs *Inside the Third Reich*, published long after he wrote these words, Speer forcefully reasserted the view he took in his 1945–46 interrogations, that bombing was ineffective in cracking Germany until the closing phase of the war. Speer was a manager, not a strategist. The balance of evidence suggests that in his Spandau writing, he overstated the importance of the German resources devoted to air defence, and underestimated the drain on the Allies of mounting the bomber offensive.

Germany's tragedy in the air war was that she lacked a coherent strategy, because of the lack of support and direction from the top. Her defences relied upon compromises and expedients. The resources that the Luftwaffe devoted to night-fighters were paltry by the standards of its own overall strength, far less when considered against the strength of the Allied air forces. Yet by the spring of 1944, in the face of every possible handicap, the German night-fighter force had inflicted a series of devastating blows on Bomber Command, culminating in the destruction of 108[25] aircraft on the Nuremberg raid of 30 March 1944.

However angered and dismayed were the leaders of Germany by Allied bombing, they never considered it sufficiently mortal a threat to order a major withdrawal of aircraft from the eastern front to meet, it. But had they done so, had they lavished a fraction of the resources devoted to futile aircraft development or even ground defences upon the night-fighters of the Reich, had Jeschonnek or Goering forcefully supported Speer and Milch in their efforts to gain priority for home-fighter defence, Bomber Command might by the winter of 1943 have suffered losses that would have brought its offensive against Germany to an abrupt conclusion.

X

Bomber Command Headquarters, Buckinghamshire, 1943–44

Even in the bleakest nights of the bomber offensive it is remarkable how little dismay rippled the calm routine of Bomber Command headquarters at High Wycombe. Looking back over the war years later, staff officers remembered the thrill of excitement and triumph that ran through them all at the news of the '1,000 Raid' on Cologne and the breaking of the Ruhr dams by 617 Squadron. In the wake of Hamburg in August 1943, there was a euphoric period 'when we really believed that we'd got it in the bag.'[1] But beyond these false dawns, there were few high surges or steep plunges of morale and enthusiasm. Week in and week out, eventually year in and year out, they walked or bicycled from their familiar billets in the morning to the quiet offices on No. 1 Site, poured forth the stream of orders and memoranda that cluttered down the teletypes to Groups and Stations to launch seven thousand young men into the night sky over Germany and the following morning garnered the paper harvest of signals and scrambled telephone messages, still-damp reconnaissance prints and provisional bomb-tonnage figures by which success or failure was measured. Their absolute remoteness from the battlefront has led some historians to compare High Wycombe with the French châteaux from which the generals of the First World War directed Passchendaele and the Somme, to liken Sir Arthur Harris to Sir Douglas Haig.[2]

Harris's eventual fall from grace was inevitable. He tossed too many hostages to fortune with his wildly exaggerated claims and promises, and attacked too many powerful interests with reckless rudeness. He was a warrior to the roots of his soul. He sought to engage and destroy the enemy by every means at his command, and it was this quality in him that undoubtedly appealed to Churchill, a like spirit. Harris had never been asked to determine the morality or desirability of a bomber offensive. He had been appointed to attack Germany. If he fought fiercely for resources and support, this was not merely his privilege, but his duty. If he lost the confidence of the Prime Minister or the Air Staff, it was their business to sack him.

It is interesting that his aircrew, who never saw him, regarded him with rueful but enduring affection. His staff at High Wycombe respected and feared but, with a few exceptions, did not like him. He was too ruthless, too impatient of failure or disagreement, too devoid of endearing weakness. The stories of his abrasive encounters with authority were legion. Striding into the Air Ministry one morning, he passed one of the most senior civil servants with a bluff greeting of 'Morning, Abrahams, and what have you done to impede the war effort today?'[3] The Foreign Office sought Harris's help: 'Sam Hoare came bleating to me for a second aircraft to carry his diplomatic bags. But it just happened that one bag had burst open in the air on a previous run, and we found it full of lackeys' uniforms. I told Hoare that I did not consider these a fit cargo for my aircraft in the middle of the war.'[4] He made no secret of his loathing for the Royal Navy, and could contemptuously reel off the details of the deluge of decorations awarded to sailors for some of their less successful operations. He said that there were three things one should never take on a yacht – a wheelbarrow, an umbrella and a naval officer. One day Churchill told Harris that Pound was deeply concerned about the continued survival of the battleship *Tirpitz*: 'Tell the First Sea Lord he need not worry,' said Harris blithely. 'I'll sink it when I have a spare moment.'

The mask never slipped from Harris, because there was no mask. Behind that unyielding visage and those piercing eyes, there was shrewdness but little tolerance. Critics like Major Morton who recoiled from his philistinism correctly perceived his lack of cultural interests. He had no small talk. He disliked physical activity – he often said that after his experience in South-West Africa in the First World War, he made up his mind never to walk again unless he had to. At the same period, he formed a deep affection for mules and their ways, a joke against himself which he enjoyed. Few men have applied themselves to their duty even in war with the single-mindedness of Harris. Portal occasionally took a few days' fishing. Yet in the course of more than three years at High Wycombe, Harris allowed himself only two weekends of holiday, with friends in Norfolk. Many of his staff officers were middle-aged men who found it possible to do their parts to a not uncomfortable routine. But Harris lived with enormous strain. He often remarked that while most commanders were required to risk their forces in battle only at intervals of months, he was staking everything almost every night. He drowned his ulcers in Dr Collis Browne's mixture, and later in a potion supplied by the Americans. He chain-smoked Camels or Lucky Strikes through a battered holder. He gave vent to his inner tensions in moments of fierce anger that exasperated his equals and thoroughly frightened his subordinates.

But those who seek to present him simply as a latter-day 'Donkey', indifferent to casualties, do him an injustice. He was passionately concerned to give every man in his command the best possible chance of survival. A senior civil servant at the Ministry of Aircraft Production described vividly[5] an occasion on which Harris arrived to denounce the Stirling bomber and demand more Lancasters: 'It's murder, plain murder to send my young men out to die in an aircraft like that!' said Harris furiously. But a good case can be made that he was slow to grasp the possibilities and limitations of the new generation of radar technology. He was one of those men who refuse to accept any lesson until they have proved it for themselves. He was not a quick or indeed a first-class mind in the academic sense, but it is debatable whether first-class minds are wanted at the summit of operational commands in wartime.

The mainspring of all that Harris did was his determination to prove the unique qualities of strategic air power. Trenchard in the end came to regard Harris as his most perfect disciple, when other bright hopes such as Portal had been infected by unbelievers. Harris was a man of immense force and directness – though a good deal less frank than he sometimes appeared – whose overwhelming advantage was that he was quite indifferent to what the world thought of him. He reserved great warmth of heart for those who inspired his respect and affection, and was unswervingly loyal to his friends and those who served him well.

But he never took the precaution of cloaking what he was doing in the formal dress of circumspection and manners that the English traditionally cherish in peace and war. His Rhodesian background may explain something of this. He seemed to delight in assaulting social convention, in expressing the realities of the bomber offensive in the most brutally literal language. 'I wonder whether in Allied headquarters, as in ours, the talk was not of victory over the enemy, but of his "extinction" or "Annihilation",' Speer mused in his cell at Spandau years later. 'How, for example, did Air Marshal Harris express himself?'[6]

Harris had performed a great service to England and to the Government in the first eighteen months of his command, when the bomber offensive was the Western Allies' greatest thrust against Germany. Now, strategic bombing had become a controversial matter. It is notable how much Churchill wrote about Bomber Command in the early chapters of his war memoirs, how little in the later. In his final volume, Harris himself is mentioned only once, *passim* and critically. It was Harris's reckless choice of language in writing and speaking of the bomber offensive during the war years that pinioned the levelling of Germany's cities to his back for good or ill for the rest of history, while men who chose their words more carefully – Churchill, Portal, even Cherwell – have somehow kept a distance from it.

From February 1942 until the end of the war Harris lived a few minutes' drive from High Wycombe, at the Commander-in-Chief's official residence, Springfield House. It was an odd *ménage*. He married his second wife Therese only in 1938, and it took her some time to shrug off her natural initial shyness, a young woman suddenly thrust amidst the summits of the Royal Air Force. Now, at Springfield, she was bringing up their small daughter Jackie and entertaining ministers and celebrities of every nation in the war. De Gaulle came, and Ellen

Wilkinson, the radical MP; there were Indians who needed special food, and Americans like Ira Eaker to be shown Harris's famous Blue Books – indeed his chief concern with every visitor was to indoctrinate them about the achievements and potential of Bomber Command. An RAF cook, Sergeant Simmonds, presided over the kitchen, although Harris himself was fond of taking over at the stove when there were no guests. There was a resident nucleus of Harris's staff. Harry Weldon, his Personal Staff Officer, was a philosophy don from Magdalen College, Oxford. It was Weldon who adapted Harris's language and sentiments into the forcefully expressed minutes and memoranda with which he bombarded the Air Ministry and the War Cabinet.

John Maze was posted to Harris at the completion of his tour of operations with 76 Squadron in the winter of 1943, one of a succession of ADCs throughout the war. Naturally nervous in his C-in-C's drawing-room after dinner, the gangling young man emptied his coffee over the pristine white carpet sent to Springfield from the *Queen Mary* when she was stripped to become a troopship. The Harrises liked to nickname the household and they knew their Damon Runyon, so Maze became 'Feets', just as Weldon was 'Harry the Horse'.

Harris's other permanent guest at Springfield was Air Vice-Marshal Sir Robert Saundby, first SASO and now Deputy C-in-C of Bomber Command. Sandy Saundby was effectively Harris's Chief of Staff, an outstanding technician who was responsible for translating Harris's target decisions into operational reality, in liaison with the Group commanders. Saundby's family lived in Berkshire, too far for him to get home for more than occasional visits, so the Harrises invited him to live with them. Second only to his dedication to the concept of strategic bombing, he was a passionate naturalist. In his spare hours at High Wycombe, he stalked the hedgerows in pursuit of butterflies and plants. There was a legendary occasion on which he was arrested up a tree with his butterfly net, suspected by a local constable of attempting to catch sparrows for the London market. Saundby was also a superb fly-fisherman, drifting across West Wycombe lake in summer, rowed by any officer who would play boatman for him. Once he brought back a basket of trout for the Harrises, unconscious of their conviction that fish were a mass of pins and cottonwool. It was Saundby's turn to shudder at dinner that night, when he found his beloved trout on the table as fishcakes.

The Deputy C-in-C's other passion was model railways. In a room above the mess at High Wycombe, he had an enormous layout on which he lavished all the attention that he could spare from nature and the bomber offensive. He was a genuine English eccentric, a placid, humorous, mild-mannered man who excelled at detail. He drove an old Rolls-Royce which he said he had bought as a lifetime investment, but never took shopping because it caused stores to overcharge him. He was almost old-maidishly careful about money, and the difficulty of catching him when it was time to buy a round of drinks was a standing joke in the mess at High Wycombe.

Saundby's crippling weakness was that he was totally in awe of Harris. A staff officer describes their relationship as that of headmaster and schoolboy.[7] It would never have occurred to Saundby to make a decision without consulting Harris, or to dispute policy with the C-in-C. Studying Bomber Command headquarters throughout the period of Harris's command, it is difficult to find evidence of any senior staff officer who took open issue with the C-in-C on a major policy matter. Harris was perfectly approachable on tactics and organization, but it would have been a brave man – and there were very few at High Wycombe – who touched the C-in-C on one of his exposed nerves. There was a chronic lack of open, critical debate. There were too many weak men and sycophants around the throne, and this situation must be attributed to Harris's choice and treatment of his subordinates. There was a fear of clear thinking if it led to unpalatable conclusions. If Harris had been able to call on more frankness from those close to him, some of Bomber Command's most serious misfortunes might have been avoided. Most important, perhaps, the Battle of Berlin might have been halted months before its eventual conclusion. 'Berlin had become a fixation with Bert, and we knew it,' said one of his staff officers thirty years later.[8] But it never occurred to himself or his colleagues to say as much to Harris at the beginning of 1944.

The routine at High Wycombe was a mirror-image of war on the stations: the day began as the crews went to bed, ended as they took off into the night. Each morning after breakfast Harris left Springfield in his black Bentley two-seater at 8.30, driven by the impeccable Maddocks, his chauffeur, with his distinctive patent-leather moustache. In his car Harris rushed everywhere, the way swept clear by the 'Cabinet Priority' badge on the bonnet, WAAFs and staff officers leaping for their lives as they saw the C-in-C's motor racing up the road of No. 1 Site. His office was situated at the corner of the solid redbrick two-storey building that housed Bomber Command's most senior officers, down the long ground-floor corridor. Lesser mortals were scattered over several acres of wartime huts. On Harris's arrival Peggy Wherry, his formidable WAAF secretary, brought him the most urgent signals and target folders. He retired to his morning ablutions to consider them, and there was often a hasty struggle to recall him when the Prime Minister came on the scrambler for details of the previous night's attack.

'I'm sick of these raids on Cologne,' growled Churchill testily one morning.

'So are the people of Cologne,' barked Harris.

If the C-in-C was not available, the call went through to some nervous staff officer in the Operations Room: 'How did the raid proceed last night?' inquired the most famous voice in England. 'Only 700 aircraft reached the target? Your C-in-C promised 800. And how many tons of bombs did you discharge?' The hesitant young man in the Ops Room might talk on for several minutes before realizing that the Prime Minister, having learnt what he wanted, had long since noiselessly hung up.[9]

At 9 am Harris left his office and was driven the few hundred yards across the base to the grass-covered mound that concealed the great underground bunker from which the bomber offensive was directed. The Operations Room, 'The Hole' as it was known, had been purpose-built for Bomber Command just before the outbreak of war. Here, at 'Morning Prayers' each day, Harris determined which city of Germany would suffer fire and high explosives that night. He took his seat at the desk in the midst of the big room, flanked by the great wall-maps of Europe and the target-priority list of dozens of cities and objectives, updated daily in accordance with the movement of the war, extensive enough to afford Harris enormous latitude. Around him stood Saundby, Magnus Spence the weather expert, the SASO, Deputy SASO, Group-Captain Operations, Group-Captain Intelligence, Navigation Officer, Captain de Mowbray of naval liaison, Colonel Carrington for the army, and a supporting cast of half a dozen wing-commanders and squadron leaders from Operations and Intelligence.

After a brief report on the previous night's operations, it was invariably Spence who commanded the attention of the meeting. He might report that a front was moving up western Germany around midnight. Harris would say: 'In that case it's obvious that Hamburg, Bremen or Wilhelmshaven are our best bet for tonight' – he pronounced German names in obstinate English, so that Wiesbaden became 'Wysbaden' – 'Can we get there in time without too early a start?' If Spence approved, there was a hasty shuffling of target folders and photographs among the staff, and the possibilities were handed forward to the C-in-C. Occasionally Saundby reminded Harris of an urgent Air Ministry or Ministry of Economic Warfare request, but there was no controversy at 'Morning Prayers'. The decisions were unequivocally those of the C-in-C. The weather was both a dominant reality and an all-embracing alibi. Whatever target lists had recently been passed down by the Combined Strategic Targets Committee, on which the Americans, the Ministry of Economic Warfare and Bomber Command were all represented – Harris could and did plead the weather as an excuse for pursuing his own intentions, although often enough it genuinely restricted his options. He seldom lingered more than a few moments over the target folders at conference before closing the issue: 'Right. We'll send 800 heavies to Hamburg. Now what about some "gardening"? What do you want "gardened", de Mowbray?' Harris could never resist teasing the naval officer, not unkindly. The moment the key decisions had been taken – targets and forces – Harris left the room and returned to his office.

It became Saundby's responsibility to organize the detailed planning of the operation. He had given every German city its piscine codename: Berlin was WHITEBAIT, Munich CATFISH, Nuremberg GRAYLING. Now he reached for the WEAVERFISH file on Hamburg. The key staff officers dispersed around the Operations Room to maps and telephones – most important, to talk to Bennett, commanding the Pathfinders, and to Cochrane, commanding 5 Group. The two men detested each other, and invariably contested any tactical suggestion offered by his rival. Bennett planned a route for his Mosquito 'Light Night Striking Force' to divert the defences. In telephone consultation with Saundby, he discussed the Main Force's course changes as they crossed Europe, aimed at concealing until the last possible moment the real objective of the attack. Addison's 100 Group was alerted to lay on its jammers and night-fighters. There might be weather problems in certain areas of England – perhaps 4 Group, in Yorkshire, was having difficulties clearing snow from its runways. On the wall, lights flickered like Christmas-tree illuminations on the great map that indicated the serviceability of Bomber Command's stations. Some squadrons might be ordered to carry extra fuel if they faced bad-weather landings on their return. Perhaps two hours after Harris left The Hole, Saundby had noted precise routes, bombloads, take-off times and aiming-points in his meticulous handwriting, ready to be typed-up for the C-in-C's final approval. Aiming-points were not infrequently changed late in the morning, as a concession to *Pointblank*. It looked better on paper to send the Pathfinders to mark an airframe plant or a tank factory, however meaningless such distinctions became over the target. Then each Group Commander addressing his own conference, mirroring Harris's 'Morning Prayers', and the High Wycombe staff dispersed to their offices under the beech trees, to fix details department by department.

For the handful of senior officers directly concerned with the planning of operations, High Wycombe was a fascinating posting at the very heart of the war. For those of less exalted rank, it was a staid, formal, claustrophobic place, darkened by the overhanging trees that dripped endlessly in the rain, corseted by the strictures of service bureaucracy. There were many elderly men like 'Daddy' Dawes, the Senior Personnel Staff Officer who controlled postings throughout Bomber Command, and relished every moment of his absolute power over so many men and women's service careers. The pace of work was hard, broken only by prolonged spells of bad weather that halted operations. There were none of the excitements and compensations of the operational stations. In their spare hours they walked across the fields to The Plough at Speen or hitch-hiked into London. Everybody who could, lived off the base. Young wing-commanders posted to High Wycombe from 'ops' yearned to escape. Their opinions and advice were seldom heeded amidst so much 'brass'.

Perhaps the most preposterously unsuitable appointment at High Wycombe throughout the war was that of the Chaplain, Rev. John Collins, in future years the arch-radical opponent of Britain's nuclear bomb, and even in wartime a permanent thorn in the side of authority.

> Bomber Command Headquarters [he wrote afterwards] was perhaps the most soul-destroying, the most depressing of the . . . places in which I had to serve. For there, in contrast with the natural beauty of the surroundings, the evil . . . policy of the carpet bombing of German cities was planned. . . . The majority of the personnel were simply clerks in uniform, for most of whom any interest or glamour in being attached to Bomber Command headquarters had long since gone; and those not of this category were mainly officers who had been taken off operational duties or deadbeats.[10]

It was Collins who invited the socialist Minister of Aircraft Production, Sir Stafford Cripps, to give a talk at High Wycombe on the unlikely theme 'Is God My Co-Pilot?', which enraged the C-in-C and his staff, because Cripps suggested that officers

> . . . should send men on a bombing mission only if, with a clear conscience, they were convinced that such a mission was morally justified as well as justified on grounds of military strategy and tactics. At question time, he was accused by one or two officers of saying things that, if heeded, might threaten discipline and hinder the war effort. . . . The chairman found an excuse to call the meeting to an abrupt end.[11]

Harris fought back by sending Harry Weldon to give a lecture on 'The Ethics of Bombing', at which according to Collins attendance by all ranks was compulsory. When it ended, Collins stood up and said that he presumed he had misunderstood Weldon's title, which should have been 'The Bombing of Ethics'. It is difficult to understand how Harris and his chaplain stood each other's company in the same camp for the remainder of the war.

On the squadrons the bomber offensive was conducted without any great emotion except that of fear. But the staff at High Wycombe sought constantly to instil in the aircrew a suitable enthusiasm for their work. The Intelligence Department issued Briefing Notes for groups and squadrons. This is a sample from September 1943:

> The history of MANNHEIM symbolizes on a small scale the evil history of Germany. The old town, decent and dignified, was

designed in the seventeenth and eighteenth centuries as a setting for a riverside castle – the largest in Germany – for one of the innumerable but reasonably inoffensive little German states. Today it is one of the most important industrial centres of Hitler's Reich, its atmosphere darkened with the smoke of engineering plants and polluted by enormous chemical works. Vital war industries which together employ one-third of the total population (430,000) of MANNHEIM and its satellite town LUDWIGSHAVEN. It is as though WINDSOR had sprouted a malignant growth of war factories, and one-and-a-half square miles of chemical works covered the playing-fields of ETON.[12]

The report goes on to assess the damage done by Bomber Command's latest attack, quoting a German broadcaster named Karl Rumpf:

> The egregious RUMPF . . . rounded off his tale of woe with a tragedy enacted in the NATIONAL THEATRE in the centre of the town. It appears that this institution opened its new season on the night preceding the attack. The first night doubtless had an enthusiastic reception, but the following night all too literally brought the house down.[13]

Reports such as this made little impact on aircrew, but perhaps did something for the enlightenment and enthusiasm of the vast army of ground staff supporting the offensive. Just as it was the ground-based men and women who wrote the poems eulogizing the deeds of the aircrew, so it was they who also took the keenest interest in the Germany that they never saw.

Target Intelligence was one of the most vital departments at High Wycombe, and because Intelligence proved to have been the cardinal weakness of Bomber Command's offensive against Germany, it is necessary to explain at some length precisely how High Wycombe assessed the success or failure of their attacks. Harris's staff share responsibility for the huge misconceptions surrounding the strategic offensive with the Air Ministry and the Ministry of Economic Warfare, which failed at the outset to grasp the complexities of the German economy; the Secret Service, which never appears to have controlled agents inside Germany capable of providing useful economic Intelligence; and the Foreign Office, which throughout the war believed that the morale of the German people was crumbling. MEW and the Air Ministry never understood how widely critical industries were scattered: only 48 per cent of plant was located in the fifty-eight towns attacked in strength by Bomber Command, and by 1943 Speer and Milch were working energetically towards still greater dispersal, and locating vital assembly-lines underground. Although Hamburg was the third city of the Greater Reich, it accounted for only 3.6 per cent of Germany's production.

By far the most effective damage-assessment organization Britain possessed was RE8, the research department of the Ministry of Home Security, which reached its conclusions by projecting the British experience of lost production, absenteeism, de-housing and wrecked services in 1940 on to Germany's cities. RE8 computed the number of German buildings lost or damaged beyond repair – 212,000 by the end of 1943 – with consistent accuracy. Its judgements on the probable injury to German production were also remarkably sound. The tragedy was that the airmen simply declined to believe them.

A typical Bomber Command Air Staff Intelligence report of February 1944, headed 'The Progress of the RAF bomber offensive against German Industry, 7 March 1943–31 December 1943' began with the following remarkable assertion: 'This paper is based on figures issued by RE8, but owing to difficulties in assessing certain factors, RE8 state that the calculated industrial loss is as much as 65 per cent underestimated.'[14]

In its six-monthly review of the achievements of the bomber offensive in mid-1943, the Ministry of Economic Warfare suggested that German production was 15 per cent down on the previous year, and in the Ruhr, 35 per cent down. By the end of 1943 it estimated that German output had fallen a further 10 per cent. As has been explained above,[15] MEW believed that this supposed loss represented a net absolute drain on war production, which was far from the truth. By mid-1944 its analysts argued that Axis war production was being destroyed faster than it could be replaced.

These figures were, of course, largely based on information provided by the Royal Air Force. Instead of grasping that aerial photographs overestimated damage – for instance by making buildings with collapsed rooves appear a total loss, while in fact the machinery beneath them could often be cleared of rubble and become operational again within days – High Wycombe argued that vertical air reconnaissance must conceal vast damage. The staff never made adequate allowance for the fact that the weight of area attacks was always directed against city centres, while industry lay in the suburbs.

It is important to remember that all but the most senior officers at High Wycombe were as much amateurs, civilians in uniform, as the men who flew the aircraft. An officer of the key Target Intelligence department INT I recalled later: 'We made up the damage-assessment techniques as we went along, because there was no precedent for what we were doing.' The fatal error by the scientists and statisticians was their determination to establish an absolute mathematical relationship between acres of urban devastation (of which they were accurately informed) and loss of production to the German war economy. Bomber Command built its great edifice of self-delusion about the plight of the German war machine on an astonishing foundation of graphs and projections. In 1943 the staff recorded that 'Efficiency' – as measured by 'acres of target devastated per ton of bombs claimed dropped' – had risen from 0.038 at the end of 1942 to 0.126 by October 1943. 'Success', measured by 'acres destroyed per acre attacked', had risen from 0.032 in 1942 to 0.249 in 1943. Reports are strewn with such headings as 'Average monthly increase in number of industrial workers attacked.' From February 1944, High Wycombe announced, 'The "Labour Target" now takes the place of the "Area Target", its dimensions being the number of industrial workers (which means exclusively factory workers) multiplied by the period of time which is being considered. . . .' Another Air Staff Intelligence report dated 19 February 1944 stated that in 1943

> . . . it will be seen that the enemy has *irretrievably lost** 1,000,000 man *years.** This represents no less than 36 per cent of the industrial effort that would have been put out by these towns if they had remained unmolested. . . . Expressing these losses in another way, 2,400,000,000 man-hours have been lost for an expenditure of 116,500 tons of bombs claimed dropped, and this amounts to an average return for every ton of bombs dropped of 20,500 lost man-hours, or rather more than one quarter of the time spent in building a Lancaster. . . . This being so, a Lancaster has only to go to a German city once to wipe off its own capital cost, and the results of all subsequent sorties will be clear profit. . . .[16]

Bomber Command Intelligence projected that by 1 April 1944, 33,760 acres – 40 per cent of 89,000 acres attacked – should have been destroyed, if average bomb tonnage remained static. But on the other hand, if the average monthly tonnage could be increased from 13,350 to 21,270, then 50 per cent of the 89,000 acres attacked could be destroyed. . . .

The samples above are typical of the acres of paper filled by the Intelligence Staffs throughout the bomber offensive, and they are a powerful indication of Bomber Command's diminishing grasp on the reality of the German economy in 1943–44. Seldom in the history of warfare have attempts been made to measure victory or defeat by such remarkable mathematical yardsticks as those conceived in the huts and bunkers under the beech trees at High Wycombe.

But long before RE8's much more modest estimates had been reached and submitted, before even High Wycombe's own projections

*emphasis in original text.

were compiled, Harris had been given an immediate provisional summary of results achieved, on the basis of reconnaissance photographs. Target Intelligence believed that the officer who presented this each day gave a persistently optimistic picture of what had been done. Harris seemed to make judgements from his own interpretation of the photographs on his desk. He frequently assessed a target destroyed which later proved to be merely damaged. Target Intelligence might suspect the truth, but its staff seem to have been unwilling forcefully to assert it. 'Has Eaker seen these?' Harris would say when some choice reconnaissance photographs of disroofed German urban areas appeared on his desk, and dispatch them for the American's delectation. Harris and his staff were guilty of the same error as those earlier generals in Flanders who were so awed by the magnificence of their own barrages that they found it inconceivable that the enemy could have survived them. Nor were these delusions confined to High Wycombe. On 2 February 1944, for instance, Air Vice-Marshal W. A. Coryton, Assistant Chief of Air Staff (Operations), wrote to Portal, commenting on a Ministry of Economic Warfare report:

> The contribution Bomber Command has made to the reduction of German Air Force production as given in paragraph 9 of the attached report is remarkably low. I suggest that we should not treat these figures as firm, since the calculations on which they are based must invariably include assumptions based on guesswork. It is inconceivable that Bomber Command, in their attacks on the major industrial centres of Germany, have not caused acute bottlenecks in the production of supply of many items of equipment, eg machine tools, of which we are not aware.

Throughout the war Harris himself was wedded to his headquarters. He seldom left his office, with its barograph on the window-sill monitoring the fickleness of the weather, its charts and graphs on the wall concealed by shutters from insecure visitors. He lunched at home, then returned to his desk. His masters seldom troubled him in the flesh. Portal never came to High Wycombe. Instead, Harris drove once a week at his usual headlong pace to the Air Ministry for a conference, not infrequently involving the latest round of his feud with Bufton and the Directorate of Bomber Operations. 'Another paper from DB Ops?' Saundby would inquire schoolboyishly, lifting Bufton's file from the desk at arm's length. 'Tweezers. Pause for nausea.' Once a month the Group commanders assembled at High Wycombe, their meetings often punctuated by angry exchanges between Bennett and Cochrane. On very rare occasions, such as that recorded at the nadir of 76 Squadron's fortunes, Harris visited a bomber station. But the vast majority of his crews never saw him. It was not a matter of conviction that he toured stations so little: it was merely that when Bomber Command was laying on a raid almost every night, there was no one at High Wycombe to whom he cared to delegate the vital decisions if he went elsewhere.

The Royal Navy's most grievous grudge against Harris was that he appeared to possess privileged access to the Prime Minister. Chequers, Churchill's official country residence, was only a few miles from High Wycombe. Perhaps once in six weeks on a weekend evening, one of the Prime Minister's staff telephoned to invite Harris to dine. But Harris asserts[17] that it was unusual for him to be closeted *tête-à-tête* with Churchill, and there is no reason to doubt this. There was usually a large dinner table and general conversation. Later the party adjourned to the house cinema to watch one of the Prime Minister's favourite films. Churchill called his C-in-C 'Bert', or 'Harris', or more ebulliently 'Bomber', according to his mood. The two men might have five or at most ten minutes' private conversation. Churchill asked how the campaign was going, and what was planned for the future. Harris certainly used these opportunities to deplore his own shortage of resources and the difficulties of meeting the claims of rival services. But Churchill never gave direct orders to Bomber Command. While Harris frequently expressed his own views on paper to Downing Street, Churchill almost invariably replied, with punctilious protocol, through Portal. Harris was sometimes irked by Churchill's impatience with his expositions: 'I wouldn't have called Winston a good listener.'[18]

The visits to Chequers gave vent to one of Harris's few private enthusiasms: driving horses. One day Churchill deplored the internal-combustion engine as the curse of the modern age. 'I entirely agree, Prime Minister,' said Harris, 'and what's more I think I'm the only man here who lives up to his principles.' He had driven himself over to lunch in a pony-trap.

But for all the courtesies between them, their respect for each other as dedicated warriors, there is no evidence of real personal warmth between Churchill and Harris, or that their meetings had any influence on the priority accorded to the bomber offensive. Harris, with his horror of 'panaceas' and his passion for the concentration of force, despaired of the Prime Minister's 'Parergonitis', as he called it, 'the search for soft underbellies' that had filled Churchill with enthusiasm for Gallipoli and North Africa. Harris would never forgive Churchill for his mute disavowal of the strategic offensive at the end of the war, when he declined to authorize a Bomber Command campaign medal.

Churchill, for his part, probably found Harris a convenient tool rather than a convivial companion. He always liked the sense of immediacy that he gained from meeting his C-in-Cs in the field. In most cases they were too far afield to be readily available, but Harris was on hand. Contrary to much that has been written in the past, there is no reason to suppose that the course of the bomber offensive would have been any different if the two men had never met. Churchill invited Harris to dine because he was a keen supporter of bombing for many reasons of his own. He did not become a supporter of bombing because the C-in-C had his ear. There is no evidence that he was impressed by Harris's extravagant promises. By the spring of 1944 his enthusiasm for bombing was already waning. Harris continued to enjoy the memory of the Prime Minister's support and protection perhaps more in the minds of others than in reality. If Portal had chosen to put the matter to the test by sacking the C-in-C of Bomber Command at any time from the spring of 1944 onwards, he might have been surprised how passively Churchill acquiesced.

Harris's working day at High Wycombe ended at the same time as that of any businessman, around 6 pm. Maddocks and the Bentley took him home to Springfield. Often there were guests to entertain, Americans or Russians to be invited to sit themselves at the stereopticon through which Harris gazed for so many hours on images of the ruined cities of Germany. Some evenings, the Harrises visited their close friends the Maurice Johns, a gynaecologist and his wife who lived next door to Springfield, with whom they could find some kind of release from the war. If they were at home and there were no guests, they dined with Saundby, Weldon and Maze, and in Harris's words, 'talked bombing until bedtime'.[19] Throughout the night the telephone by his bedside rang intermittently with reports of the night's operations. Harris had the fortunate ability to wake, listen, and instantly fall asleep again. It is one of the ironies of the bomber offensive that while the aircrew fought through the darkness over Germany, while the sleepless cities stood to their guns and searchlights and burst forth in their nightly torment of fire and blast, the Commander-in-Chief of Bomber Command lay dreamless in his bed among the Buckinghamshire woods.

XI

Conflict and Compromise, 1943–44

1. The Battle of Berlin

> 'It is my firm belief', Sir Arthur Harris wrote to Portal on 12 August 1943, 'that we are on the verge of a final showdown in the bombing war, and that the next few months will be vital. Opportunities do not knock repeatedly and continuously. I am certain that given average weather and concentration on the main job, we can push Germany over by bombing this year . . .'

It was the immoderation of Harris's expectations in the autumn of 1943 that provoked the scale of the subsequent disillusionment. If his promises had been less ambitious, his failure to fulfil them might have been forgotten. But until almost the last weeks before the invasion of Europe in June 1944, he continued to argue that Germany could be defeated by bombing alone. In the personal minute to Churchill of 3 November 1943 in which he listed the nineteen cities allegedly totally destroyed by Bomber Command, he went on to make the statement that would haunt his career to the last: 'We can wreck Berlin from end to end if the USAAF will come in on it. It will cost between 400–500 aircraft. It will cost Germany the war.'

This assertion, more than any other that he made throughout the war, surrendered Harris's reputation to his critics. It cast very serious doubts upon his judgement. Berlin was not to be wrecked 'from end to end' in the winter of 1943, and calm analysis of the tactical and industrial realities should have exploded this fantasy at birth. It is anyway a mystery why Harris supposed that the destruction of Berlin would have caused the collapse of German resistance. By proclaiming his intention to launch the full weight of Bomber Command's resources against the enemy's capital, Harris also flaunted his defiance of the *Pointblank* directive. Attacking Berlin had only the most distant relevance to the defeat of the German air force in production, which was supposed to be the first duty of the Allied air offensive. It was absurd to imagine that the Americans were likely to join an attack that would entail renouncing *Pointblank*, which they had largely created. There is some evidence that the extent of the 8th Air Force's sense of defeat in the wake of Schweinfurt a fortnight earlier was still unknown to the British, and it was only to later historians that it became clear that the winter of 1943 was the critical low-water mark of the USAAF's fortunes in Europe. But Harris knew the scale of the Americans' losses. It is remarkable that he imagined they were in the mood to embark on new deep-penetration operations against the most heavily defended city in Europe.

It says much for the respect Harris had built up for his own personality and achievements that the Prime Minister and the Air Staff did not at once lose confidence in a man capable of making such extravagant claims. On 5 November 1943, Air Vice-Marshal F. F. Inglis, Assistant Chief of Air Staff (Intelligence), wrote to Portal commenting on Harris's letter to Churchill. It is interesting to see the C-in-C's ideas interpreted by an unflinching admirer:

> We are convinced that Bomber Command's attacks are doing more towards shortening the war than any other offensive including the Russians' [began Inglis modestly]. The C-in-C's letter is the letter of a man with ONE AIM, the rightness of which is his obsession. It is necessary to take this obsession into account because, inevitably, it leads him to make statements which can be criticized even by those who are in sympathy with his plea for more help to finish the job. Its purpose is, apparently, twofold:
>
> (1) To get the Prime Minister's support to speed up USAAF concentration in the United Kingdom even at the expense of forgoing the strategic offensive from Italy.
>
> (2) To get the Prime Minister to persuade General Eaker to bomb Berlin.
>
> Our plan first to break the German air force defence and then to get on with the war does not appeal to a man who knows that it can be won by immediate offensive action long before our defensive plan has come near to completion. This is why the importance of industries in the Balkans and southern Germany does not appeal to him. Although he speaks of nine-tenths of German industry being nearer Norfolk than Lombardy, we are sure he really means that nine-tenths of the German population is nearer Norfolk, and in the light of our new morale paper which is about to be published, it is the population which is the joint in the German armour. The C-in-C's spear is in it, but it needs a jolt to drive it home to the heart. Apparently, only the Americans can provide this additional thrust, and we believe he is right to ask for it.

Harris failed to persuade Portal or the Prime Minister to press the Americans to join Bomber Command's assault on Berlin. He has since said that he would never have embarked on the Battle had he known that 8th Air Force would not take part. But it is impossible to believe that this was ever likely, or would have changed the outcome. The winter weather would have made daylight blind-bombing as indecisive as night blind-bombing, and the heavy losses the Fortresses suffered when they finally attacked Berlin with powerful fighter escort in March 1944 suggest that their casualties would have been appalling if they had begun to do so four months earlier, before the Mustang long-range escort became available in quantity.

But it would be unjust to Harris to suggest that he could have begun his assault on 18 November 1943 without the support, indeed the active encouragement, of the Prime Minister and the Chief of Air Staff. Since August 1943, Portal had been asking when a major attack on Berlin could take place. If Harris flagrantly ignored *Pointblank* to pursue his own concept of air warfare, where was Portal, his superior, the man specifically charged by the Combined Chiefs of Staff with responsibility for *Pointblank* on their behalf? Throughout the autumn American concern about lack of progress with the destruction of the German aircraft industry had been mounting. May 1944, the provisional date for the invasion, was drawing inexorably closer. As its own losses and difficulties grew, the USAAF pressed harder for the full participation of Bomber Command in attacks on the aircraft factories. On 19 October 1943, Bufton, the Director of Bomber Operations, wrote to Portal:

> Although General Eaker and the C-in-C Bomber Command had many reasons for not adhering more rigidly to the high priority German Air Force objectives in the Directive, I believe a greater concentration upon them to be possible if political pressure is brushed aside and the Commanders set their minds to the task.

A few days later Portal answered a letter from Arnold in Washington, who had been expressing his concern about the lack of concentration on *Pointblank*:

> I would say at the outset that I agree with you that there have been diversions from priority objectives as laid down by the Chiefs of Staff. I had already become apprehensive about this dispersal of our effort. Last week I had a useful meeting with Eaker and Harris and stressed to them the urgency of concentrating the maximum effort on to the defeat of the German air force.

At first, it is difficult to reconcile this letter of Portal with Harris's opening of the Battle of Berlin less than a month later. The Air Staff had repeatedly reasserted its commitment to *Pointblank*, in the directives to Bomber Command of 10 June and 3 September 1943, signed by the Deputy Chief of Air Staff, Bottomley, who increasingly shared Bufton's misgivings about Harris. Portal was not so machiavellian as wantonly to deceive Arnold about Bomber Command's intentions. How therefore did Harris defy him?

There are two answers. First, while history now sees the Battle of Berlin from November 1943 to March 1944 as a single entity – Harris's last undiluted effort to win the war by area bombing – at no time in these months did the Air Staff see the Battle in this light. A continuous struggle was being waged to induce Harris to conform to the objectives of *Pointblank*, although nowhere was it suggested that Harris could not devote part of his available effort to attacks on the German capital. There was never a conscious surrender by the Air Ministry to Harris's point of view. He staved off his opponents on a week-by-week basis: with explanations of weather and tactical difficulties, fierce argument about policy, and undisguised prevarication. Meanwhile, each night he launched his aircraft against his chosen targets. He fought with such success that it was not until the end of February 1944 that Bomber Command at last staged five operations specifically directed against elements of the German aircraft industry. But throughout the winter the Air Staff had been waiting in almost daily expectation of Harris's acquiescence to his orders.

The second critical figure in the struggle was the Prime Minister. Since Casablanca, he had displayed little interest in *Pointblank*. Bomber Command no longer occupied the prominent place in his mind that it possessed in 1940 and 1941. But he was still greatly attracted by bringing fire and the sword upon Germany's cities, and he was delighted by Harris's triumph at Hamburg. Throughout the war, Churchill pressed for more and greater attacks on Berlin. On several occasions Harris sensibly cooled his master's impatience. Now the airman promised to raze the Nazi capital. Churchill may not have shared his C-in-C's expectations about knocking Germany out of the war, but he was attracted by the vision of Berlin engulfed by a second firestorm. To a man who had not studied the difficulties closely, it seemed perfectly possible for Bomber Command, with its ever-increasing force of heavy aircraft and extraordinary new range of tactics and technology, to inflict a catastrophe on Berlin to match 'Operation Gomorrah'. By any measure, this would be a great victory, and a savage blow to the Nazi regime. Portal was increasingly dismayed by Harris's obduracy, but it was already apparent that the only way to defeat the wilfulness of Bomber Command's C-in-C was to sack him. Churchill would never have endorsed such an action in the winter of 1943. Portal knew this and Harris knew this. On 18 November, Bomber Command embarked on the Battle of Berlin.

Like the earlier 'battles' of 1943, this was not to be merely an assault on a single city, but a convenient title for a sustained struggle embracing targets all over Germany. Between the first attack on Berlin on 18 November and the end of the series at Nuremberg on 30 March 1944, Bomber Command mounted 9,111 sorties against the German capital in sixteen major attacks, and 11,113 sorties against other cities, notably

Mannheim, Stuttgart, Frankfurt, Nuremberg, Leipzig, Brunswick and Schweinfurt. Bomber Command lost 1,047 aircraft missing – 5.1 per cent of sorties dispatched – and a further 1,682 damaged or written off. After the second operation, it became apparent that it was intolerable to dispatch the wretched Stirlings against the devastating German defences, and they were removed from the attack on Berlin, as were most of the Halifaxes a few weeks later. The Stirlings were shortly afterwards withdrawn from all operations against Germany. The Battle of Berlin was fought overwhelmingly by Lancasters, with support from the Mosquitoes, which flew 2,034 sorties for the loss of only ten aircraft, an astonishing tribute to the light bomber's invulnerability.

For the crews of the Lancasters, the Battle of Berlin was a nightmare. Northern Germany seldom enjoyed clear weather in mid-winter, and that year conditions were exceptionally bad. Night after night, Bomber Command took off through the rain, sometimes through the snow, into the upper atmosphere's freak winds and sudden icing conditions, loaded to the aircraft's limits with bombs and fuel for the 1,150-mile round trip. Very early in the Battle, Pathfinders began to report seeing crews dumping their 4,000-lb 'cookies' in the North Sea to gain height and speed.

> By grossly underestimating the Germans' resilience [wrote a Pathfinder navigator] Command had given the impression that the war was almost over. Tactically, because of the longer nights, this was the only feasible time of the year for making regular deep penetrations. Psychologically and physically it was the worst. Long hours at sub-zero temperatures dulled the brain, reflexes were slowed and mistakes were made. Frostbite was common even among pilots and navigators; with the cabin that cold, conditions elsewhere in the aircraft had to be experienced to be believed . . . . If there was one time in an operational tour when the crew felt they needed the best the aircraft could offer, it was on a sortie to Berlin. Crews could get neither height nor performance with the new all-up weight, and although performance was improved by getting rid of bombs either over the North Sea or Germany, psychologically the damage was already done. Pilots had lost confidence in their aircraft, and crews who elsewhere would not have hesitated to go over the centre of the town became 'fringe merchants'.[1]

Command ordered the rewiring of bomb-release circuits so that the photoflash exploded automatically when a pilot released his 'cookie', to put an end to dumping. The heavily-laden bombers were now meeting the German night-fighter force at the summit of its wartime effectiveness and strength. An enormous effort was mounted to thwart it. 100 Group's Intruder Mosquitoes sought out the night-fighters around their airfields, while *Serrate* Mosquitoes stalked the skies equipped with radar that homed on the German *Lichtenstein* transmissions. German-speaking men and women broadcast false orders to the fighters by the *Corona* technique, attacked their radio-telephone communications with *Cigar* jamming, interrupted the controllers with *Tinsel* transmissions. Halifaxes and Stirlings flew diversionary mining operations off the coast while OTUs and HCUs sent their aircraft to make *Bullseye* training flights over the North Sea to divert German early-warning systems. Airborne and ground-based *Mandrel* jammers sought to fog enemy radar frequencies, Bennett's Mosquito Light Night Striking Force flew spoof raids, dropping fake fighter-flares and route-markers, *Window*ing their way to a city upon which they dropped Target Indicators and 4,000-lb 'cookies' to drive the population to their shelters and simulate the opening of a Main Force attack. All these techniques contributed something sometimes to diverting the defences, but none of them was sufficiently successful consistently to protect the bombers. Again and again the fighters broke into the stream and inflicted punishing casualties. Berlin, above all, was a very difficult target to conceal. For the last hundred miles of the route, it was clear that Bomber Command could be going nowhere else. The sky was lit by exploding aircraft as frozen gunners, numbed in their turrets, missed the shadow slipping below the fuselage that a few seconds later consigned them to oblivion.

But that winter, it was over the target itself that the bombers' difficulties became intolerable. Again and again, they fought their way to Berlin to find the city sheathed in impenetrable cloud. It was far beyond *Oboe* range. Unlike Hamburg, it represented no clearly defined H2S image. The difficulties of marking were enormous. The Germans had created huge, effective decoy fires. In the first attacks, the parachute sky-markers – cascading pyrotechnic candles – disappeared into the overcast within seconds. Later in the Battle, 8 Group evolved their 'Berlin Method', sustaining a barrage of both ground- and sky-markers throughout the twenty-five minutes or less of the attack. Crews were instructed to bomb on the ground-markers where they could see them, on the sky-markers where they could not. In the first six major attacks on Berlin that winter only 400 of 2,650 aircraft dispatched reported sighting the ground-markers. The remainder bombed the sky-markers – or sometimes no markers at all – and came home without glimpsing the target. More serious even than the crews' inability to see what they were attacking by night was Photographic Reconnaissance's inability to pierce the overcast by day to discover what they had or had not achieved. From November 1943 to March 1944, of thirty-seven PRU sorties to Berlin, only two were successful.

Yet throughout the battle, Bomber Command HQ continued to circulate to groups and stations the most melodramatic reports of the damage achieved in Berlin. On 29 December 1943, Air Staff Intelligence, at High Wycombe distributed a progress report which asserted that a minimum of 320,000 Berliners had been de-housed,

> . . . and the word 'minimum' cannot be repeated too often in connection with any estimates based on the present photographic cover. . . . Estimates of 500,000 to 800,000 are quite likely to be nearer the truth than the calculations made above. . . . The following paragraphs describe the damage (in central Berlin only) as a London newspaper might have described it if the Luftwaffe had succeeded in inflicting corresponding damage in the central London area:
>
> Government buildings in Whitehall have suffered severely. The Treasury is largely destroyed and the Foreign Office partially gutted. Scotland Yard is a soot-blackened ruin and so is the Ministry of Transport. The Cabinet Offices at No. 10 Downing Street are roofless, and fire has destroyed half of No. 11. Many other well-known landmarks in central London have disappeared. The British Museum Library and University buildings have been damaged. The Albert Hall and Drury Lane Theatre are smouldering wrecks. Big office blocks like Shell-Mex House and Bush House have been burnt out. The Ritz Hotel is no more, and fire has damaged part of the Savoy. The Café Royal is gutted from roof to basement. . . . Railway stations everywhere are besieged by crowds of evacuees, but many of them are so badly damaged that few trains, or none at all, are able to leave. . . . It is difficult indeed to imagine devastation on such a scale in a modern capital.[2]

High Wycombe's Intelligence Section waxed lyrical for six pages on the situation in Berlin. When Bomber Command began its great assault, it was justified on the grounds that the city contained some critical elements of the German war effort: one-tenth of all aero-engines and precision instruments, one-third of the electrical engineering output, a quarter of all tanks and half of all field artillery were built in Berlin. But the metropolitan area extended over 883 square miles. It was an impossible undertaking effectively to saturate this with bombs in winter weather amidst the most formidable defences in Europe. Ministries and other public buildings were indeed razed to the ground. The Allkett tank plants were damaged. The Siemens electrical works were hit. The leaders of Germany including Speer and Milch were initially appalled by what Bomber Command was doing and threatened to do. But Berlin's industries continued to produce war material in scarcely diminished quantities, while the wreckage of a thousand British bombers littered the north German countryside. Harris set out to achieve a second Hamburg. He came nowhere near this. Goebbels wrote on 28 November:

> The British are greatly overestimating the damage done to Berlin. Naturally it is terrible, but there is no question of 25 per cent of the capital no longer existing. The English naturally want to furnish their public with a propaganda morsel. I have every reason to want them to believe this and therefore forbid any denial. The sooner London is convinced that there is nothing left of Berlin, the sooner they will stop their air offensive against the Reich capital.[3]

Since 1943 there has been acid controversy among airmen about the Pathfinders' alleged failure to mark their targets satisfactorily that winter. In reality, 8 Group did all that could be expected of themselves and their equipment. Their crews were often little better qualified or more experienced than those of Main Force, and were almost as prone to the problem of 'Creep-back', for all Bennett's harsh comments about Main Force letting down his men by 'baulking the jump' and bombing short. Looking back on the battle a year later, Bennett claimed that Bomber Command's crews failed to destroy Berlin because they did not press home their attacks: 'There can be no doubt that a very large number of crews failed to carry out their attacks in their customary determined manner,' he wrote to Harris. The Pathfinders' AOC claimed that 50 per cent of Main Force never even troubled to use their bombsights.

It is certainly true that crews' determination suffered in the winter of 1943–44. Cochrane considered this the only moment of the bomber offensive at which morale was slipping dangerously: 'One of my squadrons had cracked and another was cracking until I took firm action.'[4] But flagging morale was not responsible for Bomber Command's failure to destroy Berlin. The truth was that the city was too sprawling to lend itself to a second 'Operation Gomorrah'; too deep in Germany to achieve the same sort of concentrated attack against heavy opposition; and too difficult to hit accurately by H2S. H2S was never an adequate tool for blind bombing, and throughout the war Bomber Command failed to achieve satisfactory results by bombing sky-markers, the 'Wanganui' technique, as Bennett had codenamed it. Even if markers were satisfactorily placed on release, in a high wind they could be miles off-target within seconds. It is unreasonable to claim that the Pathfinders were responsible for Main Force's failure, just as it was wrong for the Pathfinders to blame Main Force. The operation was simply beyond Bomber Command's capabilities.

Harris and his staff should have recognized this, but they did not. As late as 7 December 1943, when the difficulties of the task had become abundantly clear, Harris declared that by 1 April 1944 he could bring about the collapse of Germany if he was able to launch 15,000 Lancaster sorties against her vital cities. If it is necessary to acquit the C-in-C of Bomber Command of personal ambition, surely this extraordinary statement must do so. No man with the slightest instinct for professional self-preservation would have committed himself so recklessly to a specific date by which he would personally have won the war.

Harris almost got his 15,000 Lancaster sorties from the Battle of Berlin – 14,562, to be exact – but not without a bitter struggle that intensified through the winter months. Portal's concern and the pressure from the Americans was growing. There was no evidence of a collapse of the German defences, no slackening of losses, no holocaust engulfing Berlin. Yet still Harris resisted every proposal to shift the weight of his attack to those cities in which the aircraft industry was concentrated:

> It is naturally impossible to state with arithmetical precision the acreage of German built-up area which must be destroyed to produce capitulation [he wrote to the Air Ministry on 28 December 1943]. However . . . it is surely impossible to believe that an increase by more than one half of existing devastation within four months could be sustained by Germany without total collapse.

In the Air Ministry directives of 14 and 28 January and 17 February 1944, Air Marshal Bottomley yet again forcefully urged the C-in-C of Bomber Command to address himself to the aircraft industry:

> It is confirmed and emphasized that the closest co-ordination is essential to the successful prosecution of the Combined Bomber Offensive [Bottomley wrote on 14 January] and that without it, the reduction of the German fighter strength which is a prerequisite to the launching of *Overlord* as well as to the effective conduct of *Pointblank* may not be achieved in the time available. I am accordingly to request that you adhere to the spirit of the directive forwarded in the Air Ministry letter dated 10 June 1943, and that you attack, as far as practicable, those industrial centres associated with the German fighter air-frame and ball-bearing industry.

Harris's resolute refusal to attack the German ball-bearing factories at Schweinfurt had become the central *casus belli* of his escalating struggle with the Air Ministry. 'So far Bomber Command has done far more than was planned or could have been expected to give effect to *Pointblank*, he wrote. 'I cannot continue this process and in addition carry out the part of the programme specifically allocated to the Americans.'

Bufton, the Director of Bomber Operations, was now foremost among those who believed that whatever tactical difficulties they were experiencing, the Americans' concept of strategic bombing by precision attack on key industrial targets was far more promising than

Bomber Command's area offensive. He was exasperated by Harris's repeatedly successful defiance of Air Ministry instructions:

> The C-in-C states that there can be little doubt that the enemy would be caused to capitulate by the destruction of between 40 and 50 per cent of the principal German towns, and that the Lancaster force alone should be sufficient, but only just sufficient, to produce in Germany by 1 April 1944 a state of devastation in which surrender is inevitable [he wrote to Portal, early in January]. I am of the opinion that it would be sounder for Bomber Command to subordinate as far as may be necessary their efforts to achieve a quick victory in favour of helping the Americans to deploy their strength so that the Combined Bomber forces (and *Overlord*) may together achieve a certain victory.

One January morning at the Air Ministry, as Bufton waited to see the Chief of Air Staff, Portal's Personal Staff Officer, Bill Dry, emerged from the office and murmured to Bufton: 'They're all gunning for Bert Harris.' The Americans, the Ministry of Economic Warfare and key departments of the Air Ministry were growing exasperated by the C-in-C of Bomber Command. The baldness of Harris's refusals to change policy added insult to insubordination. 'What do you think about the C-in-C then, Bufton?' Portal asked the Director of Bomber Operations that morning in King Charles Street. 'Do you think it might be good to have a change?' Bufton recalls that he told Portal he was opposed to sacking Harris, which is remarkable. But the C-in-C of Bomber Command had achieved enormous prestige in the years of Hamburg and Cologne. To remove him now would be a great shock to public and service opinion. Nor was it yet apparent how far he was willing to go in defiance of orders. Harris was not sacked. Towards the end of February he grudgingly diverted his forces to carry out a series of moderately successful attacks in support of the American 'Big Week' onslaught on the German aircraft industry. But the overwhelming weight of Bomber Command's effort continued to be directed towards the area offensive.

If Portal and his colleagues had been confident of an alternative policy for Bomber Command, it is likely that Harris would have been sacked in January 1944. In the Air Ministry hostility to his behaviour was hardening. But how much visible success was an attack on the German aircraft industry under a new C-in-C likely to achieve, to compensate for the seismic shock of Harris's dismissal? What were the prospects of a definable, decisive success against key selected German industrial targets, as an alternative to Harris's assault on German cities? The Air Staff wavered on these questions. They knew that they now doubted the efficacy of area bombing, but they did not know what they should substitute for it. It was their indecision that saved Harris, the one man unswervingly certain of his objectives and intentions. It required iron resolution to dismiss him, and Portal was not the man for confrontation if it could be avoided. Harris continued his battle.

It was only because Bomber Command was now receiving plentiful supplies of aircraft and crews that he could sustain his terrible losses into the New Year and the spring. Harris's average daily availability of aircraft, almost all 'heavies', rose from 948 in November 1943 to 1,043 in March 1944. It is important to remember that losses had to fall below 4 per cent for a crew to have a favourable chance of completing a tour of operations. In January 1944, Harris was losing 6.1 per cent of aircraft dispatched to Berlin, 7.2 per cent of those which went to Stettin, Brunswick and Magdeburg. On one operation against Leipzig in February he lost seventy-eight aircraft missing, 9.5 per cent of those dispatched. On 24 March he lost seventy-two aircraft – 9.1 per cent of those dispatched – against Berlin on a night of unpredicted fierce winds that blew much of the stream over the most heavily defended flak belts in Germany. It was not an unbroken slaughter: sometimes the diversions and 'spoofs' succeeded, the night-fighters failed to engage. On the night of 26 March, 705 aircraft went to Essen and only nine were lost. On the night of 1 March, 557 went to Stuttgart and only four were lost. But on 30 March 1944, Bomber Command suffered its worst single disaster of the war, when ninety-six of the 795 aircraft dispatched to Nuremberg – 11.8 per cent failed to return. Twelve more aircraft were fatally damaged.

The Nuremberg raid is one of Harris's most bitter memories, not for itself but for what posterity has made of it. The official historians, among others, have declared that it signalled the collapse of Harris's personal attempt to defeat Germany by razing her cities to ashes. Harris remarks[5] that it is surprising that his forces did not suffer a score of Nurembergs. This was not a unique disaster, but a night on which an unhappy coincidence of clear skies to guide the fighters, and bad tactical planning that gave the German controllers an uncommonly easy task, led to losses that were statistically a little worse than those at Leipzig and Berlin in previous weeks. The Nuremberg casualties were in themselves acceptable in the context of Bomber Command's overall loss rate and the supply of replacement aircraft and crews.

But time had run out on Harris. He had commanded the centre of the stage for more than two years. Now other war machines were waiting impatiently in the wings: armies and fleets were gathering themselves for the invasion that dominated the minds of the leaders of the Grand Alliance. The generals and admirals had never cared for the 'bomber barons' and their all-consuming proposals. Now, at last, bombing operations were to be formally subordinated to the Supreme Allied Commanders to support the invasion. From 14 April 1944, Harris and Eaker would take their orders from Eisenhower.

Bomber Command conducted further spasmodic operations against Germany through the late spring and summer of 1944, and amid these Harris could comfort himself with the delusion that if the invasion had not overtaken him, his attack on Germany could have continued. Indeed it is probably true that it would have done, for a few more weeks. But at the Air Ministry's morning conferences, reports of Bomber Command's overnight casualties were greeted with growing dismay. In the year since Harris began his 'battles', Bomber Command had lost 4,160 aircraft missing and crashed in England. His failure to bring Germany to her knees, and the cost of his failure, had become embarrassingly evident to every man but himself. And in a letter to the Air Ministry on 7 April 1944, he came as close as ever in his life to conceding that he was in deep trouble.

> The strength of the German defences [he wrote] would in time reach a point at which night-bombing attacks by existing methods and types of heavy bomber would involve percentage casualty rates which could not in the long run be sustained. . . . We have not yet reached that point, but tactical innovations which have so far postponed it are now practically exhausted. . . .

This was the preamble to a demand for ten squadrons of night-fighters, to support his bombers. It was the final admission of defeat for the Trenchard doctrine. First Bomber Command, then the Luftwaffe, then 8th Air Force had proved that daylight air bombardment was intolerably costly unless air superiority had first been attained. Now Bomber Command had discovered that even night operations against Germany could no longer be continued on their existing basis unless the enemy's night-fighter force could be neutralised. The tactical possibilities of the single concentrated bomber stream protected by *Window* were exhausted. Bomber Command was in a dilemma: to achieve decisive destruction it was necessary to attack a target repeatedly. Yet to do so was tactical suicide. Only once, at Hamburg, did the debut of *Window* provide the momentary tactical advantage to make possible a succession of saturation bombardments.

To the end of his life, Harris continued to argue that, had he been given the resources he sought, and been permitted to continue his assault on Germany into the summer of 1944, the war could have been ended months sooner. But many of his fellow airmen disagreed with him. 'He was a gambler doubling up on each losing throw,' said Bufton, looking back on the Battle of Berlin.[6] 'In the operational sense, the Battle of Berlin was more than a failure. It was a defeat,' wrote Webster and Frankland.[7] 'Berlin won,' said Sir Ralph Cochrane,[8] AOC of 5 Group. 'It was just too tough a nut.'

The compulsory transfer of Bomber Command to tactical operations in support of the invasion, which Harris resisted so bitterly, saved him from confronting the reality of his own defeat. He had inflicted a series of catastrophes upon the enemy. But he had failed to achieve the decisive, war-winning thrust that lay at the heart of all his Trenchardian hopes.

2. *The American Breakthrough*

On the day of the second disastrous American Schweinfurt operation, 16 October 1943, Arnold in Washington cabled to Eaker that the Luftwaffe appeared to be on the verge of collapse. Even in the wake of Schweinfurt, Eaker claimed ungrammatically that the Luftwaffe's victory had been 'the last final struggle of a monster in his death throes'. But in reality, the Americans had suffered an overwhelming and traumatic defeat. They had lost 148 aircraft in four operations. In the face of the Luftwaffe's massed fighter assaults with cannon, rockets and bombs against their formations, the Fortresses and Liberators were taking intolerable punishment. Morale sagged in a manner unknown to Bomber Command at any period of the war. Attempts to revive aircrew spirit with periods of 'Rest and Recuperation' at Miami Beach, Atlantic City and Santa Monica were scrapped when these were found to increase men's reluctance to return to operations. The practice of force-landing damaged aircraft in neutral territory became sufficiently common to cause serious controversy – by the summer of 1944 there were 94 8th Air Force crews interned in Sweden and 101 in Switzerland.

The Norden bombsight was useless in the persistent overcast of the European winter. While Harris fought the Battle of Berlin by night, the 8th Air Force, and the newly-formed 15th Air Force operating under Spaatz's direction from Italy, were reduced to limited penetration blind-bombing missions by H2X, the American adaptation of H2S. In reality if not in theory, the Americans spent much of the winter of 1943–44 engaged in area-bombing operations. In the words of the American official historians: 'It seemed better to bomb low-priority targets frequently, even with less than precision accuracy, than not to bomb at all.'[9]

But with their limitless resources and unshakeable determination to succeed, the Americans persisted. The main handicap of their operations in the summer and autumn of 1943 had been that their fighter escort of Thunderbolts and Lightnings lacked the performance to meet the Luftwaffe on equal terms, and were compelled by lack of range to turn home at the German frontier. The Germans were thus able to choose their own time and place to fall on the bombers. But in the wake of Schweinfurt, Arnold directed that the 8th and 15th Air Forces should be given absolute priority for supplies of the remarkable new P-51B Mustang long-range fighter. The Mustang had originally been ordered from its American makers by the RAF in 1940. When it was delivered in 1942, they were disappointed by its lack of power. Rolls-Royce tried an experiment, replacing its Allison engine with one of their own Merlins. After various disappointments and modifications, they found themselves testing an aircraft that most airmen and designers had thought impossible, with the reach to fly deep into Germany equipped with disposable long-range drop-tanks, and with a speed of 455 mph at 30,000 feet that enabled the Mustang to match or out-perform every German fighter when it got there.

The Americans now began to take a keen interest in this extraordinary hybrid. The Packard company started building Merlin engines under licence, and a massive programme was undertaken to provide the USAAF with Mustangs. Progress towards a satisfactory drop-tank was hesitant, and it was not until the spring of 1944 that the Mustang element of 8th Air Force became formidable. But when it did so, the means at last existed to fight the Luftwaffe on highly favourable terms. As the tide of American aircraft production became a flood, with astonishing speed, huge Mustang escorts drove the German air force from its own skies. Whatever Speer was doing to increase German fighter-production in the factories, he could do nothing to halt the attrition of trained aircrew in the air battles. The Luftwaffe continued to offer resistance to the end, and on occasions inflicted heavy loss on the Fortresses. But within four months of Schweinfurt, the Americans had overturned the balance of war in the air.

The escort fighter was introduced to assist bomber operations. But through the spring of 1944, understanding grew among the American airmen that whatever they were or were not accomplishing against the German aircraft industry on the ground through bombing, by compelling the Luftwaffe to scramble to its defence they were winning a critical victory in the air. It was the ultimate vision of the *Circus* operations that the RAF had begun over northern France in 1941, intended to provoke the Luftwaffe to battle, but unsuccessful because the bombers' targets were not important enough to make the Germans rise to the bait. Now the Americans could compel the defenders to meet the challenge. In 'Big Week', the immense effort by 8th and 15th Air Forces against the German aircraft factories that began on 20 February 1944, 3,800 Liberators and Fortresses dropped 10,000 tons of bombs for the loss of 226 heavy aircraft – 6 per cent of sorties dispatched – and twenty-eight escorting fighters. Bomber Command's five parallel night raids against aircraft-industry targets added a further 9,198 tons of bombs for the loss of 157 aircraft, 6.6 per cent of sorties dispatched. Between them, the Allies inflicted severe blows, but production continued to rise dramatically. In the last half of 1943 Germany produced an average of 851 single-engined fighters a month. The real impact of 'Big Week' and the Americans' other daylight operations became visible in the Luftwaffe's air-loss figures: these rose from 1,311 aircraft destroyed from all causes in January 1944 to 2,121 in February, and 2,115 in March.

By March the Americans had consciously embarked on a policy of seeking targets which they knew that the Luftwaffe must defend. The skies over Germany were strewn day after day with the plunging wrecks of broken fighters and bombers, the black smears of flak, rocket trails, and amidst them all the glinting silver wings of the Fortress formations, cruising steadily onwards. Encounters continued for hours, with successive waves of Luftwaffe fighters landing to refuel and rearm, then engaging once more. On 6 March, 8th Air Force lost 69 of 660 bombers which attacked, and 11 fighters. The flak was intensifying and becoming more deadly – a quarter of all American bombers dispatched came home with shrapnel damage. But the enemy was tiring:

> Viewed in retrospect [wrote the American official historians] the preceding sixteen months of bombing by American forces became a long period of preparation. . . . The German air force could still offer serious resistance. Yet it was just such an air fight that the American commanders hoped to provoke, confident as they were in the ability of their airmen to impose a ruinous wastage upon the enemy. . . . It is difficult to escape the conclusion that the air battles did more to defeat the Luftwaffe than did the destruction of the aircraft factories.[10]

But even as the USAAF was achieving the victory over the Luftwaffe that would enable Bomber Command eventually to dominate the night skies over Germany, the controversy over Allied bombing policy entered a new phase. *Overlord*, the plan for the Normandy landings, was now the chief preoccupation of the military and political leaders of the Grand Alliance. They were determined that the invasion would receive all the air support at their command to ensure its success. From the summer of 1943 until the spring of 1944, there was constant and acrimonious debate about how this could best be achieved.

The British were dismayed by the now inescapable transatlantic domination of the war, by Washington's unconcealed determination to conduct the liberation of Europe with its commanders and by its strategy. The Americans were no longer much concerned with soothing British sensibilities. Their build-up in Britain and the Mediterranean was flooding bases, ports, airfields. Already the US bomber force outnumbered Bomber Command in aircraft, although not in bombload. American policy was to concentrate forces within highly centralized command structures, inevitably controlled by their own generals. The British squirmed furiously to prevent their own air forces from being engulfed in these monoliths. At the *Sextant* conference in Cairo in November 1943, the British were alarmed by the American announcement that they planned to place the 8th and 15th Air Forces under a single commander, and ultimately under the control of the American Supreme Commander of the invasion forces. Sir Douglas Evill, Vice-Chief of Air Staff, signalled London's reaction to Portal in Cairo in a Most Secret cipher telegram of 26 November:

> After consultation with the Secretary of State, Permanent Under-Secretary and Deputy Chief of Air Staff, we are all of us agreed that everything possible should be done to resist any proposal that would end in 8th and 15th Air Forces being placed under the command of the Supreme Allied Commander for North-West Europe. Such centralization would logically suggest inclusion of the RAF strategic night-bomber force, and there are insuperable operational and political objections to this.

There was considerable pathos in the efforts of the British to preserve their dwindling independence. One remarkable proposal to avoid placing Bomber Command under Eisenhower's control involved appointing an American Deputy Chief of Air Staff at the Air Ministry, to second Portal's direction of *Pointblank* on behalf of the Combined Chiefs of Staff. The British finally lost their fight to prevent the union of 8th and 15th Air Forces under the command of Spaatz, but they staved off a decision about Bomber Command's future place in the Allied command structure.

> We were . . . able to secure some improvements in the organization originally proposed [Portal signalled to London on 7 December 1943]. This arrangement gives us essential general control and the new Commanding General will doubtless discover soon enough the difficulties of exercising detailed control of XVth Air Force from the United Kingdom. No commitments have been entered into about the date on which command passes to the Supreme Allied Commander.

But the principal officers and ministers of the Grand Alliance were not in the mood to concern themselves with the airmens' sensitivities when *Overlord* was at stake. Eisenhower insisted that, as Supreme Commander, he must have operational control of the strategic-bomber forces. Among his colleagues even his Deputy, Sir Arthur Tedder, himself an airman, was unwilling to trust the vital invasion air-support decisions to the discretion of Harris and Spaatz.

During the winter of 1943–44, acres of Air Ministry and Bomber Command paper were dedicated to demonstrating the scale of the

British contribution to *Pointblank* against that of the Americans. Much has been made of Portal's fears that the programme for crippling the German air force before the invasion was falling behind schedule – three months was the stated lag.

> [The achievements of the USAAF and Bomber Command] had to be considered always in close relationship to the strategic timetable [write Craven and Cate]. The important thing was to determine how near the operation was to achieving its assigned objectives within the time allotted; for although it was in a sense true that the success of *Pointblank* would determine the date of *Overlord*, there was a limit to how long the invasion could be postponed while awaiting the anticipated fatal weakening of the German air force.[11]

This seems grossly to exaggerate the concern of the Allied leadership about *Pointblank*, and about the threat which the Luftwaffe presented to *Overlord* by the winter of 1943. The Russian armies had contributed immeasurably more than *Pointblank* could hope to achieve in bringing about the 'fatal weakening' of Germany in advance of the Western Allied invasion. As has been suggested earlier, the superiority of the Allied tactical air forces was already so overwhelming that neither Washington nor London would conceivably have considered postponing the invasion in the light of what *Pointblank* had or had not achieved. Naturally Eisenhower, Marshall, Brooke and others were anxious to drive the German air force from the sky, and for that matter to inflict maximum damage on Germany. But they had long since lost any hope of finding the German ability to resist *Overlord* 'fatally weakened' by bombing. It was almost embarrassing to recall the plan codenamed *Rankin*, drawn up in the full flush of the airmen's enthusiasm months earlier, for a sudden occupation of Europe if German resistance collapsed under the weight of bombing or Russian offensives.

It was because the ground commanders doubted the airmen's judgement of what constituted the critical pressure-points of German military and industrial strength that they insisted upon control of the strategic bombers being transferred to the Supreme Commander. There was a final pathetic wrangle provoked by the British, about the precise wording of Eisenhower's powers over Bomber Command: they refused to let him have 'command', but finally settled for giving him 'direction'. Then the issue was closed. From 14 April 1944 until further notice the Allied air forces would conduct strategic operations only with Eisenhower's specific consent. Their prime function would be the tactical support of the invasion. This was a total defeat for the wishes of the bomber commanders of Britain and America.

Air Chief Marshal Sir Trafford Leigh-Mallory had been appointed to nominal command of the Allied air forces at the invasion, and although he would never have the opportunity effectively to exercise this, in the winter of 1943 he drew up a plan for the bombing of key rail communications links in northern France and Belgium as a preliminary to D-Day. Professor Solly Zuckerman, co-author of the Hull and Birmingham Report which Cherwell misquoted to such effect in 1942, had subsequently been posted to the Mediterranean. There he achieved considerable influence as a scientific adviser to Tedder, Eisenhower's air chief, particularly after he planned the bombing of the island of Pantellaria, which surrendered without further ado following the air attack. When Tedder was nominated Deputy Supreme Commander for D-Day in January 1944, Zuckerman came home to serve on his staff, and in particular to devise bombing plans. Zuckerman read the Leigh-Mallory plan, concluded that it was quite inadequate, and set out to devise a comprehensive strategy for the destruction of every key rail link in northern France. The fruits of his efforts became known as the Transport Plan, and unleashed a new bombing controversy that locked the leaders of the Allied war effort in fierce conflict until the last weeks before the invasion.

The Allied planners believed that the greatest threat to the invasion would come in the build-up period after landing. Unless the Wehrmacht could be drastically impeded, the Germans would be able to concentrate divisions around the Allied bridgehead more quickly than the Allies could reinforce it. Eisenhower and Tedder were rapidly persuaded that Zuckerman's plan represented the most promising means of wrecking the German army's communications with Normandy, and the most effective use of the strategic bomber force in the weeks before the invasion. Almost all the military leaders agreed, and Portal was willing to be convinced.

But deployed against the Transport Plan were the massed ranks of the other airmen; Lord Cherwell, who was still single-mindedly dedicated to the area offensive, which he cherished as his own brainchild; and the vital figure of the Prime Minister. Churchill was appalled by initial estimates from Cherwell and RE8 that bombing the key French railway centres could kill 40,000 French civilians.* This seemed to him – the Americans were less concerned – an utterly unacceptable manner in which to begin the liberation of Europe. Harris, who was resolutely opposed to the Transport Plan for a host of his own reasons, refused to give the Prime Minister any reassurance at all about possible civilian casualties: 'I was not about to start keeping a gamebook of dead Frenchmen.'[12] Throughout February the Prime Minister remained obdurate in his refusal to sanction the railway bombing, to the increasing alarm of Eisenhower.

* In the event approximately 12,000 French and Belgian civilians were killed in the pre-invasion bombing by Allied air forces.

But it was Harris and Spaatz who unleashed the most formidable revolt against the Transport Plan, or indeed against any tactical employment of the heavy-bomber force at all. Even at this late stage, neither officer had renounced his private conviction that *Overlord* was a vast, gratuitous, strategic misjudgement, when Germany was already tottering on the edge of collapse from bombing.

> *Overlord* [Harris wrote to Portal on 13 January 1944] must now presumably be regarded as an inescapable commitment. . . . It is clear that the best and indeed the only efficient support which Bomber Command can give to *Overlord* is the intensification of attacks on suitable industrial centres in Germany. If we attempt to substitute for this process attacks on gun emplacements, beach defences, communications or dumps in occupied territories, we shall commit the irremediable error of diverting our best weapon from the military function for which it has been equipped and trained to tasks which it cannot effectively carry out. Though this might give a specious appearance of 'supporting' the Army, in reality it would be the greatest disservice we could do them. It would lead directly to disaster.

Harris professed himself unshakeably convinced that the only proper, or indeed possible use of his Command was for the area bombing of Germany. The scientists of his Operational Research Section were driven to ever more tortuous statistical efforts to demonstrate that this was indeed the case. While it may be argued that some of Harris's wartime misjudgements were only revealed with hindsight, in this matter his narrow-mindedness was astonishing. To any balanced observer of the Grand Alliance at the beginning of 1944, it was obvious that all other strategic priorities were dwarfed by the importance of *Overlord*. Any success that the bombers might achieve over Germany that spring and summer by continuing the area offensive would be swept aside by the scale of disaster if the Allies failed to get ashore in Normandy and stay there.

But Harris was not alone in his obsession. Spaatz was convinced that victory over Germany was within his own grasp. He was exasperated by the prospect of giving the Luftwaffe a long respite while his aircraft attacked the French railway system. There was also another, even more critical factor. For two years of war, the USAAF had been groping for the throat of the German war machine, and now at last Spaatz believed that they had found it: the synthetic-oil system. In 1943, Germany's synthetic-oil plants produced 6.2 million tons of petroleum products from coal, in addition to the 2 million tons imported from Hungary and Rumania. The plants were dispersed among eighty locations, of which twenty-seven were notably important. Many of the targets were within range of 15th Air Force in Italy, if not of 8th Air Force in England, but hitherto the Allies had devoted barely 1 per cent of their entire wartime bombing effort to oil targets.

Now Spaatz's staff had drawn up a plan for the systematic destruction of Germany's oil resources by precision bombing. With the coming of the spring weather, with the enormous forces at his command, and with the Mustang to carve a path to the targets, Spaatz believed that he had the means to win the war. Professional rivalry with Harris also loomed large. He was haunted by fear that Bomber Command might somehow win the laurels while his Fortresses were reduced to running a bomb shuttle for Eisenhower. 'What worries me is that Harris is being allowed to get off scot-free,' he complained bitterly to Zuckerman.[13] 'He'll go on bombing Germany and will be given a chance of defeating her before the invasion, while I am put under Leigh-Mallory's command. . . .'

By February, Tedder was in despair about the obstinacy with which each faction was fighting for its own triumph in the deployment of air resources. Like so much else to do with the strategic air offensive, the final decisions represented a compromise. In March 1944, at the insistence of Portal – who was compelled to issue a direct order to Harris to gain his co-operation – the RAF carried out a series of experiments against the marshalling yards at Trappes, Aulnoye, Le Mans, Amiens/Lougeau, Courtrai and Laon. The attacks were a triumph for the aircrew of Bomber Command, who achieved startling success while inflicting far lower civilian casualties than had been predicted. Harris stood confounded by the virtuosity of his own men. His most virulent opposition to the Transport Plan was based on insistence that his crews were incapable of carrying it out. That argument was no longer credible. Furthermore Zuckerman told Tedder that, far from Bomber Command assisting the invasion if its aircraft continued area attacks on Germany until D-Day, in his view they could only hope to reduce enemy production by a maximum of 7 per cent, which could not conceivably be decisive. Churchill persisted with his opposition to the rail bombing until May, but he was overcome by pressure from Washington: Eisenhower had formally notified Roosevelt and Marshall that he considered the Transport Plan indispensable to *Overlord*: 'There is no other way in which this tremendous air force can help us, during the preparatory period, to get ashore and stay there.' The Prime Minister at last bowed to the Americans' insistence. Bomber Command would undertake the principal burden of carrying out the Transport Plan. In March 1944, 70 per cent of British bombs were directed against Germany. In April this proportion fell to well under half; in May, to less than a quarter; in June to negligible proportions. The 'panacea merchants' had triumphed. Harris wrote artlessly in his memoirs: 'Naturally I did not quarrel with the decision to put the bomber force at the disposal of the invading army once the die had been cast; I knew that the armies could not succeed without them.'[14]

The die had been a long time casting.

But while Harris fought his battle to continue area bombing, Spaatz was arguing in London and by direct appeal to Washington to be permitted to undertake his Oil Plan. On 19 April, Eisenhower authorized him to carry out two experimental attacks against oil plants, chiefly in the hope of bringing the Luftwaffe to battle. The weather was not suitable until 12 May, when Spaatz dispatched 935 bombers and a vast force of escorting fighters, losing forty-six bombers and ten of the escort. Further attacks followed on 28 and 29 May. Speer's nightmare had at last come to pass. Spaatz had touched the vital nerve of the German economy. In the months that followed, his aircraft were chiefly committed to attacking *Crossbow* targets to impede the German V-weapon attack on England, and providing tactical support for the Allied armies. In June only 11.6 per cent of his effort was launched against oil targets, in July 17 per cent, in August 16.4 per cent. But the results were dramatic. Petroleum available to Germany fell from 927,000 tons in March, to 715,000 tons in May, and 472,000 tons in June. The Luftwaffe's supplies of aviation spirit fell from 180,000 tons in April, to 50,000 tons in June, and 10,000 tons in August. All Speer's achievements in the aircraft factories went for nothing. By the late summer of 1944 the Luftwaffe lacked the fuel to fly anything like its available order of battle.

American airmen have lamented ever since the failure of the Allied command to understand the importance of Spaatz's achievement, to press home the Oil Plan and bring victory by the end of 1944. Bufton was among those at the Air Ministry who opposed the Transport Plan in favour of the Oil Plan. He described Zuckerman's scheme as 'a national disaster'.[15] He and many other airmen believed that the French rail links could have been destroyed with far less effort, had they been given the task and left to choose their own methods of executing it, by hitting bridges rather than marshalling yards. An American air force evaluation based on railway records concluded in 1945 that 'The pre D-Day attacks against French rail centres were not necessary, and the 70,000 tons involved could have been devoted to alternative targets.' The President of SNCF, the French rail network, said that he believed bridge-breaking would have far more effective than hitting yards. The fact that the Germans indeed suffered enormous difficulties in reinforcing Normandy after D-Day must be attributed in substantial measure to the efforts of the Allied tactical air forces and the French Resistance, in addition to the strategic bombers.

But to make much of the fact that Spaatz's obsession with the Oil Plan was justified is a misuse of hindsight. By the spring of 1944 the credibility of the 'bomber barons' among the leaders of the Grand

Alliance had sunk very low. Spaatz privately considered that Harris was 'all washed up' after the failure of the Battle of Berlin.[16] The British, in their turn, noted the yawning chasm between the Americans' past promises and their achievements. The admiration of politicians and ground commanders for the airmen's powers of organization and leadership was now eclipsed by cynicism about their failures and their insatiable demands for resources. At one of the vital meetings to discuss the rival merits of the Oil and Transport Plans, Oliver Lawrence of the Ministry of Economic Warfare – who was much respected by both the British and the Americans – said that on his estimate of German oil reserves, even if Spaatz's attacks were immediately effective against the production plants, it would be four to five months before the results benefited the battlefield. This projection was enough to damn Spaatz's hopes of undivided concentration of attack. The soldiers wanted results in days and weeks, not months.

The employment of the strategic bombers in the weeks preceding D-Day, and afterwards in support of the armies in Normandy, may today seem cautious and unimaginative. But it was vital insurance, and reflected a perfectly logical view of strategic priorities by the Combined Chiefs of Staff. *Overlord* had to succeed. Bomber Command and the USAAF were directed to do all in their power to see that it did so, and worked to that end with courage, dedication and professionalism. If their leaders were heard with insufficient respect in the councils of war, they had only their own vast errors of judgement of the past to blame. It is an indulgence of historians and armchair critics to pretend that, in the spring of 1944, there was a better way.

XII

Pathfinders: 97 Squadron, Lincolnshire, 1944

'Usual flares and aircraft shot down on way in,' Flight-Lieutenant Charles Owen noted in his diary[1] after a Berlin operation on 26 November 1943:

> Target was clear and we could see fires burning from an attack on the previous night. Hundreds of searchlights and very heavy flak, firing mainly into the cones. Flew over Hanover by mistake on return journey, and was coned for seven minutes, lost height from 20,000 to 13,000 feet during evasive action. Several holes in starboard wing and roof of cockpit, and the bomb-aimer wounded slightly in the leg. Also attacked by fighter when coned, but only damage was six inches knocked off one blade of the starboard outer prop.

The night of 16 December 1943 became known as 'Black Thursday' among Bomber Command crews, when returning from Berlin they found their bases in England blanketed in impenetrable fog. Owen's note of his own and 97 Squadron's experience was typical:

> Ten-tenths cloud over target. W/T and *Gee* packed up on way home, so homed across North Sea on D/F loop, which luckily was not jammed. Homed on to base on SBA beam, breaking cloud at 250 feet to find fog, rain and visibility about 300 yards and deteriorating. R/T then packed up, so after circling for ten minutes at 200 feet, landed without permission in appalling conditions. Six other aircraft landed at base, three landed away, three crews baled out when they ran out of fuel, four crashed when trying to land, and one was missing. Quite a night. . . .

In order to understand the transformation that came over 97 Squadron and Bomber Command during 1944, the lightening of losses and the breakthrough to remarkable tactical success, it is necessary to remember the mood in which they emerged from winter, and from the Battle of Berlin. After losing one CO over Magdeburg, his successor did not live long enough to enter the squadron record book. Night after night, they took off into freak winds and fog, to face the flak and the night-fighters. A new pilot remembered arriving to join the unit at six o'clock one December evening, and moving into a hut with a crew dressing to operate that night. At 5 am he was awakened by the clatter of boots as the Service Police arrived to collect his dead room-mates' possessions. There were many acquaintances and few close friends on Bomber Command stations that winter.

97 Squadron dispatched an average of twenty Lancasters a night, and almost invariably lost one, frequently two. On 28 January, of nineteen aircraft that took off for Berlin one returned early, two were lost and one, piloted by a tough Australian named Van Raalte, came home having failed to find 'The Big City', bombed Kiel instead, and had his rear gunner decapitated by flak. In the first fortnight of February, they were briefed three times for Berlin, only to have the operations scrubbed by bad weather. When they finally went again on the 15th, they lost one out of seventeen. In March, they lost two out of fourteen against Frankfurt on the 22nd, two out of fourteen against Berlin on the 24th, two out of fourteen against Nuremberg on the 30th.

97 was a Pathfinder squadron, one of Bennett's Lancaster units, based at Bourn in Cambridgeshire, in a straggling wasteland of mud and Nissen huts, where men slept in their greatcoats to fight the all-pervading damp and cold. But like the rest of Bennett's men, they took intense pride in their membership of 8 Group, a perverse pleasure in the ban on publicity about their 'ops', in Bennett's insistence that there should be no stars or professional heroes among his officers. 'There will be no living VCs in 8 Group,' the Australian announced in 1942. His edict stood in 1944. But his men cherished the hovering eagle badge that they were forbidden to wear on operations, and the inscribed Pathfinder Certificate that survivors were awarded on completion of their double tour of forty-five operations. Bennett was a humourless, unrelenting officer whom it was hard to like, but difficult not to respect as a professional airman. It was his achievement that he created a genuine Pathfinder spirit among the men of his squadrons, pitchforked into 8 Group from every corner of Bomber Command under all manner of circumstances. They had their share of LMF cases, 'Fringe merchants', poor pilots. But for the most part they were conscientious young men. By 1944 Bomber Command's skills had come a long way from the Stone Age of 1940 and 1941. On most operations the bulk of Main Force bombed within three miles of the Target Indicators. The success or failure of a raid depended overwhelmingly on how these markers were placed, how successfully the Master Bomber corrected those that fell wide, how accurately the Supporters timed their back-up marking throughout the Main Force attack. Bennett's crews understood all this, and did their utmost to fulfil their commander's expectations.

But they were not a picked elite. 97's crews, like the rest of the Group, reached Pathfinder Force by remarkably varied routes. Some were novices who had shown exceptional promise in training. Some were on their second, even third, tour of operations, men who had become supremely proficient bomber pilots and sought only to exercise their skills as long as 'The Reaper' allowed them. The majority of recruits had done ten or fifteen operations with a Main Force squadron, then volunteered or been drafted to Pathfinders when word came down to Groups that five or ten crews were required. Bob Lasham, for instance, was a pilot at 9 Squadron when he decided to go to PFF. His bomb-aimer and wireless operator were keen – the glamour and the temporary step in rank and pay appealed to them. His gunners acquiesced without enthusiasm. His navigator would have nothing to do with a 45-trip tour, and left the crew.

Pat Turner was a 44 Squadron flight engineer when his crew heard that they were being posted to Pathfinders. They did not mind going, but were conscious that they were not outstandingly talented fliers. It

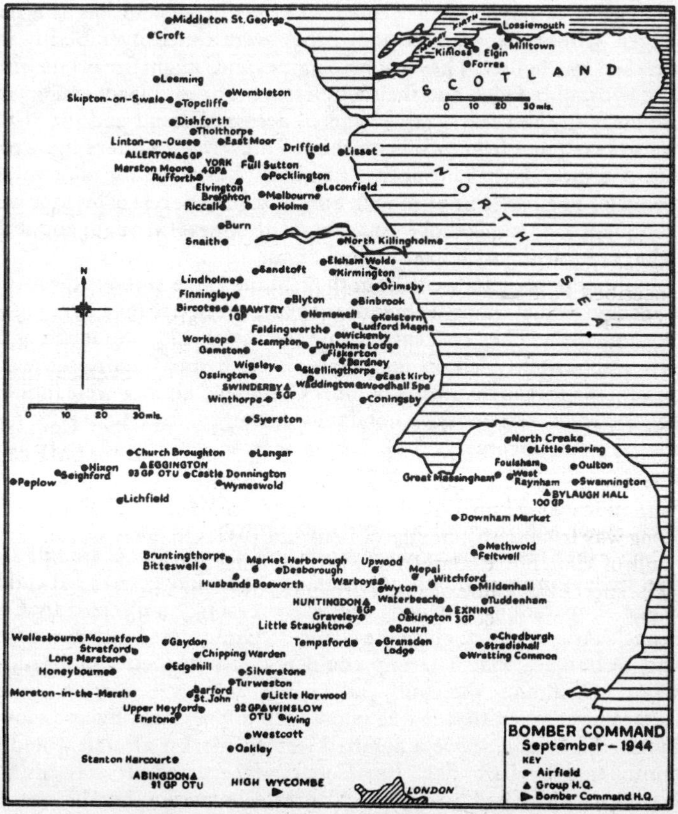

was only later that they discovered that they had been 'volunteered' by station headquarters as a simple solution to their pilot's passion for the base commander's WAAF driver.

Charles Owen, after leaving public school, was working at the Supermarine aircraft factory as a boy of seventeen in 1940, when he was badly injured in an air raid. He spent the winter in hospital, and came out at last old enough for the RAF. An exceptional pilot trainee, he was posted as an instructor, and served a year before transferring to operations with 97 Squadron, where he proved an oustanding operational captain. By 1944 he was a squadron leader, celebrating his twenty-first birthday one January night over Stettin. He ended the war as a Master Bomber with a string of decorations.

Tony Aveline left France through Dunkirk with the British army in 1940, and after an eternity at training camps in Scotland, volunteered for the RAF in 1941. He was washed out of pilot training in Florida, but qualified as a navigator in Canada. On his first operation as a passenger with an experienced crew, they were coned over Berlin and attacked by a fighter. They lost two engines and caught fire in one wing. The hydraulics failed and their wireless went dead. Blaspheming continuously in their fear, they staggered across Holland and the North Sea to crash in a field in Lincolnshire. They crawled out of the wreck and Aveline asked: 'Is it always like this?' But when his pilot volunteered for PFF, Aveline went with him, and flew the rest of his tour with 97 Squadron in a mood of cynical fatalism: 'I never thought about the value of it all. I just hoped it would end.'

Pathfinder recruits went from their Main Force stations for a two-week course in marking techniques at Warboys before they were posted to a squadron. They concentrated on the use of H2S, and much of the new responsibility fell on the bomb-aimer. Bennett addressed every new intake personally. Most Bomber Command aircrew were indifferent to which Group they nominally belonged. But Bennett's men shared with Cochrane's 5 Group an intense sense of identification, loyalty, and rivalry. At the beginning of April 1944, when 97's crews were abruptly informed that they were being transferred to 5 Group, their anger and resentment were unbounded.

Sir Arthur Harris had always mistrusted the concept of a single elite Pathfinder Group in Bomber Command. As his force expanded and its range of operations widened, he was increasingly impressed by Cochrane's insistence that given the chance, 5 Group could attempt targets and techniques that 8 Group could not. To Bennett's undisguised scorn, Cochrane forcefully advocated low-level marking. The Australian argued that it was impossible to map-read flying below a hundred feet, and above a hundred feet the marker aircraft would be annihilated by light flak. But Cochrane persisted. It was his 617 Squadron which had carried out the greatest precision-bombing feat of the war, breaking the Ruhr dams from a height of sixty feet. Despite their subsequent failure against the Dortmund–Ems Canal, during the winter of 1943, 617 carried out further experiments in bombing accuracy; on 16 December, nine of their Lancasters using the Stabilized Automatic Bomb Sight achieved an astounding error of only ninety-four yards against a V-Weapon launching site at Abbeville. On 8 February 1944, Leonard Cheshire marked the Gnome and Rhône engines factory at Limoges from a height of 200 feet, supported by Micky Martin, and the rest of 617 then demolished the works with extraordinary accuracy. They failed against the Antheor Viaduct in February, but both Cheshire and Cochrane were convinced that there was enormous scope for precision bombing guided by low-level marking, especially if Mosquitoes were available to do it. At the beginning of April, in one of his more imaginative decisions, Harris decided to give Cochrane the chance to prove his point. He ordered Bennett to transfer 627, one of his cherished Mosquito squadrons, together with 83 and 97 Lancaster squadrons, to 5 Group. They remained administratively responsible to 8 Group and retained their PFF badges and ranks. But they were to operate under Cochrane's command.

Bennett fought until the last moment to retain his squadrons, in his most bitter clash of the war with Harris. He rang Saundby at High Wycombe to demand furiously where 8 Group was to get more Mosquitoes when Cochrane's had all been shot down. Some of his staff urged him to resign, but he pointed out grimly that he had no intention of vacating his chair in order to let Cochrane move into it. In the end he swallowed his pride, but the enmity between 5 and 8 Groups was redoubled. 'I'm afraid I was rather tactless with Bennett,' admitted Cochrane afterwards.[2] But each was a dedicated man, convinced of a point of view.

97 Squadron's Movement Orders were issued and cancelled three times before they finally flew their Lancasters to Coningsby in Lincolnshire, a pre-war permanent station at the heart of a web of 5 Group airfields. There was friction at the outset: the Tannoy summoned all aircrew to the cinema, where the base commander gave them a terse talk about shedding their 8 Group habits and learning that they were in 5 Group now. A plaintive voice called from the back: 'We're fighting the Germans, you know, sir, not 5 Group.' The base commander announced that they would begin training immediately. Jimmy Carter, 97's CO, stood up and said: 'I'm sorry, sir, but my chaps were operating last night, and they're not going out to train now.'

It was weeks before the first tensions relaxed. On 17 April two pilots, one of them Charles Owen, went to the Juvisy marshalling yards with 617 Squadron, to study the 5 Group technique: 'It seemed to work well enough against no opposition,' Owen wrote presciently in his diary, 'but I decided it might not be so much fun against a heavily-defended

German target.' The essence of the 5 Group method was that no aircraft attacked until the Master Bomber was satisfied with the placing of the markers, and gave the order by radio-telephone. The hazards were that this was only practicable in clear visibility, and that it entailed delay for the bomber force in the target area. Both these difficulties would become unpleasantly apparent as summer went on.

8 Group's prestige undoubtedly declined in the shadow of 5 Group's achievements in the last year of the war, so much so that a medical officer at one of Bennett's stations considered that morale suffered.[3] He reported a conversation in the mess one day, when a group of officers were discussing whom Princess Elizabeth might marry. A voice in the corner muttered gloomily, 'It's bound to be somebody from 5 Group. . . .' But Cochrane was fortunate in his timing. Had he embarked on his low-level marking operations during the Battle of Berlin, or against heavily-defended German targets, he would almost certainly have met disaster. On 24 April 1944, Cheshire and three other 617 Squadron pilots carried out their extraordinary roof-level marking of Munich in Mosquitoes, for which Cheshire received the Victoria Cross. But Harris has remarked that 'any operation which deserves the VC is in the nature of things unfit to be repeated at regular intervals'.[4] The Munich exercise was proof of the extraordinary determination of Cochrane and his pilots, but not of the possibilities of regular low-level marking against heavy defences.

5 Group's luck was that their breakthrough came at exactly the right moment to meet the unique problem of the French invasion targets, where accuracy was vital not only to destroy the objective but to save civilian lives, and where ground defences were generally negligible. In the first month of their independent operations, 5 Group almost halved the normal 680-yard aiming error for effectively-aimed bombs dropped on *Oboe* ground marking. In May, when Cochrane introduced 5 Group's famous 'offset' technique, the average error fell to 285 yards. Cochrane was the most imaginative of Harris's Group commanders, probably the man who should have occupied Harris's chair at High Wycombe in the last phase of the war. He created 'offset' marking to contend with the problem of markers obliterated by smoke and flame in the midst of an attack. The principle was to mark a clearly visible point some distance short, beyond or wide of the target. Crews were anyway required to feed an allowance for wind into their bombsight computers. By adjusting this allowance to compensate for the markers' distance from the aiming-point according to radio-telephone instructions from the Master Bomber, the bomb-aimer could hit the aiming-point without obscuring the brilliance of the marker.

Although 5 Group continued frequently to bomb with the rest of Main Force, and although 8 Group continued to mark targets with considerable success, Cochrane had made his point. In the last year of the war, his 'Independent Air Force' became a rueful focus of controversy among those of Bomber Command who were restricted to a more pedestrian role. Cochrane introduced 'the 5 Group corkscrew', his own variation of the defensive manoeuvre against night-fighters (and compelled all his station and squadron commanders to go into the air and experience it), and 'the 5 Group quick landing scheme' to cut the delay in bringing down squadrons on their return from operations. He waged remorseless war against all that he considered undisciplined in the air and on the ground, checking navigators' logs, seeking to purge smoking on operations and intercom chatter in which crews referred to each other by their first names rather than the proper 'Captain', 'Navigator', and so on. He insisted that aircraft captains should be commissioned, to have the authority over their crews that he thought essential. This able martinet fumed when, after the introduction of 'Secretary aircraft' carrying wire-recorders to monitor radio-telephone conversation over the target, he heard the informality and unprofessionalism (as he considered it) that sometimes broke out in the stress of an operation.

But Cochrane's outstanding virtue was his receptiveness to ideas and innovations, from whatever source they came. He could behave arrogantly, but he had no professional conceit. 5 Group's unique broadcast link-up between headquarters and the squadrons made a real contribution to briefings, with flight and squadron COs encouraged to offer suggestions and tactical changes. It is hard to believe that it was coincidence that Cheshire, Gibson, Willie Tait[5] and Micky Martin were all 5 Group officers who came to the fore under Cochrane's command. He has a good claim to be considered not merely the outstanding Group AOC, but the outstanding British bomber commander of the war.

In April, 97 Squadron lost only two crews in ninety-eight sorties. After Bomber Command's early experiences against the French targets, the success in hitting the marshalling yards and the weakness of the Luftwaffe response, the spring brought lengthening odds on each man's survival. Berlin and the winter were behind them. But their spirits plunged when word came that High Wycombe planned to recognize the ease of attacking French targets by making each sortie count only one-third of an 'op' towards a man's tour. Crews with only three or four trips left were appalled by the prospect that these might stretch to nine, twelve.

Then, on 3 May, they went to Mailly-Le-Camp.

> Bright moonlight night [wrote Charles Owen] and Gerry pilots had a field day. Went in at 8,000 feet, but circled outside target at 4,000 feet waiting for order to bomb. Saw several fighters but was not attacked

> until on the bombing run at 5,000 feet. Luckily he was a rotten shot and we were able to carry on and drop our markers. We were attacked again coming out of the target, and he shot away our mid-upper turret and made a few holes elsewhere. The mid-upper gunner, miraculously, was only slightly wounded, but had to leave what was left of his turret. The fighter came in again, but the rear gunner drove him off and claimed him as damaged. I came home at 0 feet.

Of 362 aircraft that attacked, forty-two, or 11.3 per cent, were destroyed, overwhelmingly by night-fighters. One of them came from 97 Squadron. On 10 May, 5 Group sent eighty-nine Lancasters to Lille. There was a prolonged delay in the midst of the attack, when the Target Indicators were blown out and the target had to be remarked. Twelve aircraft, 13.5 per cent, were destroyed. 97 lost two out of eight dispatched. There was no more talk of French targets counting a third of an 'op'. These were two exceptionally bad nights, but they were a brutal reminder of what the Luftwaffe could still do, given the chance. Lingering around a target for accurate visual marking could be fatal.

It was the beginning of a summer of intense effort by Bomber Command, vastly different in kind and scale from everything that had gone before. In June 1944, it carried out 15,963 sorties against the 4,997 of June 1943. Huge forces of aircraft no longer attacked a single target in a concentrated stream. The new objectives required great accuracy from limited forces dispersed across France. To obscure the Allies' intentions in Normandy, it was necessary to attack marshalling yards, airfields, radar and wireless installations with equal intensity, from Belgium to the Cherbourg peninsula. There were still failures caused by weather and bad luck: on 19 May the Master Bomber cancelled the attack on Amiens as they circled the target, for lack of visibility. Three nights later, 97 Squadron went to Brunswick, a confused and unsatisfactory attack in which Cliff Chatten's aircraft was badly damaged by a night-fighter while coned over the target, and he somehow brought it home without instruments or cockpit canopy, circling the Wash until there was light enough for a crash landing. He was awarded the DSO and ceased to be a teetotaller.

On 31 May they went to a gun battery at Maisy near Cherbourg, but once again were sent home when they found the target shrouded in cloud. On 3 June they hit a wireless station at Ferme D'Urville. On the evening of 5 June they were briefed to attack a gun battery on the French coast at St Pierre du Mont. They were told nothing of the special significance of the occasion, but their orders were unusual: no aircraft was to fly below 6,500 feet; no bombs were to be jettisoned in the Channel; no IFF was to be used. In the early hours of 6 June, they flew south across the Channel, and broke cloud to see the great invasion armada below them. 'The army had pulled its finger out at last, and D-Day was on,' wrote Owen. 'We bombed at 0500 hrs just as it was getting light, and had a grandstand view of the Americans running in on the beach.' 3,467 heavy and 1,645 medium and light bombers flew in support of the landings that day. Bomber Command's Operation *Flashlamp* committed a hundred aircraft to each of ten major German coastal batteries. Some of the attacks were hampered by poor visibility and the guns went into action, but in many cases the German crews were paralysed by the bombing for long enough to enable the Allied forces to overrun them.

As 97 Squadron turned for home, its crews saw the huge formations of American aircraft following them into attack. There was a holiday excitement about the fantastic spectacle below, and perhaps this contributed to a moment of tragedy when German fighters made one of their few effective interventions of the day. Jimmy Carter, 97's CO, went down hit by a Ju88, taking with him the squadron gunnery and signals leaders. Another aircraft from 97 followed. Yet even the losses could not suppress their satisfaction at taking part in one of the great operations of the war. They turned on the mess radio as they landed at Coningsby, and hung fascinated around it all day.

On 13 June the Germans launched the first of the 30,000 V-Weapons with which they bombarded Britain before the end of the war. For the rest of the summer, Bomber Command and the USAAF added the 'ski-sites' and V-Weapons storage depots to the target list of barracks, airfields and marshalling yards that they were already attacking daily. American experiments had indicated that low-level fighter-bomber strikes were the most effective weapon against the 'ski-sites', but in its desperate anxiety to save the British people from another Blitz, the Government insisted that the 'heavies' should also be thrown into the counter-attack. Senior airmen reminded the War Cabinet that even at maximum intensity, the V-Weapons – 'those damn silly rockets', as Harris called them – could do less damage than a single Bomber Command attack on a German city. But this was no consolation to the Prime Minister. Like many aircrew, he regarded the V-Weapons as uniquely cowardly, launched by men who did not risk their own lives in the killing of others. In his anger, he seriously considered reprisal gas attacks against Germany, and several Bomber Command squadrons were specially trained to carry them out. But Eisenhower and Tedder were foremost among those who dissuaded Churchill. The V-Weapons continued to cause much pain and fear, although very limited material damage to Britain. Bomber Command continued to divert aircraft to the ineffectual counter-offensive against them, despite Harris's bitter opposition.

On 24 June, amidst one of 97's strikes against a 'ski-site' at Prouville, they met the German fighters in force. Tony Aveline suddenly felt the stink of his bomb-aimer's vomit surge up from the nose, as their pilot hurled the Lancaster into a corkscrew under attack. The squadron lost one aircraft. In the three summer months of June, July and August, barely one-sixth of Bomber Command's effort was directed against German targets, compared with more than a third of the USAAF's tonnage. Spaatz had been more successful than Harris in convincing Eisenhower that his operations against Germany would yield early dividends to the Allied armies. Harris, on the other hand, was playing his usual forceful hand in fighting off unwelcome proposals. To the C-in-C of Bomber Command, the German oil plants were merely the latest in the long line of 'panacea targets' with which so many knaves and fools sought to divert him from the task of destroying Germany. His fierce opposition to the pre-*Overlord* deployment of Bomber Command forgotten, he also expected greater public recognition of the achievements of the Transport Plan. He wrote to Portal on 1 July:

> I think you should be aware of the full depth of feeling that is being aroused by the lack of adequate or even reasonable credit to the RAF in particular and the air forces as a whole, for their efforts in the invasion. I have no personal ambition that has not years ago been satisfied in full, but I for one cannot forbear a most emphatic protest against the grave injustice which is being done to my crews – there are over 10,500 aircrew in my operational squadrons. In three months we have lost over half that number. They have a right that their story should be adequately told, and it is a military necessity that it should be.
>
> Your Ever,
> Bert

The Air Ministry asked what resources Harris would now need to destroy ten selected oil targets in the Ruhr. On 13 June, he replied that his staff estimated that 32,000 tons of bombs would be required – scarcely less than Bomber Command had dropped on all operations in the entire month of May.

Yet as a sop to the 'panacea merchants', of whom there seemed to be disagreeably many on the matter of oil, Harris verbally agreed with Tedder that Bomber Command would divert its spare effort to oil targets through the summer. On the night of 21 June, 97 Squadron was part of the force that went to the oil plants at Gelsenkirchen, their only operation against Germany between June and late August. There was a marked lack of enthusiasm among the crews for their return to the Ruhr. They bombed amidst heavy flak and thick overcast, and on the way home met the night-fighters as the moon rose. 'Not at all a nice trip, and a lot of chaps missing,' wrote Charles Owen. One of 97's aircraft failed to return, and two more were badly damaged. That month, Bomber Command launched four major attacks on German oil plants, 832 sorties in all, and paid heavily – extraordinarily so compared with casualties against the French targets. Ninety-three aircraft were missing.

Then the word came down that daylight sorties, abandoned by Bomber Command in mid-1943, were to be resumed. Training was to begin immediately. Formation-flying is a difficult art, and one which it had taken the Americans years to perfect. The British in 1944 had neither the stable, heavily armed and armoured aircraft, nor the highly trained crews to compete with the USAAF over Germany. But as the Allies approached absolute daylight air superiority over France, there was obviously a strong case for Bomber Command to take advantage of the situation, especially after Lille and Mailly-Le-Camp.

On the morning of 23 June, 97 Squadron's aircrew were in a boisterous mood as they waited for the trucks to take them to the dispersals for a formation training flight. They suddenly fell on a tiny Fiat car owned by a pilot named Perkins, and by force of fifty pairs of arms hauled it to the top of a big air-raid shelter. It was still perched there, and they were still laughing, when they took off. High over Lincolnshire they took up their unaccustomed positions in formation. Then Van Raalte momentarily allowed his Lancaster to drift into the slipstream of Bill Gee's aircraft in front. The huge bomber was tossed fiercely aside, plunging into that of Perkins beside it. The two aircraft fell steeply out of the sky, breaking up as they went. The rest of the squadron landed and walked to the air-raid shelter to lift down the little Fiat, much sobered young men. The remains of only eleven bodies were found, but they filled twelve coffins for the funerals. The twelfth turned up in a field weeks later. The thirteenth man, a wireless operator, miraculously survived. A few weeks later another crew took him into the air for a training flight. He landed shaking, and never flew again. In the first weeks after D-Day, the casualties of Bomber Command were higher than those of the British Second Army in Normandy. The scent of victory had gone out of the air again.

On 25 June the new CO arrived. Wing-Commander Anthony Heward had been commanding 50 Squadron when he was summoned to see Cochrane: 'I want you to take over at 97 and train them to concentrate on the task of target illumination,' said the AOC. He made no secret of his opinion that the squadron did not conform to the standards of discipline and efficiency that he was looking for. The taste of 8 Group was still too strong at Coningsby for Cochrane's liking. By the same token, 97 Squadron at once sensed that Heward had been sent to shape them to the 5 Group mould, and resented him accordingly. They also resisted the feeling that here was a career RAF officer, sent to impose meaningless service routines upon experienced operational aircrew. A sharp, clever, rather chilly man, who flew brilliantly when he chose to go into the air, his initial impact on Coningsby was dramatic. He sacked the squadron adjutant within hours of his arrival, and summoned the flight commanders for an icy lecture on untidiness, indiscipline and inefficiency: 'Nobody was bothering about the length of their hair. They dressed like Desert Rats, in their own idea of uniform.' Some of his officers were angry and resentful, and indeed Heward won little of their affection. He had more success in moulding novices to his ways than converting the 'Old Lags' from 8 Group. But he quickly became aware that 97 Squadron's aircrew were markedly superior to the general run of Bomber Command in ability and qualifications.

For no apparent reason, there were a surprising number of officers of private means and comfortable background among them: Charles Owen; Heward himself; Arthur Ingham, the tall, balding son of a northern wool-merchant's family who was older than most and said little about his experiences, but was respected as a superb operational captain. Lionel Wheble and Gordon Cooper, the H2S leader, were both members of Lloyd's, the London underwriters. Jock Simpson had been chief accountant of the Bank of Scotland. Most exotic of all was Pete de Wesselow, a surgeon's son of White Russian origins who had transferred to the RAF from the Brigade of Guards. The precise, immaculate de Wesselow spoke several languages fluently, collected antique glass, and could call on a rower's physique for throwing his Lancaster around the sky.

These men of unusually elegant background for Bomber Command were leavened by the host of Australians, New Zealanders, Canadians, Norwegians, South Africans and Englishmen who made every squadron such a melting-pot of youth and experience: Noel Parker, an Australian who had already been shot down over France and walked home to return to operations; 'Killer' Booth, the primeval little rear gunner who had somehow survived over a hundred operations with ruthless relish, and had an axe dripping blood painted on the wall of his billet; Pat Broome, the bombing leader, who decorated the mess with his cartoons, and who never seemed to be without his dog Virginia and the WAAF of the moment; Steve and Dave – Bowman and Crugeon – two inseparable Australians who were finally killed on the same night in different aircraft; Bill Clayfield, the debonair signals leader who raced his Singer to the Gliderdrome dancehall in Boston so many nights of Stand-Down; Watson, with the spaniel that he always took on operations, and which finally fell from the night sky over Germany beside him; Perkins's two wild Canadian gunners, who were sent to Sheffield in punishment for smashing the sergeants' mess one night and thus missed the crash that killed their pilot. These and 170 or so other aircrew made up 97 Squadron in 1944.

Coningsby was one of the crack stations of 5 Group, the hub of '54

Base'. Bomber Command had sub-divided its Groups into base commands, each centred on a station with several 'satellite' airfields. 97 shared Coningsby with 83 Squadron. The two units worked in close partnership, indeed were usually briefed together by the little base commander, Air Commodore Bobby Sharpe. There was also a tiny, elite force at Coningsby known as 54 Base Flight, which comprised 5 Group's Master Bombers. A hut on the station housed the Jordan Trainer, a highly sophisticated device for training Master Bombers. Pupils sat in their 'cockpit' in a gallery, while below them a fifteen-foot darkened model of a German city revolved to create its image as seen from a circling aircraft, with steam producing cloud, lights and small pyrotechnics imitating Target Indicators and smoke. To be a Master Bomber was intensely dangerous, circling the target throughout an attack, often descending to very low level to correct markers that had fallen wide. Visually-marked attacks depended heavily on the Master Bomber, and when he was shot down or suffered technical failure, the whole raid often ended in fiasco.

97 Squadron still carried out marking and bombing attacks according to well-established 8 Group techniques. But their most notable contribution to 5 Group's operations was as an Illuminating Force, lighting up the target for the Mosquitoes who followed them. Routines varied in detail from operation to operation, but a classic 5 Group raid in the late summer of 1944 sent selected aircraft of 83 and 97 Squadrons to open the attack by laying lines of parachute flares over the target blind by H2S, at seven-second intervals, with a margin of error seldom much above 200 yards. Meanwhile the Primary Blind Marker dropped his Target Indicators, also by H2S, to give the Mosquitoes an approximate line on the target. 627's Mosquitoes then came in low with their Target Indicators or Red Spot Fires – more precise but less brilliant markers. The first pilot to see the marking-point called 'Tally-Ho!' on the radio-telephone, and dived in to mark. It was then the Master Bomber's business to assess its accuracy and call for correction and support as required, before letting loose the Main Force. Supporting illuminators were available to reinforce the flares as necessary, but often went home without being required to act. In both 5 and 8 Groups, there was a distinct hierarchy of importance and efficiency among marking crews, who were promoted to 'Flare Force I', or demoted to become 'Supporters' according to their operational performance.

There was now an extraordinary profusion of marking and aiming techniques: visual; by *Oboe*; by H2S; by a new device called G-H, of the *Oboe* family but with greater range and capable of use by a hundred aircraft simultaneously. Often a combination of more than one of these would be employed. Sometimes the Pathfinders would decide only on the run-up to the target whether to mark visually or by radar. They were equipped with multi-stage Target Indicators which changed colour through the attack to defeat German decoys. At 97 Squadron, the bomb-aimer's vital function had become that of 'Set Operator', manning the H2S from a seat beside the navigator as the aircraft ran up to the target. Flight engineers had been retrained as 'Visual bomb-aimers', and it was they who customarily handled the Mk XIV bomb-sight on a visual attack. Almost every squadron aircraft carried its own individual combination of Target Indicators, flares, 'Wanganui' sky-markers, high-explosive bombs and incendiaries, according to its place in the attack.

At a crack Pathfinder unit there was intense professional dedication to improving technique. Gordon Cooper, the H2S leader at 97, had devised a range of new methods of handling the set. The squadron engineering officer discovered that by applying a high polish to the bulging H2S dome below the fuselage, it was possible to add 5 mph to a Lancaster's speed. Each radar set was individually tuned. Highly-skilled *Gee* operators found that they could use their equipment almost to the Ruhr despite the German jamming, getting the vital blip at extreme range by calling on their pilot to waggle his wings.

But it is important not to allow admiration for the sophistication of Pathfinder techniques at this stage of the war to obscure one central fact: Bomber Command never overcame the problem of the weather. Until the very end, there were failed attacks and unsatisfactory marking when the cloud-base was low. The weather remained almost as central an element in the bomber offensive in April 1945 as it had been in September 1939. Despite the FIDO burners that were established at key airfields to clear runways of fog, crashes on take-off and landing remained a major cause of lost aircraft. With the approach of winter, the sortie rate declined severely even in the last year of the war.

One of Cochrane's most intensely held convictions was that training must never stop, even when crews were operating constantly. Heward kept 97 Squadron in the air by day and night all that summer. They dropped bombs at Wainfleet, practised H2S technique on blind 'cross-countries', tested their gunners in the air against drogues and targets. Some of the crews resented the pressure when they felt entitled to relax between operations. Most were sufficiently dedicated to improving their art to accept it with reasonable good grace, although somebody wrote an acid note in the operational record book at the end of June: 'The Group "Exercise" which was laid on for tonight was once more cancelled at a late hour. One gets the impression that these "Exercises" are laid on and cancelled at such late hours to prevent the aircrews ever having an evening out of camp to themselves.'

Operations reached a peak of intensity in August, when they sortied by day or night on eighteen occasions. Some men found the daylight trips a pleasant change, forging across France in a great loose gaggle, gazing down at the unfamiliar sunlit scenery. Most, however, were deeply wedded to the night. They hated the sense of nakedness in daylight, the horror of watching aircraft fall from the sky in slow motion, of being able to identify each man's funeral pyre, to see the collisions, the bursting flak and attacking fighters, seldom though it was that they now encountered the Luftwaffe.

On 18 August, they were ordered to the U-boat pens at Bordeaux. They took off that morning in uncommonly easy mind. They had had little trouble with French targets for weeks, and this trip had been laid on at short notice, almost as an afterthought by High Wycombe. Then as the group of Lancasters curved in towards the town and the vast, unbroken concrete mass that housed the U-boats, a terrifying blanket of flak opened before them. Instinctively, pilots edged outwards to skirt it, their course widening away from the pens. Arthur Ingham, in 97's lead aircraft, drove unswerving onwards, calling furiously down the radio-telephone: 'Come in, come in. Support me. Support me.' The flak began to kick and rock the aircraft. Ingham locked his arms on the yoke and said grimly to his crew: 'We are going through.' There was intense nervous chatter between aircraft on the R/T, somebody calling in bewilderment: 'There are some Germans down there pushing out what looks like a wheelbarrow.' The 'wheelbarrow' erupted as its crew brought their quad AA guns into action. Beside Ingham sat Pat Turner, a flight engineer who had volunteered for Bordeaux because he was a few trips behind the rest of his usual crew, and 'this one sounded dead cushy'. The flak bracketed them in earnest as they came in to bomb, tearing through wings and fuselage, wrecking the electrics and flaps, holing five tanks, wounding the navigator and mid-upper gunner. They came home through the bright sunshine with the wind rushing through 160 holes in the aircraft, two engines gone, Pat Turner bent over the bleeding squadron navigation leader with a morphia syringe. They crashed at Fighter Command's airfield at Tangmere, where their survivors were grudgingly found sleeping space on the mess floor.

Bill Clayfield, 97's signals leader, came home in an aircraft with a badly wounded bomb-aimer. The ambulance met them as they landed, and rushed him away. Only when the others reached the mess did they realize that they were a man short. They raced back to the Lancaster, to find their mid-upper gunner slumped unconscious over his guns. He had been hit in the backside by shrapnel, but when he recovered later he said that knowing of their difficulties in the cockpit with the bomb-aimer, he had not wanted to add to these by reporting his own injuries.

It was, inevitably, a dangerous business using heavy bombers with a mean aiming accuracy of three miles to support ground operations. But that summer the Allied armies called repeatedly for assistance from Bomber Command and 8th Air Force to blast open the German lines in advance of an attack. Until the end of the war, many airmen and some thoughtful soldiers argued that it was counter-productive to send in Bomber Command, for the devastation caused serious problems for advancing armour, and bombing was not accurate enough to pinpoint German positions. And even with good marking, there were fatal errors. In an incident on 14 August during the battle for Falaise, Bomber Command hit Canadian troops, causing several hundred casualties. This was largely a failure of liaison, because the men on the ground fired Colours of the Day unknown to the airmen, but closely resembling Target Indicators. There was also some careless bombing, however, and on most ground-support sorties thereafter, there was a 'long stop' controller to ensure that no aircraft bombed beyond a certain point near the Allied lines. Tactical support bombing became a central part of the summer's operations, as the army called repeatedly for preparation by heavy bombers, if only to boost the morale of the Allied assault troops.

On 16 August, 97 Squadron carried out their first operation against a German target since June. Bomber Command dispatched 461 aircraft on a deep penetration to Stettin. While the Main Force attacked the city, 97 and 83 Squadrons went to mine the nearby Swinemunde Canal. This was an exceptionally difficult low-level operation, and before they left Coningsby they had long consultations with Guy Gibson, drawing on his dam-busting experience. Gibson recommended that the three marking aircraft make one low-level run down the canal before turning to drop their flame-float markers. At tea in the mess, there were some gloomy jokes about Heward's refusal to allow crews to take part in swimming exercises at the local baths, on the grounds that the chlorine might damage their night vision. Ed Porter, approaching the end of his second tour, was Master Bombing with a scratch crew. He would mark the middle of the canal, Parker the south end, Reid the north. Then somebody remembered that Reid could not swim. To their intense dismay, for it was to be the last trip of their tour, Harry Locke's crew were detailed instead.

Locke's aircraft lost its *Gee* on the outward run, but approached the canal dead on time at 300 feet, to find the five flak ships moored beside the channel already hosing up fire. On their second run, their flame floats had just fallen away when they were hit by ground fire, and plunged towards the water. 'Pull out,' yelled the wireless operator, Tony Boultbee, as he glanced from his window to see the water rushing up at them. They called Porter on the R/T as they climbed away: 'Permission to break off?' Porter assented. They turned for home. Crossing Denmark at 6,000 feet, they reached the English coast with leaking hydraulic fluid swamping the H2S, and all radar aids out of action. Locke belly-landed at Coningsby with the crew huddled behind the main spar, haunted by the usual terror of fire on impact. Somehow they all walked away. Locke was awarded an immediate DSO.

But the furious flak caught Portal's aircraft as he hung over the canal, coned by a dense knot of searchlights. With an unshakeable calm that every crew listening remembered for the rest of their lives, he said on the R/T: 'I'm afraid we have had it. I shall have to leave you now. Bailing out. Good luck everybody.' But they were too low for parachutes. Going home that night, one of 97's crews looked down on the bright lights of neutral Sweden, and for several minutes they talked seriously among themselves about the possibility of parachuting into internment. Later, they felt ashamed and never mentioned the conversation to each other again. But that night fear had sunk deep into their reserves of courage.

In August 1944, 97 Squadron carried out 193 sorties for the loss of only three aircraft missing. Faces that came to the squadron were now lingering long enough to become familiar. There were often more crews than aircraft for them to fly, and with an establishment of twenty, on some 'maximum effort' night, they sent out twenty-four Lancasters, some of their novices carrying bombs with Main Force. But the declining graph of losses, the rise in the fortunes of Bomber Command, were more readily apparent to the statisticians at High Wycombe than to the aircrew on the stations. The unending exhaustion, the dirtiness; the stink of aviation spirit and the lonely ride through the darkness to the dispersals; the monotony of the air broken only by moments of intense concentration or fear, felt the same in the summer of 1944 as in 1943 or 1942. It is only to historians that it is so readily apparent that the nature of the battle changed profoundly in this last year of the war.

With such a strong contingent of Colonials on 97 Squadron, Coningsby's senior officers fought a losing battle to enforce discipline on the ground. These men were not career airmen. Whatever dedication they brought to operational flying, they had no patience with rigid restriction away from their aircraft. Elsewhere in Bomber Command, disgruntled Canadians had been known to ring up their High Commission in London when confronted, for example, with official efforts to prevent NCOs from addressing officers by their christian names. 'No bullshit!' said the Canadians defiantly, and when all aircrew at Coningsby were confined to camp in punishment for the sawing-down of the base flagpole by a crew completing their tour, general impatience came close to explosion. Gordon Cooper slept with a pistol under his pillow to protect himself from the two New Zealanders with whom he shared a room, who were utterly careless whom they assaulted after a few drinks. In the early hours of one August morning after an operation, all 97's crews were hauled out of bed to take part in a post-mortem about the failure of the attack. They listened to Bobby Sharpe's incisive questioning for a few minutes, then Harry Locke, one of the Australians, called in disgust: 'This is a heap of horseshit.' They were allowed to go back to their beds.

Heward, the CO, was known as 'Smiler' in deference to the chilly mask that he presented to the world. It was said that in his days at 50 Squadron, a pilot interrupted one of the base WAAFs who said how much she would like to do something special for the war effort: 'Marry the CO, then, because he's giving us absolute hell.' Heward's crew reported for duty one morning in severe pain after a heavy social night at a local American base. His face cracked into a frosty smile: 'Fighter affiliation for us this morning, I think.' For the next hour he hurled the Lancaster through the Lincolnshire sky until the cockpit floor was awash with rebellious breakfasts. But unknown to the squadron, Heward was conducting one exercise that was quite out of step with the character they had drawn of him: laying siege to Clare Wainwright, a general's daughter who was Code and Ciphers Officer at Coningsby, and by common consent the most beautiful WAAF on the base. There was little opportunity for going out together in the town, but instead they went for long walks across the flat Lincolnshire fields. They were married late in 1944.

Coningsby had all the facilities of a pre-war station, but was grossly overcrowded with aircrew. Officers were sleeping in double-banked bunks, eating at long tables in a self-service mess, sharing a batman between six. Discomfort that would have been tolerable for men working regular hours in undemanding jobs became insufferable to aircrew permanently weary, coming and going at all hours of day and night. They discovered that the mess funds had accumulated enormously in five years of war, and threw them all into two massive parties. It was always possible to laugh and find the war funny when you were amongst a mass of apparently exuberant colleagues. But once they left the throng, most men's faces relapsed into that mask of mingled earnestness, tiredness and strain that is apparent in so many photographs of wartime briefings. On Stand Down evenings, they lounged on the grass outside the Leagate Arms in the village, conducting inter-crew drinking contests in which victory was measured by the length of each team's line of beer bottles stretching down the lawn, or dashed into Boston and Lincoln, or drank around the mess piano.

Coming out of briefing,
Get into the kites,

they sang, to the tune of *Lili Marlene*,

Down the f---ing runway,
And off into the night,
We've left the flarepath far behind,
It's f---ing dark but never mind,
We're pressing on regardless
For the Wingco's DFC . . . .

Often that summer, targets and bombloads were changed at short notice, and operations were laid on and cancelled at a few hours' warning. They played cricket in the sunshine outside the flight offices, or joined the high poker school in which Tony Aveline was a monotonously steady winner. Fewer men were dying, but the tension and discomfort of night operations were unchanged. Fred Hendry, one of the navigators, suffered chronically from air sickness, but was haunted by fear that he might be considered 'Lacking Moral Fibre'. Trip after trip, he flew with his topographical map folded into a sick-bag, throwing up his heart despite all the pills that he took before take-off, at last completing his forty-five amidst the admiration of 'the Navigators' Union'. One night Bob Lasham's flight engineer fell unconscious in the aircraft when he accidentally unplugged his own oxygen. When he was reconnected and brought round, he tried to attack the wireless operator with a fireaxe. He thought that they had crashed, and that the man bending over him was a German soldier.

Billy Russell was a Scots rear-gunner, who had come to the RAF from the mines. One night on the way to the target, his electrically-heated suit failed. On his return, he had to spend two days in hospital with frostbite. Russell flew with Noel Parker, an intensely professional Australian of much experience. On the trip to Mailly-Le-Camp, with the sky lit by tracer and exploding aircraft, Russell suddenly saw a shape in the darkness behind him, and swung his guns. He hesitated for a moment until he could see clearly, then sagged with relief, for it was another Lancaster. Back on the ground, he told Parker about the near-disaster, and was astounded by the Australian's explosion: 'You stupid bastard – you thought it was an Me110 and you hesitated. You should have fired the second you saw it!'

'But I was wrong,' said Russell in confusion.

'Next time you may not live to know that,' said Parker curtly. 'Fire every time.'

Some crews took chances and got away with it. One night, a 97 Lancaster landed back at Coningsby ahead of the Mosquitoes. At the ensuing inquiry, it emerged that its crew had ignored the stream's dog-leg route home, and flown a direct course in order to get to a mess party. Some men fell asleep in their aircraft on the way back. Others smoked, used torches carelessly to read the instruments, switched on IFF or even landing lights over enemy territory without noticing. A few came back but many of these men lie in the cemeteries of France and Germany. Billy Russell was appalled one night, coming home from a trip to Germany with a novice captain, to hear the man say: 'OK, we're over our own lines now. You can come out of the turrets and have a smoke.' Survivors of Bomber Command needed luck, but also sanity, discipline and utter concentration.

One of the saddest episodes at Coningsby that autumn concerned the station commander, the huge, popular teddy-bear figure of Group-Captain Evans Evans. Evans Evans felt a deep respect for aircrew. At Bourn, there had been a superstitious tradition that no one ever came to watch the aircraft take off, but at Coningsby 97 were surprised and at first alarmed to see Evans Evans saluting by the runway at the head of a crowd of waving WAAFs and ground staff. He was there without fail, every trip. Then one day in August, Evans made up his mind that it was his duty to fly an operation himself. He was a man of such enormous dimensions that he had difficulty getting into a Lancaster cockpit, far less controlling the aircraft. Bob Lasham's crew went to the squadron CO and flatly refused to fly with the station commander after a hair-raising cross-country flight in his hands. Instead, Evans took a scratch crew, flew to Caen and somehow came back to tell the tale. He was awarded a DFC. But instead of delighting him, this played on his mind. He felt that his 'gong' had been easily earned by comparison with those of the aircrew. He decided that he must fly another operation. He took off for Germany one night with all 97's specialist 'Leaders' in his crew, including Jock Wishart, the navigation leader, who was on his eighty-fourth trip. They somehow drifted into a 'Diver' area, where the Allied gunners had orders that any flying object must be treated as hostile. The aircraft was blown to pieces by American flak. Only the Australian rear gunner baled out in time to survive and tell the tale. Coningsby was torn between regret for Evans Evans, and sympathy for those who had been obliged to die with him.

But war on a bomber station was always a cruel business, in which the laws of natural selection were pushed to the limit. Throughout the offensive, the majority of casualties were novice crews on their first six trips. Yet because they were new to their squadrons, they found their inexperience compounded by the fact that they had to fly the aircraft nobody else wanted, the oldest and most vice-ridden. Beyond even this, by 1944 the best crews were concentrated overwhelmingly in the crack units – 8 Group, 5 Group, the Mosquito squadrons. 'Main Force' had become a term of condescension. New and mediocre crews in other Groups lacked a sufficient leavening of knowledge and experience in their flights and squadrons. It was a situation that Harris had anticipated with the formation of the Pathfinders in 1942, but which there was now no momentum in Bomber Command to reverse.

The experienced had little pity to spare for the newcomers in the mess. Statistically, seven or fourteen or twenty-one of us have to die tonight, so please God, let it be the nervous young face in the corner whom I do not know, rather than Harry, or Bill or Jack laughing at the bar, who are my friends. Thus their jokes: 'Killer' Booth walking over to the new crew having their pre-op meal in the mess at Coningsby, looking them up and down and declaring with cold certainty: 'You're for the chop tonight.' Or the familiar chestnut of putting a chopper cut out of perspex into a navigator's mapcase, for the man to find as his pilot ran up engines at dispersal. It was part of their defences against their own fear, of the schoolboy immaturity that was always close to the surface among so many young men of eighteen, nineteen and twenty, who still thought it the greatest sport in the world to pull somebody's trousers off after dinner. It was this same feather-light tread of youth that enabled so many thousands of their generation to fly for Bomber Command through six years of war, amidst the terrible reality that, statistically, most of them were dead men.

The early autumn of 1944 was the last false dawn of the war for the Allies, before the crushing disappointments of Arnhem and the German counter-offensive in the Ardennes, followed at last, belatedly, by victory. After months of delay, the armies had broken out of Normandy, sweeping across France and Belgium. It seemed perfectly possible to end the war in Europe by Christmas.

For Bomber Command, the path into Germany that had been fraught with such loss and disappointment only five months before, suddenly reopened. It was a remarkable twist of war that *Overlord*, which the airmen had sought to supplant as the key to victory, now made possible the reopening of the strategic air offensive with devastating results, at vastly reduced cost:

> The Combined Bomber offensive as planned in the spring of 1943 was . . . primarily a campaign to defeat the Luftwaffe as a prerequisite to *Overlord* [wrote Craven and Cate]. Ironically enough, it was not until the Allies had gained a firm foothold on the continent . . . that the bombing of Germany's vital industries, originally considered the purpose of a strategic bombing offensive, was systematically begun.[6]

The German early-warning radar and observer stations, together with their vital forward airfields in France, were gone. The attrition of the summer against the American strategic and the Allied tactical air forces had destroyed much of the Luftwaffe's remaining corps of trained aircrew, and wrecked its aircraft at the rate of 500 a week. The German air force continued to inflict loss on Bomber Command until the very end of the war, but Harris's casualties fell to 1 per cent of aircraft dispatched. In January 1944 he lost 314 aircraft for 6,278 dispatched. In September, losses fell to 96 missing for 6,428 night sorties, in October to 75 in 10,193 night sorties. Casualties on daylight operations were negligible.

With the benefit of hindsight, it is remarkable how much Allied nerves relaxed after the Normandy bridgehead was secured. D-Day had been the climax of so many hopes and fears. By 11 July, Portal found time to preside over a meeting at the Air Ministry to discuss, of all things, means by which the Royal Air Force might gain more publicity in the Press. The Chief of Air Staff opened the discussion himself:

> In the second stage of the war, RAF operations might be to a large extent overshadowed by army and naval operations and by the Americans, and so would receive comparatively little national publicity. There was accordingly a genuine danger that the part which it had played in the earlier part of the war would be forgotten by Ministers and by the public.
>
> The Director of Public Relations said that the Admiralty were obstructing publicity for Coastal Command. The Chief of Air Staff said that he would take this matter to the highest levels if necessary. . . .

In August the Air Ministry issued a long memorandum to all Commands concerning preparations for the end of the war. They were anxious that there should be no destructive or extravagant celebrations, and thus pointed out that it was advisable to ensure that when the time came, personnel had no unauthorized access to firearms, explosives or pyrotechnics. There was expectancy in the air at the highest levels of command: The Russians had seized great areas of Poland and Rumania including the vital oilfields, and seemed to be driving all before them. On every side there was a feeling that one more push could suffice to topple the Nazi edifice.

This impatience contributed significantly to the Allies' failure in the last nine months of war to devise and prosecute a consistent strategic-bomber strategy, with the enormous resources now at their command. Had they but known it, Spaatz's oil offensive was succeeding beyond the Americans' wildest expectations. By the end of September, German fuel supplies had fallen to less than a quarter of their January total, and a fatal crisis was threatening the German armed forces. But once again, as throughout the bomber offensive, a failure of Intelligence led to tragic misjudgements. For four years the airmen had exaggerated the achievements of bombing because they possessed no satisfactory means of assessing them. Now, Spaatz's dramatic prognostications of impending victory fell on sceptical ears, because he had no conclusive means of proving what he had done. Generals might gain ground, admirals might sink ships, but the airmen were forced back on the measurement of success or failure by aerial mosaic and mathematical projection. The Allied leadership did not dispute Spaatz's progress, nor the potential of his attacks. But they were by now far too well-versed in the apparent realities of the bomber offensive to accept that the oil attack offered a chance of early and absolute victory. Spaatz continued his campaign – with the support of Portal, of which more will be heard later. But at no point did it seem likely that the undivided weight of the Allied strategic-bomber force would be committed to the assault on the German oil industry.

By late summer many of the Allied leaders behaved as if the German military collapse was so close that it no longer mattered greatly what the bombers attacked, as long as they provided tactical support for the advancing armies on demand. In July, the British Chiefs of Staff had produced the minute to the Prime Minister which sowed the seeds of Operation *Thunderclap*, ultimately executed in a modified form against Dresden:

> The time might well come in the not too distant future when an all-out attack by every means at our disposal on German civilian morale might be decisive [they wrote] . . . . The method by which such an attack would be carried out should be examined and all possible preparations made.

The importance of this minute was not that it resulted in any immediate drastic action, but that it confirmed that the candle of support in high places for area bombing, which had all but expired in March 1944, was once again flickering by July. The fact that it was signed by all the Chiefs of Staff is a reminder that the concept of inflicting mass death and destruction on Germany's cities was not a unilateral air-force enthusiasm. The Directorate of Bomber Operations did some calculations about the possibilities of *Thunderclap*:

> If we assume that the daytime population of the area attacked is 300,000, we may expect 220,000 casualties. 50 per cent of these or 110,000 may expect to be killed. It is suggested that such an attack resulting in so many deaths, the great proportion of which will be key personnel, cannot help but have a shattering effect on political and civilian morale all over Germany. . . .

Tedder showed great interest in the possibilities of pursuing the attack on morale. Portal seemed for a time to favour it. There was intense discussion of a possible four days and nights round-the-clock air assault on Berlin, to precipitate the collapse of the Nazi regime.

The critical point is that none of the Allied leaders resolutely opposed a renewal of area bombing in some form or other, and this was more than enough of a mandate for Sir Arthur Harris. The C-in-C of Bomber Command had never lost faith in the principles on which he set out to level Germany two and a half years before. He bowed to overwhelming pressure to commit his forces to support *Overlord*, and this they had done wholeheartedly and with great effect. As the German air defences crumbled and losses fell, Harris found himself with more than a thousand first-line aircraft daily available, a surplus of crews so great that by autumn trainees found themselves employed shifting coal, and a range of devices and techniques formidable beyond the dreams of two years before.

Harris was still obliged to seek the authorization of SHAEF headquarters for every operation by his Command, but Tedder himself agreed by August that the army had become far too careless in its demands for strategic-bomber support even in the most unsuitable circumstances, and must be 'weaned from the drug'. In August, Harris gained SHAEF's approval for twelve area attacks on German cities, when his forces were not required elsewhere. The biggest raids were those of 16 August, when 809 'heavies' staged a two-pronged attack on Kiel and Stettin.

By early September, the French marshalling-yard campaign was complete, the 'ski-sites' had been largely overrun by the armies, and the Chiefs of Staff were addressing themselves to the future of the strategic air offensive. On 14 September a new bombing directive was issued, of which more will be heard later. But by the end of that month, Arnhem had ended, and the mood of the Allies was changing once more.

In the period of strategic hiatus for the airmen in late August and early September, however, they were for a few weeks astonishingly free to pursue their personal inclinations. Spaatz addressed himself to oil. On 11, 12 and 13 September, for example, he launched three great attacks on synthetic plants by 1,136,888 and 748 aircraft respectively, in which the Luftwaffe once more lost heavily in air battles, its defeat uncompromised by the half-hearted intervention of a few jet fighters. Bomber Command returned, inevitably, to Germany's cities. On 29 August its aircraft gave terrible proof of their new effectiveness in an attack on Königsberg. A mere 175 Lancasters 'de-housed' 134,000 people in a single night. They lost four aircraft.

Harris was going back to the ground that he had so reluctantly abandoned in April. He was able to do so, quite simply, because there was no one among the Allied directors of the war sufficiently determined to stop him.

XIII

'A Quiet Trip All Round': Darmstadt, 11/12 September 1944

'A quiet trip all round, with everything going according to plan.'

83 Squadron debriefing report, 12 September 1944

On the night of 11 September 1944, three days before the Combined Chiefs of Staff issued their directive restoring Bomber Command to Portal's control and establishing new priorities for the strategic offensive, 5 Group bombed the German town of Darmstadt. 218 Lancasters and 14 Mosquitoes delivered an exceptionally effective attack in which somewhere between eight and twelve thousand people – about a tenth of the town's population – were killed. In the words of the *United States Strategic Bombing Survey* in 1945:

> This was an area raid of the classic saturation type, which had so effectively razed Cologne and Hamburg. . . . The mechanics of the raid, between the 'Target Sighted' and the 'Bombs Away' were almost perfunctory, and as a consequence Darmstadt was virtually destroyed.

From the British point of view, this was not an important operation – it rates only a footnote in the four volumes of the official history. But I propose to describe it in some detail, partly to show the destruction of which Bomber Command was capable by late 1944, but chiefly to give some impression of what it was like to suffer one of the most devastating forms of assault in the history of war. I have tried to convey the courage and dedication of the aircrew who flew over Germany. In any story of Bomber Command it is also appropriate to show something of the spirit of the enemy below.

Damstadt was a prosperous provincial town set in rolling farmland studded with woods, some fifteen miles south of Frankfurt. It was primarily a residential and small-business centre, where shopkeepers and craftsmen plied their trades from stores and workshops beside their homes. The heart and pride of Darmstadt was the old town, a maze of narrow, cobbled streets radiating outwards from the seventeenth-century *landgraf*'s castle, whose grey walls and tall bell-tower overlooked the central market square. Among the gabled baroque and renaissance houses stood two theatres, a celebrated museum and a cluster of lesser palaces and great houses built in the days when Hesse was among the most notable independent German principalities. It was 'typical' in the manner that made pre-war English tourists nod and exclaim on the charm of the German bourgeoisie. It was a survivor of the greatest age of German culture and architecture.

The old town gave way at its edges to modern houses and widening streets, squares and small parks and a scattering of factories. The south suburb was the smart residential area. Most of the industrial workers lived on the north side, close to the town's two largest factories, E. Merck and Rohm & Haas, family businesses which between them employed almost half the total workforce of Darmstadt making chemicals and pharmaceuticals. A number of V-2 rocket technicians were being trained at the Technical University. Almost one in ten of the town's workers were employed in government offices; the remainder worked in shops, the printing business, or the small factories making photographic paper, leather goods and wood products. Most of the factories were working only a single eight-hour shift a day. According to the post-war USSBS survey, 'Darmstadt produced less than two-tenths of 1 per cent of Reich total production, and only an infinitesimal amount of total war production. Consequently, it had a low priority on labour and materials. Nor was the city important as a transportation centre, because it had no port and was by-passed by the principal rail arteries.' In all, 18.5 per cent of the workforce was employed on production that directly assisted the German war effort.

Being situated in western Germany, Darmstadt had always been readily accessible to Bomber Command, and indeed as early as October 1940 Portal placed it on his list of German cities suggested for proscription. In November 1943, Sir Arthur Harris included it in his great list of towns that he claimed had been damaged by Bomber Command, in his letter to the Prime Minister. But in reality very few bombs had ever hit Darmstadt, whether aimed or not. Over the years, a few crews jettisoned their loads there. There were two 'nuisance' raids against the town in the spring of 1944. On one occasion, fifteen USAAF Flying Fortresses attempted a precision attack on the Merck works, without significant effect. On the night of 25 August 1944, 202 5 Group aircraft were dispatched to bomb Darmstadt, but by a series of extraordinary flukes the Master Bomber was compelled to go home with technical failure, both his deputies were shot down en route to the target, and the Illuminating Force dropped their flares well wide. The Main Force arrived to find the VHF wavelength silent, the flare lines already dying. Most aircraft diverted to join the other Bomber Command attack of the night, on Rüsselsheim. Only five crews bombed Darmstadt itself, and a further twenty-five dropped their loads within three miles.

The Darmstadters were not even aware how close they had come to extinction that night. They assumed that the bombs which fell upon them were either jettisoned, or intended as a further nuisance raid, to drive them into the shelters. Before the night of 11 September they had suffered only 181 people killed in air raids. They were vividly aware that this was a trifle by the standards of every great city in Germany, and, to tell the truth, they had become complacent, almost careless about the peril of air attack.

The Allied armies were now scarcely a hundred miles west. To the very end of the war, few Germans sensed the depths of their Führer's alienation from them, his indifference to their suffering, his deranged determination to drag them with him to Wagnerian cataclysm. But there was little faith left in secret weapons or miraculous deliverance in Darmstadt. Its people had become fatalists, living out their lives in the hope of some ending of the war at tolerable cost in pain and pride.

But they cherished one terrible delusion. After four years of the Allied air offensive, Darmstadters believed that their town had been

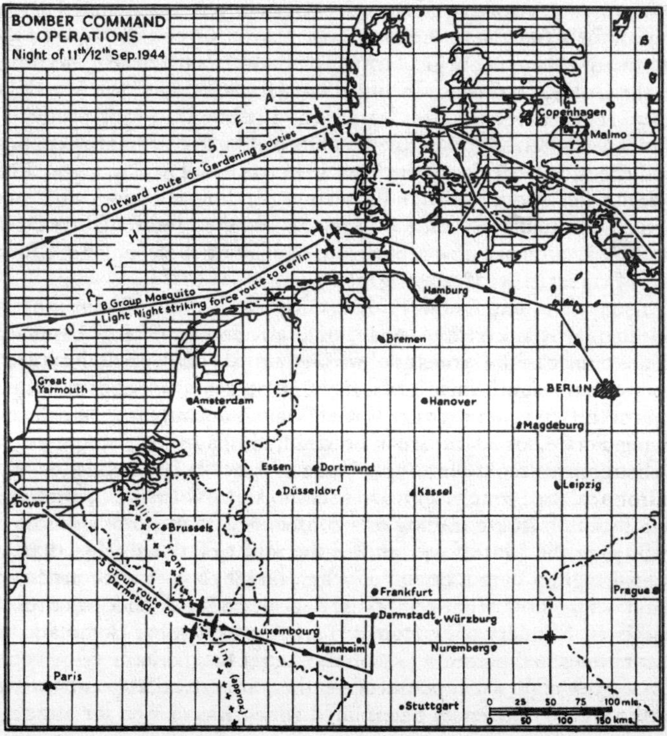

deliberately excluded from the Allied target lists. Their great treasure-trove of paintings and works of art had not been evacuated from the city. Night after night they watched the terrible fireworks displays over nearby Mannheim, Frankfurt, Ludwigshaven. They saw the great glow in the sky as other cities burned; the 'Christmas trees', as they called them, floating down from the Pathfinder aircraft cascading light; the burning bombers plunging to earth. They felt the earth shaking with the torrent of explosives falling around them. Yet Darmstadt stood, and they often discussed why. Some people said that with the Allied armies already closing on the borders of Germany, the enemy had selected certain cities to be preserved intact for headquarters and billets, and as a sop to the advocates of preserving German culture. Heidelberg, Wiesbaden and Darmstadt were said to be foremost among these. There was another quaint local theory that Darmstadt was marked for salvation because the Prince of Hesse, who was related to the British Royal Family, lived close to the town and still owned extensive property there.

In reality Darmstadt had always been on the British target lists. Like every other town of significant size in Germany, it was included in High Wycombe's *Guide to the Economic Importance of German Towns and Cities*, subtitled with macabre jocularity 'The Bomber's Baedeker'. According to the Guide, Darmstadt included one Grade I target, the Merck factory: 'It is believed that this works is now concentrating on products of direct war interest at the expense of its production of pharmaceuticals and chemicals,' declared the May 1944 edition. The Eisenwerk Eberstadt Adolf Riesterer, manufacturing grinding machines and stone saws, was listed as a Grade 3 target. So was the Motorenfabrik Darmstadt AG, 'who are now reported to be making diesel engines'. Rohm and Haas rated as a Grade 2 target.

Today it is impossible to determine exactly why Darmstadt was selected for attack on 25 August and finally destroyed on 11 September in preference to the scores of other area targets of far greater industrial and military significance. On a given night, a city was chosen from the vast target list generally after verbal discussion, and those who decided the fate of Darmstadt are now dead, or have long forgotten one unmemorable night among six years of war.[1] It is possible, as many historians have sought with Dresden, to seek evidence of a prolonged and rational debate leading to a consciously momentous decision. In reality, in the heat of war and in the midst of a campaign that was waged nightly over a period of years, target choices were made with what might now seem remarkable carelessness. A succession of Air Ministry, Ministry of Economic Warfare and Bomber Command HQ committees had placed a city on the target list, perhaps years before. On a given night a compound of weather, forces available and the state of the German defences determined which was chosen for attack. In

September 1944, 5 Group was seeking previously undamaged area targets of manageable size upon which to test the accuracy and effectiveness of various marking and bombing techniques, tolerable cost – in other words at limited penetration inside Germany. Darmstadt met all these criteria perfectly. On the night of 11 September, 5 Group experimented with a new aiming technique. Because Darmstadt had never before been seriously scarred by boming, it was ideally suited to provide a verdict on the new method and its potential. When *The Times* reported the raid the following morning, the paper stated, according to the Air Ministry public-relations brief: 'This is a centre of the enemy's chemical industry.'

Late on the morning of 11 September, the teletypes from 5 Group headquarters at Swinderby began to clatter out the long winding sheet of orders for its bases and squadrons. This was to be an operation exclusively by Cochrane's men, and thus most of the detailed planning had been done by his own staff rather than High Wycombe.

AC864 SECRET Action Sheet 11 September
Target: LUCE
8 Group to WHITEBAIT
MONICA not to be used at any time
Aim: to destroy an enemy industrial centre
2359 H Hour
Aircraft to attack between 12,500 and 16,000 feet
Main Force 1 x 4,000 lb plus maximum 4 lb incendiary clusters. . . .

5 Group's attack on LUCE – one of Saundby's countless fish codenames – was to be the main Bomber Command operation of the night. Bennett was dispatching forty-seven Mosquitoes of his Light Night Striking Force to Berlin. Seventy aircraft from 100 Group would be in the air, putting up the usual *Mandrel* radar-jamming screen, interrupting the night-fighter controllers, sending twenty-six Intruder Mosquitoes to attack the Luftwaffe airfields, and a further eighteen *Serrate* Mosquitoes to stalk the night-fighters in the sky. 3 Group would also be dispatching mining sorties to area GERANIUM, in the Baltic.

At 4 pm, 5 Group's squadron and flight commanders gathered in the operations rooms of their bases across Lincolnshire. The familiar crisp, sharp, patrician voice began to echo down the broadcast link from Swinderby: 'Good afternoon. This is the AOC. The target for tonight is Darmstadt. . . .' After Cochrane's introduction, his weather man gave the provisional forecast for western Germany: clear skies and strong westerly winds. Then the little groups of men in the ops rooms listened intently as they heard the tactical plan for the night. Darmstadt was an 900-mile round-trip from Lincolnshire as the crow flies, but their dog-leg deception course would take them 1,083 track miles there and back. They would be carrying the usual fire-raising mix of 'cookies' to blast open the walls and windows, and incendiaries to ignite the households and factories thus exposed. Darmstadt would receive in all 399 tons of high explosive and 580 tons of incendiaries.

Marking would be offset, the marking-point being an old army parade-ground, the *Kavallerie Exerzierplatz*, a mile west of the city centre. This had been chosen because its white, chalky soil showed up vividly by day or night on the reconnaissance photographs that they all had before them. But the most remarkable part of the plan was now to come: when the ten squadrons of 5 Group's Main Force ran in to bomb, rather than approaching as usual along a single common axis, tonight they would bomb along no less than seven different aiming-lines at varying heights, spreading out from the marking-point in what Darmstadters were later to call '*Der Todesfacher*' – 'The Death Fan'. Every aircraft would vary its delay in bombing after passing the marking-point by between three and twelve seconds. Instead of a single mass of devastation, tonight 5 Group sought to spread its attack evenly and fatally the entire length and breadth of Darmstadt. Finally, to ensure that the key industrial targets were destroyed, after the Main Force attack seven of 627 Squadron's Mosquitoes – the less proficient marking crews – would go in low with all-incendiary loads to deliver precision strikes on the key factories.

83 and 97 Squadrons, the Illuminating Force, took off from Coningsby a few minutes before 9 pm, 2100 hrs. Crossing the Channel, they flew down the Franco-Belgian border, high above Luxembourg, within earshot of tens of thousands of Allied and German soldiers confronting each other in the forward positions miles below. The bombers were on track for Karlsruhe, perhaps, or Mannheim or Stuttgart. German radio began its nightly running-commentary for millions of civilian listeners, huddled behind the blackout in their bedrooms or sitting-rooms, fully dressed with their suitcases and valuables beside them. Programmes were interrupted at regular intervals for the terse bulletins:

> 2216: Enemy bomber formations over and approaching Denmark in an easterly direction [this was the 'Gardening' force].
>
> The reported fast-bomber formation is still approaching Schleswig-Holstein and Denmark – [these were Bennett's Mosquitoes].

The sirens wailed in Copenhagen as people left the cinemas and bars for the shelters. The first Bomber Command casualty of the night, one of the 'gardening' Halifaxes, was hit by a night-fighter and crashed into a farmhouse near Vordinborg. Its mines blew up, killing the farmer, his wife and three children, most of their livestock and seven young Englishmen.

> 2309: The reported bomber formation is now approaching Pomerania. The reported fast bomber formation is over Mark Brandenburg. A new formation of fast bombers is approaching west Germany.

Here at last were 5 Group's marking Mosquitoes, overtaking the Lancasters and tracking fast down the Franco-Belgian frontier.

> 2332: The reported formation continues to approach Pomerania. The bomber formation reported over and approaching western Germany is now over west and south-west Germany. The reported bomber formation over Mark Brandenburg is flying off north-westerly.

Eight minutes earlier, the air-raid sirens sounded in Darmstadt, for the fourth time that day – the Americans had passed overhead during the afternoon. Wearily but without great fear, families gathered their children, their possessions, their helmets and a little food, and trooped down to the cellars, remembering to switch off the gas and unlock the emergency exits to their houses as they went. Many had been listening to the night's radio broadcast of Strauss's *Der Rosenkavalier*. They chattered to their neighbours as they slipped down from their apartments. There were the usual air-raid warning jokes.

North-west of Karlsruhe, 5 Group suddenly swung up through a steep 75-degree turn to port. Now they were tracking north, straight for Darmstadt. The city had laughed for the last time for many days.

Darmstadt had always been low on the priority list for civil defence, flak and searchlights. 'Looking back,' said Jacob Glanzer, one of the survivors of this night, 'our precautions were ridiculously dilettante.' The great cities of Germany possessed an elaborate and efficient hierarchy for the control of air-raid reporting and rescue, reaching down from each city's Police President to individual house wardens. Darmstadt possessed the structure, but not the effectiveness. Few of its children had been evacuated to rural areas. No deep public shelters had been dug. While in the embattled industrial centres the Nazi Party under the personal direction of Dr Goebbels had taken over many of the rescue and relief functions – a shrewdly-calculated propaganda move – in Darmstadt these had been left to the municipality. Communal shelters existed in the basements of offices and public buildings and in the cellars of the local brewery, but the overwhelming majority of Darmstadters relied exclusively on their own cellars for protection. Reinforced slit-trenches had been dug in and around the railway station, and 'safety holes' had been knocked through the brickwork of adjoining cellars in many rows of houses. But these things had been done without the terrible sense of urgency and expectancy that moved

Berliners and Hamburgers. Many of the flak batteries around Darmstadt had been removed to cover seriously embattled cities. The local fire-brigade was just 150 men strong, and on the night of 11 September their thirteen engines were arrayed as usual in the courtyard of the castle, ready to move on the orders of Max Jost, the fire chief, in his underground bunker. It was not unlike holding a tugboat under orders to save the *Titanic*.

At 2346 hrs, a local hairdresser named Emil Thier rang the bunker from his observer post on Hochzietsturm, to report 'Christmas trees in the west'. 17,000 feet above, 97 and 83 Squadrons' Flare Force I droned over the city, laying in their wake five lines of parachute-borne light. The green proximity Target Indicators of the Primary Blind Markers, aimed by H2S, burst on the city at the same moment. Those who were still above the ground in Darmstadt heard the flares burning. Some described a rustling sound, others a persistent hiss. The town seemed frozen in the still, icy glare. Then the light flak began to clatter angrily into the sky, the heavier 88s burst into their barrage. Somebody in the control bunker said flatly: 'Now it's us.'[2]

5 Group was not very impressed by Darmstadt's flak and searchlights. One pilot in his report described the light AA as 'meagre'. 83 Squadron assessed the heavy 88-mm fire as 'light to moderate'. The three 'Windfinder' aircraft, circling at 22,000 feet a few miles from the city with their special equipment, maintained reports to the Master Bomber on VHF, chattering a good deal too much according to the marking aircraft crews, straining to catch R/T instructions across the busy ether. The windspeed was forty-three knots, and Main Force were instructed to feed their bombsight computers accordingly. Flare Force I had scarcely begun illuminating when there was a crackled 'Tally-ho!' from one of 627's circling Mosquitoes, and the pilot swung in to mark the *Kavallerie Exerzierplatz*. Wing-Commander Woodroffe, the Master Bomber, orbited at a thousand feet. The red Target Indicators were perfectly positioned. Crews could see one German dummy green TI in the distance, perhaps ten miles westwards, and some decoy incendiaries burning furiously in a nearby wood. But none of these threatened to disturb the attack on a clear night with only the slightest haze.

Woodroffe ordered the rest of his marking pilots to back up the red TIs with greens, halted Flare Force II in the midst of their run at 2352 hrs, and a few moments later sent all the marking aircraft home. At 2356 hrs, he called in Main Force to bomb on their aiming lines as ordered, attacking by the red TIs if they could see them, by the greens if they could not. Two hours later, the Mosquitoes were back on the ground at Woodhall Spa. The Lancasters had no difficulties in bombing, but ran into night-fighter trouble as they turned away from Darmstadt. 5 Group lost twelve aircraft that night, including two crews from 97 Squadron. But those who came home described the operation without notable excitement or dismay. 'Should prove a very successful raid,' said Flying Officer Birdling of 83 Squadron at debriefing. 'Marking was done quickly and without a hitch. Opposition was slight.' 627 Squadron's report was brief and contented: 'Objective: Town centre, Darmstadt. All TIs were within 400 yards of the Marking Point. Main Force bombing was well-concentrated.' Squadron-Leader Twigge of 83 Squadron said: 'A quiet trip all round.'

The raid on Darmstadt lasted fifty-one minutes, from the fall of the first Target Indicator to the release of the last Mosquito incendiary load. In the cellars and shelters of the city, almost a hundred thousand people lay numbed by the continuous concussions, the dust swirling in through the ventilators, the roar of falling masonry all around them. The lighting system collapsed almost immediately, and as foundations trembled cellar-doors buckled, brickwork began to fall. The civil defence organization disintegrated as streets were blocked and bombs cut the vital cable links to the control centre on Hugelstrasse and the emergency control on lower Rheinstrasse. The firemen were thenceforth without orders. The fire-watching centre behind the city church was itself ablaze. Gas, water and power mains were severed. In the first minutes of the attack, the people of Darmstadt lost their coherence as a body of citizens, capable of mutual assistance. The town became a splintered, blazing, smoking battlefield upon which a hundred thousand men, women and children struggled to save themselves as best they might. This, of course, was precisely the purpose of saturation air attack on cities. But it was very rarely, even in this last year of the war, that the intention was as comprehensively fulfilled as on the night of 11 September in Darmstadt.

In the cellars, thousands of isolated clusters of humanity lay unmoving, limbs limp, stomachs shrunken by terror. The heat grew, and burning embers began to drift through the ventilators. Most people lay in silence, huddled with their private nightmares. But where Jacob Schutz sheltered, a child cried endlessly through the attack as the walls shook: 'Jesus, my Jesus, Mercy, Mercy . . .' Schutz imagined the bombers above, strewing their loads upon Darmstadt like men sowing a field. A Dutchman who had been upstairs suddenly rushed into their cellar with his hair awry shouting 'Everything, everything is burning!'

> There was a dreadful crash, the walls shook, we heard masonry cracking and collapsing, and the crackle of flames [wrote Martha Gros]. Plaster began to fall and we all thought the ceiling would collapse. . . . About thirty seconds later there was a second terrible explosion, the cellar-door flew open, and I saw, bathed in a brilliant light, the staircase to the cellar collapsing and a river of fire pouring

> down. I shouted 'Let's get out!' but the Hauptmann gripped me: 'Stay here, they are still overhead.' At that moment, the house opposite was hit. The armoured plate in front of our cellar flew up in the air, and a tongue of fire about fifteen feet long shot through at us. Cupboards and other furniture burst and fell on to us. The terrible pressure hurled us against the wall. Now somebody shouted: 'Get out and hold hands!' With all his strength he pulled me out from under the wreckage, I dropped my cash box and pulled the others with me. We climbed through the hole leading to the back. . . . More bombs were already falling into the garden. We crouched low, each of us beating out the small flames flickering on the clothes of the one in front. Phosphorus clung to the trees and dripped down on us. . . . The heat was terrible. Burning people raced past like live torches, and I listened to their unforgettable final screams. . . .

Gerhard Hartmann sat on a chair in a shelter crowded with his family's most precious furniture, a huge cupboard behind him 'rolling like a ship at every blast'. Carolin Schaefer clung to her two sons in the cellar of her home in Weiterstedtstrasse, the children burying their heads deeper in her breast at each explosion. Her husband was with the army on the western front. On most nights, they spent air-raid alarms in her father-in-law's strongly-built cellar a few streets away, but tonight they had been unable to get there in time, so they were packed into the basement of their apartment building. They shared their refuge with an elderly couple and a girl with a baby, who cried continuously about the lack of bedclothes for her child. At last Frau Schaefer passed her sons to the woman, and ran upstairs to fetch some covers. She opened the door from the cellar to be met by a cascade of flame. She seized a sand bucket and threw it in a futile gesture into the blaze. Then there was another roar of explosives as a 4,000-lb bomb exploded nearby. She fled once more to the cellar empty-handed.

In the shelter where Karl Deppert lay near the main post office, the lights survived through the first stage of the attack. Then there was a single heavy explosion, and blackness descended. There was a choked cry from the next cellar: 'Break through – we're trapped.' The men scrambled to the jumble of brickwork and struggled in the glimmering torchlight to clear a hole. After a few minutes' fevered labour, dust-covered bodies began to crawl through the wreckage. A sudden strong draught of air brought behind them a rush of smoke and sparks. Somebody yelled: 'Get out! The town's in flames!' Deppert picked up his small son in his arms, seized his wife's hands and gave her the bag holding the most vital family papers and some bread, then stumbled up the steps into the night.

All around them, flames were roaring through houses, shops, offices. Timbers sagged, window-frames and doors gaped empty, furniture blazed furiously. The 40 per cent slaked-lime fireproofing of roof timbers which had saved acres of Kassel in the great raid a year before could do nothing for Darmstadt. A paper factory crumbled and collapsed before the Depperts' eyes. They stood hesitating for a moment, uncertain which way safety lay. They thought of the castle, then saw that upper Rheinstrasse, through which it lay, was already an inferno. They began to run the other way, up Mathildenhohe. Their hair smouldered as embers fell upon their heads, and they brushed them away. A girl ran to them begging: 'Take me with you – I've just come from the pastry shop, and all the sugar is melting and no one dares to get out.' They linked arms to avoid falling among the debris, and fled through the spirals of fire and the corpses that already decked the streets.

Young Hanna Schnaebel crawled from the cellar beneath her family's little shop on Elizabethstrasse when the heat became unbearable, into that of the house adjoining, and then on down the cellars of the street. She ran up the stairs of the last one, into the midst of a shop whose counters were already on fire. An unknown man forced open the door for them to escape, then she stood alone on the streets shouting for the rest of her family and their little shopgirl, Annie. She began to run, a wet blanket over her head. She saw people crowding for shelter into a little workman's hut in the midst of the grass of the Palaisgarten. She ran to join them, and together they cowered panting and silent with their terror until someone shouted: 'The hut's on fire!' They staggered out, to find flames entirely encircling them, leaping towards the sky:

> Suddenly I saw my mother. It was a miracle. We embraced, then we got to the wall of the Palaisgarten and crept beneath it. My blanket had been swept away. I lay half across her to shield her. Suddenly the bushes around us began to burn. We crawled to a big tree. I began to shake, to feel sick. Then I was sick, and I felt better. There was a momentary blast of icy air before the heat descended again. There was a gale of ashes as houses collapsed. No one spoke. All we could hear were the terrible screams for help from the cellars of the streets around us. But no one could move. . . .

The first fatal misfortune for the people of Darmstadt after the departure of 5 Group that night was that an ammunition train in a siding near the central station began to burn. At intervals for the next hour, its cars exploded, convincing the terrified city that the bombardment was continuing either from aircraft above, or from delayed-action bombs, whose value Bomber Command had learnt from the Luftwaffe in the 1940 Blitz on Britain. Thousands of Darmstadters lay motionless, numb in their cellars when their only hope of survival lay in flight. The last of 627's Mosquitoes had dumped its incendiaries more than half an hour before the fires of the *Todesfacher*, fuelled by the superlative tinder of the old town and the stiff breeze, combined to create a firestorm.

This was the terrible hurricane of flame and wind that destroyed Hamburg, and which was to raze Dresden. As the fires leapt a mile into the sky, they sucked in cold air to bellow the blaze, sweeping from street to street in an irresistible rush of heat. Darmstadt was overwhelmed by a great roaring sound that induced deadly paralysis among the thousands in the shelters. They peered briefly out at the city, light as day amidst the flames, and lacked the will to step forth. So there, in their underground refuges, they died – whether of suffocation or by incineration it mattered little. The only people who lived that night were those who summoned the courage to fly.

Even among those who tried to escape, hundreds were sucked into the fires by the force of the wind, a snowstorm of ashes whirling around their heads. By 2 am, a Force 10 gale was driving through Darmstadt, while at the heart of the fires temperatures reached an incredible 1,500, perhaps 2,000 degrees centigrade. No one knew with certainty which way to run for safety. After Hamburg, the big city streets were everywhere adorned with arrows pointing the way to flight in a firestorm, but there were no such refinements in Darmstadt. Those who sought to carry their great bundles of possessions or pull their handcarts behind them were doomed. Many fell as they ran, and could not rise again. Their corpses sank into the asphalt as it melted, and were mummified long before morning. Jacob Schutz, the man in whose cellar a child had appealed for divine intervention, dipped his coat in the water tank in the shelter, then ran up the stairs and down the street, clutching it to his head. After a few minutes, he sank down to rest by a garden fence. Looking up past the flames, for a curiously tranquil moment he marvelled, like so many bomber crews, at the sight of the stars and the thin moon, crystal clear and wonderfully cool above Darmstad's fires. Then he regained his composure, and ran back to the cellar.

> I urged the others to move. Four women had already gone, led by another man. No one else would go. I went back to lie under a big advertising hoarding in the street. For perhaps fifteen minutes I stayed among the children there, trying to help to make them feel safe, wrapping them in blankets. Then I went to look for a better place for us. I was forced back again and again by the smoke and the flames. Then I found a wall in Heinrichstrasse where perhaps a hundred people were sheltering. When I returned to the hoarding, it was in flames. With one child in my arms and leading another by the hand, I took twenty people to the wall. I saw a few faces I knew: a husband and son who had lost his wife and daughter. A cow had wandered in from somewhere, and stood calmly among the people. . . .

Schutz found his way to a nearby fountain, and threw himself into its blissful coolness. Then he filled his helmet with water, and carried it carefully back to the beleaguered survivors in Heinrichstrasse. They dipped their scarves and handkerchieves into the water, and pressed them to their lips to deaden the terrible heat beating at their faces. Again and again Schutz made the journey to the fountain. At last, when all the group had been tended, in a moment of pity he went back once more for water for the cow. He met a friend who had recently given him two packets of precious tobacco. Now it lay in the abandoned embers of his house. They laughed absurdly about the tragic loss. Then they lay down to wait for the dawn. 'It was not death that was terrible that night,' said Schutz, 'but the fear of death – the whimpering, the shrieks, the screams. . . .'

All over Darmstadt, men, women and children were being asphyxiated where they sheltered, slowly slipping away into unconsciousness. One cellar lay beneath a house that received a direct hit from a 'cookie'. Every inhabitant was killed instantly by blast except a single survivor, a chemist. He was found later with a razor in his hands. He had slit his own throat. Fifty people took refuge in one fountain, lying amidst the surrounding smoke and flame in a few inches of water beneath a great statue of Bismarck. In the morning, twelve survived. In a communal shelter beneath an apartment block in Rheinstrasse, a central-heating boiler burst, drowning sixty people whose bodies were discovered in the morning, perfectly cooked. Two pregnant women collapsed as they fled through the streets and gave premature birth. Their bodies and those of their infants were found incinerated where they lay. Corpses were everywhere, the horror increased by the remains of long-dead Darmstadters blasted from their graves by a 4,000-lb bomb that had exploded in a cemetery. Schutz saw the body of a young woman 'lying like a statue, her cold heels in their shoes stuck up in the air, her arms raised, parts of her face still visible, her mouth and teeth gaping open so that you did not know whether she had been laughing or crying. . . .'

There were the usual multi-coloured corpses, stained every shade of the rainbow by pyrotechnics. 'One fat air-raid warden lay, his little lantern beside him, his hands peacefully folded on his enormous chest. He looked like a sleeper replete after a banquet in some wonderful country.' Since the earliest raids on Germany's cities, there were strict laws forbidding the storing of solid fuel in cellars, which had contributed to so many terrible fires in the wake of bombing. But in this as so much else, Darmstadt had been complacent. Many cellars were packed with wood, coal and coke. Now these fuelled their owners' funeral pyres.

The castle, with its priceless library, was blazing furiously. In Mathildenplatz, seven stallions which had broken out of their stables careered around the ring of flame encircling the square, maddened with

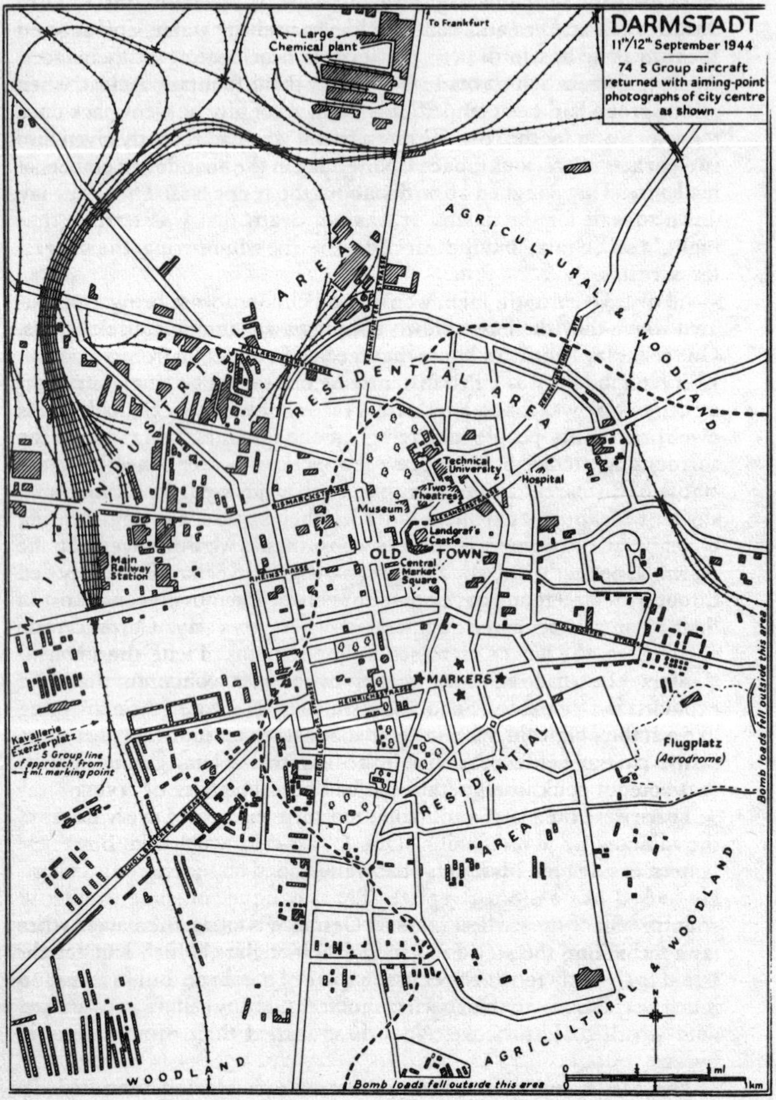
DARMSTADT
11th/12th September 1944
74 5 Group aircraft returned with aiming-point photographs of city centre as shown
To Frankfurt
Large Chemical plant
AGRICULTURAL & WOODLAND
INDUSTRIAL AREA
MAIN INDUSTRIAL AREA
RESIDENTIAL AREA
Technical University
Hospital
Two Theatres
Museum
Landgraf's Castle
OLD TOWN
Central Market Square
Main Railway Station
RHEINSTRASSE
BISMARCKSTRASSE
HEINRICHSTRASSE
MARKERS
Kavallerie Exerzierplatz
5 Group line of approach from ½ ml. marking point
Flugplatz
(Aerodrome)
Bomb loads fell outside this area
RESIDENTIAL AREA
AGRICULTURAL & WOODLAND
WOODLAND
Bomb loads fell outside this area
0
1 ml
km

terror, striving in vain to break out. Seven of Darmstadt's eight Evangelical churches were already gone, and firemen were struggling hopelessly to save the Technical University, the museum and the theatres. Georg Dumas had to watch the priceless panelling of his home in Mathildenhohe burn before his eyes. His beloved grand piano sank into the flaming floorboards 'with a final beautiful chord like the last trump'. His little dachshund crawled under the stove and whined hysterically until at last the fires silenced it. One of his neighbours cried ceaselessly for the loss of her beloved paintings, including a Tintoretto and a Salvator Rosa. It was entirely beyond her to grasp what was happening to the entire city.

In Maria Tevini's cellar, the doors burst from their frames after a near-miss early in the attack. Her eighteen-month-old son was hidden beneath a cushion in a laundry basket, while her 4½-year-old huddled beside her. She heard voices outside yelling to them to escape at once if they hoped to live. Clutching the children, she stumbled out into the garden to see their rabbit hutch and chicken-coop blazing, and molten debris from the roof of the museum next door smouldering on the grass. A fireman appeared from somewhere, and helped her to carry the children through the rubble and the flames to the Herrengarten park, fighting to walk upright in the face of the gale of wind and ash and heat.

> I saw people tearing off their clothes as they caught fire, amidst the terrible music of the storm. The Herrengarten looked like an enormous medieval military camp, inhabited by the most ragged army in the world. Incendiaries burned everywhere, and no one was certain whether they were dangerous. Our eyes smarted with the smoke. I was given a handkerchief – a great prize – to soak in the water of the fountain. My son hung motionless, silent beside me. My arms ached with the weight of the baby. Then I met some women who soothed the children, and promised that there was a house intact nearby where we could shelter. It sounded like a fairytale. . . . I found my father, sunk on a grassy bank, sleeping exhausted with his steel helmet perched on top of his hat. I should have laughed. But in the past few hours, I had forgotten how. . . .

Ludwig, Prince of Hesse, was at his castle outside Darmstadt when he heard the assault on the city begin. He went outside and stood in the darkness, watching the sky lightening into a great red and yellow glow over the town. Too old for this war, he still possessed his army uniform from the last. Now, he went indoors and put it on, together with his helmet and jackboots. There was no petrol for the cars, so he helped his old coachman Helmuth to harness the horses to a cart. They loaded two bicycles in the back. Then with great fear in their hearts, they climbed aboard and Helmuth whipped the team towards the fires.

Darmstadt Castle was still burning as they approached, beside its grey walls a huge charred Wellingtonia, decapitated by blast. 'My only satisfaction was that the New Palace which I had sold to the Gestapo was utterly destroyed. It had always been a terrible thought to me that in cellars where my brother and I had played so happily as children, people were now tortured and imprisoned. . . .' They moved among numbed survivors checking piles of corpses. One woman said, 'Is that father?' but her son shook his head: 'He was wearing different trousers.' The Prince helped an enormous old lady to clamber over a wall from the ruins of her house:

> I told her to imagine that we were both a few years younger, and that I was a charming cavalier into whose arms it would be a pleasure to fall. The old lady instinctively wanted to go to the old cemetery, where she joined hundreds of people sitting amidst the graves on rescued sofas and mattresses, gazing hypnotized into the fires. . . .

A Russian prison-camp at the edge of the town was totally destroyed. 200 Italian internees sought to escape from the Concordia Hall in Waldstrasse through a narrow archway into the street. It collapsed upon them as they battered at the doors. The town treasury was gutted. A soldier on leave from the Russian front stood crying by the burning castle: 'I have never seen this,' he said. 'This is hell.' Else-Marie Ullrich was a sixteen-year-old lawyer's daughter who had been sheltering with her parents in the basement of the Dresdner Bank, above which they had an apartment. They were a cheerful, easygoing family who seldom bothered to go down to the shelters when there was an alarm, and joked about it when they did. After attempting to escape and finding flames and debris all around them, they made a conscious decision that it was better to suffocate than to burn. One woman who tried to flee was never seen again. The others sat in silence as the air thickened and grew stifling. Else-Marie's sister suddenly blurted out: 'Oh! I've found my lucky penny! It's all right, we're all going to be all right!' But water was pouring into the cellar from the wrecked boiler-room next door. They lay on the floor, gasping for the dwindling breaths of air. One by one they lost consciousness. They were very close to death when at the imprecations of a bank employee, in the early hours of daylight, a gang of soldiers dug through the wreckage to free them. 'Many people struggled to help and gave unstintingly that night,' said Fraulein Ullrich. 'Others, who had much, offered nothing. We have forgotten neither kind.'

One of Darmstadt's principal tragedies that night was that no outside help could reach the city through the ruins and the flames until the firestorm was far beyond checking. There was an elaborate nationwide organization to support local town fire-brigades in crises such as this.

There were fifty-three Luftwaffe fire-fighting battalions, and the men of the Mobile Reserve Service – part of the Fire Protection Police – were stationed at strategic points all over Germany to race down the *autobahns* to a city under attack. There were also relief columns which went to the assistance of devastated cities with personnel and equipment capable of providing 30,000 meals a day. All these organizations worked with efficiency and dedication until the last weeks of the war, but on the night of 11 September they could do nothing. By 3 am the following morning, a great mass of vehicles and men from neighbouring towns and villages and from as far afield as Mannheim, Mainz and Frankfurt stood helpless on the *autobahn* that the Führer had opened himself almost exactly ten years before, gazing towards the tormented city. In Darmstadt itself, the fire service did its pathetic best. But they were without orders and short of petrol for their pumps. Scores of fire hydrants were blocked by rubble. Scores more were linked only to fractured mains.

In the Marienhospital in the midst of the city, doctors and nurses worked amidst the blast-broken window frames to do what they could for thousands of terribly injured Darmstadters. The hospital's patients were evacuated to the cellars when the attack began, and there in the candlelight they remained. Two babies were delivered in the basement even as 5 Group delivered their attack. Now, queues of adults and children sought treatment for eyes tormented by the smoke and fumes. The doctors worked by emergency lighting powered by batteries – mains power and water were gone. For scores of horribly burned casualties, there was nothing to be done but ease their dying. Nurses soaked their sheets in salad oil to calm the pain. Most ended their sufferings by morning.

The firestorm died around 4 am. A yellow-grey light began to break over the city. Houses and public buildings still burned, but without the ferocity of the night. Prince Ludwig met a friend near the Inselstrasse who described how his old tutor, Professor Eugen Koser, had run headlong through the blazing darkness, cursing the rulers of Germany. People began to pick their way between the smoking buildings, through the melted asphalt of the streets to their houses, searching for life or property. The first terrible discoveries were made: cellars crammed with suffocated bodies – worse still, with amorphous heaps of melted and charred humanity. There were whole families whose remains could be removed in a laundry basket. Some bodies had shrunk to a quarter of life-size. Dr Fritz Kramer had been in France with the Kaiser's army thirty years before, 'yet this was worse than anything I had ever seen in Champagne'. There were blue corpses and purple corpses, black heaps of flesh and protruding bones. Kramer saw a man carrying a sack containing the heads of his entire family; the body of a girl lay on a pavement with one naked leg broken off beside her, 'looking like some obscene joint of cold meat'. Loose hands and legs, the head of a man buried in rubble to the chin with his eyes open and empty, lay in Ludwigstrasse. Bodies were already piled in the Palaisgarten. The bleak humour of disaster began to assert itself. 'Well, at least we have nothing to worry about now,' said Ernst Luckow's wife Wilma, 'because we have nothing left at all. . . .'

Rudolf Vock ran into the Mayor of Wamboldt, which was one of the outlying suburbs of Darmstadt. 'Vock,' said the Mayor, 'you've got to get a hundred spades and go at once to the Waldfriedhof cemetery. There are a hundred Russian prisoners who've got to be started digging graves.' As he went, Vock passed a column of lorries in Rheinstrasse already piled with corpses. Two French prisoners ordered to help the sisters at the Marienhospital to remove their dead proved too nauseated by the stench to do the job, and now the nurses pushed a cartload of corpses to the Waldfriedhof themselves. At the cemetery, a silent crowd of men and women watched as the Russians unloaded the corpses, and began dumping them in hastily-dug pits, each covered with a layer of quicklime. A squad of armed SS troopers guarded the prisoners. Police detectives were stripping bodies of valuables and placing these in envelopes, labelled if there was any clue to identity. Hour after hour, the lorryloads trundled in. They laboured on, without food or rest. A gang of Gestapo prisoners were brought to reinforce the Russians, and that afternoon 5,000 men of the Wehrmacht moved into the city to support relief operations.

In four years of bombing, Germany had evolved a detailed procedure for dealing with the unspeakable realities of mass death. In the wake of the great raid on Kassel in 1943, the local Police President circulated a long list of suggestions that he believed other cities might find helpful: protective overalls, rubber gloves, goggles and disinfectants were essential for handling corpses; supplies of alcohol, candles, tobacco and torch batteries should be stockpiled for use in the first days after the raids; as many witnesses as possible should be brought to central collecting points to assist with identification of bodies. Identification teams should be equipped with shears and bolt-cutters for removing jewellery. It was useful to print in advance supplies of death-registers, corpse-cards and pro formas for individual personal descriptions, and to prepare supplies of envelopes for valuables. Bodies were best labelled in pencil, for ink ran in the rain. Dismembered corpses should be reassembled whenever possible, to avoid double-counting of loose limbs if they became separated. The Darmstadt authorities, therefore, had a useful body of case-history to draw upon. They needed it all in the days that followed.

At lunchtime on 12 September, Wilhemine Wollschrager hurried into the city from her suburban home to look for her grandparents, equipped with bread and a thermos of tea. She made her way down the narrow avenue through the rubble on Rheinstrasse, a moistened pad over her mouth amidst the lingering smoke. She was awed by the tramlines hung crazily over the road, the stream of empty-eyed refugees fleeing down the street against her, seeking the East Station. On the corners, little knots of blackened firemen and rescue workers sat exhausted, while others still laboured amidst the debris. At last she reached her grandparents' house.

> Thank God! The cellar windows were open. In my excitement I ran forward calling 'Grandmother! Grandfather!' Then I looked through the windows and saw small flames licking at the floor. Somebody pulled me back, shouting that the building could collapse at any minute. I rushed through the yards to the neighbour's house next door. I saw him lying dead in the yard, his bicycle and briefcase against a tree beside him. I never saw my grandparents again.

'There was a deathly silence in the town, ghostly and chilling,' wrote Martha Gros, the doctor's wife who had fled from her blazing cellar at the height of the attack.

> It was even more unreal than the previous night. Not a bird, not a green tree, no people, nothing but corpses. . . . We climbed over the wreckage into the garden and proceeded to the burnt-out cellar. The ashes were almost two feet deep. I found the place where I had dropped our cash box, picked it up and opened it. The 1,000 Reichsmark note which I had saved for emergencies was a heap of ashes. The little boxes of jewellery had been burned. The best piece, a large emerald, had cracked. Around our safe lay large lumps of melted silver, and in the wine-racks, there were melted bottles hanging in bizarre long ribbons. For this to have happened the temperature must have been something like 1,700 degrees.

'One was afraid of losing one's reason,' said Jacob Schutz:

> People from the rescue service were collapsing into nervous hysteria. It was a privilege to have a coffin, or even the means to make one oneself. Most of the bodies were put on a lorry or wheeled in little handcarts to the mass graves in the cemetery.
>
> The hospitals were crammed. All preparations counted for nothing. You could travel without a ticket on the train, bicycle on the pavements. There were no windows in the trains, no schools, no doctors, no post, no telephone. One felt completely cut off from the world. To meet a friend who survived was a wonderful experience. There was no water, no light, no fire. A candle was of priceless value. Little children and old people collected wood from the ruins for

cooking. Every family dug its own latrine in the garden. There was no more absolute ownership of anything. Many people moaned about their losses, yet others seemed almost relieved by their freedom from possessions. This had suddenly become a city of proletarians. . . .

Half-dressed people struggled to the stations in the great surge of anxiety to flee. Loudspeaker cars toured the city broadcasting evacuation instructions. The relations of the dozens of pregnant women who had given birth under the strain of the night sought desperately for a doctor or a midwife. Carolin Schaefer had covered the eyes of her children as they fled through the corpse-strewn streets 'because I felt that if the boys were to see this, they could never grow up to lead happy lives'. But by dawn she was compelled to abandon her efforts to save them from the sight of horror, because it was everywhere. A friend passed her in the streets pushing a bicycle, the melted rubber on its rims all that was left of the tyres. On the luggage rack was a soap box. 'Silently she embraced me. Then she began to cry, pointing to the box. "In there is my husband," she said.' Frau Schaefer's father and sister heard on the radio about the fate of Darmstadt, and travelled the breadth of Germany from their home in Chemnitz to look for her. Her husband was granted five days' leave from the front, and reached home in a Wehrmacht staff car: 'When he arrived, he said that nothing he had seen on the battlefield had ever pained him so much.' She found her father-in-law in the crowded ward of a city hospital, blind and terribly injured, 'a wreck of a man looking expressionlessly through his bandages'. He had been found wandering through the streets, dazed and unseeing.

Chalk scribbles on buildings were the only indication of the fate of thousands of Darmstadters. 'Where is Doctor Kutz?' Jacob Schutz saw scrawled on the broken wall of a house. Another hand had written briefly beneath: 'DEAD'. Men, women, children wandered the streets, searching for lost relatives and friends, struggling to save a few charred possessions from the ruins of their houses. Others were more fortunate. Passers-by were enraged to see a working-party of prisoners from the jail, under guard and in prison-striped uniform, labouring to rescue hundreds of cases of wine from the cellar of the local *Kreisleiter*'s house.

The troops who cleared the city of its corpses were openly plied with alcohol to enable them to complete their ghastly task. The living stumbled through the streets pushing handcarts laden with luggage, or piled their remaining sticks of furniture until some vehicle could break through to collect them. People of every age and background pillaged ruthlessly what they needed to survive. When Martha Gros miraculously found a coffin for one of her relations, she was compelled to chain it to the railings outside the house until they could carry out the burial.

Soup kitchens were established at strategic points, and businessmen and lawyers, shopkeepers and industrialists learnt to commute in a new pattern, from canteen to cellar, cellar to canteen. Many left the city altogether, some walking miles past the crowds of awed spectators who came from scores of surrounding villages to gaze on Darmstadt. 'And so we went like gypsies out of our dear, burning town,' wrote Hanna Schnaebel. Thousands of people clogged the railway station, where, by the afternoon of the 12th, packed refugee trains were running out of the city. Vast numbers of postcards were distributed, supposedly to let distant relatives know the fate of their families, but although they were filled in and collected for postage, none seemed to reach its destination.

At lunchtime on 13 September, to the stupefied disbelief of the survivors amidst the ruins, there was an air-raid warning. A great cry went up: 'They're coming again!' Carolin Schaefer saw the shattered faces around her in the street gaze appalled into the sky. Voices shouted in horror: 'Why have the come back?' 'What do they want?' 'There's nothing for them here.' High in the clear sky, they saw the glinting wings of a formation of the 8th Air Force's Flying Fortresses. The black puffs of flak began to burst around them. Moments later, the earth shook once more with explosions as people huddled with their hands to their ears, cowering amidst the rubble of the city, for only a few surviving deep shelters cut into rock were still of value to the people of Darmstadt.

The Americans had come for the marshalling yards, but when they bombed they were also able to destroy a pocket of housing on the north side of the city that had somehow survived the attack thirty-six hours before. Fritz Kramer noted the ironic case of a man who returned to Darmstadt on compassionate leave from the front to see his mother after the night raid. He was killed when the American bombs hit the railway station.

Psychologists who studied the effects of bombing on morale after the war concluded that it was a terrible experience to be bombed, but that once one had been bombed once, successive treatments made less and less effective impact on morale. So it seemed to be in Darmstadt. A passivity, an apathy gripped the city, as if its people were no longer capable of feeling. Overnight they had become hardened, even brutalized. Jacob Schutz met a man who had lost a son, but simply said: 'I thank God I have two more of them.' Another man was bemoaning the loss of his wife and child to an officer, who interrupted him with a shrug: 'In that cellar over there you'll find a family of ten who all caught it together.' When it rained, the hastily piled earth slipped away from some of the mass graves, exposing the bodies once more. Fungus grew upon them. It was days before anyone could be troubled to bury them again.

Bomber Command's report of the attack on Darmstadt was no more dramatic than that on scores of other targets, past and future: 'Photographic Reconnaissance Unit cover shows industrial part not covered, but remaining part shows large areas of complete devastation. Damage Assessment shows Rohm & Haas severely damaged; E. Merck – slight damage; diesel engine works has had nine buildings gutted.' On the night of 11/12 September, Bomber Command lost sixteen aircraft, including the twelve from the Darmstadt force. A *Serrate* Mosquito claimed to have shot down an Me110 north of Darmstadt. An Intruder Mosquito claimed a Ju88 damaged. A surprisingly large number of Bomber Command aircraft – forty-three in all – claimed to have seen German fighters at some point before, during or after the attack on Darmstadt. 218 of the 236 aircraft dispatched claimed to have bombed the target.

It was not until the end of the war that a scientific attempt could be made to assess the achievement of 5 Group's attack on Darmstadt, by the USSBS. Even this cannot be examined without emphasizing the degree of guesswork and statistical projection that went into the Survey's work, coupled with an enthusiasm to prove that USAAF 'precision' bombing had been more effective than British 'area' attacks. But the USSBS 'Detailed Study of the effects of the Bomber Command raid on Darmstadt' is the only collated evidence that exists, and thus it should be quoted:

> The area raid of 11/12 September came when industrial employment had already started on a general decline [stated the report]. The raid accelerated this decline. Its principal disruptive impact on the city's labour was felt in small commercial enterprises, who lost some 50 per cent of their workers. The most disruptive factor in the labour situation was not the air raids, but the withdrawal of German men into the army. . . . Industrial labour remained adequate, although a shortage of skilled labour was generally acknowledged. . . .
>
> Disruption of essential services such as gas, water, electricity and local transportation was not sufficient to interfere with production. The effects on industrial production of the 11/12 September raid were sufficient to have caused an overall production loss to the city of one month. The loss in the chemical industry was 1.4 months, and 1.1 months for the iron and metal production and fabrication industries. However, in a period of general economic decline this loss seems to be overstated in that it does not give proper weight to the downward trend which would have continued even without the raid. Therefore, by means of another computation . . . it was estimated that the overall loss can more fairly be stated as 0.4 months, ie 0.5 months for the chemical industry and 0.4 months for iron, metal production and fabrication.

Without accepting the detailed statistical conclusions of the report, it is possible to state that the raid of 11/12 September devastated the city of Darmstadt without fatally damaging the industries which theoretically prompted the bomber attack. Darmstadt's production fell from 8.3 million Reichsmarks in August 1944 to 3.7 in September, but then rose to 5.2 in October. In November it was still 4.5 million, despite the general national industrial decline, and in December 4.3. Thereafter, it collapsed completely in the wake of a further massive raid. But in the words of the USSBS: 'The production loss for the area raid of 11/12 September 1944 was remarkably small for a city experiencing a 49 per cent housing destruction.' During 5 Group's attack, the left-hand axis of attack achieved insufficient weight and concentration. While the old town was fatally hit, the industrial north-west escaped remarkably lightly, even after the low-level Mosquito attacks. It was a characteristic shortcoming of Bomber Command area raids: city centres burned readily, but the overwhelming weight of industry was in the suburbs, which were far harder to hit and destroy.

Yet there could be no doubt of the effective impact of the 5 Group attack on Darmstadt as a society. Where the abortive 25 August attack destroyed only 327 buildings, that of 11 September totally gutted 4,064 out of 8,401 dwellings. A further 462 had been rendered uninhabitable. 570 of the town's 888 shops ceased to exist. The old town was simply erased from the face of the earth. The prison and the post office were the only notable buildings to survive. From Lord Cherwell's point of view, the operation was a major success: 70,000 people were 'de-housed'. 49,200 fled the city as refugees. In 1939 Darmstadt and its outlying villages mustered a population of 115,211 people. By December 1943 conscription had reduced the total to 98,440. By 1 March 1945, there were only 51,750 people on the city's official ration strength. The remainder joined the vast army of refugees, 'displaced persons' and corpses. What was done to Darmstadt – virtually unnoticed by the Allied leadership, far less the public of Britain and America – vastly exceeded the devastation in Cologne created by the trumpeted '1,000 Raid' of 1942.

It will never be certain exactly how many people died on the night of 11 September, because so many bodies were never identified and so many records were destroyed. Contemporary Nazi statistics showed that of every 100 deaths, 15 were caused by blast, 15 by incineration, 70 by suffocation. 181 women and children died for every 100 men. One in five of the dead was a child under the age of sixteen.

The best estimate is that 12,300 Darmstadters were killed in air raids up to the end of the war, the overwhelming majority of these on the night of 11 September. In the immediate wake of the attack, the authorities counted 6,049 confirmed dead, 4,502 missing and 3,749 wounded. When the figure of those confirmed dead reached 8,433, the casualty list broke down as follows:

936 military
1,766 civilian males
2,742 civilian females
2,129 children
368 prisoners of war
492 foreign labourers

It would be absurd to imagine Darmstadt as a town somehow possessed of a unique innocence, its people free of the taint of Nazism, its factories producing cuckoo clocks or cigarette boxes. Darmstadt was an industrial town no more and no less devoted to supporting Hitler's war effort than scores of others. It was unusual only in that it was so little prepared to save and defend itself, and that its contribution to the war was slight in proportion to the Allied resources deployed to destroy it. What happened to Darmstadt was merely a supremely efficient example of the destruction meted out to so many towns for so long by the armed forces of Germany. The horrific tales of Darmstadters' experiences in September 1944 were only a late reflection of those of millions of Poles, Frenchmen, Dutchmen, Englishmen and Russians since 1939. For Bomber Command, it had now become possible to administer such blows almost nightly to the cities of Germany. It did so until the last month of the war.

The American 8th Air Force visited Darmstadt once more, on 19 September, just a week after Bomber Command. The Flying Fortresses delivered a precision attack on the Merck works, with considerable effect on production and further devastation of the pockets of buildings still standing around them. It might have seemed impossible that there now remained anything left to destroy in the city, but on 12 December the B-17s came once more – 446 of them, delivering 1,421 tons of explosives to the industrial area on the north-west of the town. The Allied armies then inherited the ruins.

A friend of Jacob Schutz, a very old man, wrote to him after the destruction of Darmstadt:

> At the turn of the century, I travelled through Germany's towns, and each one had its own soul and its own face. Shortly before the war I ventured again through the same towns, and it seemed that their souls and faces were gone, as if they were dead within themselves.
>
> Now, as I walk through the ruins of these same towns, I am overcome by the terrible awareness that they have fulfilled the promises that was made before the war. Instead of living corpses, they have become truly dead ones.

XIV

Saturation

> **You would think the fury of aerial bombardment**
> **Would rouse God to relent; the infinite spaces**
> **Are still silent. He looks on shock-pried faces**
> **History, even, does not know what is meant**
>
> **– Richard Eberhart**

In the last phase of the war, between October 1944 and May 1945, the Allied strategic-bomber forces played a dominant part in bringing the German economy to the point of collapse. Against only ineffectual resistance from the Luftwaffe, they attacked Germany by day and night on an unprecedented scale. Bomber Command alone dropped more bombs in the last quarter of 1944 than in the whole of 1943. The air forces' destruction of Germany's oil resources was chiefly responsible for the breakdown of the Ardennes offensive at the end of 1944, and must have hastened the end of the war at least by several weeks. The bomber attack on German rail and water communications was choking industry to death by the last weeks of 1944. However, it is more difficult to argue that the Transport Plan had a decisive effect, since although munitions production was doomed to extinction, the German armies continued to possess adequate supplies of arms and ammunition almost until their capitulation. The airmen's misfortune was that their triumphs came too late, in the context of the advance of the Allied armies across Germany, to be accepted as a decisive contribution to victory. By September 1944, with a degree of assistance from Bomber Command, the USAAF had brought German oil production almost to the point of collapse. Aviation spirit production, for instance, fell from 156,000 tons in May to 54,000 in June, 34,700 in July, 17,000 in August and 10,000 in September, measured against Luftwaffe consumption of 165,000 tons in April. Pilot training all but ceased; the Luftwaffe could not operate the aircraft Speer was still producing with such huge exertions. Total supplies of all fuel products had fallen to less than a third of their January levels. The German armies were largely driven back on horse-drawn transport; diesel trucks towed petrol vehicles; whole tank formations were immobilized; tactical battlefield mobility was seriously affected, and strategic fuel reserves were rapidly becoming exhausted.

But with the onset of winter weather that often made precision bombing impossible, and the herculean efforts of Speer's repair squads at the oil plants, the Allied bombing offensive lost momentum. Aviation spirit production rose to 21,000 tons in October, 39,500 in November, and 24,500 in December. Germany was able to husband the slender reserves with which it became possible to mount the Ardennes offensive. Thereafter, the bombing pressure became finally intolerable, and by the end of January 1945 the Allied victory over Germany's oil resources was all but complete. But the airmen had missed their moment. They were never to receive undisputed credit for an achievement that came so late. There has been a continuing controversy about responsibility for the failure to press home their assault in the summer and autumn of 1944, when a marginal increase in bombing effort might have tipped the balance to make the oil campaign decisive and to end the Second World War in Europe months earlier.

In previous chapters, it has been suggested that in the spring of 1944 the airmen's credibility was too low for Spaatz's enthusiasm for the Oil Plan to be wholeheartedly accepted by the Allied High Command. By autumn, however, there was widespread understanding of the success and potential of the attack on fuel. How was it, then, that against the USAAF's overall wartime effort of 131,000 tons of bombs dropped on oil targets, Bomber Command with its greater lifting capacity contributed only 94,000 tons, most of this in the last stages of the campaign?

The answer lies in the decisive breakdown of the RAF's internal command structure which took place in the winter of 1944, when the Chief of Air Staff, Sir Charles Portal, finally showed himself unable to exercise authority over Sir Arthur Harris. At the Quebec *Octagon* conference in September 1944, Portal proposed to the Combined Chiefs of Staff that the strategic air forces should be removed from control of SHAEF now that the Allied armies were fully established in Europe. The Americans demurred – they thought that Eisenhower and Tedder had directed the bombing effort admirably since June. They also believed, according to their official historians, that behind the smokescreen of British arguments about effective command, 'perhaps the crucial issue was one not mentioned in the official British proposals: a desire of the Air Ministry to re-establish its control of Harris's Bomber Command'.[1] That September, the Chiefs of Staff still envisaged the European war coasting to a reasonably smooth conclusion by Christmas. The British Air Staff were acutely conscious that Bomber Command had thus far failed to make the 'decisive' contribution to victory that they sought. They sensed time running out on them. Portal had become completely committed to the attack on German oil. He clearly believed that by re-establishing his control of Bomber Command, it might yet be possible for the RAF to play a leading part in the conclusive attack of the war on German oil supplies. Air Ministry papers of 1944 refer repeatedly to the danger that unless Bomber Command addressed itself urgently to the oil attack, 8th Air Force would complete the task single-handed. The British would be left to rest on the withered laurels of their area campaign against the cities.

Portal finally got his way in Quebec, not least because American attention was now overwhelmingly focused on the Pacific. The British, with their Bomber Command, were to have a last opportunity to make an independent contribution to the defeat of Germany. On 14 September, Arnold and Portal issued a new joint directive on behalf of the Chiefs of Staff to Sir Norman Bottomley, Deputy Chief of Air Staff, and General Spaatz, the USAAF's commander in Europe. Control of the strategic-bomber forces henceforth reverted from SHAEF to Bottomley and Spaatz as representatives of Portal and Arnold. The priority of *Pointblank* 'to bring about the progressive destruction and dislocation of the German military, industrial, and economic systems' was reasserted, save only that the Luftwaffe had ceased to be an important consideration. Support of the armies remained a major responsibility, and 'important industrial areas' were to be attacked 'when weather or tactical conditions are unsuitable for operations against specific primary objectives'.

It was a clumsy command arrangement, which placed Portal at one remove from his notoriously wayward C-in-C. But the directive issued by Bottomley on Spaatz to Bomber Command and 8th Air Force on 25 September, translating the Chiefs of Staff's instructions into formal orders, ranks among the most emphatic and specific of the war. There were no more wordy equivocations: oil became sole First Priority target, with transport links, tank and vehicle production as Second Priority. Perfunctory mention was also made of area targets, in the same terms as in the directive of 14 September.

The new orders were a disappointment to Sir Arthur Tedder, Deputy Supreme Commander at SHAEF. He had fought a fierce battle to concentrate the air attack on Germany's rail and water transport links. Tedder was persuaded by the evidence presented to him by Professor Zuckerman and others that what the pre-*Overlord* bombing had achieved in breaking French transport links could now be repeated against those of Germany, producing speedy and dramatic paralysis reaching forward to the battlefield. But to be effective, Tedder's Transport Plan called for the concentration of bomber effort. This was never achieved. During the winter of 1944 the 8th Air Force poured bombs on to marshalling yards and communication centres by H2X when the weather was too bad for oil targets, but in reality this amounted to nothing more than American participation in the area-bombing campaign on the cities. Germany's rail and water links were indeed hit with devastating effect by all the strategic air forces, including a series of notable precision attacks by Bomber Command, three of which breached the Dortmund–Ems Canal. But it was only in March 1945 that the effects of transport bombing became terminal for German industry. Most of the senior airmen and the members of the Combined Strategic Targets Committee had become wholehearted advocates of the oil offensive. It was their view which prevailed in Quebec, and to their purposes that 8th Air Force addressed its dedicated efforts in the winter of 1944.

Awareness seems only slowly to have grown on Sir Charles Portal, back in London, that Bomber Command was contributing less than its utmost energies to fulfilling the September directive. As Arnhem was fought and lost and the Allied ground offensive slithered into its wretched winter lassitude, Harris's aircraft were hitting again and again at Germany's cities. In the last three months of 1944, the C-in-C waged his last and greatest Battle of the Ruhr, with complete and terrible success within his chosen compass. 14,254 sorties were dispatched to the great industrial centres at which he had hammered for so long – Duisburg, Essen, Cologne, Düsseldorf and their lesser brethren. 60,830 tons of bombs were dropped – 85 per cent high-explosive now, for almost anything that would burn in these towns had long since gone to Harris's bonfires. Only 136 aircraft were lost. The transmitting stations for *Oboe* advanced into Europe with the armies, vastly extending the range of accurately-guided marking. With the decline in the defences, accuracy and concentration rose among the great bomber force of more than a thousand 'heavies' which now set forth nightly. With the fall in casualties, aircrew experience and competence rose.

Yet in October, 6 per cent of Harris's effort was directed against oil targets, less than in June. Between July and September 1944, 11 per cent of Bomber Command's sorties were dispatched to oil plants, 20 per cent to cities. Between October and December, 14 per cent went to oil, 58 per cent to the cities. It was impossible to believe that Harris was applying himself to the September directive. He had merely returned to the great area-bombing campaign precisely where he left it in April, despite the almost unanimous conviction of the Air Staff that the policy had long been overtaken by events. Harris now embarked on a correspondence with Portal in defence of his convictions and policy, in the course of which the Chief of Air Staff first requested, then demanded, and at last pleaded with Harris to obey the orders he had been given.

Harris fired his opening salvo in this last great bombing controversy of the war on 1 November 1944. In a letter to Portal, he violently protested the range of demands on his forces, 'the number of cooks now engaged in stirring the broth'. The Admiralty and the ball-bearing experts were tunnelling at his resources again, 'and even the nearly defunct SOE* has raised its bloody head and produced what I hope is now its final death rattle . . .'

*SOE: Special Operations Executive, for whom Harris reluctantly provided aircraft from his Special Duties squadrons to parachute arms and agents into occupied Europe.

> . . . in the past eighteen months, Bomber Command has virtually destroyed forty-five out of the leading sixty German cities. In spite of invasion diversions we have so far managed to keep up and even to exceed our average of two and a half cities devastated a month. . . . There are not many industrial centres of population now left intact. Are we going to abandon this vast task, which the Germans themselves have long admitted to be their worst headache, just as it nears completion?

To complete his great design, said Harris, all that was required was the destruction of Magdeburg, Halle, Leipzig, Dresden, Chemnitz, Nuremberg, Munich, Coblenz, Karlsruhe and the surviving areas of Berlin and Hanover. Portal replied on 5 November: 'At the risk of your dubbing me "another panacea merchant", I believe the air offensive against oil gives us by far the best hope of complete victory in the next few months. . . .' The next day, Harris dispatched a long answer in which he expressed his agreement about the importance of the oil plan, and offered tactical justification for the launching of great raids on Cologne and Bochum, which had been questioned by Portal. But, on the 12th, Portal returned to the fray:

> You refer to a plan for the destruction of the sixty leading German cities, and to your efforts to keep up with, and even to exceed, your average of two and a half such cities devastated each month; I know that you have long felt such a plan to be the most effective way of bringing about the collapse of Germany. Knowing this, I have, I must confess, at times wondered whether the magnetism of the remaining German cities has not in the past tended as much to deflect our bombers from their primary objectives as the tactical and weather difficulties which you described so fully in your letter of 1 November. I would like you to reassure me that this is not so. If I knew you to be as wholehearted in the attack on oil as in the past you have been in the matter of attacking cities, I would have little to worry about. . . .

In November the weight of bombs delivered against oil targets increased to 24.6 per cent of all Bomber Command effort, and even outstripped the 8th Air Force's tonnage at the end of the month. But by 12 December, Harris was once more writing to Portal to declare his renewed scepticism about the value of the oil offensive. 'The MEW experts have never failed to overstate their case on "panaceas". . . . The oil plan has already displayed similar symptoms.' Portal replied on 22 December that he was 'profoundly disappointed that you still appear to feel that the oil plan is just another "panacea". . . . Naturally, while you hold this view you will be unable to put your heart into the attack on oil.' Harris replied on 28 December:

> It has always been my custom to leave no stone unturned to get my views across, but when the decision is made I carry it out to the utmost and to the best of my ability. I am sorry that you should doubt this, and surprised indeed if you can point to any precedent in support of your statement. I can certainly quote precedent in the opposite sense.

This was truculence of a very high order, even by the standards of Sir Arthur Harris. Yet instead of seeking now to exert his authority, Portal chose to try to continue a rational debate with his C-in-C about the merits of razing cities: 'While area bombing, if it could have been continued long enough and in sufficient weight, might in the end have forced the enemy to capitulate,' he wrote on 8 January 1945, 'his counter-measures would have prevented us from maintaining such a policy to the decisive point.'

But for the favourable air situation created by the Americans, said Portal, 'it is possible that the night blitzing of German cities would by now have been too costly to sustain upon a heavy scale'. Here was a remarkable admission from the British Chief of Air Staff – that it was only the success of American air policy which had spared that of Britain from visible and humiliating defeat. Not surprisingly, Harris totally rejected Portal's criticism of the area campaign. He now asserted flatly that he had no faith in selective bombing, 'and none whatever in this present oil policy'.

Then he threw down the glove.

> I will not willingly lay myself open again to the charge that the lack of success of a policy which I have declared at the outset . . . not to contain the seeds of success is, after the event, due to my not having tried. That situation is simply one of heads I lose, tails you win, and it is an intolerable situation. . . . I therefore ask you to consider whether it is best for the prosecution of the war and the success of our arms, which alone matters, that I should remain in this situation. . . .

In their judgement on the C-in-C of Bomber Command, the British official historians wrote:

> Sir Arthur Harris made a habit of seeing only one side of a question and then of exaggerating it. He had a tendency to confuse advice with interference, criticism with sabotage and evidence with propaganda. He resisted innovations and was seldom open to persuasion. He was sceptical of the Air Staff in general, and of many officers who served upon it he was openly contemptuous. Seeing all issues in terms of black and white, he was impatient of any other possibility,

and having taken upon himself tremendous responsibilities, he expected similar powers to be conferred.[2]

Harris saw his own role in the ultimate Trenchardian sense, as the independent director of a campaign that he was entitled to wage in his own way for as long as he possessed the confidence of his superiors. He had now made it brutally apparent that if Bomber Command was to advance from an area force to a precision one, he himself must be sacked. The moment of truth had come for Portal.

Yet in these last months of war, how could the British public be reconciled to the dismissal of 'Bomber' Harris, whom Press, newsreel and radio publicity had built into one of the most celebrated British leaders of the war? It has been often and emphatically argued above that the great difficulty throughout the bomber offensive was to find any sensibly defined and generally acceptable criteria by which success or failure might be measured. Even after the war, it was to prove difficult to do so. For what specific defeat was Harris now to be sacked? It was unthinkable to reveal the nature, far less the course, of the dissention between the Chief of Air Staff and his C-in-C.

In all this it is important to stress what was at stake. No one familiar with the tactical and weather problems could have expected Bomber Command's aircraft to maintain an unbroken offensive against Germany's oil plants – the Americans failed to do so, despite their total commitment to the policy. Throughout the winter, the Allied armies were pressing their own urgent and almost compulsory demands on the strategic-bomber force. There were targets to be attacked at the behest of the Admiralty, alarmed by a late surge in U-boat activity, and at the urging of the politicians with their own preoccupations. Tedder himself pressed for a concentrated attack on the Ruhr in October, the *Hurricane* plan. But having made allowances for all these elements, there were still many mornings when Harris sat at his desk confronted with a long list of targets of every kind, together with a weather forecast that – as usual throughout the war – made the C-in-C's decision a matter of the most open judgement. And again and again, Harris came down in favour of attacking a city rather than oil plants. He believed that the use of massed bomber squadrons against oil installations was a waste of the power at his command.

The difference between the actual and potential effort Bomber Command concentrated on oil targets may have been only a matter of ten or twenty thousand sorties. But it is essential to reiterate what dramatic consequences might have stemmed from a real determination by Harris to put everything into oil, and even fractionally to increase Bomber Command's contribution: 'By the narrowest of margins, the strategic air offensive failed to smash Germany's economy by this one method of attack,' wrote the economist Professor Milward.[3] 'The most successful operation of the entire Allied strategical air warfare was against Germany's fuel supply,' wrote Galland of the Luftwaffe. 'Looking back, it is difficult to understand why the Allies started this undertaking so late. . . .'[4] 'Thus the Allies threw away success when it was already in their hands,' wrote Speer, of the slackening of the oil offensive as far back as the summer of 1944. 'Had they continued the attacks of March and April with the same energy, we would quickly have been at our last gasp.'[5]

Speer testifies that when Bomber Command did attack oil plants, its larger bombs caused greater damage than those of 8th Air Force. But beyond Harris's underlying contempt for the oil plan, High Wycombe also suffered grievously in the winter of 1944 from the perennial difficulty of damage assessment. Again and again oil plants were judged destroyed when Speer's extraordinarily effective repair squads had been able to restore some level of production. 18.9 per cent of RAF bombs dropped on oil plants failed to explode. The winter weather hampered effective photographic reconnaissance, just as during the Battle of Berlin a year before. When pictures did become available, Harris personally studied them, and often drew unwarrantably sanguine conclusions.

In the last quarter of 1944, 14 per cent of Harris's effort fell on oil targets against 53 per cent on cities, 15 per cent on transport targets, 13 per cent on army-support operations, 5 per cent on naval targets such as U-boat and E-boat pens. Between January and May 1945, 26 per cent of Harris's effort was directed towards oil, 37 per cent against cities. The cost of his stubbornness to the Allied war effort at this last stage was almost certainly grievous. The Oil Plan will be remembered by history as one of the Allies' great missed opportunities. Harris himself said thirty years later:[6]

> The only serious row I ever had with Portal was about the Oil Plan. I was against putting everything into oil. It was using a sledgehammer to crack a nut. I remember Portal ringing me up, the only time in the war that he lost his temper with me. I simply told him that if he didn't want me, I was quite prepared to go.

Long after the war, Portal sought to argue that his dispute with Harris was grossly exaggerated by mischievous witnesses.

> Harris's offer of his resignation (by no means the only one I had from him) was not, I knew, intended seriously, but was made in a moment of exasperation [he wrote in 1959[7]]. His good qualities as a commander far outweighed his defects, and it would have been monstrously unjust to him and to his command to have tried to have him replaced on the ground that while assuring me of his intention to carry out his

orders, he persisted in trying to convince me that different orders would have produced better results.

It is impossible to accept this view. Portal in his own wartime correspondence made it abundantly clear that he was not satisfied that Harris was wholeheartedly seeking to carry out his orders. The issue at stake was one of profound significance for the conduct of the war. The evidence is clear that Harris never conformed single-mindedly to his instructions, and the margin by which he failed to do so may have been decisive.

But the simple fact was that at the end of 1944, Harris enjoyed wider fame and greater prestige than Portal, and knew it. He believed, rightly or wrongly, that he could count on the support of the Prime Minister. He was certain of his own cause. He inspired considerable open and tacit admiration for pursuing a defiantly British policy at a moment when American dominance of the Alliance was everywhere being made painfully apparent: 'By 1945 he was one of the very few senior British officers who seemed able to ignore, let alone to deny the American predominance in the conduct of grand strategy.'[8] In those last months of the European war, it seemed to Portal that the uproar that would have surrounded Harris's removal was not justified by the strategic benefits that would result. He flinched from sacking his C-in-C, and having shown his own weakness, had no further sanctions against him. His letter of formal surrender to Harris on 20 January 1945, which effectively acknowledged his subordinate's right to continue bombing cities as he saw fit, bears a note of almost pathetic resignation:

> I willingly accept your assurance that you will continue to do your utmost to ensure the successful execution of the policy laid down. I am very sorry that you do not believe in it, but it is no use my craving for what is evidently unattainable. We must wait until after the end of the war before we can know for certain who was right, and I sincerely hope that until then you will continue in command of the force which has done so much towards defeating the enemy, and has brought such credit and renown to yourself and to the Royal Air Force.

Portal's retreat, which greatly diminishes his stature as a director of war, was the negation of all that he sought to achieve at Quebec by the transfer of authority from SHAEF. He had proved too weak to impose his will on the command structure he himself created. It is hard to believe that had Bomber Command continued under SHAEF's orders, Tedder would have tolerated the same degree of defiance from Harris. Whether or not Tedder would have insisted that Bomber Command dedicate itself single-mindedly to the Transport Plan, it is at least likely that a coherent policy would have been consistently pursued.

Harris's behaviour towards the Air Staff in this last phase almost certainly influenced the fact that he received no peerage and was offered no further employment at the coming of peace, much more than any notion of making him a scapegoat for Dresden. If he had shown sufficient flexibility in the autumn of 1944 to acknowledge that the usefulness of area bombing was ended, that his force was now capable of better and more important things, history might have judged him more kindly. But he did not. With the single-mindedness that even one of his principal supporters at the Air Ministry had termed obsession,[9] he continued remorselessly with his personal programme for the levelling of Germany's cities until the very end. In the first four months of 1945, 181,000 tons of bombs were delivered to Germany, a fifth of the tonnage dropped throughout the entire war.

No period is more resistant to setting in context than this final phase, from the winter of 1944 to May 1945. Bomber Command reached the zenith of its strength: 1,609 aircraft, drawn from a force that included 1,087 Lancasters, 353 Halifaxes, 203 Mosquitoes. Sir John Grigg, the Army Minister, said in the House of Commons in the Army Estimates debate of 1944: 'We have reached the extraordinary situation in which the labour devoted to the production of heavy bombers alone is believed to be equal to that allotted to the production of the whole equipment of the army.' Every heavy bomber was equipped with H2S, *Gee* and a mass of other sophisticated electronic equipment. Belatedly, some Lancasters were being fitted with 0.5 calibre rear-turret guns, and a handful even with gun-laying radar. The advanced successor to the Lancaster, the Lincoln, was being prepared for operations in the Far East with the RAF's 'Tiger Force' when the European war ended. There was a vast surplus of aircrew, many of whom were never called upon to fly operations. Cochrane and Carr were transferred from their Groups early in 1945, merely in order that two other promising officers might gain experience of operational command before the end. Amidst the deep weariness that afflicted Britain by 1945, Bomber Command at last tasted victory.

Until the final days, the Luftwaffe offered resistance, and Bomber Command's overall loss rate of 1 per cent masked individual nights of operations when casualties of 5 per cent, even 10 per cent were inflicted by the dwindling band of German night-fighters. But stripped of their early-warning systems and swamped by the mass of Allied jamming and radar devices, the defences were in ruins. After losing 31,000 aircrew between January 1941 and June 1944, the Luftwaffe suffered 13,000 casualties between June and October 1944 alone. In 1944, the USAAF destroyed 3,706 enemy aircraft merely in daylight operations over Germany.[10] No air force could stand losses on this scale. As Bomber Command's operations became more and more a routine exercise of technique and professionalism, amidst the monotony of the long trips to and from Germany, for the first time some crews felt sufficiently lightened of their own fear to pity those who lay beneath. Standards of marking, of bombing, of devastation had risen enormously since the previous winter of the Battle of Berlin. Huge forces of aircraft set forth, and the cities beneath were levelled in due measure. In the first four months of 1945, there were thirty-six major Bomber Command operations against German urban areas, twenty-four by night and twelve by day: 528 and 1,107 aircraft went on two nights to Dortmund, 717 and 720 to Chemnitz, 276 to Kassel, 805 to Dresden, 654 to Munich, 521 and 293 to Nuremberg, 597 to Wiesbaden, 349 to Worms, 458 to Mainz, 478 to Mannheim, and 238 to Bonn.

Night after night the huge palls of smoke and fire rose from the cities. 'The situation grows daily more intolerable and we have no means of defending ourselves against this catastrophe,' wrote Goebbels on 2 March.[11] 'Reports sound almost monotonous but they tell of so much sorrow and misery that one hardly dares think about them in detail.'[12] Had Hitler not maintained his spellbinding influence over the German people to the very end, it is impossible to believe that they would have continued the war through these months, if the opportunity had existed for them to surrender. It is almost beyond belief that the German army continued to resist so effectively even amidst the rubble of the nation. The Wehrmacht's dogged last stand, and the continued output from the factories until the last weeks, rendered the concept of morale bombing finally absurd.

Beyond the great area attacks, Bomber Command delivered 17,621 tons of bombs – more than half the total dropped by all the Allied strategic and tactical air forces – in the campaign against Germany's communications. Thousands more sorties were carried out in support of the Allied armies, although some argued that these were self-defeating, because of the mountains of rubble that they created in the path of advancing armour. On 12 November 1944 the *Tirpitz* was finally capsized in Tromsö Fjord by Lancasters of 617 and 9 Squadron – the victims of Wilhelmshaven on 18 December 1939. The *Admiral Scheer* was capsized in Kiel harbour during an attack on 9 April 1945. A vast ten-ton 'Grand Slam' bomb, created by Barnes Wallis and delivered by 617 Squadron, finally severed the Bielefeld Viaduct linking Hamm and Hanover on 14 March 1945, and 617 Squadron dropped forty more of these monstrous weapons on hitherto impregnable installations before the end of the war. Altogether in 1945, Bomber Command launched 67,487 sorties for the loss of 608 aircraft. It is a measure of the scale of the strategic air offensive in its final months that such casualties could be regarded as a small price.

There will never be a definitive judgement on the contribution of the strategic bombers to the final collapse of Germany, because there are so many impenetrable uncertainties. Speer and his army of managers and workers struggled through the winter of 1944 against the tides of disaster breaching their industrial sandcastle on every side, and by the beginning of 1945 it was clear to him that it was being overwhelmed. 'From July 1944 to May 1945 the German economy was tried with so many stresses applied from different directions that it is impossible to say which was the heaviest stress and which caused the final break,' writes Professor Milward.[13]

The advancing Allied armies had cut off Germany from the raw materials on which her industries were dependent. There would be no more chrome from Turkey. The Swedes were belatedly cutting the flow of high-grade steel to the Reich. The Rumanian oil-fields were in the hands of the Russians. Germany had been desperately short of man-power thoughout the war, but in October 1944 Hitler made clear his own priorities by decreeing the creation of the *Volkssturm* and calling up every German male between sixteen and sixty for some degree of part-time military training. Hitler and most of his colleagues perceived clearly that unless they could achieve a decisive success on the battle-field within months, the achievements of industry would become irrelevant. Thus they ignored the desperate protests of Speer about the effects of the call-up on production. After the autumn of 1944, Speer was probably the only leading man in Germany still concerned about the long-term future of the armaments industry, or indeed about any industry at all.

Beyond the final success of the oil offensive, the Allied bombing of German communications and especially of the Ruhr's rail and canal network was strangling coal output and thus steel production by the end of November 1944. It is impossible to separate the achievements of precision air attacks on rail yards, bridges and canals from those of the Allied area attacks on the Ruhr cities. The end result, in any event, was catastrophic. 80 per cent of Germany's coal came from the Ruhr, and to maintain supplies to industry it was necessary for 22,000 wagon-loads a day to leave the pits. By the end of November, this flow had been cut to 5,000 a day. In the last quarter of 1944, it was essential for Germany to produce more than 9 million tons of steel. Largely in consequence of the coal famine, less than 4 million tons were in fact produced, barely enough to sustain ammunition production, far less to create new armaments. Allied bombing of the Ruhr links relaxed sufficiently that winter to allow coal flow to increase to 8,100 wagons a day by February, but after another deluge of explosives early in March the Ruhr was totally isolated from the rest of Germany by the middle of the month, a few days before the arrival of the Allied armies.

From September 1944, Speer's economic edifice had passed its peak and was doomed to decline as labour, raw materials and plant in fallen territories were taken from him. By 30 January 1945, with remarkable courage he conceded openly to Hitler, that the game was played out: 'It is a matter of estimating with certainty the final collapse of the German economy in four to eight weeks. . . . After this collapse the war can no longer be pursued militarily.' Thereafter Speer devoted most of his labours to frustrating Hitler's orders to destroy German industry in the face of the advancing armies.

The strategic-bomber offensive contributed overwhelmingly to the destruction of Germany's ability to continue the war after the spring of 1945. It remains a matter for speculation whether the German army would have been capable of prolonging its resistance thereafter, even had it been provided with more weapons with which to do so. This seems extraordinarily doubtful. Even in the midst of disaster, tank production was maintained almost to the end, although the tactical air forces made it difficult to move finished armour from the works to the battlefield. Jet aircraft continued to be produced underground despite the best efforts of the Allied bombers, and shortage of fuel and pilots contributed more than bombing to preventing their effective use in the air.

By the end of January 1945, Germany's gas, power, water and rail systems were in chaos. Fuel of every kind was in desperately short supply on the battlefield and across the nation. Railway signalling and telephone systems and industrial communications had almost totally broken down. Yet the strategic-bomber offensive continued for ten more weeks. It became overwhelmingly an area attack in the final stages, because beyond maintaining the ruin of the oil plants there were pitifully few selective targets to justify the employment of the huge air forces available. In one of the most telling phrases of his correspondence with Portal the previous autumn, Harris declared: 'In Bomber Command we have always worked on the assumption that bombing anything in Germany is better than bombing nothing.' Whatever their post-war assertions of principle, in these months the American airmen joined wholeheartedly with the British in devastating the last remaining undestroyed cities of Germany, because to leave their great forces idle on the ground seemed an intolerable alternative.

The Americans erected a smokescreen of strategic bluster to blur their part in the area-bombing campaign, which was much less attractive than Harris's open commitment. Even before the Americans unleashed the ultimate area attacks at Hiroshima and Nagasaki, the distinction between the respective national bombing policies had grown to seem very threadbare indeed. But in January 1945 the 8th Air Force's commander, Ira Eaker, could still declare fervently that 'We should never allow the history of this war to convict us of throwing the strategic bomber at the man in the street.'[14]

General Carl 'Tooey' Spaatz, until March 1945 the senior American airman in Europe, consistently opposed proposals that were openly terroristic, such as *Thunderclap* in the summer of 1944, but proved perfectly willing to commit his aircraft to bombing cities if some credible window-dressing could be erected around their purpose, such as 'blind-bombing of transportation centres'. By early 1945 the 8th Air Force had achieved an average circular probable error of two miles on operations guided by H2S. All its blind-bombing missions through the winter of 1944, therefore, amounted in reality if not in name to area bombing. Yet still the American official historians wrote:

> It is not surprising that proposals for all-out attacks on Berlin, the Ruhr or other critical areas of Germany always seemed to come from the British, who had undergone the German raids of 1940–41, and were now enduring the punishment of V1s and V2s. All proposals frankly aimed at breaking the morale of the German people met the consistent opposition of General Spaatz, who repeatedly raised the moral issue involved, and American air force headquarters in Washington strongly supported him on the ground that such operations were contrary to air force policy and national ideals.[15]

Throughout the war the American airmen were driven by determination to win their place as an independent third service alongside the army and navy. Spaatz had gained a great degree of freedom to prosecute the war in his own way by the end of 1944, and great forces with which to set about doing so. He was determined to concede nothing to the RAF in the bombing competition that continued until the end of the war, and as Harris heaped explosives on to Germany's cities in the last stages Spaatz's bombers matched the British ruin for ruin.

It was the most futile and the most distasteful phase of the bomber offensive, and it was also that in which the airmen disastrously damaged their place in history. They did not then know the exact date upon which Germany would concede defeat, but it was apparent for months beforehand that the end was so close that the razing of cities could do nothing to hasten it. The vast American fire-raising attacks on Japan, in which Lemay's Superfortresses killed 84,000 people in a day before the atomic bomb was heard of, have somehow escaped the widespread attention of posterity. But the attacks on Dresden by Bomber Command and the American 8th Air Force between 13 and 15 February 1945, which destroyed the city and killed a minimum of 30,000 and perhaps as many as 100,000 people, aroused a revulsion even in the dying days of the war which has not been diminished by the passing of a generation.

It is ironic that while Harris and Spaatz must accept chief responsibility for continuing the area offensive after it ceased to have any strategic relevance, the Allied attack on Dresden cannot be laid at their doors. Dresden had indeed been on Harris's target lists for months, but the impetus finally to launch the raid on the great East German city came from the Prime Minister and the Chief of Air Staff. Since the end of 1943, with the exception of his role in the pre-*Overlord* debate, Churchill had displayed diminishing interest in bombing, as so many other great issues of war and diplomacy unfolded around him. He continued occasionally to invite Harris to dine,[16] but as has been suggested above, the C-in-C's real influence upon and protection from the Prime Minister may not have been nearly as great as both Portal and Harris supposed, by the winter of 1944.

Yet now, as Churchill prepared to leave for Yalta for the last major Allied conference of the European war, he turned almost impulsively to consider what evidence he could offer the Russians of Western support for their great offensives in the East. He talked to Sinclair on the night of 25 January 1945. The next day the Air Minister informed the Air Staff that the Prime Minister wanted to know Bomber Command's proposals for 'basting the Germans in their retreat from Breslau'. The old *Thunderclap* plan for delivering a series of overwhelming raids to bring about the collapse of German morale was taken out and dusted down. Yet Portal was not at all keen to divert the Allies' massed air resources from the tasks he considered pre-eminent: hitting jet-aircraft factories, and maintaining the ruin of Germany's oil plants. He said that he thought the Allies might merely commit 'available effort' to 'one big attack on Berlin, and attacks on Dresden, Leipzig, Chemnitz, or any other cities where a severe blitz will not only cause confusion in the evacuation from the east, but will also hamper the movement of troops from the west'. Sinclair submitted a long memorandum to the Prime Minister outlining these possibilities. He received a crisp reply:

> I did not ask you last night about plans for harrying the German retreat from Breslau. On the contrary, I asked whether Berlin, and no doubt other large cities in East Germany, should not now be considered especially attractive targets. I am glad that this is 'under examination'. Pray report to me tomorrow what is going to be done.

Sir Norman Bottomley forthwith dispatched an official letter to Harris, pointing out the implications of the Russian advance, and reporting that Portal favoured one big attack on Berlin, with related operations against Dresden, Leipzig and Chemnitz, 'subject to the overriding claims of oil and other approved targets within the current directive'. At Yalta on 4 February the Russians submitted a memorandum in which they formally requested strategic air attacks against Germany's eastern communications, especially such centres as Berlin and Leipzig. On 6 February, Portal signalled Bottomley that the Air Ministry proposals for the eastern air attacks had been approved by the Chiefs of Staff. Thus on the night of 13 February Bomber Command launched its great fire-raising attack on Dresden, to be followed up by those of the 8th Air Force. Little but the railway yards escaped destruction. Chemnitz was fired the next night. Berlin, already heavily attacked by the 8th Air Force earlier in the month, was hit with devastating effect on the night of 24 February by Bomber Command.

It is important to stress that to those who planned and directed it, the raid on Dresden was no different from scores of other operations mounted during the years of war. Bomber Command's attacks had reached an extraordinary pitch of technical efficiency, but it was impossible to anticipate the firestorm which developed, multiplying the usual devastation and deaths a hundredfold. To the staff at High Wycombe, Dresden was simply another German town. Here are Bomber Command's hitherto unpublished briefing notes, issued to Groups and squadrons on the eve of the Dresden raid:

> Dresden, the seventh largest city in Germany and not much smaller than Manchester, is also far the largest unbombed built-up area the enemy has got. In the midst of winter with refugees pouring westwards and troops to be rested, roofs are at a premium, not only to give shelter to workers, refugees and troops alike, but to house the administrative services displaced from other areas. At one time well known for its china, Dresden has developed into an industrial city of first-class importance, and like any large city with its multiplicity of telephone and rail facilities, is of major value for controlling the defence of that part of the front now threatened by Marshal Koniev's breakthrough.
>
> The intentions of the attack are to hit the enemy where he will feel it most, behind an already partially collapsed front, to prevent the use of the city in the way of further advance, and incidentally to show the Russians when they arrive what Bomber Command can do.[17]

Much of this, of course, was fantasy. Dresden was not a city of major industrial significance. And unlike so many of Bomber Command's targets of the past five years which had been mere names to the British public, symbols of Nazi power such as Nuremberg or of enemy industrial might such as Essen, Dresden was a city which an important section of educated Englishmen had heard of, read about, visited. Since the eighteenth century, the old town had stood for all that was finest, most beautiful and cultured in Germany, a haven where Trollopian heroines sought exile, visited by generations of young English noblemen on the Grand Tour. For the first time since the bomber offensive began, on the news of the destruction of Dresden, a major wave of anger and dismay swept through Whitehall and the Air Ministry, echoed in Parliament, and finally reached the gates of High Wycombe. Urgent questions were asked by important people about the reasons for destroying the city.

Concern was heightened by the release of an Associated Press dispatch from SHAEF on 17 February, in which a correspondent reported that 'Allied air chiefs' had at last embarked on 'deliberate terror bombing of German population centres as a ruthless expedient to hasten doom'. The attacks on Dresden, Chemnitz and Berlin had been launched 'for the avowed purpose of heaping more confusion on Nazi road and rail traffic, and to sap German morale'. This dispatch – which of course was perfectly accurate, although its news was three years old – was hastily suppressed by the censor in Britain. But it had already been widely distributed in America, causing a major public controversy whose echoes soon reached London. Popular concern might have been even greater had it been known that at the end of February the entire resources of British and American tactical and strategic air power were committed briefly to the execution of the consciously terroristic American operation *Clarion*, attacking local transport centres the length of Germany in a kind of inverted *Thunderclap*, designed to create moral collapse by bringing the war into even the smallest centres of population. *Clarion* tailed off without achieving any measurable success. Concentrated attacks on the cities, the airmen believed, were a more effective method of sowing despondency than widely dispersed local raids.

But February 1945 marked the moment when farsighted airmen and politicians began to perceive that history might judge the achievements of strategic air power with less enthusiasm than their own Target Intelligence departments. General Marshall asserted publicly that Dresden had been bombed at the specific request of the Russians. In the midst of the controversy, General Arnold cabled Spaatz, seeking to be informed of the distinction between 'morale bombing' and radar attacks on transportation targets in urban areas. Spaatz replied that 'he had not departed from the historic American policy in Europe, even in the case of Berlin, and Arnold expressed himself as entirely satisfied with the explanation'.[18] This, of course, was cant. But its incessant repetition would do much to spare Spaatz and Eaker from the criticism heaped upon Harris in the post-war era.

Churchill also sensed the new climate. On 28 March 1945 he composed a memorandum for the Chiefs of Staff Committee and the Chief of Air Staff:

> It seems to me that the moment has come when the question of bombing of German cities simply for the sake of increasing the terror, though under other pretexts, should be reviewed. Otherwise we shall come into control of an utterly ruined land. We shall not, for instance, be able to get housing materials out of Germany for our own needs because some temporary provision would have to be made for the Germans themselves. The destruction of Dresden

> remains a serious query against the conduct of Allied bombing. I am of the opinion that military objectives must henceforward be more strictly studied in our own interests rather than that of the enemy.
>
> The Foreign Secretary has spoken to me on this subject, and I feel the need for more precise concentration upon military objectives, such as oil and communications behind the immediate battle-zone, rather than on mere acts of terror and wanton destruction, however impressive.

It is impossible to regard this memorandum as anything other than a calculated political attempt by the Prime Minister to distance himself from the bombing of Dresden and the rising controversy surrounding the area offensive. The airmen were not unreasonably angered and dismayed. At Portal's insistence, Churchill withdrew his paper and substituted a new one, dated 1 April 1945:

> It seems to me that the moment has come when the question of the so called 'area bombing' of German cities should be reviewed from the point of view of our own interests. If we come into control of an entirely ruined land, there will be a great shortage of accommodation for ourselves and our Allies; and we shall be unable to get housing materials out of Germany for our own needs. . . . We must see to it that our attacks do not do more harm to ourselves in the long run than they do to the enemy's immediate war effort. Pray let me have your views. . . .

In the years that followed, many of the airmen who wrote their memoirs – Tedder and Slessor prominent among them – prevaricated about both area bombing and their own part in it. Harris alone never sought prudent cover, nor made excuse or apology for what his forces had done. 'I would not regard the whole of the remaining cities of Germany as worth the bones of one British grenadier,' he wrote to Bottomley on 29 March 1945, at the height of his anger about Churchill's draft memorandum. 'The feeling over Dresden could easily be explained by any psychiatrist. It is connected with German bands and Dresden shepherdesses.'* Alone he stood on the parapet of his trench, facing the slings and arrows of posterity with the same unflinching defiance that he had offered to his critics and enemies throughout the bomber offensive.

The Chiefs of Staff formally decreed the ending of area bombing on 16 April 1945. Yet it was intolerable to the airmen that Bomber Command should sit out the last weeks of the war in idleness. Harris's aircraft bombed Berchtesgaden and a few remaining oil plants, and the

*The letter embodying this sentiment is reproduced in full as Appendix C.

coastal guns on the north German island of Wangerooge. One of Bomber Command's last operations was carried out on 16 April 1945, against the German island fortress of Heligoland, where naval radar first detected Wing-Commander Kellett's Wellingtons before their terrible defeat five and a half years earlier.

More than 900 aircraft were dispatched, a force great enough to level three cities. There were three aiming-points: the main island, the airfield and the naval base. 'Marking, from the initial *Oboe* TIs to the last backer-up, was of a high standard, and the Master Bombers kept a tight rein on an enthusiastic Main Force,' recorded the History of 8 Group.[19] 'The next day, thirty-three Lancasters of 5 Group, six carrying Grand Slams and the remainder Tallboys, sent to flatten anything left standing, reported that the centre of the island was still ablaze.'

The means, which were for so long lacking to fulfil the airmen's great ambitions, had at last overtaken the ends.

XV
The Balance Sheet

We want – that is, the people who served in Bomber Command of the Royal Air Force and their next of kin – a categorical assurance that the work we did was militarily and strategically justified.

– Wing-Commander Ernest Millington, MP, House of Commons, 12 March 1946

At the end of the war, Bomber Command received the courtesies of victory. There was a letter from Buckingham Palace for High Wycombe, on receiving the final version of Harris's beloved Blue Books:

> The King has asked me to thank you for the two volumes of Bomb Damage Diagrams which were brought here this morning. . . . These reports have been a constant source of interest to His Majesty since they started, and provided an admirable record of the great part played by Bomber Command in winning the war. The King hopes that you will express to those who have compiled the records His Majesty's appreciation of the neatness and accuracy of the work. . . .[1]

But beneath a thin layer of perfunctory goodwill, it was soon apparent not only at High Wycombe but throughout Bomber Command, that in the safety of peace the bombers' part in the war was one that many politicians and civilians would prefer to forget. The laurels and the romantic adulation were reserved for Fighter Command, the defenders. The men of the Army of Occupation were first awed, then increasingly dismayed, by the devastation of Germany. As more pictures and descriptions of the effects of area bombing appeared in Britain, especially those detailing the destruction of Dresden, public distaste grew. Among the vanquished, those who had launched air attacks on civilians were prominent in the dock at Nuremberg. 'Was not your purpose in this attack to secure a strategic advantage by terrorization of the people of Rotterdam?'[2] asked Sir David Maxwell Fyfe damningly, as he examined Kesselring about his part in the 1940 offensive. 'I decided on Coventry because there the most targets could be hit within the smallest area,' declared Goering,[3] on trial for his life, with his direction of the Blitz on Britain among the principal prosecution issues. The Reichsmarshal was sentenced to hang. Kesselring went with Milch and Speer to begin a long imprisonment.

Sir Arthur Harris was offered no further employment in the Royal Air Force, and departed for South Africa at the end of 1945. Churchill's proposal for an honour for Bomber Command's C-in-C was rejected by the new Prime Minister, Attlee. Only in 1953 did Harris receive a baronetcy, the sort of title more frequently granted to time-serving Members of Parliament. Whatever posterity may make of Harris, he served Churchill well, and gave all that he could offer to the service of the Royal Air Force. It was an oddly ungenerous gesture by the Prime Minister, and tends to support Major Morton's contention about Churchill's lack of personal affection for the C-in-C of Bomber Command. Of the offensive as a whole, Churchill had only this to say in the final volume of his war memoirs:

> In judging the contribution to victory of strategic air power it should be remembered that this was the first war in which it was fully used. We had to learn from hard-won experience. . . . But although the results of the early years fell short of our aims, we forced on the enemy an elaborate, ever-growing but finally insufficient air-defence system which absorbed a large proportion of their total war effort. Before the end, we and the United States had developed striking forces so powerful that they played a major part in the economic collapse of Germany.[4]

By the last months of the struggle, Churchill the politician was already reasserting himself over Churchill the director of war. When the Americans began to pour thousands of economists and scientists into captured territory to compile their massive Strategic Bombing Survey, the RAF hoped to do likewise. But Churchill curtly rejected their proposals, on the grounds that they would waste skilled manpower. It is difficult to accept his argument at face value. It is easier to believe that he wished to put the strategic air offensive behind him, with as little resort as possible to further statistical fantasies and noisy claims by the airmen. The British Bombing Survey Unit was grudgingly granted token resources. American and British airmen competed for German documents and access to the top captured Nazis, above all Speer, in their anxiety to prove the triumph of 'precision' or 'area' bombing. Professor Solly Zuckerman, who wrote the final 'Overall Report' of the BBSU, had always been an advocate of attacking communications links rather than cities. When his work was completed, it was received without enthusiasm at the Air Ministry, although Zuckerman's old chief Sir Arthur Tedder was now Chief of Air Staff.

> The main fault of commission in the combined bomber offensive [wrote the scientist] would undoubtedly appear as the launching of the offensive against German aircraft assembly plants, and the

> continuation of 'area attacks' on German towns beyond the point where they were necessitated by the operational limitations of inaccuracy in navigation and bombing. Even the more accurate and devastating raids on the Ruhr that took place towards the end of the war were an extravagant means of achieving a fall in steel production compared to the direct attack on communications. . . .[5]

Originally a biologist by training, Zuckerman was staggered to discover, on arriving in Germany at the surrender, that most zoos which had not suffered direct damage were still feeding a full complement of animals. In Britain such useless mouths had been ruthlessly destroyed early in the war. This was a striking example of the gulf between the desperate plight of Germany as Allied Intelligence had perceived it and the reality as it now emerged. Zuckerman's 'Overall Report' was suppressed by the Air Ministry, as was Sir Arthur Harris's final dispatch on the work of Bomber Command 1942–45. Meanwhile, across the Atlantic a similar uncertainty and controversy about the bomber offensive broke out among Americans:

> Even General Arnold had doubts about how effective the air war had been. The British and American strategic air forces had blasted factories and cities from one end of the Reich to the other. Unquestionably the destruction had not had the effect on the enemy's war effort that Arnold had expected or hoped for, the effect 'we all assumed would result'.[6]

The Royal Air Force entered the Second World War committed to demonstrating that the air-dropped bomb was a weapon of unique capabilities. Political, social and professional pressure on the infant service drove the airmen to adopt a messianic approach, and it is precisely for this reason that some historians have argued that the RAF should never have become an independent service in 1918. The airmen, desperately jealous of their freedom, became obsessed with their need for an independent function. Only a strategic-bomber offensive seemed able to provide this.

The technical failings of Bomber Command in the first years of the war were no worse than those of the army and the Royal Navy. The bombers made an important, perhaps critical contribution in 1941 and 1942 to keeping alive the morale of the British people, and to deterring the Americans from a premature second front. The casualties suffered by the airmen would have been far exceeded by the Allied armies if they had been compelled to face the Wehrmacht head-on in 1942 or 1943.

The Allies' possession of a heavy-bomber force was an important military asset, seen to most advantage in support of *Overlord*. But Churchill made a major error of judgement in the winter of 1941–42 by committing British industry to the enormous heavy-bomber programme that came to fruition at the end of 1944. The Prime Minister could have achieved his strategic purpose with a far less extravagant outlay of resources. Instead, although they were denied their '4,000 Plan', the airmen were allowed to pursue their own ambitious and partisan war aims. Tizard said after the war: 'No one thinks now that it would have been possible to defeat Germany by bombing alone. The actual effort expended on bombing Germany, in manpower and resources, was greater than the value in manpower and resources of the damage caused.

Whether or not this is precisely true, the British investment in Bomber Command was immense. Webster and Frankland suggest that the bomber offensive employed only 7 per cent of the nation's manpower, but this figure can hardly be accepted literally, since it discounts the exceptional quality and skills of those concerned. It is difficult to compute the exact proportion of the nation's war effort that was involved, but A. J. P. Taylor, one of the critics of the bomber offensive, argues around one-third. Bomber Command took the cream of Britain's wartime high technology, and the true cost of a Lancaster fitted with H2S, *Gee*, the Mark XIV bombsight and other supporting equipment was immense. The fact that Britain was compelled to buy from America all its transport aircraft (and enter post-war civil aviation at a serious disadvantage), most of its landing craft, a large proportion of its tanks and vast quantities of ammunition stemmed directly or indirectly from the weight of British industrial effort committed to the bomber offensive. The simple fact was that only America possessed the industrial resources to embark on strategic air warfare on the necessary scale to have decisive results within an acceptable period.

Lord Trenchard is entitled to the undying gratitude of the Royal Air Force for keeping the service in being between the wars, but all the key strategic principles upon which he built air-force doctrine were found wanting. It was a terrible experience to be bombed, but German morale never came near to collapse until the very end. In any event, as Liddell Hart perceived, morale bombing was incompatible with the Allied doctrine of enforcing unconditional German surrender.

The 'de-housing' paper, a document which leaves an ineradicable sense of distaste forever surrounding the name of Lord Cherwell, was itself curiously mealy-mouthed. If moral considerations were to be discarded, the most rational policy for Bomber Command would have been to pursue a campaign overtly directed at killing the largest possible number of Germans, rather than dally with such euphemisms as making them homeless. Supplies of arms were never critically lacking in Germany, but there was a chronic shortage of hands to bear them.

By the spring of 1944, it was clear that Harris's area-bombing campaign had failed to bring Germany within even distant sight of defeat. That winter, when Harris made clear his continuing commitment to the area offensive despite the contrary directions of the Chief of Air Staff, he should have been sacked. The obliteration of Germany's cities in the spring of 1945, when all strategic justification had vanished, is a lasting blot on the Allied conduct of the war and on the judgement of senior Allied airmen. 'We had a surfeit of air staffs,' Lord Zuckerman has written,[7] 'presided over by chiefs who were not called "the air barons" for nothing. They ruled their commands like feudal allegiances. What mattered was the ability to destroy . . .' By his indecision and weakness in handling Harris and the bomber offensive in the last eight months of the war, Sir Charles Portal disqualified himself from consideration as a great, or even as an effective, commander of air forces, whatever his merits as a joint-service committee-man.

The bomber offensive compelled the Germans to divert resources from the battlefield to the defence of their cities. If Hitler had been a reasonable man, the pressure upon him to do this on a much larger scale might have had important strategic consequences. Reason demanded that major forces of day- and night-fighters should be deployed against the bomber offensive as Speer, Milch and Galland demanded. But Hitler was not a reasonable man, and did not comply with their wishes until the means to do so were gone. Economic historians agree that German industry proved astonishingly resilient in the face of bombing:

> There can be no doubt that active interference of this nature in the work of the German economy hastened the decline in production [wrote Professor Milward[8]]. But the overall importance of bombing, as well as the importance of particular aspects of the offensive, has been exaggerated, often for the purpose of demonstrating the success of different kinds of bombing policy.

The two great achievements of the Allied strategic air offensive must be conceded to the Americans: the defeat of the Luftwaffe by the Mustang escort-fighter, and the inception of the deadly oil offensive. 'The British inflicted grievous and bloody injuries upon us,' said Milch after the war, 'but the Americans stabbed us to the heart.' Even the American breakthrough came late in the overall context of the war. The most common fault among air historians since 1945 is that they have examined the strategic-bomber offensive in isolation. The course of the war must be considered in its entirety. It is gratifying to airmen, but historically irrelevant, that they had destroyed the German economy by the time the armies achieved victory on the ground. Many of their greatest feats of precision bombing such as the sinking of the *Tirpitz* – which would have been a vital strategic achievement in 1941, 1942, even 1943 – became no more than marvellous circus-tricks by the time they were achieved in 1944 and 1945. The pace of the war had left them behind.

By late 1944, Bomber Command and the USAAF possessed the means to undertake what Harris had attempted without success in 1942 and 1943: the wholesale destruction of Germany's cities. But it was too late. When they possessed the strategic justification – in 1942 and 1943 – they lacked the means. By the winter of 1944, when they had gained the means, the justification was gone, for the Allied armies were evidently on the verge of complete victory on the ground, and it was only a combination of their own shortcomings and the Wehrmacht's genius that delayed the end so long. In the last months of war Bomber Command contributed to the punishment of Germany more than to the defeat of the enemy. No one disputed Germany's guilt. Arguably, it is because of what the German people suffered from bombing in the Second World War that they are so unlikely to embark upon such a national adventure again. But it is difficult to accept in cold blood that the Allied air forces were appropriately employed as a punitive force. Contrary to the view of the British official historians, most civilized men would agree that there *is* a significant moral distinction between the incidental and deliberate destruction of civilian life in war, and it is hard to look back across a generation with any pride on such a night's work as the destruction of Darmstadt.

Bomber Command was very well served by its aircrew, and with a few exceptions very badly served by its senior officers, in the Second World War. The gulf between the realities in the sky and the rural routine of headquarters was too great for most of the staff to bridge. Cochrane and Bennett were the only men among Bomber Command's leaders to do so. High Wycombe was fatally isolated both from the front and from sharp critical debate on policy. Even after all their bitter experience in the early years of war, senior officers were unwilling to face unacceptable realities. Dr Noble Frankland has written that 'the whole belief that the bomber was revolutionary in the sense that it was not subject to the classical doctrines of war was misguided',[9] and this should have been apparent to the airmen by 1942. The air-dropped bomb had shown itself no more potent than any other explosive object. For all the technology embodied in the bomber aircraft, its load once released was an astonishingly crude and imprecise weapon.

The airmen's great error, in which they have persisted to this day, was their refusal to admit that they overstated their case. Had they chosen to stand on Bomber Command's undisputed achievements and marvellous courage, their shortcomings and excesses might have been forgotten. Instead, many prominent British airmen have fought doggedly ever since the war to prove that the bomber offensive was the decisive factor in Allied victory in 1945. Their imprecision about what they sought to achieve has persisted through the intervening generation. The four-volume official history prints forty-nine sets of statistics covering every aspect of German production, hundreds of pages of data on British aircraft and losses, and yet not a single appendix giving details or estimates of German civilian casualties or even numbers 'de-housed' by the bomber offensive. The Federal Statistical Office in Wiesbaden computed after the war that 593,000 German civilians died and 3.37 million dwellings were destroyed, including 600,000 in Berlin alone, from 1939 to 1945.

The bomber offensive partly fulfilled useful purposes for the Allied war effort. Bomber Command entirely satisfied Churchill's hopes as I have interpreted them at the beginning of 1942, by fighting a long holding-action to buy time before launching *Overlord* on overwhelmingly favourable terms. If the airmen had pitched their demands for resources, their own hopes and their subsequent claims more modestly, history might have judged them more kindly. As it was, the cost of the bomber offensive in life, treasure and moral superiority over the enemy tragically outstripped the results that it achieved.

* * *

Beyond those who died flying for Bomber Command, many more outstanding young men somehow used themselves up in the Second World War, leaving pathetically little energy and imagination to support them through the balance of their lives. Surviving aircrew often feel deeply betrayed by criticism of the strategic air offensive. It is disgraceful that they were never awarded a Campaign Medal after surviving the extraordinary battle that they fought for so long against such odds, and in which so many of them died. One night after I visited a much-decorated pilot in the north of England in the course of writing this book, he drove me to the station. Suddenly turning to me in the car, he asked: 'Has anybody else mentioned having nightmares about it?' He said that in the past ten years he had been troubled by increasingly vivid and terrible dreams about his experiences over Germany.

A teacher by profession, he thought nothing of the war for years afterwards. Then a younger generation of his colleagues began to ask with repetitive, inquisitive distaste: 'How could you have done it? How could you have flown over Germany night after night to bomb women and children?' He began to brood more and more deeply about his past. He changed his job and started to teach mentally-handicapped children, which he saw as a kind of restitution. Yet still, more than thirty years after, his memories of the war haunt him.

It is wrong that it should be so. He was a brave man who achieved an outstanding record in the RAF. The aircrew of Bomber Command went out to do what they were told had to be done for the survival of Britain and for Allied victory. Historic judgements on the bomber offensive can do nothing to mar the honour of such an epitaph.

Appendix A

Bomber Command Sorties Dispatched and Aircraft Missing and Written off, 1939–45

		Sorties		*Missing*		*Crashed*	
		NIGHT	DAY	NIGHT	DAY	NIGHT	DAY
1939	September	83	40	2	12	3	0
	October	32	0	2	0	2	0
	November	15	4	0	0	1	0
	December	40	119	0	17	0	2
1940	January	38	6	0	0	0	0
	February	54	4	1	0	2	0
	March	239	53	5	1	6	0
	April	489	167	18	15	8	0
	May	1,617	802	21	49	3	3
	June	2,484	812	26	31	7	1
	July	1,722	616	40	32	3	4
	August	2,188	417	52	18	11	0
	September	3,141	98	65	1	21	0
	October	2,242	172	27	1	32	0
	November	1,894	113	50	2	34	0
	December	1,385	56	37	2	23	0
1941	January	1,030	96	12	3	12	1
	February	1,617	124	16	2	32	2
	March	1,728	162	35	4	36	0
	April	2,249	676	56	23	12	7
	May	2,416	273	39	20	14	3
	June	3,228	531	76	22	15	3
	July	3,243	582	91	66	28	3
	August	3,344	468	121	35	45	5
	September	2,621	263	76	14	62	1
	October	2,501	138	68	17	40	1
	November	1,713	43	83	0	21	0
	December	1,411	151	28	7	16	0
1942	January	2,216	24	56	0	32	0
	February	1,162	252	18	15	14	1
	March	2,224	131	78	2	21	0
	April	3,752	246	130	13	29	2
	May	2,702	105	114	1	21	0
	June	4,801	196	199	2	39	1
	July	3,914	313	171	19	22	0
	August	2,454	186	142	10	16	5
	September	3,489	127	169	6	39	0
	October	2,198	406	89	14	27	0
	November	2,067	127	53	11	23	0
	December	1,758	200	72	16	22	2
1943	January	2,556	406	86	15	18	3
	February	5,030	426	101	6	22	3
	March	5,174	284	161	7	25	1
	April	5,571	316	253	12	24	1
	May	5,130	360	234	19	27	4
	June	5,816	0	275	0	15	0

	July	6,170	0	188		31	
	August	7,807	0	275		33	
	September	5,513	0	191		34	
	October	4,638	0	159		21	
	November	5,208	0	162		48	
	December	4,123	0	170		47	
1944	January	6,278	0	314		38	
	February	4,263	45	199	0	24	0
	March	9,031	18	283	0	39	0
	April	9,873	10	214	0	25	0
	May	11,353	16	274	0	29	0
	June	13,592	2,371	293	12	30	0
	July	11,500	6,298	229	12	29	4
	August	10,013	10,271	186	35	22	1
	September	6,428	9,643	96	41	15	0
	October	10,193	6,713	75	52	26	0
	November	9,589	5,055	98	41	34	0
	December	11,239	3,656	88	31	43	0
1945	January	9,603	1,304	121	12	57	0
	February	13,715	3,685	164	9	60	0
	March	11,585	9,606	168	47	76	10
	April	8,822	5,001	51	22	29	6
	May	349	1,068	3	2	0	1

This record is admittedly incomplete because it does not include minelaying or Special Duties sorties and casualties, and because some squadron and group record books were carelessly kept. But they are the best figures that the Royal Air Force is ever likely to compile. The statistics for crashed aircraft before February 1942 are unreliable because it is not clear which were damaged and which were totally written off.

Appendix B

Specifications and performance of the principal aircraft of Bomber Command and Luftwaffe night-fighters, 1939–45

It is impossible to detail the immense number of different Marks of each aircraft. I have therefore chosen those which relate to the events most closely described in the text. Performance figures are only the most approximate guide, since individual aircraft varied immensely in efficiency and handling. Some Lancasters, for instance, were modified to carry a bombload of ten tons, with front and mid-upper turrets removed.

British aircraft

Vickers WELLINGTON IC. Type: twin-engined medium bomber; crew: 6; length: 60.8 feet; height: 18.75 feet; wing-span: 86 feet; maximum loaded weight 30,000 lb; ceiling: 15,000 feet; cruising speed: 165 mph; maximum speed: 245 mph; bombload: 4,500 lb (with fuel for 1,200 miles)/1,000 lb (with fuel for 2,550 miles); armament: twin .303s in front and rear turrets, single free .303s on beam mountings*; engines: Pegasus XVIII.

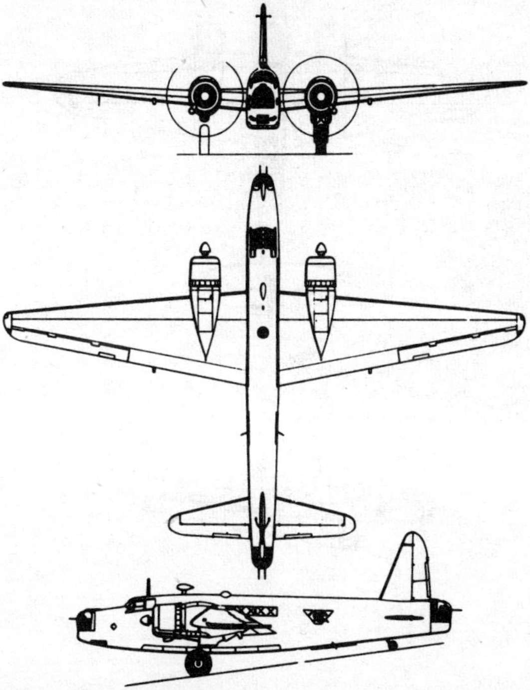

* 3 Group Wellington Is of 18 December 1939 lacked beam guns and carried only a single gun in forward turret.

Bristol BLENHEIM IV. Type: twin-engined light bomber; crew: 3; length: 40 feet; height: 9.2 feet; wing-span: 56 feet; maximum loaded weight: 15,800 lb; ceiling: 22,000 feet; cruising speed: 180 mph; maximum speed: 266 mph; bombload: 1,000 lb (with fuel for 1,460 miles); armament: twin .303s in forward under nacelle*; single .303 in rear turret, single .303 rearward fixed firing from engine nacelle; engines: Mercury XV.

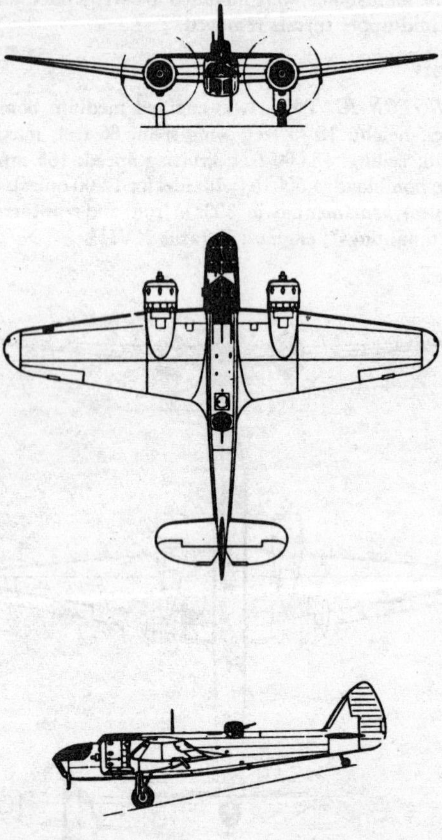

* not shown

Armstrong Whitworth WHITLEY V. Type: twin-engined medium bomber; crew 5; length: 69.3 feet; height; 12.75 feet; wing-span: 84 feet; maximum loaded weight: 33,500 lb; ceiling: 17,600 feet; cruising speed: 165 mph; maximum speed: 202 mph; bombload: 8,000 lb (with fuel for 630 miles)/3,500 lb (with fuel for 1,930 miles); armament: single free .303 in forward turret, four .303s in rear turret; engines: Merlin X.

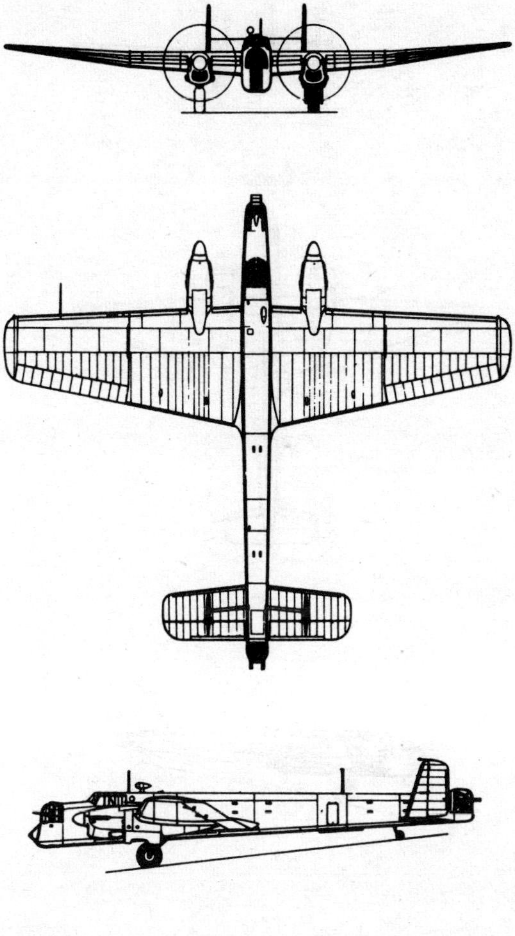

Handley Page HAMPDEN. Type: twin-engined medium bomber; crew: 4; length: 53.3 feet; height: 14.9 feet; wing-span: 69.3 feet; maximum loaded weight: 22,500 lb; ceiling: 20,000 feet; cruising speed: 155 mph; maximum speed: 243 mph; bombload: 4,000 lb (with fuel for 1,200 miles)/2,000 lb (with fuel for 1,885 miles); armament: single fixed and single free .303 in nose, single or twin free .303s in rear and mid-under positions; engines: Pegasus XVIII.

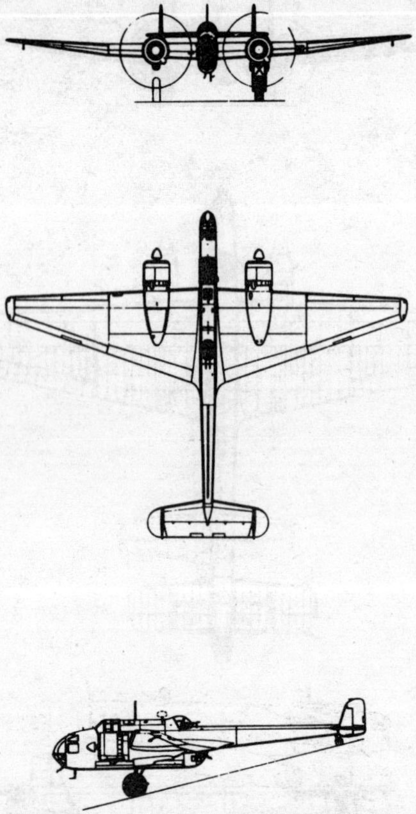

Avro MANCHESTER. Type: twin-engined heavy-medium bomber; crew: 6; length: 68.8 feet; height: 19.5 feet; wing-span: 90.1 feet; maximum weight: 50,000 lb; ceiling: 19,200; cruising speed: 185 mph; maximum speed: 258 mph; bombload: 10,350 lb (with fuel for 1,200 miles)/8,100 lb (with fuel for 1,630 miles); armament: twin .303s in front and mid-upper turrets, quad .303s in rear turret; engines: Vulture II.

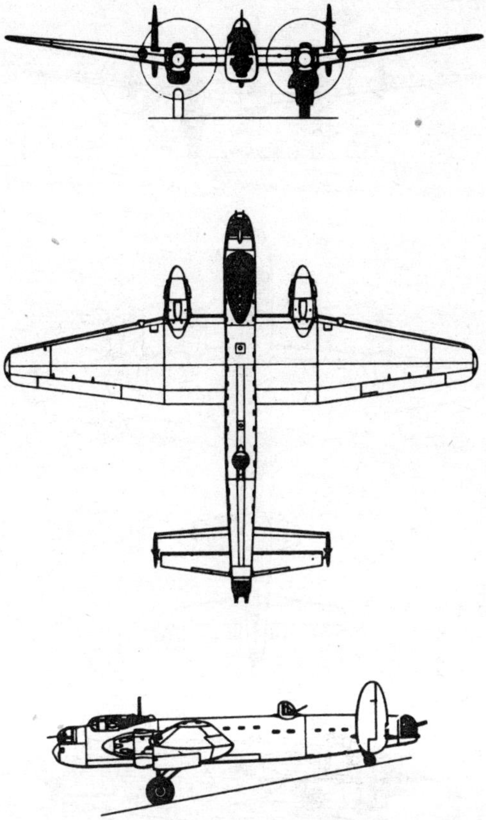

Short STIRLING III. Type: four-engined heavy bomber; crew: 7; length: 87 feet; height: 22.75 feet; wing-span: 99 feet; maximum loaded weight: 70,000 lb; ceiling: 17,000 feet; cruising speed: 200 mph; maximum speed: 270 mph; bombload: 14,000 lb (with fuel for 590 miles)/2,010 lb (with fuel for 3,575 miles); armament: twin .303s in front and mid-upper turrets, quad .303s in rear turret; engines: Hercules VI.

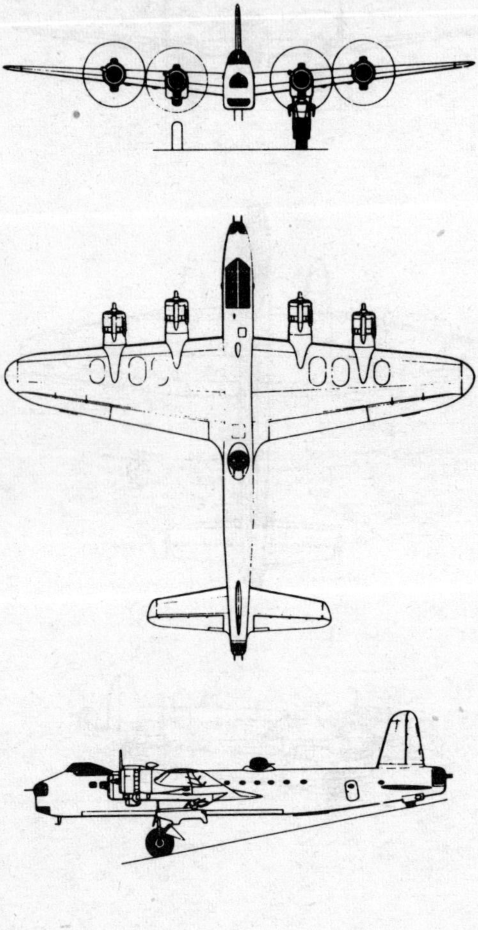

*Handley Page HALIFAX III**. Type: four-engined heavy bomber; crew: 7; length: 70.1 feet; height: 20.75 feet; wing-span: 104 feet; maximum loaded weight: 50,000 lb; ceiling: 20,000 feet; cruising speed: 225 mph; maximum speed: 277 mph; bombload: 13,000 lb (with fuel for 980 miles)/6,250 lb (with fuel for 2,005 miles); armament: single or twin .303s in front turret, quad .303s in mid-upper turret, quad .303s in rear turret; engines: Hercules XVI.

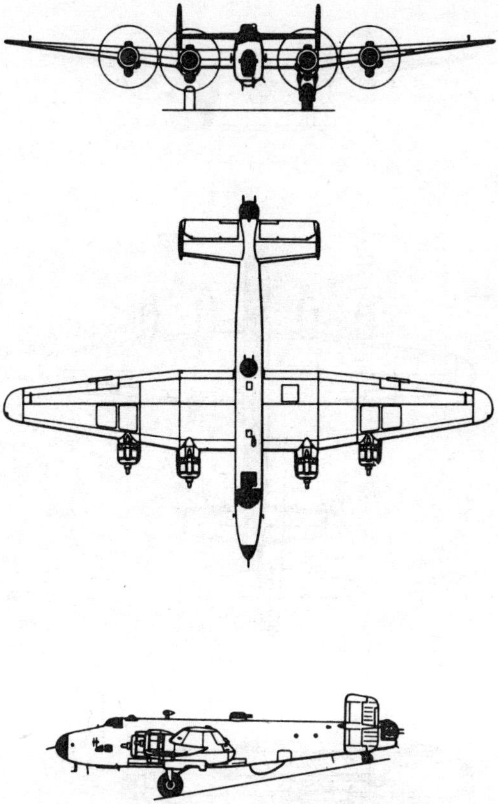

*76 Squadron in 1943 was equipped with the earlier Halifax II or V.

Avro LANCASTER I and III. Type: four-engined heavy bomber; crew: 7 (sometimes 8 in PFF aircraft and 6 Group aircraft with ventral turrets); length: 68.9 feet; height: 19.5 feet; wing-span: 102 feet; maximum loaded weight: 68,000 lb; cruising speed: 216 mph; maximum speed: 266 mph; ceiling: 20,000 feet; bombload: 14,000 lb (with fuel for 1,660 miles); armament: twin .303s in front and mid-upper turrets, quad .303s in rear turret; engines: Merlin 22, 28 or 38*.

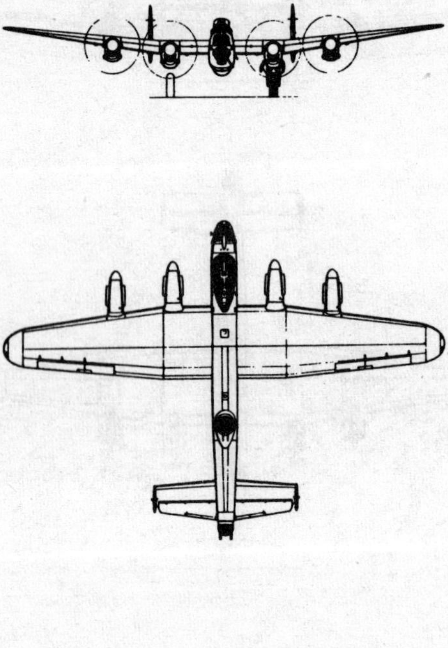

*Note H2S dome under fuselage below mid-upper turret.

De Havilland MOSQUITO Mk.IV. Type: twin-engined light bomber; crew: 2; length: 40.5 feet; height: 12.5 feet; wing-span: 54.17 feet; maximum loaded weight: 21,462 lb; ceiling: 33,000 feet; cruising speed: 265 mph; maximum speed: 362 mph; bombload: 2,000 lb (with fuel for 1,620 miles) – some aircraft were modified to carry a 4,000-lb bomb; armament: none; engines: Merlin 21 or 23.

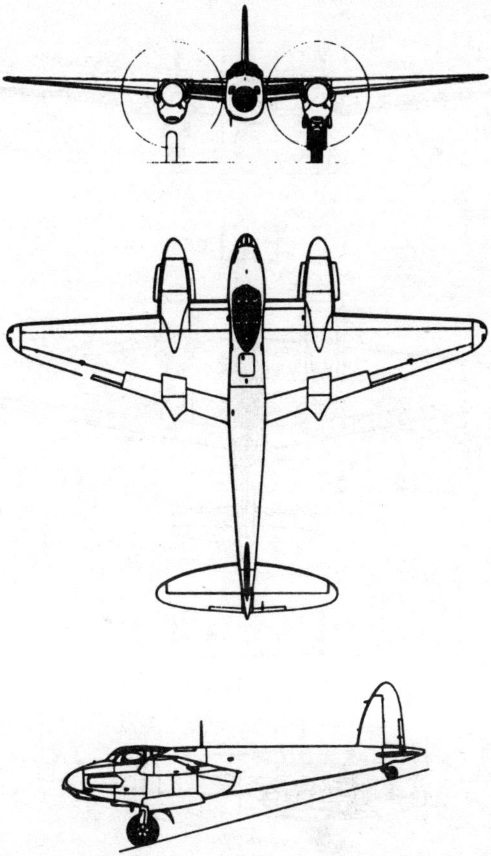

German aircraft

Messerschmitt BF 110G. Type: twin-engined night-fighter; crew: 3; length: 42.8 feet; height: 13.7 feet; wing-span: 53.4 feet; maximum weight: 21,800 lb; ceiling: 26,250 feet; cruising speed: 250 mph; maximum speed: 342 mph; range: 1,305 miles; armament: two 30-mm cannon and two 20-mm cannon in nose, twin 7.9 mm machine-guns in rear; some aircraft fitted with *schrage musik* in 1944; engines: Daimler-Benz DB 605B.*

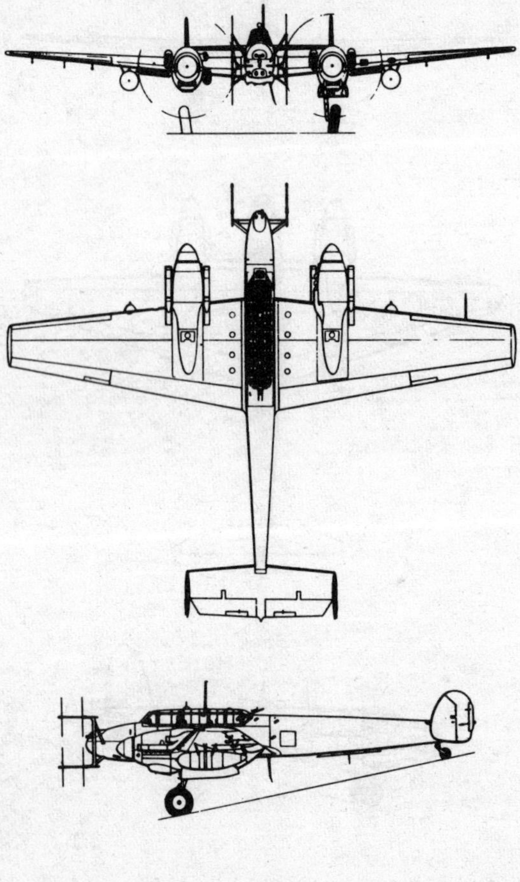

*Note *Lichtenstein* aerials at nose.

Messerschmitt BF 109G. Type: single-engined day-fighter used as 'Wild Boar', July 1943–March 1944; crew: 1; length: 29 feet; height: 8.2 feet; wing-span: 32.5 feet; maximum weight: 7,491 lb; ceiling: 37,890 feet; cruising speed: 260 mph; maximum speed: 386 mph; range: 620 miles; armament: one 30-mm cannon or one 20-mm cannon plus two 13-mm machine-guns; engine: Daimler-Benz DB 605A.

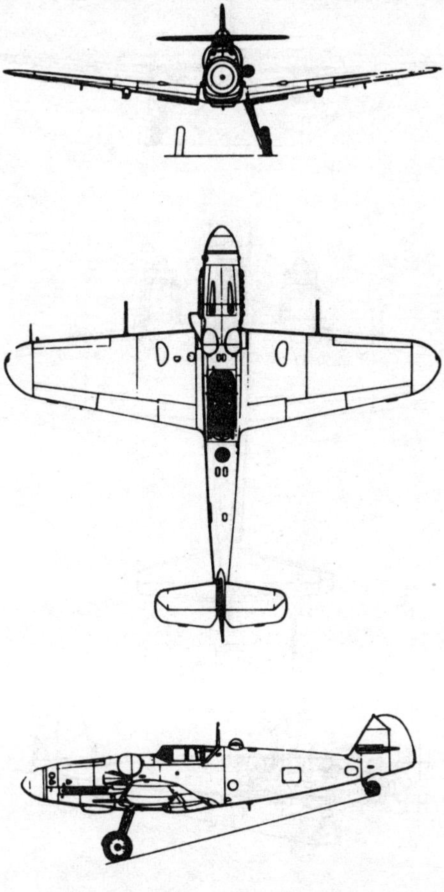

Junkers Ju88C. Type: twin-engined night-fighter; crew: 2 or 3; length: 49.4 feet; height: 16.6 feet; wing-span: 65.8 feet; maximum weight: 27,225 lb; ceiling: 32,480 feet; cruising speed: 263 mph; maximum speed: 307 mph; range: 1,230 miles; armament: three 20-mm cannon and three 7.9-mm machine-guns in nose, one 13-mm machine-gun in rear of cockpit; some aircraft in 1944 fitted with *schrage musik**; engines: 2 Junkers Jumo 211J.

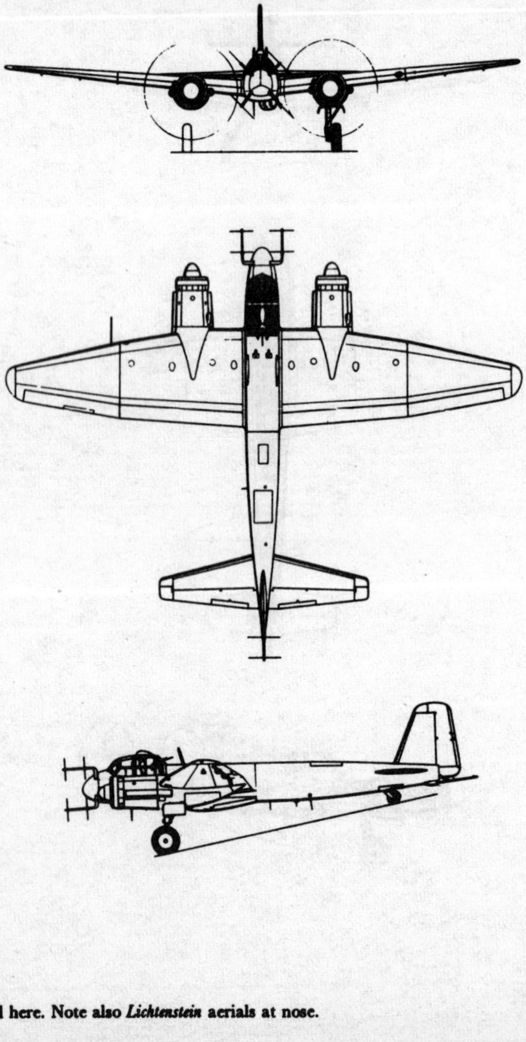

*Illustrated here. Note also *Lichtenstein* aerials at nose.

US aircraft in service with Bomber Command

*Boeing B-17 FORTRESS III**. Type: four-engined heavy bomber; crew: 6; length: 73 feet; height: 15.6 feet; wing-span: 104 feet; maximum weight: 64,000 lb; ceiling: 31,500; cruising speed: 230 mph; maximum speed: 280 mph; bombload: 12,800 lb (with fuel for 1,140 miles); armament: nine .50 in turrets and free-mounted; engines: 4 Cyclone GR1820-97.

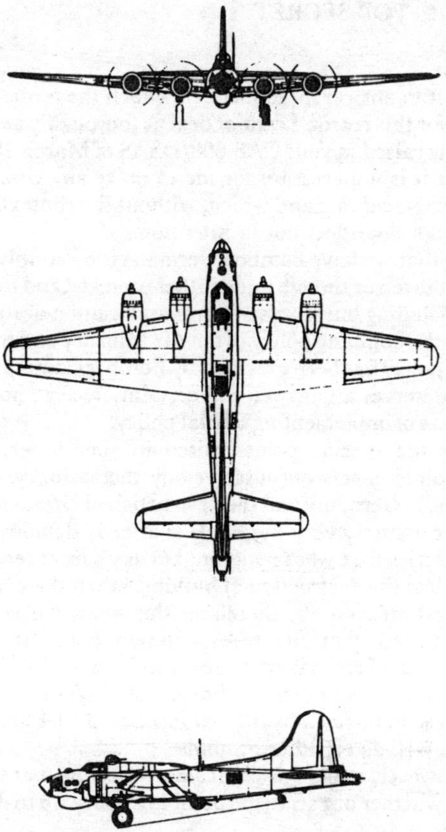

*Deployed by 100 Group, 1944–45.

Appendix C

Letter to Sir Norman Bottomly, Deputy Chief of Air Staff, from Sir Arthur Harris

AIR 20/3218
Headquarters, Bomber Command
High Wycombe, Bucks
29th March 1945

ATH/DO/4B
PERSONAL & TOP SECRET

Dear Norman

It is difficult to answer indictments of which the terms are not fully revealed and for this reason I cannot deal as thoroughly as I should like with the points raised in your CAS.608/DSAS of March 28th. I take it, however, that it is unnecessary for me to make any comment on the passages which you quote and which, without the context, are abusive in effect, though doubtless not in intention.

To suggest that we have bombed German cities 'simply for the sake of increasing the terror though under other pretexts' and to speak of our offensive as including 'mere acts of terror and wanton destruction' is an insult both to the bombing policy of the Air Ministry and to the manner in which that policy has been executed by Bomber Command. This sort of thing if it deserves an answer will certainly receive none from me, after three years of implementing official policy.

As regards the specific points raised in your letter, namely the adverse economic effects on ourselves by increasing yet further the material havoc in Germany and the destruction of Dresden* in particular the answer is surely very simple. It is already demonstrated in the liberated countries that what really makes any sort of recovery almost impossible is less the destruction of buildings than the complete dislocation of transportation. If, therefore, this objection is to be taken seriously I suggest that the transportation plan rather than the strategic bombing of cities is what needs to be considered, as I understand it has been, and for precisely that reason. You will remember that Dresden was recommended by the Targets Committee as a transportation target as well as on other grounds.

I do not, however, stress this point since I assume that what is really at issue is (a) whether our strategic bombing policy up to date has been

*The feeling, such as there is, over Dresden could be easily explained by any psychiatrist. It is connected with German bands and Dresden shepherdesses. Actually Dresden was a mass of munition works, an intact government centre, and a key transportation point to the East. It is now none of those things. [This footnote is part of the letter.]

justified (b) whether the time has now come to discontinue this policy. I will therefore confine myself to these questions.

As regards (a) I have on previous occasions discussed this matter very carefully in official correspondence with the Air Ministry and to avoid repetition I refer you to the following correspondence:

(i) Bomber Command letter BC/S.23801/Press/C.-in-C. of October 25th 1943.
(ii) Air Ministry letter CS.21079/43 of December 15th 1943.
(iii) Bomber Command letter BC/S.23801/Press/C.-in-C. of December 23rd 1943.
(iv) Air Ministry letter CS.21079 of March 2nd 1944.
(v) Bomber Command letter BC/S.31152/Air/C.-in-C. of March 7th 1944.

I have always held and still maintain that my Directive, which you quote, 'the progressive destruction and dislocation of the German military, industrial and economic systems' could be carried out only by the elimination of German industrial cities and not merely by attacks on individual factories however important these might be in themselves. This view was also officially confirmed by the Air Ministry. The overwhelming evidence which is now available to support it makes it quite superfluous for me to argue at length that the destruction of those cities has fatally weakened the German effort and is now enabling Allied soldiers to advance into the heart of Germany with negligible casualties. Hence the only question which I have to answer is this: would 'confining ourselves to more precise concentrations upon military objectives such as oil and communications behind the immediate battle zone' tend to shorten the war more than persistence in attacks on cities? The answer appears to me to be obvious; but, even if it is not, I must point out as I have frequently done before that we have by no means always a free choice in this matter. Weather conditions frequently constrain me to decide between attacking cities and not attacking at all. When this happens it is surely evident that it is expedient to attack the cities. I can only find, pinpoint and hit small targets with a small part of my force at a time, and I have not enough fighter escort to do more than two such small attacks daily.

I have thus disposed of point (a). We have never gone in for terror bombing and the attacks which we have made in accordance with my Directive have in fact produced the strategic consequences for which they were designed and from which the Armies now profit.

Point (b) is rather difficult to follow. It can hardly mean that attacks on cities no longer produce dislocation in the German war effort. Quite the contrary is the case. The nearer Germany is to collapse the less capable she is of reorganizing to meet disasters of this kind and we ought logically to make a special effort to eliminate the few cities which still remain more or less serviceable.

I therefore assume that the view under consideration is something like this: 'no doubt in the past we were justified in attacking German cities. But to do so was always repugnant and now that the Germans are beaten anyway we can properly abstain from proceeding with these attacks'. This is a doctrine to which I could never subscribe. Attacks on cities like any other act of war are intolerable unless they are strategically justified. But they are strategically justified in so far as they tend to shorten the war and so preserve the lives of Allied soldiers. To my mind we have absolutely no right to give them up unless it is certain that they will not have this effect. I do not personally regard the whole of the remaining cities of Germany as worth the bones of one British Grenadier.

It therefore seems to me that there is one and only one valid argument on which a case for giving up strategic bombing could be based, namely that it has already completed its task and that nothing now remains for the Armies to do except to occupy Germany against unorganized resistance. If this is what is meant I shall no doubt be informed of it. It does not however appear to be the view of the Supreme Commander. Until it is, I submit that the strategic bombing of German cities must go on.

Some final points. As you know Transportation targets are now largely off. Oil has had, and is getting, all we can practically give it in consideration of weather and escort factors. We answer every army support call and, as Monty tells us, in a 'decisive manner'. We have asked for more but there aren't any. H.E. is seriously limited in supply. Incendiaries are not. All these factors must therefore also be considered, and the inevitable answer is that either we continue as in the past or we very largely stand down altogether. The last alternative would certainly be welcome. I take little delight in the work and none whatever in risking my crews avoidably.

Japan remains. Are we going to bomb their cities flat – as in Germany – and give the Armies a walk over – as in France and Germany – or going to bomb only their outlying factories* and subsequently invade at the cost of 3 to 6 million casualties? We should be careful of precedents.

Yours Ever,

Bert

Air Marshal Sir Norman Bottomley, KCB, CIE, DSO, AFC,
Air Ministry, Whitehall, SW1

*Largely underground by the time we get going. [Part of original.]

Appendix D

British and German production of selected armaments, 1940–44

	1940		1941		1942		1943		1944	
	Germany	UK	Germany	UK	Germany	UK	Germany	UK	Germany	UK
Military Aircraft										
Total (numbers)	10,200	15,000	11,000	20,100	14,200	23,600	25,200	26,200	39,600	26,500
Total structural weight (million lb.)	59	59	64	87	92	133	138	185	174	208
Bombs (filled weight in 1,000 tons)		48	245	143	262	241	273	309	231	370
Armoured vehicles										
Tanks	1,600	1,400	3,800	4,800	6,300	8,600	12,100	7,500	19,000	4,600
Others	500	6,000	1,300	10,500	3,100	19,300	7,800	24,200	9,900	22,600
Wheeled vehicles (thousands)										
Heavy type		112	62	110	81	109	109	104	89	91
Light cars and vans		21		17	29	16	36	17	26	13
Motor cycles		68		71		75	38	79	33	75
Heavy guns (75 mm and over)										
Field, medium and heavy	4,400	1,000	4,700	3,800	5,100	4,000	11,700	3,000	24,900	2,800
Tank	470	–	650	–	2,200	2	9,500	4,600	20,400	7,500
Anti-tank	–	–	–	–	2,100	500	9,900	3,300	13,800	1,900
Anti-aircraft	1,400	900	2,400	1,500	4,200	2,100	6,900	1,300	8,200	200
Total	6,300	1,900	7,800	5,300	13,600	6,600	38,000	12,200	62,300	12,400
Light guns (under 75 mm, excluding 20 mm)										
Tank	–	240	100	6,000	3,000	22,000	900	10,400	700	1,700
Anti-tank	430	1,500	2,100	2,700	4,500	9,100	2,600	9,800	–	1,100
Anti-aircraft		1,100	1,200	2,700	2,100	5,300	4,600	5,600	7,700	800
Total		2,800	3,400	11,400	9,600	36,400	8,100	25,800	8,400	3,600

Appendix E

Schedule of German cities subjected to area attack by Bomber Command, 1942–45

Town	Date of First Main Force Attack	Date of Last Main Force Attack	Total Number of Main Force Attacks	Tonnages (Short) claimed dropped (including Mosquito Attacks) Jan. 1942–May 1945	Acreage 40 per cent or more Built-up (Target) Area	Acreage Destroyed in Built-up (Target) Area	Destroyed Percentage of Built-up (Target) Area
Aachen	5/6.10.42	13/14. 7.43	2	3,930	1,030	605	59
Augsburg	25/26. 2.44	–	1	2,076	1,535	445	29
Berlin	16/17. 1.43	24/25. 3.44	24	49,400	19,423	6,427	33
Bochum	29/30. 3.43	4/5.11.44	6	10,207	640	532	83
Bonn	18.10.44	4/5. 2.45	5	2,317	708	240	34
Bremen	3/4. 6.42	22. 4.45	12	9,709	1,744	1,042	60
Bremerhaven	18/19. 9.44	–	1	968	375	297	79
Brunswick	14/15. 1.44	14/15.10.44	5	6,803	1,400	655	47
Chemnitz	14/15. 2.45	5/6. 3.45	2	4,574	1,452	590	41
Coblenz	6/7.11.44	–	1	896	523	303	58
Cologne	13/14. 3.42	2. 3.45	22	28,699	3,250	1,994	61
Darmstadt	25/26. 8.44	11/12. 9.44	2	1,726	745	516	69
Dessau	7/8. 3.45	8/9. 4.45	2	2,017	542	331	61
Dortmund	14/15. 4.42	12. 3.45	9	18,295	1,720	923	54
Dresden	13/14. 2.45	–	1	2,978	2,844	1,681	59
Duisburg	13/14. 7.42	21/22. 2.45	18	29,010	2,955	1,424	48
Dusseldorf	31/1. 8.42	2/3.11.44	10	18,099	3,115	2,003	64
Emden	6/7. 6.42	6. 9.44	5	2,834	485	270	56
Essen	8/9. 3.42	11. 3.45	28	39,907	2,630	1,319	50
Frankfurt A/Main	24/25. 8.42	28/29.12.44	11	23,139	2,200	1,145	52

Freiburg	27/28.11.44	–	1	1,900	694	257	37
Friedrichshafen	27/28. 4.44	–	1	1,234	148	99	67
Gelsenkirchen	25/26. 6.43	22/23. 1.45	4	7,386	757	360	48
Giessen	2/3.12.44	6/7.12.44	2	549	398	130	33
Hagen	1/2.10.43	15/16. 3.45	4	4,515	486	325	67
Hamburg	15/16. 1.42	13/14. 4.45	17	16,089	8,315	6,200	75
Hamm	5.12.44	–	1	514	355	140	39
Hanau	6/7. 1.45	18/19. 3.45	2	3,059	275	190	69
Hannover	22/23. 9.43	25. 3.45	16	15,299	2,519	1,517	60
Harburg	11/12.11.44	–	1	–	286	153	53
Heilbronn	4/5.12.44	–	1	1,254	430	351	82
Hildesheim	22. 3.45	–	1	1,168	378	263	70
Kaiserslautern	27/28. 9.44	–	1	909	369	134	36
Karlsruhe	2/3. 9.42	2/3. 2.45	6	8,178	1,237	398	32
Kassel	27/28. 8.42	8/9. 3.45	6	6,175	905	620	69
Kiel	27/28. 2.42	23/24. 4.45	10	10,875	1,466	725	50
Konigsberg	26/27. 8.44	29/30. 8.44	2	1,053	824	435	53
Krefeld	2/3.10.42	21/22. 6.43	2	2,779	1,529	714	47
Leipzig	20.21.10.43	10/20. 2.44	3	5,714	3,183	625	20
Lubeck	28/29. 3.42	–	1	441	633	190	30
Magdeburg	21/22. 1.44	13/14. 2.45	4	4,166	1,884	774	44
Mainz	11/12. 8.42	27. 2.45	4	3,295	971	593	61
Mannheim-Ludwigshaven	14/15. 2.42	1. 3.45	13	14,319	1,911	1,213	64
Mulheim	22/23. 6.43	–	1	1,848	303	193	64
Munchen-Gladbach and Rheydt	30/31. 8.43	1. 2.45	4	4,115	1,176	633	54
Munich	19/20. 9.42	7/8. 1.45	9	8,755	3,634	1,547	42
Munster	28/29. 1.42	25. 3.45	6	3,769	997	650	65
Neuss	23/24. 9.44	28/29.11.44	4	5,744	225	17	8
Nuremberg	28/29. 8.42	16/17. 3.45	11	13,807	2,255	1,146	51
Oberhausen	14/15. 6.43	4.12.45	3	3,065	502	100	20
Osnabruck	9/10. 8.42	25. 3.45	5	4,437	658	441	67

Town	Date of First Main Force Attack	Date of Last Main Force Attack	Total Number of Main Force Attacks	Tonnages (Short) claimed dropped (including Mosquito Attacks) Jan. 1942–May 1945	Acreage 40 per cent or more Built-up (Target) Area	Acreage Destroyed in Built-up (Target) Area	Destroyed Percentage of Built-up (Target) Area
Pforzheim	23/24. 2.45	–	1	1,825	369	304	83
Plauen	10/11. 4.45	–	1	1,344	712	365	51
Potsdam	14/15. 4.45	–	1	–	559	75	13
Remscheid	30/31. 7.43	–	1	871	339	289	83
Rostock	23/24. 4.42	26/27. 4.42	4	990	634	200	32
Saarbrucken	29/30. 7.42	5/6.10.44	4	2,986	866	418	48
Schweinfurt	24/25. 2.44	26/27. 4.44	2	3,321	293	126	43
Solingen	4.11.44	5.11.44	2	2,048	343	169	49
Stettin	20/21. 4.43	29/30. 8.44	4	5,261	1,386	736	53
Stuttgart	4/5. 5.42	12/13. 2.45	18	21,246	2,514	1,152	46
Trier	21.12.44	23.12.44	2	1,436	492	48	10
Ulm	17/18.12.44	–	1	1,449	562	155	28
Wiesbaden	2/3. 2.45	–	1	2,483	605	90	15
Wilhelmshaven	10/11. 1.42	15/16.10.44	9	7,354	972	130	13
Witten	18/19. 3.45	–	1	1,081	207	129	62
Worms	21/22. 2.45	–	1	1,116	328	127	39
Wuppertal-Barmen	29/30. 5.43	13. 3.45	2	3,448	1,139	655	58
Wuppertal/Elberfeld	24/25. 6.43	–	1	1,979	929	870	94
Wurzburg	16/17. 3.45	–		1,127	477	422	89
			475,363				
All area attacks prior to January, 1942			7,074				
Total			482,437				

Source: British Bombing Survey Unit report. Figures do not seek to include tonnage dropped and damage achieved by USAAF attacks.

Appendix F

Comparative Allied and German aircraft production, 1939–45

Average monthly output		Single-Engine Fighters			Twin-Engined Aircraft*			Four-engined Aircraft		
		German	British	United States	German	British	United States	German	British	United States
1939	1st Quarter	128	70	–	219	134	–	0.5	–	Not Known
	2nd Quarter		82	–		141	–		–	
	3rd Quarter		74	–		153	–		–	
	4th Quarter		114	–		174	–		–	
1940	1st Quarter	156	155	–	382	151	24	3	–	5
	2nd Quarter		340	12		288	24		1	–
	3rd Quarter		563	91		365	28		3	6
	4th Quarter		420	156		339	20		11	9
1941	1st Quarter	160	452	146	366	375	51	5	25	8
	2nd Quarter	326	491	152	353	428	106	5	34	17
	3rd Quarter	242	550	174	454	438	169	6	50	18
	4th Quarter	221	559	320	373	407	224	3	57	64
1942	1st Quarter	396	625	395	434	465	326	12	89	125
	2nd Quarter	349	692	473	504	511	376	20	142	182
	3rd Quarter	420	681	517	521	503	526	24	191	237
	4th Quarter	449	659	484	555	517	575	27	232	329
1943	1st Quarter	642	697	525	698	488	625	31	321	457
	2nd Quarter	865	687	741	683	472	808	45	387	700
	3rd Quarter	932	672	993	743	443	707	34	383	914
	4th Quarter	763	661	1,205	663	452	1,010	54	428	1,134
1944	1st Quarter	1,236	663	1,320	567	525	1,138	64	483	1,435
	2nd Quarter	1,927	666	1,290	779	489	1,185	72	481	1,516
	3rd Quarter	2,779	563	1,394	795	476	1,067	36	460	1,383
	4th Quarter	2,645	534	1,221	554	434	908	Nil	412	1,113
1945	1st Quarter	2,078	483	1,283	492	421	837	Nil	350	1,066

Source: *BBSU Effects of Bombing the German Aircraft Industry.*

*German twin-engine aircraft were mostly bombers pre-1943 and mostly fighters thereafter.

Bibliography and a note on sources

The principal sources of original material for this book have been the AIR files in the Public Record Office, notably those of the Chief of Air Staff, the C-in-C Bomber Command, the Directorate of Bomber Operations and the Secretary of State for Air, although sadly most of the latter's papers have been lost or destroyed. I have also relied heavily on group and squadron Operational Record Books, *Bomber Command Quarterly Review*, and that stand-by of the wartime Target Intelligence department, *The Bomber's Baedeker*. At the end of the war, High Wycombe's Intelligence Section devoted great labour to compiling a remarkable two-volume file entitled 'A Review of the Work of Int I', which I can only describe as a handbook for the use of any future planner who might be called upon to organize a strategic bomber offensive. It gives a fascinating flavour of High Wycombe's staff work, and I am deeply indebted to the officer who loaned me his almost unique copy. *The United States Strategic Bombing Survey* is vast, uneven, often unreliable but indispensable. So is the British official history, *The Strategic Air Offensive against Germany*, especially the final volume of appendices, selected documents and statistics. A good study of the strategy of the campaign is Anthony Verrier's *The Bomber Offensive*, to which I am indebted for many important lines of thought. *Hansard*'s reports of the parliamentary debates on the Royal Air Force both during and immediately after the war make fascinating reading. No novelist writing of the air war from 1939–45 has matched the genius of V. M. Yeates's *Winged Victory* or Cecil Lewis's *Sagittarius Rising* on the First World War, but I have included below several works of fiction which either paint a vivid picture of operational bomber flying, or cast interesting light on contemporary wartime attitudes to Bomber Command. I have omitted many relevant volumes on the general conduct of the Second World War, which are invaluable background reading, but deal only peripherally with Bomber Command. Asterisked titles are notable for their exceptional photographs of operational aircraft.

Air Ministry, *Bomber Command* (HMSO 1941)
Bates, H. E., *The Stories of Flying Officer X* (Cape 1952)
Bekker, Caius, *The Luftwaffe War Diaries* (Macdonald 1964)
Bell, George, *The Church and Humanity* (Longmans 1946)
Bennett, D. C. T., *Pathfinder* (Muller 1958)
Birkenhead, The Earl of, *The Prof in Two Worlds* (Collins 1961)
Blackett, P. M. S., *Studies of War* (Oliver & Boyd 1962)
Bond, Brian, *Liddell Hart: A Study of His Military Thought* (Cassell 1977)
Boyle, Andrew, *Trenchard* (Collins 1962)
Bowyer, Chaz, *The Mosquito at War** (Ian Allan 1976)
——, *Hampden Special** (Ian Allan 1975)
Bowyer, Michael, *A History of 2 Group, RAF* (Faber 1974)
——, *Mosquito* (Faber 1967)
Braddon, Russell, *Cheshire VC* (Evans 1954)
Cheshire, Leonard, *Bomber Pilot* (Hutchinson 1943)
Churchill, Winston, *The Second World War* (Cassell 1948–54)

Clark, Ronald, *The Rise of the Boffins* (Phoenix 1962)
——, *Tizard* (Methuen 1965)
Collier, Basil, *A History of Air Power* (Weidenfeld 1974)
Deighton, Len, *Bomber* (Cape 1970)
——, *Fighter* (Cape 1977)
Divine, David, *The Broken Wing* (Hutchinson 1966)
Frankland, Dr Noble, *The Bombing Offensive against Germany* (Faber 1965)
Galland, Adolf, *The First and the Last* (Methuen 1955)
Garbett and Goulding, *The Lancaster at War** (Ian Allan 1971)
Gibson, Guy, *Enemy Coast Ahead* (Michael Joseph 1946)
Goebbels, Josef, *The Goebbels Diaries* (Hamish Hamilton 1948)
——, *The Goebbels Diaries: The Last Days* (Secker & Warburg 1978)
Groves, Brigadier P. R. C., *Our Future in the Air* (Harrap 1935)
Hansell, Major-General H. S., *The Air Plan that Defeated Hitler* (Atlanta 1972)
Harris, Marshal of the RAF Sir Arthur, *Bomber Offensive* (Collins 1947)
Hornsey, Denis, *The Pilot Walked Home* (Collins Blue Circle 1946)
Hyde, Montgomery, *British Air Policy between the Wars* (Heinemann 1976)
Irving, David, *The Destruction of Dresden* (Kimber 1963)
——, *Nicht Und Deutschlands Stadte Starben* (Schweitzer, Zurich 1963)
——, *The Mare's Nest* (Kimber 1964)
——, *The Rise and Fall of the Luftwaffe* (Weidenfeld 1973)
——, *Hitler's War* (Hodder & Stoughton 1977)
Jones, Geoffrey, *Raider: The Halifax and its Fliers* (Kimber 1978)
Jones, Nevill, *Origins of Strategic Bombing* (Kimber 1973)
Jones, H. A., *The War in the Air* (Oxford 1937)
Jones, R. V. *Most Secret War* (Hamish Hamilton 1978)
Lawrence, W. J., *No. 5 Bomber Group RAF* (Faber 1951)
Lee, General Raymond, *The London Observer* (Hutchinson 1972)
Lewin, Ronald, *Ultra at War* (Hutchinson 1978)
Liddell Hart, B. H., *Paris, or The Future of War* (Kegan Paul 1925)
——, *When Britain Goes to War* (Kegan Paul 1935)
——, (*and see* Bond, Brian)
Lumsden, Alex, *Wellington Special** (Ian Allan 1974)
Middlebrook, Martin, *The Nuremberg Raid* (Allen Lane 1973)
Milward, Alan, *The German Economy at War* (London University 1965)
——, *War, Economy and Society* (Allen Lane 1975)
Mosley, Leonard, *The Reichsmarschal* (Weidenfeld 1973)
Muirhead, J. T., *Air Attack on Cities* (Allen & Unwin 1938)
Musgrove, Gordon, *Pathfinder Force* (Macdonald and Janes 1976)
Price, Alfred, *Instruments of Darkness* (Kimber 1967)
Revie, Alasdair, *The Lost Command* (David Bruce & Watson 1971)
Richards, Denis, *Portal of Hungerford* (Heinemann 1978)
Richardson, Frank, *Fighting Spirit* (Leo Cooper 1978)
Roskill, Captain S. W., *Churchill and the Admirals* (Collins 1977)
Rumpf, Hans, *The Bombing of Germany* (Muller 1963)
Saint-Exupery, Antoine de, *Airman's Odyssey* (Reynal & Hitchcock, New York 1942)

Saundby, Air Marshal Sir Robert, *Air Bombardment* (Chatto and Windus 1961)
Saward, Group-Captain Dudley, *The Bomber's Eye* (Cassell 1959)
Schmidt, Klaus, *Die Brandnacht* (Reba Verlag, Darmstadt 1964)
Seversky, Major Alexander, *Victory through Air Power* (Hutchinson 1942)
Slessor, Marshal of the RAF Sir John, *The Central Blue* (Cassell 1956)
——, *Air Power and Armies* (London 1936)
Snow, Lord, *Science and Government* (Oxford 1961)
Spaight, J. M., *Air Power and Cities* (Longmans 1930)
——, *Air Power and the Next War* (Bles 1938)
——, *The Sky's the Limit* (Hodder & Stoughton 1940)
——, *Bombing Vindicated* (Hodder & Stoughton 1944)
Speer, Albert, *Inside the Third Reich* (Weidenfeld 1970)
——, *Spandau: The Secret Diaries* (Collins 1976)
Tedder, Lord, *Air Power in War* (Hodder & Stoughton 1948)
——, *With Prejudice* Cassell 1965)
Thomson, R. W., *Churchill and Morton* (Hodder & Stoughton 1976)
Verrier, Anthony, *The Bomber Offensive* (Batsford 1968)
Watson, John, *Johnny Kinsman* (Cassell 1956)
Winfield, Roland, *The Sky Belongs to Them* (Kimber 1976)
Zuckerman, Lord, *From Apes to Warlords* (Hamish Hamilton 1978)

OFFICIAL HISTORIES

The Royal Air Force 1939–45, Richards, Denis (HMSO 1953)
The War At Sea, vols I & II, Roskill, Captain S. W. (HMSO 1954 and 1956)
The Strategic Air Offensive against Germany, vols i-iv, Sir Charles Webster and Noble Frankland (HMSO 1961)
The Design and Development of Weapons, Postan, Hay and Scott (HMSO 1958)
RAF Medical Services, Rexford Welch (HMSO 1955)

It may be useful to add to the above list the following books which were published after the manuscript was completed, but which it was possible to consult while *Bomber Command* was still at proof stage. All contain important relevant material on the bomber offensive, although none caused me to wish to make significant changes to what I have written:

Dean, Sir Maurice, *The RAF and Two World Wars* (Cassell 1979)
Faber, Harold (ed.), *Luftwaffe* (Sidgwick & Jackson 1979)
Hinsley, F. H., *British Intelligence in the Second World War*, vol i (HMSO 1979)
McLaine, Ian, *Ministry of Morale* (Allen & Unwin 1979)

Notes and references

All letters and documents quoted in the text are from the AIR files in the Public Record Office unless otherwise stated.

Foreword

1 Harris, *Bomber Offensive* (Collins 1947), p. 176.
2 *Quarterly Review*, vol. 300, p. 428.

Prologue

1 3 Group report on the events of 18 December 1939.
2 Quoted Bekker, *The Luftwaffe War Diaries* (Macdonald 1964), p. 74.
3 Grant to author, July 1978.
4 Ibid.

Chapter I

1 *The Strategic Air Offensive against Germany* (HMSO 1961), vol. 1, p. 10.
2 Fuller, *Tanks in the Great War* (London 1920), p. 314.
3 Liddell Hart, *Paris* (Kegan Paul 1925), p. 47.
4 Shaw, *Adventures of the Black Girl in Search of God* (Constable 1932).
5 Spaight, *Air Power and Cities* (Longmans 1930).
6 Robert Rhodes James, *The British Revolution* (Hamish Hamilton 1977), vol. II, pp. 258–9.
7 Sir Barnes Wallis to author, 8 November 1976.
8 Slessor, *Air Power and Armies* (London 1936), p. 65
9 Quoted in the Appendices to H. A. Jones's *The War in the Air* (Oxford 1937), along with Sir Douglas Haig's equally interesting remarks.
10 R. V. Jones, *Most Secret War* (Hamish Hamilton 1978), p. 45.

Chapter III

1 Denis Hornsey, unpublished MS 'Here Today, Bomb Tomorrow'.
2 Air Vice-Marshal S. O. Bufton to the author, 12 November 1976.
3 Webster and Frankland, op. cit., vol. I, p. 154.
4 Denis Richards, *Portal of Hungerford* (Heinemann 1978), p. 166.
5 Hornsey MS, op. cit.
6 Letter to the author, March 1978.

Chapter IV

1 Churchill to John Lawrence, cited interview with the author, 7 July 1978.
2 Taylor, *The Second World War* (Hamish Hamilton 1975), p. 129. Some airmen claim that a much smaller proportion, as low as 6 per cent of the war effort, was devoted to the bomber offensive, but this is quite unconvincing.
3 Raymond Lee, *The London Observer* (Hutchinson 1972), pp. 372–3.
4 Quoted Roskill, *Churchill and the Admirals* (Collins 1977), p. 139.
5 Ibid., p. 206.
6 Quoted A. J. P. Taylor, *Beaverbrook* (Hamish Hamilton 1972)
7 Kennedy, *The Business of War* (Hutchinson 1957)
8 Craven and Cate, *The Army Air Forces in World War II* (University of Chicago Press 1949), vol. II, p. 735.
9 Roskill, op. cit., p. 137.
10 Webster and Frankland, op. cit., vol. I, p. 180.

Chapter V

1 Webster and Frankland, op. cit., vol. I, pp. 15–16.
2 Ibid., p. 336.
3 Sir Barnes Wallis conversation with the author, November 1976.
4 I must differ from the view expressed by Ronald Clark in his excellent biography of Tizard: even if Tizard was not questioning the principles on which the bomber offensive was based, he was convinced that it could not yield results in proportion to the effort being expended upon it. His disagreement with Cherwell does indeed seem 'fundamental'.
5 See Zuckerman's autobiography, *From Apes to Warlords* (Hamish Hamilton 1978), pp. 139–46.
6 Harris, op. cit., p. 147.
7. Harris conversation with the author, 25 April 1978.
8 Harris, op. cit., pp. 15 and 52.
9 Quoted Thompson, *Churchill and Morton* (Hodder & Stoughton 1976), p. 44.
10 Ibid., pp. 48 and 86.
11 Anthony Verrier, *The Bomber Offensive* (Batsford 1968), p. 4.

Chapter VI

1 The Empire Training Scheme handled 200,000 aircrew in the course of the war.
2 Owen Conversation with the author, November 1976.
3 Feelings of Esmond Romilly as quoted by Philip Toynbee, *Friends Apart* (McGibbon & Kee 1954), p. 68.
4 Harris to David Irving, 1961.
5 Webster and Frankland, op. cit., vol. I, p. 392.
6 S/Ldr Ronald Barton, *Hampdens from Swinderby* (published privately).

7 Webster and Frankland, op. cit., vol. I, pp. 394–5.
8 Dudley Saward, *The Bomber's Eye* (Cassell 1959), p. 126.
9 Lee, op. cit., pp. 378–9.
10 Ibid., pp. 379–80.
11 Hornsey MS, op. cit.
12 Yeates, *Winged Victory* (Cape 1973).
13 Information to the author from a German-speaking aircrew POW who saw story and photograph in German Press. I have interviewed a WAAF who was once taken as a passenger on an operation.

Chapter VII

1 See Anthony Trythall, *'Boney' Fuller* (Cassell 1977), p. 226.
2 See Brian Bond, *Liddell Hart: A Study of his Military Thought* (Cassell 1977), pp. 146–8.
3 Harris, op. cit., p. 58.
4 Seversky, *Victory thru Air Power* (New York 1942).
5 As far as I am aware, this remarkable paper from the 4 Group files in the PRO has never before been published. It is a major reflection on Harris's tactical judgement, and it is fortunate that he was dissuaded from pursuing his faith in daylight operations at this stage.
6 Or so the Air Ministry believed: Harris himself says that he never actually set eyes on *Pointblank* until it reached his desk in its final form in June 1943 (conversation with the author, 25 April 1978).
7 Webster and Frankland, op. cit., vol. II, p. 5.
8 Churchill, *The Second World War* (Cassell 1950), vol. II, p. 314.
9 Robert Rhodes James, *The British Revolution* (Hamish Hamilton 1976).
10 Webster and Frankland, op. cit., vol. II, p. 7.
11 Harris, op. cit., p. 143.
12 Harris, op. cit., p. 49.
13 Harris conversation with the author, 14 October 1976.
14 Bennett conversation with the author, July 1978.
15 Harris, op. cit., p. 144.

Chapter VIII

1 Craven and Cate, op. cit., vol. II, p. ix.
2 Hank Iveson conversation with the author, 17 June 1978.
3 Hornsey MS, op. cit.
4 Webster and Frankland, op. cit., vol. II, p. 142.
5 Professor Derek Jackson, one of the scientists most closely involved in wartime radar development, has stated (letter to the *Sunday Telegraph*, 12 March 1978) that insufficient supplies of *Window* existed to enable its introduction before July 1943. But Air Vice-Marshal Addison, then commanding 80 Wing, possessed supplies stockpiled in his HQ at Radlett golf club, Herts, in mid-1942 (conversation with the author 11 November 1976).

6 Sir Barnes Wallis conversation with the author, 8 November 1976.
7 Kirkham to the author, 20 March 1978.
8 Conversation with the author, February 1977.
9 Conversation with the author, February 1978.
10 Cochrane conversation with the author, November 1976.
11 Cheshire, *Bomber Pilot* (Hutchinson 1943), p. 9.
12 Kirkham to the author, 12 November 1978.
13 Hornsey did publish one book, on his escape from France after being shot down: *The Pilot Walked Home* (Collins Blue Circle 1946).

Chapter IX

1 *Goebbels Diaries* (Secker and Warburg 1978), p. 86 (9 March 1945).
2 See David Irving, *Rise and Fall of the Luftwaffe* (Weidenfeld 1973), p. 82.
3 See Appendix F for comparative figures.
4 Milward, *The German Economy at War* (London University 1965), p. 10. Milward is invaluable for any study of German industry at this period.
5 Speer, *Inside the Third Reich* (Weidenfeld 1970), p. 214.
6 Ibid., p. 284.
7 Frankland, *The Bombing Offensive against Germany* (Faber 1965), p. 76.
8 See Speer Interrogations 24.
9 Irving, op. cit., p. 230.
10 Speer, op. cit., p. 209.
11 Irving, op. cit.,
12 Speer Interrogations, op. cit.
13 Irving, op. cit., p. 230.
14 *Goebbels Diaries*, pp. 138–9.
15 Ibid., p. 208.
16 Dated 7 July 1942.
17 Speer memoirs, op. cit., p. 278.
18 Webster and Frankland, op. cit., vol. II, p. 95.
19 In his book *Most Secret War* (Hamish Hamilton 1978).
20 Galland, *The First and the Last* (Methuen 1955), p. 188.
21 Ibid., p. 198.
22 Irving, op. cit., p. 153.
23 Ibid., p. 153.
24 Speer, *Spandau: The Secret Diaries* (Collins 1976).
25 Total includes aircraft missing and crashed in England.

Chapter X

1 Former High Wycombe staff officer in conversation with the author, June 1978.
2 For instance, see Taylor, op. cit., p. 130.
3 Harris himself denies this story, but it was offered to the author by one of his personal staff who claimed to have been present.

4 Harris conversation with the author, 14 October 1976.
5 Sir Archibald Forbes to the author, November 1978.
6 Speer, *Spandau Diaries*, op. cit., p. 29.
7 To the author, May 1978.
8 Ibid.
9 Lord Elworthy conversation with the author, March 1977.
10 Collins, *Faith under Fire*, p. 69.
11 Ibid., p. 89.
12 From the original text in possession of the author.
13 Ibid.
14 From the internally circulated 1945 'Review of the Work of Int I', loaned to the author by a former High Wycombe staff officer.
15 See Chapter IX.
16 'Review of the Work of Int I', op. cit.
17 Harris conversation with the author, 25 April 1978.
18 Ibid.
19 Ibid.

Chapter XI

1 Musgrove, *Pathfinder Force* (Macdonald & Janes 1976), pp. 85 and 87.
2 From 'Review of the Work of Int I', op. cit.
3 *Goebbels Diaries*, op. cit., p. 438.
4 Cochrane conversation with the author, November 1976.
5 To the author, April 1978.
6 To the author, July 1978.
7 Webster and Frankland, op. cit., vol. II, p. 193.
8 To the author, November 1976.
9 Craven and Cate, op. cit., vol. III, p. 11.
10 Ibid., vol. III, pp. 51, 63 and 730.
11 Ibid., vol. III, p. 715.
12 Harris conversation with the author, October 1976.
13 Zuckerman, op. cit., p. 276.
14 Harris, op. cit., p. 192.
15 Bufton conversation with the author, July 1978.
16 See Zuckerman, op. cit., p. 352.

Chapter XII

1 Loaned to the Author by Group-Captain C. B. Owen.
2 Cochrane conversation with the author, November 1976.
3 8 Group post-war Station MO's report in PRO.
4 Harris, *Bomber Offensive*.
5 Tait, CO of 83 Squadron and subsequently of 617 Squadron, was among the most distinguished and decorated Bomber Command pilots of the war.
6 Craven and Cate, op. cit., vol. III, p. 666.

Chapter XIII

1 In his book *The Destruction of Dresden*, David Irving suggests that Darmstadt was bombed at the prompting of a Jewish former resident of the town, who in 1944 lived in the same Surbiton apartment block as an officer of the RAF's target selection staff. There is no reason to doubt that the refugee spoke to the staff officer, but it seems open to question whether their conversation directly provoked the attack of 11 September. The RAF had been well aware of Darmstadt's chemical plants since 1940. I am more inclined to believe that the raid was inspired by tactical considerations such as those discussed in the text.
2 Klaus Schmidt *Die Brandnacht*, Darmstadt 1965. For this and all other quotations from the stories of the people of Darmstadt in this chapter, I am indebted to the above collection of first-hand accounts, especially valuable because so many of those who contributed have since died.

Chapter XIV

1 Craven and Cate, op. cit., vol. III, p. 320.
2 Webster and Frankland, op. cit., vol. III. p. 82.
3 Milward, op. cit., p. 170.
4 Galland, op. cit., p. 279.
5 Speer, *Inside the Third Reich*, p. 286.
6 Harris conversation with the author, 14 October 1976.
7 Portal to the Air Ministry, 30 September 1959, commenting on draft of Webster and Frankland. Quoted Richards, *Portal*, op cit., p. 330.
8 Verrier, op. cit., p. 283.
9 See Chapter XI above, Inglis to Portal.
10 Milward, op. cit., p. 188.
11 *Goebbels Diaries*, ed. Trevor-Roper (Secker & Warburg), p. 24.
12 *Goebbels*, op. cit., p. 96.
13 Milward, op. cit., p. 188.
14 Eaker to Spaatz, 1 January 1945, quoted Craven and Cate, op. cit., vol. III, p. 733.
15 Craven and Cate, op. cit., vol. III, p. 638.
16 For instance, Harris to Churchill, 30 August 1944: 'I would much have liked to give you my views personally in response to your invitation to dine, but I have the sort of cold which I would not bring within ten miles of you and yours. . . .'
17 Quoted in 'A Review of the Work of Int I,' op. cit.
18 Craven and Cate, op. cit., p. 727.
19 Musgrove, op. cit., p. 181.

Chapter XV

1 Transcribed from the original in possession of S/Ldr Ronald Barton.
2 Churchill, op. cit., vol. VI, p. 434.

3 Nuremberg hearings, 13 March 1946.
4 Ibid., 15 March 1946.
5 Quoted as Appendix 5 of Zuckerman, op. cit.
6 Craven and Cate, op. cit., vol. III, p. 716.
7 Zuckerman, op. cit., p. 353.
8 Milward, op. cit., p. 163.
9 Frankland, *The Strategic Air Offensive against Germany*, p. 106.

Glossary

1. Royal Air Force commissioned ranks with their army equivalents

Marshal of the RAF	Field-Marshal
Air Chief Marshal	General
Air Marshal	Lt.-General
Air Vice-Marshal	Major-General
Air Commodore	Brigadier
Group Captain	Colonel
Wing-Commander	Lt.-Colonel
Squadron-Leader	Major
Flight-Lieutenant	Captain
Flying Officer	Lieutenant
Pilot Officer	Second Lieutenant

A British bomber squadron in the Second World War was commanded by a wing-commander with squadron-leaders as flight commanders. Fighter squadrons were commanded by squadron-leaders.

2 Abbreviations, codenames and technical terms

AOC	Air Officer Commanding
ABC	AirBorne Cigar – aircraft-mounted transmitter which jammed German fighter frequencies
AI	Airborne Interception radar equipment fitted to fighters
ASV	Air to Surface Vessel radar
Boozer	Radar warning device against fighters fitted to bombers
CAS	Chief of Air Staff
Circus (operations)	Fighter-escorted daylight bomber sorties by the RAF against short-range French targets, chiefly in 1941, intended to provoke the Luftwaffe to battle
Clarion	American plan to disrupt German communications and morale by wide-ranging bomber attacks in February 1945
Corona	Counterfeit orders to German fighters broadcast by the British 100 Group
Crossbow	Countermeasures against German V-Weapons
DR	Dead Reckoning navigation
Duppel	German word for *Window*
ETA	Estimated Time of Arrival
Fishpond	British early-warning radar against fighters, fitted to some bombers in 1944

Flak	*Fliegerabwehrkanonen* – German anti-aircraft gun
Flensburg	German radar device fitted to night-fighters, homing on British bombers' *Monica* transmissions
Freya	German early-warning radar
Gee	Radio navigational aid introduced in 1942
G-H	Blind bombing device based on ground-station transmissions to aircraft introduced in 1944
Glycol	Aircraft engine coolant
Grand Slam	22,000-lb penetrating bomb
HCU	Heavy Conversion Unit
Himmelbett	German controlled night-fighting system
H2S	British radar navigation and blind-bombing aid fitted to some bombers from 1943 onwards*
H2X	American name for H2S
Husky	Allied invasion of Sicily in 1943
IFF	Identification Friend or Foe, transmitting a blip to British radar screens.
Knickebein	German radio-beam navigational system introduced in 1940
Lichtenstein	German night-fighter radar introduced in 1941
Mandrel	British 100 Group swamping of German early-warning radar from 1944 onwards
Monica	British radar early-warning device against fighters fitted to bombers from 1943
Naxos	German night-fighter radar homing on British H2S transmissions
Newhaven	Pathfinder codename for target marking blind by H2S, supported by visual backers-up
Oboe	British blind-bombing device fitted to Pathfinder aircraft, controlled by transmissions from ground stations
OKW	*Oberkommando der Wehrmacht* – High Command of the German armed forces
OTU	Operational Training Unit
Overlord	The Allied invasion of France, 6 June 1944
Paramatta	Pathfinder codename for target marking by blind-dropped ground-markers (with prefix '*Musical*', *Oboe*-guided)

*The German habit of giving their radar appropriate-sounding codenames to suit the nature of the device was of vital assistance to British scientific Intelligence in interpreting the enemy systems. The British thus learned to be more careful about their own equipment. H2S was originally christened 'TF' until Dr R. V. Jones pointed out that this plainly stood for 'Town-Finding'. The name was changed to H2S, popularly believed to stand for 'Home Sweet Home', but in reality for Hydrogen Sulphide. It earned its evil-smelling acronym when at an early meeting to discuss its progress Lord Cherwell showed scepticism and declared gloomily, 'It stinks!'

Pointblank	The June 1943 directive from the Combined Chiefs of Staff for the Combined Bomber Offensive
PRU	Photographic Reconnaissance Unit
Razzles	Air-dropped incendiary device for igniting crops and forests, employed by Bomber Command August–September 1940
R/T	Radio/Telephone, ie voice communication
SASO	Senior Air Staff Officer
SBA	Standard Blind Approach
Schrage musik	Upward-firing cannon fitted to some German night-fighters from late 1943 onwards
Sealion	German codename for the invasion of Britain in 1940
SHAEF	Supreme Headquarters Allied Expeditionary Force 1944–
Tallboy	12,000-lb penetrating bomb developed by Barnes Wallis
Tame Boar	German tactic for guiding night-fighters from orbit around a visual beacon into bomber stream by running-commentary from ground controller
Thunderclap	1944 Allied plan to deliver overwhelming *coup de grâce* to Berlin and/or other leading German cities by sustained bomber attack.
Tinsel	Technique by which British bomber wireless-operators fed jamming noise on to German night-fighter frequencies
Torch	Allied invasion of French North Africa in 1942
VCAS	Vice-Chief of Air Staff
Wanganui	Pathfinder codename for target marking by blind-dropped sky-markers (with prefix '*Musical*', *Oboe*-guided)
Wild Boar	Freelance German single-engined fighter guided into bomber stream by ground controller's running-commentary, July 1943–spring 1944
Window	Tinfoil strips dropped by Allied bombers to fog German radar
W-Mines	Small air-dropped mines for use against locks and river traffic employed briefly by Bomber Command in 1940
W/T	Wireless transmission, ie morse signal rather than voice
Würzburg	German tactical radar for gun-laying, searchlight and night-fighter direction
X-Gerat, *Y-Gerat*	German beam-guided blind-bombing systems

Acknowledgements

I have received generous help in the writing of this book from a great range of people directly and indirectly concerned with the Royal Air Force. Among them I must mention Group-Captain E. B. Haslam, until 1978 head of the Air Historical Branch of the Ministry of Defence, and his colleague Mr Humphrey Wynn; S/Ldr 'Jacko' Jackson and the RAF's Battle of Britain Flight, who flew me in one of the few remaining airworthy Lancaster bombers, and enabled me to get the feel of the aircraft from every turret and crew position; Freddy Lambert of the Public Record Office, who was tireless in answering my endless demands; Dr John Tanner and his staff at the RAF Museum, who enabled me to explore the Wellington and the Mosquito.

The Daily Telegraph, the Pathfinder Association journal *The Marker*, the Air Gunners' Association journal *Turret*, the Australian Pathfinders' *Marker*, the RAF Association's *Air Mail*, the Goldfish Club newsletter and the RAF POW Association newsletter *Kriegie* published the appeals which enabled me to contact more than three hundred survivors of Bomber Command, over a hundred from the squadrons which I had chosen for special study.

Mrs Joan Hornsey and her daughter Mrs Carol Wain allowed me to read and to quote extensively from the late Denis Hornsey's remarkable unpublished manuscript on his service in Bomber Command, *Here Today, Bomb Tomorrow*.

This book would never have been written without the inspiration of my publisher James Wade in New York, and the support of my editor at Michael Joseph in London, Alan Samson. David Irving is one of the most controversial of contemporary historians, but he is also one of the most generous, and allowed me to borrow for many months his extensive files on the bomber war. Andrea Whittaker helped me with the German translations.

I am indebted to the following for permission to quote from published works and private letters: Lord Salisbury for the letter of the 4th Marquess of Salisbury reproduced on page 172; the Rt. Hon. Sir Geoffrey Shakespeare for his letter to Sir Archibald Sinclair on page 125; the Controller of Her Majesty's Stationery Office, for extracts from Webster and Frankland's *The Strategic Bomber Offensive against Germany*; the Keeper of the Public Record Office for documents and correspondence from the AIR files; the University of Chicago Press for extracts from Craven and Cate's *The Army Air Forces in World War II*; Messrs. Hutchinson for the extracts from General Raymond E. Lee's *The London Observer*; Oxford University Press, for permission to quote from 'Aristocrats' from *The Complete Poems of Keith Douglas*, edited by Desmond Graham; A. D. Peters & Co. Ltd, for permission to quote from *Men at Arms* by Evelyn Waugh; Faber & Faber Ltd, for permission to quote from 'Lincolnshire Bomber Station' by Henry Treece; Denis Richards and William Heinemann Ltd, for the extract from *Portal of Hungerford*; and Chatto and Windus Ltd and Richard Eberhart, for permission to quote from 'The Fury of Aerial Bombardment'. I am also indebted to Flight

International (London), for allowing me to reproduce the line drawing of a Lancaster on page 158; and to Air-Commodore John Voyce, for permission to reproduce the illustration of a 'Stand Down' night in 1944.

I would also like to thank: the Air Ministry; Michael Bowyer; Chaz Bowyer; George Carter; Keith Creswell; G/Capt. L. C. Deane; G/Capt. J. R. Goodman; the Imperial War Museum and especially their photographic library; H. M. Irwin, RN retd; Tom Jones; A. Killingley; the London Library and its indefatigable librarians; Doug McKinnon; K. J. Reinhold, editor of the *Darmstadter Echo*; Alun Richards; Captain Stephen Roskill, RN retd; T. A. Stern; W. G. Uprichard; Air-Commodore John Voyce; and John Winton.

And now for the principal witnesses of the story of Bomber Command who have assisted me in the past two years; I have omitted ranks below that of Wing-Commander, and a plethora of decorations which would otherwise overwhelm these pages.

The Air Ministry, Bomber Command and Group headquarters

Air Vice-Marshal E. B. Addison; Ronald Barton; Air Vice-Marshal S. O. Bufton; Air Vice-Marshal D. C. T. Bennett; the late Air Chief Marshal Sir Ralph Cochrane; Canon John Collins; Marshal of the RAF Lord Elworthy; Wing-Commander F. A. B. Fawsett; Marshal of the RAF Sir Arthur Harris; Air Commodore W. I. C. Inness; John Lawrence; Fred Lloyd; Miss Barbara Morton; Sir Barnes Wallis; Miss Peggy Wherry; Lord Zuckerman.

3 Group, December 1939

D. Beddow (99 Squadron); E. T. Butcher (37 Sq.); I. P. Grant (9 Sq.); J. R. Greaves (37 sq.); Frank Hargreaves (51 Sq. weather reconnaissance); H. J. Hemsleyhall (37 Sq.); L. E . Jarman (9 Sq.); Harry Jones (37 Sq.); Wing-Commander J. Lovell (9 Sq.); Air Marshal Sir Hugh Pughe Lloyd (9 Sq.); J. T. Reynolds (9 Sq.); Herbert Ruse (37 Sq.); L. Russell (pupil at North Coates); Eric Scott (115 Sq.).

82 Squadron, 1940–41

Wing-Commander L. V. E. Atkinson; J. W. D. Attenborough; the late Air Chief Marshal The Earl of Bandon; Kenneth Collins; L. C. Davey; J. Harrison-Broadley; T. C. P. Hodges; F. W. S. Keighley; W. J. Q. Magrath; D. W. McFarlane; Wing-Commander John McMichael; F. H. Miller; N. W. Orr; R. J. Rumsey; Air Vice-Marshal Ian Spencer; Air Commodore Philip Sutcliffe; George Whitehead; Mrs E. M. Wilkins.

10 Squadron, 1940–41

F. Ashworth; Bob Dodd; Peter Donaldson; Group-Captain Pat Hanafin; Norman Gregory; Wing-Commander H. J. Heal; J. M. Poole; Group-Captain A. V. Sawyer; Air Vice-Marshal W. E. Staton; A. E. Smith; P. G. Whitby.

50 Squadron, 1942

C. W. Gray; Mrs M. A. Hamilton; Stewart Harris; H. S. Hobday; Gus Macdonald; Air Marshal Sir Harold Martin; J. H. Mitchell; L. O'Brien; Ken Owen; G. A. Philipps; Reg Raynes; S. D. Stubbs; John Taylor.

76 Squadron, 1943

Sidney Ashford; V. G. Bamber; Fred Beadle; Group-Captain Leonard Cheshire; P. C. Chipping; Pamela Finch; Eric Freeman; Group-Captain D. Iveson; C. A. Kirkham; Etienne Maze; R. G. McCadden; B. McNulty; Ferris Newton; C. Rathmell; Cliff Ramsden; S. W. Palmer; E. A. Strange; A. L. Tame; Air Marshal Sir John Whitley

97 Squadron, 1944

Tony Aveline; Mrs Dorothy Bird; A. Boultbee; F. Broughton; Ron Buck; Wing-Commander W. E. Clayfield; Gordon Cooper; J. A. M. Davies; F. W. A. Hendry; Air Chief Marshal Sir Anthony and Lady Heward; R. L. C. Lasham; T. H. Makepeace; J. W. Nedwich; Group-Captain C. B. Owen; Arthur Tindall; P. R. Turner; Jack Watt.

Index

OVERLORD

D-Day and the Battle for Normandy 1944

TO HARRY

in the hope that beaches will mean no more to him than buckets and spades

Contents

List of Illustrations

MAPS

LINE DRAWINGS

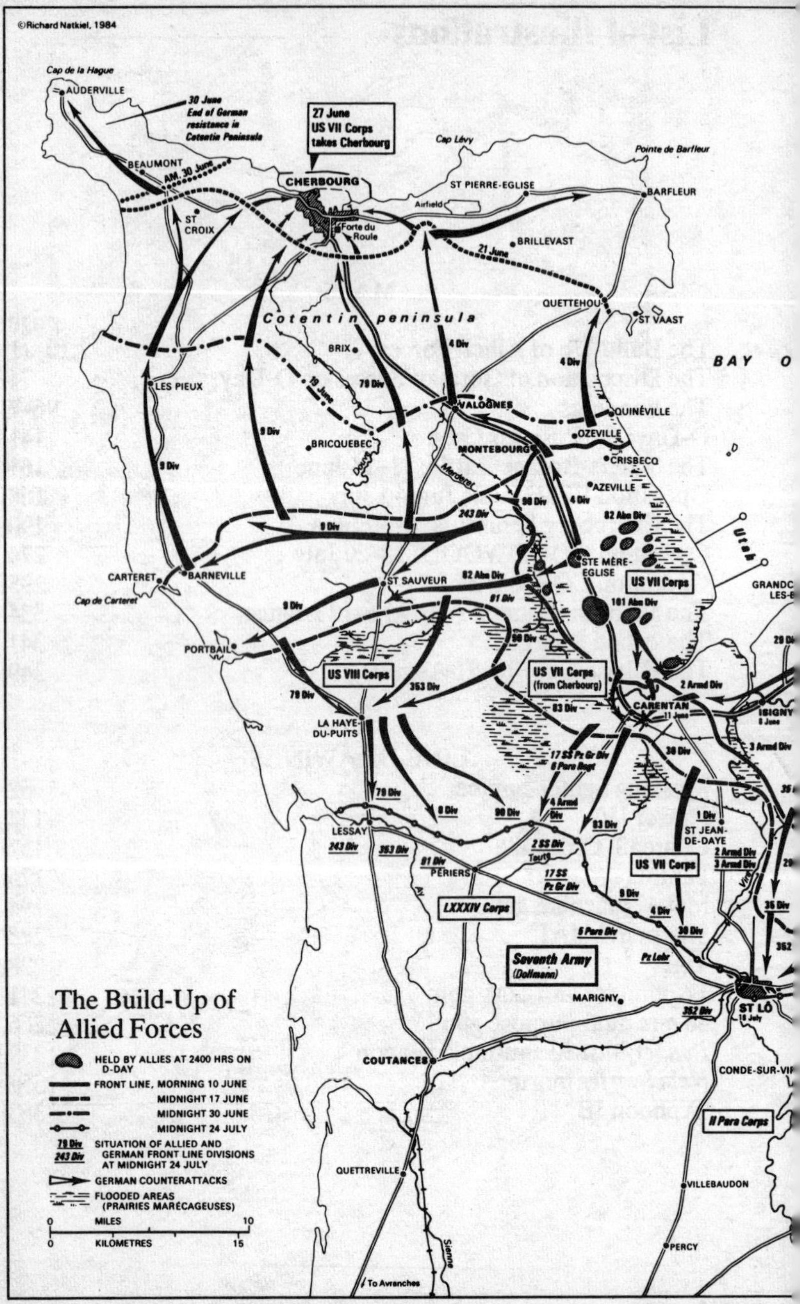
©Richard Natkiel, 1984
The Build-Up of Allied Forces
Cap de la Hague
AUDERVILLE
30 June End of German resistance in Cotentin Peninsula
27 June US VII Corps takes Cherbourg
Cap Lévy
Pointe de Barfleur
BEAUMONT
AM. 30 June
CHERBOURG
ST PIERRE-EGLISE
BARFLEUR
Airfield
ST CROIX
Forte du Roule
BRILLEVAST
21 June
QUETTEHOU
ST VAAST
Cotentin peninsula
BRIX
4 Div
BAY O
LES PIEUX
79 Div
19 June
VALOGNES
QUINÉVILLE
9 Div
BRICQUEBEC
OZEVILLE
MONTEBOURG
CRISBECQ
Douve
Merderet
AZEVILLE
90 Div
243 Div
82 Abn Div
Utah
CARTERET
BARNEVILLE
STE MÈRE-EGLISE
US VII Corps
Cap de Carteret
ST SAUVEUR
91 Div
101 Abn Div
PORTBAIL
US VIII Corps
US VII Corps (from Cherbourg)
353 Div
2 Armd Div
CARENTAN
11 June
ISIGNY
8 June
LA HAYE-DU-PUITS
17 SS Pz Gr Div
6 Para Regt
3 Armd Div
30 Div
4 Armd Div
83 Div
1 Div
ST JEAN-DE-DAYE
LESSAY
2 SS Div
2 Armd Div
3 Armd Div
PERIERS
17 SS Pz Gr Div
US VII Corps
LXXXIV Corps
35 Div
5 Para Div
Seventh Army (Dollmann)
Pz Lehr
MARIGNY
ST LÔ
18 July
COUTANCES
CONDE-SUR-VI
II Para Corps
QUETTREVILLE
VILLEBAUDON
PERCY
Sienne
To Avranches
HELD BY ALLIES AT 2400 HRS ON D-DAY
FRONT LINE, MORNING 10 JUNE
MIDNIGHT 17 JUNE
MIDNIGHT 30 JUNE
MIDNIGHT 24 JULY
79 Div / 243 Div SITUATION OF ALLIED AND GERMAN FRONT LINE DIVISIONS AT MIDNIGHT 24 JULY
GERMAN COUNTERATTACKS
FLOODED AREAS (PRAIRIES MARÉCAGEUSES)
0 MILES 10
0 KILOMETRES 15

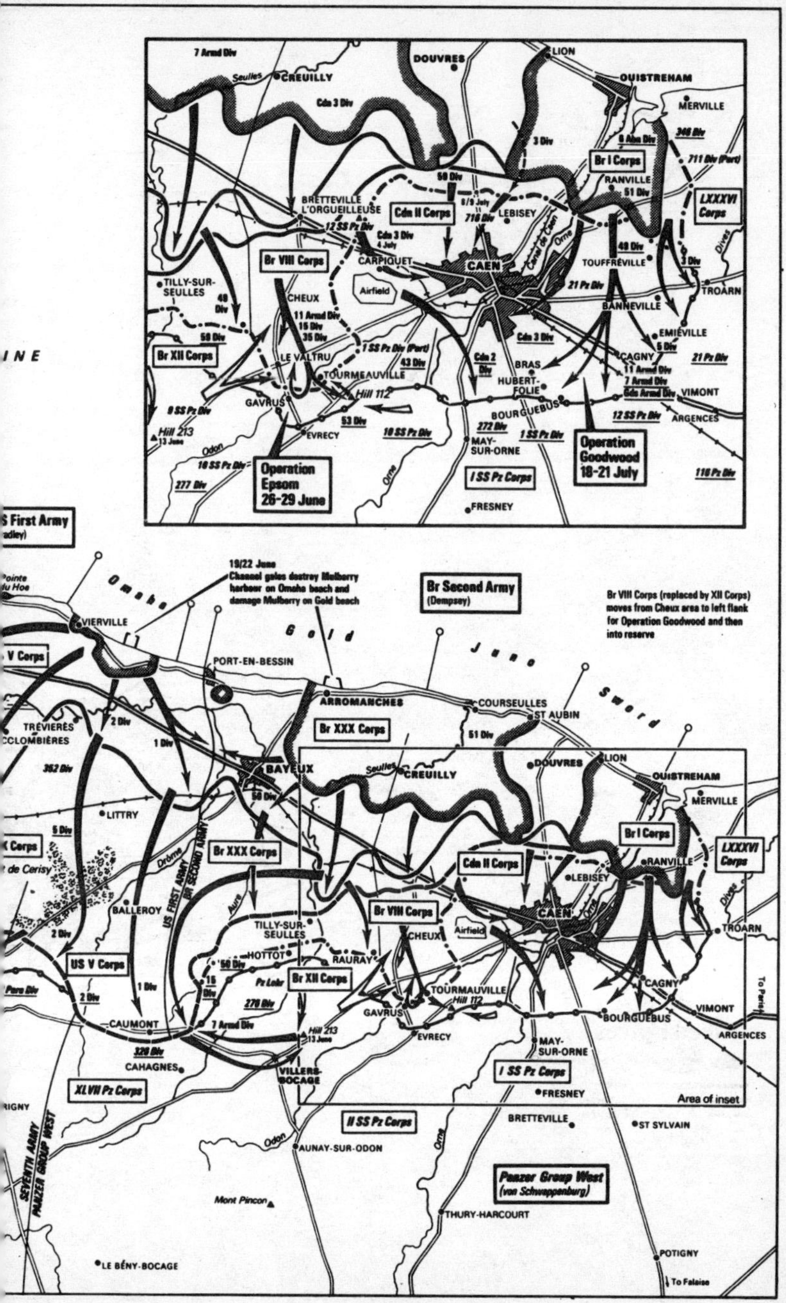

7 Armd Div
DOUVRES
LION
Seulles
CREUILLY
OUISTREHAM
Cdn 3 Div
MERVILLE
346 Div
6 Abn Div
3 Div
Br I Corps
711 Div (Part)
59 Div
RANVILLE
51 Div
BRETTEVILLE L'ORGUEILLEUSE
6/9 July
Cdn II Corps
LEBISEY
LXXXVI Corps
716 Div
12 SS Pz Div
Canal de Caen
Orne
Cdn 3 Div
4 July
49 Div
Dives
3 Div
Br VIII Corps
CARPIQUET
CAEN
TOUFFREVILLE
TILLY-SUR-SEULLES
Airfield
21 Pz Div
TROARN
49 Div
CHEUX
BANNEVILLE
11 Armd Div
15 Div
35 Div
EMIEVILLE
50 Div
Cdn 3 Div
5 Div
Br XII Corps
LE VALTRU
1 SS Pz Div (Part)
CAGNY
21 Pz Div
43 Div
Cdn 2 Div
BRAS
11 Armd Div
TOURMEAUVILLE
HUBERT-FOLIE
7 Armd Div
Hill 112
Gds Armd Div
VIMONT
GAVRUS
9 SS Pz Div
BOURGUEBUS
12 SS Pz Div
ARGENCES
53 Div
272 Div
Hill 213
13 June
EVRECY
10 SS Pz Div
1 SS Pz Div
MAY-SUR-ORNE
Operation Goodwood 18-21 July
Odon
10 SS Pz Div
Operation Epsom 26-29 June
I SS Pz Corps
277 Div
116 Pz Div
Orne
FRESNEY
INE
S First Army
radley)
19/22 June
Channel gales destroy Mulberry harbour on Omaha beach and damage Mulberry on Gold beach
Br Second Army
(Dempsey)
Br VIII Corps (replaced by XII Corps) moves from Cheux area to left flank for Operation Goodwood and then into reserve
Pointe du Hoe
Omaha
VIERVILLE
Gold
Juno
V Corps
PORT-EN-BESSIN
Sword
ARROMANCHES
COURSEULLES
ST AUBIN
TREVIÈRES
2 Div
Br XXX Corps
CLOMBIÈRES
1 Div
51 Div
LION
DOUVRES
352 Div
BAYEUX
Seulles
CREUILLY
OUISTREHAM
MERVILLE
50 Div
LITTRY
5 Div
Br I Corps
LXXXVI Corps
K Corps
Br XXX Corps
RANVILLE
Cdn II Corps
de Cerisy
Drôme
LEBISEY
US FIRST ARMY
BR SECOND ARMY
Br VIII Corps
CAEN
Orne
Dives
Aure
BALLEROY
Airfield
TROARN
TILLY-SUR-SEULLES
CHEUX
2 Div
HOTTOT
RAURAY
50 Div
US V Corps
15 Div
Pz Lehr
Br XII Corps
CAGNY
To Paris
TOURMAUVILLE
1 Div
Hill 112
Para Div
2 Div
276 Div
GAVRUS
VIMONT
BOURGUEBUS
CAUMONT
7 Armd Div
Hill 213
13 June
EVRECY
ARGENCES
326 Div
MAY-SUR-ORNE
CAHAGNES
VILLERS-BOCAGE
I SS Pz Corps
XLVII Pz Corps
FRESNEY
Area of inset
RIGNY
II SS Pz Corps
BRETTEVILLE
ST SYLVAIN
Orne
SEVENTH ARMY
PANZER GROUP WEST
Odon
AUNAY-SUR-ODON
Panzer Group West
(von Schweppenburg)
Mont Pincon
THURY-HARCOURT
POTIGNY
LE BÉNY-BOCAGE
To Falaise

Foreword

The struggle for Normandy was the decisive western battle of the Second World War, the last moment at which the German army might conceivably have saved Hitler from catastrophe. The post-war generation grew up with the legend of the Allied campaign in 1944–45 as a triumphal progress across Europe, somehow unrelated to the terrible but misty struggle that had taken place in the East. Today, we can recognize that the Russians made a decisive contribution to the western war by destroying the best of the German army, killing some two million men, before the first Allied soldier stepped ashore on 6 June 1944. It is the fact that the battle for Normandy took place against this background which makes the events of June and July so remarkable. Much has been written about the poor quality of the German troops defending the Channel coast. Yet these same men prevented the Allies almost everywhere from gaining their D-Day objectives, and on the American Omaha beach brought them close to defeat, even before the crack units of the SS and the Wehrmacht approached the battlefield. In the weeks that followed, despite the Allies' absolute command of sea and air, their attacks were repeatedly arrested with heavy loss by outnumbered and massively outgunned German units. None of this, of course, masks the essential historical truth that the Allies eventually prevailed. But it makes the campaign seem a far less straightforward affair than chauvinistic post-war platitudes suggested. Captain Basil Liddell Hart suggested in 1952 that the Allies had been strangely reluctant to reflect upon their huge superiority in Normandy and draw some appropriate conclusions about their own performance: "There has been too much glorification of the campaign and too little objective investigation."[1] Even 40 years after the battle, it is astonishing how many books have been published which merely reflect comfortable chauvinistic legends, and how few which seek frankly to examine the record.

It remains an extraordinary feature of the war in the west that, despite the vast weight of technology at the disposal of the Allies, British and American soldiers were called upon to fight the German army in 1944–45 with weapons inferior in every category save that of artillery. Only in the air did the Allies immediately achieve absolute dominance in Normandy. Yet if the massive air forces denied the Germans the hope of victory, their limitations were also revealed. Air power could not provide a magic key to victory without huge exertions by the ground forces.

Post-war study of the campaign has focussed overwhelmingly upon the conduct of the generals, and too little attention has been paid to the respective performance of German, British and American ground troops. How could it be that after the months of preparation for OVERLORD, Allied armoured and infantry tactics in Normandy were found so wanting? The British, to a far greater degree than their commanders confessed even years after the campaign, were haunted by fear of heavy infantry casualties. I believe that Brooke and Montgomery's private perceptions of the campaign – and perhaps those of Bradley, too – were profoundly influenced by the knowledge that the German army was the outstanding fighting force of the Second World War, and that it could be defeated by Allied soldiers only under the most overwhelmingly favourable conditions. In Normandy, the Allies learned the limitations of using explosives as a substitute for ruthless human endeavour. It seems fruitless to consider whether an Allied plan or manoeuvre was sound in abstract terms. The critical question, surely, is whether it was capable of being carried out by the available Allied forces, given their limitations and the extraordinary skill of their enemies.

Few Europeans and Americans of the post-war generation have grasped just how intense were the early OVERLORD battles. In the demands that they made upon the foot soldier, they came closer than any other in the west in the Second World War to matching the horror of the eastern front or of Flanders 30 years earlier. Many British and American infantry units suffered over 100 per cent casualties in the course of the summer, and most German units did so. One American infantryman calculated that by May 1945, 53 lieutenants had passed through his company; few of them left it through transfer or promotion. The commanding officer of the 6th King's Own Scottish Borderers found, when his battalion reached Hamburg in 1945, that an average of five men per rifle company and a total of six officers in the unit were all that remained of those with whom he had landed in Normandy in June 1944. "I was appalled," he said. "I had no idea that it was going to be like that." He, like the Allied nations at large, had been conditioned to believe that industrialized warfare in the 1940s need never match the human cost of the earlier nightmare in France. Yet for those at the tip of the Allied spearhead, it did so.

This, then, is a portrait of a massive and terrible clash of arms redeemed for the Allies, but not for the Germans, by final victory. The early narrative of the background to the landings and their initial stages will be familiar to some readers, but its inclusion seems necessary for the sake of completeness, and it makes such a marvellous tale that it bears retelling. Thereafter, I have tried to examine much less closely studied aspects of the armies' tactics and performance, and to consider some unpalatable truths about what took place in the summer of 1944. Because Normandy was a vast campaign, it is impossible to retrace the history of every battle and every unit in detail, without achieving the tedium and bulk of an official history. By focussing upon the fortunes of a few individuals and units at different moments of the campaign, I hope that I have been able to give an impression of the experiences and difficulties endured by thousands of others. I have described each nation's sectors of the front in separate chapters, even at the cost of some loss of chronology, because only thus can the progress of the armies be considered coherently. Where I have quoted men by name, the ranks given are those that they held at the date concerned. I have adopted American spellings for American units and direct quotations from American personnel. I have made little mention of material that is familiar to every student of war history – Group-Captain Stagg's weather forecasting problems, the commanders' formal statements, the airborne operations on D-Day – which have been exhaustively described in other books. Instead, I have concentrated upon aspects which I hope will be less familiar: the battle inland and the personal experiences of men whose stories have never been told before, above all the Germans. The German army's achievement in Normandy was very great, and I have sought out many of its survivors. I have tried to write dispassionately about the German soldier's experience without reference to the odiousness of the cause for which he fought.

I have interviewed scores of American and British veterans, and corresponded with hundreds more. I am especially indebted to Field-Marshal Lord Carver, Field-Marshal Sir Edwin Bramall, General Sir Charles Richardson, Major-General G. P. B. Roberts, Major-General Sir Brian Wyldbore-Smith, General Elwood R. Quesada, General James Gavin and Brigadier Sir Edgar Williams. I also owe much to the librarians of the London Library, the Royal United Services Institution, the Staff College Camberley and the Public Record Office. For this, as for my earlier books, *Bomber Command* and *Das Reich,* Andrea Whittaker has been a splendid German interpreter and translator. Among the host of relevant literature, I must pay tribute to Nigel Hamilton's latest volume of his official biography of Lord Montgomery, and to Carlo D'Este's important recent study of the strategy of the Normandy campaign, both of which I was able to consult in the later stages of writing this book, and which were invaluable in causing me to consider some issues and some documents which would otherwise have passed me by. As always, I owe a great deal to the patience and forbearance of my wife Tricia who, having endured in recent years my spiritual life in a Lancaster at 20,000 feet and in the midst of occupied France, has now spent many months admidst the ruins of Caen and St Lô. Carlo D'Este and Andrew Wilson MC were kind enough to read the completed manuscript and to make helpful suggestions and corrections, although of course they share no responsibility for the narrative and the judgements, which are entirely my own. I am also greatly indebted to my editor in London, Giles O'Bryen, to Philippa Harrison, and to Alice Mayhew in New York.

Perhaps I should also avow a debt of gratitude to the British Army and the Royal Navy. One morning early in April 1982, I was sitting at my desk in Northamptonshire seeking to make the leap of imagination that is essential to books of this kind, to conceive what it was like to crouch in a landing craft approaching a hostile shore at dawn on 6 June 1944. By an extraordinary fluke of history, less than two months later I found myself crouched in a British landing craft 8,000 miles away. In the weeks that followed, I had an opportunity to witness an amphibious campaign whose flavour any veteran of June 1944 would immediately have recognized, even to the bren guns, oerlikons and bofors hammering into the sky. I would like to think that the experience taught me a little more about the nature of battles, and about the manner in which men fighting them conduct themselves. It has certainly made me all the more grateful that my generation has never been called upon to endure anything of the scale and ferocity that encompassed the men who fought in Normandy.

Max Hastings
Guilsborough Lodge,
Northamptonshire
October 1983

Prologue

On the night of 9 May 1940, Lieutenant John Warner did not reach his bed until 2.00 a.m. Along with the other officers of the Royal West Kents deployed along the Belgian frontier with the British Expeditionary Force, he had been celebrating in the mess amid the traditional rituals of the British army, with the regimental bands beating retreat in the little town square of Bailleul. It was unusual for all three battalions of a regiment to be campaigning – if the "bore war" in France could be dignified as such – alongside each other, and their party did justice to the occasion.

They were asleep a few hours afterwards when they were forced to take notice of "some enormous banging all over the place".[1] The German offensive in the west had begun. As the West Kents hastily prepared to march that morning of 10 May (caching the band instruments which they would never see again) it is a measure of the British army's collective delusion that they were ordered to advance to the Scheldt and to expect to remain there for some months.

In reality, they occupied their positions on the river for just four days before a trickle, and then a stream, of Allied soldiers began to pass through them towards the rear. Rumours drifted back also that "the French had packed it in down south". Their colonel, Arthur Chitty, hated the enemy with all the fervour of a regular soldier who had been captured in the first weeks of war in 1914 and spent four years behind the wire. Now, he organized the pathetic deployment of their Boyes anti-tank rifles in an anti-aircraft role. Shortly afterwards, the Germans arrived.

The 4th West Kents were deployed along the river bank. For reasons best known to itself, the battalion on their right chose to take up positions some way back from the waterline. As a result, the enemy was quickly able to seize a bridgehead on the British side, threatening the flank of the 4th. John Warner, a 23-year-old solicitor from Canterbury with a Territorial Army commission, claimed that, "as a lawyer, I was a cautious chap who always liked to look round corners before turning them". Yet he found himself leading a succession of headlong charges against the Germans with his bren-gun carrier platoon which resulted in what he later called "a very interesting little battle", and won him the Military Cross. The West Kents held their ground, but they were outflanked and soon forced to withdraw, their rear covered by the Belgians. In the days that followed, driving and marching north-westwards along the dusty roads, they fought one more significant action against the Germans in the forest of Nieppe, but found themselves chiefly confounded by the appalling traffic jams clogging the retreat, refugees and British vehicles entangled upon roads endlessly strafed by the Luftwaffe. Warner and his carrier platoon struck off across country to escape the chaos, which was fortunate, because shortly afterwards the Germans struck the main column, capturing the entire headquarters of the 1st West Kents, just ahead of the 4th. The young officer was dismayed by a brief visit to divisional headquarters, where "control had broken down completely". Morale among his own men remained surprisingly high, but the enemy had achieved absolute psychological dominance of the battlefield. "We thought the Germans were very good. In fact, we overestimated them," said Warner. Like so many others, the West Kents bitterly cursed the absence of the Royal Air Force, and became practised at leaping into ditches at the first glimpse of an aircraft.

When they reached the Dunkirk perimeter, Warner was ordered to abandon his vehicles. But having brought them intact every yard of the way from the Scheldt, he stubbornly drove into the British line, and handed over the carriers to one of the defending battalions. For the next three days, he sat in the sand dunes waiting for rescue, with a motley group of some 60 men who had gathered around him. He thought miserably: "Here I am with an MC in the field, and now I'm going in the bag." On the third day, he wearied of hanging about where he had been told to, and marched his men determinedly onto the Dunkirk mole, where he parleyed them a passage on an Isle of Man pleasure steamer. Thus, sleeping the sleep of utter exhaustion on the sunlit decks, they sailed home to England.

Curiously enough, while senior officers and statesmen were vividly aware that Britain had suffered catastrophe, once the young men of the BEF were home, very few saw their misfortunes in such absolute terms. It is the nature of soldiers to take life as it finds them from day to day. In the months and years that followed Dunkirk, John Warner shared the British army's dramas and anti-climaxes, abrupt moves and lengthy stagnations, leaves and exercises, promotions and changes of equipment. He spent some months defending Romney Marshes, "prepared to do or die". A keen young soldier, he wrote to the legendary apostle of armoured warfare, Captain Basil Liddell Hart, explaining that he had mislaid his copy of the author's *The Future of Infantry* during the goings-on in France. Liddell Hart sent him a new one.

Warner never consciously considered the prospect of going back to fight against the German army in France until one day in 1942, when he attended an officers' conference in Doncaster addressed by his corps commander, Lieutenant-General Frederick Morgan. Morgan astonished them by expounding upon future landings across the Channel, "talking of how we were going to stream across north-west Europe with huge tank power. For the first time, we did start to think seriously about going back." The conference addressed itself to some tactical problems. An officer inquired how advancing forces would indicate their progress. "They can set fire to the villages they pass through," said Morgan unanswerably. Not only new armies, new equipment, would be critical to a landing in Europe: so also would a new spirit.

The chance of war dictated that John Warner did not remain with the 4th West Kents, which was fortunate for him, because the battalion was sent to Burma. If he had gone with it, he would probably have died, like so many others, on the tennis court at Kohima. Instead, he was posted to become second-in-command of 3rd Reconnaissance Regiment, earmarked with its division for north-west Europe. It was with 3rd Recce that in June 1944, Major Warner returned to the battlefield from which he and his comrades had been so ruthlessly ejected four years earlier. Along with a million and a half other Allied soldiers, he went to Normandy.

1 "Much the greatest thing we have ever attempted"

Not the least remarkable aspect of the Second World War was the manner in which the United States, which might have chosen to regard the campaign in Europe as a diversion from the struggle against her principal aggressor, Japan, was persuaded to commit her chief strength in the west. Not only that, but from December 1941 until June 1944 it was the Americans who were passionately impatient to confront the German army on the continent while the British, right up to the eve of D-Day, were haunted by the deepest misgivings about doing so. "Why are we trying to do this?" cried Winston Churchill in a bitter moment of depression about Operation OVERLORD in February 1944,[1] which caused in him a spasm of enthusiasm for an alternative Allied landing in Portugal. "I am very uneasy about the whole operation," wrote the Chief of the Imperial General Staff, Sir Alan Brooke, as late as 5 June 1944. "At the best, it will come very far short of the expectations of the bulk of the people, namely all those who know nothing about its difficulties. At its worst, it may well be the most ghastly disaster of the whole war."[2] Had the United States army been less resolute in its commitment to a landing in Normandy, it is most unlikely that this would have taken place before 1945. Until the very last weeks before OVERLORD was launched, its future was the subject of bitter dissension and debate between the warlords of Britain and America.

For a year following the fall of France in 1940, Britain fought on without any rational prospect of final victory. Only when Hitler invaded Russia in June 1941, the most demented of his strategic decisions, did the first gleam of hope at last present itself to enemies of the Axis. For the remainder of that year, Britain was preoccupied with the struggle to keep open her Atlantic lifeline, to build her bomber offensive into a meaningful menace to Germany, and to keep hopes alive in the only theatre of war where the British army could fight – Africa and the

Middle East. Then, in the dying days of the year, came the miracle of Pearl Harbour. Britain's salvation, the turning point of the war, was confirmed four days later by another remarkable act of German recklessness: Hitler's declaration of war upon the United States.

The outcome of the Second World War was never thereafter in serious doubt. But great delays and difficulties lay ahead in mobilizing America's industrial might for the battlefield, and in determining by what strategy the Axis was to be crushed. To the relief of the British, President Roosevelt and his Chiefs of Staff at once asserted their acceptance of the principle of "Germany first". They acknowledged that her war-making power was by far the most dangerous and that, following her collapse, Japan must soon capitulate. The war in the Pacific became overwhelmingly the concern of the United States navy. The principal weight of the army's ground forces, whch would grow to a strength of eight million men, was to be directed against Germany and Italy. This decision was confirmed at ARCADIA, the first great Anglo-American conference of the war that began in Washington on 31 December 1941. America committed herself to BOLERO, a programme for a vast build-up of her forces in Britain. Churchill, scribbling his own exuberant hopes for the future during the Atlantic passage to that meeting, speculated on a possible landing in Europe by 40 Allied armoured divisions in the following year: "We might hope to win the war at the end of 1943 or 1944."[3]

But in the months after ARCADIA, as the first United States troops and their senior officers crossed to Europe, it was the Americans who began to focus decisively upon an early cross-Channel invasion. The debate that now began, and continued with growing heat through the next 20 months, reflected "an American impatience to get on with direct offensive action as well as a belief, held quite generally in the U.S. War Department, that the war could most efficiently be won by husbanding resources for an all-out attack deliberately planned for a future fixed date. American impatience was opposed by a British note of caution: American faith in an offensive of fixed date was in contrast to British willingness to proceed one step at a time, molding a course of action to the turns of military fortune."[4] Here, in the words of the American official historian, was the root of the growing division between the Combined Chiefs of Staff throughout 1942 and much of 1943.

At first, American thinking was dominated by fear of a rapid Russian collapse unless the western Allies created, at the very least, a powerful diversion on the continent. ROUNDUP was a plan for an early invasion, with whatever forces were available, which the British speedily took pains to crush. Under strong American pressure, Churchill agreed in principle to the notion of executing ROUNDUP with 48 Allied divisions not later than April 1943. But the British – above all Sir Alan Brooke – privately continued to believe that ROUNDUP neither could nor should take place. Despite their assent to the operation, in the name of Allied solidarity, they began a successful struggle to divert resources towards much more modest – and in their view, more realistic – objectives. In the summer of 1942, the Americans reluctantly acceded to GYMNAST, an operation for the invasion of French North Africa. This was allegedly to be undertaken without prejudice to ROUNDUP, because of well-founded British fears that America would shift the weight of her effort to the Pacific if it became obvious that many months must elapse before major action took place in Europe. But as the BOLERO build-up in Britain fell behind schedule, the desert campaign dragged on without decisive result, and the tragic Dieppe raid demonstrated some of the hazards of cross-Channel operations, it became apparent in Washington as well as in London that there could be no campaign in France in 1943. GYMNAST was translated into reality by the TORCH landings of November 1942. It was at Casablanca in January 1943 that the Anglo-American leadership met for their second major conference.

This was to be the last meeting at which, by dint of brilliant military diplomacy, the British gained acceptance of their own ideas about the manner in which the war should be pursued. The Americans reluctantly accepted HUSKY, the invasion of Sicily, with the prospect of further operations in Italy. They also undertook a commitment to an even greater combined bomber offensive against Germany, POINTBLANK, designed to "weaken Germany's war-making capacity to the point to which invasion would become possible".

The American Chiefs of Staff returned to Washington irritably conscious that they had been persuaded to adopt a course they did not favour – the extension of "sideshow" operations in the Mediterranean which they believed were designed chiefly to serve Britain's imperial and diplomatic purposes. But the British had at least acknowledged that north-west Europe must be invaded the following year. Sir Alan Brooke agreed at Casablanca that "we could definitely count on re-entering the continent in 1944 on a large scale". The Americans were determined to countenance no further prevarication. Throughout the remainder of 1943 – while the British argued for extended commitments in the Mediterranean, possible operations in the Balkans, further delays before attempting to broach Hitler's Atlantic Wall – the Americans remained resolute. At the TRIDENT conference in Washington in May, the date for invasion of north-west Europe was provisionally set for 1 May 1944. This commitment was confirmed in August at the QUADRANT conference in Quebec. To the deep dismay of the British, the Americans also pursued most forcefully their intention to execute ANVIL, a landing in southern France simultaneous with OVERLORD, whatever the cost to Allied operations in Italy. This proposal was put to Stalin at the Teheran conference in November 1943; he welcomed it. Thereafter, the Americans argued that, quite apart from their own enthusiasm for OVERLORD and ANVIL, any cancellation or unreasonable postponement of either would constitute a breach of faith with the Russians.

Throughout the autumn and winter of 1943, even as planning and preparation for OVERLORD gathered momentum, the British irked and angered the Americans by displaying their misgivings and fears as if OVERLORD were still a subject of debate, and might be postponed. "I do not doubt our ability in the conditions laid down to get ashore and deploy," Churchill wrote to Roosevelt on 23 October. "I am however deeply concerned with the build-up and with the situation which may arise between the thirtieth and sixtieth days . . . My dear friend, this is much the greatest thing we have ever attempted."[5] The Prime Minister cabled to Marshall in Washington: "We are carrying out our contract, but I pray God it does not cost us dear."[6] On 11 November, the British Chiefs of Staff recorded in an aide-memoire: "We must not . . . regard OVERLORD as the pivot of our whole strategy on which all else turns . . . we firmly believe that OVERLORD (perhaps in the form of RANKIN) will take place next summer. We do not, however, attach vital importance to any particular date or to any particular number of divisions in the assault and follow-up, though naturally the latter should be made as large as possible consistent with the policy stated above."[7]

Remarks of this sort aroused the deepest dismay and suspicion among the Americans. They believed that the British were seeking grounds for further delays because they feared to meet major formations of the German army in France, with the prospect of huge casualties that the battered Empire could so ill afford. A sour memorandum prepared in the U.S. Chiefs of Staffs' office in the autumn declared that, "it is apparent that the British, who have consistently resisted a cross-Channel operation, now feel OVERLORD is no longer necessary. In their view, continued Mediterranean operations, coupled with POINTBLANK and the crushing Russian offensive, will be sufficient to cause the internal collapse of Germany and thus bring about her military defeat without undergoing what they consider an almost certain 'bloodbath'. The conclusion that the forces being built up in the United Kingdom will never be used for a military offensive against western Europe, but are intended as a gigantic deception plan and an occupying force, is inescapable."[8] This document was not a basis for action, but serves to illustrate American suspicion and scepticism at the period.

It was patently true that Britain's strength was waning, her people growing weary: "At the end of 1943, the population of Britain was . . . nearing the limit of capacity to support the Allied offensive,"[9] wrote the British official strategic historian. "The government was therefore faced by the prospect of conducting the main offensive against Germany and Japan over a period when greater casualties and further demands must lead, after a period of uneasy equilibrium, to a reduction in the war effort." By May 1944 the British army would attain the limits of its growth – two and three-quarter million men. Meanwhile, the American army would number five and three-quarter millions, still far short of its potential maximum. British production of ammunition had been falling since late 1942, of vehicles since mid-1943, of artillery and small arms since late 1943. Whereas in 1940 Britain was producing 90.7 per cent of the Commonwealth's munitions, buying 5.6 per cent from America and finding the remainder within the Empire, by 1944 Britain's share of production had fallen to 61.2 per cent, with 8.9 per cent coming from Canada and 28.7 per cent by purchase or Lend-Lease from the U.S. Britain's leaders were more and more despondently conscious of America's dominance of the Grand

Alliance and its strategy. Americans were not slow to point out either at the time or after 1945 that Alamein remained the only major land victory of the war that the British achieved unaided.

Yet the Americans, their minds fixed on the importance of concentrating effort upon a campaign that they would dominate, often judged British motives and intentions unjustly. For all Churchill's moments of irrationality, quirkiness, senility, his absurd operational proposals and flights of fantasy and depression, his brilliant instinct for the reality of war sparkles through the archives of the Second World War, and often towers over the judgements of his professional service advisers. At root, the Prime Minister never doubted the eventual necessity for a major campaign in Europe. As early as October 1941, dismissing a demand from the Chief of Air Staff for resources which Portal claimed would enable bombers alone to win the war, Churchill looked forward to "the day when Allied armies would conduct simultaneous attacks by armoured forces in many of the conquered countries which were ripe for revolt. Only in this way could a decision certainly be achieved . . . One has to do the best one can, but he is an unwise man who thinks there is any *certain* method of winning this war, or indeed any other war between equals in strength. The only plan is to persevere."[10]

Churchill's uncertainty concerned not whether to invade Europe, but when to do so. Looking back over the strategic debate that took place between 1941 and 1944, it is impossible to acquit America's leadership of naivety, just as it is difficult to deny the inability of Britain's service chiefs to match the American genius for overcoming difficulties. For the Americans, Professor Michael Howard has written, "shortages were not a problem, as for the British, to be lived with indefinitely, but a passing embarrassment which need not affect long term strategy. This view may have led them to underrate not only the problems of organizing production but the difficulties of planning, logistics and tactics which still lay in the way of bringing those resources to bear. But their British Allies were no less prone to regard as insoluble difficulties which American energy and abundance now, for the first time, made it possible to overcome."[11]

In the winter of 1943–44, the British were by no means certain that the moment had come when OVERLORD might be launched on the overwhelmingly favourable terms that they sought. They saw many hazards in haste, and great virtues in delay. The German army had already suffered vast losses in the east, and was being desperately depleted each day by the advancing Russian armies. The air forces believed that strategic bombing was rapidly eroding the ability of Hitler's industries to arm and supply his armies. Operation RANKIN, referred to above in the British Chiefs of Staffs' aide-memoire, was a plan for the occupation of the continent if the bomber offensive or dramatic developments in the east caused German resistance suddenly to collapse. Such a profoundly realistic, even pessimistic, figure as Sir Alan Brooke can never have pinned many hopes on such a remarkable turn of events. But it is a measure of lingering British wishful thinking about the avoidance of a bloody campaign in Europe that, as late as November 1943, the Chiefs of Staff could still refer even to the possibility of implementing RANKIN.

A forceful faction among post-war historians has sought to argue that Germany could have been defeated much earlier had the American strategic view prevailed from the outset and France been invaded in 1943.[12] They suggest that in that year, Allied air supremacy was already overwhelming; that Italy unliberated would have been a drain upon the Axis rather than an asset to it; that the Atlantic Wall and its garrison were visibly weaker in 1943 than the following year; and that the landing craft lacking could readily have been found by reducing the quota for the Pacific and cancelling further amphibious operations in the Mediterranean.

All of this ignores the consideration of the heart of Churchill's and Brooke's fears to the very moment of invasion – their knowledge of the immense and extraordinary fighting power of the German army. Four years of war against the Wehrmacht had convinced Britain's commanders that Allied troops should engage and could defeat their principal enemy only on the most absolutely favourable terms. Throughout the Second World War, where British or American troops met the Germans in anything like equal strength, the Germans almost always prevailed. They possessed an historic reputation as formidable soldiers. Under Hitler their army attained its zenith. Weapon for weapon and tank for tank, even in 1944, its equipment decisively outclassed that of the Allies in every category save artillery and transport.

In four years of war, Churchill had been given ample cause to doubt the ability of British troops to match those of Germany. As late as November 1943, 5,000 British troops on the island of

Leros were defeated by 4,000 German invaders during the ill-fated operations in the Dodecanese. The Germans admittedly possessed strong air support. But in the hands of the British this advantage frequently proved inadequate to ensure victory. Final Allied success in North Africa took months longer than the gloomiest prophet anticipated after Alamein. There was no evidence to suggest that the American soldier was capable of performing any more effectively than the British. Alexander wrote to Brooke from Tunisia about the Americans: "They simply do not know their job as soldiers and this is the case from the highest to the lowest, from the general to the private soldier. Perhaps the weakest link of all is the junior leader, who just does not lead, with the result that their men don't really fight."[13]

This was no fit of chauvinism, but a verdict with which most Americans in North Africa concurred. They learned a great deal in the battles of 1942–43, but there remained no evidence to suggest that they had become the equals of their German opponents. The Italian campaign became a nightmare of frustrated hopes and thwarted ambitions: even with absolute command of sea and air, the Allies proved unable to bring about the collapse of the dogged yet brilliant German fighting retreat up the length of Italy. The Anzio landings of February 1944, designed to outflank the enemy line with dramatic results, came close to ending in a major disaster for the Allies, and provoked one of Churchill's most famous, bitter sallies: "We hoped to land a wild cat that would tear out the bowels of the Boche. Instead we have stranded a vast whale with its tail flopping about in the water."[14]

Most of the German troops in Italy were line formations; only very limited numbers came from elite units. Yet in France the Allies would meet the SS Panzer divisions, the most fanatical and effective battlefield forces of the Second World War. What if the weather should close down, denying the British and Americans the air support that alone could give them a real prospect of victory? An Allied OVERLORD planner reflected in Septemer 1943 upon the difficulties in Sicily where 15 Allied divisions had faced 13 enemy divisions of which just three were German, on a battlefield of 17,000 square miles. In Normandy, he pointed out, 24 Allied divisions would confront at least 17 German formations on a battlefield of 33,000 square miles.[15] These were not, of course, the eventual numbers on the battlefield. But they were estimates which provided food for thought in London in the autumn of 1943.

The revelations since 1974 of Allied success in breaking German codes in the Second World War has created some illusions that Ultra provided a magic key, an open sesame for the Allies on the battlefield. Important as Ultra's contribution was, its supply of information was erratic and incomplete. It provided vital strategic guidance, and its forewarning of German attacks was often of immense importance to the formations seeking to parry these. But Ultra could seldom provide decisive intelligence for Allied troops going into an attack. Only fighting power could gain objectives on the battlefield. It was about this that Churchill and Brooke remained so uncertain in the winter of 1943.

Yet given impetus by American determination, the planning and preparation of OVERLORD now gained pace, and were not to slacken again. Through the winter of 1943 and even into the spring of 1944, other plans and other problems were also occupying and vexing the minds of the British and American high commands. But one by one lesser operations – CULVERIN, BUCCANEER, HERCULES, PIGSTICK – withered on the bough. One of the most divisive Anglo-American quarrels of the war, which continued until high summer of 1944, concerned the diversion of forces from Italy for the ANVIL landings in the south of France. In a moment of strategic fantasy, Roosevelt proposed that ANVIL should precede the landing in Normandy by a month. But inexorably distractions were cast into the wings. The concentration narrowed until it focussed decisively upon OVERLORD. This was an operation for which all paper estimates of strength promised Allied victory. Yet the consequences of failure were so great as to haunt the leaders of the Grand Alliance.

Lieutenant-General Frederick Morgan had been designated Chief of Staff to the Supreme Allied Commander – COSSAC – in April 1943, when there was no appointed Supreme Commander, and for the remainder of the year he and his Anglo-American staff were responsible for the outline planning for OVERLORD. He wrote in his initial report of 15 July: "An operation of the magnitude of Operation OVERLORD has never previously been attempted in history. It is fraught with hazards, both in nature and magnitude, which do not obtain in any other theatre of the present world war. Unless these hazards are squarely faced and adequately overcome, the operation cannot succeed. There is no reason why they should not be overcome, provided the energies of all concerned are bent to the problem."[16]

The COSSAC staff's crippling handicap was that without the authority of a Supreme Commander they were compelled to carry out their task within limitations laid down by the Chiefs of Staff. Morgan was instructed to plan an operation, with a specified and quite inadequate weight of resources, that would put only three divisions ashore in the first landings in France. OVERLORD, even more than any ordinary operation of war, demanded a commander who could decide what forces were necessary for its execution, and then insist that these were provided. It was not until the end of the year that the commanders were appointed; only then was sufficient authority brought to bear upon this issue to enable demands for extra men and ships to be made, and met.

Yet within the limitations of their brief, Morgan and his staff achieved a great deal. They drew upon the fruits of aerial reconnaissance and a canvass of Britain for pre-war holiday photographs of every yard of the coast line of France. The limiting factors for an invasion site were the radius of air cover (effectively the range of a Spitfire, 150 miles); the limits of beach capacity (it was scarcely possible to unload any army beneath steep cliffs); the length of the sea crossing; and the strength of the German defences. For the first three the Pas de Calais, opposite Dover, offered the most obvious advantages. To the end some soldiers, including General Patton, favoured the Pas de Calais as the shortest route to the heart of Germany. Yet Morgan and the Chiefs of Staff easily rejected this choice because of the strength of the German defences. Eyes swung west, towards the broad beaches of Brittany, the Cotentin, Normandy. Brittany lay too far away, beyond the reach of dominant air cover. The Cotentin offered the Germans too simple an opportunity to bottle up the invaders within the peninsula. Very early on, in the spring of 1943, decisive attention concentrated upon the beaches, woods and undulating fields of Normandy. "The Cotentin peninsula and the hinterland behind the Caen beaches are on the whole unsuitable for the use of large armoured forces, coming particularly to the marshy river valleys near the coast and the steep hills and narrow valleys in the Normandy highlands," reported Morgan. "The area N, NW and SE of Caen is good tank country, and in this area the enemy is likely to make best use of his panzer divisions."[17]

Throughout the spring and summer, a constant succession of meetings took place at Norfolk House, COSSAC headquarters in St James's Square. Most were attended by around 40 British and American officers of colonel's rank and above, working painstakingly through every aspect of the invasion. Despite disparaging comments made later by Montgomery and his staff about COSSAC's achievements, the contemporary minutes and memoranda are eloquent testimony to the remarkable range of difficulties they isolated and discussed. "The crux of the operation," wrote Morgan, "is . . . likely to be our ability to drive off the German reserves rather than the initial breaking of the coastal crust."[18] The order of Allied priorities must be Caen, Bayeux and the road to St Lô, followed by the road to Falaise and the port of Cherbourg. There was a danger that if Allied assault divisions pursued overly ambitious objectives inland on D-Day, they would be caught in vulnerable and over-extended positions by the inevitable German counter-attack. COSSAC identified the immense problem of beach exits – the difficulty of pushing vehicles rapidly inland from the landing craft. There were endless staff war games, such as Exercises JANTZEN and HARLEQUIN, testing possible Allied and German movements around the Norman beaches. The planners endured moments of despair. In August, aerial photographs revealed massive German flooding of river areas around Caen, which caused the Operations Division to minute: "The full implications of this have not yet been assessed, but it is quite possible that it will finally 'kill' OVERLORD."[19]

It did not of course do so, and a few days later the staff were considering and rejecting the possibility of a feint invasion: "The feint will be over by D-Day and it will be clear that it was only a feint and the threat to the Pas de Calais will have disappeared, and the enemy may move his reserves. If we are to maintain our threat, we must dispense with the feint. If we are to have the feint, we must dispense with the threat."[20] Here was the germ of FORTITUDE, the brilliant Allied deception operation which would keep the German Fifteenth Army locked in the Pas de Calais deep into July 1944.

While the planners studied beach gradients and the complexities of the French railway system, Roosevelt and Churchill considered leaders. Both Marshall and Brooke were disappointed in their passionate hopes of the Supreme Command,

Marshall because he was indispensable in Washington, Brooke because he was British. On 7 December, Roosevelt was met at Tunis airport by General Dwight Eisenhower. As soon as the two men were side by side in the back of a staff car, the President told him simply: "Well, Ike, you are going to command Overlord." Eisenhower, a 54-year-old Kansan who had risen from colonel to general in three years and who had scarcely heard a shot fired upon a battlefield, was to arouse the scorn of many more brilliant soldiers in the years that followed: "Just a co-ordinator, a good mixer, a champion of inter-Allied co-operation, and in those respects few can hold a candle to him," wrote Brooke. "But is that enough? Or can we not find all the qualities of a Commander in one man?"[21]

Eisenhower was sensitive to the well-founded charge that he was no battlefield commander: "It wearies me to be thought of as timid, when I've had to do things that were so risky as to be almost crazy."[22] But history has thus far remained confident that whatever his shortcomings as a general in the field, he could not have been matched as Supreme Commander. In 1944–45, he revealed a greatness of spirit that escaped Montgomery, perhaps every British general of the Second World War with the exception of Slim. The shortcomings of the Allied high command in north-west Europe in 1944 have provoked close critical study. Most writers have chosen to consider the successes and failures of Eisenhower and his lieutenants in isolation;[23] they have been reluctant to compare them with the collapse of so many other military alliances in other ages, or to reflect upon the vast weight of forces assembled in north-west Europe, which rendered meaningless any comparison with the command methods of Marlborough and Wellington, even those of Grant and Sherman. The most vivid contrast is that of the Allied SHAEF and the German OKW. Alongside the command structure of their enemies, that of the Allied forces was a masterpiece of reason and understanding. Eisenhower understood that in some respects his authority was that of a constitutional monarch: the power that he held was less important than the fact that his possession denied it to others. Eisenhower lacked greatness as a soldier, and tolerated a remarkable number of knaves and mischief-makers in his court at SHAEF. But his behaviour at moments of Anglo-American tension, his extraordinary generosity of spirit to his difficult subordinates, proved his greatness as Supreme Commander. His failures were of omission, seldom of commission. It remains impossible to conceive of any other Allied soldier matching his achievement.

The Americans were irked by the appointment of Englishmen to all three subordinate commands for OVERLORD – Sir Bernard Montgomery on land, Sir Bertram Ramsay at sea, Sir Trafford Leigh-Mallory for air. Yet another Englishman, Air Chief Marshal Sir Arthur Tedder, would serve as Deputy Supreme Commander, a recognition of the critical importance of the air forces to the invasion. Eisenhower quickly realized that his command difficulties with OVERLORD would be much greater than those of TORCH not merely because of the scale of the Normandy invasion, but because in North Africa "we were then engaged in desperate battling and everybody could see the sense of and the necessity for complete unification. The answer also lies partially in the fact that those three men [his deputies in the Mediterranean] were of the broadest possible calibre, while two of my present commanders, although extremely able, are somewhat ritualistic in outlook and require a great deal more of inoculation."[24] He referred to Ramsay and Leigh-Mallory; but he had also wanted Alexander instead of Montgomery as ground commander.

This was the final occasion of the war on which British officers achieved such a measure of authority over Americans, and Americans bowed to British experience and allegedly greater military wisdom. This was ironic, for the invasion was pre-eminently an American design, reflecting an American willingness to confront the enemy head-on in a collision which Britain's leaders had sought for so long to defer. But for the British people far more than for the Americans, the invasion represented a rebirth, a return, a reversal of all the humiliations and defeats that they had endured since 1939. Here, at last, the British army could resume that which it had so disastrously abandoned at Dunkirk: the battle to defeat a major German army in north-west Europe.

2 Preparations

Commanders

General Omar Bradley, Commander designate of the American First Army in north-west Europe, landed in Britain to take up his appointment on a bleak autumn morning in September 1943. Like most Americans, he did not find his spirits exalted by the renewed encounter at a northern airfield with weary, seedy, rationed, wartime Britain: "The waitress, a stocky Scottish girl with a heavy brogue, offered me a choice of two entrées – neither of which I understood. 'Let me have the second,' I replied nonchalantly. She returned with stewed tomatoes. The first choice had been boiled fish. Prestwick taught me to confine my breakfast thereafter to the U.S. army mess."[1] A steady, careful, thoughtful Missourian, like most American professional soldiers Bradley came from modest origins. His father died when he was 14, leaving his mother, a seamstress, to bring him up. He himself worked in a railway workshop until he was able to gain a place at West Point. He served as a soldier for 32 years before seeing action for the first time as a corps commander in Tunisia. Now, just eight months later, he was to bear direct responsibility for the American army's greatest operation of the war thus far. He was 50 years old. If he lacked Patton's driving force and flamboyance, he had proved himself a commander of exceptional stability and discretion, whom men liked and immediately trusted. Bradley could "read" a battle.

He had been plucked from Sicily to Washington for a briefing about his new appointment, seeing Mrs Bradley for the last time before VE Day in her modest temporary home at the Thayer Hotel in West Point. He waited a week for an appointment with General Marshall, at last finding himself squeezed in during the Chief of Staff's journey to Omaha, Nebraska, for an American Legion convention. The President met him, and talked of his fear that the Germans might develop their atomic bomb in time to influence the invasion. Then Bradley flew to Britain, and travelled to London to meet the COSSAC staff and to be briefed about the progress of planning. One morning he walked through Hyde Park and stood amongst the crowd at Speaker's Corner to listen to a soapbox orator bellowing his enthusiasm for the "Second Front Now", a catchphrase of wartime Britain so familiar that it had become a music-hall joke. "I thought of how little comprehension he had of what the 'Second Front' entailed," wrote Bradley, "of the labors that would be required to mount it,"[2] Then he drove to his new headquarters at Bristol to meet the staff with whom he must prepare the American invasion force.

Montgomery arrived in England on 2 January, and immediately began to whip up a whirlwind. He had learned of his own appointment only 10 days earlier, following a protracted period of apprehension that he might be passed over in favour of Alexander, Churchill's favourite general. Having spent the night at Claridges, at 9.00 a.m. the following morning he attended a briefing at his new headquarters, St Paul's School in Hammersmith, where he had once been a pupil. He heard the COSSAC staff outline their plan. Forearmed by a discussion with Eisenhower in Algiers and a glimpse of Churchill's copy in Tunisia a few days earlier, Montgomery found little difficulty in taking the floor when the briefers had finished and demolishing their points one by one in a 20-minute "Monty special". Like Eisenhower and Bedell Smith, he had been immediately convinced that the front was too narrow, the assault lacking in power and depth. He sent the COSSAC staff back to their offices to consider the implications of a far wider assault, perhaps reaching from Dieppe to Brittany. At the second day's session, he accepted the naval arguments against landing west of the Cotentin, but continued to insist upon a line reaching at least as far north as what became Utah beach. On the third day, he crushed formal protests from senior British and American COSSAC officers who insisted that what he wanted could not be done with the resources. The resources must be found, he declared flatly, or another commander appointed to carry out the invasion.

It was a masterly performance – Montgomery at his very best in clarity of purpose and ruthless simplicity. After months of havering among staff officers fatally hampered by lack of authority, he had sketched the design for a feasible operation of war, and begun to exercise his own immense strength of will to ensure that the resources would be found to land five divisions and secure a beachhead large enough to provide fighting room for the Allied armies. He ignored the sensibilities of the existing staff of 21st Army Group, his command for the invasion, by replacing them wholesale with his own tried and tested officers from Eighth Army – De Guingand, Williams, Belchem, Richardson and others. One of their first horrified discoveries was that the RAF had begun intensive reconnaisance of the Normandy area. The airmen were hastily persuaded to widen their operations, giving special emphasis to the Pas de Calais.

It was characteristic of Montgomery that, having achieved so much so quickly, having made a forceful and vital initial contribution to OVERLORD, he should also seek to write into history his claim that the new plan was entirely his vision and his conception. In reality, most of the staff in England had been conscious for months of the need to strengthen the attack, but lacked the authority to insist upon it. Eisenhower himself immediately grasped the problem, and had some discussion of it with Montgomery. But throughout his military career, a worm of self-destruction in the austere, awkward little man in the beret caused him to disparage the contribution of his peers, shamelessly to seize the credit for the achievements of others, and rewrite the history of his own battlefield planning to conform with the reality of what took place. These were weaknesses which would come close to destroying him, for they gained him few friends. His staff and subordinates admired and were fascinated by him; few found it possible to like him. "We never lost confidence in him," said one, talking of the Normandy period, "but we would very often say: 'Oh Christ, what's the little bugger doing now?' "[3] The support of one man, the CIGS, Sir Alan Brooke, had carried Montgomery first to the army command in which he gained fame in the desert, and then to the principal British role in OVERLORD. Without Brooke, it is unlikely that Montgomery would ever have gained the chance to display his qualities in the highest commands.

Montgomery's self-esteem, at its most conspicuous in his dealings with Americans, rested upon his faith in himself as a supreme professional, a monkish student of war who understood the conduct of military operations in a way that escaped less dedicated commanders, such as Alexander and Eisenhower, who did not aspire to his summits of military intellectualism. He would never have found himself in the headmaster's chair at St

Paul's in January 1944 had there not been much substance in his claims. In France in 1940, in England until 1942, in the Mediterranean in the 17 months that followed, he had proved himself a consummate trainer and motivator of troops, superb in his choice of subordinate staff and his organization of battles. He commanded immense respect from those who served under him for his willingness to listen to them, his directness and loyalty. Many senior officers in his armies went through the war quite unaware of the dark side of Montgomery's character, the conceit and moments of pettiness, the indifference to truth where it reflected upon himself, the capacity for malice. And perhaps these very vices contributed to Montgomery a quality lacking in many brave and famous British generals – the iron will to prevail. Wavell was an example of an officer much beloved in the British army, of whom it has been said by his best biographer[4] that he possessed the qualities for greatness in almost every sphere of human endeavour save that of high command in war. Alexander was a commander in the tradition of great Anglo-Irish military gentlemen – he lacked the intellect, the ruthless driving force that enables a general to dominate the battlefield. The very qualities that made so many German commanders in the Second World War such unpleasant personalities were also of immense value to them in battle: relentless clarity of purpose, the absolute will to win. For all Montgomery's caution in battle, the passion for "tidiness" that more than once denied him all-embracing victories, this essentially cold, insensitive man was devoted to winning. The outstanding recent American historian of the campaign in north-west Europe has written: "There is every reason to believe in retrospect, as Brooke believed then, that Montgomery not only surpassed Alexander as an operational commander, but was altogether Britain's ablest general of the war."[5]

Eisenhower reached England on 15 January, and on the 21st presided over the first meeting of his staff and commanders at Norfolk House. It was overwhelmingly Montgomery's occasion. He could claim the credit for having immensely refined the simple broad assault discussed earlier with the Supreme Commander, and was able to outline the new plan which in the weeks that followed would be transformed into the operational orders of the Allied armies. The Americans, on the right, would go for Cherbourg, Brest and the Loire ports. It was logical to land them on the western flank, because they would thus be conveniently placed to receive men and supplies arriving direct by sea from the United States. The British and Canadians on the left "would deal with the enemy main body approaching from the east and south-east". Montgomery declared: "In the initial stages, we should concentrate on gaining control quickly of the main centres of road communications. We should then push our armoured formations between and beyond these centres and deploy them on suitable ground. In this way it would be difficult for the enemy to bring up his reserves and get them past three armoured formations."[6] On 23 January, after a final effort by the COSSAC staff to impose some of their own thinking upon Eisenhower, and perhaps also to salvage a little of their deeply bruised self-respect, the Supreme Commander formally accepted Montgomery's proposals. The immense labour began of translating these into operational reality – convincing Washington of the vital need for more landing craft, devising fire plans, air support schemes, loading programmes, engineer inventories, naval escort arrangements.

Two mobile brigade groups were placed on standby in Kent and Sussex lest German commandos seek to land and dislocate the build-up. Work began on printing millions of maps in conditions of absolute secrecy, copying air photographs in their thousands, stockpiling artillery ammunition in hundreds of thousands of rounds. The vast business of marshalling American formations arriving almost weekly from across the Atlantic would continue until ports in France became available. Each armoured division required the equivalent of 40 ships, 386,000 ship tons as against 270,000 tons for an infantry division. Every formation required camps in Britain, trains to move them there, training grounds, rest areas, supplies. Tank crews must test fire their weapons, infantrymen zero their rifles. A proposed scale of one ounce of sweets, two ounces of biscuits and one packet of chewing gum for every man of the assault forces necessitated the distribution of 6,250 pounds of sweets, 12,500 pounds of biscuits and 100,000 packets of gum. Armoured units were reminded that their tanks' mileage before the invasion was to be restricted to 600 (Churchills), 800 (Cromwells and Shermans). The Air Ministry was pressed to get some of its prototype helicopters into service, although the airmen warned that none were likely to be available. Amid serious fears that the Germans might use gas against the invaders, 60 days' supply of gas shells was prepared for retaliatory use, and aircrew were specially trained for gas bombing. Training maps showing real terrain with fictitious names were issued to commanding officers. A staggering weight of orders and schedules was drawn up and sealed, a necessary security risk being taken to brief the naval units some days before the armies knew where they were to sail.

All this was completed in a mere 17 weeks before the newly-revised date for D-Day, 5 June. Its accomplishment remains the greatest organizational achievement of the Second World War, a feat of staff-work that has dazzled history, a monument to the imagination and brilliance of thousands of British and American planners and logisticians which may never be surpassed in war. At Norfolk House, a succession of 12-day courses were held for Allied supply officers, 70 at a time, to study the huge problems of the Q branch. 25 square miles of west Devon between Appledore and Woolacombe were evacuated of their entire civilian population to enable the American assault forces to rehearse with live ammunition. All over Britain exercises were held, christened with characteristic inappropriateness – DUCK I, II, III, BEAVER, FABIUS, TIGER – first for groups of specialists, then for increasingly large bodies of men, until at last entire divisions were engaged. In the assembly areas great tented encampments were created, equipped with water points, field bakeries, bath facilities, post offices, each one camouflaged with the intent of making it indistinguishable from 10,000 feet. The British devised a vehicle waterproofing compound from grease, lime and asbestos fibres. The American initial landing force comprised 130,000 men, with another 1,200,000 to follow by D+90. With them would go 137,000 wheeled and semi-tracked vehicles, 4,217 full-tracked vehicles, 3,500 artillery pieces. Week by week, the transatlantic convoys docked in British ports, unloading new cargoes of artillery shells from Illinois, blood plasma from Tennessee, jeeps from Detroit, K ration cheese from Wisconsin.

The British protested somewhat about the vast allocation of shipping that was proving necessary to provide American troops with their accustomed level of supply. Even the U.S. War Department admitted that its huge support organization was "a factor which produced problems not foreseen . . . the *matériel* needed to provide American soldiers with something corresponding to the American standard of living [caused] a prodigious growth of service and administration units."[7] The British official historian wrote more portentously: "The Americans' belief in their technical supremacy had a significant effect both on strategic thought and on its execution, while their widespread enjoyment of a high standard of living was partly responsible for a quantity of equipment which others might find extravagant, but which, in their case, may have been at the least a stimulant and at the most a necessity."[8] Each American soldier in Normandy received six and a quarter pounds of rations a day, against three and a third pounds for his German enemy. Since only four pounds per man of the American ration was consumed, it was clear that a huge and characteristic waste of shipping was involved. Meanwhile the German small-arms ammunition scale for a rifle company was more than double that of its American equivalent, 56,000 rounds to 21,000.

Throughout this period, 21st Army Group's headquarters was pre-occupied with operational planning. The specialist branches of the American and British forces were responsible for solving the technical and logistical problems of invasion. The huge, bloated staff at SHAEF circulated enormous quantities of paper between their departments – reports, minutes, studies of German reinforcement capability, French railway capacity, German coastal gun range, Allied naval bombardment power. Some of this was extremely valuable, much of it not. But it was Montgomery's staff which bore the overwhelming burden of planning the battle, using very little paper and very long hours of debate and thought. Eisenhower summarized his own preoccupations before OVERLORD as: the French political complications; the allocation of resources; air organization and planning. At 21st Army Group, the staff shared the Supreme Commander's concern about the air problem, but were chiefly haunted during those spring weeks by fear that some breach of security might compromise the landing. If it did so, there was every prospect that the Allies would learn of the enemy's knowledge through Ultra. But until the very morning of D-Day, the possibility that the Germans might secretly be waiting for the Allies in Normandy remained the overriding nightmare of the planners. Only with forewarning did the Germans possess a real prospect of turning back the invaders on the beaches.

It was agreed that gaining a foothold on D-Day was a huge organizational task, but presented no intolerable tactical risks given the weight of Allied resources. All the imponderables, the great dangers, lay in the battle of the build-up. Immense labour was devoted to comparisons of the likely Allied and German strengths. An uncommonly gloomy SHAEF estimate of April 1944 predicted that by D+14 the Germans would have 28 divisions in Normandy against 19⅓ Allied; by D+20: 30 to 24⅔; by D+30: 33 to 28⅔.[9] The differences of opinion between German commanders about the best methods of defending Normandy were known at 21st Army Group through Ultra. But as Montgomery's brilliant intelligence officer, the 31-year-old Brigadier Bill Williams, declared: "All the time we were asking ourselves: To what extent would these chaps make a good showing despite Hitler?"[10] The behaviour of the Führer himself, together with the success or failure of the Allies' FORTITUDE deception plan based upon the fictitious threat to the Pas de Calais posed by General Patton and the "First U.S. Army Group", would determine whether the German build-up attained its immensely dangerous theoretical maximum. The Allies' appreciation in April spotlighted "the grave risk of stabilization" – a euphemism for stalemate– "around D+14 . . . The greatest energy and initiative will be required at this period to ensure that the enemy is not allowed to stabilize his defence."[11]

Afterwards, there would be much discussion about how far the Allied command had anticipated the difficulties of fighting in the close country of the Norman *bocage*. The SHAEF appreciation declared: "Generally speaking the area will not be an easy one for forces to advance through rapidly in the face of determined resistance, but it will likewise be most difficult for the enemy to prevent a slow and steady advance by infiltration . . . Tanks can penetrate most of the hedgerows. It is difficult to judge whether such terrain favours defending or attacking infantry . . . The tactics to be employed in fighting through *bocage* country should be given considerable study by formations to be employed therein."[12] But they were not. The British 7th Armoured Division was preparing for D-Day amidst the flatlands of East Anglia. Most British infantry battalions knew little of the infiltration tactics in which the Germans were so skilled, and relied overwhelmingly upon the straightforward open order advance, two companies forward. Many American formations were training on Dartmoor and Exmoor. As a senior staff officer said afterwards: "We simply did not expect to remain in the *bocage* long enough to justify studying it as a major tactical problem."[13]

There were, however, no delusions among 21st Army Group

about the likely quality of resistance: "The Germans will probably base many of their main and rearguard positions on river obstacles . . . Our formations will be well-trained, but most of them will have little battle experience . . . The enemy . . . will fight fiercely in all encounters, whether major battles or battles simply to gain time for withdrawal . . . An all-out pursuit is considered unlikely until the German army is emphatically beaten in battle, and likely to come only once in the campaign. It will herald the end of the German war."[14]

The landing plan developed at St Paul's called for four corps to feed their men in columns through the five Allied beaches during the period following D-Day. On the right, at Utah beach, the U.S. VII Corps would be led ashore on D-Day by 4th Division; at Omaha, V Corps would be led by 1st and 29th Divisions; at Gold, the British XXX Corps would be led by 50th Division; British I Corps on Juno would be led by 3rd Canadian Division, on Sword by 3rd British Division. Various Ranger and Commando units would land alongside these major formations, but at no phase of the war was the high command's enthusiasm for Special Forces lower than in 1944. There was a strong feeling that these "private armies" had creamed off precious high-quality manpower, and could contribute little to the massive clash on the battlefield that was now to begin. The raiding days were over. With the sole exceptions of the American Ranger assault on the Pointe du Hoc west of Omaha, and some SAS drops deep inland to work with the Resistance on German lines of communication, the Commandos and other Special Forces were employed for normal infantry tasks on D-Day and for most of the war thereafter.[15]

Montgomery's subsequent attempts to pretend that the Normandy battle developed entirely in accordance with his own plans have distorted what was essentially a clear and simple issue. The evidence of all the planning documents before D-Day about Allied intentions is incontrovertible. The British Second Army and Canadian First Army were to "assault to the west of the R.ORNE and to develop operations to the south and south-east, in order to secure airfield sites and to protect the eastern flank of U.S. First Army while the latter is capturing CHERBOURG. In its subsequent operations the SECOND ARMY will pivot on its left (CAEN) and offer a strong front against enemy movement towards the lodgement area from the east."[16] The U.S. First Army was to capture Cherbourg, and thereafter:

> to develop operations southwards towards ST LO in conformity with the advance of Second British Army. After the area CHERBOURG-CAUMONT-VIRE-AVRANCHES has been captured, the Army will be directed southwards with the object of capturing RENNES and then establishing our flank on the R.LOIRE and capturing QUIBERON BAY.[17]

Patton's Third Army was to advance through First Army's front, clearing Brittany, seizing St Nazaire and Nantes, then covering the south flank, "while the First U.S. Army is directed N.E. with a view to operations towards PARIS." From all this, it is obvious that the eventual American movements in Normandy followed the plan created in the spring of 1944 by 21st Army Group. Where Montgomery distorted his intentions after the event, and made possible the bitter controversy that has persisted for so many years, was by pretending that the British and Canadians fulfilled their purpose by holding a line north of Caen. Indeed, they did offer a "strong front" to the great weight of German armour. But as Montgomery made abundantly clear before D-Day, he wished that "strong front" to be somewhere in the area of Falaise, which would provide adequate room for build-up and airfield construction between the perimeter and the coast. In the event, the Allies suffered severely from the lack of space within their beachhead as well as the shortage of airfield sites to increase the range of their tactical aircraft. From 6 June until the final Canadian push towards Argentan in August, Montgomery made it plain that he hoped that his troops could surpass his minimum hopes, gain more ground and break through the German front. This they were never able to do, and Montgomery's credibility with his peers and superiors diminished with each letter of intent that he dispatched before Second Army's operations, expressing ambitious hopes which were not fulfilled.

The Commander-in-Chief of 21st Army Group was justified in claiming that nothing which happened in Normandy changed the broad shape of his plan or the intended pattern of the American advance. But all those who knew him and knew the plan – not least the Americans – had a clear idea of what he wanted the British element to accomplish, and were not for a moment deluded by his evasions when these hopes were not fulfilled. Had he himself been more honest and less arrogant about his difficulties on the eastern flank as they took place – above all with

Eisenhower and Tedder – he might have avoided much of the acrimony that descended upon him.

The issue was further confused by the so-called "phase line controversy", the argument surrounding the map, drawn up by the 21st Army Group HQ at St Paul's, showing the perimeters which the Allied armies might expect to hold by given dates following the landings, concluding at the line of the Seine on D+90. Bradley was furious to see this map, and demanded the deletion of the phase lines for the American sector, to which he refused to be committed. In reality, it is difficult to attach much importance to them, or to believe that Montgomery did so either. 21st Army Group expected to fight a measured, stage by stage battle in which the Germans retreated to newly-chosen defensive positions as their front was driven in by successive Allied attacks. Some notion of where the Allies might hope to get to in the weeks after D-Day was desirable. But no general as skilled in the art of war as Montgomery could have intended that a battle lasting many weeks should be conducted *operationally* in accordance with lines on a map. Approximate phase lines were essential *logistically,* for the guidance of the supply planners, because the balance in the armies' relative requirements of ammunition and fuel would vary by many thousands of tons in accordance with their distance from the nearest offloading point, and the speed at which they were advancing. The "phase line controversy" only assumed its subsequent importance because of the tensions within the Alliance, and the willingness of mischief-makers to find a stick with which to belabour Montgomery during the weeks of wrangling that reached a pitch in high summer.

Between 15 January and 5 June – the new target date for invasion after delay became inevitable to provide sufficient landing craft – Montgomery's original concept for the assault was refined, but not altered. Enormous problems of organization and supply were overcome, difficult issues such as the role of de Gaulle and his Free French were painfully resolved[18] It was not, however, the future of the ground battle for Normandy, nor even the political future of France, which lay at the heart of the most bitter struggle within Eisenhower's command in the spring of 1944. This concerned the role and direction of the Allied air forces.

Disagreements, even full-blooded quarrels, between the services were not uncommon either in Britain or America in the Second World War. But none generated more heat and passion or diverted so much attention from the struggle to defeat the Germans than that surrounding the proper use of the Allies' vast air power in 1944.* In the First World War, aircraft were directly controlled by the armies and navies of their respective nations. In April 1918, British airmen successfully escaped the thraldom of the generals and admirals to form the Royal Air Force. In America, air power remained under the direction of the two senior services, but at no time from the 1920s onwards did the nation's leading fliers lose sight of their ambition of independence. It is impossible to escape the conclusion that, between the wars, the air forces of both countries embraced Mitchell, Douhet and Trenchard's theories of strategic air power, which claimed the bomber unsupported to be a war-winning weapon, because of their passionate anxiety to discover a role for themselves beyond that of mere flying eyes and artillery for the older services. Their enthusiasm for stragetic air power critically hampered the development of close air-ground support techniques such as the Luftwaffe took for granted from its inception. Such was the obsession of the RAF with its bomber force that during the rush to re-arm in the last years before war, the Air Ministry would have built far too few fighters to enable the Battle of Britain to be won, had it not been compelled to switch emphasis by civilian politicians more concerned with the defence of their own country than with demonstrating the potential of bombing an enemy.

Yet Britain's inability to strike directly against Germany with her ground forces between 1940 and 1944 thrust upon the RAF the opportunity to play a role of unique strategic importance. The programme for the creation of a vast heavy bomber force, conceived in the days of despair in 1940, had borne full fruit for the airmen by 1944. Each night, up to a thousand British aircraft set off for the industrial cities of Germany, to pour explosives upon them with the aid of the most sophisticated technology that the nation possessed. Air Marshal Sir Arthur Harris, the formidable Commander-in-Chief of Bomber Command, had

* For a full account of this debate, see the author's *Bomber Command* (Michael Joseph, London 1979).

become one of the best-known and most fiercely independent war leaders in Britain, waging his campaign with implacable determination, convinced that by this means alone Germany could be beaten, without recourse to a major land campaign. When the Casablanca conference committed the Allied air forces to POINTBLANK, a bombing programme specifically designed to pave the way for the invasion of Europe, Harris paid lip service, but in reality pursued uninterrupted his campaign of "area bombing" against the cities of Germany. "It is my firm belief," he wrote to Portal on 12 August 1943, "that we are on the verge of a final showdown in the bombing war . . . I am certain that given average weather and concentration on the main job, we can push Germany over by bombing this year."[1] In January 1944, almost unbelievably, Harris declared his conviction that, given continued concentration upon his existing policy, Germany could be driven to "a state of devastation in which surrender is inevitable" by 1 April.

By day, meanwhile, the American Fortresses pursued their precision bombing campaign guided by General Carl "Tooey" Spaatz, an airman who disagreed with Harris about the best means of defeating Germany from the air, but made common cause with the Englishman's commitment to independent air power. The American official historians wrote of the USAAF that it was:

> young, aggressive, and conscious of its growing power. It was guided by the sense of a special mission to perform. It had to justify the expenditure of billions of dollars and the use of almost a third of the army's manpower. It sought for itself, therefore, both as free a hand as possible to prosecute the air war in accordance with its own ideas, and the maximum credit for its performance.[2]

As the directors of OVERLORD gathered the reins of command into their hands in the first months of 1944, one of their foremost concerns was to ensure that the full weight of Allied air power was available to provide whatever support they felt need of as the campaign unfolded. Eisenhower concluded early on that the "bomber barons' " promise of goodwill would not be sufficient: the lure of their own convictions had often proved too strong in the past. Even more serious, both the British and American bomber chiefs had been proclaiming for months that they considered OVERLORD a vast, gratuitous strategic misjudgement, rendered wholly unnecessary by their own operations. Harris bombarded the Air Ministry with minutes declaring that "clearly the best and indeed the only efficient support which Bomber Command can give to OVERLORD is the intensification of attacks on suitable industrial centres in Germany . . ."[3] Spaatz's diary note of the critical 21 January Supreme Commander's meeting at which the OVERLORD framework was laid down declared only:

Nothing of note from an Air point of view except launching of OVERLORD will result in the calling off of bomber effort on Germany proper from one to two months prior to invasion. If time is as now contemplated, there will be no opportunity to carry out any Air operations of sufficient intensity to justify the theory that Germany can be knocked out by Air power. Operations in connection with OVERLORD will be child's play compared to present operations . . .[4]

As late as April 1944, the minutes of a meeting between Spaatz and General Hoyt Vandenburg, American Deputy Air Commander-in-Chief for OVERLORD, recorded:

General Spaatz stated that he feared that the Allied air forces might be batting their heads against a stone wall in the Overlord operation. If the purpose of Overlord is to seize and hold advanced air bases, this purpose is no longer necessary since the strategic air forces can already reach all vital targets with fighter cover . . . It is of paramount importance the Combined Bomber Offensive continue without interruption and the proposed diversion of the 8th air force to support of Overlord is highly dangerous. Much more effective would be the combined operation on strategic missions under one command of the 8th, 15th and 9th air forces. If this were done, the highly dangerous Overlord operation could be eliminated. It might take somewhat longer, but would be surer, whereas the proposed cross-channel operation is highly dangerous and the outcome is extremely uncertain. A failure of Overlord will have repercussions which may well undo all of the effects of the strategic bombing efforts to date. Another reason that Overlord is no longer necessary is because of the relative success of the use of H_2X [blind bombing radar equipment] operations over or in an overcast . . . Hence, the one heretofore great impediment to the strategic mission (i.e. weather) has been largely overcome and once more is an argument against mounting the Overlord operation.

If I were directing the overall strategic operations, I would go into Norway, where we have a much greater chance of ground force success and where I believe Sweden would come in with us. Why undertake a highly dubious operation in a hurry when there is a surer way to do it as just outlined? It is better to win the war surely than to undertake an operation which has really great risks . . .

In discussing future operations with General Vandenburg, Gen. Spaatz stated that all experience in Africa has indicated the inability of

American troops to cross areas heavily defended by land mines, and that the beaches of Overlord are certain to be more heavily mined than any area in Africa . . . Gen. Vandenburg cited his dissatisfaction with the plans for use of airborne troops. He stated that he has made protest a matter of record in all meetings with the Supreme Commanders [sic].[5]

This document vividly reveals, first, that two months before D-Day there were still Allied officers in high commands who were deeply sceptical about the entire operation; and, second, the messianic conviction with which the airmen opposed their own participation. It is against the background of opinions such as these that the struggles between the ground and air force commanders in the summer of 1944 must be viewed. It is a tragic reflection of the extent to which strategic bombing doctrine had distorted the thinking of so many senior air force officers in Britain and America that, on the very eve of OVERLORD, they could not grasp that this was the decisive operation of the war in the west, to which every other ambition must be subordinate.

After intense argument between London and Washington, confused by British political reluctance to surrender the independence of Bomber Command, Eisenhower had his way: direction of all the Allied air forces was placed in his hands for as long as the Chiefs of Staff deemed necessary. After a further dispute, aggravated by Churchill's fears about the level of French civilian casualties, the air forces embarked upon the huge programme of transport bombing of French rail junctions and river crossings which was to play such a critical role in restricting the movement of German reinforcements after D-Day. Its scale was intensified by the need to attack targets relating to the entire length of the Channel coast, lest concentration westwards reveal the focus of Allied intentions. Its success was a tribute to the qualities and training of the Allied aircrew, whatever the opinions of their commanders. The cost – 12,000 French and Belgian lives – was substantially lower than Churchill had feared.

Yet if the documents quoted above reveal good reasons for the ground force commanders' mistrust of the airmen, it is ironic that in the spring of 1944 Spaatz achieved one of the decisive victories of the war for the Allies, and embarked upon the course that was to lead him to a second. In fulfilment of POINTBLANK, his Fortresses and Liberators had for months been attacking Germany's aircraft factories, at a cost which compelled the Americans to accept the need for long-range fighter escorts for their daylight operations. By one of the most extraordinary paradoxes of the war, the bombing of the factories achieved only limited impact upon German aircraft production; but the coming of the marvellous Mustang P-51 long-range fighter to the skies over Germany inflicted an irreversible defeat upon the Luftwaffe, unquestionably decisive for OVERLORD. In January 1944 the Germans lost 1,311 aircraft from all causes. This figure rose to 2,121 in February and 2,115 in March. Even more disastrous than lost fighters, the Luftwaffe's trained pilots were being killed far more quickly than they could be replaced, with the direction of the air force in the enfeebled hands of Goering. By March the Americans were consciously attacking targets with the purpose of forcing the Germans to defend them. By June, the Germans no longer possessed sufficient pilots and aircraft to mount more than token resistance to the Allied invasion of France.

In May, Spaatz began attacking Germany's synthetic oil plants. The results of even a limited bombing programme, revealed after the war, were awe-inspiring. Employing only 11.6 per cent of his bomber effort in June, 17 per cent in July, 16.4 per cent in August, he brought about a fall in German oil production from 927,000 tons in March to 715,000 tons in May, and 472,000 tons in June. The Luftwaffe's aviation spirit supply fell from 180,000 tons in April to 50,000 tons in June, and 10,000 tons in August. It seems perfectly possible that had the scale of the German fuel crisis been perceived by the allied chiefs of staff and the American airmen been encouraged to pursue their oil bombing campaign with vigour through the summer of 1944, Germany could have been defeated by the end of the year.

Yet it was Spaatz's tragedy that, by the spring of 1944, his own credibility and that of the other bomber chiefs had fallen low in the eyes of the Allied high command – hardly surprising in the light of their past broken promises and wild declarations of strategic opinion. Claims of Luftwaffe aircraft destroyed had so often proved fantastic that even other leaders of the Allied air forces found it impossible to credit the extent of the Mustang's victory. For that matter, Spaatz himself remained apprehensive about the Luftwaffe's capabilities. Plans were laid for huge forces of fighters to cover the invasion, in expectation of a great battle for air supremacy over the beachhead. SHAEF estimates suggested that the Germans might still be capable of putting as many as 300 fighters and 200 bombers into the air over Normandy in a single operation. Leigh-Mallory feared that the

The American P-51 Mustang fighter made its greatest contribution to Allied victory by winning the battle for air supremacy over Germany before D-Day. In its original form, powered by the Allison engine, the fighter performed disappointingly. But when fitted with the great Rolls-Royce Merlin, it was transformed into one of the most remarkable aircraft of the war, capable of flying to Berlin and back with long-range drop tanks, and outperforming almost every Luftwaffe opponent when it got there. It was also employed over Normandy in interceptor and ground-attack roles. Normally armed with six .5 machine-guns, it possessed a top speed of 475 mph, and a ceiling of 42,000 feet.

Luftwaffe might employ new pathfinder techniques to mount night operations over the British south coast ports. Only on D-Day, when a mere 319 Luftwaffe sorties were flown, was the truth suspected; in the weeks that followed, as enemy air activity over Normandy remained negligible, it was confirmed. The critical air battle had been fought and won by the Americans over Germany weeks before the first Allied soldiers waded ashore.

In the months before the invasion, however, it was the level of mutual dissent between the Allied air chiefs which drove Tedder and Eisenhower to the brink of despair. Beyond the debate about the employment of the bombers, British and American airmen united in their hostility to Leigh-Mallory, the appointed Air Commander-in-Chief for OVERLORD. The bomber commanders flatly declined to accept their orders from him and would acknowledge only the mandate of Tedder. The fighter commanders also made clear their dislike of and lack of respect for the Commander-in-Chief. The American Brereton, an officer of limited abilities commanding IXth Air Force, and the New Zealander "Mary" Coningham, commanding the British 2nd Tactical Air Force, united in their antagonism to Leigh-Mallory, while General Elwood R. "Pete" Quesada, commanding the close-support squadrons under Brereton, was a bewildered spectator of the wrangles: "I just didn't know people at that level behaved like that. Nobody wanted to be under Leigh-Mallory, even the British."[6]

The burly Leigh-Mallory had achieved his eminence, and aroused considerable personal animosity, by intriguing successfully in the wake of the Battle of Britain to supplant its victors, Air Marshals Dowding and Park. He had directed Fighter Command – later curiously rechristened Air Defence of Great Britain – ever since, and retained this post while he acted as Air Commander-in-Chief for OVERLORD. His appointment was clearly an error of judgement by Portal, Chief of Air Staff. To his peers, he seemed gloomy and hesitant. Most of the Americans admired Tedder for his cool brain, incisive wit, and ability to rise above petty issues and work without reservation for the Allied cause. "Trivia were obnoxious to him," said one. "Though an airman, he was also a team player. He understood that war is organized confusion." But they were irked by Leigh-Mallory's pessimism and indecision. "He didn't seem to know what he wanted," said Quesada. "He couldn't get along with people. He seemed more concerned with preserving his forces than with committing them."[7] Brigadier James Gavin of the U.S. 82nd Airborne returned from his division's drop in Sicily to work on the plan for D-Day. "Now, I want you chaps to tell me how you do this airborne business," said Leigh-Mallory indulgently. He listened to them for a time, then said flatly: "I don't think anybody can do that." The exasperated Gavin exploded: "We just got through doing it in Sicily!"[8] At a meeting of the American airmen on 24 March, General Vandenburg asked Spaatz where his personal loyalties were to lie in his role as deputy to Leigh-Mallory. Vandenburg recorded in his diary that: "General Spaatz directed that the number one priority was to be the safeguarding of the interests of the American component and suggested that I make this clear to General Eisenhower and ask for his concurrence."[9]

At a time, therefore, when everywhere else within the Allied forces great and honourable efforts were being made to ensure that Anglo-American unity was a reality, the senior American airmen in Britain were conspiring – in a manner no more nor less dishonourable than that of some of their RAF counterparts – to defend the sectional interests of their own service. It remains an astonishing feature of the invasion that when it was launched the Allied air chiefs were still unwilling to accept Leigh-Mallory's orders, still disputed their proper role and employment, had still devoted only minimal thought or effort to close ground support. Forward air control techniques which had been tried and proven in the desert were not introduced in Normandy until weeks after the landings. On D-Day itself, while the Allied tactical air forces made an important contribution, they lacked forward air controllers with the leading troops ashore, who might have eased the problems of the ground battle considerably. It has become an article of faith in the history of the Normandy campaign to pay tribute to Allied air power, which indeed was critical. Yet we shall see below how many weeks elapsed before the organization – not the technology or the skill of the pilots – reached the point at which aircraft could render closely co-ordinated support to ground troops.

In the spring of 1944, the air chiefs dedicated far too much attention to disputes about their own authority and independence, and not nearly enough to considering how best they could work in harmony with the armies beneath them. The post-OVERLORD report from Montgomery's headquarters declared: "The most difficult single factor during the period of planning from the military point of view, was the delay in deciding and setting up the higher headquarters organization of the Allied air force. It is obvious that this delay was entirely an air force matter, and as such in no way the business of the military planners, but the effect was strongly felt in army planning."[10] To the dismay and near despair of 21st Army Group, the D-Day Air Plan was finally settled only 36 hours before the landings took place.

Invaders

By the spring of 1944, all of southern England and much of the rest of the country had become a vast military encampment. Under the trees beside the roads, protected by corrugated iron, stood dump after dump of artillery ammunition, mines, engineering stores, pierced plank and wire. The soldiers themselves were awed by the tank and vehicle parks in the fields, where Shermans and jeeps, Dodge trucks and artillery pieces stood in ranks reaching to the horizon. Above all, there were the men – 20 American divisions, 14 British, three Canadian, one French, one Polish, and hundreds of thousands of special forces, corps troops, headquarters units, lines of communication personnel. They were packed into Nissen and Quonset huts, tents and requisitioned country houses from Cornwall to Kent and far northwards up the length of the country. Some were homesick, some excited, a few eager to find any means of escape from the terrifying venture in front of them. Most were impatient to end the months or years of training and to begin this thing upon which all their thoughts had been focused for so long.

One of Montgomery's outstanding contributions before D-Day was his careful meshing of experienced veterans from Eighth Army with the keen, green formations that had been training and languishing for so long in England. Major-General G. P. B. "Pip" Roberts found his new headquarters at 11th Armoured Division still operating the routines and mess life of the peacetime British army. Roberts, an old desert hand, rapidly relieved them of such formalities, sacking his senior staff officer – a meticulous guardsman who affected a red light over his office door to indicate that he did not wish to be disturbed.

Lieutenant Andrew Wilson of The Buffs, a flamethrowing Crocodile tank unit of 79th Armoured Division, had watched the Battle of Britain from his home in Kent as a schoolboy, and eagerly hastened to Sandhurst and into the armoured corps at the first opportunity. Thereafter, he and the other young officers of his unit found themselves condemned to months of routine soldiering on the South Downs under the command of ageing senior officers who knew nothing of war, but were expert in the disciplines of mess life. When Wilson, in a flush of enthusiasm for Russian achievements of the kind that was so common at the time, christened his tank "Stalingrad", he was summarily ordered to unchristen it. But at the beginning of 1944, all the senior officers were abruptly removed and replaced by others from a quite different mould, who began training and exercising the regiment to the very limits of its endurance: "We suddenly knew that we were going to be put through the full Monty treatment."[1] For hours and days at a stretch, they shivered in their tanks on the hills through endless mock attacks and deployments. They did not resent this because they felt that they were learning, at last preparing in earnest for what they had to do. The dangers of taking into battle a tank towing a thinly-armoured trailer loaded with flame-throwing fuel did not greatly trouble them: "Any fears were overcome by our excitement at feeling that we were an elite."[2]

Most of the men of that English "battle school army" shared Wilson's enthusiasm. Major Dick Gosling, ex-Eton and Cambridge, commanding a battery of self-propelled 25-pounders of the Essex Yeomanry, had been waiting to see action since 1939: "We were at the very peak of enthusiasm, fitness, training."[3] Major Charles Richardson of the 6th King's Own Scottish Borderers had so far spent the war commanding a tactical school in Edinburgh, attending the Staff College and training troops amid a sense of lingering embarrassment that he had not seen a shot fired in anger, although as he later concluded: "You fight a bloody sight better when you don't know what's coming."[4]

Many of Lieutenant David Priest's men of 5th Duke of Cornwall's Light Infantry spent the weeks before D-Day attempting to master the art of wheeled warfare. They were a bicycle unit, and it was not easy for a soldier to pedal under the weight of full equipment: "the thing would rear up on you".[5] Typically, within hours of their arrival in Normandy, they were ordered to park their transport and never saw the bicycles again. Corporal Chris Portway of the 4th Dorsets claimed to find his experiences in Normandy infinitely less painful than "all those ghastly exercises"[6] which preceded them. During one in which he took part, bitter British animosity towards the French-Canadians, who were acting as the enemy, boiled over into bloodshed near Reading, with men on both sides being killed. Trooper Steve Dyson became so miserably bored with infantry soldiering in England after 1940 that in desperation he volunteered for anything that offered a chance of escape – demolition, paratroops, military police. At last he was accepted for armour, and found himself perfectly happy, for he loved his tank. Private Mick Anniwell, a 30-year-old former shoe-factory worker and scoutmaster, now posted to 2nd Royal Ulster Rifles, quite simply loved the army and everything that happened to him in it. For many working-class civilians, the 1930s had not been a happy time. In the wartime army, not a few found a fulfilment, a comradeship and sense of purpose that they would spend the rest of their post-war lives seeking to recapture.

Other men, not surprisingly, felt more resigned to their part in the invasion than exhilarated by it. Lieutenant Arthur Heal was a bespectacled 28-year-old sapper, who found that throughout his service career, "I never felt like a soldier". Heal was simply "eager to see the end of it all and be able to go home".[7] Private Charles Argent of 2nd King's Own Scottish Borderers was one of those unfortunate men who spent the war being shunted abruptly from posting to posting, each more dismal than the last, after failing to be accepted for the navy or the Parachute Regiment. In the spring of 1944, he was one morning issued with tropical kit, which was promptly withdrawn. The next day he was sent on a mortar course. At last, on the very eve of invasion, he was posted to the Lowland Division where he knew no one, and was conscious of his very un-Scottish origins. Nor, of course, was he detailed as a mortarman.

7th Armoured, 50th Northumbrian and 51st Highland Divisions had been brought home from the Mediterranean, where they had gained great reputations, specifically to provide the stiffening of experience for the British invasion force. From an early stage there were rumours among the men of 50th Division that they were expendable, that they would be used on the battlefield for tasks in which the rate of attrition would be high. Curiously enough, this did not seem greatly to dismay them, and 50th Division's record in Normandy was very good. Among the other veteran formations, however, there was cause for real concern. Lieutenant Edwin Bramall, posted with a draft of eager and untested young officers to the 2nd King's Royal Rifle Corps of 4th Armoured Brigade, found that "as a battalion, they were worn out. They had shot their bolt. Everybody who was any good had been promoted or become a casualty."[8] Many of the men from the Mediterranean, above all the old regular soldiers, were bitter that, after fighting so hard for so long, they were now to be called upon once again to bear the brunt of the battle. A staff officer described the difficulties with one unit recalled from the Mediterranean for the invasion: "The 3rd Royal Tank Regiment were virtually mutinous just before D-Day. They painted the walls of their barracks in Aldershot with such slogans as 'No Second Front', and had it not been for their new commanding officer, David Silvertop – the best C.O. of an armoured regiment that I met during the war – I really think they might have mutinied in fact." Lieutenant-Colonel Michael Carver of 7th Armoured's 1st Royal Tank Regiment found some of his senior NCOs appearing before him to protest about their role, and echoing complaints from their wives, who demanded to know why those who had sat in England for four years and had not "done their bit" could not now take over the burden. It was a sentiment shared by the Prime Minister:

It is a painful reflection [he wrote to the War Office early in 1944], that probably not one in four or five men who wear the King's uniform even hear a bullet whistle, or are likely to hear one. The vast majority run no more risk than the civil population in southern England. It is my unpleasant duty to dwell upon these facts. One set of men are sent back again and again to the front, while the great majority are kept out of all fighting, to their regret.[9]

If the Prime Minister's closing clause can be regarded with scepticism, his earlier remarks were the subject of repeated altercations with his CIGS, who patiently reminded him of the realities of modern war, of the essential need for the vast "tail" behind OVERLORD, and also of the utter exhaustion of Britain's manpower reserves. The British army that landed in Normandy would be the greatest force that Montgomery ever commanded in north-west Europe. Thereafter, as casualties mounted, its numbers must remorselessly decline. This reality was at the forefront of every British commander's mind from the first clash of arms before Caen until the last shots before Luneberg. So too was the knowledge that the early weeks in Europe would be the last of British parity with the Americans in ground-force strength. In July, the American armies would begin to outnumber the British, and thereafter their strength would rise month by month until they dwarfed those of their ally. Already many British servicemen were irked by the extraordinary social dominance the Americans had achieved within Britain, with their staff sergeants receiving the pay of British captains, their vast reservoirs of equipment for themselves, and candy for British children.

From the moment that they boarded their trains at the docks and cursed the narrowness of British carriage doors for a man in full equipment, the fresh Americans found the encounter with the tired British a strange and bewildering experience. "And where do you make your home, Colonel?" Lieutenant Julian Bach heard a newly-arrived Mississipian captain ask a somewhat frigid British officer at their first uneasy meeting over dinner. "Which home do you mean?" inquired the Colonel unhelpfully, "I have three." The Mississipian enjoyed his revenge the next morning when he watched the Englishman's expression as he poured marmalade on his porridge.[10]

Impeccably tailored American officers – and other ranks – crammed the London hotels and restaurants. Corporal Bill Preston of the 743rd Tank Battalion spent his working days practising submarine escapes from the amphibious DD tank in which he would land in Normandy – he and his crew learned that they had 20 seconds in which to get out if the Sherman foundered. But like so many young non-commissioned Americans, he confused the British by the breadth of his social connections, and found it much easier to book a table at the Mirabelle by using the name of his uncle at the U.S. Embassy than by quoting his own. General "Pete" Quesada of IXth Tactical Air Command brought a few of his pilots along whenever business took him to London, and they found no difficulty in making friends. He wrote to his mother in New York asking her to send him a monthly parcel of a box of Montecristos, six boxes of stockings and six lipsticks. Deadpan, for the rest of the war she dispatched regular consignments of men's long socks and vaseline sticks for chapped lips.

Yet if it is easy to focus upon points of friction between the Americans and their hosts, it remains far more remarkable how effectively Allied co-operation worked at every level. Beneath the tensions between governments and army headquarters on matters of high policy, officers of the two nations worked side by side with extraordinary amity in the preparations for OVERLORD. Just as there were boorish Englishmen such as the Colonel who met Julian Bach, so there were Americans of poor quality, such as General "Pinky" Bull, Eisenhower's G-3 at SHAEF, who inspired the disrespect of almost all who worked with him. But most Englishmen were deeply impressed by the energy, the willingness to learn, and the determination to finish the job of their transatlantic allies. The Americans, in their turn, respected the British forces which had been fighting for so long. Much will be said below about differences and jealousies that developed between British and Americans. Reports of these should never mask the co-operation between them, a unity between allies at working level that has seldom, if ever, been matched in war.

If several British formations that went to Normandy were already battle-weary, some of their American counterparts were alarmingly under-prepared and inadequately led for the task that they were to perform. Even though the British divisions were drawn from a citizen army, the British class system and military tradition meant that their men were far more deeply imbued with the manners and habits of regular soldiers than their

American comrades. From the first day of the war to the last, the U.S. Army could never be mistaken for anything other than what it was – a nation of civilians in uniform. Perhaps the greatest of all America's organizational achievements in the Second World War was the expansion of a tiny regular army of 190,000 men into an eight-and-a-half-million-strong host between 1939 and 1945. Even the peacetime cadre had scarcely been an impressive war machine. One cavalry division in the 1940 Louisiana manoeuvres was obliged to rent its horses, and when these poor nags proved useless, to withdraw them by truck to rest areas after the second day.

Even at war, American's ground forces – above all, her corps of infantry – remained something of a cinderella. A 1942 plan to create an army of 334 divisions, 60 of them armoured, shrivelled to a reality of 89 combat divisions by May 1944, 16 of them armoured. These might be compared with Japan's total of 100 divisions, and the Red Army's 300 – albeit smaller – formations. Huge reserves of manpower were drawn off to feed their air corps, service units, and base troops. Where officers made up only 2.86 per cent of the German army, they represented 7 per cent of the U.S. Army, many of whom never approached a front line. By 1944, it was evident to American's commanders that serious errors of judgement had been made in the mobilization of the nation. The most critical, which would markedly influence the campaign in north-west Europe, was that too little emphasis had been placed upon manning the infantry regiments at the very tip of the American spear. The air corps, the specialist branches, and the service staff had been allowed to cream off too high a proportion of the best-educated, fittest recruits. Infantry rifle companies would be called upon to fight Hilter's Wehrmacht, "the most professionally skilful army of modern times,"[11] with men who were, in all too many cases, the least impressive material America had summoned to the colours.

To some extent, this reflected the natural urge of the United States to make the utmost use of technology in fighting the war. But there was also a contrast between the social attitudes of America's "best and brightest" young men towards military service and that of their counterparts in Europe. In America, a military career has never been honourable in the European manner, outside a few thousand "army families". It has traditionally been the route by which impoverished young men – not least Eisenhower and Bradley – can carve out a career for themselves without advantages of birth. George S. Patton was a rare exception. He himself wrote: "It is an unfortunate and, to me, tragic fact that in our attempts to prevent war, we have taught our people to belittle the heroic qualities of the soldier."[12] It is striking to observe that in the Second World War, privileged young Englishmen still gravitated naturally towards rifle and armoured regiments. Their American counterparts by preference sought out exotic postings in the air corps or OSS, or managerial roles on army or diplomatic staffs. It never became fashionable for young Ivy League Americans to serve as front-line officers. This is not to deny that many did so, and fought with gallantry. But it does suggest that the American army's "teeth" elements were severely blunted because they lacked their proper share of the ablest and fittest officers and men. On a tour with General Eisenhower on 4 April, Commander Butcher recorded in his diary: "I am concerned over the absence of toughness and alertness of young American officers whom I saw on this trip. They are as green as growing corn. How will they act in battle and how will they look in three months time?"[13]

In those weeks, hundreds of thousands of young men of Bradley's assault divisions were asking themselves the same question. Private Lindley Higgins was "dumb enough not to feel the slightest trepidation. We really thought that at any moment the whole Reich was going to collapse. We saw what we had, heard what they didn't have. We really thought that we only had to step off that beach and all the krauts would put up their hands."[14] This was a delusion much more common among formations such as the 4th Division, in which Higgins was a rifleman, than among those which had fought in North Africa and Sicily. A shipping clerk from the Bronx – an uncommonly perceptive one – he went to work on 8 December 1941, listened to President Roosevelt's broadcast to the nation, and walked immediately to the army recruiting office in Whitehall Street. His father was delighted: "He thought the army would straighten me out". Higgins himself expected to be home within a few months. Instead, he spent two years practising assault landings on the American east coast, "spending a lot of time fighting the North African campaign – we kept being told that this or that would happen in the desert." The war seemed very remote from them. They felt unable to relate anything in their own experience to what was taking place in Europe and the Pacific. Even in their final pre-invasion exercises in Devon, they concentrated chiefly on the fun of firing the hayricks with tracer bullets: "We were a singularly callous and unfeeling group of young men." But now they burnt their personal papers according to orders, and speculated about where they were going. They were told that it was to be an inundated area, so Higgins said confidently: "I know geography – it's got to be Holland." Their regimental and battalion commanding officers were relieved a few weeks before the landing. At the final briefing their new CO told them that under no circumstances would they turn back after they left the landing craft. It would be a court martial offence to stop or retreat on the beach. At the assembly area outside Plymouth, as they queued for food, Higgins's friend John Schultz peered at his plate and groaned: "Boy, this is the big one. If they're starting to serve steak, we're in trouble." Higgins tried to grasp the reality of what they were about to do: "Me, Lindley Higgins, from Riverdale in the Bronx, was about to invade France. It was a problem that my mind in its then state of maturity couldn't possibly cope with."

Major Harry Herman, executive officer of the 9th Division's 2nd/39th Infantry, had a far shrewder notion of what they faced than most of the invaders. A graduate of Michigan University, his father had been killed in the First World War, his great-grandfather wounded at Gettysburg. As a student, he had read *Mein Kampf* and been a member of an anti-war group. He was earning $18,000 a year with the prosperous family business in January 1940 when, despite his pleas for a deferment, he became the 21st American to be drafted. Like hundreds of thousands of others, he endured the confusion and hardship which marked the first year of the American army's vast expansion, passed out of officer school top in weapons and tactics, bottom in personal appearance, and was shipped to Ireland with his division in October 1942. In January 1943, Herman shared the American army's bitter humiliation in the Kasserine Pass, running for his life amidst men throwing away their arms and equipment, deployed by commanders "who had no idea how to make dispositions for battle. It was awful – there were no supplies, no water, no officer leadership. But then we refitted. we went back, we did better. In a way, the North African campaign was a blessing to American troops."[15] By the time they went into Sicily, they had learned a great deal – about the need to move the ridge lines, instead of the valleys that they had been taught to use in training,[16] about leading from the front, about controlling venereal disease among the men.

Yet when the 1st and 9th Divisions were brought back from Sicily to prepare for OVERLORD, there was bitter resentment among many officers and men that they should be asked to do it all again. They felt that they had done their share, that it was time to go home and reap the glory, leaving the next battlefield to the millions of other men who had thus far endured nothing. Some officers successfully arranged transfers. "Morale was not high," said Herman. Major Frank Colacicco of the 1st Division's 3rd/18th found the same feelings among his own men: "We felt that we'd done our war, we should go home. We kept reading in the papers about the huge increase in U.S. strength."[17]

Bradley wrote: "Much as I disliked subjecting the 1st to still another landing, I felt that as a commander I had no other choice . . . I felt compelled to employ the best troops I had, to minimize the risks and hoist the odds in our favour in any way that I could."[18] Bradley and other American commanders were acutely conscious of the shortcomings of some American formations, above all of their commanders. Marshall wrote in March about the embarrassment of having been compelled to relieve a succession of generals, including two corps commanders: ". . . we couldn't relieve any more without a serious loss of prestige. What seemed to be lacking in each case was aggressive qualities . . ." As the men of the 9th and 1st – now under the command of the forceful Clarence Huebner – began to train in south-west England, as they absorbed the green replacements to fill up their ranks, "we recovered pretty quickly," in the words of one of their officers.[20] That their participation should have been thought essential to the invasion of Europe engendered a sense of pride: "We thought the outcome of the war depended on the 1st and 9th Divisions," said Harry Herman. "We felt it was inevitable that we had to do this thing. There was no way out." Herman himself had become a successful soldier who no longer looked beyond the next battlefield: "I didn't think the war was ever going to end. I thought that for the rest of our lives, we should be fighting one way or another."[21].

Like most Americans, Technical Sergeant Bill Walsh felt no great animosity towards the Germans – he merely regarded the war as a job to be got over before they could all go home. His principal concern was that the waterproofing on his tank should prove secure enough to get him ashore. A dentist's son from

New Jersey, he had joined the Essex Troop of the local National Guard in 1938. They were a mounted unit and in those days of the Depression, Walsh was among thousands of young men for whom the Guard provided a social life to which they could not otherwise have aspired. He took part in the U.S. Army's last review of mounted cavalry, and as they trotted past to the tune of *Old Grey Mare,* most the men were choking back tears. They were among the first units to ship to Europe, where they converted to tanks and began the long two-year wait before the 102nd Cavalry went into action. Walsh and his crew admitted no great apprehension to each other about D-Day: "The movies always show people talking to each other about their problems and fears before action. We never did."[22]

Corporal Dick Raymond of 3rd Canadian Division was in reality an 18-year-old American, the son of an upstate New York chicken farmer who ran away across the border to join the Canadian army – which had a reputation for not asking many questions – in January 1942, when he was 16, "an underachieving high school drop-out".[23] He was thrown out after a month, but was soon back at Niagara, greeting the recruiting sergeant, a familiar landmark of the place and the period, at the border. To Raymond, who had grown up listening to CBC Radio from Toronto, Canada sounded exciting. The Canadian army seemed full of Americans. When he was sworn in with a detail of other new recruits, they were told that Americans could keep their hands by their sides when the moment came for the oath to the King. Most of the men in the room did so. There were deserters and rejects from the American army, one or two curious fragments of human flotsam from the Spanish Civil War, and the first American negro Raymond had known, a huge, clever man, rumoured to be a lawyer from West Virginia. The young New Yorker found the army tough. When he was foolish enough to reveal that he had some money, it was quickly beaten out of him. He learned to drink and to cheat with some thoroughness. He became cynical about the manner in which the volunteer Canadian forces cleared the military prisons and hospitals in their desperate struggle to fill the ranks before the invasion. He retained a low opinion of most of the officers corps. But he loved their regimental traditions, the pipes and kilts of the Canadian Scottish units. And for all their lack of discipline, he came to admire immensely their behaviour on the battlefield.

In 1927, a 22-year-old Czech named Frank Svboda won a

scholarship to a college in Iowa, where he took a master's degree in theology, was ordained. and subsequently became a presbyterian minister among the Czech community in New York. In 1943, he volunteered to become an army chaplain – he had already done infantry training with the Czech army – and was sent for three months to the chaplain's school at Harvard. He found himself with a Jewish rabbi in the next bunk and a Catholic priest in the one below: the latter remarked cheerfully that he had never expected to find himself bedding down with heretics. Then he was posted to the 79th Division in Arizona and, in March 1944, came with them to England. They were awed by the blitzed streets of Liverpool as they marched through, and touched by the kindness of the local Cheshire families who invited so many men to tea each Sunday afternoon, despite their own desperate shortage of rations. Svboda's invasion equipment comprised a bible and a portable communion set. As a European he understood, in a way that his unblooded division did not, that the Germans would be very difficult to defeat. In the big tent that he used as a chapel before they sailed for France, he listened to men's problems – "mostly about their wives" – and held services for soldiers who filed in carrying their rifles and helmets: "They were going into battle as people go to church, with a sense of reverence. There was no rowdiness or drunkenness."[24]

It was not remarkable that the lofty sentiments about D-Day were chiefly expressed by the senior commanders. "I don't have to tell you what a big show this is, or how important," the commander of the American Western Naval Task Force, Rear-Admiral Alan Kirk, wrote to a friend in Washington on 10 March: "If this is successful the war is won, if this fails it may go on for years. Perhaps too it will settle whether we or Russia dominate the world for a while."[25] Colonel Paddy Flint, the colourful old commander of the 9th Division's 39th Infantry, wrote in a much more homespun spirit to the wife or mother of every officer under his command before D-Day. "We are sort of putting our affairs in order," he said. "Maybe it is just the spring housecleaning that we used to do under Mother's direction when I was a little boy at home. Anyway, I know you will understand. I just wanted to tell you how much we think of your son Harry in the Regiment . . ."[26]

At St Paul's School on 15 May, Montgomery presented the OVERLORD plan for the last time before the senior officers of the Allied armies, crowded on wooden benches behind the single row of chairs at the front for the King, Churchill, Smuts and Brooke. One of the greatest throngs of commanders in history was gathered in the hall for the briefing: Bradley, whom the British respected and would come to respect more as one of the Americans "who really understood the battle"; General J. Lawton Collins of VII Corps – the nervous, explosive, ambitious "Lightning Joe" who had made his reputation commanding a division on Guadalcanal; Gerow of V Corps, less impressive and untried in action; Corlett of XIX Corps; Middleton of VIII Corps. The British showed consistent concern in north-west Europe about the quality of American command and staffwork at corps and division level. Some senior Americans agreed later that this criticism had some force. There were simply not enough thoroughly trained staff officers to go round their vastly expanded army. But there were also, at St Paul's, some outstanding American divisional commanders – Huebner of 1st Division, Barton of the 4th, Eddy of the 9th.

Sir Miles Dempsey, commanding the British Second Army, was a retiring figure almost unknown to the British public, and said later to have been treated more like a corps than an army commander by Montgomery. But Dempsey was a great professional, a brilliant judge of ground, an utterly reliable agent for the execution of his Commander-in-Chief's wishes. Crocker of 1 Corps was a tough, dependable commander who never caused Montgomery unease in Normandy – unlike Bucknall of XXX Corps, about whom Brooke always had doubts, and who was destined for dismissal. Crerar, who would command the Canadian army when it followed the assault formations into the line, was considered an unimaginative, stolid administrator; Montgomery had tried hard to dispense with him, but political imperatives were too strong. Crerar's senior corps commander, Guy Simonds, was to prove one of the outstanding leaders of the campaign – a dour, direct, clever gunner upon whom Montgomery increasingly relied. For the rest, there were two verterans of the desert, O'Connor of VIII Corps and Ritchie of XII. At divisional level, with brilliant exceptions such as Roberts of 11th Armoured, the British team could better be described as solid than inspired. There were already doubts about 7th Armoured's commander, Major-General W. R. J. "Bobby" Erskine, who had been quite unexpectedly plucked from a staff job to take over the division, and was widely considered to have been promoted above his ceiling. Erskine loved and admired the men of his formation deeply, and here lay the root of much trouble in Normandy: he was too ready to accept the word of his subordinates that they had done all that could be expected of them. He was not a man to drive his command. But in war, as in all human endeavours, there are never sufficient men of a calibre perfectly suited to the demands of the hour. The shortcomings of the Allied command team from OVERLORD were mirrored by those of the Germans on the far shore.

Montgomery's presentation on 15 May, like his earlier briefing on 7 April, was acknowledged even by his critics as a brilliant performance: a display of grip, confidence, absolute mastery of the plan. He had already conducted a long session – Exercise THUNDERCLAP – with his ground force officers before the huge relief model of the battlefield, at which he threw out situations and possible setbacks to test their responses. It was Montgomery's misfortune that his very mastery of advance planning became a source of scepticism to his enemies, following the inevitable imperfections of reality on the battlefield. Throughout the Normandy campaign, Churchill never erased from his memory a paper of Montgomery's of which he received a copy, stressing the need for rapid armoured penetrations after the landings: ". . . I am prepared to accept almost any risk in order to carry out these tactics. I would risk even the total loss of the armoured brigade groups . . . the delay they would cause to the enemy before they could be destroyed would be quite enough to give us time to get our main bodies well ashore and re-organized for strong offensive action."[27] Likewise, Bradley did not forget Montgomery's remarks to him at St Paul's about the prospect of tanks reaching Falaise on D-Day "to knock about a bit down there".[28] Montgomery would have been entirely justified in saying privately to Bradley and Dempsey – above all to Churchill – that whatever exhortations he gave the troops, he did not expect deep penetrations on D-Day from inexperienced troops recovering their land legs. But he did not do so. And thus he paid a price after the event, when the hopes that he had expressed both publicly and privately, to officers both high and low, were disappointed.

In the last weeks before D-Day, the principal dissension within the Allied high command concerned not OVERLORD, but the projected invasion of southern France, ANVIL, to which the Americans were firmly committed and the British bitterly opposed, because this would certainly cripple operations in Italy. Shipping difficulties forced the postponement of ANVIL from a landing simultaneous with OVERLORD to a secondary operation ten weeks later, and the arguments between London and Washington continued until the last days before its launching. This became the first major decision of the war over which the Americans adamantly refused to bow to British pressure, and went their own way. It was an augury of other painful blows to British confidence and pride which lay ahead.

Discussion of the airborne landings in support of OVERLORD was complicated by the arrival of a delegation of staff officers direct from Marshall, to project the American Chief of Staff's strong view that, having created large and expensive airborne forces, the Allies should employ them for an ambitious envelopment plan. Marshall proposed that they should be dropped near Evreux in the "Orleans Gap" to hold a perimeter and create a major strategic threat in the German rear.[29] Eisenhower was obliged to point out painstakingly to Washington the inability of paratroops to resist armoured forces, their absolute immobility once on the ground, and the difficulties of supplying them with ammunition and heavy weapons.

More disturbingly, German reinforcement of the western Cotentin compelled Bradley to reconsider his existing plan for the American airborne drop on his flank. The two divisions were now to land on the eastern side of the peninsula only. Then it was Leigh-Mallory's turn to create difficulties. In the last days before 6 June, the airman became passionately imbued with the conviction that the American drop was doomed to disaster, with huge casualties in men and aircraft; he impressed this view upon Eisenhower. The Supreme Commander at last overruled him. But the Englishman had added to Eisenhower's huge anxieties and responsibilities at a critical moment, and further diminished confidence in his own nerve and judgement.

It was a remarkable tribute to the power of the image-builders that even among the Americans, in those last weeks before D-Day, nothing did more to boost the confidence of the men of the invasion armies than Montgomery's personal visits. From mid-May until June, he devoted his energies almost entirely to inspecting the troops under his command, whom he would never again have the opportunity to see in such numbers. The measured walk down the ranks; the piercing stare into men's eyes; the order to break ranks and gather around the general on the bonnet of the jeep; the sharp, brittle address – all were studiedly theatrical, yet defy the cynicism of history. "Even Eisenhower with all his engaging ease could never stir American troops to the rapture with which Monty was welcomed by his," wrote Bradley. "Among those men, the legend of Montgomery had become an imperishable fact."[30] Montgomery told them that the enemy had many divisions, but most of these were weak and understrength: "Everything is in the shopwindow. There is nothing 'in the kitty'."[31] He told Americans that "as a British general, I regard it as an honour to serve under American command; General Eisenhower is captain of the team and I am proud to serve under him." Lieutenant Philip Riesler and 12,000 other men of the U.S. 2nd Armored Division gathered to hear Montgomery on the football field at Tidworth camp in Hampshire. "Take off your helmets!" he ordered, and off came every helmet except that of Maurice Rose, beside the jeep. "You, too, general," said Montgomery. He paused and gazed slowly, in silence, round the great mass of men. At last he said: "All right, put them back on. Now next time I see you, I shall know you." It was brilliant stage-management.

There was less enthusiasm from the British government for Montgomery's speeches to factory-workers and railwaymen, which were also a feature of his activities at this time. These smacked too much of the national warlord, arousing the deepest instinctive fears in politicians' hearts. When he drew up a two-page outline, complete with hymns and prayers, for a proposed national service of dedication at Westminster Abbey before the invasion, the plan was speedily squashed. Montgomery would sail for France leaving behind many men who admired his skill and application in bringing the invasion to reality. Not one of his British or American critics could afterwards deny the importance of his contribution to the creation of OVERLORD; no other Allied general could have accomplished so much. But he also left behind a deep reservoir of animosity and bitterness. Morgan, who had laboured so hard and long as COSSAC, would never forgive Montgomery for ruthlessly consigning him to the backwaters of the war after his own arrival in England. Scores of other senior officers who had not belonged to Montgomery's "desert family" were also discarded – some for good reasons, others suffering merely for the misfortune of being unknown to the new Commander-in-Chief. Apart from these, there was an abundance of staff officers at Eisenhower's headquarters ready to poison the ear of the Supreme Commander towards Montgomery. As long as the Englishman remained victorious, he was invulnerable. But should the group campaign falter under his direction, he had provided many powerful hostages to fortune.

Defenders

"If they attack in the west," said Adolf Hitler in December 1943, "that attack will decide the war."[1] Whatever the shortcomings of the Atlantic Wall, Hitler's proclaimed impatience for the Allied invasion was by no means bluff. His armies in Russia were being remorselessly pushed back and destroyed; between July 1943 and May 1944 alone, they lost 41 divisions in the east. Their total manpower had fallen from over three million in July 1943 to 2.6 million in December. Thereafter, between March and May 1944, they suffered a further 341,950 casualties, and lost an additional 150,000 men in the aftermath of the Allied landings in Italy. Germany's sole conceivable chance of escaping catastrophe now lay in the destruction of OVERLORD. "Our only hope is that they come where we can use the army upon them," said General von Thoma to a comrade in captivity.[2] If the Allies could be thrown back into the sea, it was inconceivable that they should mount a new assault for years, if ever. Almost the entire strength of the German army in north-west Europe, 59 divisions, could be transferred east for a fight to the finish against the Russians. Within the year, secret weapons and jet aircraft should be available in quantity. Thereafter, Hitler reasoned, anything was possible. If it was a sketchy scenario, it was not an impossible one – granted only that the Allies could be denied a foothold in France.

In January 1944, Jodl toured the Channel coast and reported grimly on the state of its defences.[3] The perpetual bleeding of manpower from west to east had crippled every division. In the Channel Islands, 319th Division was reduced to 30 per cent of its establishment. Re-equipment was causing chaos – the artillery was armed with 21 types of gun: French, Russian and Czech. Commanders complained that they were being denied time to carry out essential training because their men were continuously employed on building fortifications. The Germans were as preoccupied as the Allies with the need to maintain air superiority over the invasion coast, yet Jodl recognized that ". . . we must not accept battle with the enemy air force".[4] The hapless Commander-in-Chief, von Rundstedt, was never consulted about what forces he deemed necessary to defeat an invasion – he was merely informed of what was to arrive. The bulk of his army was made up of the over-age and medically unfit, convalescents from the east, and an entirely unreliable rabble of Polish, Russian and Italian defectors and forced labourers. Even the majority of the first-line divisions which began to move into France in the spring of 1944, in accordance with Hitler's Directive 51 for the strengthening of the western defences, were formations shattered in the east, which would need massive reinforcement and re-equipment if they were ever to regain their old fighting power. However well Hitler recognized the need to defend against invasion, he was the victim of a remorseless imperative that demanded men and tanks to fight against the present menace in the east, rather than the prospective threat in the west.

If there was a euphoric belief among the western Allies after their victory that they had monopolized the attention and best efforts of Nazi Germany, the figures belie this. In January 1944, Hitler deployed 179 divisions in the east, 26 in south-east Europe, 22 in Italy, 16 in Scandinavia, and 53 in France and the Low Countries. By 6 June, there were 59 in France and the Low Countries – 41 of these north of the Loire – 28 in Italy, but still 165 in the east. There were 24 Panzer divisions in the east and eight elsewhere in January, compared with proportions of 18 to 15 by June. It remains astounding that after three years of devastating losses in the east and the relentless bombing of Hitler's industries, Germany could still produce and equip an army in the west capable of causing the gravest difficulties to the best that Britain and America could throw into the war. "The possibility of Hitler's gaining a victory in France cannot be excluded," wrote Brooke gloomily on 25 January. "The hazards of battle are very great."[5]

Germany's critical weakness on the Channel coast in the spring of 1944 was her blindness. The Luftwaffe had lost not only its strength, but its will. Despite the difficulties posed by Allied command of the air, some measure of air reconnaissance might yet have been possible given real determination by the German airmen. But there was no sign that they recognized the cost of their failure, or of the weakness of their photographic interpreters beside those of the Allies. "That the Luftwaffe did not carry out minimal reconnaissance of the east coast must rank as a miracle of the same dimensions as the destruction of the Armada in 1588," the historian of Allied deception planning has written.[6] The British and Americans were quick to understand the importance of impeding German weather forecasting, and seized enemy stations in Iceland, Greenland, Sptizbergen and Jan Mayen island – actions that were of decisive importance on D-Day.[7] It would have been impossible for an operation of the magnitude of OVERLORD to have sustained its extraordinary level of security had it not been launched from a sealed island. The brilliant British counter-intelligence operations had not only deprived Germany of authentic agents in Britain, but also placed the agents in whom she trusted under the control of the Allied deception planners. The Americans, surprisingly, placed little faith in deception, and showed limited interest in FORTITUDE. Yet it was the Germans' utter uncertainty about where the Allies would land that contributed decisively to their debacle in June.

There has been recent speculation[8] about the possible role of Admiral Canaris himself in Allied deception plans for D-Day. This was prompted by new discussion of the links between the British Secret Intelligence Service and a Polish woman contact of the Abwehr chief. It has been suggested that Canaris was either working actively for British Intelligence, or was at least instrumental in persuading Hitler that the Allies would land in the Pas de Calais. The evidence is overwhelmingly against either of these remarkable notions. Canaris' loyalties wavered, and he certainly leaked some useful information which reached the Allies through the Polish contact; but there is no evidence whatever that he was personally exploited by the British, or that he was privy to the fact that every Abwehr agent in Britain was in the hands of MI5.

The worst charge thus far made against the authors of the British official history of wartime intelligence is dullness. It has not been suggested that they have concealed important elements of the truth, and they have had access to all the relevant documents. They declared flatly in their second volume, published in 1981, that after 1940 the Secret Service possessed no agents whatever in Germany. Professor Hinsley, the senior historian, confirms[9] that there is still no evidence of Canaris' complicity in Allied deception plans, which relied principally on the transmission of false information through Abwehr agents in Britain controlled by MI5. By the spring of 1944, Canaris was discredited in the eyes of Hitler and OKW. In any event, for the admiral or his associates consciously to have assisted Allied deception plans, they would have needed to know the truth about Allied intentions. It is unthinkable that these could have been revealed to them. The British were successfully employing all manner of conduits to channel false information to the Germans without any need of Canaris' direct assistance. The balance of probability remains heavily in favour of the view that Hitler's intelligence departments were incompetent, not treacherous, in their assessments of Allied plans in 1944. No significant historian of the period believes otherwise, and it is only because some recent newspaper reports have insistently suggested Canaris' active involvement in the pre–D-Day deception that it becomes necessary to contradict this delusion at such length.

Many narratives of D-Day have focussed upon the German failure to heed warnings that the invasion was imminent.[10] Yet in truth, while these might have enabled more high commanders to be at their posts when the Allies landed, knowledge of *when* would have been of only the most limited strategic value as long as they remained ignorant of *where*. The confusion of German thinking in the spring of 1944 was astonishing. Hitler's instinct continued to insist that the Allies would come in Normandy. But with uncharacteristic forbearance, he did not pursue his hunch to the point of demanding special emphasis upon Normandy's defences. On 29 April, one report suggested that the Allies were concentrating in western rather than eastern England, but on 15 May "a good Abwehr source" reported the 79th and 83rd U.S. Divisions in Yorkshire and Norfolk, and XX U.S. Corps and 4th Armored around Bury St Edmunds. A report from von Rundstedt's headquarters on 21 May anticipated that the Allies would mount several simultaneous assaults, and use new weapons, including gas – this, of course, was a mirror image of the fear of the invaders. Lieutenant-Colonel Roger Michel of Rommel's intelligence staff predicted that the Allies would land 35 divisions, but Hitler's staff were studying likely figures of 85 or 90 divisions, which was not implausible if America had mobilized the same proportion of manpower for her fighting formations as Germany. Some Allied deception schemes made no impression on the Germans – for instance, the dispatch of an army pay corps lieutenant and former actor to impersonate Montgomery on a tour of the Mediterranean, and the creation of a mythical army in Scotland for the invasion of Norway. But a

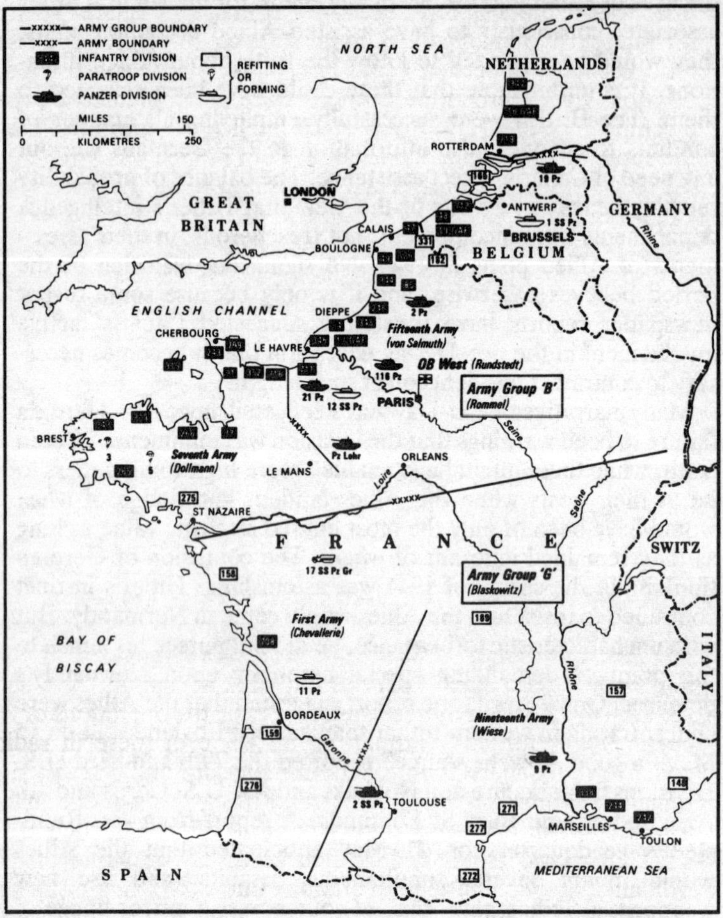

The Disposition of German Forces on D-Day

climate of uncertainty had been masterfully created, which would decisively influence German behaviour until deep into July. Its success reflected poorly both on Hitler's intelligence departments and on the enfeebled self-confidence of his commanders.

Rommel's achievement in galvanizing the building of coastal defences in the spring of 1944 was very real. But he shared the high command's indecision and lack of grip in allowing resources to be wasted building fortifications in all manner of places where it was absurd to imagine that an invasion could occur. All along the 3,000 miles of occupied coastline, bunkers were constructed, positions dug. German perceptions were much blunted by the incompetence of FHW, the western intelligence arm of OKW, the supreme command. While the eastern branch was brilliantly run by Reinhard Gehlen, the western was in the hands of Colonel Baron Alexis von Roenne. Roenne had built his reputation on a confident prediction in 1939 that the French and British armies would not attack in the west while Germany was disposing of Poland, and on his advocacy of the great Sedan thrust in May 1940. But in 1944, he was wrong on almost every vital intelligence issue. Although he never took the bait of an Allied threat to Norway, he was deceived by FORTITUDE's fantasy invasion force for the Pas de Calais. The Allies had placed General Sir Andrew Thorne in command of a fictitious British Fourth Army in Scotland, with wireless traffic to simulate a II Corps based around Stirling and a VII Corps around Dundee. But the central role in the deception operation was that of Patton, commanding the fantasy 1st U.S. Army Group in south-east England, its order of battle greater even than 21st Army Group, with a massive array of dummy landing craft, vehicles, camps and wireless communications provided by the American 3103rd Signals Service Battalion in support. MI5 and the British "XX Committee" were directing the operations of 20 captured or "turned" German agents, nine of these in radio contact with Canaris' controllers in Germany or Portugal, the remainder communicating by secret writing through the mail. The scepticism of many senior American officers about FORTITUDE was compounded by their necessary ignorance of the brilliant "XX Committee" operation. But the leading historian of wartime deception has written of "the strange reluctance among the Americans to accept that it was part of modern warfare – all the more strange since the Japanese attack on Pearl Harbor was a successful deceptive operation of the greatest magnitude."[11] Colonel W. A. Harris, the Americans' principal deception expert, was converted to belief in the value of FORTITUDE only after its success. But it is only just to concede that before the triumph of June 1944, Allied deception operations in Europe had been notably less successful than those in the Middle East. In 1943, some elaborate deceptions had been created to delude the enemy about Allied intentions, which caused OKW to move not a single man or tank.

In the wake of Germany's defeat, some bitter German commanders argued that Colonel von Roenne, one of the anti-Hitler plotters, deliberately misled them about Allied intentions. Yet it is too simplistic merely to compare the success of Allied intelligence with the failure of that of Germany, and seek conspiratorial explanations. The Allies' success depended overwhelmingly upon intelligence provided by Ultra, the kind of inspired good fortune that comes to a warring nation seldom in a century. The record of the British Secret Intelligence Service in gaining useful information about Germany from agents was lamentable. For all the nonsense written in recent years about the American wartime OSS and its chief William Donovan, their real profits from agent networks were negligible by comparison with those from decrypts. If the Allies' huge achievement in breaking the Enigma and the Japanese Magic ciphers is set aside, their agent-dependent intelligence operations appear unimpressive. There is no decisive evidence one way or the other about whether the anti-Hitler conspirators deliberately distorted German intelligence analysis. But it remains easier to believe that OKW's men were simply wrong.

Hitler's manic suspicion of his generals and his obsession with dividing authority among them to deny overall power to any one, made for a cumbersome command structure in France. In Paris, the dour, cynical, unbending von Rundstedt presided as Commander-in-Chief. "By this time his arteries were hardening," said Brigadier Williams,[12] Montgomery's principal analyst of the German army, "but they were pretty formidable arteries." At Army Group B's headquarters at La Roche Guyon, Erwin Rommel was to be responsible for directing the battle against the invaders. Yet Rommel was denied direct control of the panzer divisions of OKW reserve, and Hitler was correct in believing that his field-marshal's ability to dominate the battlefield was now deeply flawed by doubt that victory was even possible. Always highly strung, mercurial, that spring Rommel wavered between outbursts of buoyant confidence and deep depression. "If I were doing the invasion," he said laconically to his staff one morning, "I should be at the Rhine in fourteen days."[13] His driving energy was undiminished. His ability to spend hours racing from unit to unit along the coast, designing positions, hastening the erection of beach defences and glider obstacles – "Rommel's asparagus" – still aroused the wonder of his staff. But he was no longer the Desert Fox, the supremely confident Panzer leader of 1941–42. Too many defeats had intervened. Now under his command in northern France were the coastal divisions of Seventh Army in Normandy and Fifteenth Army in the Pas de Calais, together with Geyr von Schweppenburg's Panzer Group West. But while the Allies deliberated about how far Hitler would allow his generals to fight the battle in their own fashion, the Führer had already placed fatal constraints upon them. Rommel was not permitted to deploy the panzer divisions on the coast – a disposition he believed vital in view of the Allied air threat to any movement of forces – and of his armour, only 21st Panzer stood within immediate reach of the beaches, south of Caen. Had Rommel's request to place a second panzer division near St Lo been granted, the consequences for the American landings on D-Day would have been incalculable, conceivably decisive. If the Allies gained a foothold, Rommel's preference was to withdraw to a river line to hold them. Hitler's absolute determination to yield no ground precluded this. Everything would hinge upon the German's ability to halt the Allies upon the beaches. If they failed in this, the generals understood perfectly that their only choice lay between skilful retreat and inexorable destruction.

The men of the German army in France in June 1944 were sustained by a compound of fatalism and blind faith. Above all, perhaps, for most there was a sense of unreality, a comforting impossibility about the notion that their stretch of windswept dunes, their familiar billets and battery positions, should be chosen above all others by the Allies to become one of the great battlefields of history. "It wasn't in our interests to think too much about our feelings," a staff officer of 21st Panzer Division, Captain Eberhard Wagemann, said drily. "We were conscious that neither our men nor our tanks were good enough." The troops of the Division had little confidence in its commander, General Feuchtinger; Rommel still thought well of him, but this opinion was rapidly to change. 21st Panzer retained a core of veterans from its great days in Africa, but had been made up to strength with drafts of very moderate quality, and was equipped with substantial quantities of French and locally-modified equipment. Yet this division, deployed around Caen, would be the first German armoured formation to sustain the shock of the Allied landings.

"We no longer expected total victory," said Sergeant Helmut Gunther of 17th SS Panzergrenadiers, "but we still felt an absolute sense of loyalty. In Russia we had fought men against men. We knew that in Normandy it would be men against machines."[14] A bank trainee before the war, Gunther volunteered in September 1939 at the age of 20, fought across Europe until he was evacuated with frostbite before Moscow, and later served as an infantry instructor before being posted to the Panzergrenadiers in January 1944. Now, as a platoon commander in the reconnaissance battalion, he was training the big draft of 18-year-olds which had reached the unit, many of them conscripts.

One May morning, Rommel visited the 1716th Artillery Regiment in their positions around Ouistreham. He told the assembled circle of battery officers: "If they come, they'll come here."[15] Lieutenant Rudolf Schaaf did not really believe him. Twice wounded in the leg in Russia, Schaaf was one of many officers and men posted to France because they were unfit for further duty in the east – he walked with a pronounced limp. He and most of his comrades were enjoying their time in France, with plenty to eat and drink, all of it cheap. Above all, they were thankful to be out of the east. "The soldiers did as little work as possible," he said, "and we were too busy putting up wire and planting 'Rommel's asparagus' to have much time for training."[16] Private Heinz Walz, a jovial Swabian shopkeeper serving as a signaller with the 266th Artillery in the eastern Cotentin, was dismayed to hear at the beginning of June that there was to be yet another comb-out of his unit for men fit to be transferred to the eastern front. He had already served in Russia with a labour unit, and knew that he would be an obvious candidate for posting. The abrupt arrival of the Allies narrowly saved him from that.

There was a wide gulf between the men of the coastal divisions – at best cynical about their role, at worst openly defeatist – and those of the crack units. Sergeant Hans Stober of 17th SS Panzergrenadiers, a 22-year-old veteran of the East, was sent on an anti-gas course to St Lô, where he found himself alongside men of Seventh Army. The coastal troops distanced themselves from the likes of Stober, although contrary to myth there was no general animosity between soldiers of the SS and the Wehrmacht. The Russians, especially, maintained a stolid silence. Stober was amused to meet one man whom he himself had taken prisoner in 1941. A farmer's son from east Prussia, the sergeant understood that the invasion would be the decisive battle of the war. Like many men on both sides of the Channel, he found that the greatest strain was the interminable waiting for the blow to fall.

Lieutenant Walter Kruger, a signals officer with 12th SS Panzer, was an SS man in the classic mould, asserting his "absolute confidence in victory from first to last".[17] The troops of this, the Hitler Youth division, were to prove the most determined and fanatical opponents facing the Allied armies. "They had received a proper training in the Hitler Youth," said Kruger proudly. "They had a sense of order, discipline. They knew how to sing!" They had practised repeatedly the advance from their camps near Evreux to the Normandy coast. Thinking nothing of the air threat, they confidently expected to be engaged within seven hours of a movement order. Their principal problem was the lack of fuel, which hampered training, and caused such petty restrictions as the divisional mail collection being conducted by horse and cart.

In the last week of May, Kruger was one of 60 officers from his division who found themselves cursorily summoned to divisional headquarters, apprehensive about the cause. To their astonishment, they arrived to find all their wives gathered, brought up from Germany on the orders of General Fritz Witt, their commander. "Since there is going to be no leave for anybody from now on," said Witt, "you can all go to Paris for two days and then say goodbye at the Gare de l'Est." Kruger told his wife Martha that it was obvious that they were "for it". He gave her all his personal possessions to take home to Germany. "They told us that the first five days would be critical. If we could not defeat the landings by then, it would be impossible."

Much depended upon the performance of 12th SS Panzer and the other nine armoured divisions in France. General Guderian, Inspector-General of Armoured Forces, wrote: "All hopes of successful defence were based upon these."[18] Lieutenant-Colonel Kurt Kauffmann, Operations Officer of Panzer Lehr, the finest tank formation in the Wehrmacht, created from the demonstration units of the armoured corps, believed that the invasion could be defeated. Despite Panzer Lehr's lack of opportunity to exercise as a formation, 75 per cent of its men were veterans and it was superbly equipped. Kauffmann's chief worry concerned the performance of its commander, General Fritz

Bayerlein: "He was a very good soldier, but he was worn out. In Normandy he showed himself nervous and weak."[19]

Through those last weeks before 6 June, the men of the coastal units dutifully laid yet more concrete and field telephone wires, pottered between the minefields carrying their little cans of milk from the local farms, hung their washing to dry on the edge of the bunkers, and cherished their hopes that the Tommies and the Americans might come somewhere else. If high morale means the motivation to give everything for a cause or an objective, few of them possessed it. Their senior officers were haunted by the knowledge that they commanded forces inadequate for the task they might face. The highest hope of most of their men was to survive the war. For few was it to be fulfilled.

The mobile formations behind the coast exercised with varying degrees of intensity, their movements watched with deep apprehension by Allied intelligence. The Germans were carrying out their own deception operations, circulating maps showing false positions for their formations through such sources as the Japanese Ambassador to Vichy. In the face of Ultra and incessant reconnaissance, they enjoyed little success. Almost every German formation was accurately plotted on Allied maps. There were only a handful of critical uncertainties. Brigadier Williams suspected that the 352nd Division had been moved forward to the area below the elbow of the American beaches, although the evidence that he circulated proved too uncertain to disturb the American planners. When a maze of tank tracks was photographed in the coastal area of Caen, there were acute fears that 21st Panzer had been moved forward within immediate range of the beaches. In reality, after an exercise, the armour withdrew to its leaguers between Caen and Falaise.

On the afternoon of 5 June, Corporal Werner Kortenhaus, a wireless operator in the division's Panzer Regiment, took his crew's laundry to the local Frenchwoman who had been doing their washing for weeks. Sergeant Heinz Hickmann of the Luftwaffe Parachute Division, stationed outside Nevers, left his base for a relaxed evening in the local army canteen. Colonel Kauffmann of Panzer Lehr was on honeymoon near Stuttgart. Captain Wagemann of 21st Panzer was standing in as duty officer at headquarters in the absence of the division's senior staff officer in Paris, and of the divisional commander on what was believed to be private business with a female friend. Most of

Seventh Army's senior officers were attending war games in Rennes. Sepp Dietrich of 1st SS Panzer Corps was in Brussels. And Rommel had retired to Germany to celebrate his wife's birthday and to importune Hitler for a more realistic attitude to the defence of the Atlantic Wall.

3 To the far shore

The overture

Over the last few days of May and the first of June, vast columns of men and vehicles began to stream south into the assembly areas – the "sausages", as they were known, because of their shapes on the map – where the invaders were briefed and equipped before being loaded aboard the fleet. The trucks and tanks rolled through towns and villages that, to the disappointment of some, paid little heed to their passing, so accustomed had the inhabitants become to mass military movements. Although the coastal areas had supposedly been sealed off to all but local residents, in reality so many exemptions had been granted for weddings, funerals and compassionate cases that the routine of life was very little changed.

Whole divisions of the follow-up waves had been temporarily transferred from training to man the assembly areas, to feed and cosset the assault forces to the utmost extent that the circumstances allowed. The men, crowded into the tiered bunks in the huge tented camps, were issued with seasickness pills and lifejackets, new gas-protective battledress and ODs – which everybody detested because of their extra weight and smell. Each soldier was given a leaflet about getting on with French civilians which urged him to say nothing about 1940 and not to buy up everything in sight at extravagant prices: "Thanks to jokes about 'Gay Paree' etc., there is a fairly widespread belief that the French are a gay, frivolous people with no morals and few convictions. This is especially not true at the present time." More pragmatically, in the "sausages" men were issued with their ammunition and grenades, satchel and pole charges. They worked obsessively to the very last minute upon the waterproofing of their vehicles, conscious of the horror of stalling with a flooded engine under fire in the surf. The plethora of food, fruit and American cigarettes that was thrust upon them made

LAC Norman Phillips of the RAF advance party for Omaha feel "as if we were being fattened like Christmas turkeys". Despite the stringent security precautions which kept the men confined once they had entered the assembly areas, many young British soldiers slipped under the wire for a last glimpse of the pub, the village or their own families. Corporal "Topper" Brown of 5th RTR escaped from his camp near Felixstowe, stripped the unit flashes off his battledress, and travelled all the way home to Tonbridge in Kent.

The tannoy systems in the camps were seldom silent by day or night as groups of men were mustered, loaded into trucks, and driven through meticulously signposted streets to numbered docks where they joined their transports. The concentration and loading operations rank high among the staff achievements of OVERLORD. For once there was little need to motivate men to attend to their tasks: they understood that their lives depended on doing so. Dock officers later commented adversely upon the casual behaviour of the follow-up waves in contrast to that of the troops who embarked for D-Day.

Aboard the ships, each man sought to create his tiny island of privacy amid the mass of humanity crowded below decks. Officers struggled with last-minute loading problems. Lieutenant-Colonel Robin Hastings of the 6th Green Howards was enraged when an officious trade union official counted the lifeboats on his battalion's transport, declared that there were insufficient, and insisted that one vital landing craft should be left behind to make room for an extra lifeboat. The unit's chaplain, Captain Henry Lovegrove, conducted a service from the ship's bridge which men crowded onto the foc'sle to hear. Lovegrove was uncommonly respected as a padre, but he had lost some credibility during a rehearsal at sea off Hayling Island several weeks earlier, when he took as his text for morning service "The hour is now come . . .", which many men took to mean that the padre had been chosen to break it to them that they were on their way to France. In the vast anchorages off the south coast in the first days of June, many ships looked curiously unmilitary, with sailors' drying laundry draped along the rails and strung among the upperworks. A REME driver, passionately proud of his vehicle, expostulated furiously with an East End crane driver swinging his workshop's trucks into the hold of a transport, crushing wings and fenders against the hatch. "You'll be f---ing lucky if that's the worst that happens to your lot over there!" said the docker succinctly, continuing as before.

One of Montgomery's few undoubted errors of judgement during the mounting of OVERLORD was his support for a landing on 5 June despite the adverse weather forecast. Given the difficulties much less severe weather caused on the 6th, there is little doubt that a landing on the previous day would have found itself in deep trouble. For all the scorn that Montgomery later heaped upon Eisenhower's qualities as a military commander, at no single period did the Supreme Commander distinguish himself more than by his judgement and decision during the D-Day launching conferences of 3–4 June. Having unhesitatingly overridden Montgomery to postpone for the 5th, at 9.45 p.m. on the 4th Eisenhower equally firmly brushed aside Leigh-Mallory and ignored Tedder's uncertainty to confirm the decision to go for the 6th: "I'm quite positive we must give the order," he said, "I don't like it, but there it is . . . I don't see how we can possibly do anything else."[1]

The postponement much increased the mental strain and physical pressure on the men crowded in the ships. They played cards incessantly, chatted quietly, in many cases simply lay silent on their bunks, gazing up at the bulkheads. Private James Gimbert and a cluster of other RAOC men of 50th Division brewed up on a little primus stove perched atop the vast stack of ammunition cases loaded on their LST. Brigadier-General Norman "Dutch" Cota assembled his staff of the advanced headquarters group of 29th Division, of which he was deputy commander, in the aft wardroom of the U.S.S. *Carroll*. An officer of legendary forcefulness, somewhat old for his rank at 51, Cota could claim exceptional expertise in amphibious operations. He had taken part in the TORCH landings and subsequently served with Lord Mountbatten's Combined Operations HQ. Now, he addressed his team for the last time:

> This is different from any other exercises that you've had so far. The little discrepancies that we tried to correct on Slapton Sands are going to be magnified and are going to give way to incidents that you might at first view as chaotic. The air and naval bombardment are reassuring. But you're going to find confusion. The landing craft aren't going in on schedule, and people are going to be landed in the wrong place. Some won't be landed at all. The enemy will try, and will have some success, in preventing our gaining "lodgement". But we must improvise, carry on, not lose our heads.[2]

Cota and his men were to land on Omaha. On all the ships, officers and NCOs pored over the maps and photographs of their landing areas that they had at last been ordered to strip from the sealed packages: it remains one of the minor miracles of OVERLORD that although hundreds of men and women had been involved in making and printing them, there was no security leak. On every ship, some or most passengers were seasick. Apart from the assault troops, there was an extraordinary ragbag of men from all manner of units aboard the invasion fleet. On many of the transports crewed by the merchant navy, there were spcially-trained civilian aircraft recognition teams from the Royal Observer Corps. The Sicilian landings had been marred by the alarming quantity of Allied aircraft shot down by reckless ships' gun crews. Now, at the AA positions, men stood in their helmets and flash capes drinking interminable mugs of "kye" – cocoa – and peering out fascinated at the shadowy shapes of the great fleet around them in the darkness. While the soldiers below were more sombrely preoccupied by the task that awaited them on the morrow, most of the sailors felt a strong, conscious sense of pride that they were taking part in the greatest amphibious operation of all time.

One of the most curious spectators of the great invasion fleet's movement to France was an airman named Eric Crofts, seated in a caravan mounted on a turntable on a clifftop in south Devon. Crofts manned one of the RAF's centimetric radar posts, and all spring he and his colleagues had intently scanned the progress of the invasion rehearsals on their screen. Now he arrived on watch a little before midnight on 5 June to find the duty crew clustered round the set: "Large convoys of ships were creeping southward to the top of the radar screen, and small groups were coming from left to right to join the tail. Off to the east, beyond Portland, other convoys were on the move. Desperate for the relief of seeing everything pass from our range, our interest was seized later that long night by aircraft away to the east, circling but moving slowly away from us. Each dot was in a hazy cloud. We guessed, as others joined or left the group, that they were dropping metal strips of 'Window' to simulate an invasion fleet heading for the Pas de Calais. It was an anti-climax at last to see our tube empty, yet sobering to know that so many men in the ships were heading for a hell ahead of them."[3] The Germans, partly as a result of their own failures of technology, but chiefly because of damage caused by Allied bombing, possessed no sets on the Channel coast capable of showing such an accurate picture that night.

On the later afternoon of 5 June, when the men of the seaborne assault divisions had already been at sea for many hours – in some cases for days – Private Fayette Richardson of the 82nd Airborne Division was still in camp in England. He was lying on his bunk with his hands clasped behind his head, gazing up at the whitewashed ceiling and trying to exorcize from his mind the nagging beat of Tommy Dorsey's *What Is This Thing Called Love?* that had echoed out of the recreation hut every evening for weeks as the men walked to chow. A short, wiry 20-year-old from a small town near Buffalo, New York, Richardson had left home at 17 to drive an old jalopy to the west coast. He was in Seattle when Pearl Harbor was bombed, and enlisted at once "because everybody else was".[4] Like so many others, he wanted to be a pilot and was dismayed to be rejected for poor eyesight. Instead, he joined the Airborne and shipped to Northern Ireland with the 508th Regiment. There he volunteered to become a pathfinder, a decision he did not regret, because his group lived a far more independent and relaxed life than the rifle companies, spared KP and guard duties, free to come and go pretty much as they pleased after completing their special training in handling the Eureka beacon. Now, in his hut in Nottinghamshire, he stood among the rest of the team joking self-consciously with each other as they struggled to stow a mountain of personal equipment about their bodies. A 32-pound radar set was strapped below the reserve parachute on his stomach; fragmentation grenades were hooked on his harness; gammon bombs and a phosphorus grenade, chocolate D rations, fighting knife, water-bottle, anti-tank mine, a morphia syrette and an armed forces paperback edition of *Oliver Twist* were stowed about his body. Richardson, as platoon guinea pig for a morphia demonstration a few weeks earlier, had plunged the tiny needle into his leg and fallen promptly asleep, to dream in brilliant colours of sailing boats against a sunset sky, green tropical islands, flowers, rainbows.

On top of all the kit, the New Yorker was expected to carry a rifle. He decided to leave this and make do with a .45 pistol strapped to his high paratroop boot, where he could reach it easily. The pressure of the pistol belt, the tightly laced boots and equipment made him feel oddly secure, as if he was wearing armour. When the trucks came for them, the paratroopers tottered forward, floundering like men in diving suits, boosted aboard by the cooks and maintenance men who were being left behind. When the shouted messages of good luck faded away, the men in the back of the truck sat silent, scarcely able to recognize each other beneath the layer of burnt cork on their faces. Then they lay beside the fuselage of an olive-drab Dakota in the summer evening silence for almost an hour, drinking coffee and posing for an army photographer. Richardson found himself wanting to stay close to his own friends, reluctant to be alone. They were no longer excited, merely tense and thoughtful. Soon after darkness fell, they were airborne.

Jammed together in the belly of the plane, they could only talk to their neighbours by yelling over the noise of the aircraft, could see out of the windows only by squirming round inside their great clumsy burdens. Lamareux, alongside Richardson, nudged him and pointed down to the moonlight shining on the water. It seemed to the paratrooper to be frozen in smooth, unmoving ripples. The crew chief clambered down the aircraft to the rear and pulled off the door. Richardson saw a flash of light in the sky outside and understood, after a moment of puzzlement, that it was anti-aircraft fire. Then, on the shouted command, they pulled themselves clumsily to their feet and hooked static lines to the overhead cable. Now they could see streams of flashing lights coming up from the ground, making a harmless popping noise around them, like Roman candles being hosed into the sky. Each soldier felt the pressure of the man behind leaning into his pack. Then the green light came, and they began the familiar rush to the door in the paratroop one-step shuffle that they had practised so many times, at last pivoting abruptly before they hurled themselves into the slipstream and the sudden silence that followed.

At the moment "Rich" Richardson jumped over the fields of the Cotentin soon after 1.30 a.m., thousands of other Allied paratroopers were already on the ground ahead of him. Men of the British 6th Airborne Division seized the bridges over the Caen Canal and across the Orne at Ranville a few minutes after midnight. The American 101st Division began to drop at 1.30 a.m., the 82nd following at 2.30, and the bulk of the 6th Airborne – 4,800 parachutists – shortly before 1.00 a.m. A total of 8,000 British and 16,000 American airborne troops were to land by parachute and glider. The drops were marred by the poor performance of many of the Allied Dakota pilots who, by a combination of unsteady navigation and extravagant reaction to German flak, released their parachutists with near-criminal carelessness. Over both the British and American zones that night, extraordinary and undignified scenes took place in some aircraft, with paratroopers cursing the pilots as they were thrown to the floor by the frenzied weaving of their planes, officers and NCOs demanding – in several recorded instances, at gunpoint – that the airmen should resume their course and proceed with the drop rather than abort. The loss of only 30 Allied transport aircraft proved that the flak was not severe.

The glider pilots, by contrast, performed miracles of determination to crash their frail craft on their objectives, above all making possible the seizure of the British bridges after brief battles. 71 of the 196 glider pilots who landed east of the Orne on D-Day became casualties; among the Americans the proportion was even higher. The costly battle to gain the Merville Battery by the British 9th Para was a fine feat of arms, rendered anti-climatic by the discovery that the casemates mounted only 75 mm guns with slight capacity to harass the beaches. The inability of air photographs to distinguish the weapons mounted in many bunkers and casemates was a chronic problem for the planners before 6 June, and the suppression of positions such as the Merville Battery was a vital piece of insurance. The bulk of 6th Airborne struggled through the darkness and the first hours of daylight to concentrate its units, dispose of German patrols and strongpoints and create a firm perimeter east of the Orne from which to resist the powerful counter-attacks that would inevitably follow.

The American 82nd and 101st Airborne suffered even more seriously than the British from scattered dropping, and with far more deadly consequences amid the swamps and floods of the Cotentin, which drowned hundreds of men before they could even escape their harnesses. The 82nd gained one of its principal objectives, the village of St Mère Eglise, and fought to retain it against fierce German pressure. But it proved impossible immediately to secure the causeways across the Merderet. The airborne operations of D-Day emphasized painfully for the Allies the cost and difficulty inseparable from massed drops even before paratroopers could engage the enemy, and the limitations of lightly-armed formations without armoured support. Thousands of young Americans found themselves struggling, alone or with little clusters of other lonely figures, to find a path through the hedges and swamps to a rendezvous many miles from where they had been so mistakenly "given the green". It was a remarkable tribute to the 82nd and the 101st that while thousands of the men found themselves miles from their units and their objectives that night, they engaged the Germans wherever they encountered them. The great achievement of the American airborne forces on 6 June was to bring confusion and uncertainty to the Germans across the whole breadth of the Cherbourg peninsula.

Private Richardson felt a moment of pain on the inside of his thighs from his harness as the canopy jerked open, and his head and neck were jerked so sharply that he suffered a brief headache. Then he was floating rapidly down towards an orchard amid a rattle of fire from the ground. He let go the front risers of his parachute, just missed a tree, and slammed into the ground. Ears ringing, he grabbed his pistol and used his spare hand to struggle out of his harness. Then he walked cautiously towards the sound of the little metal crickets that American soldiers were snapping all over the Cotentin that night as a recognition signal. Through the darkness other men moved in to join them. They struggled to free one of the group whose parachute was caught in the top of a tree, and at last cut him down. Then they counted heads. Around half the team – including almost all the men equipped with beacon lights to back up the radar sets – were missing. These had jumped last and landed beyond a road on which the Germans were already audible, driving hither and thither searching for parachutists. Lamareux, the lead radar operator, switched on his beacon. To Richardson's chagrin, having lugged his own set so far with such sweat, he was now obliged to watch the other man pull the internal detonator to destroy it – only one set was necessary. Then the Americans dispersed hastily across the field. The one remaining tripod-mounted light was switched on. The other men pointed their torches towards the sky. Not many minutes had passed before somebody shouted, "Here they come!" They saw a new sparkle of anti-aircraft fire, moving closer and closer to them as the planes approached and local guns opened up. Then, as the first parachutes became dimly visible against the sky, the pathfinders below broke into muted but ecstatic cheers.

Hundreds of Americans who jumped that night found themselves plunged into action immediately they reached the ground, or were shot dead before they did so. After that brief moment of euphoria when the first wave over Richardson's landing zone jumped as planned, they were dismayed to see the second wave approach their signal on the same course, then drone on past the desperately flashing lights without dropping a single man. Only one plane came close to them. Flames were pouring from its starboard engine and the pilot was revving desperately as he lost height; the windows were clearly visible three or four hundred feet above them. A pathfinder sobbed desperately: "Those are our guys." Then the plane disappeared over the horizon and there was silence in the field again. The stillness persisted, for the expected third wave of aircraft never came. Instead of a powerful paratroop unit at the assembly point, there were only a few dozen men.

Richardson decided that the moment had come to make good his lack of a weapon. He picked up a machine-gun from the bundle attached to a collapsed parachute. Then another man ran over and said curtly, "That's our gun." They argued for a few moments. Richardson lost. His own company was among those which had failed to arrive, so he simply joined the nearest group of men digging slit trenches. When he had made his own foxhole, he dropped into it and fell asleep.

The German sluggishness in responding to the first Allied movements of D-Day had passed into the legend of the war. Montgomery had told his commanders: "By dusk on D-1 day the enemy will be certain that the NEPTUNE [or OVERLORD] area is to be assaulted in strength . . ."[5] Yet the astounding truth remains that even in the early hours of 6 June, the Germans were still in a condition of bewildered uncertainty. The German navy had failed to station patrols in the Channel because of its conviction that the weather was unfit for an invasion. Fifteenth Army's interception of the known BBC codeword for the French Resistance to begin their D-Day tasks was ignored. It is doubtful whether SHAEF would ever have agreed to the transmission of the BBC message on the night of 5 June, given the overwhelming probability that its significance was already compromised somewhere in France, had it not seemed inevitable that the invasion fleet would by that hour be detected.

The failures of the German navy and air force were obviously central to the defenders' lack of warning of the invasion. They had not even noticed the concentration of minesweepers operating off the Normandy coast at last light on 5 June. The lack of action following interception of the BBC message is more comprehensible, for it must be considered against the background of repeated false alarms all that spring, which had exasperated and wearied the coastal units. Neither the Germans nor SHAEF had ever taken the French Resistance entirely seriously, regarding it as a nuisance force rather than a central feature of Allied military operations. It is also important to notice that the message to the Resistance gave no hint of *where* the invasion was to take place. There was some discussion within Allied Special Forces HQ and SOE about the possibility of mobilizing only relevant sections of the Resistance, in order to reduce the possibility of bitter reprisals and long delays before liberation came to groups far from the front. But it was quickly agreed that, on grounds of security, it was vital to mobilize all *résistants* to avoid giving any clues to the Germans as to the whereabouts of the point of assault. There have been suggestions in some recent books[6] that, properly used, the BBC message could have told OKW that the Allies were going to Normandy. This notion is unfounded.

But the absence from headquarters of so many vital senior German commanders was a misfortune of critical importance. The whereabouts of General Edgar Feuchtinger of 21st Panzer have never been confirmed, but it was widely believed by his own men that he was *incommunicado* with a female friend. Rommel, of course, was in Germany, and Dollman of Seventh Army at the Rennes war games. On the night of 5 June, exploiting Rommel's absence, his Chief of Staff, General Hans Speidel, invited several of his fellow anti-Hitler conspirators to join him for drinks at the château at La Roche Guyon. It was here, after they had all dined together, that Speidel was telephone by Fifteenth Army headquarters at Turcoing and informed of the intercepted BBC message. Fifteenth Army had been placed on alert. A staff officer telephoned von Rundstedt's headquarters for a decision on whether Seventh Army should also be alerted. It was decided that it should not. Von Rundstedt's staff confined themselves to a general warning to all units that the BBC message might presage a widespread outbreak of terrorist sabotage.

Seventh Army was finally alerted at 1.35 a.m. Half an hour earlier, General Marcks had called out his own LXXXIV Corps, in the wake of the reported paratroop landings. The confusion was compounded by the Allied drop of thousands of dummies and six uncommonly brave SAS soldiers to divert the defenders inland. The discovery of the dummies doubled the Germans' uncertainty about a possible bluff. General Max Pemsel, Dollman's Chief of Staff, telephoned Rommel's headquarters and spoke to Speidel repeatedly during the night, insisting that a major Allied operation was taking place. At 3.00 a.m., von Rundstedt's headquarters reported to OKW that large-scale air landings were under way. At 4.00 a.m., General Kraiss of 352nd Division sent a regiment on bicycles in pursuit of paratroopers at a location where in reality only dummies had landed. At 6.00 a.m., Blumentritt from von Rundstedt's headquarters told OKW that a major invasion appeared to be taking place, and asked for the release of the armoured reserve, I SS Panzer Corps outside Paris. With Hitler asleep, the request was denied. It was not finally granted until ten hours later. At 6.15 a.m., Pemsel told Speidel of the opening of a massive naval bombardment and air assault on the coastal defences. At 6.45 a.m., Pemsel telephoned Fifteenth Army and told them that his forces expected to be able to cope with the situation from their own resources. Von Salmuth, Commander-in-Chief of Fifteenth Army, thereupon went to bed. So did Speidel and most of the staff at La Roche Guyon. It was after 10.30 a.m., over an hour after Allied radio had formally announced the coming of the invasion, when Rommel left his home in Herrlingen to drive headlong for his headquarters. It was almost 12 hours before he reached La Roche Guyon.

It was an impressive tribute to the success of the Allied deception plans that every key German commander greeted the news of operations in Normandy as evidence of *an* invasion, not of *the* invasion. Rommel's personal presence and energy might have galvanized the local formations to react with vigour. Most recent writers[7] have suggested that it would have availed the Germans nothing to wake Hitler in order to obtain authorization for the release of the OKW armoured reserves, because Allied air power would have prevented their movement in daylight on 6 June. This is patently untrue, since other formations, including 21st Panzer, were able to drive to the battlefield, albeit with some difficulty. The fighter-bombers and naval guns would certainly have hit hard at any German concentration of armour around the beachhead. But on 6 June forward air control and gunnery direction were not operating efficiently. The balance of probability remains that the Allies could have gained their beachhead against any German reaction on D-Day. But the early release of the armour would have made matters incomparably more dangerous for them. It was fortunate that the senior staff officers of all the major German formations behaved with a lassitude that verged upon utter incompetence.

Some subordinate German commanders, such as General Richter of 716th Division, responded more forcefully to the spectacle of enemy paratroopers dropping around them. Richter directed a battalion of infantry with an anti-tank gun and self-propelled artillery support towards Benouville to recapture the Orne and Caen Canal bridges in the early hours of the morning. But when their leading light tank was knocked out by a British PIAT and the paratroopers opened heavy fire on the counter-attacking force, the Germans contented themselves with occupying Benouville and exchanging fire with the British. 716th Division's operations were conducted with nothing like the determination that could have been expected from a top-class formation.

"You could see that the Germans were really frightened because they started being so nasty," said Nicole Ferté,[8] one of the local inhabitants of Hérouville, three miles south of the Orne bridge. "They had always been so courteous in the past." Madamoiselle Ferté, the 20-year-old daughter of a local garage owner, had lain on the floor during the bombing, sheltering her eight-year-old sister and listening spellbound to the sound of the glider tugs and transport aircraft overhead before midnight. Suddenly there was a knock at their door, and the local teacher stood outside. A wounded British soldier was in the school. Could Nicole come and interpret? Together they hurried back down the road and, in a mixture of half-remembered English, French, and even German, began to talk to the airborne soldier, lying in great pain with a broken leg. They had just given him tea when German soldiers burst in. The civilians were busquely sent to their homes, the British soldier taken away. Most of the local inhabitants hastily fled from the village, but the Fertés stayed through a week when the fighting raged to within a few hundred yards of their door, "because we were certain that liberation must come at any moment. The only other people who stayed were the girls who had been sleeping with Germans." After a week, the Germans abruptly ordered all the remaining occupants to leave Hérouville, and they endured many weeks of fear and privation before they saw the village again.

At 21st Panzer's headquarters, although two companies of infantry exercising north of Caen reported the British glider landings immediately, in the absence of General Feuchtinger and his senior staff officer the only action that could be taken was the immediate removal of divisional headquarters to its operational location. Corporal Werner Kortenhaus, wireless operator in one of the division's 127 Mk IV tanks, was out on picket with two other men when they heard the massive air activity overhead – the sound of aircraft descending, and then climbing once more as the glider tugs loosed their tows. As the panzer crew approached their platoon harbour in the darkness, they could see the shadows of men already clambering over the tanks, preparing to move off. While his own crew hastily unloaded their drill rounds and filled the turret with armour-piercing ammunition, Kortenhaus ran to the house of the Frenchwoman who did their laundry to collect their clean clothes. By 2.00 a.m., the crews were in the tanks and ready to move. Yet it was 8.00 a.m. before the 1st Tank Battalion under Captain von Gottberg began to roll north from its harbour up the long, straight road north to Caen. The 2nd Battalion under Major Vierzig did not start to move until 9.00 a.m., although that officer had held his tanks on standby since 2.20 a.m. No order had been given to them and for this failure responsibility must be shared between Speidel and Feuchtinger, who at the very least displayed an astounding lack of initiative when he arrived at his headquarters some time between 6.00 and 7.00 a.m.

Lieutenant Rudolf Schaaf, commanding a self-propelled battery of the 1716th Artillery, was telephoned at 3.00 a.m. and ordered to take his guns to join the counter-attack against the British airborne bridgehead. Yet he had driven only a few miles across country when he received a radio message recalling them to their original positions. It was clear by dawn that the seaborne menace would have to be met by every infantryman and gun that the defenders possessed.

Shortly before H-Hour, Allied bombers struck the station at Caen and soon afterwards fighter-bombers began to strafe German installations and barracks. A loudspeaker vehicle toured the streets, ordering civilians to stay in their houses. Throughout the day there were intermittent Allied air attacks. By mid-morning the first truckloads of British prisoners were being driven through the streets. The first of more than 80 ruthless executions of French civilians alleged to have assisted the invaders were taking place at the barracks. Early reports of the airborne landings and the fleet offshore were as confused as those reaching German headquarters. The overwhelming sensation among the French was terror that a landing might fail. The memory of Dieppe, the possibility that all the suffering, destruction and death might be in vain, hung heavy over Caen and all Normandy that morning and through the days that followed. A local historian described the events of the dawn of D-Day: "Thus Caen, like other towns in Normandy, passed the night of 6–7 June in fire and blood, while elsewhere in France they celebrated the invasion by drinking champagne and dancing to the gramophone."[9]

Before dawn, the invasion coast was lit by flares and flashes as the naval guns pounded the defences, explosions of every hue rippling up and down the shoreline as hundreds of launches and landing craft scuttled amid the dim silhouettes of the battleships and cruisers, transports and rocket ships a few miles out to sea. No man who saw it ever forgot either the spectacle of the vast invasion fleet crowding the Channel at first light on the morning of D-Day, or the roar of the guns rolling across the sea, or the tearing rasp of the rocket batteries firing over the heads of the men in the landing craft. Nine battleships, 23 cruisers, 104 destroyers and 71 corvettes dominated the 6,483-strong assembly of converted liners, merchantmen and tank landing craft now shaking out into their positions a few miles offshore. 4,000 landing ships – craft and barges of all sizes – would carry the troops ashore. Alongside the transports, overburdened men clambered clumsily down the scrambling nets into the pitching assault craft below. For many, this was among the most alarming experiences of the day. Thousands of men tossing upon the swell strained to make their eyes focus through binoculars upon the coastline ahead. Captain Hendrie Bruce of the Royal Artillery wrote in his notebook: "The villages of La Breche and Lion-sur-Mer are smothered with bursts, and enormous dirty clouds of smoke and brick dust rise from the target area and drift out to sea, completely obscuring our target for a time and enveloping many craft in a veritable 'fog of war'."[10] Gunnery observation

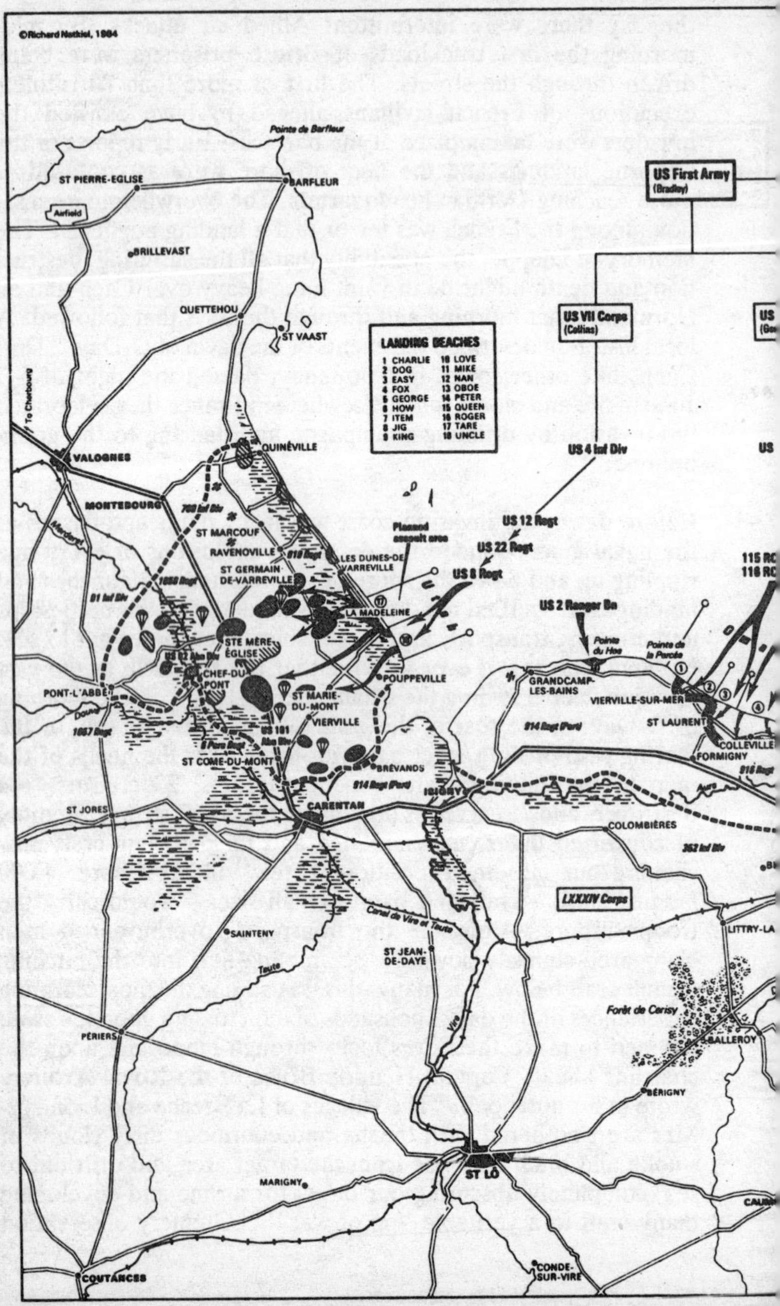
©Richard Natkiel, 1984
Pointe de Barfleur
BARFLEUR
ST PIERRE-EGLISE
Airfield
BRILLEVAST
QUETTEHOU
ST VAAST
To Cherbourg
VALOGNES
MONTEBOURG
QUINÉVILLE
709 Inf Div
ST MARCOUF
RAVENOVILLE
919 Regt
LES DUNES-DE-VARREVILLE
ST GERMAIN-DE-VARREVILLE
1058 Regt
91 Inf Div
LA MADELEINE
STE MÈRE-ÉGLISE
US 82 Abn Div
CHEF-DU-PONT
PONT-L'ABBÉ
Douve
1057 Regt
6 Para Regt
ST MARIE-DU-MONT
VIERVILLE
US 101 Abn Div
POUPPEVILLE
ST COME-DU-MONT
BRÉVANDS
914 Regt (Part)
CARENTAN
ISIGNY
ST JORES
SAINTENY
Canal de Vire et Taute
Taute
ST JEAN-DE-DAYE
Vire
PÉRIERS
MARIGNY
ST LÔ
COUTANCES
CONDE-SUR-VIRE
LANDING BEACHES
1 CHARLIE
2 DOG
3 EASY
4 FOX
5 GEORGE
6 HOW
7 ITEM
8 JIG
9 KING
10 LOVE
11 MIKE
12 NAN
13 OBOE
14 PETER
15 QUEEN
16 ROGER
17 TARE
18 UNCLE
US First Army
(Bradley)
US VII Corps
(Collins)
US 4 Inf Div
US 12 Regt
US 22 Regt
US 8 Regt
Planned assault area
US 2 Ranger Bn
Pointe du Hoe
Pointe de la Percée
GRANDCAMP-LES-BAINS
VIERVILLE-SUR-MER
ST LAURENT
COLLEVILLE
FORMIGNY
914 Regt (Part)
916 Regt
Aure
COLOMBIÈRES
352 Inf Div
LXXXIV Corps
LITTRY-LA
Forêt de Cerisy
BALLEROY
BÉRIGNY

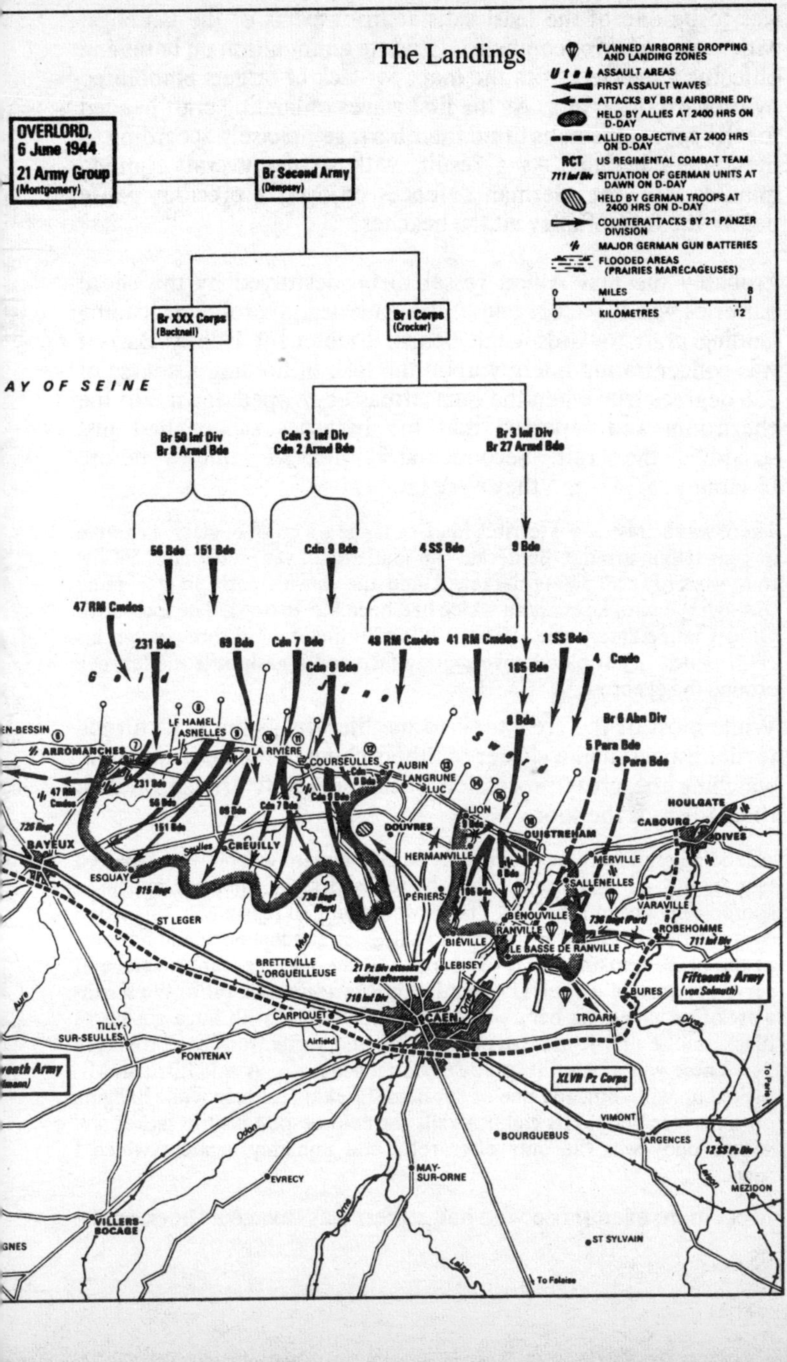
The Landings
PLANNED AIRBORNE DROPPING AND LANDING ZONES
Utah ASSAULT AREAS
FIRST ASSAULT WAVES
ATTACKS BY BR 6 AIRBORNE DIV
HELD BY ALLIES AT 2400 HRS ON D-DAY
ALLIED OBJECTIVE AT 2400 HRS ON D-DAY
RCT US REGIMENTAL COMBAT TEAM
711 Inf Div SITUATION OF GERMAN UNITS AT DAWN ON D-DAY
HELD BY GERMAN TROOPS AT 2400 HRS ON D-DAY
COUNTERATTACKS BY 21 PANZER DIVISION
MAJOR GERMAN GUN BATTERIES
FLOODED AREAS (PRAIRIES MARÉCAGEUSES)
0 MILES 8
0 KILOMETRES 12
OVERLORD, 6 June 1944
21 Army Group (Montgomery)
Br Second Army (Dempsey)
Br XXX Corps (Bucknall)
Br I Corps (Crocker)
AY OF SEINE
Br 50 Inf Div
Br 8 Armd Bde
Cdn 3 Inf Div
Cdn 2 Armd Bde
Br 3 Inf Div
Br 27 Armd Bde
56 Bde
151 Bde
Cdn 9 Bde
4 SS Bde
9 Bde
47 RM Cmdos
231 Bde
69 Bde
Cdn 7 Bde
Cdn 8 Bde
48 RM Cmdos
41 RM Cmdos
1 SS Bde
4 Cmdo
185 Bde
8 Bde
Br 6 Abn Div
5 Para Bde
3 Para Bde
Gold
Juno
Sword
EN-BESSIN
ARROMANCHES
LE HAMEL
ASNELLES
LA RIVIÈRE
COURSEULLES
ST AUBIN
LANGRUNE
LUC
LION
OUISTREHAM
HOULGATE
CABOURG
DIVES
MERVILLE
SALLENELLES
VARAVILLE
ROBEHOMME
711 Inf Div
BÉNOUVILLE
RANVILLE
LE BASSE DE RANVILLE
736 Regt (Part)
BAYEUX
726 Regt
47 RM Cmdos
231 Bde
56 Bde
151 Bde
69 Bde
Cdn 7 Bde
Cdn 8 Bde
Cdn 9 Bde
9 Bde
8 Bde
185 Bde
CREUILLY
DOUVRES
HERMANVILLE
ESQUAY
915 Regt
736 Regt (Part)
PÉRIERS
Seulles
ST LEGER
BIÉVILLE
LEBISEY
21 Pz Div attacks during afternoon
716 Inf Div
BRETTEVILLE L'ORGUEILLEUSE
Mue
CARPIQUET
Airfield
CAEN
Orne
TROARN
BURES
Fifteenth Army (von Salmuth)
Dives
Aure
TILLY-SUR-SEULLES
FONTENAY
venth Army
llmann)
XLVII Pz Corps
To Paris
VIMONT
ARGENCES
12 SS Pz Div
BOURGUEBUS
Odon
Laison
MEZIDON
EVRECY
MAY-SUR-ORNE
Orne
VILLERS-BOCAGE
GNES
ST SYLVAIN
Laize
To Falaise

was to be one of the least satisfactory aspects of the landings, with scores of ships compelled to waste ammunition on harassing objectives selected from the map, for lack of targets pinpointed by forward observers. As the first waves of landing craft headed for the shore, the guns lifted their barrage precisely according to the time schedule. As a result, with so many craft running minutes late, the German defences enjoyed a precious pause before the first infantry hit the beaches.

Probably the first Allied vessel to be destroyed by the shore batteries was PC 1261, one of the American patrol craft leading landing craft towards Utah beach. Lieutenant Halsey Barrett was concentrating intently upon the task of holding a course of 236 degrees true when the quartermaster stepped down into the chartroom and reported that the batteries ashore had just straddled the craft. Seconds later, just 58 minutes before H-Hour at 5.34 a.m., they were hit.

There was a crash – not terribly loud – a lunge – a crash of glass, a rumble of gear falling around the decks – an immediate, yes immediate, 50° list to starboard – all lights darkened and the dawn's early light coming through the pilot house door which had been blown open. The Executive Officer immediately said: "That's it", with finality and threw down his chart pencil. I felt blood covering my face and a gash over my left eye around the eyebrow.[11]

While most of the crew took to the liferafts as the craft turned turtle, Barrett and a cluster of others clung to the upturned hull, watching the great procession of landing craft driving on past them towards the shore.

A landing craft LCVP with thirty or so men aboard was blown a hundred feet in the air in pieces. Shore batteries flashed, splashes appeared sporadically around the bay. Planes were flying in reasonable formation over the beach. One transpired into a huge streaming flame and no trace of the plane remained. Aft of us an LCT lay belly skyward no trace of survivors around it. The USS battleship *Nevada* a mile off to the north-west of us was using her 14-inch guns rapidly and with huge gushes of black smoke and flame extending yards and yards from her broadside . . . There was a beautiful sunrise commencing . . . A small British ML picked up with difficulty one of our men shrieking for help while hanging on a marker buoy. His childish yells for help despite his life jacket and secure buoy was the only disgraceful and unmanly incident which I saw . . .[12]

Most men, even those who had suffered as savage a shock as the crew of PC 1261, felt reassured by the sense of the Allied armada's dominance of the sea. Barrett and the other survivors knew that somebody would pick them up as soon as they had time to spare, as indeed they did. For the men of the British and American navies, there was an overwhelming sense of relief that they faced no sudden, devastating attack from the Luftwaffe as some, despite all the reassurance of the intelligence reports, had feared they might. 'We were all more or less expecting bombs, shells, blood etc." wrote a British sailor on the corvette *Gentian*. "Dive bombers were expected to be attacking continually, backed by high-level bombing. But no, nothing like that . . . Instead, a calm, peaceful scene . . . The Luftwaffe is obviously smashed."[13]

In England early that morning, only a few thousand people knew with certainty what was happening across the Channel, and only some thousands more guessed. *The Times* news pages were dominated by the latest reports from Italy, with the Fifth Army past Rome; there was a mention of Allied bombing of Calais and Boulogne. The daily weather bulletin recorded dull conditions in the Channel on 5 June, with a south-west wind becoming very strong in the middle of the day: "Towards dusk the wind had dropped a little, and the sea was less choppy. The outlook was a little more favourable at nightfall."

Outside Portsmouth, at 21st Army Group headquarters, Montgomery's Chief of Staff, Major-General Francis de Guingand, turned to Brigadier Bill Williams and recalled the beginning of other, desert battles. "My God, I wish we had 9th Australian Division with us this morning, don't you?" he said wryly.[14] Some of the British officers at SHAEF were taken aback to discover their American counterparts reporting for duty that morning wearing helmets and sidearms, an earnest of their identification with the men across the water. Brooke described in his diary how he walked in the sunshine of St James's Park: "A most unreal day during which I felt as if I were in a trance entirely detached from the war."[15]

In his foxhole in the Cotentin, Private Richardson of the 82nd Airborne was woken by daylight, and the overhead roar of an Allied fighter-bomber. Hungry and thirsty, he munched a chocolate bar until the word came to move out. Richardson picked up a stray bazooka without enthusiasm, because he had only the barest idea of how to use it. Among a long file of men, all of them unknown to him, he began to march across the Norman fields, ignorant of where they were going. They reached a hedge by a road and halted, while at the front of the column two officers pored over a map and discussed which way to go. Suddenly everybody was signalled to lie flat. A car was approaching. They lay frozen as it approached. Richardson and the others could see the heads of its three German occupants passing the top of the ledge like targets in a shooting gallery. It seemed that no one would move against them, each American privately expecting another to be the first to act. Then one man stood up and emptied a burst of Browning automatic rifle fire at the car. It swerved off the road into a ditch, where somebody shouted, "Finish 'em!" and tossed a grenade. But the Germans were already dead. One of them was Lieutenant-General Wilhelm Falley, commanding the German 91st Division, on his way back to his headquarters from the ill-fated war games in Rennes.

Like Richardson, many of the paratroopers had never seen a man killed before, least of all on a peaceful summer morning in the midst of the countryside. They found the experience rather shocking. Leaving the Germans where they had fallen, they marched on through the meadows and wild flowers, disturbed by nothing more intrusive than the buzzing insects. They encountered another group from the 508th, presiding over 30 German prisoners, arranged in ranks by the roadside as if for a parade. Most were Poles or oriental Russians. One American threw a scene about shooting them: "The Japs killed my brother!" He was dissuaded at the time, but Richardson heard later that the whole group had been killed.

The New Yorker felt better now, because among the new group of paratroopers was one of his closest friends, a tall Oklahoman named Earl Williams, the sergeant commanding 3 Platoon. They sat and talked about money. Williams had changed $100 into francs before take-off. Richardson could not see the point of money at this stage, but Williams insisted upon giving him some. They lay in the grass chatting for what seemed a long time, conscious of the war only because of spasmodic shells falling a few hundred yards away. Finally they wrapped themselves in parachute silk, and once again fell asleep.

Richardson's experience was scarcely universal. While his group were making their way across country with little interference, many other American paratroopers were engaged in desperate battles around the causeways and hamlets of the eastern Cotentin, while the British 6th Airborne was already under fierce German pressure north-east of Caen. But the young New Yorker's story catches the dreamlike quality, the curious sense of detachment that so many men felt in those first hours after being wrenched from the peace of the English summer, and thrust onto an alien battlefield. As the days went by, the battlefield became the reality, until there came a time when they scarcely remembered that another world existed. For thousands of men, it was only when OVERLORD was behind them that they could grasp the magnitude of the events in which they had taken part. While the great drama was unfolding, it seemed a fantasy into which they had somehow slipped as spectators.

As they approached Sword beach, Lieutenant Charles Mundy's men did their best to dull their sensations with the rum rations which they had saved and bottled for three months in anticipation of this moment. They were still over a mile offshore, gazing like eager tourists towards the beach ahead, when a shell smashed through the side of their landing craft and the entire troop were ordered to close down in the tanks. Their Sherman minesweeping flails of 22nd Dragoon Guards were to lead the landing on the eastern flank. Mundy, a 31-year-old Londoner, was impressed to see that the shoreline ahead conformed precisely to the photographs that he and his men had studied so earnestly.

Some men reacted theatrically to their parts. A bugler of the East Yorkshire regiment sounded the General Salute as his landing craft passed the British command ship. Commander Angus Mackenzie, aboard the destroyer *Undaunted,* stood in his Highlander's bonnet playing the bagpipes from his bridge as the LCAs, crammed with seated infantry, ploughed by his ship towards the beach.

Private John Hein of the American 1st Division "felt a little queasy. But I trusted this vast organization – everything was so organized, so programmed that there seemed little scope for individual fear."[16] Hein was born in Germany, the son of a Jewish doctor. He and his family fled in 1936, when he was 15, and adopted their new country with the enthusiasm that only immigrants can achieve. Now, as the former music student headed towards Omaha beach, he felt only intense pride to be wearing an American uniform.

Chaplain Henry Lovegrove of the Green Howards was relieved to find that he was experienced enough not to behave as he had when, in action for the first time in North Africa, he had scrambled panic-stricken under mortar fire, crying, "Where's my helmet? Where's my helmet?" On 6 June, it was a vast reassurance to every soldier who had been in battle before to know that he was capable of doing what was asked of him. This was a consolation denied to many thousands of the men now crouched in the landing craft, bucketing towards the beaches with spray drenching themselves and their weapons.

The American beaches

Many of the defenders of Utah beach, the most westerly of the Allied landing zones just above the elbow of the Cotentin peninsula, were still helplessly stunned by the bombardment or demoralized by the spectacle before them as the first landing craft closed in. In strongpoint W 5, at the very centre of the sea wall where the 4th Division was approaching, the men of 3 Company, 919th Regiment, had lain shaking, hands pressed to their ears as 360 Marauder medium bombers attacked their positions, followed by a naval bombardment which poured down explosives around them with remarkable accuracy, destroying all the position's 50 mm guns, its 75 mm anti-tank gun and many of its bunkers. An elderly mess orderly ran out as the shelling died down, shouting desperately to his commanding officer: "Everything's wrecked! Everything's wrecked! We've got to surrender!"[1] The company commander, a 23-year-old veteran named Lieutenant Arthur Jahnke, who had won the Knight's Cross in Russia before his wounds caused him to be posted to France, pulled his garrison back into their positions. But he understood, with a sense of desperation, that he was now compelled to defend his sector of beach with only a single 88 mm gun, an old Renault tank turret dug into the sands, and a handful of machine-guns and mortars. Above all, he was shocked to gaze out at the vast armada offshore and perceive that they were attacking at low water. Every gun, every bunker had been sited to match Rommel's certain anticipation that "the Amies" would come with the high tide.

Yet now the Germans in W 5 and its adjoining positions were bewildered to see armour, Sherman tanks, rising directly from the sea and opening fire upon them. In the Renault turret, Lance-Corporal Friedrich peered through his pebble spectacles and began firing long machine-gun bursts in the direction of the waterline. A few minutes later, a direct hit from an American 75 mm tank gun destroyed his weapon and shattered his leg. W 5's 88 mm gun, damaged in the bombing, fired one round before jamming permanently. Jahnke's other positions remained in action for only a few minutes before tank fire began to focus upon them. A sudden explosion buried him in sand. He collapsed into unconsciousness, and awoke to find himself staring up the rifle barrel of an American soldier. Together with the survivors of his company, he was herded away towards imprisonment, suffering the final misery, a few moments later, of being wounded by a belated shell from the German battery inland which had been supporting his position.

Although the current off Utah swept the American landing craft 2,000 yards south of the area designated by the plan, in every other respect VII Corps' operations conformed more nearly to the timetable than those of any other Allied formation that day. 28 of the 32 amphibious DD tanks launched reached the sands. At 6.30 a.m., the three regimental combat teams of 4th Division began to come ashore under very light enemy fire. The Germans had thought it most unlikely that Allied troops would land immediately in front of the wide flooded areas beyond the beach. The navigational error caused by the current had brought the men of 4th Division into the most lightly defended sector of the entire Normandy front. As the forward infantry mopped up beach defences, the engineers began to blow up beach obstacles under only sporadic artillery fire. Vehicles and follow-up units poured in as the Americans discovered one undefended beach exit across the inundations, and the 101st Airborne secured four others at the western end. Most of the lone defending regiment of the German 709th Division surrendered as soon as the Americans came to close quarters with them.

Private Lindley Higgins waded through three feet of water to the shore in a manner that made his own invasion seem more farcical than lethal. He and other men of the 12th Regiment could hear only distant firing, but suddenly they were ordered to lie down among the organized chaos of vehicles and stores on the sand: "They're sending in artillery!" somebody shouted. As he hit the ground, Higgins felt himself being squeezed in half by an agonizing pressure at his waist. He yelled: "Aid man!" Then he saw that he had accidentally hit the release of his life jacket, which was inflating. Furious and embarrassed, he pulled his bayonet off his rifle and hacked the life jacket into submission. Then, in long straggling files, his company began to move inland.

Almost all the Americans' difficulties on Utah that day began as they left the beach. The units dispatched northwards to secure the area where the 4th Division would have landed, but for the diversion caused by the current, ran into strong resistance. When 12th Regiment and other forces striking inland clambered over the high, sandy bank looking out over the sea and began to plunge through the flat, flooded fields behind the dunes, their movement became agonizingly slow.

Captain John McGirr of the 65th Armored Field Artillery was under orders to advance with the leading elements inland, and commence acting with the 101st Airborne as a forward observer at the earliest opportunity. But he found himself lying behind the sea wall for more than two hours while waiting for his infantry unit to move off; the monotony was relieved only by a fire in an ammunition truck hit by a stray shell which he helped to fight. The guns of his battery were already coming ashore before McGirr was off the beach.

To Higgins and his companions of Company L, struggling under their impossibly heavy loads of weapons and equipment, the swamps seemed endless. Shorter men found themselves stumbling into concealed ditches that almost drowned them, and from which they had to be painfully extracted. They waded between the white tapes laid ahead of them by the engineers, rifles held high above their heads to keep dry. Higgins was carrying an entire carton of Lucky Strikes in his invasion jacket, but by evening the only smoke he managed to salvage was in the pack in his helmet. They came upon a crashed glider with a jeep still trapped inside it, which the company commander ordered them to retrieve. They hacked at the fuselage until the jeep was almost free, when suddenly a senior officer appeared and furiously ordered them to leave the vehicle and continue their advance.

All along the line, time was already slipping. The chronic problem was to maintain momentum. Yet the landing of 23,000 men on Utah, at a cost of only 197 casualties on the first day, was an almost miraculous piece of good fortune and good judgement. It seemed all the more so in contrast with the events that were unfolding that morning a few miles to the east. While the 4th Division was streaming ashore with fewer casualties than in their last exercise on Slapton Sands, on Omaha beach, where two-thirds of the entire American D-Day effort was concentrated, the 1st and 29th Divisions were enduring ten times as many losses as the 4th's, and very many times their fear and confusion.

Lieutenant Jahnke's company had been stunned and disorganized by the Utah bombardment, but the Germans manning the defences around Vierville and St Laurent had escaped almost totally unscathed. Attacking blind through cloud, the Liberator heavy bombing inevitably lacked precision. In their anxiety to avoid the risk of bombing short onto the approaching invasion fleet, the Allied aircraft poured hundreds of tons of high explosive onto the fields behind the forward defences. Here too, the Germans were defending the strongest natural positions facing the entire assault – hills and cliffs rising steeply up to 200 feet from the beach and the sea wall above it. Brigadier Williams' worst fears were confirmed. In addition to the regiment of the 716th Division defending the Omaha sector, there were strong elements of the much more formidable 352nd. The Americans below the bluffs faced by far the greatest concentration of German fire on the entire invasion front.

A little after 7.00 a.m., a 21-year-old farm boy from Metzingen named Lance-Corporal Hein Severloh had borrowed the binoculars of his battery commander, Lieutenant Frerking. He peered in fascination over the thick concrete parapet at the spectacle unfolding out to sea: "The big one is still hove to, not moving . . . More ships coming up now . . ."[2] Severloh was one of the forward observation team of 1 Battery, 352 Artillery Regiment. When the alert was called, he and the others had driven hastily to the coast from their billets in the battery position at Houteville. Now the gunners were reporting by field telephone, having suffered no hits from the bombing, "perhaps they weren't really after us . . ." Severloh began his running commentary again: "The big one's moving inshore . . . Landing craft on our left, off Vierville, making for the beach." Sergeant Krone said: "They must be crazy. Are they going to swim ashore? Right under our muzzles?" He was one of the 19 men of the 726th Grenadiers sharing position WN 62 – *Wilderstandsnesten,* "resistance nest", 62 – with the gunner OP. The telephone buzzed from regimental HQ with an order to withhold fire until the enemy touched the shore. Severloh laid aside the glasses and took up his own position at an MG 42. Frerking began telephoning fire orders to his guns: "Target Dora, all guns, range Four Eight Five Zero, basic direction Twenty Plus, impact fuse," Now there was a long, violent pause, as the naval bombardment plastering the sand and scrub around the pillboxes reached a crescendo, deafening even men behind five feet of concrete. Yet although the blasts filled the bunkers with dust, shook fragments of masonry from the ceilings, fired the scrub along the hillside at intervals above the 6,000 yards of beach where the Americans were to land, the naval shelling did no more than the bombing to reduce the fighting power of the defences. These had been constructed to be almost immune to direct fire from the sea. Now, 47 minutes after it began, the bombardment lifted as a black smoke signal curled into the sky from the command ship. There was a brief moment of silence. The grey shoals of landing craft bumped through the four-foot waves breaking onto the shore. There was only one casualty thus far in WN 62 – an NCO wounded by a shrapnel splinter tearing through a firing slit. Then the first boat dropped its ramp a few yards short of the beach and the overburdened Americans within it began to pour forward, splashing into the surf. The Germans in WN 62 and every position along the Omaha front opened fire, their machine-guns traversing steadily to and fro across the waterline, arcs of fire interlocking, occasional ricochets shrieking off the steel of the beach obstacles. Frerking called into his handset: "Target Dora – Fire!"

There is no more demanding task for infantry than to press home an attack across open ground under heavy fire, amid heavy casualties. The American assault on Omaha beach came as close as the experience of any western Allied soldiers in the Second World War to the kind of headlong encounters between flesh and fire that were a dreadful commonplace in the battles of 30 years before, and which were so grimly familiar on the eastern front. V Corps' plan for Omaha eschewed tactical subtleties, the use of British specialized armour, and any attempt to seize the five vital beach exits by manoeuvre. Instead, General Gerow committed his men to hurling themselves frontally against the most strongly defended areas in the assault zone. This was an act of *hubris* compounded by the collapse, amidst the rough weather, of all the elaborate timetables for the landing.

Whipped by a 10-knot north-westerly wind, the seas swamped at least 10 LCVPs during the run-in, drowning many of their infantry. The attempt to land artillery from amphibious DUKWs failed disastrously, and in all 26 guns from elements of five regiments were lost. The supporting rocket ships opened fire at extreme range from the shore, and most of their projectiles fell short, some landing among the assault craft. Under the impact of the waves, the flimsy canvas walls on most of the amphibious DD tanks collapsed immediately. A special kind of sacrificial heroism was demanded of the DD crews that morning when, by a serious error of judgement, 32 were launched 6,000 yards from the beach. Each one, as it dropped off the ramp of the landing craft, plunged like a stone to the bottom of the sea, leaving pitifully few survivors struggling in the swell. Yet the following crews drove on into the water undeterred by ghastly example. One commander – a certain Sergeant Sertell – insisted upon launching even after his canvas screen had been gashed open before he left the craft. Just five of this wave of DDs reached the shore. The infantry were thus called upon to storm the beach without the benefit of vital supporting armour which was intended to shoot open the way ashore. Those tanks which reached Omaha did so behind, rather than ahead of, the leading wave of eight companies – 1,450 men in 36 landing craft.

Most of the young Americans plunging into the surf had been crouched in their landing craft for some three hours, having been transferred from the transports 12 miles out from the beach rather than the seven miles the British decided upon. Many had quickly thrown up their breakfasts, and then crouched miserably in the bucketing boats, drenched in spray, paddling in vomit, as darkness gave way to the first light of dawn. Each man was grotesquely heavily loaded with gas mask, grenades, half -pound blocks of TNT, pole or satchel charges, two bandoliers of rifle ammunition, rations and waterbottle – 68 pounds in total. Now, in an instant, they were compelled to rouse themselves from the cramped, crowded stagnation of the landing craft and stumble forward into the hail of machine-gun and mortar fire from the German defences, which killed and wounded many before they even reached dry ground. Others, still groggy with seasickness, their clothes and equipment stiff and matted with salt, desperately sought cover among the beach obstacles or lay paralyzed amid the harvest of wreckage that quickly gathered on the shoreline. Early in the assault the beach was clogged with grounded and damaged landing craft, some hulks being swept broadside onto the German obstacles to create a logjam which the next wave could not pass. A flamethrower operator on one vessel suffered a direct hit on his weapon: the explosion catapulted his dying body into the sea, spewing blazing fuel over the decks. The landing craft caught fire and burnt for the next 18 hours, amid constant detonations from its 20 mm oerlikon ammunition.

The plan demanded that 270 specially-trained demolition men would follow the lead infantry onto the beach and immediately begin to blow the German obstacles, clearing the way for the great rolling succession of follow-up units before the tide covered the mines. 25,000 more men and 4,000 vehicles were due on Omaha with the second tide of the day. In the event, under the intense fire, which killed or wounded more than 40 per cent of the engineers, and the chaos of soldiers wounded or terrified behind the steel hedgehogs, only a handful of obstacles were exploded that morning. The path to the beach was forced open principally by the hulls of landing craft that rammed obstacles by accident or intent, often triggering the mines and adding more hulks to the debris on the waterline. Of 16 armoured bulldozers sent ashore, only six arrived and three of these were quickly destroyed. Among the infantry, command quickly approached collapse. Three-quarters of the 116th Regiment's radio sets were destroyed or rendered unworkable, and the unit's forward headquarters was effectively wiped out by a direct hit. Many men were confused to discover that they had been landed far from the sector for which they had been briefed and trained. Americans lay prone in the shallow water seeking cover, or dragged themselves painfully up the sand with wounds suffered before they were even out of the landing craft. Hundreds huddled beneath the sea wall at the head of the beach, seizing the only shelter Omaha offered that day, although some companies' survivors took 45 minutes to struggle even that far from the waterline. Hundreds of men were already dying or dead – there would be more than 2,000 casualties on the beach that day.

Among the living, an overwhelming paralysis set in. Much of what takes place on every battlefield is decided by example, men being driven to act in noble or ignoble fashion by the behaviour of those around them. On Omaha that morning, the inexperience of many American junior leaders made itself felt. The confused nature of the landings, with men landing by half-platoons often many yards from the boats carrying their own officers and comrades, destroyed unit cohesion. To the great majority of infantrymen looking for an example to follow out of the apparent collapse of purpose on Omaha that morning, it seemed most prudent merely to seek what shelter they could, and cling to it.

Aboard the cruiser *Augusta* offshore, General Bradley watched the events unfolding on the beaches frustrated by the paucity of communications. A steel command cabin had been built for him on deck, 20 feet by 10, the walls dominated by Michelin motoring maps of France, a few pin-ups and large-scale maps of Normandy. A row of clerks sat at typewriters along one wall, while Bradley and his personal staff clustered around the big plotting table in the centre. Much of that morning, however, the general was on the bridge, standing beside the Task Force commander, Admiral Kirk, watching through binoculars the distant smoke shrouding the shore, his ears plugged with cotton to muffle the blast of the *Augusta*'s guns, his nose swathed in plaster over an embarrassing boil that had been troubling him for days. Photographers were kept away from First Army's commander on 6 June.

The day had begun with a series of minor alarms: the sight of the swell that they knew at once would imperil the DD tanks; the report of 15 E-boats putting out from Cherbourg, sinking the Norwegian destroyer *Svenner* before they were put to flight: "As the morning lengthened," Bradley wrote, "my worries deepened over the alarming and fragmentary reports we picked up on the navy net. From those messages we could piece together only an incoherent account of sinkings, swampings, heavy enemy fire and chaos on the beaches. Though we could see it dimly through the haze and hear the echo of its guns, the battle belonged that morning to the thin, wet line of khaki that dragged itself ashore on the Channel coast of France."[3] By mid-morning the apparent collapse of the landing plan, both on and offshore, had plunged V Corps' staff into the deepest dismay. Colonel Benjamin Talley, cruising in a DUKW a few hundred yards from the beach to report directly to Gerow, told of LCTs milling around the smoke-shrouded sands "like a stampeding herd of cattle".

Bradley "gained the impression that our forces had suffered an irreversible catastrophe".[4] A situation was unfolding that came nearer than any that day to matching the terrible fears of Churchill, Brooke and Eisenhower.

Ranger Mike Rehm of C Company, 5th Battalion, landed in Dog Green sector shortly after H-Hour with 10 men, two of whom were killed and three wounded in the first hundred yards between the sea and the base of the hill. Rehm huddled for shelter behind a knocked-out DD tank, finding himself beside a Ranger whom he did not recognize, smoking a cigar. Suddenly they discovered that the tank was not knocked out, for its engine sprang into life and it began to move. The two men ran hastily towards the sea wall. After a few paces Rehm glanced around and saw that his companion lay covered in blood from the waist down. He reached the wall alone. There he lay through the two hours which followed, amidst a huddle of infantry and other Rangers representing almost every unit on the beach that morning.

A, B and C Companies of 2nd Ranger Battalion had lain offshore awaiting a signal from their commanding officer, Colonel Rudder, to land and advance through the positions of the landing force on Pointe du Hoc, if this successfully gained its objectives. But even after delaying 15 minutes beyond the appointed radio rendezvous, the men tossing in the boats had heard nothing. They were obliged to assume that the Pointe du Hoc landing had failed. They were ordered in to the western flank of Omaha beach. One LCA struck a mine as it approached, blowing off the door of the craft, killing the seaman manning it and stunning the Ranger platoon commander. His 34 men floundered out of the sinking vessel and struck out for the shore. The next platoon commander, Lieutenant Brice, waded onto the beach and turned to shout "Let's go!" to his men before falling dead in front of them. Meanwhile, A Company's craft had grounded 75 yards offshore, and many of its men died in the water under machine-gun fire. When Gerard Rotthof's mother heard that her son was to become a radioman, she said: "Well at least he won't have to carry a rifle any more." But now Rotthof lay trapped on the beach beneath the weight of his 60-pound SCR 284 set, wounded by mortar fragments in the face and back. He received the last rites twice, but somehow survived terrible internal injuries. Only 35 men of A Company and 27 from B of the 2nd Rangers reached the sea wall, out of 130 who launched from the transports before dawn.

200 yards out from the beach, Lieutenant Sid Salomon and 1 Platoon of C Company still supposed that the whole thing looked a pushover: not a single shell or small-arms round had come close to them. Then the ramp dropped and they were exposed to the full fury of the defences. An immensely tall 31-year-old graduate of New York University who enlisted in March 1942, Salomon had ordered his men to go all-out for the cliff base, under no circumstances pausing for a casualty. Yet within seconds one of his sergeants, Oliver Reed, was hit and fell beneath the ramp. Salomon could not stop himself from seizing the wounded man and dragging him through the waist-high water to the beach. Some of the platoon overtook him as he floundered, and now he passed four already dead from a mortar burst. He himself fell hit in the shoulder. Convinced that he was finished, he called to his platoon sergeant, Bob Kennedy. Reaching into his field jacket, he said: "I'm dead. Take the maps." But then a machine-gun began to kick up sand in front of them, and Salomon found that he was not only alive, but could run. At the base of the cliff he counted nine survivors of his platoon, out of 30 who left the landing craft. His old sergeant, who had left the platoon on promotion, insisted upon joining them for the assault. Salomon had placed him last out of the boat to give him the best chance of making it. But Sergeant Goales was already among the dead. All told, some two-thirds of the company were casualties.

It was a tribute to the quality of the Rangers that despite losses on a scale that stopped many infantry units in their tracks on Omaha that morning, the survivors of C Company pressed on to climb the cliffs west of the beach with bayonets and toggle ropes, clearing German positions one by one in a succession of fierce close-quarter actions with tommy guns and phosphorus grenades. Sergeant Julius Belcher charged headlong against one pillbox, tossed in a grenade and then shot down the garrison as they staggered out of the entrance. In their own area, they found later that they had killed some 60 Germans on 6 June. Yet they lacked the strength and the heavy weapons to press on westwards towards Pointe du Hoc. Towards the end of morning, Salomon stood in a captured German position, gazing down on the chaos below. "I was of the opinion that the invasion had been a failure," he said laconically.[5] He reflected that it was going to be a long swim home.

Corporal Bill Preston's DD crew of the 743rd Tank Battalion watched five of their unit's Shermans sink on launching offshore before it became obvious to the officer commanding their group of eight LCTs that the conditions were impossible. The remainder of the tanks were brought to within 250 yards of the beach before leaving the craft, very late. They glimpsed the cliffs shrouded in thick clouds of smoke as they ran in, then they were crawling out of the water among huddles of isolated infantrymen under intense small-arms fire. The tank commander, a Minnesotan farmer named Ted Geske, pressed the button to collapse their canvas screens, but nothing happened. He clambered out of the turret to do the job manually. At that moment, the waterproofing fell, and Geske was left cursing at his own vulnerability, perched on the hull in the midst of the battlefield. They saw that their tank was well to the right of its objective. They could see dead engineers floating beyond the beach obstacles, where so many wounded men also died as the tide came in over them. They later discovered to their dismay that they had run over one man, for they found his clothing jammed in their tracks. Then they saw the neighbouring platoon of Shermans brew up briskly one by one as an anti-tank gun caught them. Their battalion commander was hit in the shoulder as he stood on the sand, seeking to direct a tankdozer to clear a path for the armour through one of the beach exits.

It was obvious that something was very wrong. 21 of the unit's 51 tanks were destroyed on Omaha, and the neighbouring battalion fared even worse. Preston's crew simply took up position just above the high-water mark, and began to fire at such German positions as they could identify. These were not very many, for the tank fired only about a third of its ammunition before dusk. The 743rd remained on the beach for the next 12 hours.

Some unhappy men ended up on Omaha who should never have been there at all under such circumstances. Sergeant Andy Hertz, the Boston-bred son of a Dutch Jewish father and British mother, had been building airfields in England for almost two years with the 922nd Aviation Engineer Regiment when, somewhat to their bewilderment, he and his unit were issued with carbines, mines, bazookas and combat equipment, and loaded onto invasion transports to build airstrips in France. Aboard his liberty ship offshore, Hertz was in the galley listening to radio reports of the fall of Rome when the engineers were piped on deck. They saw the burning shore before them. A landing craft came alongside. Its skipper asked if the ship could provide any coffee, and announced that he could take in 90 men. A Ranger commanding officer sharing the ship with them declined to send his men ashore at that moment. The major responsible for the engineers shouted that they would go. Lacking assault training, they found the most frightening experience of the morning to be the descent of the scrambling nets into the pitching craft. Then, as they pulled away from the side, they saw their major waving farewell from the upper deck. He had decided to leave Hertz and the others to explore Omaha alone that day, and they never saw him again. An hour or so later, they struggled through five feet of water to the beach.

Few men or vehicles seemed to be moving. Hertz met a very frightened young 18-year-old from the 29th Division who said that he was the only survivor of his squad. The man in front of Hertz, Sergeant Valducci, suddenly fell down, screaming: "I'm shot!" A beachmaster ran to the group and demanded: "Who are you people?" Engineers, they said. "Sounds good," he replied, "we've got wire to clear here. You got bangalores?" No, they said. They were aviation engineers. "Who the hell sent you in?" They shrugged: "Some sonofabitch." And so they joined the clusters of stranded Americans on Omaha, lying behind such shelter as they could find through the hours that followed.[6]

Leading Aircraftsman Norman Phillips was one of a party of 158 British RAF personnel who were landed on Omaha: "We could see a shambles ahead of us on the beach – burning tanks, jeeps, abandoned vehicles, a terrific crossfire."[7] The captain of their LCT ordered them to offload anyway. The first vehicles found themselves driving into eight feet of water. The men struggled to the shore and formed a human chain to assist the non-swimmers. They landed on a sandspit crowded with wounded soldiers who lacked any medical attention. The British officers organized their men into salvage parties to rescue all the equipment that they could, but most had lost everything. Two RAF men were seized and taken prisoner by nervous Americans who could not identify their uniforms. By nightfall, the air force party had lost eight killed, 35 wounded, and 28 of their 35 vehicles. It was 33 days before they were issued with fresh clothing, 108 days before their lost arms and ammunition were replaced.

The reports that reached V Corps and General Bradley from Omaha that morning were not merely gloomy, but at times almost panic-stricken. Bradley's personal aide and Admiral Kirk's gunnery officer cruised close inshore aboard a PT boat and returned soaked and grim. Bradley considered halting all landings on the eastern beach and diverting the follow-up waves to Utah. A monstrous traffic jam had developed off the beach. By a serious flaw in the timetable, soft-skinned vehicles were beginning to arrive to offload in the middle of the battle. Among many naval crews who displayed exemplary courage, there were others whose lack of experience and determination magnified the confusion. The sailors manning a huge rhino raft loaded with vehicles simply abandoned it, 700 yards out, and the drivers and cargo drifted out of control until the rising tide brought them ashore. The Rangers had developed an early scepticism about naval efficiency when the officer in charge of one of their landing craft rammed a breakwater before getting out of his English harbour, and the skipper of another spent the cross-Channel voyage prostrate with seasickness. Now, one group of Rangers found themselves left to bring their landing craft in to the beach unaided. Its crew simply took to their dinghy and deserted them. In contrast to these episodes, the sailors manning two LCTs with immense courage rammed the beach obstacles head-on, and remained in position using every gun to support the infantry in their plight.

Lieutenant-Colonel John Williamson, commanding the 2nd/18th Infantry of the 1st Division, led his men into their LCVPs soon after 8.00 a.m., more than an hour late. When some craft began to swamp as they circled waiting for word that the beach was clear, the crews of others sought to begin rescue operations. After some forceful urging from Williamson, the craft began their run-in. They approached the shore not in an orderly wave, line abreast, but in a column, a queue, jostling for position on the sands. "The beach was loaded with men, tanks, DUKWs," said Williamson. "I was surprised that nobody had moved off." Major Frank Colacicco, executive officer of the 3rd/18th, stood among his men on the deck of an LCI, watching the spectacle ashore in utter bewilderment: "It was like a theatre. We could see it all, we knew that something was knocking the tanks out, but we kept asking, 'Why don't they clear the beach? Why aren't our people getting off?' " When at last their own turn came to approach the sands, Colacicco's LCI struck an obstacle whose mine blew up. Some men were hurled into the water by the blast, others found themselves struggling in the surf moments later as the craft settled. At last someone on the beach got a lifeline out to them, and the soaking men dragged themselves ashore. The major was told that Brigadier Wyman, the assistant divisional commander, wanted to see him. He reached the command post after being knocked off his feet by a mortar blast. He was told to take over the objectives of the 1st/16th, and returned to his men lying below the sea wall to point out to them, unanswerably: "We can't stay here." Slowly they began to work up the hillside, crawling over the immobile figures of men of the 116th Infantry: "They were too green to know that the closer you are to the enemy, the better off you will be." Colacicco tore a strip off one man he saw firing apparently recklessly along the hillside: "Just settle down," said the major soothingly. "That's our men over there." "But sir, they have overcoats on," insisted the soldier. Indeed they were German riflemen.

Yet although the defenders possessed the capability to maul the American landing on Omaha seriously, to impede and to disorganize it, they lacked the power to halt it absolutely. Despite the near total destruction of the first wave of invaders landing on the western flank below Vierville, despite the casualties and the terror inflicted upon thousands of green troops, a great many men survived to reach the sea wall alive – enough, finally, to swamp the vastly outnumbered German defenders. General Marcks' LXXXIV Corps reserve, the 915th Regiment, had set off in pursuit of the mythical paratroop force of Allied dummies at 4.00 a.m. on 6 June. It was hours after the seaborne landing before the 915th could be reached by dispatch rider, regrouped, and brought back from the Carentan–Isigny area on foot and by commandeered vehicle. The defenders thus lacked any force capable of mounting a co-ordinated counter-attack either against the attackers of Omaha, or against the British threat to Bayeux, further east. At Omaha, the Americans found themselves facing Germans of the 352nd Division as well as the 716th – eight battalions instead of four. The defenders possessed the strength and determination to fight doggedly from fixed positions. But where the Americans, inch by inch, gained ground, they were able to keep it. The toeholds prised out of the heights above the beach that day by a few brave men of the

Rangers, the 1st and 29th Divisions could never normally have been held against the quick local counter-attacks at which the German army excelled. But such movements did not develop. Like a trickling stream slipping between pebbles, a handful of courageous leaders and small groups of men found their way around the German strongpoints covering the beach exits, and forced a path for the American army off Omaha beach. The Corps plan for the attack was a failure. But the men on the hillside, spurred by their own desperation, found their own means to gain the high ground.

The principal problem in almost every attack on every battlefield is to maintain momentum. Every instinct, especially among inexperienced soldiers, is to take cover under fire. Instinct is reinforced when the bodies of others who have failed to do so lie all around. It requires a considerable act of will to persuade limbs to act which have suddenly acquired an immobility of their own. Inexperienced troops find it notoriously difficult to assess the extent of resistance and risk. On some occasions this can be to their advantage – or rather, that of their commanders – because it leads them to perform acts that more seasoned soldiers would not be so foolhardy as to attempt. But on Omaha the 29th Division, in its first experience of combat, deprived in the first hours of many of its officers, dismayed by its losses and confused by its predicament, became dangerously paralyzed. The veteran 1st Division, on its left, performed significantly better – indeed, most Americans later agreed that without "The Big Red One" the battle would have been lost.

It was individuals, not divisions, who determined the outcome of the day. It is arguable that as early as mid-morning, when Bradley and Gerow were still receiving deeply gloomy reports from Omaha, the real situation was much more encouraging than the view of the beach from the ships led the commanders to believe. Barely two hours after H-Hour, when the formidable network of German wire and machine-guns was still blocking all movement up the five valleys offering vehicle access from the beach, small groups of Americans had already reached the high ground to threaten the German flanks. The survivors of the 2nd Rangers' A and B Companies reached the sea wall at 7.45 a.m., and immediately began to work up the heights. Staff Sergeant William Courtney and Private First Class William Braher of A Company's 1 Platoon were probably the first Americans to reach the top of the cliff, around 8.30 a.m. When the Rangers gained the summit, they were too few in number to achieve a decisive success, although they sent word to a company of the 116th Infantry below to follow them up, and one boat section did so. But in the next two hours, a succession of similar small-scale actions took place all along the Omaha front, driving vital wedges into the German defences. 23 men of E Company, 2/16th Infantry, under Lieutenant John Spalding gained the hill and began to attack the German strongpoint which covered the east side of the St Laurent exit from the rear. After two hours of dogged fighting within the network of pillboxes and communicating trenches, the Americans cornered an officer and 20 men and forced their surrender.

Brigadier-General Norman Cota and his 29th Division command group reached the beach at 7.30 a.m. with the 116th Regiment's headquarters. The general began to move among the bewildered tangle of infantrymen, Rangers, naval beach maintenance parties and gunner forward observers. He saw one man who attempted to move up the hill shot down. The soldier lay in front of the American positions crying: "Medico, I'm hit!" repeatedly for several minutes. Then he moaned "Mama" and cried for a few moments before he died. Two of the headquarters group were killed within three feet of Cota when he established his first command post, while his signaller was hurled 20 feet up the bluff by blast. But the fiery, inexhaustible brigadier began pushing officers, urging men, seeking routes by which to break the bloody deadlock by the sea wall.

Mike Rehm of the 5th Rangers had been huddled beneath the shingle bank for two hours or more with a group of men when Cota appeared. In one of his legendary encounters of the day, the general demanded to know who they were. Rangers, he was told. "Then, godammit, if you're Rangers get up and lead the way!" exploded Cota.[8] The men began to thrust four-foot lengths of bangalore torpedo beneath the wire ahead, locking them together until they could blow a gap. In front, the entire hillside was wreathed in smoke from the blazing undergrowth. Coughing and choking, the Rangers realized that they could not run through it, but at last they pulled on their gas masks and groped forward. Some 35 men reached the metalled road at the top of the hill. Covered by 60 mm mortars firing at such short range that the tubes were almost vertical, they began to work slowly westwards. There were now Americans behind some of the most dangerous German positions covering the beach.

By 11.00 a.m., Vierville was in American hands. When Cota himself reached a house on the edge of the village, he found 70 men sheltering against the wall who shouted "Sniper! Sniper!" as he approached. The brigadier impatiently ordered them to clear the way. They closed in on the German, who threw a stick grenade down the hill towards them before being killed seconds later. Cota began to move back down the draw towards the beach. He met one of his own staff officers, Major William Bretton, clutching a briefcase and looking exceedingly angry. "Dammit, I can't get these people to move," complained Bretton. Cota called a young infantry captain and told him to get his men going off the beach. Hesitantly, they began to obey. Then Cota spotted an abandoned bulldozer loaded with TNT, desperately needed to blow obstacles down the beach. He shouted to the men lying around it for a volunteer to drive the explosives to the engineers. At last a red-headed soldier stood up and said, "I'll do it," and climbed on the vehicle. Yard by yard, the beach was unsticking.[9] At 1.30 p.m., Gerow signalled to Bradley: "Troops formerly pinned down on beaches . . . advancing up heights behind beaches."

The German strongpoints were being knocked out either by superbly vigorous gunfire from the destroyers steaming as close as 800 yards offshore, or by determined action from Rangers or infantry. Hein Severloh's battery had long since been reduced to firing single rounds in place of salvoes, for several weeks earlier half its ammunition reserve had been moved further inland as an intended precautionary measure against a direct hit. Now the gunners had no means of bringing shells forward and the only truck driver who attempted to do so was blown up on the journey by an Allied aircraft attack. By noon, Severloh himself had fired 12,000 rounds from his machine-gun, and was reduced to shooting tracer. This was helpful to his aim, for the gun's sights had been shot off by a stray bullet, but deadly in revealing his position to American spotters. WN 59 and 61 – the neighbouring "resistance nests" – had fallen silent. WN 62 had no field of fire on its west side, where the invaders were already working up to the rear. When their battery had fired all its ammunition, the gunners blew up their pieces and retreated southwards on their horsedrawn limbers. Severloh and the men in the strongpoint decided that enough was enough. They ran crouching from the entrance had began to work their way up the hill towards the rear, and safety. Only Severloh and one signaller escaped alive.

All that afternoon, Brigadier Cota moved relentlessly up and down the hillside, urging on the men clambering in sluggish files through the minefields and over the bodies of the dead. There were still perilously few heavy weapons on the higher ground to support the infantry now beginning to fight through the first hedges and fields of the *bocage*. When he found a group of Rangers claiming to be pinned down beyond Vierville, Cota himself walked ahead of them across the open ground to demonstrate that a man could move and survive. Many soldiers who attempted to set this sort of example on 6 June and in the weeks that followed were killed instantly. But Cota lived and the Rangers moved forward. Although persistent shellfire was still falling on the beach behind them, most of the Germans defending the hillside were dead or captured, and their gunnery OPs had been destroyed, removing the batteries' vital eyes. Medical corpsmen were moving among the wounded, looking out for those who had died so that they might give their blankets to men who were still living, but shivering. One of Cota's staff marvelled at the spectacle of a group of engineers sitting on the sand eating their K rations, apparently oblivious of the dead and wounded all around them. A dog, which had evidently been the pet of one of the German strongpoints, fell upon men of the 1st Division moving up the bluff with impressive enthusiasm, and had to be driven off with carbine fire. At 4.30 p.m., a staff officer of the 29th Division noted in his diary: "Prayed for the fourth time today, asking God – 'Why do these things have to be visited upon men?' " Brigadier Cota and his aide saw a soldier who appeared to be frozen with terror, praying on his knees in the scrub above the beach. But when they reached him, they saw that he was dead.[10]

On the high ground, Lieutenant-Colonel Williamson and the 2nd/18th had advanced to within a mile of their designated D-Day objectives. Like every American soldier above Omaha that day, he and his men were cursing the hedges of the *bocage*, which provided such perfect cover for snipers and were already inflicting interminable delays upon advancing units. Men sought cover whenever firing sounded nearby. Crossing a gap, the young soldier in front of Williamson was shot. The colonel put a Browning automatic rifle on top of the hedge and raked the area with fire. They moved onwards a little way without further casualties, then took up positions for the night just short of Colville. The Omaha beachhead had been secured. The Germans lacked the power and mobility to reverse the verdict of the afternoon. By nightfall, the Americans controlled a perimeter up to a mile deep beyond Omaha, while the 4th Division on Utah had linked up with General Maxwell Taylor and his men of the 82nd Airborne Division west of the causeways from the beach. Gerow of V Corps had not planned to establish his headquarters ashore until the following day. But Bradley, conscious of the urgent need to get a grip on the situation from the beach, told him to get his corps staff offloaded immediately. All the plans for a rapid supply build-up were to be sacrificed to the need to get more men onto the ground. 90 amphibious DUKWs, preloaded with ammunition, provided the vital minimum supply to sustain the forces ashore overnight. Some landing craft crews, utterly exhausted, dropped their anchors when darkness fell. Naval officers in launches hastened among them, urging the crews back into motion. That night Montgomery discussed with Dempsey the possibility of landing all further troops planned for Omaha on the British beaches. The suggestion was never pursued, but in view of the immensely dangerous gulf that such a change of plan would have exposed in the middle of the Allied line, it is a measure of the alarm surrounding the Omaha situation that it was ever discussed.

While the Utah landing had gone as nearly in accordance with planning as any commander could have expected, on Omaha the failures and errors of judgement by the staff had only been redeemed by the men on the sand. Many officers, including Brigadier Cota, believed that the American landings would have proved far easier had they been made in darkness, a possibility rejected by the navy and air force, who insisted upon the need for daylight to make best use of their bombardment power. Had elite infantry such as the Rangers led the way ashore before dawn, it is indeed likely that they would have been able to get off the beach and work in among the German positions with or without the bombardment. The events of D-Day emphasized the limited ability of high explosives to destroy strong defensive positions. But the follow-up waves and armour would have suffered immense problems attempting to get ashore under heavy fire before dawn. The timing of the landing was probably sound, although the troops could have profited immensely from continuing support fire until the moment they reached the beach, and from better gunnery forward observation thereafter. American naval reports spoke of the frustration of ships cruising silently offshore, unable to fire because of lack of identified targets.

The Americans refused to employ British-designed specialized armour – tanks throwing flame and explosive charges, and flail mineclearers. These would certainly have made a significant impact on Omaha. But they were not a magic formula for success. Given the formidable weight of German firepower concentrated against the five critical beach exits, it is likely that much of the specialized armour would have been knocked out on the beach in the same fashion as so many gun Shermans, merely contributing to the logjam of wreckage that did so much to hamper movement of vehicles and landing craft.

Chester Wilmot and others have seized upon the example of Omaha to demonstrate the supposed shortcomings of the American soldier.[12] In the weeks that followed, some American commanders, including Bradley, were to be seriously worried by the performance of some infantry units. On D-Day, there proved to be sufficient outstanding individual American soldiers and enough elite units such as the Rangers and Airborne to gain the day. Casualties on each of the Allied beaches, including Omaha, were almost exactly in proportion to the weight of unsuppressed enemy fire that the invaders met. The Americans suffered 4,649 casualties among their seaborne landing force to put ashore 55,000 men on D-Day. If the American line at midnight on 6 June was still tenuous, and fell some distance short of its planned objectives, V and VII Corps had achieved their vital strategic purposes merely by establishing themselves ashore.

It was on the British front on D-Day, where so much rested upon fast and ruthless progress inland from the beaches, that far more dramatic strategic hopes were at stake.

The British beaches

At 7.25 a.m., an hour after the Americans began landing on Omaha, the minesweeping flail tanks of the 22nd Dragoon Guards touched Sword beach at the eastern end of the Allied line, precisely on schedule. Lieutenant Charles Munday in *Leander I* drove ashore into the mortar and machine-gun fire with the hatch open as usual because of his haunting fear of fire. Some of the sappers disembarking with them were hit immediately.

Corporal Charles Baldwin watched the same instant fate befall the engineers who led his flail of the Westminster Dragoons: "They were flung about as German machine-gun fire hit them, clutching various parts of their bodies, jolting like rag dolls, then sinking out of sight into the water. I often wondered if any of those unfortunate men survived the landing. Even slightly wounded, the weight of their equipment dragged them under."[1]

Mundy's column of five Shermans clattered forward out of the landing craft and took up echelon formation to begin flailing, thrashing the sand with their great probosces of chains, creeping forward astonishingly unscathed to the metalled road, where they switched off the equipment and began engaging the German defences with their 75 mm guns. Mundy could hear screams from defensive positions above the beach as a Crocodile flame-thrower puffed its terrible jet of fire towards them. 34 of the 40 Sherman DD amphibious tanks launched against Sword also arrived as planned, ahead of the infantry, cleared the beach successfully and became heavily engaged in the dunes beyond. A few minutes later, the 20 landing craft carrying the first wave of the 1st South Lancashires and 2nd East Yorkshires dropped their ramps and launched the lead companies, followed 20 minutes later by the second wave. These point battalions suffered less severely crossing the beach than those which followed. The East Yorkshires immediately began moving off towards Ouistreham, with men of 4 and 10 Commandos. 41 Commando, which took heavy casualties in their landing, headed for Lion-sur-Mer. By 9.00 a.m. the South Lancashires were between one and one and a half miles inland, at Hermanville. Vehicles and supporting units were pouring ashore, clogging the beaches. From the outset, the Sword landing was a remarkable success. Lieutenant Arthur Heal, commanding the sapper platoon attached to the 1st Suffolks, was still congratulating himself on completing his first trip in a landing craft without feeling seasick when the order came, "Ramp down! All out!" A few moments later, having passed through the infantry on the beach and regrouped for the battalion's advance to its objectives inland, Heal was enjoying a moment of anti-climax and relief. There had been powerful rumours within the unit before D-Day that they would pay for the honour of leading the assault by accepting withering losses.

The British landing plan for each brigade front called for four LCTs carrying four DD tanks apiece to put these ashore at H−5 minutes, followed at H-Hour by four LCTs carrying the specialized armour – flails, Crocodiles, Petards and the like – with sapper groups to begin work on the obstacles. Behind them at H+7 came eight assault landing craft bearing the two leading infantry companies; at H+20 another eight LCAs followed with two more infantry companies, and at H+25 came two LCAs with the men of the beach group. At H+35 bulldozers and more specialized armour rolled ashore; at H+60 nine LCTs with self-propelled guns; at H+90 10 LCTs with a full squadron of tanks. The tenth wave, behind all these, carried more gunners and 21 amphibious DUKWs loaded with stores and ammunition. COSSAC had predicted the loss of 10 per cent of the landing craft, with a further 20 per cent damaged. In the event, the losses were less severe, but it was not remarkable that, with a landing plan of such complexity, in many places the schedule collapsed in the first half-hour and successive waves reached the shore helplessly entangled with each other – creating a great jumble of men, vehicles, landing craft and wreckage on the waterline.

Even on Sword, where the losses were slight in relation to the scale of the assault, some men paid a speedy price for the success of the 3rd Division. Two LCTs ran off course and rammed two DD tanks, which sank with merciless immediacy. The seizure of the La Breche strongpoint covering the beach took three hours, during which troops coming ashore had to struggle through fierce fire. Some men reaching the beach in Queen White sector were touched to see a lone French girl struggling in the shallows to help wounded men out of the water. Shell and mortar fire from inland continued to harass the beach for most of 6 June and the days which followed it. The South Lancashires, who bore the brunt of the La Breche battle, lost 11 officers and 96 other ranks on D-Day; the East Yorkshires about the same.

Private Len Ainslie was an anti-tank gunner of the King's Regiment, which was to provide local defence for the beach area. A regular soldier who had been in the army since 1938, if Ainslie had had his way he would have landed by glider, for he had asked for a transfer to airborne forces. But his colonel refused to forward the request because Ainslie was a battalion bugler. Now, 100 yards offshore, his landing craft was struck amidships on the starboard side by a shell. Ainslie was appalled by the trail of devastation immediately in front of him. A big cook's head vanished, the company commander's batman lost his legs. A jumble of other broken bodies drifted amid the rush of water pouring through the side. A naval officer called abruptly: "Come on, all out!" Men began to struggle over the side of the sinking hulk. Ainslie tried for a moment to help a young soldier, who remarked flatly as he lay, "I can't do anything now, can I?" Then the officer shouted to Ainslie: "Leave him." Somebody ashore hurled them a line. The survivors swam and stumbled through the dead and the wounded in the water to the beach, where they saw the battalion's commanding officer killed a few minutes later. They were all soaking wet, their battledress and boots and equipment stiff with salt for days. But Ainslie and most of his comrades felt less a sense of shock than elation at their own achievement in survival, in having made it.

Some of the fire falling upon Sword beach during the morning came from the four 150 mm self-propelled guns of 3 Battery, 1716th Artillery Regiment, firing from a position at Plumetot, 3,000 yards inland from the coast. After standing by since midnight, at dawn its commander, Lieutenant Rudolf Schaaf, walked forward a little way until he could see the great invasion fleet stretched out before him off the coast. He found the spectacle impressive rather than frightening – it all seemed somehow detached from himself. "Well," he wondered thoughtfully, "what do we do now?" Contact with the battery's forward observer in a "resistance nest" on the beach was lost soon after first light. Thereafter, the guns fired on predetermined DFs – Defensive Fire targets – measured many weeks before. Around mid-morning, Schaaf was suddenly ordered to take his guns immediately north to the coast, and counter-attack towards Lion-sur-Mer with infantry of the 3rd Battalion of 736th Regiment.

It was a pathetic episode. The first man of the battery to be killed was a taxi-driver from Leipzig who had been posted back to Germany several days earlier, but lingered in order to buy food and presents to take home. Now he died driving forward a truck loaded with ammunition. The German infantry were middle-aged men. They were strafed intermittently from the air as they advanced in open order down the gentle decline to the sea, and soon found themselves under fierce gun and small-arms fire. Schaaf's guns, astonishingly, approached Lion intact at around 10.30 a.m., and the Germans watched British infantrymen scuttling for cover, lacking heavy weapons or tanks to deal with them. As they fired into the buildings over open sights, little clusters of invaders emerged with their hands up, and were hustled to the rear. But the weight of British fire rapidly overwhelmed the infantry. When the Germans at last despaired and began to pull back, only 20 men of the 3rd/736th remained with the guns when they reached the old battery position. They examined their prisoners, and were awed by their superb maps, food and equipment. Schaaf ordered them to be herded into a shell hole. In great agitation, a German-speaking British officer produced a copy of the Geneva Convention which he waved at the artilleryman, declaring forcefully that it was illegal to shoot them. "Nobody is going to be shot," said Schaaf brusquely. A few minutes later, he was telephoned by the excitable Major Hof, his battalion commander, and ordered to advance immediately to regimental HQ, two miles away on Hill 61, and attempt to extricate them from heavy attack. Schaaf abandoned his prisoners in their shell hole, and departed south-eastwards.

On Juno beach, a few miles west of Sword, the Canadians had also broken through the coastal crust, but at heavier cost. The local naval commanders delayed H-Hour from 7.35 to 7.45 a.m., and even then many craft were late. As a result, the fast incoming tide covered an offshore reef which it had been feared would prove a serious hazard, and the first units found themselves landing right in amid the German beach obstacles. As the landing craft went astern after unloading, the coxswains could do nothing to prevent themselves from becoming helplessly entangled in mines and twisted steel. 20 of the leading 24 vessels were lost or damaged, among a total of 90 out of 306 employed on Juno that morning. Close artillery support for all the British landings was to be provided by Royal Marines manning obsolete Centaur tanks mounting 95 mm howitzers, but these proved lethally unseaworthy in landing craft. Scores capsized and were lost. Only six of 40 intended to support the Canadians reached the shore. Most of the DD tanks made it, but arrived behind the leading infantry rather than in time to provide suppressive fire ahead of them. Tanks and infantry moved inland together, becoming entangled in heavy street fighting in Courseulles that lasted well into the afternoon. The capture of St Aubin took three hours. The enemy in Bernières, where the assault company landing below the village lost fifty per cent of its strength in 100 yards, fought hard until they were outflanked. But in accordance with the plan, the Canadian follow-up units passed through the assault troops still mopping up around the beaches, ignored the snipers, who continued in action until nightfall, and pressed on towards their objectives inland.

The 50th Division attacking Gold, the most westerly of the three British beaches, ran into their first serious difficulty in front of the fortified German positions at Le Hamel. The 1st Hampshires and 1st Dorsets landed under furious fire from bunkers scarcely scarred by the bombardment, manned by Germans of 716th Division's 1st Battalion. The British supporting tanks arrived too late to give the infantry immediate support and, as on Juno, very few of the Royal Marine Centaurs arrived at all. Corporal Chris Portway, who landed with 231st Brigade HQ, was impressed above all by the sense of "noise, noise, noise", the continuous roar of gunfire, much of it from the Allied bombardment ships. Major Dick Gosling, the artillery battery commander, who landed with the Hampshires' battalion headquarters, was pleasantly surprised in his first moments ashore to find that the beach "was not the raging inferno some people had feared". Then he saw ripples of sand being pitched up all around him, and heard a noise like a swarm of angry bees over his head – his first encounter with enemy fire in six years of soldiering. Nelson-Smith, the Hampshires' fire-eating CO, who had insisted upon leading his headquarters in with the first wave, called to the others to lie down. Gosling, hopeful that the colonel knew more than he did about what to do next, dutifully prostrated himself in a foot of water. Then they all sprang to their feet and began to run for the shelter of the dunes. A blast close at hand killed a man beside Gosling, and suddenly he found that he could not walk. A mortar fragment had struck him in the leg. Somehow he reached the dunes, where he found Nelson-Smith, also wounded. Gosling began desperately scraping a hole for his head with an entrenching tool. Most of the Hampshires' wireless sets had been knocked out by the blast in the midst of the headquarters group, and the gunner found his own set so hopelessly clogged with ships' morse and other units' communications that he was unable to send a single radio message that morning to his own guns offshore. A rifleman nearby craned his head briefly to look over the rim of the dune and immediately fell back dead. Gosling looked up cautiously, and was astounded to glimpse a German only 10 yards away. He pulled out his revolver and fired a shot which discouraged the enemy soldier – no doubt as shocked as the gunner himself – from appearing again.

The sound of intense small-arms fire now seemed more distant. Gosling assumed that the Hampshires were making progress. He had been lying immobile for some time when he glimpsed the first of his own self-propelled guns coming ashore, led by his second-in-command, Vere Broke, standing proudly upright in his half-track. Gosling yelled: "Vere – get your head down, you'll get shot!" Broke studiedly tilted his helmet an inch forward on his head.

Gunner Charles Wilson, also of the 147th Field Regiment, spent most of the run-in to the beach seeking shelter from the devastating noise of four 25-pounders firing alongside each other in the landing craft. Wilson was stripped to vest, pants and gym shoes for the invasion, for he was one of a group detailed to tow ashore and release one of the huge "roly-poly" mats over which the guns would drive up the beach:

> We hit two mines going in [wrote Wilson] – bottle mines on stakes. They didn't stop us, although our ramp was damaged and an officer standing on it was killed. We grounded on a sandbank. The first man off was a commando sergeant in full kit. He disappeared like a stone into six feet of water. We grasped the ropes of the "Roly Poly" and plunged down the ramp into the icy water. The mat was quite unmanageable in the rough water and dragged us away towards some mines. We let go the ropes and scrambled ashore. I lost my shoes and vest in the struggle, and had only my PT shorts. Somebody offered cigarettes but they were soaking wet. George in the bren carrier was first vehicle off the LCT. It floated for a moment, drifted onto a mine and sank. George dived overboard and swam ashore. The battery command post half-track got off with me running behind. The beach was strewn with wreckage, a blazing tank, bundles of blankets and kit, bodies and bits of bodies. One bloke near me was blown in half by a shell and his lower part collapsed in a bloody heap in the sand. The half-track stopped and I managed to struggle into my clothes.[2]

Major Gosling eventually managed to hobble down to a German pillbox on the beach, where he sat among other casualties waiting for evacuation. The occupants had clearly been disturbed over breakfast – coffee and sausage lay on the table, a picture of Hitler on the wall. Gosling found a letter from a French girl named Madeleine, obviously addressed to one of the garrison, promising to meet him on the evening of 6 June.

It is only for commanders and historians that it is possible to say that a battle proved a great deal easier than expected, and that casualties were remarkably light. For the men taking part in the D-Day landings, there were moments of violent intensity and horror on the British beaches as shattering as anything that happened on Omaha. It would have availed them little to know that their experience was much less terrible in scale than that of the Americans, for in kind it was equally deadly. Three of the five landing craft bringing 47 Commando ashore struck mines. When the survivors who swam to the beach regrouped to begin their advance towards Port-en-Bessin, 46 men and almost every wireless set in the unit had been lost.

Most of the men of 73rd Field Company, Royal Engineers, shared a common sensation of relief on reaching a shore – even a hostile shore – after three days imprisoned on their landing craft. When the first of their LCTs lowered its ramp off Le Hamel, the leading Petard AVRE tank tipped forward into the water and jammed itself half in, half out. The craft swung slowly round with the tide until a mine exploded against its stern. With the bridge and engine badly damaged, and fire from the shore raking the crippled vessel, it lay helpless on the waterline until it could be unloaded at the next low tide at 1.00 p.m. Of the engineers aboard it, two were killed and several more wounded, including one young officer who had somehow escaped from the débacle at Singapore in 1942. A second LCT hit a mine and began to settle 300 yards offshore. One section of men was rescued by an LCT leaving the beach which, to their fury, insisted upon carrying them back to England. Another group was threatened with the same fate but, after furious protests from its NCO in charge, had themselves trans-shipped to yet another craft heading into the beach. Captain James Smith and his team had been working desperately on the beach obstacles for almost an hour when he ran to his company commander to report progress, and was killed by machine-gun fire as he reached him. For any of those ignorant of war who believed that army engineers merely built roads or bridges, 6 June revealed how the sappers were required to bear the very brunt of the battle, and the price that they paid for doing so.

The flail tanks of the Westminster Dragoons were modified to wade rather than to swim the last yards to the beach. As they tipped over the LCT ramps, the drivers saw the view through their periscopes turn dark green, then progressively lighten until the sky appeared once more and water poured off the hulls as they crawled up the shore. Captain Roger Bell halted for a

Commanders before D-Day: Tedder, Eisenhower and Montgomery (seated); Bradley, Ramsay, Leigh-Mallory and Bedell Smith (standing). *U.S. National Archives*

The air chiefs: Eisenhower with (left to right) Coningham, Leigh-Mallory, Brereton and Quesada.
General Elwood R. Quesada

Before D-Day: American Airborne pathfinders pose beside their Dakota. *Private*

Matériel massed for the invasion.
Imperial War Museum

THE 21ST ARMY

FRONT ROW: Thomas (43 Div.); Bucknall; Crerar;
MIDDLE ROW: Bullen-Smith (51 Div.); Keller (3 Cdn.
O'Connor; Barker (49 Div.); Crocker.
BACK ROW: Macmillan (15 Div.); Gale (6 Abn. Div.);

Richardson is third from the right in the second row, wearing helmet. *F.O. Richardson*

American soldiers are briefed for D-Day. *Imperial War Museum*

GROUP TEAM
Montgomery; Dempsey; Broadhurst; Ritchie.
Div.); Graham (50 Div.); Roberts (11 Armd. Div.);

Erskine (7 Armd. Div.). *Imperial War Museum*

Montgomery inspects the 5th/7th Gordons of 51st Highland Division during the run-up to OVERLORD. Lt-Col. Eric Hay walks behind the C-in-C.
Lt-Col. Eric Hay

The myth of Rommel as a 'good' German hostile to Nazism prevailed in the west for many years after the war. In reality, the C-in-C of Army Group B remained passionately devoted to Hitler until he became convinced that the war was militarily unwinnable. *U.S. National Archives*

D-Day: on the beach. *Imperial War Museum*

A fascinating glimpse of the Supreme Commander in mid-Channel; caught by the photographer looking far tougher than when pictured with the accommodating grin of the familiar Ike. *U.S. National Archives*

Beach defenders surrender to the Americans.
U.S. Army

(RIGHT) The build-up: American troops move inshore from the beaches. *U.S. Army*

US

(BELOW) George Small

(BELOW RIGHT) Phil Reisler (right, in black) with his tank crew.

Norman Cota. *UPI*

Lindley Higgins

Bill Preston

Harry Herman

Randall Bryant

Wilhelm Schickner

Hans Stober

Adolf Hohenstein

Rudolf Schaaf

(LEFT) Panzer leaders: Fritz Bayerlein, Kurt Kauffmann, Sepp Dietrich, staff officer.

Helmut Gunther

Heinz-Gunther Guderian

Austin Baker

Guy Simonds

Robin Hastings

Henry Lovegrove

Steve Dyson and (TOP) Dick Raymond

Chris Portway

(OPPOSITE) Airborne images of the battlefield: (TOP) Norman chalk pitted with foxholes *Imperial War Museum*; (LEFT) fighter-bomber's eye view of a German column after attack *U.S. Air Force*; (RIGHT) tank action among the hedges. *Imperial War Museum*

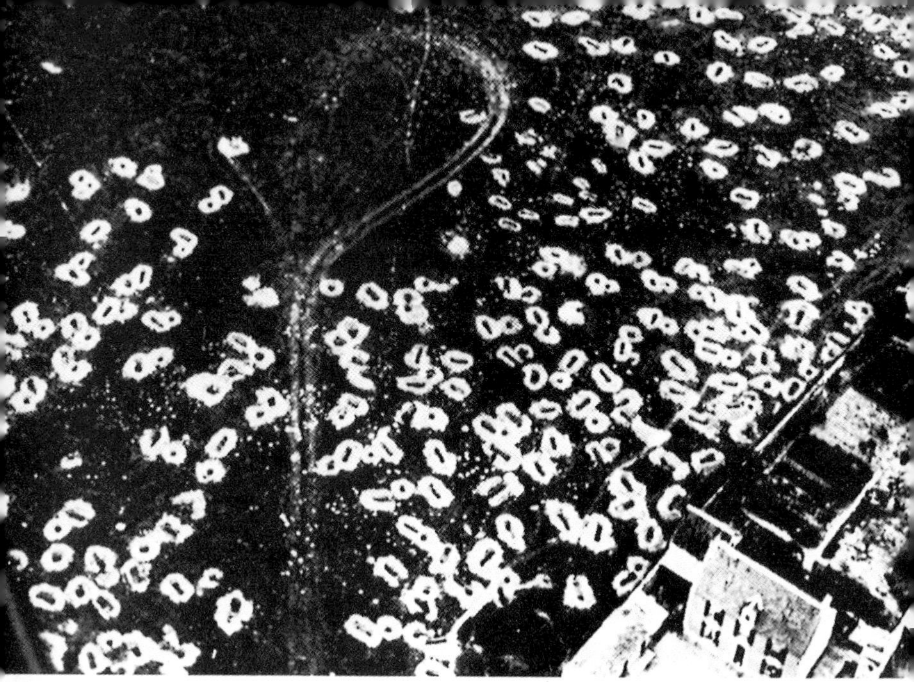

(TOP) A characteristic Normandy horizon: infantry advance through the standing corn behind a British tank. *Imperial War Museum*

(LEFT) American infantry dash between the hated hedges. Dead cows were among the most familiar landmarks of the battlefield. *Imperial War Museum*

(RIGHT) British anti-tank screen near Caen, with armoured bridging equipment in the background. *Imperial War Museum*

moment to check his position below La Rivière. His crew watched three sappers from a neighbouring AVRE Churchill clambering out onto its hull. Then there was a massive explosion, hurling sappers and fragments of tank into the air all around them and a sledgehammer thump on their own tank. For a moment they believed that they themselves had been hit by a shell, until Captain Bell reported that the engine of the exploding Churchill had struck them. They saw another tank explode. Corporal Charlie Baldwin in the co-driver's seat spotted the flash of the German gun and called over the intercom: "Eighty-eight-pillbox-eleven o'clock." They traversed rapidly and fired. "Missed," said Baldwin laconically. Jimmy Smith, the gunner, fired again and once more they assumed a miss. Bell said that they must press on anyway. They only learned later that they had destroyed the German gun. For all the attention focussed since D-Day upon the role of the specialized armour, it is striking to notice that, on the beaches, the "funnies" performing as conventional gun tanks made a markedly greater impact on the course of the battle than they did by using their engineer equipment, although this was obviously also valuable.

They began flailing at the high-water mark, and continued until they reached clear ground, where Bell pulled the pin on the green smoke canister to signal to the infantry that a lane was open. It fell on the floor of the turret, and they gasped and cursed amid the choking fumes until it could be retrieved and tossed out. Bell fought through the days that followed with his hair, face and moustache dyed a brilliant green. They drove on towards Crepon, Baldwin suddenly glimpsing three Germans cowering in a shellhole in the road. As they passed, the tank track slipped sideways into it and, over the roar of the engine, the Englishman caught the sound of the terrible screams beneath them. At their rendezvous in an orchard, they had just begun to boil a kettle when a bullet smacked against the hull beside them. They leapt quickly back into the tank and scanned the scenery. Like so many Allied soldiers in the weeks that followed, they decided that the shot could only have come from a church tower overlooking them. They worked high explosive rounds up and down the building until they were convinced that nothing inside it could have survived. Then the tanks moved on.

The 6th Green Howards, landing 1,000 yards eastwards below the German strongpoint at La Rivière, suffered the common run of small comedies, tragedies and moments of heroism. When the

LCA carrying the battalion HQ group grounded, its stern at once began to swing round towards a mined obstacle. The CO, Robin Hastings, sat on the ramp and dropped his feet cautiously into the water to explore the depth. Hitting bottom when he was only ankle-deep, the colonel paddled ashore. This was not an absurd precaution. Sergeant Hill of 16 Platoon, who had survived the entire North African and Sicilian campaigns, jumped from the ramp of another LCA into a deep shellhole, from which he could not extricate himself before the vessel ran over him.

Sergeant-Major Stan Hollis reached the beach feeling a little foolish, for he was already suffering a self-inflicted wound from a bad burn on the hand. He had carelessly seized the barrel of the bren gun with which he had been firing over the side of the craft as they closed in. His D Company advanced only a few hundred yards inland before they began to take casualties from a position to the right of the road. Major Lofthouse, the company commander, pointed it out to Hollis: "There's a pillbox in there, sergeant-major!" Without hesitating, Hollis sprang to his feet and ran 30 yards to the German position, spraying sten-gun fire as he went, until he reached the weapon slit, where he thrust in the barrel and hosed the interior with fire. Then he climbed on the roof, pulled the pin from a grenade, and leaned over to drop it through the slit. Not content with this, he began to advance alone along the communicating trench to the next pillbox. Its garrison hastily emerged and began to surrender. Hollis returned with 25 prisoners.

The sergeant-major, who performed a succession of feats of this kind in the weeks that followed, was later awarded the Victoria Cross. Every unit in every war needs a handful of men willing to commit acts of sacrificial courage to enable it to gain its objectives, and it is the nature of these that few who carry them out survive. But Hollis did, and lived to keep a Yorkshire pub after the war. Lieutenant-Colonel Hastings described him as a simple, straightforward Yorkshireman keen on horse-racing: "He was absolutely personally dedicated to winning the war – one of the few men I ever met who felt like that."

Austin Baker, wireless operator in an armoured recovery vehicle of the 4th/7th Dragoon Guards, was in an LCT which struck a mine as it manoeuvred inshore, among infantry wading up to their necks in the sea. Baker was hurled forward by the concussion, smashing a tooth on the turret hatch rim, but he managed hastily to close down the lid. The sailor directing the ramp lowering was hurled bodily into the air, and as the leading scout car drove off it was immediately knocked out by a shell. The others drove quickly off the beach, joining a procession of vehicles moving forwards between grassy banks and the skull and crossbones warnings, ACHTUNG MINEN, that were among the most familiar landmarks of every German battlefield. The village of Ver-sur-Mer had been considerably damaged in the bombardment, but a little cluster of French civilians emerged from the ruins to cheer and throw flowers. After losing their way for a time, Baker and his crew reached the inevitable orchard rendezvous. Among the other crews of the squadron, they began to exchange their excited stories of the landing while they drank tea and shared bully beef and biscuits with the crew of their wrecked landing craft, who had followed them ashore. Two tank commanders had already been killed by small-arms fire during the clearing of La Rivière. Two tanks had been swamped on the beach and a third disabled by a mine. A troop commander of B Squadron had met a self-propelled gun almost immediately after landing, and been beaten into action by the German's shot. This took off his leg, killed his operator and wounded the rest of the crew.

Yet nothing could dampen the exhilaration of those who had survived, sitting as wondering sightseers on ground that over four long years had attained for them the alien and mysterious status of the dark side of the moon. Corporal Portway of 231st Brigade thought that "once ashore, it all seemed better organised than most exercises". By 10.30 a.m., the British Second Army had landed fifteen infantry battalions, seven commandos, seven tank regiments, two engineer assault regiments, nine field artillery regiments and detachments of scores of supporting units. There had been setbacks, local failures, severe casualties to certain units, poor performance by some specialist equipment. Yet overall, the plan had succeeded stunningly well. Almost everywhere along the British line, the German coastal positions had been rolled up. It now remained to press forward to complete the second phase of the D-Day operation, to exploit German shock and surprise, ruthlessly to seize the vital ground inland.

Inland

Hitler's appointments for the morning of 6 June were not altered by the news of the Allied landings. He himself was in the Berghof at Berchtesgarten. OKW's Chief of Operations, Jodl, was in the little Reichchancellerie. For their usual midday conference that day, both men, along with their principal staff officers, were compelled to drive for an hour to Klessheim Castle, where they were officially receiving a Hungarian state visit. In a room beside the great entrance hall of the castle, Hitler was briefed on the first reports of the invasion. He approached the map of France on the wall, gazed at it for a moment, chuckled and declared in unusually broad Austrian tones: "So, we're off."[1] Then, after a few moments' further conversation with Jodl, he departed to meet the new Hungarian Prime Minister. A junior officer from Jodl's staff was dispatched to von Rundstedt to emphasize that there must be vigorous local counter-attacks against the beachhead.

Corporal Werner Kortenhaus and the rest of his company of 21st Panzer had begun to move up the Falaise–Caen road at 8.00 a.m. They were deeply unhappy, for the road ran perfectly straight and open. Moving in column in broad daylight, they felt utterly vulnerable – as indeed they were. The company was frequently halted to allow other units to speed past them. On the distant horizon, they glimpsed the smoke of the battlefield. Just south of Caen, they spotted an odd little tableau of two British soldiers standing alone in the corn by the road with their hands up, almost certainly men of 6th Airborne who had been dropped hopelessly wide. The panzers had no time to take prisoners, and hastened on. Then they learned that three companies of the regiment had been ordered to swing north-west, to move against the seaborne landings. They themselves were to head up the east bank of the Orne to engage the British airborne troops. As they moved forward, they were repeatedly compelled to pull in by the roadside and scramble beneath their tanks as Allied aircraft roared low overhead. They suffered their first casualty, a very young, half-trained replacement named Rammelkampf, who was killed by a machine-gun bullet from a strafing Typhoon. It remains one of the minor mysteries of D-Day that throughout their long drive up the road to the battlefield that morning, even after the lifting of the cloud that hampered air operations for part of the morning, 21st Panzer suffered little material damage from Allied fighter-bombers. Yet Kortenhaus and his comrades cursed the absence of the Luftwaffe as they watched the enemy overfly them with impunity. Where, they asked, were the thousands of German aircraft that they had been promised would be in the sky to support them on "The Day"?

All that morning and well into the afternoon, 21st Panzer's powerful armoured regiments – 127 Mk IV tanks and 40 assault guns – moved northwards, hampered by checks, delays and changes of orders imposed more as a result of failures of intelligence and the indecision of their own command than by Allied interference. Feuchtinger was impatient to move against the 6th Airborne bridgehead, but was frustrated by the British possession of the only bridge north of Caen by which his troops could cross the Orne. His panzergrenadiers were thus obliged to move through the city itself. The 2nd Battalion of 22nd Panzer Regi-

The Panzer IV was the most numerously-produced German tank of the war, equipping half the German tank units in Normandy. By 1944, it was obsolescent, but in its upgunned version – which the Allies called the Mk IV Special – was still a formidable enough opponent. Weighing 25 tons and moving at up to 25 mph, it carried 80 mm of frontal armour and 30 mm of side armour. Its 75-mm KwK 40 gun could penetrate 99 mm of armour at 100 yards, 92 mm at 500 yards, 84 mm at 1,000 yards. The "skirts" shown surrounding the hull in this version were designed to absorb the impact of hollow-charge projectiles, but all German armoured units in Normandy were exasperated by the manner in which these were torn off during movements among the dense hedges and orchards.

ment, 40 tanks strong, with which Kortenhaus was driving, was already approaching the paratroopers' perimeter when it was halted by orders from General Marcks at LXXXIV Corps. Marcks believed this to be a wasteful use of armour. One company only, the 4th, was left to support operations east of the Orne. The remainder were diverted to join the counter-attack west of Caen. The 1st Battalion, 80 tanks under Captain von Gottberg, was making its best speed to the startline near Lebisey, where the regimental commander, Colonel von Oppeln-Bronikowski, was already waiting with General Marcks. The corps commander had driven in person to oversee the battle. It was around 4.30 in the afternoon before this, the first major German armoured counter-attack upon OVERLORD, was ready to jump off against the British 3rd Division.

At 11.00 a.m. on the morning of 6 June, the three infantry battalions of Brigadier K. Pearce Smith's 185th Brigade were assembled exactly as planned near the village of Hermanville, ready to begin one of the most vital British movements of the day – the advance to and seizure of Caen. The 2nd King's Own Shropshire Light Infantry, who were to lead the advance on the tanks of the Staffordshire Yeomanry, had landed in better order than they did in most exercises. They warmed themselves with self-heating cocoa in an orchard near Lion, and with satisfaction discarded their first sets of maps covering the beach area, turning now to the ones covering the ground ahead, marked, like those of all the invading force, with every known German position. They marched down the road into Hermanville amid the cheers of excited local civilians, and the encouraging spectacle of clusters of German prisoners being herded in the opposite direction. Yet already the brigadier and his unit commanders were deeply concerned by the non-appearance of the tanks that were to provide vital mobility and fire support. The Staffordshires had become embroiled in the vast traffic jam on Sword beach, which was to create critical delays for the next phase of the assault. The strong onshore winds had caused an unprecedently high tide. Instead of a normal width of 30 yards of sand, that morning the incoming mass of armour and soft-skinned vehicles was attempting to manoeuvre towards the beach exits across a mere 30 feet of beach. The Staffordshires found themselves immobile for an hour before they could even reach the road. Thereafter, their progress was agonizingly slow, nose to tail on the narrow road bordered on either side by uncleared minefields. It is arguable that, if there was a serious flaw in all the Allied landing schedules, it lay in allowing too many non-essential vehicles to clog the path inland in the first hours. Inevitably, among the wreckage and under continuing German shelling, the beach-masters were unable to direct the unloading operations with precision. All along the Normandy shore by the later stages of that morning, the difficulties of getting the spearhead units off the beaches and on their way inland were snowballing into serious delays for the follow-up brigades coming ashore. There was a lull, a period of reorganization, when men were brewing up at their rendezvous, locating their units and checking vehicles and equipment, from which the momentum of the advance never recovered that day. Lieutenant-Colonel F. J. Maurice, commanding the 2nd KSLI, bicycled back to the beach to investigate the plight of the Staffordshires, then pedalled forward once more to report to Brigadier Smith at Hermanville. 185th Brigade was ordered to start its move towards Caen on foot, to be followed by the tanks as speedily as possible. It was now noon.

Meanwhile ahead of them, 8th Brigade was attempting to clear the way by destroying the two key German strongpoints, "Morris" and "Hillman". "Morris's" 65-strong garrison surrendered to B Company of the 1st Suffolks at 1.00 p.m. after a heavy bombardment. But when the battalion's A Company then attempted to seize "Hillman", a network of strongpoints some 600 by 400 yards, they were met by furious fire which caused heavy casualties. The covering wire was breached, but the infantry could not get through under the intense machine-gun fire. A tank of the Staffordshires which sought to silence the position could make no impact with its 75 mm gun. Arthur Heal, the sapper officer attached to the Suffolks, recalled afterwards that the tanks declined to mount a direct assault unless the mines had been cleared in their path. The attackers possessed no heavy artillery support, for the gunnery forward observer had been killed earlier. Heal and a lance-corporal named Bolton crawled forward under cover of smoke, each clutching a mine detector. When the sapper found the first mine, scrabbling bare-handed to uncover it, he could not recognize any known German pattern. After gazing at it apprehensively for a few moments, he pulled it out and identified an aged British Mark II, booty from Dunkirk. He returned to report that there was no threat to the tanks, and late that evening the Suffolks, led by two squadrons of

Shermans, successfully closed on "Hillman" and stormed the position, using 30-pound Beehive charges to blow open the bunkers. In Chester Wilmot's account of this battle, he is severely critical of the Suffolks for their sluggishness in taking a position that it was vital to seize quickly, at almost any cost. The battalion lost only seven killed that day. More recently, Carlo D'Este has argued that it was the fault of the planners, rather than of the infantry, who failed to assess the seriousness of the threat "Hillman" represented. But there also seem to be grounds for believing that the tanks were reluctant to force the issue. Whatever the cause, the delay in seizing the position enabled its defenders to inflict 150 casualties on the 1st Norfolks as they advanced southwards past "Hillman", following the KSLI towards Caen. The stubbornness of a handful of positions behind the coast was remorselessly reducing the strength of the British push inland.

Meanwhile the KSLI had been pressing on alone down the road to Caen, fighting a brisk battle for possession of Hill 61, whence Major Hof had telephoned Schaaf and asked him to bring his self-propelled guns to the aid of regimental HQ. Schaaf duly advanced across the cornfields. He saw the heads of the Shropshires peering at him over the standing corn, rapidly disappearing again when he opened fire. But by now, a squadron of the Staffordshire's Shermans had caught up. When Schaaf spotted these, he determined that for self-propelled guns to engage tanks was beyond the call of duty. He beat a hasty retreat. When he next found a telephone line and tried to contact regimental HQ, an English voice – presumably one of the victorious KSLI – answered the call.

The Shropshires approached Biéville later in the afternoon, having fought a succession of tough little battles against moderate German opposition. They encouraged strong enemy fire from the village. "The civilians refused to evacuate themselves," one of their company commanders, Captain Robert Rylands, wrote later, "and at that early stage we were too soft-hearted to shell their homes – a proceeding which might have facilitated our advance considerably." W Company's commander, Major Slatter, was hit in the shoulder by a sniper, but walked decisively forward to the house from which the shot had come and lobbed a grenade through its window before returning, grinning broadly, to have his wound dressed. The battalion now attacked from the flanks, sending one company forward east of the village, another west. After a fierce firefight in which they suffered heavy casualties, the Shropshire's leading Y Company approached the commanding feature of Lebisey wood. They were told that there was little more opposition ahead. They were just three miles short of Caen.

Yet it was here that the KSLI first met panzergrenadiers of 21st Panzer Division, and here, late on the evening of 6 June, that Allied hopes of reaching Caen finally vanished. Y Company's advance was stopped in its tracks, the company commander killed. At 6.00 p.m., the battalion halted under fierce German fire and the rear companies dug in for the night. Under cover of darkness, Y Company disengaged and retired into the battalion position. "We were not unpleased with ourselves," wrote Captain Rylands of W Company,[2] and indeed, at a cost of 113 men killed and wounded, their achievement had been remarkable. But a single infantry battalion with limited tank and artillery support had not the slightest hope of generating sufficient violence to gain a foothold in Caen.

From the outset, the British 3rd Division's objectives for D-Day were the most ambitious, and their achievement would have had the most far-reaching consequences. 6th Airborne, east of Orne, was expected to gain and hold a perimeter. This it did with immense courage and determination, for in addition to the static German units in their area, they found themselves facing heavy counter-attacks from elements of the 125th and 192nd panzergrenadiers of 21st Panzer. West of the Orne, however, lay the road to Caen, where, above all, Montgomery had demanded dash and determination from his commanders to carry them to the city. The first of 3rd Division's three brigades, the 8th, expended much of its strength and energy in the early operations beyond the beaches, the seizure of "Morris" and "Hillman", and the securing of Hermanville, Coleville and Ouistreham. Among 185th Brigade, which was to play such a critical role in the dash for Caen, the KSLI's advance has already been described. The 1st Norfolks and 2nd Warwicks began to move south only at around 3.00 p.m., on the left of the KSLI, and the Norfolks were severely mauled in their movement past "Hillman". By nightfall on 6 June, they were between Beuville and Bénouville. 9th Brigade, in reserve, came ashore and assembled too slowly to be sent immediately forward with the 185th. By the time they were ready to move Rennie, their divisional commander, concluded that the most urgent priority was to reinforce the bridges across the Orne and Caen canal, which were under heavy German pressure. It is no great exaggeration to say that the sole determined thrust made by 3rd Division against Caen that day was that of the KSLI, with energetic support from the self-propelled guns of 7th Field Regiment RA, and some tanks of the Staffordshire Yeomanry.

The obvious absentees from this roll-call of British units are the remaining units of 27th Armoured Brigade. Each independent armoured brigade contained 190 Shermans and 33 light tanks, giving it a greater tank striking power than many German armoured divisions. It was never realistic to imagine that the British infantry battalions could march through Caen on their feet on the same day they had landed. The only possibility of dramatic success lay in a concentrated, racing armoured thrust by 27th Brigade. Crocker had written before D-Day: "As soon as the beach defences have been penetrated, not a moment must be lost in beginning the advance inland. Armour should be used boldly from the start."[3] Yet two-thirds of 27th Brigade's strength – the tanks of the 13/18th Royal Hussars and the 1st East Riding Yeomanry – were too deeply entangled in the fighting on the beaches and immediately inland to be available for the movement south. The entire burden of the push for Caen therefore lay with the Staffordshire Yeomanry, whose tanks were rapidly dispersed to support British infantry in difficulty against objectives inland. The unit concentrated only towards evening, in the face of the sudden threat from 21st Panzer. If it is true that the British plan underestimated the difficulty of overcoming "Hillman", and failed to take sufficient account of the known presence of panzergrenadier elements north of Caen, neither of these factors alone explains the failure to reach the city. Had the KSLI, by some miracle, reached Caen on D-Day with their few supporting tanks, they would have been crushed within hours by 21st Panzer. There was nothing like enough hitting power in the vanguard of 3rd Division to occupy and organize the defence of a city against strong enemy armour, especially with 12th SS Panzer Division already on its way to reinforce. Once any hope had vanished of spearheading the British advance with strong tank forces, any British infantry who somehow made their way forward must have been pushed back with crippling loss. It is possible to criticize the lack of drive by Rennie and his brigade commanders, and a certain loss of urgency by some units after the landing. But the failure to gain Caen on D-Day was chiefly the fault of over-optimism and sloppy thinking by the planners, together with the immense difficulty of organizing a major all-arms attack in the wake of an amphibious landing.

The last important action on the British left on 6 June was the battle against 21st Panzer's armoured thrust, an action which went entirely the way of the invaders. General Marcks, on his hill above Lebisey, told 22nd Panzer Regiment's commander: "Oppeln, if you don't succeed in throwing the British into the sea, we shall have lost the war."[4] The armoured officer, a former Olympic equestrian champion, saluted and mounted his vehicle. Marcks himself drove forward from the startline with the command group of 1st/192nd Panzergrenadiers. The tanks raced north towards the sea across the open ground, driving headlong into the gap between the British and Canadian perimeters.

British troops reported several tank formations advancing towards their positions. The Germans recoiled westwards on meeting fierce fire. When at last they encountered the heavily-gunned Sherman Fireflies of the Staffordshires on Hill 61, the consequences for the Germans were devastating. 13 tanks were immediately destroyed. Only a handful of 21st Panzer's tanks and infantry reached the surviving strongpoints of the 716th Division around Lion-sur-Mer. By a dramatic coincidence, only minutes after they did so, the fly-in began of 250 gliders of 6th Airborne Division to a landing zone eastwards, around St Aubin, near the Orne bridge. This was too much for the Germans. 21st Panzer was a sound enough formation, but lacked the ruthless driving force of an SS armoured division. Arguing that the glider landings threatened them with encirclement, they withdrew up the hill towards Caen. By nightfall, they were strongly emplaced around the city with the support of their 24 88 mm guns. But they had lost 70 of the 124 tanks with which they had begun the day. For all the dash with which Marcks and von Oppeln urged 22nd Panzer Regiment into action, its belated attack had been pushed home without determination or subtlety. A gesture had been made, no more.

The leading elements of the Canadian assault force on the right of the British 3rd Division almost reached Carpiquet on the evening of D-Day. Two troops of the 1st Hussars, leaving their infantry far behind, pressed on through Bretteville along the Bayeux–Caen road until they found their loneliness too alarming and turned back. They were two miles ahead of the rest of their formation. The Canadians suffered the universal problems of congestion on their beaches, and the need to fight hard to clear isolated strongpoints. But by the night of D-Day, they had established themselves strongly up to five miles inland. Upon the Canadians, in the days that followed, would fall the principal weight of 12th SS Panzer, perhaps the most formidable of all the German units now on their way to Normandy. Having set out from Lisieux, 65 miles from Caen, late in the afternoon, its leading elements were across the Odon, south of Caen, by nightfall, and moving to take up position on the left of 21st Panzer.

50th Division, moving inland from Gold beach, had fought a succession of hard battles against elements of the 352nd Division. By evening, troops of the British 151st Brigade had reached the Bayeux–Caen road, and tanks of the 4th/7th Dragoon Guards were reporting little in front of them. Though the 50th was also short of most of its D-Day objectives, it was solidly established in the Norman hedges and fields, with only limited German forces on its front. Among fields and villages all along the coast, British and American soldiers were settling into positions for the night, mopping up stragglers, herding prisoners to the rear, pausing for the first time to absorb their surroundings. Private John Price of the 2nd Ox & Bucks was one of the men who had landed by glider to join the 6th Airborne that evening. His aircraft bucked and bumped across a field until it came to a stop in high-standing corn within reach of the sea. Price jumped down from the fuselage, and was at once confronted by three ineffectual-looking Germans, who rose at his feet and put up their hands. One had thick pebble glasses, the others looked very young and frightened. He felt somehow disappointed. These men did not look in the least like specimens of the master race. He handed them over to a nearby group of Devonshires, and walked away towards the Orne bridge in search of his own unit, past a dead German lying alone at a crossroads, and a frightened-looking French family craning out of a cottage window.

Private Len Ainslie of the 5th King's had been one of thousands of awed spectators of the airborne landing. He, and the others who had been compelled to swim the last yards to the beach, were now dug in around their anti-tank guns, seeking to dry their boots. Just beyond their position near Hermanville, they found the body of a large German officer. The platoon sergeant said off-handedly: "Just get him out of the way," and

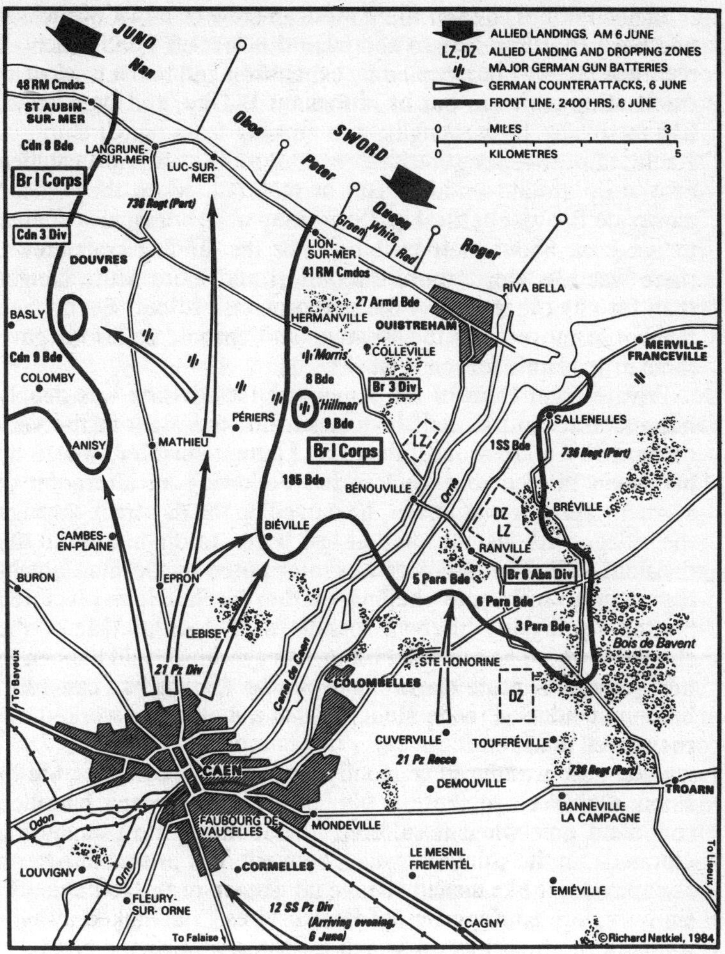

D-Day: the Push for Caen

having had no previous dealings with corpses, they threw him over a nearby hedge. One man had already been injured seeking to clean his gun. It exploded beside his face, blackening and scorching him. As darkness came, all of them began to curse the plague of mosquitoes. It was the first time that he and many other men had set foot on foreign soil. They found it very strange.

James Phillips, one of the American crew of an LCVP which had been shuttling men to and from the fleet off Utah beach all day, was chiefly preoccupied by exhaustion and hunger. Most of the landing craft ran out of rations on D-Day, and their crews had to survive by scrounging and begging from bigger ships. A British minesweeper gave Phillips' craft some stew and a canteen of brandy around midday. But at nightfall, when they closed alongside the vast battleship *Texas*, they were brusquely ordered to get back about their business. For the landing craft crews, there was less glory, more discomfort and more acute danger than for any other men in the seaborne task forces. Even when the battle moved on, the weather and chronic collisions gave them little respite for many weeks.

Private John Hein of the American 1st Division was deeply impressed to find himself bivouacked for the night in the very orchard, by a crossroads above St Laurent-sur-Mer, where he had been briefed to expect to be. Following an afternoon of alarming shelling on Omaha, he moved up the dirt track through the village with his unit, and at last begun to dig in around the divisional CP. The darkness was interrupted by German bombing activity and some shelling of the beach. Hein reassured himself by digging his own foxhole next door to that of the chaplain, where he felt that nothing very serious could happen to him. Whatever acute alarm the events on Omaha had caused to his commanders, Private Hein felt that the plan had worked out pretty well in the end.

Other men endured a much more disturbed night. Major Frank Colacicco of the 3rd/18th Infantry was in the battalion command post when it suffered a sudden night attack by the Germans, in the course of which he was taken prisoner. After a few minutes, he managed to take advantage of the confusion to leap a gully and make his escape. Back among his unit's riflemen, he began to move among them, urging the confused soldiers to bring down fire on the Germans. After 45 minutes the enemy withdrew, taking some American prisoners with them. Some manner of quiet returned to the positions.

The German battalion commander of the 3rd/716th infantry told Lieutenant Schaaf that he had been told to pull back to Caen with his 30 or so surviving men. Without orders since the fall of his regimental headquarters, Schaaf decided to do likewise: Driving south-eastwards, he lost one gun, which threw a track and became bogged down in a ditch. The drive continued without incident, until he glimpsed ahead a crude roadblock of farm implements manned by British soldiers. He ordered his men to take off their helmets, and laid a tarpaulin over the side of the hull to conceal the German black cross. As they roared past the roadblock, they could see that the British had identified them but were too surprised to intervene. They saw no more troops of any nationality until three miles on, at the outskirts of Caen, where they encountered German infantry. A stream of stragglers and survivors, men and vehicles, were making their way back into the perimeter from the coast. When Schaaf reported to the divisional artillery headquarters, he was told that his was the only battery, among 11 in the regiment, to make contact since morning. They pressed him for information about the situation forward, about which there was still terrible confusion. Then he was ordered to take up position near Epron, just north of the city. They remained in action there until, weeks later, ceaseless use had reduced their guns to wrecks.

Along 60 miles of front, men lay over their weapons peering out into the darkness lit up by occasonal flares and tracer, then slept the sleep of utter exhaustion in their foxholes or ruined cottages. Some soldiers of the British and American airborne divisions were still probing warily through the darkness miles from their own lines, wading streams and swamps on the long march from their ill-aimed dropping points. A few thousand men lay dead, others wounded in the field dressing stations or positions from which they could not be evacuated. There were already Allied stragglers and deserters, who had slipped away from their units, skulking in villages the length of the invasion coast.

In England and America, the newspapers were being printed. *The Times* for 7 June carried the headlines: "The Great Assault going well; Allies several miles inland; Battle for town of Caen; Mass attacks by airborne troops". A leading article proclaimed: "Four years after the rescue at Dunkirk of that gallant defeated army without which as a nucleus the forces of liberation could never have been rebuilt, the United Nations returned today with power to the soil of France." D-Day provoked *The Times*, along with many politicians, to a breathless torrent of verbosity. On the Letters page, a Mr R. B. D. Blakeney reminded readers that William the Conqueror had embarked for England from Dives. The *Daily Express*, characteristically, plunged into sensation: there were tales of Allied paratroopers treacherously shot in mid-air, of the glider pilot who cried as he shot up a German staff car: "Remember Dunkirk when you drove me off!" There was a photograph of a triumphant glider pilot carrying a German helmet with the words HE'S DEAD chalked upon it.

Corporal Adolf Hohenstein of the 276th Infantry Division, billeted at Bayonne, many miles from the battlefield, wrote in his diary: "A beautiful day. In the evening we hear the long-expected but still surprising news that the invasion has come. The civilians will have to pay the most dearly, and the French around here have suddenly become very quiet. They will become even quieter when this country has been devastated by Allied bombs and German shells, when they experience the full horror of war."[5]

No disappointment or setback could mask the absolute Allied triumph of establishing themselves ashore on D-Day. But the failure to gain Caen was a substantial strategic misfortune. Bradley wrote: "In subsequent days, after I had had an opportunity to study Dempsey's D-Day operation, I was keenly disappointed."[6] There is overwhelming evidence that with greater drive and energy Second Army could have "staked out claims" deeper inland on 6 June. But with 21st Panzer solidly established around Caen, it is impossible to believe that the British could have reached the city without running into deep trouble. The German coastal defenders may not have been the cream of the Wehrmacht, but they fought extraordinarily well in many places, given their isolation, the poverty of their manpower and the paucity of their equipment. Too little credit has been granted to German garrisons for their struggle with the best that the Allies could throw against them. They achieved all that Rommel could reasonably have expected – a delaying action which deprived the British advance of the momentum that it needed to reach Caen. The city was only a realistic objective for Dempsey's army if the coastal crust crumbled immediately the Allies landed. It did not. Whatever the sluggishness of some British units, Bradley was to discover ample difficulties of this kind among his own divisions in the days to come.

The Allied command of the air was plainly decisive on 6 June: "The Anglo-American air forces did more than facilitate the historic invasion," wrote the American official historians, "they made it possible."[7] The Luftwaffe put less than a hundred fighters into the sky on D-Day, and mounted only 22 sorties against shipping late that evening. Given the difficulties that the invaders suffered against the Atlantic Wall, it is difficult to imagine that they could have pierced it at all had their assault been subject to serious air attack. As it was, they were ashore. But they were still gasping to regain breath after the vast strain of getting there.

4 The British before Caen

Closing the lines

There was never any doubt in the minds of either German or Allied commanders that, in the immediate weeks of the invasion, the vital strategic ground lay in the east, where the British Second Army stood before Caen. Here, for the Germans, the threat was 50 miles closer to the heart of France, and to Germany. Here, for the British, glittered the opportunity to break into the open tank country to the south-east, freeing airfield sites and gaining fighting room before the mass of the German army could be committed to battle. By securing their beachhead ashore, the first great Allied hopes for OVERLORD had been fulfilled. Yet on the Second Army front in the weeks that followed, their second hopes – their prospects of a quick breakthrough from Normandy – died stillborn. They did so in a fashion that raised serious questions about the fighting power of the British army that had landed in France, and which demonstrated decisively the genius of the German soldier in adversity.

Between 6 June and the end of the month, Montgomery directed three attempts, first, to seize Caen by direct assault – on 7 and 8 June – and then to envelop it – the Villers-Bocage operation of 13 June, and EPSOM on 25 June. The initial operations were merely the continuation of those undertaken on D-Day. On 7 June, 185th Brigade's renewed attempt to force the direct route to the town through Lebisey, with powerful fire support, broke down after heavy casualties. 9th Brigade's battle for Cambes was at last successful after the Royal Ulster Rifles had fought their way across 1,000 yards of open ground under punishing enemy fire. But they could go no further. When the 3rd Canadian Division began to push forward, its men encountered the leading elements of 12th SS Panzer, newly arrived on the battlefield, and bent upon breaking through to the sea. Colonel Kurt "Panzer" Meyer, commanding the division's armoured regiment, directed his tanks' first actions from a superb vantage point in the tower of the Ardenne Abbey on the western edge of Caen. To cope with the immense difficulties of moving forward adequate supplies of fuel, Meyer organized a shuttle of jerry cans loaded aboard Volkswagen field cars. Throughout the 7th and 8th, the Canadians and the fanatical teenagers of the SS Hitler Jugend fought some of the fiercest actions of the campaign, with heavy loss to both sides. Lieutenant Rudolf Schaaf of the 1716th Artillery was at Corps headquarters in a mineshaft outside Caen when a swaggering colonel from 12th SS Panzer arrived to announce his intention not to halt anywhere before the sea. This, of course was the legendary Meyer, who assumed command of the division a few days later. Only 33 years old, tall and stiffly handsome, he was the archetype of the Nazi fanatic. Even as a prisoner in 1945, he told his interrogator: "You will hear a lot against Adolf Hitler in this camp, but you will never hear it from me. As far as I am concerned he was and still is the greatest thing that ever happened to Germany."[1]

"The SS showed that they believed that thus far, everybody had been fighting like milkmaids," said Schaaf.[2] He watched the bleak young men of the Hitler Jugend Division riding forward into their attack, and saw some of them return that night, utterly spent, crying tears of frustration for their failure to reach their objective. "It was a very sad chapter for them." But it had also been less than happy for the Canadian 3rd Division. By the night of 7 June, as their official historian described the situation, when the Division's forward elements had been pushed back up to two miles:

> The 9th Canadian Infantry Brigade Group had fought its first battle with courage and spirit, but somewhat clumsily. Encountering an unusually efficient German force of about its own strength, it had come off secondbest. Its advance guard had been caught off balance and defeated in detail.[3]

This was scarcely an encouraging omen for rapid progress inland. While the Germans co-ordinated armour, infantry and artillery superbly, the Canadians did not. While 9th Brigade was facing 12th SS Panzer, 8th Brigade spent the day preoccupied with mopping up strongpoints in the rear which had not been taken on D-Day. The following morning, 8 June, 7th Brigade came under heavy attack; the positions of the Royal Winnipeg

Rifles were overrun, and the Canadian Scottish were compelled to mount a major counter-attack to recover the lost ground, at a cost of 125 casualties. That night, Panthers of 12th SS Panzer, led personally by Kurt Meyer on his customary motor-cycle, hit the Canadian 7th Brigade yet again. As fires and flares lit up the area, the Regina Rifles at one stage reported 22 Panthers around their own battalion headquarters. In the confusion of the night battle, the Germans began to believe that they had broken through. A panzer officer halted a Volkswagen field car immediately outside the Reginas' command post, which was blown up seconds later by a PIAT bomb. The Canadians lost contact with all but one of their companies. "It is hard to picture the confusion which existed," said their commanding officer.[4] Six Panthers were destroyed by the Canadian anti-tank guns and PIATs before Meyer broke off the attack, and his armour squealed and clattered away into the darkness.

The Canadians were unbowed, but shaken. Corporal Dick Raymond and a draft of replacements for their 3rd Division closed on Juno beach late in the afternoon of 7 June. The landing craft dropped its ramp a hundred yards offshore, at which point the replacements flatly refused to disembark. At last, after an absurd argument, the officer in charge jumped into the chest-high water, and the men straggled ashore after him. The beach was quiet, littered with wreckage, stinking of oil. When the group had marched a little way inland, Raymond found himself suffering pains and, with his accustomed independence, fell out by the roadside. He found two drunken Canadian engineers, and joined them by a vast wine cask in a cellar. Then a half-track took the other men away, and Raymond was alone again. Having slept where he lay beside the wine cask, the next morning he met a Scottish major who had been on the landing craft with him. He learned that a random bomb from a Luftwaffe nuisance raider during the night had landed in the midst of his group of replacements, killing some 20 and wounding as many again. Still alone, he walked forward until he encountered a field artillery battery, shooting furiously in support of two infantry battalions locked in the struggle against 12th SS Panzer. Raymond spent the remainder of that day helping a gun team. At last the gunners told him to go and report to his own unit. Late that night, near Les Buissons, he found his Vickers machine-gun platoon, supporting a battalion of the Stormont,

Dundas and Glengarry Highlanders. They were utterly exhausted after the battles of the day. No questions were asked about his movements – he was simply given a shovel and told that he was with C Company. That night, the battalion was reduced to some 200 men, although more straggled in later. The next morning, Raymond found himself plunged into the bitter struggle that persisted through the days that followed: "It was just a straight shoot-out, both sides blasting at each other day and night. We used to joke about 'last man, last round'. Watching infantry advancing across those open corn fields may not have been quite as terrible as the battle of the Somme, but at times it seemed to come pretty close to it."[5] Raymond was touched by the courage of the Royal Naval gunfire forward observers, declining to wear steel helmets, being steadily killed: "They seemed to have the David Niven touch." But he was even more surprised and impressed by the performance of the Canadians. In months past, he had often been scornful of their indiscipline and doubtful of their quality, above all sceptical about their leadership: "But the strength of that Canadian army was as close-in fighters. They went at it like hockey players."

In the first six days ashore, the Canadians lost 196 officers and 2,635 other ranks, 72 and 945 of these, respectively, being killed. After the 9th, the Germans broke off their attacks for some days. The Canadians were able to consolidate their positions and plug the gaps in their line; they could draw satisfaction from beating off 12th SS Panzer's attacks. Yet if the Germans were dismayed by their failure to break through to the sea, the Canadians had also proved unable to maintain the momentum of D-Day. Meyer's panzers had successfully thrown them off balance: they now concentrated chiefly upon holding the ground that they possessed, and were most cautious about launching any attacks without secure flanks and powerful gun and tank support. They found themselves unable to advance beyond Authie.

On 7 June the British 50th Division, on the right, occupied Bayeux, which the Germans had evacuated on D-Day, and pushed forward more than three miles towards Tilly-sur-Seulles, Sully, and Longues. Yet when Montgomery himself came ashore to establish his tactical headquarters in the grounds of the château at Creully on 8 June, the leading assault units, which had landed on D-Day and been continuously in contact with the enemy ever since, were visibly weary. The prospect of breaking through the line held by 12th SS Panzer and 21st Panzer in front of Caen was very small. "The Germans are doing everything they can to hold onto Caen," Montgomery wrote to the Military Secretary at the War Office that day. "I have decided not to have a lot of casualties by butting against the place. So I have ordered Second Army to keep up a good pressure at and to make its main effort towards Villers-Bocage and Evrecy, and thence south-east towards Falaise."[6] Despite the worsening weather, which had restricted air support and delayed the progress of unloading, it is impossible now to forget Montgomery's parting address to his commanders before they sailed for Normandy:

> Great energy and "drive" will be required from all senior officers and commanders. I consider that once the beaches are in our possession, success will depend largely on our ability to be able to concentrate our armour and push fairly strong armoured columns rapidly inland to secure important ground or communications centres. Such columns will form *firm bases in enemy territory* [emphasis in original] from which to develop offensive action in all directions.[7]

For all Montgomery's declarations of willingness to regard the independent armoured brigades, with their formidable tank strength, as "expendable" in pursuit of these objectives, they had scarcely been attempted, far less attained. Second Army's efforts had been entirely absorbed by the struggle to create and hold a narrow perimeter; and this despite the overwhelming success of the FORTITUDE deception plan, and a rate of build-up by Rommel's forces as slow as the most optimistic Allied planner could have hoped for. In these first days, as much as at any phase of the campaign, the Allies felt their lack of an armoured infantry carrier capable of moving men rapidly on the battlefield alongside the tanks. From first to last, infantry in Normandy marched rather than rode, sometimes 10 or 15 miles in a day. Too many tired soldiers were asked to march far as well as fight hard. It took days for some units to re-adjust themselves after the huge psychological effort and surge of relief attached to getting ashore. In the training of paratroops, great emphasis is laid upon the fact that the act of jumping is a beginning, not an end in itself, and that their task commences only when they have discarded their harness on the ground. Yet throughout the months of preparation in England, the thoughts of the armies were concentrated overwhelmingly upon the narrow strip of fire-swept sand that they had been obliged to cross and hold on D-Day. Brigadier Williams of 21st Army Group said: "There was a slight feeling of a lack of cutting edge about operations at the very beginning after the landing."[8] A less tactful critic might have expressed the issue more forcefully, and compared the ruthlessness with which 12th SS Panzer and Panzer Lehr threw themselves into the battle with the sluggishness of Allied movements in those first, vital days before the mass of the German army reached the battlefield. The loss of momentum in the days after 6 June provided the Germans with a critical opportunity to organize a coherent defence and to bring forward reinforcements to contain the beachhead. The huge tactical advantage of surprise had already been lost.

On the evening of 9 June, Bayerlein's superb Panzer Lehr Division moved into the line on the left of 12th SS Panzer after a 90-mile drive to the front from Chartres, during which they were fiercely harassed and strafed by the Allied air force. The formation had lost 130 trucks, five tanks and 84 self-propelled guns and other armoured vehicles. But the delay and dismay it had suffered were more serious than the material damage to its fighting power, since its total complement of tanks and vehicles was around 3,000. The three panzer divisions – 21st, 12th SS and Panzer Lehr – now formed the principal German shield around Caen, supported by the remains of the various static divisions that had been manning the sector on D-Day. 21st Panzer's poor performance and reluctance to press home attacks were a source of constant complaint by Meyer's Hitler Jugend, who claimed that in several battles already they had been let down by Feuchtinger's units. But Panzer Lehr, for all their misfortunes on the road, were fighting superbly to hold the ruins of Tilly, the little town in a valley south-east of Caen which was to be the scene of some of the most bitter fighting of the campaign. Their panzergrenadier half-tracks had been sent to the rear, for they did not expect to move far or fast in any direction. Instead, the infantry were deployed in ditches and ruined houses alongside tanks employed as mobile strongpoints, meticulously camouflaged and emplaced to present only a foot or two of turret to attacking Allied armour. The tracks that they made approaching their positions were painstakingly swept away or concealed before daylight brought the spotter planes. Caked in dust, unwashed and often unfed, in the appalling heat and stink of their steel coffins, the tank crews fought through days and nights of attack and counter-attack, artillery and naval bombardment, mortaring and Allied tank fire. The panzergrenadiers found the Tilly battle especially painful because it was difficult to dig deep in the stony ground, and at times of heavy bombardment their officers had difficulty holding even Bayerlein's men from headlong flight.

For the British 50th Division also, the lyrical name of Tilly-sur-Seulles became a synonym for fear and endless death. The little fields of cowslips and buttercups, innocent squares of rural peace, became loathsome for the mortal dangers that each ditch and hedgerow concealed. The guidebook prettiness of the woods and valleys, so like those of Dorset and Devon, mocked their straining nerves and ears, cocked for the first round of mortar fire or the sniper's bullet. For the tank crews, there was the certain knowledge that a hit from a German Tiger, Panther or 88 mm gun would be fatal. The same was not true the other way around.

The tension before a set-piece attack was appalling [wrote a young Churchill Crocodile troop commander, Andrew Wilson]. When Crocodiles were used, they were generally in the lead . . . You wondered if

The Crocodile flame-throwing tank was among the best-known of the British 79th Armoured Division's "Funnies", the specialized tanks which were the brainchildren of General Sir Percy Hobart. Almost all were modified Churchills – slow infantry tanks capable of only 15 mph, five tons heavier than the Sherman, 10 tons heavier than the Cromwell. Some were modified to carry bridge-laying or ditch-filling equipment, others to lay steel track or to throw a heavy bunker-busting bomb. The Crocodile, with which two British armoured regiments were equipped, carried flame fuel in a towed trailer, and could effectively incinerate men in its path at a range of 40–50 yards. Crocodiles were normally employed in small detachments to support Allied attacks against strongly dug-in German infantry.

you'd done the reconnaissance properly; if you'd again recognise those small landmarks, the isolated bush, the dip in the ground, which showed you where to cross the start-line. You wondered if in the smoke and murk of the half-light battle, with your forehead pressed to the periscope pad, you'd ever pick out the target. And all the while you saw in your imagination the muzzle of an eighty-eight behind each leaf.

Then the bombardment grew louder, and the order came: "Advance" . . . There was the run with the blurred shape of the copse at the end. Spandaus were firing, but you couldn't see them. A Sherman officer was telling his troop to close up. The distance shortened. The Crocodiles began to speed up, firing their Besas. The objective took on detail. Individual trees stood out, and beneath them a mass of undergrowth. Something slammed through the air.[9]

He knew at once that it was an anti-tank gun. But there was nothing he could do about it. The troop ran in, pouring in the flame. Once he thought he heard a scream, but it might have been the creak of the tracks on the track guides. Suddenly it was all over. The infantry came up and ran in through the smoke. The flame-gunners put on their safety-switches, and from inside the copse came the rasp of machine-guns. A little later, when he drove back to refuel, he saw that the field was littered with dead infantry and that one of the Shermans had been hit through the turret.

Villers-Bocage

It was at this stage that Montgomery determined to commit his two veteran divisions of the old Eighth Army, 51st Highland and 7th Armoured. "You don't send your best batsman in first," he had said crisply before D-Day when one of a group of 7th Armoured officers asked – in a spirit that might not have been shared by some of his colleagues – why the formation was not to take part in the initial landings.[1] Now, he proposed to use his "best batsmen" in two major flank attacks around Caen: 51st Highland would pass through the 6th Airborne bridgehead east of the Orne; 7th Armoured would hook to the south-west. The landings of the 7th Armoured and 51st Highland had been delayed by the weather, which was also causing serious artillery ammunition shortages. Beach organization and traffic control remained a chronic problem – on Gold alone, the engineers had been compelled to deal with 2,500 obstacles, many of them mined, comprising a total of 900 tons of steel and concrete.

Nuisance night raids by up to 50 Luftwaffe aircraft constituted no major threat to the beachhead, but compounded delays and difficulties. Sword beach continued to be plagued by incoming shellfire.

Throughout these days, the German army mounted no major counter-attack. A desperate plan contrived by General Geyr von Schweppenburg of Panzer Group West was aborted by Rommel on 10 June – insufficient forces were concentrated. The following day, Geyr's headquarters were pinpointed by Allied Ultra decrypts, and put out of action by air strikes. Yet the local counter-attacks mounted by German forces in the line, above all against the paratroopers east of the Orne, were so formidable as to inflict devastating casualties upon the British paratroopers, and finally to crush 51st Highland's attack within hours of its inception on 11 June. The Germans had now deployed their 346th and 711th Divisions alongside elements of 21st Panzer and 716th on this right flank. 5th Black Watch, advancing into their first action at 4.30 a.m. that morning, suffered 200 casualties in an attempt to reach Bréville. "Every man of the leading platoon died with his face to the foe," recorded the divisional history proudly.[2] Yet General Gale, commanding 6th Airborne, concluded that it was essential to seize the village to close a dangerous gap in his own perimeter. The next night, the 12th Battalion, Parachute Regiment, in a brilliant sacrificial battle, gained Bréville at a cost of 141 casualties among the 160 men with which the unit advanced. The German 3rd/858th Regiment, which was defending the village, was reduced from 564 men to 146 in three days of fighting. Between the 11th and the 13th, other elements of 51st Highland Division sought to push southwards towards Sainte Honorine. But after a bitter series of to-and-fro actions in which every temporary gain was met by fierce German counter-attack, the British attack east of Caen petered out. The lightly-armed parachute battalions were exhausted and drained of men and ammunition. 51st Highland was unable to make progress.

"The fact must be faced," declared the divisional history, "that at this period the normally very high morale of the Division fell temporarily to a very low ebb . . . A kind of claustrophobia affected the troops, and the continual shelling and mortaring from an unseen enemy in relatively great strength were certainly very trying . . ."[3]

For the enemy also, the struggle east of the Orne remained an appalling memory. Corporal Werner Kortenhaus of 21st Panzer saw four of his company's 10 tanks brewed up in five minutes during the attack on the château at Escoville on 9 June. Again and again the Mk IVs crawled forward, supporting infantry huddled behind the protection of their hulls as they advanced into the furious British mortar and shellfire. But when the tanks reversed they were often unable to see behind them, and rolled over the terrible screams of the injured or sheltering men who lay in their path. A wounded panzergrenadier cried for his mother from no man's land all one night in front of their position. Kortenhaus, trying to sleep beneath his tank, woke in the morning to find the tunic that he had laid on the hull when he dismounted was shredded by shell fragments. The bombardment seldom seemed to pause.

On 13 June, his company lost four more tanks in the struggle against 51st Highland Division. They saved the driver and gunner of one panzer, who ran from their burning vehicle, by cramming them somehow into their own turret as they accelerated away in retreat through the cornfields. Their company commander, Lieutenant Neumann, leapt down from his own tank and led the infantry in a desperate counter-attack against the Black Watch, firing a Schmeisser. He survived, only to be hit as he climbed back into his own turret. "We became very depressed," said Kortenhaus. "We had given up any hope of victory after repeated failures in attack."[4] Yet the Germans held their ground east of the Orne despite the overwhelming superiority of the Allies in fire support.

Montgomery's 8 June concept for the envelopment of Caen included a plan to drop 1st Airborne Division behind the town when 51st Highland and 7th Armoured had made sufficient progress on the flanks. To his bitter anger, this was decisively vetoed by Leigh-Mallory, always a sceptic about parachute operations. Yet the disappointment that now attended the push by 7th Armoured on Second Army's western flank made discussion of ambitious objectives beyond Caen almost immediately irrelevant.

On 10 June, when the division moved through 50th Division's positions west of Caen, its commander Major-General Erskine could report that he "never felt serious difficulty in beating down enemy resistance". Only four tanks were lost. It thus seemed all the more remarkable that the Desert Rats made little progress, and fared no better on 11 June. British infantry who penetrated Tilly were unable to secure the town for lack of tank support.

But as opposition stiffened in front of them, Dempsey and Bucknall – XXX Corps' commander – perceived a weakness on the enemy's left – a yawning hole in the German line between Caumont and Villers-Bocage. On 12 June, they swung 7th Armoured westwards to launch a new attack on this south-easterly axis. This advance began at 3 p.m., led by the 8th Hussars, and progressed intoxicatingly well for some hours. "On arrival at Cahagnolles we meet a U.S. patrol in armoured cars and jeeps looking very dusty and excited," the Hussars CO, Lieutenant-Colonel Cuthbert Goulburn, recorded in his diary. "We are all beginning to think we have obtained a complete breakthrough." But then, at the approach to Livry, the Hussars leading tank was knocked out by a panzerfaust. In the close country, they could find no means of bypassing the village, and the motor company of the Rifle Brigade had to be called forward to clear the German outpost defending it. Meanwhile, Brigadier "Loony" Hinde, commanding 22nd Armoured Brigade, ordered Goulburn's regiment to swing east and reconnoitre a possible alternative line of advance via the village of La Croix Des Landes. "A direct advance up the road is the only way," wrote the Colonel. "So I say OK to Guy [Threlfall] and off go Talbot Harvey's troop. After two or three minutes we hear an anti-tank gun fire about three shots. Harvey goes 'off the air' and Guy gets no reply. Shortly afterwards, Harvey's troop corporal returns in his tank, very shaken and in tears, to say that both leading tanks have been 'brewed up'." Livry was by now cleared, but with darkness falling, the advance was halted. It was well into the small hours before the supply vehicles could find their way forward among the great jam of British armour clogging the narrow road to refuel and re-arm the lead squadrons. The day's events had demonstrated how readily even small numbers of Germans could hamper the movement of a British armoured division in country where it was enormously difficult to present more than one small unit at a time to the enemy.

After reveille at 4.30 a.m. on the 13th, 7th Armoured renewed their advance towards Villers-Bocage through Livry, now led by 4th County of London Yeomanry under Lieutenant-Colonel Lord Cranley. The British column clattered up the winding road among the great chestnut trees before Villers, and into the town at about 8 a.m. without meeting opposition. The bulk of the regiment halted and its crews dismounted while Cranley, with one squadron of tanks, two command vehicles, and the Rifle Brigade motor company, moved on to their objective, the high ground of Point 213, one-and-a-half miles east of the town. They passed the tantalising concrete signpost with its bald legend: CAEN 24. Cranley deployed most of his A Squadron in the fields straddling the road, facing eastwards. The balance of the tanks, followed by the half-tracks of the Rifle Brigade, halted in a long column by the roadside down the long, straight slope yards behind them. The riflemen dismounted while their officers went forward for further orders. Montgomery signalled the news to De Guingand at his main headquarters in England: "So my pincer movement to get Caen is taking good shape, and there are distinct possibilities that the enemy divisions may not find it too easy to escape; especially Panzer Lehr . . ."

Yet already nemesis was approaching every British hope around Villers, in the form of a Tiger tank commanded by Captain Michael Wittman, leader of a group of five from the 501st SS Heavy Tank Battalion. His company had left Beauvais on 7 June, and after suffering severely from an air attack near Versailles on the 8th, had travelled only in darkness to reach their present position on 12 June. They had planned to spend the 13th making repairs and urgent maintenance on their tanks. But now Wittman stood in his turret studying the halted British column beyond Villers. The Germans were some 250 yards south of the road, well behind Cranley's forward screen. "They're acting as if they've won the war already," muttered his gunner, Corporal Woll. Wittman, already celebrated on the Eastern Front as the greatest panzer ace of the war, said calmly: "We're going to prove them wrong." At about 9.05 a.m. his Tiger, two more behind it, roared forward in line ahead, parallel to the Rifle Brigade column. A horrified British dispatch rider spotted the threat: "I called to Mr de Pass and told him, and he said something like it being one of ours. At this point I decided to tell Major Wright. He calmly informed me that he knew and that they were all round us." The Tigers swung towards the British line. The rear two halted and opened fire, while Wittman himself charged forward up a farm track towards the road, to begin one of the most devastating single-handed actions of the war.

His first 88 mm shell destroyed the rearmost of 4th CLY's Cromwells, while his second hit a Sherman Firefly in front of it. Then the Tiger reached the road, swerved left towards Villers, and roared down the hill machine-gunning the Rifle Brigade and their half-tracks at point-blank range. Lieutenant de Pass jumped up saying, "We must get the PIAT," and was killed instantly as he sought to clamber on to his vehicle. A few riflemen attempted to engage the Tigers with their 6pdr anti-tank guns before being shot down. Others ran desperately for open country as machine-gun fire raked the ditch in which they had taken refuge. "Looking back down the road towards the town," wrote a British officer, "it was possible to see a long column of blazing tanks and half-tracks, which had been hopelessly surprised by the unexpected attack – a 'school solution' ambush."

Having effectively written off the motor company, Wittman reached the top of the narrow high street of Villers, where the remainder of 4th CLY's Cromwells lay wholly unawares. Here, he destroyed three tanks of the HQ group, then that of Major Carr, the 2i/c whose driver frantically reversed into a garden, unable to fire more than three rounds because his loader was dismounted. Sergeant Stan Lockwood, a 30-year-old Londoner commanding a Sherman Firefly leading B Squadron, heard shooting start nearby, then saw a scout car race around the corner towards him, the driver waving his arms in frantic warning. Lockwood's Sherman nosed cautiously around a building to see before it, 200 yards away with its turret broadside on, Wittman's Tiger apparently firing up a sidestreet. Lockwood's gunner slammed four 17-pounder shots at the Tiger, one of which caused smoke and flame to appear on the hull. Then a shot from Wittman brought half the building above the Sherman down on to its hull, and before the British had extricated themselves from the debris, the German was gone. Only superficially damaged, Wittman's tank was able to demolish a last Cromwell before reversing away. Its commander, Captain Pat Dyas, escaped with the help of a local French girl to another tank of B Squadron, from which he radioed his commanding officer Lord Cranley with a report on the disastrous events in Villers. The Colonel could only reply that he knew the situation was desperate, but that he himself, along with the tanks of A Squadron, was at that moment being engaged by other Tigers. It was the regiment's last contact with him. At 10.30 a.m. he spoke for the last time to Brigadier Hinde, then his signals to brigade ceased. The surviving tanks of 4th CLY remained in their positions with a handful of riflemen amid intermittent shellfire, hoping for rescue. The officer commanding A Squadron had been killed by shellfire. An attempt by one Cromwell to probe an escape route up a track north-eastwards was terminated abruptly by German tank fire. Thereafter, there was little movement at

Point 213 for more than two hours. Brigade assumed that the British force was already destroyed. In reality, only at 1 p.m. did new German armour reach the scene, taking prisoner almost all the British survivors, including Lord Cranley. Captain Christopher Milner of the Rifle Brigade escaped alone on foot, to rejoin his formation the next day.

Meanwhile, in the town of Villers, a day of desperate fighting had begun. Infantry of the 1/7th Queens arriving to support 4th CLY encountered a German staff car and two motor-cycle combinations head on at the western approach of the town. They staged a brisk firefight with the survivors. They then planned to advance to the relief of Point 213. Cranley vetoed this by radio. A lull ensued until about 2 p.m., when a new German armoured and infantry attack on Villers developed, and the Queens hastily deployed among the houses to meet it. This time, with PIATs and anti-tank guns, the Germans were beaten off with the loss of seven tanks, including that of Wittman, although all the German crews escaped. Brigadier Hinde sent orders that the town must be held at all costs. Yet the Germans were also desperate to destroy the threat to their line. Lieutenant-Colonel Kurt Kauffman, Operations Officer of Panzer Lehr, personally assembled two 88 mm guns, three field guns and a ragtag of rear area troops and led them into the street fighting in Villers, while infantry of 2 Panzer moved up from the south. Intermittent fierce rain showers added to the trials of the combatants. Lieutenant Cotton of the CLY, finding his 95 mm-gunned tank useless in a battle of this kind, tidily disposed of it in a nearby garage and fought on foot, clutching an umbrella. Yet as evening approached, with the Queens' battalion headquarters pinned down and his men under constant heavy shellfire, their CO reported that he could halt German infantry infiltration only with reinforcements. These were not forthcoming. Throughout 7th Armoured's sector, its units were sending back to Hinde and Erskine disturbing reports of pressure and casualties from all points of the compass. "News trickled back," wrote a British scout car commander of 1st RTR, Sergeant Peter Roach:

The leading regiment . . . had run into real trouble . . . Regiment two was sitting dangerously tight while Jerry was making his way down the flanks . . . Chalky and I sat in the shelter of our hedge and watched. Someone was reporting a man moving towards him. Was it a civilian? Perhaps it was! No, it wasn't! It must be a German infantryman.

Suddenly the colonel's voice, with a touch of weariness and exasperation, "Besa the bugger then." . . . We were all refreshed; we knew what to do and were back in reality.

"We are in a corridor with enemy on both sides", wrote Lieutenant-Colonel Goulburn of the 8th Hussars, although his German opponents were simultaneously reporting to Army Group B the acute threat presented to their front by the British penetration. Around 6 p.m. that evening, with German reinforcements still concentrating around Villers, the surviving British forces were withdrawn to positions around Tracy-Bocage, two miles west, where Hinde had created a "brigade box". The surviving tanks of the City of London Yeomanry had been warned to time their retirement precisely, for as they departed a massive bombardment was to fall on Villers-Bocage to cover them, with American support from the west. Sergeant Lockwood's Sherman moved only a few yards across the square of Villers-Bocage before it stalled. The driver reported with horror: "I can't start the bloody thing!" Then, to their enormous relief, Sergeant Bill Moore jumped down from the turret of his following tank amidst the fierce sniping and machine-gun fire, shackled his cable to their hull, and towed them out of the town minutes before the barrage erupted. "We felt bad about getting out," said Lockwood. "It made it seem as if it had been such a waste." The day's fighting had cost 7th Armoured 25 tanks and 28 other armoured vehicles.

The following morning, further east, XXX Corps launched a new series of attacks by 50th Division against 901 Panzergrenadiers in Tilly. The British were supported by 11 squadrons of fighter-bombers in an attempt to push back Panzer Lehr's units and generate sufficient pressure to enable 7th Armoured to renew its own offensive. But two brigades attacking on a 4000-yard front failed to gain ground. The Germans considered that the day was decided by the new *Panzerfaust*, the superb hand-held infantry anti-tank weapon which they were able to use to formidable effect against Allied tanks advancing in the close country. For reasons that will never be known, General Bucknall failed to ask Second Army for infantry reinforcements to provide direct support for the cut-off tanks of 7th Armoured. 1/7th Queens, which had fought so hard for Villers the previous day, had by now lost 8 officers and 120 other ranks. A massive artillery bombardment by American guns around Caumont broke up an attack on the British tank positions by 2 Panzer, but the 'brigade box' was now threatened with a serious risk of encirclement. Brigadier "Looney" Hinde drove up to his tank positions in a scout car, and began to give his officers their night orders for withdrawal, covered by the exhausted infantry of the Queens. Hinde had won his nickname in the desert both for courage and eccentricity. Now, he suddenly broke off in mid-sentence and peered fascinated at the ground. "Anybody got a matchbox?" he demanded in excitement. Amidst the acute strain of the battle, Lieutenant-Colonel Carver of 1st RTR suggested that this might not be a good moment to worry about nature. "Don't be such a bloody fool, Mike!" exploded Hinde. "You can fight a battle every day of your life, but you might not see a caterpillar like that in fifteen years!"

At the divisional commander's briefing for the withdrawal,

The Villers-Bocage battle: 11–14 June

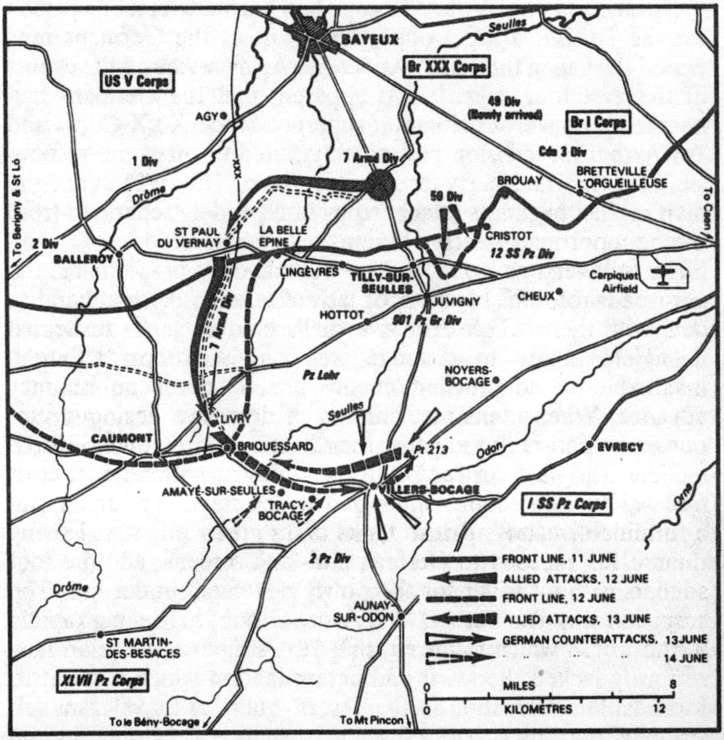

Lieutenant-Colonel Goulburn recorded the reasons given: "Firstly, 50 Div attack towards Longreves-Tilly, which commenced this morning, has made very little progress. Secondly, 2 Panzer Division has been identified on our front and it would appear that unless we can form a firm base back on our centre line with at least an infantry brigade (which we haven't got), he could cut off our communications, work round us and attack us from any direction." Early on the evening of the 14th, a heavy German attack on 22nd Armoured Brigade's "box" at Tracy-Bocage was repulsed. In its aftermath, the Germans were unable to impede 7th Armoured's disengagement and retreat under cover of darkness. They withdrew four miles to positions east of Caumont, their supporting infantry slumbering exhausted on the hulls of the Cromwells, in many cases too far gone to waken or to dismount even when they reached the safety of their new harbours.

By any measure, Villers-Bocage had been a wretched episode for the British, a great opportunity lost as the Germans now closed the gap in their line. As Second Army reviewed the events of the past four days, it was apparent that the Germans had handled a dangerous situation superbly, while XXX Corps and 7th Armoured division had notably failed to meet the responsibilities that had been thrust upon them. On 10/11 June, the division had begun its attack led by tanks widely separated from their supporting infantry. When they encountered snipers and pockets of resistance manned by only handfuls of Germans, the entire advance was blocked for lack of infantry close at hand to deal with them. High explosive shells fired by tanks possessed negligible ability to dislodge well dug-in troops, although invaluable in suppressing enemy fire to cover an infantry advance. When tanks met infantry in defensive positions supported by anti-tank weapons, their best and often only possible tactic was to push forward their own infantry within a matter of minutes to clear them, supported by mortars. Yet again and again in Normandy, British tanks outran their infantry, leaving themselves exposed to German anti-tank screens, and the foot soldiers without cover for their own movement under fire. The suspicion was also born at 21st Army Group, hardening rapidly in the weeks which followed, that 7th Armoured Division now seriously lacked the spirit and determination which made it so formidable a formation in the desert. Many of its veterans felt strongly that they had done their share of fighting in the

Mediterranean, and had become wary and cunning in the reduction of risk. They lacked the tight discipline which is even more critical on the battlefield than off it. The Tiger tank was incomparably a more formidable weapon of war than the Cromwell, but the shambles created by Wittman and his tiny force in Villers-Bocage scarcely reflected well upon the vigilance or tactics of a seasoned British armoured formation. Responsibility for the paralysis of purpose which overcame XXX Corps when 7th Armoured's tanks lay isolated at Tracy-Bocage after their initial withdrawal had to rest with its commander, General Bucknall, an officer henceforth treated with suspicion by Dempsey and Montgomery. Dempsey said:

> This attack by 7th Armoured Division should have succeeded. My feeling that Bucknall and Erskine would have to go started with that failure. Early on the morning of 12 June I went down to see Erskine – gave him his orders and told him to get moving . . . If he had carried out my orders he would not have been kicked out of Villers-Bocage but by this time 7th Armoured Division was living on its reputation and the whole handling of that battle was a disgrace.

Yet the men of 7th Armoured Division bitterly resented any suggestion that, in the Villers battle, they had given less than their best. It was enormously difficult to adjust their tactics and outlook overnight to the new conditions of Normandy after years of fighting in the desert. They were newly-equipped with the inadequate Cromwell, which many of their gunners had scarcely test-fired, after fighting with Shermans in North Africa. There had been spectacular acts of individual heroism, many of which cost men their lives. The 1/7th Queens, especially, had fought desperately to hold the town. For those at the forefront of 22nd Armoured's battle, it was intolerable to suggest that somehow an easy opportunity had been thrown away through any fault of theirs. The German achievement on 13/14 June had been that, while heavily outnumbered in the sector as a whole, they successfully kept the British everywhere feeling insecure and off-balance, while concentrating sufficient forces to dominate the decisive points. The British, in their turn, failed to bring sufficient forces to bear upon these. It seems likely that Brigadier Hinde, while a superbly courageous exponent of "leading from the front", did not handle the large brigade group under his command as imaginatively as might have been possible, and higher formations failed to give him the support he needed. It is remarkable to reflect that the men on the spot believed a single extra infantry brigade could have been decisive in turning the scale at Villers, yet this was not forthcoming. Some 7th Armoured veterans later argued that Montgomery and Dempsey should have taken a much closer personal interest in a battle of such critical importance. For whatever reasons, the only conclusion must be that the British failed to concentrate forces that were available on the battlefield at a vital point at a critical moment of the campaign.

A sour sense, not of defeat, but of fumbled failure overlay the British operation on the western flank. On 11 June, while 7th Armoured was probing hesitantly south, on its left flank the 69th Brigade of 50th Division was hastily ordered forward to exploit what was believed to be another gap in the German line, around the village of Cristot. Lieutenant-Colonel Robin Hastings of the 6th Green Howards was mistrustful of the reported lack of opposition – he anyway lacked confidence in his elderly brigadier – and was no more sanguine after his battalion had waited three hours for transport to its start-line. When the Green Howards moved off, two companies up, they were quickly outdistanced by their supporting tanks of the 4th/7th Dragoon Guards, who raced forward along through the orchards. They failed to observe the hidden positions of panzergrenadiers of 12th SS Panzer, who had been rushed forward to secure the Cristot line in the hours since the British reconnaissance. Lying mute after the passage of the tanks, the SS poured a devastating fire on the Green Howards advancing through the corn, while anti-tank guns disposed of the British armour from their rear. Only two of the nine Shermans escaped, and the advancing infantry suffered appallingly.

With one company commander dead and the other wounded, Hastings' B and C Companies were pinned down. He ordered A to move up on the right and attempt to outflank the enemy. When he himself began to go forward to sort out B and C, his battalion headquarters came under such heavy fire that he was compelled to call up D Company, his last reserve, to clear the way ahead. CSM Stan Hollis, whose courage had done so much for the battalion on D-Day, was now commanding a platoon of D. As they advanced up a sunken lane edged with trees towards the enemy, they came under fierce fire from a German machine-gun. Hollis reached in his pouch for a grenade and found only a shaving brush. Demanding a grenade from the man behind, he tossed it before he realized, to his chagrin, that the had failed to pull the pin. A second later, he concluded that the Germans would not know that and charged them, firing his sten gun while they were taking cover from the expected explosion.

Hastings found that A and B Companies had joined up amid the burning British tanks, one turning out of control in continuous circles between the trees. They gathered the German prisoners and pressed on. Then A Company commander was killed, and the attack was again pinned down. The Green Howards had lost 24 officers and suffered a total of 250 casualties. "I think there's a lot of work for you to do, padre," said Hastings wearily to Captain Henry Lovegrove, who won a Military Cross that day. The padre searched the hedges and ditches around Cristot for hours. He became a smoker for the first time in his life after a few horrific burials. Lacking armoured support and an artillery fire plan, the Green Howards could not hold their ground against German counter-attacks. Bitterly, Hastings ordered a withdrawal. The SS immediately retook possession and by nightfall were counter-attacking towards the British start-line on Hill 103.

Hastings remained bitter about the losses his men had sustained in an attack that he believed was misconceived – that was simply "not on" – a fragment of British army shorthand which carried especial weight when used at any level in the ordering of war. Before every attack, most battalion commanders made a private decision about whether its objectives were "on", and thereby decided whether its purpose justified an all-out effort, regardless of casualties, or merely sufficient movement to conform and to satisfy the higher formation. Among most of the units which landed in Normandy, there was a great initial reservoir of willingness to try, to give of their best in attack, and this was exploited to the full in the first weeks of the campaign. Thereafter, following bloody losses and failures, many battalion commanders determined privately that they would husband the lives of their men when they were ordered into attack, making personal judgements about an operation's value. The war had been in progress for a long time; now, the possibility of surviving it was in distant view. The longer men had been fighting, the more appealing that chance appeared. As the campaign progressed, as the infantry casualty lists rose, it became a more and more serious problem for the army commanders to persuade their battalions that the next ridge, tomorrow's map reference, deserved of their utmost. Hastings was among those who believed that an unnecessary amount of unit determination and will for sacrifice was expended in minor operations for limited objectives too early in the campaign. The problem of "non-trying" units was to become a thorn in the side of every division and corps commander, distinct from the normal demands of morale and leadership, although naturally associated with them.

EPSOM

The debacle at Villers-Bocage marked, for the British, the end of the scramble for ground that had continued since D-Day. The Germans had plugged the last vital hole in their line. Henceforward, for almost all the men who fought in Normandy, the principal memory would be of hard, painful fighting over narrow strips of wood and meadow; of weeks on end when they contested the same battered grid squares, the same ruined villages; of a battle of attrition which was at last to break down Rommel's divisions, but which seemed at the time to be causing equal loss and grief to the men of Dempsey's and Bradley's armies.

In the days following Villers-Bocage, unloading on the beaches fell seriously behind schedule in the wake of the "great storm" of 19/23 June, which cost the armies 140,000 tons of scheduled stores and ammunition. Montgomery considered and rejected a plan for a new offensive east of the Orne. With the remorseless build-up of opposing forces on the Allied perimeter, it was no longer sufficient to commit a single division in the hope of gaining significant ground. When Second Army began its third attempt to gain Caen by envelopment, Operation EPSOM, the entire VIII Corps was committed to attack on a four-mile front between Carpiquet and Rauray towards the thickly-wooded banks of the river Odon. Three of the finest divisions in the British Army – 15th Scottish, 11th Armoured and 43rd Wessex – were to take part, under the command of Lieutenant-General Sir Richard O'Connor, who had made a brilliant reputation for himself leading the first British campaign in the western desert. A personal friend of Montgomery since their days as Staff College instructors together in the 1920s, O'Connor had been captured and spent two years languishing in an Italian prisoner-of-war camp. This was to be his first battle since Beda Fomm in 1941. Early on the morning of 26 June, 60,000 men and more than 600 tanks, supported by over 700 guns on land and sea, embarked on the great new offensive: "The minute hand touched 7.30," wrote a young platoon commander of the King's Own Scottish Borderers:

Concealed guns opened from fields, hedges and farms in every direction around us, almost as if arranged in tiers. During short pauses between salvoes more guns could be heard, and right away, further guns, filling and reverberating the very atmosphere with a sustained, muffled hammering. It was like rolls of thunder, only it never slackened. Then the guns nearby battered out again with loud, vicious, strangely mournful repercussions. Little rashes of goose-flesh ran over the skin. One was hot and cold, and very moved. All this "stuff" in support of us! . . . So down a small winding road, with the absurd feeling that this was just another exercise.[1]

In the first hours, VIII Corps achieved penetrations on a three-mile frontage. But then, from out of the hedges and hamlets, fierce German resistance developed. Some of the great Scottish regiments of the British army – Gordons, Seaforths, Cameronians – began to pour out their best blood for every yard of ground gained. Lieutenant Edwin Bramall of the 2nd KRRC, later to become professional head of the British army, observed that a battalion of the Argylls which infiltrated forward in small groups by use of cover reached their objectives with modest casualties. But the great mass of the British advance moved forward in classic infantry formation: "It was pretty unimaginative, all the things that we had learned to do at battle school. A straightforward infantry bash."[2] That evening, the young platoon commander of the KOSB wrote again:

Rifle fire from the village periodically flared up. We were in bewildering ignorance of what was happening. The rain dripped and trickled into our slits, and there had been no hot food since before dawn. The big shells banging away on the T-roads jarred us, while the faces of the three dead Fusiliers could still be seen there as pale blobs through the gloom and rain, motionless among the shells, with their ghastly whiteness. And this, and those savage crashes, and the great spreadeagled hounds, and the grim churchyard across the wall, evoked a dull weight of depression such as one could never have dreamed. All the elation of the morning had ebbed away. It seemed there was no hope or sanity left, but only this appalling unknown and unseen, in which life was so precious where all rooted, and where all was loneliness and rain.[3]

The prose of Passchendaele seemed born again. A new experience very terrible in kind was being created in Normandy – that of the infantry soldier locked in battle of an intensity few men of

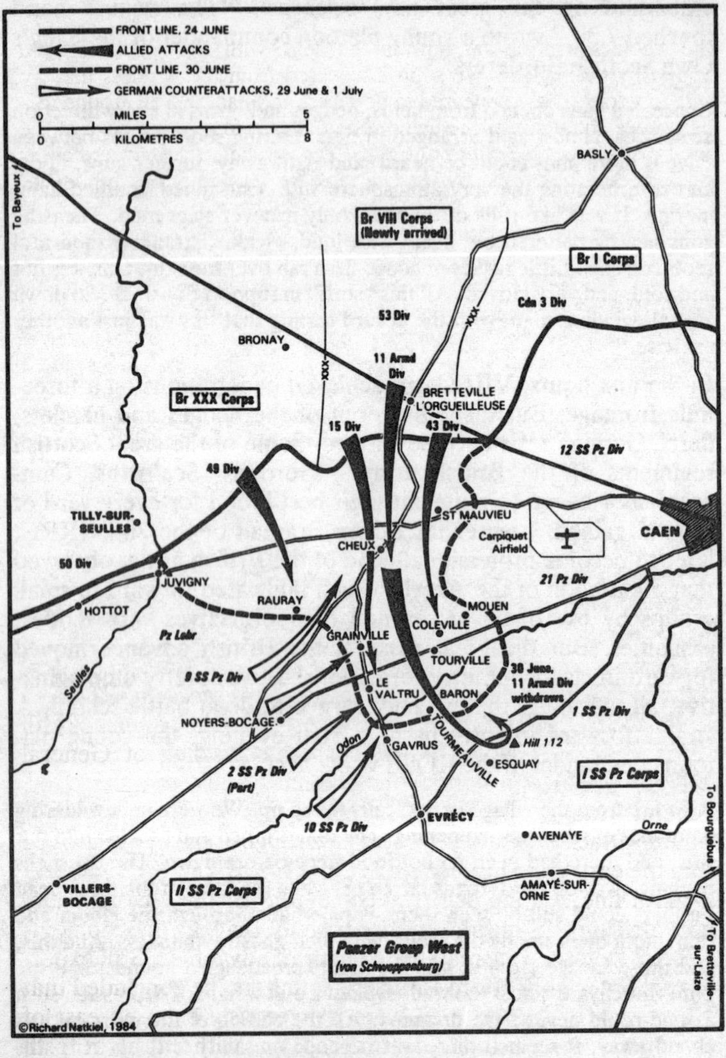

Operation EPSOM: 26 June–1 July

the Allied armies had ever envisaged at their battle schools in Britain. Nor was the struggle much less painful for the crews of the armoured units. A tank wireless-operator of the 4th/7th Dragoon Guards on the British left flank recorded in his diary the fortunes of his squadron on the morning of 26 June:

The whole squadron was now in the field, with the tanks scattered around by the hedges. We soon discovered from the wireless that we were in a trap. There appeared to be Tigers and Panthers all around us – there were about six on the high ground ahead, four in the edge of the wood just across the field to our left. Between them they covered every gap. The hours dragged by. In our tank we sat without saying much, listening intently to what was going on over the wireless. I was eating boiled sweets by the dozen and the others were smoking furiously. I didn't know how long we'd been sitting there when the tank behind us was hit. It was Joe Davis's. I saw a spout of earth shoot up near it as a shot ricocheted through it. Some smoke curled up from the turret, but it didn't actually brew up. We did not know till after that the whole turret crew had been killed. Brian Sutton and his co-driver baled out, but I didn't see them. That made six of the squadron killed already that day. In Lilly's crew Fairman had been killed inside the tank and Digger James had been blown apart by a mortar bomb as he jumped off the turret. Charrison was badly burnt and George Varley was rumoured to be dead. One of Thompson's crew, Jackie Birch, had been shot through the head by a King's Royal Rifle Corps man who mistook him for a Jerry after he baled out . . .

The Tyneside Scottish came back across the field in single file, led by a piper who was playing what sounded like a lament. I felt lucky to be alive.[4]

A German counter-attack was repulsed on 27 June. The next day, in mud and rain, tanks of 11th Armoured at last poured across the bloody stream of the Odon to gain the heights of Hill 112 on 29 June. Now, at the desperate bidding of General Dollman of Seventh Army, who committed suicide a day later, General Hausser of II SS Panzer Corps launched a major counter-attack. 9th and 10th SS Panzer Divisions, newly arrived from the east, were hurled against VIII Corps – and driven back. It was a fine fighting achievement by the British divisions and their air support, marred by the tragedy that, at this moment, General Dempsey misread the balance of advantage. Still expecting a greater effort from Hausser's Panthers, he concluded that O'Connor's exhausted men were dangerously exposed east of the Odon. On 29 June, he ordered the withdrawal of 11th Armoured to the west bank. The next day, Hill 112 was lost. Montgomery ordered that EPSOM should be closed down. VIII Corps had lost 4,020 men, 2,331 from 15th Scottish Division, 1,256 from 11th Armoured and 43rd Division.

Major Charles Richardson of 6th KOSB came out of EPSOM,

his first battle, overcome with horror and disgust after seeing his battalion lose 150 casualties. "We were one big family. I knew every man."[5] He remembered a briefing from a psychiatrist before leaving England, who said that if men wanted to talk about a terrible experience they had endured, it was essential to let them do so rather than to stifle it in their minds. Talk they now did, about the spectacle of the Royal Scots Fusiliers cresting a hill to find the Germans dug in on the reverse slope, "something we had never envisaged"; about the Germans who shot it out until the Borderers were within yards of their positions and then raised their hands, "much good it did them"; about the vital importance of keeping pace with the rolling barrage of the guns.

One of the most remarkable features of EPSOM, like almost all the Normandy battles, was that its failure provoked no widespread loss of confidence by the troops in their commanders generally, or Montgomery in particular, the one general familiar to them all. Senior officers criticized and cursed errors of tactics and judgement. The men fighting the battles became more cautious in action, more reluctant to sacrifice their own lives when told for the third, fourth, fifth time that a given operation was to be decisive. But at no time did their faith in the direction of the campaign falter. "We thought the senior officers were marvellous," said Trooper Stephen Dyson: "They had all the responsibility, didn't they?"[6] Lieutenant Andrew Wilson of The Buffs ". . . found it increasingly difficult to see how we should get out of all this – it seemed an absolute deadlock. There was some effect on morale, and places got a bad name, like Caumont. But when Montgomery passed us one day in his staff car all my crew stood up in the tank and cheered."[7] Lieutenant David Priest of 5th DCLI said: "I though it was going alright, but it might take years. We didn't seem to move very much."[8]

After the war, Montgomery said:

> Of course we would have liked to get Caen on the first day and I was never happy about the left flank until we had got Caen. But the important thing on the flank was to maintain our strength so that we could not only avoid any setback, but could keep the initiative by attacking whenever we liked. On this flank ground was of no importance at all. I had learnt from the last war the senseless sacrifice that can be made by sentimental attachment to a piece of ground. All I asked Dempsey to do was to keep German armour tied down on this flank so that my breakout with the Americans could go more easily. Ground did not matter so long as the German divisions stayed on this flank. If I had attacked Caen in early June I might have wrecked the whole plan.[9]

It was in consequence of nonsense such as this that a great professional soldier caused so much of the controversy about the Normandy campaign to focus upon his own actions. By his determination to reap the maximum personal credit for victory and to distort history to conform with his own advance planning, he also heaped upon himself the lion's share of responsibility for much that went wrong in Normandy. No sane commander could have mounted British attacks of the kind that took place in June and were to follow in July without every hope of breaking through the German defences, or at least of causing the enemy to make substantial withdrawals. Part of Montgomery's exceptional quality as a commander lay in his ability to retain an atmosphere of poise, balance and security within his armies when a less self-disciplined general could have allowed dismay and disappointment to seep through the ranks. Montgomery served his own interests and those of his men very well by maintaining his insistence to his subordinates that all was going to plan. But he did himself a great disservice by making the same assertions in private to Eisenhower, Churchill, Tedder and even his unshakeable patron, Brooke.

Even Montgomery's admirers concede the lack of concern for truth in his make-up.[10] Like Sherlock Holmes' silent dog, an interesting sidelight on the general's character is revealed by the episode of the salmon before D-Day. Visiting troops in Scotland, he cast a fly on the Spey with signal lack of success. On his return, he sent a fish to his close friends the Reynolds, who ran a school, with a note: "I have just got back from Scotland and I send you a salmon – a magnificent fish of some 18 lb. I hope it will feed the whole school."[11] It would be a natural assumption of anyone receiving such a note and such a gift to assume that the donor had caught it himself. Many men would have inserted a jesting line to explain that this was not the case. It seems typical of Montgomery that, while not positively asserting that the salmon was his own prize, he was perfectly content to leave such an assumption in the minds of the Reynolds.

Montgomery's version of the fiasco at Villers-Bocage on 12/13 June was given in an equally characteristic letter to Brooke on the 14th:

When 2nd Panzer division suddenly appeared in the Villers-Bocage–Caumont area, it plugged the hole through which I had broken. I think it had been meant for offensive action against I Corps in the Caen area. So long as Rommel uses his strategic reserves to plug holes, that is good.

Anyhow, I had to think again, and I have got to be careful not to get off balance.[12]

Montgomery was perfectly justified in telling Brooke that the German commitment of armour to create a defensive perimeter was in the long-term interests of the Allies. But it was, of course, preposterous to assert that 7th Armoured Division had "broken through" anything before it encountered Captain Wittman's Tiger tank. Only the leading elements of 2nd Panzer were deployed in the area in time to influence Erskine's withdrawal. It must be to Montgomery's credit that, while he accepted any available glory for his army's achievements, he did not seek to burden it with blame for failures. But it was rash to expect shrewd and thoroughly informed officers at the War Office and SHAEF to accept indefinitely and at face value such travesties of reality as the account above. As Villers-Bocage was followed by EPSOM, and EPSOM by GOODWOOD, it was not the doings of Second Army, but Montgomery's version of them, that became more and more difficult for his peers and critics to swallow. As early as 15 June, Leigh-Mallory recorded his reservations about the handling of the ground campaign in a fashion that was widely echoed among the other airmen, and Montgomery's enemies:

As an airman I look at the battle from a totally different point of view. I have never waited to be told by the army what to do in the air, and my view is not bounded, as seems to be the case with the army, by the nearest hedge or stream. I said as much, though in different words, to Monty and tried to describe the wider aspects of this battle as I see them, particularly stressing the number of divisions which he might have had to fight had they not been prevented from appearing on the scene by air action. He was profoundly uninterested. The fact of the matter is, however, that we have reduced the enemy's opposition considerably and the efficiency of their troops and armour even more so. In spite of this, the army just won't get on . . . The fact remains that the great advantage originally gained by the achievement of surprise in the attack has now been lost.[13]

Much attention has been focussed since the war upon the issue of whether Montgomery's strategy in Normandy did or did not work as he had intended. The implicit assumption is that if it did not, his methods were unsound. Yet his initial plan to seize Caen, and his later movements to envelop the town, seem admirably conceived. The failure lay in their execution. The focus of debate about many Allied disappointments in Normandy should not be upon Montgomery or for that matter Rommel, but upon the subordinate commanders and formations who fought the battles. How was it possible that German troops facing overwhelming firepower and air power, often outnumbered, drawn from an army that had been bled of two million dead in three years on the eastern front, could mount such a formidable resistance against the flower of the British and American armies?

The British experience during the June battles gave their commanders little cause for satisfaction about the fighting power of many of their troops, the tactics that they had been taught to employ, or the subordinate commanders at division and corps level by whom they were led. Earlier in the war Brooke wrote gloomily: "Half our corps and divisional commanders are totally unfit for their appointments. If I were to sack them, I could find no better! They lack character, drive and power of leadership. The reason for this state of affairs is to be found in the losses we sustained in the last war of all our best officers who should now be our senior officers."[14] Even in 1944, it was striking to compare the very high quality of Montgomery's staff at 21st Army Group with the moderate talents revealed by many field commanders of corps and divisions. Bucknall was already suspect as a leader of large forces. Some of those working most closely with O'Connor believed that he too fell short of the qualities needed for corps command in Europe in 1944. Much as he was liked by his staff, many of his officers believed that he had been out of the war too long now to take a grip on a vast new battlefield. At divisional level, confidence had been lost in Erskine. There were doubts about G. I. Thomas of 43rd Division – "the butcher" as he was known – one of the most detested generals in the British army. The performance and leadership of 51st Highland was the subject of deep disappointment.

> Regret to report it is considered opinion Crocker, Dempsey and myself that 51st Division is at present not – NOT – battleworthy [Montgomery cabled to Brooke in July]. It does not fight with determination and has failed in every operation it has been given to do. It cannot fight the Germans successfully; I consider the divisional commander is to blame and I am removing him from command.[15]

After paying tribute to the manner in which the Canadian 3rd Division performed on D-Day, General Crocker of 1 Corps wrote to Dempsey early in July expressing dismay about its failure in a new attempt to gain Carpiquet airfield, and deploring the manner in which since 6 June:

Once the excitement of the initial phase passed, however, the Div lapsed into a very nervy state . . . Exaggerated reports of enemy activity and of their own difficulties were rife; everyone was far too quick on the trigger, and a general attitude of despondency prevailed . . . The state of the Div was a reflection of the state of its commander. He was obviously not standing up to the strain and showing signs of fatigue and nervousness (one might almost say fright) which were patent for all to see.[16]

Early reports from Normandy about the tactical performance of British troops dwelt upon their sluggishness in attack, their lack of the flexibility and initiative which – in defiance of all the caricatures of propaganda – were such a remarkable characteristic of German operations at every level. The close country overwhelmingly favoured defence, as the Allies discovered to their advantage whenever the Germans embarked upon counter-attacks. But throughout the Normandy campaign, the strategic onus of movement lay upon the Allies, and thus their weakness in armoured-infantry co-operation told severely against them. "Armoured divisions have been slow to appreciate the importance of infantry in this type of fighting," declared an early War Office report circulated to all commanding officers.[17]

It is quite clear from even a short experience of fighting in this type of country that the tanks require a great deal more infantry than the motor battalion can provide . . . This co-operation works very well if the tank and infantry commanders of corresponding formations see the picture from the same angle and have a good knowledge of each other's role, in fact "muck in". But where such co-operation is lacking, then valuable time is wasted while higher authority is asked to adjudicate.[18]

A reasonable level of understanding between infantry and tank commanders on the battlefield was often absent. The infantry elements of British armoured divisions seldom, if ever, achieved the vital integration with their tanks that was fundamental to the German panzergrenadiers, who were also equipped with an exceptionally good armoured half-track vehicle to carry them across the battlefield. This must partly be attributed to the parochialism inseparable from the British regimental system. An immense source of strength in sustaining pride and morale, on a vast battlefield such as that of Normandy the regimental system could also become a handicap. German loyalties were to the division as a whole, and absolute mutual support within the division was bred as second nature into the German soldier. There remained a tendency among British battalions to concern themselves almost exclusively with their own affairs in battle.

The Panzer Mk V, or Panther, was the outstanding German tank of the campaign in north-west Europe, less heavily gunned but more mobile and reliable than the Tiger. One of the two tank regiments in almost every German armoured division was equipped with the Panther, which weighed 45 tons, could move at 34 mph, and carried 100 mm of frontal armour, 45 mm of side armour. Its 75 mm KwK 42 gun had a muzzle velocity of 3060 fps, and its 14-pound shell could penetrate 138 mm of armour at 100 yards, 128 mm at 500 yards, 118 mm at 1,000 yards. Its only serious weaknesses against the Sherman were indifferent periscope optics and slow turret traverse.

The infantry and armoured brigade commanders of one elite British armoured division were scarcely on speaking terms with each other in Normandy. Lieutenant-Colonel Hay of the 5th/7th Gordons was exasperated when he climbed on a young troop commander's tank during one of the desperate battles in the Orne bridgehead, and was unable to persuade the officer to advance in support because he considered the risk to his tanks too great. Conversely, following the EPSOM battle, the infantry brigade commander and two battalion COs of one British armoured division had to be sacked. Their divisional commander spoke furiously of the brigadier, "who dug a slit trench at the beginning of the battle and never left it".[19]

The SHAEF appreciation of the Normandy battlefield in April had correctly assessed the *bocage* as country in which, "it will

. . . be most difficult for the enemy to prevent a slow and steady advance by infiltration".[20] The Germans were masters of this art, working small parties behind Allied positions and forcing the defenders out by showing that their flanks were turned. Allied infantry seldom employed the technique, and thus denied themselves an important means of progress in close country. Their commanders relied almost invariably upon the setpiece battalion attack, with two companies forward. This tactic was far too rigid and predictable to defeat a determined defence. In a circular to commanding officers late in June, Montgomery made a vain effort to urge units to show more flexibility. He deplored the habit of preparing troops to fight "the normal battle". He wrote: "This tendency is highly dangerous, as there is no such thing as 'the normal battle'. Leaders at all levels must adapt their actions to the particular problems confronting them."[21] The problem had been succinctly analysed a few weeks earlier by a British corps commander in Italy:

> The destruction of the enemy was most easily achieved when we managed to keep him tired and in a state of disorganisation, which resulted in unco-ordinated defence and lack of food, petrol and ammunition. We were undoubtedly too inelastic in our methods when faced with changing conditions. After six weeks of mobile fighting, during which the enemy never launched anything bigger than weak company counter-attacks, we still talked too much about "firm bases" and "exposed flanks".[22]

It is interesting to turn to German intelligence reports of this period, such as one from Panzer Lehr which declared that "a successful break-in by the enemy was seldom exploited to pursuit. If our own troops were ready near the front for a local counter-attack, the ground was immediately regained. Enemy infantry offensive action by night is limited to small reconnaissance patrols." The Germans quickly developed the technique of holding their front line with only observation posts and a thin defensive screen, holding the bulk of their forces further back, to move forward when the huge Allied bombardments died away: "It is better to attack the English, who are very sensitive to close combat and flank attack, at their weakest moment – that is, when they have to fight without their artillery."[23] A German report from Italy at about this time is also worth quoting, for it reflects similar criticisms made by Rommel's officers in Normandy:

> The conduct of the battle by the Americans and English was, taken all round, once again very methodical. Local successes were seldom

exploited . . . British attacking formations were split up into large numbers of assault squads commanded by officers. NCOs were rarely in the "big picture", so that if the officer became a casualty, they were unable to act in accordance with the main plan. The result was that in a quickly changing situation, *the junior commanders showed insufficient flexibility*. For instance, when an objective was reached, the enemy would neglect to exploit and dig in for defence. The conclusion is: as far as possible *go for the enemy officers*. Then seize the initiative yourself.[24] [Emphases in original.]

Another German report, captured in north-west Europe, was circulated to British senior officers: "The British infantryman," it declared, "is distinguished more by physical endurance than by special bravery. The impetuous attack, executed with dash, is foreign to him. He is sensitive to energetic counter-attack."[25] It is natural that most histories of the Normandy campaign have focussed upon the many acts of courage by British troops, and said less about the occasions on which whole units collapsed under pressure. By this stage of the war, the British Army found that it never possessed as many first-rate officer's and NCOs as it wished, and the performance of some units caused deep dismay at Twenty-First Army Group. The consequence was that the best formations had to be thrust forward again and again in the heart of the battle, while others were considered too unreliable to be entrusted with a vital role in operations. On 30 June, the commanding officer of a battalion suffering serious problems in Normandy, 49th Division's 6th Duke of Wellington's Regiment, wrote a report which bears quoting in full, because it portrays so vividly the strain that the battle thrust upon units which lacked the outstanding qualities of, for instance, 6th Airborne or 15th Scottish:

1. I arrived at 6 DWR on the evening of 26 June. From am 27 June until am 30 June we have been in contact with the enemy and under moderately heavy mortar and shell fire.

2. The following facts make it clear that this report makes no reflection on the state of 6 DWR when they left UK:

a) In 14 days there have been some 23 officer and 350 OR casualties.
b) Only 12 of the original officers remain and they are all junior. The CO and every rank above Cpl (except for 2 Lts) in battalion HQ have gone, all company commanders have gone. One company has lost every officer, another has only one left.
c) Since I took over I have lost two second-in-commands in successive days and a company commander the third day.

d) Majority of transport, all documents, records and a large amount of equipment was lost.

3. *State of Men*

a) 75% of the men react adversely to enemy shelling and are "jumpy".

b) 5 cases in 3 days of self-inflicted wounds – more possible cases.

c) Each time men are killed or wounded a number of men become casualties through shell shock or hysteria.

d) In addition to genuine hysteria a large number of men have left their positions after shelling on one pretext or another and gone to the rear until sent back by the M.O. or myself.

e) the new drafts have been affected, and 3 young soldiers became casualties with hysteria after hearing our own guns.

f) The situation has got worse each day as more key personnel have become casualties.

4. *Discipline and Leadership*

a) State of discipline is bad, although the men are a cheerful, pleasant type normally.

b) NCOs do not wear stripes and some officers have no badges of rank. This makes the situation impossible when 50% of the battalion do not know each other.

c) NCO leadership is weak in most cases and the newly drafted officers are in consequence having to expose themselves unduly to try to get anything done. It is difficult for the new officers (60%) to lead the men under fire as they do not know them.

Conclusion

a) 6 DWR is not fit to take its place in the line.

b) Even excluding the question of nerves and morale 6 DWR will not be fit to go back into the line until it is remobilised, reorganised, and to an extent retrained. It is no longer a battalion but a collection of individuals. There is naturally no esprit de corps for those who are frightened (as we all are to one degree or another) to fall back on. I have twice had to stand at the end of a track and draw my revolver on retreating men.

Recommendation

If it is not possible to withdraw the battalion to the base or UK to re-equip, reorganise and train, then it should be disbanded and split among other units.

If it is not possible to do either of the above and if it is essential that the battalion should return to the line, I request that I may be relieved of my command and I suggest that a CO with 2 or 3 years experience should relieve me, and that he should bring his adjutant and a signals officer with him.

Being a regular officer I realise the seriousness of this request and its effect on my career. On the other hand I have the lives of the new officer personnel (which is excellent) to consider. Three days running a major has been killed or seriously wounded because I have ordered him to in effect stop them running during mortar concentrations. Unless withdrawn from the division I do not think I can get the battalion fit to fight normally and this waste of life would continue. My honest opinion is that if you continue to throw new officer and other rank replacements into 6 DWR as casualties occur, you are throwing good money after bad.

I know my opinion is shared by two other commanding officers who know the full circumstances.

In the field
30 June 1944 (Sgd)__________, Lt-Col., Commanding, 6 DWR[27]

If the difficulties of 6th DWR were exceptional, it is seldom that the plight of a moderate unit under pressure on the battlefield is so precisely chronicled. Montgomery, on whose desk this report finally arrived, was furious. He wrote to the Secretary of State for War, P. J. Grigg, saying that he had withdrawn 6th DWR from the 49th Division, and castigating its commanding officer: "I consider that the CO displays a defeatist mentality and is not a 'proper chap'."[28] The unit was disbanded. The Commander-in-Chief perhaps had no other option but to adopt a ruthless attitude to any manifestation of failing will at this juncture in the battle. If some divisions had proved capable of extraordinary exertions and sacrifices, in a struggle of such magnitude it was the overall quality of the army, rather than of a small number of outstanding units within it, which would determine its outcome. It was because of problems such as these that Montgomery found it necessary to keep elite formations, such as 6th Airborne, in action long after their casualties and exhaustion made them deserving candidates for relief. It must also be said that even average German formations proved capable of continuing to fight effectively when reduced to 25 per cent of their strength. None of the German formations transferred from the eastern front to Normandy were found wanting by their commanders (as 7th Armoured and 51st Highland were) because they had been over-exposed to action. When the war was over that most astringent of military critics, Captain Basil Liddell Hart, made his own comments upon the performance of British units in Normandy:

Time after time they were checked or even induced to withdraw by boldly handled pockets of Germans of greatly inferior strength. But for our air superiority, which hampered the Germans at every turn, the results would have been much worse. Our forces seem to have had too little initiative in infiltration, and also too little determination – with certain exceptions. Repeatedly one finds that big opportunities were forfeited because crucial attacks were stopped after suffering trifling casualties. That was particularly marked with the armoured formations.[29]

Montgomery's massive conceit masked the extent to which his own generalship in Normandy fell victim to the inability of his army to match the performance of their opponents on the battlefield. After all the months of meticulous training and preparation for OVERLORD, British tactics were shown to be not only unimaginative, but also inadequate to cope with the conditions of Normandy. Battalion and brigade commanders seemed capable of little beyond the conventional setpiece assault "by the book". It may be argued that it was Montgomery's business to adjust his plans to the limitations of his forces. But it was enormously difficult, indeed all but impossible, to retrain an army, to change the entire tactical thinking of a generation, in mid-campaign. Montgomery was uncommonly skilled in making the most of the units he had, discerning the qualities that suited a certain division to a certain role. It was he himself who declared that the British are a martial, not a military people. There was nothing cowardly about the performance of the British army in Normandy. But it proved too much to ask a citizen army in the fifth year of war, with the certainty of victory in the distance, to display the same sacrificial courage as Hitler's legions, faced with the collapse of everything that in the perversion of Nazism they held dear. Brigadier Williams said: "We were always very aware of the doctrine, 'Let metal do it rather than flesh'. The morale of our troops depended upon this. We always said: 'Waste all the ammunition you like, but not lives.' "[30]

But in Normandy, the Allied armies discovered the limits of what metal alone could achieve. Individual Allied soldiers proved capable of immense sacrifice and bravery; men who felt – like Sergeant-Major Hollis of the Green Howards or Corporal Kelly of the 314th Infantry at Cherbourg – that winning the war was their personal responsibility. But the British failure to gain Caen in June 1944 revealed a weakness of fighting power and tactics within the British army much more than a failure of generalship by Sir Bernard Montgomery.

5 The Americans before Cherbourg

The bocage

Something between a week and a month of intense action suffices to transform most infantryman from novices – unable to discern the source of firing, uncertain of the scale of danger, unconvinced of the need to dig deep – into veterans or casualties. In the days following 6 June, the American forces in Normandy faced few German opponents of the quality and determination of those who were already moving into battle against the British Second Army. But for the men of Bradley's divisions, fighting first to unite their beachheads, then to expand these and secure Cherbourg and the Contentin Peninsula, the first encounters with the enemy in the close confinement of the Norman *bocage* proved a testing experience. "Although there had been some talk in the U.K. before D-Day about the hedgerows," wrote Gavin of the 82nd Airborne, "none of us had really anticipated how difficult they would be."[1] The huge earthen walls, thickly woven with tree and brush roots, that bordered every field were impenetrable to tanks; each one was a natural line of fortification. In the Cotentin, the difficulties of the ground were compounded by wide areas of reclaimed marshland likewise impassable to armour, which was thus restricted to the roads. Gerow's V Corps, which had endured so much to secure Omaha beach, was fortunate during the next phase of their advance inland in meeting few German reinforcements – only the 30th Mobile Brigade began to arrive on 7 June to support the badly mauled 352nd Division. The American 29th Division, which had revealed its lack of experience on D-Day, made slow work of its move westward to link up with the survivors of the Ranger companies still holding out on Pointe du Hoc.

"Those goddam Bosch just won't stop fighting," Huebner of 1st Division complained to Bradley, when the latter hitched a lift ashore in a DUKW on the morning of the 7th.[2] But the 18th and

26th Regiments of 1st Division pushed forward to link up with the British XXX Corps across the river Drome on 8 June, and Isigny was cleared on the night of 7/8 June. The redoubtable Brigadier-General Cota of 29th Division was one of the first men into the ruined town, where the Americans found only the acrid smell of burning and the crackle of flames from buildings ignited by shells and bombs lighting up the darkness:

"Hell, they didn't even blow the bridge", Cota yelled to Col. Gill as he walked across the sturdy stone span [related the divisional after-action narrative]. Everyone was on edge waiting for sniper fire, and it was fortunate for the few prisoners that dribbled out of the ruins that they did not get shot. One of them offered to lead our men to a place where 14 of his comrades were hiding. He said they'd give up but were afraid to come out. A patrol was hastily organised, and under the prisoner's direction, rounded up his fellow soldiers.[3]

Cota dispatched a liaison officer, Lieutenant Delcazel, to report to the division that Isigny was clear. Less than a mile along the road to the division CP, his jeep was surrounded by armed men who disarmed the lieutenant and his driver and took them back to their positions. It emerged that these were not Germans, but a hodgepodge of Poles, Serbs and Russians whose officers and NCOs had fled, and who were chiefly concerned to find the means to surrender safely. They were mortally frightened of being intercepted by nearby German troops, who would shoot them at once if their intentions became apparent. After much discussion with the captured Americans, on the morning of 10 June they marched fully armed down the road towards Maisy until they encountered an astonished American half-track driver. Delcazel ran forward shouting, "Don't shoot! Don't shoot! They want to surrender.' 75 men walked forward and laid down their weapons. A squadron of impeccably-attired White Russian cavalrymen in astrakhan hats, who surrendered a few days later, sent forward a deputation to an American reconnaissance troop to demand it strength. They declared that they were eager to give up, but could only do so in the face of a substantial force. The Americans convinced them that they were in sufficient strength for honour to be served. In those first days after the landings, First Army found the quality of their opposition extraordinarily uneven: at one moment a handful of GIs were receiving wholesale enemy surrenders; at the next, an entire division was being held up by the stubborn resistance of a company of Germans with a detachment of anti-tank guns.

Following the capture of Isigny and the link-up of Omaha and Utah, the eastern American flank gave the Allied high command little anxiety in the aftermath of its troubled landings. All attention was focussed north-westwards, upon the struggle of General Collins' VII Corps to secure the Cotentin. Montgomery was eager that V Corps should press on southwards while Collins moved west and north, but Bradley told his commanders: "Nobody's going anywhere until Joe gets Cherbourg. I want to see Pete and Gee dug in solidly on their fronts. The other fellow might still hit them, and we're not going to risk his busting through to Omaha beach . . ."[4]

The German forces in the peninsula lacked the mobility and cohesion to mount a large-scale counter-attack against the Utah beachhead. But they could still defend the hedgerows and causeways with bitter tenacity, and launch a succession of local assaults in battalion or regimental strength which, at times, caused the American command much anxiety. 7 June found the airborne divisions still fighting hard to concentrate their scattered companies, and to gain the elusive passages through the floods which alone could promise Collins' corps a breakout from the beaches. Bradley told Collins to pour all the air power he wished onto Carentan, "and take the city apart. Then rush it and you'll get in."[5] It quickly emerged that by no means all the American units coming ashore could match the paratroopers' determination or skill on the battlefield. Jittery leading elements of the 90th Division moving forward from Utah encountered an approaching column of German prisoners, and opened fire upon them with every weapon they possessed. When the 325th Gliderborne Infantry were shown by Gavin and his tired soldiers where they were to make their attack, their battalion commander declared that he did not feel well, and had to be relieved. When the unit finally advanced in the face of German fire, on this first encounter with the enemy, they halted and could not be persuaded to move. Gavin was compelled to signal his paratroopers to pass through and seize the objective themselves. The airborne divisions had expected early relief after carrying out their D-Day missions – withdrawal to England to prepare for a new parachute operation. Yet because of a serious shortage of determined and competent American infantry, they were now to be called upon to fight through to the end of the battle for the Cotentin. Their experience and their achievement, lightly armed and having borne the brunt of the first fighting for the peninsula without armoured support, proved that an elite American force could match the troops of any army in Normandy. But those of them who had experienced little action before found the process of learning as painful as any line infantryman.

Private Richardson of the 82nd Airborne – who unlike most of his comrades had not seen action – was last seen asleep in a field in the midst of the Cotentin on the evening of 6 June. By the night of the 7th, he was dug into a hedgerow looking out across a field to a wood, amid the machine-gun platoon of his battalion:

> Someplace far off in the distance beyond the woods I began to hear a squeaking noise. It was the sound of a rusty wheel that needed grease, the sound of an old farm wagon I'd often heard around my farming village home. Some French farmer hauling goods? That seemed unlikely with two armies poised with uneasy fingers on the triggers of a thousand guns. Germans? That too seemed unlikely. If the Germans were moving through territory where we might be, wouldn't they be silent? Wouldn't they creep practically on tiptoe? I dismissed the idea that this distance noise meant anything dangerous, or tried to. The trouble was the noise, the only noise in the whole night around me, was coming our way. For a time there was a silence, then I heard someone shout "HALT!" and immediately a burst of fire – sub-machine gun, German. What was happening? Why wasn't the machine-gun platoon doing something? Finally there was firing from one of our machine-guns, the slower dat-dat-dat, tracer bullets though instead of being aimed were going up into the sky in a crazy wavering arc. I finally woke Johnson up and we sat there staring at the tracers flying around the sky. When the shooting stopped we could hear the Germans running around yelling and gradually moving back towards the road near the house. Then the house was on fire, and after a time the vehicle that made the squeaking noise started up again, but this time it headed down the road away from us.[6]

The Germans resumed their attack on the paratroopers' position early the following afternoon. Richardson fired only one round from the MI rifle he had picked up before it jammed, and he understood why its original owner had thrown it away. Feeling helpless and nervous, he began to shoot single rounds towards the woods from which the enemy fire seemed to be coming, pausing after each shot to ram home the sticking bolt. As a small boy, he had read a series of splendid children's adventure stories entitled *American Boys Over There*, which had planted a vivid image in his mind of big-bellied, heavy-booted "huns" or "bosch" charging across a field in spiked helmets against American doughboys, who eventually prevailed. Now, at each warning of a new German assault, he saw this picture more clearly. And at last, it became a reality. A solitary tank began to rattle slowly across the field towards the Americans, who could confront it only with fierce machine-gun fire. To their astonishment and delight, suddenly it halted. A plume of smoke rose from its turret. This was no Panther or Tiger, but some French-built makeweight. The paratroopers cheered, "like kids at a football game when their team scores". The tank turned about and lumbered away into the woods. But the defenders' exhilaration was stillborn. Moments later, very accurate mortar fire began to fall among them. "Men I had just lain shoulder to shoulder with began screaming in pain, screaming for help, hysterical helpless screams that made my stomach tighten. Because of the apparent protection of the hedgerow and our greenness, we had not realized the necessity of digging in and few of us had holes which would have saved us from all but a direct hit."[7]

Richardson remembered vividly a photograph that he had seen in a magazine, of a Russian soldier who was captioned as the only survivor of his company. Now, the young American felt that he shared the man's sensation. When his unit, and the other survivors of the airborne divisions, were withdrawn from the battle at the beginning of July, after 33 days in action, his company numbered 19 men. His division had suffered 46 per cent casualties. Lieutenant Sidney Eichen of the 30th Division's 120th Infantry was one of the men who relieved the 82nd Airborne. The green, unblooded newcomers gazed in shock and awe at the paratroopers they were to succeed:

> We asked them: "Where are your officers?", and they answered: "All dead." We asked: "Who's in charge, then?", and some sergeant said: "I am." I looked at the unshaven, red-eyed GIs, the dirty clothes and the droop in their walk, and I wondered: is this how we are going to look after a few days of combat?[8]

The 29th Division's difficulties continued throughout the first weeks in Normandy. They called for all the leadership and driving power of Brigadier Cota and a handful of other officers to keep the men moving on their push south from the beaches. In the early hours of 10 June, Cota was at the command post of the 175th Regiment in a field at Lison, when three soldiers walked in from the east and announced they were from the 2nd Battalion, which had been surrounded and wiped out. Despite the Brigadier's scepticism and efforts to calm them, the sergeant with them insisted that they were the only survivors.

We'd just gotten into our bivouac area when it all started [the sergeant described their collapse in the after-action narrative]. All of a sudden flares went up and burp guns started to fire into the big field where most of the battalion was located. We could hear the Germans yelling. Sometimes they'd yell "Surrender! Surrender!" in English. We We tried to fight back but we didn't have any firing positions. Every time we tried to move the Germans would see the movement in the bushes for flares lit up the whole field, and they'd let loose with machine gun fire. They kept shooting mortars into the field all the time. There were seven or eight of us in the little group near me. We figured a way to get out, but a couple of the boys were hit as they tried to make it.[9]

In the hours that followed, more stragglers from the battalion, including its chaplain, arrived and confirmed the NCO's story. Later in the day, Cota talked forcefully to some hundred men of the battalion who had now been reassembled.

The members of this group were visibly shaken from their experiences of the night before. One medical aid man called "Skippy" just kept repeating over and over, "That bayonet charge, that goddam bayonet charge." Cota told the group that they were under the wrong impression – that the battalion had by no means been wiped out. General Gerhardt had already appointed Lieutenant-Colonel Arthur Sheppe, who had been acting as regimental executive, to take over command. He told them that they would have an opportunity to rest, be re-equipped and would be able to go back and fight the Germans. At the moment this proposition was not accepted too warmly.[10]

The 29th Division's narrative of an action south of Lison on 11 June, when two companies of the 175th Infantry advanced across the Vire, perfectly reflects the experience of scores of units in those painful, bitter weeks in the *bocage* when every yard of ground was gained with such painful slowness:

It was with difficulty that Major Miller managed to get his heavy machine-guns up to a base-of-fire position to sweep the hedges of the suspected road. Radio channels within the company were not functioning, and the "pass-it-back" method of requesting the weapons to come forward was slow. The entire command weight of the company at this point rested upon small unit leadership. Could the sergeant make his men do what he wanted? Was the sergeant a leader? Some exemplified all the finer qualities, about one-third fell down in this respect. All were handicapped by a general lack of understanding of the situation that confronted them. The enemy never presented himself as a target in this phase, and the fire of the company had, seemingly, little effect on him. On Gen. Cota's insistence the other weapon of the infantry – movement – paid off well. Our troops continued to move into the fire by rushes, by creeping, by crawling, by ever moving forward. Result – enemy fire diminished and then stopped.

. . . Cota had advanced only 25 yards when the crisis broke. One or two burp guns, which seemed to be located behind the high hedge that bordered the left side of the road, opened up with their excited chattering. The column on both sides of the road immediately dropped into the ditch – but this ditch was a shallow affair, about 4 or 5 inches deep, and offered no natural concealment of any kind. The suddenness with which the fire started, after the intense quiet of the last 20 minutes, stunned every member of the company. They dropped there and lay still. Several men were hit by the bullets spraying along, ricocheting off the road and nipping the shrubbery. Someone yelled "Return the fire! Shoot back at the bastards!" At intervals men would rise from the ditch and try to escape from the entrapment by either scurrying to the rear, or trying to vault over the hedges. One man attempting to cross the left hedge received a blast of burp gun fire that shoved him crashing back into the road – dead . . . Shea [Cota's aide] worked his way back through the culvert to the road. Gen. Cota was standing in the shelter of a corner of the hedgerow at the road junction opposite the culvert. He was smiling. "What's this, 'Cota's Last Stand'?" he quipped. "One minute I'm surrounded by a rifle company – those birds started to shoot – and I looked around to find myself all alone."[11]

Most or all of the German 243rd, 709th, and 91st Divisions were in the Cotentin, reinforced by the 6th Parachute Regiment, the 206th Panzer Battalion, and the Seventh Army Storm Battalion. Despite the vast weight of Allied air power interdicting communications, the 77th Division was also able to reach the area virtually unscathed, and VII Corps was in consequence obliged to pay dearly to enlarge the Utah perimeter across the swamp-ridden ground northwards. Major Harry Herman, executive officer of the 9th Division's 2nd/39th Infantry, described the struggle to overcome the huge concrete casemates of Fort St Marcouf, even after it had been subjected to heavy air attack:

Not a shot is fired taking our first objective. We walk upright into the bunker through one of the doors of twisted steel, throw in a hand grenade just for luck, and rush in on the ready to be greeted only by dead jerries strewn around inside 20-foot-thick concrete walls like so many loaves of bread – concussion. It feels rather strange and eerie, all very quiet, the sea beyond the fort looking cool and green. Have the Germans pulled out? Where is the 4th division? Where is our heavy weapons company? We worm our way to the top of the bunker, get careless, stand up, loll around, planning the next jump.

While we are discussing this possibility, the entire party is suddenly lifted up and sat down hard by a blast that wounds Colonel Lockett in the head and arm. It is direct frontal fire, amazing because it gives no whistle and you find yourself out in the open with a tight exprcssion around the eyes when the thing hits. At dusk, we open up: a tremendous sight. The entire strip of beach being combed and raked by sixteen cannon, 3 and 4 inch naval guns, 8 mortars, 16 machine-guns for fifteen minutes. Then we jump off, being greeted with very heavy enfilade fire on our 15-foot wide front. The 155 mm barrage had only bounced off the fort. I send G Company on a flanking mission to the left in an effort to either divert or knock out the resistance there which is preventing any forward movement. G reports that they are up to their chests in water and can go no further. We, the remainder of E Company, start forward again after laying in that damn water for a day and a half. We inch up the road along with a tank destroyer while the first battalion is engaged in heavy rifle fire. It seemed that we would finally get to the church which was our first phase line, but sweeping machine-fire tears the road. Men will not move and finally we have to withdraw. We have taken a beating.

Several hours later, we start out again, this time with no barrage. We meet the first battalion which, in spite of mines and heavy fire, is coming up the beach. Walking "at the ready" behind our TDs, they absorb most of the hail of fire that greets us. We get to the first bunker, Sergeant Hickey with a crowbar forces open the vent and we plant a 5 lb TNT block inside, which opens a hole about the size of a man's body. Through this the TD fires 5 rounds of HE. That was that. Like killing flies with a sledgehammer. We have lost only 14 men, but the first battalion is in trouble. They lost Colonel Tinley who was first hit by a rifle bullet in the chest then while being carried on a stretcher, the litter bearers stepped on a mine. So he was buried later at St Mère Eglise. We gain the front part of the church, but jerry has the rear part and the cloisters. It is point-blank firing for a good hour until we have to get out because they got up in the rear and threw potato mashers down the belfry onto the altar where we are entrenched.[12]

The Americans gained the fort at last after blasting their way inch by inch through the defences in the manner described by Herman. The 9th Division found such fighting tolerable after all their experience in North African and Sicily, but already other, greener American formations were proving sluggish in action. Herman and his men watched the first actions of the 79th Division with deep dismay: "They were almost a cruel laugh. They had one regiment attacking through our assembly area whose commander could not read a map, and they lost more men than I've ever seen through damn recruit tricks. It is quite evident that they are not prepared for combat – a shameful waste of good American lives."[13] Major Randall Bryant, executive officer of the 1st Battalion of the 9th Division's 47th Regiment, found his unit summoned into action to relieve the 90th Division, a formation whose record was almost disastrously unsatisfactory throughout the Normandy campaign. Bryant and his men marched past the 90th's infantry, lying by the roadside behind the line: "They looked awful – unshaven, dirty, pitiful."[14]

Carentan fell only on 12 June, and it was the 13th before the two American beachheads were at last in firm contact across the great flat sweep of wetlands dividing them. That day, Taylor's paratroopers fought off a determined counter-attack by 17th SS Panzergrenadiers. Ultra intercepts had provided Bradley with warning of this German movement. Without explanation, he ordered Gerow immediately to move elements of 2nd Armored Division into the area in time to support the Airborne, and subsequently to push back the SS. In the two weeks that followed, although Gerow's V Corps progressively pushed its perimeter southwards to Caumont, American attention focussed squarely upon the drive for Cherbourg, the critical OVERLORD objective of gaining the Allies a major port. Already, the American commanders were profoundly conscious that time was slipping away, that more and more German forces were arriving on the battlefield, that ground was only slowly being gained. There was concern about the quality of infantry leadership. A forceful directive from First Army reminded all officers that they must wear badges of rank. Many had removed them, for fear of snipers. When on 14 June Gerow of V Corps told General Hodges, with some satisfaction, that his men had achieved all their objectives, Hodges reminded him with a quiet smile: "Gee, the objective of Berlin."[15] Yet the chronic shortage of supplies – above all, of artillery ammunition – was such that First Army could sustain only one major thrust at a time.[16]

Despite Collins' eagerness to strike hard and fast for Cherbourg, Bradley concluded that the risk would be intolerable unless the peninsula was first cut, to isolate the port from German reinforcements. In the first days after 6 June, the American airborne divisions fought their way forward inch by inch to consolidate the tenuous footholds they had gained in their drop, and to defeat dangerous German counter-attacks such as that on 7 June against St Mère Eglise. Then, led by the 9th and 90th Divisions and elements of 82nd Airborne, V Corps launched its drive westward, completed at the little coastal holiday resort of Barneville on 18 June. For many of the Americans, it was an exhilarating dash, infantry clinging to the hulls of the Shermans

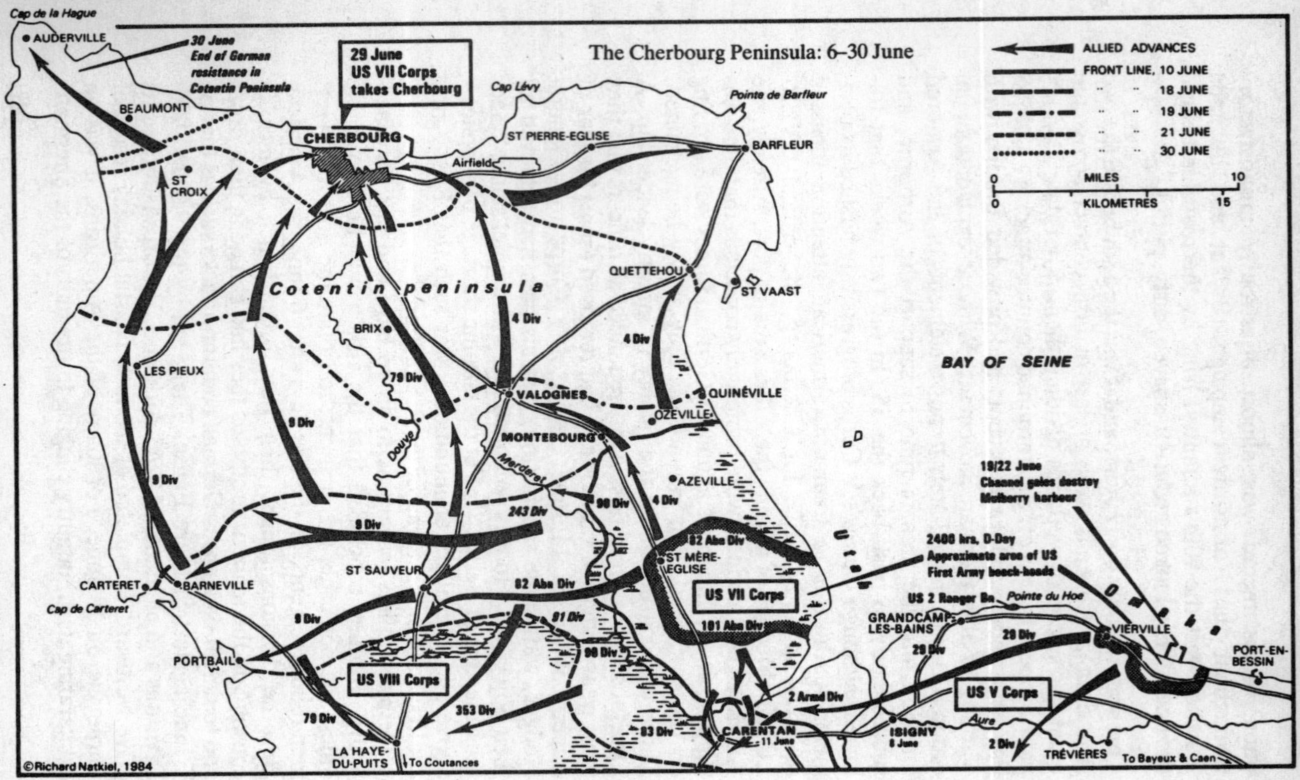
The Cherbourg Peninsula: 6–30 June
ALLIED ADVANCES
FRONT LINE, 10 JUNE
" " 18 JUNE
" " 19 JUNE
" " 21 JUNE
" " 30 JUNE
MILES
0
10
KILOMETRES
0
15
Cap de la Hague
AUDERVILLE
30 June
End of German resistance in Cotentin Peninsula
29 June
US VII Corps
takes Cherbourg
Cap Lévy
Pointe de Barfleur
BEAUMONT
CHERBOURG
ST PIERRE-EGLISE
BARFLEUR
Airfield
ST CROIX
QUETTEHOU
ST VAAST
Cotentin peninsula
4 Div
BRIX
4 Div
BAY OF SEINE
LES PIEUX
79 Div
VALOGNES
QUINÉVILLE
9 Div
OZEVILLE
MONTEBOURG
Douve
Merderet
AZEVILLE
9 Div
90 Div
4 Div
19/22 June
Channel gales destroy Mulberry harbour
243 Div
9 Div
82 Abn Div
Utah
2400 hrs, D-Day
Approximate area of US First Army beach-heads
ST MÈRE-EGLISE
ST SAUVEUR
CARTERET
BARNEVILLE
82 Abn Div
US VII Corps
US 2 Ranger Bn
Pointe du Hoe
Omaha
Cap de Carteret
9 Div
91 Div
101 Abn Div
GRANDCAMP-LES-BAINS
29 Div
VIERVILLE
PORTBAIL
90 Div
29 Div
PORT-EN-BESSIN
US VIII Corps
2 Armd Div
US V Corps
79 Div
353 Div
Aure
83 Div
CARENTAN
11 June
ISIGNY
8 June
2 Div
TRÉVIÈRES
To Bayeux & Caen
LA HAYE-DU-PUITS
To Coutances
©Richard Natkiel, 1984

and tank destroyers as they bucketed across the countryside, meeting only isolated pockets of resistance. Parties of fugitive Germans or half-hearted counter-attacks on American positions were ruthlessly cut down, although 1,500 men of the German 77th Division were able to escape southwards across country, surprising men of the 90th Division guarding a bridge over the river Olande, and taking more than 100 prisoners. The 77th was one of the few formations of reasonable quality in the Cotentin. Most of the German static units were undertrained, poorly-equipped, demoralized. Hodges' First Army diary for 16 June recorded that, "the Boche artillery extremely weak, and G-2 [intelligence] reports an increasing demoralisation because of lack of ammunition and supply." Such tanks as the Germans possessed were almost invariably captured French or Czech models. "We knew that we were not facing the top panzers," said Corporal Preston of the 743rd Tank Battalion.[17] The German units proved capable of stubborn resistance when defending prepared positions against direct assault, but lacked the will or the means to interfere with major American units manoeuvring in open country.

There was a legendary exchange between Bradley and Collins at this time, when the First Army commander received a characteristic signal from Montgomery declaring loftily that "Caen is really the key to Cherbourg." Collins exploded: "Brad, let's wire him to send us the key!"[18] Yet while the Americans interpreted Montgomery's words both as an excuse for British difficulties around Caen, and an attempt to diminish that which they themselves were seeking to accomplish in the Cotentin, Montgomery was correct. Almost every single German formation of quality was fighting against the British. There could be no comparison between the difficulty of facing 12th SS Panzer or Panzer Lehr, and that of rolling up the weak enemy divisions falling back on Cherbourg.

Not that this diminishes the qualities of speed and energy which VII Corps displayed in reaching the great port. Collins was already revealing himself as one of the outstanding personalities of the campaign. The tenth child of a Louisiana Irish family, he was 48 years old. Like so many other American career soldiers, he had spent years between the wars gaining age and enduring stagnation, seemingly without hope of glory or professional fulfilment. In 1920, when he found himself demoted to captain in the general post-war rundown of the services, he considered resignation. He was 44 before he attained a lieutenant-colonelcy, and it was January 1943 before he saw action for the first time, as a divisional commander in the Pacific. As a young man, he had considered becoming a lawyer, and possessed uncommonly catholic tastes for a soldier. He had travelled widely in Europe and the Far East, was a fine shot and an opera lover. A ruthless driver of men, he unhesitatingly sacked officers of any rank who failed to match his standards. Beyond the various divisional and regimental commanders whom he dismissed in the weeks after D-Day, he disposed of an operations officer who persisted with the fatal American army pre-war doctrine of placing unit boundaries on high ground, and an artillery commander who seemed unable to understand the vital importance of forward observation. Intolerant of excuses, he had a superb eye for an opportunity on the battlefield: American – and British – forces in Normandy sorely needed more commanders out of his mould.

Just 22 hours after gaining Barneville, having achieved an astonishingly rapid change of axis through 90 degrees, Collins' men began to push north for the port. Middleton's VIII Corps, newly operational, accepted responsibility for securing the American east-west line while VII Corps drove for the port. Collins was already agitating for a leading role in the push south when Cherbourg fell. Bradley told him: "Troy [Middleton of VIII Corps] likes to fight, too."

> General Bradley also had some definite words to say about divisions and commanders who appeared to be fighting the war for newspaper headlines alone [reported Hodges' diary]. This competition for publicity, he told General Collins, will have to cease.[19]

The intensity of rivalry between senior officers in battle is often difficult for civilians to grasp. But it is a simple fact of life that for professional soldiers, war offers the same opportunities and fulfilments as great sales drives offer corporation presidents. This is not a moral judgement, but a reality as old as war itself. All that was new in the Second World War was that unique opportunities were available to commanders on the battlefield to ingratiate themselves with newspaper correspondents, and thus to make themselves national figures. In the British Army, only an officer of Montgomery's rank could exploit this. But within the American forces in Normandy, many divisional commanders competed ferociously for publicity for themselves and their formations, and there was bitter jealousy, for instance, of the fame of "The Big Red One".

The battle for Cherbourg

At 2.00 p.m. on 22 June, preceded by a massive air bombardment, the Americans opened their attack against the three ridge lines on which the German outer defence of Cherbourg was centred. "The combat efficiency of all the [defending] troops was extremely low," admitted a German writer later.[1] Cherbourg's defences had been designed principally to meet an attack from the sea, and in an exercise early in May, General Marcks had demonstrated their vulnerability to landward assault by breaking through at exactly the points at which the Americans now attacked. Collins later expressed his astonishment that the Germans failed to make a stand on the outer range of high ground around the city, instead retiring immediately to the inner forts. They appeared to lack not only the numbers, but the will to conduct such a defence. Four German battle-groups had been formed from the remains of the units which had retreated up the Cotentin, and static defence in fortified positions is the least demanding role for poor quality troops. If the Americans were able to mount their attack without enduring forceful counterattacks, of the kind which were creating such difficulties for the British around Caen, it remained a harrowing task for infantry to advance into the intense machine-gun fire from the huge concrete bunkers.

Major Randall Bryant's battalion had fought a procession of minor skirmishes against pockets of German resistance up the peninsula, in one of which Bryant surprised himself as much as his men by successfully bouncing a bazooka round off a road into the belly of a German tank – the Americans had learned by bitter experience that direct fire would not penetrate its armour. Now, in the streets of Cherbourg, they began two days of nerve-wracking house-to-house fighting on the road to Fort du Roule. They learned by experience the techniques of covering the building opposite while squads leapfrogged forward, paving their path with grenades, for it was a skill in which they had never trained. The enemy's massive network of strongpoints had to be reduced one by one in dogged fighting, the assaulting infantry scaling the open approaches under withering machine-gun fire.

We jump off Fort Octeville [wrote Major Herman of the 39th Infantry]. A barrage pins us down initially, but men filter through somehow, running like scared rabbits directly into the fort. We stop our artillery; it falls short on G Company, knocking out a platoon. Everything seems wrong. Our supporting tanks turn tail. With my Sgt. Maachi in tow, we crawl under heavy but high machine-gun fire up to the fort that looms up like Grand Central Station. I don't quite remember what happens from here on, but piecing it together, we got two bazookas up to about sixty yards from the fort when we hit the outpost. I kneeled up to fire my MI and a burst caught me in the right hip, taking my jacket with it. I started to run towards the pillbox, firing. A potato masher tore the gun out of my hands, ripping the forearm muscles of my right arm away, but not touching the bone. My boys said that I rolled down into a ditch, unconscious.[2]

9th Division gained Octeville, and the 314th Infantry stormed Fort du Roule by other examples of the sacrificial courage which alone enables infantry to seize strongly fortified positions. When Corporal John Kelly found his platoon pinned down by machine-gun fire, he crawled forward to fix a pole charge beneath the German firing-slit, but returned to find that it had failed to detonate, and went back with another one. This time, the explosion blew off the protruding gun barrels, enabling the corporal to climb the slope a third time, reach the rear door of

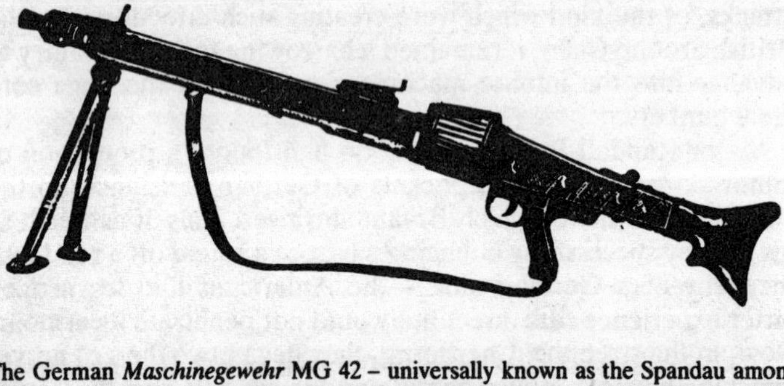

The German *Maschinegewehr* MG 42 – universally known as the Spandau among Allied troops – was a superb general-purpose machine-gun, with a startling 1,200 rpm rate of fire. It could be fed either through boxed belts or – as here – by drum for greater portability. Distributed prodigally among all German units, it contributed decisively to their ability to generate immense defensive fire-power even when positions were manned by only small numbers of men. 750,000 were made before the end of the war, and achieved a remarkable reputation for reliability – the MG 42's barrel could be changed in five seconds during periods of heavy firing.

the pillbox and grenade it into silence. Lieutenant Carlos Ogden cleared the way for his company by knocking out an 88 mm gun with a rifle grenade although already wounded in the head, ignoring a second wound to run forward with grenades and silence the supporting German machine-guns. Both Kelly and Ogden were awarded the Congressional Medal of Honor.

Underground in their tunnels and bunkers, thousands of German personnel lay crowded beneath the bombardment: naval ratings, Luftwaffe ground staff, supply units, clerks – all the rag-tag of a huge base wretchedly conscious of their isolation and disheartened by days amid the stink of their big generator motors, and the dust and cordite fumes filtering through the caverns. On a wall map in General von Schlieben's command post at St Sauveur, on the southern outskirts of the city, his operations officer, Major Forster, marked the remorseless progress of the American advance – Collins' men had unknowingly bypassed the German's switchboard bunker, leaving their communications intact. On 26 June, the unhappy von Schlieben surrendered with 800 of his men when tank destroyers began firing direct into the tunnel entrances above him. Major Randall Bryant was beside Manton Eddy, the divisional commander, when a tall, dignified German officer detached himself from the long file of surrendering defenders emerging from the arsenal and announced formally: "I am von Schlieben." The astonished Eddy showed the general to a jeep and took him away to his command post for lunch. Bradley, however, declined to entertain the German because of his anger that he had protracted Cherbourg's defence at such cost in American lives, and had finally refused to order a total surrender of the port after his capture.

Organized resistance in Cherbourg ended only on 27 June, and the 9th Division was obliged to fight hard for several days more to reduce the defences of Cap de la Hague, at the northwest tip of the peninsula. In the city, Eddy led a desperate attempt to control the men of his division as they ran riot among captured stocks of brandy, wine, champagne. At last he retired in despair, declaring, "Okay, everybody take twenty-four hours and get drunk."[3] Hundreds of cases of looted alcohol were loaded aboard captured German vehicles and followed units of VII Corps across Europe. Half a case of champagne was sent to Bradley, who touchingly sent it home to the U.S. to toast his grandson on his return in 1945. Randall Bryant's officers' club was still drinking its share of the proceeds of Cherbourg in Germany in 1946.

Bryant's battalion regretted its excesses on the morning of 28 June, when they began a long foot march towards Cap de La Hague, following the German formation signposts. They reached the entrance to a huge underground bunker without opposition, seized the single enemy sentry guarding it, and advanced warily inside, pistols in hands, towards the sound of voices. They found themselves in a room full of German officers clustered around a table laden with a large ham. Dean Vanderhouf, the battalion commander, rose to the occasion. "Stop!" he called to his astonished audience. He leaned forward to seize the ham: "I'll take that." The Americans were uncommonly lucky. Other units endured hard fights at Cap de la Hague.

In the month of June, VII Corps had captured 39,042 prisoners and achieved the first American objectives of the campaign. General Collins had proved himself an outstandingly energetic and skilful corps commander, just as General Maton Eddy had shown his capabilities at the head of the 9th Division. The reduction of a "fortress" that Hitler had ordered to resist for months gave sufficient exhilaration to the Allies to mask the disappointment of their commanders when they received the first reports from Cherbourg harbour. The port facilities of Naples had become operational just three days after the city fell, and some such new miracle had been looked for at Cherbourg. Instead, Bradley's engineers found the shambles created by one of the most comprehensive demolition programmes in the history of war. The OVERLORD logistics plan called for Cherbourg to discharge 150,000 tons of stores by 25 July. In reality, the port received less than 18,000 tons by that date. In was late September before it approached full operational capacity, by which time almost every harbour in France and Belgium was in the hands of the Allies. The drive for Cherbourg thus failed to achieve its immediate strategic purpose of accelerating and securing the Allied build-up. But of this, little needed to be said in the days of exultation following the most spectacular Allied ground gains since the landings. It was only Eisenhower, Bradley and Montgomery and their staffs who were conscious that the battle for the northern Cotentin had lasted many days longer than they had hoped or planned for and that, while it persisted, little progress was made with the drive to gain fighting room further south. On 27 June, when Everett Hughes brought Eisenhower news of a renewed delay to movement by First Army, the Supreme Commander reflected moodily: "Sometimes I wish I had George Patton over there."[4]

The men who fought the battle for the Cotentin afterwards remembered chiefly the fear and exhaustion of groping their way through the Norman hedgerows with their infantry company or tank platoon – "tiptoeing in a tank", one gunner called it – prickling with the sense of their own nakedness as they crossed each open space, cursing their inability to see the enemy mortaring or machine-gunning their advance, damning the air force, which was already revealing a disturbing inability to avoid strafing American positions. All wars become a matter of small private battles to those who are fighting them. But this was uniquely true of the struggle for Normandy, where it was seldom possible to see more than 100 or 200 yards in any direction, where forward infantry rarely glimpsed their own armour, artillery or higher commanders, where the appalling attrition rate among the rifle companies at the tip of each army's spear rapidly became one of the dominant factors of the campaign.

In this first battle in north-west Europe, the American army was given cause to regret the poor priority that it had given to infantry recruitment since the great mobilization of American manpower began in 1940. All nations in the Second World War diverted some of their fittest and best-educated recruits to the air forces and technical branches. But no other nation allowed the rifle companies of its armies to become a wastebin for men considered unsuitable for any other occupation. The infantry suffered in the services' attempts to allow men to follow specializations of their choice – of the 1942 volunteers, only 5 per cent chose infantry or armour. "By the end of 1943," confessed the official history of the training and procurement of U.S. army ground forces, "the operations of this priority and a number of other factors had reduced to a dangerously low level the number of men allotted to the ground forces who seemed likely to perform effectively in combat."[5] It was discovered that infantrymen were an inch shorter than the army's average height – a fair measure of general physique. Even more disturbing, statistics produced in March 1944 showed that while the infantry made up only 6 per cent of the army – an extraordinarily low proportion by any measure – they had suffered 53 per cent of its total battle casualties. This proportion rose to far more alarming heights in Normandy.

Great efforts began to be made in the spring of 1944 to push men of higher quality into the infantry. In March, 30,000 dismayed aviation cadets found themselves transferred wholesale to the army, almost all to ground forces. Some specialists were hastily diverted to the infantry, and the first of many comb-outs of service units took place, in search of suitable officers and men for infantry duty. But none of this came in time to assist the army that was to fight the first battles for north-west Europe. In Normandy, only 37 per cent of the replacements arriving to make good casualties were rifle-trained. First Army was suffering a desperate shortage of competent officers and NCOs. Wholesale sackings proved necessary in some units. In a situation in which junior leadership was critical, where again and again men were called up to fight beyond the control and eyes of their battalion or even company commanders, such leadership was repeatedly found wanting. The American army had determinedly eschewed the German policy of building elite and low-grade divisions to meet different requirements, and had sought instead to create a force of uniform quality. But in Normandy and after, Bradley's commanders found themselves principally dependent upon a handful of formations which proved exceptionally determined and competent – the 1st, 4th, 9th, 2nd Armored and the airborne divisions. Just as the first weeks of battle in Normandy caused the British to reach disturbing conclusions about their own tactics and about the determination of some of their principal formations, so the Americans found cause for serious concern in the performance of certain units. A First Army report on the tactical lessons of Normandy declared:

> It is essential that infantry in training be imbued with a bold, aggressive attitude. Many units do not acquire this attitude until long after their entry into combat, and some never acquire it. On the other hand units containing specially selected personnel such as Airborne and Rangers exhibited an aggressive spirit from the start. The average infantry soldier places too much reliance upon the supporting artillery to drive the enemy from positions opposing his advance. He has not been impressed sufficiently with his own potency and the effect of well-aimed, properly distributed rifle and machine-gun fire. The outstanding impression gained from a review of battle experiences is the importance of aggressive action and continuous energetic forward movement in order to gain ground and reduce casualties.[6]

Like the British, the Americans had discovered that their tank-infantry co-operation was woefully inadequate. They lacked the means for rapid communication on the battlefield between the men on the ground and those in the Shermans, battened down inside their steel hulls. They had no telephones mounted on their armour, which later enabled an infantryman to contact a tank commander without clambering up and hammering on his hatch, often under heavy fire. Officers were surprised to discover after an action how few rounds their riflemen had expended. Despite all their training in the importance of "marching fire" to suppress the defences, many infantrymen were instinctively reluctant to shoot when they could see no target, or were too concerned with hugging the earth for protection to reveal themselves and take an aim. Fieldcraft was likewise poor. A rifle company commander of the 9th Division reported: "The American soldier is too careless in unduly exposing himself when in view of the enemy. Individually he feels that some other 'Joe' will get shot and not he."[7] A report from General Mark Clark in Italy at this time stated: "The infantryman in landing operations, as in other operations, carries the heavy load, suffers the losses, and must have the guts to go forward despite danger and heavy casualties. Without question our training has not yet produced disciplined officers and disciplined men. Leaders up to and including battalion have a tendency to allow their troops to get out of control."[8]

There was interminable private debate in 1944, and there has been a great deal more in the years since, about the respective fighting power of the British and American soldier, and their shortcomings as revealed in Normandy. The truth seems self-evident – that the best British and American units were very good indeed, and perfectly comparable with each other. Each army was at times bemused by the different national approach to war of the other. Gavin wrote of the British: "In many ways they took the war far less seriously than we."[9] The British, in their turn, were sometimes scornful of the theatricality of the American style – of their generals' invariable habit of wearing helmets and personal weapons when no British commander troubled with either, of their enthusiasm for histrionics on the battlefield while the British sought always to understate the moment. But a British officer who saw much of the Americans said later that "if they were sometimes boastful, they would also go to extraordinary lengths to try to make good their boasts".[10] Gavin added to his comment on the British above: "On the other hand, on matters of discipline and combat effectiveness they set very high standards."[11]

It ill became either army in Normandy to seek to harp upon the shortcomings of the other – the British sluggishness in gaining Caen or the poor performance of some American divisions in the *bocage.* Despite the fine performance of Collins' VII Corps in gaining Cherbourg, each army at large had found it difficult to work up the driving power, the killing force, necessary to break through well-positioned German forces on the battlefield. The most important recent American historian of the campaign has written of Normandy: "There the limitations of the American army in generating sustained combat power were further to cripple the drive into the unknown, on battlefields sorely lacking in appropriate ground to apply mobility."[12]

6 The German army: stemming the tide

Soldiers

For every soldier of imagination in the German army, the battle for Normandy was the last struggle of the war which offered a frail chance of final victory. From all over Europe through the month of June, hundreds of thousands of men, thousands of tanks and vehicles, crawled painfully by the devastated rail network, and finally along roads lined with slit trenches to provide ready refuges from the inevitable fighter-bomber attacks, to bolster the precarious German line in Normandy. A 21st Army Group intelligence report of 22 June, based upon captured correspondence, found in Rommel's soldiers:

> . . . the same mixture of brash arrogance (chiefly SS), forlorn hope and outright despair that has appeared in similar collections in the past. The reprisal weapon is still the white hope and the German Air Force the main disappointment. The insistence that, despite his heavy equipment, "Tommy is no soldier" is still common.[1]

Corporal Wilhelm Schickner of the reconnaissance battalion of 2nd Panzer Division was a 25-year-old stonemason's son who had been an apprentice printer in Stuttgart when he was conscripted in March 1939 first for work service and then, a year later, for the infantry. Plunged immediately into the battle for France, like so many others he spent the next four years marching the length of Europe – with the German spearhead into Athens, to the gates of Moscow, where he was wounded in September 1942, back to Russia, to be wounded again in July 1943, and at last to join 2nd Panzer at Cambrai when he was once more fit for duty that December. On the night of 5 June, they were alerted in their positions around Amiens, and then stood down, only to be alerted again on 6 June. They moved at last on the afternoon of the 9th, reached Paris at nightfall, and drove through the empty and darkened streets to cross the Seine.

Thereafter, they leaguered all day in woodlands by the line of march, and drove only in darkness to reach Caumont around noon on 12 June. The reconnaissance battalion was immediately deployed to relieve the thin screen of defending troops covering the town. Schickner himself was ordered to take two machine-guns and one section to take over a position commanding the road 200 yards northwards. When his little party reached the spot, they found two men with a weary NCO, who said: "Thank God you're here – we're getting the hell out of it." There was no other German position to their right for some 600 yards, and little enough on their left. For half an hour, they lay patiently in the mist and waited. Then a jeep appeared in front of them, full of Americans. It stopped hesitantly, and retired abruptly when a 2nd Panzer gun crew behind them fired a 37 mm *Pak* round in its direction. Shermans appeared in the distance – Schickner counted 18 of them, and sent a runner back to report. The American tanks stopped, and began to fire HE towards the Germans. A lone GI rounded the corner of the road, helmet tilted back on his head. Behind him, Schickner could see long files of other enemy infantrymen. He sent his runner back again, and told Briese, the machine-gunner beside him, to link his belts for longer continuous fire. Then Jupp, the other gunner, called: "They're coming now," and the Americans moved confidently up the road towards them.

Schickner marvelled, because if the enemy had advanced through the fields on their flanks rather than along the road, "they could have walked into Caumont". Instead, "it was as if they were out for a Sunday stroll". Jupp asked: "Do I start now?" and settled over the butt of his MG 42. The hail of German fire scythed through the files of approaching men. It stopped, quite simply, when the two guns had fired all their available ammunition, and Schickner himself had emptied five magazines from his Schmeisser. In the silence that followed, the defenders could hear wounded Americans screaming for help from the roadside and the ditches. One of their own men, Gross, had been hit in the stomach. He could still walk, and they gave him cover while he stumbled back towards the houses. A young lieutenant appeared, who inspected the situation and declared: "You must launch a counter-attack." "What, with six men?" demanded Schickner. "Then what do you suggest?" asked the officer less confidently. "Stay put here," said the corporal. The officer disappeared, and for half an hour there was silence. The Germans lay on their weapons and smoked.

Darkness fell, and they could see the flash of firing all around them, but there was no movement on their own front. At last they received the order to pull back into the town, where they found the rest of the battalion, along with 75 mm guns of the *panzerjager* battalion, locked in a house-to-house struggle against American attacks already well inside Caumont. Their own company commander, Captain Schultz, ran from position to position telling his men, "We've got to hold the town – it's a Führer-order." After a huge effort, supported by the 50 mm guns of their big Puma half-tracks, they captured some of the lost ground in a counter-attack in the early hours of the morning. But a few hours later, American armour began pressing them relentlessly. The Germans pulled back down the hill south of the town, having suffered appalling casualties. Schickner said: "We were never told to push forward again."[2] The American official history recorded: "The 26th Infantry at the same time got one battalion to the edge of Caumont but there ran into determined resistance from an estimated two companies of Germans, giving the Americans the impression at some points that counter-attacks were in progress. Actions, however, though sometimes sharp were all local and involved few troops. The town was not cleared until the following morning."[3]

For the German soldier in the first weeks of the Normandy battle, actions such as that of 2nd Panzer's *aufklarungsabteilung* at Caumont were commonplace: a rush to the threatened sector; a fierce and expert defence against clumsy Allied tactics; growing casualties as the enemy's massed firepower was brought to bear; and at last, a retreat of a few hundred yards to the next line to be equally doggedly held with fewer men, less weapons, a slowly dwindling supply of hope. "Let's enjoy the war," ran a Wehrmacht catchphrase of the period, "because the peace will be terrible."[4]

On 6 June, the Allies had inflicted a crushing tactical surprise upon the Germans. In the weeks that followed, they maintained the greatest of all strategic deceptions by the FORTITUDE operation, which imprisoned almost the entire Fifteenth Army in the Pas de Calais until late July. Rommel's efforts were dedicated to stemming the Allied tide, throwing into the line every new unit as it reached the battlefront. Above all, he was compelled to employ his armoured forces as links of steel in the sagging chain around the perimeter, and was thus unable to concentrate them in the rear for a major counter-attack. The armoured divisions reached Normandy first, because they possessed far greater mobility than the infantry, many of whom travelled the last 50 or 100 miles to the front on foot. Tanks made immensely effective strongpoints, but were almost invariably lost wherever the Allies gained ground. They could not be replaced. If the Allies were restricted in Normandy by their perceived shortage of infantry, the Germans were much more desperately frustrated by theirs. A report by 2nd Panzer in July discussed at length the tactics the division had found it necessary to employ in holding their sector of the line against the British. It concluded bleakly: "The fact that a modern panzer division with 2 tank battalions and 2 infantry battalions with armoured half-tracks is not necessary for such fighting is another matter . . ."[5] As Bradley accurately observed, "When the tank is employed in lieu of infantry simply to hold a defensive position, it becomes a wasted and uneconomic weapon."[6]

If it is arguable that the British wasted precious time in the first days following the invasion, the Germans did no better. Rommel reached his château headquarters after his dash across France at 10.00 p.m. on 6 June, to spend most of the night trying to get a grip on his command, to learn precisely what was happening across the battle area in spite of a tangle of jammed wireless wavelengths and severed telephone links. His order for an immediate counter-attack on the 7th by 21st Panzer and 12th SS Panzer came to nothing, for Sepp Dietrich's I SS Panzer Corps were quite unable to concentrate the tanks in time. Rommel issued a prompt and formal protest to Hitler's headquarters about the lack of air and naval support for his battle, and warned Jodl that he was still convinced that the main Allied effort was to come elsewhere. It is interesting that Jodl, often a shrewd judge of strategic situation, never shared this view. But at this stage, both Berlin and Rommel were full of optimism about the prospects of throwing the Allies into the sea. Rommel's adjutant Hellmuth Lang wrote home: "There's a marvellous tranquillity shown by all concerned, particularly our chief of staff Speidel."[7] The field-marshal himself began to fight his battle with the same remorseless, restless energy that he had displayed in Africa, spending each day in headlong drives from formation to formation, inquiring, urging, demanding, galvanizing, and only returning to his headquarters at night to plan and to issue orders. It was a divisional, at most a corps commander's, style of direction.

On the afternoon of 8 June, when Rommel arrived at Panzer Group West's headquarters to find 21st Panzer and 12th SS Panzer's counter-attack against the British in serious trouble, he at once ordered Geyr von Schweppenburg to divert a powerful battle-group north-west to try to recapture Bayeux, a thrust which was broken up by massive artillery and naval gunfire. At von Rundstedt's headquarters in Paris, there was deep dismay that all the available German armour was now committed to piecemeal action, and not embarked upon a concentrated thrust. These complaints reflected sound tactical theory but ignored the desperate practical need on the battlefield to halt the enemy wherever he was pushing forward. That night, Colonel Bodo Zimmerman of Rundstedt's staff telephoned Speidel: "Rommel has got to decide whether he's going to get a big success tonight with the forces he already has. Rundstedt does not think he will, he thinks we're going to have to strip other fronts ruthlessly to provide further strength."[8] Jodl also telephoned, reasserting his conviction that the landings were indeed the sole Allied effort. "There's not going to be any second invasion."[9] Rommel dissented, declared that he was concentrating all his efforts upon preventing the link-up of the British and American beachheads, and declined to demand any weakening of Fifteenth Army in the Pas De Calais.

In the days that followed, some of his most serious losses were among corps and divisional commanders. On 12 June, the formidable old General Marcks of LXXXIV Corps set out to drive for the Carentan front when he heard that the town had fallen, and died in a strafing attack when his wooden leg prevented him from leaping from his car quickly enough to take cover. Fritz Witt of 12th SS Panzer died the same day, to be replaced by Kurt Meyer. The commander of the 243rd Infantry was killed on the 17th, that of the 77th mortally wounded on the 18th.

As Rommel strove to gain a grip of the battle, he could draw some satisfaction from the effectiveness with which the Allied thrusts southwards were being checked and even thrown back. But strategically, this was not enough. If he was frustrating the hopes of Montgomery, his own forces were nowhere within sight of the vital breakthrough to the sea. Even the fanatics of 12th SS Panzer expressed their belief that the Allied line could not be broken after their own attempts to smash through the Canadians had failed on 7 and 8 June. On 11 June, Sepp Dietrich of I SS Panzer Corps asserted that the line could be held for only three weeks. On the 14th, he told Rommel: "I am being bled and getting nowhere." Told that he must attack, he demanded: "With what? We need another eight or ten divisions in a day or two, or we are finished."[10] Wehrmacht staff officers were astonished to see Dietrich, the hoary veteran Nazi whose relationship with Hitler had alone thrust him into high command, openly derisive about their hopes of victory. "He was no soldier, but he was a realist," said one.[11]

Rommel found every counter-attack that he contemplated rendered impossible by local tactical difficulties, fuel shortages or enemy fighter-bomber attacks. Each effort to move troops west to meet the threat to Cherbourg was prevented by more urgent needs closer at hand. A sense of desperation began to overcome him. "The invasion is quite likely to start at other places too, soon," he wrote to his wife. "There's simply no answer to it. I reported to the Führer yesterday. Rundstedt is doing the same. It's time for politics to come into play. It will all be over very quickly."[12] Rommel determined on 13 June that any attempt to reinforce the divisions fighting in the Cotentin would fatally weaken the critical front opposite the British Second Army. Despite furious orders from the Berghof to defend every yard of the road to Cherbourg, he successfully extricated useful elements of the 77th Division before the Americans sealed the peninsula. "It appears dubious whether the gravity of the situation is realized up above," he wrote to Frau Rommel on 14 June, "and whether the proper conclusions are being drawn."[13]

Hitler's visit to Soissons on the 17th enabled him to work his customary magnetic spell upon his field-marshal, momentarily arresting the relentless workings of reason. Rommel "cannot escape the Führer's influence," wrote Hellmuth Lang.[14] The Commander-in-Chief of Army Group B allowed himself to be encouraged by news of the V-I offensive on England, and lifted by the promise of yet more dramatic new weapons to follow. He saw the German front stiffening and holding around Caen and Caumont, the panzer formations inflicting heavy casualties upon the Allies and parrying their attacks. Defeat was still some way off. But Rommel scornfully rejected demands from Berlin for counter-attacks in the Contentin, pointing out that he scarcely possessed the forces to hold a line. The fall of Cherbourg made little impact upon him, for he and von Rundstedt had privately written off the port from the moment Carentan was lost. He was dismayed only by the absurd orders continuing to stream forth from Hitler's headquarters, demanding that Cherbourg should be held "to the last round". The principal achievement of Operation EPSOM on the 26th was to forestall a planned counter-attack by 9th and 10th SS Panzer Divisions, newly arrived from the east, and to inflict serious losses upon them when they were belatedly thrown into the battle.

On the 28th, at the height of the struggle around the Odon, Rommel once again saw Hitler in Berlin, at the Führer's behest. Hitler's intention, plainly, was to strengthen the resolve of his commander. He was enraged when Rommel persistently attempted to bring home to him the terrible reality of the situation in Normandy. At last, Rommel said: "*Mein Führer*, I must speak bluntly. I cannot leave here without speaking on the subject of Germany." Hitler said abruptly: "Field-Marshal, be so good as to leave the room. I think it would be better like that."[15] It was their last meeting. Yet once again, the encounter had served to harden Rommel's faltering determination. He returned to Normandy to find that Geyr von Schweppenburg had persuaded Speidel of the vital importance of withdrawing from the Caen bridgehead, out of range of the Allied naval guns. In the early hours of 1 July, Rommel ordered Geyr to continue to hold his ground instead. Yet von Rundstedt had already received Geyr's report, arguing the need to pull back, and had forwarded it to Berlin with his own endorsement. Von Rundstedt had never troubled to conceal his own despair: "If you doubt what we are doing, get up here and take over this shambles yourself," he told Keitel witheringly when the OKW Chief of Staff sought to challenge his judgement by telephone from Germany.[16] Before midnight on 1 July, Hitler's order for Geyr's dismissal had reached the front. He was succeeded in command of Panzer Group West by General Hans Eberbach. Rundstedt himself resigned his command the following morning, after a peremptory hint from Berlin that his health was plainly no longer adequate to his task.

Von Rundstedt was succeeded by Field-Marshal von Kluge, a leathery Prussian veteran of the eastern front, who immediately sought to assert his own authority over Rommel and to re-establish his command's confidence in their own ability to defend

Normandy. Yet by the evening of 12 July, von Kluge was telephoning Jodl in Berlin. "I want to stress once again," he said, "that I am no pessimist. But in my view, the situation could not be grimmer."[17] Even after the removal of every open sceptic, the utmost exercise of the Führer's personal magic and force, and the commitment to battle of some of the most powerful elements of the German army, there was now no senior officer in the entire German high command in France who believed that the battle for Normandy could be won. "The tragedy of our position is this," Rommel told Admiral Ruge on 13 July: "We are obliged to fight on to the very end, but all the time we're convinced that it's far more vital to stop the Russians than the Anglo-Americans from breaking into Germany."[18] He judged, with remarkable accuracy, that the German front in Normandy must collapse within a month. At that point, the relentless attrition of men and weapons would have become intolerable. Since D-Day, he had lost 2,360 officers and over 94,000 men, while receiving only 6,000 replacements. He had lost 225 tanks and received 17, in addition to the new formations arriving at the front. The ammunition position remained critical. Yet every Allied tank and aircraft lost was replaced within a few hours. "Everywhere our troops are fighting heroically," he reported to von Kluge on 15 July, "but the unequal struggle is drawing to its close."[19]

It was at about this date that, for the first time, Rommel began to put out feelers to his commanders – notably Eberbach and Sepp Dietrich – about the possibility of their support should it prove feasible to open some form of negotiations with the Allies. Hellmuth Lang was witness to one conversation at which Dietrich – Hitler's old chauffeur and devoted follower in the Munich days of Nazism – shook Rommel's hand and declared: "You're the boss, *Herr Feldmarschall*. I obey only you – whatever it is you're planning."[20] Then Rommel and his aide climbed back into the big Horch staff car, a corporal in the back acting as the inevitable "looky-looky" for Allied aircraft, and raced away towards his headquarters. On the N179 short of Vimoutiers, at around 6.00 p.m., a British Typhoon caught them, wounding Rommel's driver and sending the car careering into a tree, throwing its passengers into the road. Rommel, terribly injured in the head, had ended his career as a battlefield commander, and would be forced to suicide three months later on the evidence of the 20 July conspirators. The field-marshal had never been party to their plans, but the evidence that they had considered him a suitable figurehead to lead negotiations with the Allies was sufficient to ensure his death sentence. Von Kluge succeeded him, remaining Commander-in-Chief West while also assuming command of Army Group B. He merely moved his own desk from Paris to Rommel's headquarters at La Roche Guyon.

Throughout his tenure of command in Normandy, Rommel directed the defence of the German front to formidable effect, filling the critical gaps and rushing forward units to stem dangerous Allied attacks. But there was no evidence in his handling of the battle of a great commander making brilliant strokes to confound the enemy. "In Normandy, there was no particular sign of Rommel's presence," said Montgomery's intelligence officer Brigadier Williams,[21] who had also watched the German general through the desert campaign. In the summer of 1944, Rommel played the part of the firefighter with all the energy at his command. It is difficult to see how any other commander could have achieved more, given the limitations of his resources and orders. His absence from Normandy on D-Day was unfortunate, but it is hard to believe that it was decisive. 21st Panzer might have intervened earlier had Rommel been present, but unsupported it could not have threatened the survival of Second Army's beachhead. At no stage in the battle did the division show anything like the determination in action of Panzer Lehr or 12th SS Panzer. It remains just possible that Rommel's personal influence would have sufficed to get Meyer and his tanks onto the battlefield on the afternoon of 6 June, in which case the British and Canadians would have been in serious trouble. But the balance of probability remains that Second Army could have established itself ashore against any available German defence. By mid-afternoon of D-Day, the excellent British anti-tank guns were already inland and deployed in strength. Just as the Allied commanders on D-Day were at the mercy of their subordinates' efficiency in executing their plan, so the German Seventh Army could achieve no more than the quality of its forces on the ground and the strength of the Atlantic Wall allowed. With or without Rommel, it lacked the mobility to concentrate for quick counter-attacks. Only the panzer divisions could execute these, and they could arrive no faster than their road speed and the Allied air forces would permit. "You know that it was my phrase

– 'The Longest Day'?" said Rommel's adjutant Hellmuth Lang. "After that day, after June 6, there was no hope of counter-attacks being decisive."[22]

Once the Allies were firmly established ashore, the only sane strategic course open to the Germans was precisely that which Hitler's madness would not allow – a progressive, carefully ordered retirement forcing the Allies to fight hard for every gain. The Germans would have been relieved of one immense handicap if they could have fought beyond the range of Allied naval gunfire. Southern France could have been abandoned, releasing the forces of Army Group G to support the decisive battle in Normandy. Some writers have sought to suggest that if the Allied FORTITUDE deception plan had been less successful, and if powerful elements of Fifteenth Army had been freed early in the campaign to fight for Normandy, the Germans might even have emerged victorious.[23] It is impossible to accept this. With stronger forces the battles would have been much harder, and Allied losses and delays even more severe. But while much has been said above about the shortcomings of British and American forces in attack, there was no doubt of their fighting prowess in defence. Then, all the terrain factors working for the Germans would operate for Montgomery's divisions, and the British army especially would fight in circumstances in which it always excelled. Overwhelming Allied air and firepower would have disposed of even the strongest German counter-attack in Normandy long before it reached the sea, although a thrust in bad weather, of the kind that crippled Allied air support in the Ardennes, could have caused the Allied high command serious concern.

Much speculation has been lavished upon the extent to which the activities of the anti-Hitler plotters, most notably Rommel's Chief of Staff, General Hans Speidel, contributed to the difficulties of the German defence. It is suggested that certain key divisions, including 116th Panzer, were kept back from the battle in the Pas de Calais to support the conspiracy. This debate was clouded by the self-serving post-war testimony of Speidel and others when they were seeking to establish their credentials as anti-Nazis. There can be no doubt of Rommel's sincerity in expecting a second Allied invasion. He devoted precious days to visiting formations of Fifteenth Army, checking their state of readiness, adjusting their deployments. 116th Panzer was edged nearer the coast in two separate moves following visits by

Rommel, which bewildered officers of the unit who expected to be ordered to Normandy, but seem most unlikely to have been related to the machinations of the 20 July plotters. Much more serious than any tampering of this kind was the vacuum in German intelligence. The second most important factor in the German defeat in Normandy, after inferiority of resources, was the blindness of the high command. Almost totally devoid of air reconnaissance, with every agent in Britain under British control, lacking any breakthrough in Allied codes and aided only by the fruits of low-grade wireless interception and prisoner interrogation on the battlefield, Rommel, von Rundstedt and von Kluge knew pathetically little of their enemies' potential strength or plans. Ignorance, plain ignorance, contributed much more to their failure than any possible acts of deliberate deceit by conspirators among the intelligence staffs. A critical contributory factor to this, as to so much else, was the dead hand of Hitler. More than any other aspect of military operations, intelligence must be conducted in an atmosphere unhampered by preconceptions. Yet Hitler's generals, above all in the latter half of the war, were never permitted to assess their predicament freely, and to act in accordance with their findings. Every act of military planning was conducted within the straitjacket of Hitler's manic instructions, which consistently ran counter to reality and logic. In such a climate, in absolute contrast to that surrounding the brilliantly conducted intelligence operations of the Allies, it becomes far less surprising that Rommel and so many of his colleagues were deluded by the fantasy of FUSAG's threat to the Pas de Calais. Their confidence, their flair and imagination, their belief in themselves, were sapped and corroded by years of serving a lunatic who lacked the military ability which served the other great dictator, Stalin, so well. The German generals were conducting a campaign in which, after the first days, they had no faith, by methods wholly inimical to all their instincts and training. It is difficult to believe that anything they might have done, in these circumstances, would significantly have altered the course of events.

The glory of German arms in Normandy – and it was glory, in however evil a cause – was won by the officers and men at divisional level and below who held the line against the Allies under intolerable conditions for more than two months. Colonel Kurt Kauffmann, operations officer of Panzer Lehr, believed that in the first few days a really determined thrust against the Americans could have driven them into the sea. Thereafter, "I realized that the situation was hopeless, with more than 40 per cent of our infantry gone and the tremendous Allied shelling and air activity."[24] Yet it was Kauffman who led the dramatically successful counter-attack into Villers-Bocage on 13 June, and Panzer Lehr which remained one of the formations most respected by their Allied opponents even after it had suffered crippling losses. "Should we win this war, Kruger," the senior signals officer of 12th SS Panzer Division remarked acidly to one of his lieutenants, "I shall write a book about why we should have lost it."[25] Yet no division fought with more fanatical tenacity than the Hitler Jugend, whose soldiers had an average age of 18½. "It was a situation for despair, but there was no alternative but to keep one's nerve," said Colonel Heinz-Gunther Guderian, son of the great panzer leader and senior staff officer of 116th Panzer Division. "One had to hold before one's eyes the memory of Frederick the Great, and perhaps also to think of the words of the American general who said that the man who wins a battle is he who can remain standing until the last five minutes."[26] Brigadier Williams said: "The Germans adjusted much better to new conditions than we did. By and large they were better soldiers than we were. The Germans *liked* soldiering. We didn't."[27] General Quesada of the American IXth Air Force found afterwards that, "One's imagination boggled at what the German army might have done to us without Hitler working so effectively for our side."[28]

Fritz Langangke's Panzer V *abteilung* of 2nd SS Panzer Division was posted at St Sauveur-Lendelin in corps reserve early in July, when it was suddenly ordered forward in a crisis move to meet a new American breakthrough. He himself was directed to take his platoon to a point on the road near St Denis, and block any enemy advance along it. He asked for the position of the HKL – the main battle line – and was told that this was unknown. Late in the evening, he led his five Panthers cautiously forward, each commander straining his eyes and ears above the roar of his engine and squealing of the track for a hint of the enemy. At last there was a rattle of small-arms fire against the hull of Langangke's tank, and he concluded that he had come far enough. The platoon pulled back to deploy on each side of the road, hull down behind a hedge. "It was a pretty tight night," said the

German. The crews sat absolutely silent in their tanks, whispering when it was necessary to report by radio, listening constantly for movement in front of them. At dawn, despite their careful camouflage, one of the ubiquitous American Piper Cubs pinpointed them, and artillery fire began to fall around the position. Towards noon, men of the division's 3rd Der Führer Panzergrenadiers belatedly arrived and began to dig in around them, while the 6th Parachute Regiment deployed on their left. Conventional wisdom demanded that the tanks should fall back at nightfall and leave the infantry to hold the positions. But Langangke understood that there could be no such refinements here, where the tanks were being employed as strongpoints, and their moral support was essential to the infantry, even of an SS division.

The tank platoon held its positions for two weeks, under constant artillery fire, protected by its very proximity to the Americans, which caused the enemy gunners to fire consistently beyond the German line. At night, when the crews risked crawling out of the vehicles for an hour or two of merciful release, they could hear the American convoys moving up with supplies, and hear American voices across the still summer air. Once, the enemy attempted an infantry attack in a fashion which astonished the German veterans. They marched forward in long, leisurely files towards the Panthers' "as if they were going to a carnival". The SS opened a withering fire, and the attack crumpled.

Langangke remembered the next attack well, for it came on his birthday, 15 July. For a time amid the shooting, he himself could see nothing from his position closed down in his tank on the left hand side of the road. At first, he could not understand why the Americans were not attacking in his sector, but he later found that the ground in front was too soft for armour. Then one of his commanders jumped on the hull and shouted: "We've had it – hit in the turret!" Langangke ordered him to pull back, and ran across the road to see for himself. Five Shermans were approaching. He dashed back to his own tank, and told the crew: "We've got to get across that road." They felt that there was only the slimmest chance of survival once they moved from their closely camouflaged position into the open. But they had to try. At full speed, the tank roared from cover and crashed across the road in front of the Americans – "the longest forty metres I travelled in the war," said Langangke. Then the driver was braking the left track to swing to face the enemy. Still undamaged despite some shellfire, they began to engage the Shermans at point-blank range. They glimpsed dead and wounded German infantry around them, and survivors running from their foxholes to shelter in the lee of the Panther. It was obvious that the foot soldiers were close to panic. The crew urged Langangke to fire on the move, but he knew that if they did so, there was little chance of a hit. Most of the Shermans had fired one or even two rounds before the Panther began to shoot, but it was the German tank which now demonstrated its legendary killing power. A few moments later, four Shermans were burning in front of them. The fifth roared backwards into the thick brush. "A thing like that puts you on an unbelievable emotional level," said Langangke. "You feel like Siegfried, that you can dare to do *anything*."

The lieutenant jumped down from his tank, to be joined by one of his other commanders, and they ran forward up the ditch by the roadside to discover what the Americans were now doing. It was common practice among tank officers of all the armies in Normandy to resort frequently to their feet, for it was too hazardous to take a tank forward among the hedges without the kind of forewarning that only ground reconnaissance could provide. The Germans found the surviving Sherman still struggling to reverse over a hedge; engine revving, it staggered backwards and forwards on the rim of the obstacle. They retired to their tanks, Langangke cursing when he tripped over an abandoned infantry *Panzerfaust* that he could have use to good effect had he noticed it on the way forward. Back in the Panther, they fired a few rounds of HE and a long burst of machine-gun fire to clear the foliage obscuring the gunner's view of the Sherman. Then they hit it once in the turret with an armour-piercing shell. The American tank brewed up in the inevitable pillar of oily, black smoke and flame. The surviving German infantry regrouped. The Americans continued shelling the area, but launched no further major attack. Langangke's platoon had fought one among a thousand similar actions in those weeks in Normandy, demonstrating the remarkable tenacity and skill of the panzer crews and, above all, the superiority of their tanks.

Yet it would be absurd to give the impression that the German soldier found Normandy an easy, or even a tolerable battle. While many men said later that it was a less terrible experience than the war in the east, from which most of them had come, even veterans were deeply shaken by the experience of hurling themselves again and again into action against the great steam-roller of Allied resources. 2nd Panzer Division reported in July on the difficulties they faced:

The incredibly heavy artillery and mortar fire of the enemy is something new for seasoned veterans as much as for the new arrivals from reinforcement units. The assembly of troops is spotted immediately by enemy reconnaissance aircraft and smashed by bombs and artillery directed from the air; and if, nevertheless, the attacking troops go forward, they become involved in such dense artillery and mortar fire that heavy casualties ensue and the attack peters out within the first few hundred metres. The losses suffered by the infantry are then so heavy that the impetus necessary to renew the attack is spent.

Our soldiers enter the battle in low spirits at the thought of the enemy's enormous superiority of *matériel*. The feeling of helplessness against enemy aircraft operating without hindrance has a paralysing effect; and during the barrage the effect on the inexperienced men is literally soul-shattering. The best results have been obtained by platoon and section commanders leaping forward uttering a good old-fashioned yell. We have also revived the practice of bugle calls.[29]

Hitler's armies had always adopted the policy of fashioning some elite divisions to provide the smashing combat power at the tip of their spear, while others – including most of the infantry formations – were equipped and manned principally to hold defensive positions between major battles. The 276th Infantry Division was a typical, moderate line formation, stationed at Bayonne on 6 June, made up to strength by combing Germany for over-age men – including many miners, who had hitherto been excused military service. Corporal Adolf Hohenstein had spent much of the war building bridges with a labour unit in Russia until he was transferred to the 276th. A 22-year-old former student mining engineer, he was much younger than most of the men around him. He found the division, "already pretty weak. We spent too much time doing old Prussian exercises rather than field training." On 16 June, they entrained for Le Mans, where they offloaded in pouring rain on the 19th. Thereafter, they marched by night to the front, advancing some 20 miles at a time, passing the days feeding the horses – upon whom they were overwhelmingly dependent for transport – among the cornfields where they halted. They loved their horses, and later were deeply depressed by the terrible casualties the animals suffered.

On 2 July, they took over a sector of the front near Villers-

Bocage from 12th SS Panzer, and spent their first days in the line laying mines and attempting to clear up the appalling wreckage of battle around them – dead men of every nationality, abandoned equipment, shattered vehicles. Harassing fire from British artillery taught them very quickly about the Wehrmacht's desperate shortage of medical supplies. Hohenstein watched his friend Heinz Alles bleed to death when an artery was severed by a bullet in the leg: "A man was lucky if he could get an injection. The doctors could only try to do something for those with a chance of life." Some men's nerve cracked very quickly. After 20 July, they convinced themselves that the shortages of supplies and ammunition and the breakdowns of administration were the fruits of treachery within their own army. In reality, of course, the entire creaking logistical machinery sustaining the German forces in Normandy was collapsing under the strain of air attack and attrition. Morale among the soldiers of the 276th ebbed steadily: "The lack of any success at all affected the men very badly. You could feel the sheer fear growing. We would throw ourselves to the ground at the slightest sound, and many men were saying that we should never leave Normandy alive."

It is important to cite the example of formations such as the 276th Infantry, indifferent soldiers, to emphasize that by no means the entire German front in France was in the hands of elite formations. Many German infantrymen were happy to seize an opportunity to be taken prisoner. They developed what they themselves called sardonically "the German look", ever craning upwards into the sky, watchful for fighter-bombers. While the Tommies played brag in their slit trenches, the Germans played "skat" in their foxholes a few hundred yards away, and listened to Lili Marlene on Radio Belgrade. They were as grateful as their Allied counterparts when, for a few days or even weeks, their sector of the front was quiet, and they endured nothing worse than harassing fire and patrols. They prayed for rain and cloud to keep the *jabos* – the *jagd-bombers* – away from them. Their greatest luxury was the capture of a few American soup cubes or tins of coffee. They pored earnestly over the English cooking instructions, and were jealously scornful of the Allies' material riches. Few German soldiers, even of moderate units, felt great respect for the fighting qualities of their enemies. Sergeant Heinz Hickmann of the Luftwaffe Parachute Division said: "We had no respect whatever for the American soldier." Colonel Kauffmann of Panzer Lehr remarked wryly that, "the

Americans started not too early in the morning, they liked a little bit too much comfort." Corporal Hohenstein reported that his men were constantly puzzled by the reluctance of the Americans to exploit their successes: "We felt that they always over-estimated us. We could not understand why they did not break through. The Allied soldier never seemed to be trained as we were, always to try to do more than had been asked of us." Here was one of the keys to German tactical success on the battlefield. Colonel Brian Wyldbore-Smith, GSO I of the British 11th Armoured Division, said: "The Germans were great opportunists. They were prepared to act – always."

It is striking to contrast the manner in which Allied units which suffered 40 or 50 per cent losses expected to be pulled out of the line, even disbanded, with their German counterparts, who were merely reassembled into improvised battlegroups – the *Kampfgruppen* – which were an essential ingredient of so many of the German army's victories, and of its very survival for so many weeks in Normandy. Cooks, signallers, isolated tank platoons, stray Luftwaffe flak units, were all grist to the mill of the *kampfgruppen*, which proved astonishingly cohesive and effective in action. When Sergeant Hans Stober of 17th SS Panzergrenadiers found the *flakabteilung* in which he served destroyed by air attack, he saw nothing remarkable in being transferred, with his surviving men, to *Kampfgruppe Ullrich*. A few weeks later, after the collapse at Falaise, he was serving with the remnants of 116th Panzer in *Kampfgruppe Fick*. In the middle of the Normandy battle, 116th Panzer's engineer battalion was drafted to fight as infantry and called upon to mount major ground attacks. The U.S. First Army were surprised to discover that one of their German prisoners in mid-July was a pay corps clerk, who had been given a week's infantry training and thrust into the line. No one could suggest that this manner of organizing an army or fighting a battle was a proper substitute for the maintenance of balanced and fully-equipped formations. But it was a critical factor in the German army's ability to avoid utter collapse even when most of its armoured and infantry formations had been battered into ruin.

The American Colonel Trevor Dupuy has conducted a detailed statistical study of German actions in the Second World War. Some of his explanations as to why Hitler's armies performed so much more impressively than their enemies seem fanciful. But no critic has challenged his essential finding that on almost every battlefield of the war, including Normandy, the German soldier performed more impressively than his opponents:

On a man for man basis, the German ground soldier consistently inflicted casualties at about a 50% higher rate than they incurred from the opposing British and American troops UNDER ALL CIRCUMSTANCES. [emphasis in original] This was true when they were attacking and when they were defending, when they had a local numerical superiority and when, as was usually the case, they were outnumbered, when they had air superiority and when they did not, when they won and when they lost.[30]

It is undoubtedly true that the Germans were much more efficient than the Americans in making use of available manpower. An American army corps staff contained 55 per cent more officers and 44 per cent fewer other ranks than its German equivalent. In a panzergrenadier division in 1944–45, 89.4 per cent of the men were fighting soldiers, against only 65.56 per cent in an American division. In June 1944, 54.35 per cent of the German army consisted of fighting soldiers, against 38 per cent of the American army. 44.9 per cent of the German army was employed in combat divisions, against 20.8 per cent of the American. While the U.S. army became a huge industrial organization, whose purpose sometimes seemed to be forgotten by those who administered it, the German army was designed solely as a machine for waging war. Even the British, who possessed nothing like the reserves of manpower of the Americans, traditionally employed officers on a far more lavish scale than the German army, which laid particular emphasis upon NCO leadership.

Events on the Normandy battlefield demonstrated that most British or American troops continued a given operation for as long as reasonable men could. Then – when they had fought for many hours, suffered many casualties, or were running low on fuel or ammunition – they disengaged. The story of German operations, however, is landmarked with repeated examples of what could be achieved by soldiers prepared to attempt more than reasonable men could. German troops did not fight uniformly well. But Corporal Hohenstein's assertion that they were trained always to try to do more than had been asked of them is borne out by history. Again and again, a single tank, a handful of infantry with an 88 mm gun, a hastily-mounted counter-attack, stopped a thoroughly-organized Allied advance dead in its tracks. German leadership at corps level and above was often little better than that of the Allies, and sometimes markedly worse. But at regimental level and below, it was superb. The German army appeared to have access to a bottomless reservoir of brave, able and quick-thinking colonels commanding battle-groups, and of NCOs capable of directing the defence of an entire sector of the front. The fanatical performance of the SS may partly explain the stubborn German defence of Europe in 1944–45. But it cannot wholly do so, any more than the quality of the Allied armies can be measured by the achievements of their airborne forces. The defence of Normandy was sustained for 10 weeks in the face of overwhelming odds by the professionalism and stubborn skills of the entire Wehrmacht, from General of Pioneers Meise, who somehow kept just sufficient road and rail links operational to maintain a thin stream of supplies to the front, to Corporal Hohenstein and his admittedly half-hearted comrades of 276th Infantry.

The German soldier was denied the sustaining force granted to the Allied armies – the certainty of final victory. But Hohenstein claimed that he and others were motivated above all by, "two words – 'unconditional surrender'. If for the rest of my life I was to chop wood in Canada or Siberia, then I would sooner die in Normandy." There is no doubt that President Roosevelt's insistence upon a public declaration of the unconditional surrender doctrine, despite Churchill's deep misgivings, was of immense value to the Nazi propaganda machine: it stifled many Germans' private hopes of some honourable escape from the war. They believed that defeat in Normandy, and beyond that defeat in Europe, would inaugurate a new dark age for Germany, a ghastly destiny for the German people. Their very sense of community with their American and British opponents, coupled with their view of the Russians as barbarians from another planet, compounded their self-delusions. To the bitter end, many German soldiers harboured a sincere belief that they could make common cause with the western Allies against the Russians. To this end, they told themselves that it was essential to sustain a front until some agreement could be achieved.

There is also little doubt of the validity of the traditional view of the German soldier as naturally obedient and dedicated, far more so than most men of the Allied armies. He was a soldier, and therefore he fought. The British had come to terms with this reality over many years, but Americans were still astonished to discover the strength of this apparently unreasoning approach.

Several times during the European campaign. [wrote Bradley] I wondered why German commanders in the field did not give up their senseless resistance. Prolonged resistance could do nothing but aggravate the disaster that had already claimed the Reich. George Patton offered an answer when he visited Army Group early in August just as we tightened our noose around the German Seventh Army. "The Germans are either crazy or they don't know what's going on," I said, "surely the professionals must know by now that the jig is up." George answered by telling the story of a German general that Third Army had captured several days before. He had been asked by G-2 why he had not surrendered before, if only to spare Germany further destruction. "I am a professional," he replied without emotion, "and I obey my orders."[31]

Most of the German army in Normandy followed his example.

Weapons

If the German army was a superb fighting instrument, a decisive factor in its ability to defend Normandy for so long, and to such effect, was the superiority of almost all its weapons in quality, if not in quantity, to those of the Allied ground forces. In the air and at sea, the Allies achieved a large measure of technological as well as numerical dominance in the second half of the Second World War. Yet the industrial resources of Britain and America were never applied to provide their armies with weapons of the same quality as those produced by German industry in the face of the Allies' strategic bombing offensive. In 1942, Albert Speer and his staff took the decision, since they could not hope to match the quantitative superiority of the Allies, to attempt to defeat them by the qualitative superiority of German equipment. Feats on the battlefield, such as Captain Wittman's ravaging of the British armoured column at Villers-Bocage, were only made possible by the extraordinary power of a Tiger tank in among even a regiment of British Cromwells. During the first weeks in Normandy, Allied tank units were dismayed to discover the ease with which their Shermans "brewed up" after a single hit, while their own shells were unable to penetrate a Panther, far less a Tiger tank, unless they struck a vital spot at close range. On 24 June, Montgomery's Chief of Staff, de Guingand, wrote to him:

"If we are not careful, there will be a danger of the troops developing a Tiger and Panther complex . . . P. J. Grigg rang me up last night and said he thought there might be trouble in the Guards Armoured Division as regards 'the inadequacy of our tanks compared with the Germans' . . . Naturally the reports are not being circulated."[1] Montgomery himself quashed a succession of complaints and open expressions of concern.

"I have had to stamp very heavily on reports that began to be circulated about the inadequate quality of our tanks, equipment, etc., as compared with the Germans . . ." he wrote to Brooke. "In cases where adverse comment is made on British equipment such reports are likely to cause a lowering of morale and a lack of confidence among the troops. It will generally be found that when the equipment at our disposal is used properly and the tactics are good, we have no difficulty in defeating the Germans."[2]

Montgomery knew that it was futile, indeed highly dangerous, to allow the shortcomings of Allied weapons to be voiced openly in his armies, for there was no hope of quickly changing them. The battle must be won or lost with the arms that the Allies had to hand. The Americans, characteristically, felt less disposed to keep silence about technical failure. On 3 July, Eisenhower complained formally to the U.S. War Department about the shortcomings of many of his army's weapons, following a meeting in France at which, "from Monty and Brooke E learnt that our AT equipment and our 76 mm in Shermans are not capable of taking on Panthers and Tigers."[3] General James Gavin of the American 82nd Airborne Division described how his men first came to understand these things in Italy:

> For years we had been told that our weapons were superior to any that we would encounter. After all, we were soldiers from the most highly industrialised and the richest nation on earth. But that very preoccupation with our advanced technology caused many to assume that technology alone would win battles – more emphasis was placed upon victory through air power than victory through better infantry . . . Our problems stemmed very often from the lack of imagination, if not lack of intelligence, of those responsible for developing infantry weapons.[4]

The Americans indeed possessed an excellent rifle in the semi-automatic Garand, and the British an adequate one in the bolt-action Lee-Enfield. But on the European battlefield, as commanders learned, men seldom fired their rifles. They had little need of accuracy when they did so, for they could rarely distinguish a target. American research showed that, in many regiments, only 15 per cent of riflemen used their weapons in any given action. What mattered was the weight of fire to saturate the battle area. For this, the Germans possessed the supreme weapons in their MG 34 and 42 machine-guns – invariably known among the Allies as Spandaus – with their fabulous rate of fire drowning out the measured hammer of the British bren or the American BAR squad light machine-gun. The MG 42's tearing, rasping 1,200 rounds a minute, against the bren's 500, proved deeply demoralizing to men advancing against it. A German infantry company carried 16 machine-guns, compared to the British 9, and the American 11, although the heavy Vickers and Brownings of the Allied support companies somewhat redressed this balance.

The handle on the German "potato-masher" hand grenade enabled it to be thrown further than its British or American counterparts. The German Schmeisser was a far superior submachine gun to the American "grease gun" or the British sten, which the War Office had ordered in quantity, in an eccentric moment in 1941, although it derived from a German patent sensibly spurned by the Wehrmacht. All the German small arms enjoyed a significant advantage over their American counterparts – in using ammunition with powder which produced less flash and smoke. It was markedly easier for a German soldier to pinpoint American fire than *vice versa*, a technological advantage upon which Marshall commented acidly in a post-war report.

The Germans had made themselves masters in the handling of mortars. Their mortar "stonks", landing without warning in the middle of Allied positions, inaudible in transit because of their slow flight, grated the nerves of every British and American unit in Normandy, and were responsible for an extraordinarily high proportion of casualties – 75 per cent for much of the campaign. Every infantry division possessed some 60 81 mm and up to 20 120 mm mortars, which could throw a 35-pound bomb 6,000 yards. The Allies also, of course, possessed mortars, but never mastered the art of concentrating them with the devastating effect that the Germans achieved. Above all, men detested the *Nebelwerfer*, the multi-barrelled projector whose bombs were fitted with a brilliantly conceived siren, causing them to wail as they flew through the air, which had an effect on those who heard them often more penetrating than their explosive power.

Nebelwerfers came in three sizes: 150 mm (75-pound bomb, 7,300-yard range); 210 mm (248-pound, 8,600-yard); 300 mm (277-pound, 5,000-yard). Each of the five regiments of these – the bulk of them concentrated in the British sector in Normandy – contained 60 or 70 projectors, some of them track-mounted. German infantry anti-tank weapons were also markedly superior. British battalions were equipped only with a spring-loaded projector named the PIAT, which threw a 2½-pound bomb 115 yards and demanded strong nerves from its aimer, who knew that if he lingered long enough to fire at his target with a chance of success, failure meant probable extinction. Even in short-range tests in England, the PIAT scored only 57 per cent hits. The American bazooka packed a wholly inadequate projectile for penetrating German tank armour. The Germans, meanwhile, were equipped in Normandy with the excellent *Panzerfaust*, the finest infantry anti-tank weapon of the war. Gavin's paratroopers seized and employed as many as they could capture.

At a higher level Allied artillery and anti-tank guns were good and plentiful. Indeed, every army fighting in Normandy singled out the British and American artillery as the outstanding arm of the Allied forces. Artillery was responsible for more than half the casualties inflicted in the Second World War. Normandy was the first campaign in which the British used the new discarding-sabot ammunition[5] for their 6 and 17-pounders, with formidable penetrating effect. But the towed anti-tank gun was of little value to troops in attack, and even very accurate artillery fire proved an uncertain method of destroying enemy troops who were well dug in. The British 25-pounder was a fine gun, out-ranging the American 105 mm by 13,400 yards to 12,200, and was immensely valuable for "keeping heads down". But it lacked killing power against defensive positions. It was essential to bring down medium or heavy artillery fire for decisive effect, and there was never enough of this to go round. Nor did the Allies possess any weapon with the physical and moral effect of the German 88 mm, the very high velocity anit-aircraft gun that had been used against ground targets with dazzling success since the early days of the war. Time after time in Normandy, a screen of 88 mm guns stopped an Allied attack dead. Firing high-explosive airburst shells, it was also formidable against infantry. The unforgettable lightning crack of an 88 mm remained implanted in the memory of every survivor of the campaign. It was a mystery to the Allied armies why their own industries failed to build a direct copy of the 88 mm, the Schmeisser, or the potato-masher.

Yet the greatest failure was that of the tank. How could American and British industries produce a host of superb aircraft, an astonishing variety of radar equipment, the proximity fuse, the DUKW, the jeep, yet still ask their armies to join battle against the Wehrmacht equipped with a range of tanks utterly inferior in armour and killing power? A British tank officer, newly-arrived in France in June 1944, recorded a conversation with his regimental adjutant about the state of the armoured battle:

"What do the Germans have most of?"

"Panthers. The Panther can slice through a Churchill like butter from a mile away."

"And how does a Churchill get a Panther?"

"It creeps up on it. When it reaches close quarters the gunner tries to bounce a shot off the underside of the Panther's gun mantlet. If he's lucky, it goes through a piece of thin armour above the driver's head."

"Has anybody ever done it?"

"Yes. Davis in C Squadron. He's back with headquarters now, trying to recover his nerve."

"How does a Churchill get a Tiger?"

"It's supposed to get within two hundred yards and put a shot through the periscope."

"Has anyone ever done it?"

"No."

If this account[6] bordered upon satire, the reality was little different – the product of an extraordinary lack of Allied foresight. A specialist who was intimately concerned in the British tank design programme from its earliest days, Colonel George Macleod Ross, suggested after the war that the War Office made a fatal error by separating the development of fighting vehicles from that of tank guns. Ross, and other experts, argued that it was vital to design the right tank gun, and then to build a suitable vehicle to carry it. Instead, throughout the Second World War, a succession of British tanks were produced in isolation from any consideration either of the enemy gun that they must expect to meet, or of the weight of armour that their own gun must expect to penetrate. Tank design was located at Chobham, while gun design was sited at Woolwich. Although the design of the superb British 17-pounder gun was approved and a prototype construc-

Defeat: a prisoner being searched by a British military policeman.
BBC Hulton Picture Library

(TOP LEFT) Digging: literally a matter of life and death, as so many troops discovered at terrible cost. *BBC Hulton Picture Library*

(TOP RIGHT) Exhaustion: a British doctor pauses between operations at a forward dressing station. *BBC Hulton Picture Library*

(ABOVE) Normandy was above all a battlefield of hedges and ditches, a succession of dashes between islands of cover, each one intensely dangerous for those making the movements. *BBC Hulton Picture Library*

(OPPOSITE) A British sniper pulls through while a young soldier grasps the most precious possession on the battlefield: sleep. *BBC Hulton Picture Library*

Behind the lines: Tommies make themselves at home in a Norman farmyard.
BBC Hulton Picture Library

The image of defeat: captured Germans and fallen horses. Note the pathetic attempt to camouflage the cart. *BBC Hulton Picture Library*

(RIGHT) Brutal encounter between a Norman shopkeeper and an abandoned Mk IV tank. *BBC Hulton Picture Library*

Glimpses in Normandy of "the most professionally skilful army of modern times" as a distinguished American historian has recently described the Wehrmacht: (OPPOSITE TOP LEFT) rearming a Panther; (BOTTOM) self-propelled *Nebelwerfers* – of all German weapons, those most detested by Allied soldiers; (THIS PAGE TOP) with *Panzerfaust*, their formidable close-quarter anti-tank weapon. OPPOSITE TOP LEFT AND RIGHT: *ADN*; OTHERS AND OVERLEAF *Ullstein Bilderdienst*.

(ABOVE) *BBC Hulton Picture Library*

(TOP) A classic propaganda image of liberators and liberated; in fact, the attitude of most Norman civilians to the Allies ranged between numbed indifference and sullen hostility.
BBC Hulton Picture Library

(ABOVE LEFT) Field Marshal von Kluge. (ABOVE RIGHT) Collins of U.S. VII Corps with von Schlieben, the captured commander of Cherbourg. *Imperial War Museum*

(BELOW) Devastation: a typical Norman street scene in the summer of 1944. *BBC Hulton Picture Library*

(TOP) German Volksgrenadier on the Western Front. *Ullstein Bilderdienst.*

(ABOVE) The battlefield: a striking view of the difficulty of movement among the closely-set farmyards of the Norman villages, ideal for defence. The bespectacled figure in the back of the Bren-gun carrier is the author's father, war correspondent for *Picture Post. BBC Hulton Picture Library*

A classic portrait of the British infantryman in Normandy. *BBC Hulton Picture Library*

The Sherman tank was the principal armoured weapon of the Allied armies, magnificently reliable and mechanically efficient, but critically handicapped by thin armour and lack of an adequate gun, save for the few British 17-pounder-mounted Sherman Fireflies. The Sherman weighed 32 tons and could move at 24 mph. It carried only 76 mm of frontal armour, 51 mm of side armour. The Mk V 75 mm gun with which most models were equipped could penetrate 74 mm of armour at 100 yards, 68 mm at 500 yards, 60 mm at 1,000 yards. Even the upgunned 76 mm and 17-pounder versions suffered problems from the fierce flash when they fired, making it difficult for the crews to observe fall of shot. Note the white star painted on the turret side, the universal identification symbol for all Allied vehicles in Europe.

ted in June 1941, it was not mounted in a tank until the first Sherman Firefly was belatedly produced in August 1943, in too small a quantity to influence OVERLORD decisively. "It is not unfair to say," declared Ross, who served for much of the war as British Technical Liaison officer to the U.S. Army Ordnance in Detroit, "that little of the labour and materials expended on the 25,000 British-built tanks helped to win the war."[7] A visit to Eighth Army in the desert by a temporary technical observer in November 1942 resulted in a disastrous report to the War Office, allegedly approved by Montgomery, asserting that "the 75 mm gun is all we require".[8] This report set the seal upon British tank gun policy for much of the rest of the war, ensuring that

6-pounder and 75 mm-gunned Churchills and Cromwells would form the basis of British tank strength. "None of our authorities seemed to understand as the Germans did", wrote Ross, "the need in war for sustained improvement of weapons."[9]

Yet the decisive force in wartime tank production, as in so much else, was the United States. Russell Weigley, an outstanding American analyst of the U.S. army in the war, has highlighted the failure of its architects to match their end – the application of concentrated power upon the battlefield – to their means: principally, the Sherman tank. Against 24,630 tanks built by the Germans and 24,843 made by the British by the end of 1944, the Americans turned out a staggering 88,410, 25,600 of which were supplied to the British. The great majority were Shermans, first produced in 1942, and dominating all Allied armoured operations in 1944–45. Two-thirds of the tanks employed by British units in Normandy were Shermans, the balance being chiefly Cromwells (7th Armoured Division) and Churchills (79th Division and independent armoured brigades). The Sherman was a superbly reliable piece of machinery, far easier to maintain and with a track life five times longer than its German counterparts. It weighed 33 tons, compared with the 43 tons of the Panther, and 56 tons of the Tiger. Its fast cross-country speed reflected the Americans' doctrinal obsession with pace in armoured operations. It possessed two important advantages over its German opponents: a faster speed of turret traverse to engage the enemy, and a higher rate of fire. Conversely, it suffered two critical weaknesses: first, its readiness to catch fire, which caused soldiers on the battlefield to christen it "the ronson" or "tommy cooker". This was a reflection upon its design and thin armour, rather than (as the U.S. War Department suggested tetchily after early complaints) because its crews were loading too much ammunition into its turret. Second, and more important, it was undergunned. Its original 75 mm gun produced a muzzle velocity of 2,050 feet-per-second against 2,900 f.p.s. of the British 17-pounder and the 3,340 f.p.s. of the German 88 mm. At a range of 200 yards, the British gun had almost thrice the penetration of the 75 mm. A Tiger could knock out a Sherman at a range of 4,000 yards, while the American tank could not penetrate a Tiger's frontal armour at all. Even when the Sherman was up-gunned with a 76 mm, it was compelled to close to within 300 yards of a Tiger to have a chance of knocking it out. "Not only do German Mk V and Mk VI tanks keep out a greater proportion of hits than Shermans," concluded a gloomy SHAEF Operational Research report in 1944, "but also they are *far less likely to brew up when penetrated*" (emphasis in original).[10] Even the much lighter 25-ton German Mk IV tank, which made up about half the tank strength of the panzer divisions, packed a KWK 40 75 mm gun with a muzzle velocity 20 per cent greater than the Sherman's 75 mm. This was capable of penetrating 92 mm of armour at 500 yards against the 68 mm of the Sherman's gun.

The American War Department could not claim ignorance of the enemy's developments in the field of gunnery. As early as May 1942, Major Jarrett of U.S. Army Ordnance shipped a captured 88 mm gun across the Atlantic with a report emphasizing its potency. There were a variety of causes for the American failure to pursue the improvement of the Sherman at once. The designers were pinning most of their hopes upon early production of an entirely new replacement tank. Enormous effort was wasted on a new model, named the T20, whose development spanned three years and seven pilots, but of which only 120 reached the battlefield at the end of the war. General Electric were labouring on a strange white elephant designated the T23. Colonel Ross wrote that "there can be no excuse for the abysmal ignorance of tank tactics generally and tank operations in Europe in particular which prompted this half-hearted attempt to design a worthy successor to the Sherman when the simple answer was to design a better gun, something infinitely easier than a tank."[11] There was undoubtedly chauvinistic resistance in the U.S. to copying either the German 88 mm or, more plausibly, the British 17-pounder. Since the first days of the war, tank design also suffered from the misconceptions of General Lesley McNair, the principal architect of the U.S. army in the Second World War. McNair believed that armoured divisions would chiefly be employed for exploitation and pursuit, and that tanks would seldom be called upon to fight other tanks. He fell victim to the same fallacies that underlay the creation of the battle-cruiser by the admirals of an earlier generation, sacrificing armour to speed only to discover that mere pace in battle is almost meaningless, unless matched by survivability.

Above all, there was a belief at the top of the American armed forces that the Allied armies possessed such a vast numerical superiority of tanks that some technical inferiority was acceptable. Yet when a Sherman tank in Normandy, or even a platoon or battalion of Shermans, found itself confronted by enemy tanks whose armour their guns could not penetrate, numerical advantage seemed to mean little. The apprehension and caution of tank crews were well founded. They knew that if they were hit, they almost certainly burned. If they burned, each crew member had only a 50 per cent statistical prospect of survival. Bradley wrote: "This willingness to expend Shermans offered little comfort to the crews who were forced to expend themselves as well."[12]

We all thought that our tanks were deficient [wrote a British tank officer], and I believe that this had a highly adverse effect on morale. In the end we all became "canny", and would obey orders only to the extent that there appeared a reasonable expectation of successfully carrying them out. There was thus a sort of creeping paralysis in the armoured units; because of the pervading fear of 88s, Panthers, Tigers and Panzerfausts, initiative was lost and squadron commanders tended

The Panzer VI, or Tiger, was the most feared German tank in Normandy, almost impenetrable by frontal Allied tank gunfire, and packing a devastating punch with its 88 mm KwK 36 gun. Muzzle velocity in all guns is chiefly a function of barrel length, and Allied troops were always shocked by their first encounters with the Tiger's gun, "as long as a telegraph pole", as so many men reported. Its 20-pound shell could penetrate 120 mm of armour at 100 yards, 112 mm at 500 yards, 102 mm at 1,000 yards. The Tiger itself carried 100 mm of frontal armour, 80 mm of side armour, weighed 54 tons and had a maximum speed of 23 mph. It was normally employed in independent battalions allocated to German corps or divisions for specific operational purposes. Its principal shortcomings were clumsiness of movement and lack of mechanical reliability.

to go to ground at the first sign of any serious opposition and call up an artillery "stonk". With any luck, as the day wore on, the battle died down and that was at least another day got through.

If the technical detail above seems laboured in a campaign narrative, it has been pursued because no single Allied failure had more important consequences on the European battlefield than the lack of tanks with adequate punch and protection. No weapon, above all no tank, is good or bad in isolation. It must be judged against the enemy weapons which it is expected to fight. Sufficient examples have been given elsewhere in these pages of encounters between German and Allied tanks in which it was not uncommon for the panzer to destroy four, five or even more Shermans before being knocked out itself. The Allies' failure to make forceful judgements about the need to match each new generation of German tanks and the blindness of the General Staffs to the need for bigger tank guns, cost them dearly on the battlefield. Even huge losses of Shermans could be made good. But the knowledge of their own tanks' weakness had a serious effect upon the confidence and aggressiveness of Allied units wherever armour met armour.

Throughout the war, the British authorities were at pains to stifle any public debate about the shortcomings of their tanks, although these were well known throughout the British army. The Labour MP Richard Stokes, who had himself fought gallantly in the First World War, was a thorn in the government's flesh on the issue of tank design, as he was also about strategic bombing, the "unconditional surrender" doctrine, and other embarrassing military matters. Stokes made himself intimately acquainted with every detail of British and German tank performance – thickness of armour, relative muzzle velocities and so on. He became the scourge of the government benches by rehearsing these unwelcome facts at every opportunity. On 30 March 1944, he requested that a Churchill and a captured Tiger tank should be brought to the House of Commons for members to judge for themselves the fighting power of each. The Prime Minister replied:

> No sir. I think the trouble and expense involved, though not very great, is still more than is justified to satisfy the spiteful curiosity of my Honourable friend.[13]

Stokes was aided and abetted by a handful of like-minded spirits. On 20 July 1944, Mr Ellis-Smith asked the Prime Minister for details of the relative performance of British and German tanks. Mr Churchill replied:

> Before the House rises I shall hope to give a solid report upon the performances of British tanks in the various theatres of war. For the present I rest on my statement of 16 March, as follows: "The next time that the British Army takes the field in country suitable for the use of armour, they will be found to be equipped in a manner at least equal to the forces of any other country in the world."

On 25 July 1944, Stokes asked the Secretary of State for War, "whether he will assure this house that our troops in Normandy are equipped with tanks at least the equal of both the German Tiger and Panther in armour and armament?" As in almost every debate in which this issue was raised, P. J. Grigg dismissed Stokes with the assurance that public discussion of this issue was not in the public interest. The backbencher denounced "the most complete humbug with which this matter is treated". On 2 August 1944, Stokes yet again savaged the government about the shortcomings of British tanks: "Relatively speaking, today, we are just as far behind the Germans as we were in 1940. I submit that this is a disgraceful state of affairs." Another MP, Rear-Admiral Beamish, leapt to the government's defence: "The Honourable member has spent his whole time in doing everything he can to lower the prestige of the British army." Stokes rejoined: "My criticisms have been based upon irrefutable facts." Hansard recorded the laughter of the House. "It is all very well for honourable members to laugh," said Stokes, "but these men are dying." He quoted a letter that he had received from a Churchill tank crewman who suggested that the Secretary of State for War should go out and fight "with one of these ruddy things". The Speaker intervened to reproach Stokes for his language: "I have heard bad language from him three times." Stokes declared that he was merely quoting the direct speech of others, from the battlefield. It was self-evident that his information, and his report on the sentiment of tank crews, were entirely well founded. But he remained a prophet without honour. The government lied systematically, until the very end of the war, about the Allies' tragic failure to produce tanks capable of matching those of the Germans.

Colonel Campbell Clarke, perhaps the foremost British ordnance expert of the war, originator of the 25-pounder and the entire range of successful anti-tank guns, wrote early in 1945:

We here in Britain have some time ago reached the stage where military weapons have developed somewhat beyond the educational capacity of the average soldier to appreciate their functional use; still more so that of the General Staff officer to direct their future lines of development for war. The inevitable consequence has been, and will increasingly be, tactical stagnation and "surprise" by an enemy who is prepared to plan new methods for their use in conjunction with a first-hand knowledge of technical possibilities and limitations.[14]

Any armoured officer fighting in north-west Europe in 1944 would have echoed his sentiments.

7 The battlefield

From the beachhead to the front

By the last days of June, the battle for Normandy had taken on the character that it was to retain for the two months that followed: a struggle involving more than 1,000,000 men pitted against each other on a front of scarcely 100 miles. By August, the numbers would be over 2,000,000. Each morning, while in the fighting areas armoured units ground forward from their night harbours and headquarters staffs plotted the hopeful course of the next battle, thousands of infantrymen lay in their foxholes scratching laconic letters home, overshadowed by a consciousness both of the censor's eye and of the desultory shell and mortar fire around them. "Dear Mum," wrote Private Sid Verrier of the 2nd Ox & Bucks on 27 June:

> I'm still feeling rather dirty after living the way I have done since D-Day and I will be very glad to have a good bath, change into civvies and go for a nice walk round the parks at home. Better than a walk would be a couple of days sleep. Still I'm not grumbling, life is too sweet . . .[1]

On the beaches, new columns of men waded ashore from their landing craft, each one awed by the feeling that he was conducting his own personal invasion, no matter how many others had gone before. Bradley, as he came ashore at Omaha on the second day, was puzzled by the sight of a broken tennis racquet and a sodden boxing glove drifting side by side amid the debris in the surf. Ceaseless columns of vehicles bumped across the piers and out of the LCTs beached on the sand, to follow the outstretched gauntlet of a military policeman towards some rendezvous inland. When Trooper Stephen Dyson drove his tank up Juno beach in the last days of June, he jumped down from the hull and filled a matchbox with French sand the moment that the Churchill had cleared the LCT. His squadron harboured alongside tanks of 11th Armoured Division, veterans of some weeks' experience. They chatted together. The 11th Armoured men derided their late appearance on the battlefield. "They told us that the Germans were very, very good."

Every man who approached the French coast that summer was amazed by the panorama of shipping that met his eye, the Rhino ferries shuttling out to the transports with cargoes of dejected German prisoners, the huge caissons and heavily gunned piers of the Mulberry harbours, whose creation had done so much to convince doubters, such as the Prime Minister, that OVERLORD was feasible. In fact, there will always be grave doubt as to whether the Mulberries justified the enormous cost and effort that was put into them. Their scale fascinated and impressed contemporary servicemen and the first generation of post-war historians, but recent researchers[2] have focussed much more closely upon the American achievement of unloading stores at a greater rate directly across the beaches than had been managed across the Mulberry before the American harbour was wrecked in the "great storm" of 19–21 June. The storm itself, treated by some chroniclers as a veritable cataclysm, has also been the subject of modern dispute. At no time, it has been pointed out, did the winds exceed force six, a moderate blow by nautical standards. The inability of the Mulberries to withstand it – for the British harbour was also severely damaged – seems to reflect more upon the strength of the structures rather than upon the nature of the gales. There was no doubt of the impact of the storm upon the Allied unloading programme, or of its serious effect upon operations at the front. But the surprise of the Allied command about the consequences of the storm was caused chiefly by their expectation that the huge Mulberry programme should have been capable of overcoming any problems of delay. It is likely that Allied unloading operations could have been shielded from the sea just as effectively merely by sinking the screen of blockships and creating a network of piers, rather than by devoting the labour of 45,000 men to building the Mulberries.[3] Some of the same doubts apply to another celebrated innovation, PLUTO – PipeLine Under The Ocean – a device for pumping petrol direct from England to the armies in France. It was 41 days before PLUTO was in position. A few weeks later its submerged couplings gave way and a new line had to be laid from Dungeness to Boulogne. This began to yield 700 tons of fuel a day only in January 1945.[4]

The slow progress inland resulted in a dramatic surplus of

vehicles ashore in the first weks after D-Day – in the first 11 days 81,000 were landed for the Americans alone. Every GI required 30 pounds of supplies per day to support him in action, compared with 20 pounds per British soldier, and a German quota that sometimes fell to four pounds. The Allied armies demanded 26,000 tons of stores *a day* to sustain them in action. By 25 July, there were 1,450,000 men ashore – 812,000 American, 640,000 British and Canadian. Amid this vast movement of humanity, some simply disappeared into the administrative jungle. General Gerow of the U.S. V Corps was compelled to make a personal visit to England to locate one unit under his command which he was persistently assured was with his corps in Normandy.

Inland from the beaches, newly arriving men gaped at the massive dumps of fuel, ammunition, supplies, the parked ranks of brand-new tanks, vehicles, guns that crowded every field. Uncamouflaged, their safety was a spectacular tribute to the Allies' absolute command of the air. As for so many others, the first impression of Major Charles Richardson of the 6th KOSB was astonishment that the beachhead was so well organized, and bewilderment about where to find a field in which to put anything. Tank tracks scarred the countryside in all directions. Unit signposts and field telephone cables were nailed to every tree by the roadside, or draped along branches and ditches. Patton, when he came, was delighted by the droll spectacle of telephone wires suspended between the crucifixes at every crossroads. The crashed aircraft that lay everywhere reminded him of "dead birds partly eaten by beetles".[5] Soldiers were puzzled, sometimes angered, by the sight of French civilians tending their fields or going about their business with their little carts, apparently indifferent to the claims of their liberators to gratitude. One morning a few days after the landing, Corporal Charles Baldwin of the Westminster Dragoons was sent back to the beaches to bring forward a draft of replacements for his squadron:

> Just after leaving Crepon by jeep, in a field on my right I noticed some dead British infantry. There were two civilians there and I pulled up. Another jeep containing a military police lance-corporal pulled up behind me. We walked towards the two men and it became apparent that they had been looting the bodies. Two had had their boots removed. The civilians started to speak quickly in French. But the military policeman simply said: "Bloody bastards" and shot them with his sten gun.[6]

Private John Price found most of the French sullen, and was struck by the predominance of the elderly – the young or middle-aged appeared to have fled. But he was touched when a kindly old clockmaker asked for a penny, and worked it into a ring for him. Many of the British, after years of privation at home, were disgusted by the abundance of food in the Norman villages. "The civilians seemed to have eaten well," said Alfred Lee of the Middlesex Regiment. "We saw no skinny ones."[7] There were persistent rumours throughout the beachhead of Fifth Column activities by local Frenchmen spying for the Germans, and these multiplied mistrust. "We almost had the feeling that these people had not been hostile to the Germans," John Hein of the U.S. 1st Division said wonderingly.[8] A captured German of 12th SS Panzer wrote cynically in his diary: "As we are marched through the town towards the port, the French insult us, shake their fists and make throat-cutting gestures. This does not really shock us. We are used to this sort of thing from the French. If it was the other way around, they would be threatening the Tommies . . ."[9] In the British sector, it was found necessary to mount pipeline patrols to prevent civilians from inserting wooden plugs at intervals along them in order to drain off fuel supplies for themselves. Most Normans treated the fighting armies with impartial disdain or occasional kindness. Helmut Gunther of 17th SS Panzergrenadiers once asked an elderly woman why she gave his men cream, and she answered gravely: "Because I have a grandson who is a prisoner in Germany, and I hope that the people there are doing the same for him."[10] It was not remarkable that so many French families were shocked and appalled by the cost of liberation to their own homes, which if anything were looted more thoroughly by the Allied than the German armies. "We have been reproached," wrote a local writer bitterly a few months later, "at least by those who regard the battle of Normandy as a military tattoo, for failing to throw ourselves on the necks of our liberators. Those people have lost sight of the Stations of the Cross that we have passed since 6 June."[11] When it began to rain early in July, the locals told the soldiers that there had not been a summer like it for 50 years. But for this, at least, they did not seek to blame the Allies. They shrugged: "*C'est la guerre.*"

A few overworked Norman prostitutes were already plying their trade. One day General Bradley was astonished to notice a village near Isigny with "Off Limits" signs posted outside it, and drove in with General "Pete" Quesada of IXth Tactical Air Command. He found a house marked "Prophylactic Station", containing three sleeping GIs, none of whom recognized their army commander when he awakened them. He inquired how much business they were doing. The medic shrugged. "Well, yesterday there was just the two for the MPs and one for me and that was it." Characteristically, Bradley moved on without inflicting the trauma of his identity upon them.[12]

It was well into July before facilities for rear-area entertainments began to be established, and few men were withdrawn from the line for long enough to enjoy them. But in the *mairie* of Balleroy, where the U.S. 1st Division had its civil affairs office issuing *laissez-passers* to civilians and supervising the blackout, a group of local inhabitants one day requested permission to hold a concert. On 2 July, a few score civilians and GIs crowded into the little auditorium for what they billed proudly as "the first cultural event in liberated France". The mayor's daughter sang a song, a succession of other local talents performed their little acts, and Leslie Bertal, a Hungarian concert pianist of some pre-war celebrity who was now serving as a prisoner-of-war interrogator, played in the oddest setting of his career. He was killed a week later, when a shell exploded in the tree above him as he was questioning a German soldier.

For most of the men fighting in France, beyond a passing curiosity about alien sights and a foreign language, life revolved around the battle and the cocoon of their units. Each squad or platoon carried its little island of east London or westside New York across Europe, the average GI only communicating with the world outside for long enough to imitate a chicken before a bewildered Frenchwoman, in an effort to persuade her to sell him eggs. They had little eye for the beauty of the creeper-clad farmhouses, the white apple and pear blossom, the golden walls of the châteaux. Most Tommies were bemused by their officers' enthusiasm for the sticky, smelly local cheese – camembert. Sergeant Andy Hertz, an American aviation engineer, was once asked to dinner by a French refugee family, fellow Jews. He said that it was his first inkling of what the Germans were doing to his people. As a souvenir, his hosts gave him one of the yellow Stars of David that they had been compelled to wear. He kept it all his life.

The rear areas were littered with signs – divisional symbols and direction markers, cautionary KEEP TO SWEPT PATH, or roughly daubed FRONT LINE NO VEHICLES FORWARD OF HERE, or simply DUST MEANS DEATH. Except when rain and the vast columns of tracked vehicles had chewed the roads into muddy ruins, one of the greatest perils was the dust thrown up by speeding convoys, bringing down a deadly rain of German artillery fire. Infantry cursed the proximity of their own tanks or artillery for the same reason, and took pains to avoid occupying positions near a major signals unit, for fear of German radio locators and the fire that they could call down. Every German signaller testified to the carelessness of Allied soldiers on the air, especially the Canadians and some American units whose easy chatter provided priceless intelligence.

Among the fighting soldiers, there was little to do between battles except stroll among the fields or visit a nearby village to buy milk or eggs; they could write home; drown themselves in the universal calvados and cider; play cards; or talk interminably. Padre Lovegrove of the Green Howards tried to get his men to speak about their civilian jobs and homes, to preserve some grip upon the world beyond the battlefield. Among themselves many men, inevitably, talked about women. But deep in their hearts most soldiers on the battlefield would readily trade a night with a woman for a hot bath, a home-cooked meal, and a safe bed in which they could merely sleep. Some found solace in religion. Frank Svboda, a presbyterian chaplain with the U.S. 79th Division, was moved by the manner in which his services were attended by Protestants, Jews, and Catholic soldiers clutching their rosaries. Before battle, he found himself administering communion of crackers and squeezed raisin juice to little clusters of 15 or 20 sombre young men in a hedgerow a few hundred yards behind the front. Good chaplains were greatly prized by their units, but bad ones – of whom there were many in the Allied armies – were detested and avoided for the hypocrisy with which they offered their blessings from the rear echelon. Frank Svboda felt that the best aid he possessed in cementing relations with his men was a little axe he had bought in England, and which they found invaluable for hacking off the stubborn hedgerow roots as they dug foxholes. "Chaplain, pass the hatchet!" became a unit catchphrase.

The Americans lived chiefly off 5-pound cartons of C rations, or the more popular three-meal K ration – 60,000,000 of them were shipped to Normandy in the first three weeks of operations. Everybody detested the powdered lemon juice, but otherwise it was the monotony of the food that men cursed, rather than its quality. One night, John Hein found himself called upon to feed four German prisoners seized by a patrol. The men wolfed their first American rations, one of them declaring courteously: "This is first-rate." British soldiers were astonished by the sheer quantity of American supplies, and by the ice cream-making machines that soon appeared in rear areas. But their own rations were of substantially higher quality than the food on which the British civilian population at home was being fed. Augmented by occasional cuts from freshly-dead cattle and produce bought or thieved from the Normans, it was tolerable enough. Almost every man smoked. The armies supplied the troops with cigarettes in prodigal profusion, as the readiest means of sustaining morale, the most portable comfort available to a soldier. For the first weeks ashore in France, their greatest craving was bread. There was none to be had until field bakeries were established in the beachhead, and as they chewed day after day on tasteless hard tack biscuits, soft white bread came to seem an unimaginable luxury.

To almost every man of the Allied armies, the predominant memory of the campaign, beyond the horror of the battle, was the astounding efficiency of the supply services. The Americans had always justly prided themselves upon their organization. But for young British soldiers, who had grown up with the legend of the War Office's chronic bungling, and of the Crimea and the Boer War, Second Army's administration in Normandy seemed a miracle. "We were all very agreeably surprised by the efficiency," said Major John Warner of 3rd Recce Regiment. "We always knew that we would receive ammunition, letters, petrol, food." Curiously enough, whatever the command shortcomings of the British Army in France in the First World War, its administration had been a supreme achievement. So it was now, and this contributed enormously to men's faith in their commanders and in final victory. "There was so much *matériel* at the back," said Alf Lee of the Middlesex Regiment. "Whenever you went to the rear and saw fields packed with petrol tins as high as a house, rows of guns in their canvas covers waiting to come up, huge dumps of shells, you couldn't doubt that we could do it. We would often fire 25,000 rounds from a Vickers gun in a single shoot. Yet we were never short of ammunition."

Few men on the battlefield read anything more demanding than comics. Private Richardson of the 82nd Airborne self-consciously carried around his U.S. army paperback edition of *Oliver Twist* until his unit was withdrawn from action, but he never looked at it. Padre Lovegrove read Housman's *A Shropshire Lad*, and some men clung to their bibles. But most merely glanced at their own unit's weekly duplicated news-sheets – if there was time for headquarters to produce such refinements – or, in the American army, leafed through *Stars and Stripes*. To Lieutenant Floyd Ratliff of the 30th Artillery, this at least "made it seem that there was some design, some grand strategy to what we were doing". Unless a man had access to radio news or headquarters gossip, he lived entirely in the tiny private world of his unit, cut off from both the successes and failures of others, and from the army of which he was a part. The sheer enormity of the forces deployed in Normandy destroyed the sense of personality, the feeling of identity which had been so strong, for instance, in the Eighth Army in the desert. The campaign in north-west Europe was industrialized warfare on a vast scale. For that reason, veterans of earlier campaigns found this one less congenial – dirty and sordid in a fashion unknown in the desert. Many responded by focussing their own loyalties exclusively upon their own squad or company. One of the chronic command difficulties of the campaign was that of overcoming the conviction of many men that another unit or another division's difficulties were entirely its own affair. The sense of detachment was inevitably strongest among the hundreds of thousands of men serving in the rear areas or on the gunlines:

> We would suddenly find ourselves put with a different army [said Ratliff of his 155 mm battery], and we would more likely hear about it on the grapevine than from orders. Much of our firing was blind or at night, and we often wondered what we were shooting at. Nobody would say down the telephone: "I can see this village and people running out." We would just hear "50 short" or "50 over" called to the Fire Control Centre. We didn't enjoy the job. It was simply something we had to do, and there was no way out except to finish it. Nobody felt much animosity towards the Germans except a couple of German-speaking Jews in our unit. What hatred there was was generated by propaganda, and didn't go deep. We didn't really know anything about the Germans, or even about their army. Most of our men were bewildered by the whole thing. They didn't understand what it was all about, although they felt that it was a just cause because of Pearl Harbor. Wherever they went they would look around and say: "This isn't the way we do things at home."[13]

For the gunners, the greatest strain lay in the shattering noise of their own pieces, and the physical sweat of shifting 95-pound

155 mm projectiles day after day, stripped to the waist and working like automatons through the bombardment before a big attack. Their risk of death or mutilation was small – very small by comparison with that of the infantry. In Ratliff's battalion in Normandy, one observation officer was lost when his Piper Cub was shot down, and a switchboard operator and his assistant were wounded by an incoming shell exploding in a tree above their foxhole. That was all.

Much the most hazardous gunnery task was that of forward observer, either working with the infantry, spotting from the steel towers erected around Caen, or flying an American Piper or British Auster. The pilots droned slowly up and down the line at 120 mph, normally 1,000 feet up and 1,000 yards behind the front. They seldom glimpsed men below, more often the quick flash of German guns or a brief movement of vehicles. Then the pilot called his battery: "Hello Foxtrot 3, I have a Mike target for you." When the guns warned him that they were ready, he called the firing order and watched the ground below for the explosions. Then he radioed "All north 400," or whatever correction was necessary until shells were bracketing the target. The aircraft was often jolted by the passage of shells through the sky around it. "But it was a very disembodied business," said a British spotter pilot, Captain Geoffrey Ivon-Jones.[14] One day he was puzzled by piles of logs lying beside a road, until he saw that they were dead Germans. He developed a personal affection for some of the batteries for which he spotted, above all the 79th Scottish Horse, which prided itself on its smartness. Circling above them in action, the pilot could see the tiny figure of the gun position officer standing with his battery, giving the signal to fire with a sweep of his white silk handkerchief.

Tragic accidents were part of the small change of the battle. One day, spotting for a warship, Ivon-Jones found that the naval gunners were reading the directional "clock" messages upside down, and shelling British positions. An Auster crew watched in horror as bombers rained explosives on friendly forces, and swung alongside to signal frantically by Aldis lamp: WRONG TARGET. On the ground, the pilots lived in foxholes beside the pits bulldozed to protect their aircraft, which took off and landed from any convenient field. Ivon-Jones, a passionate falconer, kept a sparrowhawk named Mrs Patton for some weeks, feeding her on birds and meat cut from dead cows. He and the other pilots flew perhaps four or five 40-minute sorties a day, ever

The British 17-pounder was the best Allied anti-tank gun of the war, capable of penetrating 149 mm of armour at 100 yards, 140 mm at 500 yards, 130 mm at 1,000 yards. In August 1944, small quantities of the new "Discarding Sabot" ammunition began to become available for the 17-pounder, dramatically increasing its hitting power. But throughout the campaign in north-west Europe, the Allies faced the problem that the strategic onus for attack lay upon themselves, and towed anti-tank guns were of limited value – except against German armoured counter-attacks, in which the 17-pounder proved its outstanding quality.

watchful for German fighters. Some Allied fliers became so accustomed to regarding every aircraft as friendly that the Luftwaffe could spring lethal surprises. "What are those, Geordie?" Captain Harry Bordon asked his observer. "Spitfires, sir," came the cheerful reply, seconds before five Me 109s shot them down.

Beyond the obvious dangers of enemy action, an extraordinary number of men were injured in accidents, or shot up by their own guns or aircraft. Padre Lovegrove was well behind the lines, looking for dead men of his unit from an earlier battle, when he stooped to pick up a man's web equipment, hoping to find his service number, and trod on a mine. John Price of the Ox & Bucks watched a man shake with fear when he was called for a reconnaissance patrol, then sag with relief as he returned alive. He laid down his bren, and fell asleep beneath it. A passing soldier tripped on the gun. It fired, killing its owner instantly. Hundreds of men were run over by tanks or trucks. As Stephen Dyson's tank troop halted after disembarking, the waterproof sealing on another Churchill blew up without warning, taking off the hand of the gunner beside it before he had been in France five minutes. Lieutenant Arthur Heal, having survived the storming of "Hillman" with the Suffolks on D-Day, had to be evacuated after rupturing himself. His replacement was killed within 24 hours. Lieutenant-Colonel Eric Hay of the 5th/7th Gordons had already been injured in Sicily when his own intelligence officer dropped a sub-machine gun. Now, after surviving six weeks in the Orne bridgehead, he was travelling in a staff car miles behind the forward positions when a single German shell exploded without warning alongside, wounding him badly in the head. Hundreds of soldiers paid the price of recklessly ignoring warnings about German booby-traps, failing to see tripwires between hedges, or charges linked to tempting booty on abandoned farmhouse tables.

With the coming of night, men lay down to sleep beneath the stars, wrapped in a blanket in their foxholes or the nearest ditch. Most tank crews stretched out a tarpaulin from the hulls of their vehicles and slept beneath it. Some felt safer lying under the tank itself, although enthusiasm for this practice diminished when the bad weather came and a number of men were found in the morning crushed by the vast weight of steel subsiding into the soft ground as they slept. The mosquitos plagued them, and seemed quite immune to the cream issued for their suppression. There were other natural miseries: swarms of flies and wasps; the dysentery from which so many men suffered despite the heavy use of chlorine in the water; and the lice.

> We had been spared by the felt lice but their brothers, the lovely white ones, defeated us [wrote an SS trooper, Sadi Schneid]. As if the Allied invasion was not enough! I escaped from them only when I became an American prisoner six months later. I could never understand why the Germans with all their excellent chemists could not find something effective against this plague. The only thing available was Lysol, which had no effect, and cleaning our clothes in steam baths. The result was that we had permanent lice, and our leather equipment became stiff from steam. Our pullovers were so crawling with lice that we could not bear to put them on. Those Norman civilians who found underwear missing from their cupboards must forgive me for helping myself, but the constant torture of lice was sometimes worse than the fighter-bomber attacks.[15]

With hundreds of thousands of vehicles crammed into a narrow beachhead, movement by day was hampered by constant traffic jams. In darkness it became a nightmare: columns of tanks and trucks crawled nose to tail, guided solely by a pinpoint red lamp on the tail of each one, to reach their destinations only after interminable detours and delays. The vital role of the military police in making movement to any battlefield possible in Europe in 1944 has not been sufficiently recognized, nor the dangers that they faced in doing so from the shelling of crossroads as well as chronic traffic accidents.

Each side bombarded the other with propaganda of varying effectiveness. Allied leaflets promised German soldiers who surrendered a life of comfort and safety, evidenced by photographs of grinning Wehrmacht prisoners. One German leaflet was headed, CAUGHT LIKE FOXES IN A TRAP. It demanded:

> English and American soldiers! Why has Jerry waited so long after the landings to use his so called secret weapons behind your back? Doesn't that strike you as queer? It looks very much as though after waiting for you to cross the Channel, he has set a TRAP for you. You're fighting at present on a very narrow strip of coast, the extent of which has been so far regulated by the Germans. You are using up an enormous number of men and huge quantities of material. Meanwhile the robot planes scatter over London and Southern England explosives, the power and incendiary efficiency of which are without precedent. They are cutting the bridge to your bases.

A more succinct document addressed to Bradley's men demanded: "American soldier! Are you on the wrong side of the street?" By far the most effective propaganda organ was Radio Calais, the British-run station which reached half the German army, who listened intently for the lists of prisoners which were regularly read over the air.

Although the Luftwaffe possessed no power to impede Allied operations seriously, it was still capable of causing considerable irritation, and even acute fear among men living and working on its principal targets, the beaches. Each night, up to 50 Luftwaffe aircraft droned overhead, bombing almost at random, yet with the near certainty of hitting something in the crowded perimeter. The Americans called the night visitation "Bedcheck Charlie". The men behind the beaches – a great army of support and supply troops, inevitably not the most highly-trained or best-equipped to withstand bombardment – dug themselves deeper and deeper into the dunes. "We were terrified by the bombing," said an NCO who had landed with a port construction company on 6 June, expecting to proceed immediately to Caen to reopen its facilities. Instead he and his comrades were stranded for weeks behind the beaches in bewilderment and misery. "We were so frightened, so glad to be alive every morning. We hadn't expected to be in anything like that." Each night they lay down in their gas masks, as protection from the great smokescreeen that was ignited to shroud the piers from enemy bomb aimers. "Golden City", the German pilots called the invasion coast, because of the dazzling array of tracer lacing the darkness offshore. The bald statistics of ships lost to German mines and one-man submarines in the Channel, dumps blown up by air attack, and men killed by brief strafing attacks make the Luftwaffe and German navy's impact upon the Allied build-up seem slight. But for those who were on hand to suffer these small disasters, they seemed very terrible indeed.

The great majority of Allied soldiers who went to Normandy had never before seen action. Many thousands of British troops, especially, had lingered at home through two, three, four years of training and routine. They approached the campaign with an eagerness that promised much to their commanders. "We were all very scared, but glad that we were now going into battle," said Lieutenant Andrew Wilson of The Buffs. "We had been frightened that the war would end before we were really in it. People had no great urge to kill, but they wanted to face the challenge to their manhood of being in danger."[16] Major William Whitelaw and his brother officers of the Scots Guards tank battalion were "thrilled that we were actually going to do something. We had been terrified that we weren't going to get there, and worried how we should answer that question about 'What did you do in the war, daddy?' "[17]

The first shock of battle, the first losses, however severe, did not entirely destroy the sense of wonder, exhilaration and fulfilment that was created by the consummation of months and years of training. A British infantryman wrote of the period following his first action in another theatre at this time:

> We had been in some bloody fighting and lost many men. but the sense of nastiness had been overlaid, even at the time, by an exhilarating aura of adventure. I did not of course then realise that that sense of adventure, with its supercharged impulses of curiosity and excitement, was one of the few advantages that the infantryman new to battle enjoyed over the veteran; and that it would, alas, gradually fade away. Thereafter we would become much better soldiers, hardened and more expert. But we would also, to that end, have to draw more deeply on our innermost resources of discipline, comradeship, endurance and fortitude.[18]

After the enormous initial excitement of the landings, the quick capture of Bayeux, and the dramatic American seizure of Cherbourg and clearance of the northern peninsula, the mood among the men of the Allied armies slowly changed, stiffened as the line of battle congealed. They learned the cost of digging slit-trenches beneath trees if these were struck by shellfire, the vital importance of oiling rifles to protect them from the ravages of rust that set in almost overnight, the price of leaving magazines filled too long so that in action their springs would no longer feed the weapon chambers. As most soldiers on most days found themselves holding fixed positions among the nettles and cow parsley of the hedgerows, at risk principally from mortar and artillery harassing fire, they dug deeper and adjusted to a routine of war: dawn stand-to; breakfast of tea, coffee or self-heating soup in their observation positions or foxholes or tank harbours; then the daily grind of infantry patrolling or tank deployments – for the Allied armour almost invariably withdrew from the front line during the hours of darkness. There were map shoots by the gunners or local attacks to adjust a salient or clear a start-line for major operations to come. Among the greatest strains on all the armies in Normandy was the sheer length of the summer day – from 4.45 a.m. to 11.15 p.m. in the first weeks of June. This bore especially heavily on commanders and staff officers, who were compelled to continue writing reports and issuing orders when they returned to their headquarters from the front with the coming of the brief darkness. Most commanding officers found that they could remain on their feet only by sleeping a little during the day. It was difficult to remain undisturbed. One British colonel posted a sign outside his CP: "HAVE YOU HAD YOUR ORGANIZED REST TODAY? I AM HAVING MINE NOW."[19] Men discovered that they could sleep on their feet, under bombardment, in their tanks, on the march. Fatigue, and the struggle to overcome it, ruled their lives.

For the tank crews, even in battle, there were hours sitting motionless, closed down beneath their hatches, firing an occasional shell merely to provide a receptacle into which to urinate. Inside their hulls, they were vulnerable only to direct hits from artillery or mortar fire, but they were often more ignorant than the infantry of what was taking place around them. During the critical battle for Villers-Bocage, Trooper Denis Huett of 5th RTR never saw a German. Scout cars radioed that enemy tanks were approaching, "and stuff started flying about". They once traversed their turret violently to meet an oncoming tank, to discover just in time that it was one of their own. A nearby battery of 25-pounders was firing over open sights. Three of the crew of a neighbouring Cromwell, who lost patience with all the hanging about, dismounted for a private reconnaissance beyond the hedge and did not return, for they walked 100 yards to a barn and found themselves staring into the muzzle of a

German tank commander's Schmeisser. In an uncommon moment of humanity, when he learnt that it was the lap gunner's 21st birthday, he produced a bottle of wine in celebration before sending the prisoners to the rear.

All one night and through the next day, Huett and the other crews remained in their tanks, periodically starting the petrol engines to charge the batteries, acutely watchful when darkness came and they were no longer able to pull back to harbour: "Oh gawd, we thought, and every time we saw a shadow we were sure something was out there." Somebody said that they were surrounded. They were deeply relieved on the night of 15 June when at last they retired, exhausted infantry clinging to their hulls. But of who had gone where, who had gained or lost what, they understood little. There was only the vague ranker's awareness, communicated to Corporal Topper Brown, that, "the Germans had chewed us all for arsepaper, hadn't they?"[20]

The tankmen pitied the infantry, their bodies naked to every form of high explosive, just as most foot soldiers preferred the comfort of their slit trenches to facing the enemy in a vast, noisy steel box which seemed to ignite instantly when hit. Tank crews could carry all manner of private comforts and extra rations with them, and despite strict orders against cooking inside the tanks in action, all of them did so, brewing up on the floors of the turrets. The chief handicap was the poor visibility through their periscopes with the hatches closed. Many of the best tank commanders were killed by small arms, standing up in their turrets for a wider view of the battlefield. Their greatest fear was of breakdown or throwing a track under fire, which would compel them to dismount. Corporal Bill Preston of the U.S. 743rd Battalion had been in action for 32 days when his crew came upon another Sherman bogged down in a hedgerow ditch. He was peering out of the turret watching his commander and wireless operator hitch a cable to the casualty when two German mortar rounds dropped in their midst. Of the two men on the ground, one was killed and the other wounded. Preston himself fell to the bottom of the turret paralyzed – his neck broken by a hit in the spine. "Dad's not going to like this," he thought through his coma. He spent the next six months in hospitals, and reflected more pragmatically: "Thank God I'm out of it."[21]

Every forward unit suffered a steady drain of casualties from snipers, mortaring and artillery fire, which both sides employed daily to maintain pressure upon each other, the Allies in greater volume since they possessed greater firepower. 2nd Panzer reported in July that they were receiving an average of 4,000 incoming artillery and 5,000 mortar rounds a day on their front, rising dramatically during British attacks to a total of 3,500 rounds in two hours on one occasion. It is important to remember that throughout the campaign, even in sectors where neither side was carrying out a major offensive, there were constant local attacks. To emphasize the staggering weight of firepower that the Allies employed in support of their movements, it is worth citing the example of a minor operation near Cristot on 16 June. Throughout the night of the 15th, the German positions to be attacked were subjected to harassing fire. In the early morning of the 16th, from H–35 to H–20, naval guns on the objectives. From H–15 to H-Hour, Typhoons rocketed and strafed them. A squadron of tanks provided covering fire for the assault from a hull-down position on the flank. An entire armoured regiment carried out a diversionary manoeuvre just north of the intended thrust. A company of heavy 4.2-inch mortars stonked selected German positions from H–15 to H-Hour. The operation itself was supported by seven field regiments of 25-pounders, and four regiments of medium guns. At H-Hour, noon on the 16th, the battalion of 49th Division making the attack advanced two companies forward, at the normal infantry assault pace of 25 yards a minute; a troop of tanks accompanied each company. The tanks led across the open fields beyond the start-line, then, as they approached an orchard, allowed the infantry to overtake them and sweep it for anti-tank guns, before the tanks once again took over. At 1.15 p.m. the battalion passed through Cristot, where it reorganized. They found 17 German dead in the village and two armoured cars and one soft-skinned vehicle destroyed. The British had lost three killed and 24 wounded, almost all by enemy mortars. A few hundred yards of fields and ruins had been gained, at uncommonly small cost in British life. But the extraordinary firepower that had been deployed to make this possible readily explains why the Allies in Normandy suffered chronic shortages of artillery ammunition.[22]

Every German unit reported ceaselessly on the agonizing difficulties caused by constant Allied air surveillance, even when there were no incoming air strikes. The mere presence in the sky of Allied spotting aircraft frequently reduced every nearby German gun to silence. Anti-aircraft fire was discouraged by bringing down an immediate Allied barrage upon his source.

Snipers were detested and feared as much for the strain that they caused to men's routine movements in forward areas as for the casualties that they inflicted. Their activities provoked as much irrational resentment as the killing of baled-out tank crews or parachutists in mid-descent. Both sides habitually shot snipers who were taken prisoner. "Brad says he will not take any action against anyone that decides to treat snipers a little more roughly than they are being treated at present," wrote the First Army commander's ADC in his diary: "A sniper cannot sit around and shoot and then capture when you close in on him. That's not the way to play the game."[23] It is important to distinguish here between the work of the specially-trained, superbly-camouflaged marksmen who worked with telescopic-sighted rifles between the lines during periods of static warfare, and the universal habit of describing any man hit by a small-arms round as "shot by a sniper".

One of the chronic preoccupations of Allied commanders in Normandy was the need to persuade attacking infantry to keep moving, not to cause incessant delays by taking cover whenever small-arms fire was heard in their area. For most infantrymen, when a shot came from an unseen gun – and almost every gun fired in Normandy was unseen – it was a reflex action to seek cover until the danger had been pinpointed. No habit caused greater difficulties and delays to Allied movement, nor proved more difficult to overcome when those junior leaders who resisted it and pressed on were so frequently killed. "It is a natural tendency for inexperienced troops to think that every bullet that comes over their heads is fired from about a hundred yards away," stated an acerbic British report after the early fighting in France, "whereas in fact it is probably fired from a much greater range."[24] Many units in defensive positions habitually sprayed the surrounding area – above all, nearby woods – with random gunfire at dawn to shake out any enemy who had infiltrated during the night. Commanders sought in vain to discourage this practice, which almost invariably provoked an unwanted exchange of shooting.

Casualties

There was a brutally self-evident hierarchy of risk among the armies: naturally this was lowest among lines-of-communication troops and heavy artillery, rising through field artillery and armoured units and engineers, to reach a pinnacle among infantry. Of the British forces in Normandy by August 1944, 56 per cent were classified as fighting troops rather than service elements. Just 14 per cent were infantrymen, against 18 per cent gunners, 13 per cent engineers, 6 per cent tank crews, 5 per cent signallers. Even within an infantry battalion, a man serving heavy weapons with the support company possessed a markedly greater chance of survival than his counterpart in a rifle company. It was here that the losses, turnover of officers and men, became appalling, far more serious than the planners had allowed for, and eventually reached crisis proportions in Normandy for the American, German and British armies. Before D-Day, the American logisticians had expected 70.3 per cent of their casualties to be among infantry. Yet in the event, of 100,000 American casualties in June and July, 85 per cent were infantry, 63 per cent riflemen. The British forecast casualties on the basis of staff tables known as the Evetts' Rates, which categorized levels of action as "Intense", "Normal" and "Quiet". After the army's early experiences in Normandy, it was found necessary to introduce a new scale to cover heavy fighting: "Double Intense".

Vision, for the men in the front line, narrowed to encompass only the immediate experience of life and death. "One was emotionally absorbed by the question: 'Am I going to get through tomorrow?' " said Lieutenant Andrew Wilson of The Buffs. "I really believed each time I went into action that I was going to get killed." For all his fear, Wilson was one of those young Englishmen who found the experience of war deeply fulfilling:

> I had the delayed adolescence of so many English public schoolboys. Everything I learned about things such as how not to get a girl pregnant, I learned from my tank crew. In the truest sense, I developed a love of other men such as is not possible in Anglo-saxon society in peacetime. In some ways, our emotional capability developed beyond our years at this time. But in others, in our knowledge of life outside the battlefield, we were retarded.[25]

A close friend of Wilson's, commanding another flame-throwing tank troop, was shot along with his crew when he was captured because the Germans considered that the Crocodile somehow transcended the legitimate horrors of battle. Much has been made of the shooting of prisoners – most notoriously, Canadian prisoners – by 12th SS Panzer and other German units in Normandy. Yet it must be said that propaganda has distorted the balance of guilt. Among scores of Allied witnesses interviewed for this narrative, almost every one had direct knowledge or even experience of the shooting of German prisoners during the campaign. In the heat of battle, in the wake of seeing comrades die, many men found it intolerable to send prisoners to the rear knowing that they would thus survive the war, while they themselves seemed to have little prospect of doing so. Many British and American units shot SS prisoners routinely, which explained, as much as the fanatical resistance that the SS so often offered, why so few appeared in POW cages. The 6th KOSB never forgave or forgot the action of a wounded SS soldier to whom Major John Ogilvie leaned down to give water. The German drank, then shot the British officer.

German treatment of prisoners was as erratic as that of the Allies. Sergeant Heinz Hickmann of the Luftwaffe Parachute Division was holding a crossroads with a 12-man rearguard early one morning, when he was nudged out of a doze by an urgent whisper: "Tommy's here!" They shot up the lead jeep of a convoy of 12 lorries, from which a procession of rudely-awakened British supply personnel tumbled out with their hands up. Embarrassed by the burden of 34 prisoners, Hickmann had them locked in a nearby barn, and left them there when his squad pulled out: "In Russia, we would have shot them." Some men had special reasons for fearing capture: Private Abraham Arditti of the U.S. 101st Airborne could never forget the H for Hebrew imprinted on his dogtags. But although there were well-documented instances of SS units murdering their captives, overall it seems doubtful whether this was done on a greater scale by one side than the other. Lieutenant Philip Reisler of the U.S. 2nd Armored watched infantrymen of the 4th Division carelessly shoot three wounded Germans. One of his fellow officers echoed a common sentiment in the unit: "Anything you do to the kraut is okay because they should have given up in Africa. All of this is just wasted motion." Patton described how a German soldier blew a bridge, killing several GIs after their leading elements had passed: "He then put up his hands . . . The Americans took him prisoner, which I considered the height of folly." Lindley Higgins of the U.S. 4th saw a lieutenant shout impatiently to a soldier moving off with a prisoner: "You going to take that man to the rear?", and simply pull out his pistol to shoot the German in the head. Once a definable atrocity had been discovered – as with the bodies of the Canadians killed by 12th SS Panzer – and the conscious decision taken to respond in kind, it is difficult with hindsight to draw a meaningful moral distinction between the behaviour of one side and the other on the battlefield.

Corporal Topper Brown of the 5th RTR never even knew where his tank was hit when his squadron commander in the turret said quietly: "Bale out." He found himself alone in a ditch with his mate Dodger Smith, the gunner. They could hear the Germans digging in quite close to hand, and saw some tracer overhead. But they felt desperately tired, and after lying listening for a time, fell asleep. They woke in bright sunshine to hear only birdsong around them. Cautiously they explored, and found an abandoned Cromwell. They climbed onto the hull to find it commander dead inside, and tried in vain to use the radio to contact their own unit. Then they began to walk up the road until they heard voices, and found themselves face to face with a file of Germans. They put up their hands: "We couldn't have got them no higher." Even when shells began to land nearby and the Germans took cover, the frightened young Londoners remained standing in the road with their hands in the air.

At last they were stripped of their revolvers and watches and marched to a farmhouse, where they marvelled at the superbly-camouflaged Tiger tank dug in outside. They were led down to a cellar where they were sharply questioned by an English-speaking German who said finally: "You aren't very intelligent for a British NCO, are you? You know you're not going to win, don't you?" Then they were marched round a hedge in front of their escort. Brown said nervously, "They're going to shoot us, Dodge." A moment later, overcome with relief, they saw a lorry filled with men of the Queen's and the DCLI, shouting cheerfully: "Come on, you silly buggers!" and they were driven away into captivity. Brown thought a little about escaping, but he did not feel inclined to try it alone. Most of the others seemed to take the view: "Well, that's me f—ing finished, then", without great remorse. He remained in a POW camp until 1945.

Beyond those who left the battlefield as prisoners, or never left it alive at all, hundreds of thousands of men were more or less seriously wounded. Indeed, it became an exceptional achievement for an infantryman who had landed on D-Day to remain with his unit uninjured until July. The doctors and medical teams, who handled hundreds of cases each day – aided by facilities of unprecedented quality, and above all by the miracle of penicillin – found that many lightly-wounded men were deeply relieved to have escaped the battlefield with honour. "No *Heim ins Reich* for you, Langangke," sympathized the German doctor who patched up an SS panzer lieutenant after a shell fragment had hit him in the forearm – the wound was not sufficiently serious to give him the coveted ticket home. When Corporal Bill Preston was evacuated with serious wounds, his principal sensation was relief that he had done his job without disgracing himself. For most men, the need to continue the job, to sustain their own self-respect, was the principal motive force upon the battlefield.

John Price, a medical orderly with the British 2nd Ox & Bucks, was moved to discover how desperately men wished to be reassured that they would survive, how much words meant to them even when they were suffering the most terrible injuries. For all the wealth of facilities that the Allies possessed, there was seldom a short-cut from pain. One day in the farmyard in the Orne bridgehead where he was based, Price was appalled to see a young lieutenant drive up in a jeep, shouting with the pain of terrible bowel wounds. They laid him on a stretcher on the bonnet, and Price sat beside him as they drove for the casualty clearing station, holding his hand until he died. When Robin Hastings, CO of the Green Howards, was at last wounded by mortar fragments on 27 June, Padre Lovegrove was touched that a man of such courage and forcefulness suddenly showed fearful shock at his own vulnerability, and begged the orderlies who were tending him: "Don't hurt me." Hastings's temper was not improved when he met his detested brigadier as he was being driven to the rear by jeep. The senior officer demanded furiously: "What are you doing back here? I think you're perfectly fit," which, as Hastings remarked acidly afterwards, "showed what a bloody old fool he was."

In the field hospitals, doctors and nurses toiled over the procession of ruined men laid before them in the tents, cutting away mudstained battledress and bloody boots to reveal the interminable tragedies beneath.

Stepping over splinted limbs and stretcher handles [wrote Sister Brenda McBryde] we moved to the next man, a penetrating wound of the chest, needing a large firm dressing to contain those ominous sucking noises and another pillow to keep him upright. Lieutenant-Colonel Harding, one stretcher ahead with Audrey Dare, kept up a running commentary. "Stomach here. Put him number one. Quarter of morphia, Sister. Straight away. Two pints of blood, one of plasma . . ." Gunshot, mortar blasts, mines, incendaries. Limbs, eyes, abdomen, chest. He chewed his pencil. Who had priority? Of all these desperately wounded men, whose need was the most urgent?

. . . Men brought to Resus were always in a serious condition, some of them *in extremis*, past meaningful speech or any sustained communication. Each man was an island in his own desperation, unaware of other men on other stretchers, but their utterances were all the same. There were no impassioned calls to God, no harking back to mother, only an infinitely sad "Oh dear", from colonels and corporals alike. Strangely and mercifully, I have forgotten the deaths, although one bright face I do remember. He was brought into our tent with eyes wide open, looking about him, still remembering to be polite. "I've often wondered what you sisters got up to," he said, with a brave, cheeky smile. Then a sudden look of surprise opened his eyes very wide, and he was dead, still with the smile on his lips. A captain of the Coldstream Guards, the same age as myself, he was caught unawares by death. With part of a shell buried in his back, he had suddenly tweaked his spinal cord and, in one astonished moment, he was gone.[1]

The family of a wounded British soldier received a simple roneoed sheet from the Army Records Office at Ashford. For example, a Mr Griffin of 28 Dean Drive, Stanmore, Middlesex, was addressed:

Sir,

I am directed to inform you, with regret, that a report has been received from the War Office stating that No . . . *6216504* . . . *Private George Edward Griffin, the Middlesex Regiment* . . . was wounded in the north west Europe theatre of War on *3rd August 1944*. The report also states that he sustained . . . *shrapnel wound right buttock* . . . Please accept my sympathy in your anxiety, I am, Sir,

Your obedient servant
Major, for officer i/c Infantry Records[2]

It is a measure of the relative severity of the Normandy fighting, compared with later battles, that hospital admissions as a result of enemy action comprised 9.7 per cent of British soldiers engaged in the first three months following the invasion, falling to 2.6 per cent in the autumn quarter. Accidental injuries attained a remarkable 13.2 per cent in the wake of D-Day, although many of these were very slight. Psychiatric casualties reached a high of 14 per 1,000 among the British in the same period, falling to 11 per 1,000 by winter. Although "battle fatigue" never reached epidemic proportions in the British army, every unit in Normandy suffered its share of men who found themselves utterly unwilling to endure more. One morning, as Charles Mundy and his fellow troop commanders of the 22nd Dragoon Guards stood in their turrets on the start-line before an attack, they were startled by a brief burst of sten gun fire. A man had simply shot himself in the foot rather than endure the assault. An American company commander in Major Randall Bryant's battalion reported to him to declare flatly: "I've had it. You can do anything you want, but I won't go back." Men seldom despised or scorned those who were driven to these acts – they merely pitied them, and prayed that they themselves might not be reduced to such extremities. Major Bryant was only roused to real anger years later, when the ex-company commander showed himself at a veterans' reunion.

One morning, Captain Anthony Babington of the Dorsets heard the call "Stretcher bearer!" in the midst of an incoming barrage, and was surprised to see no reaction from the medical orderly's slit trench, for the man had hitherto been uncommonly quick to reach any wounded soldier. Running across, he found the orderly lying in the bottom of the trench, crying and shaking. He asked if the man was wounded, and received no reply. When the shelling stopped, he told his CO about the stretcher bearer. "Oh, send him back with an NCO and we'll find him a job in the rear," said the colonel. All of them understood, in the Second War, something which had not been contemplated in the First – that each man possessed a limit beyond which he could not be forced. It was merely vital to ensure that such problems did not become epidemic.

A few men deliberately recoiled in disgust from the labour of destruction upon which they were engaged. Lieutenant William Douglas-Home, who was to become a distinguished British playwright and was the brother of a future Prime Minister, had told his fellow-officers for years that if he disapproved of something that was done on the battlefield, he would say so. They did not believe him. Now, in France as a Crocodile troop commander, he was appalled by the impending massed air bombardment of a town to induce its garrison to surrender. He set out on his own initiative to attempt to parley the Germans into giving up, declining to have anything to do with the attack himself. He was stopped, court-martialled, and served a term of imprisonment in Wormwood Scrubs. When it was learned that he had been threatening for months to make a gesture of this sort, his commanding officer was also sacked.

Each night, one of the most painful tasks for the commanding officer of every unit was to write to the families of his men who had died. Most widows and mothers bore the news with pathetic resignation. A few were bitter. On the way home from the Mediterranean, Padre Lovegrove of the Green Howards had listened for hours to an officer talking about the little daughter he looked forward so much to seeing. When they docked, he learnt that she had died while he was on passage. In the following months the officer suffered great strain comforting his wife. In Normandy, he too was killed. Lovegrove received a tragic, savage letter from the man's wife, demanding to know how the padre could pretend that there could be a loving God, who allowed such unspeakable miseries to occur.

That summer, there was no more pitiful measure of the enormity of what was taking place in Normandy than the death announcements in the newspapers of Britain and America: "Died of wounds", "Killed while leading his wing over Normandy", "Killed in action June 1944, aged 23". The London *Times* for 2 July reported on its news pages that "General Eisenhower may . . . look forward to the early use of a port of entry into France following the capture of Cherbourg," while "the time may be approaching when General Montgomery will be strong enough to march boldly inland." But among the columns of announcements on the front page, there were scores like this:

HORLEY – Killed in action in June 1944, Lt. Montague Bernard Horley, RTR Notts Yeomanry, elder son of the Rev. C. M. Horley, The Rectory, Bisley, Surrey, and brother of Sgt. John Midwood Horley, RAFVR, missing presumed killed in January 1942.

On the battlefield, men were reluctantly fascinated by the look of the dead. Lieutenant Wilson of The Buffs gazed down on a cluster of SS infantry, and was impressed by their physical splendour even as they lay lifeless. He was struck by the contrast between these young Nazi supermen and the usual British infantry platoon, "with all its mixtures which were a sergeant-major's nightmare – the tall and short, bandy-legged and lanky, heavy-limbed countrymen and scruffy, swarthy Brummagem boys with eternally undone gaiters."[3] How can we defeat men like these, he wondered, gazing down at the German bodies?

"To me, Normandy will always mean death," said Lindley Higgins, "that yellow-green, waxy look of corpses' hands. Anything that personalized death was upsetting, like seeing a 4th Division flash on a body's helmet."[4]

Keith Douglas, who was killed in Normandy, wrote:

Remember me when I am dead
and simplify me when I'm dead.

As the processes of earth
strip off the colour and the skin
take the brown hair and blue eye

and leave me simpler than at birth,
when hairless I came howling in
as the moon entered the cold sky.

Of my skeleton perhaps,
so stripped, a learned man will say
"He was of such a type and intelligence",
no more.

Some soldiers were supersititious about picking up a dead man's weapon, although few were above looting a German luger pistol if they found one. Almost every man had his private equivalent of touching wood, his secret luck charm. Trooper Steve Dyson of the 107th RAC, a Catholic, carried a little statuette of the Virgin in his tank, wedged between the smoke bombs. Philip Reisler's 2nd Armored tank gunner, a Polish boy from Michigan, convinced himself that he would be hit if he failed to write up his diary each night. Three times in the war when he did not do so, he was wounded. Coming out of action, the whole crew invariably sang over the intercom:

I'm going home where I came from,
where the mocking bird's sitting
on the lilac tree . . .

Men were frequently shocked by the speed at which an entire unit could be transformed into a ruin on the battlefield. One morning in mid-July, the 2nd KRRC were waiting in their half-tracks, on the reverse slope of a hill in the approved manner, to follow up the 43rd Wessex Division in an operation towards Evrecy. Lieutenant Edwin Bramall had just joined the other platoon commanders for a company Orders Group when they came under devastating fire from German self-propelled guns which had worked around to overlook them from high ground on their flank. Bramall dived under a half-track and found himself lying next to his friend Bernard Jackson, a slightly-built Old Harrovian who was senior platoon commander. "Do you think we've had it?" Jackson asked him. A moment later there was a fierce explosion as a shell hit the half-track, and Jackson lay blackened and dead. Bramall emerged from cover to find "quite a *götterdämmerung* situation, with vehicles and motor-cycles on fire everywhere." He suddenly felt a burning sensation in his side, and threw himself to the ground to extinguish flames on his clothing – he had also been hit by a shell fragment. Somehow Bramall and the other surviving platoon commander managed to shepherd the remaining half-tracks into dead ground before he was evacuated to the Regimental Aid Post. When he returned to his unit just a month later, "I found a very different battalion. There had been no dramatic heavy fighting – just a lot of casualties and a lot of shell-shock cases."[5]

The Scots Guards Tank Battalion – which numbered among its officers a future British Home Secretary, a Moderator of the Church of Scotland and an Archbishop of Canterbury – went into its first action, in support of 43rd Wessex Division in July, with all the enthusiam of novices. They gained their objective with the loss only of Major Whitelaw's tank blown up by a mine. But as they stood deployed on a ridge in the midst of virgin country they found, characteristically of many British armoured units, that they had far outstripped their infantry. The officers were assembling for an Orders Group in a wood when they heard a huge explosion and saw a pillar of smoke in the distance. The second-in-command, Major Sidney Cuthbert, said: "I'll go and see what's happening," and dashed across the ridge in his tank, followed by Whitelaw in a second. Suddenly, Whitelaw saw the turret of Cuthbert's Churchill lifted bodily into the air. In the flash of bewilderment so common to men in war, he thought: How odd that the turret should do that. In a few ruthless minutes of fire, a single German self-propelled 88 mm gun, which had stalked unseen behind the Guards' positions, destroyed six of their tanks and killed 15 men.[6]

Every infantryman feared falling victim to a TOT – Time On Target, an artillery shoot carefully synchronized to concentrate the fire of an entire battery or regiment at a precise moment. Major Randall Bryant of the U.S. 9th Division was walking across an orchard near St Lô to a battalion Orders Group, his closest friend, Captain Charles Minton, beside him: "Suddenly everything was exploding. There was blood all over me, and a helmet on the ground with a head inside it. It was Minton's. Three young 2nd lieutenants had just joined us, straight from the beach and Fort Benning. I had told them to sit down and wait to be assigned to companies. They were dead, along with six others killed and 33 wounded in a shoot that lasted only a matter of seconds."

The ambitions of most men in Normandy were pathetically simple: to survive, to finish the job, and to go home. "Everything is okay here," wrote Private Verrier to his parents in Stoke Newington on 24 July:

> and I hope the war news continues to be good. I wonder if anything very serious will come of this stir inside Germany. It may be the beginning of their collapse. I hope so. I would very much like to see this war finish much sooner than the critics estimate. I read so much in the papers, and I begin to think that Jerry is in a tough position, although he has many occupied countries in his hands. I'm quite content to sit and patiently wait for Jerry to collapse. I don't think it will be as easy as the newspapers try to make believe. Dead Germans are the best Germans, especially these fanatical Nazis about 18 to 20.
>
> I also think it is time we were given a break considering the Allies' so-called overwhelming masses of men. Many rumours go round about being sent to a rest camp, letters from Monty congratulating the division on doing such a fine job, which you have probably read in the papers, all of which are hardly worth taking any notice of as we still sit in the front line, wet dugouts, dirty clothes, no bath and very little comfort, and I'm beginning to wonder if once again we have been forgotten. I suppose one day, certain people will realise that we are human beings and not machines of war.
>
> Sam mentioned that he has applied to try to get posted to France. Gosh – if I had his opportunity now to stop in England, I know what I would do with voluntary applications. He would be crazy to come out here, with Lily expecting a baby so soon, and the flying bomb raids at home. Surely he wil not be upgraded to A1. If he does come I sincerely hope he gets a job with a GHQ well behind the line . . .[7]

Early in August, John Hein of the U.S. 1st Divison came upon three unposted letters written by German soldiers in Normandy. He never knew which unit their authors came from, what rank they held, what fate overtook them. But the densely penned scrawls seem to reflect the equally simple, troubled emotions of all but the fanatical SS, now losing ground in Normandy against appalling odds.

My Irmi-love,

. . . It doesn't look very good, that would be saying too much, but nonetheless there is no reason to paint too black a picture. You know the high spirits with which I face things, which allow me to stroll through difficult situations with some optimism and a lot of luck. Above all there are so many good and elite divisions in our near-encirclement that we must get through somehow. The most difficult thing has been and remains the enemy air force . . . it is there at dawn, all day, at night, dominating the roads. Sadly my dog was pinched yesterday by soldiers passing through. I should so like to have taken him back to Germany, but it was not to be. The last three days we have had the most wonderful summer weather – sun, warmth, blue skies – so utterly in contrast to everything else around us. Ah well, it must turn out alright in the end. Don't lose heart, I'll get through this somehow as I always do. A thousand loving kisses to you and the children, your FERD.

My darling wife,

Yet another day. Nowadays I am grateful to the good Lord for every dawn he lets me wake. When I listen to the guns at night, my thoughts wander back home to you, my dearest, and I wonder whether I shall ever see you again. You will have to be prepared not to receive any letters from me for some time. I shall have to cope with great difficulties. May the good Lord be always with me as he has been! I long for you all! How much I would now like to look at your dear pictures, but my kit is far away and I am unlikely to get it back. Should I not return home then you, my treasure, will have to bear this lot too with courage. I leave you our dear boys, in them you will have me too. Your dear little Ortwin and our little Wilfried will be your dear Karl to you. I would so like to go with you after our victory into a lovely and happy future. Many thousands of loving greetings and kisses to you, my dear, good, loyal little wife and to my dear children from your dear Daddy! Farewell! God bless you! KARL

My dear Heather-love,

Do my letters still reach you? Nonetheless I will talk to you rather than mourn to you. One day the light of truth and clarity will shine over this time of humiliation. I just went for a walk in the hot sun to Bagnoles. I did not get there. On the way, I picked a sprig of heather and wore it on my breast. All nature's creatures were out – how high and low the bees, bumblebees, insects hummed, just like in 1926. Today there is another accompaniment as well, spreading death and destruction. I am constantly surprised how calmly I take it all. Is it because of the rocklike certainty of your love? I have written a letter which you should open later, if I don't return. I don't know if it will reach you. But you know what I have to say to you and the children. I have left my affairs in order. What love can express I have already done. The children are on their way, already independent, and will find a path through whatever befalls them. It will not be easy in this chaos, but life is never handed to us on a plate.

Last night we had a little "soldier's hour" and sang our soldiers' and folk songs into the night. What would a German be without a song? The evening sky glowed with fire and explosions. One always thinks the earth brings forth new life, but now it is death. What new order will emerge from this devil's symphony? Can a vision, strong in faith, be born into a new world? The social order rooted in National Socialism cannot be delayed for ever.

Enough of that . . . What remains is great love and loyalty, the acknowledgement of the eternal source of life. I take you and the girls in my arms in gratitude for all you have given me, your FRITZ.

"It was quite against logic to suppose that you were destined to survive the war," wrote Andrew Wilson. "All the appearance of things was against it. You saw a pair of boots sticking out from a blanket, and they looked exactly like your own; there was no ground for thinking that the thing that had come to the owner of these boots was not going to come just as casually to you . . . So before going into action he would utter a phrase articulately beneath his breath: 'Today I may die.' It was a kind of propitiation; and yet he could never quite believe in it, because that would have defeated its purpose . . ."[8]

8 Crisis of confidence

The fall of Caen

By early July, the struggle for Normandy was inflicting almost equal misery upon the German, British and American armies – the first having by far greater cause for it. The defenders knew that their forces were being inexorably ground down, and that they could not hope for tolerable replacements. Many of their difficulties of manpower, armour, supplies and ammunition were known to the Allies through Ultra. Yet it was small comfort to read the Germans' gloomy signals about their predicament when, on the battlefield, the force and effectiveness of their resistance seemed quite undiminished. Meanwhile, the men of the invading army were growing weary. The summer was slipping away, and the disturbing prospect of autumn weather in the Channel lay ahead. The safe refuge of the Brittany ports still seemed many miles and many battles away. What if FORTITUDE abruptly collapsed, and Rommel brought down powerful reinforcements from Fifteenth Army? What if the German flying bomb campaign, already causing so much alarm in England, intensified and gave way to new and more deadly secret weapons? The problem of infantry casualties, a matter of concern to the Americans, had become a crisis for the British. Sir Ronald Adam, the Adjutant-General, paid a personal visit to Montgomery to warn him about the shortage of replacements. Already battalions had been broken up to fill the ranks of others in the line; now came the possibility that entire divisions might have to be disbanded.

After the excitement of the capture of Cherbourg and the northern Cotentin, on 3 July the American VIII Corps, along with a division from VII Corps, began a new southward offensive in driving rain, mist and low cloud. Within the first days, it became bogged down in the mire of now-familiar difficulties: green formations, and stubborn defensive tactics which destroyed momentum. If British commanders were too slow to sack incompetent subordinates, their American counterparts were almost too swift. Now, there was a new spate of dismissals of divisional and regimental commanders in Bradley's army. The Americans were to discover in north-west Europe that it was easier to remove officers than to find more effective newcomers to replace them. As the months went by, their enthusiasm for purges declined, and they concluded that it was more profitable to give commanders time to settle down and learn their business than to remove them immediately after their formation's first failure. Eisenhower wrote to Marshall about the stagnation of First Army's push south: "The going is extremely tough, with three main causes responsible. The first of these, as always, is the fighting quality of the German soldier."[1] The others he identified as the terrain and the weather, which was hampering air support.

Meanwhile, on the eastern flank, Second Army was fighting the tough, slow-moving battle that at last gained its men a large part of the ruins of Caen. For almost a month since the landings, the British and Canadian 3rd Divisions had endured the frustrations of static warfare around Cambes wood, Carpiquet and other landmarks that they first beheld on 6 or 7 June. On the night of 7 July, 450 heavy aircraft of Bomber Command attacked Caen, principally with delayed-action bombs, in an operation designed to clear the way for an assault by I Corps the following morning. Hundreds of thousands of men of Second Army watched in awe as the waves of bombers droned steadily over the city, letting loose their loads and turning away, some bleeding smoke and flame as they slipped from the sky. Amid the rumble of constant explosions from the city, a great pall of smoke and dust rose upwards, shrouding the houses and factories. The use of the heavy bombers reflected the belief of Montgomery and the Allied high command that they must now resort to desperate measures to pave the way for a ground assault. Afterwards, this action came to be regarded as one of the most futile air attacks of the war. Through no fault of their own, the airmen bombed well back from the forward line to avoid the risk of hitting British troops, and inflicted negligible damage upon the German defences. Only the old city of Caen paid the full price.

About a quarter of the citizens of Caen had departed before the bombers came, urged by both the Germans and the local prefect. Many more remained, fearful for their homes and possessions, and arguing that "to evacuate is only to escape Germans to meet other Germans, to avoid bombs and shells to meet other bombs and shells."[2] Nothing had prepared them to expect the devastating rain of explosives from the massed air attack. As the sound of the bombers faded, "a great silence fell over the town, broken only by the cries of the wounded and the sound of falling masonry from burning buildings."[3] The *Palais de l'Université* was in flames, the initial fires in its chemistry department having spread in minutes to other parts of the building. Hopeless little groups of firemen struggled to draw water from the Odon, since the mains had been blasted in a hundred places. 38 civilians died in one cellar, 50 were killed and wounded in a single street. The survivors were so terrorized by the destruction around them that, even as the Germans at last began to withdraw through the streets, most inhabitants clung to the shelter of their cellars.

When I Corps jumped off on Operation CHARNWOOD the next morning, the troops were heartened by the memory of the air attack. But they quickly discovered that the Germans were resisting as tenaciously as ever. Meyer's men of 12th SS Panzer remained the core of the defence, apparently indestructible even though their ranks had been decimated by weeks of heavy fighting without replacements. Two days of desperate battle cost some British infantry battalions 25 per cent of their strength. They won through to the northern bank of the Orne, in the middle of the utterly desolated city, but could go no further. The Germans still held the critical high ground of the Bourgébus Ridge to the south and, nearer at hand, the steelworks of Colombelles, from which their observation posts could mark every British movement. Too much blood had been shed and too many weeks had elapsed for possession of the shattered ruins to offer any more to most thoughtful British commanders than a ghastly echo of other ruins, other empty victories, almost 30 years before. From CHARNWOOD, there was not even the compensation of having "written down" significant German forces.

While the British and Canadian 3rd Divisions painfully battered their way into Caen, further west 43rd Wessex and its supporting armour suffered 2,000 casualties in two days of renewed fighting for Hill 112, the commanding position beyond the Odon which had been lost in the last stages of EPSOM. Once again, the formidable fighting power of 12th SS Panzer forced Thomas's men into bloody difficulties. Like so many other

British assaults, that of 10 July began well in the wake of the huge bombardment, with the leading units reaching Eterville and well up the slopes of 112 by 8.00 a.m. Corporal Chris Portway was a 21-year-old section commander in the 4th Dorsets: "They plod along and do the job – not death or glory boys like the paratroops," the sort of comment which might be made about many solidly dependable British county regiments. Urged on by their colonel's hunting horn, they reached Eterville without serious casualties. Portway fought a fierce little private battle in its churchyard, pursuing two Germans between the gravestones until he reached them with a grenade in the church itself. He was dismayed to meet his commanding officer among the ruins, asking helplessly: "What's happening, corporal?" The colonel appeared to have lost all grip on events. But the day's work had been done at tolerable cost. They were digging in around Eterville, pleased to find themselves alongside a château painted with huge red crosses, "because the Germans were usually quite good about trying not to hit hospitals,"[4] when they were suddenly summoned to a new Orders Group and told that they must press on to the next village, Maltot.

Without enthusiasm, but also without knowledge of what lay ahead except that a battalion of the Hampshires was in trouble, they advanced in extended line through the cornfields towards the village. They reached an orchard, and suddenly found themselves under intense German DF[5] fire. With flame and smoke all around them, they pressed on, to meet machine-gun and tank fire from a screen of Tigers dug into pits covering Maltot. "They knocked us down in lines . . ." Portway and other survivors took shelter for a moment in an empty tank pit, and saw a German glance over the rim and reach back to throw a grenade down on them before a quick-thinking Dorset shot him. They ran from the hole to a house in which they hastily cleared a field of fire. The corporal felt a moment of revulsion about bringing the battle into some unknown family's home: "There we were, wrecking this house, and I suddenly thought – 'How would I feel if this was mine?" Then a more pressing problem intervened. A noise upstairs showed that they were not alone. There was a fierce exchange of grenades and small-arms fire with the Germans above. They fought from house to house for some time until, without warning, a devastating artillery barrage began to fall among them. Portway learned later that it came from British guns. The order had been given for the brigade to withdraw from

Maltot, but it never reached the survivors of the Dorsets. Portway threw himself into a ditch, and a handful of others fell in on top of him. When the guns at last stopped, he wondered why nobody rose. He heard German voices, and lay motionless until he found one of the men above him being moved, and looked up into the face of the enemy. All the others on top of him in the ditch were dead. He felt a sense of unreality: "You imagine being wounded, being killed. But you never think of being captured. You think that when you've had a chat, they'll let you go home. I couldn't believe that I'd never see the unit again." The SS treated Portway unusually well, "much better than we did German prisoners. It was when one got further back that the nastiness started."

Portway's experience was almost precisely mirrored by that of Private Zimmer of 12th SS Panzer who was in Eterville the same day. Zimmer, as his narrative makes clear, was cast in a somewhat less heroic mould than some of his colleagues:

From 6.30 to 8.00 a.m. again heavy machine-gun fire. Then Tommy attacks with great masses of infantry and many tanks. We fight as long as possible but we realize we are in a losing position. By the time the survivors try to pull back, we realize that we are surrounded. In our sector, we had driven back the British infantry attack, but they had bypassed us to left and right. I moved back as fast as I could under the continuous firing. Others who tried to do the same failed. When the small-arms fire stopped our own guns got going. I lay there in the midst of it all. I still cannot understand how I escaped, with shelling falling two or three metres away, splinters tearing around my ears. By now I had worked my way to within 200 metres of our own lines. It was hard work, always on my stomach, only occasionally up on hands and knees. The small-arms fire began again, and the English infantry renewed their attack. My hopes dwindled. The advancing Tommies passed five or six paces away without noticing me in the high corn. I was almost at the end of the my tether, my feet and elbows in agony, my throat parched. Suddenly the cover thinned out and I had to cross an open field. In the midst of this, wounded Englishmen passed within ten metres without seeing me. Now I had to hurry. There were only ten metres to go to the next belt of corn. Suddenly three Tommies appeared and took me prisoner. Immediately I was given a drink and a cigarette. At the concentration point for prisoners I met my *unterscharführer* and other comrades of my company . . .[6]

It was a battle of shattering intensity even by the standards of Normandy. Brigadier Michael Carver, who had taken over 4th Armoured Brigade at half an hour's notice a few days earlier,

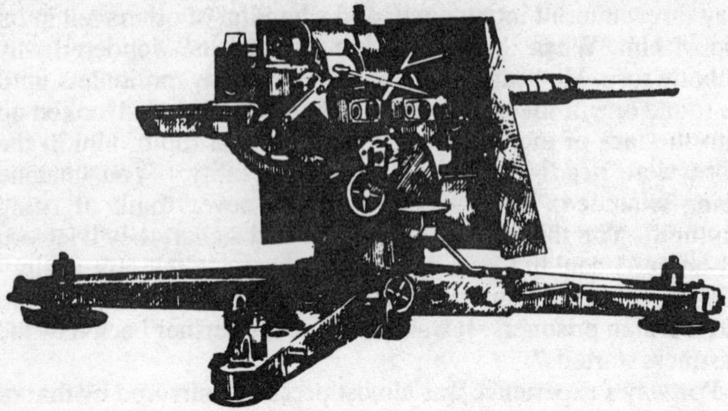

The 88 mm dual-purpose gun was the decisive force in the German destruction of many Allied tank attacks in Normandy, above all in the open country on the British flank, where its long reach could be exploited to best effect. It was, quite simply, the best gun produced by any combatant nation in the war, with a formidable killing power against all Allied tanks.

found himself compelled to draw his revolver to halt fleeing infantrymen, including an officer. Amid the blackened, leafless trees on the slopes of Hill 112 itself, the 5th Duke of Cornwall's Light Infantry attacked, two companies up, after the Somersets failed to gain the summit. Lieutenant David Priest's company commander had been killed shortly before, and he found himself leading his company forward. Their vehicles drove to the start-line over the bodies of British infantry spreadeagled across the road. They took a wrong turning and came under fire. The men dismounted and shook out for the advance. Priest had put his own platoon in the rear, but quickly found himself compelled to pass it forward when the point platoons were ravaged by mortar and machine-gun fire. Then he felt a blow. At first, it made him imagine that he had been struck with a pickaxe. Only after a few moments lying shocked on the grass did he understand that he had been hit in the chest by a machine-gun bullet. He felt somebody undoing his pouches and taking out his grenades. The he heard the acting battalion commander shouting, before he died, that he could not breathe. Priest lay gazing upwards, watching each side's mortar bombs soar unhurriedly across the sky. There was more fierce small-arms fire, and he was frightened of being hit again. When darkness came he felt a little better. He managed to drag himself back towards the British line until he was challenged by a Somersets sentry.

Yet still the nightmare was not ended. That night, 12th SS Panzer counter-attacked. Priest was waiting at the rendezvous where the carriers picked up casualties, when a German tank suddenly crashed through the trees almost on top of him. Wounded men screamed as they were crushed beneath its tracks, and flares began to burst overhead as the defenders struggled to pinpoint the threat. The tank blundered away into the darkness, and the stretcher-bearers came. Priest learned that he had a clean entry and exit wound. He felt deeply grateful that he was not maimed or disfigured. Like every rifle company officer, he had long ago accepted the inevitability of being hit somewhere, at some time. It was six weeks before he walked again, and 1945 before he returned to his battalion.

The self-propelled 17-pounder M10s of E Troop, 129th Battery, left the start-line with the Hampshires and the supporting Churchill infantry tanks at 5.30 a.m. They had landed in France ten days before, and this was their first action of the war. German mortar and artillery fire began to fall amongst them soon after they set off, and the infantrymen of the Hampshires huddled behind the Churchills and E Troop's tank destroyers as they crawled forward through the barrage. Sergeant Burnell's gun was hit a few yards beyond Eterville by a mortar bomb which landed directly in its open turret; just two of the crew escaped wounded. The troop commander's gun received a direct hit from an 88 mm shell a few yards short of Maltot. Only he himself and an NCO were able to leap down and escape alive. A third gun's turret was jammed by fire and its aerial shot away. The crew baled out, expecting it to "brew up". When it failed to do so they remounted, with the exception of the wireless operator, who declined to leave the slit trench in which he had taken refuge. Then it became obvious that the attack had failed. The two surviving guns withdrew, bringing back the survivors of the other ruined M10. Of 20 men in the guns which had gone forward, six were dead, four wounded, one missing. Sergeant Jim Stephens, who had served with the battery since 1939, was heartbroken to have been left behind with the echelon, when the troop of which he was so proud went forward for the first time.

Now, he looked appalled at the return of the survivors, and the blank and shocked face of the young troop commander, Lieutenant Wimpey. The adjutant had recovered the gun whose turret had received a direct hit. Wimpey told Sergeant Stephens that they must bury its crew. Stephens never forgot the experience.

The explosion of the mortar in that confined space had devastated everything inside. The 17 pdr and .50 calibre ammunition had gone up. Lying on the floor of the turret was what was left of the crew, burnt to a cinder with their teeth bared in some kind of grin. I cried, having known them all for so long – Jimmy Burrell, a cockney whose wife had presented him with a baby a few weeks before D-Day, who used to hang a pair of bootees in the turret every time he went out; Dick Greenwood, no more than 5′ 2″, a Devonian from Newton Abbot who used to be E troop's storekeeper, but insisted on getting aboard an M10 as a gunner; Phillips, only 18, hardly knew what it was all about. I remember him being sick on one occasion after drinking too much, and me making him clear it all up. With some reverence Lt. Wimpey and I began to lift them out and place them in blankets. In some cases we had to use a shovel to get them off the floor, for so intense was the heat that they had become fused to it. We buried them at Marcelet, by the side of the Bayeux–Caen road. The regimental padre said a few words, the battery carpenter constructed wooden crosses, a few shots were fired, and so we left them.[7]

It was a little scene played out a hundred times daily on both sides of the Normandy line. Hill 112 was held briefly by Priest's shattered battalion of the Duke of Cornwall's Light Infantry, only to be lost to a German counter-attack.

Montgomery was now compelled to endure a crisis of confidence in his leadership which would have cracked the nerve of a more sensitive man. He had always been the object of animosity within the huge headquarters staff at SHAEF in England, and unloved by many of Bradley's Americans. The tensions now broke into open criticism. Commander Butcher, the embodiment of all gossip-ridden staff officers, wrote after his first visit to France on 1 July: "Some of the people I talked to venture that Monty has been too slow to attack and thus permitted the Germans to get set in fixed positions and to bring up reserves."[8] Patton, an unconcealed enemy, wrote venomously in his diary after a trip to Montgomery's Tactical Headquarters on 7 July: "Montgomery went to great lengths explaining why the British had done nothing." Eisenhower, himself under intense pressure from Washington and his own staff, frustrated by his own inability directly to influence the events for which he bore the huge responsibility, wrote an unhappy letter to the Commander-in-Chief of 21st Army Group that day expressing his concern about the German build-up: "It appears to me that we must use all possible energy in a determined effort to prevent the risk of a stalemate or of facing the necessity of fighting a major defensive battle with the slight depth we now have in the bridgehead . . . We have not yet attempted a major full-dress attack on the left flank supported by everything we could bring to bear . . ."[9]

The American press had become openly impatient with the lack of progress in France, causing a degree of concern in Washington that, as always, far outweighed the worry the British press could cause any British government. It was being suggested that the western Allies were content to mark time while the Russians did the hard fighting to defeat Hitler's armies. Even more dangerous to Montgomery's position was Churchill's growing impatience. The Prime Minister was at pains to remind Eisenhower, a few days after the landings, that the Supreme Commander had only to express his dissatisfaction with any British officer, "no matter what his rank", for him to be removed. Churchill had convinced himself that if there was no rapid break-through after D-Day, it might be a year or more before the Allies reached the Seine. His memory of Flanders haunted all his visions of the battle for France in 1944, especially as he read the infantry casualty lists. On the night of 6 July, Churchill furiously denounced Montgomery to Brooke. He had never warmed to his cold, awkward commander: now, remembering Montgomery's bold declarations at the St Paul's briefing about rapid armoured thrusts and the urgent need to "peg out claims inland", he felt that these intentions had been betrayed. Brooke was driven to defend his protégé with equal anger: "I flared up and asked him if he could not trust his generals for five minutes instead of continuously abusing them and belittling them."[10]

The air chiefs divided their ill-will between Montgomery and the hapless Leigh-Mallory. Tedder felt a persistent lack of confidence in the Commander-in-Chief of 21st Army Group, which he displayed with all the force of his personality. "It seemed clear to me that Montgomery did not attach sufficient importance to the pressing time factor. Few weeks of summer remained. Our urgent need was to get across the Seine."[11] Tedder was a man of genuine stature, and it is impossible to saddle him with the personal malice and small-mindedness that afflicted some of his subordinates. He sincerely believed that he possessed an understanding of the priorities of the land campaign which Montgomery lacked. But as Deputy Supreme Commander, he suffered all the handicaps and frustrations that are the lot of a second-in-command in any military organization: he was privy to all debate but lacked executive power. If Leigh-Mallory was not permitted to exercise executive authority, Tedder showed a marked reluctance to do so. He was invariably consulted and frequently intervened in the air debate, but he never accepted full responsibility for air operations. His intelligence and force of personality were not in doubt, but it is questionable whether he was able to employ these to best effect as Eisenhower's deputy, and whether his understanding of the ground campaign was sufficient to justify his chronic disloyalty to Montgomery, and his promise to Eisenhower of personal support if the Supreme Commander saw fit to sack his ground-force commander.

With all these dangerous currents swirling in his rear, Montgomery sat in the camouflaged caravans of his Tactical Headquarters, surrounded by his pet puppies and canaries, and pondered the course of the battle. One of his biographers, the war correspondent Alan Moorehead, wrote of his supposed conceit and gracelessness, then added that "these vices, if they existed in him, had also distilled a virtue which was regrettably lacking at times among the officers struggling up to a high command: he was nobody's sycophant, he could not be wined and dined into an amenable frame of mind, he could not be impressed by a show of authority nor were his wits clouded by ceremony."[12] Montgomery changed his plans in Normandy, but it cannot be proved that he did so because of the pressure of his enemies and rivals. If anything, the charge against him is that he became too isolated from the political and politico-military realities, too ready to absorb himself exclusively in the battle within the monastic loneliness of his Tactical Headquarters. His Chief of Staff talked freely to the Commander-in-Chief when he saw him, but there is no evidence that Montgomery unburdened himself of his innermost thoughts and hopes to de Guingand or any other man. Yet he possessed the great virtue of accepting the battlefield as he found it, and adjusting to its exigencies without complaint. He was seen to considerable advantage at a meeting of his commanders on 10 July, at which Bradley frankly admitted that the American attack southwards had failed.

> Monty quietly replied: "Never mind. Take all the time you need, Brad." [Dempsey related later] Then he went on tactfully to say: "If I were you I think I should concentrate my forces a little more" – putting two fingers together on the map in his characteristic way. Then Monty turned to me and said: "Go on hitting: drawing the German strength, especially some of the armour, onto yourself – so as to ease the way for Brad."[13]

it seems significant that while Eisenhower became restless and unsympathetic to Montgomery as the Normandy battle developed – or rather, in the Supreme Commander's view, failed sufficiently to do so – Bradley did not complain about 21st Army Group's commander. Later, he would become one of Montgomery's most bitter critics. But "during these operations in the lodgement," Bradley wrote, "where Montgomery bossed the U.S. First Army as part of his 21st Army Group, he exercised his Allied authority with wisdom, forbearance, and restraint. At no time did he probe into First Army with the indulgent manner he sometimes displayed among those subordinates who were also his own countrymen."[14] Harmony between the two men at this stage may also have been assisted by Bradley's consciousness of the shortcomings of some of his own formations. It was only afterwards, when the Americans had carried out their sweeping dash through Brittany and across to Argentan, that exhilaration about their own achievement and British sensitivity about Second Army's painful march to Falaise fostered jealousies and resentments that persisted through the campaign.

GOODWOOD

On 7 July, the eve of CHARNWOOD, Montgomery's chief planner, Brigadier Charles Richardson, submitted a report on more far-reaching objectives than Caen. He argued, first, that it was necessary for Second Army to embark on a major offensive rather than merely to pursue a succession of limited operations; second, that in view of the desperate need to avoid heavy infantry casualties, the obvious course was to embark upon an armoured assault. Tanks were one commodity with which the British were amply provided. Indeed, there was scarcely sufficient fighting room within the beachhead for the proper employment of all the armour they possessed. At that date they outnumbered the Germans by four to one in tanks and two to one in infantry, while on the American front the ratios were eight to one and three to two. Bradley's men were holding a line 108,000 yards long, compared with the 77,500 yards in the hands of the British. On 10 July, Dempsey outlined for Montgomery a plan to employ massed armour in an attempt to break through the German defences from the constricted Orne bridgehead, still little larger than that gained by 6th Airborne Division early in June. Montgomery approved. The details of Operation GOODWOOD were settled two days later: all three British armoured divisions would attack, under the command of General O'Connor's VIII Corps, along a corridor blasted open by massed bomber forces. The aim was to strike fast through the German defences while the enemy were still reeling from the air bombardment, seize the Bourgébus ridge in the first hours and thence race on across the great sweep of open country beyond. The tanks would drive headlong for Falaise. Meanwhile, Simonds' II Canadian Corps would attack south from the centre of Caen in an effort to secure the rest of the city. I and XII Corps would launch subsidiary infantry attacks, with support from the independent armoured brigades, on the flanks.

"The Second Army is now very strong," Montgomery wrote to Brooke on the 14th, "it has in fact reached its peak and can get no stronger. It will in fact get weaker as the manpower situation begins to hit us. Also, the casualties had affected the fighting efficiency of divisions; the original men were very well trained; reinforcements are not so well trained, and the fact is beginning to become apparent and will have repercussions on what we can do . . . So I have decided that the time has come to have a real 'showdown' on the eastern flank, and to loose a corps of three armoured divisions into the open country about the Caen-Falaise road."[1] Eisenhower wrote to Montgomery of the GOODWOOD plan: "I am confident that it will reap a harvest from all the sowing you have been doing during the past weeks. With our whole front acting aggressively against the enemy so that he is pinned to the ground, O'Connor's plunge into his vitals will be decisive . . . I am viewing the prospects with the most tremendous optimism and enthusiasm. I would not be at all surprised to see you gaining a victory that will make some of the 'old classics' look like a skirmish between patrols."[2] It is interesting and important to notice that after the war Bradley, the most unlikely man to provide spurious alibis for

Montgomery, declared that he had never expected GOODWOOD to be anything other than a supporting operation for the American COBRA, which was originally scheduled to jump off at much the same time. Yet if Montgomery's hopes and objectives were really so limited, it was politically suicidal for him to allow Eisenhower, Tedder and even Brooke to be deluded about them. There was a perfectly sound military argument for the British to mount only a limited offensive. But there is no hint of evidence that Montgomery sought to explain GOODWOOD in these terms to any of his patrons in England, above all Brooke.

Every previous operation that Montgomery had mounted in Normandy was skilfully conceived, soundly based, offering a real prospect of success at its H-Hour. By the time GOODWOOD was launched, for political and moral reasons he was more seriously in need of a victory than at any time since D-Day. Yet from its inception the operation was flawed. It relied heavily upon surprise to gain the high ground which dominated the British line of advance, yet called for the movement of 8,000 tanks and armoured vehicles across the Orne to the assembly points. Until the armour had cleared the start-line, the artillery could not deploy to provide the massive bombardment which was such an important asset to any operation. Days before GOODWOOD was set in motion, 51st Highland Division's engineers had sown new minefields to cover their own positions, which could not now be properly cleared for the armoured advance. Only narrow corridors would be available through which the tanks could progress. Most damning of all, the Germans were expecting them. Sepp Dietrich claimed after the war that he had heard the British tanks coming by using an old trick he had learned in Russia, of putting his ear to the ground. Perhaps he did. But long before the tanks began to roll from the start-line, German intelligence had achieved one of its few important battlefield successes in Normandy, by alerting Rommel to the imminent British move against Bourgébus. General Eberbach of Panzer Group West reacted by adopting perhaps the most formidable defensive deployments of the entire campaign: five lines of tanks and anti-tanks guns, directly confronting VIII Corps' axis of advance. 36 hours before GOODWOOD was set in motion, Ultra interceptions revealed to the British that Field-Marshal Hugo Sperrle of Luftflotte 3 had signalled a forecast of a major British attack, "to take place south-eastwards from Caen about the night of 17–18th".

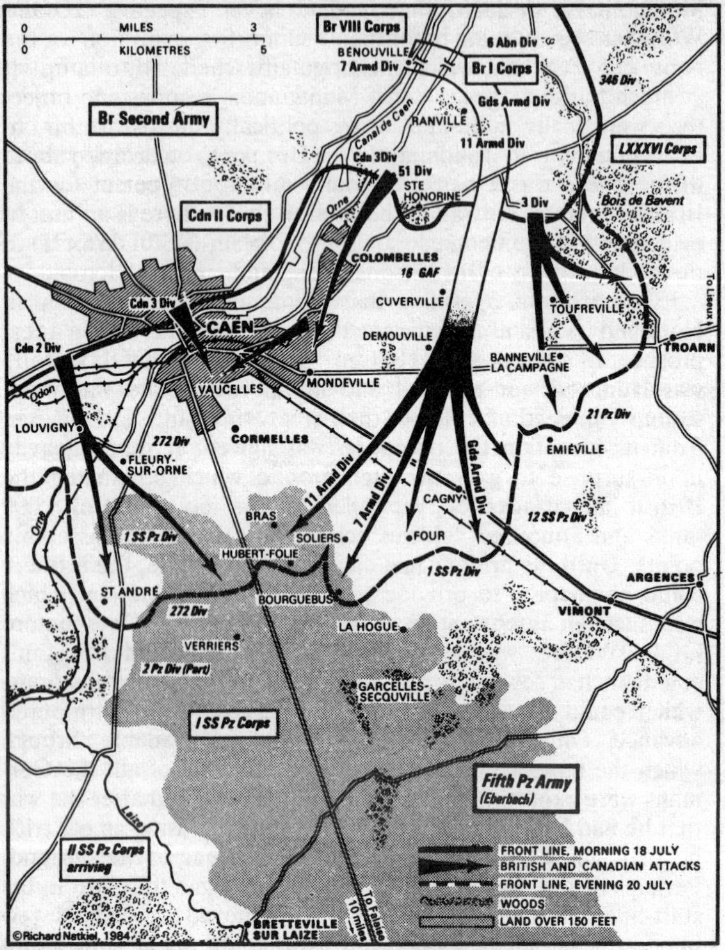

Operation GOODWOOD: 18–20 July

In Montgomery's directive to Dempsey before the battle, all mention of Falaise as an objective had vanished; a sudden onset of caution seemed to have overcome him. But Dempsey himself was still full of brilliant hopes as he transferred his Tactical HQ to a position alongside that of O'Connor, where he could oversee the battle at close quarters. "What I had in mind was to seize all the crossings of the Orne from Caen to Argentan," Second Army's commander said after the war.[3]

Carlo D'Este, the author of an important recent study of the Normandy battle, pays tribute to General O'Connor's understanding of the vital need for close armoured–infantry co-operation in GOODWOOD. O'Connor sought to employ some of the gunners' self-propelled chassis as infantry personnel carriers for the battle, and was much vexed by Dempsey's refusal to let them be used. Yet General "Pip" Roberts of 11th Armoured, probably the ablest British divisional commander in Normandy, suffered deep misgivings when he studied O'Connor's plan for GOODWOOD, and discovered that the armour and infantry had been given separate objectives. He felt so strongly about the error of this decision that he recorded his view in writing, which cause O'Connor to reply that if Roberts lacked the conviction to lead the attack according to his plan, one of the other armoured divisions could relieve the 11th as spearhead. Robert reluctantly acquiesced. But he believed that O'Connor did not understand the proper handling of armour on a European battlefield.[4] Other senior officers echoed Roberts' lack of confidence not only in the corps commander himself, but also in his staff.

Between 5.30 and 8.30 a.m. on the morning of 18 July, one of the greatest-ever air bombardments of ground forces was unleashed upon Panzer Group West by heavy and medium bombers of the RAF and USAAF. In three waves they attacked the German positions confronting O'Connor's armoured divisions: tanks were hurled bodily into the air or buried by earth and rubble; men were deafened and stunned for days or blasted into fragments; guns were wrecked and twisted on their mountings; fuel and ammunition exploded. Shortly after H-Hour, a scout car of the Inns of Court Regiment reported exultantly that it was well on the way to 11th Armoured's objectives, and could see no evidence of opposition. "I said 'Jolly good show' and didn't believe a word of it," said Roberts tersely.[5] His scepticism was rapidly justified.

One of the great surprises of warfare in the twentieth century has been the power of soldiers to survive what would seem to be overwhelming concentrations of high explosive, and emerge to fight with skill and determination. So it was now with the men of Panzer Group West. The leading units of 11th Armoured Division jumped off promptly at 7.30 a.m. and made rapid progress for the first two hours, before meeting heavy and stiffening resistance. Around the village of Cagny, just four 88 mm flak guns of the 16th Luftwaffe Field Division had escaped the air bombardment. At pistol point, Colonel Hans von Luck of 21st Panzer Division compelled their commander to abandon his delusions about his anti-aircraft role, and to engage the advancing British tanks at once. 16 of 11th Armoured's Shermans fell to these guns alone. It was 4.00 p.m. before the Guards Armoured Division entered Cagny. As other British units crossed the Caen-Vimont railway embankment and attempted to push on towards Bourgébus, they met ruthless German tank and anti-tank fire. The vehicle carrying 11th Armoured's sole RAF Forward Air Controller was knocked out in the first two hours, with the result that close air support for the advance was lost. Meanwhile, in the rear, the Guards Armoured and 7th Armoured Divisions had been seriously delayed by the huge traffic jam of vehicles moving along the corridors through British minefields. Without support, the British spearhead of 29th Armoured Brigade was already in serious trouble, only 12,000 yards from its start-line and scarcely through the crust of the deep defences. Trooper John Brown was driving a 17-pounder Sherman Firefly of the 2nd Fife and Forfar Yeomanry. He and his crew left the start-line in a mood of excited optimism, after watching the vast air bombardment, convinced that no German position could have survived such appalling punishment.

It was not long after the earlier euphoria that we realised what was in store for us – 13 tanks, one of our squadrons knocked out, some burning and what remained of their crews either walking or crawling back from the front. Our tanks reached the Caen–Vimont railway close beside a level crossing in the Cagny area. From our position we knocked out two, probably three German tanks, but it was difficult to recognise this in the carnage. We were shooting over the rear of the tank when fire broke out and the order was given to bale out. I tried my hatch but was unable to get it open. Lying on my back over the ammunition in the co-driver's position, a space of about eighteen inches between the shells and the hatch which I was able to open, I pulled myself out, falling to the ground. Lying beside the tank, we realised that it was only our equipment and bedding on the hull which was burning. Pulling this off, I said I would get back into the tank and bring it into the shelter of the house at the level crossing. I had got in and started the engine when suddenly a horrible eruption of molten metal came in through the side immediately behind the ammunition. This was like an acetylene cutter in action. Fortunately I was able to bale out faster than the first time. From there my crewmates and I made our way back to rear echelon in the glider landing fields near Ranville.[6]

Soon after noon, bitterly conscious that his attack was running out of steam, O'Connor organized a new two-pronged thrust to be carried out by 11th Armoured on the right, 7th Armoured's Cromwells on the left.

We moved well for a while [wrote a British reconnaissance vehicle commander, Corporal Peter Roach], until we came to another flat stretch littered with knocked-out Cromwell tanks extending right away to the ridge in front. Delay, frustration, ignorance of what was happening . . . Some shells landed nearby; violent black smoke with a brilliant red centre and large jagged pieces of metal tearing at the unwary. The tank I was following stopped and the commander jumped down swearing. The driver, who had his head out, was hit. I got the lead from his headphones under his arms and we tugged him through the small hatch opening, floppy and inert. Our hands were wet with blood; we laid him on the ground; from his head oozed blood and sticky brains; he quivered and made quacking noises, and then mercifully died. The officer was crying . . .

The light was going slowly and the air warm. I sat on the top of the tank as we ate cold rice pudding from a tin. I looked at my hands gory with dried blood and brains. Nearby two flail tanks were talking on the radios and coming through on my set. The commanders were tired and their nerves were frayed. I could hear the scorn in the voice of A and the almost pleading voice of B as he complained bitterly that A had "pissed off without warning". It was frightening to hear men so open in their dislike on the one hand and dependence on the other. UJ came up on the air, asking my position and then querying my reference. I too was frayed, so I asked if he thought I couldn't read a map or didn't know where I was.[7]

The only regiment of 7th Armoured to approach its point of attack, after escaping the chaos around the Orne, did not reach 29th Brigade's battered squadrons until 5.00 p.m. by which time the latter had suffered 50 per cent tank losses, 11th Armoured losing a total of 126 tanks during the day. Guards Armoured Division lost 60 tanks in this, its first battle. Roberts' foreboding about O'Connor's separation of tanks and infantry had been entirely justified: his armour received no infantry support until 5.00 p.m. Although many officers liked O'Connor, and to this day there are energetic defenders of his conduct of the battles in Normandy, the evidence suggests that he never achieved the "grip" of VIII Corps which had so distinguished his command in the desert. Montgomery's public modifications of his ambitions for GOODWOOD can hardly have critically influenced O'Connor's conduct, when Dempsey declared his own hope that VIII

Corps would get to Falaise. Colonel Brian Wyldbore-Smith, GSO I of 11th Armoured, said flatly of GOODWOOD: "We really did think that this was to be the breakout."[8] Brigadier Richardson, 21st Army Group's BGS Plans, said that "at the time, I thought Goodwood had been a tremendous flop."[9] He subsequently modified his view in the light of post-war evidence that Montgomery only sought to maintain pressure on the eastern flank. But it seems absurd to suppose that GOODWOOD could have been secretly transformed into a limited operation without the acquiescence of Dempsey, the army commander, or the knowledge of the senior staff officers charged with carrying it out.

It becomes even more difficult to believe this in the light of Montgomery's behaviour at the time. In an extraordinary moment of optimism that afternoon – of the kind that did so much to damage his credibility with less sympathetic recipients – Montgomery signalled Brooke: "Operations this morning a complete success . . . The effect of the air bombing was decisive and the spectacle terrific . . . situation very promising and it is difficult to see what the enemy can do just at present."[10] Far more serious, he read to the assembled press corps a disastrously optimistic bulletin about the progress of the attack. Brigadier Williams remembered seeing on Alan Moorehead's face "this wonderful Australian disbelief". Yet in consequence of Montgomery's remarks, on 19 July *The Times* carried the headline, "Second Army breaks through", and quoted the communiqué's assertion that "early this morning British and Canadian troops of the Second Army attacked and broke through into the area east of the Orne and south-east of Caen." Another headline read, "British army in full cry", followed the next day by "Wide corridor through German front". A "Special Correspondent" was "at pains to rebut suggestions of 'setbacks' ".

In reality, the Canadians had gained most of Caen, but the Germans remained in absolute control of the Bourgébus Ridge, which they reinforced strongly during the night. Crerar's men were perhaps more angry and bitter about the disappontments of the battle than O'Connor's patient and long-suffering British troops. "Goodwood had been sold to us as a big deal," said Corporal Dick Raymond of 3rd Canadian Division. "To see those Shermans puffing into black smoke gave us a sick feeling in the stomach. It seemed a futile, clumsy thing." ATLANTIC, the Canadian operation on the GOODWOOD flank, cost Crerar's men 1,965 casualties. Two infantry battalions alone bore the brunt of these – the South Saskatchewans, who lost 215 men, and the Essex Scottish, losing 244. Two days later, after further brutal fighting, 7th Armoured Division had gained part of the ridge, but in the heavy rain and mud which now made the closure of the operation inevitable, the German line was still unbroken. The British had suffered 5,537 casualties and lost 400 tanks, 36 per cent of their armoured strength in France, of which only a proportion could be recovered and repaired. So prodigious were Allied reserves of *matériel* that replacements reached almost every armoured division within 36 hours. The restoration of Montgomery's prestige would take a great deal longer.

In the post-mortems in the wake of GOODWOOD, all manner of suggestions were made about what had gone wrong and what could have been done better. Since the assembly of such a vast force had proved impossible to keep secret, could more have been gained by opening the attack in darkness? Would a shorter interval between the end of the air bombardment and the British approach to the German positions have been decisive? Was the Guards Armoured Division briefed to expect too easy an assault in this, its first battle, and were its units thus too readily overcome by the unexpected strength of the opposition? Could O'Connor have pushed 7th Armoured Division forward faster? Why was there still such lamentable cohesion between tanks and infantry?

The answers to all these questions partially explain the British misfortunes. Yet none of them can mask the bald truth that Second Army sought to attack powerful and skilfully-directed German defences. Major changes of British tactics would have been necessary to bring about a different outcome. A daylight infantry attack across open ground would have been cut to pieces, but a carefully-planned night assault might have yielded dramatic dividends. The airmen were vociferous in their anger about the army's failure to gain a decisive result after calling upon a vast bomber force in support. Nothing, except their own parochialism, could justify such an attitude. Even if the air attack on Caen earlier in the month was misconceived, there were major enemy concentrations to be bombed on the Bourgébus ridge, and substantial damage was inflicted upon these, moral as much as material. The GOODWOOD experience showed the limitations of massive air attack, but it also revealed its value. Only the airmen's obsessive belief that all their squadrons could meanwhile have been better employed over Germany justified their furious reaction.

In the years since the revelation of the Allies' breaking of German ciphers in the Second World War, it has sometimes been assumed that Ultra provided the Allies with absolute knowledge of enemy deployments and capabilities. This is a travesty of the truth. Ultra was of immense value, but its reliability and comprehensiveness varied greatly from day to day, according to luck, the extent to which local German units were signalling by radio rather than using land-lines, and the speed of the decrypters at Bletchley Park. O'Connor's forces embarked upon GOODWOOD with no concept of the strength of the German defences they were to engage, while the Germans had been using observation posts, prisoner interrogation and aerial reconnaissance to powerful effect. This was the first and last occasion of the Normandy campaign on which von Kluge's men were able to fight a battle on terms that suited them, albeit at a cost which they could much less well afford than the Allies.

The British were attacking across more open country than in any battle of the campaign thus far. So much has been said about the difficulties of fighting amid the hedges of the *bocage*, that it seems worth emphasizing the equal difficulties of advancing against powerful defences over an unbroken field of fire. Tanks could use open country to great advantage if they could manoeuvre around enemy positions. But where they were confronted by a continuous line of defences, even a small number of well-handled German tanks and guns could do enormous execution. Here, perhaps more than in any other battle in north-west Europe, the British paid the price for their lack of a survivable battle tank; armour of the weight of the German Tigers and Panthers might have battered a path up the Bourgébus ridge – a feat that the Shermans and Cromwells were too frail to achieve.

It has been suggested above that blame for the failure of some of Montgomery's June battles in Normandy lay more with those charged with directing and fighting them than with the planners who conceived them. Yet GOODWOOD failed because the concept, the plan, the preparations were unsound. The British were sometimes accused of being unimaginative in their use of armoured forces by comparison with the Americans. Below Bourgébus ridge in July, they attempted an extraordinarily ambitious massed tank operation which, had it succeeded, might have rivalled that of Patton a few weeks later. But there was an important difference between the British and later American operations: in the first, the German defence was unbroken: the old military axiom about the hazards of employing unsupported cavalry against an unbroken square still held good. Colonel Brian Wyldbore-Smith, GSO I of 11th Armoured, argued convincingly that it was a great mistake to launch the attack with massed tanks: "One squadron per infantry battalion would have been ample. More than that simply confused the issue." Here he touched upon the very heart of the GOODWOOD failure. The forces assembled for the operation were not those judged necessary to meet the ground or the nature of the defences, but those which the British then felt willing to expend – their tanks. The critical problem of manpower and infantry casualties thus directly influenced an important tactical decision.

As a result of GOODWOOD, Montgomery's prestige within the Allied high command suffered damage from which it never recovered. Eisenhower was disappointed and angered by the gulf between Second Army's promise and performance. His staff became genuinely concerned about the rise in the Supreme Commander's blood pressure. Butcher wrote on the 19th, referring to the tragic sudden death in France of 4th Division's deputy commander: "What a blow it would be to the world, not mentioning that to his personal followers, if he [Eisenhower] should pull a Teddy Roosevelt!"[11]

Tedder's animosity was redoubled. He considered that the air forces had been the victims of a deliberate deception by Montgomery, who had exaggerated his expectations merely to ensure that he received the support of the strategic bombers. Tedder told Eisenhower baldly: "Your own people are thinking you have sold them to the British if you continue to support Montgomery without protest." Of all the criticism heaped upon Montgomery in the course of the war, that following his handling of GOODWOOD is the most difficult to refute. He sent a limited directive to Dempsey before the battle,[12] a copy of which never reached SHAEF, who thus continued to expect more from GOODWOOD than 21st Army Group; this matter has been the subject of much speculation. Yet, directive or no directive, Montgomery could not escape the consequences of other grandiloquent declarations of expectation and achievement before and during the battle. Whatever written insurance policies he took out before 18 July, it is impossible to doubt that when he launched his three-corps attack, he hoped desperately to reach Falaise. He and his staff must have been aware of the expectations they had raised in London and Washington, and therefore of the inescapable cost of failing to meet these. After GOODWOOD, said Brigadier Richardson, 21st Army Group's BGS Plans, "we were distinctly worried. We knew Monty put on this impenetrable act of confidence, whatever was happening. But below Freddy de Guingand's level, it was difficult to judge whether this confidence was soundly based. My feeling was that we were getting into a bigger jam than he was prepared to admit."[13]

Montgomery admitted in his memoirs that he had overdone his public comment, and been "too exultant at the press conference I gave during the Goodwood battle. I realise that now – in fact, I realised it pretty quickly afterwards. Basically the trouble was this – both Bradley and I agreed that we could not possibly tell the Press the true strategy which formed the basis of all our plans. As Bradley said, 'We must grin and bear it.' It became increasingly difficult to grin."[14] It is almost tragic to behold a man of Montgomery's stature so far diminishing himself as to write such nonsense. GOODWOOD rendered great service to the American flank and to the Allied cause by maintaining pressure and by "writing down" irreplaceable German forces. But to demand that history should accept that this alone was the sum of British ambitions is to suggest that a man sows wheat to harvest straw. Montgomery, under all the pressures building up around him since early July, must have known that, had the British embarked upon an operation with such limited objectives as he afterwards attributed to GOODWOOD, the anger and impatience of the Americans towards their British allies would have become uncontainable. The truth, which he never avowed even to Brooke, yet which seems self-evident from the course of events, was that in GOODWOOD, and throughout the rest of the campaign, Montgomery sought major ground gains for Second Army if these could be achieved at acceptable cost. He forsook them whenever casualties rose unacceptably. This occurred painfully often.

When Montgomery and Eisenhower met privately on the afternoon of 20 July – one of their nine personal encounters during the campaign – it seems clear that the Supreme Commander vented his distress. It is possible, even probable, that Montgomery emphasized to Eisenhower his concern over British manpower and casualties, and said something of the Americans' greater ability to overcome these problems. For in Eisenhower's subsequent letter to his Commander-in-Chief, written the following day, he reminded Montgomery sharply that "eventually the American ground strength will necessarily be much greater than the British. But while we have equality in size we must go forward shoulder to shoulder, with honors and sacrifices equally shared."[15] Confidence in Montgomery, and in the performance of the British Second Army, had reached the lowest point of the campaign in north-west Europe among the Americans, among the airmen, and even among some of the British, including their Prime Minister. "Whatever hopes he [Montgomery] had of remaining overall ground commander died with Goodwood," Bradley believed.[16] He afterwards asserted his conviction that Eisenhower would have sacked the British general, had he felt able to do so.

Montgomery's behaviour throughout this period seems dominated by the belief that he could afford to spurn Eisenhower, whose unfittedness for field command was so apparent to every senior officer. It is undoubtedly true that even Bradley, the most loyal and patient of men, was irked by Eisenhower's inability to "read" the battle that was taking place in Normandy. As early as 7 June, Bradley was irritated by Eisenhower's sudden appearance aboard the *Augusta* in mid-Channel: "On the whole Ike's visit had been perhaps necessary for his own personal satisfaction, but from my point of view it was a pointless interruption and annoyance."[17] The First Army commander, both then and later, acknowledged the justice of Montgomery's claim that Eisenhower never understood the Allied plan in Normandy. The Supreme Commander laboured under a misapprehension that he himself could best serve the Allied cause by touring the touchline like a football coach, urging all his generals to keep attacking more or less simultaneously. Eisenhower's personal life-style, journeying between fronts with a ragbag of sycophantic staff officers, his Irish driver and mistress, occasionally his newly-commissioned son and cosseted pet dog, was more suggestive of an eighteenth-century European monarch going to war than a twentieth-century general.

Yet Dwight Eisenhower was the Supreme Commander of the Allied armies, upon whom hung the fervent hopes of two governments for the unity and triumph of their armies. His charm and statesmanship deeply impressed, even moved, all those who worked closely with him. Montgomery's inability to establish a personal relationship with the American, to confide to Eisenhower his own private hopes and fears for the battle, cost him dear. 21st Army Group's Commander-in-Chief made the immense error of believing that the Supreme Commander could be side-stepped, deluded, soft-talked into leaving himself, Montgomery, the supreme professional, to fight the war. He might indeed have been successful in this had his armies on the battlefield fulfilled his early hopes in Normandy. But when they did not, it was Eisenhower, fretting impotent in England, who bore the impatience of the American press, the doubts and fears of the politicians, the charges of failure of generalship which the ignorant associated with himself. Eisenhower might have been willing to ride passively upon a tide of success created by Montgomery. He was quite unwilling idly to accept responsibility for apparent failure and stagnation. At the time and for some years after the war, the extent of the breakdown of relations between Montgomery and Eisenhower was concealed. Today there is no doubt that by late July 1944, the American was weary to death of his ground-force commander.

Brooke urgently warned Montgomery on 19 July to drop his objections to a prime-ministerial visit to Normandy, and use the opportunity to rebuild a little of Churchill's flagging faith. The CIGS warned his friend "of the tendency of the PM to listen to suggestions that Monty played for safety and was not prepared to take risks." Brooke wrote in his diary:

> Winston had never been very fond of Monty; when things went well he put up with him, when they did not he at once became "your Monty". Just at this time Eisenhower had been expressing displeasure and accusing Monty of being sticky, of not pushing sufficiently on the Caen front with the British while he made the mericans do the attacking on the right. Winston was inclined to listen to these complaints.[18]

Brigadier Richardson said that "in strategic terms, things were going according to plan. In tactical terms, they were not." It is much easier to understand the criticisms made of Montgomery by the Americans than those made by his fellow-countrymen. Until the very end of the war, the British demanded that they should be treated as equal partners in the alliance with the United States, and vied for a lion's share of Allied command positions. They could scarcely be surprised if the Americans showed resentment when the British flinched before heavy casualties, and fought on the eastern flank with less apparent determination and will for sacrifice than the American army in the west. Whatever the Americans' weaknesses of command and tactics, their willingness to expend men to gain an objective was never in doubt. "On the whole, they were prepared to go at it more toughly than we were," said Brigadier Carver of 4th Armoured Brigade.[19]

Montgomery, however, was never allowed to forget that he was charged with responsibility for Britain's last great army, her final reserves of manpower in a struggle that had drained these to the limit. With the constant admonitions reaching him from England about casualties, he would have faced bitter criticism – from Churchill as much as any man – had losses risen steeply. It is indisputable that this knowledge bore hard upon the British conduct of operations in Normandy, from the summit to the base of the command structure. Butcher wrote on 24 July, after visiting Southwick House for an hour when Eisenhower drove there to see de Guingand:

> Bill Culver, de Guingand's American aide, in response to my pointed question as to what really stopped Monty's attack, said he felt that Monty, his British Army commander Dempsey, the British corps commanders and even those of the divisions are so conscious of Britain's ebbing manpower that they hesitate to commit an attack where a division may be lost. When it's lost, it's done and finished . . . The Commanders feel the blood of the British Empire, and hence its future, are too precious for dash in battle.[20]

With hindsight it may be easy to suggest that a more ruthless determination to break through on the British front earlier in the campaign would, in the end, have cost fewer lives. Tedder's allegation that Second Army was not trying hard enough had some foundation, but it was much easier to take this sanguine view from the distance of SHAEF – or from the perspective of history – than for Montgomery and his commanders in Normandy, who had to watch their precious army take persistent punishment. Tedder's attitude proved his claim to be an outstanding Alliance commander, with a truly Anglo-American perspective, but it showed little sympathy for valid if more parochial British sensitivities. If the British army was to achieve major ground gains on the eastern flank against the powerful German forces deployed before it, the evidence suggested that the cost would be terrible.

Montgomery is entitled to the gratitude of his country, as well as of his soldiers, for declining to yield to the temptation to mount a ruthlessly costly attack merely to stave off the political demands made upon him. He judged, correctly, that if the Allies persisted with their existing plan for pressure in the east and breakthrough in the west, the Germans would eventually crack without a British bloodbath. Yet in July as in June, he denied himself the goodwill of either American or British sceptics by creating a smokescreen of distortion and untruth to conceal his disappointment with the failure of Second Army to gain ground at acceptable cost. It is a measure of the criticism now directed against him, and of the political pressure within the Alliance, that as late as 28 July, when the American breakout was already making good progress, Brooke was writing to him:

> Now, as a result of all this talking and the actual situation on your front, I feel personally quite certain that Dempsey must attack *at the earliest possible moment* [emphasis in original] on a large scale. We must not allow German forces to move from his front to Bradley's front or we shall give more cause than ever for criticism.[21]

It is impossible to imagine that Montgomery could have been sacked – whatever Tedder's delusion on that count – without inflicting an intolerable blow to British national confidence. He whom propaganda has made mighty, no man may readily cast aside, as Portal was compelled to acknowledge a few months later in his difficulties with "Bomber" Harris. But it is difficult to guess what new pressures and directives might have been forced upon the Commander-in-Chief of 21st Army Group had not the perspective of the Normandy campaign now been entirely transformed by the American Operation COBRA.

9 The breakout

COBRA

Throughout the first half of July, while the British and Canadians were fighting their bitter battles around Caen, the Americans were enduring equal pain and frustration in their efforts to disentangle themselves from the clinging misery of the *bocage*. On 3 July, Middleton's VIII Corps attacked south towards Coutances–St Lô-Caumont. The corps commander himself was one of the most experienced fighting soldiers in the American army, having led a regiment in France in the First World War, and more recently a division in Italy. But Middleton was now seriously troubled and weakened by the pain of an arthritic knee, and his staff were conscious that this reduced his ability to concentrate upon the battle. Not that it was likely that the outcome of the early fighting would have been different had be been fit. By far the toughest initial objective was the 300-foot height of Mont Castre, dominating the Cotentin plain. After heavy fighting the superb 82nd Airborne Division, halved in strength by weeks in action, gained the hill and proved what a first-class formation could achieve even against dogged opposition. Elsewhere on the front, however, matters went much less happily. The accident-prone 90th Division made no headway, and Bradley prepared to sack yet another of its commanders, Landrum. The 79th Division suffered 2,000 casualties in the next five days to crawl forward a little over three miles. There was nothing to suggest that these difficulties were caused by command shortcomings, for when VII Corps joined the attack on 4 July under the dynamic Collins, they too found themselves rapidly bogged down. On the 7th, XIX Corps was thrown in, although Corlett, its corps commander, like Middleton was in visibly poor health, and even when fit had never been considered a driver of men. Hodges described him at the time as possessing "that hospital look".[1] Scenes of near-farce ensued when advancing elements of 30th Division became entangled with the tanks of 3rd Armored, creating terrible congestion. There was a furious confrontation between Generals Bohn and Hobbs about whose fault this was, which ended in the sacking of Bohn, the junior officer, but a tough old veteran who had started as a private soldier and risen through the ranks of the American army.

After 12 days of battle, VIII Corps had suffered 10,000 casualties to advance some seven miles. Corlett's and Collins' men had fared no better. "Thus my breakout and dreams of a blitz to Avranches failed badly," wrote Bradley, "a crushing disappointment to me personally."[2] The principal American achievement was the defeat of a counter-attack by Panzer Lehr towards St Jean-de-Daye on 11 July, which 9th and 30th Divisions threw back causing the loss of 25 per cent of the Germans' strength. Once again,.it had been demonstrated that movement by either army was the crucial difficulty in the *bocage*, and that in defence American troops could hammer the Germans as hard as Hausser's men of Seventh Army had hit the Americans when they were defending.

Enduring the pain of their own difficulties, the Americans sometimes forgot the scale of suffering that they were inflicting upon the Germans. Sergeant Helmut Gunther, of 17th Panzergrenadiers, each day watched his company of the reconnaissance battalion whittled away without hope of replacements: Hahnel, who was killed by small-arms fire in their first battle; Heinrich, his veteran chess partner, who died on the Carentan road; Dobler, who took over a platoon when its commander was killed and was shot in the head as he jumped from the ditch to lead a counter-attack. All these old friends and many more were gone: "I used to think – 'What a poor pig I am, fighting here with my back to the wall.' "[3] Yet Gunther's self-pity was mixed with astonishment that the survivors stood the strain and the losses so well, and fought on. He was astounded that the Americans did not break through their line in early July. His own company was reduced to 20 men out of 120, yet when he sought his CO's permission to withdraw 50 yards to a better tactical position, it was refused.

On 9 July, they were at last driven from their positions, and Gunther found himself staring at a Sherman tank bearing down upon him only yards away. He was working forward to throw a sticky bomb at it when a German voice called "Come back!", and he glanced round to see a German tank behind him. He stood confused and uncertain for a moment as the panzer commander shouted, "Get down, he's going to shoot!" and a shell from the Sherman blasted into the German tank, splinters ricocheting into Gunther's back. Characteristically, the panzer survived the encounter. The Sherman did not. Gunther was evacuated to hospital.

The defeat of the German counter-attacks was encouraging to the Americans, but provided little consolation for Bradley, wrestling with his fundamental problem of breaking through into Brittany. At the highest level, the Americans discussed with deep concern the problem of giving their infantry divisions something of the thrust and attacking power that so far seemed the monopoly of the Airborne. "We were flabbergasted by the *bocage*." said General Quesada of IXth Tactical Air Command, who was working daily alongside Bradley. "Our infantry had become paralysed. It has never been adequately described how immobilized they were by the sound of small-arms fire among the hedges."[4] Patton reminded an old French army friend of a remark that he had made in the First War: "He had said, 'The poorer the infantry the more artillery it needs; the American infantry needs all it can get.' He was right then, and still is."[5] First Army reported on "the urgent need for the development of an aggressive spirit by the infantry soldier . . . The outstanding impression gained from a review of battle experience is the importance of aggressive action and continuous energetic forward movement in order to gain ground and reduce casualties."[6]

It had become brutally apparent to every man in First Army that service in an infantry unit was an almost certain sentence to death or wounds. The top sergeant in Corporal George Small's anti-aircraft battalion routinely threatened jesters: "One more crack like that and you'll find yourself in the infantry."[7] The unfortunate 90th Division suffered replacement of 150 per cent of its officers and over 100 per cent of enlisted men in its first six weeks in action. Typical tank casualty figures showed that in June alone, the 712th Battalion lost 21 out of 74 in 16 days of action, the 746th 44 out of 51 in 23 days, the 747th 41 out of 61 in 10 days. In July, the 712th lost 21 out of 68 in 16 days, the 756th 51 out of 91 ins 29 days. Temporary or permanent losses from "battle fatigue" had reached an alarming 10,000 men since D-Day, around 20 per cent of all casualties. Between June and November 1944, a staggering 26 per cent of all American soldiers in combat divisions were treated for some form of battle fatigue; this was out of a total of 929,307 such cases in the U.S. Army in the Second World War. There was a real fear that "battle fatigue" was reaching epidemic proportions. The after-action medical report of First Army declared that:

. . . the rate of admission to the exhaustion centres . . . during the first weeks of operations was in accord with the estimates made previously, however, the rate thereafter increased to such proportions that it became necessary to reinforce each of the platoons operating the exhaustion centres . . . Reasons for this increase: a) addition of a number of divisions to the army in excess of original estimates, b) difficult terrain, mud, hedgerows etc, c) stiff resistance offered by the enemy in the La Haye du Puits, Carentan and St. Lô actions, d) troops remaining in combat for long periods.[8]

Every army in the Second World War recognized battle exhaustion or shell shock as a genuine, curable condition among soldiers under acute strain. But it was felt by many officers in 1944 that the U.S. Army had become too ready to allow its men to believe that battle exhaustion was an acceptable state. There is a narrow borderline between humanitarian concern and dangerous weakness. If Patton had been overharsh in his treatment of battle exhaustion in Sicily, there seemed grounds for believing that in Normandy, First Army moved too far in the opposite direction. Major Frank Colacicco of the 3rd/18th Infantry described how men appeared before him claiming battle fatigue and, if challenged, defied him to court-martial them. "What was five years in the brig? They knew that the U.S. government would fluke out." By July, the rear areas of all the Allied armies were generously populated with deserters, whom American units often treated with much greater forbearance than the British. Provost-Sergeant James Dobie of the British 5th King's Regiment was astonished to discover, when he returned two errant GIs to their unit, that "they were greeted like long-lost brothers instead of absentees." The German army's discipline was not based entirely upon natural loyalty. Between January and September 1944, the Wehrmacht executed almost 4,000 of its own men, 1,605 of these for desertion.

Some senior Americans regretted that their army had failed to adopt Montgomery's policy before D-day, of leavening untried divisions with key officers and NCOs who possessed battle experience at battalion level and below. There had also been a failure to make the men of First Army familiar with their leaders. An extraordinary number of American soldiers who fought in north-west Europe regarded the high command as impossibly remote, and Eisenhower and Bradley as hardly comprehensible figures. A few divisional commanders – Huebner, Cota, Barton, Rose, Eddy – became widely known and respected by their men. But the roll call of senior American officers found wanting and sacked in Normandy was astonishing: two successive commanders of 90th Division, Brown of 28th Division, McMahon of 8th (who told Bradley frankly, "Brad, I think you are going to have to relieve me."),[9] Watson of 3rd Armored, to name only the most prominent. Bradley found 83rd Division's leadership "uncertain", and that of the 79th and 80th suspect. Of the corps commanders, only Collins had distinguished himself. The commander-designate of First Army, Courtney Hodges, was considered by most of his peers to be an officer of limited imagination and self-effacing personality. Bradley described him as "one of the most skilled craftsmen under my entire command," but was constrained to add that he was also "essentially a military technician . . . a spare, soft-voiced Georgian without temper, drama, or visible emotion."[10]

If Bradley's personal modesty was one of his most engaging characteristics, it contributed to the impersonality of his army. Whatever men thought of Patton – and many scorned him – all of them knew who he was. Most took a pride, then and later, in serving with Patton's Army. As Montgomery understood so well, the cult of personality can be immensely valuable in war. The lack of it within the American army in Normandy – the difficulty for most infantry replacements of identifying with a man, a unit, anything human beyond their own squad save the vast juggernaut of tanks and guns with which they rolled – contributed significantly to the difficulties of the American army. Where the German army did its utmost to maintain men in regional formations, the Americans pursued a deliberate policy of dividing men from the same town or state – a legacy of the First War, when the pain of a local unit's destruction was thought to have borne too heavily upon individual communities. But even industrialized war on a vast scale needs its focus of identity, its charismatic leaders. These were instinctive human necessities that America's commanders seemed slow to understand.

Private Gerard Ascher, a 27-year-old New Yorker who worked in the family business until he was drafted in 1943, was one of countless thousands of infantry replacements shipped to Normandy in June 1944 in anonymous packages of 250 men, to be directed wherever casualties dictated. One of his group gazed around at Normandy for a few minutes after their landing, then declared decisively: "This is no place for me," and vanished from their ken for ever. Ascher reached the 357th Infantry in darkness with an unknown young Mississippian, to be greeted by a lieutenant, who said simply: "You two stay in this hedgerow – the others are in that one." The New Yorker's memories of the campaign were above all of disorientation, of utter ignorance of their purpose: "I really couldn't fathom the whole thing – I couldn't understand what it was all about. I never remembered seeing the battalion commander except at ceremonies."[11] If all infantrymen in all armies share something of this feeling, and if Ascher was uncommonly unlucky to be sent to the 90th Division, his sentiments reflected a problem that afflicted much of the American army in north-west Europe. Very many soldiers respected their NCOs. But in sharp contrast to the British army, in which most men looked up to their officers, few American rankers admitted to thinking well of theirs. Corporal George Small wrote of "this nearly universal scorn of American soldiers for most officers".[12] Above all at platoon level, the "90-day wonders" – the young lieutenants upon whom so much junior leadership depended – seldom won the confidence and respect of their soldiers.

The men of Bradley's army might not be privy to "the big picture", but in early July 1944 they felt a deep sense that much was going wrong. "We were stuck," said Corporal Bill Preston of the 743rd Tank Battalion: "Something dreadful seemed to have happened in terms of the overall plan. Things were going very awry. The whole theory of mobility that we had been taught, of our racing across the battlefield, seemed to have gone up in smoke." Sergeant Bill Walsh of the 102nd Cavalry thought that the struggle between Germans and Americans resembled "a pro fighter taking on an amateur who didn't want to fight. None of those American infantry boys wanted to be over there." Lieutenant Philip Reisler of 2nd Armored felt that the campaign had become "like an interminable succession of Thermopylaes. In every engagement, we were only able to present one tiny unit to the enemy at a time."

Yet even as First Army's difficulties seemed at their greatest, the transformation of American fortunes was at hand. Together with General Collins of VII Corps, Bradley had conceived a new plan. To clear the way for a major offensive, Collins' men began to push forward to the St Lô–Périers road. By 20 July, they had reached positions commanding it. On 18 July, at a cost of 3,000 casualties in the 29th Division and more than 2,000 in the 35th, the Americans gained the vital heights of St Lô. The battle for the shattered rubble of the town was one of First Army's outstanding feats of arms in the campaign, driving back General Eugene Meindl's II Parachute Corps yard by yard, despite constant casualties. The body of Major Thomas Howie, killed leading the 3rd/116th Infantry to the rescue of the 2nd Battalion on the outskirts of St Lô, was laid on a bier of rubble outside the church of Notre-Dame. Hill 122 joined a host of other Norman map references among the American army's battle honours. The German 352nd Division, whose presence had wrought such havoc with American plans on 6 June, was now in ruins. Even Meindl's paratroopers had cracked. The stage was set for the supreme American military achievement of the Normandy campaign, Operation COBRA.

It was symbolic of the contrasting approaches to war by the two principal Allies in Normandy that the British codenamed their greatest efforts after race meetings, while the Americans adopted a symbol of deadly killing power. Montgomery's official biographer has recently argued that it was the C-in-C of 21st Army Group who produced the essential framework for COBRA, in a declaration of future intentions dated 13 June. After discussing immediate objectives for that period, he continued:

f) to capture ST LO and then COUTANCES
g) to thrust southwards from CAUMONT towards VIRE and MORTAIN; and from ST LO towards VILLEDIEU and AVRANCHES
h) all the time to exert pressure towards LA HAYE DU PUITS and VOLOGNES, and to capture CHERBOURG.

"This was," declares Montgomery's biographer, "*town for town the layout for the American Operation 'Cobra'*."[13] [emphasis in original] If this assertion arouses ire among the ghosts of the First Army, it is also true that, after the event, Americans were too eager to write into history the view that COBRA was expected from the outset to lead inexorably to Lorient, Le Mans and Argentan, and that from its launching the rest of the campaign was preordained. In reality, of course, it would have been extraordinary to plan it as anything of the sort. It was an ambitious, well-conceived blueprint for a major offensive. Considering the proven difficulties of wrestling ground from the Germans, and the earlier failure of many equally high hopes, it could never have begun as more than that. To suggest that the Americans now consciously embarked upon a completely new phase of the campaign – "the breakout" – is to pretend that they had not been trying desperately to escape from the *bocage* for many weeks already. What took place in late July on the American flank was that First Army launched an offensive that worked, assisted by the absence of most of the best of von Kluge's army, who were engaged with the British and Canadians in the east. They then pursued and exploited their success with dramatic energy.

No earlier statement of objectives by Montgomery can diminish the personal achievement of Bradley, whose plan COBRA was. During the weeks since 6 June, there had been a subtle but steady shift in the command relationship between 21st Army Group and the Americans, reflecting both the growing weight of U.S. strength now deployed in Normandy, and the shrinking confidence of First Army in Montgomery's superior wisdom and experience. There was still the closest consultation between the Allies, and great care was taken to mesh British and American plans. Montgomery confirmed American intentions in crisply-worded written orders. There is little doubt that his *negative* authority over First Army was undiminished: he could have prevented the Americans from embarking upon a course of which he disapproved. But he could no longer expect to exercise *positive* authority, to compel them to initiate operations for which they felt disinclined. A study of Montgomery's files for this period, his successive orders to the armies, might give a different impression. But in real terms, while the Americans accepted his co-ordinating authority, it would be inaccurate to describe him as their commander, in the sense that Bradley was commander of First Army.

The American Secretary for War, Henry Stimson, visited Bradley's headquarters on 17 July, and recorded in his notes: "Plan Cobra – attack by 2 infantry divisions (30th and 9th) followed by 1st Infantry and 2nd Armoured to the left. Break through and turn to right, enveloping 5 or 6 divisions. If successful would have easy going to the SW end of the *bocage*."[14] In the event, between Stimson's visit and the COBRA jump-off, the thrust of VII Corps south-westwards from the St Lô–Périers road towards Coutances was strengthened by the addition of the 4th Division in the centre. In contrast to the usual American prefer-

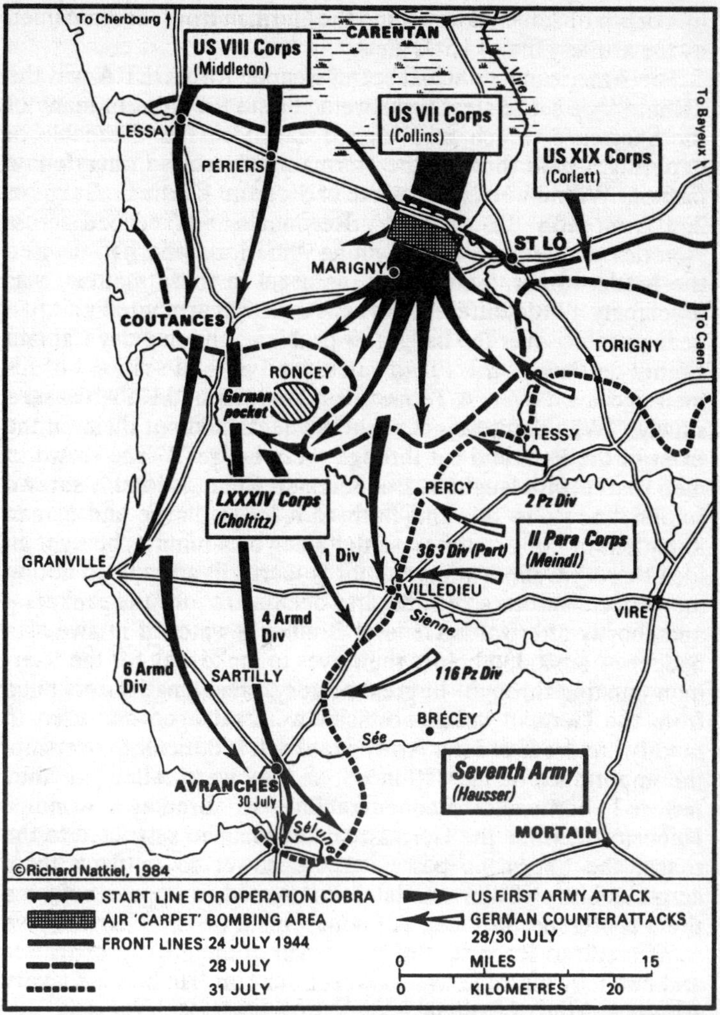

Operation COBRA: 25 July–

ence for broad front assaults, this was to be a narrow, concentrated attack on a 7,000-yard front, immediately preceded by a massive air bombardment. The fighter-bombers would concentrate on hitting forward German defences in a 250-yard belt immediately south of the road. Spaatz's "heavies" would bomb to a depth of 2,500 yards behind the German front, accompanied by the artillery fire of 1,000 guns.

The Americans' principal secret weapon for COBRA was the "Rhino" – a set of steel tusks welded onto the front of many of the Shermans, which so equipped had been found capable of battering a path through the Norman hedgerows in heartening fashion. Within weeks, the name of Sergeant Curtis G. Culin, of 2nd Armored's 102nd Cavalry Reconnaissance, echoed across America as the imaginative young American who had devised the battle-winner. The reality, as usual in these matters, was touchingly a little different. Every American armoured unit had been puzzling over the hedgerow problem, and one day Captain Jimmy de Pew of the 102nd summoned a "bull session" of his men to chew it over. A Tennessee hillbilly named Roberts asked slowly: "Why don't we get some saw teeth and put them on the front of the tank and cut through these hedges?" The crowd of men roared with laughter. But Sergeant Culin, a notably shrewd soldier known in the unit both as a chess player and a man impatient of army routines, said: "Hang on a minute, he's got an idea there." Culin it was who put Roberts' ill-articulated notion into effect, and directed the first demonstration: the tankers – and shortly afterwards General Bradley – watched in awe as a hedgerow exploded before their eyes to make way for the Sherman bursting through. In great secrecy, steel lengths stockpiled from the German beach obstacles were salvaged and used to modify hundreds of First Army's tanks. It is difficult to overstate the importance of the "Rhinos", as they were called, for they restored battlefield manoeuvrability to Bradley's armour. Henceforth, while the German tanks remained restricted to the roads, the Shermans possessed the power to outflank them across country. Culin was later summoned to appear before a press conference in Paris. An honest man, he tried hard to give some credit to Roberts. But the weight of the great propaganda and publicity machine was too much for him. He became a very American kind of national hero.[15]

Another kind of hero was lost to First Army on the very eve of COBRA – 54-year-old Colonel Paddy Flint, the hoary old commander of the 39th Infantry who had made himself legendary for the reckless courage which now killed him. Irritated by the slow progress of his 2nd Battalion approaching the COBRA start-line, he strode impatiently forward under heavy mortaring to galvanize them into life. He sent a message to his executive officer from the battalion CP: "Strangely quiet here. Could take nap. Have spotted pillbox. Will start them cooking." He reached the front line with his headquarters group to be greeted by a German with a machine pistol whose fire ripped Flint's trousers. Flint ordered a tank to move forward, and when its commander told him that he could not do so as he had turret trouble, Flint exploded: "It isn't often you'll have a colonel for a bodyguard!" The reluctant tank and a cluster of infantry advanced up the road with their colonel. At one point, when he was standing on the Sherman's hull directing the driver, German fire began to ricochet off the steel, and Flint was induced to step down into cover. The "bodyguard colonel" now advanced with his little group towards the Germans, disdaining their hand grenades: "I don't mind that – they can't hit me anyway." His driver was wounded, but while he was being taken to the rear Flint kept up heavy fire with the two carbines and M1 rifle with which he was now armed, and of which his unhappy staff officer sought to relieve him. The colonel was standing in a doorway lecturing a sergeant on infantry tactics when there was a single shot, and he pitched forward, hit in the head. The sergeant spotted the German sniper and worked forward until he shot him out of a tree. Flint was given morphia and a cigarette, and murmured as he lay: "You can't kill an Irishman, you only make him mad." He died in the field hospital. In one sense, Flint's performance was suicidal and wildly unsuited to the role of regimental commander. But in another, given the chronic difficulty of inducing the infantry to employ "Indian fighting", to get to close quarters with the enemy, it was a magnificent example. George Patton acted as one of Flint's pallbearers, and said with uncommon accuracy that he was sure that this was how his old friend would like to have gone. Flint was one of the great characters of First Army, cast in a mould of leadership that filled his men with immense pride.[16]

The launching of COBRA was delayed for some days by the same torrential rain and low cloud that sealed the fate of GOODWOOD. On 24 July, the order was given and 1,600 aircraft had already taken off for the preliminary air bombardment when the weather closed in again. Some were successfully recalled, or declined to risk bombing through the overcast atmosphere. But others again poured down explosives destined for the path of the American attack. The results were disastrously erratic. 25 Americans were killed and 131 wounded in the 30th Division, and the Germans were provided with final confirmation of the American intention to move on the St Lô–Périers front. Some enraged American units, such as the 2nd/120th Infantry, opened fire on their own aircraft, a not uncommon practice among all the armies in Normandy when suffering at the hands of their own pilots.

The next morning, the forecasters' promise of brighter weather was fulfilled. At 7.00 a.m., 901st Panzergrenadiers telephoned divisional headquarters to report: "American infantry in front of our trenches are abandoning their positions. They are withdrawing everywhere." As similar reports reached Bayerlein from all along the front, his operations officer, Kurt Kauffmann, said cheerfully: "Looks as if they've got cold feet. Perhaps Seventh Army is right after all." Hausser's staff had confidently predicted, despite every indication from Panzer Lehr to the contrary, that the major Allied attack would come south of Caen. Then the field telephones in Bayerlein's farmhouse at Canisy began to ring again, reporting: "Bombing attacks by endless waves of aircraft. Fighter-bomber attacks on bridges and artillery positions."[17] At 9.38 a.m., the fighter-bombers opened their first 20-minute assault on the German front line. Behind them, high above the dust and smoke, 1,800 heavy bombers of 8th Air Force droned slowly towards the target area, their glinting wings watched by thousands of expectant young Americans in their foxholes and tank turrets below, massed ready to move when the airmen had finished.

As we watched [wrote the war correspondent Ernie Pyle], there crept into our consciousness a realization that windrows of exploding bombs were easing back towards us, flight by flight, instead of gradually forward, as the plan called for. Then we were horrified by the suspicion that these machines, high in the sky and completely detached from us, were aiming their bombs at the smokeline on the ground, and a gentle breeze was drifting the smokeline back over us! An indescribable kind of panic comes over you at such times. We stood tensed in muscle and frozen in intellect, watching each flight approach and pass over us, feeling trapped and completely helpless.

Bradley had asked that the bombers attack east-west, out of the sun and parallel to the front on the St Lô–Périers road, to reduce the risk of "short bombing", or "creepback", as the British called it. The airmen, for their own reasons, came in north-south. Despite desperate efforts by the ground troops to identify their positions with yellow panels and smoke markers, there was wild bombing by 8th Air Force, with appalling consequences for the men below. "The ground was shaken and rocked as if by a great earthquake," said Lieutenant-Colonel George Tuttle of the 30th Division. "The concussion, even underground, felt as if someone was beating you with a club."[18] Ernie Pyle wrote of "that awful rush of wind, like the rattling of seeds in a dry gourd." Lieutenant Sidney Eichen of the 120th Infantry had stood with his men watching the bombers approach with comfortable satisfaction: "We thought – 'How gorgeous.' Then it was – 'Goddamit, they're coming for us again!' My outfit was decimated, our anti-tank guns blown apart. I saw one of our truck drivers, Jesse Ivy, lying split down the middle. Captain Bell was buried in a crater with only his head visible. He suffocated before we could get him out."[19] 111 Americans were killed, including Lieutenant-General Lesley McNair, who had come forward to watch the attack, and 490 wounded. The entire command group of the 9th Division's 3rd/47th Infantry was wiped out. Maddened men were forcibly carried to the rear. Others merely ran blindly from the battlefield. Maimed men lay screaming for aid. Brigadier-General William Harrison of the 30th Division wrote savagely home that night: "When you read of all the great glamour of our flying friends, just remember that not all that glitters is gold!"[20] Harrison won a Distinguished Service Cross that day for his part in dragging men from their shock and paralysis, pulling together shattered units, and driving them forward to press on with the attack. He told the commanding officer of the 120th Infantry: "Colonel, the attack goes ahead as scheduled. Even if you have only two or three men, the attack is to be made." Eichen saw his regimental commander running from company to company shouting: "You've gotta get going, get going!" Eichen said: "Half-heartedly, we started to move."

General Courtney Hodges, commander-designate of First Army, visited 30th Division's command post to meet its enraged commander, Hobbs, who, "was naturally terribly upset by the air show . . . 'We're good soldiers, Courtney, I know, but there's absolutely no excuse, no excuse at all. I wish I could show some of those air boys, decorated with everything a man can be decorated with, some of our casualty clearing stations.' "[21]

Amid the shambles created by the bombing of their own forward areas, VII Corps' attack began hesitantly on the 25th, men moving slowly forward to discover, to their dismay, that the

Panzer Lehr division before them was battered but still unbroken. Some German troops had even moved rapidly forward to occupy ground evacuated by the Americans to provide an air safety zone – a technique they had also adopted on the 24th. Collins' troops were even more disheartened to meet fierce artillery fire, which they had confidently expected to find suppressed by the bombing. "It was hard to believe that any living thing could be left alive in front of our positions," said Colonel Tuttle. "However on moving to enemy-held territory, our men ran into some determined resistance."[22] Units found themselves entangled in protracted firefights against strongpoints and networks of foxholes held by the customary German mix of a handful of tanks, supporting infantry, and the inevitable 88 mm guns.

Bayerlein had personally ridden forward by motor-cycle to the 901st Regiment, whose commander, Colonel von Hausser, was sitting in a cellar beneath an old stone tower. Von Hausser declared gloomily that his entire front line had been devastated. Yet the survivors resisted with all their usual stubbornness. Colonel Hammonds Birks of 120th Infantry radioed to 30th Division that "the going was very slow . . . the boche had tanks dug in, hull down, and were shooting perhaps more artillery than they had ever previously used along any American sector." First Army's diary recorded bleakly: "This day, a day to remember for more than one reason, did not bring the breakthrough for which we had all hoped . . . There was no question but that the postponement of the attack from Monday to Tuesday, plus two successive days of bombing of our own troops. took the ginger out of several of the front-line elements."

Yet even in these first encounters, General Collins found cause for encouragement. While the German positions were resisting fiercely, they did not appear to form a continuous belt of defences. They could be outflanked, bypassed. In contrast to the meticulously-prepared succession of defensive positions in depth with which the Germans on the Bourgébus Ridge met GOODWOOD, below the St Lô–Périers road on 25 July, they retained only a crust. This, despite all the warning they had received of an impending American thrust. It was a tribute to the efforts of the British and Canadians that von Kluge's fears, as well as his principal forces, were still decisively fixed upon the eastern flank. That day, the 25th, the 2nd Canadian Corps launched a new attack towards Bourgébus which quickly broke down and was counter-attacked by 9th SS Panzer. But, faced with two heavy assaults, it was to the east that von Kluge chose to go himself that day, to inspect the front. Against the 14 British and Canadian divisions, the Germans still deployed 14 of their own, including six panzer. The Americans faced only 11 seriously weakened enemy divisions, two of them armoured. The old Panzer Lehr began the COBRA battle with a strength of just 2,200 men and 45 operational armoured vehicles in the front line. Against this weary gathering of German battle-groups and depleted infantry formations, the full weight of 15 American divisions would shortly be committed. Bayerlein was enraged to receive a visit from a staff officer of von Kluge, conveying the Field-Marshal's order that the St Lô–Périers line must be held: not a single man must leave his position. A battalion of SS Panthers was on its way to provide support. Bayerlein said flatly: "Out in front every one is holding out. Every one. My grenadiers and my engineers and my tank crews – they're all holding their ground. Not a single man is leaving his post. They are lying silent in their foxholes, for they are dead. You may report to the Field-Marshal that the Panzer Lehr Division is annihilated."[23] In keeping with the occasion, at that moment a vast ammunition dump exploded nearby, hit by fighter-bombers. Bayerlein's remarks were only slightly exaggerated.

On the afternoon of the 25th, Collins learned enough about the vulnerability of the Germans to outflanking movements to risk giving the order to his mobile columns to start moving. By nightfall, elements of 1st Division were outside Marigny. The next morning, across the entire VII Corps front, units began to shake free from engagements with the defenders of Panzer Lehr and move fast across country, reporting that resistance was crumbling before them. The tank columns were slowed by the need for the "Rhinos" to spend an average of two and a half minutes cutting through each hedgerow. But delays of this order were trifling by comparison with the hours of sluggish progress under fire that had marked each battle in the *bocage* since D-Day. The entire offensive was rapidly gaining momentum. Pockets of resistance at crossroads halted the American tanks only for such time as it took the infantry to jump down and pour fire into them. Sergeant Hans Stober and his company of 17th SS Panzergrenadiers had been ordered to hold their positions for 24 hours. "But we found that American units in company strength had bypassed us. There was no choice but to order us to withdraw."[24] So it was for thousands of German soldiers the length of the line. As darkness fell on the night of the 26th, the forceful Brigadier Maurice Rose of 2nd Armored's Combat Command A – the equivalent of a British brigade group – raced on. His men's progress had been dramatically rapid, a tribute to the careful training of his tank companies before the attack, alongside the foot soldiers of 22nd Infantry. At 3.00 a.m. the next morning, they had reached the first objective of COBRA, a road junction north of Le Mesnil-Herman. By noon on the 27th, 9th Division was also clear of all organized German resistance, and moving fast. Since the rear areas were alive with German stragglers and retreating units, it proved essential to provide armoured escorts for the American supply columns racing to follow the lead troops. Everywhere behind the front, they were now meeting the chaos of German defeat – fleeing men and vehicles, enemy columns searching desperately for a route of escape.

Lieutenant Philip Reisler of 2nd Armored was sitting dozing in the turret of his Sherman on a bend in a sunken road, his crew sleeping the sleep of utter exhaustion in the hull beneath him, when he heard an unfamiliar engine sound behind him, and turned to see a German half-track driving fast in his direction, the soldiers inside it laughing, oblivious of the Americans. The vehicle smashed full-tilt into the tank and stopped dead, its radiator hissing and steaming. The horrified German driver tore his gears in a desperate effort to reverse, while Reisler fumbled equally clumsily with his machine-gun, simultaneously kicking his gunner into life. A German machine-gunner began to fire wildly, and the half-track somehow swerved around the tank. Then the Americans slammed a 75 mm at point-blank range into its rear: it slewed across the road and began to burn. Reisler's coaxial machine-gun killed the crew as they leapt out of the flames. At that moment, a second half-track rounded the corner, steered around the tank, halted behind the flaming barricade and received another 75 mm shell which blew most of its occupants alive into the road. One German walked in a daze to the Sherman and leaned against it, shaking his head. Reisler pressed the trigger of his pistol. To his dismay nothing happened. The German, however, scrambled hastily up the bank into an orchard, and infuriated the American by turning back and grinning before he walked unhurriedly away through the trees. Three more Germans marched towards the tank, hands in the air. The tank crew chatted to them by the roadside. Reisler suggested to one that he should hide his wristwatch in his sock, for otherwise the MPs would surely take it.

A few minutes later, Reisler's battalion commander walked down the road and took over the Sherman's radio. His own tank, he said, had been hit. From the orchard came a burst of sub-machine gun fire. The colonel seized a Thompson gun and emptied clip after clip into the trees until, assuaged, he stepped down and walked forward to the wreck of his own tank with Reisler. The lieutenant peered down into the driver's seat, and was appalled to find only the man's lower half remained. He looked upwards, and saw the remainder of the body hanging obscenely from the telephone wires, 20 feet above his head, one hand gently waving.

The flak battalion of the 17th SS was wiped out by air attack. "The troops had been trained to lose a battle quite calmly," said one of its survivors, Sergeant Stober, "we knew that the vital thing was to stick together. But we could see that the Americans had learnt how to break through, ignoring their flanks and pushing on to occupy crossroads and set up blocking positions so that our vehicles and heavy weapons could not get through. We lost vast quantities of *matériel*."

On 26 July, VIII Corps joined the offensive on the right. Middleton felt compelled to use the 8th and 90th Divisions to lead his attack, because their positions alone possessed clear paths in front through the floods and swamps. Both bitterly disappointed First Army by failing to gain ground. But the next morning, first light revealed that the Germans in front of them had gone, compelled to pull back because of their crumbling left flank, leaving only immense minefields to delay the advance of VIII Corps.

A sense of exhilaration such as they had not known since Cherbourg, perhaps not matched since 7 June, was now overtaking the Americans as they dashed through villages which welcomed them with all the warmth of civilians whose homes and possessions and livestock had not been destroyed. "This virtual road march was such as the American army was designed for," Russell Weigley has written, "especially the American armored divisions. Appealing also to the passion for moving on that is so much a part of the American character and heritage, it brought out the best in the troops, their energy and mechanical resourcefulness."[25] The infantry clung to the tank hulls and sat up in the trucks waving wildly to French onlookers as they raced south-westwards, blackened German vehicles by the roadside testifying to the achievement of the fighter-bombers in clearing the roads ahead of them. Despite stiffening resistance east of Coutances on the 28th, that evening the CC B of Middleton's 4th Armored swung up from the south to reach the town. "The highlight of the day", recorded First Army's diary of the 29th, "occurred when a considerable force of enemy tanks, vehicles and guns were bottled up on the Roncey–St Denis le Vêtu by-highways by elements of the 2nd and 3rd Armored Divs, and was pounded to bits by armor, artillery and aircraft." Lieutenant Eichen of the 120th Infantry said: "By now we were expecting to push them all the way through to Germany. You might come to a hill line or a road junction and find a few tanks or 88s firing from it, but for all the rest of that week it was just push and go."

The Americans destroyed two tanks within minutes of encountering Lieutenant Fritz Langangke's platoon of 2nd SS Panzer; a third bogged in a ditch. Langangke's driver, Zeeger, jumped down to fix a towing shackle to the hill of the cripple, and was immediately wounded badly in the face by shell fragments. Shocked, the man staggered into the undergrowth and vanished from sight. A retreating tank met him and got him away to the rear. Langangke leapt from his turret to the empty driving position and steered the Panther himself until, two hours later, a new driver was found for him. They all knew that the front was crumbling: "*Verloren!*"–lost!–was a word they heard much of that week.

Sergeant Helmut Gunther of 17th SS Panzergrenadiers had returned from hospital in Le Mans on the 14th after being wounded in the abortive American offensive in early July. The reconnaissance battalion with which he served was already reduced to two understrength companies, which were merged and placed under his command. They were sent together with the pioneer battalion to defend a supposedly quiet sector of the front. On the 23rd–24th, they heard the sound of fierce fighting on their right as a neighbouring paratroop unit held off a local American attack. Then, although they themselves were not in the direct path of VII Corps' assault, they were hastily ordered to fall back as the line around them cracked.

We were marching, marching back all the time. One morning we were ordered to keep a road open, but we found that the Americans had already blocked it. The roads were crowded with American vehicles, and all that we could do was to take to the fields on foot. On the fourth day, by sheer coincidence we ran into some of our own unit's vehicles, and kept going by road. But we were losing stragglers all the time – some of us later had letters from them from America. Once when we were moving to take up position an army staff car stopped beside us. I saluted. The officer in it asked me where we were going. "Have you gone crazy?" he said. "The Americans are there already." Then he drove on. In a ditch in a wood we met ten exhausted paratroopers who asked us for water. I suggested that they come with us, but they were reluctant. We moved off, and a while later heard shooting. One paratrooper caught up with us, and told us that all the rest were dead. They had tried to surrender, but it was too difficult.

We found a pig in a farm, killed it and cooked it. We took sheets from the farmhouse and laid them out on the table and prepared to eat. Suddenly a Luftwaffe man burst in shouting: "The Americans are right behind me." We grabbed the corners of the sheet with everything inside it, threw it in the back of a field car, and pulled out just as the first Sherman came in sight. Eventually we met up with our battalion headquarters, who were expecting the enemy at any moment. From then on, I could not distinguish the days. I had seen the first retreat from Moscow, which was terrible enough, but at least units were still intact. Here, we had become a cluster of individuals. We were not a battleworthy company any longer. All that we had going for us was that we knew each other very well.[26]

The offensive now entered a new and bloodier phase. As the American columns lay strung out over miles of unfamiliar country, German units began to fight with all their customary ferocity to escape entrapment. There were elements of 2nd SS Panzer, 17th SS Panzergrenadiers and the 353rd Infantry Division seeking to break free, while von Kluge was at last moving reinforcements west – 2nd Panzer and 116th Panzer under the command of XLVII Panzer Corps. A single self-propelled 88 mm gun overran two American companies near Notre Dame de Cenilly until Sergeant Robert Lotz of 41st Armored Infantry shot out its periscope, then closed in to kill its commander. A fierce counter-attack was fought off by CC B of 2nd Armored and cost the Germans dearly when Quesada's fighter-bombers were vectored onto the scene. Americans came across abandoned German vehicles whose occupants had decided to flee on foot. On the night of 29 July, elements of 67th Armored Regiment and 41st Armored Infantry found themselves fighting for their lives against a column from 2nd SS Panzer and 17th SS who smashed through their lines in the darkness near St Denis-le-Gast. Most of the Germans eventually escaped, but they left behind 500 prisoners. Other elements of the same American units were attacked near Cambry the same night, and fought for six hours. But now the commanders of First Army knew that they were dominating the battlefield and that the German assaults reflected the thrashings of desperate men, rather than a genuine threat to the American front.

Lieutenant Fritz Langangke of 2nd SS Panzer was ordered to rendezvous with a paratroop unit at a crossroads which was to be held open until evening. He arrived to find no sign of the infantry, and was reinforced only by a single tank – that of his company commander. They camouflaged the Panthers and deployed to cover the road. Their engines were switched off as the first Sherman appeared, and although they struggled to hand crank the turret they were too slow. Their first round missed. While the American seemed to hesitate, Langangke roared hastily backwards, fired again and hit. The Sherman's commander was still standing uncertainly upright in his turret when his tank caught fire; the second Panther accounted for the next two Shermans. Mist, most unusual for the season, was drifting across the road. In its midst, Langangke was shocked to see Germans moving towards the Americans with their hands up. These were the infantry he had expected to meet: "They had taken their chance to finish the war."

There was a lull in the action. American artillery fire began to fall around the orchard, and the Germans took it in turns to doze. Then a solitary Sherman raced headlong towards them, and its gun began to traverse to meet that of the Panther. The German fired first. The American tank commander leapt from his burning turret and ran for cover. The heat in the Panther was becoming intolerable, and sweat was pouring down the crews' faces. There was another pause. Then came a sudden massive explosion against the hull, and they looked out to see American infantry all around them. To their astonishment, the tank responded when they roared into reverse. But now they were clearly visible, in the open, and a succession of American tank shells hit them. The driver shouted: "I can't see! The periscope's gone!" Langangke pushed up his head and directed the driver further back. Another shell sprang open the turret welding, and they could see daylight through the steel. The crew baled out, Langangke wrenching his neck as he jumped without removing his headset.

They left their company commander still in his tank, working on a jammed gun, and ran away down the road towards the main German positions. They were in open country when a passing fighter-bomber swooped upon them, and Langangke's gunner was killed by a cannon shell. Like all soldiers attacked by aircraft, they felt a passionate hatred for the pilot: "If we had had a chance to get that man, there would have been another war crime." They walked on until they reached the headquarters of one of the division's panzergrenadier regiments, and were eventually provided with a repaired tank from the workshops, in time for the Mortain counter-attack

Corlett had been pressing Bradley for a role for his XIX Corps in the offensive. Now he gained his point. As his men began to advance on the left of VII Corps, they encountered the first German reinforcements reaching the west. West of Tessy-sur-Vire, between the 28th and 31st, they collided with 2nd Panzer and then with the newly-arrived 116th Panzer in the fiercest fighting since COBRA began. On the 30th, Brigadier-General Rose's CC A of 2nd Armored, recently attached to Corlett's command, approached the town of Percy and was attacked in the rear by German tanks and infantry.

Percy lay in a hollow surrounded by hills. At about 4.30 p.m., a cluster of Rose's tank commanders and infantry officers were at the bottom of the hill preparing to advance, ignorant of the powerful opposition in the area. Some of the tank crews were out of their vehicles, cheerfully milking cows in a field. Men of 4th Infantry lay on their backs under a hedgerow, smoking. Without warning, the entire area erupted under German mortar fire. Wounded and dying GIs lay scattered in the grass as the Americans hastily deployed to move up the hill, the tanks crawling forward at walking pace to allow the infantry to keep with them. As they paused to breast a hedge, two tanks were hit and burst into flames. The gunners poured fire into every hedge in front of them, but from his Sherman Lieutenant Phil Reisler could see infantry dropping around him:

> . . . like some terrible war film. I saw one tall, very thin man drop his rifle and start to run away down the hill. Then I caught sight of holes in his head, and he crashed full tilt into an apple tree. He was running dead, like a chicken. I'll never forget the dedication of those men of 4th Infantry walking up that hill over their dead buddies like British redcoats attacking in Revolutionary War days. It was magnificent. We got to the top with about ten tanks and about thirty-five foot soldiers.[27]

They placed two careful rounds through Percy clock tower and church and the mortaring stopped. But all that night they stood on the hill under heavy German fire, the tank crews listening unhappily to the moans and screams of wounded American infantrymen. The scene was lit by flames from the wrecked tanks, which burned through the darkness. On the radio net, they heard the infantry company commander asking repeatedly for medical support, until his unit ordered: "Quit calling. We can't get to you." At intervals, the little infantry medical corporal would run to Reisler and beg him to call through again for aid, and the tank officer pretended to do so, without pressing his transmission switch. Once the corporal laid a blanket over a man who had gone. A few hours later, the men on the hill were appalled to see the figure beneath it sit up and scream. In the morning, the six surviving American tanks out of the 15 that had driven up, together with what was left of the infantry, withdrew from the hill, the Shermans coasting in neutral so that the Germans would not know that they had gone. Later Figurski, the gunner, had to pull human remains from their bogie wheels. Reisler said: "We never did get to see any krauts. Only dead ones."

After more fierce fighting, Rose's men and the other divisions of XIX Corps threw back the Germans, inflicting heavy losses of men and tanks. Some Sherman crews kept their engines running almost continuously for seven days. In the course of the entire battle, from 26 July to 12 August, one tank battalion – the 2nd/66th – lost 51 per cent of its combat personnel and 70 per cent of its tank strength. By 31 July, after fighting off repeated German assaults, the 743rd Tank Battalion was reduced to 13 Shermans.

But the Americans could afford losses of this kind far better than 2nd and 116th Panzer. Colonel Heinz-Gunther Guderian, 116th's senior staff officer, described the desperate frustration of seeking to concentrate the division for its attack on 29 July amid incessant American fighter-bomber activity. They were expecting to go in with direct support from 2nd Panzer, but they did not receive this, for the other division had problems of its own. Their assault was postponed from the night of the 29th until the morning of the 30th, but they still had had no chance to probe the American front. On their left was relatively good tank going. Ignorant of this, they attacked with maximum weight on their right, and immediately found themselves plunged into thick *bocage*. All the frustrations that the Allies had endured in the preceding weeks overtook 116th Panzer. Unable to move across country and largely restricted to the roads, their hesitant advance struck an enemy exhilarated by success, at last gaining confidence in his own powers on the battlefield. Only one German infantry company reached the St Lô road on the 30th, and the vital tanks were still struggling far behind. By noon that day, the Germans knew that their attack had failed. From the bus which served as divisional headquarters, Guderian and the staff struggled to switch the axis of advance to the west, but they were now informed that their tank battalions were being transferred elsewhere under the direct command of LXXXIV Corps. They were being pounded remorselessly by American air and artillery. The next morning, the 31st, they were not surprised when a renewed attack failed. Their only concern now was to disengage, as the Americans began to push forward again in front of them. On the night of 1 August, they were successful. Thereafter, reduced to little more than the effective strength of a battle-group, they were moved south to support the sagging German left. Guderian confessed his own disappointment in the performance of some of the division throughout the battle: "Without proper artillery and armoured support, the panzergrenadiers would not hold. These were not the men of 1941–42."[28]

While 2nd Armored's CC A was fighting around Percy, the rest of Corlett's XIX Corps were struggling to gain ground further east. On 31 July, Sergeant Bill Walsh of 102nd Cavalry was with a mixed team of tanks and assault guns which fought a characteristic action to clear the bridge across the Vire and the high ground dominating it at the little town of Torigny, south-east of St Lô.

The American armour rattled up the ruined main street of Torigny, watched in silence by clusters of frightened French civilians, hugging their doorways. One out of three bridges across the river remained intact, and across this the vehicles rolled one by one, under fire from small arms and artillery from Germans on the ridge above, Hill 204. The Americans turned and began to advance steadily up the hill towards the enemy, dug in behind the inevitable hedgerow. To their horror, Walsh's crew found their assault gun sagging, losing grip and sinking sideways into a small swamp. They baled out hastily and ran for the shelter of a cluster of trees. As they caught their breath and watched shells bursting around the crippled gun, Walsh suggested to the driver that he might try again to unstick it. He declined. Walsh ran across, started the engines, accelerated and braked in vain for a moment or two, then fled back to the trees.

He heard an officer shout for all dismounted men to follow the tanks up the hill. He began to run with the infantry, clutching his carbine. Beside him a big, walrus-moustached mechanic called Cerbeck, who had joined the battle because he said that he wished to see what combat was like before he went home, was killed by small-arms fire along with the man beyond. Walsh made a desperate grab to clamber up on a Sherman as it paused, tracks grinding and throwing up clods of earth and stones, to smash a hedgerow with its "Rhino" prongs. He fell off as the tank broke through, and looking around saw that it was the only American vehicle to have survived the drive. Propped against the reverse bank of the hedge, he found a bareheaded German soldier sitting bleeding badly from a stomach wound, muttering feebly: "*Bitte, bitte.*"

Walsh now saw the solitary Sherman reversing hard through the hole that it had cut, evidently pulling back. He ran desperately alongside until infantrymen clinging to the hull dragged him up. They withdrew to a safer distance from the German positions, and lay down around the tank waiting for reinforcements. Walsh saw a little cluster of unhappy men gathered around a soldier he knew from B Troop, who was lying footless after stepping on a *Schuemine*. The doctor appeared and dressed the clean amputation while the others fed the man cigarettes and tried to force themselves to chat easily to him as he lay in the calm of acute shock. Exhausted and drained soldiers lay all along the hedgerow, roused to life only for a few moments of heavy firing when an officer shouted that some Germans were trying to counter-attack ahead. Then the battle seemed to peter out, the Germans disappearing beyond the reverse slope of the ridge. American vehicles clattered forward nose-to-tail across the bridge below, on the road to Vire, amid inefectual enemy artillery fire. The word came that the division had decided to bypass the Germans on the ridge rather than continue a direct assault upon them. Two days later, with the enemy long gone as the advance reached far ahead of their flanks, Walsh returned with an armoured recovery vehicle and rescued his abandoned gun. The sharp, bitter little afternoon at Torigny had cost the Americans 33 casualties, three tanks and a clutch of trucks and half-tracks.

The 82nd Reconnaissance Battalion of 2nd Armored suffered

a similar shock on the afternoon of 2 August, as it moved fast south-eastwards at the head of CC B. Led by a Sherman, its column drove up a steep winding hill through the thickly-wooded forest of St Sever towards the town of Calvados beyond. In their haste to reach their objectives, they had dispensed with infantry flank protection or advance patrols. As teh lead vehicle emerged from the wood, it was halted by a road block of trees felled across the road. The commander, a Pennsylvanian named Sergeant James Maser, dismounted to inspect the trees seconds before fire from two Tiger tanks, hull-down covering the road, destroyed his Sherman. German infantry in the woods began to bring down machine-gun and mortar fire the length of the column. Americans ran from their vehicles to try to pinpoint their attackers, but could see nothing through the trees and thick scrub. Within a few minutes, one of the survivors wrote, "it became a nightmare of embarrassing, disorganized rout." 25 Americans died in a few minutes of furious German firing, before the rest of the battalion could make their escape. Half their NCOs were lost, and two more became casualties in accidents in their assembly area that night. It was a brutal, stinging reminder of the punishment that the Germans could still inflict upon tactical carelessness. It was 7 August before 2nd Armored cleared St Sever and advanced to St Hilaire and Barenton.

As von Kluge's exhausted men at last recoiled further east, the Allies were pressing forward. On 30 July, the British VIII Corps launched Operation BLUECOAT south from Caumont towards Vire and Mont Pinçon, while the U.S. V Corps advanced on their right. V Corps' official task was merely to protect the flank of COBRA, but General Hodges told Gerow that there was nothing to stop him making all the ground that he could in the process. There was some confusion between the British and Americans about rights of access to roads, and mutual irritation when British reconnaissance vehicles found Vire empty and claimed its liberation, only to find the Americans occupying the town before British main elements could reach it. For the British, any satisfaction at the extraordinary loosening of the front that had now begun was soured by the discovery that, once again, XXX Corps and 7th Armoured Division were performing feebly. Montgomery's patience was finally exhausted: Bucknall and Erskine were sacked. The U.S. First Army's diary for 31 July reported:

Resistance in the XIX Corps sector continues to be rugged; the boche here shows no sign of demoralization, 30th division made only 300 yards, and the 29th were only able to make 800. V Corps had things a bit easier, the 2nd and 5th divisions making more than two miles, 35th div a mile. The Second British Army continued its drive, but met determined enemy resistance and consequently had to be content with a stalemate . . . Some 10,000 prisoners have been taken during the drive.

The disappointments on Gerow and Corlett's fronts could not mar the exhilaration of the vast success of COBRA to the west, the personal triumph of Collins, who played a pre-eminent role in the achievement. This passionate, intolerant, impatient soldier had once again demonstrated his outstanding qualities as a corps commander. All the American virtues of speed and energy had at last come into play on the battlefield. The plan and the army had found their moment. It is highly doubtful whether an operation resembling COBRA could have been launched earlier in the campaign. Its prerequisites were, first, a degree of battle wisdom that First Army only attained after weeks of painful experience; and second, an erosion of German strength that had taken much hard fighting to bring about. Against an army of such supreme professionalism, a prémature American dash deep into the German front might have resulted in a crushing defeat for the attackers; the Allies needed first to cripple the fighting power of the enemy and crumble their resources. Having done so, they now reaped rich rewards.

At this pivotal moment in the Allies' fortunes, the long-scheduled shift in the American command structure took effect: Lieutenant-General Courtney Hodges assumed command of First Army; Patton's Third Army formally came into being; Bradley stepped up to exercise overall command of the American forces, now designated 12th Army Group. The stage was set for one of the most dramatic American strategic movements of the war.

The limits of air power

It has become an historical cliché of the Normandy campaign to assert that Allied air power was decisive in making victory possible. This is a half-truth. Overwhelming Allied air superiority enabled the ground troops to operate with almost total freedom from Luftwaffe interference. This was the battle chiefly won by

Spaatz's Mustang fighters in the sky over Germany during the first months of 1944, and maintained until the end of the war by the vast numbers of Allied interceptors over the battlefield. A second factor, of which more will be said below, was the fighter-bombers' ability to smash German attempts to concentrate for a decisive armoured thrust. Thanks to the bombing of communications and constant fighter-bomber sweeps over the German rear areas, German daylight movement became hazardous, and was often impossible. In the first weeks of the campaign, while the air forces' claims about the level of destruction that they had inflicted upon German units advancing to the front were exaggerated, the delay and anxiety that they caused were of critical importance. The infantry suffered much more than the armoured units, since they possessed few vehicles and were almost entirely dependent upon horses for divisional transport.

Yet in Normandy, the greatest concentration of air power ever assembled in support of ground operations also revealed its limitations. It was unable to inflict sufficient damage upon German defensive positions to offer the Allied armies anywhere an easy passage, despite Sir Arthur Harris' characteristically extravagant assertion in 1945 that the air forces had given the armies in north-west Europe "a walkover". The poor flying weather – which averaged one day in three through the summer – and the hours of darkness provided the Germans with sufficient respite from air attack to move their forces more or less where they wished, and to continue bringing forward a bare minimum of ammunition and supplies. Every captured German officer in 1944–45 complained bitterly about the difficulties caused to his unit by Allied aircraft and this, together with the exaggerated claims of the airmen, caused Allied intelligence to be too uncritical in its assessments of the material damage inflicted upon enemy formations in transit. Almost all were indeed seriously delayed by the wrecked river bridges and railways and the harassment upon the roads. But careful study of German records shows that only in a very few cases was the combat power of a unit seriously diminished by air attack on the journey to Normandy. Even allowing for the early morning cloud, it is remarkable that 21st Panzer's armoured regiments were able to reach the battlefield on D-Day from their harbours around Falaise with only minimal losses from air attack. Panzer Lehr's journey was fraught with frustration and harassment, but its order of battle was diminished by less than 10 per cent. Most Germans interviewed for this narrative recall the smashed railway junctions and bridges they passed on their way to the front, but very few remember their units suffering the actual loss of more than a few trucks. The allegedly appalling journey of the 2nd SS Panzer Division from Toulouse to Normandy has passed into the legend of the Second World War, and its arrival was certainly much delayed by encounters with the Resistance and Allied air forces. But its material losses of tanks and armoured vehicles were negligible.* The truth is that tactical air power began to inflict crippling damage upon enemy transport only in the later stages of the battle for Normandy, when difficulties on the ground compelled the Germans to move in daylight, and when techniques of forward air control, which should have been available from 6 June, were at last put into practice.

The fundamental difficulty overhanging all Allied air support of operations in Normandy was that, with two very honourable exceptions of whom more will be said below, senior Allied airmen remained obsessed with their conviction that it was not the major function of the air forces to serve as flying artillery for the army. This, of course, was precisely the role in which the Luftwaffe had achieved such remarkable results for the Wehrmacht in the first half of the war. In 1944 and in their own writings after the war, Allied airmen wrote with astonishing condescension about the diversion of their forces to support ground operations.[1] Vandenburg records a conversation with a colleague on 15 June about the army's demand for a massed bomber attack, "to blast the English army from in front of Caen . . . We both agreed that the use contemplated was not proper . . ."[2] Whatever Montgomery's shortcomings in other directions, he could never be accused of failing to understand the vital importance of air support. He harangued his officers again and again about the need to live and work in the closest proximity to the airmen. It was the airmen themselves, and Air-Marshal Coningham in particular, who resolutely refused to accept a close relationship with the soldiers. Coningham had been nettled by Montgomery's supposed failure to grant sufficient credit to the air forces under his command in the desert, and he never forgave him. He saw as little of the C-in-C of 21st Army Group as he could, and physically distanced himself from the ground

*For a detailed study of 2nd SS Panzer's terrible march, and the impact of the French Resistance upon the Normandy campaign, see the author's *Das Reich* (London and New York, 1981).

headquarters. It is remarkable that Coningham's attitude and behaviour was not rewarded with dismissal. But Tedder shared many of Coningham's views, and above all sympathized with his distaste for Montgomery.

Tedder's high intelligence has often been praised by his colleagues, yet his arrogant self-assurance matched that of Montgomery. He shared the views of the "bomber barons" that air support by heavy aircraft for ground operations was a diversion from their war-winning role in attacking German industry: "I told Leigh-Mallory that he was in danger of leading the Army up the garden path with his sweeping assurances of help . . . I felt that the limitations of air support on the battlefield were not sufficiently understood; neither was the full scope of the role of air power outside the battle area sufficiently appreciated by the Army, or by Leigh-Mallory."[3]

Studying Tedder's writings, it is impossible to escape the conclusion that he suffered the same grievous handicap as most airmen of his generation – the inability to perceive that the war could only be won by the defeat of the German army upon the battlefield, an enormously difficult task to which all other operations by sea and air must be subordinated. There were grounds for much disappointment and sympathy over the failures of ground operations in Normandy in June and July. It has been suggested above that few of these were the fault of Montgomery's generalship. Yet Tedder's remorseless hostility to the Commander-in-Chief of 21st Army Group, his sniping and carping from SHAEF about the shortcomings of the soldiers, lessen his stature as a commander; although, of course, the anomaly of his position was that he could speak his mind in the highest places about any aspect of the campaign that he chose, but bore direct responsibility for none of it. Early in July, he was agreeing with Coningham "that the Army did not seem prepared to fight its own battles."[4] He persuaded Eisenhower to amend a draft letter to Montgomery promising that all the resources of the air would be available to support him: "I insisted that the Air could not, and must not, be turned on thus glibly and vaguely in support of the Army, which would never move unless prepared to fight its way with its own weapons."[5] He made common cause with two senior British officers at SHAEF known for their enmity to Montgomery – Morgan and Humphrey Gale – in discussing the possibility of removing the British general. On 20 July after GOODWOOD, "I spoke to Portal about the Army's failure. We were agreed in regarding Montgomery as the cause. We also talked about the control of the Strategic Air Forces. Portal felt that the time was drawing near when their control could revert to the Combined Chiefs of Staff exercised through himself."[6] Yet it was Portal who, during the autumn and winter, would prove wholly incapable of controlling the British strategic bomber force, to the extent that he was obliged to confess his own inability to induce Sir Arthur Harris to conform to Air Staff policy.

The airmen considered that they were on most solid ground in their complaints against the army about heavy bomber operations. The soldiers repeatedly demanded and received the support of the "heavies" in a role for which the airmen insisted they were unsuitable. The soldiers were then surprised when the bombers failed to achieve the expected results, whether against coastal positions on D-Day or tank concentrations on the Bourgébus Ridge. The bombing of Caen had accomplished nothing but the levelling of a great Norman city. The bombing before GOODWOOD had been provided, the airmen claimed, only because the army insisted that it would pave the way for a major breakthrough. This it did not. On 21 July, somewhat obscurely, Tedder "saw the Supreme Commander at once and told him that Montgomery's failure to take action earlier had lost us the opportunity offered by the attempt on Hitler's life."[7] This comment appears to reflect the airman's wholly mistaken assumption that the German army was on the brink of internal collapse.

A SHAEF Operational Research report upon the benefits of heavy bombing in support of ground operations declared that "it is the provisional opinion of the investigators that the moral effects of the bombing upon the enemy and upon Allied troops far outweigh the very considerable material effects."[8] Quesada of IXth Air Force declared that he doubted whether the American bombing before the attack on Cherbourg had killed more than 10 Germans: "Of course, our army loved to see it before they went in. But it made me more sceptical about whether we should be using the air force as a USO show. I believed in attacking specific, identifiable targets that could be destroyed by aircraft."[9]

The airmen considered that the proven inability of heavy bombers to do crippling material damage to enemy ground forces was sufficient reason to confine them to assaults upon

Germany's cities and industrial plants. Yet if massed bomber attacks provided moral benefits in the greatest campaign of the western war – which all concerned on both sides agreed that they did – it seemed reasonable to suggest that the armies were entitled to them. It was also forgotten, amidst the recriminations about "short bombing" and ground force failures, that the use of the "heavies" had in fact inflicted immense damage upon the German defences before both COBRA and GOODWOOD, even if this was not conclusive. What was gravely needed, and never achieved as a result of the lack of sympathy between the personalities concerned, was improvement in the technique of co-ordinating heavy bomber operations with ground offensives. Vandenburg recorded sourly in his diary for 27 July: "Leaving for lunch with the C-in-C and Bedell Smith, I heard Beadle tell Jimmy [Doolittle] to the effect that what was needed to correct deficiencies in strategic bombers operating with ground forces was to get a commander who could view that support sympathetically."[10] As late as November 1944, a 21st Army Group report on air support lamented that "we have lacked and still do lack high-powered air staff officers at the Army Group HQ to be in on the initial stages of planning just as the gunners and sappers are."[11] This was surely a damning reflection on the gulf between the two services even in the last months of the war. All that summer of 1944, the feuds within the air forces, which had so disfigured the Allied high command in the spring, continued unabated. Vandenburg's diary for 23 June reports: "Lunched with General Spaatz at which time he cautioned me to be very careful not to create an incident which, in his opinion, was desired by the RAF to start the disintegration of this can of worms by 'the Tedder, Coningham, Harris clique'."[12] Brereton, commanding IXth Air Force, held a press conference following the COBRA short bombing tragedy, at which he blamed COBRA's slow start upon the sluggishness of the ground troops.

Yet the sluggishness with which ground–air co-operation techniques developed in Normandy must be attributed principally to the attitudes of the airmen. Air-Marshal "Mary" Coningham, commanding the British 2nd Tactical Air Force, was a bitter enemy of Montgomery and of Leigh-Mallory. Brigadier Charles Richardson, Montgomery's very able BGS Plans, worked closely with the airmen on ground support plans, and found Coningham to be "a prima donna. He seemed to have a glorified concept of his own position, and to be too remote from the battle."[13] For many weeks, Coningham continued to direct air support from Stanmore, outside London, on the grounds that communications in France were too poor for him to command his squadrons from a headquarters with the armies. While the wide-ranging fighter-bomber sweeps carried out every day over France by Allied aircraft created great difficulties for the Germans, it was Typhoons and Thunderbolts operating in close support of the ground troops and directed by a Forward Air Controller (FAC), which could play the critical role. Requests for air support channelled through a rear staff and then passed forward with merely a map reference to the squadrons did not produce rapid or precise results. There was no lack of communications technology for Forward Air Control. Yet above all in the early stages of the battle, there were nothing like enough FACs with the front-line troops. The destruction of a single RAF vehicle in the first hours of GOODWOOD wiped out Forward Air Control for the central axis of the offensive. "As a result of our inability to get together with the air in England," wrote Bradley, "we went into France almost totally untrained in air–ground co-operation."[14] Brigadier Richardson said: "In North Africa we seemed to have got the air business right, yet we had lost some of it in Normandy."[15]

Only two senior air force officers distinguished themselves by an absolute commitment to assisting the armies, undiminished by personal hostilities or jealousies. The first was British, Air Vice-Marshal Harry Broadhurst, working alongside Dempsey's Second Army as the RAF's AOC 83 Group. Broadhurst, a fighter pilot of great experience and a veteran of the desert, earned the affection and respect of all the soldiers with whom he worked. The second was the American General Elwood R. "Pete" Quesada, a pioneering airman of Spanish extraction, quick intelligence and easy charm who commanded IXth Tactical Air Command, responsible to Bradley for close air support of the American armies.

Quesada may claim to have done more than any other airman in the Allied ranks to originate and refine techniques of ground–air co-operation, and to put them into practice. "Unlike most airmen who viewed ground support as a bothersome diversion to war in the sky," wrote Bradley, "Quesada approached it as a vast new frontier waiting to be explored."[16] The American airman had served in North Africa, where he found that the prevailing USAAF attitude "was that air forces should take care of themselves, with little consideration to the needs of the armies." Indeed, in 1943, it was Coningham – such a thorn in Montgomery's side in Europe in 1944 – to whom Quesada paid generous tribute, "for forcing the USAAF to participate in the ground battle". It was in North Africa that Quesada's undogmatic willingness to adjust command arrangements to the needs of the battle first caught the attention of Eisenhower. The airman handed over operational control of a B-24 anti-submarine wing to the navy rather than seeking to direct it himself through Casablanca, on the simple grounds that this scheme was likely to be more effective. Undramatic enough, perhaps, but his gesture should be seen in the context of a war in which most airmen fought tooth and nail to retain control of their squadrons rather than surrender direction to either of the other two services. Only 38 years old, unmarried, with a quaint enthusiasm for cabinet-making in his off-duty hours, Quesada was the embodiment of the American "can do" spirit which so attracted all those Europeans of his generation who were not intractably prejudiced.

In France – "not until Normandy did the army air force become a real participant in the ground battle" – Quesada flew a Lightning into the beachhead on D+1 to establish his own headquarters alongside that of Bradley, with whom he established a close personal relationship. It was Quesada who first mounted aircraft radios in American tanks at the time of COBRA – it was a measure of the earlier suspicions between the two services that the airman was astonished when Bradley agreed to give them to him. Thus equipped, Forward Air Controllers could direct strikes from the very tip of the front. While on the British front the RAF jealously kept forward air control in the hands of its own personnel, among the Americans, specially-designated army officers with every unit were able to call down their own support.

Lieutenant Philip Reisler of the U.S. 2nd Armored Division had begun his career as a Forward Air Controller in Sicily, "where the bombing confusion was horrible", equipped only with red and green signal lights, which were quite invisible to the pilots, and yellow smoke canisters to reveal the Allied line. The limitations of these were still apparent in Normandy. Too many troops well behind the front fired smoke or laid out identification panels, only to expose the men ahead of them to a hail of bombs and rockets. In July, Reisler at last received a radio for his Sherman with which he could talk direct to the pilots, and operate directly under the orders of his Combat Command's brigadier. A glimpse of clear skies at dawn and the words, "it looks like we're going to have air today", became one of the great morale boosters on the unit radio net. CC A headquarters would inform Reisler of fighter-bombers on the way, and at the scheduled hour he would seek contact: "Hello, Skudo leader" (or Red Flag or Back Door or whatever the air group's callsign), "this is Cutbreak. I am at co-ordinate 656474 south-east Vire." For the pilot above, conditions in the cockpit made map reading difficult, and as he reported to the soldier that he was approaching his area, Reisler would seek to call down a round or two of artillery or tank smoke to mark the target. Then he would hear the flight commander on the ground ordering his pilots in: "Jake, you go down first, Pete fly high cover . . ." As they bombed or rocketed, Reisler would correct their fire around the target. Within five minutes, the mission was over and the aircraft gone.

It was not unknown for the Germans to spot the planes and fire smoke onto the American positions, once obliging a desperate Reisler to yell, "Pull out! Pull out!" to a Thunderbolt pilot as he dived onto the Shermans. More often still, for reasons which the tank crews were never told, there was simply no air available to them. They had no power to command the presence of the fighter-bombers; they could only request them. When they did have support and it was obliged to turn home for lack of fuel, Riesler would sometimes get the planes to attack empty countryside simply to encourage the ground troops.[17] This was a practice that infuriated the pilots, for whom every ground-attack sortie was fraught with peril. If they were hit, they enjoyed very little hope of parachuting at low level. When a shortage of Typhoon pilots developed in 2nd Tactical Air Force, the RAF asked for volunteers to transfer from Spitfires. There were none. Men had to be drafted.

Quesada and Broadhurst were frequent visitors to forward areas to discover at first hand what their squadrons were achieving. One morning the American was riding a jeep in search of his old fellow pupil at the Command and General Staff School, Maurice Rose, now leading the CC A of 2nd Armored Division. Following the directions of a succession of tankers up a surprisingly silent road, 100 yards away he glimpsed a tank he took to be the brigadier's. He was driving towards it when a 75 mm shell from its turret slammed into the jeep, smashing the vehicle into a ruin and wounding Quesada's driver. It was a Panther. The two men spent an uncomfortable twenty minutes crawling away under small-arms fire. Quesada was conscious that only the previous day he himself had laughed heartily as he heard a German corps commander's aide being interrogated about the whereabouts of his general. The aide answered: "The last time I saw him, he was crawling up a ditch." Now it was the American general's turn to crawl, and he was fortunate to escape alive. Few airmen of any nationality went to such lengths to keep in touch with the realities of the ground battle.

Conversely, Quesada worked hard to keep the ground commanders up to date with the air situation. The tiny handful of Luftwaffe aircraft that ventured over the Allied lines caused wholly disproportionate distress among the ground troops, and were sometimes used as an alibi by divisional commanders to explain difficulties and failures. One morning, Quesada was compelled to listen to complaints from Bradley that the 29th Division had been harassed by enemy air attack. The airman persuaded Bradley to ride with him to see the 29th Division's commander, the excitable Gerhardt, "more like a rooster than a divisional commanding officer," suggested Quesada wryly. He demanded to know precisely what the army was complaining about. After much prevarication and inquiries down the chain of command, it transpired that a regimental commander was fulminating about an attack by two German aircraft on his command post, which had set a half-track on fire and wounded his cook. Bradley drove back in silence, to compose a letter to all divisional commanders suggesting that they should not expect to be immune to air attack. On another occasion when a similar protest was made, Quesada sent up reconnaissance aircraft to provide Bradley with two sets of photographs of the battlefield. One showed the area behind the German lines, with its empty roads and utter absence of visible movement. The other showed the Allied zone, crawling with nose-to-tail armour and transport convoys, uncamouflaged dumps in the fields, shipping unloading off the beaches. Bradley took the point.

Another personal venture by Quesada was more controversial. During one of Eisenhower's visits to France in mid-June, the airman got up from a staff meeting, declaring that he was off on a fighter sweep. In an impulsive moment, the Supreme Commander asked boyishly: "Can I come?" Equally impulsive, Quesada agreed. Within the hour he took off in his Mustang with Eisenhower crammed behind his seat in place of a 70-gallon fuel tank. "Once we were airborne, I began to realize, first, that he didn't fit – I told him that I would have to turn the plane over if we were hit – and then that perhaps this was wrong." A few miles over the lines, Quesada aborted the sweep and took the general home. This spared neither himself nor Eisenhower severe reprimands from Washington for the risk they had taken.

For aircraft, as for so much else among the Allied armies, the abundance of resources was staggering. Quesada controlled 37 squadrons of aircraft, with enough reserves to ensure that losses could be replaced immediately. He was irked to see six Lightnings on an airstrip one morning marked as unserviceable, because their canopies had been damaged by pilots forgetting to lock them down on take-off. It was the type of damage that could be repaired in hours by an air force in real need of fighters, "like putting an automobile on the junk pile with a flat tire". Pilots flew three or four days a week, perhaps five missions a day that might be as brief as 20 minutes, living between sorties in much the same mud and discomfort as the ground forces. The Normandy dust contained a hard silicon-like material that played havoc with aircraft engines running up on improvised strips. Filters were hastily designed and fitted to cope with this. "I was never consciously short of pilots or aircraft," said Quesada. British fliers were acutely nervous of their eager but inexperienced American counterparts, who were prone to attack any aircraft in the sky that they could not immediately identify. RAF Typhoons found that being attacked by Mustangs or Thunderbolts was not an occasional freak, but an alarmingly regular occurrence. So too was being fired upon by the Royal Navy over the Channel.

Despite the resentment felt towards the air forces by those Allied units which had suffered from "short bombing", the pilots earned the respect of most troops who watched them in action. Well-controlled close air support became, by late summer, one of the most formidable weapons in the hands of a unit which found itself bogged down. Yet for the fliers, ground attack enjoyed none of the glamour of high-level fighter interception, and was infinitely more hazardous. Like all low-level flying, it required unrelenting concentration and precision. A New Zealand Typhoon pilot described a morning over Normandy:

Swirling clouds of yellow dust hung over the busy roads beneath us, and further to the south-east the battered city of Caen flickered and smouldered under a huge mushroom of pink and black smoke. Southwards, in the region of Villers-Bocage, a furious gun battle was taking place, and to the west, thin streams of coloured tracer spouted into the morning sky before falling away in chains of red-hot clusters. In the more open country the fields were strewn with the bloated carcasses of hundreds of tan and white cattle. Shell craters, bomb holes and burnt-out tanks littered the tortured countryside.

To the south of Potigny we began climbing but streams of light flak came racing towards us. So I hastily sank down again to the comparative safety of the taller trees and hedgerows . . . I caught sight of the object of our early-morning mission. The road was crammed with enemy vehicles – tanks, trucks, half-tracks, even horse-drawn wagons and ambulances, nose to tail, all pressing forward in a frantic bid to reach cover before the skies once more became alive with the winged death of 2nd Tactical Air Force. As I sped to the head of this mile-long column, hundreds of German troops began spilling out into the road to sprint for the open fields and hedgerows. I zoomed up sharply over a ploughed field where 20 or 30 Germans in close array were running hard for a clump of trees. They were promptly scythed down by a lone Mustang which appeared from nowhere. The convoy's lead vehicle was a large half-track. In my haste to cripple it and seal the road, I let fly with all eight rockets in a single salvo; I missed but hit the truck that was following. It was thrown into the air along with several bodies, and fell back on its side. Two other trucks in close attendance piled into it.

. . . Within seconds the whole stretch of road was bursting and blazing under streams of rocket and cannon fire. Ammunition wagons exploded like multi-coloured volcanoes. Several teams of horses stampeded and careered wildly across the fields, dragging their broken wagons behind them. Others fell in tangled heaps, or were caught up in the fences and hedges. It was an awesome sight: flames, smoke, bursting rockets and showers of coloured tracer – an army in retreat, trapped and without air protection.[18]

Quesada believed that his British counterparts never approached tactical air support with enough imagination; for instance, they did not follow the Americans in using radar for the navigational guidance of fighter squadrons rather than merely for defensive purposes. He felt that the RAF was hampered by the incubus of its immense force of Spitfires, superb aircraft for high-level interceptor work, of which there was now almost none, but unsuited to the ground-attack task because of their small 1,000-pound payload and lack of robustness. It was essential for any close-support aircraft to be able to withstand small-arms fire. The British Typhoon carried 2,000 pounds and was a sound ground-attack aircraft, but Quesada much preferred his own Thunderbolts and Mustangs, the former also carrying 2,000 pounds.

A close personal friend of both Spaatz and General Ira Eaker, Quesada would never acknowledge any lack of enthusiasm for the support of ground forces among his USAAF colleagues. Indeed, he argued that it was precisely because of their long term ambitions for their service that "Spaatz saw that it was vital that we should do whatever we could for the land battle – it was always on his mind that after the war we must have an independent air force. We were obsessed by proving our worth."

Nothing above diminishes the claims of the Allied air forces to have made a vital contribution to the Normandy campaign. The bombers' execution of the Transport Plan was central to ensuring that the invasion forces won the battle of the build-up. The fighter-bombers' low-level operations inflicted immense damage upon the German army, above all in the later stages of the campaign. The issue is simply whether, if the leading airmen of Britain and America had devoted themselves earlier and more wholeheartedly to the support of the armies, the air forces could have provided even more effective, perhaps decisive, direct support for the ground offensives. From 1940 to 1942, the humiliations of the British army were consistently attributed to the Luftwaffe's command of the air. Yet in 1944, when the Allies possessed air forces of a strength Goering's pilots had never dreamed of, the German army continued to mount a formidable resistance until broken in bloody ground action.

10 The open flank

By the last days of July 1944, the German army in Normandy had been reduced to such a condition that only a few fanatics of the SS still entertained hopes of avoiding defeat, far less of achieving victory. Any faint prospect of replacing the huge casualties in the west vanished in the wake of the Russian offensive against Army Group Centre, which had destroyed 28 German divisions in five weeks, a blow as shattering to Hitler as that which was now befalling him in Normandy. The Allies' intelligence reports of the German order of battle flattered their opponents – or perhaps themselves by detailing the divisions still before them: Panzer Lehr, 2nd SS Panzer, 12th SS Panzer and so on. In fact, these formations were shattered ruins of their old selves, sustained by a fraction of the men and a tiny fragment of the armour and gun power that they had carried into battle weeks before. Attrition, not manoeuvre, had been decisive in reducing von Kluge's formations to a state in which they could no longer sustain the sagging line. As the tide poured over the walls of their sandcastle from Bourgébus to Rennes, they lacked both the mobility to race the Allies to the breaches and the fighting power to seal the gaps, even where they could reach these. Von Kluge reported to Hitler:

> Whether the enemy can still be stopped at this point is questionable. The enemy air superiority is terrific, and smothers almost every one of our movements . . . Losses in men and equipment are extraordinary. The morale of our troops has suffered very heavily under constant murderous enemy fire, especially since all infantry units consist only of haphazard groups which do not form a strongly coordinated force any longer. In the rear areas of the front terrorists, feeling the end approaching, grow steadily bolder. This fact, and the loss of numerous signal installations, makes an orderly command extremely difficult.[1]

Wholesale collapses in morale were resulting in the mass surrender of units swamped by the American advance. General Hausser of Seventh Army, a legendarily tough SS commander, reported that 10 of his divisions had disintegrated, leaving scattered bands of demoralized stragglers roaming north-west France without equipment or leadership. Sergeant Hans Stober admitted that even in 17th SS Panzergrenadiers, from mid-July shell-shock – hitherto an almost unrecognized condition in SS units – became a significant problem. "By this stage, the whole German army was deteriorating," said Lieutenant Langangke of 2nd SS Panzer. "We no longer had a chance to do anything big. We could only play foxes, do this or that in a small way. *Heim ins Reich* –Home to Germany– was the principal thought in many people's minds." It was astonishing that the German east–west front held together at all. Yet the surviving fragments of the old elite units still disputed the Allied advance at every stage.

The reverberations of the bomb explosion on 20 July at Hitler's headquarters echoed through the upper ranks of his army. "At one moment was to be seen a set of men and things which together formed a focal point of world events," wrote one of the survivors, Jodl's Deputy Walter Warlimont. "At the next, there was nothing but wounded men groaning, the acrid smell of burning and charred fragments of maps and papers fluttering in the wind."[2] Hitler's chronic mistrust and scorn for his generals became manic. Throughout the Normandy campaign, he had intervened in their decisions. Now he began to sweep aside the unanimous advice of men as unfailingly loyal to him in the past as Hausser, Eberbach, Dietrich, as well as the wavering von Kluge, and to direct the battle in a fashion that severed all contact with reason or reality. On 30 July Jodl placed before him an order "for possible withdrawal from the coastal sector", which was in effect a blueprint for the evacuation of France.[3] Hitler brushed this aside, saying that it was not at present necessary. Jodl anyway telephoned Blumentritt at von Kluge's headquarters and told him to be prepared to receive such an order when it came. Late on the night of 31 July, Hitler personally briefed Warlimont for the trip he was to make to France, declaring simply: "The object remains to keep the enemy confined to the bridgehead and there to inflict serious losses upon him in order to wear him down."[4] When Warlimont received his final orders at the midday conference the next morning, Hitler said irritably, "You tell Field-Marshal von Kluge to keep on looking to his front, to keep his eyes on the enemy and not to look over his shoulder."[5] Warlimont was to be Hitler's personal agent at von Kluge's headquarters, ensuring that the havering

Field-Marshal executed his orders precisely.

The Führer suffered increasingly from self-pity in the days following the assassination attempt. On hearing a recital of the sufferings of his soldiers and of the German people, he remarked crossly: "I think it's pretty obvious that this war is no fun for me. I've been cut off from the world for five years. I've not been to a theatre, a concert or a film . . ."[6] It was a remarkable irony that, at a time when his own faith in his army was crumbling, most of its officers and men in the field were shocked by news of the bomb plot, and were continuing to hold their positions despite intolerable difficulties. Colonel Heinz-Gunther Guderian of 116th Panzer was astonished and disgusted by the news from the rear: "We were not part of some South American military junta. We had the constant feeling that there were traitors in our midst." Captain Eberhard Wagemann of 21st Panzer staff had long ago concluded, in a discussion with an older officer of the division who was a personal friend of Count von Stauffenburg, that the war could not be won. But like many German officers, he felt that however hopeless the situation, "no officer, no soldier had any business to concern himself with treachery." Corporal Adolf Hohenstein of 276th Infantry retained no faith in victory, but was thoroughly dismayed by Stauffenburg's bomb. "It cost us thousands of lives at the front," he believed. A 21st Army Group intelligence report based upon prisoner interrogation following the bomb plot concluded: "The overall effect of the news on the men of fighting units was one of no excitement. One effort to end the war had been frustrated. Therefore everything was as before."[7] The same document came to the conclusion that only 5 per cent of German troops now believed in the possibility of final victory. 10th and 12th SS Panzer were the only divisions in which it could be said that morale was still high.

The principcal consequences of the bomb plot among the men in Normandy was to sow an almost poisonous mistrust within the officer corps. It was ironic that many officers whose confused sense of honour had convinced them that they should not be party to the bomb plot, now suffered bitter consequences because that same interpretation of honour had prevented them from betraying the plotters to Hitler. The Wehrmacht found itself deprived of all power or respect within the German state, subjected to the final humiliation of being compelled to adopt the Hitler salute. Relations between the SS and the *Heer* – the soldiers of the Wehrmacht – were normally good at field level.

Now a chasm widened between the fanatical loyalists and those despairing of victory and increasingly weary of defeat. In the hospital where Corporal Werner Kortenhaus of 21st Panzer was recovering from his wounds, a young soldier playing chess said as they talked about news of the bomb plot: "He'd be better dead." An SS NCO sprang to his feet and caught the speaker a furious slap across the face. Kortenhaus himself, along with most men of the *Heer*, had no illusions left: "We reckoned that the whole game was up." The SS were increasingly obsessed by the conviction that the anti-Hitler plotters were contributing directly to their misfortunes on the battlefield. "It was obvious to us that there was a lot of treachery," said Lieutenant Walter Kruger of 12th SS Panzer. Hitler raged that the lack of *Panzerfausten* in Normandy was clearly the consequence of sabotage by the Quartermaster-General, Wagner, one of the dead plotters.

After the war, when the names of those concerned with the plot were shown to include such men as Rommel's Chief of Staff, Hans Speidel, and Graf von Schwerin, commanding 116th Panzer, thousands of their former comrades sought to blame their treachery for the misfortunes that befell the German army in Normandy. Above all, they allowed themselves to be convinced that delays in moving units from the Pas de Calais and in getting ammunition and supplies to the front were the result of sabotage. There will never be conclusive evidence one way or the other. But it remains far more probable that the failures and difficulties were genuine accidents and errors of war. The plotters were guided by a desire to make peace on the best available terms with the western Allies. Nothing could have made this task more difficult than for Hitler's death to take place at a moment when the German army was in collapse after a shattering defeat. It was very much to the plotters' advantage that the line in Normandy should be stable when the Führer died. By July, some officers and men were giving less than their best efforts to the war because they were convinced of its futility. But there was a great gulf between passive defeatism of this kind, and an active attempt to sabotage the campaign. By early August, the German army in France was on the edge of catastrophe because of its ruin on the battlefield and the demented strategy of Hitler, not because it had been betrayed from within.

For the Allied armies, the battle now took on a new character. Hitherto, while generalship had naturally been important, the progress of the campaign depended above all upon the ability of

British, American and Canadian units to seize ground from their German opponents on the next ridge, in the next hedge, beyond the next road. Henceforth, while hard fighting still lay ahead, Normandy became a commanders' battle. It was the decisions of the generals that determined the manner in which events unfolded in August, their successes and failures which brought about the position that was achieved by September.

Of all the Allied movements of the campaign, few have evoked such widespread post-war criticism as the American "right turn" into Brittany at the beginning of August.[8] The German XXV Corps was known to be weak and lacking the mobility to create a major threat to Bradley's armies. Montgomery anticipated that no more than a single U.S. corps would press on west from Avranches towards Brest and the other Breton ports. In fact, two of Patton's three corps swept across the bridge at Pontaubault into Brittany, and Bradley was determined to embark on no reckless adventures south-eastwards unless he was certain of holding the Avranches "elbow" in their rear. "We can't risk a loose hinge," he said.[9] He feared a German counter-attack north-westwards, breaking through to the coast and cutting off Patton's armoured divisions from their fuel and supplies – with disastrous consequences. Bradley himself later accepted responsibility for the decision, for good or ill, to swing large American forces west into Brittany.

Patton won the admiration of the world for the energy and ruthlessness with which he forced his army through Avranches and into its dash across Brittany. "If the greatest study of mankind is man," he said, "surely the greatest study of war is the road net."[10] He wrote with justified pride of his own direction of the movement:

> The passage of Third Army through the corridor at Avranches was an impossible operation. Two roads entered Avranches; only one left it over the bridge. We passed through this corridor 2 infantry and 2 armoured divisions in less than 24 hours. There was no plan because it was impossible to make a plan.[11]

Yet for all the verve and energy of Patton's movements, of which so many other American and British commanders were envious, there is considerable force in the remarks of those veterans exasperated by the Patton legend. They declare: "He didn't break out. He walked out."[12] Bradley had no patience with Patton, dismissing one of Montgomery's wilder flights of strategic fantasy with the adjectives, "militarily unsound, Pattonesque". He wrote of Third Army's great sweep in early August: "Patton blazed through Brittany with armored divisions and motorized infantry. He conquered a lot of real estate and made big headlines, but the Brittany campaign failed to achieve its primary objectives."[13] Bradley referred, of course, to the rapid seizure of the western ports in a usable condition. The true architects of Patton's rush through Brittany were Collins and the men of his VII Corps who had broken the German line in COBRA – and the British and Canadian armies still facing the bulk of von Kluge's effective formations. It is essential to emphasize that there was no German front in the west – merely a disorganized jumble of units retreating with all the speed that they could muster into the fortified ports where they were expected to make a stand. When Patton's army later met serious German resistance, the American divisions under his command fought no better and no worse with his leadership than under that of any other commander. At the beginning of August 1944, the posturing general was the man for the hour, performing feats of movement that probably no other Allied commander could have matched. But it would be absurd to suppose that he discovered a key to the downfall of the German armies which had escaped his peers. It was they who made possible the glory that he now reaped with such relish.

The fruits of the dash into Brittany were intoxicating for the men riding the tanks and trucks – an almost unopposed swing across country already largely in the hands of the French Resistance, gaining for Gerow's 6th Armored Division 4,000 prisoners at a cost of 130 killed, 400 wounded, 70 missing. Yet most of the Germans in the region were given time to withdraw into Brest, whose garrison swelled to 38,000 men, and whose defences held until 19 September. Far more seriously, the vital turn east towards Mayenne and Alençon, intended to initiate the rolling up of the main German front in Normandy, was delayed by days.

Major-General John "P" Wood of the 4th Armored Division was one of the outstanding American commanders of the campaign. On 2 August, having advanced over 50 miles in four days, Wood and his tanks stood west of Rennes, where he had shrewdly bypassed a 2,000-strong German garrison – too weak to present a serious threat, but possibly strong enough seriously to delay a direct assault. Wood perfectly grasped the urgency of turning east. Late on the afternoon of 3 August, his tanks were more than 30 miles south of Rennes, and had cut seven of the ten major roads to the city. Wood gave initial orders for a move south-east, on Châteaubriant. Then Middleton at VIII Corps intervened. First, he ordered that Wood must not merely cut off Rennes, but capture it. This Wood's 13th Infantry achieved with a bold push for the heart of the city which prompted the defenders to withdraw during the night of the 3rd. But Middleton's eyes were still fixed west towards the sea. Quiberon Bay had been a vital Allied objective since D-Day, the intended site of a major artificial port. VIII Corps' commander drove to see Wood and insist that, rather than pressing east, where the countryside yawned empty of all significant German forces, 4th Armored must make for the coast. Early on the morning of 4 August, Middleton found Wood standing by his vehicles in a field, stripped to the waist, gazing at the maps laid out before him on the grass.

He came over and threw his arms around me. I said, "What's the matter, John, you lost your division?" He said, "Heck no, we're winning this war the wrong way, we ought to be going toward Paris."[14]

"I protested long, loud and violently," Wood said later. He believed that he could have been in Chartres in two days. "But no! We were forced to adhere to the original plan – with the only armor available, and ready to cut the enemy to pieces. It was one of the colossally stupid decisions of the war."[15] But Middleton confirmed Wood's orders, and so also did Patton's Chief of Staff, Gaffey. Gaffey told Middleton that his general "assumes that in addition to locking the roads . . . you are pushing the bulk of the [4th Armored Division] to the west and south-west to the Quiberon area, in accordance with the army plan."[16] Patton, desperately anxious not to become entangled in a wrangle with Bradley when his own position remained that of probationer, had no intention of crossing his wished. 4th Armored spent 6–10 August standing before Lorient, attempting to induce the German garrison to surrender. It was 15 August before the division was once more pushing east.

There is little doubt that the commitment of major forces in Brittany was ill-judged, when resistance was so slight and – after the example of Cherbourg – the prospect so small of the port being in early use. Bradley lies open to the charge of lack of imagination in failing to adjust the original OVERLORD plan to meet the changed situation and the great new opportunity in the west. If the Germans had now behaved rationally, recognized the threat of envelopment to their entire front and begun a full-scale retreat east, then Bradley could indeed be accused of losing his armies a great prize. But, driven on by Hitler's delusions, they did nothing of the sort. They prepared a major counter-attack and, even when it failed, were so slow to begin pulling back that Bradley's divisions had all the time that they needed to reach around behind the German rear. The diversion into Brittany may have been poor strategy, a future source of grief to staff college students. But the ultimate prize at Falaise was as great as it was ever likely to be, whatever course the American had adopted. It is also useful to remember that, while the Channel ports were in Allied hands within a month, making those of Brittany largely unnecessary, Bradley still had too much respect for the German army at the beginning of August to be confident that its collapse was total. Almost every witness at American headquarters to the events of early August agrees that their finality only became apparent later. There was no immediate conviction that the end in France had come, that von Kluge was not merely defeated, but routed. Many officers still expected to be fighting around the Seine – if not further east – come September.

On the night of 6 August, von Funck's XLVII Panzer Corps launched a major attack against the positions of the 30th Division around Mortain, which had fallen to 1st Division on the 3rd. The Germans advanced without a preparatory artillery bombardment, for they still cherished the illusion of surprise. Armoured columns of 2nd SS Panzer and 17th SS pushed forward from north and south to seize the town, and by noon of the 7th were close to St Hilaire in the south-west. Von Luttwitz's 2nd Panzer overran two companies of the American 117th Infantry. Elements of 1st SS Panzer were also committed as they arrived on the battlefield. 116th Panzer's commander pleaded the difficulty of disengaging on his existing front to explain his own formation's absence from the start-line. But within a few hours, German units were within nine miles of Avranches. If they could break through to the coast, they might cut off the 12 American divisions south of the junction from their lifeline of fuel and supplies.

Yet from the moment on the night of 6 August that Ultra

provided a brief warning to Bradley's headquarters of the Mortain counter-attack, the Americans perfectly understood this as an opportunity, not a threat. The Germans had plunged enfeebled forces into battle against powerful American formations which were not not merely confident of withstanding them, but expected to destroy them. Bradley told the visiting Henry Morgenthau: "This an opportunity that comes to a commander not more than once in a century. We are about to destroy an entire German army."[17] The veteran U.S. 4th Division, in VII Corps reserve, was deployed to seal the German flanks while 3rd Armored's CC B went to the aid of the hard-pressed 30th Division. Haislip's XV Corps was ordered to press on with its push south to Le Pau, then swing north-east to Alençon and Argentan. Third Army's great sweep was not to be impeded by the Mortain battle. Collins' VII Corps would handle the business of repelling von Funck's panzers, with formidable assistance from the Allied air forces.

Hitler had personally dispatched to von Kluge detailed plans for the armoured attack, Operation LUTTICH. "We must strike like lightning," he declared. "When we reach the sea the American spearheads will be cut off. Obviously they are trying all-out for a major decision here, because otherwise they wouldn't have sent in their best general, Patton . . . We must wheel north like lightning and turn the entire enemy front from the rear."[18] It will remain one of the great enigmas of history, not that the German generals could have accepted the invasion of Poland or the mass murder of the Jews, but that so many sane men could have borne obediently with fantasy such as this. The Commander-in-Chief of Army Group B, too weak to reject the plan as absurd, determined that if it was to be launched at all, the armour must move immediately, before the American envelopment had rendered any move impossible. He could not wait, as Hitler demanded, for the full weight of panzer forces to be transferred westwards. Of 1,400 tanks committed to battle in Normandy, 750 had already been lost. The panzer divisions initially committed to the Mortain thrust – 2nd, 1st and 2nd SS – attacked with only 75 Mk IVs, 70 Mk Vs, and 32 self-propelled guns.

From the outset, they ran into difficulties. 2nd Panzer on the right left the start-line on time, at midnight on 6 August, but 1st SS Panzer's armour was seriously delayed by a fighter-bomber which crashed onto the leading tank in a sunken lane, creating an impassable road block. It was daylight before the SS tank crews

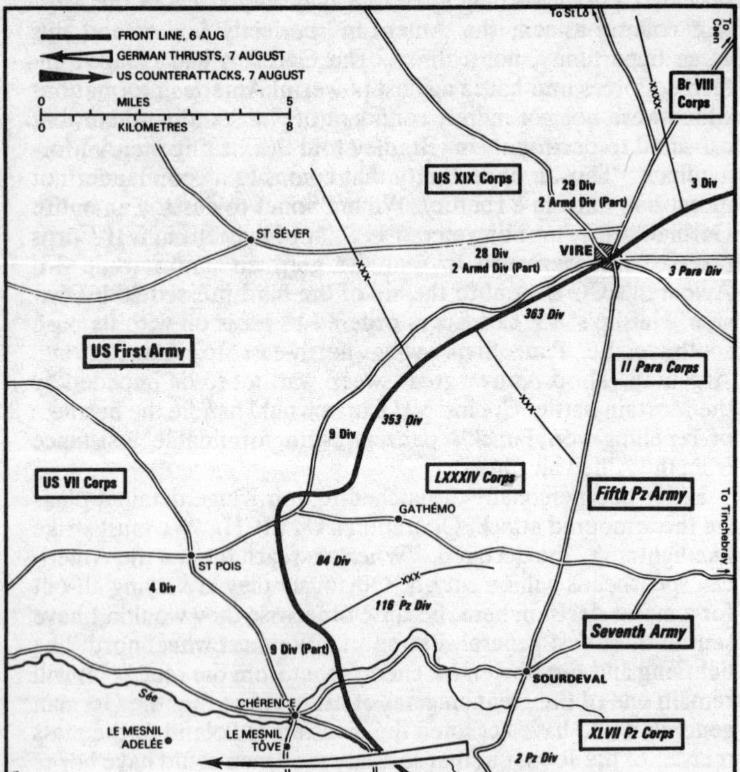

The Mortain Counter-Attack: 6–12 August

had reversed out of the shambles and found a new road to Mortain. After promising early gains beyond the little town of St Barthélémy, 1st SS met CC B of the U.S. 3rd Armored and were quickly in deep trouble. 116th Panzer, which appeared on the scene only late in the afternoon, was stopped dead by an American anti-tank screen. Only 2nd Panzer seemed to be making good progress. "Bad weather is what we need," said Luttwitz's operations officer. "Then everything will work out alright."[19] But as the early morning mist lifted, out of the sky came the first aircraft of the greatest concentration of fighter-bombers yet deployed in the west, Quesada's Thunderbolts supported by the RAF's rocket-firing Typhoons. They caught 2nd Panzer at Le Coudray. The promised Luftwaffe air cover never materialized. Almost every approaching German sortie was intercepted by Allied fighters. The ground attack, begun with little hope even among the most formidable remaining formations of the German army, foundered in disarray and destruction. Far from creating even temporary relief from the threat of encirclement, von Kluge's divisions had driven themselves deep into the destructive embrace of the Americans.

Yet for the men in the path of von Kluge's offensive that week in August, it was difficult to view the situation as enthusiastically as did Bradley's staff. Corporal George Small of 465th Anti-Aircraft Battalion, covering the Pontaubault bridges against the resurgence of Luftwaffe activity, was appalled to find his unit's triple AA guns being issued with armour-piercing ammunition: "Then we were really scared." The 30th Division bore the brunt of the German attack. Most men had been roused from their rest area on the night of the 6th, aware of a German attack but not of its details, and marched forward under the full moon to relieve infantry of the 1st Division. Guides showed them the foxholes and trenches that they were taking over. Then the men of "The Big Red One" padded away into the darkness, leaving the newcomers to meet the enemy, supported by a sprinkling of tanks and tank destroyers. On Hill 317 east of Mortain, 700 Americans of the 2nd/120th Infantry and K Company of the 3rd/120th fought surrounded for five days, supplied by erratic air drops, by the end losing 300 killed and wounded. The four rifle companies were reduced by repeated attacks to 8, 24, 18 and 100 men respectively. Men grubbed in the village gardens for radishes and potatoes when their rations were exhausted. By

3.07 p.m. on the afternoon of 7 August, the 120th's Regimental CP was reporting German tanks within 200 yards. One of them was knocked out with a bazooka by a telephone operator, Private Joe Shipley. A platoon commander of the 1st Battalion, Lieutenant Lowther, called to a driver from his company standing on the far side of a hedge to join him immediately. "I can't," the driver called back unhappily. "I'm captured." The 2nd Battalion's aid station was captured by the Germans on the night of the 8th. An SS officer carrying a white flag approached the Americans' positions on Hill 282 to demand their surrender – without success. Soon afterwards, they were called upon to withstand a fierce attack. Medical supplies were fired into the American positions by artillery shell. Brigadier-General William Harrison, deputy divisional commander, moved from battalion to battalion urging and encouraging his men as he had on the first morning of COBRA. To one of his officers, he seemed to possess "the radiant face of a confident shepherd, for that is what he was to us in those difficult, horrible days". The little stone farmhouse where he had his command post was known to the Americans as "Château *Nebelwerfer*".

At Abbaye Blanche, 150 men and the company mascot – a tiny dog named Mobile Reserve – held a junction where five roads converged. One private soldier, Robert Vollmer, used a bazooka to demolish in succession an armoured car, a motorcycle, another armoured car and a fuel truck. A soldier named Estervez was wounded by a grenade taking men to the rear in a jeep, but returned for a second journey on which he was killed. The defenders were disturbed to find small-arms fire rattling at them from the rear – a classic German infiltration movement. But they held their ground with the support of a steady trickle of stragglers who found their way into their lines. Some men found a rocky cave beside the road, and took refuge in it when the German shelling became intense. Sometimes as they lay in their foxholes they could hear the sound of German voices. Every few hours there was a grinding of tracks or wheels as a vehicle approached up the road, and a brief exchange of fire as an American tank destroyer or anti-tank gun engaged it – and almost invariably, destroyed it. One man somehow found the means to get himself hopelessly drunk. When another soldier declined to take up an exposed position, the drunk said promptly, "Sure, I'll go," and attempted to man a bazooka and a machine-gun simultaneously.

The American command handling of the battle suggested a new maturity and grip within Twelfth Army Group. From beginning to end of the German push, officers at every level responded with vigour and sureness. Hodges' First Army diary for 7 August reported: "The boche is attacking . . . The air went after the enemy armor with a vengeance . . . The general is not too worried over the situation, although there is admittedly the strongest kind of pressure." On 8 August, the diary first noted a visit from the actor Edward G. Robinson, then added: "The situation appears a bit better tonight . . . 9th Div repulsed several small local enemy counter-attacks . . . The 30th Div was heavily engaged . . . 35th Div advanced against very light resistance." Next day, Hodges was greeting Henry Morgenthau, then: "Tonight, as before, the General issued orders for all troops to 'button up tight' for the night, and be prepared for anything, although it appears to be the General's feeling that his [von Kluge's] main effort is over, and that it has been decisively broken."

On the night of 12 August, the 35th Division at last broke through to relieve the 120th. Lieutenant Sidney Eichen of the 2nd Battalion's anti-tank platoon felt overcome by a great surge of relief as the files of fresh troops marched through their positions: "What a sight they were, coming off the hill." War correspondents and photographers swarmed over the positions, eager to interview the tired survivors of the fine American stand. Around the road junction at Abbaye Blanche, they found 24 wrecked German vehicles. As the Americans cleared the Mortain battlefield, they counted over 100 abandoned German tanks.[20]

Hitler, with his unerring instinct for reinforcing failure, now did so yet again. In the south, where Haislip's XV Corps was hastening towards the Loire, for 100 miles from Domfront to Angers there was only one panzer and one infantry division in its path, along with a few security battalions. Yet Hitler ignored Hausser's vehement protests, and ordered the armoured division – 9th Panzer – shifted north for a renewed attack towards Avranches on the 10th. Hausser called this movement "A death blow not only to Seventh Army but also to the entire Wehrmacht in the west". Von Kluge said simply: "It is the Führer's order."[21] But as the new attack was about to be launched, the Caen front also began to buckle. The despairing von Kluge asked Hitler that the panzers might be "temporarily transferred from the Mortain area to . . . destroy the enemy spearheads thrusting northwards."[22] Hitler gave his grudging assent on the 11th, but still declined to countenance any general withdrawal. Von Kluge's weekly situation report declared baldly: "The enemy's first main objective is to outflank and encircle the bulk of the 5th Panzer Army and 7th Army on two sides."[23] As late as 8 or 9 August, von Kluge could readily have executed the only sane movement open to him, a withdrawal to the Seine covered by a sacrificial rearguard. Hitler, and Hitler alone, closed this option to him and presented the Allies with their extraordinary opportunity. The climate within the German high command plumbed new depths of fantasy and grotesque comedy. The Luftwaffe had been lamentably directed for years by Goering, but at last its failure at Mortain drove Hitler to turn upon his old henchman.

"Goering! The Luftwaffe's doing nothing." [Guderian reported a confrontation that August] "It is no longer worthy to be an independent service. And that's your fault. You're lazy." When the portly Reichs-marschall heard these words, great tears trickled down his cheeks.[24]

Hitler placed the principal responsibility for failure at Mortain upon von Kluge's lack of will. Yet he seemed far more depressed by small personal tragedies, such as the death of his former SS orderly, Captain Hans Junge, who was killed by Allied strafing in France. He broke the news personally to the man's widow, his youngest secretary, Traudl Junge: "*Ach*, child, I am so sorry; your husband had a fine character."[25] When von Choltitz reported to Hitler fresh from the front, he was informed that the Führer was about to hurl the Allies into the sea. The general concluded that "the man was mad".[26]

On 11 August, with Haislip's XV Corps still pushing east around Alençon, it became Montgomery's responsibility to consider setting a new boundary between the American, British and Canadian forces, which expected to meet east of the German armies imminently. Despite the changed circumstances, he declined to alter the line he had set near Argentan on 6 August. He believed that XV Corps would meet slow going on its turn north, where it re-entered the *bocage*, which the Germans could exploit to their advantage. It seemed reasonable to assume that the Canadians, pushing south across reasonably open country, would be in Argentan before Haislip. The new boundary, the

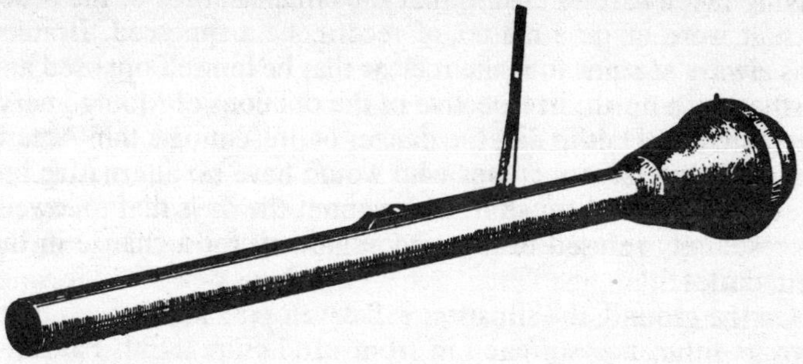

The German *Panzerfaust* was the best hand-held infantry anti-tank weapon of the war, exceptionally useful in Normandy, where the close country made it possible for its operators to reach Allied tanks at the very short ranges for which it was designed. It was a one-shot, throwaway weapon, weighing 11½ pounds. Its hollow charge could penetrate 200 mm of armour at 30 yards, and an improved version, introduced in the summer of 1944, possessed a higher velocity and was effective up to 80 yards. By contrast, the American 2.36 inch "bazooka" fired too light a projectile to be effective against the frontal armour of most German tanks. The British PIAT was moderately useful – it was effective up to 100 yards and could be used as a primitive mortar as well as against tanks. But it was twice as heavy as the *Panzerfaust*, cumbersome to carry, to cock and to fire.

point at which XV Corps would halt its advance, was therefore set just south of Argentan. Patton nonetheless warned Haislip to be ready to push up to Falaise, despite the corps commander's fears that his division would not prove strong enough to hold a trap closed in the face of the wholesale retreat of Army Group B. Patton urgently began to seek reinforcement from XX Corps and from Brittany. Just before midnight on the 12th, Haislip informed Third Army that his 5th Armored Division was just short of Argentan. Did Patton wish him to continue north to meet the Canadians? Patton now telephoned Bradley with his legendary demand: "We have elements in Argentan. Shall we continue and drive the British into the sea for another Dunkirk?"[27]

Despite Bradley's refusal, Patton anyway ordered Haislip to advance cautiously north of Argentan. Only at 2.15 p.m. on the 13th did XV Corps receive categoric orders to halt at Argentan and recall any units north of the town. Bradley's staff had consulted 21st Army Group about a possible boundary change, but were refused it. Patton wrangled with Bradley until at last, having taken care to ensure that the circumstances of the order to halt were made a matter of record, he acquiesced. Bradley was always at pains to make it clear that he himself opposed any further push north, irrespective of the opinions of Montgomery. He feared, as Haislip did, the danger of presenting a thin American front to German troops who would have no alternative but to seek to break through it. Throughout the days that followed, he resolutely refused to press Montgomery for a change in the boundaries.

On the ground, the situation was developing imperatives of its own as resistance stiffened in front of Haislip. 116th Panzer – with 15 surviving tanks – and elements of 1st SS and 2nd Panzer – with 55 tanks between them – were now deployed on his front. The Germans had still made no decision to attempt to flee the threat of encirclement. As mopping up around Mortain was concluded and forces of the U.S. First Army became available to move east, Collins' VII Corps began a rapid advance north-east from Mayenne on the 13th. At 10.00 a.m. that day, Collins telephoned First Army in a characteristically ebullient mood, asking for "more territory to take". First Army's diary recorded:

> 1st Div was, in some places, on the very boundary itself, and General Collins felt sure that he could take Falaise and Argentan, close the gap, and "do the job" before the British even started to move. General Hodges immediately called General Bradley, to ask officially for a change in boundaries, but the sad news came back that First Army was to go no further than at first designated, except that a small salient around Ranes would become ours.

Bradley, curiously enough, claimed now to be convinced that the importance of closing the trap at Falaise had diminished, because most of the Germans had already escaped eastwards, a view which neither Ultra nor air reconnaissance confirmed. For whatever reasons, he switched the focus of American strategic energy east, towards the Seine. Haislip, he told Patton, was to take two of his four divisions east, while the remainder, with VII Corps, remained at Argentan. It was almost as if Bradley had lost all interest in the "short envelopment" which he himself had proposed to Montgomery on 8 August. He now seemed determined instead to concentrate upon trapping the Germans against the Seine, the rejected "long envelopment". In these days, an uncharacteristic uncertainty of purpose, a lack of the instinct to deliver the killing stroke against von Kluge's armies, seemed to overtake Bradley. General Gerow of V Corps, sent to take

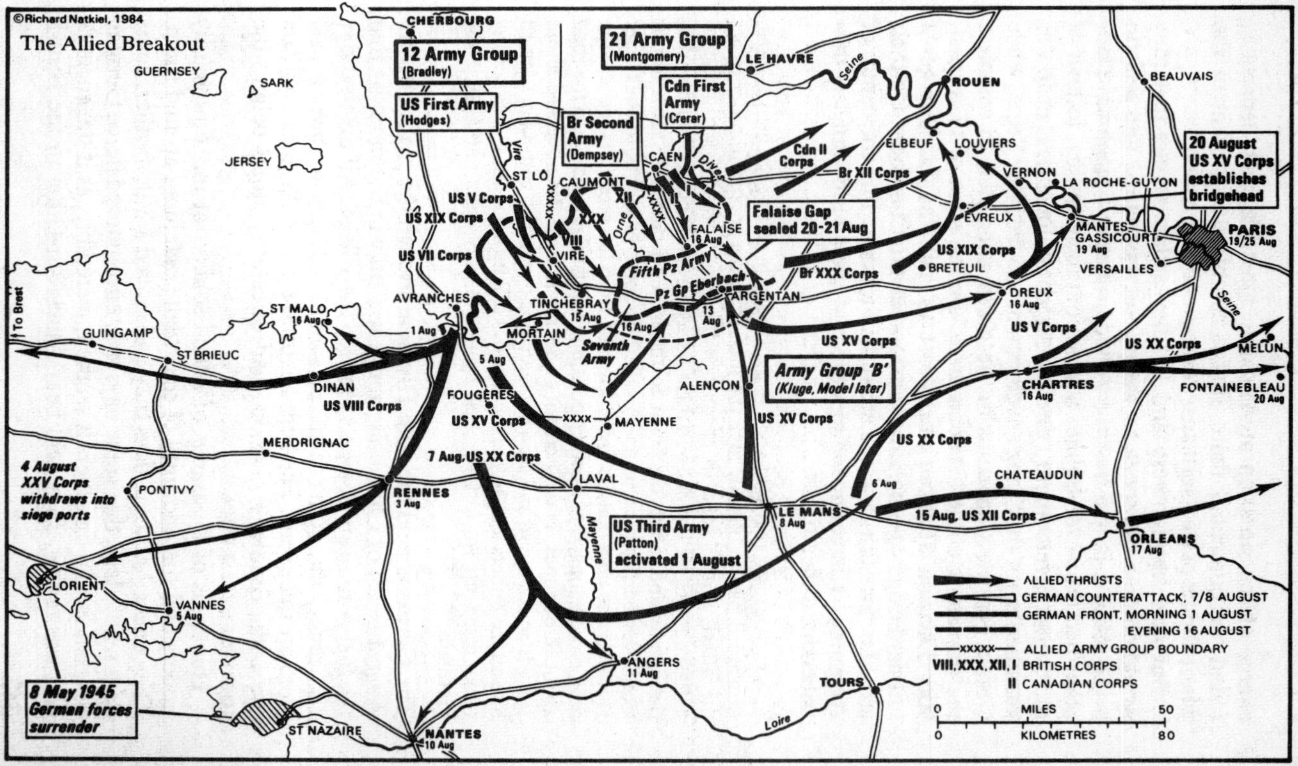

©Richard Natkiel, 1984
The Allied Breakout
12 Army Group (Bradley)
US First Army (Hodges)
21 Army Group (Montgomery)
Cdn First Army (Crerar)
Br Second Army (Dempsey)
20 August US XV Corps establishes bridgehead
Falaise Gap sealed 20-21 Aug
Army Group 'B' (Kluge, Model later)
US Third Army (Patton) activated 1 August
4 August XXV Corps withdraws into siege ports
8 May 1945 German forces surrender
CHERBOURG
GUERNSEY
SARK
JERSEY
LE HAVRE
ROUEN
BEAUVAIS
ELBEUF
LOUVIERS
VERNON
LA ROCHE-GUYON
MANTES GASSICOURT 19 Aug
PARIS 19/25 Aug
VERSAILLES
EVREUX
BRETEUIL
DREUX 16 Aug
CAEN
CAUMONT
ST LÔ
FALAISE 16 Aug
ARGENTAN
13 Aug
VIRE
TINCHEBRAY 15 Aug
16 Aug
MORTAIN
AVRANCHES
1 Aug
5 Aug
ST MALO 16 Aug
GUINGAMP
ST BRIEUC
DINAN
To Brest
FOUGÈRES
MAYENNE
ALENÇON
MERDRIGNAC
PONTIVY
RENNES 3 Aug
LAVAL
LE MANS 8 Aug
6 Aug
CHATEAUDUN
CHARTRES 16 Aug
ORLEANS 17 Aug
MELUN
FONTAINEBLEAU 20 Aug
LORIENT
VANNES 5 Aug
ANGERS 11 Aug
TOURS
ST NAZAIRE
NANTES 10 Aug
Seine
Vire
Orne
Dives
Mayenne
Loire
US V Corps
US XIX Corps
US VII Corps
US VIII Corps
US XV Corps
7 Aug, US XX Corps
US XX Corps
15 Aug, US XII Corps
US XIX Corps
Br XXX Corps
Br XII Corps
Cdn II Corps
XXX
VIII
XII
I
II
XXXX
XXXXX
Fifth Pz Army
Pz Gp Eberbach
Seventh Army
ALLIED THRUSTS
GERMAN COUNTERATTACK, 7/8 AUGUST
GERMAN FRONT, MORNING 1 AUGUST
EVENING 16 AUGUST
—XXXXX— ALLIED ARMY GROUP BOUNDARY
VIII, XXX, XII, I BRITISH CORPS
II CANADIAN CORPS
0 MILES 50
0 KILOMETRES 80

charge of the situation at Argentan after Haislip's departure, found the command there almost completely ignorant of the whereabouts of the Germans, or even of his own men.

But now Montgomery and Bradley at last agreed that they would enlarge the scope of the pocket eastwards, and seek to bring about a junction of the Allied armies at Chambois. Their plans had thus evolved into a series of compromises: instead of the "short envelopment" through Argentan-Falaise, Haislip was launched upon the "long envelopment" to the river Seine, while Gerow and the Canadians in the north attempted to complete the trap along a line between them. On the night of 17 August, 90th Division attacked north-east to gain the Le Bourge–St Leonard ridge commanding the approach to Chambois. On their left, the raw 80th Division attempted to move into the centre of Argentan. The commanding officer of their 318th Infantry described his difficulties:

> This was our first real fight and I had difficulty in getting the men to move forward. I had to literally kick the men from the ground in order to get the attack started, and to encourage the men I walked across the rd without any cover and showed them a way across. I received no fire from the enemy and it was big boost to the men. A tank, 400 yards to our front, started firing on us and I called up some bazookas to stalk him. However the men opened fire at the tank from too great a range and the tank merely moved to another position. I walked up and down the road about three times, finding crossings for my troops. We advanced about 100 yds across the rd and then the Germans opened up with what seemed like all the bullets and arty in the world. I call up my tanks . . . When my tanks came up we lost the first four with only eight shots from the Germans.[28]

The Germans held the 90th Division through the night of 18/19 August south of Chambois, and it was only in the morning that the first American elements reached the village. All the next day and night, the 90th's artillery pounded Germans fleeing east from encirclement. The 80th Division secured Argentan only on the 20th. Bradley's divisions had effectively stood behind the town for over a week.

Hundreds of thousands of Allied soldiers at this time hardly understood the enormity of the events unfolding around them. They knew that some days they had moved a little further, some days a little less; that some days they encountered fierce German resistance, and on others it seemed, incredibly, as if the enemy's will was fading. In a field near Aunay-sur-Odon in the British sector on 14 August, a tank wireless-operator named Austin Baker was camped with his squadron of the 4th/7th Royal Dragoon Guards:

We hadn't been there more than a couple of hours when everybody in the regiment had to blanco up and go over by lorry to the 13/18th Hussars area to hear a lecture by General Horrocks, who had just taken over command of XXX Corps. He was very good, and made us feel quite cheerful. He told us about the Falaise pocket – how the German Seventh Army was practically encircled and how the RAF were beating up the fleeing columns on the roads. He said that very soon we should be breaking out of the bridgehead and swanning off across France. That seemed absolutely incredible to us. We all thought that we should have to fight for every field all the way to Germany. But Horrocks was right.[29]

11 The road to Falaise

Through most of the campaign in north-west Europe, while there were tensions between the American and British high commands and each army possessed a large stock of quizzical jokes about the other, there was no real ill-will between the soldiers. "We knew that they were the chaps that mattered," said Major John Warner of British 3rd Reconnaissance Regiment about the Americans. "We couldn't possibly win the war without them."[1] But during the weeks between the start of COBRA and the march to the Seine, many men of the British Second Army and the newly-operational Canadian First Army found the blaring headlines about the American breakout, their armoured parade through Brittany and down to the Loire, a bitter pill to swallow. Much more than most armies in most campaigns, they were very conscious of the press. They received newspapers from England only a day or two after publication, and studied avidly the accounts of their own doings in Normandy. They saw photographs of jubilant American infantry, helmets pushed back and weapons slung, waving as they rode their tanks through liberated villages alive with smiling civilians. They studied the sketch maps that revealed their allies controlling tracts of country far greater than their own overcrowded perimeter. Above all, they read of the light opposition that the advance was meeting. An NCO of 6th KOSB asked his commanding officer bitterly, "if it was the high command's intention to wipe out all the British and finish the war with the Americans."[2]

For throughout the weeks of COBRA, Brittany, Mortain, almost every day the British and Canadians were pushing slowly forward on their own front with much pain and at heavy cost. The British VIII and XXX Corps were attacking on an axis south-east from Caumont, while the Canadians moved directly south from Caen towards Falaise. Second Army was still in thick country, facing an unbroken German line with far greater armoured strength and *Nebelwerfer* support than anything the American Third Army encountered. Only immediately before the Mortain counter-attack did the weight of German armour begin to shift dramatically eastwards. Most of Dempsey's men were very tired by now, above all the infantrymen of 15th Scottish, 43rd Wessex and 50th Northumbrian divisions, who had borne so much of the heaviest fighting, and continued to do so. It was a matter of astonishment to officers of other units that 43rd Division still retained any morale at all. Its commander, Major-General G. I. Thomas, was a ruthless, driving soldier for whose determination Montgomery was grateful, but who had earned the nickname "Butcher" for his supposed insensitivity to losses. The purge in XXX Corps when Montgomery sacked Bucknall, together with Erskine and Hinde of 7th Armoured, dismayed many of the 7th's men, but did not produce a dramatic improvement in performance.

The episode that prompted the sackings, the fumbling of BLUECOAT, was characterized by many of the misfortunes that befell the British that summer, and deprived them in the eyes of the Americans of the credit that was justly theirs for bearing so thankless a burden on the eastern flank. It began with the usual confident, even cocky, letter from Montgomery to Eisenhower: "I have ordered Dempsey to throw all caution overboard and to take any risks he likes, and to accept any casualties, and to step on the gas for Vire."[3] On 30 July, O'Connor's VIII Corps drove hard for Le Bény Bocage and Vire along the boundary with the American XIX Corps, while on their left XXX Corps made for the 1,100-foot summit of Mont Pinçon. Roberts' 11th Armoured – by now established as the outstanding British tank division in Normandy – made fast going and seized the high ground of Le Bény Bocage, at the vulnerable junction between Panzer Group West and Seventh Army. Boundaries are critical weak points in all formations in all armies, the seams in the garment of defence. It has been suggested in recent years[4] that Montgomery missed a great opportunity by failing to push through here, seize Vire and roll up Seventh Army instead of leaving Vire to the American XIX Corps. When 11th Armoured approached the town before obeying orders to turn south-east on 2 August, it was virtually undefended. But by the time the Americans moved against it the Germans had rushed in troops to plug the gap, mounted vigorous counter-attacks, and were only finally dispossessed on the night of 6 August. Once again, the line had congealed.

But Montgomery and Dempsey's attention in the first days of August was focussed upon the new failure of 7th Armoured. Bucknall was warned to reach Aunay-sur-Odon quickly, or face the consequences. After two days of BLUECOAT he was still five miles short. Montgomery acted at last – belatedly, in the view of much of his staff, particularly his Chief of Staff, de Guingand, who was far more sensitive than his Commander-in-Chief to the prevailing scepticism about the British at SHAEF.

In the days that followed, Second Army continued to push forward south-east of Caumont, gaining a few miles a day by hard labour and hard fighting. Tank and infantry co-operation was now much improved, with the armoured divisions re-organized to integrate tanks and foot-soldiers within their brigades. Since GOODWOOD, it had at last become accepted tactical practice for infantry to ride forward clinging to the tanks when there was suitable opportunities for them to do so. If there was less of the flamboyant spirit of the landings, there was much more professionalism. Most of the Scottish units, which in June so eagerly sent forward their pipers to lead the men into battle, had long ago dispensed with such frivolities by August. Too many pipers would never play another pibroch.

But for the men among the corn and the hedges, each morning seemed to bring only another start-line, another tramp through incessant mortar and shellfire, coated in dust, to another ruined village from which the Germans had to be forced by nerve-racking house-clearing.

The war artist Thomas Hennell wrote late in July of "the sense-haunted ground" the armies left in their wake. "The shot-threshed foliage of the apple orchards was fading and just turning rusty, fruit glowed against the sky; there were ashes of burnt metal, yellow splintered wood and charred brown hedge among the shell pits; every few yards a sooty, disintegrated hulk . . ." The equipment in the hands of von Kluge's armies was perfectly suited to generating maximum firepower with minimum manpower. The multi-barrelled mortar, employed in powerful concentrations, was a devastating weapon against advancing infantry. By August, British artillery was making intense efforts to grapple with the problem by creating specialist counter-mortar teams. The surviving German tanks were as resistant as ever to Allied penetration. A sergeant-major of the KOSB received a well-earned Military Cross for knocking out an enemy Panther which endured six hits from his PIAT before succumbing. The fields at evening were landmarked with upturned rifles jammed in the earth to mark the dead. The tank crews cursed the ripened apples that cascaded into their turrets as they crashed through orchards, jamming the traverses, while the shock of repeated impacts on banks and ditches threw their radios off net. The Germans had lost none of their skill in rushing forward improvised battle-groups to fill sudden weaknesses that were exposed. Again and again, British scout cars or tanks reported an apparent gap which might be exploited, only to find it filled before an advance in strength could be made. 15th Scottish Division signalled one of its battalions one evening that Guards Armoured had reported a withdrawal by the enemy on their front. The infantry must ensure that they patrolled to avoid losing contact. An acerbic message came back from the company commander on the front line, that since he was at that moment engaged in a fierce close-quarter grenade battle, there was scant need for patrolling to discover where the enemy was. But another German skill, much in evidence in those days, was that of disengagement: fighting hard for a position until the last possible moment, then breaking away through the countryside to create another line a mile or two back, presenting the British yet again with the interminable problems of ground and momentum.

You turn off the main road to Vire at Point 218 and go down a side road to the top of a ridge [Lieutenant Richard Mosse, commanding 1st Welsh Guards Anti-Tank Platoon, described his battalion's position on 8 August]. "Dust means shells" notices were in great evidence. It was the worst place I have ever been in. Numerous bodies of our predecessors lay in the fields between the companies, with about 25 knocked out vehicles, mostly British. A thick dust covered everything, and over it all hung that sweet sickly smell of death. By day we could not move as we were under observed mortar fire, and going up to the forward companies under machine-gun fire at times . . . August 12 brought news that our guns had opened short again, and Sgt. Lentle and one other had been killed and several wounded. Sgt. Lentle I could ill afford to lose. He was a steady, sensible man. He would not take risks, he had a wife and two boys he adored, but he would obey any order however dangerous. I could always rely on him . . . David Rhys, the mortar platoon commander, was wounded. Hugh, Fred and I were all that was left in the company, so we helped hold a bit of the line. We had advanced some half a mile; our casualties were 122, 35 killed . . . As long as I live that word *bocage* will haunt me, with memories of ruined countryside, dust, orchards, sunken lanes and the silly little shoots that were all I could find for the guns.

Mosse's description of his battalion's predicament is a sober corrective for those who suppose that by the middle days of August, with the German army in Normandy within a week of collapse, the pressure upon their opponents was easing. The pain and the constant drain of losses persisted to the bitter end.

On the night of 7 August, preceded by a massive air attack by Bomber Command, Lieutenant-General Guy Simonds launched his II Canadian Corps on a renewed offensive southwards towards Falaise: Operation TOTALIZE. Simonds, who had commanded a division in Sicily,was to prove one of the outstanding Allied corps commanders in Europe, a dour, direct officer who brought unusual imagination to bear on every operational plan for which he was responsible. It was Simonds who now decided to make his attack across open country in darkness, to use 76 converted self-propelled gun-mountings to move his lead infantry, and to employ a sophisticated range of electronics and illuminants to guide his men to their objectives through the night. There was to be no delay in following up the bombers.

Even as the planning for TOTALIZE was being carried out, von Kluge's redeployment for Mortain was taking place. 9th SS Panzer retired from the British front on 1 August, followed by 1st SS Panzer on the night of the 4th, to be relieved by 89th Infantry. A Yugoslav deserter from the 89th reached the Canadian lines almost immediately, bringing this information to Simonds. For the first time since 7 June, the weight of the German army had been lifted from the eastern flank. On Crerar's right, 43rd Division had at last cleared the heights of Mont Pinçon in a fine action on 6/7 August, and the 59th Division was across the Orne north of Thury–Harcourt. The Germans' left front was thus already under heavy pressure when the Canadians moved.

At 11.30 p.m. on 7 August, the assault forces crossed the start-line, led by navigating tanks and flails. They rumbled forward, in four columns of four vehicles abreast, into the great dust cloud raised by the bombing. Bomber Command had done its job, guided by coloured marker shells, with astonishing accuracy – there were no casualties among Allied troops and 3,462 tons of bombs had fallen on the villages in the path of the attack. There was no preliminary artillery bombardment. For the men on the ground, the spectacle was astonishing, with searchlights directed towards the clouds – "Monty moonlight" –

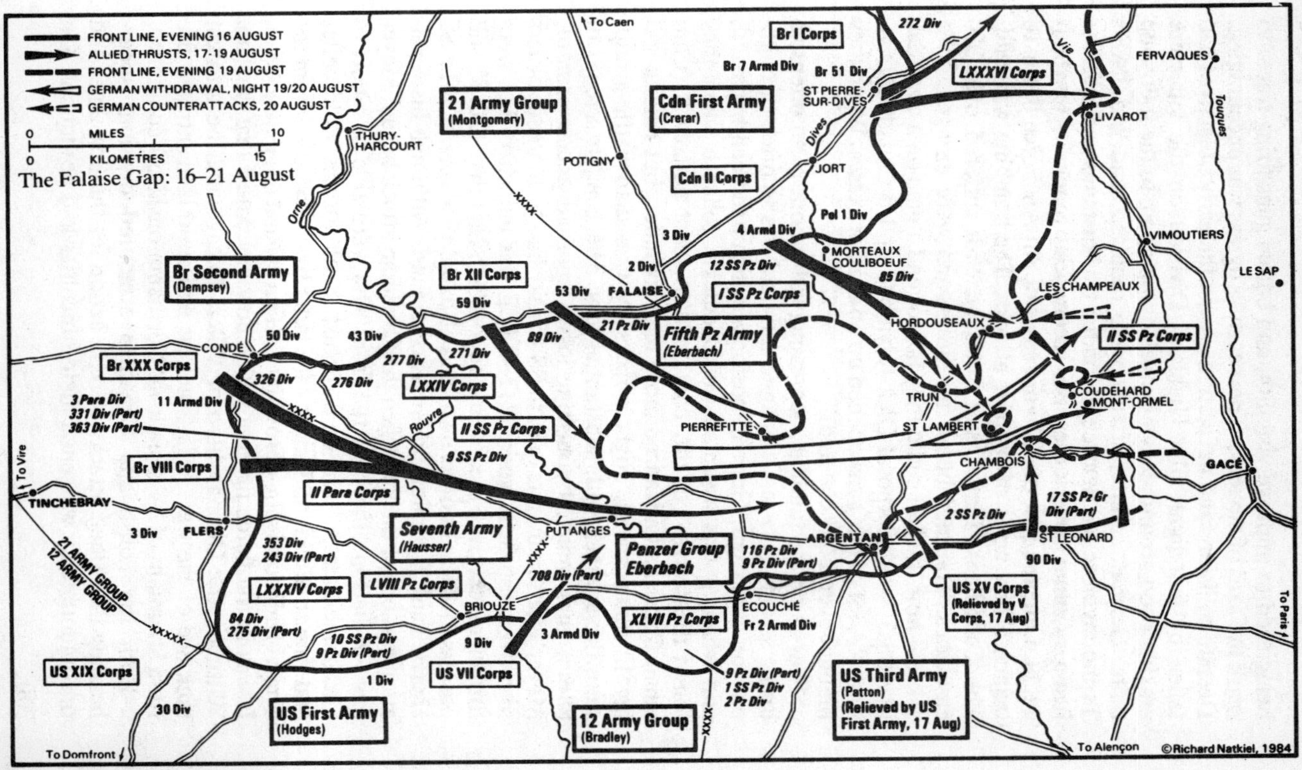

The Falaise Gap: 16–21 August

being used to improve visibility, and bofors guns firing tracer to mark the axes of advance. Their early progress was encouraging. Despite collisions and navigation errors, the early objectives had fallen by first light. 51st Highland Division on the left were making good ground, leaving much mopping-up to the follow-up units. German counter-attacks were repulsed, and 2nd TAF's Typhoons were out in strength, aided by Mustangs and Spitfires flying sweeps over German approach roads. At about 12.50 p.m., the first of 492 Fortresses of 8th Air Force began to launch a new wave of support attacks. The bombing was wild. The Canadians, British and Poles beneath suffered over 300 casualties. The men below on the ground were enraged. "We asked – how the hell could they fail to read a map on a clear day like this?" said Corporal Dick Raymond of 3rd Canadian Division. "A lot of our guns opened up on the Fortresses. When they hit one, everybody cheered."

Now came the familiar, depressing indications of an offensive losing steam. Tilly-la-Campagne still held. As so often throughout the campaign, German positions which had been bypassed, and which it was assumed would quickly collapse when they found themselves cut off, continued to resist fiercely. II Canadian Corps had advanced more than six miles, but Falaise still lay 12 miles ahead. Night attacks by Canadian battle-groups were driven back with substantial loss. The familiar screens of 88mm guns inflicted punishing losses upon advancing armour. Meyer's battered units of 12th SS Panzer had been under orders to move westwards when TOTALIZE was launched, but were thrown quickly into the line to support 89th Infantry. 12th SS still possessed 48 tanks of its own, and also had 19 Tigers of 101st SS Heavy Tank Battalion under its command. Although his formation was out of the line when the Canadian attack began, Meyer had left liaison officers at the front who were able to report to him immediately. Early on 8 August, battle-groups Waldmuller and Krause of 12th SS Panzer – the latter hastily switched from the Thury–Harcourt front – drove into action around the Falaise road. It was in the fierce fighting which now developed that Michael Wittman, the German hero of Villers-Bocage and the greatest tank ace of the war, at last met his end amid concentrated fire from Shermans of 'A' squadron, Northamptonshire Yeomanry.

Both the Polish and Canadian armoured divisions spearheading the Allied attacks were in action for the first time, and this undoubtedly worsened their difficulties and hesitations. On the night of 8 August, Simonds ordered the tanks to press on with operations through the darkness. Many units simply ignored him, and withdrew to night harbours in the manner to which they were accustomed. The few elements which pressed on regardless found themselves isolated and unsupported, and were destroyed by the German 88mm guns. On 9 August, Simonds' staff were exasperated by the persistent delays that appeared to afflict almost every unit movement, the repeated episodes of troops and tanks firing on each other, the difficulty of getting accurate reports from the front about what was taking place. A fierce German counter-attack by a battle-group of 12th SS Panzer completed the chaos. The British Columbia Regiment lost almost its entire strength, 47 tanks in the day, together with 112 casualties. The infantry of the Algonquins, who had been with them, lost 128. The Poles on the left made some progress, getting through to St Sylvain. On the night of the 9th the Canadian 10th Brigade made good progress further west. But after accomplishing little during the day of 10 August, a major night attack on Quesnay woods by 3rd Canadian Division ended in its withdrawal early the following morning.

The Canadians' enthusiasm was obviously waning; difficulties at higher headquarters compounded uncertainty on the ground. Montgomery had always lacked confidence in Crerar, the Canadian army commander, and much upset the Canadians at the outset of this, their first battle as an army, by sending his own staff officers from 21st Army Group to Canadian headquarters to oversee their performance. Crerar became locked in dispute with the rugged Crocker, the British I Corps commander, whom he attempted to sack on the spot. An impatient Montgomery sought to persuade both men to focus their animosity upon the enemy. "The basic cause was Harry. I fear he thinks he is a great soldier, and he was determined to show it the moment he took over command at 1200 on 23 July. He made his first mistake at 1205; and his second after lunch . . ."[5] It is an astounding reflection upon the relative weight of forces engaged north of Falaise that by the night of 10 August, the German tank strength was reduced to 35 (15 Mk IV, five Panther, 15 Tiger), while the Canadian II Corps, even after losses, mustered around 700. Yet on 10 August, with some German reinforcements moving onto the front, it was decided that nothing less than a full-scale, set-piece attack with massed bomber preparation would break the Canadians through to Falaise. The defenders had shown their usual skill in shifting such armour and anti-tank guns as they possessed quickly from threatened point to point, presenting strong resistance to each successive Canadian push. It was also evident that the Canadians were not performing well. Because their government, until very late in the war, would ask only volunteers to serve overseas, it had great difficulty in maintaining First Canadian Army at anything like its establishment level. Many men on the battlefield were embittered by the feeling that the Canadian nation as a whole was not sharing their sacrifice. The best of Crerar's troops were very good indeed. But his army was handicapped by its undermanning, and chronically troubled by leadership problems, which were also the cause of the notorious indiscipline of Canadian aircrew. Even the Canadian official historian ventured the opinion that their army suffered from:

> . . . possessing a proportion of regimental officers whose attitude towards training was casual and haphazard rather than urgent and scientific. Analysis of the operations in Normandy seems to support this opinion. Regimental officers of this type, where they existed, were probably the weakest element in the Army. At the top of the command pyramid, Canadian generalship in Normandy does not suffer by comparison with those of the other Allies engaged . . . The Canadian regimental officer at his best . . . had no superior . . . There still remained, however, that proportion of officers who were not fully competent for their appointments, and whose inadequacy appeared in action and sometimes had serious consequences.[6]

On 11 August, Simonds ordered his armoured divisions to pull out of the line, to be relieved by infantry formations. On the 12th, the U.S. First Army's diarist recorded sardonically: "The British are making some gains, none of them sizeable or of break-through proportions." In Paris, the press was reporting triumphant German claims to have destroyed 278 Allied tanks, and Berlin's assertion that "each foot of ground gained is being paid for with enormous losses of men and equipment."

For Montgomery, the breakdown of TOTALIZE was a disappointment, but there is no evidence that he yet perceived it as a long term threat to his hopes. It still appeared incredible to many officers that von Kluge could commit such an act of madness as to leave his forces in the closing Allied noose. There remained ample time and space for the Germans to retreat eastwards. Montgomery had always planned to swing the Canadians and the British left from Falaise across to the Seine, while the American Third Army blocked the so-called Paris–Orleans gap between the Loire and the Seine. This was what was known as the "long envelopment", designed to entrap the entire surviving German forces in western France within its grasp. But when Eisenhower telephoned Montgomery from Bradley's headquarters on the afternoon of 8 August to discuss American proposals for a "short hook", with the arms of Third Army and the Canadians and British meeting somewhere around Argentan to create a much smaller noose, Montgomery was receptive. He signalled to Brooke the next day: "There are great possibilities in the present situation. If we can get to Alençon, Argentan and Falaise fairly quickly, we have a good chance of closing the ring around the main German forces, and I am making all plans to drop an airborne division at Gacé about 15 miles east of Argentan in order to complete the block."[7] Montgomery retained some reservations about the "short hook", which were shared, unusually enough, by Patton. Both men feared that too many Germans might escape a trap closed at Argentan. They were attracted by the much more dramatic gains of ground and prisoners that might result from encircling the greater area towards Paris and Orleans. But Montgomery was uncharacteristically indecisive, and Bradley was absolutely determined on Argentan. The British general acceded. He told Brooke: "Should the Germans escape us here I shall proceed quickly with the plan outlined in M517"[8] – the "long envelopment".

It was now, on 11 August, with the Canadians bogged down north of Falaise, that Montgomery missed probably his last opportunity to conduct a major switch of forces in time to hasten the closing of the German pocket. Had he recognized that the Canadians' difficulties reflected fundamental shortcomings in unit leadership and fighting power, he might have rushed tested British formations south-eastwards to support them, or even to take over the lead. But this was not Montgomery's way. Such a course would have been exceedingly "untidy" – the word he most detested in military operations – and would have created genuine, though not insuperable, problems of movement, control and supply. It may also be that he was reluctant to impose new strains upon British divisions which had already suffered so much; or even that he doubted whether they would do any better than the Canadians. For whatever reasons, he merely ordered Dempsey's Second Army to continue pushing south-east. He left the vital operation – the drive to meet the Americans at

Argentan – entirely in the hands of Crerar's Canadian Army, which had graphically demonstrated its shortcomings in the past four days. From that moment, all that followed on the British-Canadian front was preordained.

Beyond a limited operation by 2nd Canadian Division down the Laize valley on the 12th and 13th, those days were passed entirely in preparations for another big set-piece attack on Falaise, Operation TRACTABLE. It is easy to understand the impatience of the Americans, so conscious of time slipping away. TRACTABLE at last jumped off at 11.42 a.m. on the morning of the 14th, shielded by a smokescreen which Simonds on this occasion substituted for the darkness of TOTALIZE. With the smoke compounded by the great dust cloud thrown up by the advancing armour, the Canadians found navigation difficult. The brigade commander of their leading tanks was mortally wounded in the first hour, causing acute control problems in the actions that followed. More seriously, the Germans had found a copy of Simond's orders on the body of a scout car commander killed the day before. They redeployed with exact knowledge of the Canadian lines of advance.

Most of the attack's early problems resulted from difficulties in finding paths across the little stream of the Laison, which proved a much more formidable anti-tank obstacle than had been expected. More disruptive still, "short bombing" by the RAF's Bomber Command – much of it, ironically enough, by Canadian squadrons – caused more than 300 casualties among the assault troops. By a tragic error, some ground units ignited their usual yellow identifying smoke, while Bomber Command was employing yellow target indicators. All this seemed to be yet more poisoned fruit of the lack of close liaison and staff planning between the army and the air forces. The Canadians declared that the bombing disaster had a severe effect upon the morale and determination of the troops embarking upon TRACTABLE.

On 15 August, the renewed advance still made poor progress. 4th Armoured Brigade's chaotic operations broke down after their leading units met a German anti-tank screen. 3rd Canadian Division made some headway, but lost the village of Soulangy to a counter-attack. That evening, 2nd Division reached positions a mile from the edge of Falaise only after the Germans had disengaged and pulled back in front of them. The Canadian and Polish armoured divisions were now ordered to push south-eastwards for Trun, hooking beyond the original "Falaise gap". Meanwhile, 2nd Infantry Division drove on into the shattered town, which they cleared only on the 17th. Some 50 Hitler Jugend fought to the last in the *Ecole Supérieure*. Only four were reported to have escaped from the blazing building. Two, chosen by lot from among the defenders, had slipped out the previous night to report the situation to Meyer. None surrendered. In many parts of the town, surrounded by rubble, the Canadians found it difficult to judge where the streets had run. It was hours before the bulldozers could clear a path for vehicles.

It was now, for the first time, that large elements of the German army began to retire eastwards out of the shrinking pocket. On the 16th, von Kluge at last issued the order for a full-scale retreat. It was his last act as Commander-in-Chief, almost the last of his life. On the 15th, his car had been shot up by Allied fighter-bombers, his wireless destroyed, and he was cut off from all contact with OKW or with his own forces for some hours. Hitler was convinced, fallaciously, that during his absence the Field-Marshal had been attempting to open negotiations with the Allies. At midday on the 16th, von Kluge declined to execute an order from OKW for a counter-attack, which he declared was utterly impossible. Although a withdrawal was at last authorized by order of the Führer later that afternoon, on the evening of the 17th von Kluge was relieved. On his way back to Germany to explain himself to Hitler, he killed himself. He left behind an extraordinary letter affirming his undying devotion to the Führer, a final testimony to the German officer corps' obsession with loyalty, its utter inability to grapple with any greater issues of morality, humanity, or the historic interests of the German people. Suicide, for an astonishing procession of German senior officers who failed in Normandy, became the final expression of their own retreat from reason. Von Kluge was succeeded by Field-Marshal Walter Model. The supply of senior officers willing to attempt to implement their master's deranged will seemed limitless. Model's first act was to order the immediate escape of Seventh Army and Panzer Group Eberbach, while II SS Panzer Corps (the ruins of 2nd SS, 9th SS, 12th SS and 21st Panzer) held the north against the British and Canadians, and XLVII Panzer Corps (2nd and 116th Panzer) the south against the Americans.

For the Allies, time had now become the critical factor in blocking the German army's escape. Yet while the Americans stood at

Argentan, the Canadian armour edged south towards Trun with agonizing sluggishness. Their 4th Division reach Louvières, two miles north of the village, on the evening of the 17th after delays caused as much by traffic problems in narrow village streets and at little rustic stone bridges across trickling streams, as by enemy action. At 2.45 p.m. that day, Montgomery himself telephoned Crerar's Chief of Staff to press the urgency of the situation upon him: "It is absolutely essential that both the Armoured Divs of 2 Cdn Corps close the gap between First Cdn Army and Third U.S. Army. I Polish Armoured Div must thrust on past Trun to Chambois at all costs, and as quickly as possible."[9]

Yet the Poles, too, were slow to move. Their 2nd Armoured Regiment was ordered on the evening of the 17th to push immediately for Chambois, but instead departed only early on the 18th for Les Champeaux, possibly as a result of a misunderstanding with their local French guide, who shortly afterwards disappeared. The gap through which German vehicles and infantry were pouring in headlong retreat had now narrowed to a few thousand yards. Yet the principal labour of destroying the forces within it was being borne by the Allied air force. The fighter-bombers, flying 2–3,000 sorties a day throughout this period, inflicted massive losses. There were still serious problems with identification of ground troops. The British 51st Highland Division reported 40 separate incidents of accidental air attack for 18 August alone, costing its units 51 casualties and 25 vehicles. The Poles, who had lost scores of men in the "short bombing" of the 8th and 14th, the same day lost half their petrol supplies to Allied air attack.

On the morning of the 19th, Simonds spoke personally to his four divisional commanders at the headquarters of the 4th east of Morteaux-Couliboeuf. He emphasized that their objective was to ensure that no Germans escaped from the pocket. There was fierce fighting that day in the village of St Lambert, where two Canadian infantry companies fought all morning to gain a foothold in the village, then found themselves unable to go further. They dug in, and for the rest of the day fought off successive counter-attacks as German troops struggled to hold open the road east. Extraordinary sacrificial efforts by Meindl's survivors of 3rd Parachute Division defended the path east for thousands of their comrades. Canadian units blocked enemy attempts to escape through Trun. Artillery forward observers on the high ground overlooking the gap were calling down massive fire upon

The German *Nebelwerfer* multi-barrelled mortar was one of the most formidable weapons in Normandy, the object of bitter hatred and cause of a remarkable proportion of casualties among Allied troops – some estimates attributed 75 per cent of infantry losses to German mortaring, even if many of the wounds were slight. In the last phase of the war, the Germans concentrated more and more attention upon the massed use of mortars in preference to artillery, and the *Nebelwerfer* – or "moaning minnie" as the Allies called it – proved outstandingly useful in generating defensive fire when the shortage of German infantry and guns had become a chronic problem.

every column of vehicles and infantry on the roads and in the fields. The evening, Polish and American units met in Chambois.

Yet still the gap was not closed. Both the Poles and the Canadian 4th Armoured were under ferocious pressure from elements of 2nd SS Panzer, fighting westwards to hold open the retreat of Seventh Army. 1,500 Poles and 80 tanks were cut off from their lines of communication, unable to evacuate their wounded, perilously short of fuel and ammunition. Their battle was fought out with a fury uncommon even by the standards of Normandy. Poles and Germans detested each other with real passion, and each believed that they had much to avenge, the Poles with better reason. Now, from the heights of Mont Ormel, their tank machine-gunners raking the Germans below them, they called down artillery fire on every passing column of vehicles. From their wooded ridge, they could view the battlefield for miles. Meanwhile, the Canadian 4th Armoured Division's war diary recorded: "Due to the heavy fighting, Germans attacking from both the east and the west and the numerous calls made on the div to seal off any German escape routes, the units are all mixed up and it is difficult to define any particular brigade areas."[10] The Canadians merely poured fire into German elements wherever they encountered them. "Until about 0800," (on the 21st) wrote an officer of the Cameron Highlanders of Ottawa, "the machine-gunners fired at whatever they could see. During this time a host of white flags appeared and hundreds of the enemy crowded in to surrender. Many others were unable to give up, for every move towards our lines brought bursts of fire from certain SS troops patrolling the low ground behind them in an armoured half-track."[11] Corporal Dick Raymond, one of the Camerons' Vickers gunners, said: "It was the first time we had ever seen the German army out in the open. We would see a group trying to run across a field from one wood to another, and watch some fall, some run on, some lie moaning in front of us. It was more of an execution than a battle. I remember feeling puzzled that it didn't upset me more."

Yet the pocket at Falaise was being closed too late to prevent the escape of a formidable cadre of the German army, including some of its most skilled and dedicated officers, who lived to lead men through many more battles. It was only the most determined who still possessed the will to try the gap. Few, even within the Canadians' own ranks, disputed that the principal cause of this Allied failure was the feeble performance of First Canadian Army. Characteristically, the British official history describes the advance to Falaise in terms of hard fighting, "a gruelling day for the Canadians . . . Germans fighting strongly . . . dogged resistance." All this is perfectly true, but it evades the central fact that the ragged remains of two German divisions and a handful of tanks held all Crerar's army for 13 days, from the opening of TOTALIZE to the closing of the gap at Chambois, a distance of barely 30 miles. The Canadian official historian is far more frank than his British counterpart: "A German force far smaller than our own, taking advantage of strong ground and prepared positions, was able to slow our advance to the point where considerable German forces made their escape."[12] General Foulkes of the Canadian 2nd Division said: "When we went into battle at Falaise and Caen, we found that when we bumped into battle-experienced German troops, we were no match for them. We would not have been successful had it not been for our air and artillery support."[13] The Canadians had already recognized their difficulties by replacing a long succession of officers commanding brigades and battalions since 6 June. On 21 August, Crerar sacked the commander of his 4th Armoured Division, Major-General Kitching, a ritual sacrifice to his formation's failure.

The focus of the struggle now concentrated upon a few square miles of fields and little villages in which the wreckage of a half-million-strong army was fighting for survival. Command and control by signal had been almost entirely lost. Such direction as existed was provided by German officers to whatever men they chanced to find around them. Blackened vehicles, blackened corpses, blackened buildings and hedgerows scarred every acre over which the fighter-bombers had passed. The wounded were merely gathered where they might be tended by their captors when the Allies reached them – there were no more drugs and few enough doctors. Men ate what they could find in shattered vehicles or farmhouses – every surviving building was crowded with stragglers hunting food or seeking shelter from the shelling and bombing, or merely rest from the interminable march among the dead. The Allied cordon was a swollen, bulging sac against the walls of which thousands of men were pressing and forcing their bodies in a hundred places, seeking escape and often dying to find it. Amongst a vast mass of despondent Germans who sought only to surrender, there were still some thousands who fought at Falaise with desperate courage, hurling themselves again and again against Allied positions despite ferocious artillery fire and concentrated machine-guns.

Montgomery issued a directive on 20 August urging his forces to greater efforts: "There is no time to relax, or to sit back and congratulate ourselves. I call on all commanders for a great effort. Let us finish the business in record time . . . The first task of Canadian army is to keep the Normandy 'bottle' securely corked."[14] On the 22nd, it was concluded that all significant German forces west of the Allied lines were dead or in captivity. The "cork", it was concluded, could be removed from the empty bottle. The Allied armies could make free with the ruins of St Lambert and Coudehard, Chambois and Trun, the ghastly killing ground of the Falaise Gap.

12 The Gap

Some men had already been fortunate enough to achieve their *Heim ins Reich* before the collapse in Normandy came. Corporal Schickner of 2nd Panzer was in hospital in Germany recovering from a head wound inflicted by an American sniper in July. Lieutenant Schaaf and his gunners of the 1716th Artillery had been sent back to re-equip with new guns when those which they had fired since 6 June were worn out from ceaseless use. Corporal Kortenhaus of 21st Panzer was still in hospital after catching his foot in his tank track. Captain Wagemann of 21st Panzer staff had been posted back to Germany at the end of July. But the mass of the German army in Normandy remained, to endure one of the great nightmares of military history in the Falaise Gap. Pounded by shells from north and south and fighter-bomber strikes from first light to dusk, the long columns of men, horse-drawn carts and the few surviving tanks and vehicles struggled slowly eastwards, past their unburied dead by the roads and in the fields, the stinking carcasses of countless hundreds of horses and cattle, the ruins of Panthers and half-tracks, field cars and trucks, the last hopes of Hitler's armies in France.

20 August was a beautiful summer's day. To the straggling clusters and columns of Germans moving painfully eastwards, the weather mocked them as shells searched the roads and tracks, and tore open the meadows in which so many sought safety. The detested Piper Cubs droned busily overhead, directing their destruction. Colonel Heinz-Gunther Guderian sent two officers forward to St Lambert to reconnoitre a route for the vestiges of his division. With the coming of darkness, at the head of a column of 300 men, 50 vehicles and a battery of guns, they edged cautiously forward beneath the Allied positions, moving 100 yards at a time, then halting in silence to listen, then slipping forward again. At last, after hours of desperate tension, they met panzergrenadiers of 2nd SS Panzer holding the eastern line. Guderian and his men sank wearily into oblivion by the roadside,

and slept all through the day that followed. Yet his glimpse of safety was illusory. The next morning, he was ordered to take the remnants of the formation south, to stiffen the tenuous line against American pressure. On the road in his Volkswagen field car, he was caught by an Allied fighter-bomber diving out of the sun. Guderian, hit in the shoulder, was still in the vehicle when the petrol tank exploded. He never fought again in France.

Lieutenant Walter Kruger, signals officer of 12th SS Panzer, was wounded by shrapnel as he sat in his truck in a great unmoving press of transport on the Falaise road. "Then I saw that the whole column was on fire. Everybody was running." He walked for three days, then sat by the roadside near Breteuil among the endless lines of filthy, bloody, exhausted men passing east, looking for survivors of his own unit and collecting them to continue the retreat. His divisional commander, Kurt "Panzer" Meyer, outstanding combat commander and fanatical Nazi, escaped according to his own account "guided by a French civilian". It is not difficult to picture the means of persuasion Meyer brought to bear. Yet even the iron Meyer described later how he climbed out of his vehicle amid the shambles of the Gap, "my knees trembling, the sweat pouring down my face, my clothes soaked in perspiration."[1] He and his men represented, at one level, the utmost perversion of national socialism. Yet at another, they command reluctant respect. No formation caused the Allies such deep trouble in Normandy until the end as 12th SS Panzer.

Sergeant Hans Stober of 17th SS Panzergrenadiers encountered no difficulties driving east until he and his handful of surviving men reached the Dives. There they became entangled in the chaos of the retreat. By ruthless determination they forced a way through and found a track north of Mont Ormel that remained open, and slipped past the silent Canadian army positions in darkness, with the men and even a few vehicles. "The Poles never closed that pocket for anybody who really wanted to get through," claimed Stober scornfully. Eventually they reached a reporting station near Paris, which had been set up to gather and reorganize men arriving from the west. Ten days after passing Mont Ormel they reached the Saar area, where they spent three days resting and regrouping. Then they were sent back into action with the remains of 116th Panzer in *Kampfengruppe Fick*.

General Eugene Meindl of II Parachute Corps spent two

hours hidden beneath a wrecked Polish Sherman within yards of the Allied lines, waiting for a moment to make his escape from the pocket. Like so many men in those days of turmoil, he had a succession of extraordinary personal encounters: with his own son; with a general named Eric Straube whom he was disgusted to find bivouacked in comfort with his staff, well supplied with food and wine; with a corps commander whom he did not identify, sitting weeping alone by the roadside. Meindl finally fought his way out at the head of a few score paratroopers and three tanks of 2nd SS Panzer.[2] General Hausser of Seventh Army was wounded by shrapnel as he marched amongst his men, and was carried out upon the back of a tank of 1st SS Panzer.

Lieutenant Fritz Langangke of 2nd SS Panzer had been driving since the beginning of August in a hastily-repaired tank with chronic overheating problems. Its collapse on the start-line for the Mortain counter-attack probably saved his life, and the same Panther carried him eastwards as the line crumbled, sustained by petrol drained into a canvas bucket from abandoned vehicles. In the final days of the pocket, the Panther's engine caught fire for the last time. The crew blew it up and started walking: "We just kept going along with the rest of the German army." They rejoined the remains of the division around Mont Ormel, finding their tank regiment now under the command of Major Enzerling. Their old commander, the bullet-headed Colonel Tyschen, an officer in the mould of "Panzer" Meyer, had died in the Mortain battle. The spirit of absolute doom was abroad. Enzerling solemnly visited his tank crews to say farewell to each man personally. Just west of the Seine, they were finally compelled to abandon all their vehicles, and each man to seek salvation as best he might. Langangke and eight others reached the river at Elbeuf to find French resistants already all over the town, waving tricolours and shooting at German stragglers. The lieutenant and his group hid in a house, considering their next move. There was no choice open to them save to cross the river. Neither his gunner nor his loader could swim, but they had to try. They drowned. Langangke himself reached the eastern bank clinging to the bloated body of a dead cow which was floating downriver amidst a host of other hapless animals and debris from the battlefield. He rejoined his unit at Huy-on-the-Maas, whence they were withdrawn to retrain and re-equip.

The SS and those men of the German army still determined to fight on were enraged by the wholesale collapse of will that they

The Hawker Typhoon – the 'Tiffy to all its pilots – was a big, heavy, rugged fighter-bomber which bore the brunt of the RAF's low-level ground-attack tasks over Normandy, carrying eight 50-pound rockets or 2,000 rounds of bombs. Handling a rocket-equipped Typhoon was a delicate art, since the rails reduced its speed and affected its handling. It was necessary to attack either at very low level – risking heavy punishment from ground fire – or almost vertically, as most pilots preferred. Typhoons were the principal destructors of the retreating German army at Falaise, and became legendary in the last nine months of the war for their effectiveness in the "cab rank" role, circling over advancing troops until directed onto a target by a forward air controller.

saw around them in those days. Lieutenant Ernst Krag of 2nd SS Panzer's assault gun battalion came upon a group of Wehrmacht armoured crews intent upon blowing up a company of new Panthers which they had just brought forward from Germany as replacements. The furious Krag ordered them to hand over the tanks intact to his own men, and they salvaged five. "What do you do," he demanded bitterly, "if even your commanders have begun to work according to the principle of *Heim ins Reich*?" Colonel Kurt Kauffmann, the operations officer of Panzer Lehr, who had contributed so much to the recapture of Villers-Bocage in June, walked out of the pocket in the clothes he stood up in, the entire divisional headquarters and its documents having been lost in the American breakthrough. He was posted to the eastern front for speaking openly about the hopelessness of the military situation.

Corporal Adolf Hohenstein of 276th Infantry marched eastward out of the pocket with a handful of men, having lost all contact with his unit. A general passed along the column of slow-moving soldiers, telling them that it was every man for himself – they were now encircled. Hohenstein said that this did not trouble him as much as it might, "for in Russia we had been surrounded again and again." He was one of the few who had escaped from the Sixth Army's disaster at Stalingrad, clinging to the hull of a tank. Now they came upon a château, where they paused to gaze sadly upon the wonderful library, torn open to the elements by shellfire. Around noon on 20 August, they were lying in a field wondering desperately how to cross the flat ground ahead, littered with dead horses, burning vehicles, wounded men, and still under furious shellfire. Suddenly the firing stopped. There was a rumour, probably unfounded, that a local truce had been declared while a German hospital was handed over to the Allies. They seized their moment, and hastened through the smoking chaos, wading the Dives to reach St Lambert. Many men, said Hohenstein, were no longer seeking to escape, but merely lingering in the hope of making a safe surrender. The houses of St Lambert were crowded with Wehrmacht fugitives who had abandoned their weapons and clutched only sheets to assist their efforts to give themselves up. Men said that it was no longer possible to get through to the east.

In the church, Hohenstein found scores of wounded being treated with such pathetic resources as the doctors still possessed, and a cluster of generals. The corporal met a colonel who said that he was going to take a tank through, and if the soldier wished, he could follow with his men. That night, when darkness came, they fell in behind the tank, moving eastwards. But they were deeply uneasy, travelling with the squealing monster that now seemed more a source of danger than security. They decided to separate from it and make their way alone. It started to rain, and the corporal had only a feeble torch to check their bearings. At 5.00 a.m. on the 21st, they approached the village of Coudehard, its houses burning quietly in the early morning light. They heard voices. They strained to discover from the shelter of the trees to which army the men belonged. At last they moved cautiously forward until an unmistakably German accent called "Halt!" They had reached the lines of 10th SS Panzer.

They struggled on eastwards in the days that followed, hastening to remain ahead of the Allies. In the little village of Le Sap near Vimoutiers, they found the entire population gathered around tables laid out with food and wine to greet their liberators. The exhausted, desperate Germans seized what provisions they could carry. Wary of a sudden attack by local *résistants*, Hohenstein told the frightened Frenchmen: "Me and my men just want to get through here in one piece. In a few hours you'll have a chance to find out if the other army treats you any better than ours." They marched the mayor and the curé at pistol point in front of them through the town until they were safe on the road beyond. On 25 August, they crossed the Seine at Elbeuf, sitting on a tank which was carried across on the sole surviving ferry, already under artillery fire. "After Normandy," said Hohenstein, "we had no illusions any more. We knew that we stood with our backs to the wall."

As the first Allied forces moved into the pocket, gathering up prisoners in their thousands, they were awed by the spectacle that they discovered:

The roads were choked with wreckage and the swollen bodies of men and horses [wrote Group-Captain Desmond Scott]. Bits of uniform were plastered to shattered tanks and trucks and human remains hung in grotesque shapes on the blackened hedgerows. Corpses lay in pools of dried blood, staring into space and as if their eyes were being forced from their sockets. Two grey-clad bodies. both minus their legs, leaned against a clay bank as if in prayer. I stumbled over a typewriter. Paper was scattered around where several mailbags had exploded. I picked up a photograph of a smiling young German recruit standing between his parents, two solemn peasants who stared back at me in accusation . . . Strangely enough it was the fate of the horses that upset me most. Harnessed as they were, it had been impossible for them to escape, and they lay dead in tangled heaps, their large wide eyes crying out to me in anguish. It was a sight that pierced the soul, and I felt as if my heart would burst. We did not linger, but hurried back to the sanctity of our busy airfield near Bayeux.[3]

Men moved among the bloated bodies firing bursts of sten-gun rounds to empty them of their ghastly gasses before they were burned. "Falaise was not the most frightening sight, but the most disgusting of the war," said Private Alfred Lee of the Middlesex Regiment. "The bodies crawled with blue-grey maggots. The spectacle was unspeakable when tanks drove over them. Many men had to put on their gas masks to endure getting through it." With the great burden of fear lifted from them, French civilians began to show much greater warmth and kindness to their deliverers. Trooper Dyson of the RAC, collecting replacement tanks from a depot near Villers-Bocage, was wined and dined with his mate by a French family: "They treated us like kings.

That village made us feel that we had liberated France all on our own." The last shell fell on Caen as late as 17 August. Nicole Ferté, having endured weeks as a refugee in a convent crowded with terrified and wounded civilians, had at last been forced out into countryside along with thousands of others late in July. She was living with a group of 30 in a barn, and was out scavenging for food one morning when she saw American tanks rolling down the road towards her. A GI sitting on the hull of the leading Sherman leapt down and kissed her, declaring in one of the phrases that the period of Liberation made immortal: "You look just like my girlfriend!" Ironically, on that very day of liberation, the girl was wounded in the foot by shrapnel. But she recovered to work as interpreter to the Town Major of Caen, and to experience the extraordinary life of France amid the Allied armies that summer. She said sardonically: "All the Americans thought that everybody would go with them because they had the cigarettes, the stockings, the money." Many did.

In a village south of Caen, a platoon commander of 15th Scottish Division sat with his men in their trucks:

> An enormous convoy crammed with dishevelled, dusty Wehrmacht prisoners rolls in the opposite direction: "The bastards!", wrenches out my truck driver with a sudden rush of feeling; while a great bearded Frenchman, like a ferocious dog, stands alone in the desolation of a village square, shaking his fist at the vast POW convoy and yelling after them as though his heart would break: "Kaput! . . . Kaput! . . ."[4]

Most Allied soldiers found that now, for the first time in the wake of their own crushing victory, they could spare pity for the defeated enemy. Trooper Dyson watched the lines of prisoners shuffling through the forward area, "some of them old men wearing overcoats down to their ankles." Like so many Allied soldiers, he took a German's belt for its eagle buckle, then felt ashamed because the man's trousers fell down. "I looked at them all, and somehow it seemed unbelievable that they were the Germans, the enemy – some mother's sons." Jerry Komareks's battalion of the U.S. 2nd Armored adopted a little blond 14-year-old Russian prisoner as a unit mascot. Pedro, as they called him, was given cut-down American fatigues and a pistol, then rode with them all the way to Berlin. There they were compelled to surrender him, crying bitterly, to the Russians. Presumably he was shot, like so many thousands of others turned over to the Red Army.[5]

It was only on 21 August that the Falaise Gap could properly be accounted closed, as tanks of the Canadian 4th Armoured Division linked with the Poles at Coudehard, and the Canadian 3rd and 4th Divisions secured St Lambert and the northern passage to Chambois. 344 tanks and self-propelled guns, 2,447 soft-skinned vehicles and 252 guns were counted abandoned or destroyed in the northern sector of the pocket alone. The battle for Normandy had cost the German army a total of 1,500 tanks, 3,500 guns and 20,000 vehicles. They had lost around 450,000 men, 240,000 of these killed or wounded. On 22/23 August, Army Group B reported the state of its eight surviving armoured divisions:

2 Pz: 1 infantry battalion, no tanks, no artillery
21 Pz: 4 weak infantry battalions, 10 tanks, artillery unknown
116 Pz: 1 infantry battalion, 12 tanks, approx. two artillery batteries
1st SS Pz: weak infantry elements, no tanks, no artillery
2nd SS Pz: 450 men, 15 tanks, 6 guns
9th SS Pz: 460 men, 20–25 tanks, 20 guns
10th SS Pz: 4 weak infantry battalions, no tanks, no artillery
12th SS Pz: 300 men, 10 tanks, no artillery.

Meyer's division alone had driven into Normandy with over 20,000 men and 150 tanks. Panzer Lehr had ceased to exist as a formation after COBRA, 9th Panzer was wiped out in the Mortain battle. Of the 100,000 men of First Army, facing the Bay of Biscay, who had been ordered to retire east, some 65,000 crossed the Seine, having lost most of their equipment. Only what was left of Fifteenth Army in the Pas de Calais, and Nineteenth Army, retiring north in the face of the American landings in the south of France which began on 15 August, still possessed any semblance of organization and cohesion. More than 40 German divisions had been destroyed. The Allies had achieved this at a cost of 209,672 casualties, 36,976 of these killed. British and Canadian losses amounted to two-thirds those suffered by the Americans. Some 28,000 Allied aircrew were also lost either over Normandy, during the vast campaign of preparatory bombing of communications and coastal installations, or the execution during 1943–44 of the POINTBLANK programme designed to pave the way for OVERLORD.

Few episodes in the Normandy campaign have provoked such a torrent of words since the war as the Allied failure to close the gap south of Falaise more speedily,[6] permitting the escape of a significant fragment of the German army which seemed doomed to absolute destruction, given the military situation around 7 August. Before considering the reasons for the Allied fumbling – if fumbling it was – it seems worth emphasizing that the portion of the German forces which got away was tiny by comparison with that which was destroyed. Only 24 tanks and 60 guns were ferried east across the Seine. Something over 20,000 Germans escaped the pocket, with only the clothes on their backs and personal weapons. Events around the Falaise Gap between the opening of TOTALIZE and 22 August became a source of anger and controversy much more because it appeared that Allied operations had been clumsily handled, than because any such failure cost Montgomery and Bradley important fruits of victory. The Americans were bitter because they considered that, once again, Montgomery had promised to achieve an objective on the battlefield, and failed: namely, to get the Canadians to Argentan before the Germans began to escape east. Montgomery himself implicitly acknowledged the importance of the Canadian failure to reach Falaise in time on 16 August, when he directed elements of the Canadian First Army to bend sharply south-east to Trun and Chambois, and asked Bradley to push American forces there to meet them. He hoped that by creating a wider noose the Germans could still be held within it.

A number of recent writers, including Martin Blumenson and Carlo D'Este, have noted the absurd over-simplification by critics who suggest that if Bradley's men had been set free to push north to Falaise, they would have closed the gap days earlier.[6] In reality, an American south-north line around 17 or 18 August would almost certainly have been broken by the Germans, fighting with the desperation they revealed everywhere at this period. The U.S. division which finally closed the gap at Chambois, the 90th, had shown itself to be one of the least effective formations among the Allied armies in Normandy. Meindl's paratroopers, and the survivors of 2nd SS and 12th SS Panzer, would almost certainly have cracked the 90th, inflicting an embarrassing and gratuitous setback upon the Americans. This prospect and danger must have occupied Bradley's thoughts when he declined to allow the move north, and declared that he preferred "the strong shoulder" at Argentan to "a broken neck at Falaise".[7] Bradley knew that the fleeing German army was already being devastated by air attack and pounded by artillery. His avowed reason for failing to close the gap – fear of a collision between the Allied armies – scarcely merits serious examination.

It seems far more probable that he saw a situation in which the enemy was being mauled almost to death without significant risk to the Allied armies; to slam the trap precipitately shut with ground forces and to close for a death-grapple with the desperate men fighting eastwards, offered a risk of humiliation which could not be justified by any possible tactical or strategic gain. If the man outside the thicket knows that the wounded tiger within it is bleeding to death, he would be foolish to step inside merely to hasten collection of the trophy. If this was indeed Bradley's reasoning, he was almost certainly correct.

Far too much of the controversy and criticism surrounding the Falaise Gap and other Normandy battles has focussed solely upon the generals, as if their making of a decision ensured its effective execution.[8] It seems equally important to consider whether a given option was feasible *within the limits of the capabilities of the forces concerned.* It has been the central theme of this book that the inescapable reality of the battle for Normandy was that when Allied troops met Germans on anything like equal terms, the Germans almost always prevailed. If the campaign is studied as an abstract military exercise, then all manner of possibilities become acceptable: the British could and should have got men into Caen on D-Day; they could and should have broken through at Villers-Bocage on 13 June; EPSOM and GOODWOOD should have led to decisive advances and the collapse of the German defences. As it happened, of course, nowhere did the Allies achieve decisive penetrations against high-quality German formations until these had been worn down by attrition and ruined by air attack. COBRA was a superb example of American dash and movement, but the vast American attacking force met only the shattered remains of Panzer Lehr and a few flanking battle-groups. Even these gave Collins' men a hard time on the first day. The British began to make significant ground gains in August only when the Germans in front of them were greatly outnumbered and reduced to a few score tanks and guns. It may be argued that any Allied attempt at envelopment before the German forces had been brought to the brink of destruction by attrition would have cost the attackers dear. A British or American breakthrough southwards in June might have been very heavily punished by German counter-attack.

It has become commonplace to assert that the Allies' basic difficulty was that they devoted too much thought and energy before the landings to the problems of getting ashore, not enough to what must happen thereafter. There is an element of truth in this, applicable to events on the afternoon of D-Day and on 7 and 8 June. Thereafter, however, the Allies' difficulties lay not in any lack of planning, but in the difference in fighting ability between the opposing forces on the battlefield.

The Allies in Normandy faced the finest fighting army of the war, one of the greatest that the world has ever seen. This is a simple truth that some soldiers and writers have been reluctant to acknowledge, partly for reasons of nationalistic pride, partly because it is a painful concession when the Wehrmacht and SS were fighting for one of the most obnoxious regimes of all time. The quality of the Germans' weapons – above all tanks – was of immense importance. Their tactics were masterly: stubborn defence; concentrated local firepower from mortars and machine-guns; quick counter-attacks to recover lost ground. Units often fought on even when cut off, which was not a mark of fanaticism, but of sound tactical discipline, when such resistance in the rear did much to reduce the momentum of Allied advances, as in GOODWOOD. German attacks were markedly less skilful, even clumsy. But they adapted at once to the need for infiltration in the *bocage*, a skill of which few Allied units proved capable, even at the end. Their junior leadership was much superior to that of the Americans, perhaps also to that of the British.

Few American infantry units arrived in Normandy with a grasp of basic tactics – a failure for which many men paid with their lives. The American airborne units showed what was possible on the battlefield, what the American soldier at his best could achieve. But only a handful of other formations proved capable of emulating the 82nd and 101st. The belief that firepower could ultimately save the infantry from the task of hard fighting underlay many difficulties and failures on the ground. It is interesting that Lieutenant Andrew Wilson, who fought as a British tank officer in north-west Europe and worked on occasion with American infantry, visited Vietnam a quarter of a century later as a correspondent, and noted the same carelessness on the battlefield that he had observed in 1944–45. Some more dedicated and skilful infantry fighting earlier in the Normandy campaign might, in the end, have saved a great many American lives. Both British and American commanders sometimes seemed to search for scapegoats rather than causes of poor performance by their men on the battlefield. Some of the generals sacked in Normandy (and elsewhere) were incompetent. But there was a limit to what a corps or divisional commander could achieve with the material he was given. It is striking that when Patton or Collins were given poor-qualitjy divisions with which to gain an objective, they could extract no better performance from these than less competent commanders. The same was true of the British 7th Armoured – none of its successive commanders in north-west Europe could make anything of it. The problems, where there were problems, often descended to regimental and battalion level. There were not nearly sufficient able field officers for any solution to be found in wholesale sackings.

The British were superior to the Americans in regimental leadership and staffwork. But they proved unable to generate the weight of fighting power – combat power, as the Americans call it – to smash through unweakened German defences. Germans who fought in the desert often expressed their surprise at the willingness of the British soldier to do what he believed was expected of him, and then to stop – even to surrender – when ammunition ran low, petrol ran out or he found himself encircled or deprived of officer leadership. Again and again in Normandy, British units fought superbly, with great bravery, only to lack the last ounce of drive or follow-through necessary to carry an objective or withstand a counter-attack. The inexperience of American, British and Canadian formations must be measured against the performance of 12th SS Panzer. This, too, was a "green" division, which had never fought a battle before 7 June. The Canadian official historian wrote: "One suspects that the Germans contrived to get more out of their training than we did. Perhaps their attitude towards such matters was less casual than ours."[9]

An ethos, a mood, pervades all armies at all times about what is and is not acceptable, what is expected. Within the Allied armies in Normandy in 1944–45, the ethos was that of men committed to doing an unwelcome but necessary job for the cause of democracy. The ethos of the German army, profoundly influenced by the threat from the east, was of a society fighting to the last to escape *götterdämmerung*. Lieutenant Langangke was perhaps not exaggerating when he said that as he sat in his Panther, knocking out Shermans one after the other, he felt like Siegfried. Mercifully for the future of western civilization, few men in the Allied armies ever believed for a moment that they were anyone other than Lindley Higgins from Riverdale in the Bronx, or Corporal Brown from Tonbridge. Montgomery wrote to Brooke from the desert: "The trouble with our British lads is that they are not killers by nature." Each man knew that he was a small cog in the great juggernaut of armed democracy, whose eventual victory was certain. Suicidal, sacrificial acts of courage were admired when performed by individuals and rewarded with decorations. But they were not *demanded* of whole Allied formations as they were of so many in Hitler's armies. Even Corporal Hohenstein of that very moderate organization, the 276th Infantry, never allowed himself to be troubled by encirclement because this was an experience that he, like so many others, had often overcome in Russia: they were merely expected to break out of it. The attitude of most Allied soldiers was much influenced by the belief, conscious or unconscious, that they possessed the means to dispense with anything resembling personal fanaticism on the battlefield: their huge weight of firepower. This view was not unjustified. Artillery and air power accomplished much of the killing of Germans that had to be done sooner or later to make a breakthrough possible. But it could not do all of this. It is not that the Allied armies in Normandy were seriously incompetent; merely that the margin of German professional superiority was sufficient to cause the Allies very great difficulties.

All this Montgomery and Bradley understood perfectly well, and they shaped their plans and expectations accordingly. They had not been sent to Normandy to demonstrate the superiority of their fighting men to those of Hitler, but to win the war at tolerable cost – a subtly but importantly different objective. Their business and their difficulty, while acknowledging the difference in mood and spirit between their own soldiers and those of Hitler, was to persuade their armies to do enough – albeit, just enough – to prevail on a given battlefield and in a given action. This they were at last able to do, inflicting an absolute defeat upon their enemies. Overall, it may be said that Montgomery accomplished as much in Normandy as he could with the forces available to him. He is owed a greater debt for his performance than has been recognized in recent years, when his own untruths and boastfulness have been allowed to confuse the issue; and when the root problem of the limited abilities of his troops, and the dynamism of the Germans, has often been ignored.

Much of the criticism emanating from SHAEF, the airmen and Washington was based upon the inability of men lacking direct contact with the battlefield to grasp painful truths. The American and British public had been fed for years upon a necessary diet of propaganda about the superiority of their fighting men to those of the enemy. Even some senior service officers could not now understand the difficulty of fighting the German army. Brooke did, and his awareness lay at the heart of many of his fears about OVERLORD and about the course of the campaign on the continent. He was too big a man to continue to support Montgomery blindly, merely because the Commander-in-Chief of 21st Army Group was his protégé. He backed Montgomery and sympathized with his disappointments and failures because he understood, perhaps better than any man outside France, the difficulty of arranging matters so that British and American soldiers could defeat German soldiers on the ground. Brooke knew – as surely also did Montgomery in his secret thoughts – that it was the Allies' superiority of *matériel* that enabled them to prevail at the last, assisted by competent generalship and a solid performance by most of their men on the battlefield. Patton's headlong rush around western France was a far less impressive command achievement than the cool, professional response of Bradley and his corps commanders to the Mortain counter-attack. By that first week of August, the balance of psychological advantage had at last shifted decisively. The German thrust lacked conviction – even formations such as 2nd SS Panzer fought half-heartedly. Meanwhile, the Americans had gained a new confidence in their own powers Isolated infantry units held their ground; headquarters staffs kept their nerve; the American forces dispatched to meet the Germans – with the possible exception of the 35th Division, which seemed slow to achieve the relief of the 30th – drove hard and sure to throw back the panzers.

Normandy was a campaign which perfectly exemplified the strengths and weaknesses of the democracies. The invasion was a product of dazzling organization and staffwork, and marvellous technical ingenuity. Once the armies were ashore, there was no firework display of military brilliance. Instead, for the armies, there was a steady, sometimes clumsy learning process. Each operation profited from the mistakes of the last, used massed firepower to wear down the Germans, absorbed disappointments without trauma. This last was a true reflection of the nature of the struggle: most German commanders, amidst the insuperable difficulties of grappling both with Hitler and the Allies, declined towards a state bordering on hysteria. Among the Allied armies, however, there was sometimes gloom, but never real alarm or nervousness. These symptoms were more in evidence at SHAEF, where the role of impotent spectator taxed some men, even the highest, beyond endurance. Montgomery and Bradley and their staffs and corps commanders merely fought, reconsidered, and fought again until at last their resources granted them victory. Armchair strategists and military historians can find much to look back upon and criticize in Normandy. On 22 August 1944, it is doubtful whether many regrets troubled the Allied army commanders in France.

One lesson from the fighting in Normandy seems important for any future battle that the armies of democracy might be called upon to fight. If a Soviet invasion force swept across Europe from the east, it would be unhelpful if contemporary British or American soldiers were trained and conditioned to believe that the level of endurance and sacrifice displayed by the Allies in Normandy would suffice to defeat the invaders. For an example to follow in the event of a future European battle, it will be necessary to look to the German army; and to the extraordinary defence that its men conducted in Europe in the face of all the odds against them, and in spite of their own demented Führer.

Liddell Hart described Normandy as "an operation that eventually went according to plan, but not according to timetable."[10] A good case can be made that the Allies' disappointments and delays in gaining ground eventually worked to their advantage. Just as in Tunisia, more than a year earlier, Hitler's obsessive reinforcement of failure caused him to thrust division after division into the cauldron for destruction. By the time the breakout came, no significant forces lay in front of the Allies before the German border. Paris fell on 25 August, Patton crossed the Meuse on 31 August, and was at Metz on the Moselle the next day. The Guards Armoured Division reached Brussels on 3 September, after advancing 75 miles in a single day. 11th Armoured reached Antwerp on the 4th, to find the port intact.

On 1 September, Eisenhower assumed direct control of the Allied armies in the field – to Montgomery's bitter frustration, disappointment and chagrin. The Commander-in-Chief himself was the only man at 21st Army Group unable to understand the imperative by which American dominance among the armies demanded American command in the field. Williams and de Guingand attempted to explain this reality to him, and the fact that his loss of control was inevitable, "even if the Americans thought you the greatest general in the world – which they do not."[11]

At this juncture, there were perhaps 100 German tanks on the entire western front against over 2,000 in the Allied spearheads; 570 Luftwaffe aircraft against the Allies' 14,000. By yet another herculean feat of organization, Student mobilized 8,000 men of First Parachute Army to cover a 100-mile chasm in the front. The Allies paused to regroup and resolve their immense logistical problems. By mid-September, the German line was thickening everywhere. "I left France almost convinced that Germany was through and that the war would end in 1944," wrote Gavin of the 82nd Airborne. "But many in the division felt more cautious, since the fighting at times had proved to be far more difficult and costly than we had anticipated."[12] The battles in Holland and along the German border so often seem to belong to a different age from those of Normandy that it is startling to reflect that Arnhem was fought less than a month after Falaise; that within weeks of suffering one of the greatest catastrophes of modern war, the Germans found the strength to halt the drive of Horrocks' XXX Corps in its tracks, and to prolong the war until May 1945. But if this phenomenon reveals the same staggering qualities in Hitler's armies which had caused the Allies such grief in Normandy, it is also another story.

Notes and references

All quotations in the text based upon the author's interviews with individuals are given specific references on the subject's first mention, but not thereafter unless there are grounds for confusion between personal interview quotations and those not listed in the bibliography.

FOREWORD

1 *Lessons Of Normandy*, Liddell Hart; essay in LH papers, King's College, London

PROLOGUE

1 This narrative is based entirely upon an interview with Lt-Col. John Warner, 16.vi.83

CHAPTER 1

1 Fraser, *Alanbrooke*, p. 397
2 Bryant, *Triumph in the West*, p. 205
3 Howard, *Grand Strategy* vol. iv, p. 252
4 Harrison, *Cross Channel Attack*, p. 10
5 Ehrman, *Grand Strategy*, vol. v, p. 108
6 *ibid*, p. 109
7 *ibid*, p. 109 *et seq.*
8 U.S. CoS papers, ABC 384, Europe: 5.viii.43
9 Ehrman, *Grand Strategy*, p. 43
10 Portal Papers, Christchurch College, Oxford, File 2, 2g
11 Howard (op. cit.), p. 249
12 For instance, see Grigg, *1943: The Victory that Never Was*, Walter Scott Dunn, *Second Front Now – 1943*
13 See Nigel Nicolson, *Alexander*, p. 211
14 Bryant (op. cit.), p. 160
15 Public Record Office WO205/33
16 PRO WO205/2
17 *ibid*
18 *ibid*
19 PRO WO205/33
20 *ibid*
21 Fraser (op. cit.), p. 421
22 Eisenhower, diary

23 For an extreme example, see Irving, *The War Between The Generals* (London, 1981), which highlights the squabbles within the Allied high command and the personal vices of its commanders to a degree which obscures the extraordinary co-operation on the military issues that mattered.
24 Eisenhower, diary

CHAPTER 2

COMMANDERS

1 Omar Bradley, *A Soldier's Story*, p 171
2 *ibid*, p. 176
3 Interview with the author, vi.83
4 Ronald Lewin, *Wavell: The Chief* (London, 1980)
5 Russell Weigley, *Eisenhower's Lieutenants*, p. 37
6 Quoted in Hamilton, *Montgomery: Master of the Battlefield*, p. 513
7 Palmer, Wiley & Keast, *Procurement and Training of Ground Combat Troops*, p. 258
8 Ehrman, *Grand Strategy*, p. 50
9 PRO WO205/118
10 Williams, interview with the author, 14.vi.83
11 PRO WO205/118
12 *ibid*
13 Interview with the author
14 PRO WO232/1
15 Some special forces, above all the U.S. Rangers and the French SAS parachuted into Brittany, made a notable contribution on D-Day and in the weeks that followed. But their story has been repeated so often in earlier narratives of OVERLORD that it seems redundant to retrace the story in detail here.
16 Quoted in Hamilton (op. cit.), p. 562 *et seq.*
17 *ibid*
18 See Aron, *De Gaulle Before Paris*; François Kersaudy, *Churchill and De Gaulle* (London, 1981). None of the parties concerned emerge with great credit from the pre-D-Day struggle concerning the future administration of liberated France, the Americans showing extraordinary insensitivity by their determination to treat her as if she were bankrupt stock purchased in blood from some global liquidator, rather than one of the great nations of the world.

AIRMEN

1 Harris quoted in Hastings, *Bomber Command*, p. 257
2 Craven & Cate, *The U.S. Army Air Forces in World War II*, vol. ii, p. 735
3 Hastings (op. cit.), p. 275
4 Carl F. Spaatz, diary, 21.i.44, in Spaatz papers, Box 15, Library of Congress

5 Spaatz papers, Box 14 (loc. cit.)
6 Quesada, interview with the author, 5.vii.83
7 *ibid*
8 Gavin, interview with the author, 8.vii.83
9 Vandenberg, diary, 24.iii.83, MS Division, Library of Congress
10 PRO WO216/139

INVADERS

1 Wilson, interview with the author, 20.vi.83
2 *ibid*
3 Gosling, interview with the author, 21.vi.83
4 Richardson, interview with the author, 21.vii.83
5 Priest, interview with the author (pseudonym at subject's request), 14.vi.83
6 Portway, interview with the author, 13.vii.83
7 Heal, interview with the author, 27.vi.83
8 Bramall, interview with the author, 28.vi.83
9 PRO WO216/101
10 Bach, interview with the author, 30.vi.83
11 Weigley, *Eisenhower's Lieutenants*, p. 31
12 Patton, *War as I Knew it*, p. 336
13 Butcher, diary, unexpurgated MS, Eisenhower Library
14 *et seq*. Higgins, interview with the author, 3.vii.83
15 *et seq*. Herman, interview with the author, 3.vii.83
16 Pre-war American tactical doctrine dictated that forces advance with the weight of their fighting power centred in valleys, their flanks on hilltops. This proved absurd in the face of German defenders who invariably concentrated their strength on available high ground.
17 Colacicco, interview with the author, 6.vii.83
18 Bradley (op. cit.), p. 226–7
19 Marshall, on sacking corps commanders
20 Colacicco, interview with the author (loc. cit.)
21 Herman, interview with the author (loc. cit.)
22 Walsh, interview with the author, 1.vii.83
23 *et seq*. Raymond, interview with the author, 2.vii.83
24 Svboda, interview with the author, 3.vii.83
25 Papers of Admiral Allen G. Kirk, U.S. Navy Archives, Washington DC
26 Original letter in possession of Herman
27 Quoted in Hamilton (op. cit.), p. 570
28 Bradley (op. cit.), p. 223
29 *inter alia* Gavin, interview with the author (loc. cit.)
30 Bradley (op. cit.), p. 209
31 *et seq*. Reisler, interview with the author, 5.vii.83

DEFENDERS

1 Warlimont, *Inside Hitler's Headquarters*, p. 403
2 Ehrman (op. cit.), p. 108
3 *ibid*, p. 406–7
4 *ibid*
5 To the Dominions Secretary; *Churchill*, vol. v (op. cit.), p. 602
6 Cruickshank, *Deception in World War II*, p. 186
7 German forecasting was drastically impeded by the loss of their outlying weather stations. Their blindness in meteorology, as in military intelligence, contributed directly to the German high command's unpreparedness on D-Day. Where Group-Captain Stagg and his colleagues had predicted the "window" of reasonable weather which would follow the poor conditions prevailing in the Channel on 5 June, their German counterparts had not.
8 In the British press, drawing entirely unwarranted conclusions from material contained in West, *MI6: British Secret Intelligence Service Operations 1909–45*.
9 To the author, 25.ix.83
10 Most sensationally, Irving, *The Trail Of The Fox*; Cave-Brown, *Bodyguard Of Lies*
11 Cruickshank (op. cit.), p. 213
12 To the author, 14.vi.83
13 Irving, *Trail Of The Fox*, p. 320
14 Interview with the author, 3.v.83
15 Schaaf, interview with the author, 4.v.83
16 *ibid*
17 Interview with the author, 2.v.83
18 Guderian, *Panzer Leader*, p. 332
19 Interview with the author, 6.v.83

CHAPTER 3

OVERTURE

1 Quoted in Harrison, *Cross Channel Attack*, p. 274
2 Combat narrative from Cota papers in Eisenhower Library
3 Letter to the author, 16.iii.82
4 This, and all subsequent F. O. Richardson quotations, from unpublished narrative loaned to the author, or interview of 2.vii.83
5 Quoted in Hamilton, *Montgomery: Master of the Battlefield*, p. 561
6 See note 7 to Chapter 2, DEFENDERS
7 For instance, Cooper, *The German Army: Its Political and Military Failure 1933–45*, p. 502
8 Interview with the author, 6.viii.83
9 Gosset & Lecomte, *Caen Pendant La Bataille*, p. 26
10 Extract loaned to the author
11 Barrett, privately printed narrative on *The First Ship Sunk On D-Day*, loaned to the author

12 *ibid*
13 Diary loaned to the author
14 Williams, interview with the author (loc. cit.)
15 Fraser, *Alanbrooke*, p. 423
16 Interview with the author, 4. vii. 83

THE AMERICAN BEACHES

1 Quoted in Carell, *Invasion – They're Coming*, p. 49 *et seq.*
2 *ibid*, p. 80 *et seq.*
3 Bradley (op. cit.), p. 270
4 *ibid*
5 Interview with the author, 3. vii. 83
6 Interview with the author, 1. vii. 83
7 Letter to the author
8 Rehm, interview with the author, 3. vii. 83
9 Cota papers, combat narrative (op. cit.)
10 *ibid*
11 For example, see Wilmot, *Struggle for Europe*; Howarth, *Dawn of D-Day*
12 Wilmot, *Struggle for Europe*, p. 253 *et seq.*

THE BRITISH BEACHES

1 Unpublished narrative loaned to the author
2 Unpublished narrative loaned to the author

INLAND

1 Warlimont, *Inside Hitler's Headquarters*, p. 431
2 Narrative published in the regimental magazine of the King's Own Shropshire Light Infantry
3 I Corps operational order in PRO WO171/258
4 Carell (op. cit.), p. 106
5 Diary loaned to the author
6 Bradley, *A General's Life*, p. 253
7 Craven & Cate, *The U.S. Army Air Forces in World War II*, vol. iii, p. 181

CHAPTER 4

CLOSING THE LINES

1 Quoted in Brett-Smith, *Hitler's Generals*, p. 162
2 Schaaf, interview with the author (loc. cit.)
3 Stacey, *The Victory Campaign*, vol. iii, p. 133
4 *ibid*, p. 137
5 Raymond, interview with the author, 30. vi. 83
6 Hamilton, *Montgomery: Master of the Battlefield*, p. 631
7 *ibid*, p. 596
8 Williams, interview with the author (loc. cit.)
9 Wilson, *Flamethrower*, pp. 74–5

VILLERS-BOCAGE

1 Author's interview with 7th Armoured eye-witness
2 Fergusson, *The Black Watch and the King's Enemies*, p. 206
3 Salmud, *History of the 51st Highland Division* (Edinburgh, 1953), p. 144
4 Kortenhaus, interview with the author, 6.iv.83
5 Hamilton (op. cit.), p. 649
6 Carell (op. cit.), p. 169
7 Peter Roach, *The 8.15 To War* (London, 1982), p. 138–9
8 Lockwood, interview with the author, 9.xi.82
9 Carver, interview with the author, 22.vi.83
10 Dempsey, interview with Chester Wilmot, Liddell Hart papers, King's College, London

EPSOM

1 Woollcombe, *Lion Rampant*, p. 49
2 Bramall, interview with the author, 28.vi.83
3 Woollcombe (op. cit.), p. 60
4 Baker, unpublished narrative loaned to the author
5 Richardson, interview with the author, 21.vii.83
6 Dyson, interview with the author, 28.i.83
7 Wilson, interview with the author, 14.ii.83
8 Priest, interview with the author (loc. cit.)
9 Montgomery, interview with Wilmot, Liddell Hart papers, King's College, London
10 For instance, Hamilton (op. cit.)
11 *ibid*, p. 580
12 Quoted in Ellis, *Normandy*, p. 261
13 Leigh-Mallory, diary, PRO AIR 37
14 Brooke, diary, 31.iii.43; Bryant (op. cit.), p. 297
15 PRO CAB106/1092, 15.vii.44
16 Quoted in Hamilton (op. cit.), p. 714–5
17 War Office, *Current Reports From Overseas*, 8.vii.44, Staff College Library
18 *ibid*, no. 44
19 Interview with the author, 24.vi.83
20 PRO WO205/118
21 C-in-C's order quoted in *Current Reports from Overseas* (op. cit.)
22 *ibid*, no. 54
23 PRO WO208/3193
24 *Current Reports* (op. cit.), no. 58
25 PRO WO208/393. For a further fascinating, damning but unbiased view of British tactics and of the British army's general performance in Normandy, see the notes of Brigadier James Hargest, New Zealand observer with XXX Corps, in PRO CAB 106/1060
26 Richardson, interview with the author (loc. cit.)
27 Grigg papers, Churchill College, Cambridge. The name of the com-

manding officer concerned is given in the document, but is omitted here to spare personal embarrassment.

28 *ibid*

29 *Lessons of Normandy*, Liddell Hart papers, King's College, London

30 Williams, interview with the author (loc. cit.)

CHAPTER 5

THE *BOCAGE*

1 Gavin, *On to Berlin*, p. 121

2 Bradley (op. cit.), p. 280

3 Cota papers, Combat narrative (loc. cit.)

4 Bradley (op. cit.), p. 295

5 *ibid*, p. 283

6 Richardson, narrative (loc. cit.)

7 *ibid*

8 Eichen, interview with the author, 7.vii.83

9 Cota (op. cit.)

10 *ibid*

11 Cota (loc. cit.)

12 Herman, unpublished narrative loaned to the author

13 *ibid*

14 Bryant, interview with the author, 9.vii.83

15 First Army diary, copy held in DDE Library

16 It is an apparent paradox that while all the combatants in Normandy agreed upon the prodigious scale of Allied resources, the Allied high command complained of constant difficulties with supplies, above all artillery ammunition. Many observers both at the time and since have suggested that the ammunition shortages could readily have been remedied had the vast shipments of rations, equipment, vehicles been moderated somewhat, especially on the American flank. But the scale of supplies provided for the Allied forces reflected a philosophy determined many months before D-Day.

17 Preston, interview with the author (loc. cit.)

18 Collins, *Lightning Joe*, p. 220

19 First Army diary

THE BATTLE FOR CHERBOURG

1 Carell, *Invasion – They're Coming*, p. 194

2 Herman, narrative (loc. cit.)

3 Bryant, interview with the author (loc. cit.)

4 Hughes, diary

5 Palmer, Wiley & Keast, *The Procurement and Training of Ground Combat Troops*, p. 1

6 First U.S. Army Report of Operations, p. 117

7 PRO WO205/401

8 PRO WO232/17

9 Gavin (op..cit.), p. 71
10 Interview with the author, iv.83
11 Gavin (op. cit.), p. 71
12 Weigley, *Eisenhower's Lieutenants*, p. 45

CHAPTER 6

SOLDIERS

1 PRO219/1908
2 Schickner, interview with the author, 3.iv.83
3 Harrison, *Cross Channel Attack*, p. 374
4 Kruger, interview with the author, 30.iv.83
5 PRO WO219/1908
6 Bradley (op. cit.), p. 292
7 Quoted in Irving, *Trail Of The Fox*, p. 340
8 *ibid*, p. 343
9 *ibid*
10 PRO WO205/1021 (Dietrich interrogation)
11 Kauffmann, interview with the author, 4.v.83
12 Irving (op. cit.), p. 346
13 *ibid*, p. 351
14 *ibid*, p. 353
15 *ibid*, p. 363–4
16 PRO WO205/1022 (von Rundstedt interrogation)
17 Irving (op. cit.), p. 74
18 Ruge, quoted in Irving (op. cit.), p.375
19 *ibid*
20 *ibid*, p. 376
21 Williams, interview with the author (loc. cit.)
22 Hellmuth Lang, interview with the author, 6.v.83
23 For instance, Cave Brown and Irving (op. cit.)
24 Kauffmann, interview with the author (loc. cit.)
25 Kruger, interview with the author (loc. cit.)
26 Guderian, interview with the author, 4.v.83
27 Williams, interview with the author (loc. cit.)
28 Quesada, interview with the author (loc. cit.)
29 PRO WO219/1908
30 Dupuy, *A Genius for War*, pp. 253–4
31 Bradley (op. cit.), p. 357

WEAPONS

1 PRO WO205/5b
2 Quoted in Hamilton, *Montgomery: Master of the Battlefield*, pp. 713–4
3 Kay Summersby, diary, 2.vii.83
4 Gavin, *On to Berlin*, p. 51
5 Discarding sabot was a formidable British innovation in armour-

piercing ammunition. The casing of the shell was shed after leaving the gun-barrel, and only a slender bolt of hardened steel continued to the target at very high velocity, generating unprecedented power of penetration. Discarding-sabot ammunition had been available for some time for 6-pounder guns, but became available for 17-pounders only in the summer of 1944. It has been one of the principal forms of anti-armour projectile ever since.

6 Wilson, *Flamethrower*, p. 54
7 Ross, *The Business of Tanks*, p. 153
8 *ibid*
9 *ibid*, p. 263
10 ORS reports nos. 12 & 17, Staff College Library
11 Ross (op. cit.), p. 275
12 Bradley (op. cit.), p. 320
13 *et seq.* Hansard
14 Ross (op. cit.), p. 316–17

CHAPTER 7

FROM THE BEACHHEAD TO THE FRONT

1 Letter loaned to the author by Mr James Verrier
2 See, for instance, Dunn, *Second Front Now*; Hartcup, *Code Name Mulberry*
3 *ibid*
4 See Fergusson, *The Watery Maze*
5 Patton, *War as I Knew It*, p. 101
6 Baldwin, MS (op. cit.)
7 Lee, interview with the author, 4.iii.83
8 Hein, interview with the author, 1.vii.83
9 Zimmer, diary from Hoover Institute, S644D/1.5.202
10 Gunther, interview (loc. cit.)
11 Gosset & Lecomte, *Caen Pendant la Bataille*, p. 51
12 Quesada, interview (loc. cit.)
13 Ratliff, interview with the author, 3.vii.83
14 Ivon-Jones, interview with the author, 4.ii.83
15 Sadi Schneid, *Beutesdeutscher*, p. 119
16 Wilson, interview (loc. cit.)
17 Whitelaw, interview with the author, 27.vii.83
18 Sir David Cole, *Rough Road to Rome* (London, 1982), p. 82
19 *Current Notes* (op. cit.), no. 44
20 Brown, interview with the author, 18.ii.83
21 Preston, interview (loc. cit.)
22 *Current Notes* (op. cit.) for 8.vii.44
23 Hansen, diary, U.S. Army Military History Institute
24 *Current Notes* (op. cit.), no. 54
25 Wilson, interview with the author (loc. cit.)

CASUALTIES

1 Brenda McBryde, *A Nurse's War* (London, 1979), p. 86–7
2 Copy loaned to the author
3 Wilson, *Flamethrower*, p. 70
4 Higgins, interview (loc. cit.)
5 Bramall, interview (loc. cit.)
6 Whitelaw, interview (loc. cit.)
7 Letter loaned to the author by Mr James Verrier
8 Wilson (op. cit.), p.71

CHAPTER 8

THE FALL OF CAEN

1 Quoted in Wilmot, *The Struggle For Europe*, p. 338
2 Gosset & Lecomte, *Caen Pendant La Bataille*, p. 37
3 *ibid*
4 Portway. interview with the author, 16.v.83
5 DF: Defensive Fire – a standard gunnery technique whereby batteries designate certain likely lines of enemy attack by code numbers, and range in upon them in advance. Then, when an attack develops, men in the forward positions can summon immediate artillery support at a threatened point by radioing simply to the guns for "DF63" or "DF14", rather than having to waste precious minutes correcting the gunners' aim onto map coordinates from scratch.
6 Zimmer, diary (loc. cit.)
7 Stephens, unpublished MS loaned to author
8 Butcher, diary, DDE Library
9 *Eisenhower Papers*, vol. iii, p. 1982
10 Bryant (op. cit.), p. 229
11 Tedder, *With Prejudice*, p. 555
12 *Colliers' Magazine*, 5.x.46
13 Note of 18.iii.52 in Dempsey file, Liddell Hart papers (loc. cit.)
14 Bradley (op. cit.) p. 319

GOODWOOD

1 Montgomery to Brooke, M511
2 Quoted in Pogue, *The Supreme Command*, p. 188
3 Dempsey, notes in Liddell Hart papers, "The aims of Operation Goodwood"
4 Roberts, interview with the author, 17.vi.83
5 *ibid*
6 Brown, unpublished MS loaned to the author
7 Roach, *The 8.15 to War*, p. 144–6
8 Wyldbore-Smith, interview with the author, 13.vi.83
9 Richardson, interview with the author, 21.vii.83
10 Quoted in Ellis (op. cit.), pp. 344–5

11 Butcher, diary (op. cit.)
12 Most recently by Hamilton, *Montgomery: Master of the Battlefield*, and Carlo D'Este, *Decision in Normandy*
13 Richardson, interview with the author (loc. cit.)
14 *The Memoirs of Field-Marshal Lord Montgomery*, p. 257
15 *Eisenhower Papers* (op. cit.), p. 2018–9
16 Bradley, *A General's Life*, p. 274
17 *ibid*, p. 257
18 Bryant (op. cit.), p. 235
19 Carver, interview with the author (loc. cit.)
20 Butcher, diary, DDE Library
21 Bryant (op. cit.), p. 245

CHAPTER 9

COBRA

1 First Army diary, 7.vii.44
2 Bradley (op. cit.), p. 271
3 Gunther, interview with the author (loc. cit.)
4 Quesada, interview with the author (loc. cit.)
5 Blumenson, *The Patton Papers*, vol. ii, p. 521
6 First U.S. Army report (loc. cit.)
7 Interview with the author, 2.vii.83
8 First U.S. Army report (loc. cit.)
9 Bradley (op. cit.), p. 270
10 Bradley, *A Soldier's Story*, p. 226
11 Ascher, interview with the author, 5.vii.83
12 In a letter to the author, 3.viii.82
13 Hamilton (op. cit.), p. 650
14 Stimson papers, Yale University
15 This account is derived from information provided by another NCO of 102nd Cavalry Reconnaissance, Bill Walsh.
16 Contemporary narrative by Flint's executive officer, in DDE papers no. 84, Patton G. no. 2.
17 Carell, *Invasion – They're Coming*, p. 257 *et seq.*
18 *History of the 120th Infantry Regiment* by Officers of the Regiment (Washington Infantry Journal Press, 1947)
19 Eichen, interview with the author, 26.vi.83
20 Quoted in D. Bruce Lockerbie, *A Man Under Orders*, p. 79
21 First U.S. Army diary (loc. cit.)
22 *History of the 120th* (op. cit.), p. 133
23 Carell (op. cit.), p. 259
24 Stober, interview with the author, 6.v.83
25 Weigley, *Eisenhower's Lieutenants*, p. 157
26 Gunther, interview with the author (loc. cit.)
27 Reisler, interview with the author, 4.vii.83
28 Guderian, interview with the author (loc. cit.)

THE LIMITS OF AIR POWER

1 For instance, see Tedder, *With Prejudice*; Harris, *Bomber Offensive*; and the memoirs of other more junior air force officers who wrote in a fashion that suggested it was an indulgence on the part of their service to accept any responsibility for direct support of the armies
2 Vandenberg, diary, MS Division Library of Congress
3 Tedder (op. cit.), p. 559–60
4 *ibid*, p. 557
5 *ibid*, p. 557–8
6 *ibid*, p. 562
7 *ibid*, p. 565
8 PRO WO232/51
9 Quesada, interview with the author (loc. cit.)
10 Vandenberg, diary (loc. cit.)
11 PRO WO232/51
12 Vandenberg, diary (loc. cit.)
13 Richardson, interview with the author (loc. cit.)
14 Bradley, *A Soldier's Story*, p. 249
15 Richardson, interview with the author (loc. cit.)
16 Bradley (op. cit.), p. 249
17 Account based upon Reisler interview (loc. cit.)
18 Scott, *Typhoon Pilot*, p. 120

CHAPTER 10

1 Liddell Hart papers, translations of Army Group B and C-in-C West reports, quoted in Cooper, *The German Army*, p. 507
2 Warlimont, *Inside Hitler's Headquarters*, p. 442
3 *ibid*, p. 445
4 *ibid*
5 *ibid*
6 *ibid*, p. 453
7 PRO WO219/1908
8 Among the strategic theorists, most authoritatively from Basil Liddell Hart, but also from some serving U.S. commanders, such as John "P" Wood (see text below)
9 Hansen, diary, U.S. Army Military History Institute
10 Patton, *War as I Knew It*, p. 92
11 *ibid*, p. 382
12 A remark repeatedly made to me in interviews with veterans of the U.S. First Army of all ranks.
13 Bradley, *A General's Life*, p. 285
14 Frank Price, *Middleton* (Louisiana State University, 1974), p. 188
15 *ibid*
16 Blumenson, *Breakout and Pursuit*, p. 463
17 Bradley, *A Soldier's Story*, p. 367
18 Irving, *Hitler's War*, pp. 683–4

19 Carell, *Invasion – They're Coming*, p. 278
20 The above account is compiled from the *History of the 120th Infantry* (op. cit.), interview with Sidney Eichen (loc. cit.), First Army diary (op. cit.).
21 Quoted in Wilmot, *The Struggle for Europe*, p. 404
22 *ibid*, p. 416
23 Liddell Hart papers, translations of Army Group B reports (loc. cit.) quoted in Cooper, p. 510
24 Guderian, *Panzer Leader* (op. cit.), p. 445
25 Irving (op. cit.), p. 686
26 Warlimont (op. cit.), p. 451
27 Bradley (op. cit.), p. 376
28 Blumenson, *Patton Papers* (op. cit.), vol ii, p. 521
29 Baker MS (op. cit.)

CHAPTER 11

1 Warner, interview with the author (loc. cit.)
2 Richardson, interview with the author (loc. cit.)
3 Signal M69, Montgomery papers, quoted in Hamilton, *Montgomery: Master of the Battlefield*, p. 768
4 See How, *Normandy: The British Breakout*
5 Letter to Brooke, 26.vii.83, quoted in Hamilton (op. cit.), p. 780
6 Stacey, *The Canadian Army in World War II*, vol. iii, p. 275
7 Hamilton (op. cit.), p. 779
8 *ibid*
9 Stacey (op. cit.), p. 252
10 *ibid*, p. 263
11 *ibid*
12 *ibid*, p. 276
13 *ibid*
14 *ibid*, p. 266

CHAPTER 12

1 PRO WO205/1021 (Interrogation of Meyer)
2 *ibid* (Interrogation of Meindl)
3 Scott (op. cit.), p. 129
4 Woollcombe (op. cit.), p. 107
5 Komarek, unpublished MS loaned to the author
6 For an extreme and extraordinary example of fanciful thinking about the failure wholly to destroy the German army at Falaise, see Richard Rohmer, *Patton's Gap* (London, 1981).
7 Bradley (op. cit.), p. 337
8 It is odd that while Chester Wilmot wrote with great frankness in 1952 about the difficulties and shortcomings of the Allied armies in north-west Europe, in more recent years most narratives have focussed overwhelmingly upon the alleged virtues and vices of the commanders on both sides, and lapsed into comfortable platitudes

when discussing the relative fighting performance of the armies engaged.

9 Stacey, *The Canadian Army in World War II*, vol. iii, p. 275
10 Liddell Hart, *History of The Second World War*, p. 543
11 Williams, interview with the author (loc. cit.)
12 Gavin, *On to Berlin*, p. 121

Appendix I

Glossary

ADGB	Air Defence of Great Britain
ANVIL	Codename for the Allied invasion of southern France, later designated DRAGOON
AOC	Air Officer Commanding
AVRE	Armoured Vehicle Royal Engineers — Churchill tank mounted with Petard short-range heavy mortar, and various devices for bridging and ditching
BAR	Browning Automatic Rifle — American squad light machine-gun
Battalion	Basic infantry unit of 600–1,000 men in all armies in Normandy, sub-divided into four rifle companies and a support company of 100-plus men each, with organic anti-tank guns, heavy machine-guns and mortars. Companies were divided into platoons of three or four rifle squads, each commanded by a corporal — or an NCO in the German army.
Bazooka	American infantry anti-tank rocket-projector
BEF	British Expeditionary Force
BGS	Brigadier General Staff
Bren	.303 British squad light machine-gun
Brigade	British nomenclature for a formation normally composed of three infantry or tank battalions — roughly equivalent in strength to a German or American regiment
CC	Combat Command
CIGS	Chief of the Imperial General Staff
COBRA	American breakout operation, 25–29 July
Corps	A group of divisions assembled under the command of a lieutenant-general, their number and identity varying constantly according to the task for which the corps is being employed.
COSSAC	Chief of Staff to the Supreme Allied Commander
CP	Command post
CSM	Company Sergeant-Major
DCLI	Duke of Cornwall's Light Infantry
DD	Duplex-Drive amphibious Sherman tank
DF	Defensive fire

Division	The basic formation through which all armies are controlled, commanded by a major-general and comprising 12–18,000 men. A British armoured division in Normandy normally comprised two tank brigades, one infantry. The Americans preferred to divide the armoured division into two "Combat Commands" (CC), A and B, each in the hands of a brigadier-general.
DUKW	Duplex-Drive amphibious truck
EPSOM	2nd Army's attacks to the Orne and beyond, 26 June to 1 July
Flail	Tank mounted with chains on a revolving drum for minesweeping
FORTITUDE	Allied deception plan for OVERLORD
FUSAG	First U.S. Army Group — the fictitious army commanded by Patton, whose supposed threat to the Pas de Calais was central to FORTITUDE
GOODWOOD	British attack on the Bourgébus ridge, 18–21 July
GSO	General Staff Officer (grades I, II or III)
HE	High Explosive
Kangaroo	Canadian infantry armoured personnel carrier improvised from self-propelled gun mountings
KOSB	King's Own Scottish Borderers
KRRC	King's Royal Rifle Corps
KSLI	King's Own Shropshire Light Infantry
LCA	Landing Craft Assault
LCI	Landing Craft Infantry
LCT	Landing Craft Tank
LCVP	Landing Craft Vehicle and Personnel
LST	Landing Ship Tank
ML	Motor launch
NCO	Non-commissioned officer
NEPTUNE	Naval assault phase of OVERLORD
ODs	American army combat clothing
OKW	*Oberkommando der Wehrmacht* — high command of the German armed forces
OP	Observation post
OSS	Office of Strategic Services, the American wartime foreign intelligence service
Panzerfaust	German hand-held infantry anti-tank weapon
Petard	Short-range tank-mounted heavy mortar
PIAT	Projector Infantry Anti-Tank — British hand-held platoon anti-tank weapon
POINTBLANK	Pre-OVERLORD strategic bombing of Germany
Priest	British self-propelled mounting for 25-pounder
PT	Patrol Torpedo boat
RAC	Royal Armoured Corps

RAOC	Royal Army Ordnance Corps
Regiment	American or German equivalent of a British brigade, normally composed of three battalions, commanded by an American brigadier-general or German colonel
REME	Royal Electrical and Mechanical Engineers
ROUNDUP	Plan for an Allied invasion of Europe in 1943, superseded by OVERLORD
RTR	Royal Tank Regiment
SAS	Special Air Service
SHAEF	Supreme Headquarters Allied Expeditionary Force
SOE	Special Operations Executive
Spandau	Allied shorthand for German MG 34 or MG 42 machine-guns
TOT	Time On Target concentrated artillery, a speciality of American gunners, although practised by all armies
TOTALIZE	Canadian army attack towards Falaise, 8–11 August
TRACTABLE	Canadian attack towards Falaise, 14–16 August
Vickers	British .303 water-cooled heavy machine-gun — the infantry battalion support weapon

Appendix II

Chronology of the Normandy Campaign

13 MARCH 1943	Lt-Gen. F. E. Morgan appointed COSSAC — Chief of Staff to the Supreme Commander (designate)
23 JANUARY 1944	Eisenhower approves Montgomery's plan for the landings in Normandy
7—8 APRIL	Montgomery presents the OVERLORD plan at St Paul's, and presides over Exercise THUNDERCLAP with subordinate commanders
15 MAY	Montgomery's final presentation at St Paul's
3JUNE	D-Day postponed from 5 June to 6 June
4 JUNE	D-Day ordered for 6 June
6 JUNE	Allied landings in Normandy
7 JUNE	Bayeux falls
8 JUNE	U.S. First and British Second Armies link near Port-en-Bessin
12 JUNE	Omaha and Utah beachheads united
13 JUNE	British 7th Armoured Division checked and repelled at Villers-Bocage
	Germans open V-I flying bomb offensive against Britain
18–21 JUNE	The "great storm" in the Channel
18 JUNE	U.S. VII Corps reach west coast Cherbourg peninsula at Barneville
19 JUNE	Americans take Montebourg
22 JUNE	Russians open their summer offensive against Army Group Centre with 146 infantry divisions and 43 tank brigades attacking on a 300-mile front
25 JUNE	British Operation EPSOM south-west of Caen
26 JUNE	Americans in Cherbourg
27 JUNE	Resistance in Cherbourg ends
29 JUNE	British break off EPSOM
1 JULY	Geyr von Schweppenburg sacked and replaced by Eberbach
	Americans secure Cap de la Hague
2 JULY	Von Rundstedt sacked and replaced by von Kluge
6 JULY	Flotilla of *biber* one-man submarines attack Allied shipping off the beachhead, sinking three minesweepers and damaging a Polish cruiser for the loss of seven German craft

8 JULY	British attack Caen, Americans seize La Haye-du-Puits
10 JULY	British occupy Caen
17 JULY	Rommel wounded and replaced as C-in-C Army Group B by von Kluge
18 JULY	British Operation GOODWOOD east of Caen Americans take St Lô
20 JULY	Hitler wounded by bomb at his headquarters, abortive conspiracy and its aftermath rocks the Third Reich
25 JULY	American Operation COBRA launched west of St Lô
30 JULY	British Operation BLUECOAT launched south-east of Caumont Americans "turn the corner" at Avranches
31 JULY	Russians within 10 miles of Warsaw. Uprising begins
1 AUGUST	Hodges assumes command U.S. First Army, Patton's Third Army activated, Bradley becomes C-in-C U.S. Twelfth Army Group
7 AUGUST	Germans launch Mortain counter-attack Canadian Operation TOTALIZE launched towards Falaise
10 AUGUST	TOTALIZE broken off
12 AUGUST	U.S. XV Corps takes Alençon
14 AUGUST	Canadian Operation TRACTABLE launched towards Falaise DRAGOON landings in southern France
17 AUGUST	Model assumes command German armies, orders full retreat east from Allied pocket Falaise falls
19 AUGUST	Polish Armoured Division and U.S. 90th Division reach Chambois
21 AUGUST	Falaise Gap closed
25 AUGUST	Paris falls
1 SEPTEMBER	Eisenhower assumes direct command Allied ground forces Montgomery promoted Field-Marshal
2 SEPTEMBER	U.S. First and Third Armies ordered to halt by Eisenhower in view of huge fuel and supply problems
3 SEPTEMBER	Brussels falls
16 SEPTEMBER	U.S. First Army units cross the German border near Aachen
17 SEPTEMBER	Operation Market Garden launched against Arnhem and the Maas and Waal bridges

Appendix III

PART A

Allied order of battle

SUPREME HEADQUARTERS ALLIED EXPEDITIONARY FORCE

Supreme Allied Commander
General Dwight D. Eisenhower

Chief of Staff
General Walter Bedell Smith

TWENTY-FIRST ARMY GROUP

General Sir Bernard L. Montgomery
Commander-in-Chief
Major-General Sir Francis W. de Guingand
Chief of Staff

G.H.Q. AND ARMY TROOPS

79th Armoured Division
Major-General Sir Percy C. S. Hobard

30th Armoured Brigade
22nd Dragoons
1st Lothians and Border Horse
2nd County of London Yeomanry
(Westminster Dragoons)
141st Regiment R.A.C.

1st Tank Brigade
11th, 42nd and 49th Battalions R.T.R.

1st Assault Brigade R.E.
5th, 6th and 42nd Assault Regiments R.E.

79th Armoured Divisional Signals
1st Canadian Armoured Personnel Carrier Regiment

4th Armoured Brigade
The Royal Scots Greys
3rd County of London Yeomanry (Sharpshooters) (to 28.7.44)
3rd/4th County of London Yeomanry (Sharpshooters) (from 29.7.44)
44th Battalion R.T.R.
2nd Battalion The King's Royal Rifle Corps (Motor)

6th Guards Tank Brigade
4th Tank Battalion Grenadier Guards
4th Tank Battalion Coldstream Guards
3rd Tank Battalion Scots Guards

27th Armoured Brigade (to 29.7.44)
13th/18th Royal Hussars
1st East Riding Yeomanry
The Staffordshire Yeomanry

8th Armoured Brigade
4th/7th Royal Dragoon Guards
24th Lancers (to 29.7.44)
The Nottinghamshire Yeomanry
13th/18th Royal Hussars (from 29.7.44)
12th Battalion The King's Royal Rifle Corps (Motor)

31st Tank Brigade
7th Battalion R.T.R. (to 17.8.44)
9th Battalion R.T.R. (to 31.8.44)
144th Regiment R.A.C. (23–31.8.44)

34th Tank Brigade
107th and 147th Regiments R.A.C.
153rd Regiment R.A.C. (to 24.8.44)

33rd Armoured Brigade
1st Northamptonshire Yeomanry
144th Regiment R.A.C. (to 22.8.44)
148th Regiment R.A.C. (to 16.8.44)
1st East Riding Yeomanry (from 16.8.44)

2nd Canadian Armoured Brigade
6th Armoured Regiment (1st Hussars)
10th Armoured Regiment (The Fort Garry Horse)
27th Armoured Regiment (The Sherbrooke Fusiliers Regiment)

H.Q. Anti-Aircraft Brigades
74th, 76th, 80th, 100th, 101st, 105th, 106th and 107th

Heavy Anti-Aircraft Regiments
60th, 86th, 90th, 99th, 103rd, 105th, 107th, 108th, 109th, 112th, 113th, 115th, 116th, 121st, 146th, 165th and 174th; 2nd Canadian

Light Anti-Aircraft Regiments
20th, 27th, 32nd, 54th, 71st, 73rd, 93rd, 109th, 112th, 113th, 114th, 120th, 121st, 123rd, 124th, 125th, 126th, 127th, 133rd, 139th and 149th

Searchlight Regiments
41st

56th Infantry Brigade
(Became integral part of the 49th Division from 20.8.44)
2nd Battalion The South Wales Borderers
2nd Battalion The Gloucestershire Regiment
2nd Battalion The Essex Regiment

1st Special Service Brigade
Nos. 3, 4 and 6 Commandos
No. 45 (Royal Marine) Commando

47th Special Service Brigade
Nos. 41, 46, 47 and 48 (Royal Marine) Commandos

OTHER FORMATIONS AND UNITS

Armoured
G.H.Q. Liaison Regiment R.A.C. ('Phantom')
2nd Armoured Replacement Group
2nd Armoured Delivery Regiment
25th Canadian Armoured Delivery Regiment (The Elgin Regiment)

Artillery
H.Q. Army Groups Royal Artillery: 3rd, 4th, 5th, 8th and 9th; 2nd Canadian

Heavy Regiments: 1st, 51st, 52nd, 53rd and 59th

Medium Regiments: 7th, 9th, 10th, 11th, 13th, 15th, 53rd, 59th, 61st, 63rd, 64th, 65th, 67th, 68th, 72nd, 77th, 79th, 84th, 107th, 121st and 146th; 3rd, 4th and 7th Canadian

Field Regiments: 4th R.H.A., 6th, 25th, 86th, 147th, 150th and 191st; 19th Canadian

Engineer
H.Q. Army Groups Royal Engineers: 10th, 11th, 12th, 13th and 14th; 1st Canadian

G.H.Q. Troops Engineers: 4th, 7th, 8th, 13th, 15th, 18th, 48th and 59th

Airfield Construction Groups: 13th, 16th, 23rd, 24th and 25th

Army Troops Engineers: 2nd, 6th and 7th; 1st and 2nd Canadian

2nd and 3rd Battalions Royal Canadian Engineers

Signal
Twenty-First Army Group Headquarters Signals
Second Army Headquarters Signals
First Canadian Army Headquarters Signals
Air Formation Signals, Nos. 11, 12, 13, 16, 17 and 18
1st Special Wireless Group

Infantry
4th Battalion The Royal Northumberland Fusiliers (Machine Gun)
First Canadian Army Headquarters Defence Battalion (Royal Montreal Regiment)

Royal Marine
Armoured Support Group: 1st and 2nd Royal Marine Armoured Support Regiments

Army Air Corps
Glider Pilot Regiment: 1st and 2nd Glider Pilot Wings

Special Air Service
1st and 2nd Special Air Service Regiments
3rd and 4th French Parachute Battalions

European Allies
1st Belgian Infantry Brigade
Royal Netherlands Brigade (Princess Irene's)

ARMIES, CORPS AND DIVISIONS

Second Army
Lieutenant-General Sir Miles C. Dempsey
General Officer Commanding-in-Chief
Brigadier M. S. Chilton
Chief of Staff

First Canadian Army
Lieutenant-General H. D. G. Crerar
General Officer Commanding-in-Chief
Brigadier C. C. Mann
Chief of Staff

I Corps
Lieutenant-General J. T. Crocker
The Inns of Court Regiment R.A.C. (Armoured Car)
62nd Anti-Tank, 102nd Light Anti-Aircraft, 9th Survey Regiments R.A.
1 Corps Troops Engineers
I Corps Signals

VIII Corps
Lieutenant-General Sir Richard N. O'Connor
2nd Household Cavalry Regiment (Armoured Car)
91st Anti-Tank, 121st Light Anti-Aircraft, 10th Survey Regiments R.A.
VIII Corps Troops Engineers
VIII Corps Signals

XII Corps

Lieutenant-General N. M. Ritchie

1st The Royal Dragoons (Armoured Car)
86th Anti-Tank, 112th Light Anti-Aircraft, 7th Survey Regiments R.A.
XII Corps Troops Engineers
XII Corps Signals

XXX Corps

Lieutenant-General G. C. Bucknall (to 3.8.44)
Lieutenant-General B. G. Horrocks (from 4.8.44)

11th Hussars (Armoured Car)
73rd Anti-Tank, 27th Light Anti-Aircraft, 4th Survey Regiments R.A.
XXX Corps Troops Engineers
XXX Corps Signals

II Canadian Corps

Lieutenant-General G. G. Simonds

18th Armoured Car Regiment (12th Manitoba Dragoons)
6th Anti-Tank, 6th Light Anti-Aircraft, 2nd Survey Regiments R.C.A.
II Canadian Corps Troops Engineers
II Canadian Corps Signals

Guards Armoured Division

Major-General A. H. S. Adair

5th Guards Armoured Brigade

2nd (Armoured) Battalion Grenadier Guards
1st (Armoured) Battalion Coldstream Guards
2nd (Armoured) Battalion Irish Guards
1st (Motor) Battalion Grenadier Guards

32rd Guards Brigade

5th Battalion Coldstream Guards
3rd Battalion Irish Guards
1st Battalion Welsh Guards

Divisional Troops

2nd Armoured Reconnaissance Battalion Welsh Guards
Guards Armoured Divisional Engineers
55th and 153rd Field, 21st Anti-Tank and 94th Light Anti-Aircraft Regiments R.A.
Guards Armoured Divisional Signals

7th Armoured Division

Major-General G. W. E. J. Erskine (to 3.8.44)
Major-General G. L. Verney (from 4.8.44)

22nd Armoured Brigade

4th County of London Yeomanry (Sharpshooters) (to 29.7.44)
1st and 5th Battalions R.T.R.
5th Royal Inniskilling Dragoon Guards (from 29.7.44)
1st Battalion The Rifle Brigade (Motor)

131st Infantry Brigade

1/5th, 1/6th and 1/7th Battalions The Queen's Royal Regiment

Divisional Troops

8th King's Royal Irish Hussars
7th Armoured Divisional Engineers
7th Armoured Divisional Signals
3rd and 5th Regiments R.H.A.; 6th Anti-Tank and 15th Light Anti-Aircraft Regiments R.A.

11th Armoured Division

Major-General G. P. B. Roberts

29th Armoured Brigade

23rd Hussars
2nd Fife and Forfar Yeomanry
3rd Battalion R.T.R.
8th Battalion The Rifle Brigade (Motor)

159th Infantry Brigade

3rd Battalion The Monmouthshire Regiment
4th Battalion The King's Shropshire Light Infantry
1st Battalion The Herefordshire Regiment

Divisional Troops

2nd Northamptonshire Yeomanry (to 17.8.44)
15th/19th The King's Royal Hussars (from 17.8.44)
11th Armoured Divisional Engineers
13th Regiment R.H.A.; 151st Field, 75th Anti-Tank and 58th Light Anti-Aircraft Regiments R.A.
11th Armoured Divisional Signals

3rd Division

Major-General T. G. Rennie (to 13.6.44)
Brigadier E. E. E. Cass (acting)
Major-General L. G. Whistler (from 23.6.44)

8th Brigade

1st Battalion The Suffolk Regiment
2nd Battalion The East Yorkshire Regiment
1st Battalion The South Lancashire Regiment

9th Brigade

2nd Battalion The Lincolnshire Regiment
1st Battalion The King's Own Scottish Borderers
2nd Battalion The Royal Ulster Rifles

185th Brigade
2nd Battalion The Royal Warwickshire Regiment
1st Battalion The Royal Norfolk Regiment
2nd Battalion The King's Shropshire Light Infantry

Divisional Troops
3rd Reconnaissance Regiment R.A.C.
3rd Divisional Engineers
3rd Divisional Signals
7th, 33rd and 76th Field, 20th Anti-Tank and 92nd Light Anti-Aircraft Regiments R.A.
2nd Battalion The Middlesex Regiment (Machine Gun)

6th Airborne Division
Major-General R. N. Gale

3rd Parachute Brigade
8th and 9th Battalions The Parachute Regiment
1st Canadian Parachute Battalion

5th Parachute Brigade
7th, 12th and 13th Battalions The Parachute Regiment

6th Airlanding Brigade
12th Battalion The Devonshire Regiment
2nd Battalion The Oxfordshire and Buckinghamshire Light Infantry
1st Battalion The Royal Ulster Rifles

Divisional Troops
6th Airborne Armoured Reconnaissance Regiment R.A.C.
6th Airborne Divisional Engineers
53rd Airlanding Light Regiment R.A.
6th Airborne Divisional Signals

15th (Scottish) Division
Major-General G. H. A. MacMillan (to 2.8.44)
Major-General C. M. Barber (from 3.8.44)

44th (Lowland) Brigade
8th Battalion The Royal Scots
6th Battalion The Royal Scots Fusiliers
6th Battalion The King's Own Scottish Borderers

46th (Highland) Brigade
9th Battalion The Cameronians
2nd Battalion The Glasgow Highlanders
7th Battalion The Seaforth Highlanders

227th (Highland) Brigade
10th Battalion The Highland Light Infantry
2nd Battalion The Gordon Highlanders
2nd Battalion The Argyll and Sutherland Highlanders

Divisional Troops

15th Reconnaissance Regiment R.A.C.
15th Divisional Engineers
15th Divisional Signals
131st, 181st and 190th Field, 97th Anti-Tank and 119th Light Anti-Aircraft Regiments R.A.
1st Battalion The Middlesex Regiment (Machine Gun)

43rd (Wessex) Division
Major-General G. I. Thomas

129th Brigade
4th Battalion The Somerset Light Infantry
4th and 5th Battalions The Wiltshire Regiment

130th Brigade
7th Battalion The Hampshire Regiment
4th and 5th Battalions The Dorsetshire Regiment

214th Brigade
7th Battalion The Somerset Light Infantry
1st Battalion The Worcestershire Regiment
5th Battalion The Duke of Cornwall's Light Infantry

Divisional Troops

43rd Reconnaissance Regiment R.A.C.
43rd Divisional Engineers
43rd Divisional Signals
94th, 112th and 179th Field, 59th Anti-Tank and 110th Light Anti-Aircraft Regiments R.A.
8th Battalion The Middlesex Regiment (Machine Gun)

49th (West Riding) Division
Major-General E. H. Barker

70th Brigade (to 20.8.44)
10th and 11th Battalions The Durham Light Infantry
1st Battalion The Tyneside Scottish

146th Brigade
4th Battalion The Lincolnshire Regiment
1/4th Battalion The King's Own Yorkshire Light Infantry
Hallamshire Battalion The York and Lancaster Regiment

147th Brigade

11th Battalion The Royal Scots Fusiliers

6th Battalion The Duke of Wellington's Regiment (to 6.7.44)

7th Battalion The Duke of Wellington's Regiment

1st Battalion The Leicestershire Regiment (from 6.7.44)

56th Brigade (from 20.8.44)

See under GHQ

Divisional Troops

49th Reconnaissance Regiment R.A.C.

49th Divisional Engineers

49th Divisional Signals

69th, 143rd and 185th Field, 55th Anti-Tank and 89th Light Anti-Aircraft Regiments R.A.

2nd Princess Louise's Kensington Regiment (Machine Gun)

50th (Northumbrian) Division

Major-General D. A. H. Graham

69th Brigade

5th Battalion The East Yorkshire Regiment

6th and 7th Battalions The Green Howards

151st Brigade

6th, 8th and 9th Battalions The Durham Light Infantry

231st Brigade

2nd Battalion The Devonshire Regiment

1st Battalion The Hampshire Regiment

1st Battalion The Dorsetshire Regiment

Divisional Troops

61st Reconnaissance Regiment R.A.C.

50th Divisional Engineers

50th Divisional Signals

74th, 90th and 124th Field, 102nd Anti-Tank and 25th Light Anti-Aircraft Regiments R.A.

2nd Battalion The Cheshire Regiment (Machine Gun)

51st (Highland) Division

Major-General D. C. Bullen-Smith (to 26.7.44)

Major-General T. G. Rennie (from 27.7.44)

152nd Brigade

2nd and 5th Battalions The Seaforth Highlanders

5th Battalion The Queen's Own Cameron Highlanders

153rd Brigade

5th Battalion The Black Watch

1st and 5th/7th Battalions The Gordon Highlanders

154th Brigade
1st and 7th Battalions The Black Watch
7th Battalion The Argyll and Sutherland Highlanders

Divisional Troops

2nd Derbyshire Yeomanry R.A.C.
51st Divisional Engineers
51st Divisional Signals
126th, 127th and 128th Field, 61st Anti-Tank and 40th Light Anti-Aircraft Regiments R.A.
1/7th Battalion The Middlesex Regiment (Machine Gun)

53rd (Welsh) Division
Major-General R. K. Ross

71st Brigade
1st Battalion The East Lancashire Regiment (to 3.8.44)
1st Battalion The Oxfordshire and Buckinghamshire Light Infantry
1st Battalion The Highland Light Infantry
4th Battalion The Royal Welch Fusiliers (from 5.8.44)

158th Brigade
4th and 6th Battalions The Royal Welch Fusiliers (to 3.8.44)
7th Battalion The Royal Welch Fusiliers
1st Battalion The East Lancashire Regiment (from 4.8.44)
1/5th Battalion The Welch Regiment (from 4.8.44)

160th Brigade
2nd Battalion The Monmouthshire Regiment
4th Battalion The Welch Regiment
1/5th Battalion The Welch Regiment (to 3.8.44)
6th Battalion The Royal Welch Fusiliers (from 4.8.44)

Divisional Troops

53rd Reconnaissance Regiment R.A.C.
53rd Divisional Engineers
53rd Divisional Signals
81st, 83rd and 133rd Field, 71st Anti-Tank and 116th Light Anti-Aircraft Regiments R.A.
1st Battalion The Manchester Regiment (Machine Gun)

59th (Staffordshire) Division
Major-General L. O. Lyne

176th Brigade (to 26.8.44)
7th Battalion The Royal Norfolk Regiment
7th Battalion The South Staffordshire Regiment
6th Battalion The North Staffordshire Regiment

177th Brigade (to 26.8.44)
5th, 1/6th and 2/6th Battalions The South Staffordshire Regiment

197th Brigade (to 26.8.44)
1/7th Battalion The Royal Warwickshire Regiment
2/5th Battalion The Lancashire Fusiliers
5th Battalion The East Lancashire Regiment

Divisional Troops

59th Reconnaissance Regiment R.A.C. (to 31.8.44)
59th Divisional Engineers
59th Divisional Signals
61st, 110th and 116th Field (to 31.8.44), 68th Anti-Tank (to 26.8.44) and 68th Light Anti-Aircraft (to 22.8.44) Regiments R.A.
7th Battalion The Royal Northumberland Fusiliers (Machine Gun) (to 24.8.44)

4th Canadian Armoured Division
Major-General G. Kitching (to 21.8.44)
Major-General H. W. Foster (from 22.8.44)

4th Armoured Brigade

21st Armoured Regiment (The Governor General's Foot Guards)
22nd Armoured Regiment (The Canadian Grenadier Guards)
28th Armoured Regiment (The British Columbia Regiment)
The Lake Superior Regiment (Motor)

10th Infantry Brigade

The Lincoln and Welland Regiment
The Algonquin Regiment
The Argyll and Sutherland Highlanders of Canada (Princess Louise's)

Divisional Troops

29th Reconnaissance Regiment (The South Alberta Regiment)
4th Canadian Armoured Divisional Engineers
15th and 23rd Field, 5th Anti-Tank and 8th Light Anti-Aircraft Regiments R.C.A.
4th Canadian Armoured Divisional Signals

2nd Canadian Division
Major-General C. Foulkes

4th Brigade

The Royal Regiment of Canada
The Royal Hamilton Light Infantry
The Essex Scottish Regiment

5th Brigade

The Black Watch (Royal Highland Regiment) of Canada
Le Régiment de Maisonneuve
The Calgary Highlanders

6th Brigade

Les Fusiliers Mont-Royal
The Queen's Own Cameron Highlanders of Canada
The South Saskatchewan Regiment

Divisional Troops

8th Reconnaissance Regiment (14th Canadian Hussars)
2nd Canadian Divisional Engineers
2nd Canadian Divisional Signals

4th, 5th and 6th Field, 2nd Anti-Tank and 3rd Light Anti-Aircraft Regiments R.C.A.
The Toronto Scottish Regiment (Machine Gun)

3rd Canadian Division

Major-General R. F. L. Keller (to 8.8.44)
Major-General D. C. Spry (from 18.8.44)

7th Brigade

The Royal Winnipeg Rifles
The Regina Rifle Regiment
1st Battalion The Canadian Scottish Regiment

8th Brigade

The Queen's Own Rifles of Canada
Le Régiment de la Chaudière
The North Shore (New Brunswick) Regiment

9th Brigade

The Highland Light Infantry of Canada
The Stormont, Dundas and Glengarry Highlanders
The North Nova Scotia Highlanders

Divisional Troops

7th Reconnaissance Regiment (17th Duke of York's Royal Canadian Hussars)
3rd Canadian Divisional Engineers
3rd Canadian Divisional Signals

12th, 13th and 14th Field, 3rd Anti-Tank and 4th Light Anti-Aircraft Regiments R.C.A.
The Cameron Highlanders of Ottawa (Machine Gun)

1st Polish Armoured Division

Major-General S. Maczek

10th Polish Armoured Brigade

1st Polish Armoured Regiment
2nd Polish Armoured Regiment
24th Polish Armoured (Lancer) Regiment
10th Polish Motor Battalion

3rd Polish Infantry Brigade

1st Polish (Highland) Battalion
8th Polish Battalion
9th Polish Battalion

Divisional Troops

10th Polish Mounted Rifle Regiment
1st Polish Armoured Divisional Engineers
1st and 2nd Polish Field, 1st Polish Anti-Tank and 1st Polish Light Anti-Aircraft Regiments
1st Polish Armoured Divisional Signals

LINES OF COMMUNICATION AND REAR MAINTENANCE AREA

Headquarters Lines of Communication

Major-General R. F. B. Naylor

Nos. 11 and 12 Lines of Communication Areas
Nos. 4, 5 and 6 Lines of Communication Sub-Areas
Nos. 7 and 8 Base Sub-Areas
Nos. 101, 102 and 104 Beach Sub-Areas
Nos. 10 and 11 Garrison

Engineers

Nos. 2, 3, 5 and 6 Railway Construction and Maintenance Groups
No. 3 Railway Operating Group
No. 1 Canadian Railway Operating Group
No. 1 Railway Workshop Group
Nos. 2, 6, 8, 9, 10 and 11 Port Operating Groups
Nos. 1, 2, 4 and 5 Port Construction and Repair Groups
Nos. 3 and 4 Inland Water Transport Groups
No. 2 Mechanical Equipment (Transportation) Unit

Signals

Nos. 2 and 12 Lines of Communication Headquarters Signals
No. 1 Canadian Lines of Communication Headquarters Signals

Infantry

5th and 8th Battalions The King's Regiment
7th Battalion The East Yorkshire Regiment
2nd Battalion The Hertfordshire Regiment
6th Battalion The Border Regiment
1st Buckinghamshire Battalion The Oxfordshire and Buckinghamshire Light Infantry
5th Battalion The Royal Berkshire Regiment
18th Battalion The Durham Light Infantry

UNITED STATES TWELFTH ARMY GROUP

Lieutenant-General Omar N. Bradley
Commanding General
Major-General Leven C. Allen
Chief of Staff

First Army
Lieutenant-General Courtney H. Hodges
Commanding General
(Succeeded General Bradley from 1.8.44)
Major-General William B. Keen
Chief of Staff

Third Army
Lieutenant-General George S. Patton, Jr
Commanding General
Major-General Hugh J. Gaffey
Chief of Staff

Corps

V. Major-General Leonard T. Gerow
VII. Major-General J. Lawton Collins
VIII. Major-General Troy H. Middleton
XII. Major-General Gilbert R. Cook (to 18.8.44)
Major-General Manton S. Eddy (from 19.8.44)
XV. Major-General Wade H. Haislip
XIX. Major-General Charles H. Corlett
XX. Major-General Walton H. Walker

Divisions

Armored: 2nd, 3rd, 4th, 5th, 6th and 7th; 2nd French
Infantry: 1st, 2nd, 4th, 5th, 8th, 9th, 28th, 29th, 30th, 35th, 79th, 80th, 83rd and 90th
Airborne: 82nd and 101st

PART B

Forces available in ETO for Operation "Overlord" "D" Day – 6 June 1944

PART I: LAND FORCE DIVISIONS

	INFANTRY	ARMOURED	AIRBORNE	TOTAL
United States	13	5	2	20
British	8	4	2	14
Canadian	2	1	–	3
French	–	1	–	1
Polish	–	1	–	1
TOTAL	23	12	4	39

PART II: AIR FORCES
A/C on Operational Combat Stations

A. *Summary by Types*:

		OPER & NON O	OPERAT'L	EFFECTIVE STRENGTH*
Heavy	Bombers	3,958	3,455	3,130
Med & Lt	Bombers	1,234	989	933
Ftrs & Ftrs	B^mbers	4,709	3,824	3,711
	TOTAL	9,901	8,268	7,774

B. *Summary by Command*:

VIII A/F	Hvy Bomb	2,578	2,243	1,947
	Fighters	1,144	961	961
IX A/F	Med Bomb	624	513	467
	Lt Bomb	228	165	156
	Fighters	1,487	1,132	1,123
		5,061		
BOMB CMD	Hvy Bomb	1,380	1,212	1,183
	Lt Bomb	134	98	97
2ND TAF	Med Bomb	88	67	67
	Lt Bomb	160	146	146
	Fighters	1,006	856	831
ADGB	Fighters	1,072	875	796
	TOTAL	9,901	8,268	7,774
		5,061		
		4,940		

* Operational aircraft with crews available.

PART III: NAVAL FORCES

A. *Major Combat Vessels*:

Battleships	7
Monitors	2
Cruisers	23
Gunboats	2
Destroyers	93
Sloops	15
Escorts	142
TOTAL	284

B. *Landing Craft and Ships*:

LST & LST (2)	233	
LST (1)	3	
LCT (A)	48	
LCT (R)	36	
LCT (64 flotillas)	768	
LCT (CB)	5	
LCT (HE)	16	
XAP	3	873
APA	7	
LSI (L)	18	
LSI (M)	3	
LSI (H)	18	
LSI (S)	6	
LSH (L)	5	
LSH (S)	9	
LSD	3	
LCI (L)	208	
LCI (S)	39	
LCH	18	
LCF	29	
LCA	486	
LCC	9	
LCG (L)	25	
LCE	6	
LCP (L) smoke	144	
LCA (HR)	45	
LCS (L) (2)	10	
LCS (L) (1)	4	
LCS (M)	26	
LCS (S)	36	
LCVP	839	
LCM (1)	128	
LCM (3)	358	
LBF	15	
LBV (2)	228	
LBO	100	
LBE	60	
LBW	20	
LBK	10	
TOTAL	4024	
	284	
	4308	

C. *Special Type Equipment*:

LVTs	470
DD Tanks	514
DUKWs	2583
TOTAL	3567

PART IV: STRENGTHS*

A. *Totals*: (Officers and Men)

Air	659,554
Land	1,931,885
Sea	285,000
TOTAL	2,876,439

* Officers and Men

Appendix IV

German land forces encountered by the Allies in Normandy

The composition of German armies and corps varied constantly during the campaign, but at different times part or all of the following were engaged:

Seventh, Fifteenth, Fifth Panzer (formerly Panzer Group West) and First Armies, embracing the following 13 corps and 15 divisions:

Panzer Corps: I SS, II SS, XLVII, LVIII
Infantry Corps: II Parachute, XXV, LXVII, LXXIV, LXXX, LXXXI, LXXXII, LXXXIV, LXXXVI
Panzer Divisions: 1st SS, 2nd SS, 2nd, 9th, 9th SS, 10th SS, 12th SS, 21st, 116th, Panzer Lehr
Panzergrenadier divisions: 3rd, 15th, 17th SS
Infantry Divisions: 2nd, 3rd, 5th and 6th Parachute; 16th, 17th, 18th Luftwaffe Field; 47th, 48th, 49th, 77th, 84th, 85th, 89th, 91st Airlanding, 226th, 243rd, 245th, 265th, 266th, 271st, 272nd, 275th, 276th, 277th, 326th, 331st, 343rd, 344th, 346th, 348th, 352nd, 353rd, 363rd, 708th, 709th, 711th, 716th

SS Panzer divisions were substantially larger and better-equipped than their Wehrmacht counterparts. All panzer divisions normally contained an armoured regiment of two battalions — one equipped with Mark IV tanks, the other with Panthers. Army panzer divisions also contained two infantry regiments, each of two battalions, but SS divisions mustered six infantry battalions. The average panzer division went into Normandy with 160 tanks, 700 machine-guns, 70 mortars, 37 infantry guns, 40 field and medium guns, 33 anti-tank guns and over 100 anti-aircraft guns. Each division's vehicle establishment was around 3,000. Wehrmacht divisions mustered almost 15,000 men at full strength, SS divisions up to 20,000.

Panzergrenadier divisions possessed no tanks but their infantry were fully motorized, and supported by a battalion of 45 self-propelled guns.

Of the 38 German infantry divisions that fought in Normandy, five were "static" formations comprising nine battalions, the same organization as the parachute units. The other 30 were on "1944 establishment" of six infantry battalions, with a fusilier reconnaissance battalion, often bicycle-mounted. Each division mustered, on average, 650 machine-guns, 76 mortars, 24 infantry guns and howitzers, 31 anti-tank guns and 48 medium and field guns. Transport was provided by 615 motor vehicles and 1,450 horse-drawn vehicles.

GHQ and army troops included III Flak Corps' 160 88 mm guns in a dual-purpose role facing the British front. There were three heavy tank battalions, each containing up to 45 Tigers; two battalions of *Jagdpanthers,* 88 mm tank-killing self-propelled guns; several independent towed 88 mm gun battalions and 75 mm-mounted self-propelled gun battalions. The Germans possessed relatively few field or medium guns, and only one heavy regiment of 170 mm guns.

Appendix V

Some British administrative statistics

Units

1	New Units formed in theatre	756
2	Existing Units reorganised, including 50 Div	634
3	Units disbanded	177
4	Units placed in suspended animation	33
5	Unit designation changed	270

Courts Martial Held

	Type of Offence	In respect of Officers	In respect of Other Ranks
1	Absence and Desertion	4	7,018
2	Other offences	59	3,628
3	TOTAL ALL OFFENCES	63	10,646

Admissions to Mil Prisons, Detention Barracks and Field Punishment Camps (5 May 45)

	Type of Sentence	Other Ranks
4	Penal Servitude and Imprisonment	4,032
5	Other Sentences	4,421
6	TOTAL ALL TYPES OF SENTENCES	8,453

Leave (excluding Personnel in 2 TAF)

	Type of Leave	No. of leaves granted to All Ranks
7	Privilege Leave in UK	472,000
8	Short Leave on the Continent	468,000
9	Compassionate Leave	23,600
10	TOTAL ALL TYPES OF LEAVE GRANTED	963,600

Marriages approved between British subjects and aliens 398

BATTLE CASUALTIES

As known at 2nd Echelon 12 May 45 which approximates to the situation on 30 Apr 45

		British	Canadian	Allied
1	Killed	30,289	9,872	1,421
2	Wounded	97,947	30,072	4,662
3	Missing and prisoners	15,485	2,137	418
4	TOTAL	143,721	42,081	6,501

STRENGTHS

		Strength 6 Jun 44		Strength 30 Apr 45	
		Offrs	ORs	Offrs	ORs
1	Total strength of force	37,937	680,021	46,138	792,722
2	Second Army	15,808	300,392	14,333	280,934
3	Airborne Troops	1,798	26,987	1,644	25,612
4	Allied forces under comd 21 A Gp	1,332	21,400	1,814	32,905

1	AFs B115 (Declaration of illegal absence)	3,030
2	AFs B252 (Charge Sheets—Summary Disposal)	140,508
3	AFs A3104 (Review of Sentences awarded by Courts Martial)	16,779

4	AFs A2 (Courts of inquiry re Accidental Injuries)	4,565
5	AFs B117 (Reports on Accidental Injuries)	29,613
6	Intimation received of personnel granted compassionate leave	7,270
7	Intimation received of extension of compassionate leave and extension of privilege leave granted on compassionate grounds	20,794
8	Notification to soldiers of casualties affecting their families	9,498
9	Welfare enquiries re soldiers made by their relatives	1,558
10	Marriages (abroad) registered (First ceremony conducted 3 Oct 44)	280

CHAPLAINS

Battle Casualties

	Type of Casualty	Number of Chaplains
1	Killed in action	10
2	Died of wounds	7
3	Missing	11

Religious Offices

4	Soldiers baptised	22
5	Soldiers confirmed	443
6	Soldiers admitted to the Free Churches	4
7	Soldiers seeking ordination	300
8	Marriages performed between British subjects	56

Number of New Testaments distributed 30,000

General Medical Statistics

1	Casualties cleared from Army Areas to Base Hospitals by air	36,000
2	Cases admitted to Medical Units:	
	Battle	181,695
	Non-Battle	224,393
3	Cases evacuated to UK by air	77,174
4	Cases evacuated to UK by sea	70,466
5	Attendances for dental treatment	674,958
6	New dentures supplied	29,111
7	Dentures repaired	30,458

Specialised Treatment to Casualties

8	Pints of whole blood given	85,000
9	Pints of other intravenous fluid given	165,000
10	Millions of units of penicillin used for wounded	65,000
11	Morphine—doses given	470,000
12	Bandages used (32,000,000 yards)	8,000,000
13	X-ray plates used	250,000

Incidence of Disease—Mean Monthly Rate per 1,000 Strength

	Disease	First World War 1914–1918	Second Word War Jun 44–May 45
14	Venereal Disease	2.474	2.116
15	Enteric	1.525	0.006
16	Dysentery	0.466	0.314
17	Pneumonia	0.419	0.066
18	Meningitis	0.026	0.007
19	Influenza	0.890	0.231
20	Trench Foot	0.503	0.039

	Sick and Accidentally Injured	First World War 1914–1918	Second World War Jun 44–May 45
21	Sick and accidentally injured admitted to Medical Units (per month, per 1,000 strength)	53.9	23.2

GENERAL NOTES:

(*a*) The use of penicillin, combined with close liaison between surgeons, physicians and pathologists, has been a large factor in producing a recovery rate of over 93% of all casualties who reach the Medical Unit.

(*b*) Psychiatry has been extensively used in combating cases of exhaustion and treatment of cases in Forward Areas, and also in selection of personnel for suitable employment.

(*c*) Preventive inoculations and the standard of Unit hygiene have been responsible for an almost complete absence of major infectious diseases.

PAY

1 Commencing on D+2 Field Cash Offices and Forward Base Pay Offices landed on D+6 with 6,500 million French francs weighing 120 tons. Not one franc was lost in transit.

2 Although only five currencies are current in the theatre, work has involved almost every currency in world circulation. Average weekly advances of pay to Officers and Other Ranks in these currencies approximated in sterling value one million pounds, whilst 100,000 currency exchange have been carried out weekly.

3 Impounded from enemy Prisoners of War:
12 million Francs
5½ million Reichmarks
½ million Guilders

4 20,000 British Commonwealth ex-Prisoners of War have been given advances of pay.

5 The Pay Service has been responsible for supplying cash to 5,000 British Army Imprest Holders.

PROVOST

1	Length of routes signposted in British sector—miles	4,000
2	Military police signs erected	141,800
3	Information posts manned by CMP	370
4	Arrests made of Military Personnel	2,335
5	Total arrests made	7,875
6	Summaries of charges preferred by CMP (to 31 Mar)	36,366
7	Total Special Investigation Branch cases:	
	reported	6,404
	completed	5,880
8	Specimen traffic density test—Number of vehicles which passed a CMP post in 24 hours at Antwerp	41,679
9	Value of property recovered by Provost (SIB)	£384,454

EDUCATION

1	Army Study Centres and Libraries formed	12
2	Mobile Libraries circulated among forward troops	7
3	Formation newspapers published daily	30

The first Formation newspaper was published on D+3, entitled "Triangle". The paper "Pegasus" was delivered to airborne troops east of the Rhine within 20 hours of the airborne landing.

WELFARE

1	Number of clubs opened	316
2	Personnel CVWW (British Voluntary Organisation)	584
	Personnel Voluntary Workers (Belgian Red Cross canteens)	893
3	Average daily number of men served by these clubs	420,000
4	Mobile canteens	374
	Whole-time entertainment parties:	
5	ENSA	57
6	Army	32
	Entertainment and Welfare equipment issued:	
7	Musical Instruments	10,000
8	Gramophones	500
9	Gramophone Records	35,600
10	Wireless Sets	13,600
11	Books	1,185,000
12	Magazines	4,000,000
13	Dart Sets	225,000

14	Cigarettes	41,000,000
15	Value of sales in Brussels and Bruges gift shops—Belgian francs	22,723,000
16	Cases now in hand in three Legal Aid Sections	7,000
	Army Kinema Services:	
17	Number of sections operating	20
18	Average performance per week	3,700
19	Average audiences per week	400,000
20	Public kinemas put into operation	74

TONNAGE OF STORES
landed by commodities 6 Jun 44–8 May 45

		Total Tonnage	Daily Average	Daily Average per Equivalent Div
		tons	tons	tons
1	AMN (excl. RAF)	951,865	2,825	155
2	POL (Army) (excl. bul)	632,500	1,877	103
3	POL (RAF) (excl. bulk)	92,184	274	15
4	SUPS	875,308	2,597	142
5	RE	767,383	2,277	125
6	ORD	494,853	1,468	80
7	CA (incl. wheat, edible oils)	518,041	1,537	84
8	MISC (incl. coal, RAF amn)	814,220	2,416	132
9	TOTAL	5,146,354	15,271	836

ENGINEER WORKS

1	Tons of timber felled by Forestry Coys (this does not include civilian production, captures or imports. A fifth of this was used for pitprops)	250,000
2	Miles of hutting erected (equivalent 20 ft span)	180
3	Miles of hutting manufactured locally	30
4	Tons of stone quarried	2,000,000
5	Oil: High pressure pumps installed	330
6	Tons of bulk storage in 110 tanks	101,000
7	Total pipes laid—miles	1,200
8	Total weight of equipment—tons	97,000
9	Tons of Engineer Stores imported	750,000
10	Items of Engineer Plant and Machinery imported	25,000

11	Sterling value of local production of equipment	£3,250,000
12	Electric Generators installed (this represents 10,000 horse power)	420
13	Miles of overhead electric cable erected	280
14	Miles of insulated cable installed	3,000
15	Airfields constructed or repaired (this represents an equivalent of 2,020 miles of roadway, 20ft wide)	125
16	No. of Bailey Bridges built (8% were cl. 70, 80% cl. 40, 12% less than cl. 40)	1,350
17	Miles of Bailey Bridges built	29
18	No. of FBE bridges built (cl. 9)	80
19	Miles of FBE bridges built	3

AIR FREIGHT

		tons
1	Total tonnage flown into theatre between 6 June 44 and 8 May 45	35,174

Consisting of:

Mail	1,043 tons
Newspapers	946 „
Blood	308 „
Ord stores	6,362 „
Engr stores	480 „
Currency	46 „
Maps	419 „
Airfield Track	2,421 „
Amn	10,397 „
Pet	11,612 „
Rations	539 „
Med stores	90 „
Other stores	511 „
	35,174 tons

Excluding 9,017 tons of food for HOLLAND flown by Bomber Comd and VIII USAAF between 29 Apr and 8 May 45

2	Average daily lift	107
3	Largest special lifts:	
	(*a*) Food for HOLLAND 7 May 45	1,151
	(*b*) 882 tons POL and 178 tons Amn for SECOND ARMY 29 Sep 44	1,060

SUPPLIES AND TRANSPORT
(To 8 May 45)

Transport

1	Tonnage capacity of RASC task vehicles in theatre	148,252
2	Tonnage lifted from ship to shore by DUKWs	414,509
3	Mileage run by bulk petroleum vehicles	12,831,484

Number of RASC task vehicles at 8 May 1945

4	Lorries 3–6 ton	20,788
5	Lorries 10 ton	2,959
6	DUKWs	228
7	Tippers	1,181
8	Tank Transporters	1,089
9	Troop-carrying vehicles	693
10	Tankers 800–2000 galls	981
11	Total	27,919

Supplies

12	Tonnage of supplies landed	810,305
13	Tonnage of supplies procured locally	32,500
14	Average daily feeding strength (including PW and civil mobile labour)	1,127,915
15	Maximum feeding strength (including PW and civil mobile labour)	2,113,962
16	Reserve of supplies on 1 May 45 in rations	70,145,265
17 (*a*)	Number of different ration scales for British Personnel	8
17 (*b*)	Number of different ration scales for PW and Civilian Internees	5
17 (*c*)	Number of different ration scales for animals	8
17 (*d*)	Number of different ration scales for civilian labour	2
17 (*e*)	Scale of provision of miscellaneous and disinfectant items	1
17 (*f*)	Average nett weight of rations per head Field Service Scale Fresh Items	70 ozs
17 (*g*)	Average nett weight of rations per head Field Service Scale tinned equivalents	50 ozs
17 (*h*)	Calorific value of Field Service Ration (male personnel)	3,900
17 (*i*)	Calorific value of Field Service Ration (women's services)	3,400

17 (*j*)	Calorific value of Ration Scale for European PW and Civil Internees	2,000
17 (*k*)	Calorific value of Ration Scale for civilian labour (Enrolled)	3,400
17 (*l*)	Calorific value of Ration Scale for midday meal for casual labour	800

POL

		Tons	Equivalent Gallons
18	Bulk POL imported through ports	1,020,927	306,278,100
19	Bulk POL imported through pipeline	313,596	94,078,800
20	Packed POL imported through ports	612,786	141,467,782
21	POL pumped through pipeline	746,075	223,522,500
21a	Average daily rate of construction of 6-in Victaulic pipeline	3,2 miles	
21b	Total length of pipeline laid	1,125 miles	
22	POL filled into containers by Mobile Petrol Filling Centres	549,695	164,908,500
23	Average daily issues of POL (including civil requirements but excluding aviation spirit for RAF)	4,459	1,029,392
24	Reserve of POL on 1 May 45	242,968	65,177,837
25	Average daily POL import	6,000	
26	Number of jerricans imported	15,580,000	

POL was being landed in bulk D+13. Pipeline finally ran from UK to BOCHOLT (GERMANY).

ORDNANCE

Vehicles—Total Numbers Landed

1	By Units	231,000
2	Reserve "A" Vehicles	23,000
3	Reserve "B" Vehicles	70,000
4	TOTAL VEHICLES LANDED	324,000

Ammunition

5	Total tons landed	942,562
6	Total tons expended	722,546

Ordnance Stores

7	Total tons landed	486,650
8	Average tons issued daily	1,140

ROUNDS EXPENDED

NATURE / MONTH	7.2 in How HE	155 mm Gun HE	5.5 in Gun HE	4.5 in Gun HE	25 pr all types	95 mm	77 mm
1944							
JUN (from 12th)	6166	11058	101453	20746	516400		
JUL	23547	31612	448057	23686	1934002		
AUG	12788	19510	348580	24953	1660137		
SEP	4619	9160	125444	5369	751374		
OCT	23411	24236	337155	37411	1800871		
NOV	8650	11864	202655	16787	768560		
DEC	5421	3144	60126	4150	314681		
1945							
JAN	5205	6743	169838	10849	802855	1906	
FEB	23957	7966	334985	29485	1751557	1542	661
MAR	31485	13251	328278	50864	2127072	682	
APR	12031	8314	140386	38736	1277696	9181	298
MAY (to 8th)	2618	1815	10190	4743	123754	423	
TOTAL	159898	148673	2610747	267779	13828959	13734	959

ROUNDS PER GUN

NATURE / MONTH	7.2 in How HE	155 mm Gun HE	5.5 in Gun HE	25 pr HE	95 mm	77 mm	76 mm
1944							
JUN (from 12th)	15.1	27.1	35.2	46.3			
JUL	20	26.9	45.7	70.6			
AUG	10.3	15.7	30.6	49.3			
SEP	3.8	7.6	11.4	21.7			
OCT	18.9	19.5	30.5	48.6			
NOV	7.2	9.9	19.5	20.4			
DEC	4.4	2.5	5.7	9			
1945							
JAN	4.2	5.4	16.3	21	0.6		0.4
FEB	21.4	7.1	35.6	53.5	0.5	0.3	0.5
MAR	25.4	10.7	32.9	59.5	0.2		1.2
APR	8.1	5.6	13.1	30.6	2.4		0.1
MAY (to 8th)	5.8	4.1	3.5	11	0.4		0.1
TOTAL	12.1	11.2	23.6	36.8	0.9	0.1	0.5

PER MONTH

76 mm	75 mm	17 pr	6 pr	All types 3.7 in AA	40 mm	4.2 in Mortar	3 in Mortar	Vickers .303 VIII Z
	22261	2858	7925	37588	64170	16867	224977	
	35558	6426	9735	98381	157747	131283	192881	
	58495	9288	8005	56291	54428	106943	118169	
	35827	6668	4966	35415	64183	34729	64974	
	41962	8695	8759	86019	117609	126735	148115	
	49509	7853	9884	64237	76933	87385	106057	
	29011	7360	2319	62855	79012	55375	62610	
1542	91970	14658	2192	103894	119759	73626	160251	3071354
2119	51313	20562	4016	194353	121621	75329	121647	7389561
5057	199295	18862	2526	180959	279876	76694	79159	5929800
365	139121	27389	11390	109216	187934	70268	150149	6821174
64	19345	2008	695	18194	15587	6578	6417	125750
9147	773667	132627	72412	1057402	1338899	861812	1435406	23337629

PER DAY (AVERAGE)

75 mm	17 pr	6 pr	3.7 AA HE	40 mm HE	4.2 in Mortar HE	3 in Mortar	Vickers .303 VIII Z	4.5 in Gun HE
0.7	0.3	0.5	10.5	4.0	7.5	16.9		68.2
0.5	0.3	0.3	12.7	4.0	24.9	6.7		47.8
0.9	0.3	0.2	5.1	1.1	19.8	4.1		50.3
0.6	0.3	0.2	2.2	1.5	7.1	3.2		11.2
0.6	0.3	0.3	4.8	2.4	24.8	6.5		41
0.8	0.3	0.3	3.6	1.4	16.2	4.7		17.5
0.5	0.2	0.1	3.3	1.4	10.8	2.8		4.2
1.4	0.4	0.1	4	2.2	13.4	6.4	305.8	10.9
0.8	0.7	0.1	7.4	2.5	16	5.5	814.5	32.9
3.4	0.6	0.1	6.8	5.1	14.4	3.4	589	34.9
2	0.6	0.3	5.8	3.5	10.8	5.3	596.5	16.8
1.1	0.2	0.1	5.2	1.2	3.6	0.8	38.9	6.3
1.1	0.4	0.2	5.3	2.5	15.1	5.4	532.2	24.3

REME

Repairs and Maintenance (excluding Work in LADs)

1	"A" Vehicles	40,000
2	"B" Vehicles	205,000
3	Wireless and Radar equipment	90,000
4	Small Arms and Machine Guns	650,000
5	Artillery equipment	18,500
6	TOTAL NUMBER OF EQUIPMENTS	1,003,500

LABOUR

Total effective personnel incl. train guards but excl. adm personnel and cadres

	Numbers employed	Military Labour	Civil Labour	PW Labour	Total
1	D Day	6,500	—	—	6,500
2	20 Jun 44	27,000	700	—	27,700
3	8 Sep 44	43,000	6,000	8,000	57,000
4	1 May 45	56,000 incl. Allied Pnr Coys	175,000	15,000	246,000

POSTAL

1	First delivery of inward mail made D+1	
	Daily average delivery of letters:	
2	Inward	1,000,000
3	Outward	800,000
4	Daily tonnage of parcels received	100

VETERINARY and REMOUNT SERVICES

1	Number of horses used between 6 June 44 and 8 May 45	913
	These animals were all draft horses. They were used principally at ANTWERP docks and in certain depots in the Advanced Base. Initially V and RS personnel were in charge. Later RASC personnel took over the supervising duties, with civilian labour working the horses.	
2	Number of horses captured in FRANCE	6,000
3	Number of horses captured in BELGIUM and the NETHERLANDS	4,000
4	Number of horses captured in GERMANY	794
5	Total number of horses captured	10,794

The animals captured in FRANCE, BELGIUM and the NETHERLANDS were all disposed of to farmers with the exception of those horses retained for work.

FIRE

1	Fires caused by enemy action	340
2	Fires by other causes	1,451
3	TOTAL FIRES DEALT WITH BY AFS	1,791

Q (MOVEMENTS AND TRANSPORTATION)

PORTS

Mulberry (Opened 12 Jun 44. Closed 28 Nov 44)

	Amount of traffic during period:	
1	Personnel	231,315
2	Vehicles	45,181
3	Tons of stores	628,000

Ports (Other than Mulberry)

	Port	Date Opened	Date Closed	Daily Average Tons of Stores
		1944		
4	Beaches	6 Jun	Jul–Aug 44	13,392
5	Port en Bessin	8 Jun	25 Sep 44	869
6	Caen	31 Aug	12 Mar 45	782
7	Dieppe	8 Sep	28 Dec 44	3,768
8	Ostend	26 Sep	—	2,908
9	Boulogne	13 Oct	8 Jan 45	1,422
10	Calais	6 Dec	—	156
11	Antwerp	27 Nov	—	10,203
12	Ghent	23 Feb	22 Apr 45	4,464

13	Peak day traffic of stores discharged through MULBERRY and over beaches	17,000
14	Average tons through Ports	20,517
15	Total tons through Ports (including Grain and POL)	6,720,695
16	Area dredged to open Ports—cubic yards	2,800,000

INLAND WATER TRANSPORT

1	Miles of waterways opened for traffic (this is equal to one-third of canal mileage in UK)	870
2	Average tons carried daily	8,528
3	Tons carried during peak month (Apr 45) (this is equal to more than a quarter of average monthly lift on canals in UK)	400,000
4	Number of barges brought into service	4,230

RAILWAYS

1	Number of track miles opened	7,000
2	Route miles of L of C railways at peak period	2,000
3	Present daily average personnel moving by rail	30,000
4	Total personnel carried by rail	1,750,000
	Daily average tons of stores carried:	
5	Aug 44	5,000
6	Apr 45	25,000
7	Peak period—tons of stores carried in one day	70,000
8	Tons of military stores (less coal) carried	4,500,000
9	Tons of coal carried	2,500,000
10	Tons of military stores and coal carried	7,000,000

11	Locomotives imported	1,076
12	Locomotives repaired	2,745
13	Wagons imported	3,200
14	Wagons erected	1,700
15	Wagons repaired	4,200
16	Ambulance trains imported	11
17	Bridges rebuilt	91
18	Total length of bridgework—miles	3
19	Bridges at present under construction	17

Bibliography and a note on sources

The literature of the north-west Europe campaign in general and of Normandy in particular is vast. I have omitted many battlefield reminiscences, together with the invaluable regimental and divisional histories which are available for almost every British and American formation mentioned in the text. I have also left out a number of books whose accuracy has been the subject of such severe strictures as to make them of doubtful value to students of the period. I am deeply indebted to all those men, British, American and German, who have lent me contemporary letters, diaries, and narratives.

I have learned much about contemporary attitudes to the campaign from the files of *The Times,* the *New York Times,* the *Daily Express* and *Picture Post,* for whom my father served as war correspondent in Normandy. For this as for other books of mine, I must acknowledge the generosity of David Irving in lending documents and files he had assembled for his own researches. Among original sources which have proved especially valuable, I must mention *Current Notes From Overseas,* the weekly British tactical pamphlet circulated to unit commanding officers; the diaries of General Carl Spaatz, General Hoyt Vandenburg, Captain H. C. Butcher; the papers of Sir John Grigg; copies of papers pertaining to General Walter Bedell Smith, General Everett Hughes, Air-Marshal J. M. Robb, General George Patton, General Raymond Barker held in the Eisenhower Library; the personal diary of Brigadier N. Elliott Rodger, Chief of Staff II (Canadian) Corps; the superb after-action reports of U.S. units in France; and of course, the SHAEF, War Office and War Department files in the U.S. National Archive and the Public Records Office in London.

AMBROSE, Stephen, *The Supreme Commander,* New York, 1970.
ARON, Robert, *De Gaulle Before Paris*, New York, 1962;
De Gaulle Triumphant, New York, 1964.
BATCHELOR & HOGG, *Artillery,* New York, 1973.
BELCHEM, David, *All in a Day's March,* London, 1967.
——, *Victory in Normandy*, London, 1981.
BENNETT, Ralph, *Ultra in the West,* London, 1979.
BLUMENSON, Martin, *Breakout and Pursuit*, Washington, 1961.
BRADLEY, Omar, *A Soldier's Story,* London, 1952
——, *A General's Life*, New York, 1982.

BRYANT, Arthur, *The Turn of the Tide*, London, 1957
———, *Triumph in the West*, London, 1959.
BUTCHER, Captain H. C., *My Three Years with Eisenhower*, London, 1946.
BUTLER, J. R. M., & GWYER, M. A., *Grand Stategy,* vol. iii, London, 1964.
CARELL, Paul, *Invasion — They're Coming*, London, 1962.
CHALFONT, Alun, *Montgomery of Alamein,* London, 1976.
CHURCHILL, Winston, *Triumph and Tragedy*, London, 1954.
COLLINS, J. Lawton, *Lightning Joe*, Louisiana, 1979.
COOPER, Matthew, *The German Army: Its Political and Military Failure*, London, 1978.
CRAVEN & CATE, *The U.S. Army Air Forces in World War II*, Chicago, 1951.
CRUIKSHANK, Charles, *Deception in World War II*, Oxford, 1979.
De GUINGAND, Frederick, *Operation Victory*, London, 1960.
D'ESTE, Carlo, *Decision in Normandy*, London, 1983.
DUNN, Walter Scott, *Second Front Now — 1943*, Alabama, 1980.
DUPUY, Colonel T. N., *A Genius for War*, London, 1977.
EHREMAN, John, *Grand Strategy,* vol. v, London, 1956.
EISENHOWER, Dwight, *Crusade in Europe*, New York, 1948.
———, *Papers*, vol. iii, Baltimore, 1970.
ELLIS, Major L. F., *Victory in the West*, vol. i, London, 1962.
FARAGO, Ladislas, *Patton: Ordeal and Triumph*, New York, 1963.
FARRAR-HOCKLEY, Anthony, *Infantry Tactics 1939–45*, London, 1976.
FERGUSSON, Bernard, *The Black Watch and The King's Enemies,* London, 1950.
———, *The Watery Maze*, London, 1961.
FOOT, M. R. D., *SOE in France*, London, 1966.
FRASER, Sir David, *And We Shall Shock Them*, London, 1983.
———, *Alanbrooke*, London, 1982.
GAVIN, James, *On To Berlin*, London, 1978.
GOLLEY, John, *The Big Drop*, London, 1982.
GOSSET & LECOMTE, *Caen Pendant La Bataille*, Caen, 1946.
GREENFIELD, PALMER & WILEY, *The U.S. Army in World War II: The Organization of Ground Combat Troops*, Washington, 1946.
GRIGG, John, *1943: The Victory that Never Was*, London, 1980.
GUDERIAN, Heinz, *Panzer Leader*, London, 1952.
HAMILTON, Nigel, *Montgomery: The Making of a General*, London, 1981.
———, *Montgomery: Master of a Battlefield*, London, 1983.
HARRISON, Gordon, *Cross Channel Attack*, Washington, 1951.
HASTINGS, Max, *Bomber Command,* London, 1979.
———, *Das Reich*, London, 1982.
HASWELL, J. *The Intelligence and Deception of the D-Day Landings*, London, 1979.
HINSLEY, Prof. F. H. & others, *British Intelligence in the Second World War,* vol. ii, London, 1981.

How, J. J., *Normandy: The British Breakout*, London, 1981.
Howard, Michael, *Grand Strategy*, vol. iv, London, 1972.
Howarth, David, *Dawn of D-Day*, London, 1959.
Irving, David, *Hitler's War*, London & New York, 1979.
———, *The Trail of the Fox*, London & New York, 1977.
———, *The Rise and Fall of the Luftwaffe*, Boston, 1973.
Ismay, Lord, *Memoirs*, London, 1960.
Joly, Cyril, *Take These Men*, London, 1955.
Jonson, G., & Dunphie, C., *Brightly Shone the Dawn*, London, 1980.
Keegan, John, *Six Armies in Normandy*, London, 1982.
Kohn & Harahan (eds), *Air Superiority in World War II and Korea*, Washington, 1983.
Lamb, Richard, *Montgomery in Europe*, London, 1983.
Lane, Ronald L., *Rudder's Rangers*, Manassas, 1979.
Lewin, Ronald, *Montgomery as Military Commander*, London, 1971.
———, *Ultra Goes to War*, London, 1978.
Liddell Hart, Basil, *The Other Side of the Hill*, London, 1951.
———, *The Second World War*, London, 1970.
Lovat, Lord, *March Past*, London, 1978.
Lucas, J., & Barker, J. *The Killing Ground*, London, 1978.
Macksey, Kenneth, *Armoured Crusader*, London, 1967.
Maule, Henry, *Caen: The Brutal Battle and the Break-out from Normandy*, London, 1976.
Marshall, S. L. A., *Night Drop*, London, 1962.
McBryde, Brenda, *A Nurse's War*, London, 1979.
McKee, Alexander, *Caen, Anvil of Victory*, London, 1964.
Montgomery, Earl, *The Memoirs of Field-Marshal Montgomery*, London, 1958.
———, *Normandy to the Baltic*, London, 1947.
Moorehead, Alan, *Montgomery*, London, 1947.
Morgan, F. E., *Overture to Overlord*, London, 1950.
Nelson, *Second Front Now — 1943*, Alabama, 1980.
Palmer, Wiley & Keast, *The U.S. Army in World War II: The Procurement and Training of Ground Combat Troops*, Washington, 1948.
Patton, George S., *War as I Knew it*, Boston, 1947.
Pogue, Forrest C., *George C. Marshall,* vols ii & iii, New York, 1965, 1973.
Roach, Peter, *The 8.15 to War*, London, 1982.
Rohmer, Richard, *Patton's Gap*, London, 1981.
Ross, George MacLeod, *The Business of Tanks*, London (privately printed), 1976.
Ruge, Frederich, *Rommel in Normandy*, London, 1979.
Ruppenthal, Ronald G., *The U.S. Army In World War II: Logistical Support of the Armies*, Washington, 1966.
Ryan, Cornelius, *The Longest Day*, London & New York, 1959.
Scarfe, Norman, *Assault Division*, London, 1947.

SCOTT, Desmond, *Typhoon Pilot*, London, 1982.
SEATON, Albert, *The Fall of Fortress Europe 1943–45*, London, 1981.
———, *The German Army*, London, 1982.
SHULMAN, Milton, *Defeat in the West*, London, 1948.
SPEIDEL, Hans, *We Defended Normandy*, London, 1951.
STACEY, C. P., *The Canadian Army in the Second World War*, vol. iii, Ottawa, 1960.
STRONG, Kenneth, *Intelligence at the Top*, London, 1968.
TEDDER, Lord, *With Prejudice*, London, 1966.
VAN CREVELD, Martin, *Supplying War*, London, 1978.
———, *Fighting Power: German Military Performance 1914–45*, Washington, 1980.
WARLIMONT, Walter, *Inside Hitler's Headquarters*, London, 1962.
WEBSTER & FRANKLAND, *The Strategic Air Offensive Against Germany*, vol. iii, London, 1961.
WEIGLEY, Russell F., *Eisenhower's Lieutenants*, London & New York, 1980.
WELLER, Jac, *Weapons and Tactics: Hastings to Berlin*, New York, 1966.
WEST, Nigel, *MI6: British Secret Intelligence Service Operations 1909–45*, London, 1983.
WESTPHAL, S., *The German Army in the West*, London, 1951.
WILMOT, Chester, *The Struggle for Europe*, London, 1952.
WILSON, Andrew, *Flamethrower*, London, 1974.
WOOLLCOMBE, Robert, *Lion Rampant*, London, 1970.

Acknowledgements

Then men who fought in Normandy are today 40 years older than they were in 1944, but it is astonishing how vividly retentive are their memories. All those listed below — American, British, German, French — contributed to the narrative above, either through personal interviews, diaries, contemporary letters, or correspondence. I have omitted their ranks and decorations, which would otherwise overwhelm these pages. To each of them I offer my gratitude, and my admiration for what they endured.

L. W. Ainslie 5th Kings Regiment, W. Anderson 5th Battalion, Abraham Arditti 101st Airborne Div., D. W. Armstrong REME, R. A. H. Arnold 3rd Infantry Div., G. Ascher 357th Infantry, A. Ashley 3rd Infantry Div., T. K. Atherton 93rd LAA Regt., Julian Bach, Charles F. Baldwin, S. Bamber RAMC, Alan Barber RAF, G. Barden Armoured Div. Guards, D. Barker 6th Airborne Div., C. Barnby 1st Royal Norfolks, Mrs N. F. Barnes 6th Airborne Div., H. T. W. Barter 49th Div., Bill Bartlett USAAF, Hubert S. Bass 82nd Airborne Div., T. R. Beason RE, Chris Belcher 2nd Armored Div., William T. Belvin 2nd Infantry Div., M. Bennett Royal Navy, Arthur Berry, R. L. Beverley RAF, Richard Bills U.S. Navy, D. G. Bion 5th RTR, Peter Birkett Tyneside Scottish, Norman Bishop U.S. Navy, Edward J. Bisso Jr, A. Blooman RAOC, B. Boden, Robert Bogart 1st Infantry Div., J. Bond RASC, G. A. Bone RAF, Frank Booth RASC, L. Bour 1st Infantry Div., G. A. D. Bourne Royal Navy, R. I. M. Bowen RAF, G. Braysford Royal Engineers, Dr Warren E. Breniman, C. Brewer No. 12 Field Surgical Unit, G. Brice 246th Coy RE, A. Briggs, A. D. Briggs RE, D. Brinkman, D. G. Brown 5th RTR, J. Brown 11th Armoured Div., A. J. Brown 3rd Infantry Div., John Brown 11th Armoured Div., W. Brown 3rd Canadian Div., H. Brown, G. Bruce Royal Engineers, Randall Bryant 9th Infantry Div., Mrs Jean Buck, B. E. Buck REME, Eric Bulman, M. A. Burgess, James N. Burt 2nd Armoured Div., Jesse T. Butler 9th Infantry Div., R. W. Campbell 6th Airborne Div., W. A. Carter, Arthur L. Chaitt 1st Infantry Div., Mrs M. Chandler, O. H. Clark, Roy Clark Royal Navy, S. R. Cockaday 3rd Div. Provost Coy, Al Cohn U.S. Navy, W. A. Coke Royal Marines, Frank Colacicco 1st Infantry Div., Harry Collins 6th Airborne Div., Robert L. Conway 5th Engineer Special Brigade, James William Cook Royal Navy, Leo Cooper, John Purley Cooper Jr. 29th Div., Paul W. Corrigan 3rd Armored Div., John Craig, E. A. Crofts, R. B. Crosby Essex Yeomanry, Robert Michael Crossley, Rupert Curtis Royal Navy, Milton Dank, Mrs Margaret Darley-Bentley, W. Davies RAF, Harold Davies 7th Armoured Div., William E. Davis Royal Artillery, Frederick Davis RE, E. Dearsley, Bernard W. Deehan 2nd Armoured Div., M. Delaney Armoured Div., Ronald C. Denhand RAF, James Dobie The Kings Regiment, George W. Dohmann 9th Infantry Div., H. H. Downs RAF, F. G. Dubber 165th HAA Regt. RA, G. T. Duckworth RAF, Hayes W.

Dugan 3rd Armored Div., Martin Dumoch U.S. Navy, Steve Dyson 5th RTR, C. J. Eason 2nd Lincolnshires, J. Eccles, Alec Ecclestone Royal Navy, J. Edmondson 2nd Armoured Guards Div., J. E. Edney 7th Armoured Div., Sidney Eichen 30th Infantry Div., William J. Eisemann U.S. Navy, J. H. Ellis 1st Ox & Bucks, F. K. Faulkner REME, K du B. Ferguson RAF, W. M. H. Flory RAF, Mrs M. Floyd-Norris QAIMNS/R, A. H. Forrest RASC, J. S. Forster Royal Signals, E. A. Fowles RAF, Edward T. Francis 47th Anti-Aircraft Brigade, Jerrold Freeman RAF, W. M. Frick 79th Infantry Division, R. Frith Royal Navy, Robert Frost Royal Navy, Col. William B. Gara 1st Infantry Div., Wayne Garrets 90th Infantry Div., G. George 6th Airborne Div., E. H. Gibbs 9th Beach Group, A. C. Gigg 50th Infantry Div., J. A. Gill 2nd Infantry Div., A. F. Gillespie RASC, L. C. Gimbert RASC, Doug Ginder 3rd Div., Joe Glavan 35th Infantry Div., J. G. Glixby Royal Tank Regiment, Don Gordon Royal Engineers, Richard Gosling Essex Yeomanry, J. W. Goulder Royal Navy, Henry Grant 3rd Canadian Division, Mrs M. Z. Gray, J. Greenfield 116th HAA Regt., N. Griffin Royal Signals, G. Griffin 43rd Infantry Div., L. Griffiths 2nd Army HQ, Heinz Gunther Guderian 116 Panzer Div., Helmut Gunther 17 SS Panzergren. Div., William I. Hahn U.S. Navy, L. Haines 2nd/60th Rifles, J. G. Hanson RAF, Mrs Edward W. Harrison, Robin Hastings 6th Green Howards, R. E. Hauchan Royal Navy, J. A. Hawkes Royal Marines, S. D. Hayden 49th Div., A. Heal Royal Engineers, Richard Heap, John Hein 1st Infantry Div., Pamela Hensy QAIMNS/R, Harry Herman 9th Infantry Div., Andrew Hertz 834th Engineer Aviation Battalion, Heinz Hickmann Luftwaffe Parachute Div., Lindley R. Higgins 12th Infantry Rgt., H. Highwood Queens Regiment, George Hird RAOC, R. A. Hoar Royal Artillery, H. W. S. Hodd, Dr Adolf Hohenstein 276th Infantry Div., Alan W. Holmes RASC, F. A. Honey Royal Engineers, G. B. Honour Royal Navy, S. Hooker 6th Airborne Div., Charles T. Horner, H. Horsfield Royal Marines, James Houston Royal Navy, R. A. Howard Army Air Corps, W. T. Hoy REME, D. J. Hudson ACC, B. Hudson Staffordshire Yeomanry, D. S. Huett Armoured Div., J. A. Hughes Royal Marines, G. E. Humnas RAOC, S. F. Humphrey 344th Indep. Searchlight Battery RA, J. H. Humphries 50th Div., Mrs N. S. Hyde-Ferte, H. M. Irwin, J. L. Irwin 45th RM Commando, Jackson 50th Division, Harolds L. Jett U.S. Navy, Frank A. Jobson 6th Airborne Division, Mrs Susan Johnson ATS, A. E. Johnson 4th/7th Royal Dragoon Guards, R. Johnson 24 Base Section Royal Signals, A. Johnson Durham Light Infantry, G. R. Johnson 5th RTR, Carl R. Jones USAAF, Albert M. Jordan 2nd Armored Div., T. Josephs 29th Infantry Div., Kurt Kauffman Panzer Lehr, J. E. Kean 3rd Recce Regiment, R. O. Keeffe RASC, G. Keighley Sussex & Surrey Yeomanry, Dennis Kelley 9th Infantry Div., Lt. H. G. Kenyon Royal Navy, Henry W. Kilburg 875th Ordnance Battalion, R. R. Killona 237th Engineer Combat Battalion, Jerry W. Komarek 2nd Armored Div., Vincent A. Kordack 6th Beach Battalion, U.S. Navy, Warner Kortenhaus 21st Panzer Div., Hal Kosut 979th Batt., Edward B. Kovar 110th AAA Batt., Walter Kruger 12th SS Panzer Div., D. Lancaster, Mrs J. Lang WAAF, Helmut Lang Army Group B Headquarters, Fritz Langangke 2nd SS Panzer Div., T. Langston RA, Bruce A. Larose 1st Infantry Div., J. Law 147th Regiment RAC, P. Lawton 49th West Riding Div., J. E. Leather 4th Ox & Bucks, R. D. Lee 1st Ox & Bucks, A. Lee 1st Middlesex, J. M. Leggate FRCS 46th Field Surgical Unit, Edward M. Leitch 2nd Army Troop, Andrew J. Lento 4th Infantry Div., P. Leslie 79th Armoured Div., Arthur Lester, J. Leverett 6th Airborne Div., C. T. Lightman 11th Royal Scots Fusiliers, Mrs R. Lindner QAIMNS/R, Theodore S. Liska 4th Infantry Div., Dominic J. LoPiccolo 2nd Engineer Combat Battalion, S. Lockwood 4th CLY, Donald E. Loker US Navy, Len Lomell, J. S. Longster Suffolk Regt., A. V. Looker 1st KOSB, Rev. T. H. Lovegrove 6th Green Howards, W. W. Lund 6th

Airborne Div., R. Lyon REME, P. R. MacIver 8th Armoured Brigade, James G. Macpherson Merchant Navy, Maj. Gen. John J. Maginnis, J. S. Malkin 7th Field Reg. RA, G. C. Mantripp Royal Navy, Arlo J. Markestad 29th Infantry Div., P. Marshall 78th Coy. Royal Engineers, E. A. Martin 3rd Infantry Div., W. Martin, S. B. Mason, L. F. Matthews Royal Navy, John P. McGirr 65th Armored Field Artillery Batt., John A. McAllister 29th Infantry Div., Robert McCosh, Andrew McFadzean 29th Infantry Division, Dr Marie McHugh, L. J. McLaughlin 9th Infantry Div., Alan W. McQuillin RAF, S. Mills Royal Marines, James H. Moninger, Jr. 79th Infantry Div., Bidwell Moore 1st Infantry Div., G. Moore Royal Engineers, David Morgan REME., W. T. Morgan REME, Ted Morris, H. J. Morris Jones 746th Tank Batt., G. W. Moses, R. Mosse Guards Armoured Div., Anthony Mott 500th Div. RHR, F. L. Muttor 1st Infantry Div., Lt. Gen. Samuel L. Myers, Philip D. Myers 78th Armored Field Artillery Batt., W. E. Needler, A. L. Neely, Albert E. Nelson RCAF, D. C. Newton 6th Airborne Div., Ralph A. Nichols U.S. Navy, A. E. Nicholson RAMC, Ronald N. Palmer RMAS, J. Parkinson Royal Engineers, L. S. Parnell RAOC, A. Pascarell 487th Bomb Troop, Lt. Brewster G. Pattyson U.S. Coast Guard, Joseph K. Perkins 29th Infantry Div., R. Perkins, G. J. Peters 2nd Warwicks, N. C. Phillips, James Taillie Phillips U.S. Navy Minesweep-Unit 9, M. A. Philip Royal Signals, A. G. Pickely, H. A. Pickering 3rd Infantry Div., C. Piercy-Hughes 6th Airborne Div., Brig. Gen. Allan G. Pixton 5th Engineer Special Brigade, C. J. Potter, Bill Preston 29th Div., J. K. Price 2nd Ox & Bucks, Carl D. Proffitt DSC 29th Infantry Div., Clay Purvis 29th Infantry Div., Paul J. Quaiver 326th Engineer Batt., Lt. Gen. E. R. Quesada, Daniel Quinn 9th Infantry Div., G. T. Radmore 6th Airborne Div., G. L. Ramage, George L. Ramage Royal Engineers, Edward Rapp 4th Armored Div., Mrs Margaret R. Rathbone WRNS, Floyd Ratliff 30th Artillery., Ken Rawlings 35th Infantry Div., Dick Raymond 3rd Canadian Div., Mr & Mrs L. R. Reed, Philip B. Reisler 2nd Armored Div., A. J. Rennie KOSB, L. Reynolds 6th Airborne Div., Eric Richards, A. Richardson 43rd Infantry Div., F. O. Richardson 82nd Airborne Div., Robert L. Riggs 82nd Airborne Div., G. H. Robinson 5th Dorsets, Walter Rodman 102nd Cavalry Recon., A. Rolph 50th Div., George Rosie 101st Airborne Div., S. Rossant 2nd Welsh Guards, H. Rowe Pioneer Corps, E. Royle Royal Highland Reg. of Canada, G. E. M. Ruffee 14th Field Reg. Canadian Royal Artillery, K. M. Rugman 6th Airborne Div., R. R. Rylands KSLI, A. W. Sadler RASC, Charles Salt 4th Armoured Brig., H. L. Salter, Alvin Sapinsley U.S. Army Signals Corps, Richard W. Sargent 2nd Infantry Div., Rudolf Schaaf 716th Infantry Div., R. Schafer 9th Infantry Div., Wilhelm Schickner 2nd Panzer Div., Kevin Sharkey, Carl R. Sherrets, W. P. Shines Kings' Regiment, C. Shread 69 Field Coy (RE), E. F. Siderits U.S. Navy, Frank L. Sills RAF, Lawrence Silverman 5th Amphibious Engineer Special Brigade, P. Silverman 35th Infantry Div., W. J. Skittrall Essex Regiment, George L. Small 35th Infantry Div., Lt. Col. A. T. Smith 1st Infantry Div., Henry Smith Armored Div., Anthony M. Smith 819th Av. Engineers, J. R. Smith 141st Regt. RAC, Roy Smith 4th Airborne Div., J. F. Smyth Royal Navy, Mrs Robert F. Snetzer, Henry D. Soderberg 507th Military Police Batt., Sid Solomon, Saul Solow 30th Infantry Div., Mrs A. Sowerby, E. F. Spottiswoode REME, Vernon C. Squires 81st Construction Batt., A. Stackpole, William Stelling 29th Infantry Div., J. W. Stephens 86th Anti-Tank Reg. RA, Hans Stober 17th SS Panzergren. Div., W. L. Stray KSLI, Wallace C. Strobel 101st Airborne Div., D. J. Studdard 2nd Army HQ Troops, Edward Sullivan, William A. Sutton, G. R. Tait 3rd Div., D. A. Tait 101st Airborne Div., Peter Terry 47 Commando, Peter J. Terry, Hans Teske, O. H. Thomas 5th Beach Group, G. W. Thomas RAF, Charles H. Thomas 1st Div., David E. Thomas 82nd AB Div., G. Thorn Royal Marines, John M. Thorpe 11th Armoured Div., Matt N. Touchton

U.S. Navy, Major F. B. Upfold REME, E. H. Upward Royal Navy, L. J. Verier Home Guard, Dr. Eberhard Wagemann 21st Panzer Div., P. Wagg RE, Bill Walsh 102nd Cavalry, Edward Warman, John Warner 3rd Recce Regt., Geoffrey L. Way, A. C. Webb REME, Reg. A. F. Weigall, J. M. Welch 4th Infantry Div., A. H. Wells RE, Mrs Doreen Westaway QAIMNS, John A. Wheeldon 11th Armoured Div., F. W. White 51st Highland Div., Mrs H. G. White RE, Jack D. Whiteley 9th Infantry Div., A Whittenbury RE, Dr. John S. Wier 2nd Armored Div., K. M. Wilford RAF, Cyril Wilkins Royal Navy, Harold Wilkinson 3rd Infantry Div., Col. J. B. Wilks, Mary Williams WAAF, C. A. Williams Royal Navy, J. Williamson 3rd Scots Guards Tank Batt., Col. John Williamson 1st Infantry Div., S. E. Willis Royal Navy Commandos, F. V. Wilson Royal Navy, Thomas G. Wilson Merchant Navy, George R. Wilson Royal Navy, P. C. Wixey KRRC, N. C. Wood Military Police, A. S. Woods RAF, D. A. Woods Royal Navy, T. Woodward 3rd Infantry Div., R. Wright, H. Yarwood, A. E. Younger RAF.

Index

DAS REICH

The march of the 2nd SS Panzer Division
through France, June 1944

Contents

Illustration Acknowledgments

The author and publishers would like to thank all those who gave their kind permission to reproduce photographs here. Among others, we are grateful to Miss Vera Atkins, Mrs Pilar Starr, The Hamlyn Group, Askania Verlagsgesellschaft, HMSO, Editions Daniel & Cie, Verlag K. W. Schütz KG, SOGEDIL, Sygma, Popperfoto and Keystone Press.

Illustrations

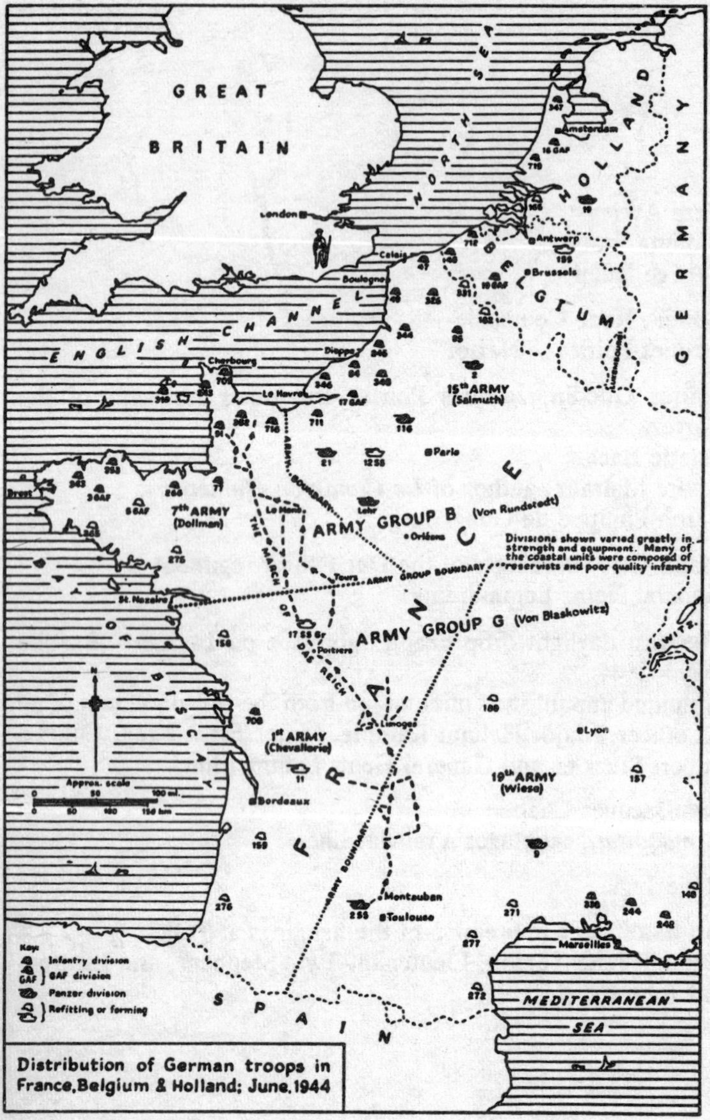

Distribution of German troops in France, Belgium & Holland; June, 1944

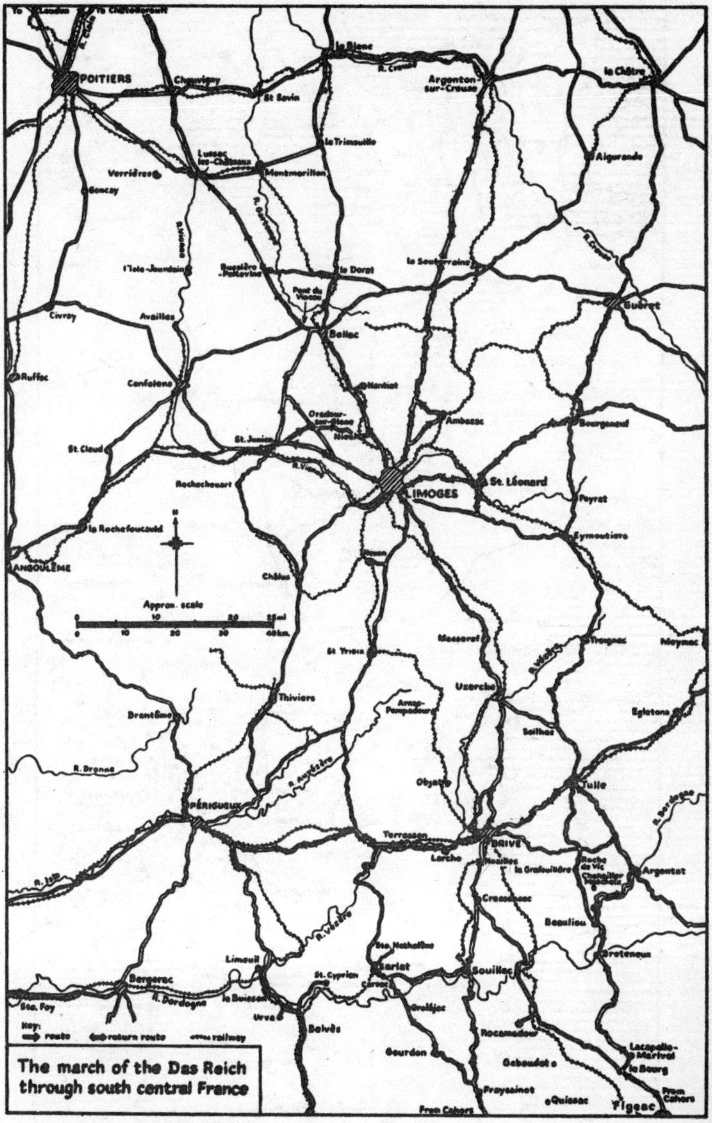

The march of the Das Reich through south central France

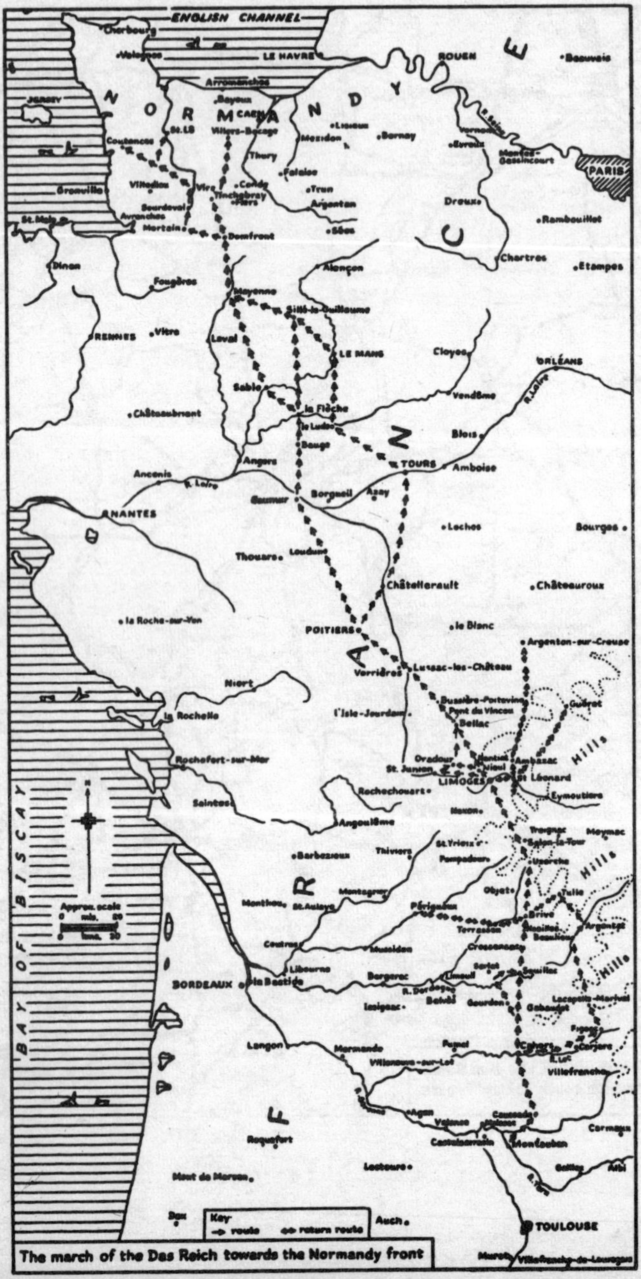

The march of the Das Reich towards the Normandy front

Foreword

On 8 June 1944, some 15,000 men and 209 tanks and self-propelled guns of the Das Reich 2nd SS Panzer Division rolled out of Montauban in southern France, and began a march that ended 450 miles northwards in Normandy more than two weeks later. In the interval the division became one of the most dreadful legends in the history of France and World War II. This book is an attempt to tell its full story for the first time.

I have always been fascinated by the controversy surrounding guerillas, special forces, and their influence upon the main battlefield. I had initially considered writing a general study of the campaigns behind the lines in France, Yugoslavia, Italy and Russia, but the story of the Das Reich continued to nag me. I concluded that I could make a more original contribution to the subject of Resistance by examining this specific episode in some detail than by attempting yet another *tour d'horizon*. In his official history of the French Section of Special Operations Executive, Professor M. R. D. Foot wrote of the Das Reich story:

> The extra fortnight's delay imposed on what should have been a three-day journey may well have been of decisive importance for the successful securing of the Normandy bridgehead. . . . Between them these [SOE] circuits left the Germans so thoroughly mauled that when they did eventually crawl into their lagers close to the fighting line . . . their fighting quality was much below what it had been when they started. . . . The division might be compared to a cobra which had struck with its fangs at the head of a stick held out to tempt it: the amount of poison left in its bite was far less than it had been.

Here, then, was my starting point: a legend of guerilla action in World War II, the boldest of claims for an achievement by special forces. Pursuing the outline of the story further, it became even more fascinating, as I studied the involvement of the

British and American Jedburgh teams in the attack on communications in the Das Reich's area; the division's capture of the British agent Violette Szabo; and the extraordinary history of some of the British and French agents most closely connected in building the Resistance groups that fought the SS.

During the months that followed, I interviewed men and women in England and America, France and Germany. It became evident that almost everything hitherto published was unreliable, and in many cases simply wrong. Accounts have been confused by the deliberate untruths of post-war German testimony in the shadow of war crimes trials, and by the fact that almost every Frenchman who fired upon a German in south-west France in June 1944 reported that he had been in action against the notorious Das Reich. Casualty figures were wildly mis-stated, and so were contemporary assessments of German plans and intentions.

I must now emphasize that the story I have written is neither full nor definitive – it could never be completely satisfactory in the absence of any but the sketchiest written records. So much has been lost with dead men, and so much forgotten with failing memories, that I have been unable to discover, for instance, which *maquis* group carried out every minor ambush, and which unit of the Das Reich returned its fire on every occasion. But I think that I have come as close to the reality as it is now possible to get.

My first source was the German war diaries and records of signal traffic in the Freiburg archives, which are an invaluable guide to what the Germans themselves believed that they were doing at the time. In the Public Record Office in London, I found the SAS files for 1944, and scores of fascinating papers on the debate in the Allied High Command before D-Day about what Resistance might and might not achieve. It is exasperating that so many relevant files – especially on war crimes investigations – are still marked 'Closed' when there can no longer be any valid security pretext. The Paris library of the *Comité de l'histoire de la deuxième guerre mondiale* was especially useful for long-forgotten books published in the wake of the Liberation, and I received much help from the *Comité*'s local correspondents in southern and central France.

I leave readers to make their own moral judgments on the actions of the SS officers and men concerned in the story. I can only record my gratitude as an author that they met and corresponded with me at such length, above all Otto Weidinger and Heinrich Wulf. Albert Stuckler, former senior staff officer of the Das Reich, has compiled a vast file on its movements in 1944 for internal circulation among its veterans, which, like Colonel Weidinger's regimental history of the Der Führer, entitled *Comrades to the End*, has been of immense value. As far as possible, I have tried to reflect the human emotions of the officers of the division in June 1944, divorcing my mind from the knowledge of the deeds with which they were associated. If I have been able to catch their mood with less fluency than that of the French and British, this may be because in my interviews with them, when certain questions had to be asked and answered, our conversations became stilted and distant.

The Veterans of the OSS in New York helped me to trace relevant survivors. I am deeply indebted to Captain John Tonkin and the other survivors of the ill-fated Bulbasket SAS mission who gave so much time and assistance.

Of the distinguished survivors of Special Operations Executive, a full list follows in the Acknowledgements, but I must especially mention Maurice Buckmaster, Vera Atkins, Selwyn Jepson, the later George Starr, Annette Cormeau, Jacques Poirier, Baron Philippe de Gunzbourg, and Mrs Judith Hiller, who lent me the fascinating and moving tapes and notes compiled by her husband, the late George Hiller, for a memoir he did not live to complete.

For this book, as for my earlier *Bomber Command*, Andrea Whittaker proved a brilliant German translator and interpreter. Juliette Ellison gave me invaluable help interviewing former *résistants* – among whom I must single out M. René Jugie – in the hills of the Corrèze, the Dordogne and Haute Vienne through the long, wet June of 1980.

Above all, I must express my gratitude to Professor M.R.D. Foot, doyen of British and American historians of Resistance, former Intelligence Officer of the SAS Brigade in 1944, and one of the regiment's few survivors of German captivity. He not only gave me hours of help and guidance as I researched this book, but later read the manuscript and provided scores of invaluable comments and corrections. None of this, of course, burdens him with responsibility for my errors or judgments.

In the text, I have taken for granted a little knowledge of Vichy, the Nazi Empire and the SS, and I have not retraced ground that seems to me well-travelled concerning special operations, the training of agents for SOE and so on. There are a host of admirable personal memoirs by former agents, some of which I have listed in the Bibliography. In this book I have sought to tell some of the unknown stories of the secret war.

This is not a history of Resistance or special operations. It is intended to be a portrait, at a critical moment of the war, of one of their great dramas. It is an attempt to establish the context of events. What manner of men and women on both sides did these things? How and why did they do them? There is much stupidity, cruelty and tragedy below, but there are also great heroism and achievement. Some people protest today that too many books continue to appear about World War II. I believe that those of us who write them have no cause to be ashamed as long as such extraordinary stories as this one are still untold.

Max Hastings
Guilsborough Lodge,
Northamptonshire
May 1981

Prologue: London and France, 5/6 June 1944

At 9.15 pm on 5 June 1944, as the first ships of the Allied invasion fleet came within sight of the Normandy shore, the French Service of the BBC began to broadcast its customary *messages personnels*. Through more than three years of tragedy, pessimism, defeat and occupation, through the long struggle to create an armed opposition movement within France, the *messages personnels* had been among the most vital, emotion-charged weapons of Resistance. In flats and farmhouses in the cities and countryside of France, little knots of men and women clustered to listen, at risk of their lives, amidst the static and crackle of distance and German jamming, to the voice of London: '*Charles est très malade. . . . Marcel aime Marceline. . . . Il n'y a pas de bananes. . . . La guerre de Troie n'aura pas lieu. . . . Yvette a dix doigts. . . .*' Some of these phrases were as meaningless as they seemed. But many others each night gave *résistants* from Brittany to the Pyrenees, from the Vercors to the Ardennes, their private, prearranged signal to expect a rendezvous with a Lysander on a field outside Paris, a parachute arms drop on a hillside in the Corrèze, or a new wireless operator's arrival in the Gers.

On 1 May 1944 a most unusual set of *messages personnels* were broadcast. They covered the whole of France, and indicated that the Second Front could be expected within weeks. On 1 June, a second series was transmitted, giving a warning of days. On the afternoon of 5 June, the chief of Special Operations Executive, General Gubbins, and the London chief of the American Office of Strategic Services, Colonel David Bruce, called together on General Koenig, the Free French officer designated chief of all Resistance operations in France after the invasion. They went through the formality of asking his assent to the transmission of the 'Action Messages' that night.

For the rest of their lives, former Allied agents and *résistants* would forget much about World War II, but none would ever forget his or her 'action message' on the night of 5 June 1944. George Starr's message was '*Il a un voix fausset.*' It was his wireless operator, a little English WAAF named Annette Cormeau, who came down from the bedroom where she kept her set to report the news to the little group in the kitchen of a farmhouse at Castelnausur-l'Avignon, in the heart of Gascony. Starr – SOE's Hilaire – was sitting among the Laribeau family, with whom he lived. He was a laconic, iron-tough mining engineer from Staffordshire who in the past twenty months had built one of the largest SOE networks in France. He was not given to extravagant displays of emotion. He simply grinned and said: 'That's it, then', and began to summon men from other houses in the lonely little hamlet to drive and ride into the night, passing word. Within a few hours, the first explosions on the railways indicated the opening of the attack on communications. As the night advanced, men began to arrive on foot, by bicycle, and charcoal-driven *gazogène*. Exhilarated chatter and laughter echoed among the houses as they broke out the arms hidden in the church and began to pass them out, filling magazines and stripping Brens and Stens of their protective greasing.

Jacques Poirier's message was '*La girafe a un long cou*'. He received it among the *maquis* with whom he was quartered in the lonely dignity of the Château Le Poujade, high above the Dordogne valley. The Germans had relinquished control of much of the Dordogne many months before, confining themselves to occasional punitive sorties. Under his codename Nestor, Poirier was SOE's agent for eastern Dordogne and Corrèze, in which he had arranged arms drops for several thousand *maquisards*, most of whom were now bursting to make use of their weapons. Poirier immediately took to his car. That night of 5 June, and through the days that followed, he raced from *maquis* to *maquis* in the woods and hills, pressing on them the request he had been making for weeks. 'Make as much mess as you can.'

Most of the *résistants* to whom he spoke had never in their lives heard of the Das Reich, the 2nd SS Panzer Division some eighty miles southwards around Montauban in the Tarn-et-Garonne. It was only on the rarest occasions that SOE's agents, far less *maquisards*, had access to military intelligence from

London. They had no means of communicating with other groups except with chronic delay, by courier or personal visit. On the morning of 6 June, the thousands of *résistants* gathering with their arms in the Lot, the Dordogne, the Corrèze and the south-west knew little except that '*Le Jour-J*' had come. They expected to fight but few guessed against whom.

Captain Marius Guedin, lately of the French 60th Infantry Regiment, was one of the few Resistance leaders who had been convinced for months what his men should do. He was a native of Brive-la-Gaillarde, the beautifully named town at the foot of the hills of the Corrèze to which he had returned in 1942 from captivity in Germany. Guedin had been one of the first to begin working towards creating a local Resistance movement, and although he had the bespectacled appearance of a diffident university don, he pursued his plans with fierce single-mindedness. He developed a close relationship with a succession of British agents who came to his area, of whom Jacques Poirier was the latest. He rejected the overtures of De Gaulle's agents who came to see him, and who sought to exert a measure of direction over the local *Armée Secrète*. By June 1944, his chief in the departmental AS, Colonel René Vaujour, claimed to have some 5000 *maquisards* and secret *résistants* under his control. Guedin was effectively their field commander. He was convinced that, when the invasion came, the Das Reich would move north through his sector to reinforce the German counter-offensive. In March 1944 he gave orders to his men: on D-Day, they would deploy company by company to cover the bridges of the river Dordogne in south Corrèze and northern Lot. In the early hours of 6 June, throughout the region men who had been secret *résistants* for months or years left their homes and their families and began to walk or bicycle to the various rendezvous. Guedin's *maquisards*, already living openly without the law, broke their camps and moved to join them as his couriers brought the news.

But many others who were to meet the Das Reich Division had no foreknowledge. All through the afternoon of 5 June, at a splendid Georgian mansion in Bedfordshire named Hasell's Hall, a pretty, dark-haired girl and a cheerful young man in battledress chattered, laughed and pieced jigsaws together without knowing each other's names. The man was a twenty-two-year-old officer of the Special Air Service named John Tonkin, who had already fought in North Africa and Italy, and made a remarkable escape from German hands to rejoin his regiment. Now he was to be parachuted into France to prepare a landing ground for forty of his men to follow, and attack German communications from a base far behind the lines, south of Poitiers. The house, he wrote later in a letter to his mother,

> . . . was the 'last resting place' for all agents to enemy countries. We were very well looked after by ATS. The only operational people there were Richard and I and the Jedburgh team for Operation Bulbasket, two of our officers for Houndsworth, two for Titanic, and four agents, of whom two were surprisingly beautiful girls. We had checked and rechecked everything and packed our enormous rucksacks about fifty times. Finally, there was nothing more to do, so we spent the time very profitably with the girls, doing jigsaw puzzles.

It was an odd little fluke of war that Tonkin's men should within the week have directed an air attack on petrol trains intended to move the Das Reich, while the girl, twenty-four years old and with one mission to France already behind her, should have been captured and sent on the road to execution by the division. Her name was Violette Szabo.

Vera Atkins, one of the most celebrated of SOE's Baker Street staff, also spent the long day at Hasell's Hall, after the postponement of the invasion, and thus of their drop, for twenty-four hours. That night, she drove with the girls to the secret aerodrome at Tempsford. Violette Szabo, she said, '. . . looked incredibly beautiful, in white marguerite earrings and a marguerite clip that she had bought in Paris on her last mission. . .' One of the SAS officers approached Vera as they waited, and asked her to take his cufflinks and send them to his mother. Then the Halifaxes taking the British officers and agents to their several destinations disappeared into the darkness at the end of the runway; Vera returned to her car, and at last to Baker Street. There was no celebration of D-Day. They were all much too tired.

At the headquarters of the Der Führer Panzergrenadier Regiment, one of the two armoured infantry brigades of the 2nd SS Panzer Division, on the morning of 6 June a brief signal was received from divisional headquarters at Moissac: 'Since the early hours of the morning, the invasion has been taking place on the Channel coast. Preparations are to be made for a march.'

1 2nd SS Panzer Division: Montauban, Tarn-et-Garonne, May 1944

In the early afternoon of 6 April 1944, in the conference room of his headquarters in East Prussia, Adolf Hitler and his staff discussed what further units they dared strip from the Eastern Front to reinforce France against Allied invasion. The transcript of their conversation is mangled, but when they begin to discuss the future of the 2nd SS Panzer Division, the Das Reich, the import is clear.

WARLIMONT: This movement of the 12 SS Div in this area is also under way, though for the moment they can't be replaced. On the other hand, Student's paratroop replacement and training division, which has about 12,000 men, is going into southern Holland . . . being built up there . . . Reich has. . . . Now the . . . please, that he should be able to do with tanks . . . because here . . . can be moved here . . . as well as . . . and the front on the south coast. . . .

FEGELEIN: When contact to 1st Panzer Army has been established, the Reich Battle Group can presumably be withdrawn?

THE FÜHRER: Of course it should be pulled out – it should move over here.

FEGELEIN: It could be put together quickly.

THE FÜHRER: How strong is this battle group?

KEITEL: Fifteen or sixteen hundred men.

FEGELEIN: No, it's a bit bigger: 2,500 men. They weren't too badly mauled. That's the hard core.

THE FÜHRER: For over there, it's nothing. But if they're put here, you've immediately got 15,000 men. Then in no time. . . .

FEGELEIN: The Das Reich Division has 15,385 men altogether.

BUHLE: The battle group and that?

FEGELEIN: No, that alone.

THE FÜHRER: Then it's ready! Then it's a division again – in fact an old division!

Thus it was that some 2,500 survivors of Battle Group Lammerding, rump of one of the finest armoured divisions, Nazi

Germany had created, found themselves ordered to abandon the mud and floods of Russia in the spring thaw, and entrain for a move across Europe that would finally lead them to Tulle, Oradour-sur-Glane and Normandy. They left behind their few remaining tanks, vehicles and guns, together with the memory of countless thousands of their dead in frozen graves from the Pripet marshes to the Cherkassy pocket. With infinite gratitude for their deliverance, they began to roll away through East Prussia, on the long journey from the eastern to the western extremity of Hitler's empire.

It was the high point of German fortunes in the East in 1944. The weather had forced a temporary halt in campaigning. The Russians decided to defer their next offensive until the Allies landed in France. Hitler had a priceless opportunity to shorten his line, to withdraw to defences in depth while he moved men to meet the threat in the West. Instead, as always, he held his ground. His shrinking armies straggled along a front of 1,650 miles. In the centre, divisions averaging only 2,000 men were holding sixteen-mile sectors of the line. Between July 1943 and May 1944, Germany lost forty-one divisions in Russia – almost a million casualties between July and October 1943 alone, 341,950 men between March and May 1944. Even in the months following the Allied invasion in Normandy, German casualties in Russia continued to average four times the number in the West.

Hitler's *Führerdirectiv* No.51 of November 1943 gave first priority to strengthening the western defences against the Allied invasion. Yet in reality the East continued to consume the overwhelming proportion of men and resources. Divisions sent to France had either been ruined in Russia, were untrained or medically inferior. Special battalions were formed from the deaf and diseased. The ranks were filled with Russian, Hungarian and Romanian subjects of Hitler's empire – even some defectors from POWs of the Indian Army. Von Rundstedt had demanded seventy full-strength divisions to defend the West. By 6 June 1944, he had only fifty-nine woefully under-strength ones – 850,000 men and 1,552 tanks. By contrast, there were 156 German divisions in Russia and twenty-seven in Italy. 'Often I would be informed that a new division was to arrive in France direct from Russia, or Norway, or central Germany,' Rundstedt wrote acidly. 'When it finally made its appearance in the West, it would consist, in all, of a divisional commander, a medical officer, and five bakers.'

The 2nd SS Das Reich Armoured Division was not quite such a shadow when it arrived in Bordeaux from the East, but it was nothing like the superb all-volunteer force that had swept into Russia with the Wehrmacht in June 1941. The High Command in the East had ruthlessly stripped its surviving 'teeth' formations to strengthen the sagging line on the Dnieper. Only a few thousand support personnel had been sent to France, to wait re-equipment with every kind of weapon and vehicle. To fill the ranks, 9,000 replacements flooded into the division's barracks and lagers: untrained boys, almost all seventeen or eighteen, many of them *Volksdeutsche* – Hungarians, Romanians and a large contingent of Alsatians, twelve nationalities in all. Three months before they were plunged into one of the great battles of history, in the woods and fields of south-western France, the raw recruits were firing their Mauser K98s for the first time, practising the naming of parts on the MG42, and receiving their introduction to the Pak 75 anti-tank gun.

In April, they moved south-eastwards to a rendezvous with the survivors of the division's battle group, at last released to join them from the East. They formed one of the three armoured, one motorized and thirteen infantry divisions of General Von Blaskowitz's Army Group G, responsible for the defence of southern France. The point on the map that Hitler's forefinger had stabbed on 6 April was the town of Montauban, just north of Toulouse. There, his staff suggested, the Das Reich could not only prepare for battle in a quiet area, but stand poised to intervene on the north or south coasts of France, when the Allies landed. If the disturbing terrorist situation in central France which was already irritating Von Rundstedt continued to worsen, the Das Reich could guarantee communication between Army Groups G and B.

Throughout the last two years of the war, the deployment of the SS divisions consumed countless hours at Hitler's Führer conferences. His faith and pride in their power were unshakable. Again and again throughout the war in the East, SS units had defied his generals' predictions of the possible, broken through the unbreakable, or held the untenable. The Das Reich had fought with distinction through the great summer battles of 1943, above all in the slow fight back to the Dnieper in August. In November, the SS Leibstandarte Division spearheaded the counter-attack that smashed the Russian armoured corps after its breakthrough near Kiev. In April 1944, it was the SS Panzer Corps under Hausser that launched a brilliant flank attack to save the 1st Panzer Army from certain destruction in the Cherkassy pocket.

The SS had become the fire brigade of Hitler's empire, rushed to every crisis. In the last two years of the war, the Leibstandarte Division moved seven times between the Eastern and Western Fronts. Himmler exaggerated only a little when he said in January 1944: 'So far, the Waffen SS has never under any circumstances caused disappointment, and it will not – even under the most severe hardships yet to come – disappoint in the future.' Since October 1943, seven crack Panzergrenadier units, includ ing the Das Reich, had been redesignated as Panzer divisions. With an establishment of over 20,000 men and 200 tanks, each was almost twice the strength of a Wehrmacht Panzer division. These seven units, together with another five or six SS divisions of slightly lesser quality, were at the forefront of Hitler's operational plans until the end of the war. It is a measure of his strategic priorities that, until June 1944, only one SS division was engaged with the Western Allies, in Italy. The remainder of this vast personal army – thirty-eight divisions and 600,000 men at its zenith – was committed in Russia or refitting.

Of the ten Panzer divisions in France on D-Day, three were SS. The only unit in a position to provide immediate support for the weak static infantry divisions defending the Normandy beaches was 21 Pz. Rommel had already protested repeatedly to Hitler against the policy of holding the bulk of the armour at least fifty, in some cases 150 miles behind the coast. When the Allies landed, it was evident to every senior German commander that their air power would create immense difficulties for German reinforcements seeking to move forward. The Das Reich Division at Montauban, like 9 Pz further east on the Rhône, was some 450 miles from the north coast.

But whatever the difficulties in the forward areas, it seemed reasonable to expect that it would be possible to move an armoured division from southern France at least as far north as the Loire before encountering serious enemy interference. Even the British, with their huge programme of transport bombing, assumed that the Das Reich would be available for a German counter-thrust against the beachhead within a few days of 5 June: '2nd SS Panzer Division will . . . be concentrating in a forward area by D+3,' argued a British Intelligence assessment of German armoured capability, drawn up three weeks before Overlord. The Allies expected, and indeed greatly feared, that the 2nd SS and its 209 tanks and assault guns – one-tenth of the entire German armoured strength in the West – would be playing a prominent role in the Normandy battle by 9 or 10 June. Most of the officers of the Das Reich Division were of the same opinion.

In this fifth year of the war, Hitler deceived himself when he spoke of the Das Reich as 'an old division'. The ranks of the units training around Montauban were overwhelmingly filled by conscripts of a kind the 'old' SS of 1939 would never have glanced at. A veteran NCO laughed scornfully when Sadi Schneid, a young Alsatian recruit who joined them at Bordeaux in February, complained of toothache and appeared on his first parade with his front tooth missing, after a visit to the dentist. The old Waffen SS, the legion of pre-war National Socialist supermen, rejected every recruit with the slightest physical imperfection, even a single dental filling.

Schneid himself was a boy of seventeen whose mother, a fervent Nazi, had caused his father to be sent to an internment camp by denouncing him as a former Alsatian autonomist. His elder brother had already joined the SS as an alternative to ten years' forced labour for black marketeering. It is a measure of the confusion of Alsatian loyalties that one of his younger brothers later joined the French Resistance, and one of his sisters broke off her engagement to a German tank officer because of his ardent Nazi sympathies. An officer of the Das Reich wrote later: 'It was a terrible mistake to send men from Alsace to fight in the West when they had such strong links with France. . . . The effects were not only military. There was a rapid increase in crime requiring severe punishment.' From the moment that they arrived in Bordeaux, the young Alsatians were incited by local French people to desert. On his second day in camp

Schneid was offered an escape route to the *maquis* by a French girl dental assistant. He did not take it, but, to the fierce bewilderment of SS officers who had never encountered such a problem before, others did.

Even the German soldiers lackeo the passionate fervour of four years earlier. A Panzergrenadier officer named Major* Otto Weidinger wrote:

With the increasing bombing attacks on German towns, and the heavy civilian losses, the morale of troops is badly affected. Every day, soldiers receive news of the destruction of their homes, the tragic death of wives and children. They return from leave depressed. The pressure is increased by the treacherous campaign waged by the *maquis*, which is not fought according to the Hague Convention, and which makes every man a target at any time. Every soldier lost through these mean and unsoldierly methods increases the unit's bitterness. The years of fighting bolshevism in Russia have also affected the men's nerves.

Yet despite the diminished quality of recruits and major shortages of fuel, transport and equipment that hampered training through the spring of 1944, the Das Reich was still a formidable fighting force. Whatever the ghastly record of the SS and of Hitler's Germany, nothing can diminish their military achievements. Unit for unit – above all in the last years, 1943–5 – the German army proved itself the greatest fighting force of World War II. Neither the British nor the American nor even the Russian Army could have matched its performance outnumbered, starved of fuel and supplies, faced by overwhelming air power. Even in 1944–5, diluted by the *Volksdeutsche* recruits, the SS divisions performed miracles. 'The military significance of the Waffen SS is to be found not so much in its accomplishments during the years of German victory, as in its victories during the years of German defeat,' the most objective post-war historian of the SS has written. Germany's methods of manning her armies in 1944–5 were little worse than those by which the Roman Empire filled its legions. According to veterans, among the officers and NCOs of the Das Reich at Montauban in May 1944 10 or even 20 per cent were obviously inadequate to their

* Throughout the text, I have omitted the unwieldy SS ranks, ie Major-Sturmbannführer, except on rare occasions when they seem necessary to make a point. Ranks given are those held in June 1944.

task. But so were an equal or greater proportion of junior leaders in most Allied units. The overwhelming majority of the Das Reich's regimental officers and NCOs were experienced, battle-hardened veterans who would fight to the end.

To understand the officers of the SS, and some of the things that were done by the Das Reich Division in June 1944, it is essential to realize what Hitler's Germany had given them. Almost all were of lower middle-class or working-class origins, men whom the old German Army would never have considered commissioning. Fritz Langangke, a tank lieutenant, was a miner's son. Major Gunther-Eberhardt Wisliceny, commanding the Deutschland Panzergrenadier regiment, looked the image of a tall, stiff Prussian *Junker*. Yet in reality he had served for three years as a miner in Upper Silesia before joining the army. His family had lost everything in 1918, when his grandfather's estates near Posen (Poznan) became part of Poland. Major Weidinger's father was a post office worker. He himself was rejected by both the army and the police before being accepted by the SS. This tough, impressionable young man embraced his new life passionately, above all the emphasis on athletics. When he was commissioned, he and his fellow-officers loved the gentlemanly rituals of the mess, to which men of their class could never have aspired in the Wehrmacht. Weidinger met his wife Annelise, a pharmacist's daughter, at a regimental drag hunt ball in November 1938. He would end the war with a brigade command at the age of thirty – scarcely an officer in the Das Reich Division was over thirty-two years old in 1944. Major Heinrich Wulf, commanding the reconnaissance battalion, was the thirty-year-old son of a North German worker who died as a conscript in Flanders in 1917. His mother became a waitress in a cavalry mess at Lüneburg. He himself left school at sixteen, was rejected by the army, and became a clerk. In 1934 he joined the SS – as a ranker, like every recruit – and was commissioned four years later.

Those pre-war years had been a glorious time for all of them: the comradeship, the discipline and supreme shared physical fitness of the training camps; officer school and the affectations of the mess with full-dress uniform and the adulation of so many girls. Then came the triumphal sweep into Poland, the exhilaration of discovering that they could crush the best that the enemy could send against them. Wulf was on his honeymoon when he heard that the attack on France was to begin: he raced to his unit still in full-dress uniform with his ceremonial dagger at his hip, terrified that he might miss the battle. After France, Wulf remained an instructor at the famous SS officer school at Bad Tolz in Bavaria until July 1943, because of his wife's persistence in producing daughters. As the only male in his family, SS rules decreed that he could not return to the front until he had a son. In October 1943, this duty accomplished, he took command of the Das Reich reconnaissance battalion in Russia.

It remains a common delusion among the people of Britain and America that World War II was fought in conditions far less terrible than those of World War I, and indeed from their own point of view this is perfectly true. But the huge, primeval struggle waged for four years between the German and Russian armies exceeded in scale and horror the worst of the 1914–18 battles for France. New standards of brutality in warfare were achieved by both sides. To understand how the officers of the Das Reich Division behaved in June 1944, it is essential to remember what they had spent three years learning in Russia. Each man who emerged from that campaign to fight again in the West counted his survival a miracle of odds.

The conditions of war in the East defied description. In winter weapons, vehicle bearings, engines, horses and men were relentlessly destroyed by the cold. Soldiers trudged through the snow with their boots wrapped in straw, their bodies lined with straw and newspapers beneath their greencoats, their faces almost invisible lest some chink in their armour allow frostbite to attack. The cold, the lice, malaria, frostbite, fever, hunger and partisan attack all took their toll of health and morale. Fritz Langangke once stood shivering beside a railway siding as a Panzer unit's train drew up and a contingent of young tankers jumped down, fresh from France: 'They laughed at our rags. We shouted to them to cover their noses, their ears. They just joked and laughed and chattered. Then the tips of their noses and ears began to turn white before our eyes. . . .'

They abandoned shaving for weeks on end to protect their skin, forgot mail from home, for it never came, grew accustomed to seeing their own ranks shattered in battle, rebuilt and shattered once again until their old units were unrecognizable. Casualties provoked meteoric promotions to fill the gaps. Heinrich Wulf found himself commanding a battalion reduced to a tenth of its establishment, yet when he himself left Russia, only one in ten of those men was left. 'Our only concern was not to be captured,' he said. The two armies rivalled each other in ruthlessness. One night Wulf's young ordnance officer, Hubseh, was captured by a Russian patrol. At dawn, as the light revealed the Russian lines two hundred yards away, they saw the German lashed to a haystack. A few moments later, a Russian loudhailer broadcast simple terms: surrender within ten minutes, or watch the haystack fired. The haystack was fired. Karl Kreutz – by June 1944 the Das Reich's artillery commander – remembered the discovery of an ambulance column, with forty German wounded systematically butchered by the Russians with their doctor. The order came down from division to take no prisoners for eight days. Was the order obeyed? 'Of course.'

There was no peace in darkness, for the Russians were masters of night-fighting. After the first months of the 1941 campaign, when herds of bewildered, untrained Russian soldiers were driven by their leaders on to the German guns, Stalin's commanders learned quickly. Every German who fought in the East returned with a profound respect for his enemy. There was no German tank to match the Russian T-34. By 1943, the Germans were awed by the huge artillery barrages laid down before the Russian attacks. Red infantry, sometimes stupefied with alcohol and driven on by their commissars at gunpoint, pressed home their assaults with the fury of despair.

Nor were the Russians always ignorant slaves. Fritz Langangke remembered a night in a hut, huddled over a little 'Hindenburg light' stove, when two Russian girls who spoke German talked to them for hours about the war: 'They were so intelligent, they said with such certainty that we lacked the fervour to match theirs. . . . That night I almost became a bolshevik,' said Langangke wryly. He was a man of unusual imagination and sensitivity for an SS officer. But another Das Reich tank man, Otto Pohl, was also deeply impressed by a badly wounded Russian sergeant whom they blew out of his bunker with grenades: 'We asked him his unit number. He replied simply: "An NCO of the Russian Army does not give information." '

It was the iron toughness of the Russians that they admired, and later compared so favourably with the qualities of the Americans. Some Russians were fighting just as doggedly beside the Germans, against their fellow-countrymen. Every German unit had its contingent of 'Hi-Wis' – Russian prisoners or renegades who served as batmen, stretcher bearers, ammunition carriers and scouts. Hi-Wi patrols would slip out of the German lines every night, returning at dawn with often vital intelligence, until the inevitable morning when they failed to come back. They were utterly expendable, easily and casually replaced.

Through those years in Russia, few German fighting soldiers expected to come home. There was a catchphrase among them about 'Living like God in France'. The West came to seem almost a dream world. To the men of the Das Reich who emerged from the East in 1944, the rich fields and vineyards of south-west France brought them back to the glorious, happy memories of 1940. Yet they found that much had changed. Those who served there in 1940–1 had found most of the French people astonishingly relaxed and friendly. They now discovered that in public civilians addressed them coldly, or not at all. There was less to eat. The terrorist threat meant that it was impossible for vehicles or men to travel alone outside city centres. Even in Toulouse, the officers' messes and the *Soldatenheim* were faced with wire mesh against grenade attack.

Almost all of them took it for granted that within a matter of months they would be committed to battle against an Allied invasion, probably in the north. Over wine in the cafés, the officers reminisced endlessly about Russia, and speculated about the British and Americans whom they had never seen. 'We thought of the Americans as children,' said one of them. An officer who had been in North Africa with the Wehrmacht described how the British would sometimes surrender simply because they had run out of petrol. 'But we knew that their air forces would be a terrible problem. We were not frightened of their men, but of their material. . . .'

Ever since the first winter in Russia, 1941, when the German Army suffered privations of Crimean proportions because of supply failures and military misjudgments in Berlin, many even among the SS had been puzzled by the High Command's omissions and failures. By 1944 some, like Wisliceny, had long since abandoned hope of winning the war militarily, but still hoped for some political settlement at tolerable cost. Others, like the twenty-four-year-old veteran Otto Pohl, not only loved their tanks and their division, but cherished ambitions to reach high command, and never thought of defeat. 'Until the very end in 1945, I was sure that it would be all right for us,' he said. Pohl was a son of one of the old German elite who had transferred his allegiance very early to the new aristocracy. His father had been an officer in the Kaiser's navy who joined Hitler in the 1920s, and was now an SS general. Young Pohl was educated at one of the special Young Socialist cadet schools, volunteered for Russia in 1941, and somehow survived there for three years. Some officers, like Otto Weidinger, had been troubled about the logic of invading Russia, but not Pohl: 'A soldier never asks himself whether an operation is a good idea. Fighting is his business.' When they asked themselves why they were sent the wrong type of ammunition, why there were desperate fuel shortages, why they were sometimes compelled to suffer terrible losses to no purpose, scarcely a man in the division considered fixing the blame on Adolf Hitler. Some said that the Führer simply did not know of these things. Others, that he was badly advised by those around him, above all by Bormann and Ribbentrop.

But it is essential to perceive that, in many respects, these young soldiers of the SS – and the divisional commander was their only officer older than thirty-two – had much in common with the men of other armies. The SS newspaper prided itself on the freedom with which it criticized the failings of the organization. Officers and men shared a far closer relationship than those of the British Army. They inflicted their arrogance upon the outside world, not upon each other. Among junior officers, there was a hoary joke whenever some supreme organizational disaster was inflicted upon them: '. . . *Wenn der Führer wüsste!*' – '. . . If only the Führer knew!' When they sang, it was seldom the *Horst Wessel* song, more often a number like *Waldeslust*:

I don't know my father,
I'm not loved by my mother,
But I don't want to die so young. . . .

In the privacy of their billets, most of them enjoyed a reasonably civil relationship with the French civilians who were obliged to house them. A Frenchwoman who provided quarters for six men of the Das Reich in Montauban in 1944 described how one of them with punctilious correctness brought her a 1,000 franc note that he had found in his room. It was a matter of pride within the SS that no man was permitted to lock up his possessions in barracks, although some of them stole petrol from the unit stocks to get to the brothels in Toulouse. The SS officers were elaborately, Germanically courteous to the wives and daughters of their enforced hosts. They considered themselves, indeed, to be the very pattern of chivalry. An officer of the Das Reich cited to the author an example of his division's gentlemanly code: in Russia, a colleague was found to have committed some aberration with a Russian woman, and was at once ordered to go to his quarters and shoot himself. He did so.

Yet these young men, so careful in their private courtesies and honesty, were also profoundly flawed. It is unnecessary to review in detail the principles of National Socialism, the anti-semitism, the uncritical devotion to Hitler – it can be taken for granted that almost every officer of the Das Reich shared all these, not least from practical gratitude for what Hitler's Germany had done for his career. The only acceptable salute in an SS unit was '*Heil Hitler*'. Otto Pohl readily forgave his father-in-law and two brothers-in-law dead in Russia, Karl Kreutz his home in Berlin destroyed by bombing and his family refugees in Silesia, Ernst Krag his six wounds, and the half of his class comrades at officer school already dead.

The aspect of their conditioning that is most relevant to this story is the extraordinary respect with which they had been imbued for the virtues of strength, of ruthless dedication to the task in hand, and the equally extraordinary indifference to the claims of the weak and the innocent. All their virtues were reserved for others within their closed society. They possessed neither charity nor mercy for any who were not deemed to have deserved it by their own code. It is striking that when the survivors of the British First Airborne Division at Arnhem found themselves in the hands of the SS, they expected to be shot. Instead, they were treated with the respect due to heroes. According to the SS code of chivalry, these were fellow-knights worthy of their highest honour. Yet as we shall see below, those whom the SS did not deem worthy of its respect – above all, enemy civilians – were treated with unflinching ruthlessness. The young leaders of the SS had been educated and trained to believe that only one principle mattered – the interests of Germany as they themselves and their commanders saw fit to interpret them. They did not spurn morality or justice or process of law – these were simply forgotten or unknown concepts to them. If the *Einsatzgruppen* – the SS extermination squads – or the concentration camps ever passed through their consciousness, they never allowed these mildly distasteful matters to linger. They were part of the natural machinery of the state, and no concern of theirs.

The greatest fear of an SS officer was that he might be considered guilty of weakness or cowardice. He could never be wrong if he adopted or accepted the most drastic solution to a problem. From the first appearance of the Waffen SS in the war, it had been made apparent that superior officers would always pardon an excess of zeal in the right direction. In September 1939, a member of an SS artillery regiment in Poland herded fifty Jews into a synagogue and shot them. The prosecuting officer at his court martial appealed for the death sentence, and the man was indeed sentenced to a term of imprisonment. But then Berlin intervened. An appeal hearing was held, at which the presiding judge said that the accused '. . . was in a state of irritation as a result of the many atrocities committed by Poles against ethnic Germans. As an SS man, he was also particularly sensitive to the sight of Jews and the hostile attitude of Jewry to Germans; and thus acted quite unpremeditatedly in a spirit of youthful enthusiasm.' The sentence was quashed. The SS never looked back. Throughout the next four years of conquest and struggle, above all on the Eastern Front, the Waffen SS shot whomsoever they wished, whenever they wished. Within two weeks of the invasion of Russia, the SS Wiking Division had killed 600 Galician Jews 'as a reprisal for Soviet cruelties'. The Leibstandarte Division found six of its men brutally killed by Russian troops, and shot every prisoner for three days, a total of about 4,000 men. In September 1941, a support unit of the Das Reich assisted an SS extermination squad to kill 920 Jews near Minsk. Mass killing in pursuit of state policy never became the professional business of the Waffen SS – the *Einsatzgruppen* looked after all that sort of thing. But there can have been few experienced officers and men in the Waffen SS by June 1944 who did not regard it as a perfectly legitimate exercise to carry out mass reprisals and wholesale killings if the situation seemed to justify them.

The qualities that the SS most signally failed to foster were intelligence and imagination, probably because these characteristics would have rendered their possessors unfit for service in its ranks. Throughout its history, the Waffen SS produced an extraordinary corps of soldiers and regimental officers, but failed to throw up a single outstanding higher commander. At divisional level and above, the Waffen SS was lamentably directed. Only Paul Hausser, the venerated Panzer commander who once led the *Verfügungstruppen* from whom the Das Reich derived, has any claim to military brilliance, and he was a product of the old German Army. The SS fought and died bravely, often fanatically. They can expect no higher epitaph.

General Heinz Bernard Lammerding, commanding officer of the Das Reich Division in June 1944, was a typical product of the new Nazi aristocracy. He was born in Dortmund, qualified as an engineer, and became an early convert to National Socialism. He took a job as director of an SA engineering school, and worked in various capacities for the organization until 1935. He then became SS member no. 247062. He was a Waffen SS engineer captain at the outbreak of war, served on the staff of the *Verfügungstruppen* division from November 1940 to August 1942, then took command of an infantry regiment. After a brief period on an armoured corps staff, in July 1943 he became chief of staff to General von der Bach-Zelewski. This officer was directing with legendary ruthlessness anti-partisan operations in the rear of the German armies in Russia. Lammerding's signature appeared on several appalling documents, ordering the wholesale destruction of entire villages and towns which were judged guilty of assisting partisans. At the end of 1943, Lammerding took command of troops of the Das Reich Division operating against partisans in its rear areas, and on 25 January 1944, of the division itself. On 22 May 1944, while the division was at Montauban, it was announced with suitable celebration that Lammerding had been awarded the Knight's Cross for his work in Russia. He was still only thirty-eight.

Few of the surviving officers of the Das Reich Division have much to say in favour of Lammerding as a commander. He lacked personal presence, and possessed none of the obvious gifts of a leader of men. He was a curiously colourless, forceless figure, whose greatest merits were administrative competence and friendship with Heinrich Himmler. It was rumoured in some Das Reich officers' messes that it was this personal alliance which had secured him command of the division. Himmler paid them a personal visit in the spring of 1944: 'It was obvious that Lammerding and Himmler got on well, although I couldn't say whether this affected Lammerding's career,' said his senior staff officer, Major Albert Stuckler. 'After all, Lammerding had been a good engineer.' But the impression emerges of Lammerding from all the accounts of June 1944 of a man overpromoted and quite unsuited to a fighting command, who would have been much more at ease on Himmler's staff.

In May 1944 Fritz Langangke was suddenly ordered to carry out a major rail reconnaissance for his tank regiment: 'I had always wanted to have a railway since I was a little boy, and suddenly I was given one. I was provided with a special train with a saloon car and a carriage full of Russian soldiers as escort, and ordered to check every possible rail route for the division to the front.' For two idyllic weeks, he coasted comfortably around southern France, measuring tunnel heights, checking bridge capacities and road connections. The train was commanded by a major who had been a pre-war wine merchant, and used the trip to shuttle hundreds of cases of black market wine hither and thither about his domains: 'These fellows, they had already forgotten about the war. For me, coming from Russia, it was a revelation. For the first time I thought – "Oh yes, this is going to go. . . . We can lose. . . ." '

Langangke found most of the French railway officials almost unctuously friendly and hospitable, complaining bitterly about the damage being done to the nation's transport system by Allied bombing, which was indeed provoking passionate hostility to the Allies in many great cities of France. But in the house where he was billeted with an elderly aristocratic lady, her nephew sometimes called to talk. One evening this man said to Langangke: 'You poor devils made a big mistake when you joined the Waffen SS, you're going to be the first to catch it when the time comes.' The man offered to smuggle him to Algeria. Langangke said: 'What would you do in my place?' The Frenchman remained silent. Langangke never saw him again.

The Das Reich's training programme was lamentably behind schedule, yet all that spring it was continually interrupted in order that units could take part in sweeps and punitive operations against the French Resistance. Week by week, around the huge area in which the division was encamped in its fifty barracks and lagers, the campaign of sniping, roadblocking and sabotage intensified. For a vast fighting machine such as an armoured division, the terrorists represented no substantial threat. But they obliged every unit to put its quarters under guard, every man to carry a weapon at all times, every ration truck to travel with an escort. Otto Pohl became so exasperated by the need to keep a four-man picket on the house in which he was billeted that he moved into quarters in the centre of Caussade with his men. Sadi Schneid's anti-tank platoon found themselves the subject of a furious unit investigation one morning when it was learned that a stock of mines had been stolen from their store. Even Karl Kreutz's gunners were periodically diverted from training to sweep stretches of the countryside where there were reports of arms being parachuted to *maquisards*. Sometimes they found odd containers in the woods or fields, but more often than not the operation was in vain.

In the month of May 1944, according to Albert Stuckler, the division lost some twenty men and a hundred vehicles to terrorists. A soldier was shot with his wife who was visiting him in their hotel room in a village near Caussade. An NCO coming out of a café in Figeac was killed by a burst of Sten gun fire. Any vehicle travelling alone was liable to ambush.

In those last weeks before D-Day, the 2nd SS Panzer Division made the price of Resistance very clear to the surrounding countryside. Reprisals were on a scale modest enough compared with Russia, but thus seemed savage enough at the time. On 2 May, one of the tank battalions was training near the small town of Montpezat-de-Quercy when an SS patrol was fired upon a mile to the south-west. The SS swept through Montpezat, setting fire to several houses, looting extensively and assaulting several civilians who seemed slow to acquiesce. On 11 May men of the Der Führer Panzergrenadiers conducted a series of sweeps in the Lot. Twenty-four people, including four women, were seized for deportation in St Céré, forty from Bagnac. In Cardaillac, two women were shot, of whom one died. In Lauze, fifty-year-old Mme Moncoutre and her twenty-year-old daughter Berthe were shot among their sheep. Orniac was comprehensively looted. On 1 June, a tank unit moving north of Caylus machine-gunned six civilians in Limonge, one at Cadrieu and two at Frontenac. On 2 June, after a *maquis* attack in the countryside, twenty-nine farms were burned, along with the entire village of Terrou, whose 290 inhabitants became refugees. On 3 June, after an SS truck was attacked near Figeac, two men of twenty-two and seventy-four were shot on the spot, and six men and a woman from nearby Viazac were taken out and shot. The most massive action by the Das Reich before D-Day was a raid on Figeac, in which the Germans discovered a Resistance arms dump including sixty-four rifles, three Bren guns, thirty-one Stens and a bazooka. The town paid a terrible price: more than a thousand people were arrested and deported to Germany. Forty-one were killed.

Yet for all the thoroughness with which the Das Reich approached these operations when ordered to carry them out, they were a matter of exasperation to the divisional staff, anxious about its training programme. Several protests were made to 58 Corps and Army Group G about this use of *Frontsoldaten* against communist bandits. 'We were completely unsuited in character and mentality to this sort of warfare,' said Major Stuckler. 'There were specially trained units for this type of work.' Training was also being hampered by the chronic shortage of fuel. Although they exercised intensively at company and battalion level, they lacked opportunity to manoeuvre as a division. Communication and liaison between units was poor. Many of the raw recruits who had joined them in February and March were scarcely past basic training. They were still acutely short of transport – above all trucks for the infantry units and tractors for the towed artillery. Deliveries of tanks were proceeding slowly. On 16 May, they had received thirty-seven Panzer Vs and fifty-five Panzer IVs towards their new reduced establishment of sixty-two of each. But they possessed a full complement of thirty of the superb *Sturmgeschützen* – assault guns that were in effect turretless tanks, with a low silhouette that made them very difficult targets for enemy fire. The two *Panzergrenadier* regiments – each in British parlance a brigade – were at full strength, but under-trained. Major Weidinger, casting a critical eye upon his men, believed that they were capable of fighting a limited battle. His fear was that in a prolonged action, under continuous strain for a period of weeks, their inexperience and lack of training would tell against them.

Then Heinz Guderian, the godfather of all German armoured forces, arrived on an inspection tour. For three days he watched their exercises, above all the night movements which they knew would be critical against Allied air power, the 'walking forest' – heavily camouflaged advances of the tank units who had been warned that there would be none of the great sweeps across open plains that had been possible in Russia. Guderian pronounced himself reasonably satisfied. On his last evening, the officers arranged a dinner for him in their mess at a nearby château. Silver candles and linen tablecloths were found, the black market was swept for food, and that night a circle of dress-uniformed young tankmen and gunners sat down to dinner with the general at the head of the table. He was at his most affable and talkative. He told one of his favourite stories:

> How long have infantry existed? Four thousand years! And in all that time, no one has been able to invent a useful pair of infantry boots. They are always too long or too short. How long have cavalry existed? More than four thousand years! And in all that time, they have never been able to invent a useful lance – they are always too long or too short! How long has artillery existed? Five hundred years. I suggested to our designers a revolutionary measure. They answered: 'My dear Oberst Guderian, you may be a very good tankman, but you know nothing about artillery. Artillery has been pointing backwards for five hundred years! Now you say you want a gun that will go into action pointing forward!'

The officers of the *Sturmgeschützabteilung* laughed with the rest at his version of the development of their self-propelled guns.

With the benefit of hindsight, the success of the Allied landings in Normandy, against indifferent and poorly directed German resistance, seems inevitable. It did not seem so to either side at the time. Even a sceptic such as Fritz Langangke said: 'It did not seem impossible that we could defeat the invasion. We did not then realize that not all Germany was fighting as we were.' It has sometimes been suggested that the Das Reich in June 1944 was so weakened by its large intake of recruits of doubtful enthusiasm that it could have played no important role in Normandy, even had it arrived much earlier on the battlefield. In reality, its deficiencies of training and equipment were no worse than those of most other Panzer divisions in France at that period. It was better equipped with tanks and assault guns than most of its counterparts. Lammerding reported to Army Group G that 2nd SS Panzer was 'conditionally ready for battle'.

Sadi Schneid, the young Alsatian recruit who wrote a fascinating personal memoir after the war for SS veterans' consumption, testifies that many of the Alsatians were indeed lukewarm in their enthusiasm for the war, but intensive training and the fierce spirit of the SS had imbued an astonishingly high proportion with a determination to do whatever was expected of them. He described an evening in their barracks, when his company of the reconnaissance battalion returned from an anti-terrorist sweep. Their senior NCO, Hauptscharführer 'Hascha' Kurz, a formidable veteran of the Eastern Front, was relieved and delighted that not one of his motley crew of *Volksdeutsche*, former prisoners of war and green Alsatians had attempted to desert while they had the chance to do so, in open country. He made a speech to them:

'Boys, if the Americans land one day, they won't be throwing potatoes, and I'm going to need all of you. That's why I keep emphasizing to you that I don't need dead heroes but live ones. Remember everything I've taught you in training. A fraction of a second's carelessness at the front, and it'll do for you. Once again, I urge you – trust me. If you do what I do, you've got a chance of coming out of it. Always obey my finger and my eye, and you'll thank yourselves later. I'll guarantee to do everything I can to keep your skins in one piece. Can I count on you?'

'JAWOHL, HAUPTSCHARFÜHRER!', we shouted in chorus, from the bottom of our hears. 'SIEG HEIL! SIEG HEIL! SIEG HEIL!'

One might have imagined us at Munich, after an oration from Hitler himself.

2 SOE: Baker Street

For the men and women of the French Resistance, D-Day was the decisive moment of the war. After years in which their potential power and enthusiasm had been doubted and disputed in London and Washington, now they were to be put to the test. Resistance did not wage a continuous four-year guerilla struggle against the Germans. Only late in 1941 and early in 1942 did a small number of French people begin to stir from the terrible lethargy and trauma of defeat. Clandestine opposition newspapers were printed. There were cautious meetings of handfuls of like-minded enemies of Vichy. Very many of these courageous pioneers were caught and shot, but others followed. The early handfuls began to grow into a hundred, a thousand independent Resistance groups and escape lines. Each began to develop its own links with one of many interested organizations in London – The British-run French Section of SOE, MI6, MI9, De Gaulle's BCRA and later the American OSS. These links, often forged by the chance of a brief encounter or an exchange of names, determined whether a circuit spent the remainder of the war gathering information, assisting escaping prisoners or preparing for open battle against the Germans. Despite the brief effective existence of a National Council for Resistance under the brilliant Jean Moulin in 1943, after his capture the quest for unity flagged, and in the interests of security this was probably fortunate. Until the end, Resistance remained a patchwork of overlapping and often mutually hostile independent networks. The British and French officers parachuted to provide arms and liaison with London could seldom do more than paper over the cracks of local rivalries, and try to steer the movement towards a broad common policy.

This policy was, quite simply, to direct every effort towards creating a clandestine army to rise on D-Day and cause the maximum difficulty for the Germans behind their lines. In 1942 and early 1943 the *Armée Secrète* – The AS as it was referred to – was composed of Frenchmen continuing their ordinary lives – *les légaux* who had agreed that when the signal was given they would drop their cover and take up arms. The seizure of Unoccupied France by the Germans in November 1942 gave the AS an important boost. Many officers and men who had served with Pétain's Armistice Army, now disbanded, became *résistants*. Some, chiefly in the south, were able to bring arms with them. Then the German introduction of deportation for forced labour – the detested *Service de Travail Obligatoire* – gave Resistance a vast pool of recruits to which it could never otherwise have aspired. Hundreds of thousands of young men who would never have contemplated taking up arms against the Germans now found themselves compelled to do so. The only alternative to the STO was escape into the countryside, either to become a refugee in a remote community or to join a *maquis*. By the end of the war, the Germans had successfully carried away 17 per cent of the youth of France to the factories of the Reich. But they paid for this by inflating Resistance in a matter of months from a slight faction into a mass movement of young men, with millions of their worker and peasant parents bitterly alienated from Vichy and the Occupiers.

The general instruction to all the men of the AS and those *maquis* under the influence of De Gaulle or of British officers – around two-thirds of all *résistants* – was that they should fight the Germans only when they were compelled to do so. There was a limited programme of sabotage of vital industrial targets. But between 1942 and June 1944 most Resistance groups fought gun battles only when themselves attacked, or when a minor action seemed essential to maintain morale and stave off boredom.

The remaining one-third of *résistants*, the communists of the *Francs-Tireurs et Partisans* who scorned De Gaulle or any authority other than their own, pursued an entirely different policy. They were committed to an internal liberation of France by her own people – and of course to their own political glory in the process. From late 1942 onwards, they sought to damage the Germans wherever and whenever they could be attacked, at whatever cost in reprisals, and whatever the strategic futility of their actions. They captured or stole arms from Vichy, the

Germans and non-communist Resistance groups with equal energy. The attacks on the Das Reich Division's area around Montauban in the spring of 1944 were almost entirely the work of FTP groups. They despised the *Armée Secrète's* policy of *attentisme, immobilisme*. 'The French know that a citadel is never so readily taken as from within,' wrote their leader, Charles Tillon, 'and that none has ever successfully resisted attack from without and within. This is why they are so astonished to be so poorly encouraged and assisted to play a decisive role. . . .'

Many FTP *maquis* achieved a terrible reputation in their regions as little better than bandits, murdering alleged collaborators with a ruthlessness that earned as much enmity from respectable Frenchmen as the reprisals of the Das Reich and the Gestapo. But there were also many non-communists who admired the energy with which the FTP inflicted violence on the Germans. 'If there is no violence, how is France to know that there is a Resistance?' ran their argument. It possessed considerable force. The momentum that Resistance had attained by June 1944 owed more than its survivors may care to accept to the actions of the FTP – and to the hatred of the Germans which reprisals had inspired among workers and peasants who would otherwise have remained indifferent neutrals.

But London's policy was still single-mindedly directed towards D-Day. The success of Resistance, in the eyes of the Allied governments and the chiefs of staff, would be determined by the scale of difficulty that it then caused to the Germans – above all, the delay it could impose on the movement to Normandy of reinforcements. Among these, outside northern France the 2nd SS Panzer Division was the most formidable formation.

For the French Section of Special Operations Executive 6 June was the beginning of the end of four years of extraordinary labour. There was a rush to dispatch the last batch of agents to the field. A quarter of all the arms parachuted into France since 1941 were dropped in the single month of May 1944. For months, an acrimonious struggle for control of SOE operations in France had been approaching a crisis. It had been agreed that the Free French, in the person of General Koenig, should take command of French Section from the British once the Allies had landed. But to their bitter resentment neither Koenig nor De Gaulle himself was to be allowed more than a few hours' notice of the invasion. The private view at the top of SOE was that the vital work of French Section would be finished after D-Day. Once Resistance became an open rather than a secret army the alleged insecurity of the Free French could do no harm. Within 'F', however, there was persistent bitterness about the new command structure. Vera Atkins flatly refused to leave Baker Street for the move to Koenig's headquarters in Bryanston Square, and indeed she never did so. This last unseemly wrangle somehow sullied their four years of passionate, dedicated struggle towards the great moment of the Allied return to France.

They held no celebration in the austere rooms at Norgeby House in Baker Street. They were too busy. Signals traffic and demands for supplies continued to pour into the office. In any event, throughout the war they had neither celebrated their secret triumphs, nor wept for their secret tragedies: 'There was no place for emotional scenes. It would have seemed to cheapen what we were doing,' said one of them. For four years they had worked to build an underground circulation system in France, to provide the lifeblood of arms, explosives and communications for the Resistance. Now, the body was coming to life. From D-Day onwards, French Section could do little to steer the battle – it could only report and support it.

Special Operations Executive had been created in the depths of Britain's strategic impotence in 1940 'to set Europe ablaze', in Churchill's memorable phrase. Ironically enough, it was that man of peace Neville Chamberlain who was responsible for drawing up its original charter for '. . . a new organization . . . to co-ordinate all action by way of subversion and sabotage, against the enemy overseas'. To understand SOE, and to judge what the French Resistance did and did not achieve in 1944, it is essential to remember that throughout its history the organization was dogged by controversy and scepticism in London. The Chiefs of Staff disliked and distrusted it. Beyond their instinctive distaste for irregular warfare, they considered it – like all 'private armies' – a drain of resources from the main battlefields, above all a waste of precious aircraft. In 1942–3, much of the material parachuted to Resistance movements in

Europe was from captured Italian stocks, simply because these were all that the War Office would release. Sten guns were unsuitable for guerilla operations in open country, because they were short-range weapons wasteful of ammunition in unskilled hands. But they were dropped into France in vast numbers because they were cheap and plentiful.

In February 1941, the Chief of Air Staff, Sir Charles Portal, one of the principal architects of area bombing, attempted to insist that one of the first SOE parties sent into France should be dropped in uniform: 'I think that the dropping of men dressed in civilian clothes for the purpose of attempting to kill members of the opposing forces is not an operation with which the Royal Air Force should be associated. . . .' Portal never lost his scepticism about SOE, even when he was confronted with such achievements as the halting of tank production at the Peugeot factory in 1943, one of the great sabotage coups of the war. 'I am not at all clear,' he wrote acidly on 27 February 1944, 'how far the promises and claims of SOE have been fulfilled or substantiated. I have in mind as a typical instance the Peugeot factory at Montbéliard. There must be many others. I believe SOE claims to have put this plant out of action by the sabotage of a single individual. . . . I should gravely doubt its being true.'

MI6, the professional Secret Intelligence Service, had obvious cause to dislike its amateur rival because SOE's campaign to make conspicuous trouble for the Germans made the work of SIS agents, who were seeking to gather intelligence as unobtrusively as possible, substantially more difficult. There was also jealousy. All the evidence now available suggests that SIS achieved little through its agents in Occupied Europe in World War II, and certainly less than SOE. The prestige of SIS in 1945 stemmed almost entirely from the work of the Ultra decrypters at Bletchley Park, whom that skilful courtier Sir Stewart Menzies, head of SIS, had contrived to keep within his own empire. 'C', as Menzies was known, together with his deputy Sir Claude Dansey, met the chiefs of SOE regularly throughout the war. But SIS was never better than a suspicious neutral in the Whitehall struggle for resources and support.

The fiercest battle of all, of course, was that fought by General De Gaulle, who claimed the right to control all agents and Resistance operations on French soil. To his bitter resentment, he was merely permitted to drop his own arms and agents through SOE's RF Section, created specifically to maintain control over Free French activities and communications. RF worked parallel to but with somewhat fewer resources than the British-run F Section. F's officers maintained regular contact with the Free French through meetings with 'Colonel Passy', the austere young Captain André Dewavrin who commanded De Gaulle's *Bureau Central de Renseignements et d'Action militaire* – the BCRA – from Duke Street, behind Selfridge's department store. Although the British found little to like about Dewavrin, they respected his brains and did much informal business without friction. 'But any time that Passy came to Baker Street in uniform, we knew that we were in for trouble,' according to an SOE officer. When Passy spoke as the voice of De Gaulle, it was seldom without bitterness. It is a measure of the General's attitude that after the Liberation, on several occasions when he met a French Section officer in France he sought to have him immediately ejected from the country. It is a measure of British regular army feeling towards SOE that, after the war, General Sir Colin Gubbins – the Highland soldier who directed the organization with distinction from September 1943 – found his career permanently blighted by his association with the 'irregulars' and died a disappointed man.

But SOE also had powerful friends, above all the Prime Minister. Churchill seldom informed himself about the details of SOE operations in Europe, but his spirit was deeply moved by the ideal of Resistance. His support for Gubbins was strengthened by a number of meetings at Downing Street with British agents who had worked in France, above all Wing-Commander Yeo-Thomas of RF Section. When Lord Selborne became Minister of Economic Warfare in February 1942, with responsibility for SOE, he used his personal friendship with Churchill to some effect, especially in the struggle with Sir Arthur Harris and Bomber Command for supply-dropping aircraft. SOE's senior officers never felt much warmth for Major Desmond Morton, the former Secret Service officer who served as Churchill's personal aide and mediated when necessary between 'C' and Gubbins. But one of the chiefs of SOE always believed that Morton made a decisive personal contribution in persuading Churchill that it was essential to support De Gaulle as the unchallenged leader of Free France. Had that decision not been taken, the course of events in France both before and after D-Day would have been even more complex and possibly disastrous.

By June 1944, SOE had grown into an organization of almost 14,000 people, running a chain of agent schools in England and Scotland, dropping arms by sea and air almost nightly across Europe. Its formal title had also changed, to become SOE/SO. It was now officially a joint Anglo-American organization – the SO stood for Special Operations, an arm of General Donovan's Office of Strategic Services. An American officer had been placed alongside each of the senior British executives as part colleague, part understudy. To the Americans' chagrin, the British had largely excluded their men from an operational role in France until after D-Day. But they shared in the fierce debate about the role of Resistance that preceded the invasion, and which began with the establishment of a formal SOE/SO Planning Group on 30 August 1943.

Until the last weeks before the landings on 6 June, Yugoslavia was overwhelmingly the most important theatre of operations for SOE, where it was effectively sponsoring a full-scale war. More than twice as many weapons were being delivered to Yugoslavia as to France, chiefly because it was possible to land cargoes from the sea. But all over Europe, SOE's agents were becoming legends in the closed world of secret operations: Harry Rée, who organized the destruction of the Peugeot tank plant; Michael Lis, who pursued a charmed life through Hungary and Poland; Paddy Leigh-Fermor, who kidnapped the German general commanding in Crete; Alfgar Hesketh-Pritchard, who sent a last message from his doomed position in the mountains of Yugoslavia: 'Give all my love to all at White's. This is no place for a gentleman. . . .'

Those with the best prospect of survival on SOE operations were the most ruthless and untrusting. But however strongly their instructors discouraged it, there was also a romantic, buccaneering streak about the organization that brought into its ranks many men and women who would never have become professional spies for SIS. Although reared as a regular gunner, General Gubbins himself had always been suspected of unorthodox tastes. He wrote an important pamphlet on guerilla warfare in the 1930s, and commanded the Independent Companies in Norway in 1940, winning a DSO. But he incurred the lasting enmity of the Brigade of Guards in Scandinavia by sacking one of its battalion commanders on the battlefield. Animosity from some of the most senior soldiers in Whitehall dogged him for the rest of the war. 'Gubbins had all the outward affectations of a regular Highland officer,' said Selwyn Jepson, French Section's recruiting officer who later became his friend, 'but underneath it all, there was great sensitivity.'

After Yugoslavia, France was always Gubbin's overwhelming preoccupation, '. . . because the Allies were obviously going to have to land somewhere there in the end', in the words of Colonel Dick Barry, his chief of staff. From October 1941 until 1945 the French Section of SOE was commanded by Colonel Maurice Buckmaster, with a staff of some thirty men and women in Baker Street, supported by hundreds of training instructors, signals and supply personnel at 'the stations' all over England and Scotland. Like most of SOE, Buckmaster was not a professional soldier – indeed his only military experience had been gained as a cadet in the Eton Officers' Training Corps, on an Intelligence course in 1940, and as a liaison officer with the Free French on the Dakar expedition. Before the war, he had been a senior executive of Ford in France, and one of his staff said, not without respect, that 'he brought the optimism of a sales director into Baker Street'. His enthusiasm and energy made a great contribution to French Section's success, although the reverse of these qualities as a certain lack of scepticism: 'He believed that all his geese were swans,' according to a senior SOE officer. Buckmaster's deep respect and feeling for the agents whom he sent into France were shared by all his staff. They never achieved a battlefield commander's resigned detachment about losses. When mistakes were made, it was almost always because French Section had been too ready to believe that too much was being achieved in the field. Their greatest difficulty throughout the war was accurately to assess the achievements and potential of networks in the field when there were no troops to inspect, no battlefields upon which to measure yards won or lost. Colonel Barry said: 'One would hear that such-and-such a network was very efficient, but it was all hearsay. One never saw the bloody thing.'

French Section has been the subject of some misunderstanding since the war. General Gubbins and the operational chief of the Western Europe department, Robin Brook, exercised rather more control of operations in France, and Colonel Buckmaster perhaps a little less, than has generally been recognized. F played the central role in sending officers to France to assess the capabilities of Resistance groups and to arrange arms deliveries to them. By June 1944 there were some forty French Section networks each operating with at least one British-trained agent. But throughout most of France, British officers did not control the Resistance or lead it into action. It was not their business to use a gun, except in self-defence. Their vital function was to act as a catalyst for Resistance, to make it possible for Frenchmen to translate their own will into action. They sought to teach, to encourage, and to convey the hopes and wishes of London. Most lacked the temperament or training to act as military commanders in the field, a function that former French regular soldiers undertook in most areas.

The operations of the Das Reich Division involved five of French Section's networks in southern and central France, and it will become apparent that in almost all their areas, as throughout the rest of France, the impetus for Resistance came from within. To the end, local commanders jealously guarded their right to command their own men. Some surrendered it latterly to De Gaulle's French nominees. Very occasionally, they accepted the direction of an Englishman of outstanding personal force, such as George Starr. But throughout the war, the most important function of the British staff in Baker Street was to search out, train and dispatch men and women of exceptional character, capable of moving others by sheer force of personality. In the early years of F Section, they were obliged to select agents who were capable of living a cover story, of acting as something close to the traditional image of the spy. By late 1943 and early 1944, as the para-military role of the Resistance developed, agents who could scarcely speak more than schoolboy French were being dispatched to the wilder rural regions. From beginning to end, the agents who failed were almost all those who lacked the inner strength, the lack of need to confide in others while themselves encouraging confidences, that was essential to their curious calling. Yet it is striking to notice that there was absolutely no common denominator between the men and women of SOE beyond their courage. There was no *genus* agent as there was a *genus* Guards officer, bomber pilot, even *résistant*. Each was entirely an individual, often whimsical and elusive.

Once these agents had gone to France, Baker Street could seldom give them useful tactical instructions about what to attack or where to go. The staff knew too little about conditions on the spot. Signals traffic was generally restricted to brief practical messages about the number of men an agent believed could be mobilized in a given area, and about rendezvous for the dropping of arms, explosives and money – the last always an essential lubricant in making local Resistance groups susceptible to reason. F section knew a great deal about the conditions of life in France – ration cards, train times, German repressive measures – but very little about the detailed military situation. While SIS, through Ultra, was reading many German troop deployments and readiness states, virtually no military intelligence was passed on to French Section. Resistance was regarded as a strategic weapon. Baker Street was seldom brought into Allied planning debates, and Gubbins never achieved the place that he sought on the Chiefs of Staff Committee.

A perceptive SOE officer who served with distinction in France remarked that 'there was no atmosphere of brilliance in Baker Street – just shrewd, sensible people working very hard indeed'. Beyond Buckmaster, the most familiar figures were Gerry Morel, the Operations Officer – thought by some to be a trifle lightweight for his role; 'BP' – Bourne-Paterson, a professional accountant who handled finance; Selwyn Jepson, a successful novelist who fulfilled the critical role of recruiting officer; and Vera Atkins, wryly pseudonymized by George Millar in his excellent book about his SOE experiences, *Maquis*, as 'the intelligent gentlewoman'. Coolly handsome, very tough, shrewd, quick, Miss Atkins (for she held no rank until she became a WAAF squadron-leader in August 1944 and seldom wore a uniform) was regarded by many people as the critical force in French Section. In Baker Street's years of almost chronic crisis, Vera was the woman never seen to lose her head.

Her father had been in the timber business. She was largely educated in France, and travelled widely in Europe before the war, learning to take shorthand in three languages. In 1940 she was living at home with her mother and working in Civil Defence when the superb British facility for word-of-mouth recruiting sought her out for French Section. She came to Baker Street as a secretary on a month's trial, and ended the war with an absolute grasp of every aspect of F's affairs. It was Vera who kept the signal log and card index that were almost the only written records. Much of the Section work seemed to be done at night, and again and again she, Buckmaster or Morel would find themselves catching two or three hours' sleep on a camp bed in the office before waking to read the latest signals brought by dispatch rider from the huge radio stations at Crendon and Poundon on the Oxfordshire–Buckinghamshire border. In a very English way, although they worked in conditions of such intimacy, they saw little of each other outside the office. Vera's mother was allowed to know nothing of the reasons for her endlessly absent lifestyle. One morning when she came home from Tempsford at breakfast time, Mrs Atkins said with a sigh: 'Well, I hope at the end of all this he makes an honest woman of you, dear.' A Frenchman who was trained in England by F Section was among those who much admired Vera. He nerved himself to make a pass, but in the end could not go through with it – he was too frightened of her.

At the beginning of 1944, French Section faced a crisis: hundreds of thousands of Frenchmen were now believed to be ready to join an uprising when the Allies landed, but there were arms for only a tiny fraction of them. It required an average of twenty-five RAF bomber sorties to drop arms for 1,000 *résistants*. Each night, the RAF was dispatching enough bombers on a single raid to Germany to arm 30,000 *résistants*, but the Air Staff and Sir Arthur Harris resolutely refused to divert more than twenty-three Halifaxes to the needs of SOE throughout north-western Europe. The Chiefs of Staff showed little interest in the problem: they regarded General De Gaulle and the Resistance as a potential political liability, rather than an actual military asset. During the February moon period, against 1,500 tons of arms landed in Yugoslavia, France received only 700 tons. In desperation, the Free French and SOE for once made common cause in turning to the Prime Minister.

Churchill did not disappoint them. He had already been influenced by impressive pleas from leading Frenchmen, among them Emmanuel d'Astier de la Vigerie. At a meeting on 27 February attended by Selborne, Sinclair the Air Minister, and representatives of Gubbins and De Gaulle, Churchill over-rode the airmen, and decreed that supply-dropping to France should become the second priority of Bomber Command, whenever aircraft could be spared from the Battle of Berlin. In the last quarter of 1943, the RAF had dropped 139 tons of arms into France. In the first quarter of 1944, this rose to 938 tons. In the second quarter, with American help, it reached 2,689 tons. Just over half of all these weapons went to F Section circuits, the remainder to those liaising with RF.

But the Allied invasion planners at SHAEF were less than delighted by the Prime Minister's intervention. 'We cannot hope to equip all the Resistance bodies to the extent we wish to,' said a SHAEF memorandum of 28 February. For the purposes of the invasion, all Allied Resistance and behind-the-lines commando operations were being co-ordinated by Special Forces headquarters, a specially created body answerable to Eisenhower, despite protests from Koenig. Throughout the winter of 1943 and the spring of 1944, the representatives of SFHQ debated plans for the participation of Resistance in Overlord. But to their increasing dismay, they found that the planners at SHAEF took little interest in the hopes and ambitions of guerillas and saboteurs. 'It is unfortunate that Resistance only gets "support by results",' wrote SHAEF's G-3 Operations Department in answer to a protest from SFHQ, 'and never ahead of results. The fact remains that owing to the nature of its indefinite contribution, Resistance has to prove itself before getting the support necessary. . . .'

After the initial Allied landing in Normandy, the decisive problem was to prevent the Germans from building up their counter-attack against the beach-head more rapidly than the Allies could move reinforcements across the Channel to strengthen it. If the Germans could move unimpeded, predicted the Joint Planning Staff, by D+60 they could have a theoretical fifty-six divisions (with a strength equivalent to thirty-seven Allied units) deployed against thirty-six Allied divisions in France. SHAEF Intelligence staffs had created a mass of detailed projections of German troop movements in the first days after the Allied landings:

> . . . Assuming seventy trains are required to move a Panzer division; that it will take six hours to collect the trains; four hours to load; that forty-eight trains can move in twenty-four hours, given two main lines, ninety-six trains can move in twenty-four hours . . . one and a half hours' minimum move-off time. . . . Assume two hours to pass a point . . . tracked vehicles are unlikely to move over 100 miles by road, or wheeled vehicles more than 150. . . .

Through Ultra, they were reading almost every German monthly equipment state. They knew, for instance, that '2 Sugar Sugar Panzer Div', as the decrypters incongruously recorded the Das Reich, was short of 257 trucks, had only two of a complement of seventeen tracked artillery tractors, and was 2,001 rifles and 546 machine pistols short of complement. But SHAEF consistently overestimated both the speed at which the German units in the West would be ordered to Normandy, and the pace at which they would move once they had been set in motion.

They had to. It was their business to plan for a 'worst case' situation. After much argument among the airmen and heart-searching by the Prime Minister about the cost in civilian life, it was agreed that Allied bombers should carry out an intensive bombardment of seventy-two critical railway junctions in France during the months before D-Day. To conceal the location of the landings, the attacks would be spread throughout the north and centre of the country. Air Chief Marshal Tedder, Deputy Supreme Commander, rejected proposals for concentrating the attack on rail bridges, on the ground that these were too difficult to hit. The bombers would go for major rail centres, on the basis that even those which missed their aiming point would probably damage other rail installations.

The Free French, appalled by the prospective casualties, considered the possibility that the rail system could be immobilized by a general strike of SNCF workers from D-Day. But the idea was rejected not only because of the difficulty of carrying it out, but because it was essential to maintain some communication with the great cities of France in order to feed their populations: 'It was unthinkable to compel 400,000 people to take to the *maquis* . . . and the total strangulation of the network would cause a famine.' Contrary to the accounts of some Resistance historians, it was never intended that the entire rail network of France should come to a halt after D-Day.

But the other obvious course, keenly advocated by SOE, of attacking the railways by sabotage at minimal risk to civilian life, was politely brushed aside by the planners. 'The weight of air effort necessary to produce results comparable to those achieved by the SOE/SO option would certainly be very considerable,' wrote Kingston McLoughry, Air Commodore Plans and Operations at Allied Air Forces HQ, on 10 February. He went on:

However, since these operations must necessarily involve a large measure of chance, it would be unwise to rely on their success to the extent of reducing the planned air effort. Furthermore, the cutting of railway tracks produces only a temporary effect which could not contribute materially to the general disruption of the enemy's rail communications. For these reasons the results of SOE/SO operations should be regarded only as a bonus, although this may admittedly be a valuable one.

General Morgan added a note to the same file: 'I agree with you entirely that we must continue to do as we have in the past, and treat any dividend we may get out of SOE as a windfall. . . .'

Through all the debates that continued until the eve of D-Day about the role of the French Resistance, this was the unchanging view of the Allied planners. The Resistance should be encouraged to create whatever havoc it could for the Germans, but no part of the Overlord plan should be made dependent on Resistance success. This attitude must have been reinforced by a modest experiment carried out in southern France in December 1943. Local Resistance groups were allotted fifty rail targets, to be attacked on receipt of an 'Action Message' from London, of the kind that would be transmitted across all France on D-Day. The message was duly sent. A few weeks later a full report reached London. Of the fifty targets specified, fourteen had been attacked, together with a further twelve chosen on local initiative by *résistants*. SHAEF was not greatly impressed. One of the officers who served in SHAEF's G-3 division in 1944, liaising with SOE and SFHQ, remarked:

In the normal course of events, if one makes a military plan, provides the forces and avoids some Act of God, there is a good chance that the plan will be carried out. But in the case of guerillas, there is never any certainty whatever that the plan will be carried out. It is unthinkable to make a major military operation dependent on irregular co-operation.

But to the Free French, the role of Resistance on D-Day was not a mere matter of military judgment: it was the critical moment in the resurrection of France. The overwhelming concern of De Gaulle's staff was to ensure the liberation of the largest possible area of their country as rapidly as possible. They were deeply dismayed by the great Allied transport bombing programme. The lawyer Marcel Brault, alias Jérôme, who came to London from the Rhône Valley early in 1944 and played a leading role in persuading the Prime Minister to reinforce the Resistance, wrote in February:

The French population has become very discouraged by the postponement of the invasion which had been expected last autumn, by the Vichy propaganda which has called attention to the terrorism in the Resistance groups, and finally by the slow progress of the Allied armies in Italy. It could become absolutely apathetic if aerial bombing is intensified without a clear indication of its necessity.

Colonel Passy was among the pessimists about the real prospects of a mass uprising in France on D-Day. But many others among De Gaulle's men had a spectacular vision of open insurrection in southern and central France, where the Germans were thinly spread and great tracts of broken country lent themselves readily to guerilla warfare. There was discussion of possible Resistance 'redoubts' in which great masses of *maquisards* might assemble, and to which they might withdraw if they were driven back on to the defensive by German counter-attacks. Although all these misconceived notions were finally quashed, one of the most serious errors of omission in the weeks before D-Day was that *résistants* were not discouraged with nearly sufficient force from concentrating in arms when the Action Messages came. Some groups were even left by London and Algiers with a clear idea that they were expected to gather *en masse*. This confusion in high places was caused by doubt about just what would happen when the Action Messages were sent. It was indirectly responsible for the tragedies of the Vercors, the Glières and several lesser slaughters inflicted upon *résistants*.

On 7 May 1944 Churchill cabled President Roosevelt:

Massigli handed me this morning a memorandum concerning Allied bombardments of French targets, expressing the serious psychological effect they are having on the French Resistance groups when the loss of human life obtained does not seem to correspond with the results obtained, notably in the case of stations and factories in occupied districts. It is suggested that sabotage operations would achieve a better result without risk of life.

The President disagreed, and the Allied military commanders almost unanimously followed him. A senior British staff officer scribbled upon the Free French blueprint for Resistance and D-Day:

This plan gives the impression that the object of Overlord is to support the operations of the French Resistance, eg by drawing off enemy armour from freed zones, and not the other way round. . . .

The French at all times keep in mind the fact that they have the economy of their country to maintain during the period of military operations and after the war. They tend to put this consideration before military requirements.

The Allied air assault on the French transport system continued until and after D-Day on the 'worst case' assumption, that Resistance could contribute nothing to the dislocation of the communications. Between 9 February and 6 June 75,000 tons of bombs were dropped in 21,949 sorties by Bomber Command and the USAAF. The overwhelming consensus at SHAEF was that, when Resistance mobilized, its men should remain in small groups, and at all costs avoid concentrating in large bodies that invited German attack. However, the Allied commanders were obviously content to approve any Resistance plan that did not increase their commitment, and promised to cause difficulty to the Germans. The Free French had devoted enormous labour to compiling detailed plans for the destruction of key rail, road and telecommunications links on D-Day – Plans *Vert*, *Tortue* and *Violet*, in which both RF and F Sections had become deeply involved. SHAEF accepted these, on the basis that they cost nothing.

At a meeting at Special Forces headquarters on 20 May, Allied policy crystallized thus:

The immediate offensive task of Resistance will be to give every assistance possible towards the build-up of the lodgement area:

a) by the delaying of, and interference with, the movement of enemy reinforcements towards the area, and subsequently by attacks on his lines of supply.

b) by creating, in areas remote from the lodgement area, diversionary threats that the enemy cannot afford to neglect, thereby tying down a proportion of his available forces.

It must also be envisaged that, even in districts of vital importance to the enemy, the population may not remain inactive. Spontaneous popular activity may combine with the efforts of remaining Resistance to develop to a design of individually small but widespread guerilla activity.

An SFHQ memorandum of 4 June said: 'It cannot be foreseen how Resistance will react to Overlord. It is clear that we must, generally speaking, reinforce where Resistance is most strong. Our policy will therefore be largely opportunist.'

One critical dilemma was unresolved until the last moment: whether to attempt a selective mobilization of Resistance, sparing those areas most remote from and irrelevant to the Normandy battle from the inevitable consequences of German counter-attack. The overwhelming conclusion was that it was neither desirable nor possible to restrain whole areas of France from taking part at the great moment: 'In view of the fact that the spirit of Resistance groups throughout France is keyed up to a high pitch, and that a wave of patriotic enthusiasm is likely to sweep the country on D-Day, it is considered that any restraint placed on certain areas of organized Resistance on D-Day would only meet with partial success.'

Thus it was agreed that at the moment of the landings, all the *résistants* of France would be called to arms. Beyond the practical difficulties of restraining them, it was vital to keep the Germans in doubt for every possible day about the prospect of further Allied landings. Colonel Barry of SOE said: 'We were, in an absolutely hard-headed way, sacrificing Frenchmen to that purpose.' The Allied staffs expected that any benefits from Resistance would continue at best for a few days. 'It is probable that action . . . will be taken for a few days, after which stores and enthusiasm will begin to run low unless further instructions, backed by supplies, are speedily issued,' ran an SFHQ memorandum. By the end of May, there were believed to be around half a million active *résistants* in France. Of these, 10,000 were estimated to be already armed by RF Section in Region R5 – comprising the Dordogne, Corrèze, Haute-Vienne and Creuse – the principal battleground of the Das Reich, and some 9,000 in R4, south-westwards from the Lot; 16,000 men in R4 and 2,500 men in R5 were believed to be already armed by F Section. According to SFHQ figures, 75,975 Sten guns, 27,025 pistols, 9,420 rifles, 2,538 Brens, anti-tank rifles and bazookas, 285,660 grenades and 183 tons of explosives and ammunition had been dropped to the Resistance, of which a significant but unknown proportion had been unrecovered by reception committees or lost to the Germans. There was a chronic shortage of ammunition of all types. Most *résistants* possessed two, three, sometimes only a single magazine for their arms, and there were few reserves. They had no heavy weapons beyond a few bazookas, despite constant pleading from the bigger groups in the field. But there were excellent reasons for this. Heavy weapons required training and transport, to neither of which most *maquisards* had access. To be effective, they required stocks of ammunition which it would have been immensely difficult to drop and handle on the ground. The other serious obstacle to any complex or co-ordinated manoeuvre by large groups of *maquisards* was the complete absence of short-range radios.

Yet even with hindsight, it is difficult to fault the attitudes or the conduct of those in London who were responsible for organizing Resistance for D-Day. SOE and the Free French, concerned with supporting Resistance, had done everything possible with the resources they were granted. The Allied commanders charged with responsibility for Overlord were also eminently reasonable. Despite the claims of enthusiasts, a guerilla struggle in a major international war must always be a campaign on the margin. If the likely contribution of guerillas to victory is doubtful, then so also must be the resources expended upon them. General De Gaulle's preoccupation with restoring the soul of France could only be courteously acknowledged at SHAEF. In the spring of 1944 it would have been unthinkable, indeed hopelessly irresponsible, to cancel or curtail the transport bombing offensive which cost 12,000 French and Belgian civilian lives, in favour of reliance on the Resistance.

If there was a failure, it was in frankness towards the networks in the field. Inevitably, *résistants* were given an exaggerated notion of the importance of their role in the attack on communications. But it was less necessary that most were allowed to believe that Liberation would inexorably follow invasion within weeks, if not days; and that the creation of Resistance armies would be rewarded from London by massive supplies of arms and ammunition, probably also by reinforcements of regular parachutists.

SHAEF confidently expected that the Germans would throw every man, tank and gun they could bring to bear into the struggle to defeat the Allied armies on the beaches of Normandy. To any commander with a clear grasp of strategy, this was the overwhelming priority. Fundamentally it could not matter to the Germans what Resistance achieved in the Vercors, the Dordogne, or other areas remote from the north coast. Any insurrection could be crushed at leisure once the Allies were thrown back into the sea. If they secured a lodgement, then the loss of southern France scarcely mattered. The simple truth was that French Resistance was strongest in areas that strategically mattered least to the Germans – the Massif Central, the southwest, the Dordogne, the Corrèze and the Haute-Vienne. An important SHAEF paper of 28 February 1944 assumed that in their response to the Allied landings, '. . . the Germans will ignore local Resistance'. This was a fundamental – albeit perfectly rational – misjudgment of German thinking. Hitler's obsession with retaining every foot of his empire once again betrayed him. The Germans would deploy resources to repress Resistance on a scale the Allies had never conceived possible. In the first, vital days after the Allied landings, the German struggle to hold France against Frenchmen employed forces – above all, the 2nd SS Panzer Division – that could have made a vital contribution on the battlefield in Normandy. There are many tales of tragedy, reckless error and even absurdity among *résistants* in the chapters that follow. It must never be forgotten that the Germans' response was absurd only in its cost to their battle for France.

3 SOE: Southern France

Few of the British and French agents parachuted into France fired a shot in anger during the battles of June 1944. Their names will seldom recur during the story of the Das Reich's march through their sectors. But to understand what Resistance was on D-Day, and how it came to be what it was, it is essential to know something of the men and women who made it possible. For thousands of *résistants* taking up their Sten guns and their gammon bombs and embarking upon open warfare, D-Day was a beginning. But for the agents of SOE and De Gaulle's BCRA, it was the flowering of four years' labour, the end of the most difficult and nerve-racking period of Resistance. The British agent George Hiller exulted in the sense of release that D-Day brought: 'The beauty of life, the joys of spring, the stream of men and cars, the relief of being armed.'

Hiller was French Section's officer in the Lot, the region dominated by high limestone plateaux thick with scrub oak and sheep grazing that lies between the Dordogne and the Tarn, on the Das Reich division's direct route north. With his twenty-one-year-old wireless operator, Cyril Watney, he had been parachuted into France in January 1944 to make contact with a socialist Resistance organization named the Groupes Vény. Its tentacles were reported to extend through southern France from Marseille and Toulouse to the Lot and Limoges. Hiller's business was first to assess their potential, then to organize and arm the *résaux* – the networks – in the Lot.

He was born in Paris, the son of an English father and French mother, educated at *lycées* in Paris and London, then at Exeter College, Oxford. He had planned a career as a diplomat when the war intervened. Like a significant number of future French Section recruits, in 1939 he was a near-pacifist, and he joined the medical corps because he disliked the idea of killing people. Only in 1942 did he modify his opinions sufficiently to pass through Sandhurst and become an army officer. Then SOE's recruiters found him. He told his parents that he was being posted to the Middle East, but on the night of 7 January 1944, at the age of twenty-eight, this highly intelligent, sensitive, rather reserved young man landed near Quatre Routes high in the hills of the Lot to begin his career as a secret agent.

Like most F Section officers, Hiller and Watney suffered a severe shock of disorientation and bewilderment when they landed. Only moments after the reception committee had greeted them, the two Englishmen were appalled to see the headlights of a car approaching up the road. They flung themselves into a ditch as it passed, then were bemused to see the little group of *résistants* still standing nonchalantly by the roadside in its headlights. Sten guns under their arms. The two Englishmen agreed that there was a wide gulf between security as taught at their tradecraft school at Beaulieu and as practised in France. From the dropping zone they were driven to Quatre Routes. They spent their first nights in a creamery at the edge of the little village, until Watney was moved to a safe house from which he could transmit, and Hiller began his travels among the *résistants* of the Lot.

Like many men who found themselves behind enemy lines in World War II, Hiller was profoundly moved by his experience in the spring and summer of 1944. In the timescale of those days, Liberation still seemed far away and the German command of France still appeared unshakable. Many Frenchmen and women – especially among the business and official classes – had long since come to terms with their Occupiers, and feared and hated the Resistance as communist bandits who threatened the peace and stability of their communities. By no means all the girls who slept with the men of the Das Reich and others of the occupying army did so for money. Since the end of World War I, France had been a bitterly divided and fragmented society. 'Her position', Sir Denis Brogan has written, 'was unique. She was a victor, but she had in many ways the psychology of a defeated nation.' Many, perhaps most, French bourgeois in the 1930s feared fascism far less than communism. Peasants were profoundly embittered by the ceaseless betrayals of their politicians. Their distaste for authority extended from contempt for Paris to hatred of their local landlords and parish priests.

Religion was a waning influence in much of southern France by the 1940s. Most peasants, phlegmatically ploughing the fields and driving the oxen on their meagre farms, seemed to have set themselves apart from the war – indifferent both to the Allies and the Germans, concerned only with the crops and the seasons.

Yet beyond all these people, an utterly dedicated minority risked their lives, their families, everything they possessed to further the cause of Resistance. These were the men and women, whom he had never met before, to whom Hiller entrusted his own life. He was deeply moved by the strength of the bond created by the relationship between the hiders and the hidden. There was no common denominator among the *résistants*, except perhaps that their leaders in the Lot and the Dordogne seemed to come chiefly from the professional and small business classes, and were politically of the Left.

Jean and Marie Verlhac, already in their forties during the Occupation, were legendary *résistants*. Of fifty *parachutages* in their region, Jean organized the reception of nineteen. His wife Marie, a teacher who had been active for years in the trade union movement, was one of the brains and principal driving forces behind the growth of Resistance in the Lot. It was at their house that within days of his arrival Hiller prepared the charges for a local *résistant* to lay at the Ratier airscrew factory in Figeac, one of F Section's most successful acts of sabotage of the war. In the weeks that followed, Hiller was passed on from the hands of the Verlhacs to those of other men and women who sheltered him as he travelled through the region, meeting contacts and assessing the prospect of building upon them.

He spent many nights at the home of Georges Bru, a teacher in the little town of St Céré, a blunt, stocky figure with a genius for organizing and providing the unexpected. Late on those icy winter nights, Hiller would watch Bru come home blue with cold, his body wrapped with newspapers under his coat, after riding for hours around the region on his little moped on the business of the *réseau*. Despite an endless procession of clandestine visitors, his wife kept a spotless home, in which she seemed to be eternally cooking for her unexpected guests. Hiller watched fascinated as their two children did their homework at one end of the kitchen table, while the other was littered with explosives and Sten gun magazines. Sometimes the children cycled through the streets to look out for Germans or *miliciens*. It was uncanny how young they learned the reflexes of secrecy. One night, at the home of another schoolteacher in Figeac, named Odette Bach, Hiller was sitting in the kitchen when there was a knock at the front door. Pierrette, the Bach's five-year-old daughter, opened it to find a *gendarme* outside. He demanded whether anyone was at home. The child shook her head and replied unhesitatingly, '*Non*, *Monsieur*.' The *gendarme* departed. Hiller breathed again. Even thirty-five years later, Pierrette could not explain how she had known that she must lie except to shrug: '*Il y avait un ambiance* . . .' And she was still enough of a child to enjoy herself immensely one day when Hiller took her to the circus.

He marvelled at all these people, conscious of their fear, of all that they risked. The Bachs always seemed to him to be making a great effort to conceal their nervousness, yet their flat was known locally as 'the stray dogs' home' because Odette would never turn away a fugitive from Vichy or the Germans. Odette and Hiller talked for hours about their common pacifist backgrounds. Then it would be time for her to leave to go to her class. It was difficult to come to terms with the relative normalcy of life: taxes were paid, people were married and baptized, the peasants continued their simple lives sleeping on mattresses filled with maize, working in the fields in their blue smocks and black hats, shaving once a week on Sunday, baking bread in great wheels two feet across. Yet amidst all this, for Hiller and the *résistants* there was unceasing danger, the extra layer of clandestinity to add to all the practical difficulties of finding enough food to eat, renewing the endless permits for every aspect of daily life, and queueing for the simplest commodities.

The Germans were seldom seen outside the big towns. Occasionally a black Citroën would race down the road, and the village postmistress would telephone her counterpart a few kilometres away to warn her that Germans were on the way. Only Germans or agents of Vichy or the local doctor had access to petrol-driven cars. Perhaps twice a year, a village might suffer the passage of one of the notorious German punitive columns sent into the countryside wherever Resistance activity became conspicuous. The Dordogne suffered terribly from the attentions of Division B in 1943, and the Corrèze and Creuse from those of the Jesser column. That year 40,000 French men and women were arrested under suspicion of Resistance activities, and many of them had been deported to Germany, never to return. The risks for a British agent in the Lot or the Dordogne were less great than in Paris or Lyon. But the tension and fear, the certain knowledge of the price of capture, never altogether faded even in the happiest and most romantic moments of their secret lives. In notes for an uncompleted memoir of his experience with Resistance, Hiller scribbled long afterwards: 'Explain how very ordinary people can do it. . . . Many people were lifted out of their little lives, to be dropped down again afterwards. . . . Show the mixture of tension and light fantastic. . . . The extraordinary brotherhood, the immense enjoyment of being together, among ourselves, like children.'

Hiller likened his first weeks in France to learning to ride a bicycle – there was 'a quality of strangeness and uncertainty, everyone working in a fog'. He was dismayed by the lack of force displayed by some of the senior leaders of Resistance in the region, but conscious of his own lack of authority. His only influence sprang from his ability to conjure up money and arms. 'We were working on a number of uncertain variables: The weather. The amount available for the drop. The lack of information about what was going on around us. . . . The sense of isolation from London. The poor security.' He found himself frustrated by the immense effort and time that had to be wasted upon petty personal logistics – finding safe houses for Watney and his transmitter; getting a *gazogène* charcoal-burning car for travel; passing messages and receiving answers even over short distances when he was constantly on the move. It took weeks to lose the screaming self-consciousness that afflicted him in a public place: 'As I walked down the muddy high street with the debonair Jean at my side, I felt that everyone down to the dogs was staring at me. Loudspeakers were shouting: "Look at the Englishman, freshly arrived, there in the grey check suit with the brand-new beret!" '

Soon after his arrival, one of the Groupes Vény's colonels took him northwards to Limoges, the great grey metropolis of china manufacture, to talk to its local supporters. It was the first of many such trips: 'Limoges was a dangerous town – small enough for most people to know each other, yet large enough for strangers to pass unobserved. And Limoges was plentifully supplied with Gestapo agents, not all of them natives of the town.' Taillaux was the Groupes Vény's principal contact in Limoges,

> . . . a very cautious man, thoroughly drilled in clandestine work, he carried even into his discussions the habit of keeping negotiations on various subjects separate, and of telling no one more than they needed to know. . . .

The Taillaux, like all people who continued to lead legal lives, were continually on the alert. If the German or French police wanted to arrest them, they had only to come and pick them up. They were well-known local figures leading busy working lives, yet somehow into these they had to fit in their clandestine work and meetings. And yet like many thousands of others, they carried on, because as normal citizens they were able to do things that would no longer be possible if they went underground.

Hiller and the colonel slept at the railway station, inconspicuous among hundreds of other stranded wartime travellers and the incessant clanking of rolling stock through the night. The Englishman dozed, gazing at the colonel asleep beside him: 'This old man with his patched-up body could have chosen to live on his pension in his flat in Nice, yet here he was with his worn shoes and his battered overcoat, sleeping in railway waiting-rooms and dodging the Germans. Luckily, he looked a harmless enough figure as he slept with his head near the red rosette of the Legion of Honour. . . .'

As the weeks went by, Hiller's admiration for the *résistants* did not diminish, but he began to perceive that their networks were far less powerful than London had supposed: 'I had been there long enough for my initial optimism to have worn off. The whole organization was much weaker than I had imagined.' As they built up the clandestine arms dumps with the fruits of the *parachutages*, he became conscious that there was no precise plan as to how they were to be used: 'It was all rather vague, but then so were our ideas of what would happen after D-Day.'

Many of the *résistants* were simply not by temperament warlike people. They were men and women of great moral courage who sought to do whatever they could to oppose the Germans. But neither by background nor inclination were they killers. 'It was not, on the whole, a heroic area,' wrote Hiller. By this, of course, he did not seek to diminish the courage of local *résistants*, but to describe the difficulty of rousing the sleepy, rustic communities of the Lot to violent action. Hiller wrote later that he regretted wasting so much time on the movement's internal quarrels and jealousies. Perhaps he should have 'started fewer schemes and followed them through; should have been more concrete; [adopted] a more aggressive policy, more firmness and ruthlessness'. He was too hard on himself. He did not know that his were the fortunes and difficulties of most Allied agents all over France.

Hiller also encountered the universal difficulty in handling the *maquis* – the groups of young *résistants* who lived entirely outside the law in the woods and hills. Most were young evaders from the STO, and some were more enthusiastic about avoiding forced labour than about taking part in positive action against the Germans. In the Lot, the most active and numerous *maquis* were those of the communist FTP, to whom many of the wilder spirits defected, tiring of the AS policy of patience until D-Day. Hiller wrote:

Organizing the *maquis* was difficult. Getting boys together in twos and threes; stealing camping equipment from government stocks; buying food. Getting a lorry made available for hasty flight. Large and regular supplies of tobacco were essential if morale was to remain good. The boys were often slovenly, and few had done military service. They wanted immediate raids. They had no amusements. Occasionally, on a very rare night, there might be an operation, yet every night in the moon period we were out on the dropping ground. The boys were pathetically grateful when they were given a small job in the outside world. Once a drunk and bored boy simply emptied his pistol into the air.

After a while, we got used to it all. We lived with the moon and the weather. Hopelessly and impatiently waiting during the non-moon periods, then full of hope at the beginning of the new moon, when the weather prospects would be earnestly discussed. The precious days would pass, and there would be no BBC messages for us. Sometimes the weather was obviously bad, sometimes it was fine and we had to tell everybody that the weather was bad over London. . . . At other times, there would be a great many messages, although none for us. We were envious of others, and wondered if we were not being forgotten. . . . We never managed to become indifferent to the moon periods, but we forgot all about hard and fast plans and just tackled things as they came. But I sometimes thought how nice it would be for a change to have to deal with a situation in which all the factors were readily ascertainable, and predictable in their development.

The Groupes Vény's strength in the Lot had grown from twelve in January 1941 to forty-eight in January 1942, 401 in July 1943 with eighty-five *maquis*, and 623 in January 1944 with 346 *maquisards*. It achieved a peak in July 1944 of 156 AS and 2,037 *maquisards* after the great D-Day mobilization. To the Frenchmen with whom he worked, Hiller was the very image of an English gentleman of *L'Intelligence Service*, to which all France was convinced that every British agent belonged. He became much liked and respected in his area. While many agents had no contact whatever with neighbouring circuits, in the late spring of 1944 he began to work increasingly closely with his neighbours in the Dordogne and Corrèze. When he wrote of his assignment's extraordinary combination of tension and 'the light fantastic', he must have been thinking of such moments as Soleil's banquet in the heart of the Dordogne.

Soleil was a ferocious, semi-literate, twenty-three-year-old communist, originally from Avignon and more recently from the darker corners of Marseille. His real name was René Cousteille. 'Fearless and unscrupulous, a born leader, small, dark, twitching with energy', in Hiller's words, the little tough had formed a *maquis* on the south side of the Dordogne river, close to the marvellous golden hilltop village of Belvès. From his camps, he ruled a great swath of the region. He had forced every inhabitant of the neighbouring hamlets to conceal some of his petrol and oil reserves, according to Hiller to ensure that all of them would suffer if any was indiscreet. In the spring of 1944, a young Englishman named Peter Lake – 'Jean-Pierre' of F Section – toured Soleil's *maquis* in miserable discomfort on the pillion of a '*moto*', holding weapon training classes for an eager audience. Jean-Pierre was not happy with the young bandits. He sensed that the slightest misplaced word could cause him to disappear rapidly and painfully. Soleil had already threatened to kill his SOE colleague, 'Commandant Jack', if he cut off supplies of arms. His *maquis* was feared and detested throughout most of the surrounding countryside for the ruthless killing of any man suspected of collaboration, and Soleil's orders to his men to seize whatever they needed from whoever possessed it. But Commandant Jack respected Soleil's courage and toughness, and armed his men because he believed that they would excel where it mattered – in fighting the Germans. The *maquis* prospered, and one night Hiller found himself solemnly invited by the young killer to a formal banquet, with after-dinner entertainment in the form of a lecture on small arms by Jean-Pierre.

The castle chosen by Soleil's nineteen-year-old deputy, the Baron, was a fine example of late eighteenth-century Gothic, hidden away in a wood on the banks of the Dordogne. As we approached, we were repeatedly challenged, and we found that detachments of Spaniards armed with numerous Bren guns guarded all the approaches. Their French was poor, and they did their job so conscientiously that we were glad to get inside the castle. There we found the village leaders, some fifty fat, middle-aged men, dressed in their Sunday best. Jean-Pierre fussed around like a good lecturer making sure that all the exhibits were ready. Against a background of tapestries and wrought iron stood a U-shaped table covered with linen and flowers and candelabra and fine porcelain. In front of each plate was a menu bearing the badge of the Groupe Soleil, a flaming sun and an inscription recording the occasion. The Baron, once he had been duly congratulated, explained that he had had great difficulty in finding a competent sign writer. For the rest, he merely told the butler and his wife, who lived there permanently, that the castle was requisitioned for the night, and there would be so many guests. They in turn prepared everything as if it were a formal peacetime dinner party. The service was perfect, and the butler and his staff impassive. But we could not help trying to guess from the fleeting expressions on his face what was going on in his mind as he leaned forward to pour the wine. He was probably scandalized at the way these ruffians had invaded the house, to which they would never have been invited before the war. He was probably frightened, too, that the dinner might end with a surprise raid by the Germans. Then, as the dinner went on, he seemed to thaw as he listened to the quiet conversation of these people who all appeared too young or too old to be terrorists. In the end, he was listening with interest to the panegyric on the Sten.

The inaugural lecture began very late. Some of us, in fact, thought that it would never take place after so many speeches and toasts. But we had counted without Jean-Pierre's determination, or the surprising resilience of the village's leaders, who had taken the banquet in their stride. Not only was the lecture a great success, but when we went off to bed in the small hours, Jean-Pierre and the fat men were still busy arguing about some of the finer points of the Bren gun.

Jean-Pierre – Peter Lake – was a twenty-nine-year-old diplomat's son who had been a merchant banker in West Africa when the war began, and took part in an early SOE operation in that area before being transferred to French Section and parachuted near Limeuil on Easter Sunday 1944. His French was very poor, but by that stage F was not dropping secret agents, but paramilitary instructors. A more serious deficiency in all F's training, however, was that in the interests of remaining apolitical they gave agents no briefing whatever on the intricacies of local Resistance politics, and many of them were confused and bewildered to discover the byzantine complications in the field. Lake was taken from his landing ground to the home of a carpenter named Charles Brouillet – '*Le bolshévik*', as he was known locally – in the enchanting village of Siorac-en-Périgord. It was a picaresque introduction to Resistance, eating a splendid 4 am breakfast with the recklessly confident *résistants*. '*Ha, ha, mon cher Jean-Pierre*', said Brouillet happily. '*Siorac a deux mille habitants, et sur ces deux mille habitants, il y a deux mille résistants!*' He confided that many of their arms were stored in the roof of the church: '*Tu vois, à l'église, c'est sous la protection du bon Dieu!*'

Yet in catching the genuine, extraordinary romance of secret survival and the preparations for war in one of the most beautiful regions of all France, it is essential never to forget its darker face. Those whom Soleil's men threatened or robbed hated him as bitterly as the Germans. Each of those at that exotic banquet could never entirely erase from his mind the fear of betrayal, the knowledge that capture meant certain imprisonment and torture, concluded only by an appallingly lonely death. So much sentiment has been expended upon British agents and *résistants* killed by the Germans that it is sometimes forgotten that the Germans were perfectly entitled by the laws of war to shoot them. It was the fact that execution was invariably accompanied by such ghastly cruelty that made their fate seem so intolerable. Commandant Jack had only succeeded to responsibility for the eastern Dordogne and Corrèze in March, after the capture in

Brive-la-Gaillarde and dispatch to Buchenwald of his commanding officer, one of SOE's greatest agents, Harry Peulevé.

Commandant Jack – officially Nestor – was a big, robust, handsome, compulsively adventurous twenty-two-year-old who was assumed by all the *maquis* to be a British officer. In reality, he was the Frenchman Jacques Poirier, who concealed his nationality until the moment of Liberation to safeguard the lives of his family. He was one of those fortunate spirits blessed with the ability to inspire laughter and affection wherever he went. It was Poirier who, with Peulevé, armed most of the *maquisards* of the Corrèze and Dordogne who met the Das Reich division after 6 June.

Poirier had reached SOE after an odyssey remarkable even by Baker Street standards. He had been destined for a career in the air force, following his father, until the war intervened and the family retreated into the Unoccupied Zone near Nice. Young Jacques was running small errands for the local Resistance when he encountered Harry Peulevé, making a painful escape to England after being badly injured parachuting into France as one of SOE's wireless operators. Poirier formed an immediate intense admiration for the Englishman, and offered to go with him across the Pyrenees. After many adventures, the two men reached Gibraltar and Peulevé was at once flown back to England. Poirier had to wait rather longer for transport. When at last he arrived in Bristol, to his intense fury he was detained for five days for screening. He was then taken to London as a prisoner, before being handed over to SOE.

He never remembered asking to go back to France – he always took it for granted, just as he assumed and insisted that it would be with Peulevé. French Section put him through the usual training courses under the name of Peters. He had some cheerful evenings in London, some of them with Violette Szabo. Then, one night late in 1943, he found himself at Tempsford airfield, being handed the customary gold cigarette case as a parting present from Buckmaster, *en route* to join Peulevé in the Corrèze.

Poirier reached the soil of France to find that his dropping aircraft had ejected him more than 100 miles from the rendezvous. He walked for some hours to reach a station, survived asking for a ticket in English, and fell asleep on the train to wake up surrounded by a compartment full of Germans. They mercifully ignored him, and within a few hours he found himself in the substantial town of Brive-la-Gaillarde, deserted in Sunday silence. He could think of no less conspicuous refuge than a church, and sat through four masses before slipping discreetly out of the town to a nearby hillside for the night. The next morning, he found Peulevé.

In the months that followed, Poirier and his commanding officer travelled ceaselessly through the eastern Dordogne and Corrèze, meeting the men of the AS and the FTP, arranging *parachutages* and holding weapon training classes. Roger Beauclerk – 'Casimir' – was parachuted to act as Poirier's wireless operator, and settled down to the usual nerve-racking, monotonous existence. The operators suffered terribly from boredom between transmissions, unable to wander because of their schedules, moved constantly from safe house to safe house to avoid the risk of German direction-finding, and thus never able to relax amidst established relationships. They had too much time to think, and too few of the compensations of the agents. Many found the strain intolerable unless, like Cyril Watney, they were blessed with unshakeable patience and good nature.

In March 1944 Poirier slipped away for a few days to visit his mother, now living in the foothills of the Pyrenees. By the merest chance, one night he was sitting in the kitchen listening with half an ear to the BBC *messages personnels* – which it was wildly unlikely would bear any special signal for him – when he caught an electrifying phrase: '*Attention à Nestor! Message important pour Nestor! Ne retournez pas chez vouz! Jean est tres malade!*' Peulevé and his wireless operator Roland Malraux had been arrested – by terrible ill luck, denounced by a neighbour as suspected Jewish black marketeers. George Hiller heard the news, and with immense effort and ingenuity managed to have the warning broadcast to Poirier. Jacques took the train to Martel, high in the Lot, and sought out the Verlhacs who were astounded to see him, because they believed that he had already been taken by the Germans.

Contrary to popular belief, it is never expected that an agent will tell his captors nothing. The most critical achievement that is expected of him is silence for forty-eight hours, until warnings can be circulated and men take to hiding. Then he can begin to reveal small things, odd names and places. Eventually, under extreme duress, it is recognized that he may begin to talk of more vital matters. Peulevé revealed nothing important under torture in Fresnes prison, or later in Buchenwald. But the Germans had a description of Poirier. He vanished into hiding while they combed every possible contact point in Corrèze and east Dordogne for him.

Roland Malraux's brother André said that the region was obviously too hot to hold Poirier for the time being. He suggested a cooling-off period, in Paris. This young, still impressionable ex-student found himself hiding in the flat of André Gide, with its window looking out on the courtyard of Laval's Interior Ministry. He walked by the Seine between Malraux and Albert Camus. To his lifelong regret, he never remembered a word of what either man said.

Of all the extraordinary figures who held the stage in the Resistance of Dordogne and Corrèze in the summer of 1944, none surpassed André Malraux. Young men like Poirier, Hiller, Lake – so worldly about so much in their secret lives – found themselves awed and fascinated by this mountebank of genius who thrust himself upon them. He was already a legend – the author of *La Condition Humaine*, exotic traveller, film-maker, commander in Spain of the Republican fighter squadron he himself had raised, *Malraux-le-rouge* who had his uniforms tailored by Lanvin.

Yet his record as a *résistant* from 1940 to 1944 had not been impressive. After serving with a French tank unit in the débâcle of 1940, he retired to the Côte d'Azur to work – though he wrote nothing of merit – and to reflect, in circumstances of sybaritic ease by the standards of the world in those days. In September 1941, Jean-Paul Sartre and Simone de Beauvoir cycled the length of France to appeal for his support in Resistance. 'They lunched on chicken Maryland, exquisitely prepared and served. Malraux heard Sartre out very courteously, but said that for the time being at any rate, action of any sort would be quite useless. He was relying on Russian tanks and American planes to win the war.' Later, when the *Combat résistants* also approached him, he asked simply: 'Have you arms? No? Have you money? No? Then it's not serious. . . .' Towards the end of 1943, he moved with his mistress Clara to a comfortable little château on the Dordogne. Still he showed no urge to have any part of Resistance.

Yet when his brother Roland was captured – his other brother Claude was also working for SOE – Malraux presented himself to the Resistance of Dordogne and Corrèze, quite without humility, as a man ready to take command. He was forty-two. It is a remarkable tribute to his force of personality that 'Colonel Berger', as he styled himself after the hero of one of his novels, quickly persuaded Poirier, Hiller and others to treat him as an equal in their counsels. He began to travel with them around the region, addressing *maquisards* and attending conferences. He created the notion of a joint Anglo-French (and later, with the coming of OSS agents, American) council to bring together the Resistance groups of the region, with himself at its head. Malraux had left behind the mood of 1941, when he wrote that 'a German defeat would be a victory for the Anglo-Saxons, who will colonize the world and probably France. . . .' But he was still Red enough to give the clenched fist salute. Chain-smoking English cigarettes from *parachutages* (a status symbol among *maquisards*), he would talk off-handedly yet at breakneck speed about 'old man Churchill', 'that chap De Gaulle , Chinese art, the acoustics of a château dining-room, 'occasionally interjecting "Your turn now!", which it was as well not to take too literally as an invitation to reply'. When later captured, he claimed to have declared himself to the Germans as 'the military chief of this region. . . . I have nothing to confess. I have been your opponent since the day of the Armistice.' He also convinced himself that his captors were of the notorious Das Reich Division, although by then they were a month gone from the department.

The FTP regarded Malraux with withering scorn and took no notice whatever of his opinions, and even the AS had their reservations about him. But Malraux visibly enjoyed the confidence of the F Section officers, and encouraged the *résistants* to believe that he himself was an SOE-trained officer with important influence on *parachutages* and weapons and money supplies. By the summer of 1944, he had become a familiar figure to the *résistants* of the region.

Asked many years later about the lack of substance in Malraux's claims and achievements as a *résistant*, Jacques Poirier paused for a moment. Then he said: 'There are a few people born in every century who are important not for what they do, but for what they say. Malraux was one of those.' All of them were mesmerized by his obsessive fluency, the torrent of ideas that flooded over their heads in conversation. Visiting the camps of bored young *maquisards* in the torrid heat of the summer woods, Poirier knew how to talk pragmatically to their leaders. But he watched fascinated as Malraux leaped on to the roof of a *gazogène* and harangued the guerillas about the glory of France, the dignity of struggle, the nobility of sacrifice. It was irresistible, and it brought tears to their eyes. Poirier quoted a favourite word of Malraux's – *un farfelu*, a compulsive activist who is also half-crazy. Malraux had for years been obsessed with the story of Lawrence of Arabia, and had himself always been a compulsive role-player. There is no doubt that while other Frenchmen in the woods of the Corrèze in 1944 thought of the next *parachutage*, the next cigarette, Malraux saw himself acting out a great heroic drama.

Some *maquisards* joked about his unsoldierly appearance – a certain physical clumsiness, one eye chronically weeping, Basque beret tilted, the constant sniffing. Poirier admitted that it was difficult to concentrate Malraux's attention on practical military problems. The SOE officer would urge: 'André, we must discuss the blowing of that bridge.' But Malraux would say: 'No, tonight I think I would prefer to hear Casimir play the piano.' And in the château that was now their headquarters, in the failing summer evening light Malraux would sit lost in thought, gazing at the ceiling, while their wireless operator played his brilliant repertoire of classical music surrounded by a little group of half-naked, half-literate *maquisards* lying beside their weapons.

But Malraux's personal courage was beyond question. One day, he and Poirier were driving together down a road when they were hailed by a *maquisard* who warned them of German vehicles ahead. Neither man wished to be the first to suggest turning back. Poirier drove nervously but defiantly onwards, until inevitably they rounded a bend to meet a German tank. Poirier desperately swung the car in a screaming turn. Malraux seized the small automatic pistol from his belt and absurdly – yet to Poirier, also nobly – stood up and emptied it at the tank.

Miraculously they escaped to tell the tale, although later that summer Malraux was less fortunate. He was with George Hiller in a car that ran headlong into a German column. Malraux was slightly injured and captured. Hiller was terribly wounded and was rescued, close to death, by Cyril Watney and a group of *maquisards*. He was operated upon under the most primitive circumstances in an abandoned presbytery high in the hills of the Lot, and narrowly survived. Malraux was delivered unscathed from imprisonment at the liberation of Toulouse, not without incurring the scepticism of some *résistants* who inquired acidly how he had 'conned' the Germans out of a firing squad.

That April with Poirier in Paris, Malraux had been as flamboyant as ever. He took him to dine at Prunier, relishing his immediate recognition by the head waiter. He introduced the young Frenchman to Camus as a British officer. Poirier began to be infected by the other man's style. One morning, walking up the Champs-Elysées, he saw a huge German shepherd dog in the window of a pet shop, and knew instantly that he had to possess it. Ten minutes later and 10,000 francs of SOE's money the poorer, he was leading it past the Arc de Triomphe when he met Malraux. Even the *farfelu*'s sense of discretion was appalled: 'Jack, you're crazy – you're in Paris to *hide*.' But Poirier would not be parted from the dog. He arranged for it to be taken down to the Dordogne, and all through that wild summer of 1944, Dick the dog rode with him on the wing of his car, trotted behind him through the camps in the woods, and slept in his room at the château where, with increasing confidence in their own power, the *maquisards* made their headquarters.

'I was always a château type at heart,' said Poirier wryly. In the weeks before D-Day, he and a band of Soleil's *maquisards* took over the lovely Château le Poujade, set high on a hill above Urval, overlooking the great river and its irregular patchwork of fields and vineyards in the distance. Only once were they disturbed by the Germans. Early one morning, a *maquisard* guard burst in to report that a German column led by armoured cars was crawling up the long, narrow road towards the château. Hastily they seized their weapons and took up position covering the approaches, conscious that their situation was desperate. But to their astonishment, halfway up the hill the Germans halted, paused, and then turned their vehicles and drove away. It seemed almost certain that they had seen the *maquisards*' movements. Yet by that phase, the Occupiers had become less than enthusiastic about meeting them head on, in battle. A large part of the contempt with which crack units such as the Das Reich regarded local garrison troops stemmed from the tacit enthusiasm of most security regiments for a policy of 'live and let live' with the Resistance. To German fighting units and to the zealots of the Gestapo, local German commanders often appeared absurdly anxious to placate French opinion, and contemptibly preoccupied with shipping produce and loot back to the Reich.

Poirier survived a dozen narrow escapes that spring. *Maquisards* in their camps in the woods were comparatively safe except in action. It was organizers and couriers, who were compelled to travel, who constantly risked capture. Meetings of any kind were a deadly risk: in November 1943, eleven local Resistance chiefs had been captured at a single conference in Montpazier.

There was a delicate balance to be struck between the need for speed and that for security. To walk or cycle was safer, but much too slow for the huge area Poirier had to cover. He generally employed *gazogènes*, which were designed by a Brive engineer, Maurice Arnhouil, who was one of the *maquis*'s most enthusiastic – although also least discreet – supporters. Even the *gazos* were maddeningly sluggish, often needing to be pushed uphill by the combined efforts of every passenger except the driver. Once, stopped at a German roadblock, Poirier fed all his incriminating papers into the charcoal burner under the pretext of filling it with fuel. Although the Germans seldom now ventured far from main roads and towns unless in punitive columns, as the aggressiveness of the Resistance increased, so did the enemy's nervousness and ferocity. 'From February 1944 onwards,' said Poirier, 'it became highly dangerous for anyone to fall into the hands of the German Army.' Racing through the sunlit hills, among the chickens scratching in the dust, the enchanting creeper-clad villages, it was easy to forget the terrible nature of their war. But when Poirier's friend and comrade Raymond Maréchal was seized by the Germans, they forced his hands into the charcoal furnace of a *gazogène* and held him against the burner until he died. They burned a hotel which they searched in vain for Poirier a few hours after he left it, on an inexplicable impulse, at 5 am one day.

The romantic aura surrounding Resistance, together with Poirier's gift for laughter, made it easy for him to attract girls but only very rarely did he sleep with those who were deeply involved in Resistance and utterly secure, 'more or less for health reasons, you know'. George Starr, his F Section counterpart further west, had no sexual relationship with any woman during his two years in Gascony, because he considered the security risk too great.

It is only human nature that, after the war, these men forgot the months of chronic tension, the habit that dogged Poirier for months after the Liberation of watching his back everywhere that he walked. They remembered the absurd moments. An excited *résistant* who had been a French air force pilot came to Poirier one day and reported that he had found an abandoned and forgotten Maubussin light aircraft at the nearby Belvès flying club. One extraordinary spring day, the two men took off in the aircraft and circled over Périgueux, hurling out propaganda leaflets. They returned to Belvès with the exulting pilot leapfrogging the Dordogne bridges. The terrified Poirier demanded to get out, and was duly landed. The pilot took off again and made a dramatic swoop upon the river bridge. Poirier heard the terrible noise of the crash, and raced miserably to the scene to drag out the pilot's body. Instead, he found the nonchalant young man sitting on the bridge, smoking a cigarette and surveying the ruins of the aircraft: 'The Dordogne air force had made its first and last sortie.'

All the months that he had been in England and with Peulevé, Poirier had assumed that his father Robert, another dashing spirit who became a racing driver for a time after leaving the air force, was somewhere working for Resistance. But the two had no contact until one day Poirier was informed that he was to meet a man at the *bloc-gazo* works in Brive whom local *résistants* thought could be helpful. To his utter astonishment, he walked into the room to find himself face to face with his father. His first thought was to mutter urgently: 'Say nothing about our relationship!' He had concealed his real French identity very closely, even from Malraux. The two talked earnestly. Poirier's last words that night, before they went to bed, were: 'Father, if you stay to work with me, you must accept that I am the boss.' The next morning his father's first words were '*Bonjour, mon capitaine.*' For the rest of the war Robert Poirier acted as secretary and administrative assistant to his son, without either man betraying a hint of the relationship to their colleagues.

As he toured the *maquis*, Poirier was indifferent to the political allegiances of each camp. Unlike some SOE officers, who would arm only those who would accept a measure of direction, and above all those who were not communist, Poirier cared only about how energetically they seemed likely to fight Germans. He overlooked the banditry by which some *maquis* existed, unless it appeared to threaten their security. Indeed, he was appalled one day to visit a *maquis* of Spaniards high in the hills – there were thousands of refugees from the Civil War all over southern France – and found them attempting literally to live off the land. They seemed to exist chiefly on nuts and wild plants. They were desperately hungry and passionately eager to fight fascists. At the end of the war, Poirier was deeply moved when their commander said to him: 'And now, *mon commandant*, will you ask Baker Street to begin their *parachutages* to us in Spain?' He loved the Spaniards, and went so far as to relay their doomed request to London, deadpan.

'For a long time, those who had least were the best *résistants*,' said Poirier. The poor and the radical, those whom respectable citizens dismissed as troublemakers and drifters, sowed the seeds of Resistance. If there was a hierarchy of courage, those who came to Resistance in 1942 or 1943 – above all, before the great flood of recruits after D-Day – were at its summit. It may seem cynical or trite to remark that it is easier to abandon a workman's flat or a peasant cottage than a château, in order to become a *maquisard*, but it proved overwhelmingly true. Those who possessed most had most to lose from German revenge. Many of the aristocrats who owned the châteaux of the Dordogne detested and feared the Resistance. Many of the bourgeoisie, deeply frightened by the Popular Front government of 1936, the 1½ million votes cast for the communists, the coming of such revolutionary spectres as paid holidays for workers, feared the *maquisards* as the harbingers of revolution. And indeed many *maquisards* themselves – not all of them communists – regarded Resistance as a revolutionary act, the spur to radical change in their society: 'After the war, it will all be different. . . .' In French bourgeois terms, as Poirier remarked wryly, Robin Hood had been a dangerous bolshevik. Many small businessmen passionately believed that the experience of the 1930s had shown democracy to be a failure in France, a path to anarchy. German occupation was perfectly acceptable if it produced social and economic stability. Anti-semitism had always been deeply rooted in French society. Hatred of the British remained very strong among a signficant number of Frenchmen throughout World War II, especially in French naval circles after the destruction of their fleet at Mers-El-Kebir. Beyond even those who were ideologically sympathetic to the Germans – a significant minority – a much larger number profited financially from coming to terms with the Occupation – the contractors, the black marketeers. Great landowners with estates held in their families for generations were passionately committed to preserving them, even at some small moral cost. Unjust as it may seem, those among the aristocracy, the professionals, the bourgeois, the factory owners and the officials who supported Resistance must be awarded greater moral credit than their humbler countrymen, because they were few, and because they acted against the spirit and inclination of their class.

One of the most remarkable of these *résistants* was Poirier's professional neighbour in the Dordogne, known throughout the countryside as 'Edgar', but in reality Baron Philippe de Gunzbourg. The de Gunzbourgs were a Russian Jewish family, bankers and landowners who acquired a Hessian title and moved to Paris in the early years of the century. Philippe's grandfather achieved an enormous coup by taking a founding interest along with the Rothschilds in the Dutch Shell company. His father consolidated the fortune by marrying an immensely rich bourgeois wife. Philippe himself, born in 1904, grew up rich, spoilt and essentially rootless, torn between his French and Jewish loyalties. There was a procession of family tragedies: his brother died, a sister was killed in a riding accident in England. Philippe was destined for Eton, but after a family change of heart went to a Paris *lycée*, and later spent a few terms at Oxford. In his early twenties he married a *demi-mondaine* twenty years older than himself, an absurd alliance which was quickly terminated. He explored all the traditional extravagances of rich, reckless young men, flying aircraft and racing cars between bursts of high living. He married a second time, more happily, a French Jewish girl with whom he went on a prolonged round-the-world honeymoon and had four children. Then he began to lead a more settled existence, with a Paris house and a large ugly mansion which he bought in the Lot-et-Garonne because he felt a growing sympathy for the countryside and its peasants.

But as he approached forty, he felt no closer to achieving an identity. The most consistent strand in his life was his feeling for England. He had been reared by an English nanny, taken constantly to England on visits, bought all his clothes in London, and had been taught by his father 'to believe that England, and the British Empire, were the greatest institutions in the world'. He was living in the Lot-et-Garonne – in the Unoccupied Zone – when the Germans swept across France, and the rest of his family prudently fled to America. One of their English nannies remained defiantly at their Paris house throughout the war on the grounds that she had to protect the family's possessions, and twice defied arrest and interrogation by the *milice*. In the south, the de Gunzbourgs listened reverently to the BBC each night, and shared the house with 'the living embodiment of the British Empire', their own nanny Alice Joyce who regarded all Germans with withering scorn, and throughout the war declined to speak any tongue but her own.

As the months passed, de Gunzbourg reflected more and more deeply about his own position. He became convinced that he must play some active role in the struggle against the Germans and Vichy. He contacted like-minded friends in Toulouse, and one day in September 1942 one of them telephoned and asked him to come down: 'There's somebody here that I think you should meet.' In the back room of a scruffy little bar in Toulouse, he was introduced to an intensely English young man lolling back in his chair who asked him simply: 'Why do you want to help?'

'Because for me, England is the only country in the world,' said de Gunzbourg, 'above all the only one fighting the Germans.' He talked of his own horror of the French elite – the politicians, the magistrates, the generals. Two weeks later, he heard that he had been successfully 'checked out' by the Englishman, one of SOE's early agents in the region, Maurice Pertschuk, 'Eugène'. De Gunzbourg entered the secret war, carrying messages and seeking out recruits. Eugène began to visit de Gunzbourg's home. He loved to eat Yorkshire pudding made by Nanny, and beyond this it became rapidly apparent that the young Englishman was obsessed with de Gunzbourg's beautiful wife, Antoinette. The Frenchman was less disturbed by this than by the agent's reckless lack of security. They began to hear stories of the leaders of the *réseau* sharing noisy tables at the best black market restaurants in Toulouse, of Pertschuk's wireless operator living with his girlfriend in a château outside the city. It was an operational style which could lead to only one conclusion: Pertschuk, his wireless operator and several of their key colleagues were betrayed, captured, and killed in a German concentration camp.

De Gunzbourg survived, but he was now a fugitive. He dispatched his wife and children to safety in Switzerland, and began a life that was to continue until the Liberation as a gypsy without a home, without possessions, whose only life was that of Resistance. This playboy who before the war had driven only the fastest cars that money could buy began to travel south-west France by bicycle, covering 15,000 miles before the war was over. In the first months of 1943, he could achieve little amidst the wreckage of Pertschuk's circuit. But one evening in May, in the house of a little railway worker in Agen, he met French Section's new agent in Gascony. This was a man of utterly different stamp from Pertschuk, the extraordinary George Starr, 'Hilaire', who by the Liberation controlled a vast sweep of Gascony. A chunky former mining engineer from north Staffordshire whose false teeth gave him a permanent twisted grin, Starr inspired immediate confidence despite his atrocious French accent.

De Gunzbourg became his principal organizer in the Dordogne, while the Englishman concentrated his efforts on the Gers and the Landes. He learnt to assemble *plastique* charges, and arranged the first of many major sabotage operations against locomotives at Eymet, Bergerac and other key rail centres on New Year's Eve 1943. He taught dozens of eager little groups of *résistants* the techniques of receiving *parachutages*, lighting bonfires to a prearranged pattern on a receipt of a *message personnel* from the BBC (and by now each night scores of unarmed *résistants* the length of France lit bonfires whenever they heard an aircraft, in the hope of intercepting a silken bounty). Maurice Loupias, 'Bergeret', a local official in Bergerac who became one of the key AS leaders of the region, has vividly described 'a farmhouse with twenty silent peasants listening in religious silence to Philibert explaining *parachutage* drill, puffing their pipes by the fireplace as he described the method of folding the canopies'. Bergeret called de Gunzbourg 'the principal artisan of our victory'.

De Gunzbourg also believed from what Starr had told him that they could expect parachute landings by Allied troops within days of the main invasion. Whether or not his understanding was correct, in his own mind the importance of seizing and holding a perimeter on D-Day became as dominant as among the *maquisards* of the Vercors. Like most Allied agents, de Gunzbourg found his recruits willing enough to listen to any man who could influence the coming of arms and money. Some were irked by his open devotion to the English – after the invasion, there were some sour jokes about his appearance in British boots. There were still many Frenchmen who wished to keep the British at arm's length. Despite his codename, de Gunzbourg was obviously an aristocrat and a Jew, and there were many *résistants* who loathed both. Some also felt that he was too assertive in giving orders. But it is a remarkable tribute to his dedication and personality that he was able to co-ordinate Resistance in the western Dordogne so effectively, without training or military experience.

Some regarded the latter as a positive merit: 'We'll follow you because you're less of a "*con*" than the others,' shrugged one group of peasant recruits, but they added – 'if you start using the *naphtalinés*, we will never go with you!' One of the strongest prejudices among many French *résistants* was that against the 'mothball brigade', former French officers who sought to take belated command of *maquis* now that the tide had turned decisively towards the Allies. The ORA, the Resistance movement founded by former officers, never achieved much support or success, and survived until the Liberation only because the Americans developed an unfounded faith in its future. It is also worth remembering that not all *résistants* in early 1944 were enthralled by De Gaulle, and many did not even know what he looked like. But some did. De Gunzbourg never forgot a *résistant's* wife declaring to him passionately one night, '*Oh, M. Philibert, je suis amoureuse, je suis amoureuse de Général De Gaulle!*'

For all its discomforts and dangers, and the months spent in peasant cottages and workmen's flats without even a passing encounter with a man or woman with whom he might find enough in common to relax socially or mentally, de Gunzbourg enjoyed his war: 'I had thought that I was incapable of doing anything with my life, and I discovered that there was something I could contribute. It gave me a purpose.' He developed great respect for the peasants of south-west France, and above all for their wives, whose discretion and influence were so formidable. By the spring of 1944, de Gunzbourg was in touch with *réseaux* from Bergerac in the west to Sarlat in the east, and south towards Toulouse and Auch. It is a measure of the isolation in which most circuits worked that, although he was sometimes within a few miles of Jacques Poirier, neither man was aware of the other's legitimacy. Each simply heard reports of another alleged agent operating in what he considered his own territory. Starr told de Gunzbourg laconically that if the mysterious 'agent' who was said to be causing difficulties over-reached himself, it might be simplest to have him killed. By the same token, Soleil was enraged to hear that de Gunzbourg was 'poaching', and swore that he would shoot him if they met. The only relevance of these mildly silly exchanges is that they show the fog and confusion in which Resistance existed. Each group was an uncharted island upon an ocean. It was safer so, but it caused much bewilderment.

Over most of the south-west, George Starr had fewer such problems because he was unchallenged overlord, with half a dozen British-trained couriers and instructors, and a much greater degree of control over local Resistance than most of F's agents achieved. He was also an exceptional personality – '*un homme du métier*', de Gunzbourg called him, '*un grand chef, de la classe de Lawrence*.'

Starr was the son of an English mother and American father who owned a circus which travelled the length of Europe. He was educated at Ardingly public school, and studied mining at London University. He was a cosmopolitan, but he retained the accent and earthy hardiness of northern England. Through the 1930s he travelled Europe as a mining engineer, providing occasional reports to British Intelligence as a sideline. On 10 May 1940 he was down a mine near Liège when the Germans invaded Belgium. He beat a hasty retreat to England through Dunkirk, joined the army, and spent a year as a sergeant commanding the carrier pigeon section of Phantom, the GHQ Reconnaissance Unit based in St James's Park in London. It was there that he received a summons to Selwyn Jepson of SOE, who asked if he would go to France. 'Only if I choose where I go,' said this dour little man. He refused to work in an area where he had friends, and might be recognized. After the usual training in the black arts, one night early in November 1942 he landed by felucca on the Mediterranean coast of France, near Marseille. On the beach to meet him he found his own brother, John, who was already an F Section agent, and who presented him with a ration card and other essential forged paperwork.

George Starr had been ordered to go to Lyon, '. . . but I didn't like the look of it. The whole situation had the wrong smell about it.' His instincts were correct. The network to which he had been assigned was extensively penetrated by the Germans, and was crumbling rapidly. At the suggestion of Peter Churchill, Starr instead moved west, into the Lot-et-Garonne. These were still the most dangerous days of the Resistance, when agents were compelled to feel their way through France 'by guess and by God'. Each man embarked on a process of exploring initial contacts, as sensitive and dangerous as dismantling an unexploded bomb. An agent's most priceless gift was luck, as again and again he exposed himself to men and women of unproven loyalty. To touch the wrong connection was usually fatal. There were occasional sabotage operations and spasmodic arms drops, but most of the work in 1942–3 was a long, unglamorous struggle to turn a thousand isolated groups of Frenchmen hostile to the Nazis into a coherent underground movement.

Starr's luck held. He reached Lot-et-Garonne with one contact address, which proved welcoming. He began to meet potential local helpers. His first priority was to gain radio contact with London – he had brought with him only an S-phone, by which he could establish short-range voice communication with an overhead aircraft. With some difficulty, he passed a message to London through another, distant agent, giving a rendezvous. Gerry Morel, F's operations officer, flew in person over the dropping zone and talked to Starr on the S-phone. When he asked for some evidence of identity, the blast of Staffordshire blasphemy satisfied him. Starr got his radio, and soon began to receive arms.

One of the key rules of clandestine life was 'Keep moving'. But Starr broke it successfully when he set up his headquarters in the little corner house by the church in the hamlet of Castelnau-sur-l'Avignon, some twenty-five miles west of the Das Reich Division's cantonment area. Gascony had a deep-rooted tradition of resistance to authority, even from Paris. The peasant smallholders who farmed their tobacco among the gentle hills, living in villages without paved roads or piped water, were intensely hostile to the Germans. Starr's host, the taciturn, moustachioed Roger Laribeau, was mayor of Castelnau. He made Starr, in his cover as Gaston, a retired Belgian mining engineer, deputy mayor. This chiefly gave him access to the immense range of permits needed for the smallest action or movement in Occupied France. The Englishman began to travel the countryside by train, bicycle, and '*peut-peut*' motor bicycle, as far eastwards as Toulouse, west into the coastal forests of the Landes, north to Bergerac. When he met *résistants*, he tried to convey an impression that he merely bore orders from a senior officer, but they knew him always as '*Le Patron*'. He had a strong streak of peasant cunning himself, and the maturity and judgment gained in twenty years of directing mining operations. 'Building a network,' said Starr, 'is like making a ladder. You fix one rung. You stand on it. You jump on it. If it holds, you build the next one. It takes time. The people who wanted to do it in five minutes got caught. I was bloody lucky.'

Baker Street soon recognized the quality of the circuit Starr was creating – Wheelwright, as they knew it. In August 1943 a thirty-four-year-old WAAF named Annette Cormeau was parachuted to join him as a wireless operator. She was the daughter of a British consular official who had been educated in Europe and was working as a secretary in Brussels in 1937 when she met and married a half-Belgian, half-English accountancy student. They had a daughter in 1938, and she was expecting another baby when a German bomb struck their flat in London in November 1940. Her husband, by then a British soldier, was killed. She herself was badly injured and miscarried. When she recovered, she joined the WAAF, and was serving in the operations room of a bomber station when she was called to London to see Selwyn Jepson.

She was troubled about leaving her daughter, but very eager to play a larger part in the war. She joined a training course with a group of F Section girls, most of whom were later killed by the Germans. They were worked hard. In their free time, 'we used to discuss very feminine things – would we be able to carry off wearing high heels after so long in flat service shoes? We spent a lot of time talking to exiled Frenchmen on the course about conditions in France. We had our pub crawls, and sometimes everybody went haywire, but generally the atmosphere was very serious.' There was a three-week wireless course at Thame Park – 'Station 52' – then the tradecraft course in security at Beaulieu in Hampshire, which Annette found less exacting than she had expected – 'They didn't want to frighten us off.' Every few weeks, she took a train to Bristol to see her five-year-old daughter. One day the little girl came to London, to wave her mother goodbye as she got into a taxi. There were no tears, for no one told her that it would be more than a year before they met again, and that from the taxi Annette was to be transferred to a car for Tempsford, and then France.

Much has been written about the dangers of life as a secret agent – and it must be remembered that, statistically, F Section's men and women fared rather better for casualties in France than a front-line infantry battalion. But little has been said about the tedium and discomfort of living for months in humble surroundings, without personal friends, with only peasant hosts for company. Starr scorned any notion of finding romance in his work, and although it was part of their cover that Annette was his mistress, their relationship was entirely professional. Selwyn Jepson said that when he chose agents, he looked for people who had seen something of the world, discovered their own strengths and limitations, and learned self-reliance. Annette sometimes found the boredom of the tiny hamlet stifling. She helped with the cows and the babies and the housework, and dressed in the same simple peasant clothes. She and Starr were exasperated by a courier once sent from London, a very pretty girl who insisted on wearing high Paris fashion at every opportunity. The most important element in their security was inconspicuousness. Most nights Annette listened to the radio to stay awake until the time came for her own transmitting schedule. She picked up South American stations, and sometimes RAF weather aircraft in the Bay of Biscay. 'Air temperature L-Love', they reported cryptically. She never discovered whether this was hot or cold. Then, at the prearranged moment, she tapped out her own message of 100 or 150 words – fifteen or twenty minutes of transmission time. The set, hidden behind her bed, was powered by six-volt car batteries, because the Germans had an irksome habit of switching off power in rotation to every village when their direction finders picked up a transmission. If there was a break in the morse, they had pinpointed their set.

Unlike Annette, Starr seemed to enjoy the long evenings at the kitchen table, sitting with his head in his hands while the soup pot simmered over the huge fireplace, talking about crops, beasts and wine. Sometimes he lent a hand at the back-breaking business of tending the tobacco fields. He had a bottomless stock of anecdotes about England and earthy jokes that delighted the villagers. Sometimes, when there was urgent work to be done, he tugged insistently at his beret in tension and excitement. But never, even after the fiercest evening with the villagers and their formidable capacity for Armagnac, did he betray the slightest indiscretion. Starr was a natural secret agent.

There is just one other Englishman to be mentioned here – of them all, the agent closest to the heart of the Das Reich Division, indeed the only one who had walked and driven past the lagers and vehicle parks of 2nd SS Panzer Division in the months that they lay around Montauban. One night, Germans interrupted a *parachutage*, and he was compelled to spend hours taking refuge in a tree while they talked and searched beneath him. The troops were very probably of the Das Reich. The agent was a twenty-two-year-old veteran named Tony Brooks.

Brooks was an Englishman brought up in Switzerland and living in the Jura at the outbreak of war. Like Jacques Poirier, he became involved in an escape line, in his case in Marseille, and himself walked over the Pyrenees in the autumn of 1941, reached England and offered himself to SOE. In July 1942, just turned twenty, he was given a crash course in French trades unionism and parachuted into France with instructions to explore the creation of a *réseau* based on the railway workers of southern France. He spent the next two years – an extraordinary lifespan for an agent in Occupied territory – establishing a marvellously successful network among the *cheminots* who, all over the country, provided some of the most dedicated recruits for Resistance.

The Germans fought unceasingly and unsuccessfully to stop the railways being used for the transport of fugitives on engines and as centres of sabotage. Every rail yard in France bore signs: 'AVERTISSEMENT: PEINE DE MORT CONTRE LES SABOTEURS. POUR LE PAYS, POUR TA FAMILLE, POUR TON RAVITAILLEMENT, POUR TOI, CHEMINOT, IL FAUT ENGAGER ET GAGNER LA LUTTE CONTRE LA SABOTAGE.' The rail workers were the most valuable saboteurs of all, because they knew exactly what to hit to achieve most damage without permanently wrecking the railways of France, as opposed to the Allied bombings 'which did more harm than good', as their official historian remarked acidly. They were also exasperated by the extravagant, irrelevant demolitions of the FTP, which destroyed viaducts and installations which would take literally years to rebuild. They believed there was a better way.

Brooks was blessed with a natural sense of security, working with small cells each of which remained unaware of each other's existence. He preserved one refuge for himself in Lyon of which he informed not a single soul. 'So English, so careful,' said a respectful French officer who met him 1944. Weeks before D-Day, Brooks had established that the key to the movement of heavy armour from southern France by rail was the limited stock of flatcars capable of passing under the nation's bridges laden with tanks. He had pinpointed the whereabouts of most of them. In the days before 6 June, he and some of his enthusiastic *cheminots* spent many hours of many nights working on their axle bearings with abrasive paste supplied from London. They were now incapable of travelling more than a matter of miles before seizing. Like Starr and de Gunzbourg, Brooks had also briefed his saboteurs in great detail about *Plan Vert*. At his safe house in Toulouse in the first days of June 1944, Brooks felt tolerably confident that if German reinforcements were moving north in the wake of D-Day, it was most unlikely that they would be doing so by train.

4 The Road

Within hours of the Allied landings on the morning of 6 June across the Lot and Corrèze and Dordogne, as across the rest of France, men were streaming on foot and by car and truck and bicycle to collect their arms and take to the *maquis*. Odette Bach was in the hairdresser's in Souillac when she heard the news, and bicycled thirty miles home to Figeac, bursting with exhilaration. Her husband abandoned his job as a cashier at the local Crédit Lyonnais – with a doctor's certificate to enable him to continue to be paid – and joined his group. Jean Sennemaut, commanding the AS detachment at Bellac, north-west of Limoges, took his wife, Sten gun and grenades, left their nine-month-old daughter at her grandmother's, and abandoned their home for the farmhouse seven miles into the countryside which he had designated weeks before as the group's rendezvous on mobilization. In the Corrèze, especially, men began to flock to the various rendezvous of the *Armée Secrète*. Many of them had no previous connection with Resistance, and there were not remotely enough weapons to arm them. When Deschelette, De Gaulle's *Délégué Militaire Régional*, heard of the great concentrations moving to join Vaujour and Guedin's companies, he was deeply concerned, for he feared the consequences of massing more men than they could possibly arm and control. But it seemed unthinkable to turn them away, and their leaders were that day a little drunk with the exhilaration of the moment. Deschelette, whom some of his subordinates found an ineffectual figure, was soon much preoccupied with reports of a major FTP action around the town of Tulle, and an even more alarming AS concentration developing around Bergerac in the Dordogne. In the Corrèze, Marius Guedin's AS companies deployed as he and Vaujour had arranged weeks before, on the bridges across the Dordogne and the key junctions west of Brive.

The Resistance made no direct assault on the German garrison of Bergerac in the days following 6 June, but the entire countryside surrounding the town rose in open insurrection. De Gunzbourg took command of the *résistants* south of the Dordogne river, and Bergerac – Maurice Loupias – of those to the north. They reckoned that they had some 2,800 Stens, 450 rifles, 100 Brens and twenty anti-tank weapons. With these arms, they believed that they could cut off the Germans in Bergerac and control the eastern Dordogne until the expected Allied parachutists arrived. In the area he had chosen as a landing ground, de Gunzbourg was directing hundreds of men who had arrived in trucks from all over the department to distribute weapons, clear obstacles and cut down trees on the field, then set up an all-round defence to cover it. There was one predictable disappointment when the local FTP, whom they had armed, refused to have any part in the AS uprising. But Soleil arrived with sixty of his *maquisards* and took up position at Mouleydier, on the direct route between Bergerac and Brive-la-Gaillarde. 'Barricades are a great tradition in France,' said de Gunzbourg. Barricade fever seized the area, and he wrote:

With immense enthusiasm the whole region put itself in a state of war. Bridges were blown, roads blocked with tree trunks, wagons and so on. The obstacles were mined at points I had chosen in advance. Some men were deployed for guerilla action. Others patrolled the roads and made all civilian movement impossible without papers being checked. Indeed, people overdid the roadblocking, and Jean and I had the greatest difficulty in dissuading them. . .

It was Bergeret's proudest hour – he himself publicly proclaimed the Fourth Republic. From a distance, Poirier at Belvès was horrified to hear of all these events. The *résistants* of western Dordogne had created a static threat to German control which it seemed impossible for them to ignore. The ingredients were assembled for a tragedy which could have been as horrific as that of the Vercors, where 2,000 *maquisards* died in the hopeless attempt to defend a 'redoubt' against the Germans in July 1944. This was not at all what London had in mind.

As Starr's men assembled and armed in the Gers and the Landes, the first rail demolitions were taking place. Brooks' *cheminots* cut the vital line north from Montauban to Brive-la-Gaillarde. Starr and de Gunzbourg's team hit the lines westwards to Bordeaux, and Peter Lake several of those in the eastern Dordogne. At Brive, a taciturn, soberly Catholic SNCF engineer named Jean Marsat directed his *cheminot* resisters in cutting the lines to Tulle and to the south and west. In the first week following D-Day, 960 of 1,055 rail cuts scheduled under *Plan Vert* were carried out.

It is essential, however, to keep a sense of perspective about rail sabotage. Even SNCF's official historian remarks that 'in spite of the active help of the *cheminots*, the execution of *Plan Vert* was only partial on D-Day. . . .' The Allied commanders' objections to dependence on sabotage had partly stemmed from the knowledge that explosions on stretches of main line could be repaired within sixteen to forty-eight hours. More sophisticated attacks on points and turntables by *cheminots* could do much more damage, but these accounted for only a minority of D-Day targets. The greatest weakness in the execution of the sabotage plan was that it placed insufficient emphasis on repetition at almost daily intervals. Contrary to the assertions of many *résistants* and Resistance historians, the Germans continued to run some trains on the lines that they considered vital across most of France after D-Day. A group of Guedin's *maquisards* was in action against a German armoured train which arrived to repair a line cut at Noailles, south of Brive, on 7 June. Two were killed and one was captured. He was burnt to death in the furnace of the locomotive.

But the evidence is overwhelming that, from 7 June, it was impossible to move the Das Reich Division at any speed by direct routes north or north-west from Montauban. A little of the credit for this undoubtedly belongs to the Allied air forces, as do all of the laurels for their difficulties north of the Loire, but it was principally the achievement of Brooks, Starr, de Gunzbourg and other SOE officers, together with the Frenchmen whom they had equipped and instructed. Without SOE, Resistance could have achieved nothing.

At 6 pm on 6 June, General De Gaulle broadcast to France from the BBC: 'The supreme battle has begun. . . . For the sons of France wherever they may be, whatever they may be, the simple and sacred duty is to fight the enemy by every means at their command.'

The first of scores of G-3 SHAEF daily bulletins on the development of Resistance reported that, despite heavy German short-wave jamming, the Action Messages had been generally well received on the medium wave: 'General reports indicate that the *maquis* are increasing in strength earlier than anticipated, without much interference from the Germans.'

The news of the Allied landing trickled erractically to the officers of the Das Reich. Many men heard it for the first time from exulting or nervous French civilians on the streets of Montauban or the villages in which they were quartered. Among most veterans, it inspired a sense of relief that at last the waiting and uncertainty were ended. The decisive battle had begun. But most unit commanders were acutely conscious of their shortages of equipment and transport, and the inadequate training of the new drafts. Ernst Krag, commanding the assault gun battalion, had been retraining an infantry company to make up his shortage of gunners. Heinrich Wulf's reconnaissance battalion was still awaiting an entire company's complement of heavy armoured cars.

Karl Kreutz, commanding the artillery, heard of the landings at the little château where he had his headquarters from his adjutant Gerstenburger, a middle-aged reserve officer who had been a bank clerk before the war. Kreutz, a robust, jovial man unlike any stereotype of an SS officer, began urging his batteries into activity: 'We knew that every single day was vital, every day lost was a day won for the Allies.' His 105 mm battalion's gunners were sadly under-trained. One entire unit lacked towing vehicles. In some of the division's dispersals, on their own initiative officers ordered drivers to begin requisitioning French civilian trucks and cars to make good the transport shortages. Some officers and men were absent on courses and on leave. Borkmann, adjutant of Otto Pohl's tank unit, was still on his way back from his own wedding in Silesia, and did not rejoin them until four days later, having hitch-hiked perilously in their wake. One entire tank company was absent in Germany, collecting new Panzer Vs.

As the news from Normandy filtered through the camps and parks around Montauban, there was little doubt in any man's mind that within hours they would be ordered to entrain for a move 450 miles north to support the counter-offensive in Normandy. Yet all through that critical day of 6 June no orders from Army Group G reached the Das Reich. One of the decisive factors in the triumph of the Allied landings was the hesitant, poorly co-ordinated German response in the first hours of D-Day, and for that matter in the days that followed. As wave after wave of British, American and Canadian forces advanced across the beaches, the four weak infantry and one armoured division of Dollman's 7th Army were left alone to man the defences. OKW* prevaricated, hypnotized by the spectre of a second landing conjured up by the brilliant Allied deception operation.

The SD's† interception of the Resistance Action Messages was ignored. At 4 am, Von Rundstedt requested Berlin's assent to move the Panzer Lehr and 12th SS Armoured Divisions against the beach-head, but received it only twelve hours later. At 6.30 am, 21st Panzer was only fifteen miles from the coast and ready to move, but at 10 am it was ordered to shore up the defence of Caen. That afternoon, 21 Pz launched the only armoured counter-stroke of the day, without support. Its tanks reached the coast at one point before they were driven back, having lost a quarter of their strength. At 4.55 pm, Von Rundstedt telephoned 7th Army HQ, and

> . . . emphasized the desire of the Supreme Command to have the enemy in the bridgehead annihilated by the evening of 6 June, since there exists a danger of additional sea and airborne landings. In accordance with an order by General Jodl, all units will be diverted to the point of penetration in Calvados. The beach-head there must be cleaned up not later than tonight. The Chief of Staff answers that such action would be impossible. . . .

At 5 pm, Sepp Dietrich's 1st SS Panzer Corps was given its first orders since the landing – to prepare to counter-attack west of Caen at first light on 7 June. In the event, Allied air and artillery action, together with the fuel shortages that crippled every German troop movement, prevented the Panzer Corps from passing its start line on the seventh. Its first, belated assault was launched the following day, 8 June. All over northern France the destruction of the rail system, the Allied fighter bomber attacks

* *Oberkommando der Wehrmacht* – German Army High Command.

† The *Sicherheitsdienst*, or security service, an arm of the Gestapo.

and the chronic petrol problem left units straggling over hundreds of miles of road and track as they crawled forward to the battle zone.

Yet while the signals centres of Army Group B were swamped by ill tidings of Allied success in the north, so those of Army Group G at Toulouse were receiving a torrent of messages from isolated German garrisons all over south and central France, announcing the uprising of Resistance:

Impression growing that the *maquis* are a strictly organized military force, and effective action against them possible only with mobile heavy weapons. . . .

Tarbes infested with guerillas. . . .

OKW to C-in-C West: vital importance to protect wolfram mines east of Limoges. . . .

Two trucks of 2nd SS Pz pioneer battalion attacked by guerillas in lorry with machine gun at approaches to Figeac. Enemy lorry destroyed by gunfire. 5 enemy killed, 2 SS killed, driver taken prisoner. . . .

First Army signalled from Bordeaux: 'The departments of Dordogne and Corrèze are held by terrorists. Part of the department of the Indre and the town of Tulle are dominated by gangs.* The town of Limoges is beseiged. Périgueux and Brive are expecting attacks by gangs. Tulle has been under attack with mortars and artillery since last night (information from the SD).'

It had been obvious for many months to the abler German commanders – above all Rommel and Von Rundstedt – that an attempt to hold every yard of Occupied France once the invasion began would be militarily disastrous, and would merely cause weakness everywhere. Yet as late as 16 June, when Von Rundstedt urged OKW to abandon all France south of the Loire and bring the sixteen infantry divisions then in southern France to join the line in Normandy, this idea was rejected as 'politically impossible' by Berlin.

If OKW and Army Group G had kept their heads, withdrawn their weak, and obviously panicky, local garrisons and abandoned large tracts of southern France to the Resistance, it would have avoided immense problems. The *résistants* posed no military threat to major formations, and could be disposed of at leisure once the vital battle in Normandy had been won. Instead,

* *Banden* – the customary Wehrmacht term for Resistance groups.

Army Group G now deployed piecemeal every man, gun and vehicle that could be scraped together to counter-attack *résistants* wherever they had massed. Not even the most optimistic Allied planner before the invasion had anticipated that the German High Command would be so foolish as to commit major fighting formations against *maquisards*. Perhaps the greatest contribution that Resistance made to D-Day was now to goad the Germans into deploying against the *maquis* forces out of all proportion to the real threat that they represented. General Heinz Lammerding had argued even before D-Day that it was essential to retain control of south central France, and to suppress the *maquis*. On 5 June 1944 he drafted a memorandum to 58th Corps which bears heavily on much that followed:

SUBJECT: Anti-terrorist measures.

The development of the *maquis* situation in the zone Cahors–Aurillac–Tulle represents a threat which, in the event of a landing, could adversely influence operations. The majority of the terrorists are pursuing the objectives of communisim and destruction. The population only assists them under duress (especially the moneyed and official classes). The measures taken so far against the terrorists have not had much success. . . .

Lammerding suggested a forceful propaganda offensive to drive home to the population that the miseries of repression were brought upon them by the actions of the terrorists. He proposed a wholesale seizure of vehicles and petrol stocks throughout the terrorist area, intensive sweeps and checks on movement, and the occupation of Cahors, Figeac and Brive by powerful units. Then, most formidably:

On 15 June, I propose that we should round up 5,000 male suspects in the Cahors–Aurillac–Tulle area and deport them to Germany. The terrorists, according to local reports, have enlisted the classes of 1945 and 1946 in this region. If one removes that number of men, the terrorist organization will lose the elements to make any major expansion of their strength possible.

[I propose] the freeing of a member of a family or a friend taken prisoner, in return for information about arms dumps or *maquis* leaders; to make it known that for every German wounded, three terrorists will be hanged (and not shot), and for every German killed, ten terrorists will be hanged. . . .

The division is convinced that if these steps are taken, the area will be pacified, and there will be no further problems for operations in the event of an invasion. . . .

Lammerding's memorandum was forwarded to Army Group G by 58th Corps endorsed by its commander: 'With reference to the punitive and reprisal measures proposed by 2nd SS Pz, the general commanding heartily concurs.'

Early on 7 June, Army Group G dispatched a long signal to 58th Corps which began:

The development of the gang situation in the Massif Central demands immediate and unhesitating action by major formations. To this effect, on the orders of OB West and with the agreement of Führer headquarters, the 189th Infantry Division and the 2nd SS Panzer Division are immediately placed under the orders of 66th Reserve Corps. The 2nd SS Armoured Division thus reassigned is to deploy in the Tulle–Limoges area, where substantial formations of gangs appear to be gathered. . . .

In other words, despite the onset of invasion, a version of Lammerding's own plan was to be put into immediate effect. It was an extraordinary decision, and one which OKW would quickly regret.

At 11.15 on the morning of 7 June, signals were at last dispatched to all elements of the Das Reich warning that a move was imminent. Unit commanders were summoned to the villa on the edge of Montauban where Lammerding's headquarters stood festooned with its aerials, busy with scurrying clerks and signallers. All that day and far into the night, around the divisional area men laboured filling tanks, assembling fuel and ammunition, checking guns and vehicles. Most of the local population were heartily glad to see them preparing to go. But there were also partings with girlfriends, and sincere expressions of good wishes. A few girls tied flowers to the radiators of trucks and half-tracks. One gave Private Schneid a paper bag full of biscuits for the march: 'Did her compatriots later cut off her hair for that gesture?' he mused afterwards. Some of the SS gave the civilians with whom they had been billeted their unused ration books. Ernst Krag was saddened that he would no longer hear the elderly doctor with whom he had been billeted play the piano so beautifully. Whatever hatred the German Occupiers inspired as a mass, it is absurd to imagine that there were not moments of private sympathy, even warmth. Several German officers found that the families with whom they lodged apologized in private for being unable to greet them in public. Marguerite Rollet, one of the Frenchwomen who had a group of troopers billeted in her house, was struck by the irony that they would bring her food to supplement the rations and behaved with perfect courtesy in the house. Meanwhile, they returned from anti-partisan sweeps laden with booty from bicycle parts to the ducks and chickens of the hapless households through which they had passed.

For the divisional staff, the movement order created immense problems. Every armoured formation takes it for granted that its tracked vehicles move between battlefields by rail or transporter, for they are chronically prone to breakdown if driven for long distances on their caterpillars. On receipt of the warning order from 58th Corps, Major Stuckler at once signalled a routine request to the Corps for rail space for his tanks and assault guns, which could be of no possible value to anti-terrorist operations. To his utter astonishment it was peremptorily refused, without explanation. A heated exchange of signals followed as he remonstrated with Corps about the consequences to the tank units of a long road movement. But the order stood. The tanks and assault guns were to drive north via Figeac and Tulle. This was the first important, direct achievement of the Resistance rail-cutting operations, of the havoc wreaked by Brooks and his men with the precious flatcars.

Next came a further furious message from the division to 58th Corps about wheeled transport. Weeks earlier they had been assured that, when the day came, they could count upon the provision of a pool of requisitioned French vehicles, sufficient to move an entire battalion. The staff had repeatedly warned Corps that unless pre-emptive action was taken, these vehicles would mysteriously disappear when they were needed. Now, indeed, their fears were fulfilled. The vehicles were gone, and every local Frenchman denied knowledge of them. Worse still, to the fury of the unit transport officers who had requisitioned vehicles on their own initiative, they were now ordered to return these. The local commander, desperate to maintain some *modus vivendi* with the local population after the Panzers had gone, insisted that no transport was to be arbitrarily commandeered. To the SS, it was another example of the feeble attitudes of local garrisons. They complied sullenly, and divisional headquarters began the difficult struggle to reorganize its formations for movement.

Stuckler, the division's 1a or senior staff officer, was an effective administrator. A thin, sombre man of thirty-one, the son of a works manager who had been an air force NCO in World War I, he had yearned to be a pilot himself, but the family had lacked the money. Instead he had joined the Bavarian police, and three years later, in 1935, the new Wehrmacht. After five years as a gunner, he was put through the superb General Staff course and was serving as a Corps staff officer in January 1944 when he found himself transferred to 2nd SS Panzer.

His first problems now were the two Panzergrenadier brigades. Both were desperately short of transport and contained too many under-trained recruits. A drastic solution was decided upon. The Deutschland regiment would hand over its best battalion – the 1st – and all regimental transport to the Der Führer. The Der Führer would transfer its least effective battalion – the 2nd – to the Deutschland. The weaker Deutschland brigade would remain at Montauban, together with the least equipped artillery battalion and a rag-tag of support units until their training and transport position improved. After a further exchange of signals with 58th Corps, the Deutschland under Major Wisliceny was ordered to form a 600-man battle group from its better-trained elements to operate in a local security role under the orders of Toulouse. This force achieved its own terrible notoriety in south-west France in the weeks that followed, but its operations in Gascony have no part in the story that follows.

At dawn on 8 June, the great columns of vehicles and armour began to roar into life in lagers for thirty miles around Montauban. Lurching forward with their great clatter and screeching of tracks, they started to swerve out on to the roads, tearing up the asphalt behind them as they moved north through the sharp early morning light. It was an immensely complex manoeuvre to organize some 15,000 men and over 1,400 vehicles in order of march. Wulf's reconnaissance unit, the *Aufklärungsabtei-*

lung, was a few minutes late. The headquarters groups of the Der Führer, led by the inevitable motor cyclists, impatiently rolled away up the Cahors road without waiting for them. Behind, throwing a long, pursuing dust cloud into the sky, came the trucks and half-tracks and field cars.

In the heavily armed armoured cars and gun-mounted half-tracks of the reconnaissance group, the men ate cherries and sausages purchased with the last of their ready money from the fat, blackhaired grocer's wife in Beaumont-de-Lomagne where they had been billeted. Every vehicle had been ordered to maintain 100-metre spacing in case of air attack. Karl Kreutz, the artillery commander, sat beside his driver with a Sten gun between his knees, souvenir of an Allied container drop captured by his men. It was a tradition that, on anti-terrorist sweeps, they kept what they found. While any Allied officer would have willingly thrown away his Sten in exchange for the much superior German Schmeisser, in the way of soldiers it pleased Kreutz to carry a captured weapon. Behind him and his elderly driver, Feldwebel Lehmann, sat their 'looky-looky', the man nominated in every vehicle in the division to search the sky for enemy aircraft. From the moment that they crossed the Loire, the 'looky-lookies' would have plenty to do.

Far behind the towed artillery and the assault gun battalion, divisional headquarters and the flak units, came the two tank battalions, which were to swing eastwards at Cahors, taking the D940 north to Tulle. On exercises, engineer squads followed the armoured columns, repairing the havoc that they had wrought with the road surfaces. Today there were no such refinements. The tank squadrons were not expecting action. Two forty-gallon petrol drums were lashed to each hull – an essential measure when fuel supplies were uncertain, but unthinkable if there was a risk of gunfire. Within a few hours, as the sun came up, the heat and dirt and stink within the tanks were becoming intolerable. They moved far more slowly than the lighter elements, and halted every two hours to rest and make running repairs. Within a few miles of leaving Montauban, the maintenance crews were under pressure: the pins connecting the tracks snapped with heart-breaking regularity. Corth, the *Schirrmeister* or maintenance king of Pohl's company, raced up and down the column with his men, sweat pouring down their bodies as they laboured over the roasting steel. They were grateful that Corth had wangled MAN engines for their entire company's Panthers. Other, less fortunate units, equipped with the notoriously unreliable Daimler-Benz engine, suffered ceaseless problems. Major Tyschen, with his bullet head and the appalling scar on his chin, moved from company to company in his Volkswagen, checking tanks and driving their commanders. Already it was apparent that for the tank crews the road march would be a nightmare.

The division rolled without incident down the long, straight road beside the railway from Montauban to Caussade, and began the winding climb into the hills. It was open country here, unsuited to ambushes or sniping. The men relaxed and sang as they lay against the guns or clung to the supports of their trucks. They breasted the ridge and saw the road fall away to Cahors, down a long avenue of plane trees, past the great rail viaduct, and then across the river into the medieval town. A number of isolated civilians were already dead, killed by fire from one or other of the columns on pretexts that will never be known. It may have been enough that they were under orders that this was to be a *ratissage* – a clearance and demonstration of dominance of the countryside which would not be complete without a heavy blood price. The reconnaissance battalion, the Der Führer regiment, the towed artillery and divisional headquarters – followed by the support units of the division – pressed straight on northwards, towards Souillac and Brive. The heavy armour branched east, to Figeac and St Céré. An hour up the road, Major Dickmann and his 1st battalion of the DF turned west at Gourdon. They were to swing through the eastern Dordogne, taking up their final position on the flank of the division in the Limousin. Ten miles up the road, at the tiny hamlet of Groslejac, the Das Reich Division began to fight.

Local Resistance histories record formally an action by '3rd Section, Company Rémy, Ace of Hearts *maquis*'. One of the survivors saw the day more simply. At 7 am on the morning of 8 June, Marcel Vidal, a stonemason who was also mayor of Groslejac, received a visitor. It was a woodseller named Victor, who was also an enthusiastic *résistant*, one of Guedin's men. Germans were expected to pass through the village, said Victor, on their way north to fight in Normandy, and the order was that everybody must do everything possible to delay or to stop them. Vidal and Victor left the house, and began hastily knocking on doors up and down the village. There was a sharp difference of opinion among the men. Was it really worth it? What reprisals would the Germans take? How many of them would come, and was Victor sure that they would only be in lorries? . . . But one by one they dug out their weapons and walked, still arguing heatedly, towards the old bridge across the Dordogne that lay at the north end of the village. Marcel Malatrait, the butcher who was also a radical socialist like so many of the people of the Lot, took command. There were two men from one of Soleil's *maquis* who had come down from nearby woods where they were camped. One of them took his post on a rock overlooking the road, to fire a warning shot as the signal that the Germans were approaching. Ironically enough, Vidal had been given a revolver by the Germans as a mark of his status as mayor. Like most of the others there that day, he also possessed a 1914 vintage French Army rifle and bayonet. Each man held two grenades, from Resistance supplies. Almost all of them had served their time in the French Army – Vidal in the Alpine Infantry. But before that day, not one of them had seen action. The *maquisards* brought with them a single Bren gun. Fifteen men in all, they crouched and lay around the short, narrow bridge, and began the long wait in the sunshine. A few more wore the brownish tunics affected by some AS men. Most were in everyday peasant blue with berets. None really possessed the slightest hint of what was about to happen to them.

At around 8.30 am, they heard the warning shot from the rock. Up the single village street, round the curve towards the bridge swept the leading armoured half-tracks of Major Dickmann's battalion of Panzergrenadiers. The little cluster of Frenchmen began to fire. The German vehicles slammed to a halt. Helmeted, camouflage-smocked infantry spilled out, racing for the cover of houses and trees, working swiftly round to outflank the defenders clustered at the bridge. A devastating hail of automatic fire poured on to the French position, answering the single shot, bolt-action rifles. René Lacombe, thirty-one, was mending his car outside his house, absurdly seeking to ignore the intruders, when German fire killed him as he stood. The Hôtel Jardel, just short of the bridge, was hit by

Vera Atkins, regarded by many as the critical force in the French Section

Violette Szabo

George Hiller, French Section's officer in the Lot

left 'Soleil', René Cousteille, leader of the Groupe Soleil

opposite left Marius Guedi (right), Jacques Poirier (second right) and other *résistants* of the Corrèze

opposite right Odette Bach, who kept the 'stray dogs home' in Figeac

left Jacques Poirier – 'Nestor – who, with Harry Peulevé, armed most of the *maquisards* of the Corrèze and Dordogne who met the Das Reich division after 6 June

opposite left André Malraux, author of *La Condition Humaine* and one of the most extraordinary figures who held the stage in the Resistance of the Dordogne and Corrèze in 1944

opposite right Baron Philippe de Gunzbourg on the bicycle on which he travelled more than 15,000 miles on his missions for Wheelwright in the Dordogne, often with *plastique* on the carrier

above left Major Otto Weidinger of the Der Führer regiment of which he assumed command on 16 June 1944

above right General Hienz Lammerding with one of the division's Panzers in the background

opposite above One of the most famous *parachutages* of the war – a vast daylight drop near Loubressac on 14 July – Bastille Day – 1944, which provided huge supplies of arms for the *maquis* of the Corrèze, Lot and Dordogne

opposite below A unique unpublished photograph from the private album of an SS officer: as the march north from Montauban began, (left to right) Major Helmut Kampie, Major Ernst Krag, Colonel Albert Stuckler and General Heinz Lammerding

Jean-Jacques Chapou, known as 'Philippe' in the Lot and 'Kléber' in the Corrèze

opposite right René Jugie, of the Corrèze AS, who blew the Uzerche line on the night of 8 June 1944

A *maquisard* sabotages a railway line

An SS officer's impression of the hangings at Tulle, sketched on the same day and perhaps the only contemporary visual evidence of the atrocity

Captain John Tonkin, who commanded the SAS Bulbasket mission; Lieutenant Twm Stephens, in the civilian clothes which he wore on his mission to pinpoint the petrol trains; and Lieutenant John Crisp

cannon fire and began to billow flames. A gaggle of civilians fled hopelessly through the front door and were shot down as they ran. Louis Cauquil, one of the men on the bridge, tried to bolt across it as the Germans advanced, and was blown dead into the roadway. The remainder of the Frenchmen, without lingering to try conclusions with their hand grenades, scrambled hastily down the river bank and fled towards the woods. The gunfire ceased. The Germans remounted their vehicles, leaving the French dead where they lay. The convoy rolled on over the Dordogne, with slight loss. Groslejac lay in silence again. Only the flames rising from the hotel and the bodies beside the road showed that there had been a battle. This mad, absurdly courageous act of defiance had lasted perhaps twenty minutes, and cost the lives of five of the defenders and five non-combatants. Today, a plaque beside the bridge records their names above the inscription: 'It was here, on 8 June 1944, that a German column suffered an appreciable delay due to the sacrifice of these patriots.'

North of the river, the column approached the hamlet of Carsac. As they crossed a little bridge, they met a truck bearing five astonished *résistants*. One fled, pursued by fire. The other four were shot down at point-blank range. Dickmann had now intended to turn right, and move along the river to rejoin the main road at Souillac. Here, on 6 June, Guedin's men had attacked a German outpost just after an armoured train had arrived to resupply it. The French had lost three wounded, and the region was duly marked down on the German maps as a hotbed of Resistance.

On 8 June, at Carsac, the SS briefly took the wrong road, and moved through the village towards Sarlat, firing as they went. Thirteen people died in as many minutes, including a Jewish refugee doctor, the eighty-year-old blacksmith Pierre Trefail, and a man driving oxen in the fields. Several houses were set on fire. The Germans then turned their vehicles, and disappeared down that most beautiful riverside road towards the east.

At Rouffilac, *maquisards* enthusiastically assisted by local civilians had erected a huge barricade across the road. The French later claimed to have killed the motor cyclist leading the column and hit an armoured car with a bazooka rocket before the Germans broke through, killing one *maquisard* and wounding two who were later taken to the hospital at Sarlat. Fifteen civilians also died. Little more than a mile further on, at Carlux, the Germans shot two women at the approach to the village. They then rejoined the main road at Souillac, rather later than they had intended, without further incident. The Occupying army had reminded the eastern Dordogne of the cost of rebellion.*

It should be noted that all the active *résistants* mobilized in the Lot that day were either directed by the Corrèze *Armée Secrète*, or belonged to the FTP *maquis*. The Groupes Vény were simply unaware that the German forces were upon them until it was too late. George Hiller wrote:

> The first we knew of the movement of the Das Reich was when its advance columns rattled up the roads in the Lot. They met with little opposition except at Bretenoux. The Germans were quickly able to open themselves a passage. For a couple of days after, one heard the rattle of armoured vehicles on the road, and at night saw farmhouses set alight in reprisals. In the Dordogne the *maquis* were much more successful, partly owing to their greater determination, and partly to more favourable terrain.

The most pathetic tragedy of the day was at the little hamlet of Gabaudet, a few miles south of Gramat in the heart of the Lot. Among hundreds of local young men who were streaming into the countryside from their homes to join the *maquis* after D-Day, a large party gathered in a farm at Gabudet – it is thought *en route* to join the FTP group led by Robert Noireau, 'Colonel Georges'. That evening, Noireau heard of their coming, and drove to join them. He and his colleagues were half a mile away when they heard heavy automatic fire, and prudently halted. Later, when silence fell and they could see only the smoke from

* Many historians of Resistance have mentioned a battle between local *résistants* and the Das Reich at Souillac during its advance. There was certainly a clash on 6 June. I have been unable to trace a further action on the eighth in German records, or from the information that I received from local Resistance sources. However, because of the uncertainty of evidence, it remains just possible that there was a minor brush that I have failed to discover.

During all the actions described in this chapter, the Germans suffered a total of around a dozen killed according to their casualty reports, which will be discussed below. It is impossible to determine which were caused in which battles on the road.

the burning hamlet, they went into Gabaudet. An unknown unit from the right flank column of Das Reich had chanced upon the gathering of would-be *résistants* – which included a number of *gendarmes* – while patrolling up a side road. Ten boys and men, together with one girl, were shot on the spot. Eighty others were seized and driven off for deportation to Germany. To their overwhelming relief and astonishment, they were later released on the road to Tulle. Noireau's men subsequently executed a French *gendarme* who was said to have informed the Germans of the gathering at Gabaudet.

The Ace of Hearts *maquis*, under Guedin's command, was deployed across the southern Corrèze and northern Lot. Most were somewhat better armed than the little band at Groslejac, but like them they lacked the vital discipline and confidence that can only come with long training and experience as a unit. Very few *résistants* understood fire discipline – wasting ammunition is a chronic vice of guerillas. It is worth quoting the report of Maurice Parisot, commander of the Armagnac battalion, the most effective Resistance fighting group operating with George Starr, after their first action:

> The men shoot too much, without sighting and often without a target. This is unacceptable – we are short of ammunition. Even if one is surprised, it is essential to fire from the shoulder and not to shoot beyond the range of your weapon (Sten 75 or 80 metres, rifle 300 metres, Bren, 1,000 metres, revolver 15 metres). Men don't know how to use shelter or cover; they expose themselves and don't understand fire and movement. Instructors must immediately drum into them these basic rules of tactics. . . . Men must 'keep their cool' in action. It is essential for them to keep in closer touch with their commanders.

These injunctions and failings applied to almost every Resistance group in France. On the N20, up which the Der Führer and reconnaissance battalion were advancing, Guedin's men had wasted hours felling trees and placing carts across the road, ignoring the vital precept of roadblocks – that to be effective they must be covered by fire, since otherwise any convoy with heavy vehicles can sweep them aside with contemptuous ease. So it was with the Das Reich, that long afternoon of 8 June. The Germans were irritated, even outraged. But they were not seriously hampered. The headquarters group of the Der Führer, including its commander Colonel Stadler in his staff car, were still cruising at the head of the division when they reached the little village of Cressensac, ten miles north of the Dordogne river.

It is a pretty, creeper-clad place with a single wide main street dusty in the June sun. It had been the scene of a minor action on 31 March, in which two *résistants* had been killed by the detested Vichyite *Garde Mobile de Réserve* – the GMR. On the afternoon of 8 June, the first vehicles of the Der Führer suddenly found themselves swept by a long burst of fire at the approaches of the village, which hit several men and caused the Germans to leap in confusion from their soft-skinned vehicles. The trucks laden with infantry pulled in beside the road, and for a few minutes both sides exchanged fire without effect. But the infantry, to their considerable fury, found themselves pinned down. Then the huge armoured vehicles of the reconnaissance battalion roared up the road, past the trucks and the headquarters group. Wulf and his men enjoyed the spectacle of the infantry officers crouching in the ditch as the price of their impatience in driving ahead of them. They moved into the village, spraying cannon and machine gun fire into the *maquisard* positions. A 75 mm Pak gun started to blast the houses from which fire was being directed, and blew a hole in the church spire. The *résistants* began to break east and westwards into the countryside, leaving four dead behind them. The Germans mounted their vehicles again, and prepared to move on, this time with Wulf's half-tracks undisputed in the lead. It was around 4 pm.

Eight miles further north, at Noailles, on the crest of the hill that guards the approach to Brive-la-Gaillarde, a little group of men of the 1st section, 6th company of the Ace of Hearts covered the crossroads, listening to the gunfire. Their leader, Commandant Romain, had been talking to them when he heard the shooting at Cressensac. He hurried away down the road on his little *moto*, just too late for the action, and narrowly avoided encountering the Das Reich. The Noailles party had just been reinforced by a group of nine defectors from the GMR, whose men had been hastening to join the Resistance in large numbers since D-Day. Several of these *Gardes*, including their leader, a man named Lelorrain, were still beside their vehicle when they heard '*un bruit infernal*', in the words of one of the survivors.

The first of Wulf's vehicles ground over the crest and instantly opened fire, hitting Lelorrain and several others with the first burst. Some of the *résistants* fired a few shots, but more scattered among the houses and gardens by the road. After just three hours' service to the Allied cause, the GMR leader lay dying by the roadside, along with several other dead or mortally wounded Frenchmen. The long hill into Brive lay open to the Germans. Through the evening and far into the night their vehicles crawled onwards through the little villages, each successive unit speculating idly about the source of the flames that still played through the ruins of houses fired in the little skirmishes, and the wreckage of bullock carts and fallen trees from barricades swept aside by the half-tracks as they advanced up the road. Guedin's *maquisards* could consider it their principal achievement that it had taken the Das Reich Division six hours, rather than perhaps three, to cover the last forty miles to Brive-la-Gaillarde. A young Swiss girl from the Château de Noailles and a grocer's daughter named Denise Neymarie ran out into the gardens to do what they could for the *maquis* wounded, bleeding behind the trees on the hilltop.

The small town of Bretenoux, a medieval *bastide* founded in 1277, stands beside the upper Dordogne at a point where the great river has dwindled to resemble a mellow Hampshire chalk stream, with a race and a graceful weeping willow below its ridge. The old timbered shuttered houses slope to a walled quay on the southern bank, from which generations of townspeople have nursed their fishing rods.

On the morning of 9 June, the 1st Section of the 3rd Company of the Ace of Hearts *maquis* guarded the bridge under the command, ironically enough, of a young Alsatian named Sergeant Frédéric Holtzmann – 'Fred' to most of his men. He was twenty, tall and fair, the sort of young man who might have been drafted into the SS had he remained at his home on the German border. In the early hours of the morning, word reached the village – probably by telephone from the St Céré area where the Das Reich armoured column had lagered for the night – that a German convoy was approaching. Many of the townspeople, roused from their beds, prudently departed into the woods and fields for safety. One young *résistant*, seeing a friend on his way to join them, embraced him emotionally in farewell. Then the twenty-six Frenchmen under Holtzmann, armed with rifles and a scattering of Brens and Stens, deployed around the bridge and on the roofs of the houses covering its approaches.

At about 6.30 am the first German vehicles approached the bridge down the main street of Bretenoux. Two *maquisards* who had ridden their *moto* towards St Céré to reconnoitre were fired upon, and hastily fled. The *maquisards* around the bridge began to use their own weapons, and a stubborn little battle began. For the next three hours the Germans fought for possession of the road, while the *résistants* clung to their river bank. At his headquarters at Montplaisir, Marius Guedin heard the gunfire, and sent a *sousofficier* and a party of men to investigate. They reached the outskirts of Bretenoux to find that there was no means of reaching the bridge. They lay watching and listening as the Germans began to use mortars. Guedin himself arrived to join them. There was nothing to be done. The SS had at last forded the river and worked around the flanks of the *résistants*. Holtzmann himself was badly wounded and could not move had he wished to. Most of the others had left it too late to withdraw. Several houses and three German vehicles were in flames. Eighteen of the twenty-five defenders of the bridge were dead. After the Liberation, Sergeant Holtzmann was awarded a posthumous Médaille Militaire.

Five miles further north, at the village of Beaulieu, another group of Guedin's men exchanged fire briefly, and lost three killed. One last section, at the crossroads of la Grafouillère still further up the road, saw the armour approaching and decided that discretion demanded that they hold their fire. The right flank of the Das Reich reached the summit of the hills, and began the long descent into Tulle without further interruption

Resistance estimates of the casualties they had inflicted upon the Das Reich between Montauban and Brive/Tulle on 8 and 9 June ran into hundreds, and as such were written into many regional histories. In addition to the actions reported above, Colonel Kreutz was dismayed to discover that a small maintenance party who were left behind the main body of the column to repair a disabled vehicle had been fallen upon and killed by a Resistance group. There is room for doubt about an additional one or two German casualties. The armoured column was engaged in a further battle, which will be described in the account of the Allied Jedburgh operations. But there seems no reason to doubt the overall German casualty report to 66th Reserve Corps for the fighting on that first march – some fifteen men killed and more than thirty wounded. French dead, as we have seen, were already over a hundred.

A signal was drafted that day from OKW's Operations Department, concerning the situation in Corrèze, Dordogne and Lot:

> Reports coming in on the secret army and acts of terrorism in the area show that *maquis* actions are reaching considerable proportions. The 66th Reserve Corps with the 2nd SS Panzer Division which are placed under the orders of the military command in France must immediately pass to the counter-offensive, to strike with the utmost power and rigour, without hesitation. The outcome of these operations is of the utmost importance to other operations in the West.
>
> In those areas partly infested, it is necessary to use intimidatory measures against the inhabitants. It is necessary to break the spirit of the population by making examples. It is essential to deprive them of all will to assist the *maquis* and meet their needs. . . .

From the high plateaux of the Lot, the road falls steeply into the spacious town of Brive-la-Gaillarde – 'Brive the Bold', named for its many gallant defences during the wars of the Middle Ages. In 1944 it possessed some 30,000 inhabitants, better fed than much of France at the period thanks to the fruit-growing and market-gardening of the area. Its central streets and squares suggest respectability and prosperity rather than beauty, but Brive has always enjoyed a reputation as a cheerful, welcoming place. Here, on the evening of 8 June, the first vehicles of the Das Reich swept down the road from Noailles and the south. 'Brive was like a beehive,' said Heinrich Wulf. Civilians crowding the street corners to exchange rumours and fears fled into their houses when they saw the column approach. As the most powerful German formation the town had ever seen roared up the road to the *Ortskommandantur*, they peered bleakly through the shutters. Some vehicles showed scars of battle. All of them were caked in dust and crowded with grim, camouflage-smocked troopers. A grisly souvenir was draped across the bonnet of one of the half-tracks – the body of a *maquisard*, Maurice Vergne, picked from the roadside in Cressensac.

The local German headquarters received them as an American western fort beleaguered by Indians might have greeted the coming of the cavalry. For two days they had clung to the safety of the *Kommandantur* building, protected by sandbagged emplacements, convinced that an attack by several thousand *maquisards* was imminent. They had received word of an attack on Tulle on 7 June, but there had been silence from the town all day on the eighth. Most of the Brive garrison and administrative staff were reservists ten, twenty, even thirty years older than the SS troopers. Beneath the universal coalscuttle helmets and detested uniforms of the Occupiers, had the inhabitants of Brive known it, there were several hundred very frightened and unenthusiastic enemies.

Major Wulf, Major Stuckler, Colonel Stadler and Major Weidinger strode into the Brive headquarters at the Hôtel de Bordeaux less than impressed by what they saw. They had always regarded the terrorists with contempt, and been convinced that aggressive, decisive military action could drive them headlong back into their woods. Nothing that they had seen that day at Cressensac or Noailles altered that view. The *maquis* were an infernal nuisance to regular military operations, but it was absurd that they had been allowed to achieve such psychological dominance over local German garrisons. The SS forcefully suggested to Colonel Luyken and the Brive command staff that a more active policy, with intensive sweeps and patrolling, would have prevented the partisans from achieving the concentrations that now threatened Tulle, Brive, and even – it was being reported from the Haute-Vienne – Limoges. In the view of the officers of the Das Reich, all this was the fruit of the infirmity of policy and weakness of execution.

There was a brief discussion of how best to deploy the division's teeth elements to meet the situation. Divisional headquarters under Stuckler – more than a hundred men and thirty vehicles – were already intending to pass the night in Tulle, and Stuckler himself was supposed to pay a liaison visit to 66th Reserve Corps at Clermont-Ferrand the following day. If there was trouble in Tulle – and panic-stricken messages from the garrison had talked of encirclement and crisis – then Wulf's reconnaissance battalion with its armoured vehicles and 75 mm guns should be more than competent to dispose of any *maquis* force. The artillery, flak and interminable tail units would lager along the Brive–Limoges road as they arrived, and General Lammerding proposed to supervise their disposal personally. The Der Führer regiment, as planned would continue immediately to Limoges and deploy around the town in support of the local garrison. The heavy armour, of course, was still far to the south-east, making sluggish progress up the road south of St Céré.

While the officers of the Das Reich were making their dispositions in the *Ortskommandantur*, among the little crowd of French civilians gazing stonily at the ranks of German vehicles in the Grand' Place was a young man named René Jugie, who had been following their progress with the keenest interest since the first word of their coming reached him early that morning of 8 June. Jugie was a member of the Corrèze committee of MUR – the *Mouvement Uni de Résistance*, intended to co-ordinate the activities of all the department's fragmented *réseaux* and *maquis*. He was himself the founder of one of them, which bore his codename, 'Gao'; he was also a great admirer of De Gaulle and a close associate of the SOE officers in the area – first Peulevé and now Poirier and Hiller.

Jugie took his codename from that of the air squadron to which he had been attached in 1940. He himself was thirty, a voluble, compulsively energetic Brive businessman of more prosperous bourgeois origins than the general run of *résistants*. He became involved in Resistance as early as 1942, when they were gathering such weapons as they could collect or steal from private and Armistice army sources, and assisting young men to escape from forced labour for Vichy. At that time, some communists worked with him despite the party's official refusal to have anything to do with Gaullist Resistance. Jugie took part in a few early sabotage operations of 1942–3, killing collaborators and organizing *parachutages*, while continuing to live publicly as a respectable citizen of Brive. He was one of many AS men who throughout the war had to overcome the emotional misgivings of his wife about the risks that he was taking. On one occasion when he was questioned by the *milice*, he escaped only because his appearance was so shrunken by the consequences of a stomach ulcer that he bore little resemblance to the description of the fleshier figure whom they sought.

One night a team of which Jugie was a member shot a local *milicien* and informer in a Brive bar. They were horrified to discover that the ambulance had removed him to hospital still breathing, possibly able to identify them. It was Jugie who had to snatch an excuse to visit the clinic, where he exchanged condolences with the chief local *milicien*, with whom he had played rugger before the war. It was appalling, this 'terror on the streets'. Yes, tragically the young man died without regaining consciousness.

Some of their efforts, however, verged on farce. A two-man 'hit team' dispatched to the office of a prominent local industrialist and collaborator emptied an entire pistol magazine at him and bolted, only to discover later that not a single shot had struck the target.

By the summer of 1944 the efforts of Peulevé, Poirier and the BCRA had brought thousands of weapons to the Corrèze, and the enthusiasm of the local Resistance had created one of the most numerous departmental movements in France. The British and Malraux had devoted great efforts to persuading the disparate groups to work with each other, and the existence of MUR meant that they were at least aware of each other's major plans. But the division between the Gaullists and the FTP was beyond bridging. Guedin was among those who bitterly attacked the British agents for arming the FTP, furthering their own entirely selfish ends. Some 5,000 *maquisards* in the hills of the upper Corrèze accepted the direction of the French communist party, and had no interest whatever in the wishes or instructions of London.

In the weeks before D-Day, the split became decisive. On Sunday 28 May, Jugie – as the representative of MUR – met 'Laurent', a cool, dark teacher from Marseilles who was a dedicated communist and the FTP's delegate to MUR. 'Laurent declared that he had given orders to his men to attack [the main centres of Vichy and German activity] in Brive on the night of 30 May,' the horrified Jugie reported to Emile Baillely, departmental chief of the *Combat* Resistance movement, and of MUR. He continued:

I told him that we had received formal instructions from Algiers and from London to launch attacks only in open country and at the Dordogne bridges, while carrying out the prearranged rail cuts according to *Plan Vert*, on receipt of the 'action messages'. Laurent replied that the Allies would never land in France, and that only by taking an independent initiative ourselves could we drive them to parachute us arms and material. Laurent said that he had received no orders from London or Algiers, but that he obeyed the orders of his superior party chiefs. He insistently demanded that I cause the units of my group, both the *légaux* and the *maquis*, to join his troops' attack on Monday. Naturally I refused. . . . I believe it is a matter of urgency to make Laurent's chiefs see reason. . . .

In the days that followed, there was intensive secret discussion between the two factions. The AS leaders made it clear that they would have no part of an attack on Brive, which could provoke horrific reprisals, and contravened London's repeated injunctions to make no attempt to seize towns at such risk. At another meeting, on 30 May, the FTP renounced the attempt to organize an attack on Brive, but made it apparent that they would be proceeding with their own attack on Tulle, with or without AS support. Amidst considerable rancour on both sides, the factions went their way to prepare for action.

On 7 June, Jugie passed a report from Tulle to Baillely:

FTP forces have attacked the German garrison in Tulle. Losses are heavy on both sides. The Ecole Normale where the enemy was billeted has been destroyed. Edith* and Maes,* on missions to Tulle during the attack, met Laurent at the head of his men. Laurent told Maes that an attack on Brive had been scheduled for the next day, 8 June. I think it is *urgent* to get the Comité départementale to intervene, because Guy I* and Pointer* say that armoured units are moving north-westwards, and threaten to pass through our region. . . .

Further frenzied activity by the MUR committee members ensured that no AS units made any move to take part in an attack on Brive, although it was learnt that a few groups in the north-east had joined the FTP attack on Tulle. By the morning of 8 June it was apparent that the FTP were too heavily committed in that town to have any chance of moving on to Brive.

* *Noms de guerre* for AS agents.

But the German garrison had heard enough from its own informers to be in the state of acute alarm that the SS found on their arrival.

At 9.30 am on 8 June, as Guedin's *maquisards* lay in their positions covering the Dordogne bridges, a prominent Vichy official who was one of the most vital sources of Resistance intelligence reported to Jugie that German armoured elements were moving north towards Corrèze to conduct a *ratissage*. He had heard directly from Colonel Bohmer, commanding the German 95th Security Regiment, that the first units were expected in Brive around 2 pm. A prominent Brive *milicien* named Thomine had also remarked briefly to another Resistance informant that 'Tulle will pay very dearly for the town terrorists' little joke.'

At 5 pm that afternoon, Jugie passed a further message:

> Pierre has just told me that companies Rémy, Désiré, Bernard and Gilbert are in action in the south of the sector against armoured elements of the Das Reich Division. It seems that this column will reach Brive towards 6 pm, because our men cannot hold for long against heavy tanks. I hope you will make Laurent and his friends see reason before it is too late.

The Corrèze committee held a secret rendezvous early that evening at the monastery of St Antoine on the edge of Brive, under Emile Baillely's chairmanship. Jugie noted:

> Some of *Laurent*'s friends insist that the plan for an uprising in Brive be immediately and vigorously implemented, so that it may be liberated like Tulle, and as Limoges may be this evening. . . . Baillely, armed with the latest information on the imminent arrival of the Das Reich – delayed on its march by the heroism of the AS–MUR Corrèze brigade – succeeded in dissuading Laurent's friends from any further folly. Some minutes after the meeting, the first elements of the Das Reich arrived in Brive.

Jugie's notes gave an indication of the bitterness with which the argument raged through those days, with mutual charges of betrayal and cowardice flung and contradicted, when the AS refused to fight in Brive to relieve the pressure on the FTP in Tulle. It is an interesting aside on the nature of Resistance in the days after the Allied landing that none of the local SOE officers was invited to take any part in the debate. These decisive questions were fought out entirely between Frenchmen. Before the event and subsequently, French Section's agents discussed, advised, persuaded and argued, but neither here nor in any but a handful of departments of France did the British or Americans have a chance to exercise executive authority. In the Corrèze, indeed, they firmly resisted the efforts of De Gaulle's BCRA to take a hand in directing their operations.

Reading Jugie's report, it is also essential never to lose sight of the chasm between his impressive references to companies and brigades and the reality on the ground of clusters of half-trained, half-armed boys among whom it was intensely difficult to maintain discipline in camp, far less in action. Rather than diminishing their achievements, these difficulties only serve to enhance them.

Early that evening of 8 June, at the Café des Sports in the centre of Brive a courier from Marius Guedin reached Jugie. He reported that the AS officer was furious to hear that trains were still running on the line north of the town, towards Uzerche. Would 'Gao' act immediately to halt them? Jugie fetched his bicycle and began a long ride around the town. First, he briefly visited three men of his circuit – Lescure, Briat and Chauty. They would meet him outside the town. Then he rode a mile or two to the farm of a man named Levet. Levet was one of many thousands of Frenchmen who did nothing spectacular or worthy of decoration during the Occupation, yet took terrible risks to support Resistance. Under the straw in his barn was a dump of explosives and detonators. Jugie rapidly assembled four 'loaves' of around a quarter of a pound of *plastique* apiece, and took a bunch of the deadly little grey detonators. Strapping his cargo in the bag on the carrier of his bicycle, he rode briskly to the rendezvous with the others. Well-distanced to avoid suspicion, they hastened onwards through the soft evening sunshine to a point where the railway dropped into a wood.

They passed a squad of French workmen working under German guard to repair the last section of line they had attacked. A mile or so beyond, they reached their target. Briat and Chauty held the bicycles and kept watch while Lescure and Jugie worked the charges under the track, one set to each of the north- and south-bound lines. They pushed the detonators into the soft lumps of explosive, connected them with bickford cord, and scrambled hastily into the wood, trailing cable to the electric detonator. Suddenly, to their consternation, they saw a peasant leading an ox cart across the line only yards away. He had resolutely resisted the pleas of Briat and Chauty to halt, insisting dourly that he was only going about his business. Moments passed, and a girl rode up on a bicycle. She was the daughter of the railway-crossing keeper, and Jugie had known her brother in the army. She said that she could hear gunfire in the distance. Jugie waited a few moments for her to disappear from sight, then twisted the exploder. One charge detonated hurling a twisted section of line into the air, but the other failed to go off. They ran to it, fumbled hastily to replace the cord, and fell back. They were careless. Jugie was slow to take cover as he fired the charge, and the blast, together with a deluge of stones from the permanent way, caught him where he crouched. He lost his hearing in one ear for life. But the line was blown, and there was still no sign of any Germans. The four men slipped swiftly back into Brive. The forward elements of the Das Reich had moved on. The Der Führer regiment was rolling up the long hill that led the way to Limoges, where its tired troopers arrived at last in the early hours of 9 June. The guns and miles of supporting vehicles were still moving steadily through Brive, towards their lagers on the Uzerche road. Major Heinrich Wulf's reconnaissance battalion, the *Aufklärungsabteilung*, followed by Colonel Stuckler and divisional headquarters, was closing rapidly upon Tulle.

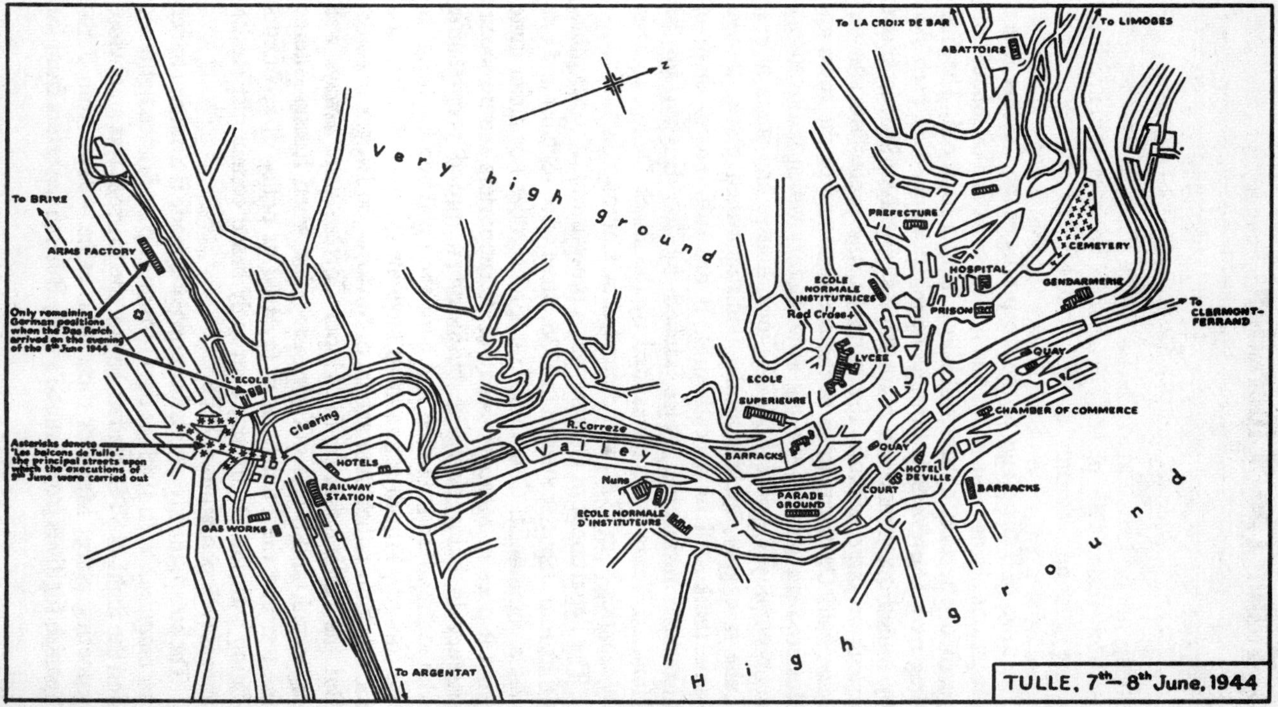

TULLE, 7th–8th June, 1944

5 Tulle: The 'Liberation'

The town of Tulle clings to the steep hills of the Corrèze like a precarious alpinist, the shops and houses of its 21,000 inhabitants perched wherever nature will allow them a foothold. The bustling river Corrèze falls through its midst, banked on each side by walled quays and the main streets. On the hillsides above rise three large schools, the barracks, the prefecture and the town hall. On the plateau at the southern end of the town are clustered the station, the big arms factory which is the town's main employer, and a knot of shops, houses and small hotels. Tulle is a grey, architecturally undistinguished place, though some think well of its cathedral. It has suffered its share of historical misfortune: twice sacked by the English in the Hundred Years War, devastated by the Black Death, retaken by Charles V in 1370, and defended by Catholics in 1585.

The department of Corrèze was a pre-war radical stronghold. Of its four deputies elected in 1936, three were socialist and one was a communist. Communism in France does not mean quite what it does in Moscow. Many of its supporters see no inconsistency in being energetic businessmen, proud *propriétaires* who are married in church and have their children baptized. In the country, French communists have always been 'leaders of a local faction rather than agents of Moscow', in Brogan's words. But the communists of the Upper Corrèze were always well organized, and it was not surprising that when Russia entered the war and the French party reversed its policy of accommodation with the Occupiers, a strongly based communist Resistance developed around Tulle.

The steep, thickly wooded countryside made it a natural haven for *maquisards*. In 1943, as the German grip on France tightened and the flight of STO evaders began, the Corrèze was an obvious gathering place. Many of those who came – Jews from Paris, Spanish fugitives from Franco's rule, Russian deserters from the

German Army, teenagers from half the departments of France, were not themselves communists, but they were willing to accept the energetic leadership of the local FTP. Among the Spaniards especially, it became common to find the absurd ideological rag-bag that Robert Noireau noted among one of his groups in the Lot: 'orthodox communists of PCE, anarchists of FAI, anarcho-syndicalists of CNT. Trotskyites of POUM and Catalan socialists. . . .' Few of them troubled much about politics in the *maquis*, and the zealots soon learned to hold their meetings unobtrusively. Only the jargon and the utter ruthlessness with which the FTP removed anyone – including a number of would-be defectors to the AS – whom they considered a threat made life for a rank-and-file FTP *maquisard* any different from that of a Gaullist. By the winter of 1943, perhaps 2,000 *maquisards* were grouped under FTP control in the Corrèze. The number had more than doubled by D-Day.

The communists' reputation for action appealed to enthusiastic spirits. They set up roadblocks and wrecked trains (George Hiller once found himself exchanging expressions of outrage with other, German passengers on a train which the FTP hijacked from under them). Between 27 April and 25 May 1944, the Tulle *gendarmerie* recorded seventy-eight terrorist outrages, almost all the work of the communists: fourteen were against railways, eight road attacks, seventeen against police, one factory sabotage, nineteen phone line cuts, seven attacks on *milice* and two on Germans, the remaining ten being thefts of food and material. The local population paid a terrible price in reprisals: after one minor FTP attack on a patrol near Camburet, the Germans burnt twenty-nine farms. Civilian hostages of all ages and both sexes were routinely seized and shot on the sites of ambushes. It is not surprising that Resistance only became a source of general national enthusiasm in France after the Liberation.

But the Germans were compelled to recognize that they no longer controlled large areas of the countryside. In March 1944, the Prefect of Corrèze estimated that seventeen cantons of the department were in the hands of the *maquis*, against nine held by the Germans and Vichy. The German garrison of elderly reservists in Tulle and Brive was supported by a *Sicherheitsdienst* security police and intelligence team and a detested following of several hundred armed Vichyites of the GMR and the Bony–Lafont gang – recruited chiefly from Parisian and North African criminals. The Hôtel St Martin, in which they were based, became notorious for the torture sessions customarily conducted in its baths. From time to time punitive columns took to the country, distributing violence with or without provocation. But for weeks on end *maquisards* on foot or in their *gazogène* trucks possessed unchallenged passage through the villages and countryside. Hundreds more secret FTP members awaited the call to mobilize from their jobs in the shops and factories of Tulle. There was even a 300-strong Young Communist group, led by a fifteen-year-old cadre.

Until the winter of 1943 the FTP was receiving only a trickle of arms, organized either by SOE's Harry Peulevé, or by a BCRA agent who was transmitting for a time from the church spire of Tulle. But in the six months before D-Day, a deluge of weapons began to reach the *maquisards*: Stens, Brens, gammon grenades, rifles and a handful of mortars and bazookas. For a time these were stockpiled in secret caches in the forests, but the frustration and insistent demands of the *maquisards* persuaded their leaders to issue them directly to the groups. They had no London-trained instructors, and were compelled to teach themselves by laborious study of the pamphlets supplied with the containers, and sometimes at bitter cost in accidents. One man made himself horribly ill by eating off a knife that he had last used for cutting *plastique*. Two *maquisards* named Pagat and Rozier made their first essay in throwing a gammon bomb, only to find that it refused to detonate. They threw stones at it until it exploded, slashing their faces with pebbles and debris. More serious, however, was the shortage of ammunition which made it impossible for most men to have live firing practice until they did so against the Germans. Contrary to popular belief, using a Sten or Bren gun effectively is not a knack as naturally acquired as riding a bicycle.

Food and boredom were the greatest problems of the *maquis*. The Corrèze had none of the natural abundance of Gascony or the great truffle region of the Périgord. Local sympathizers gave what they could, and the *maquis* stole everything they could lay their hands on from Vichy and the Germans. Noireau's group in the Lot once captured an entire lorryload of *foie gras*, and declared cheerfully every time they opened a tin: 'Here's one the Boche won't enjoy!' In the Corrèze there were seldom such extravagances. The *maquis* relied heavily upon raids on farms and villages which made some groups as detested as the Germans, whether or not they left promissory notes behind them. The borderline between Resistance and banditry was often thin. It was widely crossed all over France that winter of 1943–4. London, conscious of the problem, contributed what little it could by filling every spare corner of parachute containers with small blue tins of vitamin pills. But tobacco remained the greatest difficulty. A *maquis* with cigarettes retained some cohesion and morale. A *maquis* without them often came close to collapse. Very few FTP groups were led by men with any experience of command. It was hard to teach hungry, frustrated teenagers sleeping under parachute silk in a muddy clearing in the woods the need to wash, to dig latrines, to make route marches to maintain fitness, to post efficient sentries. Again and again, *maquis* were surprised by German patrols, sometimes undoubtedly tipped off by disgruntled peasants. A party of twenty-two was caught asleep at dawn one April morning in a wood near Roux. Only four escaped. On 5 May, two men were killed in another surprise attack, and the nearby village of Bordes was burned.

The drops from England or Algeria were the outstanding highlights of *maquis* life. 'Those *séances de parachutage* remain for me the finest memories of the *maquis*,' wrote Robert Noireau. 'Feats of patience and dreaming, of exhilaration at the idea of this contact between those in the interior and those who had chosen exile, the better to fight. Ah! Those February nights when one had to remain motionless on the landing ground, swept by the icy winds from the Massif Central!'

With the coming of spring and warmer weather, conditions improved in the *maquis*. Leaf on the trees increased their protection from observation, above all from the air. Throughout south central France, the FTP made increasingly daring demonstrations, holding parades through villages with flags and arms. The leader of the Lot FTP, a teacher named Jean-Jacques Chapou, achieved an immensely admired coup when he occupied the small town of Carjac on 10 April, the day of its fair, executed three alleged local collaborators, and telephoned the

Cahors Gestapo in the name of the mayor, demanding urgent help. When the Germans approached, the *maquisards* shot up their convoy before retiring. He attempted to lay the same trap in Gramat on May Day, but the Germans failed to respond. 'The first of May was a success throughout the region,' reported the Corrèze party chief, Louis Godefroy, who had organized other demonstrations like that of Carjac and Gramat. 'The departmental headquarters showed a spirit of initiative and enthusiasm which surpassed all our hopes. The prospects for this month of May are rich with promise for the success of the continuing offensive.' Early in May, the Corrèze FTP received a directive from Limoges, reporting the communist national military committee's commitment to preparation for 'a national insurrection. . . . The uprising was forcefully advocated as the only means of self-defence. When the Allies landed, how else could the Nazi armies be prevented from carrying out massive internments and massacring millions of Frenchmen? Best not to take that risk. The national uprising is "the supreme wisdom".'

The communist leadership in the Corrèze considered itself uniquely well-placed to liberate its own territory. 'Our forces, our weapons, the intelligence we possess about the enemy forces stationed in the area, the very favourable mood of the population' all gave confidence to André Odru, a twenty-two-year-old teacher who was their 'commissar for the fighters'. He wrote:

> We also know the strength of armed Resistance in the neighbouring departments. In the north, the forces of Guingouin and the *maquis* of the Creuse; in the south, the FTP activists of the Lot; in the west the Dordogne, which will assist a mass uprising of fighters; in the east, the highlands of the Massif Central and their *maquis*. We cannot believe that the Nazi forces are stronger than our own. It is in these conditions that the inter-regional military committee decided a long time ago to strike a major blow, when conditions became favourable, against Tulle – the very heart of the area.

Louis Godefroy, the short, stocky, thirty-year-old sanitary worker codenamed 'Rivière', who was their party chief, argued that it would be easy to cut off Tulle by isolating its road and rail links; that enemy morale was low; the garrison weak; and popular support for the *maquis* overwhelming. Much impressed by Jean-Jacques Chapou's achievements in the Lot, they now persuaded him to move to the Corrèze as the FTP's military commander. 'Kléber', as he was known, was a slim, austere figure of considerable personal force but limited military understanding. With some 5,000 men in the department, he and the others believed that they could easily dispose of the garrison of Tulle, whose strength they estimated at 250 Germans and 400 GMR. In reality, there were 700 Germans of the 3rd battalion of the 95th Security Regiment, 500 *miliciens* and a substantial number of SD, field police and German civilian and military administrators.

On 26 May Godefroy, the dynamic prime mover among them, made a discreet reconnaissance trip to Tulle with Albert Faucher, their quartermaster commissar. He claimed later that in the back room of a café full of local people, they were goaded and incited to act decisively. Both then and subsequently, Godefroy sought to escape acknowledging that he knew at the end of May that the FTP of the Limousin had decided not to attack Limoges. One of their most flamboyant leaders, the formidable and murderous Georges Guingouin, had shown surprising moderation when the Limoges project was being discussed. Perhaps, like some other FTP leaders, he had already determined to hold back the bulk of his strength for the moment when the Germans retreated from the city, and the communists could seize undisputed power. In any event, he declined to have any part in a *coup de main* against Limoges. Although rumours of its imminence panicked the German garrison, the Haute-Vienne Resistance continued to confine themselves to local attacks.

The Germans were correctly informed, however, that a crisis was imminent at Tulle. On the morning of 6 June, Pétain's detested deputy Pierre Laval personally telephoned Prefect Pierre Trouillé to discuss the threat. On the afternoon of the sixth, the schools closed early and remained shut through the days that followed. The same day, among the street posters inciting young Frenchmen to 'Join the Waffen SS', a new Vichy notice appeared: 'In the event of fighting or shooting in the street, shutters must be closed and civilians must remain in their own houses.'

The FTP organized their attack before the Allied landings, as soon as they knew from the *messages personnels* that D-Day was imminent. They believed that Liberation would follow invasion within weeks, if not days. If they did not seize their opportunity, communism in the Corrèze might be swamped by the tide of history. In defiance of every order they had received through London, every protest of the *Armée Secrète*, every rule of guerilla warfare and common prudence, they attempted to seize and hold the town of Tulle.

A few minutes after 5 am on the morning of 7 June, the flat crump of a bazooka rocket explosion echoed through the sleeping streets of Tulle. A thin plume of smoke rose from the Champs de Mars barracks where it had detonated. It was the signal for the attack. Threading their way down the hills and into the streets came the first columns of guerillas clad in blue tunics and berets, draped in haversacks and bandoliers, clutching their Stens and Brens, carrying bazooka rounds and mortar bombs in makeshift harnesses, exultantly conscious that they had reached a turning point of their war. The Germans and *miliciens* in their barracks and the schools in which they were billeted dragged on their clothes and equipment and began returning the *maquis* fire from windows and rooftops. Street by street and house by house, Chapou's men advanced into Tulle.

Assaulting a strongly held city without artillery or air support is one of the most difficult operations of modern war. It calls for surprise, close co-ordination, resolution and highly trained men. Not one of these advantages did the FTP possess. In the first hour, they threw away surprise. The signal bazooka was fired forty-five minutes before the main attack was launched. It had already been postponed by twenty-four hours at the request of some units who had many miles to cover on foot to the rendezvous. Many of those in the assault force knew neither the town nor the way to it, and had to be led by local guides. Two hours after the first shot, barely half the guerilla army was engaged. All that day, little columns were trickling belatedly into Tulle to join the attack. Without radio or telephone links, each company fighting in the dense streets had no means of judging the progress of others, of summoning help or ammunition or medical aid.

The first hours gave the *maquisards* a terrible lesson in war. Among the Germans and the *miliciens*, even the reservists were trained soldiers with plentiful ammunition, firing from solidly constructed buildings. The *maquisards* had been led to suppose that when the enemy saw the forces deployed against them, they would quickly surrender or flee. But when a young man named Marcel Chrétien leaped upon the *Monument aux Morts* and called to the *miliciens* in the billets opposite to surrender, he received only a fierce burst of fire. Few of the attackers had any experience of using firearms in action, far less of accurate marksmanship. From their street corners and doorways they blazed at the German positions 100, perhaps 200 yards distant. They lacked the cohesion to get to close quarters and mount a determined assault. After some painful early casualties, most preferred to hold their positions and exchange fire. In the first hours, ammunition began to run short in many companies. Many wounded men lay where they had fallen. From their first, dashing descent on Tulle, the *maquisards* found themselves pinned down in a deadly street fight. One of them, Roger Simonot, described an experience that morning.

We are cut off. The *feldgendarmes*, firing from the Hôtel La Tremolière and its gardens, bar our escape route. The situation is difficult. From my doorway, I can clearly hear a Nazi working the bolt of his rifle after each shot. I decide to break out towards the top of the Rue d'Epierre. The section leader motions me to move and covers me with his Thompson. A rush, then in the exchange of fire, I get through. A few seconds later Jean Bordas follows me. Alas, he is hit and falls in the midst of the road. My other companions abandon the initiative, and remain trapped. . . .

Jean-Jacques Chapou and Louis Godefroy had moved swiftly to the town hall when the attack began and established their headquarters in the council chamber. It was there that Constant Magnac, a twenty-nine-year-old teacher among the attackers, came to report:

I find a perplexed Kléber. Things are not going as well as he thought. I have seen Alfred and Luc in the Rue Louis-Mie, and they are no longer in dashing spirits. Albert Faucher is dead. Communications are very bad, and there is an almost total blackout of news from the north and north-east of the town. Have the units of Sub-Sector B arrived, and are they in place? Is Sub-Sector A here and in position? I learn that the

GMR stationed at the Champs de Mars barracks are still holding out. . . . Kléber cannot satisfy my request for reinforcements for the south and south-east of the town. . . .

'Towards 8 am,' wrote Chapou himself, 'after two hours of heavy fighting, none of the runners whom I had sent to the battalion commanders had returned. . . . The enemy maintained a heavy fire.' Francesco Molinari, a young Italian communist who had won a Croix de Guerre fighting with the French Army in 1940 and was now an STO evader, shot his way into the Hôtel Moderne in the midst of the quays at the head of a group of *maquisards*, to be met by fierce resistance from the opposite end of the bar and the stairs. The attackers hurled themselves behind overturned marble tables to return the fire. Table by table they worked across the bar, one man crawling behind them, feverishly refilling Sten magazines from loose rounds in his haversack. At last the Germans retreated up the stairs. Molinari seized a bottle from the bar and raised it to his throat, only to have a bullet smash it from his grasp. Furiously he dashed for the stairs, firing as he ran. The Germans had escaped through the back door. He caught a glimpse of himself and his men reflected in a huge mirror on the landing, and they laughed at the image: filthy, exhausted, bearded, their clothes torn and their arms scratched and bleeding. They moved warily out of the hotel, and on down the street.

At about 11 am, a civilian approached a *maquisard* company commander in the street. He brought a message from the GMR and the gendarmes beleaguered in the Champs de Mars barracks. They had had enough. Could they withdraw up the road to Limoges under a flag of truce? Grudgingly the *maquisard* assented. Not long after, one by one a cautious procession of trucks emerged from the barracks yard, each one bearing a white flag. They were not fired upon. In haste and intense relief, the Vichyites retreated northwards towards the hills and Limoges. Some of the *maquisards* who saw them depart were infuriated, above all that the enemy had been allowed to take their weapons. But by now the FTP's leaders were under no illusions. The GMR would never have handed over their arms, given the *maquis*'s disposition to '*bouziller les gars*' – eliminate

Vichy's agents out of hand. Chapou's difficulties were more than great enough that day. Any diminution of the number of defenders must be welcomed on any terms.

When the first euphoria of the battle had receded, fatigue came quickly to the *maquisards*. Many had marched on foot for hours to reach the rendezvous, before they began to fight. They lacked the mutual confidence that supports trained units. Their clumsiness with their weapons caused repeated accidents. 'Fanny', a boy loading one of the bazookas, was horribly burned on the face as he lay carelessly in the path of its back blast when the gunner fired. A few moments later, a well-timed stick grenade from a window above a florist's caught the injured boy again, agonizingly, together with two other men beside him. A few hundred yards away, another group was attempting to drive the Germans off the roof of the Ecole Supérieure with smoke and shrapnel rifle grenades. Two men were terribly wounded by premature explosions as they pressed their triggers. The others abandoned using rifle grenades.

The only German sally of the day took place at the bottom of the town at about 1.30 pm, when a party broke out of the buildings they were holding opposite the station, and took up positions on the platforms. In a waiting-room they burst in on eighteen nervous young French line guards who had taken refuge out of the line of fire. The Germans shot three immediately. When they withdrew to the hotel, they herded the other Frenchmen with them. One managed to break away and escape. The other fourteen were killed at once.

The afternoon wore on without decision. The *maquisards* now occupied most of the town, but the Germans were still holding out in the Ecole Normale, the arms factory and a school just in front of it. Two reconnaissance aircraft droned overhead, inspecting the town and raking the *maquisards* with desultory machine gun fire as they scuttled beneath. As evening approached, it was still impossible to move freely along the quays, because of the Germans' commanding positions on the heights above. The attackers were tired, hungry, and depressed by their losses. Kléber and the others in the council chamber weighed the events of the day: 'Positive – the Germans are reduced to a cautious defensive (if one excludes their determined counter-attack on the station); negative – disastrous communications. Obvious lack of training among the men. Insufficient caution, lack of heavy weapons and shortage of ammunition. . . .' The *maquisards*' best chance against the arms factory would probably have been a forceful night attack, but as darkness fell they had no spirit for such adventures. Most men slept where they stood, or slipped into the bedrooms of houses from which they had been firing, in some of which the terrified inhabitants still lingered amidst their possessions.

That evening, a car bearing couriers from Godefroy slipped out of Tulle and raced north to the château in the forests south-east of Limoges where Georges Guingouin had his headquarters. Like so many Resistance leaders, he had awarded himself colonel's rank and shoulder pips on his uniform, and hugely enjoyed playing the part of military commander. The FTP visitors from Tulle were exasperated by the patronizing, bombastic reception they received from 'this great devil of a man, brandishing his pistol at intervals to emphasize his remarks'. They heard a lecture on the folly of their action, and the flat rejection of their request for arms, ammunition or men.

At first light on the morning of 8 June, the firing resumed in Tulle – sporadically at first, then with more purpose as each side reawakened to its role in the drama. It continued hour after hour, with occasional casualties among attackers and defenders. The *maquis* had learned more caution, and showed no urge to storm the remaining enemy positions. The Germans appeared content to stand the siege until help came. But by early afternoon the *maquisards* had worked close enough to the Ecole Normale to use smoke grenades and incendiaries. After repeated efforts they succeeded in setting fire to one corner of the building, and soon the blaze was out of control. Smoke was pouring from the windows, and the *maquisards* perceived the enemy's fire slackening.

At 4 pm, to the delight of the exultant besiegers, a white flag appeared at the door. It was carried by Louise Boucheteil, a girl courier for the FTP who had been captured ten days earlier and held prisoner in the cellars of the building with some twenty other *maquisard* captives, expecting death at any time. Now, behind her from the school, unarmed and with their hands on their heads, came some forty Germans in uniform and civilian clothes. They had had enough. The jubilant *maquisards* seized their weapons and equipment and herded away the prisoners. One of those in civilian clothes was spotted by a *maquisard* who shouted, 'I've seen you before – in the Hôtel St Martin!' It was a Gestapo agent, who instantly broke from the column and ran for his life. A hail of fire belatedly pursued him. A *maquisard* ran down the hill in his wake, at last overtook the agent and shot him.

Now the only German garrison left in Tulle was pinned in the arms factory and the school in front of it. The Germans' fire effectively covered only a few streets, and they showed no desire to assert themselves. Through the rest of Tulle, as silence overtook the town, one by one frightened and exhausted families began to emerge from their homes, nervously to congratulate the victors, bring out what little food and drink they had, tend the wounded and carry away the dead. One of the *maquis* leaders, a twenty-one-year-old farmworker named Elie Dupuy, told Prefect Trouillé defiantly: 'If the Germans counter-attack, we shall ambush and beat them just as we have done in the past two days. In any case, we are perfectly certain that the armed struggle will bring about the liberation of our department – and of France!'

The cost had been high, but the great objective was all but gained. Excepting only the impotent huddle of Germans in the arms factory, the communist *Francs-Tireurs et Partisans* had by their own efforts liberated the town of Tulle and brought its Occupiers to naught. Kléber, Godefroy, Dupuy and their men exulted in their triumph as they counted the dead and began to clear the wreckage, discussing how best to quell the fires that were still burning around the Ecole Normale. André Odru drove a few miles out of town on the road eastwards to visit his outlying pickets, puttering triumphantly up the hill in a borrowed *gazogène*.

He returned shortly after 9 pm. As his car approached the station, a knot of frightened townspeople flagged him down in the street. 'The Germans are there!' they shouted, gesturing towards the town centre. 'Run for it!' Odru hastily reversed the car. A few moments later the first flares began to burst over

Tulle. Once again, the hammer of machine gun fire and the crump of heavier shells and mortars began to echo through the town. The Das Reich Division had entered the reckoning.

6 Tulle: The Price

When Major Heinrich Wulf's reconnaissance battalion – some hundred half-tracks and trucks bearing more than 500 men, even without their armoured car squadron – clattered out of Brive-la-Gaillarde at around 7 pm on the evening of 8 June, its officers were not in the best of tempers. They were irritated, almost affronted by the division's losses during the afternoon, doubly so because some of them had heard General Eisenhower's broadcast demanding full combatant status for *résistants* in arms. They were irked by the panic-stricken behaviour of the local garrison in Brive. So feeble was the German Empire's grasp on the Corrèze, it seemed, that an SS Panzer *Aufklärungsabteilung* had now to be deployed to rescue the Tulle garrison from a band of half-armed communist terrorists. Neither they nor their men had much hint of what to expect when they reached the town.

The road from Brive to Tulle winds steeply upwards, overlooked by cliffs and woods for much of its course. Had the FTP possessed the smallest sense of self-preservation or tactical judgment a small force of *maquisards* posted to cover it could have felled trees across the road and delayed the advance of any German force for hours with Brens and gammon grenades. Yet the watchful Germans in the leading half-tracks observed nothing for mile after mile except a hint of smoke from the hills masking Tulle. When Wulf saw from his map that they were within two or three miles of the town, he raised his arm to signal the convoy to halt. With unknown assailants ahead, it was time to close up, and take the opportunity to refuel the vehicles from their jerrycans. They could still hear no sound of firing, but it seemed possible that the noise of battle was being muffled by the hills which encircled the town.

The evening light was softening now, as they mounted the half-tracks again, and swept round the last bends and past the first houses of Tulle. Every man crouched with his weapon raised and cocked, mutely cursing the clatter of the tracks that made it impossible to hear shooting. They reached the approaches to the station, and still they did not see a soul. Every door and shutter was closed. The column swerved contemptuously around a single felled tree trunk in the road. There was a brief burst of fire in their direction which died within seconds. Wulf motioned his driver to halt. He jumped down from the half-track. Seeing nothing, he ordered the man to switch off the engine. There was still silence. Cautiously, with an NCO and his runner behind him, he moved on foot down the street, searching for signs of life and seeing none. He walked perhaps a hundred yards, then turned back to order his adjutant to deploy the companies around the town. He was still a street's width from the column, when, as if at a signal, a barrage of gunfire burst around them. Brens, Stens and the crash of grenades echoed through the houses. The Germans in the half-tracks began to pour back fire. Wulf and his two men crouched for a moment against a bus shelter, then dashed back to cover behind their own armour. He was rapidly briefing his company commanders for the advance through the town when a single elderly, obviously terrified German NCO scuttled across the street towards him. He had been sent from the beleaguered garrison in the school in front of the arms factory 200 yards away. When they heard the approaching vehicles, they had guessed that it must be a relief column. With three of his own men behind him, Wulf and the NCO zigzagged from cover to cover down the street and into the shelter of the school.

Wulf could scarcely credit the picture he saw before him inside: fifty or more elderly reservists, blazing nervously at shadows from their windows; a handful of wounded on the floor; the men so shaken that they could not dispose of *maquis* sniper firing from a position thirty yards away. Wulf curtly ordered his men to silence the enemy weapon, which ceased fire after a few moments. Then he turned to the cluster of delighted old men gathering around him, all talking at once. They were members of the 95th Security Regiment, and were commanded by Captain Reichmann, a fifty-five-year-old dentist from Baden-Württemberg. Wulf said:

They were sitting there like mice in a trap. They all started stammering at me, so that it was impossible to get any description of the situation. They said that they had heard nothing from the garrison in the other school for two days, yet they had made no attempt to make contact. I couldn't understand how they had allowed this situation to happen. It was a sad place, with these frightened old men who had had no sleep for two nights. I stayed only two minutes, then ran back to my adjutant at the vehicles. I felt outraged that we had been diverted from the battle in Normandy to deal with this nonsense. My immediate aim was simply to sort out the town before it became completely dark. . . .

Wulf reached his half-track to find Albert Stuckler arrived beside it at the head of the divisional headquarters column. They could plainly see *maquisards* moving on the hillsides above the town, and hear firing from the other end of Tulle. The first priority, clearly, was simply to sweep them from the streets.

The *maquisards* scattered through Tulle never organized a coherent defence against Wulf's companies. Many were at the limit of exhaustion and had no more ammunition. At the sound of heavy firing, they began to trickle away into the hills. One party was counting the German dead at the Ecole Normale when someone shouted that enemy vehicles were approaching. They gave their only bazooka to a young Parisian watchmaker renowned as a marksman, and watched the German convoy crawl towards them. A motor cycle and sidecar passed, then the watchmaker fired at the half-track behind. The rocket exploded against it, and the column stopped abruptly. The partisans began a hasty retreat from the town, leaving only a handful of bolder spirits who stayed long enough to fire off the last of their ammunition at the Das Reich.

Private Sadi Schneid, one of the young Alsatians who had been posted to the battalion anti-tank company at Bordeaux, crouched nervously with his fellow-recruits in their half-track as they moved into the streets of Tulle amid sporadic gunflashes. Their senior NCO, their almost worshipped Hauptscharführer – 'Hascha' – Kurz was the only man in the vehicle who knew his business perfectly. 'We've got to make that machine gun shut up!' he shouted, slamming the driver on the shoulder to make him halt. As the engine cut, for the first time they heard the gunfire. The men leaped down, unlimbered their towed Pak 75, and swung it towards the hillside from which a *maquisard* was using a Bren. The gunlayer, another raw recruit, was still peering intently through the eyepiece when, in a moment of black comedy, the gun fired and he was hurled bodily from his seat. On the asphalt road, the spades that stemmed the recoil could not grip. The 'Hascha' swore violently, the team pulled itself together and fired again. There was no sign of an explosion from the hill. The 'Hascha' cursed again: 'That clumsy hippopotamus' – this to the loader – 'is feeding us solid anti-tank rounds instead of shrapnel!' When the Pak crew fired again, the *maquisard* ceased fire.

Another of the company's vehicles roared up to them, bearing two dejected prisoners with FTP arm brassards. An NCO stood up in the back and shouted a question to the 'Hascha' about what was to be done with them. Nobody knew. The half-track clattered away. Another followed with a shaken crew. A *maquisard* bullet had caught one of the young Alsatians in the eye, killing him instantly as he crouched covering their rear. The 'Sani' – the company medical orderly – confided to Schneid that he was feeling unhappy because he had killed a woman as they drove up the street. He saw a curtain move, fired at the window, and saw a middle-aged Tulle housewife topple forward over the sill. Another half-track returned with a man dead and another wounded. A *maquisard* had lain poised above it to lob a gammon grenade into the interior as it passed.

But Wulf's companies suffered very few casualties that night. There was no serious resistance to the reoccupation of Tulle. Within twenty minutes of the Das Reich beginning to deploy around the town, their dominance was complete. Dejected files of evicted *maquisards* were trudging away into the hills, bearing such wounded as they could carry off. 'It was a Dante-esque spectacle,' wrote one of them, Elie Dupuy. 'Flares being fired from all directions, bursts of machine gun fire, cannon and mortar explosions overwhelming every other sound. Tired, beaten, our units and our men see all their efforts, their sacrifices and their hopes evaporate in a matter of minutes. . . .'

The Germans, now unchallenged, deployed around the town for the night. Every wall in the centre was hacked and pock-marked by gunshots; windows stood shattered, shutters hanging torn and loose, glass strewn in the street. The townspeople remained closely hidden behind their doors, many already terrified by the prospect of German vengeance. Private Schneid slipped into a garage close to his platoon position, in search of some tools to repair a panel on the half-track damaged when the Pak gun recoiled into it. Suddenly he found himself overshadowed by an enormous, menacing figure – a '*Kettenhunde*,' a 'chained dog', one of the *Feldgendarmes* so called because of the chains of office around their necks. 'And what are you doing here?' demanded the man fiercely, and led Schneid, protesting, to his company commander to report a suspected looter. The officer sent the *Feldgendarme* on his way. It is an odd aside on the events of Tulle that such a matter at such a moment attracted the attention of German authority.

Hungry – for they had no more rations – and exhausted by the first encounter with live ammunition for many of them, the SS lay by their weapons, dozing and standing guard through the brief summer night of 8 June.

Shortly after midnight, Wulf was called to divisional headquarters, temporarily established in a hotel at the foot of the town. Stuckler was furious. While the division had suffered only three killed and nine wounded in retaking the town, the body count among the German garrison showed that 139 men had been killed and forty wounded by the *maquis*. At first light, Wulf was to send one company to a point some twelve miles from Tulle which was reported to harbour the French headquarters and arms dump. The other two companies, less those men essential to control the perimeter, were to sweep the entire town, house by house. They were to seize any hidden weapons, and bring every male Frenchman in Tulle to the courtyard of the arms factory for an identity check. As a convenient starting point, any man without papers could be assumed to be a terrorist.

It was the beginning of the day that Tulle would never forget. From first light, files of SS troopers marched rapidly through the streets, hammering on doors, ordering out their terrified inhabitants, forming the first pitiful huddles of civilians to be herded towards the arms factory. The Prefect, Pierre Trouillé, had come close to summary execution himself when a case of grenades was found in his office, but he convinced the Germans that he had been an innocent spectator of the FTP takeover. Now, he asked Major Kowatsch, the divisional 1c or third-ranking staff officer, if there were to be any reprisals. He pointed out with perfect justice that the citizens of Tulle had been totally uninvolved in the events of the past two days. Kowatsch told both Trouillé and the German-speaking secretary-general, Maurice Roche, that no punitive action would be taken. This assurance was echoed at more junior levels. Private Schneid was summoned to interpret for one of his company officers who was commandeering a schoolteacher's house for quarters. In answer to her frightened question, the officer said that reprisals had indeed been considered, but had now been decided against. Kowatsch told Trouillé that a decisive factor in the decision to show mercy was the care with which German wounded had been treated in the town hospital.

Yet at 10 am, with some 3,000 Frenchmen of every age standing bewildered in the yard of the arms factory under the guns of the SS, a new order was given. There would, after all, be reprisals. Schneid and an SS detail were ordered to escort the town fire engine as its crew drove through Tulle reading a terrible proclamation at the street corners. Clinging to the back of 'this antediluvian machine' as it rang its bell to seize the attention of the citizens, they set off through the streets. The chief fireman – in tears according to Schneid – declaimed a brief German announcement which the soldier recalled as follows: 'Because of the indescribable murder of forty German soldiers by communist *maquisards*, the German authorities have decided that three Frenchmen will pay for each German killed, as an example to all France.' Within the hour, a formal proclamation copied by a local printer, hauled from his home, was being posted on the walls of Tulle:

CITIZENS OF TULLE!

Forty German soldiers have been murdered in the most abominable fashion by the communist gangs. The peaceful population has submitted to terror. The military authorities wish only for order and tranquillity. The loyal population wishes this equally. The appalling and cowardly fashion in which the German soldiers have been killed proves that the instruments of communist destruction are at work. It is most regrettable that there were also policemen and French *gendarmes* who, abandoning their posts, did not follow their orders and made common cause with the communists.

For the *maquis* and those that help them, there is only one penalty, the hangman's noose. They do not recognize open combat, they have no feelings of honour. Forty German soldiers have been murdered by the *maquis*. 120 *maquis* or their accomplices will be hanged. Their bodies will be thrown in the river.

As a warning, for every German soldier wounded, three *maquis* will in future be hanged. For every German soldier killed, ten *maquisards* or an equal number of their accomplices will be hanged. I expect the loyal co-operation of the civil population in fighting the common enemy, the communist bands.

Tulle, 9 June 1944
The General Commanding the German troops

It was now that the most dreadful drama of Tulle began, which to this day remains shrouded in controversy. The precise truth is beyond discovery. It is only possible to report the accounts given by the surviving participants.

Heinrich Wulf and his SS colleagues say that, early on the morning of 9 June, the senior divisional doctor who had been collecting the German dead from the battle arrived at headquarters to report that a single group of forty bodies had been discovered, horribly mutilated. Their faces had been stove in, and their testicles cut off and stuffed in their mouths. It was for this act, the Germans alleged, rather than for the Resistance attack, that reprisals were to be taken. Private Schneid claims to have heard the same story from his friend the 'Sani', the company medical orderly. He and his platoon went to the cemetery to bury their two men killed the previous night:

We arranged ourselves in front of the grave, each avoiding the eye of his neighbour because we were all crying silently. Our eighteen-year-old (minus three months) hearts could not restrain the emotion welling in our throats. I don't know if my comrades were praying, but for my part, I saw myself at the bottom of that grave, and if I recited a prayer, I don't know whether it was for the comrades at my feet, or for myself. . . .

As soon as they had fired their ceremonial volley over the grave, he and the others were ordered to form a burial detail to carry away the corpses of the forty dead Germans:

> We refused to look closely at these bloody corpses. Was it fear of death, or did we refuse to admit to ourselves that Frenchmen could do such a barbaric thing? The German soldiers had always behaved correctly to the French population – why then this fury, to massacre Germans in this fashion? Couldn't they wait for the chance to join the regular liberation army . . . which would permit them to join a decent war of revenge, with prisoners protected by the Geneva Convention?

One of the prime movers among the Germans for wholesale reprisals was Lieutenant Walter Schmald of the Tulle SD, the security police. Schmald had been in the Ecole Normale throughout its siege. He was a mechanic's son from St Vith, in Belgian territory that had shuttled between German and Belgian possession since before World War I. A former chemistry student, he had served with the SS on the Russian front, transferred to the SD, and had been based in Tulle for five months. He and his colleague, Lieutenant Beck, knew that they had no hope of mercy from the FTP. When fire overtook the school and the garrison prepared to surrender, Beck put a pistol to his head and shot himself. Schmald found a hiding place in the kitchens, and far into the night of 8 June he lay suffocating amidst the smoke and ruins of the school, barely clinging to life. When he staggered from his refuge to meet the relief column, he was consumed with bitterness. He claimed that most of those who had surrendered were now among the mutilated bodies found by the SS. But for the persuasion of Maurice Roche, pleading urgently with the German divisional staff, if Schmald had had his way the Germans would have been preparing to hang several hundred Frenchmen.

When the war crimes tribunals were examining the '*affaire de Tulle*' years afterwards, the SS witnesses concocted various alibis to excuse or conceal their own role. French historians have always assumed that the supposed murder of German prisoners was a Nazi fabrication, and indeed it may have been. The FTP insisted that when they evacuated the town, they released several large groups of prisoners, having no means of holding them.

Nothing can excuse what the Das Reich did in Tulle, but it is important at least to consider the motives that the Germans advanced. Both in the past and the future, *maquisards* – above all those of the FTP – frequently shot German prisoners out of hand. The author, during his researches for this book, never credited the possibility of the truth of the German allegations until the subject was raised in conversation with a former leading member of the *Armée Secrète* in the Corrèze, who since the war has done much research on local Resistance history. He told me:

> Ah, yes, the business of the mutilated and executed prisoners. I have written and said many times since the war that it is unthinkable that *résistants* could have behaved in this fashion. However, I have spoken to many of those who were in Tulle during the battle, and there is no doubt that it was true. The Spaniards among them, you know. . . . I tell you this because I, as a Frenchman, can never say it. For you, as an Englishman, it may be of interest. But should you ever suggest that I was the source of this assertion, of course I shall deny it absolutely. . . .

It would be absurd to accept the truth of the SS allegations on the unsupported private testimony of one man who was not an eyewitness. There was intense bitterness and ill-will between the AS and FTP in the Corrèze, as we have seen, and it is possible that this coloured the willingness of an AS veteran to believe the worst of the communists. But I am impressed by another, admittedly circumstantial piece of evidence. The FTP claim to have lost seventeen killed and twenty-one badly wounded in the original Tulle attack. Yet there were 139 German corpses. Is it really possible to believe that the garrison, fighting from strong defensive positions, in a battle which the FTP themselves admitted did not go as they had planned it, suffered such disproportionate loss in action? The balance of suspicion must be that the FTP indeed executed a substantial number of Germans who had surrendered to them.

The second significant controversy concerns the source of the order for mass reprisals in Tulle. Throughout the long post-war struggle to indict Lammerding for war crimes, from his secret refuge in Germany the general asserted repeatedly that he did not even arrive in Tulle until the later afternoon of 9 June, when the reprisals were already ended: 'I am still ignorant of the source of the order for executions in Tulle,' he said, 'but I do not think that it was given by a higher authority.' The hangings were, therefore, entirely the responsibility of his senior staff officer, Major Albert Stuckler. General Lammerding's alibi rested upon the interesting claim that at the time of the hangings in Tulle, he himself was in Uzerche, conducting an entirely separate hanging of his own.

Uzerche is a small town on the Limoges road twenty-five miles north of Brive-la-Gaillarde. After many hours visiting the scattered lagers of his units, up and down the main road, Lammerding passed the night of 8 June in the flat above the shop of a tanner named Laporte. Early on the morning of the ninth, one of his officers reported to him with three *maquis* prisoners. When the Das Reich advanced into Tulle the previous evening, the Frenchmen had escaped north-westwards in a Citroën van. At the outskirts of the town, they were flagged down by two frightened girls, who begged a lift. Uzerche is only fifteen miles distant by the direct road, and they were approaching the town when an SS patrol surrounded and seized them. The two girls, it transpired, were the mistresses respectively of Lieutenant Schmald and the late Lieutenant Beck of the SD, and they immediately denounced the young Frenchmen. Then, damningly, it was discovered that one of them was carrying three *Feldgendarmes*' neck shields, which in a moment of madness he had retained as souvenirs.

The young men were brought before Lammerding himself. The Laporte family were bewildered by the courtesy with which he received them. He offered, one, Raymond Monteil, a cigarette. The boy declined, saying that he was too hungry to smoke. Lammerding ordered food to be brought. There was no debate about the future of the *maquisard* who had been found in possession of the *Kettenhunden* chains. A rope was tossed over an electric pylon, and he was hanged. The two women pushed and twisted the body as it swung, joking with the SS executioners. Raymond Monteil and the other *maquisard* were spared, for deportation to Dachau where they died, not yet twenty.

According to Lammerding's later testimony, he had had no radio communication with his headquarters in Tulle since the previous evening because of the steep hills intervening. Only late in the afternoon of the ninth did he leave for the town, travelling because of the security situation, via Brive in a slow-moving armoured vehicle rather than taking the direct route in a staff car. Lammerding also drew particular attention to the fact that the proclamation of Tulle's doom was signed by 'The General Commanding the German Troops'. If it had been his own signature, he said, he would have naturally have signed himself 'Lammerding'.

Colonel Stuckler and Major Wulf – not surprisingly, whatever the truth of the matter – testify emphatically that Lammerding reached Tulle about 1 pm, and personally ordered the executions. The balance of probability favours this version. It is difficult to imagine a conscientious staff officer like Stuckler giving such an order entirely on his own initiative without consulting his commanding general. It is also significant that Stuckler testifies that 'there was no specific order to carry out hangings from 66th Reserve Corps'. Had he wished to shift responsibility from himself, the least difficult means of doing so would have been to cite the order of a higher formation. There was ample encouragement from OKW and Army Group G to carry out ruthless reprisals. Finally, however, the printed proclamation bears the authentic odour of Lammerding, as witnessed by his memorandum to 58th Corps of 5 June. If anyone still doubts that the reprisals in Tulle were a cold-blooded act of divisional policy, for which Lammerding bore full moral and military responsibility, it only remains to read the text of the division's memorandum on anti-guerilla operations, issued to all units that day of 9 June, and published here as Appendix A. It is extraordinary that a senior SS officer who had commanded anti-partisan operations in Russia could have attempted to persuade a post-war generation that he did not authorize a divisional mass execution.

It is at this point in the narrative that a sullen, grudging tone enters the voices of the surviving SS witnesses. Major Wulf claims to have been affronted when he was ordered to assemble an execution squad: 'I protested that this sort of thing was the responsibility of the *Feldgendarmerie*.' But the battalion found the men anyway. Private Schneid reported:

> 'Hascha' Kurz took me with him to the headquarters of the adjutant who was talking to the company NCOs. It was a matter of finding volunteers to act as hangmen. . . . Execution was to be by hanging, because it was more humiliating than a firing squad. . . . Executioners

were chosen from among the pioneer company, composed principally of native Germans, with the balance from men of our company who had recently joined us from the Russian front when their units were disbanded. It proved difficult to find enough volunteers. . . . But they were reminded what these *maquisards*, these communists had done to their fellow-countrymen.

Schneid claims to have seen a fellow-Alsatian named Pierre walk away in tears 'saying that he could not do "that" '. He himself was told by an NCO who despised '*Franzenköpfe*' like himself 'that if I did not have the courage to do some hanging, I could at least act as an escort'. So Schneid and some twenty of his fellow-troopers took up position on the street at the lower end of Tulle, close to the courtyard of the arms factory, for the odious tragedy that now unfolded.

All that morning, Lieutenant Schmald and his colleagues had been screening the great crowd of Frenchmen in the courtyard of the arms factory. Many had been allowed to depart. By early afternoon something over 400 remained, and they were becoming increasingly apprehensive. Schmald strode among them, asking acid questions: 'Why are your shoes so dirty? If you were a decent citizen, they would be clean. You must be a *maquisard*.' He did not conceal his personal craving for revenge for the days of terror that the *maquis* had inflicted upon him: 'I am one of the few survivors of yesterday's battle,' he told the Abbé Espinasse, the tall, slender almoner of the *lycée* who had been allowed to remain with the captives. 'We were almost all Rhine Catholics. We would very much have liked a priest to comfort us.' As soon as it became known that many of the prisoners were to die, Herr Brenner, the German director of the arms factory, intervened. Some of the men in the courtyard were key workers, almost irreplaceable. Surely they could be excluded? His interpreter, a thirty-two-year-old Ulm woman named Paulette Geissler, moved busily through the ranks, selecting a man here and another there, and gesturing to the SS to release him. Twenty-seven in all were allowed to go. Then Fräulein Geissler joined Schmald and a little group of other Germans at a table outside the Café Tivoli, where they could watch the balance of the afternoon's activity in comfort – some witnesses later claimed to the music of a gramophone.

The essential difficulty facing the Germans was that among all the men in the courtyard, only two were indeed *maquisards*. Among all the remainder, there was not even a shred of evidence to implicate them as accomplices of the FTP. Schmald was compelled to resort to methods arbitrary even by SD standards. One by one, the young, the dirty and the unshaven were ordered to join a group at the side of the courtyard. They were men like Louis Chieze, twenty-six, hairdresser; Marcel Demaux, thirty, a teacher married to another teacher, with a child of four; Georges Gloria, forty, fitter in a bicycle works; Raymond Le Souef, forty, manager of a *gazogène* works; Guy Peuch, twenty, a worker in the arms factory; and his brother André, twenty-three, a restaurant-owner; Jean-Marius-Joseph Rochedix, nineteen, a tramway employee compulsorily transferred to the Tulle armament factory. . . . And so on, 120 men in all, of whom the youngest was seventeen and the oldest forty-two.

The first group of some fifty victims was marshalled in the courtyard. The Abbé Espinasse was permitted to address them: 'My friends, you are going to appear before God. There are Catholics among you, believers. Now is the time to commend your souls to the Father who will receive you. Make an action of contrition for all your sins, and I will give you absolution.' An SS officer read the order for their execution in German, incomprehensible to most of them. At a gesture from the officer, the guards began to move the group out of the yard, round the corner into the street that passes over the river Vézèré at the southern end of the town. Schneid, watching them come with their hands tied behind their backs, was struck by the absurdity that some still carried loaves of bread or coats tucked under their arms, because when they left home that morning, they had not known whither they were to go. A squad of young Vichyite *chantiers de la jeunesse* had been recruited by the Germans to help with the arrangements – gathering ladders and ropes from the town when it was found that the cables on the SS vehicles were too heavy for the purpose. 'Hascha' Kurz nudged Schneid and pointed to the tall, blond French teenager at the head of the *chantiers* squad: 'You see this boy, Schneid? These are the sort of men we need – I'd make a fine Waffen SS of him!'

The operation was commanded by Major Kowatsch, a big man of around thirty who had been in the police for some years before joining the SS. Several witnesses claimed that Kowatsch taunted the condemned men before their execution. The hangings themselves were carried out by a pioneer NCO of thirty-one from the Saar, named Otto Hoff. 'Because our wounded were so well-treated,' Kowatsch told Prefect Trouillé, 'we shall be merciful and not burn the town.'

The captives were halted by the first lamp post in the street, from which a noose already dangled, and against which two ladders stood, one for the victim and one for the hangman. The first Frenchman mounted, Hoff adjusted the noose and pushed him off. He moved on to the next lamp post and repeated the process. A routine was established. Some of the pioneers laughed as they worked, but even among the SS most found silence less disturbing. As the lamp posts filled, they began to tie nooses a yard or two apart on the first-floor balconies overhanging the street. A few prisoners sobbed as they waited, but most mounted the ladder submissively enough. Some died instantly. Others twisted and twitched convulsively for several minutes, occasionally irritating a German into delivering a brief burst as a *coup de grâce*. There were brief moments of drama. A man suddenly broke free from his group and sprang over the bridge into the rock-strewn river below. An NCO emptied his Schmeisser from the parapet, and the Frenchman's body drifted down to the lodge against the foot of the bridge. Some men leaped from their ladders with deliberate force, to end their suffering instantly. One of these caused his own rope to snap. He fell heavily onto the road. His neck was broken, and the Germans saw him twist and shake as he staggered to breathe. After a pause that seemed to Schneid interminable as he gazed on the man's 'terrible look of mute supplication', one of them shot him. He lay still. Then a prisoner fell from his ladder, apparently accidentally, and dropped into the river. He was dispatched with two pistol shots. Another suddenly sprang from his waiting group and darted to a body already swinging from a balcony, to shake it by the hand. Was it his brother, mused Schneid? He was instantly shot down.

The hangings had begun at around four in the afternoon. At about 7 pm, Schneid was dispatched to the arms factory courtyard to report that if there were many more to come, there would not be enough rope. He looked about him, at the score or so of condemned men remaining, and the 300 almost equally terrified captives still under guard. Ninety-nine men had been hanged. The Germans decided that enough was enough.

It has never become clear why the Germans suddenly decided to halt the executions and reprieve the remaining twenty-one condemned men. Some witnesses have claimed that the pleas of the Abbé Espinasse for the Germans to show mercy were granted. Others suggest that the secretary-general of Corrèze, Maurice Roche – who possessed the priceless asset of fluent German – persuaded the divisional staff to desist. In any event, the last twenty-one men were sent to join the 300 captives now incarcerated in the arms factory. Later that evening, they were all loaded on to trucks and taken away. They were told that they were merely being driven to the Hôtel Moderne for further identity checks.

The *chantiers de la jeunesse* were ordered to cut down the bodies of the ninety-nine hanged men and load them on to lorries. French officials persuaded Major Kowatsch that if the SS carried out their promise to throw the bodies into the river, they would pose a threat to hygiene that might ultimately affect the garrison as well. Instead, they were tossed on the town rubbish dump on the Brive road, and later buried there. Thirty-six years later, Major Wulf said that 'French officials expressed their satisfaction that the business had been correctly and cleanly carried out.'

It is interesting that every single officer of the Das Reich interviewed in the researching of this book, including several who had no part in the extravagances of the division if only because of technical responsibilities, approved the action at Tulle as a correct and proper response to the FTP's actions. Major Wulf was mystified by the energy with which war crimes charges were later pursued against himself and others for that day's work. 'We let them have a priest,' he said. 'Where else have you heard of people being hanged in the war who were allowed a priest before they died?' It was Himmler who had given them their cue. 'One basic principle must be the absolute rule for the SS man,' he said. 'We must be honest, decent, loyal and comradely to members of our own blood and to nobody else. What happens to a Russian, to a Czech, doesn't interest me in the slightest.'

Lammerding transferred divisional headquarters to a villa on the road out of Tulle towards Clermont-Ferrand. A series of urgent conferences began, to discuss the division's next movement. Stuckler was still scheduled to drive himself to Clermont-Ferrand to hold a liaison meeting with 66th Reserve Corps, but with the road threatened by *maquisards* it was unthinkable to proceed without a strong escort. Perhaps they should conduct a major operation to clear the route to Clermont-Ferrand? Wulf was sent for. He was instructed to prepare his companies to advance eastwards at first light on 10 June.

Half an hour later, the order was cancelled. OKW and Army Group B had come to their senses. As the battle in Normandy consumed its appalling daily toll of tanks, guns and men, it had at last dawned upon their commanders that it was madness to deploy an SS Panzer division to pursue terrorists across the Corrèze. The OKW War Diary reported:

> The third day was again distinguished by the continuous activity of the enemy air forces which swept the forward area and deep into the support areas, suffocating our tank attacks. . . . Reinforcements were brought in from the west and from the Reich. . . . But it was evident that these forces would not be sufficient to drive the enemy back into the sea. So the Führer ordered the following units to be moved in: 2 Pz Div, I Pz Regt of the 116 Pz Regt, 2 SS Pz Div (which had been on clearance operations in southern France). . . .

The signals hastened from OKW to Army Group G, from Toulouse to 58th Panzer Corps, even as the hangman in Tulle was doing his business:

> 2nd SS Pz Div will temporarily be tactically subordinated to Army Group B. General commanding 66th Reserve Corps has received orders to remove the parts of the division under its control from present operations by 1200 on 11 June, and to send its wheeled elements overland direct to Army Group B in Normandy. Tracked vehicles of the division are to be entrained *immediately*, regardless of present operations. The planned entraining areas are: for full tracks – the Périgueux area; for half-tracks – the Limoges area.

In other words, Von Rundstedt was in desperate need of the Das Reich's heavy armour. But his orders were much more easily issued than executed.

7 The Jeds

Before following the Das Reich Division onwards north and west, there is one further piece of unfinished business concerning the movement of the armoured columns on the eastern axis from Cahors, which did not bring even the leading elements into Tulle until late on the evening of 9 June. At almost exactly the moment that the first companies of the Der Führer regiment were crawling wearily into Limoges on the night of 8 June, above a dropping zone in south Corrèze a few miles from Aurillac three parachutes blossomed from a Liberator bomber. They began to drift slowly earthwards to add modestly to the difficulties of 2nd SS Panzer Division.

A few moments later, an excited *maquisard* ran across the field proudly leading his newly arrived charges, and shouting to the rest of the reception committee: 'We've got a French officer and he's brought his wife with him!' The officer was introduced as 'Aristide' – Aspirant Maurice Bourdon of the French Army. His real name—which none of them learned until after the war – was Prince Michel de Bourbon, nephew of the Pretender to the French throne. His 'wife', however, was the commanding officer of the team, the splendidly kilted Highland officer Major Tommy Macpherson, among the most single-minded warriors that the war can have produced. They were accompanied by a British wireless operator, Sergeant Brown, and a load of arms and explosives with which to equip the local *maquis*. Their orders were 'to assist Resistance teams in the Lot, to stimulate guerilla action along the lines of communication between Montauban and Brive, and to cut the RN20', along which the Das Reich had been pouring all day. Two nights later another team, led by Captain Macdonald Austin of the American Army, parachuted into the Dordogne 100 miles further west, with orders to carry out the same mission from the opposite flank. Unlike French Section's agents, Austin had been specifically informed of the presence of the Das Reich and instructed to do everything possible to impede it.

These were the first of the inter-Allied 'Jedburgh' teams, of which ninety-three were to be parachuted into France before the Liberation. Their arrival acknowledged the new phase of Resistance, open guerilla war. They were dispatched in uniform, and while they had been trained in some of the skills of clandestine war, they were sent to serve as commando officers in the field, not as secret agents. Their arrival in uniform was intended – as indeed it succeeded – to boost the morale of the *maquis*.

The origins of the Jedburghs were, however, overwhelmingly political rather than military. The Free French and above all the Americans were seeking a larger share in behind-the-lines operations in Europe. General Donovan and his American OSS had been disappointed, and indeed infuriated, by the reluctance of the British to see its men dropped into France.

SOE in their turn pointed out that while OSS had sent a handful of American-controlled Frenchmen into France, the prospective agents of American nationality all spoke French with an instantly recognizable accent, and few showed much aptitude for living a cover story successfully. Although most of the British liked and admired Colonel David Bruce, the elegant OSS chief in London, they were unimpressed by General Donovan, whom they judged an ambitious empire-builder. 'The British kept tactfully reminding us that they had been in the intelligence business since Queen Elizabeth's day,' said the British-educated American Henry Hyde, who joined the intelligence branch of OSS in April 1942. ' "Those naive Americans," they said, and by and large we were a naive lot. Americans are naive. But I felt that the American Army was entitled to its own sources of information. We said: "We're not that much stupider than you. If we're taught properly, we can do it." '

After much discussion and argument, a compromise was agreed. On the intelligence side, OSS would continue to build up its modest network of French agents reporting to SI – there were twenty-seven of them by D-Day. At the suggestion of the British SIS – frankly desperate for joint Allied projects which would not interfere with their existing networks in France – a project codenamed Sussex was created, to drop fifty two-man

SIS/OSS teams into northern France from May onwards, to provide tactical intelligence for the Allied armies. But once again, the OSS agents would have to be Fenchmen.

Americans could only take their part in France, the British insisted, after the transition from secret to open guerilla war, when they would no longer be compelled to live a cover story. The Jedburgh training programme would be established under the auspices of SOE. A mixed group of 250 American, French and British trainees was assembled, to be parachuted to support Resistance in rural areas that lent themselves to guerilla war. 'The Jeds', said one of their British recruits, 'plainly represented the enormous power and interest of America in the European war.'

Tommy Macpherson reached the organization after a war that would already have sated most men. He was the youngest of seven children of a judge. In May 1939, at the age of eighteen and before he had even technically finished at Fettes public school, he took a commission in the Cameron Highlanders. In June 1940 he joined the Scottish Commando, and after training went to the Middle East with Layforce. He took part in two raids on Crete, and was then detailed to reconnoitre the landing area for Major Geoffrey Keyes on his famous mission to kill Rommel at his headquarters in North Africa. Macpherson had already developed a low opinion of the staff work for commando raids of the period, '. . . and it stuck out a mile that this was an absolute disaster'. Rommel was not even at the headquarters, Keyes was killed in the attack, and Macpherson was captured soon afterwards, attempting to walk back to the British lines through the desert.

He was sent to Italy, to one of the 'naughty boys' ' establishments, Camp 5, which he found 'quite an enjoyable place to be, because there was so much going on'. He escaped, was recaptured and sent to a camp in Austria. He escaped again with two New Zealanders, and made his way to northern Italy before being recaptured. This time he was sent to 'a very nasty sort of interrogation centre' in East Prussia, and thence to the Polish–Silesian border. He and a New Zealander exchanged identities with two private soldiers in order to be able to join an outside working party, and crawled away under the wire of the commandant's rabbit farm. They caught a train to Danzig, where they arrived in the middle of an air raid one night in October 1943. They hitched a lift to Gdynia from a sympathetic Pole, and hid up all day until they were smuggled aboard a Swedish ship carrying coal dust. They lay deep in the cargo while German guards and dogs searched the ship, and surfaced when they were safely at sea. The Swedes briefly detained them, but they were finally allowed to catch a Liberator to England. On 4 November, two years to the day after his capture, Macpherson landed home. At his debriefing, he was asked if he would like to join SOE. It seemed that General Gubbins, a family friend, had suggested him. He toyed briefly with the idea of a quiet holiday in a staff job, then took the SOE job. Early in December 1943, a captain with the Military Cross, he reported to the Jedburgh training centre at Milton Hall, the Fitzwilliam stately home in Northamptonshire.

Many of the Frenchmen who joined the Jedburghs were also veterans, or had escaped from France after desperate adventures. But Prince Michel de Bourbon had been taken to America in 1940, and was still there in 1943 when he ran away from school to enlist at the age of sixteen and a half. The French Military Mission in New York had an arrangement by which their nationals could be trained by the US Army, and de Bourbon (or Bourdon, as he should henceforth be called) was sent to an officer training school at Fort Benning, Georgia. From there he was plucked out by OSS recruiters, who sent him to their spy schools for three months to learn the usual routines of shooting, sabotage, unarmed combat and morse. After so many changes of environment, he found that he had ceased to think as a Frenchman, and identified more easily with Americans or Englishmen, although he was disconcerted by those American trainees who admired the Germans and were naive enough to say so. They seemed to possess an engaging, innocent enthusiasm for adventure ahead, rather more so than the other Frenchmen on the course, most of whom had been recruited from exiles in North and South America and seemed happy to remain as far as possible from the war.

On 23 December 1943, Bourdon landed in Glasgow from the *Queen Elizabeth*, and was promptly assigned to spend Christmas with a local surburban family who owned a circus. They found this obscure French teenager somewhat uncouth, and gave him stern advice about the proper use of a knife and fork. Early in the New Year, he was sent on a British-run selection course to assess his suitability for commando or clandestine operations. To his utter dismay, he was rejected as too young, and had to launch a furious campaign to change the authorities' minds. At last he succeeded, and was one of only two Frenchmen from his course in the US who were accepted for operations. The rest of the French Jedburghs were recruited from Free French officers in England.

Macdonald Austin, universally known as 'Mac', was a quiet-spoken southerner who failed to win a regular West Point cadetship before the war, and was studying accountancy at the University of Florida with a reserve commission when he was suddenly summoned to active duty. One day in 1943, at the age of twenty-six, he was instructing parachute infantry at a vast tented camp of 100,000 men in Georgia when a mysterious civilian from Washington arrived. The man interviewed Austin and several other jump-qualified officers. His file showed that he had some high school French; was he interested in volunteering for a dangerous mission that involved being dropped deep behind enemy lines in France? He was. The volunteers were shipped to Washington, where an extraordinary selection process took place. A French-speaking captain announced in French: 'All those who can understand what I'm saying go to the end of the room.' Austin and about half the others moved smartly. They were considered sufficiently proficient to train as guerillas for France. The failures were sent on language courses.

In the weeks that followed, about half Austin's companions were weeded out in training. Those who were left were amused and bemused by the OSS passion for melodramatics. Their school was situated at the Congressional Country Club outside Washington, and whenever they went into the city, the students were given strict orders not to move publicly in groups. The notion of secrecy, of unobtrusiveness, seemed alien and funny to the young officers. Even as they plunged through the two-week commando course at Arisaig in Scotland, and afterwards during initial Jedburgh training at Hatherop Castle in Gloucestershire, they could not escape a sense of fantasy, even absurdity.

At Milton Hall, where they came together and began their training in earnest, the British and French with their seriousness about the war – and in many cases experience of battle – found the Americans touchingly gauche. After years of stringent rationing, Macpherson and the others 'were shattered to see bacon, waffles, marmalade, scrambled eggs provided because we had an American contingent. And they had this mania for surrounding themselves with weapons.' The Americans, with their easy conversation and high poker games, found most of the Frenchmen tense and uncommunicative. Experienced British officers like Tommy Macpherson were effectively horonary instructors. Harry Coombe-Tennant had also escaped from Germany. Geoffrey Hallowes had survived ten days in a rowing boat, adrift off Sumatra. One elderly trainee who was thought to be too well known to be allowed to drop into France had his face altered by plastic surgery while on leave, and returned claiming that he had been in a car smash.

These men were bemused by such exotic American recruits as René Dusacq, who had been a Hollywood stuntman; Prince Serge Obolensky, a former New York socialite; 'Baz' Bazata, a red-haired adventurer who addressed all colonels as 'sugar'; and several near-gangsters. There were some good ex-West Point regulars, and serious students such as William Colby, future head of the CIA, who spent much of his spare time at Milton Hall pouring over *Seven Pillars of Wisdom*. But while the British admired American organization and equipment, they doubted whether they possessed the instinct for improvisation in the field. Many seemed to be acting out a role. 'The great thing in this game is that you may have a letter in your pocket signed personally by De Gaulle – as we all did when we landed in France,' said Tommy Macpherson, 'but you are in fact, in yourself, nothing. Success depends on the moral hold you can establish upon the people you are working with.'

Brigadier Mockler-Ferryman, commanding Special Forces HQ, came down to address them. Denis Rake, a wonderfully courageous and unashamedly high camp F Section wireless operator, delivered a brilliant and witty talk about life in Occupied France. The French treated all their training with desperate earnestness. 'They were very conscious of the débâcle of 1940,' said Geoffrey Hallowes. 'The idea that France should be liberated without their help was intolerable to them.'

Towards the end of the spring, the 'mating period' began. The students were told to sort themselves into pairs, and to choose an NCO wireless operator. Macpherson took Bourdon, whom he liked although he found him very immature and desperately anxious to prove his courage. Sergeant Brown, their wireless operator, was a tall, fair Londoner with no battle experience and no French, but technically highly competent. 'Mac' Austin teamed himself with a former regular French Army gunner, Raymond Leconte, a roundfaced man who seemed slow-witted, but was in reality extremely sharp. Their wireless operator, Jack Berlin, was a thickset, bespectacled eighteen-year-old Jewish boy from Brooklyn who had worked his way through high school, and regarded the war as a personal crusade.

Early in April 1944, there was one of the endless wartime 'flaps' at Milton. Without warning, fifteen teams were detailed to move to North Africa. Austin, Macpherson and the others found themselves trans-shipped to Oran on the liner *Capetown Castle*, and thence into the Algerian mountains for joint exercises with French commandos and Spahis to sharpen their wits before action. The Frenchmen among them exulted to be once more on their own soil. Michel de Bourbon met his father, Prince René, who was serving with the Foreign Legion. His sister, the ex-Queen of Romania, was driving an ambulance for Leclerc, and his other brother was in the Norwegian Air Force. The Bourbons considered that they had gone some distance towards redeeming themselves from the traditional suspicion of the French nation towards their family.

One night, the teams had been on an exercise high in the mountains, from which they had to march back to a grid co-ordinate. At 3 am on 5 June 1944, they pulled themselves wearily aboard the pick-up truck and found that they were being driven straight to Blida airfield. Major James Champion of SOE told Austin: 'You're going tonight.' They had a few hours' sleep, then the long briefing began. Austin was told that he was being dropped to a reception committee of George Starr's Wheelwright circuit, south of Sarlat. They were taking weapons for two groups of twenty men apiece. For the rest of the day, they rested and prepared their equipment, along with Macpherson's men, who were also to go that night. All the other teams had been given leave in Algiers so that they should not notice the departure of their colleagues.

That night, however, the teams stood by in vain. SHAEF had insisted that no Jedburgh should be dropped into France in uniform until the moment of invasion. When the landing was postponed for twenty-four hours, so were Austin and Macpherson. To the intense chagrin of Austin and his team, the following night also ended in anti-climax. Their Halifax failed to locate the dropping zone, and they returned crestfallen to Blida, to face much teasing from their comrades: 'Did you freeze in the door, then?' On the night of 8 June they found the dropping zone, but the pilot reported that the reception committee was flashing the wrong code letter. The Jedburgh was more than willing to risk the drop, but the airman was not. Once again they returned to Blida. It was the sort of difficulty that dogged all wartime operational flights by SOE and OSS, and caused such a high proportion of abortive missions, with all the strain and risk both for those in the aircraft and the reception committee on the ground.

By now Henry Hyde, OSS Special Intelligence chief in Algiers, had received a signal from one of his French agents, a regular army major named Jean Lescane, that the Das Reich was moving. Hyde was a lawyer like so many OSS men, twenty-nine, and educated in England at Charterhouse and Trinity College, Cambridge. To his chagrin, although he had been born in Paris and was married to a daughter of a French baron, he was turned down for agent training, and took over SI in Algiers instead. Now, the message from Lescane north of Agen was funnelled into the military intelligence machine. Austin was told that there might still be time to interdict the movement of some elements of 2nd SS Panzer.

A few minutes after midnight on 10 June, Austin's Jedburgh at last saw the green light flash above the exit hole of their Halifax. After the heat and noise of the fuselage, the American was delighted by the cool fresh air and silence of the June night above the Dordogne. He landed neatly, just behind his French colleague, Ray Leconte. A shadowy figure loomed out of the darkness. Austin unburdened himself of the French phrase he had been practising for days for this moment: 'We've come to fight on your side.'

'So – you're an American, are you?' said an unmistakably American voice from the darkness. The *maquisard* was a middle-aged civilian named Dick Andrews who had been brought up in France, educated at Cornell and served in the US Corps of Engineers in World War I. He was demobbed in France, and settled down to spend the rest of his life in the country. When the Germans took over the Unoccupied Zone in 1943, Andrews sent his family to a safe refuge abroad, and joined a *maquis*.

They cleared the dropping zone and sat down to breakfast on an omelette made from fresh eggs and truffles. Jack Berlin thought some pieces of charcoal from the fire had fallen into his omelette, and carefully picked out the truffles and put them beside his plate. It was also Berlin's misfortune to dislike wine, which caused him some privation in the weeks ahead. There was nothing else to drink.

Austin began to get the measure of the *résistants*, and of the situation in the area. He was astonished to discover that the Germans were nowhere to be seen, and that the *maquisards* moved freely along the roads by *gazogène* and truck. The French talked much and bitterly about the German atrocities, but in the peace of the woods south of the Dordogne it was hard for the Americans to be infected by their anger. They found it impossible to hate the enemy. Later, when they saw a few prisoners, Austin found that he felt only curiosity. Among the *maquisards*, those with military training responded readily enough to his proposals, but the remainder were difficult to influence and impossible to order. He found his high school French confounded by their heavily accented slang. It is a measure of the isolation of the different *maquis* that this one, commanded by a Sarlatais named Albert, seemed to know nothing about the Das Reich, or about the dramatic situation unfolding not far westwards, around Bergerac. Austin proposed that they should establish some roadblocks, but the idea met with little enthusiasm, and anyway there was little enemy traffic. On the one occasion that they went to reconnoitre the Brive–Montauban road, they saw no sign of movement. Leconte started to travel the countryside setting charges on small bridges and culverts that it seemed useful to destroy. Austin began to instruct Albert's men in the use of the weapons that he had brought. There was one unseemly interruption, when the *maquisards* tortured a local man they had brought in, suspected of treachery. He died, and they sent apologetic word to his father. The man was not appeased, and passed word to the Germans, giving the location of the little château by the river where the group was based. The Americans were elsewhere when the German armoured cars arrived. The *maquisards* beat a hasty retreat, the Germans burned the château, and thereafter they all lived in the woods. To his astonishment, Austin found himself desperately wishing that he had brought some books to read. Of all his apprehensions before he parachuted into France, the prospect of boredom had never been among them.

Austin learnt a great deal about guerillas in the weeks that followed – above all about their absolute unpredictability. He moved westwards and began attacking railways himself. On one notable day he was up a ladder fixing an explosive charge to the Bordeaux–Agen line beneath a bridge. He had posted a Bren gunner to cover him, a hundred yards up the track. Suddenly, he found a German bicycle patrol dismounting a stone's throw up the road, and opening a furious fire. The *maquis* party escaped in confusion, but intact. Austin learned that the Bren gunner, lulled by the hot sun, had simply gone to sleep: 'Sometimes they would do marvellous things,' he said, 'but one had to realize that on the next operation it would suddenly turn out that they had forgotten to crank up the *gazogène*.'

Fundamentally, from the moment that he landed Austin found himself unable to carry out the job that he had been sent to do, because of the lack of Intelligence and enthusiasm among the *maquis*, and the feud between the Wheelwright circuit and the *maquis* of Soleil and the AS, armed by Poirier, which kept him ignorant and isolated for many days. Above all, the Jedburgh had come too late. The strategic decision to send the teams on D-Day may have made sense for security reasons, but was a critical handicap in tactical terms, on the ground. No man could arrive in the middle of France without previous combat experience or knowledge of the country and immediately conduct a coherent military campaign. For all their courage and enthusiasm to get into action, Austin and his colleagues were at a loss:

'I didn't really know what to do. The target that I was to go after wasn't there any longer. I thought that the best thing I could do was to get on with training the *maquisards*, and go round the country meeting people until I could formulate some sort of plan. It was not what I expected it to be. . . .'

Major Tommy Macpherson jumped from his Halifax over the Corrèze on the night of 8 June with the overwhelming advantage that he spoke competent French and possessed the confidence of a man with great experience of battle and of life behind enemy lines. He had long ago shed his 1941 'infinite capacity for belief in the infallibility of planners'. He landed into the hands of an AS leader named Bernard Cournil, who was mayor of the tiny village of Le Rouget and owned a local garage. Macpherson gave Cournil the codename of the *maquis* leader he had been instructed to contact – 'Droite'. The Frenchman said that he had never heard of him. He himself controlled only a small group of poorly armed *résistants*, and was delighted to have suddenly acquired his own personal Allied mission. Bourdon did not much interest him – the French boy seemed disappointingly young, and was obviously from an entirely alien social background. Sergeant Brown, the wireless operator, spoke no French at all, and found himself condemned to spend most of his stay in France making tea beneath damp parachute canopies in the woods, between radio schedules. Macpherson made his own assessment of the situation:

With hindsight, it was obvious that we had been very poorly briefed. The impression in London was that the *maquisards* were all keen volunteers, but it was immediately obvious that 90 per cent of them were there to stay away from the Germans, not to fight them. There was also a pretty false idea at home about what the *maquis* were for – there was too much Secret Army stuff, rather than concentration on hit and run attacks by small groups. The men we found when we landed were neither equipped nor trained for action. It was only later that we began to get a flow of genuine volunteers who wanted to fight. I had not been given the faintest idea until I landed that there was a split between the AS and the FTP.

But Macpherson embodied the exact spirit that SHAEF had intended to send with the Jedburghs. He had no interest in clandestine life – he considered that his business was to make as much open trouble for the Germans as possible. Thus he wore his uniform and kilt wherever he went. When he acquired a Citroën car, he decorated the bonnet with the Union Jack and Tricolour. Thus also, he moved at once to take into action what men he could muster. His attitude exasperated local SOE agents, who had spent months working in great secrecy, and above all with concern for the welfare of the French people among whom they lived. Macpherson troubled himself only about attacking Germans, and wasted no time brooding about possible reprisals. He considered his instructions: 'The theme of our training had been that we were to use our own judgment to create whatever mayhem could tie down enemy forces, and build up a trained nucleus of *résistants* for the "phase of Liberation".' In the little cluster of huts in the woods in which the *maquis* lived, he reviewed Cournil's little group. Between them, they had a few old French army rifles and one light machine gun. But Macpherson and his team had come with superb personal equipment – much of it American and extending to a money-belt laden with gold sovereigns for each man. They had also brought Brens, gammon bombs and explosives. Within a few hours of landing – and chiefly to put some life into the *maquisards* – Macpherson had mined and blown an unguarded bridge on the Aurillac–Maurs railway line, where it crossed a country road. They were short of food. Macpherson stopped a civilian lorry and hijacked four sacks of sugar. A German ration truck drove down the road shortly afterwards, and they shot it to pieces. In the back, they found two tons of chestnut purée. They carted it back to the camp.

Until the moment of the Liberation, Macpherson waged an ambitious and ruthless campaign against the Germans across the region – attacking trains and convoys, rail links and roads with remorseless energy. He was determined to compel the French to decide which side they were on. One day he drove into Decazeville and invited the mayor to join him for a drink at the café in the main square. The trembling Frenchman talked to him for a few minutes before there was a sudden shout that a German convoy was approaching. Macpherson and his *maquisards* leaped into the car and drove furiously out of the town, pursued by an armoured car. When they reached the bridge over the road, Macpherson leapt out, climbed on to the parapet, and lobbed a gammon bomb neatly on to the German vehicle as it passed underneath, instantly halting and wrecking it.

I felt that I had a clear role of tip-and-run disruption, getting morale right locally. I viewed part of my job as being to move the psychology of the people. The vast bulk of the people were scared stiff to help us. I remember once stopping late at night to ask somebody to come down and show us the way. 'No, *m'sieu*, I cannot – the curfew', the man called from the window. The Germans correctly judged that this was the way to deal with a guerilla movement – to make people more frightened of the penalties than of the guerillas.

The team rapidly became cynical about some of their own men. After one or two bad experiences at *parachutages*, Macpherson insisted that all containers were opened in front of himself or Bourdon. There were some *maquisards* – a small but energetic minority – who stole substantial fortunes in the course of the war by deflecting SOE money from *parachutages*, or by selling off material. In Macpherson's view – which would be fiercely contested by many *résistants* and some of SOE's officers – 'If it hadn't been for the British officers there, the *maquis* would have done nothing. They were concerned with the necessities of life, and with establishing a power base.'

To the anger of some SOE officers, Macpherson worked closely with Robert Noireau and the local FTP, simply because he felt that these men were most committed to killing Germans. Local *résistants* were also exasperated by Macpherson's assertion that, in the first weeks after his arrival, most of the local railway system was 'working quite normally – indeed it was the only means by which the Germans could still move supplies' – no doubt assisted by the fact that they had now begun to place a flatcar loaded with very old or very young French hostages in front of most of their engines.

The young Scot was a trained soldier, who regarded the situation in southern France without sentiment, merely as a military problem. He made a fine contribution to the guerilla war in the region. It is not surprising that, in doing so, he aroused fierce controversy.

But this account must focus upon Macpherson's first days in France and his contribution to the battle against the Das Reich.

Shortly after they returned to the *maquis* camp with their load of captured chestnut purée – still little more than hours after their landing – word reached the Jedburgh that armoured elements of the Das Reich Division were still moving up the Figeac–Tulle road. Macpherson learned later to mistrust much of the intelligence he received: 'If an armoured car and a truck moved into a town, we were always told it was a battalion. If it was two half-tracks, we heard it was a Panther regiment.' But for once, the news was accurate. That evening the Scot drove to within sight of the road, and glimpsed a lagered tank. He retreated to the camp: 'I thought we'd better make a little bit of a show,' he said. But with what? They had used most of their explosives to blow the rail bridge. They had no bazookas. Macpherson thought that they might be able to weaken a small bridge, and cover it for long enough to compel the Germans to dismount from their vehicles, with all the delay that this entailed. It was time rather than casualties that they could cause the Germans to lose.

Very early the next morning, Macpherson descended to the road with twenty-seven *maquisards*. At his bidding, two men had wrapped wet cloths around the barrels of their Stens. He had learned on the ranges in England that this caused them to sound like heavy machine guns. The men were in buoyant spirits because, unlike Macpherson, they did not appreciate the extreme peril they were about to face. They were all peasants, some wearing fragments of battledress and old French Army uniforms, surmounted by the inevitable berets. A few had put on FFI armbands. Bourdon and Brown remained in camp – there was no merit in risking the entire Jedburgh. Macpherson personally positioned each man, explaining as undramatically as possible what he wished them to do. On one side trees came close to the road; the Scot tied small charges to a succession of trunks, wired them together and gave the exploder to a *maquisard* with orders to twist it when the Germans reached the bridge. He placed ten men with himself around the bridge, and the others among the trees. On the other side, the ground was flat and open. Here, when the Germans tried to deploy upon it, he planned to have his killing ground. There was a solitary cottage by the bridge. They told the old peasant who occupied it to lose himself as rapidly as possible. Then they settled down to wait. There had been rain in the night, and in the first hours after dawn the ground was cold and wet. It was three hours before they heard the shrieking clatter of the approaching column.

It was headed by two motor cyclists, followed by a half-track and a procession of tanks, with trucks in the rear. Macpherson blew the bridge under the leading half-track, which burst into flames. Germans leaped from the wreckage and dashed back down the column. Amidst the barrage of small arms fire the first tank, battened down, paused for a moment to reflect and then crept forward. Macpherson had left a man with a gammon grenade just behind the bridge for this moment. The gammon exploded at the rear of the tank, rupturing a track. The road was blocked.

The tanks further back along the column began to shell their position around the bridge, lumbering off the road into cover. German infantry began to work forward through the trees from the rear. There was a volley of explosions as the mined trees fell. The action lasted perhaps half an hour before Macpherson saw the infantry closing in around their flanks. He signalled the surviving *maquisards* to withdraw, supporting their walking wounded. At a rendezvous a few hundred yards away, their old lorry was waiting. They retreated to the camp.

The official report of their Jedburgh, Quinine, compiled after the Liberation, states that in their action against the Das Reich, twenty out of twenty-seven *maquisards* were killed. Macpherson's recollection thirty-six years later was that casualties were less severe. But the same lack of fieldcraft and tactical training that cost Guedin's men so dear further north and west made the Jedburgh action expensive. The *maquisards* simply did not understand the simplest principles of crossing ground under fire.

Macpherson was at pains later to remark that he did not make a practice of embarking on actions against such odds, and indeed he never did it again. It was the urgent need to make an impact on the *maquisards* and on the region, above all upon the Germans, that drove him to stage the ambush. 'The Germans didn't suffer much,' he admitted, beyond the damage to their leading vehicles and an hour or two's frustration and delay clearing up the mess and replacing tracks. But it was from a thousand such actions the length of France in June 1944 that the confusion and strategic misjudgments of the German High Command concerning Resistance were created, and the passage of the Das Reich to Normandy delayed.

8 'Panzer divisions are too good for this. . .'

On 10 June 1944, as General Heinz Lammerding reviewed the position of his division and the orders he had received for its urgent movement, he found little cause for satisfaction. Elements of the Das Reich were sprawled across the Lot, Corrèze, and Haute-Vienne. Broken-down tanks and assault guns were lying by the roadside from Tulle to Montauban. All the staff's warnings about the technical cost of moving heavy armour by the road had been justified. The Panzergrenadier brigade was deployed in a ring covering Limoges against the terrorist attack that the panicky *Kommandantur* in the city considered imminent. The steep hills and woods made communication between all these units erratic and uncertain. The report which Lammerding now transmitted to the general commanding 58th Panzer Corps is a great tribute to the climate created by Resistance after D-Day, and a measure of the Germans' calamitous error in committing an SS Panzer division to anti-terrorist operations. It is worth quoting in full:

STATE OF THE DIVISION

The lack of adequate transport, the substantial distances to be covered in unfavourable terrain, the dispersal of units over 300 kilometres and the lack of advance preparation for operational and supply measures has weakened the strength of the division out of all proportion during the past eight days.

Unserviceability among tanks is 60 per cent, towing vehicles and half-tracks 30 per cent. The majority of the unserviceable vehicles can only be moved again when we receive the spare parts which are still missing, despite repeated requests. The division has been compelled to establish six support points in the Figeac–Tulle–Brive–Cahors area which require strong infantry protection because of the gang situation. The opportunities for commandeering additional wheeled vehicles from the gang area are negligible, because predictably the terrorists have beaten the liaison staff to it. Adequate fuel supplies depend on the arrival of the fuel convoy, which is nowhere in sight.

Only the division's wheeled elements can begin to move to Normandy on schedule. The tanks and towing vehicles require at least four days for repairs, even assuming that the requested spare parts reach the division early on 11 June. Presumably the complete crippling of rail movement by the terrorists will anyway prevent an earlier entrainment. More long marches in this sort of country can only be undertaken at further heavy cost. The Figeac–Clermont-Ferrand–Limoges–Gourdon area is completely in the hands of the terrorists. Local German posts and garrisons are surrounded, in many cases besieged and often reduced to company strength. The French Government's forces have been completely paralysed by the terrorists. The paralysis of the German posts is quite disgraceful. Without determined and ruthless action the situation in this area will develop until a threat exists whose proportions have not yet been recognized. In this area a new communist state is coming to life, a state which rules without opposition and carries out co-ordinated attacks.

The task of eliminating this danger must be transferred to the local divisions. Panzer divisions in the fifth year of the war are too good for this. In the division's opinion, the local forces are quite capable of maintaining order if they are pulled together sharply, given transport, and led energetically. Their present isolation is a standing invitation to the terrorists. Necessary specific measures have already been reported by the division.

In view of the overall situation, the division requests emphatically:

a) that the cutting-off of German outposts should be prevented.
b) that vital spare parts for movement to Normandy be provided.
c) that the special difficulties of the division in its present state of reconstruction, together with its supply and equipment problems, be taken into account when movement and operational orders are being issued.

Signed: Lammerding

Lammerding's report provoked a flurry of signals between the German command headquarters of France. Army Group G sent an urgent request to OKW for reinforcements to replace 2nd SS Pz on its withdrawal from Corrèze and Dordogne. They reported that, as an emergency measure, they were assembling a battle group from 11 Pz Div composed of two infantry battalions, one artillery battery and an anti-tank company: 'The commander of the battle group will make personal contact with the staff of 2nd

SS Pz in Tulle. His mission – restoration of peace and order and its maintenance by the strongest measures in the departments of Corrèze and Dordogne. . . .' A further signal to OKW, also dispatched on 10 June, indicated that 'in view of the transport situation, entrainment of tracks 2 SS Pz Div Das Reich at earliest 12.6.44 at 00:00 Périgueux'. This was a reflection of the desperate flatcar shortage and the rail cuts. Yet before the tanks could even reach Périgueux, the spare parts were essential. On 11 June, Army Group G was signalling again to OKW: 'High transport losses of 2nd SS Pz Div – immediate supply of following parts to Tulle essential. . . .' There followed a list that included twelve complete tank engines, two assault gun engines, and a vast array of wheels, tracks, sprockets and oxyacetylene equipment: 'Arrival of parts essential to avoid delays in transport of division's tanks. . . .' In short, the Das Reich Division was moving nowhere in a hurry.

Lammerding and his staff spent the day of 10 June at their headquarters in a villa on the Clermont-Ferrand road out of Tulle, grappling with their huge administrative problems, above all the recovery of the disabled armour on the road from Figeac.

The reconnaissance battalion, which now possessed unchallenged control of Tulle, organized several fruitless sweeps in search of terrorists north and south of the town, which achieved no more than the burning of a few farms and the execution of a handful of peasants who were slow to remove themselves from the Germans' path. The companies remaining in Tulle set about comprehensively looting the town's shops and houses while conducting further arms searches. Private Schneid and his section suffered the embarrassment of being billeted in the home of one of the previous day's widows: 'Our hostess, still ignorant of her husband's death, asked us for news of him. We were cowards enough to pretend that he was not among the condemned, although he had been hanged at the corner of the next street. . . .' It was an interesting day. Ransacking one house, Schneid found an aged, mothballed blue *poilu*'s uniform in a tin trunk. An elderly woman appeared at the door. He suggested that she should dispose of her husband's old souvenirs lest another less charitable searcher take it for a *maquis* uniform. The 'Hascha' appeared in high spirits, driving a splendid grey car that he had liberated. Another trooper carried off a motor cycle and sidecar. One man found a gramophone with a pile of Tino Rossi records: 'Ah, Tino Rossi, if you only knew how often you enabled some young Waffen SS men to forget the war. Everybody adored your voice and hummed your songs. Later there was a rumour that after the surrender of Paris the partisans had killed you, you and Maurice Chevalier. Even the Germans were horrified. . . .' Above all, the troopers seized food, and revelled in breakfast with coffee: 'The last of that Tullois salami lasted us as far as St Lô. . . . We drank the last of the coffee in front of Mons.'

At 2.10 am on the tenth, the Das Reich issued the following tactical report to 58th Panzer Corps:

1. Area Souillac–Figeac–Clermont-Ferrand–Limoges in the hands of gangs, stubborn and well-armed.
   Souillac–Limoges and Figeac–Tulle roads cleared.
2. Bulk of division in area Brive–Tulle–Limoges. Target for 10.6.44 Clermont-Ferrand.
   Enemy losses: 500 dead, 1500 prisoners
   Own losses: 17 killed, 30 wounded
   Heavy transport losses.

The figures for enemy losses included not only civilians shot on the road, but the ninety-nine civilians hanged in Tulle. The figure for prisoners included many Tullois men who had now been released. The decision to push east to Clermont-Ferrand was, as has been shown, almost immediately reversed. The Germans were now much more concerned about the situation westwards. The garrisons of Bergerac, Périgueux and Bordeaux were struggling to deal with the uprising inaugurated by Loupias and Philippe de Gunzbourg. They had already launched one modest attempt to relieve Bergerac from the west, which had been repulsed by the *résistants*. Now they were moving up heavier metal. Much closer to the Das Reich, on the road to Périgueux which the armoured columns must travel to reach their railhead, there was a report of a strong FTP presence blocking the highway at Terrasson, a small town on the Vézère, sixteen miles west of Brive. Army Group G reported to OKW that it was essential to move to clear this gang from Terrasson at first light on 11 June. Elements of the Das Reich would do the job.

Terrasson is a pretty little town of some 3,000 people with a twelfth-century bridge, a fifteenth-century church and a prosperous peacetime trade in truffles and walnuts. Since early 1944, the FTP *maquisards* in the hills to the south-west had found it a convenient target for demonstrations and limited raids without risking an encounter with major German formations, which normally arrived only after their departure, in time to conduct reprisals against the townspeople. By June 1944, these hapless scapegoats were at their wits' end. The mayor, Georges Labarthe, proprietor of a small sweet shop, recorded the events in an unhappy letter to his mother in Paris on 4 June:

Towards 11 pm on Wednesday evening we were woken by explosions and shooting. The town was in the hands of about a hundred men of the *maquis*, out on a punitive expedition. All the roads, all the paths were guarded, electricity cut, railways blown up. From behind our shutters, we saw men festooned with weapons moving in all directions, deploying to whistle blasts. The family in the house opposite our own were beaten and compelled to hand over their goods. It was the same at the shoe merchant's and a bicycle shop. Meanwhile they had blown open the door of the *gendarmerie* and disarmed our eighteen *gendarmes*, whose rifles and revolvers they took away. They relieved the Post Office of 150,000 francs. They went to the house of the local Pétainist Legion chief. They blew open the door and shot him. He had been threatened and accused of informing a long time before, on many people's testimony. From there they went to a glassmaker whom they shot with his wife. She was accused of informing to the Gestapo. The whole business lasted until four in the morning. At a whistle blast everybody got back in the lorries and went away. I leave you to imagine the terror of the inhabitants. Having received the blows of one side, here one was getting them from the other. . . . I could have wished that there was no funeral [of the Legion chief], or at least that it was only a family affair, as was arranged for the *mairie* secretary. That was the accepted practice for victims of 'happenings' as one now calls them (we have had fifteen). But the Prefect, consulted by telephone, wanted normal obsequies.

Ah! For the flexibility of a Talleyrand who survived the whole revolutionary process after occupying every position in sight!

But the troubles of the Mayor of Terrasson were to extend

beyond agonizing about whether it was safe to attend a Vichy funeral. While the FTP's battle for Tulle was at its height, Hercules, the FTP commander below Terrasson, returned to the town at the head of his men and began setting roadblocks and putting the approaches in a state of defence. When a few local townspeople sought to remonstrate with them, Hercules shouted contemptuously: 'Terrasson has 3,000 inhabitants and France 40 million! What can these here matter?' The Fourth Republic was proclaimed in the central square. Local civilians were summoned to fell trees. The FTP took away a group of 'suspects', who were not seen again.

Mercifully for Terrasson, the German operation to clear the road on 11 June was not protracted. When the *maquisards* found themselves confronted by armour, and under shellfire from the SS vehicles, they retreated to their trucks, and to the hills, leaving a score of burning buildings, screaming women and children, and tumbled masonry beside the *mairie* where it had been struck by a 75 mm shell. The Germans burnt a house adorned with a red flag by the *maquis*, and discovered only afterwards that it was the property of Denoix, the departmental *milice* chief. The entire population was then assembled in the main square, covered by smocked and helmeted troopers. They knew what had happened in Tulle, and they were certain that they were to share its fate.

The unit doctor, who to the mayor's relief spoke fluent French, pointed to the body of a *maquisard* which the SS had tossed down before them: 'Does anyone recognize this man?' No one admitted to doing so. The tension increased. They watched the doctor talking to the German commander and a group of officers. Suddenly the commander laughed. The doctor turned to the mayor: 'The CO is in a good mood today, because it's his wedding anniversary,' he explained. Their only *maquisard* prisoner was publicly hanged, but Terrasson was spared. All that night and through the next day, as German columns rumbled through the town on the road towards Périgueux, the local firemen struggled to put out the last of the fires. To the town's utter horror, towards evening a group of *maquisards* reappeared, demanded to know what had happened, and to recover the body of their dead man. They were urged, implored and finally persuaded to leave. In an account composed on 13 June the mayor wrote:

I profit from an armoured train which is going to Périgueux to dispatch this letter. We have seen some horrors. We are all safe, but the cost is terrible: four killed, three wounded, the *mairie* burnt, eight houses destroyed by flames or tank gunfire, the population terrorized. We have lived through two hours of terror with the whole population gathered in the square covered by machine guns, a man hanged from the next-door balcony. God willed that I maintained a superhuman calm. . . .

In a vivid afterthought, written on 9 July, Labarthe added:

The cycle is simple, and repeated every time: the *maquis* conduct an operation, the Germans arrive, the *maquis* disappears once more into the woods with slight losses, the civil population pay the tariff, the Germans go away and the *maquis* reappear. Where there are casualties among the Germans, the retribution is terrible. I must confess that in the circumstances it is hard to be the representative and the defender of the people!

The day that the Das Reich cleared Terrasson, 11 June, another FTP *maquis* attacked an armoured train at Mussidan station, south-west of Périgueux. They were beaten off with the loss of nine killed and eight wounded. In reprisal local German forces shot fifty-two hostages, including the mayor. Army Group G was now asserting itself to restore control of the main roads and towns throughout the Dordogne. On 12 June, as the first armoured elements of the Das Reich reached Périgueux, a German column smashed eastwards through the *maquis* cordon around Bergerac, killing twenty *résistants* and burning much of the village of Mouleydier. To the increasing despair of Bergeret and de Gunzbourg, it was becoming apparent that there would be no Allied parachute landings to support them. Martial, De Gaulle's departmental representative, was furious about the suicidal concentration of *résistants* facing inevitable destruction. In London, General Koenig was sufficiently alarmed by the great concentrations of *résistants* reported to be gathering that on the tenth he broadcast a somewhat clumsy request to restrain their activities: 'Break contact everywhere to enable a phase of reorganization. Avoid large concentrations: form small, isolated groups.' De Gunzbourg wrote:

At the end of four or five days I admitted to myself that we would receive no Allied support, and the situation threatened to become tragic. I had to send back the men in their trucks to their various departure points, and I was constantly woken in the night by panic-stricken people.

He was doubly depressed when a *résistant* from the Gers told him that his beloved *patron*, Starr,

. . . was displeased with me, and that I had not understood the orders given to me. Useless to say that I had suffered morally through a scarcely describable period when I believed that the country was going to liberate itself within a day or so, that the Allies had not kept their promises, that the various political factions were beginning to surface, and to dispute my action, that their leaders were seeking their own advancement through the Resistance. . . .

Thousands of men and women took to the *maquis* rather than risk remaining in their homes and face German reprisals. The great concentration of *résistants* melted away into the countryside, and the German columns smashed the roadblocks and shot down anyone foolish enough to remain visible in their path. 'The British had once again become *perfide Albion*', said de Gunzbourg sadly. 'My own prestige and command of the region never recovered from their failure to arrive to support us.'

Yet the people of the western Dordogne were fortunate, had they but perceived it. The Germans had neither the forces nor the time to pursue massive, systematic reprisals for the attempted uprising. The Dordogne suffered, and the *résistants* had suffered some 200 killed, but they escaped the terrible fate of Vercors a month later, where in a precisely comparable situation the victorious Germans meted out wholesale slaughter and destruction. If the attempt to liberate the region had been ill-judged, the isolation of its communications had critically hampered the Germans. The first of the Das Reich's tank trains, bearing the heavy armour north from Périgueux towards Normandy, was unable to assemble, load and depart until the evening of 15 June, although, as has been shown, OKW had demanded its movement five days earlier.

It is now time to return to the night of 8 June, to rejoin the Der Führer Panzergrenadiers crawling wearily into Limoges after their long drive north from Montauban. The city sprawls grey and unlovely on the hills above the north bank of the Vienne. Limoges is more than twice the size of Brive, an industrial metropolis dedicated to porcelain, enamel and shoe-making. Renoir made his living here for a time, painting porcelain, but it is difficult to imagine that he enjoyed himself. In AD 250, St Martial came to convert the region to Christianity, but some ungrateful citizens of Limoges had him cast into captivity. Tradition relates that an ethereal light promptly overtook the prison, aweing his jailors and the local inhabitants, who freed Martial to stride to the temple and cast down the false idols.

No such heavenly deliverance was granted to the Limousin in June 1944. The German garrison considered itself in a state of siege. The Der Führer arrived with orders to sweep the region, clear the vital road links, and destroy *maquis* concentrations wherever they could be found. The town's railway junctions had been badly affected by determined action by *cheminot* saboteurs after D-Day. On the afternoon of the eighth the Gestapo and local garrison troops moved on the main rail depot, seeking to arrest suspected *résistants*. They opened fire, killing one apprentice and wounding another, shooting a wanted man who attempted to bolt. There had also been a string of *maquis* attacks on isolated German vehicles, whose occupants when captured had almost all been shot out of hand. At about 2 am on the ninth, the first vehicles of the Der Führer reached the nervous town, and Colonel Stadler and Major Weidinger drove to local headquarters for news. 'The regiment is greeted with general relief,' states Weidinger's history. 'All the Germans in the town hope that it will remain as long as possible. They have been cut off for two days from the outside world. Not a single vehicle had got through the circle of *maquisards*, either entering or leaving. There is talk of a converging *maquis* attack on the town. . . .' Stadler set up his headquarters in the Hôtel Central, and gave his battalion commanders their orders. The 1st battalion, under Dickmann – which was many hours late and had not yet arrived – would take up position on the western side, based on St Junien. The 1st battalion of the Deutschland would cover the south. The 3rd battalion under Major Kampfe would take the east. Kampfe's initial task, at first light on 9 June, would be to push north-north-east, towards Argenton-sur-Creuse where the *maquis* were said to be in control, and north-west to Guéret, where there was word of heavy fighting and beleaguered German troops.

The AS and FTP had planned a joint attack on Argenton but, as so often, co-operation broke down. Eighty AS men from Châtillon-sur-Indre, who were intended to occupy and hold the approaches to the town, were diverted to another operation at Chauvigny. Fifty men of the FTP under Henri Lathière attacked alone. They seized two petrol trains in sidings at the station, blew the railway in several places, and moved the passengers of a blocked through train into the local school. They took prisoner twenty-three Germans from the local garrison, who surrendered promptly, and established defensive positions. They then sat down to see what happened next.

At 6.15 pm on the evening of 9 June, shooting was heard from the Limoges road. The 15th company of the Der Führer advanced into the town, firing as they came. Henri Rognon, a twenty-year-old former Vichy soldier who had joined the Resistance only on 6 June, shot it out until the house in which he lay was blown down on him. Most of the FTP retreated hastily from the area. As usual, it was the population of Argenton who bore the price for their liberation. Three elderly inhabitants of homes on the Avenue Victor Hugo died where they sat. The Germans conducted a swift and ruthless house-clearing operation. One party burst into the homes of the Vilatte family, where a mother and her two daughters were at supper. The first burst killed Gisèle, thirteen, and a second disposed of her mother as she dragged her other daughter, Nicole, seventeen, wounded to the sofa. Nicole died in hospital two days later. The SS then gathered a hundred people found in the area, including the passengers from the stranded train. Six men were taken from the group and shot at once. Another group of ten, whose papers were not in order, was held aside. One of them was a sixteen-year-old *gendarme*'s son. His elder brother, who had been questioned and released, asked to stay with the younger boy. His request was granted and the two were shot together, along with the others. A total of fifty-four people died during and after the recapture of Argenton.

Meanwhile, further south the rest of the 3rd battalion under Major Kampfe was advancing from Limoges to Guéret, which had been in *maquis* hands since 6 June. On the road, they had a sudden encounter with two lorries moving southwards towards them. *Maquisards* in one vehicle opened fire at once, severely wounding the officer in the leading German half-track. They then abandoned the trucks, and fled through fierce German fire. When the SS reached the French vehicles they found that these contained German soldiers and officials, together with several French collaborators captured by the *maquis* in Guéret. Two of the Germans were now dead, several wounded, and a Frenchwoman had a severe stomach wound. Putting the casualties at the rear of the convoy, the battalion moved on through the thick woods and steep hills of the Creuse. Just beyond Bourganeuf, they encountered another Resistance convoy. This time the Frenchmen surrendered, and twenty-nine were immediately shot.

There was a *Garde Mobile de Réserve* training school in Guéret, whose pupils defected *en masse* to the Resistance on 6 June. The former Prefect, who had been deposed by Vichy, was reinstalled. The town celebrated. Then, on the morning of the eighth, it was subjected to heavy German air attack. Wehrmacht units moved up from Montluçon with air support, and by the time Kampfe's men arrived at 5.30 pm on the afternoon of the ninth, the Germans had already re-established control.

The SS moved the wounded Frenchwoman to the local hospital. Kampfe then ordered Muller, the battalion doctor, to put the rest of the wounded in a half-track and return to Limoges as rapidly as possible. He left two platoons of his support company in Guéret to bolster the German perimeter. Then the rest of the battalion, tired and not a little exasperated, swung themselves back into their vehicles, and turned once more towards Limoges.

At about 8 pm, Dr Muller's half-track was clattering along the road when it was overtaken at speed by Major Kampfe's open Talbot. The CO, in a hurry to return to headquarters after a frustrating day, waved carelessly and swept on. He was one of the stars of the division, a thirty-four-year-old former printer and Wehrmacht officer who had transferred to the SS in 1939. Tall, very strong, and a keen athlete, he had fought with distinction and won the Knight's Cross in Russia.

At dusk on 9 June, as his car approached a road junction at

the tiny hamlet of La Bussière, fifteen miles short of Limoges, he saw a lorry approaching and flashed his lights in greeting. With extraordinary lack of prudence, he halted and found himself surrounded by a ring of armed men, led by a miner from the nearby town of St Léonard, Sergeant Jean Canou, who was returning to an FTP *maquis* after blowing up a bridge at Brignac. The group had been travelling by side roads, and were cautiously crossing the main D941 when they chanced upon Kampfe, whom they claimed later was accompanied by a driver (German accounts hold that he was alone). Canou was not highly esteemed by his fellow *maquisards* for his brainpower, but he knew a splendid catch when he found one. Kampfe was bundled into the lorry. They could do nothing with his Talbot, for the Frenchman at the wheel of the truck was the only one among them who could drive. They said later that Kampfe showed no sign of fear, but seemed arrogantly confident that he would soon be free, no doubt because he expected to meet his own men on the main road. Within a few minutes the incident was over. Canou and his men turned up a narrow dirt road towards their camp at Cheissoux. They testified after the war that they handed Helmut Kampfe to another *maquis*, and never saw him again. To this day there is no reliable evidence of the major's fate. The only certainty is that some time after his disappearance he was killed by the *maquis*. It is a matter for speculation whether this took place immediately, or following the events of the next few days. SS records listed him: 'Missing in southern France in action against terrorists.'

Colonel Stadler's first knowledge of the disappearance of one of his battalion commanders – more than that, a close friend who had served as his adjutant in Russia – came with the arrival of a grim Dr Muller. He could report only that he had found Kampfe's car, engine running and doors open, a Schmeisser without a magazine lying beneath it, but no signs of blood or violence. The battalion adjutant, Captain Weinrauch, was leading the men in a sweep of the woods around the long, straight avenue of fir trees in the middle of which Kampfe had been seized. The SS were bitterly angry. All night, frightened local peasants heard the roar of vehicles grinding down the tracks through the woods, occasionally firing flares to light the area. Two farmers from the hamlet of La Bussière, Pierre Mon Just and Pierre Malaguise, each in his forties and the fathers of five children, proved unable to provide any useful information and were shot in the ditch by the roadside. The Malaguise farmhouse was ransacked. The Germans sent for help from the Limoges *milice*, who could provide specialized local knowledge to strengthen the search.

At regimental headquarters, frustration was compounded by their inability to communicate directly either with the 3rd battalion's search parties, or with divisional HQ in Tulle. Stadler ordered Weidinger to leave at once in a Volkswagen field car with strong motor cycle escort, and report personally to Lammerding in Tulle. It was a nervous journey through the darkness. They travelled in a long, dispersed column, never faster than 30 mph for at any moment they expected to meet a terrorist roadblock. Shortly before 1 am, to their overwhelming relief they saw ahead the knife-rests and parked vehicles of the German outpost at the entrance to Tulle. They were waved through to the divisional headquarters, along the silent, heavily patrolled streets. In the lobby of the hotel where Stuckler had established his offices, among the orderlies and staff still sobered by the events of the day, Weidinger found Lammerding. He recollects only that Lammerding ordered the regiment to pursue the search for Kampfe with the utmost vigour. For the first time, Weidinger learned of the events in Tulle, and endorsed the staff view that reprisals had been entirely justified. Then he set off back to Limoges in the first light of dawn. At 6 am, he was with Stadler again.

The regimental commander's night had not been dull. In the early hours of the morning, the *Sturmgeschützabteilung*'s ordnance officer, Lieutenant Gerlach, had arrived exhausted at Stadler's headquarters dressed only in his underwear. On the morning of the ninth, Gerlach had driven with six men in three cars to reconnoitre billets for his unit in Nieul. Finding insufficient space, they moved on towards the next town. Gerlach had been specifically warned by Stadler about the terrorist menace, but raced ahead of the other cars, accompanied only by his driver. They soon found themselves alone. Becoming nervous, they turned the car and started back towards Limoges. A few minutes later, they were forced to halt in the middle of the road, and surrounded by *maquisards*. They were stripped, not gently.

One *maquisard* strained his knowledge of German to shout repeatedly into their faces 'SS! All kaputt!', and made unmistakable slicing gestures at their throats. They were then forced back into their car and driven away. The little convoy stopped and started several times that afternoon as they moved Gerlach and his driver across the Limousin countryside. They were bound for some time, according to the German, but were later untied. Then the Frenchmen stopped at the edge of a wood, and gestured the Germans to move into the trees. Gerlach testified that they were both certain that they were about to be shot. The driver began to struggle. Seizing the moment while the Frenchmen's attention was diverted, Gerlach ran headlong for the trees, pursued by a ragged fusillade. After some hours' walking, he reached the Bellac–Limoges railway line, and stumbled down it until he reached the city, and at last his commanding officer. Stadler sent him to bed. Gerlach awoke to find another officer standing over his bed – Major Otto Dickmann, CO of the 1st battalion. Dickmann handed Gerlach the map. According to the ordnance officer's subsequent evidence, the major demanded to be shown the exact route down which he had been taken by the *maquis* from the moment of his capture to that of his release.

Every available man of the Panzergrenadier brigade was combing the Limousin on the morning of 10 June for any trace of Major Kampfe. Shortly after 10 am, at the village of Salon-la-Tour some twenty miles south of Limoges near the Tulle road, soldiers – probably from the 1st battalion of the Deutschland regiment – were approaching the village. They saw a large black Citroën approaching them, then pull up abruptly. A young boy got out and raced away into the fields. Then a man and a girl, both carrying submachine guns, broke away from the car and began to run. The Germans opened fire, and a running battle developed. A woman tending her cows by a nearby farmhouse was killed instantly by a German burst. The boy escaped, and the man vanished in the maze of dense hedges and ditches that ran back from the road. They pinpointed the girl, firing a Sten gun from the base of an apple tree at the edge of a cornfield. They worked in towards her until her gun was empty.* Then, limping from a twisted ankle and with a slight flesh wound in her arm, she was led forward and put in a staff car to be taken to Limoges. The divisional interpreter, Dr Wache, was called to her initial interrogation by Major Kowatsch – the same Kowatsch who the previous day had acted as master of ceremonies in Tulle. She admitted that she was English, and that she had been parachuted into the area on the night of 6 June. In a subsequent statement, the interpreter claimed: 'She was treated with great politeness and supplied with clean clothes. She was then passed to the SD in Limoges. I know nothing further of the treatment of this agent.'

Violette Szabo had been desperately unlucky. For months, the *maquis* had travelled with impunity by car and truck across the Limousin and the Corrèze. The FTP *maquis* in the area had no knowledge of the presence of the Das Reich and, as so often, their lack of Intelligence was fatal. The new arrivals from French Section were driven gaily through the night of 6 June from the dropping zone to the little village of Sussac, some twenty-five miles south-east of Limoges. There they were lodged above a grocer's shop. Staunton, the commander of her party, wrote later in his report:

When I left London I was given to understand that I would find on arrival a very well-organized *maquis*, strictly devoid of any political intrigues, which would constitute a very good basis for extending the circuit throughout the area. On arrival I did find a *maquis*, which was roughly 600 strong, plus 200 French *gendarmes* who joined up on D-Day. But these men were strictly not trained, and were commanded by the most incapable people I have ever met, as was overwhelmingly proved by the fact that none of the D-Day targets had been attended

* Some former *résistants* and members of SOE were irritated by the romantic popular accounts of Violette Szabo's career which were published and filmed in the 1950s. They have suggested that she was in fact captured without having the opportunity to use a weapon. Neither German records nor surviving residents of Salon-la-Tour offer any decisive evidence one way or the other on the matter. I have therefore accepted the story of Mrs Szabo's use of her Sten given in R. J. Minney's biography *Carve Her Name with Pride*. I have been unable to find any record of German casualties from the incident in the Das Reich files, although I did locate the previously unpublished statement of the divisional interpreter concerning Mrs Szabo's interrogation.

to, and that each time it took me several hours of discussion to get one small turn-out, either to the railway or the telephone line.

Sussac was in the area dominated by 'Colonel' Georges Guingouin, among the most ruthless of communist leaders, in his French Army tank helmet and sheepskin jacket a familiar and feared figure throughout the Limousin. Of all the Resistance leaders in the region, he was among the least susceptible to the influence of London.

The *maquisards* of the Châteauneuf forest around Sussac did not take to Staunton any more than he took to them. They considered that he behaved too much as an English 'officer and gentleman', though in reality he was a Frenchman. They preferred Bob Mortier, the more easy-going 'Canadian' with him, although Mortier also was French. Staunton decided that it was essential for the mission to make contact with some of the more amenable *maquis* of the Corrèze and Dordogne. It has been suggested that he also wanted to make direct contact with Jacques Poirier. He explained that he wanted to send Violette Szabo, his courier, to liaise with them. One of the section leaders, a wild, brave young man named Jacques Dufour – 'Anastasie' – volunteered to take her to a contact at Pompadour, some thirty miles south, from whence she could be passed on to local leaders.

Anastasie had a reputation for recklessness, but no one suggested to Staunton that his courier might be safer with a more prudent guide. Around 9.30 on the morning of the tenth, the two set off in the petrol-driven Citroën. One of the *maquisards* wives suggested to Violette that she would be better off with flat shoes than her high heels, but there was nothing to be done about that there. 'She looked like a little doll,' the woman said, 'but she had a lot of guts.' They waved the Citroën off. A few miles on, Anastasie stopped to pick up a twelve-year-old boy, the son of a friend who wanted a lift into the Corrèze. They strapped his bicycle on the back of the car and drove cheerfully onwards, singing and chatting. Violette was the daughter of a Frenchwoman who married a British soldier named Bushell during World War I. She was brought up a cockney and worked as a shopgirl until she met and married a French officer in 1940. He was later killed in the desert. When French Section approached her, she left a three-year-old daughter to go to France. She was adored by the men and women of SOE, both for her courage and for her endless infectious cockney laughter.

Anastasie chattered enthusiastically about the countryside through which they passed and his own boyhood. He was still talking when they came to their fatal rendezvous with the Das Reich, combing the countryside for Major Kampfe. After Violette damaged her ankle and Anastasie perfectly properly abandoned her, he hid beneath a log pile for many hours until the Germans were gone. Eventually he made his way back to the *maquis*. His boy passenger also escaped.

The *maquis* of south-east Haute-Vienne learned the identity of their latest enemies only twenty-four hours later, when one of their section commanders was examining the contents of a truck stolen from the Germans. In a crate in the back, he found a uniform bearing SS runes and the wristband of the Das Reich.

On the day after Kampfe's capture – the same 10 June on which Violette Szabo was captured – Major Stuckler issued a divisional Order of the Day to the men of the Das Reich:

> In the course of its advance, the division has already dealt with several Resistance groups. The armoured regiment has succeeded, thanks to a neatly executed surprise attack, in carrying out a knife stroke – a '*coup de filet*' – against a band organized in company strength [at Bretenoux].
>
> The division is now proceeding to a rapid and lasting clean-up of these bands from the region, with a view to becoming speedily available to reinforce the fighting men and join the line on the invasion front.

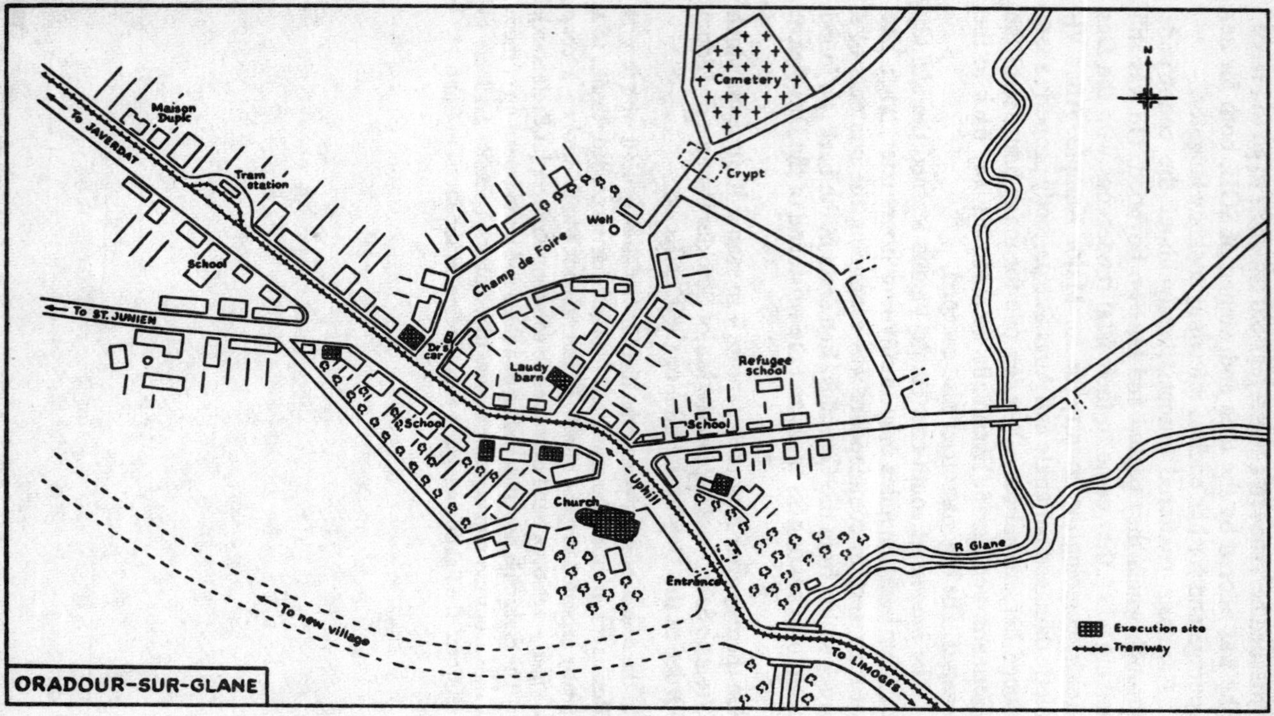
ORADOUR-SUR-GLANE
N
Cemetery
Crypt
Maison Dupic
To JAVERDAT
Tram station
School
To ST. JUNIEN
Well
Champ de Foire
Dr's car
Laudy barn
Refugee school
School
School
Church
Uphill
Entrance
To new village
R Glane
To LIMOGES
Execution site
Tramway

9 '. . . a rapid and lasting clean-up. . .': Oradour

Major Otto Dickmann, commanding the 1st battalion of the Der Führer regiment, had already fought through the *résistants* defending the bridge at Groslejac on the morning of 8 June, and he and his column had subsequently killed several *maquisards* and rather more innocent bystanders as they advanced through the eastern Dordogne. More recently it was Dickmann who had personally awakened Lieutenant Gerlach early on the morning of the tenth, to hear the tale of his experiences. Major Kampfe, Dickmann's counterpart of the 3rd battalion, was a close personal friend, and Dickmann was desperate for any clue to the missing officer's whereabouts.

The 1st battalion only reached Limoges, late and exhausted, at around 6.30 am on the 9 June, four hours after the rest of the regiment. 'It was very rough,' Dickmann told Weidinger. 'After many delays and a terrible journey,' states the regimental history, whose account of this, as of many other episodes, is enigmatically terse, 'the 1st battalion arrives at Limoges in the morning and then moves to its deployment area. . . . During its covering movement on the left flank, it had encountered several heavy shooting attacks . . . and suffered its first losses. Many tree barriers had to be removed. The commander, Sturmbannführer Dickmann, seemed tense and strained.' As soon as he had confirmed his orders, the major climbed wearily back into his car, and led the battalion south-westwards out of Limoges to the town of St Junien, some twenty miles distant.

The German dominance of the Limousin had been as rudely challenged since D-Day as that of the Dordogne and Corrèze. On the night of 7 June, *maquisards* sabotaged and severely damaged the railway viaduct carrying the Limoges–Angoulême main line through St Junien, a town of some 20,000 people notable for its tanneries and glovemakers. The attackers conducted a symbolic occupation of the *mairie* early on the morning of 8 June, and then took up positions covering the viaduct. That evening, a train from Angoulême halted at the southern end, and passengers began to walk across the weakened span to join another train sent from Limoges to meet them. Among them were ten German soldiers, two of whom were killed when the *résistants* opened fire. Five ran back to the Angoulême train, and three forward to go on to Limoges, where they urgently phoned their headquarters. By the time an armoured train arrived in St Junien at 9 am the next day, bearing a Wehrmacht detachment and Lieutenant Wickers of the Gestapo, the *maquis* had prudently vanished. The troops deployed through the town, and Wickers gave orders to the mayor that a hundred able-bodied civilians were to be assembled at once with picks and spades to dig trenches round the approaches. This was a combination of precaution and punishment. Some fifty mostly elderly men eventually gathered, and dug reluctantly under the eyes of their guards until about 1 pm.

At 10 am, Wickers had received a message from his headquarters in Limoges, informing him that the SS would be relieving the Wehrmacht as soon as they could get down to the town. At 10.30, the long file of Dickmann's trucks and half-tracks crawled into St Junien. Dickmann dismounted, exchanged brief words with Wickers and several nervous local French officials, then set up his command post in the Hôtel de la Gare. He had brought with him a notorious Limoges Gestapo officer named Joachim Kleist, a Gestapo interpreter and four *miliciens*. By the standards of the Das Reich, St Junien escaped lightly. Germans commandeered all the petrol they could find in local garages, and conducted a grenade-throwing competition to amuse themselves. As a security precaution, all the officers slept together under heavy guard.

Early the next morning – the tenth – Dickmann was back at Der Führer HQ in Limoges. According to Weidinger's narrative:

> . . . He arrives in an excited state and reports the following: in St Junien, two French civilians had approached him and told him that a high German official was being held by the *maquisards* in Oradour. That day he was to be executed and publicly burnt amidst celebrations. The whole population was working with the *maquis*, and high-ranking leaders were there at that very moment. At about the same time, the Limoges SD informed the regiment that according to Intelligence from their own

local informers, there was a *maquis* headquarters in Oradour. Sturmbannführer Dickmann requests permission from the regimental commander to take a company there to free the prisoner. In his opinion it must be Sturmbannführer Kampfe, who was a close personal friend of his. The regimental commander then informs Dickmann of the other events in the Oradour area on the previous day [the capture of Gerlach], and immediately grants permission for this plan with the additional order that Dickmann must try above all to take *maquis* leaders prisoner in case Kampfe was not found. He intended to use any prisoners for negotiations with the Resistance to release Kampfe in an exchange. . . .

Dickmann also spoke directly to Gerlach, from whom, according to post-war testimony, he received an indication that he believed his own captors had taken him through Oradour. In the regimental history, Weidinger also recounts a bizarre attempt to make contact with the *maquis* and bargain for the release of Kampfe by freeing a prisoner held by the Limoges SD. Weidinger claims that the freed *maquisard* telephoned once to say that he was doing his best to find Kampfe, but was then never heard from again.

Dickmann was back in St Junien by mid-morning. He held some discussion with Kleist of the Gestapo and the *milice*, then ordered his 3rd company, commanded by Hauptsturmführer Kahn, to prepare to move out for an operation. At about 1.30 pm Dickmann, Kahn and 120 men in a convoy of two half-tracks, eight trucks and a motor cycle drove eastwards out of St Junien on an indirect route to Oradour-sur-Glane, via St Victorien. Dickmann himself rode in his commandeered Citroën *deux chevaux* with his young Alsatian driver and his adjutant, Lange. According to some – not surprisingly hesitant and confused – post-war testimony, they halted *en route* for Dickmann to give a cursory briefing for a 'search and destroy' operation of the kind that they had several times undertaken from Montauban. But an NCO named Barth was said to have implied that this would be something special when he declared buoyantly: 'You're going to see some blood flow today!' to a group of young recruits, adding: 'And we'll also find out what the Alsatians are made of.'

There is today no longer any prospect of discovering the definitive truth about Dickmann's motive in moving against Oradour-sur-Glane. Some of those who knew are dead. Others, in the shadow of war crimes trials, have always had the strongest possible motives for lying. There are survivors of Dickmann's company alive and living in Germany today who undoubtedly know some of the answers, but will never reveal them. Some of those with whom the author corresponded in researching this book know the whereabouts of men who were in the convoy that left St Junien that afternoon, but they have no intention of disclosing them.

Certain key points can, however, be brought into focus. First, it has sometimes been alleged that a tragic error was made – that Dickmann's men moved against Oradour-sur-Glane, whereas the *maquisards* whom they sought were to be found around Oradour-sur-Vayres, twenty miles south-westwards near the forest of Rochechouart where the FTP had killed a number of German soldiers in recent weeks. There is no evidence to support this view. Oradour-sur-Vayres is geographically even more distant than Oradour-sur-Glane from the seizure of Kampfe and all the activity concerning the Das Reich. Second, some Germans allege to this day that the *maquis* had perpetrated an abominable atrocity against Wehrmacht soldiers – some say against an ambulance convoy – near Oradour. Had this been the case, it is unthinkable that the Das Reich and for that matter the propaganda apparatus of Berlin would have failed to proclaim the fact at the time, as they did the alleged killing of prisoners at Tulle. This possibility can be discounted. Third, the evidence is overwhelming that there was no *maquis* presence in or around Oradour-sur-Glane. The nearest *maquis* camp was some seven miles south-westwards.

Yet it is impossible to believe that French historians have been justified in asserting so often since the war that Oradour was the victim of an entirely arbitrary, blind stroke of savagery by the Germans. Even at their most ruthless moments, the SS contrived to pursue a policy that in their own terms possessed some logic. With so many scores of villages from which to choose for Dickmann's purge – many of them with well-known links with the *maquis* – why should he have chosen Oradour? It seems most probable that Dickmann acted upon misplaced intelligence received from some deluded or malignant French source. The Germans, in their mood of frustration that day, were questing urgently for a clue to a target. Someone in Limoges or St Junien placed the finger upon Oradour. Once the hint had been given, Dickmann showed no interest in confirming its accuracy. A pretext was enough. It seems almost certain that his officers expected Dickmann to do little more to Oradour than they had done to scores of suspect French villages that summer – search, and make an example with a clutch of salutary executions and burnings. But from the unhesitating conduct of the major that afternoon of 10 June, it seems equally clear that, in his own mind, Dickmann drove into Oradour knowing precisely what he proposed to do.

Englishmen or Americans would describe Oradour-sur-Glane as a small town rather than a village. Its 254 buildings included two small hotels and more than a score of shops. The tramway to Limoges, built in 1911, had marred the appearance of the main street, the Rue Emile Desourteaux, with overhanging cables and pylons, but it had also provided electricity and brought the village within easy commuting distance of Limoges. It was a community of twentieth-century suburban architecture and privet hedges – never beautiful, but set in the perfectly rural woods and fields of the flat countryside west of Limoges.

There was a strong leavening of bourgeois and professional families among its inhabitants – some of them were lingering over an expansive Saturday lunch at the Hôtel Milord on the afternoon of 10 June, for the black market ensured that there was no shortage of food for those able to pay for it. In the past four years of war, the population had become swollen with the sort of ragtag of refugees who had descended upon even the most remote French rural communities to escape persecution, or to put as much distance as possible between themselves and Allied bombing targets. The BBC French Service had been warning since 16 April that 'all vital points on the railways in Belgium and France will be subjected to attack in the coming weeks. Get away from them.' Some of those in Oradour on 10 June had paid heed. There were Jews and Alsatians; Parisians and Lorrainers; a group of thirty Spaniards, flotsam of the Civil War who had taken local manual jobs. The town was crowded, and not discontented. Like every other community in France, it had received the news of the Allied landings as the promise of an end to the long struggle, and the fighting was far enough distant to present no threat or cause for fear. Many people had drifted into the village to collect their tobacco ration, issued every ten days, or to do the weekly shopping. The three schools were full, because it was the day of a medical inspection and vaccination. The boys' schools opposite the tram section held sixty-four children, while the girls' – divided into three classrooms – held 106. There was also a special school for the little Lorrainer refugees.

Every circumstance conspired to ensure that Otto Dickmann found the village crowded with people. By early afternoon the farmworkers had come in from the fields. A few weekend fishermen had ridden the tram from Limoges to try their luck on the Glane. There was the usual Saturday foraging party from the city, seeking food that was more readily available in the countryside. The streets were still damp from a morning shower, but the sky had cleared and the sun was shining, warming the grey, creeper-clad houses. Oradour was a drab, unprepossessing place, but in the midst of war, Occupation and so many troubles and uncertainties it seemed a haven of sanity. 'This place', a young refugee named Michel Forest wrote in his diary, 'is pervaded by a classical tranquillity, in which one can live as a human being should. Everything here is done in moderation in the best sense of the word.'

He was a twenty-year-old law student, the son of a philosophy teacher, Professor Forest, who had been born in Oradour, and had now returned to find some peace and quiet with five of his six children – the eldest was an STO evader with a *maquis* in George Starr's area. In March 1944 the Germans had closed all the universities in France, and Professor Forest moved into the pleasant little Château de Laplaud, a mile west of Oradour, rented to him by a family friend, the Vicomtesse de Saint-Venant. Michel, a deeply religious young man, was to take his first communion on 11 June. On the afternoon of the tenth he walked into Oradour with his six-year-old brother Dominique – the family favourite – to get a haircut and see his grandfather. Professor Forest took the other three children with him on the tram to Limoges.

An insurance agent from Avignon was also on the Limoges tram that afternoon. M. Levignac had just moved his sons to Oradour because of the intense Allied communications bombing. An overshoot from the railway yards killed their neighbours in their own home, and M. Levignac decided that enough was enough. His eldest son Serge, sixteen, was now billeted with a farmer on the edge of Oradour, and the younger Charles, twelve, was staying with two elderly women. M. Levignac himself had travelled up from Avignon on the afternoon of the ninth to visit the boys, and had spent the night in the Hôtel Avril. He scribbled his wife a postcard to say how well he found them: 'I feel I am giving our sons life itself.' Then he left them for a couple of hours, promising to be back by early evening.

Another refugee was the wife of Robert Cordeau, a French POW working as a forced labourer near Danzig. The family came from Paris, but found life there very difficult during the Occupation. Mme Cordeau originally came from Oradour and after discussing the matter in letters with her husband, she decided to return to the Limousin. She found a job as secretary to a Limoges doctor, and her sixteen-year-old daughter Bernadette began to learn dressmaking in Oradour. On the afternoon of the tenth Bernadette was in the village, while her mother was in Limoges because the doctor was on call.

Denise Bardet, a twenty-four-year-old teacher at the girls' school, was one of the few people in Oradour who knew that the SS were in the area. The previous day she had boarded the rickety *gazogène* bus to St Junien with a little group of her girls who had to sit an examination in the town. They arrived to find a company of the Der Führer billeted in the classrooms, and SS troopers striding through the playground. The first thought of any woman in France when she saw Germans sweeping the district was fear for the men – they could be seized as hostages or carried off for forced labour. Denise Bardet was engaged to a young man in Limoges, and her brother was at the teacher training college there. She returned safely to Oradour on the evening of the ninth, but lay awake for hours in the big bed that she shared with her widowed mother in her cottage outside the village, discussing the alarming scene in St Junien. The next day she was at school as usual. She returned home for lunch, then mounted her bicycle and pedalled unhurriedly back to the classroom to supervise the afternoon medical check.

Here then, at 2.15 on the afternoon of 10 June, the tableau is frozen for the rest of history: an undistinguished Limousin town, its normal population of 330 swollen to some 650 by the pressures of war, lingering over the remains of its lunch on a sunny early summer afternoon; a community that had hitherto glimpsed the German Occupiers only as a convoy roaring past upon the main road, or a handful of officers slipping out from Limoges for dinner at the Hôtel Emile. There had been no battles around Oradour, no descents by the Gestapo, no brutalities. Insofar as life in France in June 1944 could anywhere be declared to be normal, in Oradour it was so. The men tilled the fields beyond the little back gardens of the town with their two-seat privies and neatly tended bushes. The women eked out the erratic food supplies and complained about the chronic queues and shortages, but there was no real hardship in Oradour.

Two young trainee teachers from the college in Limoges finished lunch at the Hôtel Milord and strolled to the edge of the village together before one, who was on an assignment with one of its schools, turned back to her classroom. The other making for a hamlet a little way off, waved, turned, and disappeared down the road. She was the last French civilian to leave Oradour at peace that afternoon.

The spectacle of Otto Dickmann's trucks and half-tracks grinding up the main street of Oradour, laden with helmeted and camouflaged-smocked infantry covering the houses with their weapons, caused immediate astonishment and bewilderment. 'Let's hide,' said a motor mechanic named Aimé Renaud to his elderly wine merchant friend M. Denis. 'I am not afraid of the Germans,' replied Denis phlegmatically. 'They're only ordinary men like us, and anyway I am too old to be frightened any more.'

But some people in Oradour had reason to be terrified by the very sight of Germans. Martial Brissaud was a teenager from Les Bordes, just arrived to visit a friend, and appalled by the thought of being seized for forced labour. Dr Desourteaux, mayor of Oradour like his father before him, sought to reassure the boy when he ran to him in the street, but Brissaud was not persuaded. He fled homewards and took refuge in the loft. He tried in vain to persuade his family that they were all in urgent danger, then took to the fields and stayed there all afternoon.

Other parents were more prudent. 'Hide! Hide!' shouted Mme Belivier to her eighteen-year-old son, who also fled into the fields. A Jewish couple staying at the Hôtel Avril frantically drove their two daughters of eighteen and twenty-two, together with their nine-year-old son, into a bolthole under the staircase just by the garden door. A Jewish dentist from Rennes named Lévy ran for his life to the fields. His wife was already in a concentration camp. His lunch companion, a Mme Jeanne Leroy from St Malo, remained composedly at her table. Her papers were perfectly in order – she had been driven out of St Malo when her home was taken over by German workmen strengthening the fortifications. She had nothing to hide or fear.

One of Dickmann's men led Dr Desourteaux to the major, who spoke briefly to him. M. Depierrefiche, the town crier, was hastily dispatched through the handful of streets escorted by two SS troopers, beating his drum and calling on the entire population to assemble instantly in the Champ de Foire, the little central square, bringing their identity papers. Apprehension gave way to relief and irritation. After all, it was only another identity check.

But as the troopers fanning out through the town began to fire in the air, to hammer doors with their rifle butts and push and jostle families through the streets, uncertainty increased again. A strange convoy appeared at the end of the road: families from outlying farms and hamlets were being herded towards the Champ de Foire – a pretty enough place with its trees and a covered well – by impatient, dead-eyed infantry. A local tenant farmer named Jean Rouffranche was in the crowd with his wife Marguerite, their son Jean and their daughters Amélie and Andrée – Amélie pushed a pram bearing her seven-month-old daughter, and behind her came their eighty-year-old grandmother. The Le Lamand family came with their small grandson and granddaughter, maid and elderly mother. Their son and daughter were away at a wedding. Other men were being driven in from the fields. Mme Binet, the principal of the girls' school, was ill in bed, but now appeared with a coat thrown over her nightdress. Another sick old man was carried by his two sons. The Abbé Lorich, the Lorrainers' own priest, was pushed out of his house with his sister and a friend.

SS troopers burst into the school classrooms calling '*Alle 'raus!'* The teachers hurriedly mustered their charges and bustled them in orderly crocodiles towards the square. Some cried, but they were hurried onwards, because everyone in Oradour that afternoon was desperate to be compliant. It is a rule of civilized or even semi-civilized existence that if threats and provocation are met only by submissiveness, the aggressor has no pretext for resorting to violence.

When a seven-year-old boy named Roger Godfrin shouted to his sisters in the rush from the classroom that they should all bolt, he was ignored. He himself ran away: 'I was very frightened, because I was from Lorraine and I knew what they were like.' He lost a shoe scrambling through a hedge at the edge of the schoolyard, then found himself pursued by a volley of shots. He rolled over and lay limp. A soldier kicked him in casual confirmation of death and moved on. The boy, uninjured, lay motionless, listening to more shooting. Then he leaped to his feet and fled onwards out of the village. He glimpsed a mechanic named Poutaraud being shot by two soldiers, sagging to the ground at the foot of a fence. One of the Germans saw the boy, and fired again. But Roger Godfrin scampered on and on until he reached the river, and fell panting under the safety of its bank. There he lay until silence fell, many hours later, and he crept on through the woods until he reached a farmhouse where he found safety.

It was now about 2.45. The entire population of Oradour except a few of the old, the crippled or the fugitive, who still lingered in their beds or hiding places, faced each other across the Champ de Foire, men on one side, women and children on the other. German machine gun teams had set up their Spandaus covering the square, the gunners lying at their weapons, ammunition belts curling into the breeches. Some of the women and children were crying noisily, but many simply stared in bewilderment, clutching each other's hands.

The men stood in their faded blue peasant overalls, grey or black suits, much-mended shoes. The local *gendarme*, Duquerry, was in uniform. Boucholle, the old baker, had come directly from his ovens and stood naked to the waist, covered in flour, impatient to be back at his business. After a few minutes, he asked a German NCO if he could go back and do something about the pastry that was still baking. 'Don't worry, we'll take care of that,' said the soldier shortly. Suddenly, into the centre of the assembly drove Dr Jean Desourteaux, the mayor's son, back from visiting a patient. Covered by an SS man, he hurried from his car to the corner where his father was talking to an officer, probably either Kahn or Dickmann. A witness afterwards claimed to have heard the German demanding that the mayor select thirty hostages. In the background, all of them could hear sporadic shooting. They could not know that isolated civilians were already dying, but they were acutely conscious of danger.

The Germans suddenly began to move decisively. All the women and children were to be taken to the church, they announced. Herded by an SS detail, rifles at the port, the long procession of old and young, mothers clutching their babies and grandmothers supported by their families, shuffled across the road and a few yards down the hill to the tall church with its red Romanesque tiles and turreted spires, its crucified Christ upon the outer wall. Inside, it was cool and dim, but bright with flowers for next day's first communion. Oradour was not a notably religious community – indeed, for years attendance at Sunday services had been sparse. Abbé Chapelle was old and sick, and had few personal friends in the village. Each day he walked three miles in all weathers to his other parish, Javerdat, to hold its masses. Ironically enough, he had always spoken warmly of Marshal Pétain from his pulpit, and offered prayers for the victims of Allied bombing. Now, while he waited with the men, the nave and altar steps of his church filled with women and children, and their nervous cries and whispers echoed from the walls.

The men were ordered to seat themselves in three rows, facing the wall of the houses flanking the Champ de Foire. An SS trooper, probably an Alsatian, shouted in fluent French: 'There are concealed weapons and stocks of ammunition in this town that have been hidden by terrorists. A house-to-house search will be conducted. While this is going on, you will be assembled in barns and garages to facilitate operations. If you know of any place in which weapons are stored, you must report the fact immediately!' An elderly farmer named Jean Lamaud called out that he possessed a shotgun and a police permit for it. 'We're not interested in that,' said the trooper. The men were ordered to their feet. Forty and fifty at a time, they were marshalled by the Germans and led briskly out of the Champ de Foire. One party was directed into Mme Laudy's big coach house fifty yards up the street. One by one, the other groups filed into five other garages and barns whose doors had been thrown open to make way for them. They huddled together, like all threatened animals, at the furthest end from their captors. It was about 3.30. There was a single shot from the square. Shouting like men advancing to the charge against the enemy, the Germans began to pour fire into the crowds of Frenchmen in their execution chambers.

An eighteen-year-old boy named Yves Roby had been seized as he cycled up the road past Oradour. He was one of those herded into the Laudy barn. He became one of the only five male survivors of the executions who lived to testify about events in Oradour that afternoon:

> As soon as we got there the Germans made us haul away two carts that stood in the way of the doors. Then they forced us at gunpoint to go inside, and four soldiers covered us with their machine gun. We reckoned this was to keep us from running away. They talked to each other and laughed as they checked their weapons. Five minutes after we had entered the coach house . . . the soldiers began howling, and opened fire on us.

The first men to fall were protected from the shots that followed by the bodies of those who fell over them. Roby threw himself flat on his stomach and hid his head in his arms. As the roar of gunfire echoed ceaselessly through the coach house, the air filled with choking brick dust, fragments from the ricochets, and wounded men's screams for their wives, mothers and children.

Then the shooting stopped. The Germans strode forward to the mound of prostrate bodies, and began shooting with pistols each one that moved or groaned. Roby lay terrified, waiting for the shot that he expected to finish him. It caught his left elbow. He lay motionless until at last the groaning died away and the shooting stopped. Soldiers began to move around them again, dragging in straw, hay, brushwood and saddlery and heaping it upon the bodies. Then they tossed down a match and left the building, closing the doors. Flames began to race through the coach house.

Roby found himself fighting to pull his body from the weight of those above it, as a handful of other survivors did likewise. Several more lay badly wounded and covered with blood, yet visibly alive. There was nothing to be done for them. Struggling frenziedly despite his smashed arm, Roby at last fought free. He clambered to his feet, expecting a shot, and saw that the Germans had gone.

It was now becoming impossible to breathe, but I found a gap in the wall, quite high up. I slipped through it and hid in the next door barn. There I found four friends – Broussardier, Darthout, Hebras and Borie. I crawled under a pile of straw and beans. Borie and Hebras hid behind a wood pile. Broussardier huddled in a corner. Darthout had four bullet wounds in the legs, and was bleeding from all of them. He asked me if there was room for him beside me. We huddled together like brothers, and lay listening carefully to every sound from outside.

A German suddenly stepped into the barn, put a burning brand to the straw that covered them, and walked out again. The Frenchmen lay motionless as flames leaped up, scorching Roby's feet. He cautiously put up his head, to see Broussardier dashing across the barn – he had seen a way out. The two men dashed through a rear door, and found themselves in a tiny yard containing a big rabbit hutch. They crawled into it, and burrowed deep into the earth and straw at its base. There they lay for three hours.

But the fires now enveloping Oradour at last reached the rabbit hutch. Almost choked with smoke, brushing away burning fragments that singed his hair, Roby forced his way out, followed by the coughing, spluttering Broussardier. They crept furtively towards the Champ de Foire. Broussardier slipped forward to look for Germans. He saw none. The two men burst into a run, fleeing towards the graveyard, and at last into the safety of thick undergrowth. 'We were so overjoyed at coming back to life that we kissed each other. I spent the rest of the night in a rye field, and returned home to Basse-Forêt the following day, Sunday, at about eleven o'clock.'

Jean Darthout, the man shot in both legs, also miraculously survived with two others. But many more who had neither been killed in the initial firing, nor dispatched by *coup de grâce*, died in the flames that were now enveloping Oradour. German troopers ran from house to house, starting fires. Here and there they discovered fugitives who had escaped the initial round-up. Some were dispatched where they lay. A few belatedly discovered women and children were pushed into the burning barns and shot, their bodies falling among those of the men. Five young men and a girl, seized when they cycled up just as the executions began, were shot against the wall of the forge.

The three young Jews who had hidden under the stairway of the Hôtel Avril were driven to bolt from their refuge when flames and smoke overwhelmed the building. Late in the afternoon, surrounded by the horror of the burning town, they ran across the yard behind the hotel and into the arms of an SS trooper. The oldest girl asked him simply: 'What are we to do?' The soldier stared down at her for a moment in silence, then swept his arm aside in an urgent gesture of dismissal. The three ran through the houses, across the fields, and many hours later to a château where they found shelter. It was an almost unique gesture of mercy among the events of the afternoon.

The Beaubreuil boys were the children of the local carpenter and, since one of them was an STO evader, their father hid them immediately under the living-room floor when he heard that the Germans were in Oradour. There they lay listening in terror to the sound of boots, shouted commands and shots. They heard a neighbour cry: '*Nous sommes perdus!*' There were screams. There was a smell of petrol or paraffin, and suddenly choking flames. The boys crawled from their refuge, and ran four miles to St Victorien without stopping, and miraculously without encountering a German soldier.

Hubert Desourteaux, a twenty-nine-year-old car dealer and escaped prisoner of war, had also hidden under a stairwell when he heard the Germans arrive. He was the only survivor of the mayor's family. His mechanic, Aimé Renaud – the man who scented danger the moment he saw Dickmann's convoy roar up the main street – had hidden with his wife in the yard behind the Desourteaux' house. They lay there all that afternoon and into the night, listening to the screams, the gunfire, and later the explosion of grenades. They were convinced that they were to die. Jeannine Renaud's mother and her four-year-old daughter were with the other women in the church.

Something over 400 women and children were crowded into the church by the time the doors were slammed upon them. Two SS remained inside, covering them, until the doors opened again to admit a group of soldiers carrying a heavy box. One woman, Marguerite Rouffranche, was struck by how very young they looked. They dumped their load at the intersection of nave and chancel, lit the fuse protuding from it, and retired down the church. Thick black smoke began to pour from the box, which appeared to contain some incendiary device. Women and children screamed and started to struggle for refuge. The Germans at the west end of the church cocked their weapons and stripped the tape from their grenades. As the first bursts of fire echoed through the town from the barns where the men were dying, the SS began hurling grenades and emptying gunfire into the great throng of women, children and babies. To their anger, they suddenly saw that the door to the vestry lay open. Fugitives were fighting their way through it. Troopers ran forward, firing as they came. They pushed through the door and began machine gunning those lying and crouching inside. Mme Rouffranche saw her daughter fall dead. She herself slipped to the ground and lay still. Two boys of ten and twelve who ran into the confessional were shot in the neck at point-blank range. One Levignac boy had already died with the men in the barns. The other, along with little Dominique Forest, the four-year-old Renaud girl, Lucien and Marcel Boulestin whose mother had scrubbed them in the tub under the apple trees to be clean for medical inspection, Bernadette Cordeau, Roger Joyeux, four, Henri Joyeux, five, eighteen members of the Bardet family aged from sixty-four to four months, Marie Claude Milaud, four months, Mme Leroy whose papers were in order, Mme Belivier who had sent her sons to hide, the Jewish mother who had left her children beneath the stairway – died with some 400 others that afternoon in the church.

Prams, chairs and the confessional were riddled with bullet holes, the walls pock-marked with gunfire in the dreadful cacophony of screams and shooting. Women and children with their clothes on fire ran shrieking hopelessly in search of refuge. The SS heaped straw and chairs upon the bodies of the dead and wounded, fired it, and finally departed. The flames spread rapidly, and soon the entire building was blazing, the roof timbers cracking and collapsing into the nightmare spectacle beneath.

One woman, Mme Rouffranche, escaped. Behind the high altar she noticed three windows. Hauling herself up on a stand upon which the Abbé stood to light his candles, she climbed on to a buttress above it and flung herself from the window. She fell ten feet, and looked up to see another woman attempting to jump behind her. Henriette Joyeux was clutching her seven-month-old baby. Suddenly it slipped from her grasp, fell and screamed. The Germans turned, caught the scene and fired at once. Mme Joyeux fell back dead into the church, and the child was killed where it had fallen. Marguerite Rouffranche fled for her life along the chancel wall, stumbling as bullets struck her – she was hit five times – but scrambled frenziedly on. Between the rows of peas in a tiny vegetable garden she found a refuge and literally buried herself in the earth until, many hours later, the silence of death descended upon Oradour.

In the countryside around the town the distant sound of gunfire and the columns of smoke from the village of fire aroused puzzlement rather than alarm. There was no *maquis* anywhere near the village, so there could scarcely be a battle. The fires appeared to be burning in the woods beyond Oradour. Towards late afternoon, the mystery deepened. Where were the children, due back from school? Little knots of mothers began to gather and chatter at the roadside, gazing towards the distant smoke. Mme Forest, at the Château de Laplaud, waited at the tea table with her husband for Michel, Dominique and their grandfather. A certain M. Deschamps had the most extraordinary, almost spectral experience of the afternoon. When he came in from the fields to his home at La Fauvette and found his wife beginning to worry about the children, he walked into Oradour to look for them. At the moment that he reached the school on the eastern edge, the Germans were fully occupied in the centre. He found the school deserted, the children's possessions still in their places, their caps and satchels in a neat row on their pegs, yet no sign of life. It seemed that Oradour had been evacuated. He glimpsed German soldiers at the other end of the street, and beat a prudent retreat.

A little later another parent, Mme Demery, mother of three children at the schools, had almost the same experience. She too visited the schoolhouses and escaped unmolested. But by this time she saw flames and heard screams and shooting. The news that she carried back across the fields heightened the growing alarm.

Other intruders were less fortunate. A young miller named Antoine cycled towards Oradour despite warnings from the roadside – 'Don't go into the town! They're shooting in there!' Antoine shrugged cheerfully: 'The Germans had me as a prisoner of war. I know them – they don't frighten me.' Waving his white handkerchief high in one hand, he rode towards a German picket covering the approach to the village. There was a single shot and he fell. A trooper finished him with a pistol.

Around 6 pm, when the shooting had subsided, Marie-Léon Foussat walked towards Oradour, despite advice to stay away. He also waved a handkerchief. He also was shot. So was the driver of a small maintenance tram who arrived from Limoges late in the afternoon. Jacques Boissou, a farmer from Mas de l'Arbre, was fired upon as he approached the village, and pursued as he fled. He lay in a little stream until nightfall, seeing one man killed as he did. When he returned to his own home, he found that his mother and grandmother had gone to Oradour. Blanche Taillander had an extraordinary escape. Dickmann's men burst into the house where she was having lunch with a woman friend, shot the friend, but spared Mme Taillander because her identity card showed that she was from Paris.

When the tram bearing M. Levignac and all the other weekend shoppers back from Limoges reached the edge of Oradour, they gazed up the hill in utter horror at the palls of flame and smoke, and the infantry still moving briskly among the houses, tossing in grenades. A German picket boarded the tram and began to check papers. When he found a man whose card showed that he lived in Oradour, the German said briefly: 'That's bad.' Another SS trooper doubled away up the hill, obviously for orders. He returned a few moments later: 'All residents of Oradour must dismount. All others will remain in the car and return to Limoges.'

Twenty-two terrified men and women dismounted slowly and walked into a ring of SS men around the car. They were separated by sexes and their papers were inspected again. Then they were put together once more. There was a heated debate between several of the Germans. The agonized minutes dragged on. It was hideously apparent that the lives of the tram passengers were at stake. Suddenly a German turned to them and shouted: 'Disappear! Into the country – not into Oradour!' Another French-speaking trooper cried after them: 'You're being let off! Believe me, you're lucky!' There was a last, grotesque afterthought. A German noticed from one girl's papers that she lived many miles away. Picking up a bicycle that he had seized from one of the doomed houses of Oradour, he offered it to ease her journey.

M. Levignac, the insurance agent from Avignon, dismounted from the tram as soon as it was once more out of sight of Oradour, and lingered on the road in an agony of terror for his children. Professor Forest, the philosopher, walked from Laplaud to Oradour at about 7 pm. The church and much of the town were still burning fiercely. He approached a sentry and asked in German where his children might be. The trooper – probably an Alsatian – replied in French, to Forest's surprise, that all the women and children were off in the woods: 'They're safe.' They were standing twenty-five yards from the church, perhaps fifteen from Mme Rouffranche's hiding place. Professor Forest turned and walked uncertainly back to Laplaud.

All that night, frightened mothers scoured the woods around Oradour for their missing children. The conviction that they were somewhere in the countryside was strengthened when the exhausted Aimé and Jeannine Renaud, escaped from their hiding place in the Desourteaux yard, stumbled into a farmhouse at La Place and announced simply: 'All the men were shot, and all the women and children were led away.'

Very early on the morning of the eleventh, a handful of brave and intolerably apprehensive people made their way towards Oradour, determined to get news. M. Lévèque, at Orbagnac, was missing not only his children but his brother and the family maid. He was one of the first to return from the terrible scene with a blurred but definite picture: everyone in Oradour had been killed. Professor Forest made his second journey at about 5 am. 'Where are the children?' he asked a sentry. '*Alles kaputt*', said the German succinctly. M. Levignac reached the house where his eldest son had been staying and found it intact, but abandoned and looted. The couple who had gone to a wedding returned to their home to find the table still set for lunch, but their parents and children nowhere to be found.

At about 11 am on Sunday morning, Dickmann's men drove out of Oradour, their vehicles loaded with loot and livestock. One truck was towing a car taken from the street which suddenly snapped its cable, careered into a pylon and crashed, injuring the SS driver. Then they were gone, and the last vestiges of doubt about what had taken place were removed from the minds of the region's inhabitants. A farmer from Le Breuil named Hyvernaud, with two sons of thirteen and six at the school in Oradour, made his way into the smoking, deserted church;

> I went to hunt for my children, and I actually found one of the boys. He was my youngest. He lay on his side and was half-charred. . . . He still had one of his wooden shoes on. His other leg was completely out of joint and twisted behind his back. His throat was half cut through.

Hyvernaud walked home to Le Breuil, gathered his wife and some sheets, and returned to the church to fetch back the little body.

> . . . I went on searching for my other son. I knelt down and peered at the stiffened faces of the children, one after another, wherever there were features that could be recognized. But I did not find my older boy. Behind the altar, crammed closely together, lay at least twenty small children who had tried to find shelter there. . . . They had all been suffocated by smoke or burned to death. I also saw prams with dead infants in them. Some were burned, others were riddled with bullets. Then I went home. That evening we dug a grave for André in our little yard.

On the morning of Monday, 12 June as the news of Oradour spread by word of mouth across the horrified Limousin, a Wehrmacht convoy drove into Oradour and worked for some hours digging two mass graves, and carrying into them some of the bodies. Towards lunchtime the Germans departed, taking with them many of the loose beasts and fowls not already appropriated by the Der Führer. That afternoon, the first of many volunteers from among local doctors and sanitary workers, civil defence teams and priests moved into Oradour and began the dreadful task of removing and identifying the bodies, already corrupted by two days of warm sunshine, or crumbling to ashes at the touch. Even for experienced medical teams it was a terrible task to work among the debris of an entire community – its burnt-out cars and sewing machines, crockery and cutlery, scorched living-rooms and charred bedding, straying cats and dogs, discarded children's toys. At one moment, the medical team saw that another lorryload of Germans had halted in the middle of the main street, and were busy loading the Frenchmen's bicycles, lying against the houses. The Germans obviously imagined that previous looters had overlooked these. The medical team remonstrated with them. The Germans unloaded the cycles and drove away.

10 Excess of Zeal

For what it is worth, this is the manner in which the regimental history of the Der Führer, compiled by Major Weidinger, records the first news of Oradour:

Late in the afternoon the same day [10 June], Sturmbannführer Dickmann returns to the regiment and reports the following: the company had met resistance in Oradour and had come across several bodies of murdered German soldiers. The company then occupied the town and had promptly started a search of the houses. Unfortunately they had not found Kampfe, though they had discovered hidden ammunition and weapons. So Dickmann had all the men of the town who could be identified as *maquisards* shot.

The women and children had been locked into the church during this time. Then the town had been set on fire; in nearly all the houses hidden ammunition had exploded. The fire then suddenly spread to the church, which also had ammunition hidden in its steeple. The church burnt down very quickly, and the women and children died.

Staf. Stadler is deeply shocked at this report and tells Dickmann: 'Dickmann, you could pay heavily for this. I shall request that you be court-martialled immediately by the division! I cannot let something like this rest on the shoulders of the regiment!'

Staf. Stadler was also furious that Dickmann had not carried out his orders to bring back *maquis* prisoners should Kampfe not be found. Deeply disturbed, he sends Dickmann away to draw up a detailed report. Dickmann does not defend himself, but obviously expects to do so at the military hearing. Immediately after the arrival of the divisional commander, Brigadeführer Lammerding, Stadler reports the events in Oradour-sur-Glane and requests the court-martial of Dickmann. This is promised as soon as the situation allows for a trial to be arranged. . . .

The 1c [Kowatsch] overhears a radio message sent by a senior *maquis* staff officer after the events of Oradour and Tulle, ordering that all fighting against the Germans is to cease until the division Das Reich has left central France. Resistance has become pointless in the face of the great sacrifices which it has provoked in Tulle and Oradour. These sacrifices bore no relation to successes achieved. Another message on an enemy wavelength claims that Kampfe has been shot to avenge the destruction of Oradour. . . .

. . . The fact that Dickmann went far beyond his commander's orders and took a personal initiative can no longer be regarded as an excess. First, it must be realized that Dickmann wanted to free his friend Kampfe. If he did not find Kampfe and did not take hostages, as he had been told to, he must have concluded that Kampfe could no longer be alive and therefore could not be released. . . . In his judgment Dickmann also had to consider the general instruction of OB West [the Sperrle order] and the special order of the corps concerning terrorists. Eye witnesses reported that Dickmann did not take the decision lightly. . . . The destruction of Oradour cannot, therefore, be blamed upon the leadership of the Der Führer regiment, or of the Das Reich Division, or on any other German authority.

The logic of these remarks may be judged by the reader. Only two points of substance need to be made. First, since no Resistance group possessed radio-telephone, it is impossible that Kowatsch could have intercepted such messages. It is possible, though unlikely, that he could have intercepted Free French signals to or from London, but there is no evidence that any traffic of this nature was ever passed. Second, although Dickmann was indeed brought before a court-martial (which never reached a verdict) in Normandy, he remained in command of his battalion until his death. The first action of a commander in any army who is seriously displeased by the action of a subordinate is to relieve him of his command. Stuckler asserts that he never heard of events in Oradour until he arrived in Normandy. The Der Führer's war diary, and the situation reports signalled to division, assert blankly that 'the town of Oradour-sur-Glane was surrounded, and ammunition found stored in almost every house. Results: 548 enemy dead. Our casualties: one dead, one wounded.' In reality, as far as the investigators were ever able to ascertain, 393 residents, 167 people from the surrounding countryside, thirty-three from Limoges and fifty-five from other places were killed – only fifty-two bodies were identifiable. Remarkably enough, Dickmann's detachment had indeed suffered casualties: falling masonry from the church injured one man and killed another, Lieutenant Knug. He was reported to his family as: 'Died for the fatherland'.

The balance of circumstantial evidence suggests that the Das Reich Division made nothing of Dickmann's doings at Oradour until forceful inquiries from Vichy officials and army headquarters caught up with them in Normandy. The local garrison commander in Limoges, General Gleininger, realized as he heard the news that the SS had over-reached themselves at Oradour, and offered effusive apologies to the Bishop of Limoges and other local dignitaries. The Germans also made clumsy attempts to conceal the nightmare. The local censor imposed a blanket ban on publication of any news of Oradour's fate in the region's newspapers. The Gestapo instituted a mercifully unsuccessful search for survivors. They realized, as the officers of the Das Reich did not, that this had been something special.

Dickmann and his battalion spent the night of 11 June in new billets at Nieul, six miles east of Oradour, attracting nervous local attention by their conspicuous array of loot. While the 1st battalion was at Oradour, Kampfe's 3rd battalion had been engaged in a number of minor skirmishes with *maquisards* as they patrolled the area east of Limoges. The *maquis* situation all over southern and central France was causing acute concern. On 12 June, General Von Blaskowitz, commanding Army Group G, took over personal tactical direction of the anti-partisan war, and requested OKW that the south-west be formally designated a battle zone. On the eleventh – before divisional headquarters became aware of Oradour – the 2nd SS Pz signalled Army Group G: 'Mopping up operations in the region Limoges, St Léonard, Ambazac, Bellac, Rochechouart. Provisional balance sheet: 337 killed, 36 prisoners. The road Tulle–Seilhac–Uzerche free of the enemy.'

That day, the units of the Das Reich in Tulle abandoned the town – they were relieved by the battle group from 11th Panzer division – and moved north to Limoges, laden with loot from the town. Early on the morning of the twelfth, once again preceded by the reconnaissance battalion, the roadborne elements of the division moved north out of Limoges, under orders to proceed with all speed to Normandy via Poitiers and Tours.

The scale of the tragedy at Oradour dwarfed other, isolated killings by the division on 10 and 11 June: Jean-Baptiste Legressy, a thirty-four-year-old workman; Charles Prima, a farm-worker, twenty-four; Roger Bayard; Henri Dijoux, nineteen; Adrian Girette, twenty-one, tortured and hanged at Buissière-Poitevine; Marchal Roger, thirty-five; Achille Maren, forty-six; Henri Villesange, a coachbuilder's apprentice, sixteen. The last, alone among all these, identified himself as a *résistant*, a member of an FTP *maquis*. Exact responsibility for their deaths cannot be pinpointed within the division. It is known only that the Frenchmen were shot by members of the Das Reich in the performance of their duties. Major Weidinger's account declares simply:

> There are further concentrations, attacks and losses. Only in the area of the 1st battalion of the Deutschland is there complete peace. . . . The 3rd battalion carried out one more operation, in search of an armed French *gendarmerie* unit which had defected to the *maquis*. The approach of German troops had obviously been noticed and reported by civilians. When they reached the camp in the forest, they were able only to arrest two or three Frenchmen and release several German soldiers. The bulk of the *gendarmerie* unit had escaped. The rest of the day was spent preparing for the march. . . .

It would be absurd not to acknowledge that the efforts of the Das Reich made a profound impression upon the population of Haute-Vienne. On the morning of 12 June, Gaston Hyllaire – 'Léonie' – the departmental commander of the *Armée Secrète*, paid a secret personal visit to Oradour. Major Weidinger was perfectly correct in asserting that a strong body of opinion among the local Resistance commanders now held that no gesture in arms was worth such a terrible price. Jean Sennemaut, commanding the AS unit around Bellac to the north-west, recalled that until the moment of Liberation, senior local AS officers opposed any attempt unilaterally to seize and free towns, lest the horror of Oradour be repeated. The FTP – and above all Guingouin's *maquisards* south-east of Limoges – were rather less troubled by these risks. But it is surely significant that while the communists of Haute-Vienne had been discussing a full-scale attack on Limoges for months, in the event they did not move to take over the town until the Germans were in full retreat from the region. 'Action taken during the passage of the Das Reich Armoured Division through Limoges and its surrounding countryside has made a visible impression on the population,' noted the war diary of the 19th SS police regiment, based on Limoges. Painful though it may be for humanitarians to accept, a policy of unlimited repression can be formidably effective. Oradour made a lasting mark on the Haute-Vienne. If the exercise had a weakness from the SS point of view, it is that it was not publicly announced as a reprisal for the seizure of Major Kampfe. It seems certain that if the Das Reich had been available to continue carrying out such appalling acts in reprisal for every operation carried out by the AS or the FTP, *maquis* commanders would have come under enormous pressure from the local population to desist absolutely from attacks. Mercifully, however, the Das Reich was compelled to move on.

The division suffered only one further clash with *maquisards* after moving north from Limoges. Jean Sennemaut's AS company, deployed in the north-west of Haute-Vienne through which the divisions passed, was not even aware of its existence until, early on the morning of 12 June, their commander risked slipping home to Bellac from his *maquis* in the woods to collect some clothes. He heard the clatter and roar of a large German convoy moving up the *route nationale*, and at one point a burst of firing. He vanished hastily back into the fields, towards his *maquis*.

An hour or two later a small group of FTP *maquisards*, approaching a junction just north of Bellac in a lorry, glimpsed a German truck halted on the main northbound road. Only a short stretch of the highway was visible to them, and thus they could not see the great mass of German vehicles halted on each side. The *maquisards* dropped from their lorry and closed upon the single parked truck, firing as they came. Their Moroccan Bren gunner fired only one burst before his gun jammed. He then turned to his haversack of grenades, and hurled one at the truck. But now, to their consternation and dismay, the little group of Frenchmen – commanded, ironically enough, by yet another Alsatian – found themselves engulfed by the ferocious return fire of several hundred extremely wakeful Germans of Wulf's *Aufklärungsabteilung*. Five *maquisards* were killed in a matter of moments, before the others fled back into the woods, abandoning their vehicle.

When the shooting began, Private Schneid and his young

comrades of the anti-tank platoon hurled themselves for cover behind the body of their half-track. The furious 'Hascha' hurled them bodily from this refuge and made them deploy to return the fire. 'We won't win the war with soldiers who hide behind their vehicle at the first shot!' he shouted. Then he motioned Schneid to follow him, and as the *maquisards* retreated, slipped forward into the fields to reconnoitre. They found a dead man on his front in the grass, a bandolier over his shoulder. 'Turn him over,' said the 'Hascha'. He picked up the Sten that lay under the man's body, and gazed at the dead face. 'They're all the same, these bloody characters. . . .', Kurz muttered to Schneid, who was surprised to notice in his voice '. . . a kind of respect. . . .' They picked up the bandolier. Then the two men strode briskly back to their half-track and, at a signal from the front, the column rolled slowly away again towards Poitiers.

One eddy from the wake of the Das Reich's operations reached the city a few hours before them. The 311 men who had been loaded into the lorries in the courtyard of the Tulle arms factory on 9 June, informed that they were being taken to the Hôtel Moderne, were in reality driven to the old cavalry barracks in Limoges, where they arrived at 3 am on the tenth. For the remaining hours of the night they were obliged to stand under the guns of the SS guards while their fate was discussed. Then the Wehrmacht relieved the sentries, and conditions improved. The prisoners were allowed to sit down, to eat and to receive visits from French Red Cross nurses. In whispered snatches of conversation, they heard for the first time that the Allied beach-head in Normandy was now firmly established. Towards 5 pm, the SS and a group of *miliciens* reappeared. The senior *milicien* announced: 'The German authorities have allowed us to collaborate with them to separate the corrupt elements from the town of Tulle. We have done this work as good Frenchmen. *Vive le maréchal! Vive Darnand! Vive le milice! Vive la France!*' It never proved possible to discover by what process of logic 162 of the detainees were now released, while the other 149 were selected for deportation. These were loaded aboard trucks once more, and driven north to Poitiers on the evening of the twelfth to await entrainment for Germany.

They joined some 250 other Frenchmen, already herded for the night in the courtyard of Gestapo headquarters at 13 Rue des Ecossais. At about 1 am, the RAF's Bomber Command attacked Poitiers railway yards, causing panic and substantial damage to the town. Not surprisingly, as bombs rained down within a few hundred yards of their prison, the desperate French captives tried to fight their way over the railings, or at least into the shelter of the building. The SS guards opened fire at once from the cover of the headquarters, killing six and wounding thirty-five. Four others were wounded by bomb fragments. Order was thus restored, and the prisoners were left to their own devices without food, water or medical assistance until 2 pm the following afternoon. On the evening of 13 June they were transferred to Compiègne, and taken from there by rail to concentration camps in Germany, arriving at Dachau on 5 July; 980 of the 2,521 prisoners on the train died during the three-day journey. In all, of 149 Tullois deported, forty-nine lived to come home in 1945.

The German-controlled press reminded the citizens of Poitiers in forceful terms of the source of their troubles. *Centre et Ouest* headlined its account of the RAF raid: 'POITIERS PAYS ITS OWN TRAGIC TRIBUTE TO THE WAR.' Its front-page story went on:

> At 1.30 am today Poitevins were brutally hauled from their slumbers by huge pillars of fire which embraced the city. You will remember the pamphlet dropped upon Billancourt two years ago that proclaimed, 'Don't be afraid, we know our business'? They knew it so well that, two hours later, there were six hundred dead. At Poitiers also, the Anglo-American pilots knew their business so well that today we are celebrating the 'final liberation' of about a hundred of our people. . . .

On the night of 12 June, on a hill a few miles outside the city, Major Heinrich Wulf and his men lay beneath the camouflage nets covering their lagered vehicles, watching the flashes and shock waves enveloping Poitiers. Somebody murmured: 'Well, let's thank God we're not down there. . . .' In the woods just a mile or two away, another little uniformed group also saw the distant raid. Much the same thoughts passed through their minds. These were officers and men of the British 1st Special Air Service Regiment, who were to cause the Das Reich Division its last significant inconvenience before it became enveloped in the battle for Normandy.

11 The SAS: Bulbasket

If the Allied staff at SHAEF headquarters had been given a free choice in the matter, it is unlikely that the forty men of D Squadron, 1st SAS would have been anywhere near Montmorillon on the night of 10 June. The roadborne elements of the Das Reich would have reached Normandy one, perhaps two or three days ealier than they did. SAS operations against the rail links south of Poitiers must also have contributed to the interminable delays suffered by the 2nd SS Pz tanks on the move from Périgueux via the city. An SAS-directed attack on the petrol dump at Châtellerault destroyed huge reserves upon which the Wehrmacht had relied to refuel the Das Reich's wheeled elements for the last phase of their march to the coast.

An impeccably-bred Englishman who fought with distinction in Europe said afterwards: 'The great thing about the 1939–45 war was that everybody did what they liked.' By this he really meant that a few thousand Englishmen with access to the bars of the great St James's clubs proved able to organize their own military destinies – sometimes even their own campaigns – in a manner impossible in any war before or since. The Special Air Service was among the most celebrated of the array of 'private armies' that emerged during the war. Almost all were conceived and partly officered by those with privileged access to high places. A posting to Phantom or the commandos was passionately coveted by a dashing young man. If the risks were greater than those of regimental soldiering, so were the fun and the company and the opportunity for extraordinary adventures.

In 1940–1, the 'private armies' were tolerated by the service hierarchies as playthings for the Prime Minister and some irregularly minded generals. But as the great confrontations of massed armies upon the battlefield developed, so did the impatience of the staff with the pirate forces on the fringes. Critics claimed that they threatened service discipline; were a grossly uneconomic drain on resources, even unto warships and air transport; and employed thousands of outstanding officers and men who might otherwise have stiffened rifle and armoured regiments on the main battlefield.

All these criticisms had some weight. The contribution of special forces of all kinds was always marginal. It is not surprising that in 1944, as SHAEF prepared for one of the great battles of history, its planners had little time or enthusiasm for any force that threatened to divert attention or resources.

Like the Special Boat Service, Popski's Private Army, the Long Range Desert Group and the Special Interrogation Group, SAS was spawned in the desert, that happy hunting-ground of buccaneers and individualists. David Stirling conceived his force in 1941, to bring havoc to the enemy rear areas. In fourteen months of spectacular activity, he and a handful of other daring spirits destroyed hundreds of enemy aircraft on their landing grounds and created a legend throughout North Africa. Stirling himself was captured in February 1943, but the SAS had by then expanded into a force of two regiments, one of them commanded by his brother Bill. They were among the first Allied troops ashore in Sicily and Italy.

Early in 1944, the survivors were brought home to prepare to take part in the invasion of France. Reinforced by volunteers from Home Forces, they were now designated the SAS Brigade, with strong French and Belgian elements. They were based in central Ayrshire in Scotland, and put under the command of Brigadier Roderick McLeod, a regular gunner. In the Scottish mountains they began intensive fitness, parachute and battle training in readiness to go into Europe.

But where and for what to send them? General Montgomery inspected SAS without enthusiasm one morning. He was shown the Phantom GHQ reconnaissance squadron, attached to provide radio links for SAS in the field. 'Don't use 'em!' snapped the general, and passed on. Beyond the conventional sceptics, there were other thoughtful officers who believed that if 'private armies' were to make an economic contribution to the war, they must be kept small and intimate. David Lloyd Owen, the brilliant commander of the Long Range Desert Group, wrote of SAS in North Africa: 'I believe that after David Stirling began to expand the SAS, the balance sheet showed too great an excess of expenditure over achievement.' John Hislop, who parachuted into France with an SAS Phantom team in 1944, wrote later:

> When small successful private armies such as the SAS in its early stages, come into being, two tendencies in particular emerge: they expand beyond their capacity to keep up the necessary standard of personnel; and the army, which has never viewed unorthodox forces with favour, takes a closer hold upon them. In the first case the private armies become less effective, and in the second their flair is liable to be hamstrung by red tape.

Hislop suggested that Brigadier McLeod in the spring of 1944 was 'quite out of his depth with SAS officers and men, and simply did not know what had hit him when he took over'.

Any regular officer might have been forgiven for finding difficulty coming to terms with such men as the commanding officer of the 1st SAS, Lieutenant-Colonel Paddy Mayne. A pre-war rugger international of enormous size, physical strength and courage, Mayne had personally destroyed more German aircraft than any British wartime fighter ace in his raids on the African airfields with Stirling. He treated the regiment as his personal fiefdom. Those of his men who did not adore Mayne were utterly awed by him. He landed on the fire-swept beach in Italy at the head of his unit, with his hands in his pockets. Sober, with his slow upper-class Irish drawl, his Irish songs and sentimentality, his charm was famous. Drunk, he could be ruthless and very dangerous. 'Where's so-and-so?' he asked mildly, looking around one evening in the mess to find an officer missing. 'Has he gone to bed without saying goodnight?' He led the others purposefully upstairs, slipped into the room of the sleeping officer, lit a bonfire under the bed and opened the betting on how long it would take the man to wake up. Under Maynes' captaincy, regimental football games were fought out with terrible violence. He was one of the great fighting machines of the war, a man who found himself perfectly in his element at the head of men in battle.

'He was everything that we all wanted to be,' said one of his men, Corporal Sam Smith. Smith was another soldier who had achieved complete happiness in the SAS. A tough young Liverpudlian who left school at fourteen, he escaped a court-martial after a brawl by volunteering for the commandos, and later transferred to SAS in Egypt. He became almost a professional 'only survivor' of operations. On one occasion, he and another man were left alone in a sandstorm with a broken-down vehicle, to discover later that the other twenty-five men in their party had all been captured or killed.

It was a ruthless war. One day, they stopped a truckload of Italian soldiers, searched their vehicle, and then allowed it to proceed. But they had quietly dropped two Mills bombs in the back as it drove off. Smith remembered a morning in Italy, with the troop pinned down by fire on a hillside. A brick-tough former booth boxer lying beside him suddenly noticed all the women of the nearby village sheltering under a bridge fifty yards away. Scorning shouted protests, the man 'belted for the bridge, had one of the women, and was back inside three minutes'. Their small arms instructor punctuated his lectures with shots into the ceiling, and once indented for the use of some nearby Italian prisoners for target practice (he was refused). Their pride in their unit, and in their style of warfare, was intense. Sam Smith, a veteran at twenty-one, was perfectly content: 'I was in love with the SAS. It was my life. Our greatest fear was that we might be sent back to our units.'

But many of the men posted to the SAS Brigade early in 1944 had no battle experience. At thirty-two, Lieutenant Peter Weaver was older than most. His father, a regular Indian Army officer, had been killed in World War I. After public school, he enjoyed a chequered career through the 1930s, trying various small businesses, a spell as a private soldier in the army (from which he bought himself out) and a great deal of rugger and cricket, to which he was devoted. 'The war came as a great relief to me,' he said. He was briefly commissioned in the Dorset Regiment in 1940 before being transferred to one of the secret auxiliary units that were formed as 'stay-behinds', to continue resistance to a German invasion if the regular army had to give ground. They were intensively trained in fieldcraft and demolition, but as the threat of invasion receded, monotony set in. In vain they sought a transfer to the commandos. At the beginning of 1944, when they were at last given the chance to go to SAS, Weaver and most of his men seized it eagerly.

But as the Brigade entered its last weeks of training at Darval, the argument at SHAEF and at Special Forces HQ about its employment continued more fiercely than ever. SHAEF was consumed by one overwhelming preoccupation: the need to get the Allies ashore on 5 June, and to keep them there. For security reasons, 21st Army Group would not entertain any plan that involved putting uniformed Allied troops into France before D-Day. But when the moment came, the French Resistance could not be expected to concentrate to much effect in the immediate battle area. Small groups of highly trained SAS dropped into Normandy on the night of D-Day might wreak havoc behind the immediate fighting front.

It was a clearly suicidal assignment, and senior Special Forces officers argued that it was not even the most useful way of employing SAS troops. All forms of irregular warfare must be regarded as strategic, not tactical weapons. SAS should be dropped far behind the lines, where they would have the freedom and flexibility to operate for months, attacking the enemy's communications with the front. SHAEF now asked what SAS could do to interdict the first, critically important German units expected to move towards the battlefield, the Das Reich prominent among them. '2nd SS Panzer Division will be concentrating in a forward area by D+3,' argued a pessimistic SAS appreciation of 19 May, 'and SAS troops cannot affect that move unless dropped on D-1, which is impossible.' The SHAEF proposal that SAS should impede the German armour by defending road blocks with small arms exasperated the Brigade.

In the middle of the row Bill Stirling, the volatile CO of 2nd SAS, was compelled to resign. One of his officers, Roy Farran, wrote:

> This was a serious situation for a volunteer unit, since our main allegiance was to our Colonel. . . . It was ridiculous to think that scattered parties of parachutists could do anything much to delay the arrival of panzer divisions. Perhaps we might have caused some confusion for a day or two, but there was no way in which we could have been resupplied so close to the front, and we would therefore have soon become ineffective. . . . These arguments proved such lack of understanding of our role that our confidence in the new command was severely shaken.

In the last days before D-Day, plans for the use of SAS changed repeatedly. Bill Stirling's resignation stood. But only a handful of men – five three-man Titanic teams – were to be dropped immediately behind the beaches to spread confusion among the defences. A larger (finally costly but useful) operation was to be mounted by 115 men of the French SAS Regiment in the Breton peninsula, to cause maximum uncertainty to the enemy about Allied intentions. The bulk of SAS was to be dropped deep behind the lines as aircraft became available after D-Day.

Something of the flavour of the argument about the use of the Airborne Army in the last months of 1944 had crept in. SAS were demanding to be employed because they were ready and keen. The case for the French operation in Brittany was self-evident. But the rest of the Brigade were to be used as large-scale Jedburghs – stiffening Resistance forces and carrying out sabotage and target-finding missions. The value of small parties of officers and NCOs in this role was obvious. But the decision to drop SAS squadrons in parties large enough to attract urgent German attention, but too small to be capable of self-defence, flew in the face of every principle of irregular warfare. It was the end-product of a succession of bad-tempered arguments and compromises. After many months in which other units had prepared for their invasion role in minute detail the Brigade moved to Fairford in Gloucestershire at the end of May in the confusion of a first-rate 'flap'. They were imprisoned under tight security in a heavily wired camp close to their airfield, still ignorant of their part in the assault on Europe.

For Captain John Tonkin, the young officer who spent the evening of D-Day making jigsaws with Violette Szabo, the monotony of idle waiting was broken on the morning of 30 May. Paddy Mayne informed him that he was to be dropped with his troop of four officers and thirty-nine men, a five-man Phantom wireless team and an RAMC corporal, near Poitiers, in the Vienne. The SAS's 'Amended Instruction No.6' ordered: 'You will now concentrate on building up secure bases in the area north-east of Château Chire, codename Houndsworth, and west of Châteauroux, codename Bulbasket, from D-Day onwards with a view to strategic operations against the enemy lines of communication from the south of France to the Neptune area as occasion may occur, or as developments in the main battle may dictate. . . .' Tonkin was about to start briefing his men when another 'flap' broke out. He was summoned to the CO and told that he himself would be dropped into France that evening with Lieutenant Richard Crisp, as a reconnaissance party. They worked far into the night, drawing and preparing equipment, maps and money. Then they received the message: 'All scrubbed.' The Titanic teams were also told that their operations were cancelled. Tonkin and his colleagues who had been telling the young Titanic officers for days how much they envied their exciting assignment, at last dropped the mask and shared their relief that these suicidal missions had been dropped. Then two Titanic commanders were told that they were 'on' again. 'I can remember the two of them coming out of Paddy's tent as white as sheets,' wrote Tonkin. Of six SAS men who dropped with an army of parachute dummies at the south-east corner of the Cherbourg Peninsula to double-bluff the German defences, three miraculously survived. They diverted an entire German brigade for the morning of 6 June.

Tonkin and Crisp were sent to London with other key SAS officers destined for France, to be briefed by some of SOE's experts. John Hislop remembered being invited to choose equipment from an exotic assortment of edible papers and pens that used invisible ink – 'as if, when a boy, I had been taken into the novelties department of a large store and been give *carte blanche*'. Tonkin and Crisp, each escorted everywhere by a security officer, were told to memorize the faces and codenames of SOE agents whom they would meet in central France. A Jedburgh team was being parachuted with them, but would operate independently on the ground. A middle-aged Frenchman who was in London 'resting' talked to Tonkin for some hours about the laws of survival in Occupied France: 'He gave me much useful advice that I recognized as being from the horse's mouth, and paid good heed to.' Hold a gun in your right hand and a bar of chocolate in your left, advised the Frenchman figuratively. If you must seek help or advice from a farm, wait for the old mother of the family; do not accost the young. Expect nothing from those *maquisards* who are merely avoiding the STO; look to the FTP and AS to do the fighting, but remember the mutual jealousy and ambition that dog them.

On 3 June Tonkin, Crisp and a handful of other SAS officers who were being dropped in advance of their main parties moved to Hasell's Hall, the house near Sandy in Bedfordshire from which SOE dispatched so many of its agents into Europe. There they waited through the three long days of expectation and postponement, to final departure. 'The fifth came, and we learned that Titanic and ourselves were definitely "on". It was a horrible day for a jump – low dark clouds and far too strong a wind – but the complete absence of any sign of activity, our peaceful house with its jigsaw puzzles, and the general holiday atmosphere made the greatest operation in history seem completely unreal,' Tonkin wrote afterwards. At 8 pm the cars came to take them to Tempsford. The RAF dispatchers fitted their parachutes and equipment. Then they waddled out to the waiting Halifax. In the darkness of the fuselage, they lay drinking coffee and chewing sandwiches as the aircraft slowly gathered height over the Channel, and below them the vast invasion armada closed upon the coast of Normandy.

For Tonkin, there was no novelty about going into action. At twenty-three he was a veteran of extraordinary adventures with the SAS in Italy. He had been born in Singapore of Huguenot stock, studied civil engineering at Bristol University, and volunteered for the Royal Engineers in 1939. He spent a frustrating three years searching in vain for action – with the RE, the Northumberland Fusiliers, and the Middle East Commando. Then in June 1942 he joined 1st SAS in North Africa. He spent four months on raids behind enemy lines in the desert, and later took part in four assault landings in Sicily and Italy. On the last of these, at Termoli in October 1943, his squadron was cut off after pushing too deep behind the German lines. They were surrounded by the German 1st Parachute Division, and compelled to surrender when they ran out of ammunition. To Tonkin's astonishment, as a fellow-parachutist he was invited to dine with General Heidrich, the German divisional commander, who talked for hours about the Russian campaign, and how the British withdrawal from Crete began just after he had ordered his own men to start pulling out of the bloody battle. Then Tonkin was removed to another headquarters. A German major told him: 'It is my unfortunate duty to inform you that we have orders that we must obey, to hand you over to our special police.

I must warn you that from now on the German Army cannot guarantee your life.' It was the first that Tonkin knew of Hitler's 'commando' order. He realized that he must escape, or die. The following night, when the lorry carrying him northwards up the frozen mountain roads stopped for a moment in the darkness, he slipped through the canvas at the front, on to the cab, and away into the hills. He walked for two weeks towards the sound of gunfire before he heard feet stumble on rocks, and a single brief English obscenity. He had walked into a British night attack. A few weeks later, he was back with 1st SAS.

The men who remember Tonkin from those days speak of him as 'the classic English public schoolboy'; a keen shot and rugger player, compulsively energetic and cheerful, an enthusiastic practical joker off-duty. Like all the SAS, he was immensely fit, and bursting to carry the war to the Germans.

A few minutes after 1 am on 6 June, the mid-upper gunner of the Halifax slipped from his turret and moved up the fuselage, softly shaking the five men awake. They finished their coffee, climbed to their feet, and fitted the huge rucksacks to the quick-release clips below their knees. Tonkin, the first man out, groped his way to the jump hole in the floor of the aircraft. Gazing below him in the light of the brilliant moon, he began to identify the ground details he had spent so many hours memorizing. The engines cut, and the aircraft started to glide. The gunner shouted the 'Go' signal and swept down his arm. Tonkin slid forward:

> It was the nicest exit I've ever had. Before I knew I was out of the plane, I felt the 'chute tugging at my shoulders and then I was swinging in the air in the bright moonlight, with only a faint breeze to mar the dead silence. I lowered the rucksack and then had a look round for the other four and the containers. They were dropping into a wood. . . . I was drifting into a tree-edged lane. For a moment I thought I was going to land in a tree, but I just missed it. My parachute caught, and I came to rest with my feet just touching the ground. I doubt if I'd have broken an egg if I'd landed on it.

The reception committee was just three men – the farmer who owned the land, his son and a farmhand. They were nervous about interference from a nearby German night-fighter field, and indeed they had scarcely finished bundling and hiding the great white parachute canopies when an aircraft droned overhead, and circled for several minutes. The team dozed in a barn through the dawn of D-Day. At around 7 am, a quiet dark-haired young man carrying a Sten gun arrived. There followed one of those conversations that always made those taking part feel slightly absurd. 'Is there a house in the wood?' asked Tonkin in French. 'Yes, but it is not very good', answered the visitor.

Tonkin had recognized him from a photograph he had seen in London, even before he heard the password. This was 'Samuel', one of SOE French Section's outstanding agents. Major Amédée Maingard de la Ville-ès-Offrans was a twenty-five-year-old Mauritian of aristocratic background, who had been studying accountancy in London when war broke out. He volunteered at once for the 60th Rifles, and it was there that Selwyn Jepson's talent scouts sought him out and asked if he would go to France. He was parachuted into the Indre in April 1943 to assist 'Hector' – Maurice Southgate. After Southgate's arrest, Samuel and the redoubtable Pearl Witherington divided his area between them, and built up two of the most effective networks in SOE, blowing scores of rail links on the eve of D-Day and in the weeks that followed.

That D-Day morning, news of the invasion had still not reached Samuel or his assistants. For some hours, after so many months of impatience and disappointment, they were frankly disbelieving of the parachutists' report that the invasion had begun. But Samuel was due to receive a *parachutage* many miles away that night, and Tonkin and Crisp and the Jedburgh team were to receive a further SAS party on the night of 7 June. At 7.30 am that morning they left the farm by car – two hours before German troops arrived to comb the area unsuccessfully for evidence of a drop. On 7 June, some forty miles south-eastwards, Tonkin was joined by Lieutenant Twm Stephens and eight more SAS. The Jedburgh team moved east, to begin demolition and *maquis* training around Leblanc. The SAS, eleven strong, then moved a few miles by truck to yet another dropping zone, this time close to the main Limoges–Poitiers road, south of Montmorillon.

Tonkin now spent the first of many hours with Samuel and local Resistance leaders, emphasizing the urgency of concentrating attacks on railways and petrol supplies, and discussing how best to assist the training of the *maquis*. There were some 2,800 FTP and 6,400 Gaullist *maquis* in the Vienne, most of them under-armed and all of them under-trained. Before D-Day, the local Resistance had concentrated upon assisting the escape of shot-down Allied aircrew, and there had been little sabotage. The flat, open country did not lend itself to guerilla war as in the Dordogne and the Lot, until the Germans had been thrown decisively on to the defensive. Colonel Bernard, the local AS chief, seemed to many *résistants* too regimental and orthodox to make the best use of his forces. He had attempted some measure of co-operation with the communists but relations between the FTP and the AS were as usual jealous and fractious.

To the British soldiers, among whom only Tonkin possessed any command of French, the *maquis* seemed exotic and somewhat bewildering. John Hislop, further east with another SAS unit, described them bluntly as 'obscure of purpose, jealous of their position and unco-operative'. The Bulbasket team were chiefly perturbed by the excessive French zeal to get into action. Tonkin, in a strange country and utterly unfamiliar conditions, quickly decided that the only reasonable course was to trust the *maquis* in almost everything. He and Samuel took a conscious decision that, since it was impossible to keep secret the arrival of a large body of uniformed men, they should seek to capitalize upon it for intelligence, propaganda and prestige. Samuel believed that his men could keep the railways cut east of Poitiers. The SAS would concentrate on the vital Poitiers–Bordeaux and Poitiers–Tours lines south of the city. The SAS would camp with groups of *maquisards*, to whom they could give weapon training, and rely on the *résistants* and local people for warning of a German attack.

On the morning of 10 June, in Tonkin's words 'a small, very frightened and therefore highly courageous French civilian (I think he was a railway employee) arrived at our newly established base. He told us that there were eleven petrol trains on a well camouflaged and heavily guarded series of sidings about a kilometre south-west of Châtellerault.' London had told them repeatedly that petrol was a priority target. But before calling for an air strike, it was essential to pinpoint and confirm the existence of the trains.

Lieutenant Twm Stephens was a fierce, wiry little Welsh regular soldier who had transferred to the SAS after meeting John Tonkin in a transit camp in North Africa after his escape in Italy. Stephens, too, had been a prisoner of war. He came to France with a passionate hatred of all things German, and a determination to erase the indignity of surrender. Although he spoke no French it was agreed that he should accompany the railwayman and another *résistant* to reconnoitre the petrol trains. A civilian suit was found for him. Despite Stephens's withering comments on French transport, he accepted the loan of a bicycle. The three men set off on the thirty-five-mile ride to Châtellerault.

They returned, exhausted, late the following morning. At 5.17 that afternoon, Special Forces HQ logged a cipher message from Bulbasket, giving the map reference of the petrol trains. The message was at once passed to 2nd Tactical Air Force. Shortly after 8 pm that night, twenty-four Mosquitos of 487 RNZAF, 464 RAAF and 107 RAF squadrons took off from their bases in south-east England to attack the sidings at Châtellerault

Late that evening, Tonkin and his men stood by the unlit bonfires on the dropping zone, ready to receive the main party of SAS. To their consternation, they saw approaching northwards on the main road from Limoges a great column of lights It was clearly a major German troop movement. There was a quick debate. They decided that if they moved quickly to clear the DZ, there was just time to handle the drop. The drone of the Stirlings closed on the field. The fires were lit and parachutes began to bloom above them. Then, to their horror, they saw coloured lights suddenly burst forth on the containers in the sky. It was the fruit of an ill-conceived technical innovation in England, to make containers immediately visible on the ground. The lights were supposed to switch on only at impact, but something had gone disastrously wrong. As the containers touched, soldiers ran desperately forward to smash the light bulbs. *Résistants* urged forward the bullock carts to move the great 500 lb containers, 16 tons of supplies in all. On the road, the German convoy had extinguished its lights. They were vehicles of the Das Reich. Mercifully for the British, they made no move to intervene.

Tonkin met Sergeant Jessiman, commanding the new arrivals.

There had been yet another change of plan, reported the NCO. There had been a request from SHAEF for attacks on the railways west of Poitiers, too distant for Bulbasket to reach. Two officers and fourteen men had therefore been dropped 'blind' on the vital lines, with orders to march to join Tonkin after they had laid their charges. As Tonkin's men settled for the remainder of the night in a farmyard, they could see the great glow in the sky to the north-west, from the flames of Poitiers. Still further north, beyond their vision, more fires were burning. 2nd TAF's Mosquitos had attacked Châtellerault in three waves at very low level with cannon, forty-eight 500 lb bombs, and perfect accuracy. The petrol trains, more precious than gold to Germany's battle for Normandy and to the movement of the Das Reich, were blazing beyond salvage.

The RAF's 38 Group made disappointing practice of dropping the four SAS 'blind' parties. Lieutenant Morris landed to find one of his troopers missing – he was never seen again, and they assumed a parachute failure. Sergeant Holmes landed successfully near Airvault, blew a stretch of rail and joined Tonkin later. Corporal Kinnevane and his team were dropped, disastrously, in the middle of the town of Airvault. One man vanished and was never heard of again. The others were compelled to abandon all their explosives and equipment in order to escape. They reached Tonkin only much later.

Lieutenant Peter Weaver, with three men from his old auxiliary unit, landed almost 100 miles from Tonkin's camp. They were equipped with pistols, wireless and explosives, but no food. They were told that they could live off the country. Weaver asked for portable bicycles to be dropped with them, but the request was refused. None of his party spoke a word of French, but they were ordered to communicate with the French only in emergency. As soon as they landed, they discovered that they were many miles off target. They hid up through the hours of daylight, then walked all night towards the railway. At dawn, they heard the sound of a train. Once more they took cover through the day, in a cornfield where they had the disturbing experience of watching the farmer harvesting around them, until they were left at dusk like rabbits in the tiny patch remaining. In the darkness, they slid down to the line, laid their charges, and retreated a few hundred yards. They waited hours before they were rewarded with an explosion, the hiss of steam and much shouting from the line. Then they set off eastwards towards Tonkin.

They had been told to walk through the fields and avoid roads, but in darkness they found this much too slow. They marched for ten nights, growing very hungry. Occasionally they would separate for an hour, each foraging in a different direction. Once, one of them found a goose, but more often it was only an egg or a few vegetables. One day, in a wood, they were astounded to hear American voices. They stepped cautiously into a clearing and found a major and sergeant in American uniforms sitting alone, surrounded by a great mass of equipment, food, wireless gear and, above all, money – they had a fat chest of French francs, Swiss francs and American dollars. They said that they had been sent to supply money to the Resistance, but had yet to find any suitable beneficiaries. They asked the British if they would like some. Weaver politely declined, on the grounds that they were overloaded already. They marched on.

When at last they reached the rendezvous, to their dismay they found no sign of Tonkin and his men. Desperately, they approached a farmhouse and asked for news. They were lucky in their choice. The farmer pedalled off on his bicycle, and some time later a car loaded with heavily armed *maquisards* raced up in a cloud of dust. They were taken to a local village, where a crowd fell upon them. Girls kissed them, wine was thrust upon them, and their desperate hunger was appeased. 'Don't worry about the Germans, they're all in Poitiers', said a *résistant* lightly when Weaver showed his unease. They were carried in triumph to the *maquis* camp, and at once put to work instructing the Frenchmen in small arms: 'They hardly knew how to throw a grenade,' said Weaver. They had weapons, but little idea what to do with them. For four days, the *maquisards* insisted that they knew nothing of any other British soliders. Then it dawned on Weaver that the French were simply so delighted to have acquired a private weapon-training team that they were concealing the truth. The SAS insisted upon being taken to the rendezvous. Very well, said the *résistants* flamboyantly, but on the way they would attack a café that the Germans used. They crowded into their cars and set off. To the intense relief of the British, the café proved empty. They drove without incident to the SAS camp.

For almost three weeks, Tonkin and his men had been among the *maquis*. Four jeeps armed with Vickers K machine guns had been parachuted to them. By night, they patrolled the area or carried the sabotage teams to within easy reach of rail targets perhaps twenty miles away. They had attacked the lines a dozen times. Richard Crisp, young and perhaps too gentle for this kind of war, had nonetheless taken out successful expeditions to mine the roads for German convoys, spreading dirt across the road at intervals in front of the mines, to compel the enemy to stop and sweep constantly after the first explosion. Tonkin himself went out repeatedly to lay charges. The one serious mishap was that the Phantom team, dropped at a DZ some miles away on 12 June, had failed to link up with Tonkin's men, and were reportedly stockpiling weapons for the *maquis* from their own base. Tonkin unsuccessfully tried to get them to join him, but was able to maintain contact with London through his own wireless operator, Corporal Chick.

Tonkin's officers and NCOs were working desperately hard at all hours of day and night. But for the men, many of whom did not go out on the sabotage operations, the greatest problem was the boredom of life in the camps. They ate eternal tinned steak and kidney puddings, varied with some local produce. Once they bought a calf, although nobody enjoyed the necessity of clubbing it to death and butchering it, to avoid the noise of a gunshot. They learned to light fires with the ferocious local spirit, *gnole*, and to barter with soap, which was almost non-existent in the area. They found that hard cash was also an essential lubricant to Resistance co-operation. They cooked, occasionally patrolled, but mostly lay on their backs smoking, talking to the *maquisards* in broken French or English among the trees. They thought little about the distant battle in Normandy, but took it for granted that they would be overrun by the advancing Allies within a matter of weeks. They lived in their own private world. The chief excitements of each day came at radio schedule time. As their code tune, 'Sur le Pont d'Avignon', echoed across the clearing, it became a standing joke for the men to jive to the beat.

John Tonkin himself was very tired and some of his men thought that he tried to do too much. The size of the party made it essential for him to spend much of his time grappling with administration and supply problems. 38 Group missed half Bulbasket's resupply drops during their time in France. Petrol for the jeeps was always chronically short, and so sometimes were explosives. They found that the German habit of running either an empty wagon or an explosives scoop in front of their railway engines made impact detonators useless. The lines could be very quickly repaired. Instead, Tonkin or one of his men would lie, sometimes for hours, with an ear to the line listening for a train, before connecting a pull switch to be fired from cover, or setting a timer. Then one of the jeeps overturned after a brief clash with a German patrol. The driver, O'Neill, badly injured his hand. Tonkin's medical orderly amputated some mangled fingers with a pair of scissors, but the wound became gangrenous. In desperation one night, Tonkin, a local Resistance leader named Jean Dieudonné and one other trooper drove O'Neill by jeep into Poitiers to leave him with a doctor. As they drove home, they stopped to wire up a railway bridge on the edge of the city with explosives and time pencils.

They moved camp four times, when the *maquis* said that the Germans were coming too close. The British had been warned at briefings that informers were a deadly threat, and they saw five alleged double agents shot by the *maquis* during their time in France. For some days, a girl who had fraternized with the Germans was held prisoner in the camp. She was in her thirties, a graduate of Poitiers University who spoke perfect English. She had no great fear for her own fate, for she did not think her crime serious. She sewed shirts from parachute silk for some of the SAS men, and they chatted amicably enough to her. Then early one morning a *maquisard* woke Sam Smith and asked if he wanted to see an execution. They walked to a clearing where the *maquisards* dug two graves. The girl was brought first. She simply asked that her ring be given to the local farmer's wife. Then a Belgian prisoner was brought, dragged screaming on his knees for mercy. When he realized that there would be none, he stood up quite calmly and said: 'Don't shoot me in the throat.' Then five *maquisards* shot them with rifles. Smith felt guilty later that he had watched without attempting to stop the executions, but at that moment he was merely a spectator of other men's war. The *maquisards* often remarked that it was easy for the SAS to be merciful, for if they were captured they faced only a POW camp. For themselves, capture meant death. Smith tried to show solidarity by sewing FFI flashes in his tunic.

Perhaps the root error that the British made was to think of themselves simply as soldiers doing an exciting and romantic job. They had scarcely glimpsed a German since arriving in France. They found the French that they met overwhelmingly friendly, despite all the cautious advice they had received before leaving England. Their Phantom officer wrote a charming and enthusiastic description in his report of a characteristic evening with the *résistants*.

There was nothing clandestine about my first what the French call '*un parachutage*'. Once the containers were released from the aircraft there was considerable drama. Albert (the local *maquis* chief) began the proceedings by shouting '*Attention!* Everyone! The *bidons* descend.' Everyone present repeated this advice to Bobo or Alphonse or Pierre, or whoever was nearest, to 'have a care that the sacred *bidons* do not crush thee!'

Once the containers had landed the parachute stakes were on. The winner was whoever could roll and hide away the most parachutes before being spotted by someone else. The bullock carts then came up with much encouragement from the drivers such as: 'But come, my old one, to the *bidons* advance.' Then began the preliminary discussions as to how the first container would be hoisted on to the cart and who should have the honour of commencing. I found that I had to go through the motions of beginning to hoist one end myself before, with loud cries of 'But no, my captain! Permit!' or for example 'My captain, what an affair!', my helpers would then get on with the job.

Once, however, the drill for clearing the DZ was understood, the helpers were of the greatest value, and we succeeded one night in clearing the DZ in seventy minutes. This was very good as it included four containers that had fallen in trees.

The *maquis* 'should be treated unreservedly as friends and Allies', the same officer continued in his report, 'and the greatest trust can be put in them. Any mistakes they make are from over-enthusiasm and willingness to help.' Once Weaver and two others went to attend the funeral of three Canadian airmen of Bomber Command whose bodies had been found near a village thirty miles away. They were deeply moved to find the entire community in the little street, following three oxcarts heaped with flowers to the graves. The Germans now appeared confined to the major roads and cities, overwhelmingly preoccupied with the battle for Normandy. Tonkin wrote in his report:

One point to be watched carefully is the general state of alertness. It often happened that we went for several days without a flap. When driving around in daylight all the villages were very friendly, and the girls looked very nice. No Jerry was seen in the area, consequently the men tended to forget they were behind the lines and liable to be attacked at any moment. They wanted to stop in the villages and there was a general tendency to relax. . . . The highest discipline must be maintained to prevent them wandering away from camp. The British soldier's aptitude for scrounging will make him see no harm in going to the nearest farm for eggs, whereas such a thing is highly dangerous. . . . The chief danger is that the locals' talk will reach the enemy through the village collaborator. . . .

There were breaches of security that might have been acceptable in the inaccessible reaches of the Lot, but were highly dangerous in the Vienne. A local Resistance leader reported to Tonkin that two SAS men had wandered into a local café for a glass of wine. The SAS, in holiday mood, photographed each other around the camp. Much more seriously, one night when Sergeant Eccles and two troopers attempted to place charges at a railway junction just south of Poitiers, the NCO returned to report that the other two had disappeared, and almost certainly been taken prisoner.

One evening, Sam Smith and two troopers were driven by jeep with a Resistance guide to a drop-off for another railway attack. Smith and his mate, Trooper Fielding, had approached Tonkin, and asked to be allowed to take on a demolition job to relieve the monotony of the camp. Tonkin warned them: 'You may be flogging a dead horse, because the Resistance say there are no trains running on the line.' But they set off with rucksacks and explosives and their pistols. To their fury they found that the jeep driver had lost his way, and put them down even further from their target than the camp. They began walking fast, soon leaving their guide far behind – they never saw him again. They passed a black-pudding factory. Once they saw a man lowering his trousers in a field, who glared up in astonishment as he saw them. They caught sight of a patrolling German, riding a white horse. Then, as they approached the railway line in the darkness, there was a sudden hammer of machine gun fire close at hand. They beat a hasty retreat, and lay up for the rest of the night and through the following day. The next evening, Smith worked his way to the edge of a cutting some way south of their original attempt. The next sensation he remembered was waking from a doze to find that he had slipped over the edge, and was rolling down the bank. He heard feet moving towards him, set his charges, broke the time pencils, and ran for it. Like most of the SAS railway attacks, this one only damaged a straight stretch of line which could be repaired in a few hours. But Tonkin had concluded that stations and junctions were now too dangerous to attack. It was the repetition of attacks – for Samuel's *maquisards* were maintaining a steady flow of rail-wrecking operations parallel with those of the SAS – that interrupted traffic. The wilder claims of the *maquis*, that rail traffic had stopped altogether, usually proved unfounded. Some trains carrying priority loads almost always kept moving. But German schedules and troop movements were hopelessly dislocated.

The three Englishmen began the long walk back to the camp. They found it hard to keep to their road, for the *maquis* had turned around many signposts to confuse the Germans. When Smith knocked on farmhouse doors to ask for directions, to his fury the inhabitants again and again closed them in his face. But at dawn, in the garden of a house they saw a group of civilians deep in conversation, and asked for help. The French told them simply that they should not go near the camp in the forest of Verriers, because there had been trouble there. After some discussion, they set off for a farmhouse near the drop zone for their jeeps, where they assumed that they would find friends and news. Smith knocked. An almost hysterical woman appeared. She identified them, and shouted something about her son having been caught and shot with the British. Then she slammed the door. They were walking away, confused and alarmed, when by extraordinary good fortune a car loaded with *maquisards* overtook them. They hailed it, and were taken at once to a farmhouse where they found Samuel, a group of Resistance leaders and a wretched captured *milicien* pedalling the generator for the SOE wireless. They fell asleep in the barn. When they woke, one by one a handful of other SAS men arrived to join them, and reported the news of the catastrophe that had overtaken Bulbasket.

Tonkin had always been aware of the dangers of remaining too long in one place, where rumour and German radio direction-finding might pinpoint the camp. But he was restricted by the need to remain within reach of supply dropping grounds, and the difficulty of finding camps close to water for a hundred men, in that exceptionally dry summer, for there were anything up to a hundred *maquisards* with them at any one time. Tonkin had also summoned all the shot-down Allied airmen from camps in the area, and offered them the chance to join the SAS. One, an American fighter pilot named Bradley, at once volunteered for operations: 'Captain, I see no reason why the lack of an aircraft should stop me fighting', he told Tonkin, and became a popular and respected member of the unit. Most of the others preferred either to return to the *maquis* camps from which they had come, or to press on down the escape line towards Spain. But when disaster struck there was one American, Lieutenant Lincoln Bundy, in the SAS camp, along with thirty-nine British soldiers and some fifty *maquisards*.

They had been camped for some days in the forest of Verriers, in a thinly wooded valley beside a stream. They moved for security reasons to another base, only to find the lack of water a chronic problem, so they moved back to Verriers. Tonkin went out to reconnoitre a site for a new base, and did not return until the small hours of morning.

Soon after first light, mortar bombs began to burst upon the men in their sleeping bags, and machine gun fire started slashing through the trees. Peter Weaver sprang up to see a cook running half naked through the trees, shouting: 'They're coming! They're coming!' Tonkin, followed by Weaver and Jean Dieudonné, ran to the edge of the trees and saw scores of German troops working rapidly along the hedges towards them, under heavy covering fire. Tonkin dashed back into the camp and shouted to his men to scatter and make their own way to safety. By one of most extraordinary, indeed almost fantastic misjudgments of the operation, the entire SAS party had been sent from England with only .45 pistols as personal weapons. Beyond the Vickers guns on their jeeps, they had no means whatever of resisting the German attack. Weaver glimpsed Richard Crisp bandaging a wounded man's leg, and heard somebody shout to him that there was no time for that – it was every man for himself now. Of the fifty-odd *résistants* in the camp, seven were killed in that panic-stricken action in the wood. Many more, with most of the SAS troopers, disappeared in a milling herd into the valley and into the arms of the German cordon. Almost all surrendered.

Tonkin broke the time pencils into their explosives bin, and vanished westwards into the forest. He lay motionless behind a rock as a line of advancing Germans passed before him, listening to the bursts of fire in the woods as little parties of *maquisards* and British troopers were rounded up. Two other officers and six men who made a dash for safety uphill, away from the stream in the same manner as Tonkin, also escaped. Peter Weaver watched his section run downhill with the main body, but himself moved in the opposite direction. At the edge of the trees he met Twm Stephens 'almost berserk with rage'. Weaver said to him: 'There's nothing we can do. I'm going through this cornfield.' They parted, and Weaver crawled into the wheat as a line of Germans began sweeping towards him. They fired. He ran zig-zagging into some trees, the Germans in his wake. He felt a passionate thirst. Jumping a stile, he saw a small waterfall before him and paused for a second to splash his face in the blessed cool water. He was revived. Choosing a thick thorn bush he scrambled into its centre. There he lay for many hours, pistol in hand, 'feeling that I was prepared to stay there for the rest of the war'. Night came. It began to rain. He crawled across a field, and suddenly found himself eyeball to eyeball with a large dog. He moved hastily away into cover, and fell mercifully asleep.

When he awoke, it was a beautiful morning. He climbed to his feet and walked into the yard of a nearby farmhouse to find, to his astonishment, John Tonkin. 'Thank God you got through,' said Tonkin. Only eight of his men had survived. Thirty-one – four of them wounded, including Richard Crisp – had been taken prisoner, together with Lieutenant Bundy of the USAAF, and the two SAS troopers captured four days earlier on the railway. The next afternoon Tonkin walked into the village of

Verriers, almost dazed with shock, to find that the Germans had gone, taking their prisoners. Twm Stephens had been wounded and captured. The Germans tied him to a tree, paraded the village past and then beat him to death with their rifle butts. The other SAS prisoners, together with Lieutenant Bundy, were executed on 7 July, presumably in accordance with Hitler's 'Commando order'. Their secret mass graves were uncovered after the Liberation. In all, of 100 SAS captured by the Germans in France during the operations after D-Day, only six survived.

John Tonkin wrote thirty-six years later: 'I have always felt that the Geneva Convention is a dangerous piece of stupidity, because it leads people to believe that war can be civilized. It can't.' There were many paradoxes about Bulbasket. Trooper John Fielding remembered that when they were briefed before they dropped, the SAS were clearly informed that they could not take prisoners, because there were no means of holding them. It is extraordinary, first, that no one reflected that such a policy might be reciprocated; and second, that the SAS were allowed to drop into France under the illusion that the war they were being sent to join had something to do with ordinary soldiering. Special Forces HQ failed to emphasize to the SAS their likely fate if they were captured. Had they been aware of it, it is unlikely that so many men would have surrendered.

SOE agents who met SAS parties in the field, notably Philippe de Vomécourt, considered that they behaved with some carelessness in the thick of enemy territory. They were sent knowing little of France or of the Resistance war, and according to Colonel Barry of SOE, regimental pride made them reluctant to accept over-much guidance from Baker Street. The SAS of that period were better trained and certainly men of higher abilities than British line infantry, but they were not remotely comparable in quality and expertise with the post-war SAS. Bulbasket's lack of armament is a measure of the misconceptions surrounding the operation. John Tonkin said: 'We were simply not intended to fight pitched battles with the Germans.' But it was absurd to imagine that a party of fifty men in enemy territory ran no risk whatever of encountering the enemy. The *maquis* lacked the training and ability to protect them. After the disaster at Verriers, the British searched bitterly for evidence from which they could pin blame for their betrayal. John Tonkin believes to this day that a foreign-born officer of the SAS (not mentioned in this story) betrayed Bulbasket to the Germans to take pressure off his own team. John Fielding thinks that two men on a motor cycle who passed the camp one day when he was on guard were in reality German agents.

The truth will never be known. But it seems much more likely that, when thousands of villagers over a wide area knew of the existence of the SAS party, the Germans received a local tip-off. Resistance historians in the Vienne who have studied the episode remark that the SAS were incautious, for instance in taking a jeep into Poitiers. The Germans at that period were not seeking confrontation with the Resistance unless it was thrust upon them, but the presence of a uniformed British force, flaunting its presence around the country, was evidently an intolerable challenge to their authority. It cannot have required very ingenious intelligence work to locate the camp at Verriers, when the SAS had been there on and off for eight days. Although contemporary SAS reports speak of the final attack being carried out by SS units, Resistance historians say that, in reality, Verriers was taken by the 158th Security Regiment from Poitiers. Seizing thirty-three men armed only with pistols was scarcely a demanding task, and it was a tribute to the Germans' fumbling that Tonkin and eight others escaped.

The survivors of Bulbasket, at last joined by the Phantom team, remained in France for almost five weeks after the disaster at Verriers. For much of that time they were awaiting fresh supplies of explosives and equipment from England. The shock of the attack lifted surprisingly quickly from the minds of the eighteen young Englishmen who survived, but their mission's back was broken. 'We'd written ourselves off,' Weaver said. 'I never expected to get back to England.' Tonkin, unfailingly energetic, made four more railway attacks, but with only one jeep – which had escaped Verriers because it was away for repairs – they lacked mobility for more ambitious operations. On 7 and 10 August the SAS group, together with Samuel and eight USAAF aircrew, were evacuated to England in two airlifts by Hudson, from an improvised landing ground.

Contemporary opinion on Bulbasket was divided. In a War Office report dated 10 August 1944, the Director of Tactical

Investigation who compiled after-action assessments wrote brusquely:

In comparison with the achievements of the other SAS groups, Bulbasket has not, on the evidence available, been so successful as a source of information. This group has from time to time reported a few bombing targets, and also the results when the targets were taken on by the RAF. There is nothing to show that SAS troops have taken any part in arming or organizing the *maquis* in this area.

But he added:

Bulbasket has, however, played an important part in making the movements of German troops in the area difficult, in conjunction with RAF bombing. . . . They have also employed many German troops in action.

Hindsight suggests that the report should have been inverted: Bulbasket probably did little more to occupy the attention of German troops in the Vienne than the Resistance could have done without them. But Stephens's pinpointing of the German petrol trains at Châtellerault was a classic example of liaison between an air force and behind-the-lines observers.

Yet could not Tonkin with a tiny handful of officers and NCOs have accomplished as much, or more, without risking the disaster that took place at Verriers chiefly because a large body of men required a conspicuous fixed base? Hislop wrote, after his own experience with SAS in France: 'In retrospect, it seemed to me that the same result could have been achieved with fewer and more carefully selected men.' There was a fundamental confusion among the planners who deployed uniformed regular soldiers – albeit with special forces training – in a profoundly irregular situation.

But war is about the balance of advantage, the final net gain or loss when the casualty returns are in. The Director of Tactical Investigation did not possess the advantage of seeing the desperate signal intercepted by the British Ultra decrypters at Bletchley Park: 'Urgent request for allocation of fuel for 2 SS Pz Div from army fuel depot Châtellerault addressed to AOK I at 1100, 13 June.' In the cold accountancy of battle, this alone was an achievement purchased cheaply by the loss of a platoon.

12 Normandy

The Das Reich Division's battle against Resistance effectively ended at Bellac, on the road to Poitiers. *Maquis* groups further north did not attempt to attack such an overwhelmingly powerful force in unfavourable country. London had never expected that *résistants* would be able to achieve much against major formations in areas approaching the battlefront. The division was not even aware of the existence of the SAS detachment which caused the destruction of their petrol depot. To most of the men of the Das Reich, there was simply another of the interminable checks and delays which had wasted so much time since Montauban.

Now, as the division approached the Loire, they entered the region of France in which most havoc was being achieved by the Allied communications bombing. 'Our operations in Normandy', wrote Rommel, 'are rendered exceptionally difficult, and in part impossible to carry out, by the . . . overwhelming superiority of the enemy air force.' Between 6 March and D-Day, the Allied air forces had poured 62,000 tons of bombs on to the ninety-three key rail centres chosen for attack by Eisenhower's air and transport specialists. By ruthlessly sweeping aside civilian traffic throughout the French rail network, the Germans continued to be able to run some priority trains, but the chaos and delays were appalling. All the lower Seine bridges were destroyed. 2nd Panzer Division arrived in Normandy only on 13 June after a journey of 150 miles, and required a further seven days to regroup before going into action; 17th SS Panzergrenadiers did not arrive until 17 June, having struggled the 200 miles from Bayonne; 9 and 10 SS Panzers arrived from the Eastern Front only on 25 June. German wireless networks were overwhelmed with pleas for fuel, transport, new routings, bridge repairs and locomotives. The Wehrmacht was bleeding terribly in Normandy, losing an average of 2,500 and 3,000 men a day, yet the reinforcements were crawling across France with fatal sluggishness, lapsing into confusion after they crossed the Loire and entered the most deadly fighter bomber target zone. The Allies were dispatching an average of almost 600 fighter bomber sorties a day on roving commission to attack moving trains and convoys wherever they were found in northern France. These inflicted terrible damage on the Germans. North of the Loire, the Germans were compelled to resort almost exclusively to the roads for the last phase of their forward movement, becoming even more vulnerable to air attack. Almost every German who fought in Normandy conceded that the Allied air attack was the decisive factor in the Wehrmacht's defeat. It was the air forces which inflicted the most important delays upon most German reinforcements approaching Normandy. No other major battlefield formation was permitted to waste as much time upon Resistance as the 2nd SS Panzer.

The Das Reich Division trickled into the rear areas of the battlefront piecemeal, between 15 and 30 June 1944. The elements which had remained at Toulouse under Major Wisliceny followed on 7 July. To the intense chagrin of its officers, units were committed independently to shore up the sagging German front. The division did not begin to fight as an integral force under Lammerding's command until 10 July, by which date it had already suffered heavy losses.

Sufficient petrol was found to move the reconnaissance battalion and the Der Führer regiment across the Loire on 13 June, by the bridges at Saumur and Tours, which were still intact despite the intensive Allied air bombardment. Other units followed as they could over the next week. The tank units did not even begin to move from Périgueux until 15 June, a great tribute to Resistance and the Allied air forces. On the sixteenth, a SHAEF G-3 report stated: 'In spite of our efforts to delay it, Panzer division Das Reich, units of which reported Périgueux, left in fifteen trains, thirteen last night, two this morning, for Poitiers.' Their progress up the railway was painfully slow. Fritz Langangke, coming from Germany with his newly equipped Panther company, travelled a great circle around France for a fortnight before catching up with them. The tanks were compelled to detrain at Angers, more than a hundred miles from the battlefront, and to move forward by night, with all the delays and breakdowns made inevitable by another prolonged road march.

From the moment that they crossed the Loire the Germans were appalled by the utter dominance of Allied air power, the '*Jabo** fairground in the sky', as Ernst Krag called it. In Russia, the enemy air force had presented no serious threat to movement. But in France, questing fighter bombers fell on them ceaselessly. The convoys of the Das Reich were compelled to abandon daylight movement after Saumur and Tours, and crawl northwards through the blackout. At dawn on 14 June they were halted by the roadside near La Flèche. A signal was handed to Colonel Stadler. The commander of the 9th SS Hohenstaufen Panzer Division had been killed in action. Stadler was to replace him immediately, handing over command to Major Weidinger. The headquarters group were making hasty arrangements for the transfer when an Allied fighter bomber section smashed into the column, firing rockets and cannon. Within minutes, as men struggled to train the light flak guns and swing the vehicles under cover, sixteen trucks and half-tracks were in flames. Thereafter, they camouflaged the vehicles with deadly care. The tanks moved only as a 'walking forest', as they called it, blanketed in foliage. When Otto Pohl's company lagered in an orchard, he had his men scythe the grass behind the tanks to conceal the tracks. The crews cursed that 'they couldn't even step into a field for a crap' without drawing a *Jabo*. Again and again, as they inched forward through the closely set Norman countryside, the tankmen were compelled to leap from their vehicles and seek cover beneath the hulls as fighter bombers attacked. Their only respite came at night. To their astonishment, after Russia where much of the most bitter fighting took place at night, they found that 'after 10 pm the Americans left us strictly alone'. In the merciful peace of darkness they could redeploy, rest and re-arm until daybreak brought the return of shelling and the fighter bombers. There were other lessons about a new kind of war. Moving into action in his Panther for the first time in Normandy, the young Das Reich tank officer Fritz Langangke swung around the corner of a building to find an extraordinary

* *Jagdbomber* – fighter bomber.

panorama stretched out before him: a Norman village street littered with the debris of fierce fighting – burning vehicles, American and German infantry and anti-tank guns confronting each other 200 yards apart. But not a man was firing. Between the lines, American and German stretcher-bearers were scuttling to and fro, removing the wounded. 'It was the first hint that this war would be different,' said Langangke. 'In Russia, we would have driven straight over them. . . .'

Weidinger and other veterans arrived in Normandy expecting to take part in a great counter-attack to force the Allies back into the sea. To their astonishment and dismay, they were ordered simply to plug a gaping crack in the line, alongside the remains of the superb Panzer Lehr Division commanded by Bayerlein. Bayerlein laughed when they talked to him about their hopes of taking the offensive. 'It will be a miracle if we can stand where we are,' he said laconically. The Das Reich's divisional staff had wanted time for a few hours' tactical training behind the line, or at least a spell in a quiet sector. But there were no quiet sectors. 'Where is the German Air Force?' men asked those who had arrived before them in Normandy: 'There is no more German Air Force.' The newcomers were dismayed to see the exhaustion and sagging morale of units coming out of the line – the open defeatism and crippling casualties, the strain of incessant bombardment and the roaring – like so many trains – as the huge shells from the warships offshore tore past them into the rear areas. Experienced officers were shocked to discover that they had a significant desertion problem, chiefly among the Alsatians.

But it would be false to suppose that the Das Reich was an enfeebled fighting unit in Normandy. The only redeeming merit of the SS was that they were among the most dogged, fanatical soldiers in the world. Fritz Langangke, sitting battened down in the turret of his Panther under artillery fire one afternoon, cursed the code of his corps when he saw the Volkswagen field car of their commander, Tyschen, dashing up the lane towards him, with the major standing erect and exposed behind the windscreen. Langangke was compelled to leap down from his turret and stand at attention before Tyschen to receive his orders while shells shattered around them.

The Der Führer regiment lost 960 men – almost half its

strength – in the first four days of battle. Shelling accounted for most of them; regimental headquarters received a direct hit which killed nine men and a visiting war correspondent. They became unwilling to gather company commanders for briefings in case they should all die under a single hit. Runners had to carry all messages between positions. The use of radio appeared to be instantly detected by Allied locators and met with artillery fire. It was futile to lay telephone wires under constant bombardment. Major Stuckler came to visit them in their positions, and was appalled by what he found. With Pak guns and Teller anti-tank mines, they halted one British tank attack within yards of regimental headquarters. Just as in Russia, they found that the postal service collapsed, and they spent weeks without letters from home, with all the corrosive consequences for morale.

It was in the line in Normandy that the division at large learned some of the details of the reconnaissance battalion and the Der Führer's accomplishments at Tulle and Oradour. Unheard-of requests for inquiries and courts-martial were being forwarded through Army Group B. But in the first weeks in Normandy there were two very convenient casualties in the Der Führer regiment. Captain Kahn was in a group of men hit by shellfire, and was badly wounded, losing an arm. He disappeared from the division and was never traced again. On 30 June Major Otto Dickmann foolishly moved outside his bunker one morning without his helmet, and was caught by a shell splinter in the head which killed him instantly. There was some speculation among his comrades that Dickmann had lost the will to live, to commit such a suicidal act. It is difficult to imagine that he was stricken by remorse. But it is possible that he was exasperated by the inquiries being pursued into his actions. With his death, these could reasonably be allowed to lapse, to the relief of the Das Reich and, no doubt, of Army Group B.

The thirtieth was the day of Von Rundstedt's celebrated telephone conversation with Führer headquarters. Keitel asked: 'What shall we do? What shall we do?' Von Rundstedt replied: 'Make peace, you idiots – what else can you do?' and was replaced three days later. Did not even the SS now begin to feel that their lives were being sacrificed in a hopeless struggle? 'Could we allow anyone to say that we were only willing to fight abroad, that we would not fight on in defence of our own country?' asked Weidinger. 'The English would have done the same.'

Wisliceny's regiment met sixty-four American attacks in eleven days, fifty-six of these without armoured support. There was a chronic shortage of Pak anti-tank ammunition. The stench of dead cows made the forward positions almost intolerable in the summer heat. The men read, talked, and played chess and scat between attacks. Lammerding was wounded by a splinter in an air attack, and relinquished command of the division.

Major Heinrich Wulf's reconnaissance battalion went into action for the first time to reinforce the western flank against an American attack. A reserve infantry regiment was cracking under pressure. Three times Wulf and his men with their armoured vehicles persuaded the infantry to move back into positions from which they had retreated, and three times they did so under intense shelling. On 8 July, Wulf reported to Stuckler that he had only 200 men left: 'If we do this again, you'll be looking for a new CO.' Stuckler brushed aside his fears. If they could simply restore the line once more, he promised Wulf, the battalion could be relieved. A few hours later, Wulf and his staff were at their headquarters in a dairy when a 105 mm shell blew off the roof, wounding almost every man in the building. A splinter severed the nerves in Wulf's left leg, while another tore off a finger. Wulf never fought again on the Western Front.

Only one man in three from the Das Reich Division came out of Normandy with his unit. They suffered terribly at Falaise, where among many others one of the hangmen of Tulle was blown up while asleep in a barn, beside a half-track loaded with Teller mines which was hit. Fritz Langangke ended up swimming the Seine to escape, leaving his gunner and loader dead behind him. Otto Pohl was in his Panther when it was blown bodily from the road by a Wehrmacht anti-tank mine, killing his driver. 'At Falaise', wrote Eisenhower, 'the SS element fought to annihilation.'

Not long after, Colonel Karl Kreutz was handed a signal by his adjutant announcing that he had been awarded the Knight's Cross. Kreutz remained expressionless. 'Aren't you pleased?' asked his adjutant, puzzled. Kreutz pointed to the skyline, torn open by one of the great American bombardments. 'Pleased? How can I be pleased? Look at that.'

'For the first time,' he said thirty-six years later, 'I knew that we had lost.'

The march of the Das Reich Division to Normandy began to achieve the status of a legend as early as 16 June 1944, when the daily Intelligence summary to SHAEF G-3 reported: 'An organization in the field claims that Resistance succeeded in delaying the departure of 2 SS Pz Div for over a week. . . . The results achieved by the FFI have far surpassed those generally expected. Wherever armament is sufficient, they have displayed unity in action and a high fighting spirit.'

'The movements of German formations to the battle area have tended to be slow on the whole,' wrote the British War Office Director of Tactical Investigation in a report in August 1944. 'In the south and south-west, the reason had been, for the most part, effective action on the part of French Resistance groups, while in the case of those divisions obliged to cross the line of the rivers SEINE and LOIRE, the hindrance has been bomb damage to bridges etc. . . .' The same report, turning to information derived from prisoner interrogation, gave the first hints of the troubles of the Das Reich on its journey northwards: 'It is estimated that on this move, most elements took twice, and some thrice as long as the distance warranted. Considerable delay was caused to the rail party by the bridge at TOURS being damaged by bombing. On 7 June a company of the Panzer Grenadier Regt was attacked by partisans at SOUILLAC, and a similar incident occurred to this unit on 11 June. Casualties were suffered, and troops deployed to deal with the partisans. . . .'

After the Liberation, the story achieved a special place in the canon of Resistance. Characteristically, it was André Malraux's vision which scaled the highest peaks of rhetoric, when he delivered the oration at the tomb of Jean Moulin:

Poor tortured king of the shades, see your shadowy people rising in the June night. . . . Listen to the roar of the German tanks moving up towards Normandy amidst the long-drawn out complaints of the awakened cattle; thanks to you, those tanks will not arrive in time. . . . Look, fighters, at your own rabble crawling out of their oak *maquis* and with their peasant hands trained in the use of bazookas, holding up one of the foremost armoured divisions of the Hitlerian empire – the Das Reich. . . .

For many years there has been a misunderstanding, that on 8 June 1944 the 2nd SS Panzer division left Montauban under orders to proceed immediately to Normandy. This was not so. There has also been an attempt to give solely to Resistance (or for that matter, by passionate advocates of air power, to the RAF and USAAF) the credit for the crippling of movement to Normandy. But as Churchill wrote in one of his most brilliant commentaries on the nature of war: 'All things are always on the move simultaneously.' It is impossible precisely to divide credit for Allied victory in Normandy between the Allied deception plans, the invading troops and their commanders, the blunders of the German High Command, the air forces and the achievements of Resistance.

French historians and former *résistants* have wildly exaggerated the material damage inflicted upon the Das Reich in action against *maquisards*. There is no reason to doubt the division's casualty return for 8–9 June – the days on which it was most heavily engaged – of seventeen killed and thirty wounded. Even adding Kampfe, Knug, Gerlach's driver and a generous allowance for Terrasson and other minor incidents on the road in the days that followed, it is easy to believe that the SS lost no more than thirty-five killed in all, out of some 15,000 men.

But casualties and material damage were never the matters at issue. The highest ambition of the Allied commanders before D-Day was that Resistance might unbalance the German forces in France, delay the passage of reinforcements and divert strength from the Normandy battle. In all these things the *résistants* of the Lot, Corrèze, Dordogne and Limousin succeeded. If the German decision to commit the Das Reich to a *ratissage* operation two days after the invasion was profoundly foolish, it was a decision to which they were goaded by Resistance. The *maquis* and the AS created a climate before and after D-Day which provoked the Germans to divert eight divisions – admittedly, as Professor Foot has said, their worst eight – to suppress the 'terrorists'.

The officers of the Das Reich today make light of their difficulties on the march, and the OKW War Diary professed that internal guerilla war in France after D-Day developed less dramatically than the staff had expected: 'The terrorist movement which had already crippled parts of France before the invasion did not increase to the extent expected.' But the scale of the German response and the almost hysterical note of some of the German signal traffic emanating from Army Group G belie these statements. SHAEF Intelligence wrote of the Das Reich's march from Montauban: 'It has been estimated that on this movement, most elements took twice and some thrice as long as the distance warranted under favourable conditions.' It is difficult to follow Professor Foot so far as to suggest that the arrival of the Das Reich in Normandy ten days earlier might have tipped the balance of the battles against the Allies, but it would certainly have made their task significantly harder. This book does not attempt to assess the overall achievement of Resistance. But it is useful to stress that its contribution to Allied victory in France must be judged chiefly by what it did in the first weeks after D-Day, and not by its later and more glamorous successes. Much nonsense has been written about the Resistance 'Liberation' of cities and departments in August and September 1944. These achievements were generally made possible simply by German withdrawals. Most of the garrisons that surrendered to *résistants* were low-grade reserve troops, unlikely to be missed.

But the story of the Das Reich Division may have helped to demonstrate the courage – the often reckless sacrifice – with which the Resistance compensated for its lack of military skill. It is worth noting the total wartime casualties of *résistants* in Region R5, where most of the actions with the Das Reich were fought: Corrèze: 248 killed, 481 deported; Creuse: 123 killed, 190 deported; Dordogne: 771 killed, 308 deported; Haute-Vienne: 957 killed, 373 deported. Lest anyone should imagine that Oradour and Tulle were entirely isolated occurrences, the following numbers of hostages and prisoners were executed by the Germans: in and around Paris: 11,000; Lille: 1,113; Angers: 863; Orléans: 501; Reims: 353; Lyon: 3,673; Nice: 324; Limoges: 2,863 – and so on across France. In all, 100,000 French men and women died in Resistance activities and German reprisals.

Because the FTP's ruthlessness and political objectives

seemed so distasteful, I believe that they have been given insufficient credit for their contribution to Resistance's achievements. It was their relentless, widespread campaign of violence in the Corrèze and the Limousin before D-Day which provoked the Germans to dispatch the Das Reich. The restrained military policy of the *Armée Secrète* was more rational, and sought to spare the civil population from many terrible reprisals. But I believe that it contributed less to the climate of chaos which so exasperated the Germans around D-Day. When *résistants* embarked on major military operations – as admittedly the FTP attempted in Tulle – they usually failed, or provoked a catastrophe. They could never face crack trained troops. But when, in Jacques Poirier's perfectly apposite phrase, they simply set out to 'make a mess', the Germans were often goaded beyond endurance. 'Resistance is small business', said Macdonald Austin reflectively, recalling his Jedburgh experience. 'Any attempt to make it anything more than that is bound to go wrong.' General Dick Barry, Gubbins's former chief of staff, looked back on the entire effort of SOE/SO and said: 'It was only just worth it.'

But Barry was considering merely the military balance sheet. Much more than this, much more than the number of days that the *maquis* delayed the Das Reich, every man and woman who played his part and survived was exalted by the experience even through the terrible layer of pain. The great contribution of Resistance – that which justified all that SOE did and made worthwhile the sacrifice of all those who died – was towards the restoration of the soul of France.

There is one further matter upon which there should be some reflection here: the conduct of the Das Reich Division in southern France. It is ironic that, to find a ready historical parallel for the way in which Hitler's army sought to suppress Resistance in Occupied France, it is necessary to look back to the manner in which Masséna's army dealt with the guerillas of Spain in 1808–9: 'In Spain . . . The French military leadership responded as leadership always will. It resorted, when it seemed profitable, to terror,' in the words of a modern historian. The French today display an undiminished reverence for the memory of Napoleon and his armies. Yet until the coming of Hitler no leader in modern European history had ruled conquered people with such savagery, or inflicted such misery.

Regular armies have always detested guerillas. In the Franco-Prussian War, some 58,000 French *franc-tireurs* killed around 1,000 Germans, and compelled the Prussians to deploy 120,000 men – a quarter of their army – to cover the lines of communication. 'We are beating them down pitilessly,' declared Bismarck. 'They are not soldiers. We are treating them as murderers.'

A British liberal historian, Thomas Arnold, wrote in 1842:

> The truth is, that if war, carried out by regular armies under the strictest discipline, is yet a great evil, an irregular partisan warfare is an evil ten times more intolerable; it is in fact to give licence to a whole population to commit all sorts of treachery, rapine and cruelty, without any restraint; letting loose a multitude of armed men, with none of the obedience and none of the honourable feelings of the soldier. . . .

Field-Marshal Bernard Montgomery, commanding the British 21st Army Group in 1944, was a Brigade-Major fighting the Irish guerillas in 1921. 'My whole attention was given to defeating the rebels,' he wrote, 'and it never bothered me a bit how many houses were burned. Any civilian or Republican, soldier or policeman, who interferes with any officer or soldier is *shot at once*.'* Until domestic public opinion compelled them to rescind the order, the British employed a policy of Official Reprisals against the rebels, including the burning of houses of those who assisted them. General Maxwell executed the leaders of the 1916 uprising, and sent their followers to camps in England. 'My own view', Montgomery reflected later on his Irish experience, 'is that to win a war of that sort you must be ruthless; Oliver Cromwell, or the Germans, would have settled it in a very short time.'

It is interesting that while General Eisenhower paid fulsome tribute to the contribution of the French *résistants* after the Liberation, Montgomery never displayed either interest in or respect for them. He always seemed to retain the regular soldier's distaste for irregulars, whatever they fought for. He might

* Montgomery's emphasis.

have felt a sneaking sympathy for those Wehrmacht officers who asked during the Occupation in France why, if it was just for the British to shoot Sinn Feiners in 1921, it was unacceptable for the Germans to shoot French *résistants* bearing arms when their own government had signed an armistice with Germany?

This, of course, was the professed opinion of the SS in France in 1944. It is worth recalling that not all their dreadful killings were illegal by the accepted usage of war. General Eisenhower could not reasonably expect the Germans to accept his broadcast demand that all captured *maquisards* be treated as prisoners of war. Historically, civilians in arms have always been liable to summary execution, whatever the Hague Convention may say in defence of those equipped with brassards or other distinguishing marks. The Das Reich was within its rights, for instance, to shoot the captured twenty-nine *résistants* on the road to Guéret; to hang the captured *maquisard* at Terrasson. The Germans were entitled to execute Violette Szabo and any other SOE agent who fell into their hands. It would be foolish to make too much of German looting – horrible though it was for the communities that had to endure it – when Allied forces were equally liable to appropriate anything not nailed down or within immediate sight of its owner. The Liberating armies were no more popular with civilians in many parts of France – above all, Normandy – than were the Occupiers, 'levelling everything in front of them on the ground, towns, villages, monuments; and distributing to the civil population in the same breath chocolate and phosphorus shells,' as Tillon wrote acidly.

Yet beyond all this, when every conceivable allowance has been made for the circumstances of war, the march of the Das Reich will always be remembered among the most dreadful episodes of World War II.

There is not a great deal that anyone other than a philosopher or a psychiatrist can say about the men who carried out the massacre at Oradour. To those with knowledge of Buchenwald and Auschwitz, it is not surprising that the leaders of the SS detachment, Dickmann and Kahn, were capable of ordering such an act. They were young men who since their earliest years had been imbued with the spirit of Nazism and of the SS. Dickmann was a product of a National Socialist cadet school, said by his comrades to have a pleasantly infectious laugh. Long before his operations on the road through the Dordogne on 8 June, he had commanded a *ratissage* at Fraysinnat-le-Gelat, when the Das Reich was still quartered at Montauban; 400 civilians had been assembled in the central square in much the same fashion as Oradour. A frightened old woman who fired a shotgun at the German intruders was hanged, along with the two nieces who shared her house. Their bodies were thrown into the flames when it had been fired. Ten hostages were chosen and shot, and when a father among them asked permission to embrace his fifteen-year-old son for the last time, the imaginative Kahn shot them together as they stood in each other's arms.

It seems almost certain that neither General Lammerding nor Colonel Stadler gave Dickmann an order that could be said to have authorized the destruction of Oradour. But throughout their years in the SS, Dickmann and his fellow-officers and NCOs had been shooting civilians as an almost routine exercise. On 3 February 1944, Field-Marshal Sperrle signed a notorious order to the Occupation forces in France, decreeing the most ruthless attitude to civilians at the slightest sign of attack or recalcitrance: 'There will be an immediate return of fire . . . immediate burning down of the houses. . . . If thereby innocent people are hit that is regrettable, but entirely the fault of the terrorists.' General Lammerding had issued repeated orders demanding savage reprisals in terrorist areas.

No authority had ever suggested to Dickmann or his colleagues that there was a precise moral and military limit, beyond which a certain number of executions or burnings became unacceptable. In Fraysinnat, Dickmann had killed thirteen people and this had been considered a proper performance of his duty. In Tulle, the division had hanged ninety-nine people without a single officer suggesting that this was unreasonable. Why should Dickmann have supposed that if he killed 642 people in Oradour, he would be considered to have exceeded his discretion?

It has been found surprising that Dickmann's soldiers, many of them young recruits, so readily carried out his terrible orders on 10 June. But many of these, too, had previous experience of shooting civilians, albeit in smaller numbers. Again and again it has been shown that the chief motive forces in war are the example of one's fellows, and the fear of revealing weakness before them. These were seen in the most grotesque form at Oradour. Even young Alsatians – half-countrymen of those they killed – found it easier to press their triggers alongside their comrades than to show revulsion or to flinch from the slaughter. Had they done so, they knew that it was possible – even probable – that they themselves would have been before a firing squad within hours. The SS made a fetish of toughness from the moment that a young recruit joined their ranks. It made them the most formidable fighting soldiers of World War II, and its perversion on such occasions as 10 June 1944 also made them the most detested. Again and again the SS showed that there were no limits to their concept of their own duty, or to their ruthlessness. I have made little in the account above about some of the more extraordinary stories told of Oradour: the baby said to have been burnt in the baker's oven, the breaking open of the champagne in the grocer's shop and the round of accordion music as the troopers waited for the fires to finish their work, the grazing horse left tethered to the outstretched arm of M. Poutaraud's corpse, because, as with all horrifying historical events, the story of Oradour was allowed to grow extravagant sideshoots and to develop its own emotional myths as the tale was told afterwards. I have omitted a number of stories and remarks which seem to bear the scent of retrospective garnishing. And yet all the evidence of SS history shows that the story of the baby in the oven could conceivably be true. Even thirty-seven years later, I find myself hoping desperately that it is not.

In the years after Oradour, countless acres of paper were filled and gallons of ink spilt in exploring the motives of the men who did these things. Even after so many other terrible tragedies that were inflicted upon France in World War II, this one developed a fascination of its own. I will quote only one passage from the trial at Bordeaux in 1953 of twenty-one men of Dickmann's company. Joseph Busch from Strasburg was a former Hitler Youth, forced by his father – an ardent Nazi – to join the Waffen SS in February 1944. He subsequently deserted from the Das Reich Division in Normandy in July.

'When we were one kilometre from Oradour, all the officers and NCOs were called forward to Major Dickmann and Captain Kahn, from whom they got instructions.'

'What instructions?' asked the Court President.

'We couldn't hear what was said. But some papers were passed to them.'

'Then what?'

'My squad drove directly to the market place. We picked up the people we met along the way, and then we helped separate them into groups and stood guard over them. I was there when a group was led off to Desourteaux' barn. We had orders to shoot when Captain Kahn fired his pistol.'

'And then you fired?'

'Yes, Herr President – three or four times.'

'You obeyed orders like a machine, like a mechanism that someone else operates?'

'Yes, Herr President.'

'Then what happened?'

'Well, people fell over.'

'Yes, but what did you do next?'

'Well, then we threw the timber and brushwood in on top of the people.'

'Were these people still alive?'

'Well, they may have been, Herr President. I didn't pay too close attention. . . . I was not especially interested.'

'Then you started the fire?'

'Yes, sir, Herr President.'

'All in accordance with orders?'

'Yes, sir, Herr President.'

'Then what?'

'We were ordered to go to the church, where I was placed on guard duty.'

'Did you see anything there?'

'Yes. Two women came looking for their children. We told them to get out of there, or they'd be shot. But then Sergeant Boos and a German came along. They dragged the women into a barn and shot them.'

It is important to remember that if Oradour was an exceptionally dreadful occurrence during the war in the West, it was a trifling sample of what the German Army had been doing on a national scale during the war in the East, since 1941. Of Russia's 20 million war dead, a countless number were killed during massacres as terrible as Oradour. Russia was where Otto Dickmann had learnt his soldiering, and become accustomed to the manner in which Hitler's Germany fought its wars.

To emphasize this, it is worth reporting a conversation that I had with an SS officer – of the Death's Head, not of the Das Reich Division – while writing this book. He told me that, long after the war, he met a fellow SS veteran who had taken part in the destruction of Oradour. The other man spoke of his astonishment about the international uproar which followed the revelation of the massacre. Speaking as one old SS man to another, said Dickmann's officer confidentially, '. . . in our circle, Herr Muller, it was *nothing*'.

General Lammerding's defence of his own and of his division's conduct, made after the war to his former subordinate Colonel Weidinger, is worth quoting only for the record:

It was necessary to provoke terror among the *maquisards* to deprive them of the support of the civil population. The remedial method was cruel, but it was war, and I do not know any army in the world which would have done otherwise in a similar situation. . . . I assume that it is useless to recall that the Geneva Convention formally forbids the actions of *franc-tireurs*, and warns that all will be shot. I assume that it is equally useless to recall that General Sperrle . . . had given precise instructions for reprisals to be carried out in areas where the civil population attacked the German military. . . . It was a matter of life or death for the German Army, and I approve of Dickmann's action in shooting the men and burning the houses in which *maquisards* had hidden, or in which arms and ammunition had been stored, conforming to the orders of General Sperrle. But Dickmann also left several hundred women and children to burn in the church, and that I cannot accept. It was a crime. I recognize it.

At the time of a post-war trial, a Swiss writer was among those who considered the guilt of the Das Reich with most sympathy. In a long, carefully reasoned essay in *Monde Nouveau* in March 1953, Pierre Boisseau wrote:

It is impossible to say that Oradour was 'useless'. Let us recall a few facts: on 6 June 1944 the Allied landed on the coast of Normandy. The 2nd SS Das Reich . . . received the order to move towards the enemy. They were delayed for four days on their march by incessant guerilla attack by a clandestine army, ubiquitous, impossible to engage, which caused explosions, hit outposts, cut communications. . . . This division defended itself by the only available means which would act quickly and effectively against the partisans: they took reprisals on such a scale as to convince everyone that any further operation would be to the disadvantage of those who attempted it. We know today that the terrifying example of Oradour added to that of Tulle prevented a surely successful attack that the *maquis* had planned on Limoges. We may assume that it also prevented many other *coups de main*.

. . . From two points of view one must choose one: either all violence is always part of the one vast unity – thus, there is no longer any question of war crimes. There is the crime of war which begins with the mere bearing of arms. All recourse to force is forbidden and punishable.

. . . Alternatively, two or several sovereign states employ violence against each other, and thus the ruins of Oradour are paid for by those of Berlin, Dresden, Hamburg, by the labour of prisoners of war, by the political division of Germany, by the dismantled factories, by Occupation, by the children of France well-fed in the Black Forest, by a certain number of summary executions, by the last mopping-up operations of the war.

It might have been worthwhile to offer, in 1945, to all those gentlemen dressed in black who are presiding at the Oradour trial, a trip to Germany. They would have seen enough ruins, widows, orphans to assess sufficient reparations and return with dry eyes.

In short, could the bombers of Dresden justly try the destroyers of Oradour? But that is a dilemma of morality, not of history, which I am grateful to be able to leave the reader to resolve.

13 Afterwards

Most of the survivors of the Das Reich Division were in Hungary or Austria when the war ended, still fighting alongside such flotsam of the Third Reich as a unit of Dresden firefighters, who said that there was nothing useful left for them to do at home. Some of the SS reacted to news of the surrender like Ernst Krag's wireless operator, who put one pistol bullet into his set and a second into his own head. Many others began an epic struggle to fight their way alone across Europe to their families – and out of the path of the Russians. Most were rounded up by the Allies and imprisoned. The French, naturally, claimed most survivors of the Das Reich, and several hundred were held in the prison ships at Bordeaux until the late forties or early fifties, awaiting trial or release. Otto Pohl, the young tank officer, found himself acting as assistant to the prison dentist, Captain Reichmann, late of the 95th Security Regiment in Tulle. Pohl's father, the SS Inspector-General of Concentration Camps, was hanged at Nuremberg.

The war crimes trials of the 2nd SS Panzer Division, when they were finally held in 1951 and 1953, proved unsatisfactory to everyone concerned. Twenty-one NCOs and men of the 1st battalion of the Der Führer were indicted for their part in the massacre at Oradour. But Dickmann was dead, and Kahn could not be found. More senior officers such as Stadler were never tried.

Even more embarrassing from the French point of view, fourteen of the accused were Alsatian. A formidable protest movement was launched in Alsace, so lately and uneasily reunited with France. The Alsatians castigated the French Government for permitting the trial of young men whom they considered almost as much the victims of Nazism as the dead of Oradour. Six of the fourteen had surrendered to the British in Normandy and told everything they knew about the massacre. Two had subsequently served with the French Army in Indochina.

On 12 February 1953, after weeks of horrifying evidence, the Military Tribunal at Bordeaux delivered its verdict. An Alsatian volunteer named Sergeant Boos was sentenced to death; nine other Alsatians received hard labour and four prison terms, none exceeding eight years. A German warrant officer, Lenz, was sentenced to death. One German was acquitted and the remaining five received prison terms of ten to twelve years. Forty-two other Germans were sentenced to death *in absentia*. France was racked by the storm that now followed – first from the relatives and survivors of Oradour, outraged by the leniency of the sentences, and second from the people of Alsace-Lorraine, convinced that their young men were being made scapegoats.

It was all too much for a French government struggling weakly to re-create national unity. All the Alsatians except Boos were amnestied. Both death sentences were commuted. Five of the seven Germans sentenced were repatriated at once, having already served more than their time while awaiting trial.

Only three people were available for trial for their part in the hangings at Tulle: Major Heinrich Wulf, the hangman Otto Hoff, and the interpreter Paulette Geissler. The defence – the only conceivable defence – was that the executions were an unfortunate but justifiable act of war. Private Schneid gave evidence of his own role, and felt that the court missed the point. He demanded of the official interpreter: ' "Ask the court if they knew what an order was in the German Army. . . ." He told me that he could do nothing about it, that justice must take its course.' Wulf was sentenced to ten years, Hoff to life, Geissler to three years. All were set free within a matter of months, in 1952.

If the leniency of the courts in 1951 and 1953 seems remarkable, it is necessary to remember the mood of the time. The world had been sated with international justice and ritual retribution at Nuremberg. There was growing doubt and uncertainty about matters of absolute right and wrong, when the Russians had been allowed to sit in judgment on the Germans for barbarities which scarcely rivalled their own. There was a sense that somewhere, the search for the guilty must stop, that the time had come to look forward, rather than forever back. Above all, perhaps, there was the embarrassing knowledge that the most notorious figures had not come before the Tribunal. General Lammerding and Major Kowatsch were sentenced to death *in absentia*. Some SS men claimed that Kowatsch had died in Normandy. But it was well known that Lammerding was alive and well and building a prosperous engineering business in Düsseldorf. He sent a sworn statement to the Military Tribunal during the Oradour trial, before taking temporary refuge in Schleswig-Holstein. He then moved to the American zone until the hunt for his life had abated, and finally returned to Düsseldorf where he remained in prosperous security until his death in 1971. The British would take no action to extradite Lammerding or other wanted Nazis to France 'unless there is incontestable evidence that the accused has committed murder.' In Lammerding's case, there was thought to be doubt.

Most of the Das Reich officers who survived the war are today prosperous and vigorous men for their age: Weidinger, Stadler, Wulf, Stuckler, Krag and Kreutz – to name only the most senior. They keep in regular contact with each other, and argue with fierce passion that there is nothing in their wartime service for which they have cause to reproach themselves.

Most of the survivors of Resistance have also prospered. In the years after the war, a record as a prominent local *résistant* proved a passport to commercial and professional success for many Frenchmen (although it is interesting to notice how many Vichy officials were able to continue their careers uninterrupted by the Liberation). Over the years it has been forgotten who joined Resistance in the dark days of 1942 and 1943, and who came hastily to the cause in June and July 1944.

But it should also be remembered that some Frenchmen still harbour a bitter private hatred for the *maquis*. One afternoon in June 1980, I sat in a pleasant house in the Dordogne hearing an elderly *vicomtesse* explode with passion about her memories of the depredations and murders allegedly committed by local *maquisards*. I heard of a priest in Brive, not many days later, who rendered great assistance to Resistance by bearing messages and concealing explosives. After the war, it is said that he was denied a bishopric because the church hierarchy so vividly remembered his activities during the Occupation.

After the Liberation, Prince Michel de Bourbon was summoned hastily to the *château* of one of his relations on the Loire, which the local Resistance were ransacking on the grounds that its owner had been a collaborator. De Bourbon, in uniform, produced his credentials, signed personally by De Gaulle. He demanded that they desist. Their leader tore up the letter, imprisoned him in a barn and promised to shoot him the next day. De Bourbon was fortunate to escape during the night.

Jacques Poirier was summoned equally urgently from Paris one day after the Liberation, by a prominent Limoges businessman who had provided Poirier with a safe house for many months, while posing as a collaborator. Now, George Guingouin's men had promised to kill him. Poirier arrived in Limoges too late to prevent the blowing-up of the man's garage business, but in time to save his life by some very tough talking to Guingouin and his cohorts.

There was a terrible national settling of scores in the months following the Liberation. M. Robert Aron suggests a total of more than 20,000 summary executions, most of them the work of former *résistants*. Simply to have served in the Resistance was not enough to provide safety in many regions – it was necessary to have been with the right faction.

Among the most prominent characters in this book, Jean-Jacques Chapou, who led the FTP attack on Tulle, was killed in action a few weeks later. Lieutenant Walter Schmald was captured by *résistants* in July and shot – some say more painfully killed. Soleil, Georges Guingouin and Robert Noireau are all alive, after quarrelling for years after 1945 with the French communist party. Violette Szabo was shot at Ravensbruck concentration camp early in 1945. Anastasie was killed in Indochina. Harry Peulevé survived Buchenwald.

Maurice Buckmaster became a successful businessman. George Hiller took up the diplomatic career that he had promised himself before the war, and served as a British ambassador before his death in 1973. Jacques Poirier and Peter Lake accepted the surrender of Brive in August 1944, while George

Starr drove into Toulouse with his *maquisards* as the Germans abandoned it. Poirier became an oil company executive, retiring in 1980. He now lives with his beautiful wife in a delightful flat in Paris. André Malraux, of course, became De Gaulle's Minister of Culture before his death. Baron Philippe de Gunzbourg still lives in enviable splendour, and has not lost his affection for Britain, while lamenting her decline. Peter Lake and the late George Starr became consular officials. In 1945, Starr had the satisfaction of entertaining to lunch his former commanding officer from the days when he was sergeant in charge of Phantom's pigeons in 1940. His CO had finished the war as a major. Starr was a colonel. Several other members of the French Section transferred to the Secret Intelligence Service after the war. It would be tactless to say which.

René Jugie lives in a large house on the edge of Brive crammed with documents on Resistance and such sentimental keepsakes as a gammon grenade, detonator and Schmeisser sub-machine gun. Marius Guedin retired from the French Army as a general. The Verlhacs are dead, but the Brus are still in the enchanting village of St Céré, and Odette Bach and her family prosper in Souillac.

Prince Michel de Bourbon was parachuted into Indochina in 1945, handed over to the Vietminh by the Japanese, and held prisoner until he escaped and walked for weeks through the jungle to Thailand. He now lives in a house at Versailles lavishly decorated with photographs of his relations among the royal families of Europe. Tommy Macpherson transferred immediately from France after the Liberation to further adventures in the Italian campaign. 'Mac' Austin lives on Hilton Head island, South Carolina. His wireless operator, Jack Berlin, is an ordained Baptist minister.

John Tonkin of the SAS travelled compulsively after the war, and took part in an expedition to Antarctica with Paddy Mayne, who later died of a heart attack. Tonkin is now a businessman in Australia. Sam Smith runs a café in Liverpool. John Fielding is an estate agent in Norwich. Peter Weaver lives in retirement on the south coast. Amédée Maingard built a large business in his native Mauritius before his death in 1980. Almost all those named above were decorated for their deeds in 1944.

*

The ruins of Oradour-sur-Glane have been preserved as they lay on 10 June 1944, a French national monument. A sadly drab new village has been built near by, in which, astonishingly enough, Mme Rouffranche chose to spend the rest of her life.

In the town of Tulle, on 9 June each year a visitor will notice garlands hanging from many balconies and lamp posts. This is not a gesture to decorate the streets. Each one marks the spot upon which a citizen of Tulle was hanged by the Das Reich Division in 1944. Tulle has not forgotten, even though each year now a great army of German tourists passes through the Dordogne and Corrèze; as far as anyone can observe, without a hint of self-consciousness.

Appendix A

2 SS-PZ Division
Das Reich

Order of the Day — Divisional HQ, 9 June 1944

The Position with Regard to Guerilla Bands and Tactics for Combatting Them

1. The guerillas have occupied the area Figeac–Clermont-Ferrand–Limmoges– Gourdon which, until now, has only been weakly held by German troops. The *maquis* who have appeared there have exclusively communistic tendencies. The small number of *Armée Secrète* are also communists and are also to be treated as gangs [*Banden*]. All instructions, orders, etc. should aim to incite the civilian population against these guerilla bands and make our action appear protective. The threat from these gangs can have the most far-reaching consequences if we are unable to instil it into the minds of the population that these men have no national feeling, and also impress upon them that they are nothing more than highway robbers. On the other hand, it is necessary that our own troops behave in such a way that the civilian population is convinced of our good intentions and also of the character of our Division as an elite formation. Looting will, if necessary, be prevented by force. In every case regimental or battalion commanders will decide what is to be done with captured material. Standing orders regarding dress, behaviour on vehicles, maximum speed, maintenance of vehicles, remain in force. To minimize casualties, personnel will remain seated in recce cars.

2. The following special instructions are laid down:
   (a) Curfew from 2100 to 0600 hours. Handing in of all arms under

threat of death penalty. Orders concerning the provision of supplies are to be enforced in all places.

(b) The mayor and police are to be reinstated in all areas and will be made personally responsible for carrying out orders.

(c) Houses from which shots have been fired, together with the neighbouring houses, will, in every instance, be burned to the ground

(d) Captured documents will not be destroyed but will be handed in to the Division.

(e) Persons whose participation in Resistance is undoubted will be treated as criminals. It may be a good idea to throw them in irons in the sight of civilian population.

(f) The inhabitants of every community will be assembled together for a count, and will be treated during this process as prisoners.

(g) In every instance units will hold the following as prisoners:

All men who have reached the area only a short time ago.

All men whose identity cards or worker's cards are obviously faked.

All those who can be proved to be members of gangs.

After examination, the men should generally be released. Prisoners should be handed over to the local army establishments concerned with the movement of workers to the Reich, for employment there (via Limoges and Montauban).

(h) In all cases attempts at escape must be made more difficult by removing the men's braces etc. Permanent and adequate pickets must be established. Whenever possible, rooms on the first floors of houses should be used. Windows will be nailed up. The local mayor must be made responsible for supplying food to prisoners.

(i) Executions are to be carried out on the order of regimental or other commanders by hanging, only in such places where guerilla units fight to hold up our troops or commit atrocities (shameful treatment of wounded or dead, use of dum-dum bullets, etc.). As a rule, the proportion to be applied is as follows:

For every wounded soldier . . . . 3 guerillas

For every dead soldier . . . . 10 guerillas

(j) Executions are in no way a public spectacle, but a punitive measure. Troops must therefore be kept at a distance until the order for the execution is carried out. Orders should be given at short notice to detail men for execution squads, and a public announcement should be made. Priests may attend executions and carry out their religious functions, provided these are not of a demonstrative character (this is very important in France).

3. Operations:
Guerilla units are highly mobile and can withdraw quickly. The only effective tactic against this is to surround and surprise them, working round their flanks and rear while pinning them in front by fire. Their objective is invariably to pick off isolated soldiers and to seize weapons and supplies. Operations which fail because inadequate forces are employed should be avoided. It is vital to ensure that German soldiers do not fall into the hands of guerillas because of careless security measures on the march, or when men are acting as couriers or sentries.

Appendix B

Principal Weapons of the *maquis* and the 2nd SS Panzer Division

The Maquis

The Bren: (Fig. 1) by general consent the finest light machine gun in the world of its period, and the most useful weapon provided to the *maquis*. A .303 gas-operated gun fed by a 30-round magazine, it was accurate up to 1,000 metres, and could withstand immense maltreatment and unskilled use. *Résistants* were constantly pleading for maximum drops of Brens.

1

The Sten: (Fig. 2) the standard British sub-machine gun of the war, a 9 mm blowback-operated gun fed by a 32-round magazine. The Sten was highly unreliable, prone to jamming, and inaccurate beyond 30 metres. It was unsuitable for guerilla operations in open country because it encouraged waste of ammunition, and was useless at average battle range. But it was easy and cheap to produce – a gun was said to cost fifteen shillings – and was supplied to the Resistance in huge quantities.

2

3

The Gammon grenade: (Fig. 3) an improvised hand-thrown bomb used by the Home Guard, the Special Air Service and the Resistance, especially suitable for the destruction of aircraft or vehicles. An explosive charge was wrapped in fabric and sewn to an impact fuse that detonated on sharp contact.

Resisters were also supplied with large quantities of British and captured Italian rifles of varying efficiency; revolvers and automatic pistols; the British 36 grenade – the Mills bomb – the standard anti-personnel shrapnel weapon; and modest quantities of plastic explosive. They also made extensive use of French Army rifles and light machine guns, mainly stolen or retained from Armistice Army stocks, and captured German 9 mm Schmeisser SMGs. One of the most serious problems for all Resistance groups was the disparate range of arms for which ammunition had to be found.

2nd SS Panzer Division

The Panther V, (Fig. 4) of which the Das Reich had an establishment of 62 in 1944, was one of the outstanding battle tanks of the war. Weighing almost 45 tons, with a crew of 5 and a 75 mm gun, it was first introduced in 1942 as a counter to the Russian T-34. It remained at the forefront of German armoured units until the end of the war.

4

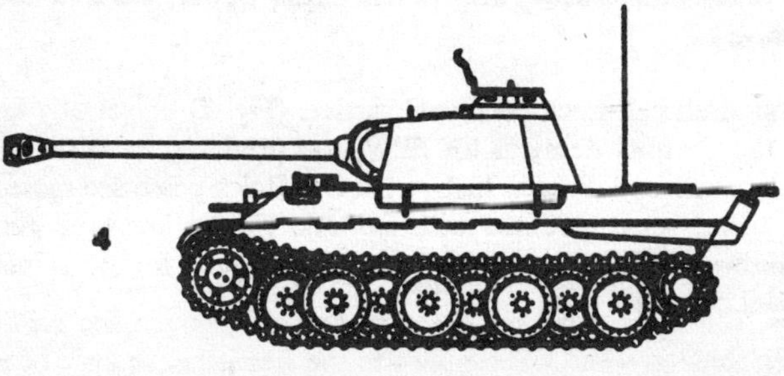

The *Panzer IV*, (Fig. 5) of which the DR had an establishment of 64, was the most widely produced German tank of the war. It weighed 23 tons, with a maximum road speed of 25 mph against the 34 mph of the Panther. By the opening of the Normandy campaign, the *Panzer IV* was obsolescent, but from necessity the Germans continued to use it extensively. The upgunned version, with a 75 mm gun, remained a very powerful weapon.

5

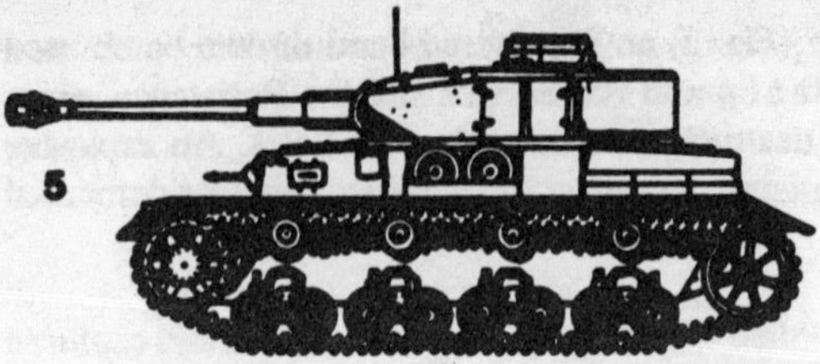

6

The *Sturmgeschütz III* (Fig. 6). This self-propelled assault gun, with which one battalion of the DR was equipped, was essentially a turretless tank, constructed upon the chassis of the *Panzer III* tank. Armed with a 75 mm gun, it provided close fire support for the infantry. Although produced principally as a 'poor man's tank', a cheap substitute when attrition on the Eastern Front began to destroy armour faster than Germany's factories could make *Panthers* and *Panzer IVs*, the *Sturmgeschütz*, with its low silhouette that provided a difficult target for enemy tanks, and its heavy armour and hitting power, was a formidable weapon.

The armoured half-track personnel carrier, (Fig. 7) universally known within the German Army as the SPW, was produced in scores of variants. An armoured division such as the Das Reich possessed more than 300 of them, some mounted with mortars, 75 mm anti-tank guns or flamethrowers, others armed only with machine guns, for use as infantry personnel carriers.

7

The *Schwerer Panzerspähwagen* (Fig. 8) was armed with a 20 mm cannon, carried a crew of 4 and possessed a maximum speed of more than 50 mph. The DR's *Aufklärungsabteilung* possessed one company of these armoured cars.

8

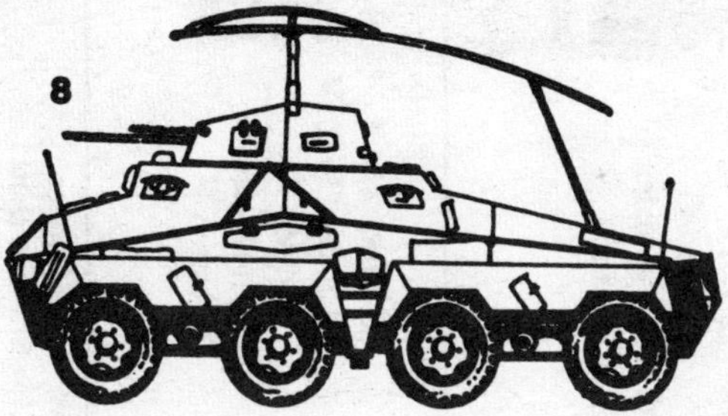

In addition to the above armoured vehicles, the DR possessed a further armoured battalion of *Panzerjaeger* self-propelled anti-tank guns, 4 battalions of self-propelled guns and howitzers, 1 self-propelled anti-aircraft gun battalion, and some 50 towed flak and field guns. The division had a total establishment of more than 3,000 vehicles, 359 of them armoured, in addition to the tanks.

2nd SS Panzer Division Das Reich, Spring 1944

Div. HQ	SS-PZ Regt 2	SS-Pz-Gren Regt 3 'Deutschland'	SS-Pz Art Regt 2	SS-PZ Jäg Abt 2	SS-Recce Abt 2
8 × M/C	62 × PzKw V	88 × M/C	12 × 17 cm G/H	31 × 7.5 cm SPG	13 × 7.5 cm SPG
32 vehicles	64 × PzKw IV	6 × 15 cm G/H	6 × 15 cm SPG	12 × Pak 40	35 × 20 mm Pak
141 men	8 × 3.7 cm Flak	12 × 10.5 cm G/H	12 × 15 cm G/H	17 × M/C	6 × F/T
	6 × 20 mm Flak	24 × F/T	12 × 10.5 cm SPG	135 vehicles	22 × M/C
	53 × M/C	12 × 12 cm Mor	12 × 10.5 cm G/H	513 men	193 vehicles
	313 vehicles	527 vehicles	40 × M/C		942 men
	2,401 men	3,242 men	534 vehicles		
			2,167 men		

SS-Pi Abt 2	SS-Sig Abt 2	SS-Pz-Gren Regt 4 'Der Führer'	SS-Flak Abt 2	SS-StuG Abt 2	SS-NblW Abt 2
3 × 20/28 mm Pak	14 × M/C	As above	12 × 8.8 cm	30 × StuG III/IV	18 × NblW
3 × 20 mm Pak	114 vehicles		18 × 20 mm	11 × M/C	8 × M/C
20 × F/T	515 men		16 × M/C	100 vehicles	107 vehicles
52 × M/C			181 vehicles	344 men	473 men
212 vehicles			824 men		
984 men					

Abbreviations

Pz = Panzer
M/C = motorcycles
men = officers, NCOs and men
Regt = Regiment
Abt = Abteilung (Battalion)
Pz = Panzer-Grenadier
G/H = Gun/Howitzer
F/T = Flamethrower
Mor = Mortar
Art = Artillery
SPG = Self-propelled gun
NblW = Nebelwerfer
StuG = Sturmgeschütz
Recce = Reconnaissance
Pi = Pioneer
Sig = Signals

Note: These figures are for the division at full establishment. In June 1944 the DR's vehicle strength was substantially lower. Excluded are medical and MP units, etc.

Bibliography and a Note on Sources

The principal sources for this book have been interviews with the survivors of those whose story it is. Some inner files of SOE remain closed in perpetuity, but I am grateful to the Foreign Office archivist, Colonel E. G. Boxshall, for providing the answers to certain specific questions from these records, and above all for copies of the relevant Jedburgh team after-action reports. The German Army's archives at Freiburg supplied the surviving relevant signal traffic and situation reports from the War Diaries of Army Group G, 66th Reserve Corps and 58th Corps. The Public Record Office contains many of the files of Special Forces HQ, G-3 SHAEF and the SAS Regiment, including the reports and signal logs of Bulbasket. I have made extensive use of scores of regional Resistance publications, especially the journal *R4*. Baron Philippe de Gunzbourg loaned me a copy of his unpublished memoir *Souvenirs du Sud-Ouest*. Mrs Judith Hiller allowed me to read and hear the marvellous notes and tapes that her husband George made for his unwritten memoir.

The books listed below are not a comprehensive guide to Resistance literature, which would be enormous, but a selection of those which I have found most helpful. Their inclusion is not an indication of merit – indeed some are wildly inaccurate – but merely a guide to their relevance.

ANON, *Dordogne martyre*, Paris, 1945.

ANON, *Maquis de Corrèze*, Paris, 1975.

ANON, *Mémorial de la Résistance et des victimes du nazisme en Haute-Vienne*, Limoges, 1975.

ARON, Robert, *De Gaulle Before Paris*, Putnam, 1963.

——, *De Gaulle Triumphant*, Putnam, 1964.

ASTIER DE LA VIGERIE, Emmanuel d', *Les Dieux et les Hommes*, Paris, 1952.

BEAU AND GAUBUSSEAU, *R5: Les SS en Limousin, Périgord et Quercy*, Paris, 1969.
BECK, Philip, *Oradour*, Leo Cooper, 1979.
BENNETT, Ralph, *Ultra in the West*, Hutchinson, 1979.
BERGERET AND GREGOIRE, *Messages Personnels*, Bordeaux, 1945.
BEST, Geoffrey, *Humanity in Warfare*, Weidenfeld and Nicolson, 1980.
BROGAN, D. W., *Development of Modern France 1870–1939*, Hamish Hamilton, 1940.
BUCKMASTER, Maurice, *They Fought Alone*, Odhams, 1958.
CALMETTE, A., *Les Equipes Jedburgh dans la Bataille de France*, Paris, 1966.
CAVE-BROWN, Anthony, *Bodyguard of Lies*, W. H. Allen, 1976.
CHURCHILL, Peter, *Of Their Own Choice*, Hodder, 1952.
COLBY, William, *Honourable Men*, Hutchinson, 1978.
COOKRIDGE, E. H., *Inside SOE*, Arthur Barker, 1966.
COOPER, Matthew, *The German Army 1933-1945*, Macdonald and Janes, 1976.
——, *The Phantom War*, Macdonald and Janes, 1979.
DELARUE, Jacques, *Trafics et Crimes sous l'Occupation*, Paris, 1968.
DURAND, P., *Histoire de SNCF pendant la Guerre*, Paris, 1968.
EHRLICH, Blake, *The French Resistance*, Chapman & Hall, 1966.
FARRAN, Roy, *Winged Dagger*, Collins, 1948.
FOOT, M. R. D., *Resistance*, Eyre Methuen, 1976.
——, *Six Faces of Courage*, Eyre Methuen, 1978.
——, *SOE in France*, HMSO, 1966.
GUICHETAU, Gérard, *La Das Reich et le Coeur de la France*, Paris, 1974.
GUINGOUIN, Georges, *Quatre Ans de Lutte sur le Sol Limousin*, Paris, 1974.
HARRISON, D. I., *Such Men are Dangerous*, Cassell, 1957.
HARRIS SMITH, R., *OSS: The History of America's First CIA*, University of California, 1972.
HINSLEY, F. H., *British Intelligence in World War II*, HMSO, 1979.
HISLOP, John, *Anything but a Soldier*, Michael Joseph, 1965.
KRUUSE, Jens, *Madness at Oradour*, Secker and Warburg, 1969.
LACOUTURE, Jean, *André Malraux*, Deutsch, 1975.
LANGELAAN, George, *Knights of the Floating Silk*, Hutchinson, 1959.

MACKSEY, Kenneth, *The Partisans of Europe in World War II* Hart-Davis MacGibbon, 1975.
MALRAUX, André, *Antimémoires*.
MICHEL, Henri, *Histoire de la Résistance en France*, Paris, 1972.
——, *The Shadow of War: Resistance in Europe 1939–45*. Deutsch, 1972.
MILLAR, George, *Maquis*, Heinemann, 1956.
MINNEY, R. J., *Carve Her Name with Pride*, Newnes, 1956.
MORGAN, William, *The OSS and I*, New York, 1957.
MOUNTFIELD, David, *The Partisans*, Hamlyn, 1979.
NOGUERES, Henri, *Histoire de la Résistance en France*, Paris, 1968–75.
NOIREAU, Robert, *Le Temps des partisans*, Paris, 1978.
PASSY, Colonel, *Souvenirs: 2me Bureau, Londres*, Monte Carlo, 1947.
——, *Souvenirs: 10 Duke Street*, Monte Carlo, 1947.
——, *Souvenirs: Missions secrètes*, Paris, 1951.
PAXTON, Robert, *Vichy France*, Barrie and Jenkins, 1980.
QUAY, Bruce, *Das Reich*, Osprey, 1978.
REMY AND BOURDELLE, *Les Balcons de Tulle*, Paris, 1963.
SCHNEID, Sadi, *Beutedeutscher*, Askania, 1979.
SCHRAMM, Percy (editor), *The OKW War Diaries*, 4 vols., Frankfurt, 1961.
SHULMAN, Milton, *Defeat in the West*, Heinemann, 1963.
SOULIER, A., *Le Drame de Tulle*, Tulle, 1971.
SPEIDEL, Hans, *We Defended Normandy*, Herbert Jenkins, 1953.
STEIN, George, *The Waffen SS at War*, Oxford, 1966.
TERRAINE, John, *The Smoke and the Fire*, Sidgwick and Jackson, 1980.
TILLON, C., *Les FTP*, Paris, 1962.
TROUILLÉ, Pierre, *Journal d'un Préfet pendant l'Occupation*.
VOMÉCOURT, Philippe de, *Who Lives to See the Day*.
WALTERS, Anne-Marie, *Moondrop to Gascony*, Macmillan, 1946.
WARNER, Philip, *The Special Air Service*, Kimber, 1972.
WEIDINGER, Otto, *Kameraden bis zum Ende*, Oldendorf, 1978.
WHITE, Frieda, *Three Rivers of France*, Faber, 1952.
ZUCKERMAN, S., *From Apes to Warlords*, Hamish Hamilton, 1978.

Acknowledgments

I am indebted to many people whom I met or with whom I corresponded during the writing of this book. Some I have already mentioned in the Foreword. Here, I should begin with my wife Tricia and Alan Samson, my editor at Michael Joseph, who endured the trauma of gestation with characteristic patience and understanding. The London Library was as splendid as always. In England I also received generous help or suggestions from Joan Bright Astley, Len Deighton, Geoffrey Lucy, Charles Wintour and the RUSI Library. Without the intervention of David Irving, my inquiries in Germany about the whereabouts of survivors of the Das Reich would have continued to meet with courteous declarations of ignorance from the relevant veterans' organizations.

In France, I am indebted above all to M. and Mme Louis Bach, M. and Mme Georges Bru, Marius Guedin, Baron Philippe de Gunzbourg, René Jugie, Pierre Péré, Marcel Racault, Marguerite Rollet, Rojé Raveux, Jean Razier, Julien Rouzier, Jean Sennemaut and Marcel Vidal. There are many others, too numerous to list, whom I had the privilege of meeting in southern and central France in 1980.

Among the former staff of SOE in Baker Street: Sir Robin Brook, General Dick Barry, Maurice Buckmaster, Vera Atkins and Selwyn Jepson.

Former agents of SOE in France: Annette Cormeau, the late Amédée Maingard, Peter Lake, Paddy O'Sullivan, Jacques Poirier, the late George Starr, Cyril Watney.

The Jedburghs and OSS: Macdonald Austin, Prince Michel de Bourbon, William Colby, Geoffrey Hallowes, Henry Hyde, Tommy Macpherson

The SAS: John Fielding, Sam Smith, John Tonkin, Peter Weaver.

The SS: Ernst Krag, Karl Kreutz, Fritz Langangke, Otto Pohl, Theo Sorg, Silvester Stadler, Albert Stuckler, Herbert Taege, Otto Weidinger, Gunther-Eberhardt Wisliceny, Heinrich Wulf.

Almost all of these received decorations from their respective nations for their services in World War II.

Glossary

BCRA: *Bureau Central de Renseignements et d'Action*, the Central Bureau for Intelligence and action set up in November 1940 by Captain André Dewavrin, alias Colonel Passy, at Free French headquarters in London. The BCRA assumed responsibility for all intelligence and sabotage operations in French territory carried out under General De Gaulle's auspices.

Chantiers de la Jeunesse: a Vichy Government-sponsored organization which ran compulsory forest work camps for all twenty year olds, at which they were subjected to intensive political indoctrination.

Cheminots: Railway workers.

DMR: *Délégué Militaire Régional*. De Gaulle's headquarters in London appointed six DMRs to act as General Koenig's on-the-spot representatives and deputies in the six Military Regions into which France was divided for the purposes of FFI direction and administration.

FFI: *Forces Françaises de l'Intérieur*. The title given by Free French headquarters in London to all Resistance forces in arms in France under Gaullist command. The FFI allegedly included the men of the Communist FTP, but in reality these almost everywhere preserved their own command and title independent of the FFI. In March 1944, General Marie Pierre Koenig was designated FFI commander, a role he exercised from London. After the liberation of France, 140,000 men of the FFI were inducted into the French First Army. Most of them spent the last months of the war blockading the remaining German garrisons in the French ports.

FTP: *Francs-Tireurs et Partisans*, the Communist *résistants*, who took their title as 'free shooters' from the roving bands of French guerillas who harassed the invaders' lines of communication in the 1870 Franco–Prussian war. Most FTP groups for most of the war accepted orders only from the French Communist Party, although they sometimes formed local tactical alliances with the Armée Secrète or agents from London in order to gain access to parachuted arms and money.

GMR: *Garde Mobile de Reserve*, a Vichyite para-military force.

MUR: *Mouvement Uni de Résistance*, a loose alliance of three non-communist Resistance groups that had developed in the Unoccupied Zone of France – *Liberation*, *Combat* and *Franc-Tireur* (not to be confused with the FTP). In the Corrèze the council of MUR included representatives of several other local groups.

Milice: Originally a para-military arm of the Vichy Government in the Unoccupied Zone of France. When the detested Joseph Darnand became Vichy's Secretary-General for the Maintenance of Order – in other words, police minister – in December 1943, he expanded the *milice* into a national para-military force to combat the Resistance, and recruited some 45,000 French volunteers. The *milice* were especially feared by the Resistance because of their local knowledge, and especially detested for their ruthlessness and treachery, although many of their recruits came forward to avoid forced labour in Germany. Some historians suggest that in the spring of 1944 at least as many Frenchmen were working actively to combat Resistance as were working with the FFI and FTP.

ORA: *Organisation de Résistance de l'Armée*, a Resistance group which was originally created within the Intelligence Service of the Vichy Armistice Army, and expanded after the disbandment of the Armistice Army when the Germans took over Unoccupied France in November 1942. It was a non-Gaullist body which accomplished little, but for a time enjoyed the enthusiastic support of the Americans. Many Frenchmen despised the ORA because of its overwhelming dependence on former regular army officers, whom they considered bore a large share of responsibility for the plight of France, and had no claim upon the support of civilians.

OSS: The American Office of Strategic Services created by General William Donovan in July 1941 to build a new Secret Service and sabotage organization to replace that disbanded in November 1942. OSS was the forerunner of the modern

Central Intelligence Agency, and after some early blunders and mishaps caused by the absolute lack of experienced personnel, it developed into a useful weapon of war. Its senior ranks were dominated by lawyers educated at the great American universities – Harvard, Princeton, Yale. Allen Dulles, later director of the CIA, was probably the most successful OSS organizer of the war, running his networks from Switzerland. OSS was dissolved in September 1945.

Plastique: Plastic explosive, the soft, malleable putty-like substance developed by the British and widely used for demolition because of its power and flexibility; charges could be moulded into any shape. They were exploded by the insertion of a detonator which in turn was ignited either by electrical impulse or delay fuse.

RAMC: Royal Army Medical Corps.

Resau: network, the standard word for one of the chains of agents created by SOE and the BCRA, meaning a linked group of people rather than a geographical area.

SA: *Sturmabteilung*, the brownshirt 'storm-troops', the original élite strong-arm force of Hitler's National Socialist Party, purged and broken in June 1934 when their leader Ernst Rohm was killed.

SAS: The British Special Air Service regiment.

SD: *Sicherhéitsdienst*, the SS Security Service operating under the orders of Himmler. The SD possessed some 6,000 agents throughout Europe, and was closely linked with the Gestapo. Most Frenchmen referred to all German police agents as Gestapo.

SHAEF: Supreme Headquarters Allied Expeditionary Force, the controlling staff for the Allied landings in Normandy and the subsequent campaign in North-West Europe, under the command of General Eisenhower.

SNCF: *Société Nationale de Chemins de Fer*, the national railway organization of France.

SOE: The British Special Operations Executive, forerunner and counterpart of the American OSS's Special Operations department.

STO: *Service de Travail Obligatoire*. The detested forced-labour programme introduced in Occupied France in August 1942, and throughout the country from February 1943. Initially the

Germans sought French volunteers to man their factories, but although they recruited with some success, the supply of labour was far below their requirements, and compulsion was introduced. By November 1943, 1.34 million Frenchmen were working in German factories (along with millions more Belgians, Dutchmen, Russians, Poles and other defeated nationals). In January 1944 the Nazis launched a new programme to recruit a further million Frenchmen, but they met with negligible success, since most of those eligible took to the *maquis*, or went into hiding.

Notes and References

p. 13 Some 15,000 men and 209 tanks: The division's total strength on 6 June 1944 was just over 19,000 officers and men. Of these more than 15,000 – it is impossible to be more precise – moved north on 8 June. The balance were either in Germany collecting new equipment, or remained at Montauban for training or local security duties. All elements were reunited in Normandy by early July.

p. 13 Professor M. R. D. Foot wrote: *SOE in France* pp. 397, 399

p. 22 Adolf Hitler and his staff discussed: see *Hitler's Führerconferences*, OUP 1950

p. 26 A British Intelligence assessment: PRO (Public Record Office) WO218/114

p. 26 It was a terrible mistake: Weidinger, *Kameraden bis zum Ende*

p. 27 'The military significance . . .': Stein, *The Waffen SS*, p. 288

p. 29 'They laughed at our rags . . .': Author interview with Fritz Langangke, 23 April 1980

p. 30 'Our only concern . . .': Author interview with Heinrich Wulf, 21 April 1980

p. 30 'They were so intelligent . . .': Langangke *loc. cit.*

p. 30 'We asked him his unit . . .': Author interview with Otto Pohl, 23 April 1980

p. 31 Every *résistant* is a terrorist to his enemies, a guerilla to his allies. I have used each word according to the perspective from which the relevant passage is written.

p. 31 'We thought of the Americans . . .': Langangke *loc. cit.*

p. 34 'was in a state . . .': Quoted Stein *op. cit.* p. 271

p. 36 'After all, Lammerding . . .': Author telephone interview with Stuckler, 11 October 1980

p. 36 'I had always wanted . . .': Langangke *loc. cit.*

p. 38 'We were completely unsuited . . .': Stuckler *loc. cit.*

p. 39 'On his last evening . . .': Author interview with Karl Kreutz, 22 April 1980

p. 40 Fritz Langangke said: Langangke *loc. cit.*

p. 40 He described an evening: Sadi Schneid, *Beutedeutscher*
p. 43 'The French know . . .': Tillon, *Les FTP*. p. 284
p. 44 'There was no place . . .': Author interview with Selwyn Jepson, 4 June 1980
p. 44 'a new organization . . .':Quoted Foot *op. cit*. pp. 8, 9
p. 45 'I think that the dropping . . .': Ibid. p. 153
p. 45 'I am not at all clear . . .': PRO AIR8/1187
p. 46 One of the chiefs of SOE: Sir Robin Brook
p. 47 SOE's agents were becoming: See Howarth, *Undercover*
p. 48 'Gubbins had all . . .': Jepson *loc. cit.*
p. 48 'because the Allies . . .': Author interview with General Barry, 4 June 1980
p. 48 'He believed that all . . .': Private comment to author
p. 48 'One would hear that . . .': Barry *loc. cit.*
p. 50 money, the last always: By December 1943 £250,000 a month was being dropped into France.
p. 50 'There was no atmosphere . . .': Hiller, unpublished notes
p. 51 'Well, I hope . . .': Author interview with Vera Atkins, 27 March 1980
p. 52 'It is unfortunate . . .': PRO WO219/2388
p. 53 'Assuming 70 trains . . .': PRO WO219/1892
p. 53 Through Ultra they were reading: PRO DEF3/44
p. 53 'It was unthinkable . . .': Durand, *SNCF pendant la Guerre*, p. 437
p. 54 'The weight of air . . .': PRO WO219/82
p. 54 'In the normal course . . .': Author interview with Major C. V. Wintour, 20 May 1980
p. 55 The Glières: The plateau in Haute-Savoie where German and Vichy troops attacked a concentration of *maquisards* in March 1944, killing 155 and capturing 175.
p. 56 'Massigli handed me . . .': PRO AIR8/1190
p. 56 'This plan gives . . .': Lt. Gen. J. A. H. Gammell in PRO WO219/2387
p. 56 Plan Vert: The principal architect of the railway sabotage plan was an enigmatic railway expert named René Hardy, who was acquitted, in an extraordinary French post-war trial, of betraying fellow-*résistants* to the Nazis.
p. 57 'The immediate offensive . . .': PRO WO219/2388
p. 57 'It cannot be foreseen . . .': PRO WO219/2388
p. 57 'In view of the fact . . .': PRO WO219/2397
p. 57 'We were,' said Colonel Barry: Barry *loc. cit.*
p. 57 'It is probable that . . .': PRO WO219/2388

p. 58 half a million active Resisters: For details, see PRO WO219/2387

p. 59 'The Germans will ignore . . .': PRO WO219/2442

p. 60 'The beauty of life . . .': Hiller, unpublished ms.

p. 61 'Her position . . .': Brogan, *Development of Modern France*, p. 543

p. 62 An utterly dedicated minority: It is important to notice that even at the summit of Resistance activity after D-Day, only an estimated 2 per cent of the French population was taking any active role, measured by the numbers decorated after the Liberation: 130,000 as *résistants*, 170,000 deportees and the estimated 100,000 who died. It is reckoned that in the spring of 1944, substantially more French men and women were engaged in the struggle to combat Resistance than were working for the Allied cause. See Robert Paxton, *Vichy*.

p. 63 'Il y avait . . .': Author interview with Pierrette Bach, 12 June 1980

p. 64 'Explain how very ordinary . . .': Hiller notes *op. cit.*

p. 64 'A quality of . . .': Ibid.

p. 64 'We were working . . .': Hiller ms. *op. cit.*

p. 65 'Limoges was a dangerous . . .': Ibid.

p. 66 'started fewer schemes . . .': Hiller notes *op. cit.*

p. 66 'Organizing the *maquis* . . .': Hiller ms. *op. cit.*

p. 67 The Groupes Vény's strength. For details, see the magazine *R4*, July 1979, article *Les Groupes Vény et leur Secteur du Lot*

p. 67 'tension and the light . . .': Hiller notes *op. cit.*

p. 67 'The castle chosen . . .': Hiller tapes

p. 69 'Ha, ha, mon cher . . .': Quoted from author interview with Peter Lake, 9 January 1980

p. 70 across the Pyrenees: It is estimated that some 30,000 fugitives successfully crossed the Pyrenees between August 1940 and the Liberation, about one-third of all those who made the attempt. Many reached Spain only to suffer miserably in one of Franco's internment camps.

p. 72 'They lunched on . . .': Quoted Simone de Beauvoir, *The Price of Life*

p. 72 'Have you arms?': Quoted Lacouture, *André Malraux*, p. 288

p. 73 'a German defeat . . .': Lacouture *op. cit.* p. 297, quoting Roger Stephane

p. 73 'old man Churchill . . .': Ibid. p. 309, quoting Pierre Viansson-Ponte

p. 73 'the military chief . . .': Malraux, *Antimémoires*

p. 74 'There are a few people . . .': Author interview with Jacques Poirier, 21 March 1980
p. 74 Poirier quoted . . .: Ibid.
p. 74 'André, we must discuss . . .': Ibid.
p. 75 'Jack, you're crazy . . .': Ibid.
p. 75 'I was always . . .': Ibid.
p. 76 'From February 1944 . . .': Ibid.
p. 77 'More or less . . .': Ibid.
p. 77 'The Dordogne air force . . .': Ibid.
p. 77 'Say nothing . . .': Ibid.
p. 78 'And now, mon commandant . . .': Ibid.
p. 78 'For a long time . . .': Ibid.
p. 80 'There's somebody here . . .': Author interview with Philippe de Gunzbourg, 11 March 1980
p. 80 'Because for me . . .': Ibid.
p. 82 'a farmhouse with twenty . . .': Bergeret, *Messages Personnels*, p. 66
p. 82 'the principal artisan . . .': Ibid.
p. 82 'We'll follow you . . .': de Gunzbourg *loc. cit.*
p. 83 'Oh, M. Philibert . . .': Ibid.
p. 83 'Un homme du métier . . .': de Gunzbourg unpublished ms, *Souvenirs du Sud-Ouest*
p. 84 'Only if I choose . . .': Author interview with George Starr, 24 April 1980
p. 84 'But I didn't . . .': Ibid.
p. 85 'Building a network . . .': Ibid.
p. 86 'We used to discuss . . .': Author interview with Yvette (Annette) Cormeau, 14 May 1980
p. 86 Selwyn Jepson said . . .: To the author, *loc. cit.*
p. 87 veteran named Tony Brooks: Information here from Foot *op. cit.* It is a matter of regret that the author was only able to have one brief meeting with Brooks.
p. 88 'AVERTISSEMENT . . .': see Durand *op. cit.* p. 440
p. 88 'Which did more harm . . .': Ibid.
p. 88 'So English, so careful . . .': Author interview with Prince Michel de Bourbon, 18 June 1980
p. 91 'Barricades are a great . . .': de Gunzbourg *loc. cit.*
p. 91 'With immense enthusiasm . . .': de Gunzbourg ms. *op. cit.*
p. 92 'In spite of the active . . .': Durand *op. cit.* p. 436
p. 93 'General reports indicate . . .': PRO WO219/2342
p. 93 'We knew that every single day . . .': Kreutz *loc. cit.*
p. 94 OKW. It is pertinent to the story of the Das Reich to under-

stand that orders descended from OKW – Hitler's Supreme Command – to Von Rundstedt's Army Group B (responsible for the defence of northern France) and Von Blaskowitz's Army Group G (responsible for the south). Within Army Group G, the Das Reich was tactically subordinated to 58th Panzer Corps, also based in Toulouse, and later briefly to 66th Reserve Corps, based in Clermont-Ferrand. On moving north to Normandy, the Das Reich naturally transferred to Army Group B's command, fighting chiefly under the orders of 2nd SS Panzer Corps.

p. 94 'emphasized the desire . . .': Quoted by Shulman, *Defeat in the West*, p. 106

p. 95 'impression growing . . .': Army Group G War Diary, Appendix 153

p. 95 'The departments of Dordogne . . .': Ibid.

p. 96 'Subject: Anti-Terrorist Measures . . .': Ibid., Appendix 339/44g Kdos

p. 97 'The development of the . . .': Ibid.

p. 104 'The first we knew . . .': Hiller tapes *op. cit.*

p. 105 'The men shoot too much . . .': Report loaned to author by regional historian M. Pierre Péré.

p. 106 'Un bruit infernal . . .': Report loaned to author by M. René Jugie

p. 109 'Reports coming in . . .': Army Group G War Diary

p. 112 'Laurent declared . . .': Minutes loaned to author by M. René Jugie

p. 113 'FTP forces . . .': Ibid.

p. 114 'Tulle will pay . . .': Ibid.

p. 114 'Pierre has just told me . . .': Ibid.

p. 114 'Some of Laurent's friends . . .': Ibid.

p. 118 'leaders of a local faction . . .': Brogan *op. cit.* p. 646

p. 119 'orthodox communists . . .': Noireau, *Le Temps des Partisans*, p. 141

p. 119 security police and intelligence: The Gestapo/SD had 131 local branches in France; the army's rival intelligence service, the Abwehr, 69.

p. 121 'Here's one . . .': Noireau *op. cit.* p. 149

p. 121 'Those séances . . .': Ibid. p. 158

p. 122 'The first of May . . .': *Maquis de Corrèze*, p. 300

p. 122 'We also know . . .': Ibid. p. 343

p. 125 'We are cut off . . .': Ibid. p. 351

p. 125 'I find a perplexed . . .': Ibid. p. 352

p. 126 'Towards 8 am . . .': Ibid. p. 355
p. 128 'This great devil . . .': Ibid. p. 357
p. 129 'If the Germans . . .': Ibid. p. 373
p. 133 'They were sitting there . . .': Wulf *loc. cit.*
p. 133 'We've got to make . . .': Schneid *op. cit.*
p. 134 'It was a Dante-esque . . .': *Maquis de Corrèze*, p. 379
p. 135 'And what are you doing . . .': Schneid *op. cit.*
p. 137 'We arranged ourselves . . .': Ibid.
p. 138 'We refused to look . . .': Ibid.
p. 139 'Ah yes,' he said: Private information to author
p. 139 'I am still ignorant . . .': Quoted from Weidinger unpublished ms.
p. 141 'There was no specific . . .': Stuckler *loc. cit.*
p. 141 'I protested that . . .': Wulf *loc. cit.*
p. 141 'Hascha Kurz . . .': Schneid *op. cit.*
p. 142 'Why are your shoes . . .': Soulier, *Le Drame de Tulle*
p. 142 'I am one of the . . .': Ibid.
p. 143 'My friends . . .': Ibid.
p. 143 'You see this boy . . .': Schneid *op. cit.*
p. 144 'Because our wounded . . .': Soulier *op. cit.*
p. 144 'Terrible look . . .': Schneid *op. cit.*
p. 145 'One basic principle . . .': Stein *op. cit.*
p. 146 '2nd SS Ps . . .': Army Group G War Diary, Appendix 180
p. 147 'We've got a French . . .': Author interview with Tommy Macpherson, 1 June 1980
p. 148 'The British kept . . .': Author telephone interview with Henry Hyde, 8 November 1980
p. 149 'plainly represented . . .': Author interview with Geoffrey Hallowes, 13 May 1980
p. 149 'and it stuck out . . .': Macpherson *loc. cit.*
p. 151 'All those who can . . .': Author interview with Macdonald Austin, 6 November 1980
p. 152 'were shattered to see . . .': Macpherson *loc. cit.*
p. 152 'The great thing . . .': Macpherson *loc. cit.*
p. 153 'They were very conscious . . .': Hallowes *loc. cit.*
p. 156 'Sometimes they would do . . .': Austin *loc. cit.*
p. 157 'I really didn't know . . .': Ibid.
p. 157 'Infinite capacity for . . .': Macpherson *loc. cit.*
p. 157 'With hindsight it was . . .': Ibid.
p. 159 'I felt I had a clear . . .': Ibid.
p. 160 'If an armoured car . . .': Ibid.
p. 161 'The Germans didn't suffer . . .': Ibid.

p. 163 'State of the division . . .': Army Group G War Diary, Appendices 195 and 326
p. 165 'In view of the transport . . .': Ibid.
p. 165 'High transport losses . . .': Ibid.
p. 166 'One man found . . .': Schneid *op. cit.*
p. 166 '1 Area Souillac . . .': Army Group G War Diary, Appendices 27 and 356
p. 167 'Towards 11 pm . . .': Quoted Beau & Gaubusseau, p. 383
p. 167 'Terrasson is a pretty little . . .': Ibid. p. 384
p. 169 'I profit from an armoured . . .': Ibid. p. 385
p. 169 'the cycle is simple . . .': Ibid. p. 385
p. 170 'At the end of . . .': de Gunzbourg ms. *op. cit.*
p. 171 'The regiment is greeted . . .': Weidinger *op. cit.*
p. 174 The account of Kampfe's kidnapping and the events leading to the massacre at Oradour are drawn from Weidinger's history, interviews with surviving second-hand French contemporary sources, and the principal published French accounts of Delarue and Beau & Gaubusseau.
p. 177 'She was treated . . .': Quoted by Wache in a sworn statement loaned to the author by Herbert Taege
p. 177 'When I left London . . .': Staunton is quoted by Minney in *Carve Her Name With Pride*
p. 178 'She looked like a little doll . . .': Author interview with an eyewitness in Limoges, 23 June 1980
p. 178 'In the course of . . .': Army Group G War Diary
p. 181 'It was very rough . . .': Quoted from author interview with Weidinger, 11 April 1980
p. 181 'After many delays . . .': Weidinger *op. cit.*
p. 182 'He arrives in an excited . . .': Ibid.
p. 183 The surviving witnesses of the massacre at Oradour were exhaustively examined by post-war tribunals and historians. All quotations in this section unless otherwise stated are drawn from testimony given at the 1953 war crimes trial, or statements recorded in Jens Kruuse's *Madness at Oradour*. I have relied principally upon the published French sources, with some collaborative details from my own interviews in France and Germany, and of course a visit to the ruins of Oradour.
p. 201 'Late in the afternoon . . .': Weidinger *op. cit.*
p. 203 'Mopping up operations . . .': Army Group G War Diary, Appendix 199
p. 204 'There are further . . .': Weidinger *op. cit.*

p. 204 'Action taken during the . . .': Quoted Delarue, *Trafics et Crimes sous l'Occupation*
p. 206 'Turn him over . . .': Schneid *op. cit.*
p. 206 'The German authorities . . .': Quoted by Soulier *op. cit.*
p. 207 'dropped on Billancourt . . .': A reference to a major raid by RAF Bomber Command against the Renault factory, on 9 March 1942.
p. 207 'At 1.30 am . . .': News cuttings from private collection of Marcel Racault
p. 207 'Well, let's thank God . . .': Wulf *loc. cit.*
p. 208 'The great thing . . .': Sir Henry d'Avigdor-Goldsmid, quoted Hislop *Anything but a Soldier*, p. 3
p. 209 'Don't use 'em . . .': Ibid. p. 124
p. 209 'I believe that after . . .': Lloyd-Owen, *Providence Their Guide* (Harrap 1980) p. 120
p. 210 'When small successful . . .': Hislop *op. cit.* p. 67
p. 210 'Quite out of his depth . . .': Ibid. p. 125
p. 210 'Where's so and so . . .': Author interview with Peter Weaver, 11 August 1980
p. 210 'He was everything . . .': Author interview with Sam Smith, 6 August 1980
p. 211 'Belted for the bridge . . .': Ibid.
p. 211 'I was in love . . .': Ibid.
p. 211 'The war came . . .': Weaver *loc. cit.*
p. 212 '2nd SS Panzer . . .': PRO WO218/114
p. 212 'This was a serious . . .': Farran, *Winged Dagger*, p. 222–3
p. 213 'You will now concentrate . . .': PRO WO218/114
p. 214 'I can remember . . .': Tonkin in a letter to the author, 11 October 1980
p. 214 'As if, when a boy . . .': Hislop *op. cit.* p. 126
p. 214 'He gave me much . . .': Tonkin letter *op. cit.*
p. 215 'The 5th came . . .': Tonkin contemporary letter to his mother, loaned to author
p. 215 'It is my unfortunate . . .': Tonkin to author, *op. cit.*
p. 216 Hitler's Commando Order: Following the discovery of a German sentry who had been bound and shot by a British commando raiding party in the Channel Islands in 1942, Hitler decreed that all members of the Commandos, SAS and paratroopers captured operating behind the lines were to be treated as saboteurs and shot, whether or not in uniform. More than 200 mostly British prisoners suffered this fate, although the

'commando' order was erratically executed. It is only just to add that when operational requirements made it embarrassing to take or hold prisoners, Allied Special Forces were not unknown to kill them. In recent years, there have been an increasing number of revelations of mass executions of German prisoners by Allied units during World War II. The US 45th Division machine-gunned one large group during the summer of 1944. On 4 January 1945, General Patton wrote in his diary: 'The 11th Armoured Division is very green and took unnecessary losses to no effect. There were also some unfortunate incidents in the shooting of prisoners (I hope we can conceal this).' The purpose of these remarks is not to excuse the German shooting of prisoners in contravention of the laws of war, but to try to place the matter in a more objective context than was possible in the first, chauvinistic years following the end of the war when many books suggested that only the Wehrmacht and the SS were guilty of breaching the Geneva Convention.

p. 216 'It was the nicest . . .': Tonkin to mother *op. cit.*

p. 218 'A small, very frightened . . .': Tonkin to author *op. cit.*

p. 221 'They hardly knew . . .': Weaver *loc. cit.*

p. 224 'There was nothing . . .': Captain John Sadoine report in PRO WO218/114

p. 224 'should be treated . . .': Ibid.

p. 225 'One point to be . . .': Tonkin report PRO WO218/114

p. 225 Sergeant Eccles . . .: On 28 June 1944

p. 225 Sam Smith and two: On 30 June 1944

p. 227 Soon after first light: On 3 July 1944

p. 228 'almost berserk . . .': Weaver *loc. cit.*

p. 229 'I have always felt . . .': Tonkin to author *op. cit.*

p. 230 'We'd written ourselves . . .': Weaver *loc. cit.*

p. 231 'In comparison with . . .': PRO WO219/2389

p. 231 'In retrospect, it seemed . . .': Hislop *op. cit.* p. 67

p. 231 'Urgent request for . . .': PRO DEF3/171

p. 233 'In spite of efforts . . .': PRO WO219/2342

p. 234 'They couldn't even . . .': Author interview with Ernst Krag, 12 April 1980

p. 234 'After 10 pm the Americans . . .': Author interviews with DR survivors

p. 235 'It was the first hint . . .': Langangke *loc. cit.*

p. 235 'It will be a miracle . . .': Quoted Weidinger *loc. cit.*

p. 235 'Where is the Luftwaffe . . .': Author interviews with DR survivors

p. 236 'Could we allow . . .': Weidinger *loc. cit.*
p. 237 'If we do this . . .': Wulf *loc. cit.*
p. 237 'At Falaise . . .': quoted Stein *op. cit.* p. 225
p. 237 'Aren't you pleased . . .': Kreutz *loc. cit.*
p. 238 'An organization in the . . .': PRO WO219/2342
p. 238 'The movements of . . .': PRO WO219/2389
p. 238 'Poor, tortured . . .': Malraux, *Antimémoires*, p. 213
p. 239 'All things . . .': Churchill to Portal, 2 October 1941, quoted Hastings, *Bomber Command*, p. 141
p. 239 As Professor Foot has said: Foot *op. cit.* p. 441
p. 240 'It has been estimated . . .': PRO WO219/1975 (8 July 1944)
p. 241 'It was only just . . .': Barry *loc. cit.*
p. 241 'In Spain the French . . .': Best, *Humanity in Warfare*, p. 115
p. 242 'We are beating them . . .': See Howard, *The Franco-Prussian War*, p. 251
p. 242 'The truth is . . .': Quoted Best *op. cit.* p. 120
p. 242 'My whole attention . . .': Quoted Nigel Hamilton, *Monty: The Making of a General* (Hamish Hamilton) p. 158
p. 242 'My own view . . .': Quoted Hamilton *op. cit.* p. 160
p. 243 'Levelling everything . . .': Tillon *op. cit.* p. 364
p. 247 'It was necessary . . .': Lammerding post-war written statement to Weidinger, provided to author
p. 250 'Ask the court . . .': Schneid *op. cit.*

Index